Lecture Notes in Computer Science 13409

More information about this series at https://link.springer.com/bookseries/558

Clemente Galdi · Stanislaw Jarecki (Eds.)

Security and Cryptography for Networks

13th International Conference, SCN 2022
Amalfi (SA), Italy, September 12–14, 2022
Proceedings

Editors
Clemente Galdi
Università degli Studi di Salerno
Fisciano, Italy

Stanislaw Jarecki
University of California at Irvine
Irvine, CA, USA

ISSN 0302-9743 ISSN 1611-3349 (electronic)
Lecture Notes in Computer Science
ISBN 978-3-031-14790-6 ISBN 978-3-031-14791-3 (eBook)
https://doi.org/10.1007/978-3-031-14791-3

This Springer imprint is published by the registered company Springer Nature Switzerland AG
The registered company address is: Gewerbestrasse 11, 6330 Cham, Switzerland

Preface

The 13th Conference on Security and Cryptography for Networks (SCN 2022) was held in Amalfi, Italy, during September 12–14, 2022. The conference has traditionally been held in Amalfi, with the exception of the 5th edition, held in the nearby town of Maiori, and the 12th edition in 2020 that, due to COVID-19 restrictions, was held as a virtual event. After the editions of 1996, 1999, and 2002, the conference has been organized biennially. SCN 2022 was organized in cooperation with the International Association for Cryptologic Research (IACR).

The SCN conference is an international meeting which focuses is on the cryptographic and information security methodologies needed to address the challenges arising in the modern digital society. SCN allows researchers, practitioners, developers, and users interested in the security of communication networks to meet and exchange ideas in the wonderful setting of the Amalfi Coast.

In this edition we received 101 submissions of exceptional quality, authored by 273 authors from 27 countries. Reviewing and selection among the very high-quality submissions was a challenging task. Each submission was assigned to at least three reviewers, whereas submissions authored by Program Committee (PC) members received four reviews, for a total of 310 submitted reviews. The single-blind reviewing process was carried out by the Program Committee, consisting of 33 members from 14 different countries, with the help of 87 external reviewers. Program Committee members received, on average, 10 papers to review. This process allowed us to select 33 papers to be presented at SCN 2022 and to be included in this proceedings. We are grateful to the PC members and external reviewers for their hard and careful work.

The conference program also included invited talks by Eli Ben Sasson and Marshall Ball.

We sincerely thank all the authors who submitted papers to this conference, the Program Committee members and all reviewers, the Organizing Committee members, colleagues, and student helpers for their valuable time and effort, and all the conference attendees who made this event truly intellectually stimulating through their active participation.

September 2022

Clemente Galdi
Stanislaw Jarecki

Organization

Program Committee Chair

Stanislaw Jarecki	University of California, Irvine, USA

General Chair

Clemente Galdi	Università di Salerno, Italy

Steering Committee

Carlo Blundo	Università di Salerno, Italy
Alfredo De Santis	Università di Salerno, Italy
Ueli Maurer	ETH Zurich, Switzerland
Rafail Ostrovsky	University of California Los Angeles, USA
Giuseppe Persiano	Università di Salerno, Italy
Jacques Stern	ENS Paris, France
Gene Tsudik	University of California, Irvine, USA
Moti Yung	Google, USA

Program Committee

Masayuki Abe	NTT Corporation, Japan
Manuel Barbosa	University of Porto (FCUP) and INESC TEC, Portugal
Dario Catalano	Università di Catania, Italy
Geoffroy Couteau	CNRS, IRIF, Université Paris Cité, France
Jintai Ding	University of Cincinnati, USA
Juan Garay	Texas A&M University, USA
Niv Gilboa	Ben Gurion University, Israel
Julia Hesse	IBM Research Zurich, Switzerland
Harish Karthikeyan	New York University, USA
Aggelos Kiaiyas	University of Edinburgh and IOHK, UK
Russell W. F. Lai	FAU Erlangen-Nürnberg, Germany
Steve Lu	Stealth Software Technologies, Inc., USA
Tal Malkin	Columbia University, USA
Chan Nam Ngo	Kyber Network, Vietnam
Omkant Pandey	Stony Brook University, USA
Giuseppe Persiano	Università di Salerno, Italy
Krzysztof Pietrzak	ISTA, Austria
Antigoni Polychroniadou	JPMorgan AI Research, USA
Mike Rosulek	Oregon State University, USA
Arnab Roy	Alpen-Adria-Universität Klagenfurt, Austria

Alessandra Scafuro	North Carolina State University, USA
Dominique Schröder	FAU Erlangen-Nürnberg, Germany
Yannick Seurin	ANSSI, France
Abhi Shelat	Northeastern University, USA
Nigel Smart	Katholieke Universiteit Leuven, Belgium
Martijn Stam	Simula UiB, Norway
Mehdi Tibouchi	NTT Corporation, Japan
Daniele Venturi	Sapienza University of Rome, Italy
Damien Vergnaud	Sorbonne University, France
Jiayu Xu	Algorand, USA
Sophia Yakoubov	Aarhus University, Denmark
Vassilis Zikas	Purdue University, USA

Local Organizing Comittee

Luigi Catuogno	Università di Salerno, Italy
Giuseppe Fenza	Università di Salerno, Italy
Graziano Fuccio	Università di Salerno, Italy
Francesco Orciuoli	Università di Salerno, Italy
Rocco Zaccagnino	Università di Salerno, Italy

Additional Reviewers

Abdelrahaman Aly
Arasu Arun
Christian Badertscher
Rishabh Bhadauria
Adithya Bhat
Olivier Blazy
Xavier Bonnetain
Joppe W. Bos
Mariana Botelho da Gama
Katharina Boudgoust
Konstantinos Brazitikos
Hongyuan Cai
Pedro Capitao
Pyrros Chaidos
Suvradip Chakraborty
Rohit Chatterjee
Clémence Chevignard
Valerio Cini
Kelong Cong
Elizabeth Crites
Luca De Feo
Nico Döttling
Julien Duman
Christoph Egger
Antonio Faonio
Pooya Farshim
Peter Fenteany
Pouyan Forghani
Sanjam Garg
Gayathri Garimella
Romain Gay
Irene Giacomelli
Aarushi Goel
Eli Goldin
Vincent Grosso
Felix Günther
Hao Guo
Mohammad Hajiabadi
Akinori Hosoyamada
Martha Norberg Hovd
Andreas Hülsing
Muhammad Ishaq
Eli Jaffe
Zhengzhong Jin

Matthias J. Kannwischer
Marcel Keller
Thomas Kerber
Elena Kirshanova
Karen Klein
Lisa Kohl
Sebastian Kolby
Liliya Kraleva
Xiao Liang
Zeyu Liu
Florette Martinez
Pratyay Mukherjee
Michael Naehrig
Ryo Nishimaki
Sabine Oechsner
Miyako Ohkubo
Emmanuela Orsini
Elisabeth Oswald
Morten Øygarden
Giorgos Panagiotakos
Mahak Pancholi
Jeongeun Park
Guillermo Pascual-Perez
Alain Passelègue
Rutvik Patel
Maxime Plancon
Bernardo Portela
Jean-René Reinhard
Siavash Riahi
Luigi Russo
Peter Scholl
Peter Schwabe
Sina Shiehian
Jaspal Singh
Luisa Siniscalchi
Sri Aravinda Krishnan Thyagarajan
Bogdan Ursu
Hendrik Waldner
Yu Wei
Ivy K. Y. Woo
Dongyu Wu
Thomas Zacharias
Shang Zehua
Bingsheng Zhang
Vincent Zucca

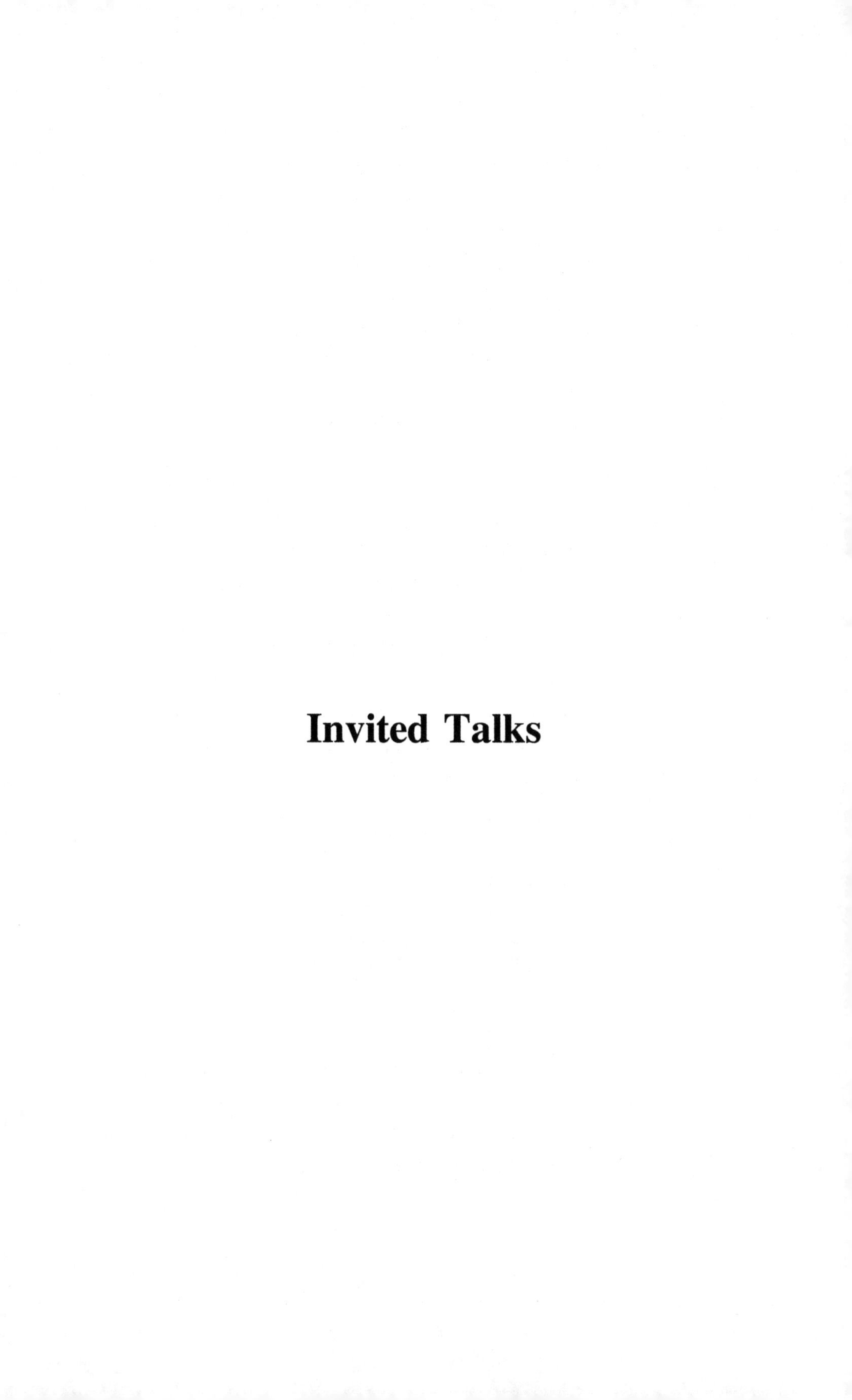

Invited Talks

How to Do Cryptography

Even When Cryptography Doesn't Exist

Marshall Ball

New York University, New York City, USA

Abstract. Over the past half century remarkable progress has been made on "provably secure" cryptography. At the heart of this progress is a clear, compelling, and convenient formalism of an adversary as a probabilistic polynomial time algorithm. Unfortunately, it remains unclear if such a cryptography is indeed possible.

We survey some recent work that studies relaxed security notions where an adversary is only moderately more powerful than honest parties. Notably, such security notions may be achievable even if classical cryptography does not exist.

Keywords: Theory of cryptography · Computational complexity · Fine-grained Cryptography

> Cryptographers seldom sleep well. Their careers are frequently based on very precise complexity-theoretic assumptions, which could be shattered the next morning.
>
> *Joe Kilian quoting Silvio Micali, 1988 [1]*

In the past decades, tremendous progress has been made characterizing the minimal assumptions necessary for a myriad of classical cryptographic objects. Nonetheless, the possibility still remains that all of this work is for nought and not even minimal cryptographic assumptions, such as the existence of one-way functions, hold true! This state of affairs is distressing not just for those of us with careers in cryptography, but our entire information infrastructure whose integrity is founded upon the security of various cryptographic protocols and primitives.

A common explanation given for the failure to prove, unconditionally, the existence of classical cryptographic objects such as symmetric key or public key encryption, is that any such proof must also prove that $\mathtt{P}$ does not equal $\mathtt{NP}$, a Millennium Prime Problem that seems to be beyond the reach of current techniques available in the larger mathematical community. Moreover, even if $\mathtt{P} \neq \mathtt{NP}$ it is still quite plausible that classical cryptography does not exist. If indeed classical cryptography does not exist, is there any hope of recovering some notion of security in a formal sense?

In more detail, classical cryptography (one-way functions, pseudorandom generators, public key encryption, etc.) formulates an adversary as any (randomized) algorithm that runs in polynomial time, n^c steps for *any* constant c. The effectiveness of this model of an adversary cannot be overstated; it is central to our ability to reason about security. Unfortunately, its generality makes it beholden various barriers.

In recent years, a variety of works (often under the heading of *fine-grained cryptography*) have proposed looking at more restricted notions of adversarial behavior which retain reasonable adversarial guarantees while skirting classical barriers. Importantly, these adversarial abstractions remain theoretically robust and simple enough to be useful.

For example, an algorithm that requires n^{1000} steps of work is already intractable to run for even nation-state level adversaries. A variant of public key encryption secure against n^{1000} time adversaries would give a robust notion of security and could conceivably exist even if $\mathtt{P} = \mathtt{NP}$ and classical cryptography does not.

In the setting of massive data (and massive n), even n^2 can be infeasibly huge. Additionally in such a setting, it may be reasonable to restrict consideration to adversaries with a sub-linear amount working memory. In certain hardware settings, it may be reasonable to consider even simpler adversarial models.

For some security notions, it is critical that the adversarial model restricted. Proofs of Work, a critical ingredient in Bitcoin and related protocols in permissionless distributed computing, can be produced with a certain amount of work and cannot computed with less. Proofs of Work, and related primitives such as verifiable delay functions and memory-hard functions necessitate precise adversarial restrictions.

To be clear, unconditional guarantees in most of these settings are well beyond the current state of computational intractability. However, recent works have shown how some of these objects can be constructed from well-studied conjectures in computational complexity that plausibly hold even if classical cryptography is impossible. This opens the door to a robust, tailor-made theory of cryptography. Despite progress, this area remains nascent; we are still only beginning to develop cryptographic theory in these settings.

Reference

1. Kilian, J.: Founding cryptography on oblivious transfer. In: Simon, J. (ed.) Proceedings of the 20th Annual ACM Symposium on Theory of Computing, 2–4 May 1988, Chicago, Illinois, USA, pp. 20–31. ACM (1988). https://doi.org/10.1145/62212.62215

From Galactic PCP Theory to Scaling Blockchains with ZK-STARKs

EliBen-Sasson

Starkware, Netanya, Israel
eli@starkware.co

Abstract. There's a beautiful story to be told about how theoretical "galactic" algorithms involved in the PCP Theorem got reduced to practice and are the main contender for scaling blockchains. This story will be the topic of this talk.

Contents

Authentication and Signatures

Multiparty Computation

Ciphers, Cryptanalysis, Defenses

Decoding McEliece with a Hint – Secret Goppa Key Parts Reveal Everything

Elena Kirshanova[1,2(✉)] and Alexander May[3]

[1] Immanuel Kant Baltic Federal University, Kaliningrad, Russia
[2] Technology Innovation Institute, Abu Dhabi, UAE
elenakirshanova@gmail.com
[3] Ruhr University Bochum, Bochum, Germany
alex.may@rub.de

Abstract. We consider the McEliece cryptosystem with a binary Goppa code $C \subset \mathbb{F}_2^n$ specified by an irreducible Goppa polynomial $g(x) \in \mathbb{F}_{2^m}[X]$ and Goppa points $(\alpha_1, \ldots, \alpha_n) \in \mathbb{F}_{2^m}^n$. Since $g(x)$ together with the Goppa points allow for efficient decoding, these parameters form McEliece secret keys. Such a Goppa code C is an $(n - tm)$-dimensional subspace of $\mathbb{F}_2^n$, and therefore C has co-dimension tm. For typical McEliece instantiations we have $tm \approx \frac{n}{4}$.

We show that given more than tm entries of the Goppa point vector $(\alpha_1, \ldots, \alpha_n)$ allows to recover the Goppa polynomial $g(x)$ and the remaining entries in polynomial time. Hence, in case $tm \approx \frac{n}{4}$ roughly a fourth of a McEliece secret key is sufficient to recover the full key efficiently.

Let us give some illustrative numerical examples. For ClassicMcEliece with $(n, t, m) = (3488, 64, 12)$ on input $64 \cdot 12 + 1 = 769$ Goppa points, we recover the remaining $3488 - 769 = 2719$ Goppa points in $\mathbb{F}_{2^{12}}$ and the degree-64 Goppa polynomial $g(x) \in \mathbb{F}_{2^{12}}[x]$ in 60 s.

For ClassicMcEliece with $(n, t, m) = (8192, 128, 13)$ on input $128 \cdot 13 + 1 = 1665$ Goppa points, we recover the remaining $8192 - 1665 = 6529$ Goppa points in $\mathbb{F}_{2^{13}}$ and the degree-128 Goppa polynomial $g(x) \in \mathbb{F}_{2^{13}}[x]$ in 288 s.

Our results also extend to the case of erroneous Goppa points, but in this case our algorithms are no longer polynomial time.

Keywords: Classic McEliece · Code-based cryptogrpaphy · Cryptanalysis · Partial key exposure

1 Introduction

Partial Key Exposure Attacks. Some cryptosystems are known to allow for full key recovery from only a fraction of the secret key. As an example, let (N, e) be an RSA public key with corresponding secret key (d, p, q). A famous result of Coppersmith [8] shows that N can be factored efficiently if half of the bits of p are given, thereby revealing the complete secret key. Boneh, Durfee, and Frankel [6] showed that for small e a quarter of the bits of d also suffices to reconstruct

C. Galdi and S. Jarecki (Eds.): SCN 2022, LNCS 13409, pp. 3–20, 2022.
https://doi.org/10.1007/978-3-031-14791-3_1

the complete secret key. This kind of attacks are often referred to as *Partial Key Exposure* attacks, and there is a long line of research for RSA [11,19,20,28].

However, the existence of polynomial time Partial Key Exposure attacks is usually considered a typical RSA vulnerability. It is widely believed that for discrete logarithm problems g^x leakage of a constant fraction of bits of x does not degrade the problem [15,23].

The situation seems to be similar for post-quantum cryptosystem. For most schemes, no vulnerabilities are known in the sense that leakage of a constant fraction of the secret key leads to full secret key recovery. In fact, some cryptosystems are believed to be somewhat robust against Partial Key Exposure attacks [9].

Among the literature on post-quantum Partial Key Exposures is an NTRU attack by Paterson and Villanueva-Polanco [24], and attacks of Villanueva-Polanco on BLISS [29] and LUOV [31]. The PhD thesis of Villanueva-Polanco [30] contains a more systematic study of partial key exposure attacks, including also McEliece. However, none of these attacks is polynomial time for a known constant fraction of the secret key bits. To the best of our knowledge the only exception is a recent result of Esser, May, Verbel, Wen [12] that recovers BIKE keys from a constant fraction of their secret key.

McEliece Cryptanalysis. Since the McEliece cryptosystem was proposed more than 40 years ago, it faced a lot of significant cryptanalysis efforts [3,13]. However, most cryptanalysis concentrated on *information set decoding* algorithms [2,4,18,21,25], basically trying to decoding McEliece instances as if they where instances of random codes with Goppa code parameters, thereby completely ignoring the Goppa code structure hidden in McEliece public keys.

When McEliece is instantiated with other codes, e.g. generalized Reed-Solomon codes, there have been devastating attacks breaking the scheme in polynomial time [27]. However, for the originally suggested binary subfield Goppa codes very little structural attacks are known, besides for distinguishers for high-rate Goppa codes [14] and for very special choices of Goppa code parameters [17], both cases being far off typical cryptographic parameter selection.

Our Results. We show surprisingly elementary facts about McEliece keys that strongly exploit the Goppa code structure. Our attacks imply a clear warning that one should well protect McEliece secret keys, e.g. against side-channels, since leaking even a small fraction of the key in *any* known positions already allows to efficiently recover the complete secret key.

Let us be a bit more precise what we show in this work. Binary Goppa codes $C \in \mathbb{F}_2^n$ of length n and co-dimension tm are defined via an irreducible *Goppa polynomial* $g(x) \in \mathbb{F}_{2^m}[x]$ of degree-t with $tm < n$, and *Goppa points* $(\alpha_1, \ldots, \alpha_n) \in (\mathbb{F}_{2^m})^n$. In fact, the parity check matrix defining a Goppa code C is a function of a Goppa polynomial and a tuple of Goppa points. Therefore, a McEliece secret key consists of $g(x)$ and $(\alpha_1, \ldots, \alpha_n)$, whereas a McEliece public key H^{pub} is a scrambled form of a parity check matrix.

It is a folklore result that $(\alpha_1, \ldots, \alpha_n)$ allows to efficiently recover $g(x)$. We give a more formal proof of this folklore result in Sect. 3.1, since it is the starting point for our more involved algorithms.

1. We show in Sect. 3.2 that any $tm + 1$ points α_i allow to efficiently recover $g(x)$.
2. We show in Algorithm 3.3 that any $tm+1$ points α_i together with $g(x)$ allow to recover in polynomial time all the remaining Goppa points, provided that the submatrix formed by the columns of H^{pub} indexed by α_i has full rank.

Both results together imply that with constant probability any $tm+1$ Goppa points suffice to recover the complete McEliece secret key in polynomial time.

We support our claims by implementing our algorithms, and successfully running them on McEliece parameters proposed in [1]. Our non-optimized implementations are available at https://github.com/ElenaKirshanova/leaky_goppa_in_mceliece.

The results are provided in Table 1. On input of $tm+1$ Goppa points, our algorithm KEY-RECOVERY for all 2000 instances succeeded to recover the degree-t Goppa polynomial $g(x)$ in $\mathbb{F}_{2^m}[x]$ and all remaining $n - (tm + 1)$ Goppa points in averaged run times between 1 and 5 mins.

Table 1. Experimental results for Classic McEliece KEY-RECOVERY (Algorithm 3.4), averaged over 2000 instances. The middle column refers to the number of Goppa points the algorithm receives as input.

(n, t, m)	$tm + 1$	Time
$(3488, 64, 12)$	769	**60 s**
$(4608, 96, 13)$	1249	**184 s**
$(6960, 119, 13)$	1548	**258 s**
$(8192, 128, 13)$	1665	**288 s**

Typical McEliece instantiations have $tm + 1 \approx \frac{n}{4}$ showing that knowledge of only a quarter of the secret key suffices to efficiently recover the whole. Somewhat interestingly, current McEliece instantiations explicitly choose small co-dimension $tm \ll n$ to guard against information set decoding attacks. Our results in turn benefit from small co-dimension.

Technically, our results heavily use the structure imposed by Goppa codes, and thus can be considered as one of the very few structural non-generic McEliece attacks. At the heart of our algorithms lies a simple routine that constructs — with the help of the McEliece public key— codewords with at most the Hamming weight tm of the co-dimension.

Impact on Classic McEliece. Classic McEliece [1, Section 2.5.2] proposes to store the secret key as a so-called *in-place Beneš network* in which neither $g(x)$, nor $(\alpha_1, \ldots, \alpha_n)$ are stored explicitly. It is an open question whether our attacks also apply to this setting.

2 Preliminaries

Notation. We let $\mathbb{F}_2$ denote the binary field and let $\mathbb{F}_{2^m}$ be a finite extension of $\mathbb{F}_2$ of degree $m > 1$. We denote by γ a primitive element of $\mathbb{F}_{2^m}$, i.e., field elements of $\mathbb{F}_{2^m}$ are of the form $\sum_{i=0}^{m-1} a_i \gamma^i$, $a_i \in \mathbb{F}_2$. We further let $n \leq 2^m$ denote some positive integer, and let $L = (\alpha_1, \ldots, \alpha_n) \in \mathbb{F}_{2^m}^n$ be our list of *Goppa points* with distinct points $\alpha_i \neq \alpha_j$ for $i \neq j$. We denote by $g(x)$ our *Goppa polynomial* – an irreducible polynomial of degree t in $\mathbb{F}_{2^m}[x]$.

Let $H = (\mathbf{h}_1 \ldots \mathbf{h}_n) \in \mathbb{F}_2^{tm \times n}$ be a matrix with n columns $\mathbf{h}_i \in \mathbb{F}_2^{tm}$. Let $I \subset \{1, \ldots, n\}$ be an index set. Then we denote by $H[\mathcal{I}]$ the projection of H's to the columns defined by $\mathcal{I} = \{i_1, \ldots, i_\ell\}$, i.e.,

$$H[\mathcal{I}] = (\mathbf{h}_{i_1}, \ldots, \mathbf{h}_{i_\ell}).$$

Analogous for a code $C \subseteq \mathbb{F}_2^n$ and some $\mathcal{I} \subseteq \{1, \ldots, n\}$ we denote by $C[\mathcal{I}]$ the projection to the coordinates in $\mathcal{I} = \{i_1, \ldots, i_\ell\}$, i.e.,

$$C[\mathcal{I}] = \{(c_{i_1}, \ldots, c_{i_\ell}) \in \mathbb{F}_2^\ell \mid (c_1, \ldots, c_n) \in C\}.$$

For a matrix A, we denote its transpose by A^{t}.

Definition 1 (Goppa code). *Let $L = (\alpha_1, \ldots, \alpha_n) \in \mathbb{F}_{2^m}$ be Goppa points and $g(x) \in \mathbb{F}_{2^m}[x]$ be an irreducible, degree-t Goppa polynomial. Then we define a Goppa code*

$$C(L, g) = \left\{ \mathbf{c} \in \mathbb{F}_2^n \ : \ \sum_{i=1}^{n} \frac{c_i}{x - \alpha_i} \equiv 0 \mod g(x) \right\}. \tag{1}$$

For a codeword $\mathbf{c}$, we define its support as $supp(\mathbf{c}) := \{i \in \{1, \ldots, n\} \mid c_i \neq 0\}$.

Let us consider $\overline{H}_{\mathsf{Goppa}}(L, g) \in \mathbb{F}_{2^m}^{t \times n}$ of the form

$$\overline{H}_{\mathsf{Goppa}}(L, g) = \begin{pmatrix} 1 & 1 & \ldots & 1 \\ \alpha_1 & \alpha_2 & \ldots & \alpha_n \\ \vdots & \vdots & \ddots & \vdots \\ \alpha_1^{t-1} & \alpha_2^{t-1} & \ldots & \alpha_n^{t-1} \end{pmatrix} \cdot \begin{pmatrix} g^{-1}(\alpha_1) & 0 & \ldots & 0 \\ 0 & g^{-1}(\alpha_2) & \ldots & 0 \\ \vdots & \vdots & \ddots & \vdots \\ 0 & 0 & \ldots & g^{-1}(\alpha_n) \end{pmatrix}.$$

From $\overline{H}_{\mathsf{Goppa}}(L, g) \in \mathbb{F}_{2^m}^{t \times n}$, we construct the parity-check matrix $H_{\mathsf{Goppa}}(L, g) \in \mathbb{F}_2^{mt \times n}$ by applying the bijection $V : \mathbb{F}_{2^m} \to \mathbb{F}_2^m$, that represents $\mathbb{F}_{2^m}$ as an m-dimensional vector space over $\mathbb{F}_2$, i.e, $\sum_{i=0}^{m-1} a_i \gamma^i \mapsto [a_0, \ldots, a_{m-1}]$.

With constant probability $H_{\mathsf{Goppa}}(L,g)$ has rank full rank tm. Throughout this paper we only consider full rank parity check matrices —the standard cryptographic case. For full rank $H_{\mathsf{Goppa}}(L,g)$ the Goppa code $C(L,g) \subset \mathbb{F}_2^n$ is a binary code of co-dimension tm and therefore of dimension $n - tm$.

In Classic McEliece [1], the echelon form of H_{Goppa} defines the public key H^{pub}, while (L,g) is the secret key. Knowledge of (L,g) allows for efficient decoding of up to t errors [7,16].

Definition 2 (Syndrome). *For* $\mathbf{y} \in \mathbb{F}_2^n$*, the* syndrome *of* y *is defined as*

$$s_{\mathbf{y}} := \sum_{i=1}^{n} \frac{y_i}{x - \alpha_i} = \sum_{i=1}^{n} y_i \prod_{j \neq i} (x - \alpha_j) \bmod g(x). \tag{2}$$

From Definition 1 and Definition 2 we see that $\mathbf{y} \in C(L,g)$ iff we have syndrome $s_{\mathbf{y}} = 0 \mod g(x)$.

The following lemma, see [5,10,16], shows that a Goppa polynomial $g(x)$ and its square $g^2(x)$ define the same code. We will use this property in our algorithms for recovering the correct Goppa polynomial. We include a proof for completeness.

Lemma 1. *[16] The binary irreducible Goppa code* $C(L,g)$ *satisfies*

$$C(L,g) = C(L,g^2).$$

Proof. Since $s_{\mathbf{c}} \equiv 0 \bmod g(x)^2$ we have $s_{\mathbf{c}} \equiv 0 \bmod g(x)$. The inclusion $C(L,g^2) \subset C(L,g)$ follows.

To show $C(L,g) \subset C(L,g^2)$, for any $\mathbf{c} \in C(L,g)$ define

$$f_{\mathbf{c}}(x) := \prod_{i \in \mathsf{supp}(\mathbf{c})} (x - \alpha_i) \text{ with derivative } f'_{\mathbf{c}}(x) = \sum_{i \in \mathsf{supp}(\mathbf{c})} \prod_{j \neq i} (x - \alpha_j).$$

From Definition 2 it follows that $s_{\mathbf{c}} \equiv f'_{\mathbf{c}}(x)/f_{\mathbf{c}}(x) \bmod g(x)$. Since $g(x)$ is irreducible of degree $t > 1$, we have $\gcd(f_{\mathbf{c}}(x), g(x)) = 1$ and hence $f_{\mathbf{c}}(x)$ is invertible modulo $g(x)$. Therefore

$$\mathbf{c} \in C(L,g) \Leftrightarrow s_{\mathbf{c}} \equiv 0 \bmod g(x) \Leftrightarrow f'_{\mathbf{c}}(x) \equiv 0 \bmod g(x).$$

Notice that $f'_{\mathbf{c}}(x) = \sum_{i=1}^{n} i f_i x^{i-1}$ and thus for even i we have $i f_i x^{i-1} = 0 \bmod 2$. Therefore, only x^i-terms with even degree remain. Thus,

$$f'_{\mathbf{c}}(x) = \sum_{i \equiv 0 \bmod 2}^{n} f_i (x^{i/2})^2 = \left(\sum_{i \equiv 0 \bmod 2}^{n} f_i (x^{i/2}) \right)^2 \bmod 2.$$

This implies that $f'_{\mathbf{c}}(x)$ is a square. Hence every irreducible divisor of $f'_{\mathbf{c}}(x)$ has to appear with even multiplicity, implying that $g^2(x)$ divides $f'_{\mathbf{c}}(x)$. Therefore, $\mathbf{c} \in C(L,g^2)$. □

Algorithm 2.1. TEST-GOPPA-POLYNOMIAL

Input: $f(x)$, Goppa points $\alpha_i \in \mathbb{F}_{2^m}$ with $i \in \mathcal{I} \subset \{1, \ldots, n\}$, index set $\mathcal{I}$ with $|\mathcal{I}| := \ell$, generator matrix $G \in \mathbb{F}_2^{j \times \ell}$ of $C(L, g)[\mathcal{I}]$

Output: 1 indicating that $f(x)$ might be $C(L, g)$'s Goppa polynomial, or 0

1: **for** all j rows $\mathbf{g}$ of G **do**
2: Compute $s_{\mathbf{g}}(x) = \sum_{i \in \mathcal{I}} \frac{g_i}{x - \alpha_i}$ mod $f(x)$ from Eq. (2).
3: **if** $s_{\mathbf{g}}(x) \not\equiv 0$ mod $f(x)$ **then**
4: Return 0
5: Return 1

The following algorithm TEST-GOPPA-POLYNOMIAL (Algorithm 2.1) tests whether a potential Goppa polynomial satisfies Eq. (1) for all codewords in the span of some projected Goppa code. We shall make use of this algorithm in the next section.

Throughout the paper, we need that some projected random submatrices have full rank. The following lemma states the probability for this event.

Lemma 2. *Suppose we obtain* $\mathbf{u}_1, \ldots, \mathbf{u}_k \in \mathbb{F}_2^\ell$, $\ell > k$ *drawn independently at uniform from* $\mathbb{F}_2^\ell$. *Then* $\mathbf{u}_1, \ldots, \mathbf{u}_k$ *are linearly independent with probability* $\prod_{i=0}^{k-1} 1 - 2^{i-\ell}$.

Proof. Let E_i, $0 \leq i \leq k$ be the event that the first i vectors $\mathbf{u}_1, \ldots, \mathbf{u}_i$ form an i-dimensional space. Define $\Pr[E_0] := 1$.

Let $p_1 = \Pr[E_1]$ and $p_i = \Pr[E_i \mid E_{i-1}]$ for $2 \leq i \leq k$. Then $p_1 = 1 - \frac{1}{2^\ell}$, since we only have to exclude $\mathbf{u}_1 = 0^\ell \in \mathbb{F}_2^\ell$. Moreover for $1 < i \leq k$, we have

$$p_i = 1 - \frac{2^{i-1}}{2^\ell},$$

since $\mathbf{u}_i$ should not lie in the $(i-1)$-dimensional span $\langle \mathbf{u}_1, \ldots, \mathbf{u}_{i-1} \rangle$. We obtain

$$\begin{aligned} \Pr[E_k] &= \Pr[E_k \mid E_{k-1}] \cdot \Pr[E_{k-1}] = \ldots = \prod_{i=1}^{k} \Pr[E_i \mid E_{i-1}] \\ &= \prod_{i=1}^{k} p_i = \prod_{i=1}^{k} 1 - 2^{i-1-\ell} = \prod_{i=0}^{k-1} 1 - 2^{i-\ell}. \end{aligned}$$

□

3 Some Parts of a Secret Goppa Key Reveal Everything

Our first result states that the knowledge of all Goppa points $\alpha_1, \ldots, \alpha_n \in \mathbb{F}_{2^m}$ together with the public key $H^{\mathsf{pub}} \in \mathbb{F}_2^{tm \times n}$ allows to recover the secret Goppa polynomial $g(x)$. This result seems to be folklore knowledge and is mentioned e.g. in [22, Section 4.3] and in [1]. However, we are not aware of an algorithm, let alone a formal proof, showing such a result. We will close this gap for completeness, and also because recovery of the full secret key from *all* Goppa points is the starting point for our more advanced results that recover the secret key from only a *small fraction* of all Goppa points.

3.1 Key Recovery from ALL Goppa Points

Idea of Goppa Polynomial Recovery Algorithm for All Points. Recall from Eq. (1) that

$$C(L,g) = \left\{ \mathbf{c} \in \mathbb{F}_2^n \,:\, \sum_{i=1}^{n} \frac{c_i}{x-\alpha_i} \equiv 0 \mod g(x) \right\}.$$

Thus, for every codeword $\mathbf{c} = (c_1, \ldots, c_n) \in C(L,g)$ we have

$$\sum_{i=1}^{n} c_i \prod_{1\le j\le n, j\ne i} (x-\alpha_j) \equiv 0 \bmod g(x). \tag{3}$$

Observe that the left-hand side of Eq. (3) is a multiple of the desired Goppa polynomial $g(x)$.

The public key H^{pub} allows to easily compute a generator matrix of the code, from which we can sample random codewords $\mathbf{c} \in C(L,g)$. Our algorithm Basic-Goppa (Algorithm 3.1) now computes from a random $\mathbf{c}$ the left-hand side of Eq. (3), factors the resulting polynomial in irreducible factors, and in case there are several degree-t factors, chooses the correct Goppa polynomial using the test from Algorithm 2.1.

Algorithm 3.1. Basic-Goppa

Input: public key $H^{\mathsf{pub}} \in \mathbb{F}_2^{tm\times n}$, Goppa points $\alpha_1, \ldots, \alpha_n \in \mathbb{F}_{2^m}$
Output: Goppa polynomial $g(x)$

1: Compute a generator matrix $G \in \mathbb{F}_2^{n\times(n-tm)}$ of C as the right kernel of H^{pub}.
2: Generate $\mathbf{c} \in C \setminus \{0\}$: for some non-zero $\mathbf{m} \in \mathbb{F}_2^{n-tm}$ set $\mathbf{c} = \mathbf{m}G^{\mathsf{t}} \in \mathbb{F}_2^n$.
3: Compute $f(x) = \sum_{i=1}^{n} c_i \prod_{1\le j\le n, j\ne i}(x-\alpha_j) \in \mathbb{F}_{2^m}[x]$, see Eq. (3).
4: Factor $f(x)$ into irreducible factors over $\mathbb{F}_{2^m}$.
5: **for** all irreducible degree-t factors $\hat{g}(x)$ such that $\hat{g}(x)^2$ divides $f(x)$ **do**
6: **if** Test-Goppa-Polynomial($\hat{g}(x), \{1, \ldots, n\}, G^{\mathsf{t}}$) $= 1$ **then** output $\hat{g}(x)$.

Theorem 1. *On input of* $H^{\mathsf{pub}} \in \mathbb{F}_2^{tm\times n}$ *and all Goppa points* $\alpha_1, \ldots, \alpha_n \in \mathbb{F}_{2^m}$, *algorithm* Basic-Goppa *recovers the Goppa polynomial* $g(x)$ *in* $\widetilde{\mathcal{O}}(n^3)$ *operations in* $\mathbb{F}_{2^m}$.

Proof. From the discussion before we know that the polynomial $f(x)$ in line 3 of BASIC-GOPPA is a multiple of the Goppa polynomial $g(x)$. By Lemma 1 we know that $C(L,g) = C(L,g^2)$, and thus not only $g(x)$, but also $g^2(x)$ divides $f(x)$.

Among all potential irreducible candidates $\hat{g}(x)$ of degree t whose square divide $f(x)$, we look for a Goppa polynomial that generates our code $C(L,g)$. To this end we use TEST-GOPPA-POLYNOMIAL that checks whether all codewords generated by the basis G^{t} are in $C(L,\hat{g})$ from Eq. (1), which implies $C(L,\hat{g}) = C(L,g)$. This in turn means that $\hat{g}(x)$ defines the desired Goppa code.

This completes correctness of BASIC-GOPPA, it remains to show the run time. Using Gaussian elimination, the generator matrix G can be computed in time $\mathcal{O}(n^3)$.

The polynomial $f(x) \in \mathbb{F}_{2^m}[x]$ is of degree $n-1$. Thus, $f(x)$ can be factored in time $\widetilde{\mathcal{O}}(n^3 + n^2 \log|\mathbb{F}|) = \widetilde{\mathcal{O}}(n^3)$ operations in $\mathbb{F}_{2^m}$ [26, Section 20]. □

3.2 Goppa Polynomial Recovery from only $tm+1$ Goppa Points

In this section, we show that only $tm+1$ Goppa points together with the public key $H^{\mathsf{pub}} \in \mathbb{F}_2^{tm \times n}$ suffice to recover a list of candidate polynomials that contain the Goppa polynomial $g(x)$. Since $tm+1 \ll n$ this improves significantly over the results of the previous Sect. 3.1. For typical McEliece parameters we have $tm+1 \approx \frac{n}{4}$, i.e. only a quarter of the Goppa points suffice to recover the Goppa polynomial. In the subsequent Sect. 3.3, we further show how to efficiently compute the remaining Goppa points, thereby identifying the correct $g(x)$ and recovering the complete McEliece secret key.

Idea of Goppa Polynomial Recovery Algorithm from $tm+1$ Points. Recall from Definition 1 of a Goppa code and Eq. (1) that all Goppa codewords $\mathbf{c} = (c_1, \ldots, c_n) \in \mathbb{F}_2^n$ satisfy

$$\sum_{i=1}^{n} \frac{c_i}{x - a_i} = \sum_{i \in \mathsf{supp}(\mathbf{c})}^{n} \frac{c_i}{x - a_i} \equiv 0 \bmod g(x),$$

where $\mathrm{supp}(\mathbf{c}) = \{i \in \{1,\ldots,n\} \mid c_i \neq 0\}$ denotes the index set of non-zero coordinates in $\mathbf{c}$, called $\mathbf{c}$'s support. We conclude that

$$\sum_{i \in \mathsf{supp}(\mathbf{c})} c_i \prod_{j \in \mathsf{supp}(\mathbf{c}) \setminus \{i\}} (x - \alpha_j) \equiv 0 \bmod g(x). \tag{4}$$

Assume now that we know the Goppa points α_j within an index set $j \in \mathcal{I} \subseteq \{1,\ldots,n\}$. If we succeed to construct a codeword $\mathbf{c}$ with $\mathrm{supp}(\mathbf{c}) \subseteq \mathcal{I}$, then we can efficiently compute the left-hand side of Eq. (4).

Our main observation is that for any index set $\mathcal{I}$ with $|\mathcal{I}| > tm$ we can easily construct a non-zero codeword $\mathbf{c}$ with $\mathrm{supp}(\mathbf{c}) \in \mathcal{I}$. In a nutshell, we project the Goppa code $C(L,g)$ to the coordinates in $\mathcal{I}$. The details are provided in ADVANCED-GOPPA (Algorithm 3.2).

Algorithm 3.2. ADVANCED-GOPPA

Input: public key $H^{\mathsf{pub}} \in \mathbb{F}_2^{tm \times n}$, index set $\mathcal{I} \subset \{1, \ldots, n\}$ with $\ell := |\mathcal{I}| > tm$, Goppa points $\alpha_i \in \mathbb{F}_{2^m}$ with $i \in \mathcal{I}$

Output: list $\mathcal{L}$ of all potential Goppa polynomials $\hat{g}(x)$ with $g(x) \in \mathcal{L}$

1: Let $H^{\mathsf{pub}}[\mathcal{I}] \in \mathbb{F}_2^{tm \times \ell}$ be the projection of $H^{\mathsf{pub}} \in \mathbb{F}_2^{tm \times n}$ to the ℓ columns from $\mathcal{I}$.
2: Compute $G[\mathcal{I}] \in \mathbb{F}_2^{\ell \times (\ell - \mathsf{rank}(\bar{H}))}$ as the right kernel of $H^{\mathsf{pub}}[\mathcal{I}]$.
3: For some non-zero $\mathbf{m} \in \mathbb{F}_2^{\ell - \mathsf{rank}(H^{\mathsf{pub}}[\mathcal{I}])}$ set $\bar{\mathbf{c}} = \mathbf{m}(G[\mathcal{I}])^{\mathsf{t}} \in \mathbb{F}_2^{\ell}$.
4: Construct $\mathbf{c}$ by appending to $\bar{\mathbf{c}}$ zeros in all positions $\{1, \ldots, n\} \setminus \mathcal{I}$.
5: Compute $f(x) = \sum_{i \in \mathsf{supp}(\mathbf{c})} c_i \prod_{j \in \mathsf{supp}(\mathbf{c}) \setminus \{i\}} (x - \alpha_j) \in \mathbb{F}_{2^m}[x]$, see Eq. (4).
6: Factor $f(x)$ into irreducible factors over $\mathbb{F}_{2^m}$. Set $\mathcal{L} = \emptyset$.
7: **for** all irreducible degree-t factors $\hat{g}(x)$ such that $\hat{g}(x)^2$ divides $f(x)$ **do**
8: **if** TEST-GOPPA-POLYNOMIAL$(\hat{g}(x), \mathcal{I}, \bar{G}[I]^{\mathsf{t}}) = 1$ **then** $\mathcal{L} := \mathcal{L} \cup \hat{g}(x)$.

Theorem 2 (Goppa polynomial). *On input of $H^{\mathsf{pub}} \in \mathbb{F}_2^{tm \times n}$, an index set $\mathcal{I} \subset \{1, \ldots, n\}$ with $\ell := |\mathcal{I}| > tm$, and Goppa points $\alpha_i \in \mathbb{F}_{2^m}, i \in \mathcal{I}$, algorithm* ADVANCED-GOPPA *computes a list $\mathcal{L}$ with the Goppa polynomial $g(x) \in \mathcal{L}$ in $\widetilde{\mathcal{O}}(n^3)$ operations in $\mathbb{F}_{2^m}$.*

Proof. The correctness and run time proof for ADVANCED-GOPPA follows mostly the reasoning in the proof of Theorem 1. In addition, we have to show that ADVANCED-GOPPA constructs a non-zero codeword $\mathbf{c} \in C(L, g)$ with $\mathsf{supp}(\mathbf{c}') \in \mathcal{I}$.

Since $\ell > tm$ we have $\ell - \mathsf{rank}(\bar{H}) \geq \ell - tm > 0$. Thus, there exists some non-zero $\mathbf{m} \in \mathbb{F}_2^{\ell - \mathsf{rank}(H^{\mathsf{pub}}[\mathcal{I}])}$, and in turn some non-zero $\bar{\mathbf{c}} \in \mathbb{F}_2^{\ell}$. Since $\mathbf{c}$ is constructed from $\bar{\mathbf{c}}$ by appending zeros in positions outside $\mathcal{I}$, we have $\mathsf{supp}(\mathbf{c}) \subseteq \mathcal{I}$. Since $\bar{\mathbf{c}}$ is from the right kernel of $H^{\mathsf{pub}}[\mathcal{I}]$ we have $H^{\mathsf{pub}}[\mathcal{I}]\bar{\mathbf{c}} = 0^{tm}$, and since we append only zeros, also $H^{\mathsf{pub}}\mathbf{c} = 0^{tm}$. This shows that $\mathbf{c} \in C(L, g)$ is indeed a codeword with $\mathsf{supp}(\mathbf{c}) \in \mathcal{I}$. □

Remark 1 (less Goppa points). In the proof of Theorem 2 we construct a polynomial $\bar{\mathbf{c}}$ with Hamming weight at most ℓ, and expected Hamming weight only $\frac{\ell}{2}$. Assume that we are given an oracle $\mathcal{O}(i)$ that returns α_i. Then we could ask $\mathcal{O}(\cdot)$ on $\bar{\mathbf{c}}$'s support, i.e., on expectation only $\frac{tm+1}{2}$ Goppa points would be sufficient.

Experiments. In Table 2 we show the results of running the ADVANCED-GOPPA algorithm on Classic McEliece parameter sets, implemented in SageMath (version 9.4). For each parameter set we generated 20 different McEliece public keys, and for each key, we ran ADVANCED-GOPPA on 100 different index sets $\mathcal{I}$.

Observe from Table 2 (columns 3 and 5) that ADVANCED-GOPPA already for the minimal $\ell = tm+1$ usually only outputs the desired $g(x)$. When we increased to $\ell = tm + 2$ we never found a polynomial $\hat{g}(x) \neq g(x)$.

Larger ℓ helps TEST-GOPPA-POLYNOMIAL (Algorithm 2.1) to exclude faulty $\hat{g}$. For $\ell = tm + 1$ we have $\mathsf{rank}((G[\mathcal{I}])^{\mathsf{t}}) = 1$ with high probability, and hence there is only a single non-zero $\mathbf{c}$ in the code generated by $(G[\mathcal{I}])^{\mathsf{t}}$. In this case

Table 2. Experimental results for ADVANCED-GOPPA(Algorithm 3.2).

(n,t,m)	$\ell = tm+1$	$\|\mathcal{L}\| = 1$	$\ell = tm+2$	$\|\mathcal{L}\| = 1$	Av. time
$(3488, 64, 12)$	769	97%	770	100%	18 s
$(4608, 96, 13)$	1249	99%	1250	100%	54 s
$(6960, 119, 13)$	1548	99%	1549	100%	91 s
$(8192, 128, 13)$	1665	99%	1666	100%	105 s

TEST-GOPPA-POLYNOMIAL cannot exclude any false positive $\hat{g}$. However, for $\ell = tm+2$ we might have $\text{rank}((\bar{G})) = 2$, which lets TEST-GOPPA-POLYNOMIAL exclude faulty $\hat{g}$'s.

Our run time (last column) is averaged over all 2000 runs. Our single-threaded experiments were conducted on Intel Xeon(R) E-2146G CPU 3.50 GHz $\times$ 12, 64GiB, Ubuntu 20.04. We see that our non-optimized implementation finds the Goppa polynomial $g(x)$ for all parameter sets in a matter of seconds.

3.3 Reconstruction of the Remaining Goppa Points

In Sect. 3.2, we showed that $\ell > tm$ Goppa points are sufficient to efficiently reconstruct the Goppa polynomial $g(x)$ (or a list $\mathcal{L}$ containing $g(x)$). In this section, we show that $g(x)$ together with $\ell > tm$ Goppa points are sufficient to recover all n Goppa points from H^{pub}. This in turn implies that $\ell > tm$ Goppa points are sufficient to efficiently recover the complete McEliece secret key.

Idea of Goppa Points Recovery Algorithm from $g(x)$ and $tm+1$ Points. Assume that we know α_i for an index set $\mathcal{I}$ of size $\ell := |\mathcal{I}| > tm$. Our goal is to compute α_r for some $r \notin \mathcal{I}$.

Our idea is to construct a codeword $\mathbf{c} \in C(L, g)$ with $\text{supp}(\mathbf{c}) \setminus \mathcal{I} = \{r\}$, i.e., $\mathbf{c}$ has all but a single 1-coordinate $c_r = 1$ inside $\mathcal{I}$.

From the definition of a Goppa code in Eq. (1) we obtain

$$\sum_{i \in \mathcal{I}} \frac{c_i}{x - \alpha_i} \equiv \frac{1}{x - \alpha_r} \mod g(x). \tag{5}$$

Knowing the left-hand side and $g(x)$ enables us to compute α_r.

The high-level idea of constructing $\mathbf{c} \in C(L, g)$ with $\text{supp}(\mathbf{c}) \setminus \mathcal{I} = \{r\}$ is to express the r-th column of H^{pub} as an $\mathbb{F}_2$-sum of the ℓ columns in $H^{\mathsf{pub}}[\mathcal{I}]$. This amounts to solving a system of linear equations. The details are given in GOPPA POINTS (Algorithm 3.3) and the analysis in Theorem 3.

Theorem 3 (Goppa points). *On input $H^{\mathsf{pub}} \in \mathbb{F}_2^{tm \times n}$, the Goppa polynomial $g(x)$, an index set $\mathcal{I} \subset \{1, \ldots, n\}$ with $\ell := |\mathcal{I}| > tm$ such that* $\text{rank}(H^{\mathsf{pub}}[\mathcal{I}]) =$ *tm, and Goppa points $\alpha_i \in \mathbb{F}_{2^m}, i \in \mathcal{I}$, algorithm* GOPPA-POINTS *outputs in time $\mathcal{O}(n^4)$ all Goppa points $\alpha_1, \ldots, \alpha_n$.*

Algorithm 3.3. GOPPA-POINTS

Input: public key $H^{\mathsf{pub}} \in \mathbb{F}_2^{tm \times n}$, Goppa polynomial $g(x)$,
index set $\mathcal{I}$ with $\ell := |\mathcal{I}| > tm$ and $\text{rank}(H^{\mathsf{pub}}[\mathcal{I}]) = tm$,
Goppa points $\alpha_i \in \mathbb{F}_{2^m}$ with $i \in \mathcal{I} \subset \{1, \ldots, n\}$

Output: all Goppa points $\alpha_1, \ldots, \alpha_n \in \mathbb{F}_{2^m}$ or FAIL

1: **while** $\mathcal{I} \neq \{1, \ldots, n\}$ **do**
2: Pick $r \in \{1, \ldots, n\} \setminus \mathcal{I}$.
3: Find $\mathbf{c} \in \mathbb{F}_2^{|\mathcal{I}|}$ that solves the linear equation system $H^{\mathsf{pub}}[J]\mathbf{c} = H^{\mathsf{pub}}[\{r\}]$.
4: Compute $f(x) = \left(\sum_{i \in \mathcal{I}} \frac{c_i}{x - \alpha_i}\right)^{-1} \bmod g(x)$ using Eq. (5).
5: **if** $f(x)$ is of the form $x - \alpha_r$ **then** output α_r,
6: **else** output FAIL.
7: Set $\mathcal{I} \leftarrow \mathcal{I} \cup \{r\}$.

Proof. Let us first address the correctness of GOPPA-POINTS. Since we require $\text{rank}(H^{\mathsf{pub}}[\mathcal{I}]) = tm$ the linear equation equation system $H^{\mathsf{pub}}[J]\mathbf{c} = H^{\mathsf{pub}}[\{r\}]$ in line 3 is always solvable.

Thus, GOPPA-POINTS constructs a solution $\mathbf{c} \in \mathbb{F}_2^{|\mathcal{I}|}$. Define $\mathbf{c}'$ by appending to $\mathbf{c}$ a 1-coordinate in the r position, and 0-coordinates in all positions from $\{1, \ldots, n\} \setminus \{\mathcal{I} \cup \{r\}\}$. By construction $H^{\mathsf{pub}}\mathbf{c}' = 0^{tm}$, and therefore $\mathbf{c}' \in C(L, g)$ with $\text{supp}(\mathbf{c}') \in \mathcal{I} \cup \{r\}$. This allows us to solve for α_r using Eq. (5) in line 4.

By Eq. (5) we always have $f(x) = x - \alpha_r$, and thus we output another Goppa point in line 5. The purpose of the else-Statement in line 6 is to identify incorrect inputs, either incorrect $\hat{g}(x)$ or faulty Goppa points $\tilde{\alpha}_i$. We come back to this issue in Sect. 3.4 and Sect. 4.

GOPPA-POINTS's runtime is dominated by running Gaussian elimination in line 3 for computing $\mathbf{c}$. Gaussian elimination runs in $\mathcal{O}(n^3)$ steps in each of the $n - \ell$ iterations, resulting in total run time $\mathcal{O}(n^4)$. □

Table 3. Experimental results for GOPPA-POINTS (Algorithm 3.3).

(n, t, m)	$\ell = tm + 1$	time
$(3488, 64, 12)$	769	42 s
$(4608, 96, 13)$	1249	130 s
$(6960, 119, 13)$	1548	167 s
$(8192, 128, 13)$	1665	183 s

Experiments. Table 3 shows how Algorithm 3.3 performs in practice.

Analogous to the experiments in Sect. 3.2, we generated 20 different McEliece public key, and for each of them we ran 100 experiments with different index sets $\mathcal{I}$. We averaged the run time over all 2000 experiments.

Again, we see that recovering all remaining $n - \ell$ Goppa points is with our (non-optimized) implementation realized in a matter of seconds.

Remark 2 (Non-full rank). The condition $\text{rank}(H^{\mathsf{pub}}[\mathcal{I}]) = tm$ in GOPPA-POINTS is required to solve the equation system in line 3. However, we would like to stress that GOPPA-POINTS allows to successfully recover some Goppa points even in the case $\text{rank}(H^{\mathsf{pub}}[\mathcal{I}]) < tm$. In this case, the equation system in line 3 is solvable by the famous Rouché-Capelli theorem iff

$$\text{rank}(H^{\mathsf{pub}}[\mathcal{I}]) = \text{rank}(H^{\mathsf{pub}}[\mathcal{I} \cup \{r\}]). \tag{6}$$

Thus, we can modify Line 2 such that we choose only r satisfying Equation (6). All corresponding α_r can still be computed by GOPPA-POINTS. E.g. for $\text{rank}(H^{\mathsf{pub}}[\mathcal{I}]) = tm - 1$ we expect that GOPPA-POINTS still computes $\frac{n-\ell}{2}$, i.e., half of all remaining Goppa points.

Remark 3 (Probability of full rank). Assume that we obtain an index set $\mathcal{I}$ of size $\ell \geq tm + 1$ chosen uniformly at random from $\{1, \ldots, n\}$. Under the assumption that H^{pub} behaves like a random matrix over $\mathbb{F}_2$, Lemma 2 shows that we are in the full-rank case $\text{rank}(H^{\mathsf{pub}}[\mathcal{I}]) = tm$ with probability at least

$$\prod_{i=0}^{tm-1} 1 - 2^{i-\ell} \geq \prod_{i=0}^{tm-1} 1 - 2^{i-tm-1} = \prod_{i=2}^{tm+1} 1 - 2^{-i} \geq \lim_{n \to \infty} \left(\prod_{i=2}^{n} 1 - 2^{-i} \right) \approx 0.58.$$

3.4 Full Key Recovery from $tm + 1$ Goppa Points

Combining Theorem 2 and Theorem 3, we obtain a full key recovery algorithm from at least $tm + 1$ Goppa points. The algorithm KEY-RECOVERY that successively runs ADVANCED-GOPPA and GOPPA-POINTS is described in Algorithm 3.4.

Theorem 4 (Key Recovery). *On input of $H^{\mathsf{pub}} \in \mathbb{F}_2^{tm \times n}$, an index set $\mathcal{I} \subset \{1, \ldots, n\}$ with $\ell := |\mathcal{I}| > tm$ such that $\text{rank}(H^{\mathsf{pub}}[\mathcal{I}]) = tm$, and Goppa points $\alpha_i \in \mathbb{F}_{2^m}, i \in \mathcal{I}$, algorithm KEY-RECOVERY outputs in time $\mathcal{O}\left(\frac{n^5}{t}\right) = \mathcal{O}(n^5)$ the Goppa polynomial $g(x)$ and all Goppa points $\alpha_1, \ldots, \alpha_n$.*

Proof. Let us first show correctness. KEY-RECOVERY calls ADVANCED-GOPPA Algorithm 3.2 and recovers a list $\mathcal{L}$ that contains the correct Goppa polynomial $g(x)$. Then for every candidate $\hat{g}(x)$ in line 3 KEY-RECOVERY tries to recover all remaining Goppa points. Usually, GOPPA-POINTS immediately fails on incorrect $\hat{g}(x)$.

Notice that the correct polynomial $g(x)$ is always contained in $\mathcal{L}$, thus by Theorems 2 and 3 the loop in line 3 recovers at least one key candidate k_i.

Algorithm 3.4. KEY-RECOVERY

Input: public key $H^{\mathsf{pub}} \in \mathbb{F}_2^{tm \times n}$,
index set $\mathcal{I}$ with $\ell := |\mathcal{I}| > tm$ and $\text{rank}(H^{\mathsf{pub}}[\mathcal{I}]) = tm$,
Goppa points $\alpha_i \in \mathbb{F}_{2^m}$ with $i \in \mathcal{I} \subset \{1, \ldots, n\}$

Output: Goppa polynomial $g(x)$, all Goppa points $\alpha_1, \ldots, \alpha_n \in \mathbb{F}_{2^m}$

1: Run $\mathcal{L} \leftarrow$ADVANCED-GOPPA$(H^{\mathsf{pub}}, \mathcal{I}, \{\alpha_i\}_{i \in \mathcal{I}})$
2: $i := 0$
3: **for** every $\hat{g}(x) \in \mathcal{L}$ **do**
4:     **if** GOPPA-POINTS$(H^{\mathsf{pub}}, \hat{g}(x), \mathcal{I}, \{\alpha_i\}_{i \in \mathcal{I}}) \neq$ FAIL **then**
5:         $i \leftarrow i + 1$
6:         $k_i \leftarrow (\hat{g}(x), \alpha_1, \ldots, \alpha_n)$
7: **if** $i = 1$ **then** output $k_1 = (\hat{g}(x), \alpha_1, \ldots, \alpha_n)$.
8: **else** check $k_1, \ldots, k_i$ via a transformation to public key and comparison with H^{pub}.

Thus, we either output the correct key in line 7, or find among more than one candidate k_i the correct key in line 8. Our check in line 8 uses McEliece's deterministic transformation from secret to public key, and thereby assures that we output the correct key.

Let us consider run time. ADVANCED-GOPPA factors in Eq. (4) polynomials of degree at most $\ell \leq n$. A candidate polynomial $\hat{g}(x)$ from $\mathcal{L}$ must have degree t, and appear as a square in the factorization. Thus, $|\mathcal{L}| = \mathcal{O}(n/t)$. KEY-RECOVERY's run time is dominated by the loop in line 3, running GOPPA-POINTS in time $\mathcal{O}(n^4)$ for $|\mathcal{L}|$ iterations. The run time follows. □

Experiments. Run times of our KEY-RECOVERY (Algorithm 3.4) experiments are provided in Table 1. Since almost always $|\mathcal{L}| = 1$, i.e., ADVANCED-GOPPA finds only the correct Goppa polynomial, KEY-RECOVERY's runtime is mainly the sum of the runtimes of ADVANCED-GOPPA and of GOPPA-POINTS (compare with Tables 2 and 3).

We would like to stress that we never found an example of more than a single key k_1, thus we never had to apply the key check in line 8 of KEY-RECOVERY.

4 Correcting Faulty Goppa Points

Error Model. In practice, one might be able (e.g. via some side-channel) to obtain erroneous Goppa points. Assume the following simple error model. An attacker obtains erroneous Goppa points $\tilde{\alpha}_1, \ldots \tilde{\alpha}_n$, where each $\tilde{\alpha}_i \in \mathbb{F}_{2^m}$ is correct with probability $1 - p$, and faulty with probability p for some constant $0 < p < 1$. In case $\tilde{\alpha}_i$ is faulty, we assume that $\tilde{\alpha}_i$ is uniformly distributed (among all incorrect values). More precisely, for all $1 \leq i \leq n$ we have

$$\Pr[\tilde{\alpha}_i = \alpha_i] = 1 - p \text{ and } \Pr[\tilde{\alpha}_i = y \mid \tilde{\alpha}_i \neq \alpha_i] = \frac{1}{2^m - 1} \text{ for all } y \in \mathbb{F}_{2^m} \setminus \{\alpha_i\}.$$

We now show that our algorithm KEY-RECOVERY nicely extends to the error scenario, but we have to sacrifice polynomial run time.

Idea of Faulty Goppa Point Correction. Recall that KEY-RECOVERY from Sect. 3.4 requires only $tm + 1 \ll n$ correct Goppa points to recover the secret key. The basic idea of our correction algorithm is to guess a size-$(tm + 1)$ subset of $\tilde{\alpha}_1, \ldots \tilde{\alpha}_n$ that contains only correct Goppa points. Thus, our algorithm is reminiscent of Prange's *information set decoding* [25].

To this end we have to be cautious, since the correctness proof of KEY-RECOVERY only guarantees that KEY-RECOVERY outputs the correct key when run on error-free α_i's. Therefore, we modify KEY-RECOVERY to FAULTY-KEY-RECOVERY that also handles erroneous inputs.

FAULTY-KEY-RECOVERY (see Algorithm 4.1) provides the following additional checks. Line 2 aborts, when ADVANCED-GOPPA does not find a candidate for the Goppa polynomial. This usually happens for faulty α_i, since Eq. (4) only holds for correct Goppa points. Moreover, line 5 aborts, when GOPPA-POINTS fails, because Eq. (5) does not hold for incorrect Goppa points. We build in additional checks in lines 8 and 9 in order to prove correctness of our Goppa point correction algorithm. However, we experimentally observe that lines 2 and 5 seem to capture already all faults in practice.

Algorithm 4.1. FAULT-KEY-RECOVERY

Input: public key $H^{\mathsf{pub}} \in \mathbb{F}_2^{tm \times n}$,
index set $\mathcal{I}$ with $\ell := |\mathcal{I}| > tm$ and $\text{rank}(H^{\mathsf{pub}}[\mathcal{I}]) = tm$,
Goppa points $\alpha_i \in \mathbb{F}_{2^m}$ with $i \in \mathcal{I} \subset \{1, \ldots, n\}$

Output: Goppa polynomial $g(x)$, all Goppa points $\alpha_1, \ldots, \alpha_n \in \mathbb{F}_{2^m}$ or FAIL

1: Run $\mathcal{L} \leftarrow$ADVANCED-GOPPA$(H^{\mathsf{pub}}, \mathcal{I}, \{\alpha_i\}_{i \in \mathcal{I}})$
2: **if** $|\mathcal{L}| = 0$ **then** output FAIL.
3: $i := 0$
4: **for** every $\hat{g}(x) \in \mathcal{L}$ **do**
5:     **if** GOPPA-POINTS$(H^{\mathsf{pub}}, \hat{g}(x), \mathcal{I}, \{\alpha_i\}_{i \in \mathcal{I}}) \neq$ FAIL **then**
6:         $i \leftarrow i + 1$
7:         $k_i \leftarrow (\hat{g}(x), \alpha_1, \ldots, \alpha_n)$
8: **if** $i = 0$ **then** output FAIL.
9: **else** check $k_1, \ldots, k_i$ via a transformation to public key and comparison with H^{pub}. If none of $k_1, \ldots, k_i$ is the correct key, output FAIL.

Our algorithm FAULTY-GOPPA (Algorithm 4.2) now calls FAULT-KEY-RECOVERY to check for error-freeness of the chosen size-$(tm+1)$ subset of Goppa points, and recovers the key for an error-free subset.

Theorem 5. *On input $H^{\mathsf{pub}} \in \mathbb{F}_2^{tm \times n}$, and erroneous Goppa points $\tilde{\alpha}_1, \ldots \tilde{\alpha}_n$, where pn α_i are faulty and $n(1-p) \geq tm+1$,* FAULTY-GOPPA *outputs the Goppa polynomial $g(x)$ and the Goppa points $\alpha_1, \ldots, \alpha_n$ in expected time*

Algorithm 4.2. FAULTY-GOPPA

Input:	public key $H^{\mathsf{pub}} \in \mathbb{F}_2^{tm \times n}$, erroneous Goppa points $\tilde{\alpha}_1, \ldots, \tilde{\alpha}_n \in \mathbb{F}_{2^m}$
Output:	Goppa polynomial $g(x)$, Goppa points $\alpha_1, \ldots, \alpha_n$

1: **repeat**
2: Choose uniformly $\mathcal{I} \subset \{1, \ldots, n\}$, $|\mathcal{I}| = tm + 1$ s.t. $\text{rank}(H^{\mathsf{pub}}[\mathcal{I}]) = tm$.
3: **until** FAULTY-KEY-RECOVERY$(H^{\mathsf{pub}}, \mathcal{I}, \{\alpha_i\}_{i \in \mathcal{I}}) \neq$ FAIL.

$$T = \mathcal{O}\left(n^5 \cdot \frac{\binom{n}{tm+1}}{\binom{n(1-p)}{tm+1}}\right).$$

The run time can only be proven under the assumption that H^{pub} behaves like a random matrix over $\mathbb{F}_2$.

Proof. Let us first show correctness. Theorem 4 ensures that KEY-RECOVERY and therefore also FAULTY-KEY-RECOVERY outputs the correct key when run on an error-free Goppa point subset $\{\alpha_i\}_{i \in \mathcal{I}}$, since the additional checks in lines 2, 5, 8 and 9 never apply. Moreover, these checks guarantee that FAULTY-KEY-RECOVERY either outputs FAIL, or the correct secret key.

Let us now prove FAULTY-GOPPA's expected run time. The input contains $n(1-p)$ correct Goppa points, and the probability that we choose an index set $\mathcal{I}$ of size $tm + 1$ with only error-free Goppa points is

$$p_0 := \Pr[\{\alpha_i\}_{i \in \mathcal{I}} \text{ error-free}] = \frac{\binom{n(1-p)}{tm+1}}{\binom{n}{tm+1}}.$$

By Lemma 2, we have $\text{rank}(H^{\mathsf{pub}}[\mathcal{I}]) = tm$ with probability at least $\frac{1}{2}$, if H^{pub} behaves like a random matrix. Thus, we have to run an expected number of $\mathcal{O}(p_0^{-1})$ iterations, until we discover an error-free Goppa point subset. Since in each iteration we run FAULTY-KEY-RECOVERY, and FAULTY-KEY-RECOVERY has the same asymptotic run time $\mathcal{O}(n^5)$ as KEY-RECOVERY, the run time follows. □

Run Time Discussion. Assume that $tm + 1 = cn$ for some constant c, typically $c = \frac{1}{4}$ for McEliece instantiations. Using Stirling's formula and the binary entropy function $\mathcal{H}(\cdot)$, one can express FAULTY-GOPPA's run time T in Theorem 5 (neglecting polynomial factors) as the *exponential run time*

$$2^{\left(\mathcal{H}(c) - \mathcal{H}\left(\frac{c}{1-p}\right)(1-p)\right)n}.$$

Experiments. In our experiments, we wanted to understand which checks of FAULTY-KEY-RECOVERY lead to FAIL. To this end, for each Classic McEliece parameter set we started with error-free Goppa points $\alpha_1, \ldots, \alpha_n$, chose a size-$(tm+1)$ subset thereof, and injected a single faulty $\tilde{\alpha}_i$ in this subset. We consider this the hardest case for letting FAULTY-KEY-RECOVERY fail. We ran FAULTY-KEY-RECOVERY on 100 of these injected faulty instances. We then repeated the experiments with two injected faults.

Our results are presented in Table 4. We provide the percentages of FAIL events caused by either line 2 or line 5 of FAULTY-KEY-RECOVERY. All faulty keys were detected by these two checks, the additional checks of lines 8 and 9 were never applied.

From Table 4 we observe that if we run FAULTY-KEY-RECOVERY with a single injected fault, it still recovers the correct Goppa polynomial $g(x)$ with probability roughly 1/2. This happens, since a codeword $\mathbf{c}$ constructed inside ADVANCED-GOPPA may have a 0-coordinate on the position of the faulty $\tilde{\alpha}_i$. This probability drops to at most 29%, when the input set has two faulty Goppa points, since now ADVANCED-GOPPA needs a $\mathbf{c}$ with 0-coordinates on these two faulty positions. However, our subroutine GOPPA-POINTS inside FAULTY-KEY-RECOVERY eventually detected all faulty inputs via Eq. (5) in our experiments.

Table 4. Occurrences of two FAIL events in FAULTY-KEY-RECOVERY, when either 1 (left part), or 2 (right part) faulty α's are injected in the index set.

(n, t, m)	1 fault in $tm + 1$ points		2 faults in $tm + 1$ points	
	line 2	line 5	line 2	line 5
$(3488, 64, 12)$	46%	54%	71%	29%
$(4608, 96, 13)$	50%	50%	80%	20%
$(6960, 119, 13)$	51%	49%	83%	17%
$(8192, 128, 13)$	52%	48%	84%	16%

Acknowledgments. Elena Kirshanova is supported by the Young Russian Mathematics scholarship and by the Russian Science Foundation grant N 22-41-04411, https://rscf.ru/project/22-41-04411/. Alexander May is funded by the Deutsche Forschungsgemeinschaft (DFG, German Research Foundation) – grants 465120249; 390781972.

References

1. Albrecht, M.R., et al.: Classic McEliece: Conservative Code-Based Cryptography (2020). https://classic.mceliece.org/nist/mceliece-20201010.pdf
2. Becker, A., Joux, A., May, A., Meurer, A.: Decoding random binary linear codes in $2^{n/20}$: how $1 + 1 = 0$ improves information set decoding. In: Pointcheval, D., Johansson, T. (eds.) EUROCRYPT 2012. LNCS, vol. 7237, pp. 520–536. Springer, Heidelberg (2012). https://doi.org/10.1007/978-3-642-29011-4_31
3. Bernstein, D.J., Lange, T., Peters, C.: Attacking and defending the McEliece cryptosystem. In: Buchmann, J., Ding, J. (eds.) PQCrypto 2008. LNCS, vol. 5299, pp. 31–46. Springer, Heidelberg (2008). https://doi.org/10.1007/978-3-540-88403-3_3

4. Bernstein, D.J., Lange, T., Peters, C.: Smaller decoding exponents: ball-collision decoding. In: Rogaway, P. (ed.) CRYPTO 2011. LNCS, vol. 6841, pp. 743–760. Springer, Heidelberg (2011). https://doi.org/10.1007/978-3-642-22792-9_42
5. Bernstein, D.J., Lange, T., Peters, C.: Wild McEliece. In: Biryukov, A., Gong, G., Stinson, D.R. (eds.) SAC 2010. LNCS, vol. 6544, pp. 143–158. Springer, Heidelberg (2011). https://doi.org/10.1007/978-3-642-19574-7_10
6. Boneh, D., Durfee, G., Frankel, Y.: An attack on RSA given a small fraction of the private key bits. In: Ohta, K., Pei, D. (eds.) ASIACRYPT 1998. LNCS, vol. 1514, pp. 25–34. Springer, Heidelberg (1998). https://doi.org/10.1007/3-540-49649-1_3
7. Chou, T.: McBits revisited. In: Fischer, W., Homma, N. (eds.) CHES 2017. LNCS, vol. 10529, pp. 213–231. Springer, Cham (2017). https://doi.org/10.1007/978-3-319-66787-4_11
8. Coppersmith, D.: Small solutions to polynomial equations, and low exponent RSA vulnerabilities. J. Cryptol. **10**(4), 233–260 (1997)
9. Dachman-Soled, D., Gong, H., Kulkarni, M., Shahverdi, A.: (In)security of ring-LWE under partial key exposure. J. Math. Cryptol. **15**(1), 72–86 (2021)
10. Engelbert, D., Overbeck, R., Schmidt, A.: A summary of McEliece-type cryptosystems and their security. J. Math. Cryptol. **1**(2), 151–199 (2007)
11. Ernst, M., Jochemsz, E., May, A., de Weger, B.: Partial key exposure attacks on RSA up to full size exponents. In: Cramer, R. (ed.) EUROCRYPT 2005. LNCS, vol. 3494, pp. 371–386. Springer, Heidelberg (2005). https://doi.org/10.1007/11426639_22
12. Esser, A., May, A., Verbel, J., Wen, W.: Partial key exposure attacks on BIKE, Rainbow and NTRU. In: CRYPTO. Lecture Notes in Computer Science. Springer (2022)
13. Esser, A., May, A., Zweydinger, F.: McEliece needs a break-solving McEliece-1284 and quasi-cyclic-2918 with modern ISD. In: Dunkelman, O., Dziembowski, S. (eds.) EUROCRYPT 2022. LNCS, vol. 13277, pp. 433–457. Springer, Cham (2022). https://doi.org/10.1007/978-3-031-07082-2_16
14. Faugère, J., Gauthier-Umaña, V., Otmani, A., Perret, L., Tillich, J.: A distinguisher for high rate McEliece cryptosystems. In: ITW, pp. 282–286. IEEE (2011)
15. Gennaro, R.: An improved pseudo-random generator based on the discrete logarithm problem. J. Cryptol. **18**(2), 91–110 (2005)
16. Goppa, V.D.: A new class of linear correcting codes. Probl. Peredachi Inf. **6**, 207–212 (1970)
17. Loidreau, P., Sendrier, N.: Weak keys in the McEliece public-key cryptosystem. IEEE Trans. Inf. Theor. **47**(3), 1207–1211 (2006)
18. May, A., Meurer, A., Thomae, E.: Decoding random linear codes in $\tilde{\mathcal{O}}(2^{0.054n})$. In: Lee, D.H., Wang, X. (eds.) ASIACRYPT 2011. LNCS, vol. 7073, pp. 107–124. Springer, Heidelberg (2011). https://doi.org/10.1007/978-3-642-25385-0_6
19. May, A., Nowakowski, J., Sarkar, S.: Partial key exposure attack on short secret exponent CRT-RSA. In: Tibouchi, M., Wang, H. (eds.) ASIACRYPT 2021. LNCS, vol. 13090, pp. 99–129. Springer, Cham (2021). https://doi.org/10.1007/978-3-030-92062-3_4
20. May, A., Nowakowski, J., Sarkar, S.: Approximate divisor multiples – factoring with only a third of the secret CRT-exponents. In: Dunkelman, O., Dziembowski, S. (eds.) EUROCRYPT 2022. LNCS, vol. 13277, pp. 147–167. Springer, Cham (2022). https://doi.org/10.1007/978-3-031-07082-2_6

21. May, A., Ozerov, I.: On computing nearest neighbors with applications to decoding of binary linear codes. In: Oswald, E., Fischlin, M. (eds.) EUROCRYPT 2015. LNCS, vol. 9056, pp. 203–228. Springer, Heidelberg (2015). https://doi.org/10.1007/978-3-662-46800-5_9
22. Overbeck, R., Sendrier, N.: Code-based cryptography. In: Bernstein, D.J., Buchmann, J., Dahmen, E. (eds.) Post-Quantum Cryptography, pp. 95–145. Springer, Heidelberg (2009). https://doi.org/10.1007/978-3-540-88702-7_4
23. Patel, S., Sundaram, G.S.: An efficient discrete log pseudo random generator. In: Krawczyk, H. (ed.) CRYPTO 1998. LNCS, vol. 1462, pp. 304–317. Springer, Heidelberg (1998). https://doi.org/10.1007/BFb0055737
24. Paterson, K.G., Villanueva-Polanco, R.: Cold boot attacks on NTRU. In: Patra, A., Smart, N.P. (eds.) INDOCRYPT 2017. LNCS, vol. 10698, pp. 107–125. Springer, Cham (2017). https://doi.org/10.1007/978-3-319-71667-1_6
25. Prange, E.: The use of information sets in decoding cyclic codes. IRE Trans. Inf. Theory **8**(5), 5–9 (1962). https://doi.org/10.1109/TIT.1962.1057777
26. Shoup, V.: A Computational Introduction to Number Theory and Algebra. Cambridge University Press, Cambridge (2005)
27. Sidelnikov, V.M., Shestakov, S.O.: On insecurity of cryptosystems based on generalized Reed-Solomon codes. Discrete Math. Appl. **2**, 439–444 (1992)
28. Suzuki, K., Takayasu, A., Kunihiro, N.: Extended partial key exposure attacks on RSA: improvement up to full size decryption exponents. Theor. Comput. Sci. **841**, 62–83 (2020)
29. Villanueva-Polanco, R.: Cold boot attacks on bliss. In: Schwabe, P., Thériault, N. (eds.) LATINCRYPT 2019. LNCS, vol. 11774, pp. 40–61. Springer, Cham (2019). https://doi.org/10.1007/978-3-030-30530-7_3
30. Villanueva-Polanco, R.: Cold boot attacks on post-quantum schemes. Ph.D. thesis, Royal Holloway, University of London, Egham, UK (2019)
31. Villanueva-Polanco, R.: Cold boot attacks on LUOV. Appl. Sci. **10**(12), 4106 (2020)

Cost-Asymmetric Memory Hard Password Hashing

Wenjie Bai, Jeremiah Blocki[✉], and Mohammad Hassan Ameri

Purdue University, West Lafayette, IN 47907, USA
{bai104,jblocki,mameriek}@purdue.edu

Abstract. In the past decade billions of user passwords have been exposed to the dangerous threat of offline password cracking attacks. An offline attacker who has stolen the cryptographic hash of a user's password can check as many password guesses as s/he likes limited only by the resources that s/he is willing to invest to crack the password. Pepper and key-stretching are two techniques that have been proposed to deter an offline attacker by increasing guessing costs. Pepper ensures that the cost of rejecting an incorrect password guess is higher than the (expected) cost of verifying a correct password guess. This is useful because most of the offline attacker's guesses will be incorrect. Unfortunately, as we observe the traditional peppering defense seems to be incompatible with modern memory hard key-stretching algorithms such as Argon2 or Scrypt. We introduce an alternative to pepper which we call Cost-Asymmetric Memory Hard Password Authentication which benefits from the same cost-asymmetry as the classical peppering defense i.e., the cost of rejecting an incorrect password guess is larger than the expected cost to authenticate a correct password guess. When configured properly we prove that our mechanism can only reduce the percentage of user passwords that are cracked by a rational offline attacker whose goal is to maximize (expected) profit i.e., the total value of cracked passwords minus the total guessing costs. We evaluate the effectiveness of our mechanism on empirical password datasets against a rational offline attacker. Our empirical analysis shows that our mechanism can significantly reduce the percentage of user passwords that are cracked by a rational attacker by up to 10%.

Keywords: Memory Hard Functions · Password Authentication · Stackelberg Game

1 Introduction

In the past decade data-breaches have exposed billions of user passwords to the dangerous threat of offline password cracking. An offline attacker has stolen the cryptographic hash $h_u = H(pw_u, salt_u)$ of a target user (u) and can validate as many password guesses as s/he likes without getting locked out i.e., given h_u

C. Galdi and S. Jarecki (Eds.): SCN 2022, LNCS 13409, pp. 21–44, 2022.
https://doi.org/10.1007/978-3-031-14791-3_2

and $salt_u$[1] the attacker can check if $pw_u = pw'$ by computing $h' = H(pw', salt_u)$ and comparing the hash value with h_u. Despite all of the security problems text passwords remain entrenched as the dominant form of authentication online and are unlikely to be replaced in the near future [17]. Thus, it is imperitive to develop tools to deter offline attackers.

An offline attacker is limited only by the resources s/he is willing to invest in cracking the password and a rational attacker will fix a guessing budget to optimally balance guessing costs with the expected value of the cracked passwords. Key-Stretching functions intentionally increase the cost of the hash function H to ensure that an offline attack is as expensive as possible. Hash iteration is a simple technique to increase guessing costs i.e., instead of storing $(u, salt_u, h_u = H(pw_u, salt_u))$ the authentication server would store $(u, salt_u, h_u = H^t(pw_u, salt_u))$ where $H^{i+1}(x) := H(H^i(x))$ and $H^1(x) := H(x)$. Hash iteration is the traditional key-stretching method which is used by password hashing algorithms such as PBKDF2 [27] and BCRYPT [36]. Intuitively, the cost of evaluating a function like PBKDF2 or BCRYPT scales linearly with the hash-iteration parameter t which, in turn, is directly correlated with authentication delay. Cryptocurrencies have hastened the development of Application Specific Integrated Circuits (ASICs) to rapidly evaluate cryptographic hash functions such as SHA2 and SHA3 since mining often involves repeated evaluation of a hash function $H(\cdot)$. In theory an offline attacker could use ASICs to substantially reduce the cost of checking password guesses. In fact, Blocki et al. [13] argued that functions like BCRYPT or PBKDF2 cannot provide adequate protection against an offline attacker without introducing an unacceptable authentication delay e.g., 2 min.

Memory-Hard Functions (MHFs) [35] have been introduced to address the short-comings of hash-iteration based key-stretching algorithms like BCRYPT and PBKDF2. Candidate MHFs include SCRYPT [35], Argon2 (which was declared as the winner of Password Hashing Competition [2] in 2015) and DRSample [5]. Intuitively, a password hash function is memory hard if any algorithm evaluating this function must lock up large quantities of memory for the duration of computation. One advantage of this approach is that RAM is an expensive resource even on an ASIC leading to egalitarian costs i.e., the attacker cannot substantially reduce the cost of evaluating the hash function using customized hardware. The second advantage is that the Area-Time cost associated with a memory hard function can scale quadratically in the running time parameter t. Intuitively, the honest party can evaluate the hash function $\mathsf{MHF}(\cdot; t)$ in time t, while any attacker evaluating the function must lock up t blocks of memory for t steps i.e., the Area-Time cost is t^2. The running time parameter t is

[1] The salt value protects against pre-computation attacks such as rainbow tables and ensures that the attacker must crack each individual password separately. For example, even if Alice and Bob select the same password $pw_A = pw_B$ their password hashes will almost certainly be different i.e., $h_A = H(pw_A, salt_A) \neq H(pw_B, salt_B) = h_B$ due to the different choice of values and collision resistance of the cryptographic hash function H.

constrained by user patience as we wish to avoid introducing an unacceptably long delay while the honest authentication server evaluates the password hash function during user authentication. Thus, quadratic cost scaling is desireable as it allows an authentication server to increase password guessing costs rapidly without necessarily introducing an unacceptable authentication delay.

Peppering [32] is an alternative defense against an offline password attacker. Intuitively, the idea is for a server to store $(u, salt_u, h_u = H(pw_u, salt_u, x_u))$. Unlike the random salt value $salt_u$, the random pepper value $x_u \in [1, x_{max}]$ is *not* stored on the authentication server. Thus, to verify a password guess pw' the authentication server must compute $h_1 = H(pw', salt_u, 1), \ldots, h_{x_{max}} = H(pw', salt_u, x_{max})$. If $pw' = pw_u$ then we will have $h_{x_u} = h_u$ and authentication will succeed. On the other hand, if $pw' \neq pw_u$ then we will have $h_i \neq h_u$ for all $i \leq x_{max}$ and authentication will fail. In the first case (correct login) the authentication server will not need to compute $h_i = H(pw', salt_u, i)$ for any $i > x_u$, while in the second case (incorrect guess) the authentication server will need to evaluate h_i for every $i \leq x_{max}$. Thus, the expected cost to verify a correct password guess is lower than the cost of rejecting an incorrect password guess. This can be a desirable property as a password attacker will spend most of his time eliminating incorrect password guesses, while most of the login attempts sent to the authentication server will be correct.

A natural question is whether or not we can combine peppering with Memory Hard Functions to obtain both benefits: quadratic cost scaling and cost-asymmetry.

Question 1. Can we design a password authentication mechanism that incorporates **cost-asymmetry** into ASIC resistant Memory Hard Functions while having the benefits of **fully quadratic cost scaling** under the the constraints of authentication delay and expected workload?

Naive Approach: At first glance it seems trivial to integrate pepper with a memory hard function $\mathsf{MHF}(\cdot)$ e.g., when a new user u registers with password pw_u we can simply pick our random pepper $x_u \in [1, x_{max}]$, salt $salt_u$, compute $h_u = \mathsf{MHF}(pw_u, salt_u, x_u; t)$ and store the tuple $(u, salt_u, h_u)$. Unfortunately, the solution above is overly simplistic. How should the parameters be set? We first observe that the authentication delay for our above solution can be as large as $t \cdot x_{max}$ since we may need to compute $\mathsf{MHF}(pw, salt_u, x; t)$ for every value of $x \in [1, x_{max}]$ and this computation must be carried out sequentially to reap the cost-asymmetry benefits of pepper. Similarly, the Area-Time cost for the attacker to evaluate $\mathsf{MHF}(pw, salt_u, x; t)$ for every value of $x \in [1, x_{max}]$ would scale with $t^2 \cdot x_{max}$. This may seem reasonable at first glance, but what if the authentication server had not used pepper and instead stored $h_u = \mathsf{MHF}(pw_u, salt_u; t \cdot x_{max})$ using the running time parameter $t' = t \cdot x_{max}$? In this case the authentication delay is identical, but the attacker's Area-Time cost would be $t'^2 = t^2 \cdot x_{max}^2$—an increase of x_{max} in comparison to the naive solution. Thus, the naive approach to integrate pepper and memory hard functions loses much of the benefit of quadratic scaling.

Halting Puzzles: Boyen [18] introduced the notion of a halting puzzle where the "pepper" value is replaced with a random running time parameter. In particular, when a new user u registers with a password pw_u we can pick our random running time parameter $t_u \in [1, t_{max}]$ along with $salt_u$ and store $(u, salt_u, h_u)$ where $h_u = \mathsf{MHF}(pw_u, salt_u; t_u)$. Given a password guess pw' the authentication server will locate $salt_u, h_u$ and accept if and only if $h_u = \mathsf{MHF}(pw', salt_u; t)$ for some $t \in [1, t_{max}]$. All memory hard functions $\mathsf{MHF}(w;t)$ we are aware of generate a stream of data-labels $L_1, \ldots, L_t$ where $L_i = \mathsf{MHF}(w;i)$ and L_{i+1} can be computed quickly once the prior labels $L_1, \ldots, L_i$ are all stored in memory e.g., we might have $L_{i+1} = H(L_{i-1}, L_j)$ where $j < i-1$ and H is the underlying cryptographic hash function. Thus, whenever the user attempts to login with password pw'_u the honest server can simply start computing $\mathsf{MHF}(pw'_u, salt_u; t_{max})$ to generate a stream of labels $L'_1, L'_2, \ldots$ and immediately accept if the server finds some label $i \leq t$ which matches the password hash i.e., $L_i = h_u$. Observe that whenever the user enters the correct password $pw'_u = pw_u$ the honest authentication server will be able to halt early after just $t_u \leq t_{max}$ iterations. By constrast, the only way to definitely reject an incorrect password pw'_u is to finish computing $\mathsf{MHF}(pw'_u, salt_u; i)$. The authentication delay is at most t_{max} and it seems like the attacker's area-time cost will scale quadratically i.e., t^2_{max}. Thus, the solution ostensibly seems to benefit from quadratic cost scaling and cost-asymmetry.

However, we observe that an attacker might not choose to compute the entire function $\mathsf{MHF}(pw', salt_u; t)$ for each password guess. For example, suppose that, as proposed in [18], the running time parameter t_u is selected uniformly at random in the range $[1, t_{max}]$, but for each password guess pw' in the attacker's dictionary the attacker only computes $\mathsf{MHF}(pw', salt_u; t_{max}/3)$ to compare the stolen hash h_u with the first $t_{max}/3$ labels. The attacker's area-time cost per password guess $(t^2_{max}/9)$ would decrease by a factor of 9, but the attacker's success rate only diminishes by a factor of 1/3—the probability that $t_u \in [1, t_{max}/3]$. Motivated by this observation there are several natural questions to ask. First, can we model how a rational offline attacker would adapt his approach to deal with halting puzzles? Second, if t_u is picked uniformly at random is it possible that the solution could have an adverse impact i.e., could we unintentionally *increase* the number of passwords cracked by a rational (profit-maximizing) attacker? Finally, can we find the optimal distribution over t_u which minimizes the success rate of a rational offline attacker subject to constraints on (amortized) server workload and maximum authentication delay.

1.1 Our Contributions

We introduce Cost-Asymmetric Memory Hard Password Hashing, an extention of Boyen's halting puzzles which can only *decrease* the number of passwords cracked by a rational password cracking attacker. Our key modification is to introduce cost-even breakpoints as random running time parameters i.e., we fix m values $t_1 \leq \ldots \leq t_m = t$ such that $t^2_m = t^2_i(m/i)$ for all $1 \leq i < m$. Now instead of selecting x_u randomly in the range $[1, t]$ (time-even breakpoints) we pick $x_u \in \{t_1, \ldots, t_m\}$. We can either select $x_u \in \{t_1, \ldots, t_m\}$ uniformly at random or, if desired, we can optimize the distribution in an attempt to minimize the expected number of passwords that the adversary breaks. Then the authentication server computes $h_u = \mathsf{MHF}(pw_u, salt_u; x_u)$ and store the tuple $(u, salt_u, h_u)$ as the record for user u.

We adapt the Stackelberg game theoretic framework of Blocki and Datta [12] to model the behavior of a rational password cracking attacker when the authentication server uses Cost-Asymmetric Memory Hard Password Hashing. In this model the attacker obtains a reward v for every cracked password and will choose a strategy which maximizes its expected utility—expected reward minus expected guessing costs. One of the main challenges in our setting is that the attacker's action space is exponential in the size of the support of the password distribution. For each password pw the attacker can chose to ignore the password, partially check the password or completely check the password. We design efficient algorithms to find a locally optimal strategy for the attacker and identify conditions under which the strategy is also a global optimum (these conditions are satisfied in almost all of our empirical experiments). We can then use black-box optimization to search for a distribution over x_u which minimizes the number of passwords cracked by our utility maximizing attacker.

When $x_u \in \{t_1, \ldots, t_m\}$ is selected uniformly at random we prove that cost-even breakpoints will only reduce the number of passwords cracked by a rational attacker. By contrast, we provide examples where time-even breakpoints increases the number of passwords that are cracked—some of these examples are based on empirical password distributions.

We empirically evaluate the effectiveness of our mechanism with 8 large password datasets. Our analysis shows that we can reduce the fraction of cracked passwords by up to 10% by adopting cost-asymmetric memory hard password hashing with cost-even breakpoints sampled from uniform distribution. In addition, our analysis demonstrates that the benefit of optimizing the distribution over x_u is marginal. Optimizing the distribution over the breakpoints $t_1, \ldots, t_m$ requires us to accurately estimate many key parameters such as the attacker's value v for cracked passwords and the probability of each password in the user password distribution. If our estimates are inaccurate then we could unintentionally increase the number of cracked passwords. Thus, we recommend instantiating Cost-Asymmetric Memory Hard Password Hashing with the uniform distribution over our cost-even breakpoints $t_1, \ldots, t_m$ as a *prior independent* password authentication mechanism.

1.2 Related Work

Trade-off between usability and security lie in the core of mechanism design of password authentication. Users tend to pick low-entropy passwords [16], leaving their accounts insecure. Convincing them to select stronger passwords is a difficult task [19,29]. Password strength meters are commonly embedded in website in the hope that users would select stronger passwords after the strength of their original passwords being displayed. However, it is found that users are often not persuaded by the suggestion of password strength meters [20,39]. In order to encourge users to pick high-entropy passwords some sites mandate users to follow stringent guidelines when users create their passwords. However, it has been shown that these policies can incur undesirable usability costs [3,24,26,37], and in some cases can even lead to users selecting weaker passwords [14,29].

Password offline attacks have been a concern since the Unix system was devised [34]. Various approaches are developed to expedite the cracking process by the adversary or model password guessability by the hoesty party. Tools like Hashcat [1] and John the Ripper [23] enumerate combinations of tokens as dictionary candidates and are widely used by real-world attackers. Liu et al. [30] analyzed these tools using techniques of rule inversion and guess counting to retrive guessing number without explicit enumeration. Probabilistic models like Probabilistic Context-Free Grammars [28,43], Markov models [21,22,31] have been applied and analyzed in password cracking. Character-level text generation with Long-Short Term Memory (LSTM) recurrent neural networks is fast, lean and accurate in modeling password guessability [33].

Memory-Hard Functions (MHF) is a key cryptographic primitive. Evaluation of MHF requires large amount of memory in addition to longer computation time, making parallel computation and customized hardware futile to speed up computation process. Candidate MHFs include SCRYPT [35], Balloon hashing [15], and Argon2 [11] (the winner of the Password Hashing Competition[2]). MHFs can be classified into two distinct categories or modes of operation—data-independent MHFs (iMHFs) and data-dependent MHFs(dMHFs) (along with the hybrid idMHF, which runs in both modes). dMHFs like SCRYPT are maximally memory hard [7], but they have the issue of possible side-channel attacks. iMHFs, on the other hand, can resist side-channel attakcs but the aAT (amortized Area Time) complexity is at most $\mathcal{O}(N^2 \log\log N/\log N)$ [4]—a combinatorial graph property called depth-robustness is both necessarily [4] and sufficient [6] for constructing iMHFs with large aAT complexity. Ameri et al. [8] introduced the notion of a computationally data-independent MHF (ciMHF) which protects against side-channel leakage as long as the adversary is computationally bounded and constructed a ciMHF with optimal aAT complexity $\Omega(N^2)$.

2 Background and Notations

Password Dataset. We use $\mathbb{P}$ to denote the set of all possible passwords, the corresponding distribution is $\mathcal{P}$. The process of a user u choosing a password for his/her account can be viewed as a random sampling from the underlying distribution $pw_u \xleftarrow{\$} \mathcal{P}$. It will be convenient to assume that the passwords in $\mathbb{P}$ are sorted such that $\Pr[pw_1] \geq \Pr[pw_2] \geq \ldots$. Given a password dataset D of n_a accounts, we can obtain empirical distribution $\mathcal{D}_e$ by approximating $\Pr_{pw_i \sim \mathcal{D}_e}[pw_i] = \frac{f_i}{n_a}$, where f_i is the frequency of pw_i and n_a is the number of accounts present in D. Often the empirical distribution can be represented in compact form by grouping passwords with the same frequency into an *equivalence set* i.e., $D_{es} = \{(f_1, s_1), \ldots, (f_i, s_i), \ldots, (f_{n_e}, s_{n_e})\}$, where s_i is the number of passwords which appear with frequency f_i in D and n_e is the total number of equivalence sets and, for convenience, we assume $f_1 > f_2 > \ldots > f_{n_e}$. We use $es_i = (f_i, s_i)$ to describe the ith equivalence set. In empirical experiments it is often more convenient to work with the compact representation D_{es} of password distribution. In addition, we use n_p to denote the number of distinct passwords in our dataset D. Observe that for any dataset we have $n_a \geq n_p \geq n_e$. In fact, we will typically have $n_a \gg n_p \gg n_e$.

Computation Cost of an MHF. The evaluation of $\mathsf{MHF}(x;t)$ produces a sequence of labels $L_1, L_2, \ldots, L_t$ where the last label generated L_t is the final output. Once $L_1, \ldots, L_{i-1}$ are all stored in memory it is possible to compute label i by making a single call to an underlying cryptographic hash function H e.g., we might have $L_i = H(L_j, L_k)$ where $j, k < i$ denote prior labels. We can also define $\mathsf{MHF}(x;i) = L_i$ for $i < t$. Thus, we can obtain all of the values $\mathsf{MHF}(x;1), \ldots, \mathsf{MHF}(x;t)$ in time t. We model the (amortized) Area-Time cost of evaluating $\mathsf{MHF}(\cdot;t)$ as $c_H t + c_M t^2$, where c_H and c_M are constants. Intuitively, c_H denotes the area of a core implementing the hash function H and c_M represents the area of an individual cell with the capacity to hold one data-label (hash output). Since the memory cost tend to dominant, we ignore the hash cost as simply model the cost as $c_M t^2$.

3 Defender's Model

In this section, we present the model of the defender. In particular, we describe how passwords are stored and verified on the authentication server.

Account Registration. When a user u registers for a new account with a password pw_u the authentication server randomly generates a $salt_u$ value, samples a running time parameter $t_u \in T$ from our set of possible running time breakpoints $T = \{t_1, t_2, \ldots, t_m\}$ (we let $q_i = \Pr[t_i]$ to denote the probability that $t_u = t_i$) and stores the tuple $(u, salt_u, h_u)$ where $h_u = \mathsf{MHF}(pw_u, salt_u; t_u)$. Note that the salt value $salt_u$ is recorded while the running time parameter t_u is discarded.

Password Verification. When a user u attempts to login to his/her account by submitting (u, pw'_u), the authentication server would first retrieve record $(u, salt_u, h_u)$, calculate $h_1 = \mathsf{MHF}(pw'_u, salt_u; t_1)$ and compare h_1 with h_u. It they are equal, login request is granted. Otherwise, the server would continue to calculate $h_2 = \mathsf{MHF}(pw'_u, salt_u; t_2)$, compare h_2 with h_u, so on and so forth. If any of h_i matches h_u, then user u successfully logs in his/her account. However, if for all possible running time parameters $t \in T$ we have $h_u \neq \mathsf{MHF}(pw'_u, salt_u; t)$ then the login request is rejected.

Defender Action and Workload Constraint. The defender's (leader's) action in our Stackelberg game is to select the probability distribution $q_1, \ldots, q_m$ over the running time breakpoints. The goal is to pick the distribution $q_1, \ldots, q_m$ to minimize the percentage of passwords cracked by a rational adversary subject to constraints on the expected server workload. Whenever user u logs in with the correct password pw_u the authentication server will incur cost $c_M t_u^2$. Since $t_u = t_i$ with probability q_i the expected cost of verifying a correct password is $\sum_{i=1}^{m} q_i c_M t_i^2$. Thus, given a maximum workload parameter C_{max} we require that the distribution $q_1, \ldots, q_m$ are selected subject to the constraints that $q_i \geq 0$, $q_1 + \ldots q_m = 1$ and

$$\sum_{i=1}^{m} q_i c_M t_i^2 \leq C_{max}. \tag{1}$$

4 Attacker's Model

In this section, we first state the assumptions we use in our economic analysis. Then we show how a rational attacker who steals the password hashes from the server would run a dictionary offline attack. Finally, we present the Stackelberg game in modeling the interaction between the defender and the attacker within the framework of [12].

4.1 Assumptions of Economics Analysis

We assume that the attacker is rational, knowledgeable and untarteged. By rationality, we mean that the attacker will attempt to maximize its expected utility i.e., the value of the cracked password(s) minus the attacker's guessing costs. By knowledgeable we mean that by Kerckhoffs's principle the attacker knows the exact distribution $\mathcal{P}$ from which the user's password was sampled. In practice, an attacker would not have perfect knowledge of the distribution $\mathcal{P}$, but could still rely on sophisticated password cracking models e.g., using Neural Networks [33], Markov Models [22,40] or Probabilistic Context-Free Grammars (PCFGs) [28,42,43]. Finally, we assume that the attacker is untargetted meaning we assume that each account has the same value v for the attacker and the attacker does not have background information about the passwords that individual user's may have selected. One can derive a range of estimates for v based on black market studies e.g., Symantec reported that passwords generally sell for \$4—\$30 [25] and [38] reported that Yahoo! e-mail passwords sell for $\approx$ \$1.

4.2 Cracking Process

We now specify how an offline attacker would use the stolen hash to run a dictionary attack. The password distribution and the breakpoint distribution induce a joint distribution over pairs $(pw, t) \in \mathbb{P} \times \{t_1, \ldots, t_m\}$ where we have $\Pr[(pw_i, t_j)] = \Pr[pw_i] q_j$.

The adversary's strategy is to formulate a checking sequence $\pi = \{(pw_i, t_j)\}$ with the purpose of finding the target (pw_u, t_u). An instruction (pw_i, t_j) in π means the adversary selects pw_i as current guess and compute the jth label for pw_i i.e., evaluate $\mathsf{MHF}(pw_i, salt_u; t_j)$. The cracking process terminates when

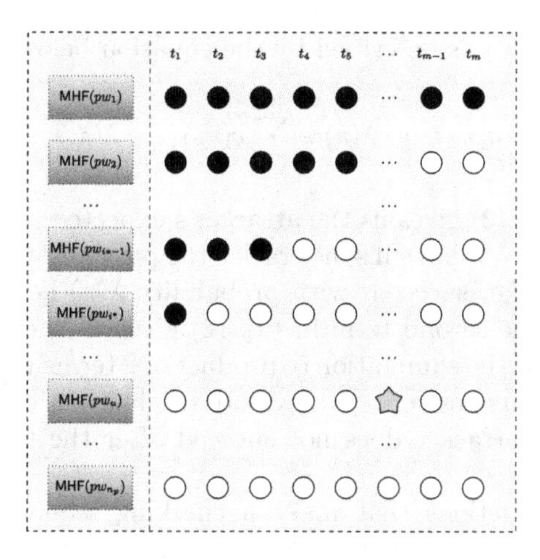

Fig. 1. Password Cracking Process. Black nodes denote current checking sequence π. White nodes denote unchecked instructions $\Pi(n_p, m) - \pi$. Star denotes unknown target (pw_u, t_u).

the adversary found the hidden target $(pw_u,\, t_u)$ or timeout. Thus, the order of instructions in a checking sequence π can impact the attackers expected cost.

A checking sequence is subject to *legit restrictions*:

1. *Small label first.* If $(pw_i,\, t_{j_1})$ appears before $(pw_i,\, t_{j_2})$ in π, then it should be the case $t_{j_2} > t_{j_1}$.
2. *Label backward continuity.* If $(pw_i,\, t_j) \in \pi$ then $(pw_i, t_1), \ldots, (pw_i, t_{j-1}) \in \pi$.
3. *No inversions.* Inversions in the form of $(pw_{i_1},\, t_{j_1}), (pw_{i_2}, t_{j_2}), (pw_{i_1}, t'_{j_1})$ where $t'_{j_1} > t_{j_1}$ are not allowed.

The first two restrictions state that the attacker cannot advance to a larger label without computing all previous labels. The third is an assumption that we made. Intuitively, the assumption is justified because an attacker who computes labels for pw_{i_2} while storing labels for pw_{i_1} will incur extra memory cost which is undesirable for a rational attacker. The cracking process is illustrated in Fig. 1.

4.3 Attacker's Utility

After specifying the restrictions for a legit checking sequence, we can formulate the the attacker's utility. Suppose the kth instruction in checking sequence π is $\pi_k = (pw_i, t_j)$, then the probability that the attacker succeeds on step k is $\Pr[\pi_k] = \Pr[pw_i] \cdot q_j$. Let $\lambda(\pi, B) \doteq \sum_{k=1}^{B} \Pr[\pi_k]$ denote the attacker's probability of success after the first $B \leq |\pi|$ instructions and let $\lambda(\pi) \doteq \lambda(\pi, |\pi|)$ denote the attacker's overall probability of success. Recall that the overall cost to compute $\mathsf{MHF}(\cdot; t_j)$ is $c_M t_j^2$. After computing $\mathsf{MHF}(pw_i; t_{j-1})$ the *additional* cost of executing instruction π_k to compute $\mathsf{MHF}(pw_i; t_j)$ is denoted $c(\pi_k) \doteq c_M(t_j^2 - t_{j-1}^2)$. For notational convenience, we define $t_0 \doteq 0$.

The attacker's utility is described by the equation below:

$$U_{adv}(v, \vec{q}, \pi) = v \cdot \lambda(\pi) - \sum_{k=1}^{|\pi|} c(\pi_k)\left(1 - \lambda(\pi, k-1)\right). \tag{2}$$

The first term in Eq. (2) gives us the attacker's expected reward. In particular, the attacker will receive value v if s/he crack's the password and, given a checking sequence π, the attacker succeeds with probability $\lambda(\pi)$ i.e., in expectation the reward is $v \cdot \lambda(\pi)$. The second term in Eq. (2) gives us the attacker's expected guesing costs, which is the summation of product of 2 terms where the probability that the attacker incurs cost $c(\pi_k)$ to evalute the instruction π_k is given by the probability that the attacker does not succeed after the first $k-1$ steps i.e., $1 - \lambda(\pi, k-1)$.

Besides legit restrictions that make a checking sequence valid a rational attacker would restrict its attention to checking sequences π that satisfy the following *opt restrictions*:

1. *Popular password first.* If (pw_{i_1}, t_j) appears before (pw_{i_2}, t_j), then $\Pr[pw_{i_1}] \geq \Pr[pw_{i_2}]$.
2. *Password backward continuity.* If $(pw_i, t_j) \in \pi$ for some j, then $(pw_{i-1}, t_{j'}) \in \pi$ for some j'.
3. *Stop at equivalence class boundary.* If (pw_i, t_j) is the last instruction in π where $pw_i \in es_k$, then $pw_{i+1} \in es_{k+1}$.

It can be easily proved that an attacker who violates opt restrictions will suffer utility loss. Legit restrictions, together with the first 2 opt restrictions, determine a complete ordering, which we call *natural ordering*, over all instructions $\{(pw_i, t_j)\}$, namely,

$$\begin{cases} (pw_{i_1}, t_{j_1}) < (pw_{i_2}, t_{j_2}), & \text{if } \Pr[pw_{i_1}] > \Pr[pw_{i_2}], \\ (pw_i, t_{j_1}) < (pw_i, t_{j_2}), & \text{if } j_1 < j_2. \end{cases} \tag{3}$$

We use $\Pi(n, m)$ to denote the sequence of all instructions for top n passwords with respect to natural ordering,

$$\Pi(n, m) := (pw_1, t_1), \ldots, (pw_1, t_m), \ldots, (pw_n, t_1), \ldots, (pw_n, t_m). \tag{4}$$

We say a sequence containing consecutive instructions for a single password is a *instruction bundle*, which is denoted by

$$\varpi_i(j_1, j_2) := (pw_i, t_{j_1}), \ldots, (pw_i, t_{j_2}). \tag{5}$$

Specifically, $\varpi_i(j_1, j_2) = \emptyset$ when $j_1 = j_2 = 0$. Then the attacker's strategy π is a sub-sequence of $\Pi(n_p, m)$ (recall that n_p is the number of distinct passwords) in the form of

$$\pi = \oplus_{i'=1}^{\mathsf{Len}(\pi)} \varpi_{i'}(1, \tau_{i'}) := \varpi_1(1, \tau_1) \circ \varpi_2(1, \tau_2) \circ \cdots \circ \varpi_{\mathsf{Len}}(1, \tau_{\mathsf{Len}}), \tag{6}$$

where $\circ$ denotes the concatenation of two disjoint instruction sequence and $\mathsf{Len}(\pi)$ is the largest index of password for which the attacker would check at least one label, which depends on the associated checking sequence, when the context is clear it is just written as Len. Because of opt restriction 3, Len can only take values in $\{0, |es_1|, |es_1| + |es_2|, \ldots, \sum_{k=1}^{n_e} |es_k|\}$. Notice that π is fully specified by the largest label index τ_i for pw_i.

4.4 Stackelberg Game

We use Stackelberg game to model the interaction between the attacker and defender. The defender (leader) fixes a distribution $\vec{q}$ over the breakpoints $\{t_1, \ldots, t_m\}$. The attacker (follower) responds by selecting checking sequence $\pi^* = \arg\max U_{adv}(v, \vec{q}, \pi)$ to maximize its utility.

Define server's utility to be $U_{ser}(v, \vec{q}) = -\lambda(\pi^*)$, where π^* is the attacker's best response to defender's strategy $\vec{q}$ given password value v. At equilibrium no player has the incentive to deviate form her/his strategy, thus equilibrium profile $(\vec{q}^*, \pi^*)$ satisfies,

$$\begin{cases} U_{adv}(v, \vec{q}, \pi^*) \geq U_{adv}(v, \vec{q}, \pi), \ \forall \pi, \\ U_{ser}(v, \vec{q}^*) \geq U_{ser}(v, \vec{q}), \ \forall \vec{q}. \end{cases} \tag{7}$$

The defender's goal is try to find a distribution $\vec{q}$ which minimizes $\lambda(\pi^*)$ subject to the constraint that the rational attacker responds with its utility optimizing strategy π^* given the breakpoint distribution $\vec{q}$ and value parameter v. Thus, before the defender can attempt to optimize $\vec{q}$ we need to be able to compute the attacker's response π^*.

5 Computing the Attacker's Optimal Strategy

As we noted in the previous section a rational attacker will use its utility optimizing strategy $\pi^* = \arg\max U_{adv}(v, \vec{q}, \pi)$. In this section, we show how to compute the attacker's optimal strategy π^* for both time-even breakpoints and cost-even breakpoints.

Before we introduce our algorithm used to find the optimal checking sequence, let us see why the native brute force algorithm is computationally infeasible. If the attacker chose to check top Len passwords; for each password pw_i the attacker has m possible choices for each password i.e., select $\tau_i \in \{1, \ldots, m\}$ and evaluate $\mathsf{MHF}(pwd_i; t_{\tau_i})$. Thus the native brute force algorithm runs in time $\mathcal{O}\left(\sum_{\mathsf{Len}=1}^{n_p} m^{\mathsf{Len}}\right) \subseteq \mathcal{O}(m^{n_p})$ with a very large exponent ($n_p \approx 2.14 \times 10^7$ for our largest dataset Linkedin, and $n_p \approx 3.74 \times 10^5$ for our smallest dataset Bfiled). This is why we need to design polynomial time algorithms.

In the following subsections, we first specify a superset[2] of π^*, setting a boundary within which we will gradually extend the checking sequence from an empty one. Then we introduce our local search algorithm which finds the optimal

[2] We use the concept and notation of subset and superset for ordered sequences the way they were defined for regular set. If all elements of sequence A are also elements of sequence B regardless the order, we say $A \subseteq B$.

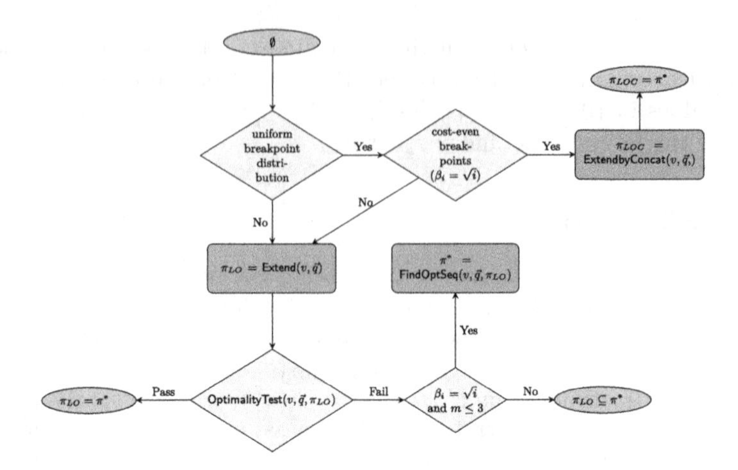

Fig. 2. Algorithm Flowchart

checking sequence most of the time. Our key intuition in designing algorithms is that an unchecked instruction bundle should be included into the optimal checking sequence if it provides non-negative marginal utility. Generally there are two local search directions, either concatenate instructions at the end of current checking sequence or insert instructions in the middle of current checking sequence. After the local search algorithm terminates we reach a local optimum π_{LO}. Finally we design algorithms to verify if the local optimum is also global optimum or promote the local optimum to global optimum under specifc parameter settings. As a overview we briefly summarize our results (also demonstrated in the flowchart, see Fig. 2) in this section as follows:

- When we use cost-even breakpoints sampled from uniform distribution, namely, $\beta_i = \sqrt{i}$ and $q_i = \frac{1}{m}$, we have a local search algorithm ExtendbyConcat $(v, \vec{q}, \emptyset)$ which iteratively considers instruction bundle that can be concatenated, ExtendbyConcat$(v, \vec{q}, \emptyset)$ runs in time $\mathcal{O}(n_p m)$ and gives optimal checking sequence;
- When breakpoints are cost-even ($\beta = \sqrt{i}$) but the distribution is non-uniform, we design an algorithm Extend$(v, \vec{q})$ which returns a locally optimal checking sequence π_{LO} in time $\mathcal{O}(n_p m)$. By locally optimal we mean that advancing any number of labels for any single password on the basis of π_{LO} will decrease attacker's utility.
  After obtaining π_{LO}, we can run a polynomial algorithm OptimalityTest$(v, \vec{q}, \pi_{LO})$ to check if π_{LO} is also a global optimum. If OptimalityTest$(v, \vec{q}, \pi_{LO})$ returns PASS, we know for sure that $\pi_{LO} = \pi^*$; otherwise, no conclusion can be drawn. If $m \leq 3$ we will use an efficient brute force algorithm FindOptSeq $(v, \vec{q}, \pi_{LO})$, which runs in time $\mathcal{O}(n_p^2)$, to the reach global optimum.
- When $\beta \neq \sqrt{i}$, regardless of the breakpoint distribution we can still run Extend$(v, \vec{q})$ to obtain locally optimal π_{LO}, and feed π_{LO} to OptimalityTest $(v, \vec{q}, \pi_{LO})$. If OptimalityTest$(v, \vec{q}, \pi_{LO})$ returns PASS, again we have $\pi_{LO} =$

π^*; if $\mathsf{OptimalityTest}(v, \vec{q}, \pi_{LO})$ returns FAIL, we cannot deduce any information about the global optimality of π_{LO}; in this case, confirm that $\pi_{LO} = \pi^*$ or promote π_{LO} to π^* will take exponential time.

5.1 Marginal Utility

Since we are going to use marginal utility as metrics of state transition in local search, we first specify how to compute marginal utility.

Definition 1. *Fixing v and $\vec{q}$, define $\Delta(\pi_1, \pi_2)$ to be marginal utility from strategy π_1 to π_2, namely,*

$$\Delta(\pi_1, \pi_2) := U_{adv}(v, \vec{q}, \pi_2) - U_{adv}(v, \vec{q}, \pi_1). \tag{8}$$

For most of the time π_2 is the result of modifying π_1 which is called *base*, in order to avoid redundantly repeating base we often write $\Delta^{\circ}(e \mid \pi_1)$ and $\Delta^{+}(e \mid \pi_1)$ to denote $\Delta(\pi_1, \pi_1 \circ e)$ and $\Delta(\pi_1, \pi_1 + e)$, respectively, where e is some ordered set of instructions, referred to as *extension*. Recall that $\circ$ is concatenation operation, here we formally introduce insertion operation $+$.

Definition 2. *Given a checking sequence $\pi = \oplus_{i=1}^{\mathsf{Len}} \varpi_i(1, \tau_i)$ and an instruction bundle $\varpi_{i'}(j_1, j_2)$, define operation $\pi + \varpi_{i'}(j_1, j_2)$ to be the checking sequence*

$$\pi + \varpi_{i'}(j_1, j_2) := \oplus_{i=1}^{i'} \varpi_i(1, \tau_i) \circ \varpi_{i'}(j_1, j_2) \circ \oplus_{i=i'+1}^{\mathsf{Len}} \varpi_i(1, \tau_i).$$

We discard superscript and comprehensively write $\Delta(e \mid \pi)$ to denote the marginal utility by including e into π, either through concatenation or insersion. Operations are valid only if the extension is *compatible* with the base. By compatible we mean the resulting checking sequence also satisfy both legit restrictions and opt restrictions.

When e is a singleton, from Eq. (2) we can derive the marginal utility by inserting instruction $e = (pw_i, t_j) \notin \pi$ to base π,

$$\Delta^{+}(e \mid \pi) = \Pr[pw_i] q_j \left(v + \sum_{e' > e, e' \in \pi} c(e') \right) - \left(1 - \sum_{e' < e, e' \in \pi} \Pr[e'] \right) c_M (t_j^2 - t_{j-1}^2). \tag{9}$$

where $\Pr[pw_i] q_j \sum_{e' > e, e' \in \pi} c(e')$ is the influence of e on future instructions since it eliminates some uncertainty about the user's password pw_u thus reduces the *expected* cost for future trials.

When e is a singleton, marginal utility upon concatenation has no future influence, hence,

$$\Delta^{\circ}(e \mid \pi) = \Pr[pw_i] q_j v - (1 - \lambda(\pi)) c_M (t_j^2 - t_{j-1}^2). \tag{10}$$

When e consists of multiple consecutive instructions, the marginal utility can be computed by iteratively applying Eq. (9) and (10). Namely,

$$\Delta(e \mid \pi) = \sum_{i=1}^{|e|} \Delta(e_i \mid \pi \cup \{e_0, \ldots, e_{i-1}\}), \tag{11}$$

where $e_0 = \emptyset$, e_i is the ith instruction of e and $\cup$ denotes inclusion (whether through concatenation or insertion) while maintaining natural ordering.

5.2 A Superset of the Optimal Checking Sequence

Before we present our algorithms we first show how to prune down the search space for π^*. Particularly, fixing v and $\vec{q}$ we find an index Len_{max} such that $\pi^* \subseteq \Pi(\mathsf{Len}_{max}, m)$ i.e., π^* will not even partially check passwords with rank larger than Len_{max}. Thus there is no need to consider any instructions beyond $\Pi(\mathsf{Len}_{max}, m)$ in construction of the optimal checking sequence.

Lemma 1. $\Delta^\circ\left(\pi_3 \,|\, \pi_1\right) \leq \Delta^\circ\left(\pi_3 \,|\, \pi_2\right),$ *if* $\lambda(\pi_1) \leq \lambda(\pi_2)$.

Definition 3. *Fixing* v *and* $\vec{q}$ *we define*

$$\mathsf{Len}_{max} := \begin{cases} \max_i\{i : F(v, \vec{q}, i) \geq 0\}, & \textit{if such } i \textit{ exists}, \\ 0, & o.w. \end{cases}$$

where

$$F(v, \vec{q}, i) := \begin{cases} \max_{1\leq j\leq m}\{\Delta\left(\emptyset, \varpi_i(0, j)\right)\}, & \textit{if } i = 1, \\ \max_{1\leq j\leq m}\{\Delta^\circ\left(\varpi_i(0, j) \,|\, \Pi(i-1, m)\right)\}, & o.w. \end{cases}$$

Intuitively, Len_{max} is the largest possible password index for which at least one of instruction bundles $\varpi_{\mathsf{Len}_{max}}(1, j), 1 \leq j \leq m$ provide non-negative marginal utility no matter what previous instructions are. We remark even though there is no theoretical proof of monotonicity of $F(v, \vec{q}, i)$, we have verified that $F(v, \vec{q}, i)$ is decreasing in i for our empirical password distribution. Note that by Lemma 1 we have

$$\Delta^\circ\left(\varpi_i(0, j) \,\middle|\, \oplus_{i=1}^{i-1}\varpi_i(1, \tau_i)\right) \leq F(v, \vec{q}, i),$$

if $F(v, \vec{q}, i) < 0$, then $\varpi_i(0, j)$ would certainly provide negative marginal utility, thus cannot be included in π^*. It is described in the following theorem.

Theorem 1.

$$\pi^* \subseteq \Pi(\mathsf{Len}_{max}, m).$$

5.3 Extension by Concatenation

We have established a superset of π^* in last subsection, now we design a local search algorithm that gives us a checking sequence π_{LOC} which is a subset of π^*. Here, LOC stands for "locally optimal with respect to concatenation." The sequence π_{LOC} will be helpful to further prune down the search space for π^*. In fact, in the special case where the breakpoint distribution is uniform ($q_i = \frac{1}{m}$) and cost-even breakpoints ($\beta_i = \sqrt{i}$) are used, we can prove that equality holds i.e., $\pi_{LOC} = \pi^*$ *is* the optimal solution.

To find our sequence π_{LOC} we start with the empty sequence of instructions and repeatedly include instructions that provide non-negative marginal utility upon concatenation to the current solution. We design a local search algorithm $\mathsf{ExtendbyConcat}(v, \vec{q}, \emptyset)$ to find a checking sequence π_{LOC}. Our local search algorithm $\mathsf{ExtendbyConcat}(v, \vec{q}, \emptyset)$ terminates after at most n_p rounds.

After the $i-1$th round we have $\pi_{LOC} \subseteq \Pi(i-1, m)$ i.e., the current solution only includes checking instructions for the first $i-1$ passwords. In the ith round we find an instruction bundle for password i which maximizes (marginal) utility upon concatenation. More specifically, in round i we compute $\tau_i = \arg\max_{0 \le j \le m}\{\Delta^\circ(\varpi_i(0,j) \mid \pi_{LOC})\}$ and append this instruction bundle to obtain an updated checking sequence $\pi_{LOC} = \pi_{LOC} \circ \varpi_i(0, \tau_i)$. Details can be found in Algorithm 1.

Algorithm 1: ExtendbyConcat($v, \vec{q}, \pi$)

Input: v, $\vec{q}$
Output: π_{LOC}

```
1  π_LOC = π;
2  start = i*(π_LOC);
3  for i = start : n_p do
4  |   for j = 0 : m do
5  |   |   Compute Δ° (ϖ_i(0, j) | π_LOC);
6  |   end
7  |   τ_i = arg max_{0≤j≤m}{Δ° (ϖ_i(0, j) | π_LOC)};
8  |   if τ_i > 0 then
9  |   |   π_LOC = π_LOC ∘ ϖ_i(1, τ_i);
10 |   |   else break;
11 |   end
12 end
13 return π_LOC
```

We can use Eq. (10) to compute the marginal utility in time $\mathcal{O}(1)$ by caching previously computed values of $\lambda(\pi)$. Thus, ExtendbyConcat($v, \vec{q}, \emptyset$) runs in time $\mathcal{O}(\mathsf{Len}_{max} m) \subseteq \mathcal{O}(n_p m)$, recall that n_p is the number of distinct password.

Theorem 2.

$$\pi_{LOC} \subseteq \pi^*.$$

From Theorem 1 and Theorem 2, it is easy to derive the following corollaries.

Corollary 1.

$$\mathsf{Len}(\pi_{LOC}) \le \mathsf{Len}(\pi^*) \le \mathsf{Len}_{max},$$

and

$$\mathsf{Len}(\pi_{LOC}), \mathsf{Len}(\pi^*), \mathsf{Len}_{max} \in \{x_0, x_1, \dots, x_{n_e}\},$$

where

$$x_k = \begin{cases} 0, & \textit{if } k = 0, \\ \sum_{k'=1}^{k} |es_{k'}|, & \textit{if } k = 1, \dots, n_e. \end{cases} \tag{12}$$

Corollary 2.

$$\lambda(\pi_{LOC}) \le P_{adv} = \lambda(\pi^*) \le \lambda\left(\Pi(\mathsf{Len}_{max}, m)\right).$$

Now we have a polynomial algorithm that returns a checking sequence π_{LOC} locally optimal with respect to concatenation. The following theorem states that $\pi_{LOC} = \pi^*$ if breakpoints are cost-even and follow uniform distribution.

Theorem 3. *When* $q_i = \frac{1}{m}$ *and* $\beta_i = \sqrt{i}$, $\mathsf{ExtendbyConcat}(v, \vec{q}, \emptyset)$ *returns the optimal checking sequence, i.e.,* $\pi_{LOC} = \pi^*$.

Even though the attacker behaviors optimally—following strategy π^*. We can guarantee that our mechanism results in lower (or equal if no passwords are cracked) percentage of cracked passwords than deterministic cost hashing, which is captured by Theorem 4.

Theorem 4. *When* $\beta_i = \sqrt{i}$ *and* $q_i = \frac{1}{m}$ *then,* $\lambda(\pi^*) \leq P^d_{adv}$, *where* P^d_{adv} *is the percentage of cracked passwords in traditional deterministic cost hashing.*

We have shown that our mechanism configured with cost-even breakpoints sampled from uniform distribution will only decrease the percentage of cracked passwords. In the next subsections we consider how the attacker would react to general configuration of the mechanism.

5.4 Local Search in Two Directions

In the previous section we introduced an algorithm $\mathsf{ExtendbyConcat}(v, \vec{q}, \emptyset)$ to produce a locally optimal solution π_{LOC} with respect to concatenation. We showed the instruction sequence π_{LOC} is a subset of the instructions in π^* and argued that in specific cases the algorithm is guaranteed to find the optimal solution. However, in more general cases the local optimum may not be globally optimum. One possible reason for this is that there may be a missing instruction from π^* that we would like to insert into the middle of the checking sequence π_{LOC}, while our local search algorithm $\mathsf{ExtendbyConcat}(v, \vec{q}, \emptyset)$ only considers instructions that can be appended to π_{LOC}.

In this subsection we extend the local search algorithm to additionally consider insertions. Note that we can still use local search to test if inserting instruction bundle $\varpi_i(j_1, j_2)$ improves the overall utility, i.e., $\Delta^+ (\varpi_i(j_1, j_2) \,|\, \pi) \geq 0$. We design an algorithm $\mathsf{ExtendbyInsert}(v, \vec{q}, \pi)$ which performs such an update. Combining $\mathsf{ExtendbyConcat}(v, \vec{q}, \pi)$ and $\mathsf{ExtendbyInsert}(v, \vec{q}, \pi)$, we design an Algorithm $\mathsf{Extend}(v, \vec{q})$ to construct a checking sequence π_{LO} (LO=Locally Optimal) which is locally optimal with respect to both operations: concatenation and insertions. Specifically, after each call of $\mathsf{ExtendbyInsert}(v, \vec{q}, \pi)$ we immediately run $\mathsf{ExtendbyConcat}(v, \vec{q}, \pi)$ to ensure that the solution is still locally optimal with respect to concatenation. See Algorithm 3 for details. The algorithms still maintain the invariant that π_{LO} is a subset of π^*—see Theorem 5.

Given π_{LOC} computed in time $\mathcal{O}(n_p m)$, the number of unchecked instructions is upper bounded by $|\Pi(\mathsf{Len}_{max}, m)| - |\pi_{LOC}|$. By caching the probability summation of previous and future instructions at each insertion position, verify if an instruction bundle is profitable and update the checking sequence take time $\mathcal{O}(1)$. One pass of `repeat` loop of Algorithm 3 takes time $\mathcal{O}(|\Pi(\mathsf{Len}_{max}, m)| - |\pi_{LOC}|) \subseteq \mathcal{O}(n_p m)$, the number of `repeat` loop execution is finite (in experiment it terminates after at most 3 passes). Therefore, $\mathsf{Extend}(v, \vec{q})$ runs in time $\mathcal{O}(n_p m)$.

Algorithm 2: ExtendbyInsert$(v, \vec{q}, \pi)$

Input: v, $\vec{q}$, π
Output: π_{LOI}

```
1 π_LOI = π;
2 while e exists such that Δ+(e | π_LOI) ≥ 0 do
3 |   π_LOI = π_LOI + e
4 end
5 return π_LOI
```

Algorithm 3: Extend$(v, \vec{q})$

Input: v, $\vec{q}$
Output: π_{LO}

```
1 π_LO = ExtendbyConcat(v, q⃗, ∅);
2 repeat
3 |   π_LO = ExtendbyInsert(v, q⃗, π_LO);
4 |   π_LO = ExtendbyConcat(v, q⃗, π_LO);
5 until no single profitable instruction bundle exist;
6 return π_LO
```

Lemma 2. *If* $\pi \subseteq \pi^*$ *and* $\Delta^+(e \,|\, \pi) \geq 0$ *then* $\pi + e \subseteq \pi^*$.

Lemma 2 guarantees that + operation preserves the invariance that our construction is subset of π^*. Naturally follows Theorem 5, which states the output of Extend$(v, \vec{q})$ is a subset of π^*.

Theorem 5. *Let* $\pi_{LO} =$ Extend$(v, \vec{q})$, *then* $\pi_{LO} \subseteq \pi^*$.

Since we are using local search to construct π_{LO}, together with Theorem 5 we know π_{LO} is a local optimum. When Algorithm 3 terminates, advancing any number of labels for any single password cannot improve the overall utility, but there is no guarantee of utility reduction upon inclusion of multiple instruction bundles that associated with different passwords. In the next subsection we will discuss how to verify if the local optimum π_{LO} is indeed the global optimum and design an efficient brute force algorithm that improves local optimum to global optimum under specific parameter settings.

5.5 Optimality Test and Globally Optimal Checking Sequence

In the previous subsections, we designed a polynomial algorithm Extend$(v, \vec{q})$ to construct locally optimal checking sequence π_{LO} with respect to insertions and concatenation. We also proved that the sequence π_{LO} is a subset of the optimal sequence π^*. In practice we find that it is often the case that $\pi_{LO} = \pi^*$ and we give an efficient heuristic algorithm which (often) allows us to confirm the global optimality of π_{LO}. In particular, our procedure will never falsely indicate that $\pi_{LO} = \pi^*$ though it may occasionally fail to confirm that this is the case. When our optimality test fails, we design algorithms to promote locally optimal solution to globally optimal solution for cost-even breakpoints and $m \leq 3$, see full version of this paper [10] for details.

6 Defender's Optimal Strategy

When making decisions about breakpoint distribution, the defender will take attacker's best response into consideration. Specifically, the defender would choose $\vec{q}^* = \arg\min \lambda(\pi^*)$ where $\pi^* = \arg\max U_{adv}(v, \vec{q}, \pi))$. Formally, the optimization problem (OPT) is

$$\begin{aligned} \min_{\vec{q}} \quad & \lambda(\pi^*) \\ \text{s.t.} \quad & 0 \leq q_i \leq 1, \ \forall 1 \leq i \leq m, \\ & \sum_{i=1}^{m} q_i = 1, \\ & \sum_{i=1}^{m} q_i c_M t_i^2 \leq C_{max}, \\ & \pi^* = \arg\max U_{adv}(v, \vec{q}, \pi)) \end{aligned} \tag{13}$$

The optimization goal is to minimize attacker's success rate. The first two constrains guarantee q_i are valid probabilities. The third constraint forces that the expected cost does not exceed maximum workload C_{max}. The last constraint states that the attacker responds optimally given password value v and the defender's strategy $\vec{q}$. Since there is no closed form expression of $\lambda(\pi^*)$ we use heuristic black box optimization solvers to optimize $\vec{q}$. We refer to the black box solver as FindOptDis(). This heuristic algorithm is parametrized by the attacker's value v and by the password distribution $\mathcal{P}$ and outputs a distribution $\vec{q}$. As a caveat our heuristic algorithm is not absolutely guaranteed to find the optimal breakpoint distribution $\vec{q}^*$. Detailed discussion about FindOptDis() can be found in the full version of this paper [10].

7 Experiments

7.1 Experiment Setup

In this section, we evaluate the performance of our mechanism using empirical password datasets. Due to length limitations we only report results for the two largest datasets: Linkedin ($1.74*10^8$ accounts with $5.74*10^7$ distinct passwords) and Neopets ($6.83*10^7$ accounts with $2.8*10^7$ distinct accounts). In the full version [10] we include results for 6 additional password datasets (Bfield, Brazzers, Clicksense, CSDN, RockYou and Webhost)[3].

[3] The password datasets we analyze and experiment with are publicly available and widely used in literature research. We did not crack any new passwords. Thus, our usage of the datasets would not cause further harm to users.

For each dataset we derive the corresponding empirical distribution $\mathcal{D}_e$ (namely, $\Pr_{pw \sim \mathcal{D}_e}[pw] = f_i/n_a$ where f_i is the frequency of pw) and analyze the attacker's success rate under this password distribution. The drawback is that the tail of empirical distribution $\mathcal{D}_e$ can significantly diverge from real distribution $\mathcal{P}$. We follow the approach of [9] and use Good-Turing Frequency estimation to upbound the CDF divergence E between $\mathcal{D}_e$ and $\mathcal{P}$. In particular, we use yellow (resp. red) to denote the unconfident region where the empirical distribution might diverge significantly from the real distribution $E > 0.01$ (resp. $E > 0.1$).

We plot the attacker's success rate $\lambda(\pi^*)$ as the ratio v/C_{max} varies under different conditions. In Fig. 3 we consider time-even breakpoints with uniform distribution over breakpoints. Similarly, Fig. 4 considers cost-even breakpoints under the uniform distribution as the number of breakpoints m varies. In Fig. 5, we fix $m = 3$ continue to use cost-even breakpoints, and run our algorithm FindOptDis() (implemented with BITEOPT [41]), to optimize the breakpoint distribution.

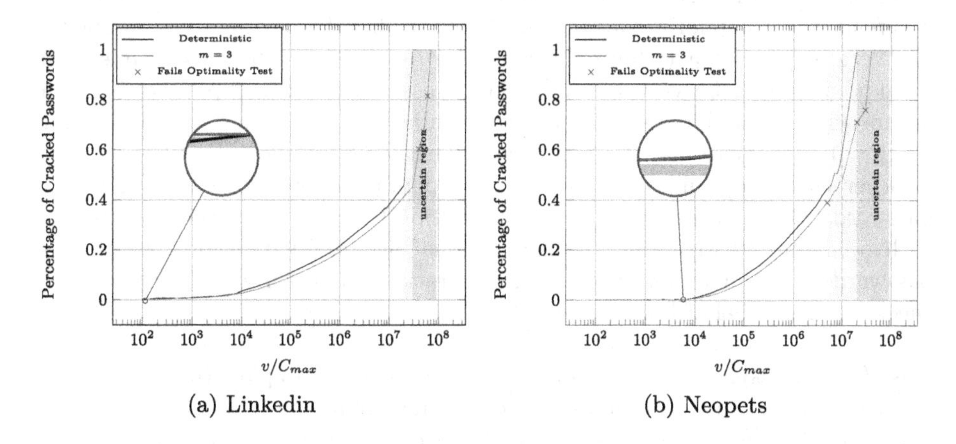

Fig. 3. Time-Even Breakpoints, Uniform Breakpoint Distribution

7.2 Experiment Analysis and Discussion

Time-Even Breakpoints with Uniform Distribution. Fig. 3 plots the attacker's success rate (vs. v/C_{max}) when we use time-even breakpoints with the uniform distribution i.e., Boyen's Halting puzzles [18]. In most parameter ranges the usage of Boyen's Halting puzzles reduces the % of cracked passwords in comparison to using deterministic (cost-equivalent) memory hard functions. However, one significant observation is that for some parameters v/C_{max} (highlighted with amplified circles on the plots) using Boyen's halting puzzles can actually increase the percentage of cracked passwords. Take LinkedIn as example, when $v/C_{max} = 100$ using time-even breakpoints increases the % of cracked passwords from 0% (determistic MHF) to 0.2%. Similar phenomenon can be observed in

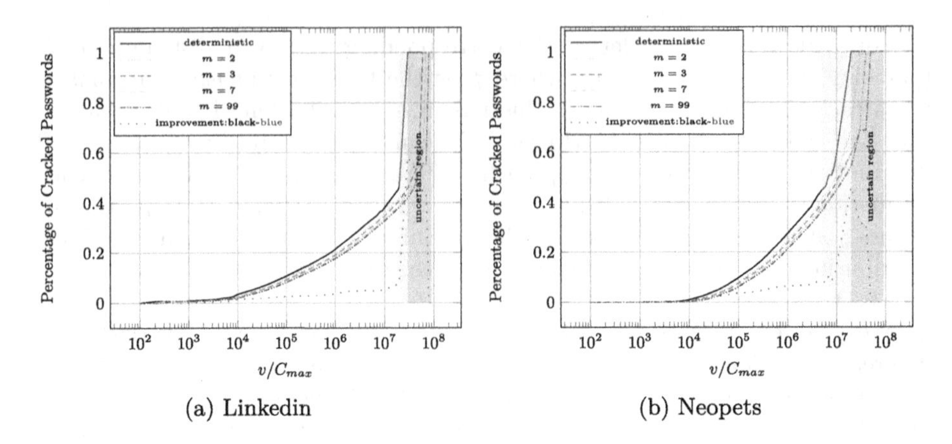

(a) Linkedin

(b) Neopets

Fig. 4. Cost-Even Breakpoints, Uniform Breakpoint Distribution

other datasets. Intuitively, these findings are explained by the observation that it is relatively cheap for the attacker to check the first few cost-even breakpoints.

We also provide a (admitedly contrived) example to show that time-even breakpoints could be very harmful. Suppose a dataset has 2 passwords, each occurs with probability $\frac{1}{2}$, and password value $v = 1.45$, and cost parameter $C_{max} = 1$. With deterministic MHFs a simple calculation shows that the rational attacker's utility optimal strategy is to give up immediately without checking any passwords. On the other hand, if we use Halting Puzzles (time-even breakpoints with a uniform distribution) then a rational attacker will recover the user's password with probability at least $\frac{1}{4}$ e.g., a rational attacker will always want to check the first label of both passwords.

Cost-Even Breakpoints and Uniform Distribution. Figure 5 plots the success rate of the rational adversary when we use cost-even breakpoints with the uniform distribution. Our results are consistent with Theorem 4 where we proved that cost-even breakpoints with the uniform distribution can *never* increase the attacker's success rate. In Fig. 5 we also explore the impact of increasing the number of breakpoints m. We find that increasing m decreases the attacker's success rate although the impact dimishes as m increases—see the [10] for additional discussion. When $m = 99$ we find instances where the attacker's success rate is decreased by an additive factor of 10%.

Optimized Distribution and Cost-Even Breakpoints. Continuing to use cost-even breakpoints we attempted to optimize the breakpoint distribution using BITEOPT[41]—see Fig. 5. In all instances we only obtained marginal reductions in the attacker's success rate when compared to the uniform distribution over breakpoints. Furthermore, optimizing the breakpoint distribution $\vec{q}$ requires the defender to know the password distribution and the attacker's value v a priori. In practice there is a very real risk that we would optimize $\vec{q}$ with respect to

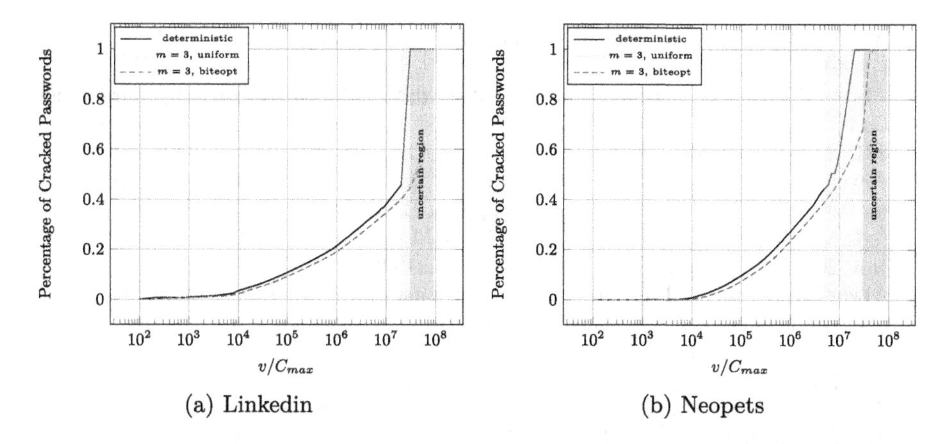

Fig. 5. Cost-Even Breakpoints, Optimized Breakpoint Distribution

the wrong distribution or value v. Thus we recommend to use cost-even break points with uniform distribution as this solution can be implemented *without* any knowledge of v or the password distribution.

8 Conclusion

In this paper, we introduce cost-asymmetric memory hard password authentication, a prior independent authentication mechanism, to defend against offline attacks. As traditional hash function are replaced by memory hard functions, we propose to use random breakpoints in evaluation of an MHF in order to have the benefit of both cost asymmetry and cost quadratic scaling. The interaction between the defender and the attacker is modeled by a Stackelberg game, within the game theory framework we formulate the optimal strategies for both defender and attacker. We theoretically proved that cost-asymmetric memory hard password authentication with cost-even breakpoints sampled from uniform distribution will reduce attacker's cracking success rate. In addition we set up experiments to validate the effectiveness of our proposed mechanism for arbitrary parameter settings, experiment results show that the reduction of attacker's success rate is up to 10%.

Acknowledgments. The research was supported in part by the National Science Foundation under awards CNS #2047272 and by IARPA under the HECTOR program. Mohammad Hassan Ameri was also supported in part by a Summer Research Grant from Purdue University.

References

1. Hashcat: advanced password recovery. https://hashcat.net/hashcat/
2. Password hashing competition. https://password-hashing.net/

3. Adams, A., Sasse, M.A.: Users are not the enemy. Commun. ACM **42**(12), 40–46 (1999)
4. Alwen, J., Blocki, J.: Efficiently computing data-independent memory-hard functions. In: Robshaw, M., Katz, J. (eds.) CRYPTO 2016. LNCS, vol. 9815, pp. 241–271. Springer, Heidelberg (2016). https://doi.org/10.1007/978-3-662-53008-5_9
5. Alwen, J., Blocki, J., Harsha, B.: Practical graphs for optimal side-channel resistant memory-hard functions. In: Thuraisingham, B.M., Evans, D., Malkin, T., Xu, D. (eds.) ACM CCS 2017, pp. 1001–1017. ACM Press, Dallas, TX, USA, 31 Oct–2 Nov 2017. https://doi.org/10.1145/3133956.3134031
6. Alwen, J., Blocki, J., Pietrzak, K.: Depth-robust graphs and their cumulative memory complexity. In: Coron, J.-S., Nielsen, J.B. (eds.) EUROCRYPT 2017. LNCS, vol. 10212, pp. 3–32. Springer, Cham (2017). https://doi.org/10.1007/978-3-319-56617-7_1
7. Alwen, J., Chen, B., Pietrzak, K., Reyzin, L., Tessaro, S.: `Scrypt` is maximally memory-hard. In: Coron, J.-S., Nielsen, J.B. (eds.) EUROCRYPT 2017. LNCS, vol. 10212, pp. 33–62. Springer, Cham (2017). https://doi.org/10.1007/978-3-319-56617-7_2
8. Ameri, M.H., Blocki, J., Zhou, S.: Computationally data-independent memory hard functions. In: Vidick, T. (ed.) ITCS 2020. vol. 151, pp. 36:1–36:28. LIPIcs, Seattle, WA, USA, 12–14 Jan 2020. https://doi.org/10.4230/LIPIcs.ITCS.2020.36
9. Bai, W., Blocki, J.: DAHash: distribution aware tuning of password hashing costs. In: Borisov, N., Diaz, C. (eds.) FC 2021. LNCS, vol. 12675, pp. 382–405. Springer, Heidelberg (2021). https://doi.org/10.1007/978-3-662-64331-0_20
10. Bai, W., Blocki, J., Ameri, M.H.: Cost-asymmetric memory hard password hashing (2022). https://arxiv.org/abs/2206.12970
11. Biryukov, A., Dinu, D., Khovratovich, D.: Argon2: new generation of memory-hard functions for password hashing and other applications. In: Security and Privacy (EuroS&P), 2016 IEEE European Symposium on, pp. 292–302. IEEE (2016)
12. Blocki, J., Datta, A.: CASH: a cost asymmetric secure hash algorithm for optimal password protection. In: IEEE 29th Computer Security Foundations Symposium, pp. 371–386 (2016)
13. Blocki, J., Harsha, B., Zhou, S.: On the economics of offline password cracking. In: 2018 IEEE Symposium on Security and Privacy. pp. 853–871. IEEE Computer Society Press, San Francisco, CA, USA, 21–23 May 2018. https://doi.org/10.1109/SP.2018.00009
14. Blocki, J., Komanduri, S., Procaccia, A., Sheffet, O.: Optimizing password composition policies. In: Proceedings of the Fourteenth ACM Conference on Electronic Commerce, pp. 105–122. ACM (2013)
15. Boneh, D., Corrigan-Gibbs, H., Schechter, S.: Balloon hashing: a memory-hard function providing provable protection against sequential attacks. In: Cheon, J.H., Takagi, T. (eds.) ASIACRYPT 2016. LNCS, vol. 10031, pp. 220–248. Springer, Heidelberg (2016). https://doi.org/10.1007/978-3-662-53887-6_8
16. Bonneau, J.: The science of guessing: analyzing an anonymized corpus of 70 million passwords. In: 2012 IEEE Symposium on Security and Privacy, pp. 538–552. IEEE Computer Society Press, San Francisco, CA, USA, 21–23 May 2012. https://doi.org/10.1109/SP.2012.49
17. Bonneau, J., Herley, C., van Oorschot, P.C., Stajano, F.: The quest to replace passwords: a framework for comparative evaluation of web authentication schemes. In: 2012 IEEE Symposium on Security and Privacy, pp. 553–567. IEEE Computer Society Press, San Francisco, CA, USA, 21–23 May 2012. https://doi.org/10.1109/SP.2012.44

18. Boyen, X.: Halting password puzzles: hard-to-break encryption from human-memorable keys. In: Provos, N. (ed.) USENIX Security 2007, pp. 6–10, Boston, MA, USA. Aug, USENIX Association (2007)
19. Campbell, J., Ma, W., Kleeman, D.: Impact of restrictive composition policy on user password choices. Behav. Inf. Technol. **30**(3), 379–388 (2011)
20. Carnavalet, X., Mannan, M.: From very weak to very strong: analyzing password-strength meters. In: NDSS 2014. The Internet Society, San Diego, CA, USA, 23–26 Feb 2014
21. Castelluccia, C., Chaabane, A., Dürmuth, M., Perito, D.: When privacy meets security: leveraging personal information for password cracking. arXiv preprint arXiv:1304.6584 (2013)
22. Castelluccia, C., Dürmuth, M., Perito, D.: Adaptive password-strength meters from Markov models. In: NDSS 2012. The Internet Society, San Diego, CA, USA, 5–8 Feb 2012
23. Designer, S.: John the ripper password cracker (2006)
24. Florêncio, D., Herley, C., Van Oorschot, P.C.: An administrator's guide to Internet password research. In: Proceedings of the 28th USENIX Conference on Large Installation System Administration, pp. 35–52. LISA 2014 (2014)
25. Fossi, M., et al.: Symantec report on the underground economy (2008). Accessed 1 Aug 2013
26. Inglesant, P.G., Sasse, M.A.: The true cost of unusable password policies: password use in the wild. In: Proceedings of the SIGCHI Conference on Human Factors in Computing Systems, pp. 383–392. CHI 2010, ACM, New York, NY, USA (2010). https://doi.org/10.1145/1753326.1753384
27. Kaliski, B.: Pkcs# 5: password-based cryptography specification version 2.0 (2000)
28. Kelley, P.G., et al.: Guess again (and again and again): measuring password strength by simulating password-cracking algorithms. In: 2012 IEEE Symposium on Security and Privacy, pp. 523–537. IEEE Computer Society Press, San Francisco, CA, USA, 21–23 May 2012. https://doi.org/10.1109/SP.2012.38
29. Komanduri, S., et al.: Of passwords and people: measuring the effect of password-composition policies. In: CHI, pp. 2595–2604 (2011). http://dl.acm.org/citation.cfm?id=1979321
30. Liu, E., Nakanishi, A., Golla, M., Cash, D., Ur, B.: Reasoning analytically about password-cracking software. In: 2019 IEEE Symposium on Security and Privacy (SP), pp. 380–397. IEEE (2019)
31. Ma, J., Yang, W., Luo, M., Li, N.: A study of probabilistic password models. In: 2014 IEEE Symposium on Security and Privacy, pp. 689–704. IEEE Computer Society Press, Berkeley, CA, USA, 18–21 May 2014. https://doi.org/10.1109/SP.2014.50
32. Manber, U.: A simple scheme to make passwords based on one-way functions much harder to crack. Comput. Secur. **15**(2), 171–176 (1996)
33. Melicher, W., et al.: Fast, lean, and accurate: modeling password guessability using neural networks. In: Holz, T., Savage, S. (eds.) USENIX Security 2016, pp. 175–191. USENIX Association, Austin, TX, USA, 10–12 Aug 2016
34. Morris, R., Thompson, K.: Password security: a case history. Commun. ACM **22**(11), 594–597 (1979)
35. Percival, C.: Stronger key derivation via sequential memory-hard functions. In: BSDCan 2009 (2009)
36. Provos, N., Mazieres, D.: Bcrypt algorithm. USENIX (1999)

37. Steves, M., Chisnell, D., Sasse, A., Krol, K., Theofanos, M., Wald, H.: Report: authentication diary study. Technical report NISTIR 7983, National Institute of Standards and Technology (NIST) (2014)
38. Stockley, M.: What your hacked account is worth on the dark web (2016). https://nakedsecurity.sophos.com/2016/08/09/what-your-hacked-account-is-worth-on-the-dark-web/
39. Ur, B., et al.: How does your password measure up? the effect of strength meters on password creation. In: Proceedings of USENIX Security Symposium (2012)
40. Ur, B., et al.: Measuring real-world accuracies and biases in modeling password guessability. In: Jung, J., Holz, T. (eds.) USENIX Security 2015, pp. 463–481. USENIX Association, Washington, DC, USA, 12–14 Aug 2015
41. Vaneev, A.: BITEOPT - derivative-free optimization method (2021). https://github.com/avaneev/biteopt. c++ source code, with description and examples
42. Veras, R., Collins, C., Thorpe, J.: On semantic patterns of passwords and their security impact. In: NDSS 2014. The Internet Society, San Diego, CA, USA, 23–26 Feb 2014
43. Weir, M., Aggarwal, S., de Medeiros, B., Glodek, B.: Password cracking using probabilistic context-free grammars. In: 2009 IEEE Symposium on Security and Privacy, pp. 391–405. IEEE Computer Society Press, Oakland, CA, USA, 17–20 May 2009. https://doi.org/10.1109/SP.2009.8

Memory-Hard Puzzles in the Standard Model with Applications to Memory-Hard Functions and Resource-Bounded Locally Decodable Codes

Mohammad Hassan Ameri, Alexander R. Block, and Jeremiah Blocki(✉)

Purdue University, West Lafayette, IN 47907, USA
{mameriek,block9,jblocki}@purdue.edu

Abstract. We formally introduce, define, and construct *memory-hard puzzles*. Intuitively, for a difficulty parameter t, a cryptographic puzzle is memory-hard if any parallel random access machine (PRAM) algorithm with "small" cumulative memory complexity ($\ll t^2$) cannot solve the puzzle; moreover, such puzzles should be both "easy" to generate and be solvable by a sequential RAM algorithm running in time t. Our definitions and constructions of memory-hard puzzles are in the standard model, assuming the existence of indistinguishability obfuscation ($i\mathcal{O}$) and one-way functions (OWFs), and additionally assuming the existence of a *memory-hard language*. Intuitively, a language is memory-hard if it is undecidable by any PRAM algorithm with "small" cumulative memory complexity, while a sequential RAM algorithm running in time t can decide the language. Our definitions and constructions of memory-hard objects are the first such definitions and constructions in the standard model without relying on idealized assumptions (such as random oracles).

We give two applications which highlight the utility of memory-hard puzzles. For our first application, we give a construction of a (one-time) *memory-hard function* (MHF) in the standard model, using memory-hard puzzles and additionally assuming $i\mathcal{O}$ and OWFs. For our second application, we show any cryptographic puzzle (e.g., memory-hard, time-lock) can be used to construct *resource-bounded locally decodable codes* (LDCs) in the standard model, answering an open question of Blocki, Kulkarni, and Zhou (ITC 2020). Resource-bounded LDCs achieve better rate and locality than their classical counterparts under the assumption that the adversarial channel is resource bounded (e.g., a low-depth circuit). Prior constructions of MHFs and resource-bounded LDCs required idealized primitives like random oracles.

1 Introduction

Memory-hardness is an important notion in the field of cryptography that is used to design egalitarian proofs of work and to protect low entropy secrets (e.g., passwords) against brute-force attacks. Over the last decade, there has

C. Galdi and S. Jarecki (Eds.): SCN 2022, LNCS 13409, pp. 45–68, 2022.
https://doi.org/10.1007/978-3-031-14791-3_3

been a rich line of both theoretical and applied work in constructing and analyzing memory-hard functions [2–8,16,25,28,34,43]. Ideally, one wants to prove that any algorithm evaluating the function (possibly on multiple distinct inputs) has high cumulative memory complexity (cmc) [7] (asymptotically equivalent to the notions of (amortized) Space-Time complexity and (amortized) Area-Time complexity in idealized models of computation [4]). Intuitively, the cmc of an algorithm A_f evaluating a function f on input x (denoted by $\mathsf{cmc}(A_f, x)$) is the summation of the amount of memory used by A_f during every step of the computation. Currently, security proofs for memory-hard objects rely on idealized assumptions such as the existence of random oracles [5–8] or other ideal objects such as ideal ciphers or permutations [34]. Informally, a function f is memory-hard if there is a sequential algorithm computing f in time t, but any parallel algorithm computing f (possibly on multiple distinct inputs) has high cmc, e.g., $t^{2-\varepsilon}$ for small constant $\varepsilon > 0$. An important open question is to construct provably secure memory-hard objects in the standard model.

In this work, we focus specifically on *memory-hard puzzles*. Cryptographic puzzles are cryptographic primitives that have two desirable properties: (1) for a target solution s, it should be "easy" to generate a puzzle Z with solution s; and (2) solving the puzzle Z to obtain solution s should be "difficult" for any algorithm $\mathcal{A}$ with "insufficient resources". Such puzzles have seen a wide range of applications, including using in cryptocurrency, handling junk mail, and constructing time-released encryption schemes [41,60,77,83]. For example, the well-known and studied notion of *time-lock puzzles* [19,29,44,73,74,83] requires that for difficulty parameter t and security parameter λ, a sequential (i.e., non-parallel) machine can generate a puzzle in time $\text{poly}(\lambda, \log(t))$ and solve the puzzle in time $t \cdot \text{poly}(\lambda)$, but requires that any parallel algorithm running in sequential time significantly less than t (i.e., any polynomial size circuit of depth smaller than t) cannot solve the puzzle, except with negligible probability (in the security parameter). In the context of memory-hard puzzles, we want to ensure that the puzzles are easy to generate, but that any algorithm solving the puzzle has high cmc. More concretely, we require that the puzzles can be generated (resp., solved) in time $\text{poly}(\lambda, \log(t))$ (resp., $t \cdot \text{poly}(\lambda)$) on a sequential machine while any algorithm solving the puzzle has cmc at least $t^{2-\varepsilon}$ for small constant $\varepsilon > 0$. We remark that any sequential machine solving the puzzle in time at most $t \cdot \text{poly}(\lambda)$ will have cmc at most $t^2 \cdot \text{poly}(\lambda)$ so a lower bound of $t^{2-\varepsilon}$ for the cmc of our puzzles would be nearly tight.

In this work, we ask the following questions:

Is it possible to construct memory-hard puzzles under standard cryptographic assumptions? If yes, what applications of memory-hard puzzles can we find?

1.1 Our Results

We formally introduce and define the notion of *memory-hard puzzles*. Inspired by time-lock puzzles and memory-hard functions, we define memory-hard puzzles *without* idealized assumptions. Intuitively, we say that a cryptographic puzzle is memory-hard if any parallel random access machine (PRAM) algorithm with "small" cmc cannot solve the puzzles. This is in contrast with time-lock puzzles which require that any algorithm running in "small" sequential time (i.e., any low-depth circuit) cannot solve the puzzle. For both memory-hard and time-lock puzzles, the puzzles should be "easy" to generate; i.e., in sequential time $\mathrm{poly}(\lambda, \log(t))$.

Similar to the time-lock puzzle construction of Bitansky et al. [19], we construct memory-hard puzzles assuming the existence of a suitable *succinct randomized encoding scheme* [11,12,17,19,46,58,70], and the additional assumption that there exists a language which is "suitably" memory-hard. Towards this end, we formally introduce and define *memory-hard languages*: such languages, informally, require that (1) the language is decidable by a family of *uniformly succinct circuits*—succinct circuits which are computable by a uniform algorithm—of appropriate size; and (2) any PRAM algorithm deciding the language must have "large" cmc. We discuss the technical ideas behind our construction in Sect. 2.2 and present its memory-hardness in Theorems 3 and 2.

We stress that our construction does not rely on an explicit instance of a memory-hard language: the *existence* of such a language suffices to prove memory-hardness of the constructed puzzle, mirroring the construction of [19]. We use succinct randomized encoding scheme of Garg and Srinivasan [46], which is instantiated from indistinguishability obfuscation ($i\mathcal{O}$) for circuits and somewhere statistically binding hash functions [57,67,78].[1] We remark that our constructions are primarily of theoretical interest, as known constructions of randomized encodings rely on expensive primitives such as $i\mathcal{O}$ [1,13,14,33,45,59,67,69]. We make no claims about the practical efficiency of our constructions.

It is important to note that even if we defined memory-hard puzzles in an idealized model (e.g., the random oracle model), memory-hard functions do not directly yield memory-hard puzzles. Cryptographic puzzles stipulate that for parameters t and λ the puzzle generation algorithm needs to run in time $\mathrm{poly}(\lambda, \log(t))$. However, using a memory-hard function to generate a cryptographic puzzle would require the generation algorithm to compute the memory-hard function, which would yield a generation algorithm running in time (roughly) proportional to $t \cdot \mathrm{poly}(\lambda)$.

Application 1: Memory-Hard Functions. We demonstrate the power of memory-hard puzzles via two applications. For our first application, we use memory-hard puzzles to construct a (one-time secure) *memory-hard function* (MHF) in the standard model. As part of this construction, we formally define (one-time) memory-hard functions in the standard model, without idealized primitives; see Definitions 7 and 8. We emphasize that all prior constructions

[1] Such hash functions generate a hashing key that statistically binds the i-th input bit. For example, a hash output y may have many different preimages, but all preimages have the same i-th bit. Construction of such hash functions exist under standard cryptographic assumptions such as DDH and LWE, among others [78].

of memory-hard functions rely on idealized primitives such as random oracles [2–8,16,25,28,43] or ideal ciphers and permutations [34]. In fact, prior definitions of memory-hardness were with respect to an idealized model such as the parallel random oracle model, e.g., [7].

Recall that a function f is memory-hard if it can be computed by a sequential machine in time t (and thus uses space at most t), but any PRAM algorithm evaluating f (possibly on multiple distinct inputs) has large cumulative memory complexity (cmc); e.g., at least $t^{2-\varepsilon}$ for small constant $\varepsilon > 0$. One-time security stipulates that for any input x, any attacker with low cmc cannot distinguish between $(x, f(x))$ and (x, r) with non-negligible advantage when r is a uniformly random bit string.[2] Assuming the existence of indistinguishability obfuscation, puncturable pseudo-random functions, and memory-hard puzzles, we give a construction of one-time secure memory-hard functions. We discuss the technical ideas of our MHF construction in Sect. 2.3 and present its memory-hardness in Theorem 4.

We stress that, to the best of our knowledge, this is the *first* construction of a memory-hard function under standard cryptographic assumptions and the additional assumption that a memory-hard puzzle exists. Given our construction of a memory-hard puzzle, we construct memory-hard functions from standard cryptographic assumptions additionally assuming the existence of a memory-hard language. or ideal cipher and permutation models.

We also conjecture that our scheme is multi-time secure as well: if an attacker with low cmc, say some g, cannot compute $f(x)$ for given input x, then an attacker with cmc at most $m \cdot g$ cannot compute $f(x_i)$ for m distinct inputs $x_1, \ldots, x_m$. However, we are unable to formally prove this due to some technical barriers in the security proof. At a high level, this is due to the fact that allowing the attacker to have higher cmc (e.g., $m \cdot g$) eventually leads to an attacker with large enough cmc to simply solve the underlying memory-hard puzzle that is used in the MHF construction, thus allowing the adversary to distinguish instances of the MHF instance. See Sect. 2.3 for discussion.

Application 2: LDCs for Resource-Bounded Channels. We use cryptographic puzzles to construct efficient *locally decodable codes for resource-bounded channels* [26]. A (ℓ, δ, p)-locally decodable code (LDC) $C[K, k]$ over some alphabet Σ is an error-correcting code with encoding function $\mathsf{Enc}\colon \Sigma^k \to \{0,1\}^K$ and probabilistic decoding function $\mathsf{Dec}\colon \{1, \ldots, k\} \to \Sigma$ satisfying the following properties. For any message x, the decoder, when given oracle access to some $\tilde{y}$ such that $\Delta(\tilde{y}, \mathsf{Enc}(x)) \leqslant \delta K$, makes at most ℓ queries to its oracle and outputs x_i with probability at least p, where Δ is the Hamming distance. The *rate* of the code is k/K, the *locality* of the code is ℓ, the *error tolerance* is δ, and the *success probability* is p. Classically (i.e., the adversarial channel introducing errors is computationally unbounded), there is an undesirable trade-off between the rate k/K and locality, e.g., if $\ell = \text{polylog}(k)$ then $K \gg k$.

[2] Our one-time security definition differs from those in prior literature (e.g., [6,7]), and is, in fact, stronger. See Sect. 2.3 for discussion.

Modeling the adversarial channel as computationally unbounded may be overly pessimistic. Moreover, it has been argued that any real world communication channel can be reasonably modeled as a resource-bounded channel [26,71]. A *resource-bounded channel* is an adversarial channel that is assumed to have some constrained resource (e.g., the channel is a low-depth circuit), and a resource-bounded LDC is a LDC that is resilient to errors introduced by some class of resource-bounded channels $\mathbb{C}$. Arguably, error patterns (even random ones) encountered in nature can be modeled by some (not necessarily known) resource-bounded algorithm which simulates the same error pattern, and thus these channels are well-motivated by real world channels. For example, sending a message from Earth to Mars takes between (roughly) 3 and 22 min when traveling at the speed of light; this limits the depth of any computation that could be completed before the (corrupted) codeword is delivered. Furthermore, examining LDCs resilient against several resource-bounded channels has led to better trade-offs between the rate and locality than their classical counterparts [15,24,50,71,76,84]. Recently, Blocki, Kulkarni, and Zhou [26] constructed LDCs for resource-bounded channels with locality $\ell = \text{polylog}(k)$ and constant rate $k/K = \Theta(1)$, but their construction relies on random oracles.

We use cryptographic puzzles to modify the construction of [26] to obtain resource-bounded LDCs without random oracles. Given any cryptographic puzzle that is secure against some class of adversaries $\mathbb{C}$, we construct a locally decodable code for Hamming errors that is secure against the class $\mathbb{C}$, resolving an open problem of Blocki, Kulkarni, and Zhou [26]. We discuss our LDC construction in Sect. 2.4 and present its memory-hardness in Corollary 1. We can instantiate our LDC with any (concretely secure) cryptographic puzzle. In particular, the time-lock puzzles of Bitansky et al. [19] directly give us LDCs secure against small-depth channels, and our memory-hard puzzle construction gives us LDCs secure against any channel with low cmc. Our LDC construction for resource bounded Hamming channels can also be extended to resource-bounded insertion-deletion (InsDel) channels by leveraging recent "Hamming-to-InsDel" LDC compilers [20,21,80]. See discussion in Sect. 2.4 and Corollary 2.

Challenges in Defining Memory-Hardness. Defining the correct machine model and cost metric for memory-hard puzzles is surprisingly difficult. As PRAM algorithms and cmc are used extensively in the study of MHFs, it is natural to use the same machine model and cost metric. However, cmc introduces subtleties in the analysis of our memory-hard puzzle construction: like [19], we rely on parallel amplification in order to construct an adversary which breaks our memory-hard language assumption. While parallel amplification does not significantly increase the depth of a computation (the metric used by [19]), any amplification *directly increases* the cmc of an algorithm by a multiplicative factor proportional to the number of amplification procedures performed. This requires careful consideration in our security reductions.

One may also attempt to define memory-hard languages as languages with cmc at least $t^{2-\varepsilon}$, for small constant $\varepsilon > 0$, that are also decidable by single-tape

Turing machines (à la [19]) in time t, rather than by uniformly succinct circuit families. However, we demonstrate a major hurdle towards this definition. In particular, we show that any single-tape Turing machine running in time t can be simulated by any PRAM algorithm with cmc $O(t^{1.8} \cdot \log(t))$; see Sect. 2.1 for discussion and Theorem 1 for our formal theorem. Taking this approach, we could not hope obtain memory hard puzzles with cmc at least $t^{2-\varepsilon}$ for small ε as we can rule out the existence of memory-hard languages with cmc $\gg t^{1.8}$. To contrast, under our uniformly succinct definition, we can provide a concrete candidate language with cmc plausibly as high as $t^{2-\varepsilon}$ such that the language is also decidable by a uniformly succinct circuit family of size $\widetilde{O}(t)$.[3] Furthermore, we show that our definition is essentially minimal, i.e., we can use memory-hard puzzles to construct memory-hard languages under the modest assumption that the puzzle solving algorithm is uniformly succinct; see discussion in Sect. 2.1 and Proposition 1.

1.2 Prior Work

Cryptographic puzzles are functions which require some specified amount of resources (e.g., time or space) to compute. Time-lock puzzles, introduced by Rivest, Shamir, and Wagner [83] extending the study of timed-released cryptography of May [75], are puzzles which require large sequential time to solve: any circuit solving the puzzle has large depth. [83] proposed a candidate time-lock puzzle based on the conjectured sequential hardness of exponentiation in RSA groups, and the proposed schemes of [29,44] are variants of this scheme. Mahmoody, Moran, and Vadhan [73] give a construction of *weak* time-lock puzzles in the random oracle model, where "weak" says that both a puzzle generator and puzzle solver require (roughly) the same amount of computation, whereas the standard definition of puzzles requires the puzzle generation algorithm to be much more efficient than the solving algorithm. Closer to our work, Bitansky et al. [19] construct time-lock puzzles using succinct randomized encodings, which can be instantiated from one-way functions, indistinguishability obfuscation, and other assumptions [46]. Recently, Malavolta and Thyagarajan [74] introduce and construct homomorphic time-lock puzzles: puzzles where one can compute functions over puzzle solutions without solving them. Continued exploration of indistinguishability obfuscation has pushed it closer and closer to being instantiated from well-founded cryptographic assumptions such as learning with errors [59].

Memory-hard functions (MHFs), introduced by Percival [81], have enjoyed rich lines of both theoretical and applied research in construction and analysis of these functions [2–8,16,25,28,34,43]. The security proofs of all prior MHF candidates rely on idealized assumptions (e.g., random oracles [5–8,27]) or other ideal objects (e.g., ideal ciphers or permutations [34]). The notion of *data-independent* MHFs—MHFs where the data-access pattern of computing the function, say, via a RAM program, is independent of the input—has also been widely explored.

[3] In fact, one can provably show that the cmc is $t^{2-\varepsilon}$ in the random oracle model.

Data-independent MHFs are attractive as they provide natural resistance to side-channel attacks. However, building data-independent memory-hard functions (iMHFs) comes at a cost: *any* iMHF has amortized space-time complexity at most $O(N^2 \cdot \text{loglog}(N)/\log(N))$ [2], while data-dependent MHFs were proved to have maximal complexity $\Omega(N^2)$ in the parallel random oracle model [6] (here, N is the run time of the honest sequential evaluation algorithm). Recently, Ameri, Blocki, and Zhou [10] introduced the notion of *computationally data-independent* memory-hard functions: MHFs which appear data-independent to a computationally bounded adversaries. This relaxation of data-independence allowed [10] to circumvent known barriers in the construction of data-independent MHFs as long as certain assumptions on the tiered memory architecture (RAM/cache) hold.

LDC constructions, like all code constructions, generally follow one of two channel models: the Hamming channel where worst-case bit-flip error patterns are introduced, and the Shannon channel where symbols are corrupted by an independent probabilistic process. Probabilistic channels may be too weak to capture natural phenomenon, while Hamming channels often limit achievable code constructions. For the Hamming channel, the channel is assumed to have unbounded power. Protecting against unbounded errors is desirable but often has undesirable trade-offs. For example, current constructions of LDCs with efficient (i.e., poly-time) encodings an obtain any constant rate $R < 1$, are robust to $\delta < (1 - R)$-fraction of errors, but have query complexity $2^{O(\sqrt{\log n \log\log n})}$ for codeword length n [65]. If one instead focuses on obtaining low query complexity, one can obtain schemes with codewords of length sub-exponential in the message size while using a constant number $q \geqslant 3$ queries [40,42,87]. These undesirable trade-offs have lead to a long line of work examining LDCs (and codes in general) with relaxed assumptions [15,24,50,71,76,84]. Two relaxations closely related to our work are due to Ostrovsky, Pandey, and Sahai [79] and Blocki, Kulkarni, and Zhou [26]. [79] introduce and construct *private* Hamming LDCs: locally decodable codes in the secret key setting, where the encoder and decoder share a secret key that is unknown to the (unbounded) channel. Blocki, Kulkarni, and Zhou [26] analyze Hamming LDCs in the context of *resource-bounded channels*. The LDC construction of [26] bootstraps off of the private Hamming LDC construction of [79], obtaining Hamming LDCs in the random oracle model assuming the existence of functions which are uncomputable by the channel.

While Hamming LDCs have enjoyed decades of research [40,42,61,62,65,66, 86–88], the study of *insertion-deletion* LDCs (or InsDel LDCs) remains scarce. An InsDel LDC is a LDC that is resilient to adversarial insertion-deletion errors. In the non-LDC setting, there has been a rich line of research into insertion-deletion codes [32,35–39,47–49,51–56,64,68,72,85], and only recently have efficient InsDel codes with asymptotically good information rate and error tolerance been well-understood [47,52–54,72]. Ostrovsky and Paskin-Cherniavsky [80] and Block et al. [21] give a compiler which transforms any Hamming LDC into an InsDel LDC with a poly-logarithmic blow-up in the locality. Block and Blocki [20] extend the compiler of [21] to the private and resource-bounded settings.

Recently, Blocki et al. [22] give lower bounds for InsDel LDCs with constant locality: they show that (1) any 2-query InsDel LDC must have exponential rate; (2) 2-query linear InsDel LDCs do not exist; and (3) for any constant $q \geqslant 3$, a q-query InsDel LDC must have rate that is exponential in existing lower bounds for Hamming LDCs.

2 Technical Overview

Our construction of memory-hard puzzles relies on two key technical ingredients. First we require the existence of a language $\mathcal{L} \subseteq \{0,1\}^*$ that is suitably *memory-hard*. Given such a language, we additionally require *succinct randomized encodings* [17,46,70] for succinct circuits. With these two objects, we construct *memory-hard puzzles*. Both of our memory-hard objects are defined with respect to *parallel random access machine* (PRAM) algorithms and *cumulative memory complexity* (cmc). We say that an algorithm A is a PRAM *algorithm* if during each time-step of the computation, the algorithm has an internal state and can read from multiple positions from memory, perform a computation, then write to multiple positions in memory. Recall that $\mathsf{cmc}(A, x)$ is the summation of the memory used by $A(x)$ during every time step of the computation, and $\mathsf{cmc}(A, \lambda) = \max_{x\colon |x|=\lambda} \mathsf{cmc}(A, x)$. Moreover, for a function y, we say that $\mathsf{cmc}(A) < y$ if $\mathsf{cmc}(A, \lambda) < y(\lambda)$ for all $\lambda \in \mathbb{N}$. We note that even though we define cmc as a maximum, in all of our memory-hard definitions we quantify over all adversaries, and thus capture worst-case hardness.

We discuss the key ideas and present our main results in the remainder of this section. Section 2.1 presents our formal definition of memory-hard languages and a discussion on the plausibility and necessity of this assumption. Section 2.2 presents our formal definition of memory-hard puzzles and presents an overview of our construction assuming the existence of a memory-hard language and a succinct randomized encoding scheme. Section 2.3 presents an overview of our construction of a (one-time secure) memory-hard functions assuming the existence of indistinguishability obfuscation, one-way functions, and memory-hard puzzles. Finally, Sect. 2.4 presents our construction of resource-bounded locally decodable codes from any cryptographic puzzle.

2.1 Memory-Hard Languages

Our definition of memory-hard languages is inspired by the notion of non-parallelizing languages,[4] which are required by Bitansky et al. [19] to construct time-lock puzzles (also using succinct randomized encodings). We define our memory-hard languages with respect to a particular language class that requires the notion of *uniformly succinct circuits*. Informally, a circuit family $\{C_{t,\lambda}\}_{\lambda \in \mathbb{N}}$ is *succinct* if there exists a smaller circuit family $\{C'_{t,\lambda}\}_{\lambda \in \mathbb{N}}$ such that for every

[4] Informally, a language is non-parallelizing if any polynomial sized circuit deciding the language has large depth.

$t \in \mathbb{N}$: (1) $|C'_{t,\lambda}| = \text{polylog}(|C_{t,\lambda}|)$; and (2) on input gate number g of $C_{t,\lambda}$ the circuit $C'_{t,\lambda}(g)$ outputs the indices of the input gates of g and the function f_g computed by gate g. Furthermore, we say that a succinct circuit family is *uniformly succinct* if there additionally exists a sequential algorithm running in time $\text{poly}(|C'_{t,\lambda}|)$ that outputs the description of the succinct circuit $C'_{t,\lambda}$ for every λ. We capture the formal definitions below, beginning with succinct circuits.

Definition 1 (Succinct Circuits [18,46]**).** *Let $C\colon \{0,1\}^n \to \{0,1\}^m$ be a circuit with $N - n$ binary gates. The gates of the circuit are numbered as follows. The input gates are given numbers $\{1, \ldots, n\}$. The intermediate gates are numbered $\{n+1, n+2, \ldots, N-m\}$ such that for any gate g with inputs from gates i and j, the label for g is bigger than i and j. The output gates are numbered $\{N-m+1, \ldots, N\}$. Each gate $g \in \{n+1, \ldots, N\}$ is described by a tuple $(i, j, f_g) \in [g-1]^2 \times \mathsf{GType}$ where the outputs of gates i and j serve as inputs to gate g and f_g denotes the functionality computed by gate g. Here,* GType *denotes the set of all binary functions $f : \{0,1\}^2 \to \{0,1\}$.*

We say that the circuit C is succinct *if there exists a circuit C^{sc} such that on input $g \in \{n+1, N\}$ outputs description (i, j, f_g) and $|C^{\mathsf{sc}}| < |C|$.*

For notational convenience, for any circuit C^{sc} that succinctly describes a larger circuit C, we define $\mathsf{FullCirc}(C^{\mathsf{sc}}) := C$ and $\mathsf{SuccCirc}(C) := C^{\mathsf{sc}}$. Next we give the definition uniformly succinct circuit families.

Definition 2 (Uniform Succinct Circuit Families). *We say that a circuit family $\{C_{t,\lambda}\}_{t,\lambda}$ is* succinctly describable *if there exists another circuit family $\{C^{\mathsf{sc}}_{t,\lambda}\}_{t,\lambda}$ such that $|C^{\mathsf{sc}}_{t,\lambda}| = \text{polylog}(|C_{t,\lambda}|)$*[5] *and $\mathsf{FullCirc}(C^{\mathsf{sc}}_{t,\lambda}) = C_{t,\lambda}$ for every t, λ. Additionally, if there exists a PRAM algorithm A such that $A(t, \lambda)$ outputs $C^{\mathsf{sc}}_{t,\lambda}$ in time $\text{poly}(|C^{\mathsf{sc}}_{t,\lambda}|)$ for every t, λ, then we say that $\{C_{t,\lambda}\}_{t,\lambda}$ is* uniformly succinct.

Given the notion of uniformly succinct circuits, we define our language class SC_t.

Definition 3 (Language Class SC_t). *Let t be a positive function. We define SC_t as the class of languages $\mathcal{L}$ decidable by a uniformly succinct circuit family $\{C_{t,\lambda}\}_\lambda$ such that there exists a polynomial p satisfying $|C_{t,\lambda}| \leqslant t \cdot p(\lambda, \log(t))$ for every λ and $t := t(\lambda)$.*

Given Definition 3, we define *memory-hard languages*. Intuitively, a language $\mathcal{L} \in \mathsf{SC}_t$ is memory-hard if any (PRAM) algorithm $\mathcal{B}$ that ε-decides $\mathcal{L}$ must have large cmc, where ε-decides here informally means that any probabilistic algorithm can decide the language $\mathcal{L}$ with advantage at least ε.

Definition 4 ((g, ε)-Memory Hard Language). *Let t be a positive function. A language $\mathcal{L} \in \mathsf{SC}_t$ is a (g, ε)-*memory hard language *if for every PRAM algorithm $\mathcal{B}$ with $\mathsf{cmc}(\mathcal{B}, \lambda) < g(t(\lambda), \lambda)$, the algorithm $\mathcal{B}$ does not $\varepsilon(\lambda)$-decide $\mathcal{L}_\lambda$*

[5] For our purposes, we require the size of the succinct circuit to be poly-logarithmic in the size of the full circuit. One can easily replace this requirement with the requirement presented in Definition 1.

for every λ. *If* $\varepsilon(\lambda) = \mathsf{negl}(\lambda)$, *we say* $\mathcal{L}$ *is a* g-strong memory-hard language. *If* $\varepsilon(\lambda) \in (0, 1/2)$ *is a constant, we say* $\mathcal{L}$ *is a* (g, ε) -weakly memory-hard.

Note that one may define a weak memory-hard language with respect to $\varepsilon(\lambda) = 1/\operatorname{poly}(\lambda)$; however, this turns out to be essentially equivalent to $\varepsilon(\lambda) \in (0, 1/2)$. See the full version of our work [9] for a discussion. Moreover, our definition of memory-hard languages is essentially minimal, as one can construct memory-hard languages from memory-hard puzzles under the modest assumption that the puzzle solving algorithm is uniformly succinct. We prove the following proposition in the full version of our work [9].

Proposition 1. *Let* $\mathsf{Puz} = (\mathsf{Puz.Gen}, \mathsf{Puz.Sol})$ *be a* (g, ε)*-memory hard puzzle such that* $\mathsf{Puz.Sol}$ *is computable by a uniformly succinct circuit family* $\{C_{t,\lambda}\}_{t,\lambda}$ *of size* $|C_{t,\lambda}| \leqslant t \cdot \operatorname{poly}(\lambda, \log(t))$ *for every* λ *and difficulty parameter* $t := t(\lambda)$. *For language* $\mathcal{L}_{\mathsf{Puz}} := \{(Z, s) \colon s = \mathsf{Puz.Sol}(Z)\}$, *we have that* $\mathcal{L}_{\mathsf{Puz}} \in \mathsf{SC}_t$ *and is a* (g, ε)*-memory hard language.*

Plausibility of Memory-Hard Languages. We complement our definition of memory-hard languages by providing a concrete construction of a candidate memory-hard language. We define a language $\mathcal{L}_\lambda = \mathcal{L} \cap \{0, 1\}^\lambda$ that is decidable by a uniformly succinct circuit $C_{t,\lambda}$ of size $t^2 \cdot \operatorname{polylog}(t)$. Our language relies on a hash function H, and under the idealized assumption that H is a random oracle, $\mathcal{L}_\lambda$ is provably memory-hard with cumulative memory complexity at least $t^2/\log(t)$.

Key to defining $\mathcal{L}_\lambda$ is a recent explicit construction of a depth-robust graph due to Blocki, Cinkoske, Lee, and Son [23]. Depth-robustness is a combinatorial property which is sufficient for constructing memory-hard functions in the parallel random oracle model [4]. Crucially, this graph is explicit and deterministic, and can be fully encoded by a uniformly succinct circuit. We remark that other randomized constructions of depth-robust graphs such the one used in the DRSample memory-hard function [3] cannot be used to construct memory-hard languages as the graphs are not uniformly succinct. We defer the reader to the full version of our work for more discussion [9].

We acknowledge that we only know how to prove our candidate language is memory-hard in the random oracle model or other idealized models of computation, which we are trying to avoid in our memory-hard puzzle construction. However, our memory-hard puzzle construction- does not require an explicit memory-hard language and our security proof holds as long as some memory-hard language exists. Thus, our goal is simply to establish a plausible candidate for such a language. We conjecture that our defined language will remain memory-hard when the random oracle is instantiated with a concrete cryptographic hash function such as SHA3. Proving that the conjecture holds in the standard model, however, would require major advances in the difficult field of complexity theory and circuit lower bounds. Moreover, assuming that all of our cryptographic assumptions hold, a concrete attack against our memory-hard puzzle construction would directly show that memory-hard languages do not exist, which is presumably a difficult problem in complexity theory.

PRAM Algorithms versus Turing Machines. One might try to define memory-hard languages to require they be decidable by a single-tape Turing machine rather than a PRAM algorithm. However, we show that if we require our memory-hard language to be decidable by a single-tape Turing machine in time $t = t(\lambda)$, then the language is only secure against PRAM algorithms with cmc *less than* $\widetilde{O}(t^{1.8})$. We show this by proving that any single-tape Turing machine running in time $t = t(\lambda)$ for λ-bit inputs can be simulated by a PRAM algorithm in time $O(t)$ using with space at most $O(t^{0.8} \cdot \log(t))$. As cmc is upper bounded by the maximum space of a computation times the maximum time of a computation, this implies that cmc is at most $O(t^{1.8} \cdot \log(t))$. We prove the following theorem in the full version of our work [9].

Theorem 1. *For any language $\mathcal{L}$ decidable in time $t(n)$ by a single-tape Turing machine for inputs of size n, there exists a constant $c > 0$ such that $\mathcal{L}$ is decidable by a PRAM algorithm with* cmc *at most* $c \cdot t(n)^{1.8} \cdot \log(t(n))$.

It is an interesting open question if such a reduction holds for multi-tape Turing machines; in particular, showing such a reduction for two-tape Turing machines would only strengthen our definition due to the reduction from multi-tape to two-tape Turing machines [82].

2.2 Memory-Hard Puzzles

We formally define *memory-hard puzzles.* Intuitively, a memory-hard puzzle is a cryptographic puzzle which requires any PRAM algorithm solving the puzzle to have large cmc. We give two flavors of memory-hard puzzles and begin with an asymptotically secure memory-hard puzzle.

Definition 5 (g-Memory Hard Puzzle). *A puzzle* $\mathsf{Puz} = (\mathsf{Puz.Gen}, \mathsf{Puz.Sol})$ *is a* g -memory hard puzzle *if there exists a polynomial t' such that for all polynomials $t > t'$ and for every PRAM algorithm $\mathcal{A}$ with* $\mathsf{cmc}(\mathcal{A}) < y$ *for the function* $y(\lambda) := g(t(\lambda), \lambda)$, *there exists a negligible function μ such that for all $\lambda \in \mathbb{N}$ and every pair $s_0, s_1 \in \{0,1\}^\lambda$ we have* $|\Pr[\mathcal{A}(Z_b, Z_{1-b}, s_0, s_1) = b] - 1/2| \leqslant \mu(\lambda)$, *where the probability is taken over* $b \xleftarrow{\$} \{0,1\}$ *and* $Z_i \leftarrow \mathsf{Puz.Gen}(1^\lambda, t(\lambda), s_i)$ *for* $i \in \{0,1\}$.

Note that for any difficulty parameter $t := t(\lambda)$ for security λ, we assume that $\mathsf{Puz.Sol}$ is computable in time $t \cdot \text{poly}(\lambda)$ on a sequential RAM algorithm. This implies that there exists a PRAM algorithm A computing $\mathsf{Puz.Sol}$ has $\mathsf{cmc}(A, \lambda) \leqslant (t \cdot \text{poly}(\lambda))^2 = t^2 \cdot \text{poly}(\lambda)$. This yields an upper bound on the function g of Definition 5: take t to be any (large enough) polynomial. Then suitable values of g (ignoring poly(λ) factors) include $g = t^2/\log(t)$ or $g = t^{2-\theta}$ for small constant $\theta > 0$. In particular, we cannot expect to design g-memory hard puzzles for any function $g = \omega(t^2 \cdot \text{poly}(\lambda))$ (by our definitions).

We complement Definition 5 with the following concrete security definition.

Definition 6 ((g, ε)-Memory Hard Puzzle). *A puzzle* $\mathsf{Puz} = (\mathsf{Puz.Gen}, \mathsf{Puz.Sol})$ *is a* (g, ε)-memory hard puzzle *if there exists a polynomial* t' *such that for all polynomials* $t > t'$ *and every PRAM algorithm* $\mathcal{A}$ *with* $\mathsf{cmc}(\mathcal{A}) < y$ *for* $y(\lambda) := g(t(\lambda), \lambda)$*, and for all* $\lambda > 0$ *and any pair* $s_0, s_1 \in \{0,1\}^{\lambda}$*, we have* $|\Pr[\mathcal{A}(Z_b, Z_{1-b}, s_0, s_1) = b] - 1/2| \leqslant \varepsilon(\lambda)$*, where the probability is taken over* $b \xleftarrow{\$} \{0,1\}$ *and* $Z_i \leftarrow \mathsf{Puz.Gen}(1^{\lambda}, t(\lambda), s_i)$ *for* $i \in \{0,1\}$*. If* $\varepsilon(\lambda) = 1/\mathrm{poly}(\lambda)$*, we say the puzzle is* weakly memory-hard.

Similar to Definition 5, suitable values of g for Definition 6 include $g = t^2/\log(t)$ and $g = t^{2-\theta}$ for small constant $\theta > 0$, as any PRAM algorithm with cmc larger than $t^2 \cdot \mathrm{poly}(\lambda)$ can trivially break puzzles security simply by running the algorithm $\mathsf{Puz.Sol}$.

We note that in our security definition the adversary is given two puzzles Z_b, Z_{1-b} in random order along with both solutions s_0, s_1 (in the correct order). An alternate security definition would only give the adversary one puzzle, Z_b, and the solutions s_0, s_1. We remark that our security definition is at least as strong since the attacker can simply choose to ignore Z_{1-b}. It is an open question whether or not there is reduction in the other direction establishing tight concrete security guarantees. Thus, we choose to use the stronger definition.

We construct memory-hard puzzles by using succinct randomized encodings for succinct circuits and additionally assuming that a (suitable) memory-hard language exists. Informally, a succinct randomized encoding for succinct circuits consists of two algorithms $\mathsf{sRE.Enc}$ and $\mathsf{sRE.Dec}$ where $\widehat{C}_{x,G} \leftarrow \mathsf{sRE.Enc}(1^{\lambda}, C', x, G)$ takes as input a security parameter λ, a succinct circuit C' describing a larger circuit C with G gates and an input $x \in \{0,1\}^*$ and outputs a randomized encoding $\widehat{C}$ in time $\mathrm{poly}(|C'|, \lambda, \log(G), |x|)$. The decoding algorithm $\mathsf{sRE.Dec}(\widehat{C}_{x,G})$ outputs $C(x)$ in time at most $G \cdot \mathrm{poly}(\log(G), \lambda)$. Note that the running time requirement ensures $\mathsf{sRE.Enc}$ cannot simply compute $C(x)$. Intuitively, security implies that the encoding $\widehat{C}_{x,G}$ reveals nothing more than $C(x)$ to a computationally bounded attacker. Due to space constraints, we defer the formal definitions of both asymptotically secure and concretely secure succinct randomized encodings to the full version of our work [9].

We extend ideas from [19] to construct memory-hard puzzles from succinct randomized encodings; the formal construction is presented in the full version of our work [9]. The generation algorithm $\mathsf{Puz.Gen}(1^{\lambda}, t, s)$ first constructs a Turing machine $M_{s,t}$ that on any input runs for t steps then outputs s, where $t = t(\lambda)$ and $s \in \{0,1\}^{\lambda}$. This machine is then transformed into a succinct circuit $C'_{s,t}$ (via a transformation due to Pippenger and Fischer [82]), and then encodes this succinct circuit with our succinct randomized encoding; i.e., $Z = \mathsf{sRE.Enc}(1^{\lambda}, C'_{s,t}, 0^{\lambda}, G_{s,t})$. Here, $C'_{s,t}$ succinctly describes a larger circuit $C_{s,t}$ which is equivalent to $M_{s,t}$ (on inputs of size λ) and has $G_{s,t} := |C_{s,t}|$ gates. The puzzle solution algorithm simply runs the decoding procedure of the randomized encoding scheme; i.e., $\mathsf{Puz.Sol}(Z)$ outputs $s \leftarrow \mathsf{sRE.Dec}(Z)$.

Security is obtained via reduction to a suitable memory-hard language $\mathcal{L}$. If the security of the constructed puzzle is broken by an adversary $\mathcal{A}$ with small cmc, then we construct a new adversary $\mathcal{B}$ with small cmc which breaks the memory-hard language assumption by deciding whether $x \in \mathcal{L}$ with non-negligible advantage. Suppose that $Z_0 \leftarrow \mathsf{Puz.Gen}(1^\lambda, t, s_0)$, $Z_1 \leftarrow \mathsf{Puz.Gen}(1^\lambda, t, s_1)$, b is a random bit, and $t := t(\lambda)$. If $\mathcal{A}(s_0, s_1, Z_b, Z_{1-b})$ can violate the MHP security and predict b with non-negligible probability, then we can construct an algorithm $\mathcal{B}$ with similar cmc that decides our memory-hard language. Algorithm $\mathcal{B}$ first constructs a uniformly succinct circuit $C_{a,a'}$ such that on any input x we have $C_{a,a'}(x) = a$ if $x \in \mathcal{L}$; otherwise $C_{a,a'}(x) = a'$ if $x \notin \mathcal{L}$. Our definition of memory-hard languages ensures that $C_{a,a'}$ is uniformly succinct and has size $G = t \cdot \mathrm{poly}(\lambda, \log(t))$. Let $C'_{a,a'}$ denote the smaller circuit that succinctly describes $C_{a,a'}$. The adversary computes $Z_i = \mathsf{sRE.Enc}(1^\lambda, C'_{s_i, s_{1-i}}, x, G)$ for $i \in \{0, 1\}$, samples $b \xleftarrow{\$} \{0, 1\}$, and obtains $b' \leftarrow \mathcal{A}(Z_b, Z_{1-b}, s_0, s_1)$. Our adversary $\mathcal{B}$ outputs 1 if $b = b'$ and 0 otherwise.

Observe that if $x \in \mathcal{L}$ then $\mathsf{Puz.Sol}(Z_0) = s_0$ and $\mathsf{Puz.Sol}(Z_1) = s_1$; otherwise if $x \notin \mathcal{L}$ then $\mathsf{Puz.Sol}(Z_0) = s_1$ and $\mathsf{Puz.Sol}(Z_1) = s_0$. By security of sRE, adversary $\mathcal{A}$ cannot distinguish between $Z_i = \mathsf{sRE.Enc}(1^\lambda, C'_{s_i, s_{1-i}}, x, G)$ and a puzzle generated with $\mathsf{Puz.Gen}$. Thus on input (Z_b, Z_{1-b}, s_0, s_1), the adversary $\mathcal{A}$ outputs $b' = b$ with non-negligible advantage. By our above observation, we have that $\mathcal{B}$ now (probabilistically) decides the memory-hard language $\mathcal{L}$ with non-negligible advantage. To obtain an adversary $\mathcal{B}'$ that deterministically decides $\mathcal{L}$, we use standard amplification techniques, along with the assumption of $\mathcal{B}'$ being a non-uniform algorithm (à la the argument for $\mathsf{BPP} \subset \mathsf{P}/\mathrm{poly}$). Whereas amplification—when performed in parallel—does not significantly increase the total computation depth, *any* amplification increases the cmc of an algorithm by a multiplicative factor proportional to the amount of amplification performed. Intuitively, this is because the cmc of an algorithm A is equal to the sum of the cmc of all sub-computations performed by A. We defer formal details to the full version of our work [9].

The memory-hardness of our construction relies on the particular succinct randomized encoding scheme used, and the existence of an appropriately memory-hard language. We again stress that the memory-hardness of our construction does not rely on an explicit instance of a memory-hard language, and the existence of such a language is sufficient for the above reduction to hold. We show that our construction satisfies two flavors of memory-hardness. First, given an asymptotically secure succinct randomized encoding scheme sRE and the existence of a *strong* memory-hard language, we show that there exists is an asymptotically secure memory-hard puzzle.

Theorem 2. *Let* $t := t(\lambda)$ *be a polynomial and let* $g := g(t, \lambda)$ *be a function. Let* $\mathsf{sRE} = (\mathsf{sRE.Enc}, \mathsf{sRE.Dec})$ *be a succinct randomized encoding scheme. If there exists a* g'*-strong memory-hard language* $\mathcal{L} \in \mathsf{SC}_t$ *for* $g'(t, \lambda) := g + 2p_{\mathsf{sRE}}(\log(t), \lambda)^2 + 2p_{\mathsf{SC}}(\log(t), \log(\lambda))^2 + O(\lambda)$, *then there exists a* g*-memory hard puzzle. Here,* p_{sRE} *and* p_{SC} *are fixed polynomials for the runtimes of* $\mathsf{sRE.Enc}$ *and the uniform machine constructing the uniform succinct circuit of* $\mathcal{L}$*, respectively.*

To get a handle on Theorem 2, consider a large enough polynomial t such that $t \gg p_{\mathsf{sRE}}(\log(t), \lambda)$ and $t \gg p_{\mathsf{SC}}(\log(t), \log(\lambda))$. Then if there exists a g'-strong memory-hard language for $g'(t, \lambda) = t^2/\log(t)$, we obtain a g-memory hard puzzle for $g(t, \lambda) = (1 - o(1)) \cdot g'(t, \lambda)$ (i.e., there is little loss in the memory-hardness of the constructed puzzle).

Next, assuming a concretely secure succinct randomized encoding scheme sRE and the existence of a *weak* memory-hard language, then there exists a weakly-secure memory-hard puzzle.

Theorem 3. *Let $t := t(\lambda)$ be a polynomial and let $g := g(t, \lambda)$ be a function. Let* $\mathsf{sRE} = (\mathsf{sRE.Enc}, \mathsf{sRE.Dec})$ *be a $(g, s, \varepsilon_{\mathsf{sRE}})$-secure succinct randomized encoding scheme for $g := g(t, \lambda)$ and $s(\lambda) := t \cdot \mathrm{poly}(\lambda, \log(t))$ such that p_{sRE} is a fixed polynomial for the runtime of* sRE.Enc. *Let $\varepsilon := \varepsilon(\lambda) = 1/\mathrm{poly}(\lambda) > 3\varepsilon_{\mathsf{sRE}}(\lambda)$ be fixed. If there exists a $(g', \varepsilon_{\mathcal{L}})$-weakly memory-hard language $\mathcal{L} \in \mathsf{SC}_t$ for $g'(t, \lambda) := [g + 2p_{\mathsf{sRE}}(\log(t), \lambda)^2 + 2p_{\mathsf{SC}}(\log(t), \log(\lambda))^2 + O(\lambda)] \cdot \Theta(1/\varepsilon)$, and some constant $\varepsilon_{\mathcal{L}} \in (0, 1/2)$, then there exists a (g, ε)-weakly memory-hard puzzle. Here, p_{SC} is a fixed polynomial for the runtime of the uniform machine constructing the uniform succinct circuit for $\mathcal{L}$.*

Notice here we lose a factor of $\Theta(1/\varepsilon)$ when compared with Theorem 2. Concretely, using our same example from Theorem 2, if t is sufficiently large such that $t \gg p_{\mathsf{sRE}}(\log(t), \lambda)$ and $t \gg p_{\mathsf{SC}}(\log(t), \log(\lambda))$, and if $\varepsilon = 1/\lambda^2$, then for $g' = t^2/\log(t)$ we obtain a (g, ε)-weakly memory-hard puzzle for $g = g' \cdot \Theta(\lambda^2)$. This loss is due to the security reduction: our adversary performs amplification to boost the success probability of breaking the weakly memory-hard language assumption from ε to the constant $\varepsilon_{\mathcal{L}}$. To achieve constant $\varepsilon_{\mathcal{L}}$, one needs to amplify $\Theta(1/\varepsilon)$ times. As discussed previously, amplification directly incurs a multiplicative blow-up in the cmc complexity of a PRAM algorithm performing the amplification.

2.3 Memory-Hard Functions from Memory-Hard Puzzles

Using our new notion of memory-hard puzzles, we construct a one-time memory-hard function under standard cryptographic assumptions. To the best of our knowledge, this is the first such construction in the standard model; i.e., without random oracles [7] or other idealized primitives [34]. Recall that informally a function f is memory-hard if any PRAM algorithm computing f has large cmc. We define the *one-time* security of a memory-hard function f via the following game between an adversary and an honest challenger. First, before the game begins an input x is selected and provided to the challenger and the attacker. Second, the challenger computes $y_0 = f(x)$ and samples $y_1 \in \{0,1\}^\lambda$ and $b \xleftarrow{\$} \{0,1\}$ uniformly at random, and sends y_b. Then the attacker outputs a guess b' for b. We say that the adversary wins if $b' = b$, and say that f is (t, ε)-*one time secure* if for all inputs x and all attackers running in time $\leqslant t$ the probability that the attacker outputs the correct guess $b' = b$ is at most $\varepsilon(\lambda)$. Note that this definition differs from prior definitions in the literature (e.g., [6,7]), and is in fact stronger than requiring that an adversary with insufficient resources cannot compute the MHF. However, we remark that in the random oracle model, for random oracle H, any MHF f immediately yields a function $f'(x) = H(f(x))$ which is indistinguishable from random to any adversary that cannot compute $f(x)$. We provide two definitions of one-time memory-hard functions in the standard model. First, we present a simplified definition of asymptotic security for MHFs (see [9] for the complete formal definition).

Definition 7 (One-Time g -MHF). *For a function $g(\cdot,\cdot)$, we say that a memory hard function* MHF = (MHF.Setup, MHF.Eval) *is* one-time g -memory hard *if there exists a polynomial t' such that for all polynomials $t(\lambda) > t'(\lambda)$ and every adversary A with $\mathsf{cmc}(A) < y$ for $y(\lambda) := g(t(\lambda), \lambda)$, there exists a negligible function $\mu(\lambda)$ such that for all $\lambda \in \mathbb{N}$ and every input $x \in \{0,1\}^\lambda$, we have $|\Pr[A(x, h_b, \mathsf{pp}) = b] - 1/2| \leqslant \mu(\lambda)$, where the probability is taken over $\mathsf{pp} \leftarrow \mathrm{MHF.Setup}(1^\lambda, t(\lambda))$, $b \xleftarrow{\$} \{0,1\}$, $h_0 \leftarrow \mathrm{MHF.Eval}(\mathsf{pp}, x)$, and $h_1 \xleftarrow{\$} \{0,1\}^\lambda$.*

We complement the above definition with a concrete security definition.

Definition 8 (One-time (g,ε)-MHF). *For a function $g(\cdot,\cdot)$, we say that a* MHF = (MHF.Setup, MHF.Eval) *is a* one-time (g,ε) -MHF *if there exists a polynomial t' such that for all polynomials $t(\lambda) > t'(\lambda)$ and every adversary A with area-time complexity $\mathsf{cmc}(A) < y$, where $y(\lambda) = g(t(\lambda), \lambda)$, and for all $\lambda > 0$ and $x \in \{0,1\}^\lambda$ we have $|\Pr[A(x, h_b, \mathsf{pp}) = b] - 1/2| \leqslant \varepsilon(\lambda)$, where the probability is taken over $\mathsf{pp} \leftarrow \mathrm{MHF.Setup}(1^\lambda, t(\lambda))$, $b \xleftarrow{\$} \{0,1\}$, $h_0 \leftarrow \mathrm{MHF.Eval}(x, \mathsf{pp})$ and a uniformly random string $h_1 \in \{0,1\}^\lambda$.*

We give a memory-hard function construction that relies on our new notion of memory-hard puzzles, and additionally uses indistinguishability obfuscation ($i\mathcal{O}$) for circuits and a family of puncturable pseudo-random functions (PPRFs) $\{F_i\}_i$ [30,31,63]. Informally, PPRFs are pseudo-random functions that allow one to "puncture" a key K at values $x_1, \ldots, x_k$, where the key K can be used to evaluate the function at any point $x \notin \{x_1, \ldots, x_k\}$ and hide the values of the function at the points $x_1, \ldots, x_k$.

We formally present our memory-hard function in the full version of our work [9] and provide a high-level overview of the construction here. During the setup phase we generate three PPRF keys K_1, K_2, and K_3 and obfuscate a program $\mathsf{prog}(\cdot,\cdot)$ which does the following. On input $(x, \perp)$, prog outputs a memory-hard puzzle $\mathsf{Puz.Gen}(1^\lambda, t(\lambda), s; r)$ with solution $s = F_{K_1}(x)$ using randomness $r = F_{K_2}(x)$. On input (x, s'), prog checks to see if $s' = F_{K_1}(x)$ and, if so, outputs $F_{K_3}(x)$; otherwise $\perp$. Given the public parameters $\mathsf{pp} = i\mathcal{O}(\mathsf{prog})$, we can evaluate the MHF as follows: (1) run $\mathsf{pp}(x, \perp) = i\mathcal{O}(\mathsf{prog}(x, \perp))$ to obtain a puzzle Z; (2) solve the puzzle Z to obtain $s = \mathsf{Puz.Sol}(Z)$; and (3) run $\mathsf{pp}(x, s) = i\mathcal{O}(\mathsf{prog})(x, s)$ to obtain the output $F_{K_3}(x)$. Intuitively, the construction is shown to be one-time memory-hard by appealing to the memory-hard puzzle security, PPRF security, and $i\mathcal{O}$ security.

We establish one-time memory-hardness by showing how to transform an MHF attacker $\mathcal{A}$ into a MHP attacker $\mathcal{B}$ with comparable cmc. Our reduction involves a sequence of hybrids H_0, H_1, H_2 and H_3. Hybrid H_0 is simply our above constructed function. In hybrid H_1 we puncture the PPRF keys $K_i\{x_0, x_1\}$ at target points x_0, x_1 and hard code the corresponding puzzles Z_0, Z_1 along with their solutions—$i\mathcal{O}$ security implies that H_1 and H_0 are indistinguishable. In hybrid H_2 we rely on PPRF security to replace Z_0, Z_1 with randomly generated puzzles independent of the PPRF keys K_1, K_2 and hardcode the corresponding solutions s_0, s_1. Finally, in hybrid H_3 we rely on MHP security to break the relationship between s_i and Z_i; i.e., we flip a coin b' and hardcoded puzzles $Z'_0 = Z_{b'}$ and $Z'_1 = Z_{1-b'}$ while maintaining $s_i = \mathsf{Puz.Sol}(Z_i)$. In the final hybrid we can show that the attacker cannot win the MHF security game with non-negligible advantage.

Showing indistinguishability of H_2 and H_3 is the most interesting case. In fact, an attacker who can solve either puzzle Z_b or Z_{1-b} can potentially distinguish the two hybrids. Instead, we only argue that the hybrids are indistinguishable if the adversary has small area-time complexity. In particular, if an adversary with small cmc is able to distinguish between H_2 and H_3, then we construct an adversary with small cmc which breaks the memory-hard puzzle.

Our main result is that given a concretely secure PPRF family and a concretely secure $i\mathcal{O}$ scheme, if there exists a concretely secure memory-hard puzzle (Definition 6), then there exists a concretely secure memory-hard function.

Theorem 4. *Let $t := t(\lambda)$ be a polynomial and let $g := g(t, \lambda)$ be a function. Let $\mathcal{F}$ be a $(t_{\mathrm{PPRF}}, \varepsilon_{\mathrm{PPRF}})$-secure PPRF family and* iO *be a $(t_{i\mathcal{O}}, \varepsilon_{i\mathcal{O}})$-secure $i\mathcal{O}$ scheme. If there exists a $(g, \varepsilon_{\mathrm{MHP}})$-memory hard puzzle for $g \leqslant \min\{t_{\mathrm{PPRF}}(\lambda), t_{i\mathcal{O}}(\lambda)\}$, then there exists one-time $(g', \varepsilon_{\mathrm{MHF}})$-MHF for $g'(t, \lambda) = g(t, \lambda)/p(\log(t), \lambda)^2$, where $\varepsilon_{\mathrm{MHF}}(\lambda) = 2 \cdot \varepsilon_{\mathrm{MHP}}(\lambda) + 3 \cdot \varepsilon_{\mathrm{PPRF}}(\lambda) + \varepsilon_{i\mathcal{O}}(\lambda)$ and $p(\log(t), \lambda)$ is a fixed polynomial which depends on the efficiency of underlying puzzle and* iO.

To get a handle on Theorem 4, consider the following parameter settings. Let $\theta > 0$ be a small constant and suppose that t is suitably large such that $p(\log(t), \lambda)^2 = \Theta(t^c)$ for some suitably small constant $0 < c < \theta$. Then for $g(t, \lambda) = t^{2-\theta+c}$, $\varepsilon_{\mathrm{MHP}} = (1/6) \cdot 2^{-\lambda}$, $\varepsilon_{\mathrm{PPRF}} = (1/9) \cdot 2^{-\lambda}$, and $\varepsilon_{i\mathcal{O}} = (1/3) \cdot 2^{-\lambda}$,[6] our theorem yields a $(g', \varepsilon_{\mathrm{MHF}})$ for $g'(t, \lambda) = \Theta(t^{2-\theta})$ and $\varepsilon_{\mathrm{MHF}} = 1/2^{\lambda}$. Note that the exact parameters of the constructed MHF depend explicitly on the parameters of the underlying primitives used in the construction. Due to space constraints, we defer the formal definitions of concretely secure PPRF families and $i\mathcal{O}$ to the full version of our work [9].

Note that for any instantiation of $i\mathcal{O}$ that we are aware of, our construction is also a (computationally) *data-independent* MHF [10], i.e., the memory access pattern is (computationally) independent of the secret input x. This is a desirable and useful property that provides natural resistance to side-channel attacks.

Remark 1. One may attempt to construct memory-hard puzzles directly from memory-hard functions in a natural way. For example, for a memory-hard function f, one could define $\mathsf{Gen}(x) = r \| x \oplus f(r)$ for random $r \xleftarrow{\$} \{0,1\}^*$ and $\mathsf{Sol}(Z)$

[6] In this example, we assume sub-exponentially secure $i\mathcal{O}$.

such that first Z is parsed as $Z = r' \| y'$ and then returns $y' \oplus f(r')$. Clearly computing $\mathsf{Sol}(Z)$ is memory-hard, but $(\mathsf{Gen}, \mathsf{Sol})$ is not a cryptographic puzzle by our definitions since Gen violates the efficiency constraints of cryptographic puzzles.

Barriers to Proving Multi-Time Security. While we conjecture that our MHF construction achieves stronger multi-time security, we are unable to formally prove this. An interesting aspect of our final hybrid is that indistinguishability does not necessarily hold against an attacker with higher cmc who could trivially distinguish between (s_0, s_1, Z_0, Z_1) and (s_0, s_1, Z_1, Z_0) by solving the puzzles Z_0 and Z_1. However, once the cmc of the attacker is high enough to solve one puzzle, then we cannot rely on the MHP security for the indistinguishability of the final two hybrids. Proving multi-time security would involve proving that any attacker solving m distinct puzzles has cmc that scales linearly in the number of puzzles; i.e., any attacker with $\mathsf{cmc} = o(m \cdot g(t(\lambda)))$ will fail to solve all m puzzles. In particular, even though we expect the cmc of the attacker to be too small to solve all m puzzles, the cmc will become large enough to solve *at least one* puzzle, which allows the attacker to distinguish between the hybrids in our security reduction. See the full version [9] for more details.

2.4 Resource-Bounded LDCs from Cryptographic Puzzles

Recall that a resource-bounded LDC is a (ℓ, δ, p) locally decodable code that is resilient to δ-fraction of errors introduced by some channel in some adversarial class $\mathbb{C}$, where every $\mathcal{A} \in \mathbb{C}$ is assumed to have some resource constraint. For example, $\mathbb{C}$ can be a class of adversaries that are represented by low-depth circuits, or have small cumulative memory complexity. In more detail, security of resource-bounded LDCs requires that any adversary in the class $\mathbb{C}$ cannot corrupt an encoding $y = \mathsf{Enc}(x)$ to some $\tilde{y}$ such that (1) the distance between y and $\tilde{y}$ is at most $\delta \cdot |y|$; and (2) there exists an index i such that the decoder, when given $\tilde{y}$ as its oracle, outputs x_i with probability less than p.

We construct our resource-bounded LDC by modifying the construction of [26] to use cryptographic puzzles in place of random oracles. In particular, for algorithm class $\mathbb{C}$, if there exists a cryptographic puzzle that is unsolvable by any algorithm in $\mathbb{C}$, then we use this puzzle to construct a LDC secure against $\mathbb{C}$. See the full version of our work for the formal definitions of a $(\mathbb{C}, \varepsilon)$-hard puzzle and a $\mathbb{C}$-secure LDC [9].

Our construction crucially relies on a *private LDC* [79]. Private LDCs are LDCs that are additionally parameterized by a key generation algorithm Gen that on input 1^λ for security parameter λ outputs a shared secret key sk to *both* the encoding and decoding algorithm. Crucially, this secret key is hidden from the adversarial channel. See [9,26,79] for formal definitions.

We provide a high-level overview here of our LDC construction and defer the formal construction to the full version of our work [9]. Let $(\mathsf{Gen}, \mathsf{Enc}_\mathsf{p}, \mathsf{Dec}_\mathsf{p})$ be a private Hamming LDC. The encoder Enc_f, on input message x, samples random coins $s \in \{0,1\}^\lambda$ then generates cryptographic puzzle Z with solution s.

The encoder then samples a secret key $\mathsf{sk} \leftarrow \mathsf{Gen}(1^\lambda; s)$, where Gen uses random coins s, and encodes the message x as $Y_1 = \mathsf{Enc_p}(x; \mathsf{sk})$. The puzzle Z is then encoded as Y_2 via some repetition code. The encoder then outputs $Y = Y_1 \circ Y_2$. This codeword is corrupted to some $\widetilde{Y}$, which can be parsed as $\widetilde{Y} = \widetilde{Y_1} \circ \widetilde{Y_2}$.

The local decoder $\mathsf{Dec_f}$, on input index i and given oracle access to $\widetilde{Y}$, first recovers the puzzle Z by querying $\widetilde{Y_2}$ and using the decoder of the repetition code (e.g., via random sampling with majority vote). Given s, the local decoder is able to generate the same secret key $\mathsf{sk} \leftarrow \mathsf{Gen}(1^\lambda; s)$ and now runs the local decoder $\mathsf{Dec_p}(i; \mathsf{sk})$. All queries made by $\mathsf{Dec_p}(i; \mathsf{sk})$ are answered by querying $\widetilde{Y_1}$, and the decoder outputs $\mathsf{Dec_p}(i; \mathsf{sk})$. The construction is secure against any class $\mathbb{C}$ for which there exist cryptographic puzzles that are secure against this class. For example, time-lock puzzles give an LDC that is secure against the class $\mathbb{C}$ of circuits of low-depth, and memory-hard puzzles give an LDC that is secure against the class $\mathbb{C}$ of PRAM algorithms with low cmc.

Security is established via a reduction to the cryptographic puzzle. Suppose there exists an adversary $A \in \mathbb{C}$ which can violate the security of our LDC. The reduction relies on a two-phase hybrid distinguishing argument [26]. Fix $(\mathsf{Enc_f}, \mathsf{Dec_f})$ to be the encoder and local decoder constructed above. We define two different encoders to be used in the hybrid arguments. First the encoder $\mathsf{Enc_0} := \mathsf{Enc_f}$ is defined to be exactly the same as our LDC encoder. Second, the encoder $\mathsf{Enc_1}$ is defined to be identical to $\mathsf{Enc_f}$, except with the following changes: (1) $\mathsf{Enc_1}$ receives both a message x and some secret key sk as input; (2) $\mathsf{Enc_1}$ encodes x as $Y_1 = \mathsf{Enc_p}(x; \mathsf{sk})$; and (3) $\mathsf{Enc_1}$ samples some $s' \xleftarrow{\$} \{0,1\}^\lambda$ that is uncorrelated with its input sk, computes puzzle $Z' \leftarrow \mathsf{Puz.Gen}(s')$, and computes Y_2 as the repetition encoding of Z'.

We now construct our attacker B which violates the security of the cryptographic puzzle as follows: B is given (Z_b, Z_{1-b}, s_0, s_1) for uniformly random bit b, where Z_i is a puzzle with solution s_i as input. Then B fixes a message x and encodes x as follows. (1) Using puzzle solution s_0, generate secret key $\mathsf{sk} \leftarrow \mathsf{Gen}(1^\lambda, s_0)$. (2) Compute Y_2 as the encoding of Z_b (i.e., its first input) using the repetition code. (3) Compute $Y_1 \leftarrow \mathsf{Enc_p}(x; \mathsf{sk})$. (4) Set $Y = Y_1 \circ Y_2$. With Y in hand, the adversary B simulates adversary A to obtain $\tilde{Y} = \tilde{Y_1} \circ \tilde{Y_2} \leftarrow A(x, Y)$. Finally, B outputs $b' \leftarrow \mathcal{D}(x, \mathsf{sk}, \tilde{Y_1})$. Here, the distinguisher $\mathcal{D}$ is given $\tilde{Y_1}$, the secret key $\mathsf{sk_0}$, and message x as input; additionally, it can simulate the local decoding algorithm $\mathsf{Dec_p}$. In particular, the distinguisher $\mathcal{D}$ is defined as follows: (1) sample an index $i \xleftarrow{\$} \{1, \ldots, |x|\}$ uniformly at random; (2) compute $\tilde{x}_i \leftarrow \mathsf{Dec_p}^{\tilde{Y_1}}(i; \mathsf{sk_0})$; and (3) output $b' = 0$ if $x_i \neq \tilde{x}_i$ and $b' = 1$ otherwise.

Intuitively, if $b = 1$ then $Y_1 = \mathsf{Enc_p}(s; \mathsf{sk_0})$ where the secret key $\mathsf{sk_0}$ is information theoretically hidden from A when the corrupted private-key codeword $\tilde{Y_1} \leftarrow A(x, Y)$ is produced. Private key LDC security ensures that, except with negligible probability, $\mathsf{Dec_p}^{\tilde{Y_1}}(i; \mathsf{sk_0})$ will output the correct answer $\tilde{x}_i = x_i$ and $\mathcal{D}$ will output the correct answer $b' = 1$. On the other hand if $b = 0$ we have $Y = \mathsf{Enc_0}(x)$ and $\tilde{Y} \leftarrow A(x, Y)$ so that the probability that $\mathsf{Dec_p}^{\tilde{Y_1}}(i; \mathsf{sk}_b)$ outputs the wrong answer $x_i \neq \tilde{x}_i$ will be non-negligible—at least $1/|x|$ times the advantage of A in the LDC security game. Thus, the probability that $\mathcal{D}$ outputs the correct answer $b' = 0$ is also non-negligible. It follows our adversary B outputs the correct bit $b = b'$ with non-negligible advantage violating security of the underlying memory hard puzzles. See [9] for formal details.

Our main result is that given any private Hamming LDC, if there exists a memory-hard puzzle, then there exists a resource-bounded LDC that is secure against the class of PRAM algorithms, where the parameters of the resource-bounded LDC are comparable to the parameters of the private LDC.

Corollary 1. *Let g be a function, let $\mathbb{C}(g) := \{\mathcal{A}\colon \mathcal{A}$ is a PRAM algorithm and $\mathsf{cmc}(\mathcal{A}) < g\}$, and let $C_{\mathsf{p}}[K_{\mathsf{p}}, k_{\mathsf{p}}, \lambda]$ be a $(\ell_{\mathsf{p}}, \delta_{\mathsf{p}}, p_{\mathsf{p}}, \varepsilon_{\mathsf{p}})$-private Hamming* LDC. *If there exists a (g, ε')-memory hard puzzle then there exists a $(\ell, \delta, \varepsilon)$-resource bounded* LDC *$C[\Omega(K_{\mathsf{p}}), k_{\mathsf{p}}]$ that is secure against the class $\mathbb{C}(g)$ with parameters $\ell = \Theta(\ell_{\mathsf{p}})$, $\delta = \Theta(1)$, $p = 1 - \mathsf{negl}(\lambda)$, and $\varepsilon = \Theta(\varepsilon_{\mathsf{p}} + \varepsilon')$.*

Actually, in the full version of our work [9], we prove a more general theorem which utilizes any private LDC in conjunction with a more general $(\mathbb{C}, \varepsilon)$-hard puzzle (i.e., the puzzle is secure against the class of adversaries $\mathbb{C}$, which allows us to construct a resource-bounded LDC that is secure against the class $\mathbb{C}$.

Resource-Bounded LDCs for Insertion-Deletion Errors in the Standard Model. Recently, Block and Blocki [20] proved that the so-called "Hamming-to-InsDel" compiler of Block et al. [21] extends to both the private Hamming LDC and resource-bounded Hamming LDC settings. That is, there exists a procedure which compiles any resource-bounded Hamming LDC to a resource-bounded LDC that is robust against *insertion-deletion errors* such that this compilation procedure preserves the underlying security of the Hamming LDC. We apply the result of Block and Blocki [20] to our construction and obtain the first construction of resource-bounded locally decodable code for insertion-deletion errors in the standard model. We remark that the prior construction presented in [20] was in the random oracle model.

Corollary 2. *Let $\mathbb{C}(g) = \{\mathcal{A}\colon AisaPRAMalgorithmand \mathsf{cmc}(\mathcal{A}) < g\}$ and let $C_{\mathsf{p}}[K_{\mathsf{p}}, k_{\mathsf{p}}, \lambda]$ be a private Hamming* LDC. *If there exists a (g, ε')-memory hard puzzle and a $(\ell, \delta, p, \varepsilon)$ resource-bounded* LDC *that is secure against the class $\mathbb{C}(g)$, then there exists a $(\ell', \delta', p', \varepsilon'')$-*LDC *$C[n, k]$ for insertion-deletion errors against class $\mathbb{C}(g)$, where $\ell' = \ell \cdot O(\log^4(n))$, $\delta' = \Theta(\delta)$, $p' < p$, $\varepsilon'' = \varepsilon/(1 - \mathsf{negl}(n))$, $k = k_{\mathsf{p}}$, and $K = \Omega(K_{\mathsf{p}})$.*

Acknowledgments. Mohammad Hassan Ameri was supported in part by NSF award #1755708, by IARPA under the HECTOR program, and by a Summer Research Grant from Purdue University. Alexander R. Block was supported in part by NSF CCF #1910659. Jeremiah Blocki was supported in part by NSF CNS #1755708, NSF CNS #2047272, and NSF CCF #1910659 and by IARPA under the HECTOR program.

References

1. Agrawal, S., Pellet-Mary, A.: Indistinguishability obfuscation without maps: attacks and fixes for noisy linear FE. In: Canteaut, A., Ishai, Y. (eds.) EUROCRYPT 2020. LNCS, vol. 12105, pp. 110–140. Springer, Cham (2020). https://doi.org/10.1007/978-3-030-45721-1_5
2. Alwen, J., Blocki, J.: Efficiently computing data-independent memory-hard functions. In: Robshaw, M., Katz, J. (eds.) CRYPTO 2016. LNCS, vol. 9815, pp. 241–271. Springer, Heidelberg (2016). https://doi.org/10.1007/978-3-662-53008-5_9
3. Alwen, J., Blocki, J., Harsha, B.: Practical graphs for optimal side-channel resistant memory-hard functions. In: CCS, pp. 1001–1017. ACM (2017)
4. Alwen, J., Blocki, J., Pietrzak, K.: Depth-robust graphs and their cumulative memory complexity. In: Coron, J.-S., Nielsen, J.B. (eds.) EUROCRYPT 2017. LNCS, vol. 10212, pp. 3–32. Springer, Cham (2017). https://doi.org/10.1007/978-3-319-56617-7_1
5. Alwen, J., Blocki, J., Pietrzak, K.: Sustained space complexity. In: Nielsen, J.B., Rijmen, V. (eds.) EUROCRYPT 2018. LNCS, vol. 10821, pp. 99–130. Springer, Cham (2018). https://doi.org/10.1007/978-3-319-78375-8_4
6. Alwen, J., Chen, B., Pietrzak, K., Reyzin, L., Tessaro, S.: Scrypt is maximally memory-hard. In: Coron, J.-S., Nielsen, J.B. (eds.) EUROCRYPT 2017. LNCS, vol. 10212, pp. 33–62. Springer, Cham (2017). https://doi.org/10.1007/978-3-319-56617-7_2
7. Alwen, J., Serbinenko, V.: High parallel complexity graphs and memory-hard functions. In: STOC, pp. 595–603. ACM (2015)
8. Alwen, J., Tackmann, B.: Moderately hard functions: definition, instantiations, and applications. In: Kalai, Y., Reyzin, L. (eds.) TCC 2017. LNCS, vol. 10677, pp. 493–526. Springer, Cham (2017). https://doi.org/10.1007/978-3-319-70500-2_17
9. Ameri, M.H., Block, A.R., Blocki, J.: Memory-hard puzzles in the standard model with applications to memory-hard functions and resource-bounded locally decodable codes. IACR Cryptology ePrint Archive, p. 801 (2021)
10. Ameri, M.H., Blocki, J., Zhou, S.: Computationally data-independent memory hard functions. In: ITCS. LIPIcs, vol. 151, pp. 36:1–36:28. Schloss Dagstuhl - Leibniz-Zentrum für Informatik (2020)
11. Applebaum, B.: Garbled circuits as randomized encodings of functions: a primer. In: Tutorials on the Foundations of Cryptography. ISC, pp. 1–44. Springer, Cham (2017). https://doi.org/10.1007/978-3-319-57048-8_1
12. Applebaum, B., Ishai, Y., Kushilevitz, E.: Cryptography in NC^0. SIAM J. Comput. **36**(4), 845–888 (2006)
13. Barak, B., et al.: On the (im)possibility of obfuscating programs. J. ACM **59**(2), 6:1–6:48 (2012)
14. Bartusek, J., Ishai, Y., Jain, A., Ma, F., Sahai, A., Zhandry, M.: Affine determinant programs: a framework for obfuscation and witness encryption. In: ITCS. LIPIcs, vol. 151, pp. 82:1–82:39. Schloss Dagstuhl - Leibniz-Zentrum für Informatik (2020)
15. Ben-Sasson, E., Goldreich, O., Harsha, P., Sudan, M., Vadhan, S.P.: Robust PCPs of proximity, shorter PCPs, and applications to coding. SIAM J. Comput. **36**(4), 889–974 (2006)
16. Biryukov, A., Dinu, D., Khovratovich, D.: Argon2: new generation of memory-hard functions for password hashing and other applications. In: EuroS&P, pp. 292–302. IEEE (2016)

17. Bitansky, N., Garg, S., Lin, H., Pass, R., Telang, S.: Succinct randomized encodings and their applications. In: STOC, pp. 439–448. ACM (2015)
18. Bitansky, N., Garg, S., Telang, S.: Succinct randomized encodings and their applications. IACR Cryptology ePrint Archive, p. 771 (2014)
19. Bitansky, N., Goldwasser, S., Jain, A., Paneth, O., Vaikuntanathan, V., Waters, B.: Time-lock puzzles from randomized encodings. In: ITCS, pp. 345–356. ACM (2016)
20. Block, A.R., Blocki, J.: Private and resource-bounded locally decodable codes for insertions and deletions. In: ISIT, pp. 1841–1846. IEEE (2021)
21. Block, A.R., Blocki, J., Grigorescu, E., Kulkarni, S., Zhu, M.: Locally decodable/correctable codes for insertions and deletions. In: FSTTCS. LIPIcs, vol. 182, pp. 16:1–16:17. Schloss Dagstuhl - Leibniz-Zentrum für Informatik (2020)
22. Blocki, J., Cheng, K., Grigorescu, E., Li, X., Zheng, Y., Zhu, M.: Exponential lower bounds for locally decodable and correctable codes for insertions and deletions. In: FOCS, pp. 739–750. IEEE (2021)
23. Blocki, J., Cinkoske, M., Lee, S., Son, J.Y.: On explicit constructions of extremely depth robust graphs. In: STACS. LIPIcs, vol. 219, pp. 14:1–14:11. Schloss Dagstuhl - Leibniz-Zentrum für Informatik (2022)
24. Blocki, J., Gandikota, V., Grigorescu, E., Zhou, S.: Relaxed locally correctable codes in computationally bounded channels. IEEE Trans. Inf. Theory **67**(7), 4338–4360 (2021)
25. Blocki, J., Harsha, B., Kang, S., Lee, S., Xing, L., Zhou, S.: Data-independent memory hard functions: new attacks and stronger constructions. In: Boldyreva, A., Micciancio, D. (eds.) CRYPTO 2019. LNCS, vol. 11693, pp. 573–607. Springer, Cham (2019). https://doi.org/10.1007/978-3-030-26951-7_20
26. Blocki, J., Kulkarni, S., Zhou, S.: On locally decodable codes in resource bounded channels. In: ITC. LIPIcs, vol. 163, pp. 16:1–16:23. Schloss Dagstuhl - Leibniz-Zentrum für Informatik (2020)
27. Blocki, J., Ren, L., Zhou, S.: Bandwidth-hard functions: Reductions and lower bounds. In: CCS, pp. 1820–1836. ACM (2018)
28. Blocki, J., Zhou, S.: On the depth-robustness and cumulative pebbling cost of Argon2i. In: Kalai, Y., Reyzin, L. (eds.) TCC 2017. LNCS, vol. 10677, pp. 445–465. Springer, Cham (2017). https://doi.org/10.1007/978-3-319-70500-2_15
29. Boneh, D., Naor, M.: Timed commitments. In: Bellare, M. (ed.) CRYPTO 2000. LNCS, vol. 1880, pp. 236–254. Springer, Heidelberg (2000). https://doi.org/10.1007/3-540-44598-6_15
30. Boneh, D., Waters, B.: Constrained pseudorandom functions and their applications. In: Sako, K., Sarkar, P. (eds.) ASIACRYPT 2013. LNCS, vol. 8270, pp. 280–300. Springer, Heidelberg (2013). https://doi.org/10.1007/978-3-642-42045-0_15
31. Boyle, E., Goldwasser, S., Ivan, I.: Functional signatures and pseudorandom functions. In: Krawczyk, H. (ed.) PKC 2014. LNCS, vol. 8383, pp. 501–519. Springer, Heidelberg (2014). https://doi.org/10.1007/978-3-642-54631-0_29
32. Brakensiek, J., Guruswami, V., Zbarsky, S.: Efficient low-redundancy codes for correcting multiple deletions. IEEE Trans. Inf. Theory **64**(5), 3403–3410 (2018)
33. Brakerski, Z., Döttling, N., Garg, S., Malavolta, G.: Candidate iO from homomorphic encryption schemes. In: Canteaut, A., Ishai, Y. (eds.) EUROCRYPT 2020. LNCS, vol. 12105, pp. 79–109. Springer, Cham (2020). https://doi.org/10.1007/978-3-030-45721-1_4

34. Chen, B., Tessaro, S.: Memory-hard functions from cryptographic primitives. In: Boldyreva, A., Micciancio, D. (eds.) CRYPTO 2019. LNCS, vol. 11693, pp. 543–572. Springer, Cham (2019). https://doi.org/10.1007/978-3-030-26951-7_19
35. Cheng, K., Guruswami, V., Haeupler, B., Li, X.: Efficient linear and affine codes for correcting insertions/deletions. In: SODA, pp. 1–20. SIAM (2021)
36. Cheng, K., Haeupler, B., Li, X., Shahrasbi, A., Wu, K.: Synchronization strings: highly efficient deterministic constructions over small alphabets. In: SODA, pp. 2185–2204. SIAM (2019)
37. Cheng, K., Jin, Z., Li, X., Wu, K.: Deterministic document exchange protocols, and almost optimal binary codes for edit errors. In: FOCS, pp. 200–211. IEEE Computer Society (2018)
38. Cheng, K., Jin, Z., Li, X., Wu, K.: Block edit errors with transpositions: deterministic document exchange protocols and almost optimal binary codes. In: ICALP. LIPIcs, vol. 132, pp. 37:1–37:15. Schloss Dagstuhl - Leibniz-Zentrum für Informatik (2019)
39. Cheng, K., Li, X.: Efficient document exchange and error correcting codes with asymmetric information. In: SODA, pp. 2424–2443. SIAM (2021)
40. Dvir, Z., Gopalan, P., Yekhanin, S.: Matching vector codes. SIAM J. Comput. **40**(4), 1154–1178 (2011)
41. Dwork, C., Naor, M.: Pricing via processing or combatting junk mail. In: Brickell, E.F. (ed.) CRYPTO 1992. LNCS, vol. 740, pp. 139–147. Springer, Heidelberg (1993). https://doi.org/10.1007/3-540-48071-4_10
42. Efremenko, K.: 3-query locally decodable codes of subexponential length. SIAM J. Comput. **41**(6), 1694–1703 (2012)
43. Forler, C., Lucks, S., Wenzel, J.: Memory-demanding password scrambling. In: Sarkar, P., Iwata, T. (eds.) ASIACRYPT 2014. LNCS, vol. 8874, pp. 289–305. Springer, Heidelberg (2014). https://doi.org/10.1007/978-3-662-45608-8_16
44. Garay, J.A., MacKenzie, P.D., Prabhakaran, M., Yang, K.: Resource fairness and composability of cryptographic protocols. J. Cryptol. **24**(4), 615–658 (2011)
45. Garg, S., Gentry, C., Halevi, S., Raykova, M., Sahai, A., Waters, B.: Candidate indistinguishability obfuscation and functional encryption for all circuits. SIAM J. Comput. **45**(3), 882–929 (2016)
46. Garg, S., Srinivasan, A.: A simple construction of iO for Turing machines. In: Beimel, A., Dziembowski, S. (eds.) TCC 2018. LNCS, vol. 11240, pp. 425–454. Springer, Cham (2018). https://doi.org/10.1007/978-3-030-03810-6_16
47. Guruswami, V., Haeupler, B., Shahrasbi, A.: Optimally resilient codes for list-decoding from insertions and deletions. IEEE Trans. Inf. Theory **67**(12), 7837–7856 (2021)
48. Guruswami, V., Li, R.: Polynomial time decodable codes for the binary deletion channel. IEEE Trans. Inf. Theory **65**(4), 2171–2178 (2019)
49. Guruswami, V., Li, R.: Coding against deletions in oblivious and online models. IEEE Trans. Inf. Theory **66**(4), 2352–2374 (2020)
50. Guruswami, V., Smith, A.D.: Optimal rate code constructions for computationally simple channels. J. ACM **63**(4), 35:1–35:37 (2016)
51. Guruswami, V., Wang, C.: Deletion codes in the high-noise and high-rate regimes. IEEE Trans. Inf. Theory **63**(4), 1961–1970 (2017)
52. Haeupler, B.: Optimal document exchange and new codes for insertions and deletions. In: FOCS, pp. 334–347. IEEE Computer Society (2019)
53. Haeupler, B., Rubinstein, A., Shahrasbi, A.: Near-linear time insertion-deletion codes and $(1+\varepsilon)$-approximating edit distance via indexing. In: STOC, pp. 697–708. ACM (2019)

54. Haeupler, B., Shahrasbi, A.: Synchronization strings: explicit constructions, local decoding, and applications. In: STOC, pp. 841–854. ACM (2018)
55. Haeupler, B., Shahrasbi, A.: Synchronization strings: codes for insertions and deletions approaching the singleton bound. J. ACM **68**(5), 36:1–36:39 (2021)
56. Haeupler, B., Shahrasbi, A., Sudan, M.: Synchronization strings: list decoding for insertions and deletions. In: ICALP. LIPIcs, vol. 107, pp. 76:1–76:14. Schloss Dagstuhl - Leibniz-Zentrum für Informatik (2018)
57. Hubácek, P., Wichs, D.: On the communication complexity of secure function evaluation with long output. In: ITCS, pp. 163–172. ACM (2015)
58. Ishai, Y., Kushilevitz, E.: Randomizing polynomials: a new representation with applications to round-efficient secure computation. In: FOCS, pp. 294–304. IEEE Computer Society (2000)
59. Jain, A., Lin, H., Sahai, A.: Indistinguishability obfuscation from well-founded assumptions. In: STOC, pp. 60–73. ACM (2021)
60. Jakobsson, M., Juels, A.: Proofs of work and bread pudding protocols. In: Communications and Multimedia Security. IFIP Conference Proceedings, vol. 152, pp. 258–272. Kluwer (1999)
61. Katz, J., Trevisan, L.: On the efficiency of local decoding procedures for error-correcting codes. In: STOC, pp. 80–86. ACM (2000)
62. Kerenidis, I., de Wolf, R.: Exponential lower bound for 2-query locally decodable codes via a quantum argument. J. Comput. Syst. Sci. **69**(3), 395–420 (2004)
63. Kiayias, A., Papadopoulos, S., Triandopoulos, N., Zacharias, T.: Delegatable pseudorandom functions and applications. In: CCS, pp. 669–684. ACM (2013)
64. Kiwi, M., Loebl, M., Matoušek, J.: Expected length of the longest common subsequence for large alphabets. In: Farach-Colton, M. (ed.) LATIN 2004. LNCS, vol. 2976, pp. 302–311. Springer, Heidelberg (2004). https://doi.org/10.1007/978-3-540-24698-5_34
65. Kopparty, S., Meir, O., Ron-Zewi, N., Saraf, S.: High-rate locally correctable and locally testable codes with sub-polynomial query complexity. J. ACM **64**(2), 11:1–11:42 (2017)
66. Kopparty, S., Saraf, S.: Guest column: local testing and decoding of high-rate error-correcting codes. SIGACT News **47**(3), 46–66 (2016)
67. Koppula, V., Lewko, A.B., Waters, B.: Indistinguishability obfuscation for Turing machines with unbounded memory. In: STOC, pp. 419–428. ACM (2015)
68. Levenshtein, V.I.: Binary codes capable of correcting deletions, insertions and reversals. Soviet Physics Doklady **10**(8), 707–710 (1966). Doklady Akademii Nauk SSSR, **163**(4), 845–848 (1965)
69. Lin, H., Matt, C.: Pseudo flawed-smudging generators and their application to indistinguishability obfuscation. IACR Cryptology ePrint Archive, p. 646 (2018)
70. Lin, H., Pass, R., Seth, K., Telang, S.: Output-compressing randomized encodings and applications. In: Kushilevitz, E., Malkin, T. (eds.) TCC 2016. LNCS, vol. 9562, pp. 96–124. Springer, Heidelberg (2016). https://doi.org/10.1007/978-3-662-49096-9_5
71. Lipton, R.J.: A new approach to information theory. In: Enjalbert, P., Mayr, E.W., Wagner, K.W. (eds.) STACS 1994. LNCS, vol. 775, pp. 699–708. Springer, Heidelberg (1994). https://doi.org/10.1007/3-540-57785-8_183
72. Liu, S., Tjuawinata, I., Xing, C.: On list decoding of insertion and deletion errors (2020)
73. Mahmoody, M., Moran, T., Vadhan, S.: Time-lock puzzles in the random oracle model. In: Rogaway, P. (ed.) CRYPTO 2011. LNCS, vol. 6841, pp. 39–50. Springer, Heidelberg (2011). https://doi.org/10.1007/978-3-642-22792-9_3

74. Malavolta, G., Thyagarajan, S.A.K.: Homomorphic time-lock puzzles and applications. In: Boldyreva, A., Micciancio, D. (eds.) CRYPTO 2019. LNCS, vol. 11692, pp. 620–649. Springer, Cham (2019). https://doi.org/10.1007/978-3-030-26948-7_22
75. May, T.C.: Timed-release crypto (1993). http://cypherpunks.venona.com/date/1993/02/msg00129.html
76. Micali, S., Peikert, C., Sudan, M., Wilson, D.A.: Optimal error correction against computationally bounded noise. In: Kilian, J. (ed.) TCC 2005. LNCS, vol. 3378, pp. 1–16. Springer, Heidelberg (2005). https://doi.org/10.1007/978-3-540-30576-7_1
77. Nakamoto, S.: Bitcoin: a peer-to-peer electronic cash system. Decentralized Bus. Rev., 21260 (2008)
78. Okamoto, T., Pietrzak, K., Waters, B., Wichs, D.: New realizations of somewhere statistically binding hashing and positional accumulators. In: Iwata, T., Cheon, J.H. (eds.) ASIACRYPT 2015. LNCS, vol. 9452, pp. 121–145. Springer, Heidelberg (2015). https://doi.org/10.1007/978-3-662-48797-6_6
79. Ostrovsky, R., Pandey, O., Sahai, A.: Private locally decodable codes. In: Arge, L., Cachin, C., Jurdziński, T., Tarlecki, A. (eds.) ICALP 2007. LNCS, vol. 4596, pp. 387–398. Springer, Heidelberg (2007). https://doi.org/10.1007/978-3-540-73420-8_35
80. Ostrovsky, R., Paskin-Cherniavsky, A.: Locally decodable codes for edit distance. In: Lehmann, A., Wolf, S. (eds.) ICITS 2015. LNCS, vol. 9063, pp. 236–249. Springer, Cham (2015). https://doi.org/10.1007/978-3-319-17470-9_14
81. Percival, C.: Stronger key derivation via sequential memory-hard functions. In: BSDCan 2009 (2009)
82. Pippenger, N., Fischer, M.J.: Relations among complexity measures. J. ACM **26**(2), 361–381 (1979)
83. Rivest, R.L., Shamir, A., Wagner, D.A.: Time-lock puzzles and timed-release crypto. Technical report, USA (1996)
84. Shaltiel, R., Silbak, J.: Explicit list-decodable codes with optimal rate for computationally bounded channels. Comput. Complex. **30**(1), 3 (2021)
85. Sima, J., Bruck, J.: Optimal k-deletion correcting codes. In: ISIT, pp. 847–851. IEEE (2019)
86. Sudan, M., Trevisan, L., Vadhan, S.P.: Pseudorandom generators without the XOR lemma. J. Comput. Syst. Sci. **62**(2), 236–266 (2001)
87. Yekhanin, S.: Towards 3-query locally decodable codes of subexponential length. J. ACM **55**(1), 1:1–1:16 (2008)
88. Yekhanin, S.: Locally decodable codes. Found. Trends Theor. Comput. Sci. **6**(3), 139–255 (2012)

RAMus- A New Lightweight Block Cipher for RAM Encryption

Raluca Posteuca[1(✉)] and Vincent Rijmen[1,2]

[1] imec-COSIC, Department of Electrical Engineering (ESAT), KU Leuven, Leuven, Belgium
{raluca.posteuca,vincent.rijmen}@esat.kuleuven.be
[2] Department of Informatics, University of Bergen, 5020 Bergen, Norway

Abstract. Over the past decades, there has been a dramatic increase of the attacks recovering the data from the RAM memory. These have heightened the need for new solutions and primitives suitable for the encryption of this information. In this paper we introduce RAMus, a new tweakable lightweight block cipher whose properties support its usage for securing the RAM memory. In this sense, RAMus attains all the requirements provided by the (German) Federal Office of Information Security (BSI) in the domain of encryption algorithms suitable for RAM and memory encryption. The design strategy of RAMus is inspired from the LS-approach. Compared to the literature, in our proposal the linear layer is replaced by a second Sbox layer. In RAMus, the diffusion is ensured by the Sbox layers, which use Sboxes with a non-trivial branch number.

Keywords: RAMus · RAM encryption · Branch number · 2S-strategy

1 Introduction

The security of a personal device, such as a smartphone or a laptop, is one of the most analyzed topics in the domain of cryptography, security, and privacy. Even though most of the vulnerabilities arise from the online behavior of the device's user, in the last decade special attention was given to the security of the data stored in the memory of the device. The attacks aiming at recovering the data from the RAM, such as the cold boot attack [26] or the direct memory access attack [40], proved the increasing importance of protecting this information. In order to increase the security of the data stored in the RAM memory, both the academia and the industry invested their resources in designing a series of solutions. While the resulted proposals employ different techniques to ensure the security of the cryptographic secrets, most of them are based on one of the following block ciphers: AES [23], Prince [19], Qarma [10] or ASCON [24].

In order to support the development of RAM encryption solutions, The (German) Federal Office of Information Security (BSI) published, in 2013, a methodology for cryptographic rating of memory encryption schemes used in smartcards and similar devices [1]. According to this methodology, an algorithm suitable for

C. Galdi and S. Jarecki (Eds.): SCN 2022, LNCS 13409, pp. 69–92, 2022.
https://doi.org/10.1007/978-3-031-14791-3_4

memory encryption schemes should exhibit small area for its implementation, while having high speed, which is translated in our work by both low latency and high throughput. Furthermore, the methodology recommends the use of a tweakable block cipher, where the tweak is parameterised with the memory address of the plaintext. Last but not least, the methodology discusses the necessary security of a suitable block cipher with respect to the known attacks. While linear and differential cryptanalysis are considered critical, the methodology considers less relevant the security against related-key attacks. The methodology also discusses the impact of side-channel attacks, noting that this type of attacks could lead to critical vulnerabilities in some particular scenarios.

Our Contribution. In order to contribute to the efforts of the cryptographic community in the area of secure memory encryption, we propose RAMus, a new lightweight tweakable block cipher. The design of RAMus follows the *2S-strategy*, a new design framework introduced in this paper. The cipher satisfies the constraints imposed by the BSI methodology, while ensuring that its *threshold implementation* against side-channel attacks does not have any overheads. RAMus is a tweakable block cipher, with a tweak space of 2^{64}. Therefore, for the 32- and 64-bit systems, it allows the usage of the same symmetric key for the entire RAM memory, without the vulnerabilities induced by the ECB mode of operation and the overhead of other modes of operation, such as XEX or XTS.

In order to ensure low area of the implementation of RAMus, the round function, tweak update function and key schedule use only two basic operations: one 8-bit Sbox and the XOR addition. To ensure good diffusion through the cipher, the Sbox was designed such that it has good cryptographic properties, while having non-trivial linear and differential branch numbers.

The latency of the cipher is closely related to the number of non-linear operations used for the round function. We note that the chosen Sbox can be implemented with only 8 non-linear gates, the minimum number of non-linear gates of an 8-bit Sbox with good cryptographic properties. Moreover, the strategy used for the design of the Sbox ensures resistance against side-channel attacks according to the literature [20,32].

Related Work. The related work covers two areas. The first one regards the block ciphers that are used for RAM encryption solutions, while the second one refers to the design and usage of Sboxes with non-trivial linear and differential branch number.

Block Ciphers Suitable for RAM Encryption. The most common block ciphers used to design RAM encryption solutions include AES, Prince, Qarma and ASCON. Although the security of all these ciphers was subjected to extended analysis (especially in the case of AES, which was selected as a NIST standard, and ASCON, which is part of the final portofolio of the CAESAR competition and a finalist of the NIST Lightweight competition), we remark that none of these ciphers fulfill all the requirements presented in the BSI methodology. Note that AES, Prince and ASCON are not tweakable, while the Sbox of Qarma does not lend itself easily to a lightweight side-channel resistant implementation.

Sboxes with Non-trivial Branch Numbers. Through the last decades, the problem of linear and differential branch numbers of an Sbox caught the attention of the cryptographic community. The first step in this direction regards the design and analysis of 4-bit Sboxes with non-trivial differential branch number, such as the Sboxes of Serpent [15] or PRESENT [18]. The natural extension of this field was proposed in [36], which presents the classification of all 4-bit Sbox equivalence classes with respect to the differential branch number. The next step of this research was the design and analysis of 5-bit Sboxes with non-trivial branch numbers, such as the Sbox of ASCON which has both linear and differential branch number 3. This work was continued in [37], which proposes new design strategies for 5-bit and 6-bit Sboxes with non-trivial branch numbers.

Further, [28] introduces the unbalanced-bridge approach, a technique suitable for the design of 8-bit Sboxes with linear and differential branch number 3. Such Sboxes have good cryptographic properties, while allowing for bit-slice implementations which use at least 11 non-linear gates. Using this type of Sboxes, the authors propose the block cipher PIPO, which follows the LS-design framework. We note that the authors also present a series of 8-bit Sboxes with differential branch number 4, but with non-linearity 0, concluding that this type of Sboxes would induce vulnerabilities with respect to linear cryptanalysis.

Structure of the Paper. The rest of this paper is organized as follows: in Sect. 2 we present some terminology regarding linear and differential cryptanalysis, the branch number of an Sbox and the LS-design framework. In Sect. 3 we introduce the 2S-strategy, a new design technique inspired by the LS-design framework. Section 4 introduces the RAMus block cipher, as a parameterization of the 2S-strategy, and Sect. 5 discusses the design rationale of RAMus. Section 6 presents the security analysis of RAMus with respect to the most important cryptanalytic techniques, while in Sect. 7 we discuss the performance of RAMus in hardware implementations.

2 Preliminaries

Linear Cryptanalysis. Linear cryptanalysis [31] was introduced in 1993 by Matsui as an attack against DES [6]. This approach aims at finding linear approximations between the bits of the plaintext and the ciphertext. In order to exploit such approximations, it is necessary that the associated probability is different from 0.5, i.e.

$$Pr = \#\{p \in \mathbb{F}_2^n | \bigoplus_i p_i \oplus \bigoplus_j c_j = 0\}/2^n \neq 0.5,$$

where p_i and c_j represent the ith bit of the plaintext and the jth bit of the ciphertext, respectively. The quality of a linear approximation defines the success rate of the future attack, and in this paper it is measured by the correlation of the linear approximation, which is defined as $corr = 2 \cdot Pr - 1$.

The most common approach to finding such approximations is by using a divide-and-conquer approach. Matsui's strategy was to identify linear approximations between the input and the output of each operation and further connect them, resulting in the *linear trail*. The analysis of every operation can be performed by following the rules of propagation of linear trails introduced in [14,21,22]. If the case of the propagation through linear layers can be considered straightforward, the case of non-linear layers is more involved. In particular, for the analysis of the Sbox with respect to linear cryptanalysis the standard approach is to compute the corresponding Linear Approximation Table (LAT).

Definition 1. *Let S be an Sbox of size n and "·" be the standard inner product. Then, the LAT of an Sbox S represents the matrix defined as follows:*

$$LAT_S[\alpha, \beta] = \#\{x | \alpha \cdot x \oplus \beta \cdot S(x) = 0\} - 2^{n-1}.$$

The maximum absolute value of LAT_S is called the *liniar uniformity* of the Sbox S and it defines the quality of the Sbox with respect to linear cryptanalysis.

Differential Cryptanalysis. Differential cryptanalysis [16] was introduced in 1990 by Biham and Shamir, also as an attack on DES. This attack aims at analysing the propagation of differences from a plaintext pair to the corresponding ciphertext pair. The approach is similar to the one presented above, involving the analysis of the propagation through the particular operations of a cipher and further connect them, resulting in the *differential characteristic*. Usually, the difference is considered with respect to the XOR operation and in this paper we conform to this. While the difference propagation through the linear layers are straightforward, the analysis of the differences' propagation through a non-linear layer involves the computation of its corresponding Differential Distribution Table (DDT).

Definition 2. *The DDT of an Sbox S represents the matrix of integers defined as follows:*

$$DDT_S[\delta, \Delta] = \#\{x | \Delta = S(x) \oplus S(x \oplus \delta)\}.$$

The maximum value of DDT_S is called the *differential uniformity* of the Sbox S and it defines the quality of the Sbox with respect to differential cryptanalysis.

Branch Number. The main criteria in the design of a block cipher is represented by the properties of confusion and diffusion. In most of the ciphers from literature, the confusion is ensured by the choice of the non-linear (Sbox) layer, while the diffusion is often ensured by the linear layer(s) of the cipher. The most common technique to measure the diffusion of a cipher is given through the means of the branch number of the underlying operations. For the purposes of this work, we only discuss the concept of the branch number associated to an Sbox. Let us denote the Hamming weight of a byte x by $wt(x)$.

Table 1. The properties of the DDT and the LAT of an Sbox

Any Sbox	Invertible Sbox
If $DDT(0, \Delta) \neq 0$, then $\Delta = 0$.	If $DDT(\delta, 0) \neq 0$, then $\delta = 0$.
If $LAT(\alpha, 0) \neq 0$, then $\alpha = 0$.	If $LAT(0, \beta) \neq 0$, then $\beta = 0$.

Definition 3. *The differential and linear branch numbers of an Sbox S, denoted by BN_d and BN_l respectively, are computed as:*

$$BN_d(S) = \min\{\text{wt}(\delta) + \text{wt}(\Delta) | DDT_S(\delta, \Delta) \neq 0\}$$
$$BN_l(S) = \min\{\text{wt}(\alpha) + \text{wt}(\beta) | LAT_S(\alpha, \beta) \neq 0\}$$

Note that the LAT and the DDT of an Sbox have the properties described in Table 1.

A consequence of these properties is that the minimum value of the linear and differential branch number of an invertible Sbox is 2, therefore we consider this to be the trivial linear and differential branch number. Frequently, the design of the non-linear layer consists of independent, parallel applications of one or more Sboxes on partitions of the internal state. In this case, the branch number of the entire non-linear layer is given by the lowest branch number of the underlying Sboxes.

Bounds on Linear and Differential Branch Number. In [38] the authors present the bound on linear and differential branch number of permutations. We summarize their results in Lemma 1.

Lemma 1. *Let $S : \mathbb{F}_2^n \to \mathbb{F}_2^n$ be a non-linear permutation. Then,*

- $BN_l(S) \leq n - 1$
- *if* $n = 4$, $BN_d(S) \leq 3$
- *if* $n \geq 5$, $BN_d(S) \leq \lceil 2\frac{n}{3} \rceil$

In particular, the maximum differential branch number for an 8-bit Sbox is 6, while the maximum linear branch number is 7. [30] presents a technique of designing non-linear layers with maximum differential branch number. The goal of this paper was to introduce new non-linear diffusion layers, therefore the resulting permutations have trivial linear and differential uniformity.

The LS-Design Framework. Nowadays, one of the goals of cryptographers is to analyse and propose different design strategies meant to ensure the security of the future symmetric primitives against the most important attacks. In order to ensure the resistance of a cipher against the two most significant mathematical attacks, namely linear and differential cryptanalysis, Daemen and Rijmen proposed the wide-trail strategy [23].

In the last decades, the scientific community focused on analysing the security of a block cipher against side-channel attacks [27]. One of the approaches to ensure the security of a cipher against such attacks is to implement the so called masking techniques [34]. While these techniques can ensure the needed level of security, they highly influence the costs of implementing a block cipher. In order to address this issue, Grosso et al. introduced the LS-design framework [25].

The internal state of a cipher based on the LS-design framework is viewed as a $l \times s$ matrix. The round function, apart from the key and constant addition, consists of two operations: a non-linear layer defined by the parallel application of an Sbox on each row of the matrix, and a linear layer in which a linear function is applied independently on each column. For more details regarding the properties of these two operations and possible parameterizations we refer the reader to the original paper.

3 The 2S-Strategy

In this paper we introduce the *2S-strategy.* The aim of this strategy is to lead to the design of a tweakable block cipher which is designed only by using non-linear operations. This design strategy is inspired by the LS-strategy described in Sect. 2. In order to ensure the diffusion through the cipher, we design non-linear layers with non-trivial linear and differential branch numbers.

3.1 Notations

The internal state of a cipher based on the 2S-strategy is viewed as an $r \times c$ matrix of bits. While the values of r and c can be chosen by the designer, in this paper, we consider $r = 8$ and $c = 8$, therefore the internal state contains 64 bits, indexed as described in Fig. 1. In this paper we consider the rows indexed top-to-bottom, while the columns are indexed left-to-right, i.e. the first row and the first column are the ones containing the bit indexed 1. For the bytes composition, we use the big-endian order. More specifically, for the first row the bit in position 8 represents the least significant bit, while in the first column the bit in position 1 represents the most significant one.

Throughout this paper we would refer to two manners in which a byte array could be extracted from the 8×8 matrix of bits s. We denote by $v_R(s)$ the array containing the bytes composed by the rows of the matrix, while $v_C(s)$ denotes the bytes read at a column level. More precisely, the first value of $v_R(s)$ is the byte composed by the bits indexed from 1 to 8, while the last component of the $v_C(s)$ is represented by the bits indexed by the values multiple of 8. A description of how the arrays $v_R(s)$ and $v_C(s)$ are obtained from the internal state s is described in Fig. 1.

We also introduce the inverse operations of v_R and v_C, which take a byte array as input and return an 8×8 matrix, as follows:

$$s^R(v_R(s)) = s, \qquad s^C(v_C(s)) = s$$

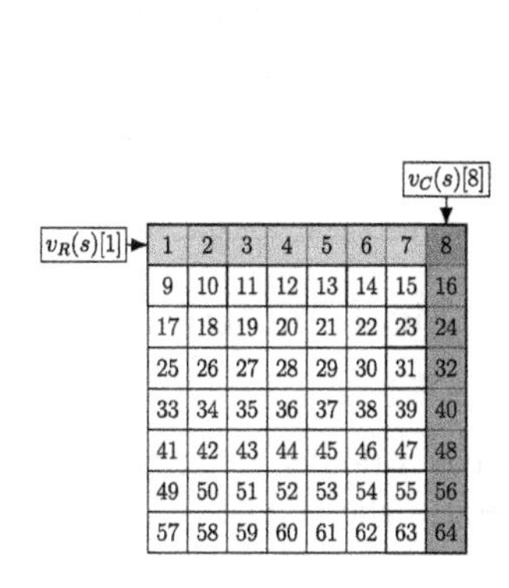

Fig. 1. The indexes of the internal state and the $v_R(s)$ and $v_C(s)$ functions' application.

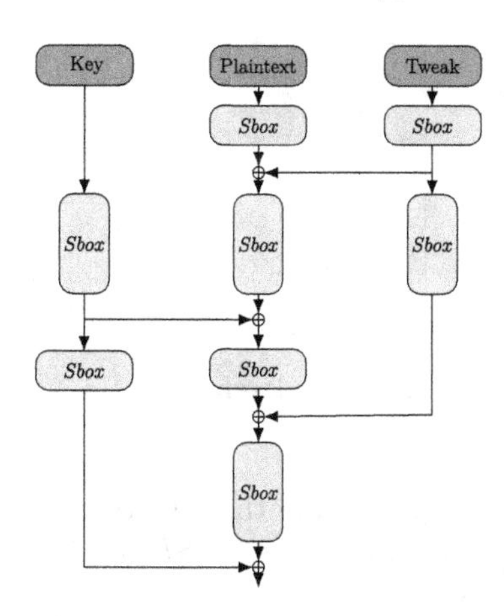

Fig. 2. Two consecutive rounds of the cipher. The lying rectangles represent the first non-linear layer, while the standing rectangles represent the second one.

3.2 The Round Function

The round function of the cipher is described by two Sbox layers, one tweak and one key addition. More precisely, the round function assumes the following operations: first, an Sbox S is applied on every row of the internal state; secondly, the round tweak is added to the internal state by the use of bitwise XOR; thirdly, the same Sbox S is applied on every column of the internal state; finally, the round key is added to the internal state. The description of the first two rounds of such a cipher is depicted in Fig. 2. We underline that, depending on the use case, more than one Sbox could be used in order to design a block cipher based on the 2S-strategy. However, the use of multiple Sboxes could have several drawbacks. Firstly, the chosen Sboxes must be designed such that they exhibit non-trivial linear and differential branch numbers, while having non-trivial uniformities. Secondly, the use of different Sboxes leads to an increase in the area needed for the implementation of the cipher.

The Sbox Layers. The diffusion of most ciphers in the literature is ensured by using linear layers with non-trivial branch numbers. In the case of the 2S-strategy, both the confusion and the diffusion of the cipher are ensured by using two non-linear layers in each round of the cipher. Both layers assume the parallel application of an Sbox on partitions of the internal state. For the first layer, denoted SB_R, the Sbox is applied on each row independently, while for the second layer, denoted SB_C, the Sbox is applied on each column. The index denotes the manner in which the inputs were chosen, where the indexes "R" and "C" marks the appliance of the Sbox on rows and columns, respectively. Figure 3 and Fig. 4 describe the manner in which the non-linear layers SB_R and SB_C

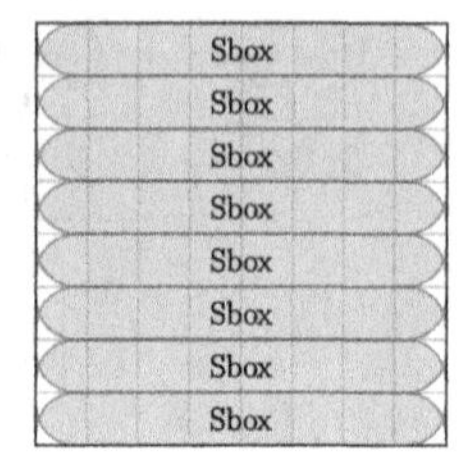

Fig. 3. The layer SB_R.

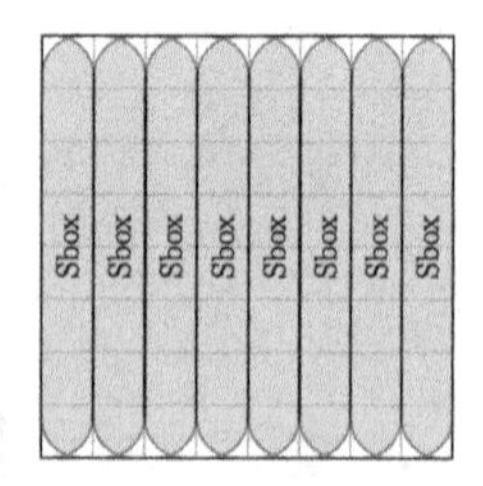

Fig. 4. The layer SB_C.

are applied. We note that the two layers are affine equivalent functions, defined by the relation $SB_R(s) = SB_C(s^T)^T$, where s^T denotes the transposition of the matrix s.

In order to ensure the security of a cipher based on the 2S-strategy, the chosen Sboxes need to have good cryptographic properties, such as good linear and differential uniformity. Moreover, in order to ensure the diffusion through the non-linear layer, the Sboxes must also have non-trivial linear and differential branch numbers. In Sect. 5 we propose a parameterization for the Sbox S, we discuss the properties of an Sbox suitable for the 2S-strategy and we describe a design strategy that leads to the design of an Sbox with the suitable properties.

Key Schedule and Tweak Update Function. In order to ensure a small area of the hardware implementation of a cipher based on the 2S-strategy, we designed the key schedule and the tweak update function by using the same non-linear layers as the round function. The choices of these two functions determine the efficiency of the cipher in practice, in the use scenario. Usually, the encryption of the RAM data is performed using the same symmetric key, therefore the key derivation function can be performed only once, in the initialization phase of the system. In this phase, all the round keys can be computed and stored in a secure register or device.

In order to ensure a higher resistance of a cipher based on the 2S-strategy against linear, differential and related-key attacks, we designed the key schedule and the tweak update function by using one non-linear layer in each round. Moreover, we designed these functions such that in two consecutive rounds different non-linear layers are applied.

The tweak update function is designed as follows: in the odd indexed rounds, the Sbox is applied on each row of the current tweak, while in the even numbered rounds, the Sbox is applied on every column. Note that the first round is indexed by 1. A pseudocode of this function is given in Algorithm 1.

Algorithm 1: The tweak update function for round r

```
Result: The round tweak
if ((r % 2) == 1) then
  | tweak_r = SB_R(tweak_{r-1});
else
  | tweak_r = SB_C(tweak_{r-1});
end
```

Algorithm 2: The key schedule for the round r

```
Result: The round key
if ((r % 2) == 0) then
  | key_r = SB_R(key_{r-1});
else
  | key_r = SB_C(key_{r-1});
end
```

A similar approach is used for designing the key schedule, where the operations on the even and odd rows are performed in reverse. More precisely, in the odd indexed rounds, the Sbox is applied on the columns of the current key, while in the even indexed rounds the Sbox is applied on the rows.

A pseudocode of the key schedule algorithm is described in Algorithm 2.

Round Constants. The round constants could be added either on the round function, the tweak update function or the key schedule, depending on the goals, in terms of performance, of the new designed block cipher. While in Sect. 4 we propose an algorithm for the generation of the round constants, we entrust the future designers to create personalized algorithms which accomplish this purpose.

4 The Description of RAMus

The RAMus cipher represents a practical parameterization of the 2S-strategy. RAMus is a tweakable lightweight block cipher with 64 bit block and 128 bit key and 17 rounds. The cipher attains all the requirements provided by the (German) Federal Office of Information Security (BSI) in the domain of encryption algorithms suitable for RAM and memory encryption.

The Sbox Layers. As mentioned in Sect. 3.2, an Sbox suitable for the 2S-strategy needs to have good cryptographic properties, together with non-trivial linear and differential branch numbers. In Sect. 5 we propose a design strategy which could be used to generate Sboxes that fulfill all the necessary properties. By following this strategy, we designed an Sbox which has differential branch number 4 and linear branch number 3, while both the linear and differential uniformities are 64. To the best of our knowledge, this is the first published Sbox with differential branch number 4 and non-trivial linear and differential uniformities.

Moreover, given the use case of RAMus, in the design of the Sbox S we used a supplementary constraint regarding the optimization of Sbox's implementation with respect to the number of non-linear gates. We discuss the design rationale of the Sbox in Sect. 5, while the full description of the Sbox, given through a look-up table, is given in the Appendix, in Table 4.

Algorithm 3: The key schedule - computing the key for the rth round

```
Input: The (r − 1)^th round key rk_{r−1}
Output: The r^th round key rk_r
x_r = r/2;
// Defining the round constants' associated initial array RC[8]
for i = 0 to 3 do
 | RC[(x_r + i)%8] = 4 · x_r + i;
end
// Computing the round constant rc_r and the round key rk_r
if ((r % 2) == 1) then
 | rc_r = SB_R(s^R(RC));
 | rk_r = SB_R(rk_{r−1}) ⊕ rc_r;
else
 | rc_r = SB_C(s^C(RC));
 | rk_r = SB_C(rk_{r−1}) ⊕ rc_r;
end
```

Key Schedule, Tweak and Round Constants Addition. The 2S-strategy defines a key schedule in which the key has the same length as the block - in the case of RAMus 64 bits. In order to design a block cipher with a master key of length 128, we use the same approach introduced by the authors of the Prince cipher [19]. More precisely, we split the 128-bit master key k into $k = (k_0, k_1)$, where k_0 and k_1 represents the first and the last 64 bits of the key, respectively. The key is then extended from 128 bits to 192 bits as follows:

$$(k_0, k_1) \rightarrow (k_0, (k_0 \gg 1) \oplus (k_0 \gg 63), k_1),$$

where $x \gg y$ defines the circular shift of the 64-bit word x with y positions. The first two keys are used for the initial and final whitening, while the key k_1 represents the input of the key schedule of RAMus.

In order to minimize the storing space and the latency of the cipher, we chose to add the round constants to the key schedule, instead of adding them to the round function. In this way, an implementation that precomputes the round keys needs to add the round constants during the precomputations only. The constants are generated depending to the current round index, and they are obtained after applying one Sbox layer. A pseudocode of the key schedule is described in Algorithm 3. We note that, for the first round, the key rk_{r-1} represents the master key of the cipher.

In each round i, the constants rc_i are added to 4 different and consecutive rows or columns, depending on the round index. More precisely, in the odd indexed round $2 \cdot r + 1$, the constants are added to the columns $r, r+1, r+2, r+3$, while in the rounds $2 \cdot r$, the constants are added to the rows $r, r+1, r+2, r+3$. Therefore, in every round, four constant bytes are added to the internal state of the key schedule. These bytes are computed by applying the Sbox on the values

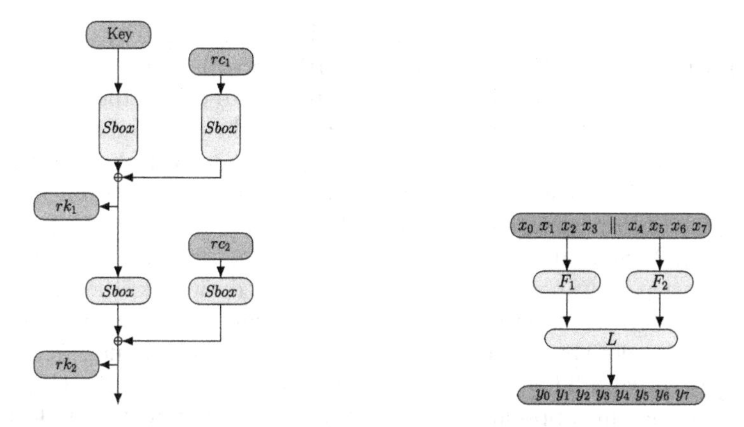

Fig. 5. The first two rounds of the key schedule of RAMus.

Fig. 6. The SPN design strategy for Sboxes

$4 \cdot r$, $4 \cdot r + 1, 4 \cdot r + 2$ and $4 \cdot r + 3$. Figure 5 describes the first two rounds of the key schedule of RAMus.

The tweak update function follows accurately the corresponding description of the 2S-strategy, which is described in Sect. 3.2 and in Algorithm 1.

5 Design Rationale

Linear vs. Non-linear Layers. The linear layer is considered a core component of the ciphers based on the SPN, LS or ARX strategies. Many papers aimed at introducing different strategies for the design of the linear layer, both from a security and efficiency perspective (e.g. [23], [7]). The general goal of the linear layer is to ensure the diffusion through the round function. Usually, the design of optimal linear layers assumes the search of linear functions that have a high branch number, while allowing for an efficient implementation. Recent works such as [28,35] introduced methods to design Sboxes with non-trivial linear and differential branch number. The non-linear layer of RAMus represents a trade-off between the constraints of a good linear and a good non-linear layer, allowing for a design following the 2S-strategy (with no linear layers).

Sboxes with Non-trivial Branch Number. The design of the Sbox S followed three main goals. The first goal of our design strategy was to optimize the linear or the differential branch number of an Sbox, while ensuring the fact that the linear and differential uniformities are non-trivial. The second goal was to ensure, by design, the resistance of RAMus against power analysis, i.e. to ensure that RAMus has an efficient masked implementation. The third goal was to ensure the low latency of the cipher, in the masked implementation, therefore we aimed at optimising the number of non-linear gates of S. In order to ensure these three goals, our approach was to identify the design strategies for designing an Sbox with a known, masking-friendly, design strategy, as the ones presented in [20,32]. The Sbox S follows the SPN Sbox design strategy, which is depicted in Fig. 6. The main idea of this strategy is to divide the 8-bit input into two equal parts of 4 bit each, i.e. $x = x_1||x_2$. Then x_1 and x_2 are used as inputs for two 4×4 non-linear functions F_1 and F_2, respectively, resulting in $y = F_1(x_1)||F_2(x_2)$. The result y is then used as an input for an 8-bit linear layer L. Formally, the Sbox S can be described as $S(x_1||x_2) = L(F_1(x_1)||F_2(x_2))$.

While the SPN Sbox design strategy facilitates the design of Sboxes with resistance against power analysis, it has an important drawback: the linear and differential uniformities of the resulting Sbox are determined by the properties of F_1 and F_2. Let us denote by δ_f and l_f the differential and linear uniformity of the function f, respectively. Then: $\delta_S = 16 \cdot \max\{\delta_{F_1}, \delta_{F_2}\}, l_S = 16 \cdot \max\{l_{F_1}, l_{F_2}\}$. Therefore, by using this approach the lowest linear and differential uniformity of S is 64.

Since one of the goals of our design strategy was to optimize the differential branch number, we analysed the properties of the non-linear functions F_1 and F_2, together with the properties of the linear layer L. Our design strategy is based on the following observation.

Observation 1. *Let L be the identity function. Then*

$$BN_d(S) = \min\{BN_d(F_1), BN_d(F2)\}$$

According to the literature [36], the highest differential branch number for a 4-bit Sbox is 3. Therefore, Observation 1 provides us a method to design 8-bit Sboxes with the non-trivial differential branch number 3.

In order to design S such that it is also optimised with respect to the number of necessary non-linear gates, we parameterize the functions F_1 and F_2 with the PRESENT Sbox, which can be implemented with only 4 non-linear gates, according to [33]. Note that this is in fact the minimum number of non-linear gates that can be used in the implementation of any 4-bit Sbox with good cryptographic properties. Moreover, according to [17,33], the Present Sbox also allows for a 3-share TI implementation.

For the design of the linear function L, we opted for a particular function with branch number 4 such that will ensure that the final differential branch number of S is 4. The linear function L was designed using three rotations, as follows $L(x) = \text{rot}(x, 1) \oplus \text{rot}(x, 2) \oplus \text{rot}(x, 5)$, where by $\text{rot}(x, i)$ we denote the circular left shift of the byte x by i positions. By using this design strategy, with different parameterizations for the non-linear function F_1 and F_2 and for the linear function L, different Sboxes with similar properties can be designed.

6 Security Analysis of RAMus

Our analysis included a series of adversarial models, depending on the capabilities of the adversary. Depending on the attack scenario, the adversary can control the plaintext or the plaintext and the tweak (known- or chosen-plaintext attack), or he can even control the master key (related-key attack).

Given the use case of RAMus (RAM encryption solutions), the most suitable adversarial model is the one in which the adversary can fully control the plaintext. While the tweak value cannot be fixed, the adversary can choose the tweak difference, since the tweak represents the memory address associated to the plaintext. We consider less relevant the related-key scenario in this use case, since all the encryptions are performed using the same, fixed, master key.

6.1 Theoretical Proven Bound

In order to compute the theoretical upper bound of any differential characteristic or linear trail, we use the method introduced by the wide trail strategy. We bound the number of active Sboxes by using *The 2-round Propagation Theorem* provided by Daemen and Rijmen in [23].

Theorem 1 (The 2-Round Propagation Theorem). *For a key-alternating block cipher with a $\gamma\lambda$ structure, the number of active bytes of any two round trail is lower bounded by the (branch) number of λ.*

In [23], γ represents a local non-linear transformation, in which any output bit is influenced only by a set of input bits, while λ represents a linear mixing transformation with high diffusion. Classically, the γ function is represented by an Sbox layer, in which the Sbox is applied on partitions of the input bits, while the λ function is designed such that it has a high branch number. We underline that, since the number of active Sboxes is not influenced by the γ function, Theorem 1 in fact computes the number of active Sboxes of the $\gamma\lambda\gamma$ function. According to Sect. 5, the non-linear layer of RAMus satisfies both criteria: it represents a local non-linear transformation, while it has a non-trivial linear and differential branch number.

In order to compute the lower bound of the number of active Sboxes in 2 rounds of RAMus we apply Theorem 1 twice, with different correspondence between the γ and λ functions and the two non-linear layers SB_R and SB_C.

In order to compute the number of active Sboxes of the first non-linear layer, we identify γ to SB_R and λ with SB_C. According to the theorem, the number of active Sboxes of SB_R, in two rounds of RAMus is given by the branch number of SB_C. Accordingly, the number of active Sboxes of the second non-linear layer is bounded by the branch number of SB_R. Figure 7 describes these associations.

Therefore, the minimum number of active Sboxes in two rounds of RAMus can be computed as $B = B_1 + B_2$, where B_1 and B_2 represent the branch number of SB_R and SB_C respectively.

Since the branch number of both SB_R and SB_C are equal to the branch number of the Sbox S, the number of active Sboxes in two rounds of RAMus is equal to twice the branch number of S. Therefore, for 2 rounds of RAMus, the minimum number of active Sboxes is 8 for differential cryptanalysis and 6 for linear cryptanalysis. This analysis is performed in the fixed tweak scenario, in which the attacker can control both the plaintext and the tweak.

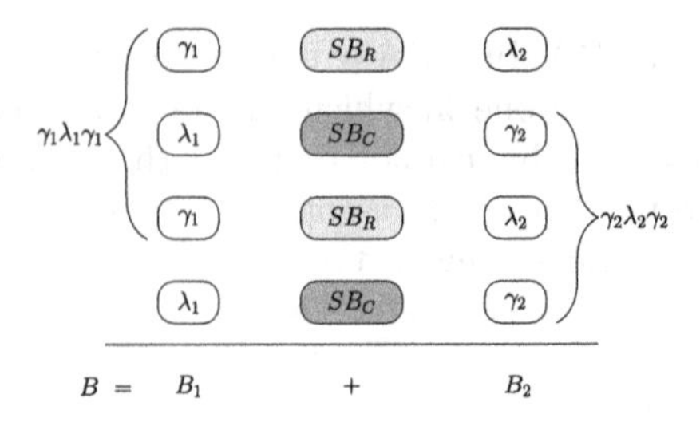

Fig. 7. The two associations between SB_R and SB_C to the γ and λ functions

Table 2. The minimum number of active Sboxes, in different scenarios

Round nr.		1	2	3	4	5	6	7	8	9	10	11	12	13	14	15	16	17
Fixed tweak	Diff sk	2	8	10	16	18	24	26	32	34	40	42	48	50	56	58	64	66
	Diff rk	1	6	9	14	17	22	25	30	33	38	41	46	49	54	57	62	65
	Lin	2	6	8	12	14	18	20	24	26	30	32	36	38	42	44	48	50
Not fixed tweak	Diff sk	2	6	10	15	18	22	26	31	34	38	42	47	50	54	58	63	66
	Diff rk	1	6	9	14	17	22	25	30	33	38	41	46	49	54	57	62	65
	Lin	3	8	12	16	20	24	28	32	36	40	44	48	52	56	60	64	68

6.2 SAT-Based Analysis

The second step of our analysis was to use SAT-based methods to evaluate the security of RAMus against linear and differential cryptanalysis. In our analysis we used the ARXpy tool [11].

We performed our analysis in two main scenarios, depending on the capabilities of the adversary to control the tweak input. Therefore, in our first scenario the tweak is constant in all the encryptions, while for the second scenario the tweak is different, but the adversary can observe the values of the tweaks, and, therefore, their difference. For these scenarios, we analysed the propagation of differences in the single key (Diff sk) and related-key (Diff rk) scenarios, together with the propagation of the linear masks (Lin). The results are presented in Table 2. We note that the table presents the minimum number of possible active Sboxes after applying any number of rounds of RAMus between 1 and 17.

Moreover, we mention that all our experiments were performed by using a generic implementation table of the Sbox S, which does not represent a real Sbox, but imposes the constraints that its properties, such as the linear and differential branch numbers and uniformities, are the same as the Sbox S presented in Sect. 5. We stress that our experiments did not take into account neither the particular LAT, nor the DDT of the Sbox S. Therefore, the results obtained by using this approach represent only a lower bound of the number of active bits. In practice, the minimum number of active Sboxes could be higher.

The attentive reader will notice that, while the number of active Sboxes in the two scenarios are similar with respect to differential cryptanalysis, in the case of linear cryptanalysis the number of active Sboxes is quite different (favouring our use case). The reason for this difference can be explained by the different propagation of linear approximations through the XOR operation.

The number of active Sboxes, together with the particular cryptographic properties of the associated Sbox, leads to an estimation of the security level of the cipher against linear and differential cryptanalysis. In our analysis, we evaluate the security of RAMus by using the assumption that all the Sboxes are independent. From this point of view, our analysis follows the same approach used to assess the security of the CS-cipher [39,42]. Moreover, we mention that this assumption is also used to assess the security of a series of permutation-based algorithms, such as the NIST LWC submissions SpoC [8] or SPIX [9].

Resistance of RAMus Against Differential Cryptanalysis. The most common approach in the security evaluation of a cipher against differential cryptanalysis is to upper bound the probability p of any differential characteristic. If the bound is smaller than 2^{-k}, where k denotes the size of the key, then an attack based on differential cryptanalysis is not feasible. Under the independence assumption, the probability p is computed by $p = p_S^s$, where s represents the number of active Sboxes and p_S is the highest probability associated to an active Sbox. Note that p_S can be computed using the differential uniformity δ_S.

In the particular case of RAMus, $p_S = 2^{-2}$ and, according to Table 2, $s > 64$ in all the scenarios based on differential cryptanalysis. Therefore

$$p < (2^{-2})^{64} \Rightarrow p < 2^{-128}$$

Therefore, an attack based on differential cryptanalysis against RAMus is unfeasible, thus we consider RAMus to be secure against the attacks based on differential cryptanalysis, in both the single-key and the related-key scenario.

Resistance of RAMus Against Linear Cryptanalysis. In general, in order to distinguish a linear trail with correlation c, an adversary needs to encrypt at least c^{-2} plaintexts. According to [14,31], the larger the size of the data sample, the more accurate the results are. In the case of RAMus, the full codebook contains up to 2^{128} (plaintext, tweak) pairs. Therefore, RAMus can be considered vulnerable against an attack based on linear cryptanalysis only if the absolute value of the correlation of its best linear trail is higher than 2^{-64}.

The correlation of the best linear trail of a cipher is computed as $c = c_S^s$, where c_S represents the best correlation associated to one active Sbox and s is the number of active Sboxes. In the particular case of RAMus, $c_S = \pm 2^{-1}$ and, according to Table 2, $s > 64$ in Scenario 2. Therefore

$$|c| < (2^{-1})^{64} \Rightarrow |c| < 2^{-64}.$$

Hence, an attack based on linear cryptanalysis against RAMus is unfeasible, thus RAMus is secure against such an attack.

6.3 The Security of RAMus Against Integral Cryptanalysis and the Division Property Attacks

Integral Cryptanalysis. Integral cryptanalysis, also known as the square attack or the saturation attack, was introduced by Knudsen in [29]. An integral attack exploits the existence of an integral distinguisher defined as follows. An adversary chooses a set of plaintexts such that a set of the bits are constant, while the remaining bits (called active bits) vary through all possible values. The goal of the adversary is to find an indexing of the active bits such that the XOR sum of the corresponding ciphertexts equals to zero in some particular indexes, with probability 1. The set of plaintexts for which this property holds is called an integral distinguisher.

To design such distinguishers, the most common approach is to analyse the propagation of different properties of parts of the internal states, such as whether they are "constant" (C), "active" (A), "balanced" (B) or with the "unknow" property (U) (i.e. a property different from the previous three ones). Note that, if components of the ciphertexts are "constant", "active" or "balanced", the XOR sum of these components results in a 0 value with probability 1. Opposed to this scenario, in the case in which components of the ciphertext have the "unknow" property, the XOR sum will be 0 with a probability less than 1.

In order to analyse the security of RAMus against integral cryptanalysis, we analyse the behaviour of the internal states in different scenarios, depending on the choice of the "active" bits. The best distinguisher identified in our analysis covers 3 rounds of RAMus. In this scenario, we consider the sets of plaintexts such that all the bits in a row have the A property. For simplicity and without loss of generality, we assume that the "active" bits are in the first row. Moreover, we impose the additional constraint that the tweak is equal to the plaintext. In this case, after the appliance of the first non-linear layer and the tweak addition, all the internal states are "constant" and each position equals to 0 (due to the cancellation between the internal state and the round tweak). After the appliance of the second non-linear layer, the state will have a "constant" value equal to $SB_C(\mathbf{0}) \oplus key$, where $\mathbf{0}$ represents the state with all 0 positions and key represents the round key. Furthermore, after the appliance of the following SB_R function, all the internal states would still have the C property.

By looking only at the tweak update function, we notice that, for the first non-linear layer, the "active" row will propagate to another "active" row, while the remaining part will be "constant". In the second round of the tweak update function, since the Sboxes are applied on a column level, each active bit will influence the properties of each corresponding column. In particular, the bits in positions 3, 4, 5, 6 will have the B property, while the remaining positions will be "constant". Therefore, the addition of the tweak in the second round would transfer the properties from the tweak to the internal state. At the end of the second round, each position of the internal state will be "balanced", a property which is also preserved through the third round. The first appliance of the non-linear layer of the 4th round will determine that all the positions of the internal state will have the "unknow" property. Therefore, in this scenario, a 3-round distinguisher could be designed, as depicted in Fig. 9 in the Appendix. Thus, even if the key-recovery phase of the attack could cover another 4 rounds, we consider that RAMus is resistant to integral cryptanalysis.

The Division Property. As a new distinguishing property against block ciphers, the division property was introduced by Todo in [41] and it represents a generalization of both the integral attack and the higher-order differential cryptanalysis. In [43], the authors introduce a division property analysis technique based on the Mixed-Integer Linear Programming (MILP) problem. Since publication, this tool was used to analyse the resistance against the attacks based on the division property of several modern block ciphers, such as Princev2 [19] or GIMLI [13]. By employing the same technique, we searched for the existence of integral distinguishers based on the division property for RAMus. The best distinguisher that we found covers 3.5 rounds and the data complexity required for an attack based on this distinguisher is 2^{63} plaintexts. Note that our analysis covered both the fixed-tweak and the variable-tweak scenarios.

7 Performance

In this section we present the results of our measurements or estimates regarding the performance of the hardware implementation of RAMus and we compare them with the performance of PRINCEv2 [19], QARMA-64 [10], PRESENT [18] and SKINNY [12]. We excluded from this comparison the other two block ciphers which are frequently used in RAM encryption solutions, AES and ASCON, due to the difference in their parameters' lengths.

Setup of the Experiments. Depending on the application, a dedicated hardware implementation is performed usually on Field-Programmable Gate Arrays (FPGA) or Application-Specific Integrated Circuits (ASIC). While ASICs are designed for a sole purpose, and the implementation is permanently drawn into silicon, the FPGAs can be reprogrammed to satisfy different purposes sequentially. Due to the versatility of the latter, all of our hardware implementations were run on the FPGA of the ZedBoard™ development kit, which uses the Xilinx Zynq®-7000 All Programable SoC (APSoC).

The first step was to identify an approach which facilitates the comparison of the hardware performance between the five targeted ciphers. In this sense, we chose to use Xilinx's Vivado High-Level Synthesis (HLS), an automated tool which transforms a high-level functional specification (such as a C or C++ implementation) into an optimized register-transfer level (RTL) descriptions, which contains the hardware implementation of the initial C/C++ code. While for RAMus we use our own C implementation, for PRINCEv2, Qarma, PRESENT and SKINNY we used the public C implementations provided by [2–4] and [5] respectively. Note that for PRINCEv2 and SKINNY we used the reference implementation provided by the authors of the ciphers.

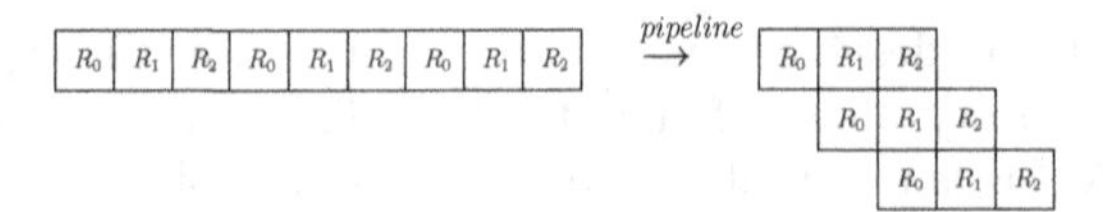

Fig. 8. The pipeline implementation of three encryptions of a 3-round block cipher. Note that the pipeline implementation is similar to a 5-round encryption.

After generating the RTL module, we used Xilinx's Vivado IP integrator to configure the hardware design, by connecting default modules (such as the Zynq architecture) with the previously generated custom one. Finally, we used Xilinx Software Development Kit (SDK), which allows for the development of embedded software applications for the hardware design formerly created.

Latency vs. Throughput. The performance of a hardware implementation can be evaluated with respect to several different criteria: the latency of the implementation (the speed of one encryption), its throughput (the amount of data processed in a fixed period of time), the area needed for the implementation or the power consumption.

In a sequential approach, the relation between the latency and the throughput of an implementation is given by the following formula: $N/l = t$, where N represents the amount of data to be processed, and l and t represent the latency and throughput, respectively. The most common approach to increase the throughput of an implementation is to use parallelization, therefore using multiple threads which perform, in parallel, the same process. This type of parallelism increases the throughput, but, in the same time, it increases the resource (CPU or area) consumption.

On the other hand, the parallelism of an FPGA, called pipelining, involves the usage of the hardware components in an optimal manner in which several instructions are overlapped during execution. The main idea behind pipelining is that a process can be divided into a set of instructions such that the output of one instruction is the input of the next one and each instruction is implemented on an independent hardware component. As soon as an instruction finishes processing an input, it is ready for the next one. Therefore, different instructions could be performed simultaneously.

For simplicity, let Enc represent a block cipher with 3 rounds, denoted R_0, R_1 and R_2. An intuitive description of the pipelining parallelism over three encryption instances can be depicted from Fig. 8. In a sequential implementation the second encryption instance will start after the first one finishes. In contrast, in the case of a pipelined implementation, the output of R_0 is transmitted as an input for R_1, while R_0 can be used in parallel for the encryption of the second plaintext. Assuming that all three rounds have the same latency, performing the encryption of three plaintexts in the pipelined implementation will have the same latency as an encryption with 5 rounds in the classical implementation.

Table 3. The performance comparison between the five targeted block ciphers. LUT, FF and BRAM stands for LookUp Table, FlipFlops and Block RAM, respectively.

	Non-pipelined			Pipelined			Throughput (KB/sec)
	Latency (μs)	Area	Power (mW)	Latency (μs)	Area	Power (mW)	
PRINCEv2	12.1	1991 LUT 2395 FF 0 BRAM	14	4.772	5730 LUT 4756 FF 0 BRAM	1705	7.29
Qarma-64	29.8	2353 LUT 3281 FF 3 BRAM	35	0.873	1050 LUT 1498 FF 0 BRAM	1682	7.95
PRESENT	25.6	1096 LUT 1320 FF 1.5 BRAM	17	9.1*	1096 LUT* 1320 FF* 1.5 BRAM*	1693*	6.75*
SKINNY	163	1210 LUT 1443 FF 2 BRAM	17	1.695	1211 LUT 1770 FF 1 BRAM	1686	7.63
RAMus	46.3	1038 LUT 1285 FF 2 BRAM	13	1.059	5065 LUT 5228 FF 0 BRAM	1669	8.00

*the PRESENT implementation contained several functions that could not be pipelined

The Results of Our Experiments. In our work, we used the pipeline parallelization in two different manners. Firstly, we used the pipeline pragma provided by Vivado HLS for generating the pipelined implementation of all three targeted ciphers. We note that for the pipelined implementation of PRINCEv2 we modified the `prince_s_layer` function such that it will not be parameterized with the corresponding Sbox. Secondly, we used the pipeline pragma to estimate the throughput of the three targeted ciphers. In this sense, we measured the latency of a single pipelined round of the corresponding ciphers and we computed the total number of rounds that need to be performed for the processing of 128 encryptions (1 KB of data). Then we computed the throughput as $t = 128/(l \cdot n_r)$, where t and l represent the throughput and the latency, respectively, while n_r represent the total number of rounds.

Note that both PRINCEv2 and Qarma-64 have a self-reflection property, thus the rounds are not identical. In order to estimate the throughput for these two ciphers we individually measured all the individual rounds. We measured the middle rounds in both cases as a single round. Our estimates use the round with the highest latency, due to the fact that the processing through a lower latency round will start after the high latency one finishes.

In our experiment, we measured the latency, area and power consumption of both the pipelined and non-pipelined implementations of all five ciphers and we estimated the throughput as presented above. Table 3 presents the results of our experiments. While the results for latency, power consumption and throughput can be easily inferred from Table 3, the area of a hardware implementation is more involved. In an FPGA, a LookUp Table (LUT) stores a custom truth table which is set to simulate logic gate combinations. A flip-flop (FF) is used to store the results of LUTs, while a block RAM (BRAM) is a larger bank of RAM which is used for storing higher amounts of data inside the FPGA.

As depicted in Table 3, in the scenario of non-pipelined implementations, RAMus exhibits the lowest area and the lowest power consumption, whereas in the case of pipelined implementations, RAMus has the lower power consumption, a higher latency than PRINCEv2 and SKINNY while the area is lower than the one of PRINCEv2. Moreover, from our estimates, the throughput of RAMus is comparable with the one of Qarma-64, both being above the throughput of the other three ciphers.

Throughout performing these experiments we were surprised by the high latency of the pipelined implementation of PRINCEv2. Nonetheless, we did not find any argument which could invalidate the correctness of our experiments.

Appendix 1. The Byte Description of the Sbox S

Table 4. The Sbox S. The output associated to the hexadecimal input xy can be depicted from the intersection of the row $x0$ and the column $0y$. For example, $S(c2) = 5d$.

	00	01	02	03	04	05	06	07	08	09	0a	0b	0c	0d	0e	0f
00	33	24	4e	c1	8d	9a	e7	15	f0	7f	59	ab	02	68	bc	d6
10	42	55	3f	b0	fc	eb	96	64	81	0e	28	da	73	19	cd	a7
20	e4	f3	99	16	5a	4d	30	c2	27	a8	8e	7c	d5	bf	6b	01
30	1c	0b	61	ee	a2	b5	c8	3a	df	50	76	84	2d	47	93	f9
40	d8	cf	a5	2a	66	71	0c	fe	1b	94	b2	40	e9	83	57	3d
50	a9	be	d4	5b	17	00	7d	8f	6a	e5	c3	31	98	f2	26	4c
60	7e	69	03	8c	c0	d7	aa	58	bd	32	14	e6	4f	25	f1	9b
70	51	46	2c	a3	ef	f8	85	77	92	1d	3b	c9	60	0a	de	b4
80	0f	18	72	fd	b1	a6	db	29	cc	43	65	97	3e	54	80	ea
90	f7	e0	8a	05	49	5e	23	d1	34	bb	9d	6f	c6	ac	78	12
a0	95	82	e8	67	2b	3c	41	b3	56	d9	ff	0d	a4	ce	1a	70
b0	ba	ad	c7	48	04	13	6e	9c	79	f6	d0	22	8b	e1	35	5f
c0	20	37	5d	d2	9e	89	f4	06	e3	6c	4a	b8	11	7b	af	c5
d0	86	91	fb	74	38	2f	52	a0	45	ca	ec	1e	b7	dd	09	63
e0	cb	dc	b6	39	75	62	1f	ed	08	87	a1	53	fa	90	44	2e
f0	6d	7a	10	9f	d3	c4	b9	4b	ae	21	07	f5	5c	36	e2	88

Appendix 2. The Integral Distinguisher Described in Sect. 6.3

We recall that, for this distinguisher, the first row is "active", with the additional constraint that the tweak is equal to the plaintext.

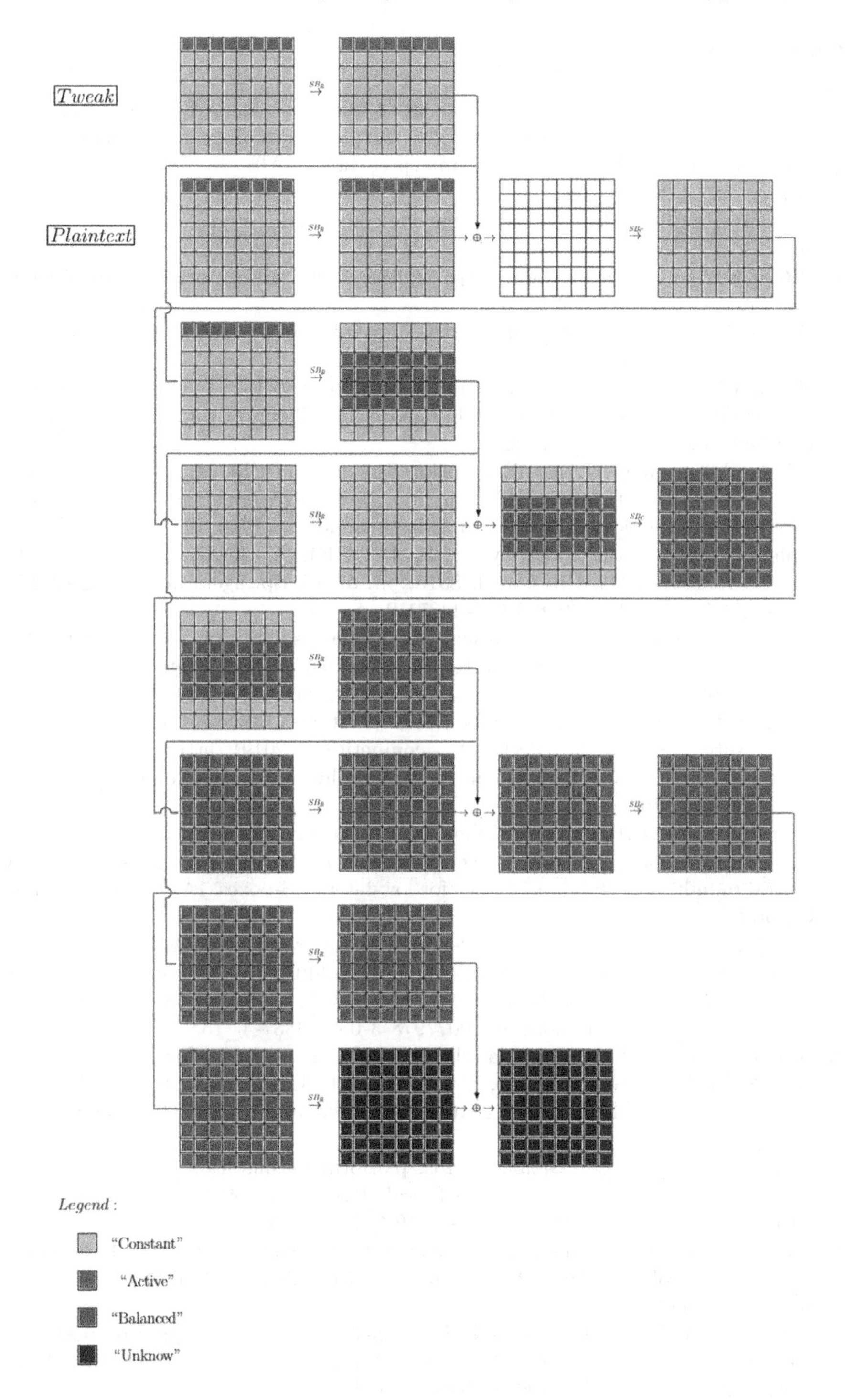

Fig. 9. The 3-round integral distinguisher described in Sect. 6.3.

References

1. Methodology for cryptographic rating of memory encryption schemes used in smartcards and similar devices. https://www.bsi.bund.de/SharedDocs/Downloads/DE/BSI/Zertifizierung/Interpretationen/AIS_46_MEGuide_e_pdf.pdf. Accessed 20 Feb 2022
2. Present C implementation. https://github.com/kurtfu/present. Accessed 23 Feb 2022
3. PRINCEv2 C implementation. https://github.com/rub-hgi/princev2/tree/main/code. Accessed 14 Nov 2021
4. Qarma-64 C implementation. https://github.com/Phantom1003/QARMA64. Accessed 14 Nov 2021
5. Skinny C implementation. https://docs.google.com/viewer?a=v&pid=sites&srcid=ZGVmYXVsdGRvbWFpbnxza2lubnljaXBoZXJ8Z3g6NTEwY2I1MGFkZGNjMDU0MQ. Accessed 23 Feb 2022
6. FIPS Publication 46–3, Data Encryption Standard (DES). https://csrc.nist.gov/csrc/media/publications/fips/46/3/archive/1999-10-25/documents/fips46-3.pdf
7. Albrecht, M.R., Driessen, B., Kavun, E.B., Leander, G., Paar, C., Yalçın, T.: Block ciphers – focus on the linear layer (feat. PRIDE). In: Garay, J.A., Gennaro, R. (eds.) CRYPTO 2014. LNCS, vol. 8616, pp. 57–76. Springer, Heidelberg (2014). https://doi.org/10.1007/978-3-662-44371-2_4
8. AlTawy, R., et al.: SpoC: an authenticated cipher submission to the NIST LWC competition (2019). https://csrc.nist.gov/CSRC/media/Projects/lightweight-cryptography/documents/round-2/spec-doc-rnd2/spoc-spec-round2.pdf
9. AlTawy, R., Gong, G., He, M., Mandal, K., Rohit, R.: Spix: an authenticated cipher submission to the NIST LWC competition (2019). https://csrc.nist.gov/CSRC/media/Projects/Lightweight-Cryptography/documents/round-1/spec-doc/spix-spec.pdf
10. Avanzi, R.: The QARMA block cipher family. Almost MDS matrices over rings with zero divisors, nearly symmetric Even-Mansour constructions with non-involutory central rounds, and search heuristics for low-latency S-boxes. IACR Trans. Symm. Cryptol., 4–44 (2017)
11. Azimi, S.A., Ranea, A., Salmasizadeh, M., Mohajeri, J., Aref, M.R., Rijmen, V.: A bit-vector differential model for the modular addition by a constant. In: Moriai, S., Wang, H. (eds.) ASIACRYPT 2020. LNCS, vol. 12491, pp. 385–414. Springer, Cham (2020). https://doi.org/10.1007/978-3-030-64837-4_13
12. Beierle, C., et al.: The SKINNY family of block ciphers and its low-latency variant MANTIS. In: Robshaw, M., Katz, J. (eds.) CRYPTO 2016. LNCS, vol. 9815, pp. 123–153. Springer, Heidelberg (2016). https://doi.org/10.1007/978-3-662-53008-5_5
13. Bernstein, D.J., et al.: Gimli: a cross-platform permutation. In: Fischer, W., Homma, N. (eds.) CHES 2017. LNCS, vol. 10529, pp. 299–320. Springer, Cham (2017). https://doi.org/10.1007/978-3-319-66787-4_15
14. Biham, E.: On Matsui's linear cryptanalysis. In: De Santis, A. (ed.) EUROCRYPT 1994. LNCS, vol. 950, pp. 341–355. Springer, Heidelberg (1995). https://doi.org/10.1007/BFb0053449
15. Biham, E., Anderson, R., Knudsen, L.: Serpent: a new block cipher proposal. In: Vaudenay, S. (ed.) FSE 1998. LNCS, vol. 1372, pp. 222–238. Springer, Heidelberg (1998). https://doi.org/10.1007/3-540-69710-1_15

16. Biham, E., Shamir, A.: Differential cryptanalysis of DES-like cryptosystems. J. Cryptol. **4**(1), 3–72 (1991)
17. Bilgin, B., Meyer, L.D., Duval, S., Levi, I., Standaert, F.: Low AND depth and efficient inverses: a guide on s-boxes for low-latency masking. IACR Trans. Symm. Cryptol. **2020**(1), 144–184 (2020)
18. Bogdanov, A., et al.: PRESENT: an ultra-lightweight block cipher. In: Paillier, P., Verbauwhede, I. (eds.) CHES 2007. LNCS, vol. 4727, pp. 450–466. Springer, Heidelberg (2007). https://doi.org/10.1007/978-3-540-74735-2_31
19. Borghoff, J., et al.: PRINCE – a low-latency block cipher for pervasive computing applications. In: Wang, X., Sako, K. (eds.) ASIACRYPT 2012. LNCS, vol. 7658, pp. 208–225. Springer, Heidelberg (2012). https://doi.org/10.1007/978-3-642-34961-4_14
20. Boss, E., Grosso, V., Güneysu, T., Leander, G., Moradi, A., Schneider, T.: Strong 8-bit Sboxes with efficient masking in hardware extended version. J. Cryptogr. Eng. **7**, 1–17 (2017)
21. Chabaud, F., Vaudenay, S.: Links between differential and linear cryptanalysis. In: De Santis, A. (ed.) EUROCRYPT 1994. LNCS, vol. 950, pp. 356–365. Springer, Heidelberg (1995). https://doi.org/10.1007/BFb0053450
22. Daemen, J., Govaerts, R., Vandewalle, J.: Correlation matrices. In: Preneel, B. (ed.) FSE 1994. LNCS, vol. 1008, pp. 275–285. Springer, Heidelberg (1995). https://doi.org/10.1007/3-540-60590-8_21
23. Daemen, J., Rijmen, V.: The Design of Rijndael. Springer, Heidelberg (2020). https://doi.org/10.1007/978-3-662-60769-5
24. Dobraunig, C., Eichlseder, M., Mendel, F., Schläffer, M.: ASCON v1. 2. Submission to the CAESAR Competition (2016)
25. Grosso, V., Leurent, G., Standaert, F.X., Varc, K.: LS-Designs: bitslice encryption for efficient masked software implementations, vol. 8540 (2014)
26. Gruhn, M., Müller, T.: On the practicability of cold boot attacks. In: 2013 International Conference on Availability, Reliability and Security, pp. 390–397 (2013)
27. Joy Persial, G., Prabhu, M., Shanmugalakshmi, R.: Side channel attack-survey. Int. J. Adv. Sci. Res. Rev. **1**(4), 54–57 (2011)
28. Kim, H., et al.: A new method for designing lightweight S-boxes with high differential and linear branch numbers, and its application. IACR Cryptol. ePrint Arch. **2020**, 1582 (2020)
29. Knudsen, L., Wagner, D.: Integral cryptanalysis. In: Daemen, J., Rijmen, V. (eds.) FSE 2002. LNCS, vol. 2365, pp. 112–127. Springer, Heidelberg (2002). https://doi.org/10.1007/3-540-45661-9_9
30. Liu, Y., Rijmen, V., Leander, G.: Nonlinear diffusion layers. Des. Codes Cryptogr. **86**(11), 2469–2484 (2018)
31. Matsui, M.: Linear cryptanalysis method for DES cipher. In: Helleseth, T. (ed.) EUROCRYPT 1993. LNCS, vol. 765, pp. 386–397. Springer, Heidelberg (1994). https://doi.org/10.1007/3-540-48285-7_33
32. Meyer, L.D., Varici, K.: More constructions for strong 8-bit S-boxes with efficient masking in hardware (2017)
33. Mourouzis, T.: Optimizations in algebraic and differential cryptanalysis. Ph.D. thesis, UCL (University College London) (2015)
34. Nikova, S., Rechberger, C., Rijmen, V.: Threshold implementations against side-channel attacks and glitches. In: Ning, P., Qing, S., Li, N. (eds.) ICICS 2006. LNCS, vol. 4307, pp. 529–545. Springer, Heidelberg (2006). https://doi.org/10.1007/11935308_38

35. Ruisanchez, C.P.: A new algorithm to construct S-boxes with high diffusion. Int. J. Soft Comput. Math. Control (IJSCMC) **4**(3), 41–50 (2015)
36. Saarinen, M.-J.O.: Cryptographic analysis of All 4× 4-bit S-boxes. In: Miri, A., Vaudenay, S. (eds.) SAC 2011. LNCS, vol. 7118, pp. 118–133. Springer, Heidelberg (2012). https://doi.org/10.1007/978-3-642-28496-0_7
37. Sarkar, S., Mandal, K., Saha, D.: On the relationship between resilient boolean functions and linear branch number of S-boxes. In: Hao, F., Ruj, S., Sen Gupta, S. (eds.) INDOCRYPT 2019. LNCS, vol. 11898, pp. 361–374. Springer, Cham (2019). https://doi.org/10.1007/978-3-030-35423-7_18
38. Sarkar, S., Syed, H.: Bounds on differential and linear branch number of permutations. In: Susilo, W., Yang, G. (eds.) ACISP 2018. LNCS, vol. 10946, pp. 207–224. Springer, Cham (2018). https://doi.org/10.1007/978-3-319-93638-3_13
39. Stern, J., Vaudenay, S.: CS-Cipher. In: Vaudenay, S. (ed.) FSE 1998. LNCS, vol. 1372, pp. 189–204. Springer, Heidelberg (1998). https://doi.org/10.1007/3-540-69710-1_13
40. Stewin, P., Bystrov, I.: Understanding DMA malware (2012)
41. Todo, Y.: Structural evaluation by generalized integral property. In: Oswald, E., Fischlin, M. (eds.) EUROCRYPT 2015. LNCS, vol. 9056, pp. 287–314. Springer, Heidelberg (2015). https://doi.org/10.1007/978-3-662-46800-5_12
42. Vaudenay, S.: On the security of CS-cipher. In: Knudsen, L. (ed.) FSE 1999. LNCS, vol. 1636, pp. 260–274. Springer, Heidelberg (1999). https://doi.org/10.1007/3-540-48519-8_19
43. Xiang, Z., Zhang, W., Bao, Z., Lin, D.: Applying MILP method to searching integral distinguishers based on division property for 6 lightweight block ciphers. In: Cheon, J.H., Takagi, T. (eds.) ASIACRYPT 2016. LNCS, vol. 10031, pp. 648–678. Springer, Heidelberg (2016). https://doi.org/10.1007/978-3-662-53887-6_24

Higher-Order Masked Saber

Suparna Kundu(✉), Jan-Pieter D'Anvers, Michiel Van Beirendonck, Angshuman Karmakar, and Ingrid Verbauwhede

imec-COSIC, KU Leuven, Kasteelpark Arenberg 10, Bus 2452, 3001 Leuven-Heverlee, Belgium
{suparna.kundu,jan-pieter.danvers,michiel.beirendonck, angshuman.karmakar,ingrid.verbauwhede}@esat.kuleuven.be

Abstract. Side-channel attacks are formidable threats to the cryptosystems deployed in the real world. An effective and provably secure countermeasure against side-channel attacks is masking. In this work, we present a detailed study of higher-order masking techniques for the key-encapsulation mechanism Saber. Saber is one of the lattice-based finalist candidates in the National Institute of Standards of Technology's post-quantum standardization procedure. We provide a detailed analysis of different masking algorithms proposed for Saber in the recent past and propose an optimized implementation of higher-order masked Saber. Our proposed techniques for first-, second-, and third-order masked Saber have performance overheads of 2.7x, 5x, and 7.7x respectively compared to the unmasked Saber. We show that compared to Kyber which is another lattice-based finalist scheme, Saber's performance degrades less with an increase in the order of masking. We also show that higher-order masked Saber needs fewer random bytes than higher-order masked Kyber. Additionally, we adapt our masked implementation to uSaber, a variant of Saber that was specifically designed to allow an efficient masked implementation. We present the first masked implementation of uSaber, showing that it indeed outperforms masked Saber by at least 12% for any order. We provide optimized implementations of all our proposed masking schemes on ARM Cortex-M4 microcontrollers.

Keywords: Post-quantum cryptography · Higher-order masking · Saber · Key-encapsulation mechanism

1 Introduction

The security of public-key cryptography (PKC) is dependent on the computational intractability of some underlying mathematical problems. The current most widely used public-key cryptographic algorithms RSA [44] and elliptic curve cryptography (ECC) [37] are based on the hardness of large integer factorization problem and elliptic curve discrete logarithm problem respectively. Unfortunately, both of these hard problems can be solved in polynomial time with large-scale quantum computers by using Shor's [46] and Proos-Zalka's [41] algorithm. Post-quantum cryptography (PQC) is a branch of PKC that focuses

C. Galdi and S. Jarecki (Eds.): SCN 2022, LNCS 13409, pp. 93–116, 2022.
https://doi.org/10.1007/978-3-031-14791-3_5

on designing cryptographic algorithms whose underlying mathematical problems remain hard even in the presence of large quantum computers. Considering the fast evolution of quantum computers and their impending threat to our current public-key infrastructure, the National Institute of Standards and Technology (NIST) started a procedure to standardize post-quantum public-key cryptographic primitives such as digital signatures, public-key encryption, and key-encapsulation mechanism in 2016 [39].

In 2020, NIST announced four finalists and five alternative candidates for the post-quantum key-encapsulation mechanism (KEM) category, that advanced to the 3rd round [2]. Three of the four finalist KEMs: Saber [19], Kyber [10], and NTRU [26], are lattice-based. NTRU is an NTRU-based KEM, whereas Kyber and Saber are based on variants of the learning with errors (LWE) problem. The security of Kyber can be reduced to module learning with errors (MLWE) problem, and the security of Saber is based on module learning with rounding (MLWR) problem. The hardness of both LWE and LWR problems are dependent on the difficulty to solve a set of noisy linear equations. This noise is explicitly added for a LWE problem but is implicitly generated in a LWR problem using the round-off of a few least significant bits.

Initially, the main focus of the NIST post-quantum standardization procedure was the mathematical security of the schemes, together with the performance, and the memory footprint of the cryptographic implementation in embedded devices. With the advancement of the standardization process, the focus was broadened to take into account the implementation-security of the schemes also. Side-channel attacks (SCA) [34] are a well-known type of physical attacks against implementations of cryptographic algorithms. These attacks exploit leakage of information, such as timing information, power consumption, electromagnetic radiation, etc., which leaks information from the physical device which runs the algorithm to extract the secret key.

Silverman et al. [47] first showed a timing attack on quantum secure lattice-based cryptographic protocol NTRUEncrypt [28] by exploiting the non-constant time implementation. To prevent the timing attack, most of the cryptographic protocols use constant-time implementation, including Saber and Kyber. In recent years, many works [3,24,29,42,50] showed SCA on lattice-based cryptographic schemes with the help of power consumption and electromagnetic leakage information. A provably-secure countermeasure against these kinds of SCA is masking [13].

The masking technique can also provide security against higher-order attacks, where the adversary can use the power consumption information of multiple points. However, the performance cost of the masked scheme increases with the order of SCA. Reparaz et al. [43] were the first to introduce a first-order SCA resistant masked implementation of chosen-plaintext attack (CPA) secure ring-LWE based decryption. Nevertheless, real-world applications use chosen-ciphertext attack (CCA) secure cryptosystems. Lattice-based quantum secure KEMs such as Saber and Kyber achieve CCA security by using a variant of Fujisaki-Okamoto transformation [30] on their CPA secure design. Oder et al. [40] proposed a 1st-order CCA secure masked Ring-LWE key decapsulation and reported an overhead factor of 5.2x in performance over an unmasked implementation on an ARM Cortex-M4.

Van Beirendonck et al. [6] proposed the first-order SCA secure implementation of Saber with an overhead factor of 2.5x. This performance was achievable because of the power-of-two moduli and efficient utilization of masking techniques specifically aimed at first-order security [48]. Heinz et al. [25] presented an optimized first-order masked implementation of Kyber with an overhead factor of 3.4x compared to the unmasked implementation of Kyber. Fritzmann et al. [21] proposed first-order masked implementations of Kyber and Saber with instruction set extensions, and Bos et al. [11] proposed higher-order masked implementations of Kyber.

First-order masked implementations of schemes are typically vulnerable against higher-order side-channel attacks [36,49], i.e., the attacks that exploit side-channel leakages of multiple intermediate values. Ngo et al. [38] proposed an attack on the first-order masked Saber using a deep neural network constructed at the profiling stage. This attack does not violate the assumption of the first-order masked Saber but exploits higher-order side-channel leakages. Higher-order masking increases the noise level exponentially and prevents attacks that exploit higher-order side-channel leakages.

In the third-round of the NIST submission, the Saber team introduced uSaber as a variant of Saber. In uSaber, the secrets are sampled from a uniform distribution instead of a centered binomial distribution as used in Saber. The authors claim that the advantage of this modification is twofold. First, it makes the scheme simpler since sampling from a uniform distribution is more straightforward than sampling from a centered binomial distribution, and it also reduces the modulus by a factor of two. Second, this change allows a very efficient masking of the secret values. However, this claim is yet to be proven as there exists no masked implementation of uSaber to corroborate this claim.

Contribution. In this work, we provide arbitrary-order masked implementations of Saber and uSaber, and we compare their performances with the state-of-the-art masked implementations of Saber and Kyber. We are the first to propose a higher-order masked implementation of uSaber. For this, we present a masked centered uniform sampler which is then applied to uSaber instead of Saber's centered binomial sampler. We generally take advantage of Saber's power-of-two moduli to mask both Saber's and uSaber's decapsulation algorithm, and we compare different recently proposed algorithms for ciphertext comparison in higher-order masked settings.

We implement and benchmark our higher-order masked Saber and uSaber on an ARM Cortex-M4 microcontroller using the PQM4 framework. The first-, second-, and third-order masked decapsulation algorithm of Saber has an overhead factor of 2.7x, 5x, and 7.7x over the unmasked implementation, respectively. In uSaber, the overhead factor for first-order is 2.3x, second-order is 4.2x, and third-order is 6.5x compared to the unmasked version. We include the performance results and requisite of the random bytes during masking for each masked primitive of first-, second-, and third-order masked Saber and uSaber.

Our implementations are available at https://github.com/KULeuven-COSIC/Higher-order-masked-Saber.

Finally, we compare the performances of our higher-order masked implementations of Saber and uSaber with the higher-order masked implementations of Kyber and Saber presented in [11,12]. We demonstrate that the performances of masked Saber implementations outperform masked Kyber implementations. Further, we show that the performance of masked uSaber is better and requires fewer random bytes than masked Saber and Kyber for any order.

2 Preliminaries

2.1 Notation

We denote the ring of integers modulo q by $\mathbb{Z}_q$ and the quotient ring $\mathbb{Z}_q[X]/(X^{256}+1)$ by R_q. We use R_q^l to represent the ring which contains vectors with l elements of R_q. The ring with $l \times l$ matrices over R_q is denoted by $R_q^{l\times l}$. We use lower case letters to denote single polynomials, bold lower case letters to denote vectors and bold upper case letters to denote matrices. The j-th coefficient of the polynomial c is represented as $c[j]$, where $j \in \{0, 1, \ldots, 255\}$. The j-th coefficient of the i-th polynomial of the vector $\mathbf{b}$ is represented as $\mathbf{b}[i][j]$, where $j \in \{0, 1, \ldots, 255\}$ and $i \in \{0, 1, \ldots, l-1\}$. Sometimes the set of $(n+1)$ elements $\{x_0, x_1, \ldots, x_n\}$ from the same ring R is denoted by $\{x_i\}_{0\leq i\leq n}$.

The rounding operation is denoted by $\lfloor\cdot\rceil$, and it returns the closest integer with ties rounded upwards. The operations $x \ll b$ and $x \gg b$ denote the logical shifting of x by b positions left and right, respectively. These operations are extended on polynomials by performing them coefficientwise.

We denote $x \leftarrow \chi(S)$ when x is sampled from the set S according to the distribution χ. We use the notation $x \leftarrow \chi(S, seed_x)$ to represent that x belongs to the set S and is generated by the pseudorandom number generator χ with the help of seed $seed_x$. To represent the uniform distribution we use $\mathcal{U}$. The centered binomial distribution is denoted by β_μ with standard deviation $\sqrt{\mu/4}$. The centered uniform distribution is expressed as $\mathcal{U}_u$, when it samples uniformly from $[-2^{(u-1)}, 2^{(u-1)}-1]$. We use $\texttt{HW}(x)$ to represent the Hamming weight of x.

2.2 Saber

In this section, we introduce the Saber encryption scheme. The parameter set of Saber includes three power-of-two moduli q, p and t, which define the rings R_q, R_p and R_t used in the algorithm. From these moduli, one can calculate the number of bits of one coefficient as $\epsilon_q = \log_2(q)$, $\epsilon_p = \log_2(p)$ and $\epsilon_t = \log_2(t)$. The parameter set also includes a vector length l, which increases with increase in security, and an integer μ defining the coins of the secret distribution β_μ. Given a set of parameters, the key generation, encryption, and decryption of Saber are shown in Fig. 1. For an in-depth review of the Saber encryption scheme, we refer to the original paper [19,20].

2.3 uSaber

uSaber or uniform-Saber was proposed in third round NIST submission [20] as a variant of Saber. The principal alteration in uSaber from Saber is that it uses a centered uniform distribution $\mathcal{U}_u$ for sampling secret vectors instead of the centered binomial distribution β_μ. The coefficients in polynomials of secret vector are from $[-2^{(u-1)}, 2^{(u-1)} - 1]$ rather than $[-\mu/2, \mu/2]$. Due to this modification, uSaber receives approximately the same level of security as Saber with a slightly reduced parameters set as shown in Table 1.

Saber.PKE.KeyGen()

1. $seed_{\boldsymbol{A}} \leftarrow \mathcal{U}(\{0,1\}^{256})$
2. $\boldsymbol{A} := \mathcal{U}(R_q^{l \times l}; \text{seed}_{\boldsymbol{A}})$
3. $r := \mathcal{U}(\{0,1\}^{256})$
4. $\boldsymbol{s} := \beta_\mu(R_q^{l \times 1}; r)$
5. $\boldsymbol{b} := ((\boldsymbol{A}^T \boldsymbol{s} + \boldsymbol{h}) \bmod q) \gg (\epsilon_q - \epsilon_p) \in R_p^{l \times 1}$
6. **return** $(pk := (seed_{\boldsymbol{A}}, \boldsymbol{b}), sk := (\boldsymbol{s}))$

Saber.PKE.Enc($pk = (seed_{\boldsymbol{A}}, \boldsymbol{b}), m \in R_2; r$)

1. $\boldsymbol{A} := \mathcal{U}(R_q^{l \times l}; \text{seed}_{\boldsymbol{A}})$
2. **if:** r is not specified:
3. $\quad r := \mathcal{U}(\{0,1\}^{256})$
4. $\boldsymbol{s}' := \beta_\mu(R_q^{l \times 1}; r)$
5. $\boldsymbol{b}' := ((\boldsymbol{A}\boldsymbol{s}' + \boldsymbol{h}) \bmod q) \gg (\epsilon_q - \epsilon_p) \in R_p^{l \times 1}$
6. $v' := \boldsymbol{b}^T (\boldsymbol{s}' \bmod p) \in R_p$
7. $c_m := (v' + h_1 - 2^{\epsilon_p - 1} m \bmod p) \gg (\epsilon_p - \epsilon_t) \in R_t$
8. **return** $c := (c_m, \boldsymbol{b}')$

Saber.PKE.Dec($sk = \boldsymbol{s}, c = (c_m, \boldsymbol{b}')$)

1. $v := \boldsymbol{b}'^T (\boldsymbol{s} \bmod p) \in R_p$
2. $m' := ((v - 2^{\epsilon_p - \epsilon_t} c_m + h_2) \bmod p) \gg (\epsilon_p - 1) \in R_2$
3. **return** m'

Fig. 1. Saber.PKE

Table 1. Parameters of Saber and uSaber with security and failure probability

Scheme	Parameters			Post-quantum Security	Failure Probability	NIST Security Level
	Identical	Different				
		q	Secret Distribution			
uSaber	l = 3, p = 2^{10} n = 256, t = 2^4	$\mathbf{2^{12}}$	$\mathcal{U}_2$	2^{165}	2^{-167}	3
Saber		$\mathbf{2^{13}}$	β_8	2^{172}	2^{-136}	3

2.4 Fujisaki-Okamoto Transformation

The encryption scheme outlined in the previous section only provides security against passive attackers (IND-CPA security). One can obtain active security (IND-CCA) security by using a generic transformation such as a post-quantum version of the Fujisaki-Okamoto transformation [22,27]. The idea is that the encapsulation encrypts a random input, and also uses this input as a seed for all randomness. The decapsulation can then decrypt the seed from the ciphertext and recompute the ciphertext. This recomputed ciphertext can then be used to check if the input ciphertext is generated correctly. The Fujisaki-Okamoto transformation transforms the encryption scheme into a key encapsulation mechanism (KEM). Given hash functions $\mathcal{F}$, $\mathcal{G}$ and $\mathcal{H}$, the saber KEM is given in Fig. 2. Again, we refer to the original Saber paper [19,20] for a more detailed description.

Saber.KEM.KeyGen()

1. $(seed_{\boldsymbol{A}}, \boldsymbol{b}, \boldsymbol{s}) =$ Saber.PKE.KeyGen()
2. $pk = (seed_{\boldsymbol{A}}, \boldsymbol{b})$
3. $pkh = \mathcal{F}(pk)$
4. $z = \mathcal{U}(\{0,1\}^{256})$
5.

return $(pk := (seed_{\boldsymbol{A}}, \boldsymbol{b}), sk := (\boldsymbol{s}, z, pkh))$

Saber.KEM.Encaps$(pk = (seed_{\boldsymbol{A}}, \boldsymbol{b}))$

1. $m \leftarrow \mathcal{U}(\{0,1\}^{256})$
2. $(\hat{K}, r) = \mathcal{G}(\mathcal{F}(pk), m)$
3. $c =$ Saber.PKE.Enc$(pk, m; r)$
4. $K = \mathcal{H}(\hat{K}, c)$
5. **return** (c, K)

Saber.KEM.Decaps$(sk = (\boldsymbol{s}, z, pkh), pk = (seed_{\boldsymbol{A}}, \boldsymbol{b}), c)$

1. $m' =$ Saber.PKE.Dec$(\boldsymbol{s}, c)$
2. $(\hat{K}', r') = \mathcal{G}(pkh, m')$
3. $c_* =$ Saber.PKE.Enc$(pk, m'; r')$
4. **if:** $c = c_*$
5. **return** $K = \mathcal{H}(\hat{K}', c)$
6. **else:**
7. **return** $K = \mathcal{H}(z, c)$

Fig. 2. Saber.KEM

2.5 Higher-Order Masking

Masking is a widely used countermeasure against side-channel attacks. The nth-order masked scheme can provide security against at most nth-order differential power attacks. The general idea of nth-order masking is to split the sensitive variable x into $n+1$ shares and then perform all the operations of the algorithms on each of the shares individually. The shares of the sensitive variable look uniformly random and the sensitive information can only be retrieved after combining all the $n+1$ shares. Moreover, if an adversary can get side-channel information from at most n points, he will not learn anything about the sensitive variable. In an nth-order masked implementation, linear operations typically duplicate $(n+1)$ times, and non-linear operations need to use more complex and costlier methods. As a consequence, the performance cost of a nth-order masked implementation increases at least by a factor of $(n+1)$.

There are several methods for masking. We primarily deal with two kinds of masking techniques: arithmetic masking and Boolean masking. For both the masking techniques, in order to obtain nth-order security, the sensitive variable $x \in \mathbb{Z}_q$ needs to be split into $n+1$ independent shares $x_0, x_1, \dots, x_n \in \mathbb{Z}_q$. In arithmetic masking, the relation between the sensitive variable x and the $n+1$ shares of x is $x = x_0 + x_1 + \cdots + x_n \bmod q$. Whereas, in Boolean masking the sensitive variable x and its $n+1$ shares are related as $x = x_0 \oplus x_1 \oplus \cdots \oplus x_n$.

The arithmetic masking is advantageous for protecting arithmetic operations such as addition, subtraction, multiplication. For example, to protect the modular addition $z = x + y \bmod q$ against n-order attacks, when only x contains sensitive data, we split x into $n+1$ shares $\{x_i\}_{0 \le i \le n}$ such that $\sum_{i=0}^{n} x_i \bmod q = x$, then the shares of $z = \sum_{i=0}^{n} z_i \bmod q$ are:

$$z_i = \begin{cases} x_i + y \bmod q, & \text{if } i = 0 \\ x_i, & \text{if } 1 \le i \le n \end{cases}.$$

If x and y both contains sensitive data, we split y together with x into $n+1$ shares $\{y_i\}_{0 \le i \le n}$ such that $\sum_{i=0}^{n} y_i = y \bmod q$, then the shares of $z = \sum_{i=0}^{n} z_i \bmod q$ are:

$$z_i = x_i + y_i \bmod q, \ 0 \le i \le n.$$

To securely compute the multiplication $z = x \cdot y \bmod q$, when x only contains sensitive data, we create $n+1$ shares $\{x_i\}_{0 \le i \le n}$ for x such that $\sum_{i=0}^{n} x_i \bmod q = x$, then the shares of $z = \sum_{i=0}^{n} z_i \bmod q$ are:

$$z_i = x_i \cdot y \bmod q, \ 0 \le i \le n.$$

We prefer Boolean masking for variables that undergo bitwise operations. For example, if we want to perform logical shift operation $z = x \gg l$ securely, write x into $n+1$ shares $\{x_i\}_{0 \le i \le n}$ such that $\oplus_{i=0}^{n} x_i = x$, then calculate $z_i = x_i \gg l, \forall i$ to obtain the shares of $z = \oplus_{i=0}^{n} z_i$.

3 Masking Saber

In a key encapsulation mechanism (KEM), the secret key remains fixed for a significant amount of time. Specifically, the decapsulation algorithm uses the non-ephemeral secret key $\mathbf{s}$, and therefore it is the most susceptible operation against side-channel attacks. In this paper, we focus on protecting the non-ephemeral secret key of Saber during the decapsulation. We introduce a masked decapsulation algorithm for Saber, which can resist higher-order side-channel attacks. The decapsulation procedure of Saber can be partitioned into three segments, namely decryption, re-encryption, and ciphertext comparison. For visualization, we present the flow of Saber's decapsulation algorithm in Fig. 3. Here, all the modules that process sensitive data due to the involvement with the secret have been marked grey. These modules are vulnerable from the perspective of side-channel attacks and need to be masked. In this section, we describe all the masked primitives that are used in the higher-order masked decapsulation procedure of Saber. We also present a new algorithm to perform the ciphertext comparison component in the masked setting. We will go through each part of the decapsulation algorithm of Saber chronologically and explain the methods we have used to mask them.

3.1 Arithmetic Operations

The decapsulation algorithm of Saber is heavily dependent on polynomial arithmetic, such as polynomial addition/subtraction and polynomial multiplication. We use arithmetic masking to protect these operations. As shown in Fig. 3, the decapsulation algorithm requires the following operations: addition between one masked and another unmasked polynomial, addition between two masked polynomials, and multiplication between one masked and another unmasked polynomial. For masking these operations, we follow the methods described in Sect. 2.5.

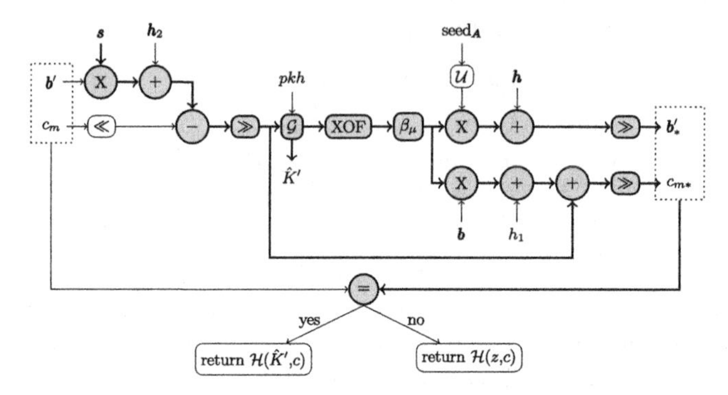

Fig. 3. Decapsulation of Saber. In grey the operations that are influenced by the long term secret $\boldsymbol{s}$ and thus vulnerable to side-channel attacks [6].

To perform the polynomial multiplication, the original unmasked Saber multiplication uses a hybrid multiplication, a combination of Toom-Cook-4, 2 levels of Karatsuba, and school-book multiplication [19,33,35]. We use this same multiplication technique in our masked implementation. Chung et al. [14] have recently introduced an efficient method to perform polynomial multiplication by using the number-theoretic transform. The same method could be used for the implementation of masked Saber to provide a significant performance improvement [12]. However, this is not the goal of our work and we keep this as future work.

3.2 Compression

In the last step of `Saber.PKE.Dec`, m is computed by calculating the most significant bit (`MSB`) for each coefficient. It compresses each coefficient of the polynomial $(v - 2^{\epsilon_p - \epsilon_t} c_m + h_2) \bmod p$ to produce a polynomial m where each coefficient is one bit long.

The logical shift operation is easy on Boolean shares. In this situation, we need to apply a logical shift operation on each share separately. Unfortunately, computing this logical shift operation on arithmetic shares is not trivial. This fact is discussed elaborately in [6] for the case of first-order masking, and the similar issue arises for higher-order masking also.

We compute `MSB` on arithmetic shares by taking the following steps: first, convert arithmetic shares to Boolean shares (A2B conversion), second, perform logical shift operation on Boolean shares, and finally, return to arithmetic domain with the Boolean to arithmetic (B2A) conversion. As $m \in R_2$, the resultant polynomial after compression is a polynomial with 1 bit coefficients. Here, the Boolean shares of m act like arithmetic shares of m. Therefore, we do not need the B2A conversion step.

Bitslicing is a technique that helps to improve the performance of bitwise operations. We have opted for the algorithm proposed in [15] using the bitsliced implementation of [17] for the A2B conversion of our implementations.

3.3 Masked Hashing

In Saber, the hash function $\mathcal{G}$ and the pseudo-random number generator `XOF` are realized by using `SHA3-512` and `SHAKE-128`, respectively. Both are different instances of the sponge function `Keccak-f[1600]` [7]. It has been shown that this construction is easy to protect by using Boolean masking [23].

`Keccak-f[1600]` permutation has five steps: θ, ρ, π, χ and ι. In between these θ, ρ, π are linear diffusion steps and ι is a simple addition. As all of these four are linear operations on Boolean shares, we just need to apply them for each share. χ is a degree 2 non-linear mapping and therefore requires extra attention to apply masking. Gross et al. [23] developed a technique to implement χ in the higher-order mask setting. We have adopted their technique in our implementations.

3.4 Masked Centered Binomial Sampler

`Saber.PKE.Enc` uses the centered binomial sampler for sampling the vector $\mathbf{s}'$. This sampler outputs the result of $\mathtt{HW}(x)-\mathtt{HW}(y)$, where x and y are pseudo-random numbers of bit length four. These pseudorandom numbers are generated by using `SHAKE-128`. As mentioned in Sect. 3.3, `SHAKE-128` is protected by using Boolean masking. After the generation of $\mathbf{s}'$, polynomial multiplications with $\mathbf{s}'$ (e.g. $\mathbf{A}\mathbf{s}'$ and $\mathbf{b}^T\mathbf{s}'$) take place. `SHAKE-128` creates Boolean shares, but polynomial multiplication is an arithmetic operation that is less expensive with arithmetic shares. To mitigate this issue, we need to include a conversion algorithm that converts Boolean shares into arithmetic shares (B2A conversion) in the masked centered binomial sampler.

Schneider et al. [45] propose two efficient higher-order masked centered binomial samplers: $sampler_1$ computes masked shares bitwise, whereas $sampler_2$ uses the bitslicing techniques to improve throughput. We have adopted the implementation of $sampler_2$ together with the modification made by Van Beirendonck et al. [6] specifically for Saber.

To convert shares from Boolean to arithmetic, we use the B2A algorithm proposed in [8]. The details have been provided in the Algorithm 1. In this Algorithm, `SecBitAdd` calculates shares of $\mathtt{HW}(x)$ and `SecBitSub` takes shares of $\mathtt{HW}(x)$ and shares of y as inputs and outputs shares of $z = \mathtt{HW}(x) - \mathtt{HW}(y)$. The function `SecConstAdd` adds $\mu/2 = 4$ with the shares of z to avoid any negative value that can occur after `SecBitSub`. In the next step the `B2A` function converts all the Boolean shares of z to the arithmetic shares of A and the last step converts shares of A from $\{0, 1, \ldots, 8\}$ to $\{-4, -3, \ldots, 3, 4\}$.

Algorithm 1: Masked centered binomial sampler [45]

Input : $\{x_i\}_{0\leq i\leq n}, \{y_i\}_{0\leq i\leq n}$ where $x_i, y_i \in \mathbb{R}_2^{\kappa}$ such that $\bigoplus_{i=0}^{n} x_i = x, \bigoplus_{i=0}^{n} y_i = y$

Output : $\{A_i\}_{0\leq i\leq n}$ where $A_i \in \mathbb{R}_q$ and $\sum_{i=0}^{n} A_i = (\mathtt{HW}(x) - \mathtt{HW}(y)) \bmod q$

1 $\{z_i\}_{0\leq i\leq n} \leftarrow$ `SecBitAdd`$(\{x_i\}_{0\leq i\leq n})$ [6]
2 $\{z_i\}_{0\leq i\leq n} \leftarrow$ `SecBitSub`$(\{z_i\}_{0\leq i\leq n}, \{y_i\}_{0\leq i\leq n})$ [45]
3 $\{z_i\}_{0\leq i\leq n} \leftarrow$ `SecConstAdd`$(\{z_i\}_{0\leq i\leq n})$ [6]
4 $\{A_i\}_{0\leq i\leq n} \leftarrow$ `B2A`$(\{z_i\}_{0\leq i\leq n})$ [8]
5 $A_1 \leftarrow (A_1 - \mu/2) \bmod q$
6 **return** $\{y_i\}_{0\leq i\leq n}$

3.5 Masked Comparison

The masked ciphertext comparison component is required to check the equality between masked ciphertext generated from re-encryption and the public ciphertext. This step performs the equality check $c \stackrel{?}{=} c^*$ of the `Saber.KEM.Decaps` algorithm in the masked domain.

An easy but efficient method for the first-order masked comparison is introduced by Oder et al. [40]. Unfortunately, this hash-based method is limited to first-order masking, and cannot be generalized to check ciphertext equality in the higher-order masked settings.

Different approaches for higher-order masked comparison were recently analyzed thoroughly by D'Anvers et al. [17]. In general, there are four approaches. The *simple method* originally due to Barthe et al. [5] groups individual bits into a large `SecOR` operation. This requires a pre-processing step to handle ciphertext compression that is straightforward to mask for Saber, but more complex for Kyber [21]. The *arithmetic method* was developed in a series of works [4,9,18], and aims to reduce the total number of comparisons by grouping coefficients into a random sum. The *decompression method* [11] developed for Kyber avoids masking the compression of the re-encrypted ciphertext, by decompressing the input ciphertext instead. Finally, the *hybrid method* [16] introduced the idea of using different of the previously discussed methods for the different components of the ciphertext. All of these approaches rely on A2B conversions, which can be heavily optimized using bitslicing [12,17].

In this section, we will discuss two of these different approaches to higher-order masked comparison. The first one is the Saber-adapted decompression method, which was not considered in [17]. The second one is the simple method, which was found to be the most efficient method for Saber in that same work. For both methods, we consolidate concurrent A2B optimization techniques proposed in [12,17].

3.5.1 Decompressed Masked Comparison Algorithm

Bos et al. [11] introduced a new method based on A2B conversion for the masked comparison algorithm for Kyber, in order to reduce the cost of the Boolean equality check circuit. This method does not perform the compression operation on

Algorithm 2: Decompressed masked comparison algorithm

Input : $\{\mathbf{b}'_i\}_{0 \le i \le n}$ where each $\mathbf{b}'_i \in \mathbb{R}^l_{2^{\epsilon_q}}$ and $\bigoplus_{i=0}^n \mathbf{b}'_i = \mathbf{b}'$, $\{c'_i\}_{0 \le i \le n}$ where each $c'_i \in \mathbb{R}_{2^{\epsilon_p}}$ and $\bigoplus_{i=0}^n c'_i = c'$, publicly available $\mathbf{b}$ and c_m

Output : $\{bit_i\}_{0 \le i \le n}$ with each $bit_i \in \{0,1\}$ such that $\bigoplus_{i=0}^n bit_i = 1$ iff $\mathbf{b} = \mathbf{b}' \gg (\epsilon_q - \epsilon_p)$ and $c_m = c' \gg (\epsilon_p - \epsilon_t)$, else 0

1 //For $\mathbf{b}$ part of ciphertext
2 $\mathbf{s_b} \leftarrow (\mathbf{b} \ll (\epsilon_q - \epsilon_p)) - 1$ //Decompression operation on $\mathbf{b}$
3 $\mathbf{e_b} \leftarrow (\mathbf{b} \ll (\epsilon_q - \epsilon_p)) + 2^{(\epsilon_q - \epsilon_p)}$
4 $\{\mathbf{b}''_i\}_{0 \le i \le n} \leftarrow \{\mathbf{b}'_i\}_{0 \le i \le n}$
5 $\mathbf{b}''_1 \leftarrow \mathbf{b}'_1 - \mathbf{s_b} + 2^{(\epsilon_q - 1)}$
6 $\mathbf{b}'_1 \leftarrow \mathbf{b}'_1 - \mathbf{e_b}$
7 $\{\mathbf{y}'_i\}_{0 \le i \le n} \leftarrow \mathtt{A2B}(\{\mathbf{b}''_i\}_{0 \le i \le n})$
8 $\{\mathbf{y}_i\}_{0 \le i \le n} \leftarrow \mathtt{A2B}(\{\mathbf{b}'_i\}_{0 \le i \le n})$
9 $\{\mathbf{y}_i\}_{0 \le i \le n} \leftarrow \mathtt{MSB}(\{\mathbf{y}_i\}_{0 \le i \le n}) || \mathtt{MSB}(\{\mathbf{y}'_i\}_{0 \le i \le n})$
10 //For c_m part of ciphertext
11 $s_{c_m} \leftarrow (c_m \ll (\epsilon_p - \epsilon_t)) - 1$//Decompression operation on c_m
12 $e_{c_m} \leftarrow (c_m \ll (\epsilon_p - \epsilon_t)) + 2^{(\epsilon_p - \epsilon_t)}$
13 $\{c''_i\}_{0 \le i \le n} \leftarrow \{c'_i\}_{0 \le i \le n}$
14 $c''_1 \leftarrow c'_1 - s_{c_m} + 2^{(\epsilon_p - 1)}$
15 $c'_1 \leftarrow c'_1 - e_{c_m}$
16 $\{x'_i\}_{0 \le i \le n} \leftarrow \mathtt{A2B}(\{c''_i\}_{0 \le i \le n})$
17 $\{x_i\}_{0 \le i \le n} \leftarrow \mathtt{A2B}(\{c'_i\}_{0 \le i \le n})$
18 $\{x_i\}_{0 \le i \le n} \leftarrow \mathtt{MSB}(\{x_i\}_{0 \le i \le n}) || \mathtt{MSB}(\{x'_i\}_{0 \le i \le n})$
19 //Boolean circuit to test all bits of each coefficient of $(\mathbf{y}, x)$ is 1
20 $\{bit_i\}_{0 \le i \le n} \leftarrow$ **BooleanAllBitsOneTest** $(\{\mathbf{y}_i\}_{0 \le i \le n}, \{x_i\}_{0 \le i \le n}, 2, 2)$
21 **return** $\{bit_i\}_{0 \le i \le n}$

the recomputed ciphertext, but performs a decompression operation on the public ciphertext instead. Then, the comparison is performed in the uncompressed domain. The decompressed operation is less costly to apply on public ciphertext, as it is public and so this operation can be performed unmasked.

Let us assume the public ciphertext be $c = (\mathbf{b}, c_m)$, where $\mathbf{b}$ be the key contained part and c_m be the message contained part of the ciphertext c. In Saber, the compression operation is applied to generate the ciphertext during encryption, and this operation is a many-to-one operation. In this process, each coefficient of b loses three bits, and each coefficient of c_m loses six bits. So, as compensation for the masked comparison, we use a decompression operation, which outputs an interval of integers for each coefficient of the public ciphertext. Let, $c[j]$ be a coefficient of the public ciphertext c, and the corresponding output of decompression operation be $(s_c[j], e_c[j])$. This implies every element in between the interval $(s_c[j], e_c[j])$ becomes $c[j]$ after the compression operation.

Next, we verify that each coefficient of the shared uncompressed ciphertext of c^* which is generated from the re-encryption, lies in the corresponding decom-

Algorithm 3: BooleanAllBitsOneTest

Input : $\{\mathbf{y}_i\}_{0\le i\le n}$ where each $\mathbf{y}_i \in \mathbb{R}^l_{2^{\text{bmod1}}}$ and $\bigoplus_{i=0}^n \mathbf{y}_i = \mathbf{y}$, $\{x_i\}_{0\le i\le n}$ where each $x_i \in \mathbb{R}_{2^{\text{bmod2}}}$ and $\bigoplus_{i=0}^n x_i = x$, bmod1, and bmod2

Output : $\{bit_i\}_{0\le i\le n}$ with each $bit_i \in \{0,1\}$ such that $\bigoplus_{i=0}^n bit_i = 1$ iff each bit of every coefficients of $\mathbf{y}$ and x is 1, else 0

```
1  for j1 = 1 to l do
2      for s = 1 to bmod1 do
3          {u_i[s][j1]}_{0≤i≤n} ← Bitslice({y_i^(s)[j1]}_{0≤i≤n})
4  for s = 1 to bmod2 do
5      {v_i[s]}_{0≤i≤n} ← Bitslice({x_i^(s)}_{0≤i≤n})
6  //Secure And on both
7  {w_i}_{0≤i≤n} ← {v_i[1]}_{0≤i≤n}
8  for s = 2 to bmod2 do
9      {w_i}_{0≤i≤n} ← SecAnd({w_i}_{0≤i≤n}, {v_i[s]}_{0≤i≤n})
10 for j = 1 to l do
11     {y_i[j]}_{0≤i≤n} ← {u_i[1][j]}_{0≤i≤n}
12     for s = 2 to bmod1 do
13         {y_i[j]}_{0≤i≤n} ← SecAnd({y_i[j]}_{0≤i≤n}, {u_i[s][j]}_{0≤i≤n})
14     {w_i}_{0≤i≤n} ← SecAnd({w_i}_{0≤i≤n}, y_i[j]}_{0≤i≤n})
15 for j = log2(256) − 1 to 0 do
16     {w'_i}_{0≤i≤n} ← w_{0≤i≤n} ≫ 2^j
17     {w_i}_{0≤i≤n} ← w_{0≤i≤n} mod (2^(2^j))
18     {w_i}_{0≤i≤n} ← SecAnd({w_i}_{0≤i≤n}, {w'_i}_{0≤i≤n})
19 {bit_i}_{0≤i≤n} ← {w_i}_{0≤i≤n}
20 return {bit_i}_{0≤i≤n}
```

pressed interval. Let $c^*[j]$ be the arithmetically masked uncompressed ciphertext coefficient corresponding to the public ciphertext coefficient $c[j]$. Now, if $c^*[j] \in (s_c[j], e_c[j])$ for all coefficients j, then the comparison returns success and outputs the shared valid key else returns a random invalid key. The test $c^*[j] \overset{?}{\in} (s_c[j], e_c[j])$ is realized by checking whether $c^*[j] - s_c[j]$ is a positive number and whether $c^*[j] - e_c[j]$ is a negative number. We have adopted this method for performing the higher-order masked ciphertext comparison in Saber as shown in Algorithm 2.

In Algorithm 2, lines 2–3 and 11–12 compute the start-point and the end-point of the interval for each coefficient of the key contained part $\mathbf{b}$ and the message contained part c_m of the public ciphertext c, respectively. The MSB of any number acts as a sign bit, i.e., if the MSB is 1 then the number is negative, else the number is positive. As in an ideal case, $c^*[j] - s_c[j] > 0$ and $c^*[j] - e_c[j] < 0$, so the $\texttt{MSB}(c^*[j] - s_c[j])$ should be 0 and the $\texttt{MSB}(c^*[j] - e_c[j])$ should be 1. In order to avoid two different kinds of checking for $c^*[j] - s_c[j]$ and $c^*[j] - e_c[j]$, we need to add a constant l with $c^*[j] - s_c[j]$ such that its MSB becomes 1. The value of l is $2^{(\epsilon_q-1)}$ and $2^{(\epsilon_p-1)}$ for $\mathbf{b}$ and c_m part of c, respectively. We compute the MSB of an arithmetically masked variable in the following way: we convert the arithmetic shares to Boolean shares using A2B conversion, and then we use a shift operation to extract the masked shares of MSB. Finally, Algorithm 2 uses Algorithm 3, the `BooleanAllBitsOneTest` function to combine the output bits of all coefficients and returns a single-bit indicating success or failure.

3.5.2 Simple Masked Comparison Algorithm

Next, we describe the simple method as given in [17]. Note that the re-encrypted ciphertext c^* is arithmetically masked and uncompressed, but the public ciphertext c is unmasked and compressed. As mentioned earlier, our task is to verify whether c equals c^* after compression. In this method, we perform the following steps: firstly, we transform arithmetic shares of c^* to Boolean shares by using A2B conversion algorithm, secondly, we compress the re-encrypted Boolean masked ciphertext c^* by using coefficientwise logical right shift, thirdly, we subtract the public ciphertext c from the compressed and masked re-encrypted ciphertext c^*. This method is shown in Algorithm 4.

Algorithm 4: Simple masked comparison algorithm [16]

Input : $\{\mathbf{b}'_i\}_{0\le i\le n}$ where each $\mathbf{b}'_i \in \mathbb{R}^l_{2^{\epsilon_q}}$ and $\bigoplus_{i=0}^{n} \mathbf{b}'_i = \mathbf{b}'$, $\{c'_i\}_{0\le i\le n}$ where each $c'_i \in \mathbb{R}_{2^{\epsilon_p}}$ and $\bigoplus_{i=0}^{n} c'_i = c'$, publicly available $\mathbf{b}$ and c_m

Output : $\{bit_i\}_{0\le i\le n}$ with each $bit_i \in \{0,1\}$ such that $\bigoplus_{i=0}^{n} bit_i = 1$ iff $\mathbf{b} = \mathbf{b}' \gg (\epsilon_q - \epsilon_p)$ and $c_m = c' \gg (\epsilon_p - \epsilon_t)$, else 0

1 //For $\mathbf{b}$ part of ciphertext
2 $\{\mathbf{y}_i\}_{0\le i\le n} \leftarrow$ A2B($\{\mathbf{b}'_i\}_{0\le i\le n}$)
3 $\{\mathbf{y}_i\}_{0\le i\le n} \leftarrow (\{\mathbf{y}_i\}_{0\le i\le n} \gg (\epsilon_q - \epsilon_p))$
4 $\mathbf{y}_1 \leftarrow \mathbf{y}_1 \oplus \mathbf{b}$
5 //For c_m part of ciphertext
6 $\{x_i\}_{0\le i\le n} \leftarrow$ A2B($\{c'_i\}_{0\le i\le n}$)
7 $\{x_i\}_{0\le i\le n} \leftarrow (\{x_i\}_{0\le i\le n} \gg (\epsilon_p - \epsilon_t))$
8 $x_1 \leftarrow x_1 \oplus c_m$
9 //Boolean circuit to test all bits of each coefficient of $(\mathbf{y}, x)$ is 0
10 $\mathbf{y}_1 \leftarrow \neg\mathbf{y}_1$
11 $x_1 \leftarrow \neg x_1$
12 $\{bit_i\}_{0\le i\le n} \leftarrow$ `BooleanAllBitsOneTest` $(\{\mathbf{y}_i\}_{0\le i\le n}, \{x_i\}_{0\le i\le n}, \epsilon_p, \epsilon_t)$
13 **return** $\{bit_i\}_{0\le i\le n}$

3.5.3 Bitsliced A2B

Both the decompression method and the simple method rely heavily on A2B conversions. Throughout the implementations, we use the bitsliced A2B conversion [17] for further speed-up. Moreover, A2B conversions use the SecAdd subfunction to perform masked addition. Bronchain et al. [12] proposed a SecAdd which uses $k-1$ SecAnd operations for k-bit inputs, as opposed to $2k-3$ SecAnd operations required in [17]. We included this technique into the implementation of [17] to receive better performance.

4 Masking uSaber

In uSaber, the coefficients of the secret vector are sampled according to the centered uniform distribution $\mathcal{U}_u$ instead of the centered binomial distribution β_μ. Here, the hamming weight computation of the centered binomial distribution is replaced by the sign extension of u bits to ϵ_q bits, to generate a sample in $[-2^{(u-1)}, 2^{(u-1)}-1]$ from u uniformly random bits. This secret vector sampler is the only component that differs between Saber and uSaber. A main advantage of uSaber is that the centered uniform sampler has fewer operations compared to the centered binomial sampler and therefore, is easier to mask.

Similar to the centered binomial sampler, the centered uniform sampler takes pseudorandom Boolean-masked bits as input that are produced by the masked SHAKE-128 function. Our simple higher-order masked centered uniform sampler is shown in Algorithm 5. We base it on SecConsAdd in the masked centered binomial sampler, mentioned in Sect. 3.4. First, we use xor to transform a negative number into a positive number. Second, we apply B2A conversion algorithm to convert Boolean shares to arithmetic shares. Third, we subtract 2^{u-1} from the arithmetic shares to map them from $[0, 2^u-1]$ back to $[-2^{(u-1)}, 2^{(u-1)}-1]$. This masked sampler does not require SecBitAdd and SecBitSub which are used in masked centered binomial sampler. The centered uniform sampler is simpler and requires fewer masked operations than the centered binomial sampler.

Algorithm 5: Masked centered uniform Sampler

Input : $\{x_i\}_{0\le i\le n}$ where $x_i \in \mathbb{R}_2^u$ such that $\bigoplus_{i=0}^n x_i = x$
Output : $\{A_i\}_{0\le i\le n}$ where $A_i \in \mathbb{R}_q$ and $\sum_{i=0}^n A_i = (x \oplus 2^{u-1}) - 2^{u-1} \mod q$

1 $\{z_0\} \leftarrow (\{z_0\} \oplus 2^{u-1})$
2 $\{A_i\}_{0\le i\le n} \leftarrow \text{B2A}(\{z_i\}_{0\le i\le n})$ [8]
3 $A_1 \leftarrow A_1 - 2^{u-1} \mod q$
4 **return** $\{y_i\}_{0\le i\le n}$

5 Performance Evaluation

To demonstrate the performance of all of the proposed methods, we implement them on a 32-bit ARM Cortex-M4 microcontroller, STM32F407-DISCOVERY development board. We adopt the widely used PQM4 [32] post-quantum cryptographic library and benchmarking framework for performance evaluation. In this framework, the system timer (SisTick) is used to measure the cycle counts. This framework uses a 24 MHz main system clock and a 48 MHz TRNG clock. We take advantage of the on-chip TRNG for sampling masking randomness instead of generating in advance and storing random bits in a table like Kyber [11]. This TRNG generates 32 random bits per 40 TRNG clock cycles, which is equal to 20 main system clock cycles. We include the cost of randomness sampling with the benchmarks. We use `arm-none-eabi-gcc` version `9.2.1` to accomplish the measurements of our implementations.

5.1 Performance Analysis of Comparison Algorithms for Saber

We present the cycle counts of the implementation for arbitrary order masked comparison algorithms of Saber. In Saber, the parameters are: $\epsilon_q = 13$, $\epsilon_p = 10$, $\epsilon_t = 4$ and $l = 3$. We break down the cycle counts into three parts: spent during all the `A2B` conversion, spent in computing the function `BooleanAllBitsOneTest` for the corresponding parameter, and spent in performing all other operations. Table 2 contains the performance details of masked ciphertext algorithms presented in Sects. 3.5.1 and Sects. 3.5.2.

In Table 2, we include two versions of the decompressed comparison algorithm and the simple comparison algorithm. We use the bitsliced `A2B` conversion technique of masked simple comparator proposed in [17] for the first version, and we improve this bitsliced `A2B` converter by employing the technique introduced in [12]. It can be seen from the table the performance of the decompressed comparison algorithm gains 9%, 16%, and 17% improvements for first-, second-, and third-order masking after using [12], respectively. Side by side, the improved decompressed comparison algorithm requires 21% fewer random bytes for any order masking. The performance of the simple comparison algorithm improves by 8%, 15%, and 16% for first-, second-, and third-order masking after using [12], respectively. The improved simple comparison algorithm requires approximately 19% fewer random bytes for any order masking.

As we can see from the table, the cycle count for all `A2B` conversions employed in the decompressed comparison algorithm is almost double for all orders compared to the simple comparison algorithm. However, for all the orders, the clock cycle required to compute the function `BooleanAllBitsOneTest` with corresponding parameters is approximately one-fourth in the decompressed comparison algorithm than the simple comparison algorithm. As we can see from Table 2, the improved simple comparison algorithm is approximately 43% faster and employ roughly 42% fewer random bytes than the improved decompressed comparison algorithm for any order masking of Saber. Similar results can be found for the higher-order masked uSaber. So, we use the improved simple comparison algorithm in our higher-order masked Saber and uSaber decapsulation algorithms.

5.2 Performance Analysis for Masked Saber Decapsulation

We present the performance cost of the Saber algorithm for higher-order masking in Table 3. This table also provides the breakdown of the performance cost of the higher-order masking for all the modules of the masked Saber decapsulation algorithm. As mentioned earlier, for masked Saber implementations we use the hybrid polynomial multiplication, a combination of Toom-Cook-4, Karatsuba, and schoolbooks multiplication. Therefore, we use the Saber implementation which uses the hybrid polynomial multiplication to get the overhead factor for n-th order masked Saber. To maintain simplicity, most of the implementation is written in C. Only the hybrid multiplication is in assembly and generated by using the optimal implementation proposed in [31].

From Table 3, we can see that the performance overhead factor of masked Saber decapsulation implementation for first-order is 2.69x, for second-order is 4.96x, and for third-order is 7.71x. From the table, we can see that the overhead factor for arithmetic operations approximately is $(n+1)$ for nth-order masking due to $n+1$ time repetitions of each operation. On the other hand, the non-linear operations on arithmetic shares, for example, hash functions, binomial sampler, compression operation, and ciphertext comparison, have much larger overhead factors in the masked setting. To maintain the security assumption, we need to use random bytes in some masking algorithms (example: SecAnd, SecAdd, SecRefresh, etc.). Table 4 shows random bytes requirements for all the components of the

Table 2. Performance breakdown of the implementation of masked comparison algorithms in the Cortex-M4 platform.

Masked Comparator	CPU [k]cycles		
	1st	2nd	3rd
Decompressed comparison [This work]	651	2,107	3,606
all `A2B` conversion	612	2,047	3,518
`BooleanAllBitsOneTest`	9	29	50
Other operations	28	31	37
# random bytes	12,048	47,920	95,840
Improved decompressed comparison [This work]	**588**	**1,756**	**2,962**
all `A2B` conversion	549	1,696	2,875
`BooleanAllBitsOneTest`	9	29	50
Other operations	28	31	37
# random bytes	**9,424**	**37,424**	**74,848**
Simple comparison [17]	363	1,160	1,992
all `A2B` conversion	308	1,023	1,766
`BooleanAllBitsOneTest`	38	117	202
Other operations	16	19	24
# random bytes	6,992	26,864	53,728
Improved simple comparison [This work]	**331**	**985**	**1,671**
all `A2B` conversion	276	848	1,444
`BooleanAllBitsOneTest`	38	117	202
Other operations	16	19	24
# random bytes	**5,680**	**21,616**	**43,232**

Table 3. Performance cost of all the modules of the higher-order masked decapsulation procedure of Saber.

Order	No mask	1st		2nd		3rd	
	CPU [k]cycles						
Saber-Decapsulation	1,121	3,022	(2.69x)	5,567	(4.96x)	8,649	(7.71x)
CPA-PKE-Decryption	129	297	(2.30x)	527	(4.08x)	775	(6.00x)
Polynomial arithmetic	126	237	(1.88x)	349	(2.76x)	464	(3.68x)
Compression	2	59	(29.50x)	178	(89.00x)	310	(155.00x)
Hash $\mathcal{G}$ (SHA3-512)	13	123	(9.46x)	242	(18.61x)	379	(29.15x)
CPA-PKE-Encryption	853	2,477	(2.90x)	4,670	(5.47x)	7,370	(8.64x)
Secret generation	69	909	(13.17x)	1,995	(28.91x)	3,561	(51.60x)
XOF (SHAKE-128)	63	611	(9.69x)	1,210	(19.20x)	1,887	(29.95x)
CBD (Binomial Sampler)	6	297	(49.50x)	785	(130.83x)	1,674	(279.00x)
Polynomial arithmetic	783	1,235	(2.00x)	1,688	(3.41x)	2,136	(4.86x)
Polynomial Comparison		331		985		1,671	
Other operations	126	126	(1.00x)	126	(1.00x)	126	(1.00x)

Table 4. Randomness cost of all the modules of the higher-order masked decapsulation algorithm of Saber.

Order	# Random bytes 1st	2nd	3rd
Saber-Decapsulation	12,752	43,760	93,664
CPA-PKE-Decryption	928	3,712	7,424
Polynomial arithmetic	0	0	0
Compression	928	3,712	7,424
Hash $\mathcal{G}$ (SHA3-512)	192	576	1,152
CPA-PKE-Encryption	11,312	38,512	83,168
Secret generation	5,952	17,856	41,856
XOF (SHAKE-128)	960	2880	5,760
CBD (Binomial Sampler)	4,992	14,976	36,096
Polynomial arithmetic	0	0	0
Polynomial Comparison	5,680	21,616	43,232
Other operations	0	0	0

higher-order masked Saber decapsulation algorithm. It can be seen from Table 4 that the random bytes requirement increases with the order. The first-order implementation requires 12k random bytes, the second-order and third-order implementations require 43k (3.43x) and 93k (7.34x) random bytes, respectively.

5.3 Performance Analysis for Masked uSaber Decapsulation

The performance cost and breakdown of the performance cost of the higher-order masking for all the modules of the masked uSaber decapsulation algorithm are presented in Table 5. As we mentioned before, the main advantage of uSaber against Saber is the coefficients of the secret vector are sampled from $\mathcal{U}_2$ instead of β_8. Thanks to the parameter choice of secret distribution in uSaber, it needs fewer numbers of pseudorandom bits than Saber. This fact reduces the cycle cost of XOF by almost 60% for the unmasked version of uSaber compared to Saber. Another advantage is that the hamming weight computation of μ bits in the centered binomial sampler β_μ is swapped by the sign extension of u bits in the centered uniform sampler $\mathcal{U}_u$. It reduces the performance cost of the secret sampler in unmasked uSaber by 50% compared to Saber. Altogether, the secret generation is almost 59% faster for the unmasked decapsulation algorithm of uSaber compared to Saber. The performance cost of the secret generation is lower in uSaber compared to Saber also after integrating masking. The performances of the secret generation in masked uSaber are 55%, 52%, and 45% faster compared to masked Saber for first-, second-, and third-order, respectively. Additionally, the value of q for uSaber is 2^{12}, whereas it is 2^{13} for Saber. This factor reduces one bit in the A2B conversion for uSaber during the masked polynomial comparison. It makes the masked polynomial comparison 5%, 5%, and 2% faster in uSaber than Saber for first-, second-, and third-order, respectively.

As we can observe from Table 5, the approximate performance overhead factor of masked uSaber decapsulation implementation for first-order is 2.32x, for second-order is 4.19x, and for third-order is 6.54x. Table 6 presents random bytes requirements for all the segments of the higher-order masked uSaber decapsulation. We obtain from Table 6 that here also the random bytes requirement grows with the order of masking. The first-order implementation needs 10k random bytes, the second-order and third-order implementations use 36k (3.49x) and 79k (7.57x) random bytes, respectively.

Table 5. Performance cost of all the modules of higher-order masked decapsulation procedure of uSaber.

	CPU [k]cycles						
Order	No mask	1st		2nd		3rd	
uSaber-Decapsulation	1,062	2,473	(2.32x)	4,452	(4.19x)	6,947	(6.54x)
CPA-PKE-Decryption	130	297	(2.28x)	527	(4.05x)	775	(5.96x)
Polynomial arithmetic	128	237	(1.85x)	349	(2.72x)	464	(3.62x)
Compression	2	59	(29.50x)	178	(89.00x)	310	(155.00x)
Hash $\mathcal{G}$ (SHA3-512)	13	122	(9.38x)	242	(18.61x)	379	(29.15x)
CPA-PKE-Encryption	791	1,928	(2.43x)	3,556	(4.49x)	5,667	(7.16x)
Secret generation	28	400	(14.28x)	954	(34.07x)	1,928	(68.85x)
XOF (SHAKE-128)	25	245	(9.80x)	484	(19.36x)	756	(30.24x)
Uniform distribution	3	155	(51.66x)	469	(156.33x)	1,172	(390.66x)
Polynomial arithmetic	763	1,214	(2.00x)	1,667	(3.40x)	2,114	(4.89x)
Polynomial Comparison		313		934		1,623	
Other operations	126	126	(1.00x)	126	(1.00x)	126	(1.00x)

Table 6. Randomness cost of all the modules of higher-order masked decapsulation algorithm of uSaber.

Order	# Random bytes		
	1st	2nd	3rd
uSaber-Decapsulation	10,544	36,848	79,840
CPA-PKE-Decryption	928	3,712	7,424
Polynomial arithmetic	0	0	0
Compression	928	3,712	7,424
Hash $\mathcal{G}$ (SHA3-512)	192	576	1,152
CPA-PKE-Encryption	9,104	31,600	69,344
Secret generation	4,032	12,096	30,336
XOF (SHAKE-128)	960	2880	5,760
Uniform distribution	3,072	9,216	24,576
Polynomial arithmetic	0	0	0
Polynomial Comparison	5,392	20,464	40,928
Other operations	0	0	0

5.4 Comparison with State-of-the-Art

In this section, we compare our masked Saber and uSaber implementations with the state-of-the-art masked implementations of Saber and Kyber. We present the performances of our masked implementations in the Cortex-M4 platform and present them in Table 7. Bronchain et al. [12] introduced faster implementations of higher-order masked A2B and B2A conversion utilizing bitsliced techniques and used these conversions to propose higher-order masking implementations of Saber and Kyber. The performances of Bronchain et al.'s masked Saber and Kyber implementations in the Cortex-M4 platform are presented in Table 7. As we mentioned before, the integration of NTT multiplication in masked Saber can provide a significant performance boost. In [12], authors use NTT multiplication for Saber to receive better performance. In order to use NTT multiplication, the authors use a multi-moduli approach that extends the modulus [1]. Even so, the performance of our 1st, 2nd and 3rd order masked implementations of Saber achieve 39%, 23%, and 13% improvement than their masked implementation of Saber, respectively.

In [11], Bos et al. proposed higher-order masked implementations of Kyber. The masked kyber implementation in [11] is faster and uses fewer random bytes than the implementation of masked kyber presented in [12] only for first-order because this masked Kyber uses an optimized implementation for first-order, while Bronchain et al.'s one uses the generalized one. The performance for 2nd and 3rd order masked implementations of Kyber in [12] receives 73% and 85% improvement over the masked Kyber of [11], respectively. However, our implementation of masked Saber is faster than masked Kyber presented in [12] 60% for first-order, 53% for second-order, and 48% for third-order. Also, the performance of our first-order masked Saber is 3% faster than the optimized implementation of the first-order masked Kyber presented in [11]. In terms of random bytes requirement, our masked Saber receives factor 20.61x and 25.98x improvement over the masked Kyber in [11] for 2nd and 3rd order masked implementations, respectively.

As discussed in Sect. 4, masked uSaber uses less number of operations and random numbers than masked Saber due to the choice of secret distribution and parameters in uSaber. Table 7 shows the performances of higher-order masked implementations of uSaber. Further, this table contains the performance of first-order masked Saber [6] and first-order masked Kyber [25], which are specially optimized to prevent the first-order differential power attacks. We can observe from Table 7 that our generalized implementation of first-order masked uSaber is 12% faster than the optimized implementation of masked Saber and is 16% faster than the optimized implementation of masked Kyber. The implementation of masked uSaber is faster than the fastest implementation of higher-order masked Saber 20% for second-order and 19% for third-order. Masked uSaber also needs 15% less random numbers for second-order and 14% less random numbers for third-order over masked Saber. In conclusion, we observe from the reported results of Table 7 that higher-order masked uSaber achieves better performance and needs fewer random bytes than masked Saber and Kyber for any order.

Table 7. The comparison between Saber and Kyber regarding the performance and the random bytes requirement.

Scheme		Performance CPU [k]cycles				/ Random bytes		
		Unmask	1st	2nd	3rd	1st	2nd	3rd
uSaber	This paper	1,062	**2,473**	**4,452**	**6,947**	**10,544**	**36,848**	**79,840**
Saber	This paper	1,121	**3,022**	**5,567**	**8,649**	**12,752**	**43,760**	**93,664**
	[12]	773	5,027	7,320	9,988	-	-	-
	[6] †	1,123	2,833	-	-	11,656	-	-
Kyber	[11] †	882	3,116*	44,347	115,481	12,072*	902,126	2,434,170
	[12]	804	7,716	11,880	16,715	-	-	-
	[25] †	816	2,978	-	-	-	-	-

†: measurements are taken from the paper
*: uses optimized implementation for first-order masking

6 Conclusions

Saber is often touted as very helpful for masking because of its two unique design components, the power-of-two moduli, and the MLWR problem. Van Beirendonck et al. [6] showed the first-order masked Saber receives better performance and needs fewer random bytes than the first-order masked Kyber. In our work, we substantiated this claim for arbitrary higher-order masking and show that the higher-order masked Saber also acquires better performance and requires fewer random bytes for its design decisions.

The third round submission document of Saber claims that the design decisions behind uSaber will be further beneficial for masking even compared to Saber. This work first concretely justifies those design decisions.

Furthermore, integrating our methods of masking is not dependent upon the underlying polynomial multiplication, which is one of the computationally expensive components. Our masked implementations can be adapted for Saber or uSaber that use the NTT multiplication instead of the hybrid multiplication.

Acknowledgements. This work was supported in part by CyberSecurity Research Flanders with reference number VR20192203, the Research Council KU Leuven (C16/15/058), the Horizon 2020 ERC Advanced Grant (101020005 Belfort) and SRC grant 2909.001.

Jan-Pieter D'Anvers and Angshuman Karmakar are funded by FWO (Research Foundation - Flanders) as junior post-doctoral fellows (contract numbers 133185/1238822N LV and 203056/1241722N LV). Michiel Van Beirendonck is funded by FWO as Strategic Basic (SB) PhD fellow (project number 1SD5621N).

References

1. Abdulrahman, A., Chen, J., Chen, Y., Hwang, V., Kannwischer, M.J., Yang, B.: Multi-moduli NTTs for saber on Cortex-M3 and Cortex-M4. IACR Trans. Cryptogr. Hardw. Embed. Syst. **2022**(1), 127–151 (2022). https://doi.org/10.46586/tches.v2022.i1.127-151
2. Alagic, G., et al.: Status Report on the Second Round of the NIST Post-Quantum Cryptography Standardization Process (2020). https://nvlpubs.nist.gov/nistpubs/ir/2020/NIST.IR.8309.pdf
3. Amiet, D., Curiger, A., Leuenberger, L., Zbinden, P.: Defeating NewHope with a single trace. Cryptology ePrint Archive, Report 2020/368 (2020). https://ia.cr/2020/368
4. Bache, F., Paglialonga, C., Oder, T., Schneider, T., Güneysu, T.: High-speed masking for polynomial comparison in lattice-based KEMs. IACR Trans. Cryptogr. Hardw. Embed. Syst. **2020**(3), 483–507 (2020). https://doi.org/10.13154/tches.v2020.i3.483-507
5. Barthe, G., et al.: Masking the GLP lattice-based signature scheme at any order. In: Nielsen, J.B., Rijmen, V. (eds.) EUROCRYPT 2018, Part II. LNCS, vol. 10821, pp. 354–384. Springer, Cham (2018). https://doi.org/10.1007/978-3-319-78375-8_12
6. Beirendonck, M.V., D'Anvers, J.P., Karmakar, A., Balasch, J., Verbauwhede, I.: A side-channel resistant implementation of SABER. Cryptology ePrint Archive, Report 2020/733 (2020). https://ia.cr/2020/733
7. Bertoni, G., Daemen, J., Peeters, M., Van Assche, G.: Keccak. In: Johansson, T., Nguyen, P.Q. (eds.) EUROCRYPT 2013. LNCS, vol. 7881, pp. 313–314. Springer, Heidelberg (2013). https://doi.org/10.1007/978-3-642-38348-9_19
8. Bettale, L., Coron, J., Zeitoun, R.: Improved high-order conversion from Boolean to arithmetic masking. IACR Trans. Cryptogr. Hardw. Embed. Syst. **2018**(2), 22–45 (2018). https://doi.org/10.13154/tches.v2018.i2.22-45
9. Bhasin, S., D'Anvers, J., Heinz, D., Pöppelmann, T., Beirendonck, M.V.: Attacking and defending masked polynomial comparison for lattice-based cryptography. IACR Trans. Cryptogr. Hardw. Embed. Syst. **2021**(3), 334–359 (2021). https://doi.org/10.46586/tches.v2021.i3.334-359

10. Bos, J., et al.: CRYSTALS - Kyber: a CCA-secure module-lattice-based KEM. Cryptology ePrint Archive, Report 2017/634 (2017). https://ia.cr/2017/634
11. Bos, J.W., Gourjon, M., Renes, J., Schneider, T., van Vredendaal, C.: Masking Kyber: first- and higher-order implementations. IACR Cryptology ePrint Archive, p. 483 (2021). https://eprint.iacr.org/2021/483
12. Bronchain, O., Cassiers, G.: Bitslicing arithmetic/Boolean masking conversions for fun and profit with application to lattice-based KEMs. Cryptology ePrint Archive, Report 2022/158 (2022). https://ia.cr/2022/158
13. Chari, S., Jutla, C.S., Rao, J.R., Rohatgi, P.: Towards sound approaches to counteract power-analysis attacks. In: Wiener, M. (ed.) CRYPTO 1999. LNCS, vol. 1666, pp. 398–412. Springer, Heidelberg (1999). https://doi.org/10.1007/3-540-48405-1_26
14. Chung, C.M., Hwang, V., Kannwischer, M.J., Seiler, G., Shih, C., Yang, B.: NTT multiplication for NTT-unfriendly rings new speed records for saber and NTRU on Cortex-M4 and AVX2. IACR Trans. Cryptogr. Hardw. Embed. Syst. **2021**(2), 159–188 (2021). https://doi.org/10.46586/tches.v2021.i2.159-188
15. Coron, J.-S., Großschädl, J., Vadnala, P.K.: Secure conversion between Boolean and arithmetic masking of any order. In: Batina, L., Robshaw, M. (eds.) CHES 2014. LNCS, vol. 8731, pp. 188–205. Springer, Heidelberg (2014). https://doi.org/10.1007/978-3-662-44709-3_11
16. Coron, J.S., Gérard, F., Montoya, S., Zeitoun, R.: High-order polynomial comparison and masking lattice-based encryption. Cryptology ePrint Archive, Report 2021/1615 (2021). https://ia.cr/2021/1615
17. D'Anvers, J.P., Beirendonck, M.V., Verbauwhede, I.: Revisiting higher-order masked comparison for lattice-based cryptography: algorithms and bit-sliced implementations. Cryptology ePrint Archive, Report 2022/110 (2022). https://ia.cr/2022/110
18. D'Anvers, J.P., Heinz, D., Pessl, P., van Beirendonck, M., Verbauwhede, I.: Higher-order masked ciphertext comparison for lattice-based cryptography. Cryptology ePrint Archive, Report 2021/1422 (2021). https://ia.cr/2021/1422
19. D'Anvers, J.-P., Karmakar, A., Sinha Roy, S., Vercauteren, F.: Saber: module-LWR based key exchange, CPA-secure encryption and CCA-secure KEM. In: Joux, A., Nitaj, A., Rachidi, T. (eds.) AFRICACRYPT 2018. LNCS, vol. 10831, pp. 282–305. Springer, Cham (2018). https://doi.org/10.1007/978-3-319-89339-6_16
20. D'Anvers, J.P., et al.: SABER. Technical report, National Institute of Standards and Technology (2020). https://csrc.nist.gov/projects/post-quantum-cryptography/round-3-submissions
21. Fritzmann, T., et al.: Masked accelerators and instruction set extensions for post-quantum cryptography. IACR Trans. Cryptogr. Hardw. Embed. Syst. **2022**(1), 414–460 (2021). https://doi.org/10.46586/tches.v2022.i1.414-460. https://tches.iacr.org/index.php/TCHES/article/view/9303
22. Fujisaki, E., Okamoto, T.: Secure integration of asymmetric and symmetric encryption schemes. In: Wiener, M. (ed.) CRYPTO 1999. LNCS, vol. 1666, pp. 537–554. Springer, Heidelberg (1999). https://doi.org/10.1007/3-540-48405-1_34
23. Gross, H., Schaffenrath, D., Mangard, S.: Higher-order side-channel protected implementations of Keccak. Cryptology ePrint Archive, Report 2017/395 (2017). https://ia.cr/2017/395
24. Guo, Q., Johansson, T., Nilsson, A.: A key-recovery timing attack on post-quantum primitives using the Fujisaki-Okamoto transformation and its application on FrodoKEM. Cryptology ePrint Archive, Report 2020/743 (2020). https://ia.cr/2020/743

25. Heinz, D., Kannwischer, M.J., Land, G., Pöppelmann, T., Schwabe, P., Sprenkels, D.: First-order masked Kyber on ARM Cortex-M4. IACR Cryptology ePrint Archive, p. 58 (2022). https://eprint.iacr.org/2022/058
26. Hoffstein, J., Pipher, J., Silverman, J.H.: NTRU: a ring-based public key cryptosystem. In: Buhler, J.P. (ed.) ANTS 1998. LNCS, vol. 1423, pp. 267–288. Springer, Heidelberg (1998). https://doi.org/10.1007/BFb0054868
27. Hofheinz, D., Hövelmanns, K., Kiltz, E.: A modular analysis of the Fujisaki-Okamoto transformation. In: Kalai, Y., Reyzin, L. (eds.) TCC 2017. LNCS, vol. 10677, pp. 341–371. Springer, Cham (2017). https://doi.org/10.1007/978-3-319-70500-2_12
28. Howgrave-Graham, N., Silverman, J.H., Whyte, W.: Choosing parameter sets for NTRUEncrypt with NAEP and SVES-3. Cryptology ePrint Archive, Report 2005/045 (2005). https://ia.cr/2005/045
29. Huang, W.L., Chen, J.P., Yang, B.Y.: Power analysis on NTRU prime. Cryptology ePrint Archive, Report 2019/100 (2019). https://ia.cr/2019/100
30. Jiang, H., Zhang, Z., Chen, L., Wang, H., Ma, Z.: IND-CCA-secure key encapsulation mechanism in the quantum random oracle model, revisited. Cryptology ePrint Archive, Report 2017/1096 (2017). https://ia.cr/2017/1096
31. Kannwischer, M.J., Rijneveld, J., Schwabe, P.: Faster multiplication in $\mathbb{Z}_{2^m}[x]$ on Cortex-M4 to speed up NIST PQC candidates. Cryptology ePrint Archive, Report 2018/1018 (2018). https://ia.cr/2018/1018
32. Kannwischer, M.J., Rijneveld, J., Schwabe, P., Stoffelen, K.: PQM4: post-quantum crypto library for the ARM Cortex-M4. https://github.com/mupq/pqm4
33. Karmakar, A., Mera, J.M.B., Roy, S.S., Verbauwhede, I.: Saber on ARM CCA-secure module lattice-based key encapsulation on ARM. IACR Trans. Cryptogr. Hardw. Embed. Syst. **2018**(3), 243–266 (2018). https://doi.org/10.13154/tches.v2018.i3.243-266
34. Kocher, P.C.: Timing attacks on implementations of Diffie-Hellman, RSA, DSS, and other systems. In: Koblitz, N. (ed.) CRYPTO 1996. LNCS, vol. 1109, pp. 104–113. Springer, Heidelberg (1996). https://doi.org/10.1007/3-540-68697-5_9
35. Mera, J.M.B., Karmakar, A., Verbauwhede, I.: Time-memory trade-off in Toom-Cook multiplication: an application to module-lattice based cryptography. IACR Trans. Cryptogr. Hardw. Embed. Syst. **2020**(2), 222–244 (2020). https://doi.org/10.13154/tches.v2020.i2.222-244
36. Messerges, T.S.: Using second-order power analysis to attack DPA resistant software. In: Koç, Ç.K., Paar, C. (eds.) CHES 2000. LNCS, vol. 1965, pp. 238–251. Springer, Heidelberg (2000). https://doi.org/10.1007/3-540-44499-8_19
37. Miller, V.S.: Use of elliptic curves in cryptography. In: Williams, H.C. (ed.) CRYPTO 1985. LNCS, vol. 218, pp. 417–426. Springer, Heidelberg (1986). https://doi.org/10.1007/3-540-39799-X_31
38. Ngo, K., Dubrova, E., Guo, Q., Johansson, T.: A side-channel attack on a masked IND-CCA secure saber KEM implementation. IACR Trans. Cryptogr. Hardw. Embed. Syst. **2021**(4), 676–707 (2021). https://doi.org/10.46586/tches.v2021.i4.676-707
39. NIST: Post-Quantum Cryptography Standardization. https://csrc.nist.gov/Projects/Post-Quantum-Cryptography/Post-Quantum-Cryptography-Standardization
40. Oder, T., Schneider, T., Pöppelmann, T., Güneysu, T.: Practical CCA2-secure and masked ring-LWE implementation. IACR Trans. Cryptogr. Hardw. Embed. Syst. **2018**(1), 142–174 (2018). https://doi.org/10.13154/tches.v2018.i1.142-174

41. Proos, J., Zalka, C.: Shor's discrete logarithm quantum algorithm for elliptic curves. Quantum Inf. Comput. **3**(4), 317–344 (2003). https://doi.org/10.26421/QIC3.4-3
42. Ravi, P., Bhasin, S., Roy, S.S., Chattopadhyay, A.: Drop by Drop you break the rock - exploiting generic vulnerabilities in Lattice-based PKE/KEMs using EM-based Physical Attacks. Cryptology ePrint Archive, Report 2020/549 (2020). https://ia.cr/2020/549
43. Reparaz, O., Sinha Roy, S., Vercauteren, F., Verbauwhede, I.: A masked ring-LWE implementation. In: Güneysu, T., Handschuh, H. (eds.) CHES 2015. LNCS, vol. 9293, pp. 683–702. Springer, Heidelberg (2015). https://doi.org/10.1007/978-3-662-48324-4_34
44. Rivest, R.L., Shamir, A., Adleman, L.M.: A method for obtaining digital signatures and public-key cryptosystems. Commun. ACM **21**(2), 120–126 (1978). http://doi.acm.org/10.1145/359340.359342
45. Schneider, T., Paglialonga, C., Oder, T., Güneysu, T.: Efficiently masking binomial sampling at arbitrary orders for lattice-based crypto. In: Lin, D., Sako, K. (eds.) PKC 2019. LNCS, vol. 11443, pp. 534–564. Springer, Cham (2019). https://doi.org/10.1007/978-3-030-17259-6_18
46. Shor, P.W.: Algorithms for quantum computation: discrete logarithms and factoring. In: 35th Annual Symposium on Foundations of Computer Science, Santa Fe, New Mexico, USA, 20–22 November 1994, pp. 124–134. IEEE Computer Society (1994). https://doi.org/10.1109/SFCS.1994.365700
47. Silverman, J.H., Whyte, W.: Timing attacks on NTRUEncrypt via variation in the number of hash calls. In: Abe, M. (ed.) CT-RSA 2007. LNCS, vol. 4377, pp. 208–224. Springer, Heidelberg (2006). https://doi.org/10.1007/11967668_14
48. Van Beirendonck, M., D'Anvers, J.P., Verbauwhede, I.: Analysis and comparison of table-based arithmetic to Boolean masking. **2021**(3), 275–297 (2021). https://doi.org/10.46586/tches.v2021.i3.275-297. https://tches.iacr.org/index.php/TCHES/article/view/8975
49. Waddle, J., Wagner, D.: Towards efficient second-order power analysis. In: Joye, M., Quisquater, J.-J. (eds.) CHES 2004. LNCS, vol. 3156, pp. 1–15. Springer, Heidelberg (2004). https://doi.org/10.1007/978-3-540-28632-5_1
50. Xu, Z., Pemberton, O., Roy, S.S., Oswald, D., Yao, W., Zheng, Z.: Magnifying side-channel leakage of lattice-based cryptosystems with chosen ciphertexts: the case study of Kyber. Cryptology ePrint Archive, Report 2020/912 (2020). https://ia.cr/2020/912

Approximate Distance-Comparison-Preserving Symmetric Encryption

Georg Fuchsbauer[1], Riddhi Ghosal[2(✉)], Nathan Hauke[3], and Adam O'Neill[4]

[1] TU Wien, Vienna, Austria
georg.fuchsbauer@tuwien.ac.at
[2] UCLA, Los Angeles, USA
riddhi@cs.ucla.edu
[3] Georgetown University, Washington D.C., USA
nah52@georgetown.edu
[4] Manning College of Information and Computer Sciences,
University of Massachusetts, Amherst, USA
adamo@cs.umass.edu

Abstract. We introduce *distance-comparison-preserving* symmetric encryption (DCPE), a new type of property-preserving encryption that preserves relative distance between plaintext vectors. DCPE is naturally suited for nearest-neighbor search on encrypted data. To boost security, we divert from prior work on Property Preserving Encryption (PPE) and ask for *approximate comparison*, which is natural given the prevalence of approximate nearest neighbor (ANN) search. We study what security approximate DCPE can provide and how to construct it.

Based on a relation we prove between approximate DCP and *approximate distance-preserving* functions, we design our core approximate DCPE scheme for Euclidean distance we call *Scale-And-Perturb* (SAP). The encryption algorithm of our core scheme processes plaintexts on-the-fly. To further enhance security, we also introduce two preprocessing techniques: (1) *normalizing* the plaintext distribution, and (2) *shuffling*, wherein the component-wise encrypted dataset is randomly permuted. We prove that SAP achieves a suitable indistinguishability-based security notion we call *real-or-replaced* indistinguishability (RoR). In particular, our RoR result implies that our scheme prevents a form of *membership inference attack*. Moreover, we show for i.i.d. multivariate normal plaintexts, we get security against *approximate frequency-finding attacks*, the main line of attacks against property-preserving encryption. This follows from a *one-wayness* (OW) analysis. Finally, carefully combining our OW and RoR results, we are able characterize *bit-security* of SAP.

Overall, we find that our DCPE scheme not only has superior bit-security to Order Preserving Encryption (OPE) but resists relevant attacks that even ideal order-revealing encryption (Boneh *et al.*, EUROCRYPT 2015) does not.

C. Galdi and S. Jarecki (Eds.): SCN 2022, LNCS 13409, pp. 117–144, 2022.
https://doi.org/10.1007/978-3-031-14791-3_6

1 Introduction

1.1 Background and Motivation

The paradigm of *secure outsourced databases* refers to a setting where a client transmits its database to an untrusted server that hosts it. The goal of such a protocol is to protect information about the database from the server to the extent possible, while maintaining the ability for the client to issue queries. This paradigm was first introduced in the database community by [28] and has received intensive study since then (see [34]) from the database and cryptographic community.

An attractive approach to constructions, which has already seen real-world deployment, is the emerging notion of *function-revealing encryption* (FRE) (*e.g.*, [5,9,12,33,48]). A (private-key) function-revealing encryption scheme for a function f allows anyone from the encryptions $c_1, \ldots, c_n$ of $m_1, \ldots, m_n$ respectively to compute $f(m_1, \ldots, m_n)$. The terminology is important here: *function* may be replaced by *property*, which refers to the case that f is a predicate;[1] *revealing* can be replaced by *preserving*, where the way of computing the above output of f is itself $f(c_1, \ldots, c_n)$. FRE is attractive because it allows the construction of outsourced database protocols that let the server index and process queries almost exactly the same way as for unencrypted data (in fact, exactly in the function-preserving case).

So far, FRE-based protocols have mainly been built for running queries on encrypted SQL databases. The types of FRE used here are *order-revealing* (ORE) and *order-preserving* encryption (OPE) [1,9,10,12], in which plaintexts are numbers and f is the comparison predicate $p_{\mathsf{comp}}(x, y) = 1$ iff $x < y$; and *deterministic encryption*[2] (DE) [2,5], which is the function-preserving case where f is the equality predicate $p_{\mathsf{eq}}(x, y) = 1$ iff $x = y$. Combined with some other schemes and tricks, DE and ORE/OPE give rise to outsourced database protocols for most SQL queries, such as the CryptDB system [50].

Unfortunately, even when these underlying FRE schemes are ideal, this approach is subject to attacks in the outsourced database setting ([7,19,26,47,52] in the "snapshot" setting, where the adversary sees one snapshot of the encrypted database, and [24,25,36,39,41] in the "persistent" setting, where the adversary observes the query processing over time,—see below). This has created a viewpoint that the FRE approach in such a higher-level applications is inherently insecure. Indeed, existing positive results for FRE-based protocols have major restrictions: they either assume uniform, high-entropy plaintexts [10] or an unknown prior on the data [13], neither of which seems likely to hold in practice. Other work introduces high overhead for practical datasets [42,51].

1.2 Our Results

Overview. In this work, we move to FRE for *non-SQL* databases. In particular, we treat the case of spatial or vector databases supporting approximate nearest

[1] Property-preserving encryption (PPE) is a special case that our construction actually falls into, but we stick with FRE terminology for generality.

[2] In our terminology, it could also be called equality-preserving encryption.

neighbor (ANN) search. We put forth a new type of FRE for this setting and a construction, achieving novel security guarantees in the "snapshot" setting.

(Approximate) Distance-Comparison Preserving Encryption. Nearest neighbor search is fundamental in spatial and vector databases. In fact, it is common to return the *approximate* nearest neighbor instead of the exact value [3,46]. Indeed, ANN is very useful for high-dimensional data due to "curse of dimensionality" [6,31]. (In higher dimensions, the notion of exact distances between points becomes less significant, thereby making it difficult for exact algorithms to converge). It has also recently become popular in information retrieval [30,38,58]. The first step of our work is to identify the "core operation" that ANN search algorithms use. This turns out to be *distance comparison* (cf. [18,57]), which gives rise to the need for *distance-comparison preserving* and *distance-comparison revealing* encryption (DCPE/DCRE) FRE for the ternary predicate $p_{\mathsf{dist\text{-}comp}}(x, y, z) = 1$ if $\mathsf{dist}(x, y) < \mathsf{dist}(x, z)$ and the predicate evaluates to 0 otherwise. As the goal is ANN, we actually consider "approximate" DCPE/DCRE, where the predicate evaluates to 1 if $\mathsf{dist}(x, y)$ and $\mathsf{dist}(x, z)$ are sufficiently far. We show approximate DCPE preserves the approximation factor of the overlying ANN search algorithm.

Relation to Approximate Distance-Preserving Encryption. In order to get a handle on an approximate DCPE construction, we would like to understand the "structure" of DCP functions—what do they look like? To this end, we prove that approximate DCP is approximate *distance-preserving* (DP) with a related approximation factor. To make this precise, let us call an encryption function β-DCP if

$$\mathsf{dist}(x, y) < \mathsf{dist}(x, z) - \beta \implies p_{\mathsf{dist\text{-}comp}}(c_x, c_y, c_z) = 1,$$

where c_x denotes a ciphertext of x. Let us call a function (α, β)-DP if

$$\alpha\, \mathsf{dist}(x, y) - \beta \leq \mathsf{dist}(c_x, c_y) \leq \alpha\, \mathsf{dist}(x, y) + \beta.$$

Although, our definitions are compatible with any distance measure, our main result in this part is that, for *Euclidean distance*, all functions which are β-DCP satisfy the notion of (α, β')-DP for some β' which depends on α and β. A detailed analysis of these relations can be found in the full version of the paper [22].

The Scale-and-Perturb (SAP) Construction. Inspired by the above results, our "core" approximate DCPE scheme for Euclidean distance is called the "Scale-and-Perturb" (SAP) scheme. It works as follows. The encryption algorithm scales the plaintext by a factor held in the secret key followed by adding a random perturbation factor. Note that this does not allow decryption, hence we apply a pseudorandom function to derandomize the perturbation step. The parameters are drawn from a uniform distribution, which is inspired by previous works [23,32,35]. Namely, we sample the perturbation from a uniform distribution within a sphere. The radius of the sphere determines the maximum permissible approximation for distance comparison. The choice of uniform distribution for noise will be crucial to prevent averaging out the noise by an adversary, thereby preventing trivial *known plaintext attacks*.

Preprocessing Techniques. While our core encryption scheme can encrypt any individual message given only the secret key, we propose preprocessing steps which enhance the security guarantees and utility of our scheme. The preprocessing steps assume additional knowledge when encrypting. The first idea is *shuffling*. Here, the entire dataset is encrypted component-wise at once, after the plaintexts are shuffled according to a random permutation. This can be achieved efficiently as shown in [8,40]. To our knowledge, this technique is new in property-preserving encryption (PPE). The second idea is *normalization*, which converts the plaintexts to a normal distribution. This can be done by applying standard statistical tools like the BoxCox transform [53]. In our results we sometimes assume that such preprocessing techniques have been applied; in particular, our results based on one-wayness apply to plaintexts (*i.e.*, vectors) following a multivariate normal distribution. Many natural statistics already follow a normal distribution as well in which case, we can skip the normalization stage altogether. Indeed, such a pre-processing enables us to bypass uniform data assumption in [10] which does not hold for most general datasets.

Indistinguishability-Based Security and "ideal DCPE" A natural type of security notions to consider here is "indistinguishability-based." Indeed, as DCPE is a special case of property-preserving encryption (PPE), the Left-or-Right (LoR) security notion of [15,48] applies. Roughly, LoR considers an adversary making queries $(x_0^1, x_1^1), \ldots, (x_0^q, x_1^q)$ to an oracle returning encryptions of either the left messages or the right messages. For the given predicate p, it is further required that $(x_b^1, \ldots, x_b^q)$ have the same "p-equality pattern" for $b \in \{0, 1\}$. This restriction ensures that the functionality of the scheme does not allow the adversary to trivially win the game and that *only* p leaks. We show that it follows from structural results discussed above that this notion is not achievable for approximate $p_{\mathsf{dist\text{-}comp}}$ with practical approximation factors. (We leave open whether it is possible using preprocessing on the entire dataset simultaneously).

Faced with this impossibility result, we move toward using the above-mentioned preprocessing techniques and considering other security notions to analyze guarantees for our scheme. We show security against three types of attacks that have been influential in prior work.

First Target: Security Against Membership Inference. Our first target is security against *membership inference (MI)* attacks, in which the adversary tries to determine whether an individual is in the database or not after seeing the encrypted database. Often, MI refers to making this determination after seeing a machine learning model (see *e.g.* Yeom *et al.* [60]). In that respect, one can think of our goal as to *immunize* a model against black-box MI by encrypting its outputs under DCPE.

Our "real-or-replaced" (RoR) notion exactly captures these attacks as it deals with indistinguishability of datasets that differ at exactly one point aka.

neighboring datasets, following the formalization of [60] but assuming the differing points are sufficiently close (so it is not a "full-fledged" MI attack, security against which is unachievable for us). As mentioned, a crucial technique we use to achieve it is that of a *shuffle* outputting a random permutation of the ciphertexts. Shuffling has become a state-of-the-art technique for security amplification in this setting for differential privacy and we observe similar results in our case as well. We stress that via shuffling we obtain a *negligible* security bound rather than a *moderate* one as one might expect from [60], which would give our result a questionable interpretation.

In more detail, in RoR the adversary chooses a dataset and sends it to an oracle which does either of the two things with equal probability—(1) Creates a random permutation of the dataset, encrypts it, (2) Chooses one point in the dataset at random, replaces it with another point chosen uniformly within a bounded distance (parameter of the security notion) from the to-be-replaced point, generates a random permutation of the modified dataset and encrypts it. The encrypted points are then returned to the adversary whose goal is to identify which dataset was encrypted.

Second Target: Frequency-Finding Security. Here, we target security against *frequency-finding* (FF) attacks, where the adversary tries to estimate how many times some element appears in the database. In our formulation, the adversary need not even know which element it is and tries to guess an *approximate* frequency. Leakage of frequency information about the plaintext has proved to be the Achilles' heel of previous works in property-preserving encryption schemes (for instance, OPE/ORE and even ideal ORE) [26,47]. Such attacks have successfully reconstructed (partially or completely) the messages encrypted under the aforementioned schemes by exploiting this leakage. Thus, it is imperative we ensure that similar attacks to do not apply.

In Theorem 6 we prove that *such leakage does not occur for* SAP (for multivariate normal data). This is proven by a reduction from a new security notion in the spirit of *one-wayness*. In particularly, we generalize the window one-wayness (WOW) notion of [10] to higher dimensions, calling it *attribute* window one-wayness AWOW and prove it holds for SAP relative to a *message* oracle, which takes as input a distribution chosen by the adversary and outputs the encryption of a randomly sampled message from the said distribution. The reduction to FF exploits the fact that a frequency table (histogram) can be used to construct the Empirical Cumulative Distribution Function (ECDF), which in turn provides vital information about the high-density points in the support of the underlying distribution. As a conclusion, the FF results say that it is impossible to guess approximate frequencies for any attribute occuring with significantly high probability from a message space sampled from a multivariate gaussian distribution.

In order to help readers have a clearer understanding of the concrete security values that we achieve and show the dependence of various parameters on the security bounds, we give some values in Tables 1 and 2 for reference.

Third Target: Bit Security. Finally, we aim to characterize *bit-security* of the plaintexts. This effort, inspired by [10,54], is motivated by the fact that while DCPE inherently cannot hide all partial information, it may still protect some "physical bits" of the plaintexts that represent important partial information in practice. To explain bit-security more precisely, let x be a plaintext in a dataset sampled from some distribution (in our results it is multivariate normal). Fix some stretch of bit-positions of x. We call the stretch OW if given the encryption of the dataset it is hard to compute that stretch of bits of x. We call the stretch pseudorandom if given the encryption of the dataset one cannot distinguish that stretch of bits from random. Intuitively, this means all partial information about these bits is hidden.

To characterize bit security, we go through several steps. First, we introduce an experiment called *Hardcore Bits* (HCB) which enables us to talk about one-wayness and pseudorandomness of lower order bits for the same message. HCB creates a hybrid to compose the RoR result atop OW. We prove the lower $\log \delta$ bits are pseudorandom, where δ is the distance parameter for RoR. Further, *at least* half the lower half of the bits are one way. Concretely the number of one way bits of a n bit string is $\frac{n}{2} + k$, where k is directly proportional to the approximation factor β. The latter beats the result for OPE [10]; the OPE scheme also does not have hardcore bits. See Fig. 2 for a depiction of our result.

1.3 Discussion

From DCPE *to Approximate Nearest Neighbour (ANN).* Any standard Exact Nearest Neighbour algorithm can be applied to a database encrypted using our scheme in a modular way to obtain ANN. We show in Sect. 3.2 that using this approach, any β-DCPE scheme yields an ANN with worst-case approximation factor of β.

Overall Security Assessment. We have chosen the three types of attacks we consider as representative of the security desired in practice and find it very encouraging that our scheme defends against them. It should however be noted that security against these attacks does not yet imply our scheme is safe to use in a particular application. PPE has been a notoriously murky area but has also been extremely influential in practice, making forward progress essential. Overall, we hope that with time the community vets our scheme and creates a more complete understanding of it, as well as extends it in directions mentioned below to further increase its security.

An Example Application. The above caveat notwithstanding, one example application where our scheme may be suitable is where the dataset consists of information of people from various demographics. The census data is a well-known example of such a dataset which is used widely for similarity search. Nearest Neighbour Search is a state-of-the-art algorithm in such a setup. In such an application, it might be acceptable to differentiate people based on zip code but the identity of a person must be indistinguishable from others living in the same zip code. Our RoR results guarantee strong security while ensuring utility in such setting.

Setting the Parameters. Overall, the choice of β is pivotal in balancing security and utility. Hence, a natural question to ask is what value of β should be chosen for some application? Unfortunately, there is no single answer, as the parameters needed would vary based on the size of the domain and tolerable error in the application. For instance, if we have a dataset where the message-space for each component is $(-N, N)$, and the ANN can tolerate an error up to $E_{\max} \leq N$, then $\beta \leq E_{\max}$ will ensure that the error is within the specified limit. (Refer to Sect. 3.2 for details). From a security perspective, Tables 1 and 2 suggest taking $\beta \geq \sqrt{N}$. Hence, we are looking at the range $\sqrt{N} \leq \beta \leq E_{\max}$. Note, that this is a contradiction if $E_{\max} \leq \sqrt{N}$. This suggests our scheme should not be used in such a case, *i.e.* maximum tolerable error must be at least square-root the domain size.

Fruitful Future Directions. A step forward in this direction would be generalizing SAP schemes to make them compatible with other metric spaces. Distance-comparison-*revealing* encryption (DCRE) is also a compelling subject of study. Recall a DCPE evaluation algorithm takes as input a set of three plaintexts and outputs the pairwise distance comparison between them. This primitive can exhibit security improvements over DCPE, similar to the effect of ORE [11,16] over OPE [9,10].

Another future direction is to combine *sketching* algorithms [37,55] with our scheme. A sketch of some data set with respect to a function f is a compression (*e.g.*, dimension reduction) which allows users to (approximately) compute f by having access to the sketch alone. Such compression approaches are intuitively expected to be effective techniques to significantly improve bit-security.

1.4 Further Related Work

The only previous FRE scheme that works on higher-dimensional vectors is the scheme of [27] for partial ordering. "Left-or-right" ORE [43] is designed to immunize ORE-based protocols against snapshot attacks but suffers the drawback that the support of efficient higher-level protocols afforded by plain ORE is no longer present. Non-FRE based protocols such as Arx [49] or essentially any structured encryption scheme [14] are semantically secure in the snapshot attack model, but also do not carry the practical benefits of using FRE, namely avoiding implementing an entirely different backend. Non-FRE based protocols for secure nearest-neighbor search have been widely addressed by the database community, although they are rather *ad hoc* or insecure (see [59] and references therein).

2 Preliminaries

We mostly use standard notation. A detailed description of the notations, some standard cryptographic primitives, and mathematical background needed for our technique is given in the full version [22].

We specialize some notions relevant to our setting. A dataset is composed of a list of vectors, which we refer to as messages $\mathbf{m} = (m[1], \ldots, m[d])$, Messages $\mathbf{m}$ lie in a bounded d-dimensional discrete space $\mathcal{M}$. We denote by $|\mathsf{D}|$ the number of messages in D. Component $m[i]$ is also referred to as the ith *attribute* of $\mathbf{m}$. Mostly plaintext space ($\mathcal{M}$) and ciphertext space ($\mathcal{C}$) are of the form $[-M, M]^d$ and $[-C, C]^d$ respectively where $M, C \in \mathbb{N}$, i.e. a d dimensional space with each dimension being $[-M, M]$.

In all our results, messages will be sampled independently from a *multivariate* distribution $\mathcal{MD}$ with support $\mathcal{M}$ (note the attributes in a given message may still depend on one another). If there is a dataset D, where each message $\mathbf{m} \in \mathsf{D}$ follows distribution $\mathcal{MD}$ (denoted by $\mathsf{D} \sim \mathcal{MD}$). At times, we take the liberty to refer to it as a distribution $\mathcal{MD}$ of a dataset D. Furthermore, each attribute $m[i]$ is assumed sampled from a distribution $\mathcal{D}_i$ defined on $[-M, M]$. Thus, $\mathcal{MD} = (\mathcal{D}_1, \ldots, \mathcal{D}_d)$. Again, we might drop the subscript and write only $\mathcal{D}$ when appropriate.

3 Approximate Distance-Comparison-Preserving Functions and Their Properties

Before turning to corresponding encryption schemes, we give definitions of distance-comparison-preserving functions and related notions. Our central notion is that of approximate distance preservation and others will serve as related auxiliary notions. Note that the definitions have been presented in a generalized form. The domain, range and parameter space can be easily chosen as per need.

3.1 Notions Considered

Below, functions can be randomized. If $f : \mathcal{X} \to \mathcal{Y}$ is a randomized function then when $f(x)$ occurs in an equation it means the equation should hold for any possible outcome of the coins. Note that in this subsection, we use generic symbols, as these notions can be applied on a variety of domains. For instance, x, y can be vectors or numbers. In particular, for generality of definitions we use $\mathsf{dist}(\cdot, \cdot)$ to denote any metric, we but our results concern the case of Euclidean distance, which we denote by $|| \cdot ||$.

Distance-Preserving (DP) Function: A function $f : \mathcal{X} \to \mathcal{Y}$ is said to be DP if

$$\forall x, y \in \mathcal{X} : \mathsf{dist}(x, y) = \mathsf{dist}(f(x), f(y)).$$

Approximate-Distance-Preserving ((α, β')-DP) Function: Let $\alpha \in \mathbb{R}, \beta' \in \mathbb{R}^+$. A function $f : \mathcal{X} \rightarrow \mathcal{Y}$ is said to be (α, β')-DP if

$$\forall x, y \in \mathcal{X} : \alpha\,\mathsf{dist}(x, y) - \beta' < \mathsf{dist}(f(x), f(y)) < \alpha\,\mathsf{dist}(x, y) + \beta'.$$

Distance-Comparison-Preserving (DCP) Function: A function $f : \mathcal{X} \rightarrow \mathcal{Y}$ is said to be DCP if

$$\forall x, y, z \in \mathcal{X} : \mathsf{dist}(x, y) < \mathsf{dist}(x, z) \implies \mathsf{dist}(f(x), f(y)) < \mathsf{dist}(f(x), f(z)).$$

Approximate-Distance-Comparison-Preserving (β-DCP) Function: For $\beta \in \mathbb{R}^+$, a function $f : \mathcal{X} \rightarrow \mathcal{Y}$ is said to be β-DCP if

$$\forall x, y, z \in \mathcal{X} : \mathsf{dist}(x, y) < \mathsf{dist}(x, z) - \beta \implies \mathsf{dist}(f(x), f(y)) < \mathsf{dist}(f(x), f(z)).$$

Note that a function f is 0-DCP $\iff$ f is DCP.

We point out that that these notions are intricately related to each other. A detailed analysis can be found in the full version [22] for lack of space. Notably, we roughly show that *approximate distance-comparison-preserving functions are approximate distance-preserving.*

Using encryption systems that are exactly distance-preserving has been proven to be highly insecure [44,56]. Hence we introduce further notions which help to achieve the necessary security requirements. The reason we concentrate on approximate-distance-comparison-preserving functions over DCP functions is that the former comprises of functions whose formulations are independent of the dataset. This is because we set the approximation fator as a constant independent of the underlying dataset. Exact distance comparison-preserving encryptions need to have parameters that depend on particular datapoints in the message space. The notion of β-DCP does not have any such restrictions as the bounds on the perturbations are independent of the dataset on which it is being applied.

3.2 Accuracy of Nearest Neighbors for β-DCP Functions

When using an existing nearest-neighbor search algorithm with a β-DCP function, our goal is to guarantee some reasonable bounds on the accuracy of the algorithm. The following claim proves that any nearest-neighbour search algorithm run on a set of points after post processing by a β-DCP function returns a point whose plaintext distance from the user query is no more than β larger than the distance to the actual nearest neighbour.

Let NN be a Nearest-Neighbor algorithm that is given query q and a set of points P and $\mathsf{NN}(q, \mathsf{P})$ returns $s \in \mathsf{P}$ if $\forall x \in P : \mathsf{dist}(q, s) \leq \mathsf{dist}(q, x)$, *i.e.*, s is the nearest neighbor for q.

Let f be a β-DCP function. Consider a run of NN with query $f(q)$ and set $f(\mathsf{P})$. Let s^* be such that $\mathsf{NN}(f(q), f(\mathsf{P})) = f(s^*)$ (which exists since NN returns a value in $f(\mathbf{P})$).

Claim. $\forall x \in \mathsf{P} : \mathsf{dist}(q, s^*) \leq \mathsf{dist}(q, x) + \beta$.

Proof. Assume that for some $x \in \mathsf{P}$ we had $\mathsf{dist}(q, s^*) > \mathsf{dist}(q, x) + \beta$, that is, $\mathsf{dist}(q, x) < \mathsf{dist}(q, s^*) - \beta$. Since f is β-DCP, this implies $\mathsf{dist}(f(q), f(x)) < \mathsf{dist}(f(q), f(s^*))$. But since $\mathsf{NN}(f(q), f(\mathsf{P})) = f(s^*)$, and thus $\mathsf{dist}(f(q), f(s^*)) \leq \mathsf{dist}(f(q), f(x))$, this is a contradiction.

We stress that β is the worst-case error in predicting the nearest neighbors.

(Approximate-)Distance-Comparison-Preserving Encryption ((β-) DCPE): We say that a symmetric key encryption scheme $\mathcal{SE} = (\mathcal{K}ey\mathcal{G}en, \mathcal{E}nc, \mathcal{D}ec)$ with plaintext and ciphertext spaces $\mathcal{X}$ and $\mathcal{Y}$ is (approximate-)distance-comparison-preserving if $\mathcal{E}nc(K, \cdot)$ is a (β-)DCP function from $\mathcal{X}$ to $\mathcal{Y}$ for all K output by $\mathcal{K}ey\mathcal{G}en$.

3.3 Impossibility of Ideal Security

As in the study of its predecessor OPE [9], a first question about β-DCPE is whether it can achieve "ideal" security, meaning it leaks *only* the approximate distance comparisons between the plaintexts. As in the case of OPE, the answer is "no". (However, there is a caveat, hence we refer readers to Remark 1). Toward this end, we first introduce the relevant definition.

Indistinguishability-Based Security of Approximate DCPE

Definition 1. *Let $\mathcal{SE} = (\mathcal{K}ey\mathcal{G}en, \mathcal{E}nc, \mathcal{D}ec)$ be a β-DCPE scheme with message space $\mathcal{M} = [-M, M]^d$ and ciphertext space $\mathcal{C} = [-C, C]^d$. For an* LoR compatible *adversary A, define its* LoR*-advantage*

$$\mathbf{Adv}_{\mathcal{SE}}^{\mathsf{LoR}}(A) = 2 \cdot \mathbf{Pr}\left[\mathbf{Exp}_{\mathcal{SE}}^{\mathsf{LoR}}(A) = 1\right] - 1$$

where the experiment above is defined as follows:

Experiment $\mathbf{Exp}_{\mathcal{SE}}^{\mathsf{LoR}}(A)$:
- $K \xleftarrow{\$} \mathcal{K}ey\mathcal{G}en$
- $b \xleftarrow{\$} \{0, 1\}$
- $b' \xleftarrow{\$} A^{\mathsf{LR}(\cdot,\cdot)}$
- *If* $b == b'$
  - *return 1*
- *Else return 0*

Oracle $\mathsf{LR}(\mathbf{m}_0, \mathbf{m}_1)$:
- $\mathbf{c} \xleftarrow{\$} \mathcal{E}nc_K(\mathbf{m}_b)$
- *Return* $\mathbf{c}$

Let $(\mathbf{m}_1^0, \mathbf{m}_1^1), \ldots, (\mathbf{m}_q^0, \mathbf{m}_q^1)$ be a sequence of queries made by A to its oracle. We call A an LoR compatible *adversary if for every such sequence the following holds for all $i, j, k \in [q]$:*

$$\mathsf{dist}(\mathbf{m}_i^0, \mathbf{m}_j^0) \leq \mathsf{dist}(\mathbf{m}_j^0, \mathbf{m}_k^0) - \beta \;\Rightarrow\; \mathsf{dist}(\mathbf{m}_i^1, \mathbf{m}_j^1) \leq \mathsf{dist}(\mathbf{m}_j^1, \mathbf{m}_k^1) - \beta.$$

This can be seen as a special case of the notion introduced by [48]. We say that $\mathcal{SE}$ is *ideal-secure* if $\mathbf{Adv}_{\mathcal{SE}}^{\mathsf{LoR}}(A)$ is small for every efficient LoR-adversary A.

Impossibility Result

We show that no β-DCPE scheme for Euclidean distance is ideal-secure unless β is likely too large to be useful in applications. The proof relies on a "Big-jump" style attack as in [9] that uses only two pairs of oracle queries.

Theorem 1. *Let $\mathcal{SE} = (\mathcal{K}ey\mathcal{G}en, \mathcal{E}nc, \mathcal{D}ec)$ be a β-DCPE scheme with plaintext space $\mathcal{M} = [0, M]$. If $\beta < \frac{M}{4}$ then there is an LoR-adversary A such that $\mathbf{Adv}^{\mathsf{LoR}}_{\mathcal{SE}}(A) = 1$.*

Proof. Consider the following adversary:

Algorithm 1. Big-Jump Adversary

```
procedure A_BigJump
    N ← LR(M, M); α ← N/M; β' ← 2αβ
    c^b ← LR(0, M)
    If dist(N, c^b) < β', then return b' ← 1
    Return b' ← 0
```

It is vacuously true that A_{BigJump} is LoR. We now argue that $\mathbf{Adv}^{\mathsf{LoR}}_{\mathcal{SE}}(A_{\mathsf{BigJump}}) = 1$. Before that we state the following theorem whose proof can be found in the full version [22].

Theorem 2 (1-Dimension). *Let $N \in \mathbb{R}, M \in \mathbb{N} \cup \{0\}$, if $f : \mathbb{N} \to \mathbb{R}$ is a β-DCP, and $f(0) = 0, f(M) = N$, then $\forall x, y$ such that $0 < x, y < M$,*

$$\frac{N}{M}(\mathsf{dist}(x, y) - 2\beta) \leq \mathsf{dist}(f(x), f(y)) \leq \frac{N}{M}(\mathsf{dist}(x, y) + 2\beta).$$

In other words, if f is β-DCP, then f is (α, β')-DP, where $\alpha = \frac{N}{M}$ and $\beta' = 2\frac{N}{M}\beta$.

Theorem 2 tells that that any β-DCP function is (α, β')-DP, where $\alpha = \frac{N}{M}$ and $\beta' = 2\frac{N}{M}\beta$, i.e. for any $m_1, m_2 \in \mathcal{M}$ and any possible corresponding ciphertexts (for any possible key and randomness of the encryption) c_1, c_2 we have

$$\frac{N}{M} \cdot \mathsf{dist}(m_1, m_2) - 2\frac{N}{M}\beta \leq \mathsf{dist}(c_1, c_2) \leq \frac{N}{M} \cdot \mathsf{dist}(m_1, m_2) + 2\frac{N}{M}\beta.$$

If c^b corresponds to the encryption of M, the above expression gives us $\mathsf{dist}(c^b, N) \leq 2\frac{N}{M}\beta$. Whereas $\mathsf{dist}(c^b, N) \geq N - 2\frac{N}{M}\beta$ when 0 is encrypted by LR.

If $\beta < \frac{M}{4}$, then $2\frac{N}{M}\beta < N - 2\frac{N}{M}\beta$, and thus $\mathbf{Adv}^{\mathsf{LoR}}_{\mathcal{SE}}(A_{\mathsf{BigJump}}) = 1$.

This impossibility result can easily be extended to multiple dimensions.

Remark 1. This proof does not necessarily hold if the data is subjected to preprocessing on the entire database before encryption. One such example of preprocessing is *shuffling* which has been explored in Sect. 4.2. It must be noted that shuffling does not contradict this proof. However there is no guarantee that there does not exist *any* preprocessing method which can bypass this result. In the case of OPE, with preprocessing ideal security *can* be achieved. We are unsure if this can be achieved for DCPE using some preprocessing and leave this for future work.

4 The Scale-and-Perturb (SAP) Scheme

We first give our core encryption scheme and then discuss additional preprocessing techniques.

4.1 Our Core β-DCPE Scheme

We now propose our core β-DCPE scheme for Euclidean distance based on our prior characterization of approximation distance-comparison preserving functions. We will suggest data preprocessing techniques in Sect. 4.2 in addition. Let $\mathcal{M} = [-M, M]^d$ be a *discrete* message space of dimension d. Let $\mathsf{PRF}\colon \{0,1\}^k \times \{0,1\}^\ell \to \{0,1\}^*$ be a function family for some $k, \ell \in \mathbb{N}$. We leave the number of output bits implicit in our algorithms for simplicity. The scheme is also parameterized by β which can take any non negative value less than $2M\sqrt(d)$. In the algorithm below, $\mathcal{U}, \mathcal{N}$ denote a uniform and gaussian distribution respectively.

The keyspace is denoted by S, where $|\mathsf{S}| \leq 2^\lambda$, where λ is the security parameter. Define the "Scale-And-Perturb" (SAP) encryption scheme on $\mathcal{M}$ as

$$\mathsf{SAP} = \mathsf{SAP}[\mathsf{PRF}, \beta, \mathsf{S}] = (\mathcal{K}ey\mathcal{G}en_{\mathsf{SAP}}, \mathcal{E}nc_{\mathsf{SAP}}, \mathcal{D}ec_{\mathsf{SAP}})$$

as shown in Algorithm 2.

Scheme Overview: The coins generated using the PRF are used for decryption. They provide a unique identity to each plaintext-ciphertext pair which makes decryption possible. The $\mathsf{TapeGen}$ PRF from [9] can be a candidate PRF. Of course, security of our scheme also depends on the chosen PRF. For simplicity, we do not talk about the PRF in the remainder, analyzing the core (no-decrypt) scheme. Our results all then transfer to the scheme described above *mutatis mutandis.*

The scaling factor is selected uniformly at random from the keyspace S (Line 1 of $\mathcal{K}ey\mathcal{G}en_{\mathsf{SAP}}$). The choice of the size of S does not affect utility but has an influence on the one-wayness bounds. Specific values of the size would vary based on applications and we have tabulated some results in Table 2. Take note that λ (which we sometimes denote as $\lambda_{\mathbf{m}}$ since it is chosen independently for each message $\mathbf{m} \in \mathcal{M}$) is a d-dimensional vector whose norm has an upper bound of $\frac{s\beta}{4}$. We sample it in such a way that λ_m is chosen uniformly from the

Algorithm 2. The SAP scheme.

```
procedure KeyGen_SAP()
  s <-$ S
  K <-$ {0,1}^k
  return (s, K)

procedure Enc_SAP((s, K), m)
  n <-$ {0,1}^ℓ
  coin_1 || coin_2 <- PRF(K, n)
  u <- N(0, I_d; coin_1)
  x' <- U(0, 1; coin_2)
  x <- (sβ/4)(x')^(1/d) ; λ_m <- ux/||u||
  c <- sm + λ_m
  return (c, n)

procedure Dec_SAP((s, K), (c, n))
  coin_1 || coin_2 <- PRF(K, n)
  u <- N(0, I_d; coin_1)
  x' <- U(0, 1; coin_2)
  x <- (sβ/4)(x')^(1/d)
  λ_m <- ux/||u||
  m <- (c - λ_m)/s
  return m
```

d-dimensional ball of radius $\frac{s\beta}{4}$ (Line 6 of $\mathcal{E}nc_{\mathsf{SAP}}$). To do so, we first generate a vector from a multivariate normal distribution with mean $\mathbf{0}$ and variance I_d, which is a d-dimensional identity matrix. The uniform point inside the ball is generated by multiplying the standardized version (point divided by its norm) of this point with the dth root of a uniformly generated point from $[0,1]$ followed by re-scaling with the radius of the ball. This mechanism ensure that the each point inside the ball can be sampled with uniform probability [29].

Claim 2: For any scaling factor $s \in \mathsf{S}$, $\mathcal{E}nc_{\mathsf{SAP}}(s,\cdot)$ is β-DCP wrt. Euclidean distance.

Proof. Denote $\mathcal{E}nc_{\mathsf{SAP}}(s,\cdot)$ by $f(\cdot)$ for notational simplicity. Let $\mathbf{x},\mathbf{y},\mathbf{z} \in \mathbf{M}$. Suppose $\|\mathbf{x}-\mathbf{y}\| < \|\mathbf{y}-\mathbf{z}\| - \beta$. $f(\mathbf{x}) = s\mathbf{x}+\lambda_{\mathbf{x}}$. $f(\mathbf{y}) = s\mathbf{y}+\lambda_{\mathbf{y}}$. $f(\mathbf{z}) = s\mathbf{z}+\lambda_{\mathbf{z}}$.
Hence,

$$
\begin{aligned}
&\|f(\mathbf{x}) - f(\mathbf{y})\| \le \|f(\mathbf{x}) - s\mathbf{x}\| + \|s\mathbf{x} - s\mathbf{y}\| + \|f(\mathbf{y}) - s\mathbf{y}\| && (1)\\
&= \|\lambda_{\mathbf{x}}\| + s\|\mathbf{x}-\mathbf{y}\| + \|\lambda_{\mathbf{y}}\| < \|\lambda_{\mathbf{x}}\| + \|\lambda_{\mathbf{y}}\| + s(\|\mathbf{y}-\mathbf{z}\| - \beta) && (2)\\
&= \|s\mathbf{y} - s\mathbf{z}\| - s\beta + \|\lambda_{\mathbf{x}}\| + \|\lambda_{\mathbf{y}}\| < \|s\mathbf{y} - s\mathbf{z}\| - s\beta + s\beta/4 + s\beta/4 && (3)\\
&= \|s\mathbf{y} - s\mathbf{z}\| - s\beta/2 < \|s\mathbf{y} - s\mathbf{z}\| - (\|\lambda_{\mathbf{z}}\| + \|\lambda_{\mathbf{y}}\|) \le \|s\mathbf{y} - s\mathbf{z}\| - (\|\lambda_{\mathbf{z}} - \lambda_{\mathbf{y}}\|) && (4)\\
&\le \|(s\mathbf{y} - s\mathbf{z}) - (\lambda_{\mathbf{z}} - \lambda_{\mathbf{y}})\| = \|f(\mathbf{y}) - f(\mathbf{z})\| \ .
\end{aligned}
$$

where (1) Triangle Inequality, (2) by assumption, (3) $\|\lambda_{\mathbf{x}}\|, \|\lambda_{\mathbf{y}}\| < s\beta/4$ and (4) Triangle Inequality.

Thus, $\|\mathbf{x}-\mathbf{y}\| < \|\mathbf{y}-\mathbf{z}\| - \beta \implies \|f(\mathbf{x}) - f(\mathbf{y})\| < \|f(\mathbf{y}) - f(\mathbf{z})\|, \therefore f$ is β-DCP.

4.2 Two Preprocessing Algorithms

To boost security and compatibility for real life application of SAP, we now propose two additional preprocessing algorithms. The first operates on the entire dataset D. The second only needs to know the *distribution* of D and can otherwise operate on the data on-the-fly. Thus, both of the transforms make stronger assumptions about the model.

Shuffle(dataset): On input dataset D which has n entries $(\mathbf{m}_1, \mathbf{m}_2, \ldots, \mathbf{m}_n)$, sample a random permutation $\Pi\colon [n] \to [n]$. Output the transformed dataset D′ that is $\mathbf{m}_{\pi(1)}, \mathbf{m}_{\pi(2)}, \ldots, \mathbf{m}_{\pi(n)}$.

Such a shuffle can be implemented using a mix network (mixnet). Very efficient implementations of mixnets handling large data exist [8,40].

Shuffling enhances the security because it hides the identity of the ciphertext from an adversary. By looking at a set of ciphertexts, the adversary cannot map it to the plaintext even if it knows them in advance. It enables security improvements without adding much computational overheads. Shuffling has been recently employed in differential privacy works [4,17,21] to achieve security enhancements while maintaining utility, which is our goal as well.

Normalize($\mathbf{m}$, $\mathcal{MD}$): On input $\mathbf{m}$ a data point coming from a multivariate distribution $\mathcal{MD}$, apply algorithm BoxCox [53] (state-of-the-art normalization algorithm) to input $\mathbf{m}$ and output the result.

Intuitively, BoxCox is a transformation which takes as input the distribution of the dataset, and makes a transformation using maximum likelihood estimation. This step can be considered as a heuristic as we do not rigorously deal with the error on our analyses.

This preprocessing step will be used because our security analyses assume the data follows a multivariate normal distribution. Such an assumption has practical significance as a large number of data available in practice [45] either follow this distribution or can be easily simulated as per the above if not. Note that if the data is naturally normally distributed this preprocessing step is not needed.

To combine these preprocessing steps with encryption, the idea is that the SAP is then applied to each data point output by the transformation; in the shuffling case this means the dataset is encrypted and sent all together. Naturally, the transforms can also be composed.

5 Real-or-Replaced Indistinguishability for Neighboring Datasets

To allow for the shuffling preprocessing step described in Subsect. 4.2, we introduce the notion of security to accommodate the adversary querying an *dataset* rather than many points individually. In essence, we define a "real-or-replaced" (RoR-type) definition where the oracle either shuffles and encrypts: (1) the dataset D provided by the adversary or (2) the dataset D with a random plaintext resampled uniformly below a certain distance threshold relative to the original. We thus have security wrt. "neighboring databases" (as in [20,60]), speaking to the adversary's ability to infer whether information of a particular individual is present in the dataset. Shuffling plays a key role in our analysis here.

Real-or-Replaced Indistinguishability. Let $\mathcal{SE} = (\mathcal{K}ey\mathcal{G}en, \mathcal{E}nc, \mathcal{D}ec)$ be a symmetric key encryption scheme. Let $\mathcal{MD}$ be the distribution from which the plaintext is sampled. In our results, *the adversary makes a single* Swap *oracle query only.*

We say that $\mathcal{SE}$ is (r, ε)-RoR-secure for $\mathcal{MD}$ if for every δ-RoR adversary A against $\mathcal{SE}$, its advantage

$$\mathbf{Adv}^{\delta-\mathsf{RoR}}_{\mathcal{SE},\mathcal{MD}}(\mathsf{A}) = 2 \cdot \mathbf{Pr}\left[\mathbf{Exp}^{\delta-\mathsf{RoR}}_{\mathcal{SE},\mathcal{MD}}(\mathsf{A}) = 1\right] - 1 \leq \varepsilon,$$

where the experiment $\mathbf{Exp}^{\delta-\mathsf{RoR}}_{\mathcal{SE},\mathcal{MD}}(\mathsf{A})$ is defined as follows (where some of its algorithms are defined below it):

Experiment $Exp^{\delta-\mathsf{RoR}}_{\mathcal{SE},\mathcal{MD}}(A)$:
- $K \xleftarrow{\$} \mathcal{K}eyGen$
- $\mathsf{Ctxt} \leftarrow \emptyset$
- $b \xleftarrow{\$} \{0, 1\}$
- $b' \leftarrow \mathsf{A}^{\mathsf{Swap}(\cdot)}$
- If $b == b'$ return 1
- Else return 0

Oracle $\mathsf{Swap}(\mathsf{D}_0)$:
- $i \xleftarrow{\$} |\mathcal{D}|$; $b \xleftarrow{\$} \{0.1\}$
- $\mathsf{D}_1 \xleftarrow{\$} \mathsf{Resamp}(D_0, i, \delta)$
- $\mathsf{D}'_b \xleftarrow{\$} \mathbf{shuffle}(\mathsf{D}_b)$
- For all $\mathbf{m} \in \mathsf{D}'_b$
  - $\mathsf{Ctxt} \leftarrow \mathsf{Ctxt.append}(\mathcal{E}nc(K, \mathbf{m}))$
- return Ctxt

We stress that Ctxt is a list because the order in which the ciphertexts are presented to the adversary is important. Above, we define $\mathsf{Resample}(\mathsf{D}, i, \delta)$ to be the algorithm that on input a dataset D, an index i that denoted which message in D must be replaced and parameter δ follows the following steps:(1) Picks up the ith message in D, call it $\mathbf{m}_i$. (2) Construct a d dimensional sphere of radius δ $\mathcal{B}(\mathbf{m}_i; \delta)$ around $\mathbf{m}_i$. (3) Samples a point at random inside $\mathcal{B}(\mathbf{m}_i; \delta)$ and return it. The final step can be done efficiently in the same way in which the perturbation factor is chosen for our encryption scheme.

Additionally, note that the **shuffle** step in the Swap oracle models this pre-processing step being applied.

5.1 δ-RoR Security Bounds

The following is the main result which upper bounds the δ – RoR adversary's advantage.

Theorem 3. *Let $\delta \leq \frac{\beta}{2}$. For any δ-RoR adversary A generating its query D of size N according to distribution $\mathcal{MD}$,*

$$\boldsymbol{Adv}^{\delta\text{-}\mathsf{RoR}}_{\mathsf{SAP}}(A) \leq \frac{2(2-p)}{N(1-p)} \left(1 - \frac{pT}{2}\right)^{N-1}$$

where $p = \left(\frac{h}{\mathsf{rad}+\frac{\delta}{2}}\right)^d$, $\mathsf{rad} = \frac{\beta}{4}$, $a = \sqrt{\mathsf{rad}^2 - \frac{\delta^2}{4}}$, $\cos(\theta) = \frac{2\mathsf{rad}^2 - 4a^2}{2\mathsf{rad}^2}$, $h = a\tan(\frac{\theta}{4})$ *and* $T = \mathbf{Pr}\left[\|X - Y\| \leq \delta\right], (X, Y) \sim \mathcal{MD}$.

The proof of this theorem requires a cumbersome analysis, hence we shift it to the full version [22]. As a brief sketch, we first reduce any δ-RoR adversary A to a canonical adversary which behaves in a pre-determined manner. Then, we proceed to prove an upper bound on the advantage of the said canonical adversary using a geometric approach along with standard set theoretic and probabilistic arguments. Intuitively, each message has a region where its ciphertext might lie based on the secret key and randomization. Ciphertexts corresponding to different messages are indistinguishable if their "ciphertext region" overlap with one another, and the distinguishing advantage of a adversary is computed by calculating the fraction of these regions which overlap with others. This along with the shuffling operation ensures that any canonical RoR adversary has negligible advantage.

Table 1 shows a few values for $\mathbf{Adv}_{\mathsf{SAP}}^{\delta-\mathsf{RoR}-\mathsf{D}}(\mathsf{A})$.

6 Security Against Approximate Frequency-Finding Attacks

Here we define security against an adversary that tries to approximately guess any one element of the *histogram* corresponding to an attribute of the plaintext. We call it the Freq-Find (FF) notion.

We proceed to state some definitions which will be useful in the formal security analysis.

Table 1. Some concrete parameters and upper bounds on $Adv_{\mathcal{SE}}^{\delta-\mathsf{RoR}-\mathsf{D}}(A)$.

N	dim	δ	β	$Adv_{\mathcal{SE}}^{\delta-\mathsf{RoR}-\mathsf{D}}(A)$
100	3	2^6	2^{15}	2^{-47}
300	5	2^5	2^{10}	2^{-96}
1000	5	2^6	2^{10}	2^{-116}
1000	10	2^9	2^{14}	2^{-217}
5000	5	2^8	2^{11}	2^{-154}
5000	8	2^8	2^{12}	2^{-160}

Attribute Histogram: For a list of attributes $\mathsf{L}_{\mathsf{attr}} = (a_1, \cdots, a_n)$, let $(a'_1, \cdots, a'_{n'})$, $n' \leq n$ be the set of all unique elements in $\mathsf{L}_{\mathsf{attr}}$. We define the *histogram* of $\mathsf{L}_{\mathsf{attr}}$ as a list denoted by $\mathsf{Hist}(\mathsf{L}_{\mathsf{attr}})$, with each element $\mathsf{Hist}(\mathsf{L}_{\mathsf{attr}})[j], j \in [n']$ as,

$$\mathsf{Hist}(\mathsf{L}_{\mathsf{attr}})[j] = \sum_{i=1}^{n} \mathbb{1}\{a_i = a'_j\}.$$

Most Likely Attribute Histogram: For a set of ciphertexts $\mathsf{L}_{\mathsf{ctxt}} = (\mathbf{c}_1, \cdots, \mathbf{c}_n)$, the most likely attribute histogram for the jth attribute, $\mathsf{j} \in [d]$ is a list denoted by $\mathsf{Hist}(\mathsf{L}_{\mathsf{ctxt}}^{\mathsf{j,ml}})$, where $\mathsf{L}_{\mathsf{ctxt}}^{\mathsf{j,ml}} = (m_1^{\mathsf{j,ml}}, \cdots, m_n^{\mathsf{j,ml}})$. $m_i^{\mathsf{j,ml}}$ is the jth attribute of the most likely guess for message m_i corresponding to c_i, $\forall\, i \in [n]$.

γ-Approximate Histograms: A most likely histogram Hist is called a γ-Approximate Histogram for the actual histogram $\mathsf{Hist}(\mathsf{L})$ if $\forall i$,

$$\mathsf{Hist}[i] \in [\mathsf{Hist}(\mathsf{L})[i] - \gamma, \mathsf{Hist}(\mathsf{L})[i] + \gamma].$$

In our case, the goal of the adversary is to guess *an entry* of *γ-approximate histogram* of the plaintext histogram.

Up next, we take a detour to introduce an intermediate security notion which is pivotal in proving the security against FF attacks.

6.1 Window One-Wayness Security Notion

In this section, $\mathcal{MD}$ is $\mathcal{MVN}(\boldsymbol{\mu}, \boldsymbol{\Sigma})$, such that, $\boldsymbol{\mu} = (\mu[1], \ldots, \mu[d])$ and $\boldsymbol{\Sigma}$ is the $d \times d$ covariance matrix. Naturally, $\mathcal{D}_i$ becomes $\mathcal{N}(\mu[i], \sigma_1^2)$, where σ_i^2 is the ith diagonal entry of $\boldsymbol{\Sigma}$. For some theorems (specifically AWOW) which deal with attribute space, the subscript has been dropped for ease of reading.

We introduce an intermediate *Window One-Wayness* based security notion which was introduced by [10]. It measures the probability that an adversary, given a set of ciphertexts corresponding to messages chosen at random from the underlying plaintext distribution decrypts one of them. The definition considers a general scenario that asks the adversary given some inputs to guess an interval (window) within which the underlying challenge plaintext lies. They do not need to point out which plaintext they intend to guess the window around. The size of the window and the number of challenge ciphertexts are parameters of the definition.

We analyze the security of individual attributes for each plaintext. This is much stronger that than looking at the security of a plaintext as a whole as window one-way security of each attribute implies one-wayness security for the whole point. The converse need not be true.

Attribute Window One-Wayness: Let $\mathcal{SE} = (\mathcal{K}ey\mathcal{G}en, \mathcal{E}nc, \mathcal{D}ec)$ be a symmetric key encryption scheme. Let $\mathcal{MD}$ be a stateful "plaintext sampler" that on input $(\mathsf{state}, \mathsf{d}^*)$ (due to ease of notation, we drop state in some function definitions) outputs a plaintext $\mathbf{m}$ whose a^{th} attribute is denoted by $m[a]$ along with the updated state. Let $r \in \mathbb{N}$. In our case, $\mathcal{MD}$ will denote a multivariate distribution sample whose i^{th} attribute follows a univariate gaussian (denoted by $\mathcal{D}_i$).

We say that $\mathcal{SE}$ is $(r, \varepsilon) - \mathsf{AWOW}$-secure for $\mathcal{MD}$ if for every r-AWOW adversary A against $\mathcal{SE}$, *i.e.*, obeying the restrictions given below, its advantage

$$\mathbf{Adv}_{\mathcal{SE},\mathcal{MD}}^{r-\mathsf{AWOW}}(A) = \mathbf{Pr}\left[\mathbf{Exp}_{\mathcal{SE},\mathcal{MD}}^{r-\mathsf{AWOW}}(A) = 1\right] \leq \varepsilon,$$

where the experiment $\mathbf{Exp}_{\mathcal{SE},\mathcal{MD}}^{r-\mathsf{AWOW}}(A)$ is defined as follows:

Experiment $Exp_{\mathcal{SE},\mathcal{MD}}^{r-\mathsf{AWOW}}(A)$:
$K \xleftarrow{\$} KeyGen$
$\mathsf{S}'_M \leftarrow \emptyset$
$(m_L, m_R) \xleftarrow{\$} A^{\mathsf{Msg}()}$
If $\exists \mathbf{m} \in \mathsf{S}'_M$ such that
for some $a \in [d]$, $m_a \in [m_L, m_R]$
return 1
Else return 0

Oracle $\mathsf{Msg}(d^*)$:
$(state, \mathbf{m}) \xleftarrow{\$} \mathcal{MD}(d^*)$
$\mathsf{S}'_M \leftarrow \mathsf{S}'_M \cup \{\mathbf{m}\}$
$\mathbf{c} \xleftarrow{\$} \mathcal{E}nc_K(\mathbf{m})$
return $\mathbf{c}$

Restrictions on the Adversary: An (r, ε) – AWOW adversary A must obey the following rules:

– For any output (m_L, m_R), $|m_L - m_R| \leq r$.

We now define an alternate r – AWOW security experiment. Here, define that on input $(\mathsf{state}, \mathsf{d}^*, N)$, the stateful sampler $\mathcal{MD}$ outputs a dataset D of size N from this distribution.

The experiment $\mathbf{Exp}_{\mathcal{SE},\mathcal{MD}}^{r-\mathsf{AWOW}-1}(A)$ where the adversary has the same restrictions as above is defined as follows:

Experiment $Exp_{\mathcal{SE},\mathcal{MD}}^{r-\mathsf{AWOW}-1}(A)$:
$K \xleftarrow{\$} KeyGen$
$\mathsf{S}'_M, \mathsf{C}_D \leftarrow \emptyset$
$(m_L, m_R) \xleftarrow{\$} A^{\mathsf{Msg}(\cdot)}$
If $\exists \mathbf{m} \in \mathsf{S}'_M$ such that
for some $a \in [d]$, $\mathbf{m}_a \in [m_L, m_R]$
return 1
Else return 0

Oracle $\mathsf{Msg}(d^*, N)$:
for $i \in [N]$
$(state, \mathbf{m}_i) \xleftarrow{\$} \mathcal{MD}(d^*)$
$\mathsf{S}'_M \leftarrow \mathsf{S}'_M \cup \{\mathbf{m}_i\}$
$\mathbf{c} \xleftarrow{\$} \mathcal{E}nc_K(\mathbf{m})$
$\mathsf{C}_D \leftarrow \mathsf{C}_D \cup \mathbf{c}$
return **shuffle**(C_D)

Lemma 1. *If in* $Exp_{\mathcal{SE},\mathcal{MD}}^{r-\mathsf{AWOW}}(A)$ *the adversary makes* N *queries to* Msg *and a single oracle query in* $Exp_{\mathcal{SE},\mathcal{MD}}^{r-\mathsf{AWOW}-1}(A)$, *then we have*

$$\mathbf{Pr}\left[\boldsymbol{Exp}_{\mathcal{SE},\mathcal{MD}}^{r-\mathsf{AWOW}}(A) = 1\right] = \mathbf{Pr}\left[\boldsymbol{Exp}_{\mathcal{SE},\mathcal{MD}}^{r-\mathsf{AWOW}-1}(A) = 1\right].$$

Note that the Experiment $Exp_{\mathcal{SE},\mathcal{MD}}^{r-\mathsf{AWOW}-1}(A)$ captures the case where **shuffle** has been applied to the dataset whereas Experiment $Exp_{\mathcal{SE},\mathcal{MD}}^{r-\mathsf{AWOW}}(A)$ is the scenario where messages are encrypted on-the-fly without shuffle.

Proof. Since each message belonging to the dataset are independently generated, the messages sampled by Msg oracles for both the experiments follow the same distribution. Moreover, all random permutations are identically distributed so the oracle's output for both experiments will also be identically distributed. Hence the lemma follows.

Thus, we see that the shuffle does not have any influence on the r-AWOW security bounds. From now on, we use $Exp_{\mathcal{SE},\mathcal{MD}}^{r-\mathsf{AWOW}-1}(A)$ and $Exp_{\mathcal{SE},\mathcal{MD}}^{r-\mathsf{AWOW}}(A)$ interchangeably as per convenience.

We say that such $\mathcal{MD}$ is multivariate *Gaussian* if $\forall$ state, d^*, every i^{th} attribute follows a univariate distribution $\mathcal{D}_i$, where $\mathcal{D}_i$ is $\mathcal{N}(\mu_i, \sigma_i^2)$.

6.2 One-Wayness Bounds

Refer to the full version [22] for detailed proofs.

We pay attention to the case when the adversary looks to decrypt the ciphertext to come with a correct guess for the "*most likely*" plaintext.

Most Likely Plaintext. Fix a symmetric encryption scheme $\mathcal{SE} = (\mathcal{K}eyGen, \mathcal{E}nc, \mathcal{D}ec)$. For given $\mathbf{c} \in \mathbf{C}$, if $\mathbf{m}_c \in \mathbf{M}$ is a message such that

$$\Pr_{K \xleftarrow{\$} \mathcal{K}eyGen} [\mathcal{E}nc(K, \mathbf{m}) = c] .$$

achieves a maximum at $\mathbf{m} = \mathbf{m}_c$, then we call $\mathbf{m}_c$ a (if unique, "the") *most likely* plaintext for $\mathbf{c}$.

An Upper Bound on the r-AWOW Advantage. The following theorem states an upper bound on any AWOW adversary against SAP.

Theorem 4. *For any r-AWOW adversary A making at most z Msg oracle queries*

$$\boldsymbol{Adv}_{\mathsf{SAP},\mathcal{MVN}(\boldsymbol{\mu},\boldsymbol{\Sigma})}^{r-\mathsf{AWOW}}(A) \leq z(1-p)^{|\mathsf{M}|} \frac{|\mathsf{S}|+1}{2|\mathsf{S}|} \sum_m \left(\left(\frac{2rm - \beta m}{m^2 - r^2} - \frac{\beta}{m} \right) \binom{|\mathsf{M}|}{m} \right). \quad (1)$$

where $\mathsf{M} = [-M, M]$ is the attribute-space of SAP *and* S *is the keyspace. Here, p is the parameter of the Binomial Distribution (denoted by $Bin(|\mathsf{M}|, p)$) which is used to approximate $\mathcal{N}(\mu, \sigma^2)$, which is the univariate distribution of the chosen attribute. Hence, $|\mathsf{M}|p = \mu$, $|\mathsf{M}|p(1-p) = \sigma^2$. For simplicity, we use m to denote an attribute instead of $m[a]$ which is an abuse of notation.*

The proof for this theorem is obtained using straightforward algebraic manipulation and probabilistic arguments (cf. [22]). To help understand the bounds, we present some values in Table 2. In the table, message space $\mathcal{M} = [-2^{80}, 2^{80}]^d$ and $|S| = 2^{30}$.

A Lower Bound on Large Attribute Window One-Wayness. Here we show that there exists an efficient adversary attacking the window one-wayness of SAP for a sufficiently large window size.

Table 2. Upper and Lower Bounds on r, 1-AWOW Advantage

d	r	β	r, 1-AWOW Upper Bound	r, 1-AWOW Lower Bound
1	$\frac{\beta}{2^4}$	2^{15}	2^{-32}	2^{-35}
2	$\frac{\beta}{2^5}$	2^{20}	2^{-40}	2^{-43}
4	$\frac{\beta}{2^5}$	2^{20}	2^{-51}	2^{-55}
6	$\frac{\beta}{2^8}$	2^{25}	2^{-62}	2^{-66}
10	$\frac{\beta}{2^{10}}$	2^{30}	2^{-76}	2^{-78}

Theorem 5. *For any* r-AWOW *adversary* A*, with* $r \geq \frac{\beta}{2}$*,*

$$\boldsymbol{Adv}^{r-\mathsf{AWOW}}_{\mathsf{SAP},\mathcal{MVN}(\boldsymbol{\mu}.\boldsymbol{\Sigma})}(A) \geq \frac{r}{2\sqrt{|\mathsf{M}|}} \ln \frac{1-p}{1-2p}. \quad (2)$$

where $\mathsf{M} = [-M, M]$ *is the attribute-space of* SAP *and* S *is the keyspace. Here,* p *is the parameter of the Binomial Distribution (denoted by* $Bin(|\mathsf{M}|, p)$*) which is used to approximate* $\mathcal{N}(\mu, \sigma^2)$*, the univariate normal distribution corresponding to the chosen attribute. Hence,* $|\mathsf{M}|p = \mu$, $|\mathsf{M}|p(1-p) = \sigma^2$.

Refer to the full version [22] for proofs.

6.3 Security Against Freq-Find Adversaries

The adversary wins the game if it can guess *an entry* HistEntry of a γ-approximate histogram, which occurs at most ψ times. We say that $\mathcal{SE}$ is $(\gamma, \psi, \varepsilon) -$ FF secure for $\mathcal{D}$ if the $(\gamma, \psi, \varepsilon) -$ FF advantage of an adversary A against $\mathcal{SE}$ is,

$$\mathbf{Adv}^{(\gamma,\psi)-\mathsf{FF}}_{\mathcal{SE},\mathcal{MD}}(A) = \mathbf{Pr}\left[\mathrm{Exp}^{(\gamma,\psi)-\mathsf{FF}}_{\mathcal{SE},\mathcal{MD}}(A) = 1\right] \leq \varepsilon,$$

where the experiment $Exp^{(\gamma,\psi)-\mathsf{FF}}_{\mathcal{SE},\mathcal{MD}}(A)$ is defined as:

Experiment $Exp^{(\gamma,\psi)-\mathsf{FF}}_{\mathcal{SE}}$(A):
$K \xleftarrow{\$} KeyGen$
$h \leftarrow A^{\mathsf{Msg}(\cdot)}$ // a guess for any element of the approx. histogram
$count \leftarrow 0$
for i in 1 to n
  for j in 1 to d
    If $h \in [\mathsf{Hist}(\mathsf{S}'^{j}_{M})[i] - \gamma, \mathsf{Hist}(\mathsf{S}'^{j}_{M})[i] + \gamma]$ // (1)
      $count \leftarrow count + 1$ // (2)
If $0 < count \leq \psi$ // (3)
  Return 1
Else return 0

Above, the Msg oracle is exactly the same as in the r-AWOW experiment.

1. Check if the guess within γ approx. of an histogram entry. $\mathsf{Hist}(\mathsf{S}'^{j}_{M})$: histogram for the list of jth attribute of elements in the list S'_{M}.
2. Track the number of times the guessed frequency occurs.
3. Make sure that this guessed frequency occurs at most λ times.

Parameter ψ is an essential parameter which depends on the underlying plaintext distribution. It prevents the adversary from trivially winning the game by guessing a frequency value which has a very high number of occurrence in the histogram. For example, a dataset from a well spread distribution will have plenty of points sampled only once. In that case, the adversary can win the game easily by guessing 1.

Upper Bound on the Freq-Find Advantage:

Theorem 6 *(Main result). Let A be a (γ, ψ)-FF adversary. Then there exists a $\frac{\gamma}{\psi}$-AWOW adversary B making at most q_m queries to the* Msg *oracle such that and $\mathcal{D} \sim \mathcal{N}(\mu, \sigma^2)$ is the univariate distribution for the chosen attribute.*

$$\boldsymbol{Adv}^{(\gamma,\psi)-\mathsf{FF}}_{\mathsf{SAP},\mathcal{MD}}(A) \leq \frac{1}{0.5(\frac{0.39\gamma}{\psi\sigma} - 2e^{\frac{-0.5}{q_m}})} \boldsymbol{Adv}^{\frac{\gamma}{\psi}-\mathsf{AWOW}}_{\mathsf{SAP}}(B).$$

We now define an AWOW adversary B in Algorithm 3 that simulates adversary A. Refer to full version [22] for proofs.

Algorithm 3. $\frac{\gamma}{\psi}$-AWOW Adversary

```
procedure B^Msg(·)
    Run A
        On Message oracle query
            (state, x) <-$ MD(d*)
            Sim <- Sim ∪ {x}
            Return Msg
    Until A outputs HistEntry*
    count <- 0
    If ∃i, j HistEntry* ∈ [Hist(Sim^j)[i] − γ, Hist(Sim^j)[i] + γ]
        count <- count + 1
    If 0 < count ≤ ψ
        Return OptInt(HistEntry*, Sim) // As calculated in the subsection below
    Else Return ⊥
```

Optimal Attribute Interval. Let $\mathsf{Hist}(\mathsf{S}'^{j}_{M})$ be the histogram for the list of jth attributes of elements in the list S'_{M}. Let X be the random variable used to denote an attribute following distribution $\mathcal{D}$ ($\mathcal{D}$ is a Normal Distribution in our case) over the attribute space. Let HistEntry be any arbitrary guess by the Freq − Find adversary.

The optimal attribute interval for such guess for a γ-approximate histogram *entry*, is denoted by $\mathsf{OptInt}(\mathsf{HistEntry}, \mathsf{S}'_M) = [m_{L_{opt}}, m_{R_{opt}}]$ such that $m_{R_{opt}} - m_{L_{opt}} = r$ and

$$\left| \Pr_{X \xleftarrow{\$} \mathcal{D}} [l_i \leq X \leq m_i] - \frac{\mathsf{HistEntry}}{|\mathsf{S}'_M|} \right| = \min_{j: m_j - l_j = r} \left| \Pr_{X \xleftarrow{\$} \mathcal{D}} [l_j \leq X \leq m_j] - \frac{\mathsf{HistEntry}}{|\mathsf{S}'_M|} \right|.$$

where r is the attribute window length defined in the AWOW experiment.

Intuitively, the above equation selects the interval of length r among all possible intervals whose sampling probability is closest to the guess of the FF adversary.

To better understand the bound, we demonstrate a graph in Fig. 1 to show how the leading multiplicative constant decays, thus giving a tight bound.

Some Practical Parameters: We present a graph (cf. Fig. 1) to demonstrate the trend of $\frac{1}{(\frac{0.39\gamma}{\psi\sigma} - 2e^{\frac{-0.5}{q_m}})}$, the multiplicative constant Theorem 6 with respect to the parameter. (It is log scaled for better visuals). This has been done as the expression is difficult to analyse and very high values of this constant would indeed make our reduction meaningless.

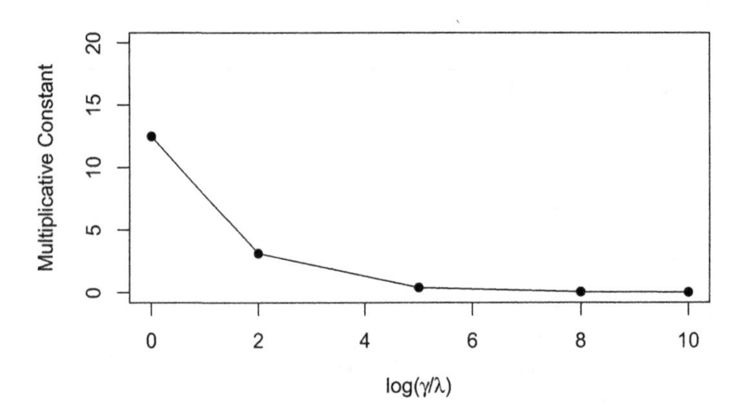

Fig. 1. $\frac{1}{(\frac{0.39\gamma}{\psi\sigma} - 2e^{\frac{-0.5}{q_m}})}$ vs $\log_2(\frac{\gamma}{\psi})$, when $\sigma = 1,\ q_m = 2^5$

7 Bit Security

In this section, we are concerned with characterizing *bit security* of the plaintexts. We define a *Hardcore Bits* experiment which enables us to comment on the *one-wayness* and *pseudorandomness* of different bits from the same message. The hardcore bits notion actually considers a specific hardcore function and differs from the classical such notion in that the adversary may request multiple challenges on related messages. We give a reduction from this notion to δ-RoR.

Theorem 7. *For any adversary B, playing the Experiment* HCB *(Hardcore bits) there exists an* δ-RoR *adversary A*

$$\boldsymbol{Adv}^{\mathsf{HCB}}_{\mathsf{SAP},\mathcal{MD}}(B) \leq \boldsymbol{Adv}^{\delta-\mathsf{RoR}}_{\mathsf{SAP},\mathcal{MD}}(A). \tag{3}$$

Experiment HCB:
- $K \xleftarrow{\$} \mathcal{K}eyGen$
- $S'_M \leftarrow \emptyset$
- $b \xleftarrow{\$} \{0,1\}$
- $b' \xleftarrow{\$} A^{Msg()}()$
- If $b' == b$ return 1
- Else return 0

Oracle $\mathsf{Msg}(d^*, N)$:
- for $i \in [N]$
  - $(state, \mathbf{m}_i) \xleftarrow{\$} \mathcal{MD}(d^*)$
  - $S'_M \leftarrow S'_M \cup \{\mathbf{m}_i\}$
  - $\mathbf{m}_i \xleftarrow{\$} \mathcal{E}nc_K(\mathbf{m}_i)$
  - If $b = 0$
    - $\mathsf{bits} \leftarrow$ right most $\log_2 \delta$ bits of m_i
  - Else
    - $\mathsf{bits} \xleftarrow{\$} \{0,1\}^{\log_2 \delta}$
  - $C \leftarrow C \cup \mathbf{c}_i \| \mathsf{bits}$
- return C

Let A be an adversary taking part in δ-RoR-Experiment. We reduce adversary B to A. Algorithm 4 gives a perfect simulation by A using its oracle for the queries made by B. Thus,

$$\mathbf{Adv}^{\mathsf{HCB}}_{\mathcal{SE}}(B) \leq \mathbf{Adv}^{\mathsf{RoR}}_{\mathcal{SE}}(A).$$

Hence, Theorem 7 follows.

Algorithm 4. RoR Adversary A

```
procedure A^Msg
    Run B
    On Msg oracle query (d*, N)
        S_D ← S_D ∪ {d*}
        for i ∈ [N]
            (state, m_i) ←$ MD(·, d*)
            S'_M ← S'_M ∪ {m_i}
            bits_i ← m_i[log_2 δ ···] // Right most log_2 δ bits
            Bits ← Bits ∪ bits_i
        C ←$ Swap_b(S'_M)
        Return C & Bits to B
    Repeat until B outputs guess bit b'
    Return guess bit b'
```

Note that the reduction holds because $\|m - m'\| \leq \delta$. It is clear that A succeeds in breaking the δ-RoR experiment if B breaks the HCB experiment. The ciphertexts generated for both the messages are identically distributed because the lower order bits are masked using a uniformly distributed noise. □

Note: It must be pointed out that the HCB experiment has been carefully crafted to ensure that one can comment on the one-wayness and pseudorandomness of bits on the *same* message. To achieve this, the standard Msg oracle has been modified to append the rightmost $\log\delta$ bits of a message (or random $\log\delta$ bits) along with the ciphertext for the particular message. The one-wayness of the bits follows directly from the AWOW results. Experiment HCB allows us to create a hybrid that can process indistinguishability on top of one-wayness.

Claim. For any message $\mathbf{m}$ following $\mathcal{MVN}((\mu, \Sigma))$ whose components are n bit long encrypted by SAP,

1. The lowest $\log_2\delta$ bits are pseudorandom (*i.e.*, hardcore).
2. The number of left most bits leaked (*i.e.*, efficiently computed) is strictly less than $\frac{\log_2 |M|}{2}$ (half the higher order bits).
3. If we remove the left-most k bits from the lowest $\frac{\log_2 |M|}{2}$ bits, the advantage of guessing the remaining lower order bits decreases by a multiplicative factor of 2^k.

The proof can be found in the full version [22].

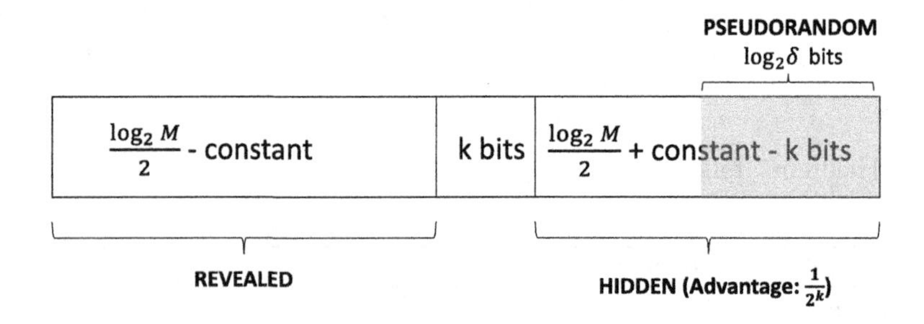

Fig. 2. Demonstrating the bit security.

This shows that SAP scheme leaks strictly less than half of the total bits and the number of total bits leaked is a decreasing function of the approximation factor β. More precisely, increasing the approximation factor by k times decreases the number of bits leaked by $\log_2 k$. This is an improvement over at least half bits leaked by its predecessor OPE [10].

References

1. Agrawal, R., Kiernan, J., Srikant, R., Xu, Y.: Order preserving encryption for numeric data. In: SIGMOD (2004)
2. Amanatidis, G., Boldyreva, A., O'Neill, A.: Provably-secure schemes for basic query support in outsourced databases. In: Barker, S., Ahn, G.-J. (eds.) DBSec 2007. LNCS, vol. 4602, pp. 14–30. Springer, Heidelberg (2007). https://doi.org/10.1007/978-3-540-73538-0_2
3. Arya, S., Mount, D.M., Netanyahu, N.S., Silverman, R., Wu, A.Y.: An optimal algorithm for approximate nearest neighbor searching fixed dimensions. J. ACM (JACM) **45**(6), 891–923 (1998)

4. Balle, B., Bell, J., Gascón, A., Nissim, K.: The privacy blanket of the shuffle model. In: Boldyreva, A., Micciancio, D. (eds.) CRYPTO 2019, Part II. LNCS, vol. 11693, pp. 638–667. Springer, Cham (2019). https://doi.org/10.1007/978-3-030-26951-7_22
5. Bellare, M., Boldyreva, A., O'Neill, A.: Deterministic and efficiently searchable encryption. In: Menezes, A. (ed.) CRYPTO 2007. LNCS, vol. 4622, pp. 535–552. Springer, Heidelberg (2007). https://doi.org/10.1007/978-3-540-74143-5_30
6. Beyer, K., Goldstein, J., Ramakrishnan, R., Shaft, U.: When is "nearest neighbor" meaningful? In: Beeri, C., Buneman, P. (eds.) ICDT 1999. LNCS, vol. 1540, pp. 217–235. Springer, Heidelberg (1999). https://doi.org/10.1007/3-540-49257-7_15
7. Bindschaedler, V., Grubbs, P., Cash, D., Ristenpart, T., Shmatikov, V.: The Tao of inference in privacy-protected databases. Proc. VLDB Endow. **11**(11), 1715–1728 (2018)
8. Bittau, A., et al.: Prochlo: strong privacy for analytics in the crowd. In: Proceedings of the 26th Symposium on Operating Systems Principles, pp. 441–459 (2017)
9. Boldyreva, A., Chenette, N., Lee, Y., O'Neill, A.: Order-preserving symmetric encryption. In: Joux, A. (ed.) EUROCRYPT 2009. LNCS, vol. 5479, pp. 224–241. Springer, Heidelberg (2009). https://doi.org/10.1007/978-3-642-01001-9_13
10. Boldyreva, A., Chenette, N., O'Neill, A.: Order-preserving encryption revisited: improved security analysis and alternative solutions. In: Rogaway, P. (ed.) CRYPTO 2011. LNCS, vol. 6841, pp. 578–595. Springer, Heidelberg (2011). https://doi.org/10.1007/978-3-642-22792-9_33
11. Boneh, D., Lewi, K., Raykova, M., Sahai, A., Zhandry, M., Zimmerman, J.: Semantically secure order-revealing encryption: multi-input functional encryption without obfuscation. Cryptology ePrint Archive, Report 2014/834 (2014). http://eprint.iacr.org/2014/834
12. Boneh, D., Lewi, K., Raykova, M., Sahai, A., Zhandry, M., Zimmerman, J.: Semantically secure order-revealing encryption: multi-input functional encryption without obfuscation. In: Oswald, E., Fischlin, M. (eds.) EUROCRYPT 2015, Part II. LNCS, vol. 9057, pp. 563–594. Springer, Heidelberg (2015). https://doi.org/10.1007/978-3-662-46803-6_19
13. Cash, D., Liu, F.-H., O'Neill, A., Zhandry, M., Zhang, C.: Parameter-hiding order revealing encryption. In: Peyrin, T., Galbraith, S. (eds.) ASIACRYPT 2018, Part I. LNCS, vol. 11272, pp. 181–210. Springer, Cham (2018). https://doi.org/10.1007/978-3-030-03326-2_7
14. Chase, M., Kamara, S.: Structured encryption and controlled disclosure. In: Abe, M. (ed.) ASIACRYPT 2010. LNCS, vol. 6477, pp. 577–594. Springer, Heidelberg (2010). https://doi.org/10.1007/978-3-642-17373-8_33
15. Chatterjee, S., Das, M.P.L.: Property preserving symmetric encryption revisited. In: Iwata, T., Cheon, J.H. (eds.) ASIACRYPT 2015, Part II. LNCS, vol. 9453, pp. 658–682. Springer, Heidelberg (2015). https://doi.org/10.1007/978-3-662-48800-3_27
16. Chenette, N., Lewi, K., Weis, S.A., Wu, D.J.: Practical order-revealing encryption with limited leakage. In: Peyrin, T. (ed.) FSE 2016. LNCS, vol. 9783, pp. 474–493. Springer, Heidelberg (2016). https://doi.org/10.1007/978-3-662-52993-5_24
17. Cheu, A., Smith, A., Ullman, J., Zeber, D., Zhilyaev, M.: Distributed differential privacy via shuffling. In: Ishai, Y., Rijmen, V. (eds.) EUROCRYPT 2019, Part I. LNCS, vol. 11476, pp. 375–403. Springer, Cham (2019). https://doi.org/10.1007/978-3-030-17653-2_13
18. Cunningham, P., Delany, S.J.: K-nearest neighbour classifiers. Multiple Classifier Syst. **34**(8), 1–17 (2007)

19. Betül Durak, F., DuBuisson, T.M., Cash, D.: What else is revealed by order-revealing encryption? In: Weippl, E.R., Katzenbeisser, S., Kruegel, C., Myers, A.C., Halevi, S. (eds.) ACM CCS 2016, pp. 1155–1166. ACM Press (2016)
20. Dwork, C.: Differential privacy: a survey of results. In: Agrawal, M., Du, D., Duan, Z., Li, A. (eds.) TAMC 2008. LNCS, vol. 4978, pp. 1–19. Springer, Heidelberg (2008). https://doi.org/10.1007/978-3-540-79228-4_1
21. Erlingsson, Ú., Feldman, V., Mironov, I., Raghunathan, A., Talwar, K., Thakurta, A.: Amplification by shuffling: from local to central differential privacy via anonymity. In: Chan, T.M. (ed.) 30th SODA, pp. 2468–2479. ACM-SIAM (2019)
22. Fuchsbauer, G., Ghosal, R., Hauke, N., O'Neill, A.: Approximate distance-comparison-preserving symmetric encryption. Cryptology ePrint Archive (2021)
23. Ghosal, R., Chatterjee, S.: Privacy preserving multi-server k-means computation over horizontally partitioned data. In: Ganapathy, V., Jaeger, T., Shyamasundar, R.K. (eds.) ICISS 2018. LNCS, vol. 11281, pp. 189–208. Springer, Cham (2018). https://doi.org/10.1007/978-3-030-05171-6_10
24. Grubbs, P., Lacharité, M.S., Minaud, B., Paterson, K.G.: Pump up the volume: practical database reconstruction from volume leakage on range queries. In: Lie, D., Mannan, M., Backes, M., Wang, X. (eds.) ACM CCS 2018, pp. 315–331. ACM Press (2018)
25. Grubbs, P., Lacharité, M.S., Minaud, B., Paterson, K.G.: Learning to reconstruct: statistical learning theory and encrypted database attacks. In: 2019 IEEE Symposium on Security and Privacy, pp. 1067–1083. IEEE Computer Society Press (2019)
26. Grubbs, P., Sekniqi, K., Bindschaedler, V., Naveed, M., Ristenpart, T.: Leakage-abuse attacks against order-revealing encryption. In: 2017 IEEE Symposium on Security and Privacy, pp. 655–672. IEEE Computer Society Press (2017)
27. Haagh, H., Ji, Y., Li, C., Orlandi, C., Song, Y.: Revealing encryption for partial ordering. In: O'Neill, M. (ed.) IMACC 2017. LNCS, vol. 10655, pp. 3–22. Springer, Cham (2017). https://doi.org/10.1007/978-3-319-71045-7_1
28. Hacigümüş, H., Iyer, B., Li, C., Mehrotra, S.: Executing SQL over encrypted data in the database-service-provider model. In: SIGMOD (2002)
29. Harman, R., Lacko, V.: On decompositional algorithms for uniform sampling from N-spheres and N-balls. J. Multivar. Anal. **101**(10), 2297–2304 (2010)
30. Hofstätter, S., Lin, S.C., Yang, J.H., Lin, J., Hanbury, A.: Efficiently teaching an effective dense retriever with balanced topic aware sampling. In: Diaz, F., Shah, C., Suel, T., Castells, P., Jones, R., Sakai, T. (eds.) SIGIR 2021: The 44th International ACM SIGIR Conference on Research and Development in Information Retrieval, Virtual Event, Canada, 11–15 July 2021, pp. 113–122. ACM (2021)
31. Indyk, P., Motwani, R.: Approximate nearest neighbors: towards removing the curse of dimensionality. In: Proceedings of the Thirtieth Annual ACM Symposium on Theory of Computing, pp. 604–613. ACM (1998)
32. Jagannathan, G., Pillaipakkamnatt, K., Wright, R.N.: A new privacy-preserving distributed k-clustering algorithm. In: 2006 SIAM International Conference on Data Mining 2006, pp. 494–498. SIAM (2006)
33. Joye, M., Passelègue, A.: Function-revealing encryption. In: Catalano, D., De Prisco, R. (eds.) SCN 2018. LNCS, vol. 11035, pp. 527–543. Springer, Cham (2018). https://doi.org/10.1007/978-3-319-98113-0_28
34. Kamara, S.: How to search on encrypted data (2015). https://cs.brown.edu/seny/slides/encryptedsearch-full.pdf

35. Kargupta, H., Datta, S., Wang, Q., Sivakumar, K.: Random-data perturbation techniques and privacy-preserving data mining. Knowl. Inf. Syst. **7**(4), 387–414 (2004). https://doi.org/10.1007/s10115-004-0173-6
36. Kellaris, G., Kollios, G., Nissim, K., O'Neill, A.: Generic attacks on secure outsourced databases. In: Weippl, E.R., Katzenbeisser, S., Kruegel, C., Myers, A.C., Halevi, S. (eds.) ACM CCS 2016, pp. 1329–1340. ACM Press (2016)
37. Kenthapadi, K., Korolova, A., Mironov, I., Mishra, N.: Privacy via the Johnson-Lindenstrauss transform. arXiv preprint arXiv:1204.2606 (2012)
38. Khattab, O., Zaharia, M.: Colbert: efficient and effective passage search via contextualized late interaction over BERT. In: Huang, J., et al. (eds.) Proceedings of the 43rd International ACM SIGIR Conference on Research and Development in Information Retrieval, SIGIR 2020, Virtual Event, China, 25–30 July 2020, pp. 39–48. ACM (2020)
39. Kornaropoulos, E.M., Papamanthou, C., Tamassia, R.: The state of the uniform: attacks on encrypted databases beyond the uniform query distribution. In: 2020 IEEE Symposium on Security and Privacy, pp. 1223–1240. IEEE Computer Society Press (2020)
40. Kwon, A., Lazar, D., Devadas, S., Ford, B.: Riffle: an efficient communication system with strong anonymity. PoPETs **2016**(2), 115–134 (2016)
41. Lacharité, M.S., Minaud, B., Paterson, K.G.: Improved reconstruction attacks on encrypted data using range query leakage. In: 2018 IEEE Symposium on Security and Privacy, pp. 297–314. IEEE Computer Society Press (2018)
42. Lacharité, M.-S., Paterson, K.G.: Frequency-smoothing encryption: preventing snapshot attacks on deterministically encrypted data. IACR Trans. Symm. Cryptol. **2018**(1), 277–313 (2018)
43. Lewi, K., Wu, D.J.: Order-revealing encryption: new constructions, applications, and lower bounds. In: Weippl, E.R., Katzenbeisser, S., Kruegel, C., Myers, A.C., Halevi, S. (eds.) ACM CCS 2016, pp. 1167–1178. ACM Press (2016)
44. Liu, K., Giannella, C., Kargupta, H.: An attacker's view of distance preserving maps for privacy preserving data mining. In: Fürnkranz, J., Scheffer, T., Spiliopoulou, M. (eds.) PKDD 2006. LNCS (LNAI), vol. 4213, pp. 297–308. Springer, Heidelberg (2006). https://doi.org/10.1007/11871637_30
45. Toby Mordkoff, J.: The assumption (s) of normality. Dostupno na: goo.gl/g7MCwK (Pristupljeno 27 May 2017) (2016)
46. Muja, M., Lowe, D.G.: Scalable nearest neighbor algorithms for high dimensional data. IEEE Trans. Pattern Anal. Mach. Intell. **36**(11), 2227–2240 (2014)
47. Naveed, M., Kamara, S., Wright, C.V.: Inference attacks on property-preserving encrypted databases. In: Ray, I., Li, N., Kruegel, C. (eds.) ACM CCS 2015, pp. 644–655. ACM Press (2015)
48. Pandey, O., Rouselakis, Y.: Property preserving symmetric encryption. In: Pointcheval, D., Johansson, T. (eds.) EUROCRYPT 2012. LNCS, vol. 7237, pp. 375–391. Springer, Heidelberg (2012). https://doi.org/10.1007/978-3-642-29011-4_23
49. Poddar, R., Boelter, T., Popa, R.A.: Arx: an encrypted database using semantically secure encryption. PVLDB **12**(11), 1664–1678 (2019)
50. Popa, R.A., Li, F.H., Zeldovich, N.: An ideal-security protocol for order-preserving encoding. In: 2013 IEEE Symposium on Security and Privacy, pp. 463–477. IEEE Computer Society Press (2013)
51. Pouliot, D., Griffy, S., Wright, C.V.: The strength of weak randomization: easily deployable, efficiently searchable encryption with minimal leakage. In: Dependable Systems and Networks, DSN 2019, pp. 517–529. IEEE (2019)

52. Pouliot, D., Wright, C.V.: The shadow nemesis: inference attacks on efficiently deployable, efficiently searchable encryption. In: Weippl, E.R., Katzenbeisser, S., Kruegel, C., Myers, A.C., Halevi, S. (eds.) ACM CCS 2016, pp. 1341–1352. ACM Press (2016)
53. Sakia, R.M.: The box-cox transformation technique: a review. J. Roy. Stat. Soc.: Ser. D (Statistician) **41**(2), 169–178 (1992)
54. Teranishi, I., Yung, M., Malkin, T.: Order-preserving encryption secure beyond one-wayness. In: Sarkar, P., Iwata, T. (eds.) ASIACRYPT 2014, Part II. LNCS, vol. 8874, pp. 42–61. Springer, Heidelberg (2014). https://doi.org/10.1007/978-3-662-45608-8_3
55. Tropp, J.A., Yurtsever, A., Udell, M., Cevher, V.: Practical sketching algorithms for low-rank matrix approximation. SIAM J. Matrix Anal. Appl. **38**(4), 1454–1485 (2017)
56. Turgay, E.O., Pedersen, T.B., Saygın, Y., Savaş, E., Levi, A.: Disclosure risks of distance preserving data transformations. In: Ludäscher, B., Mamoulis, N. (eds.) SSDBM 2008. LNCS, vol. 5069, pp. 79–94. Springer, Heidelberg (2008). https://doi.org/10.1007/978-3-540-69497-7_8
57. Anthony Wong, M., Lane, T.: A kth nearest neighbour clustering procedure. J. Roy. Stat. Soc.: Ser. B (Methodological) **45**(3), 362–368 (1983)
58. Xiong, L., et al.: Approximate nearest neighbor negative contrastive learning for dense text retrieval. In: 9th International Conference on Learning Representations, ICLR 2021, Virtual Event, Austria, 3–7 May 2021. OpenReview.net (2021)
59. Yao, B., Li, F., Xiao, X.: Secure nearest neighbor revisited. In: 29th IEEE International Conference on Data Engineering, ICDE 2013, pp. 733–744 (2013)
60. Yeom, S., Giacomelli, I., Fredrikson, M., Jha, S.: Privacy risk in machine learning: analyzing the connection to overfitting. In: 2018 IEEE 31st Computer Security Foundations Symposium (CSF), pp. 268–282 (2018)

Public Key Encryption

Key-Policy ABE with Switchable Attributes

Cécile Delerablée[1], Lénaïck Gouriou[1,2](✉), and David Pointcheval[2]

[1] Leanear, Paris, France
lg@leanear.io
[2] DIENS, École normale supérieure, CNRS, Inria, PSL University, Paris, France

Abstract. This paper revisits Key-Policy Attribute-Based Encryption (KP-ABE), allowing delegation of keys, traceability of compromised keys, and key anonymity, as additional properties.

Whereas delegation of rights has been addressed in the seminal paper by Goyal *et al.* in 2006, introducing KP-ABE, this feature has almost been neglected in all subsequent works in favor of better security levels. However, in multi-device scenarios, this is quite important to allow users to independently authorize their own devices, and thus to delegate their initial rights with possibly more restrictions to their everyday-use devices. But then, one may also require tracing capabilities in case of corrupted devices and anonymity for the users and their devices.

To this aim, we define a new variant of KP-ABE including delegation, with *switchable* attributes, in both the ciphertexts and the keys, and new indistinguishability properties. We then provide a concrete and efficient instantiation with adaptive security under the sole SXDH assumption in the standard model. We eventually explain how this new primitive can address all our initial goals.

1 Introduction

Multi-device scenarios have become prevalent in recent years, as it is now quite usual for people to own multiple phones and computers for personal and professional purposes. Users manage multiple applications across different devices, which brings forth new kinds of requirements. One must be able to granularly control what each of his devices can do for numerous applications, with a cost that is minimal for the user and the overall system. In particular, it is expected that one can control what each of its devices can access, for example restricting the rights to read sensitive documents from a professional laptop or phone during travel. Furthermore, if one suspects a key to be compromised, it should be possible to trace and change it without impacting the service. At the same time, these operations must happen transparently between different devices from the perspective of the user. This means each device should be autonomously configurable with regards to interactions with a central authority or to other devices. Eventually, one may also expect the delegated keys to be unlinkable, for some kind of anonymity for the users, even when devices are explored or corrupted by an adversary.

C. Galdi and S. Jarecki (Eds.): SCN 2022, LNCS 13409, pp. 147–171, 2022.
https://doi.org/10.1007/978-3-031-14791-3_7

Usual current authentication means defining a unique account for the user, providing the same access-rights to all the devices, is equivalent to a key-cloning approach, where the user clones his key in every device. In this case, all the devices of the same user are easily linked together, from their keys. This also prevents countermeasures against specific devices.

Key-Policy Attribute-Based Encryption (KP-ABE), in the seminal paper of Goyal *et al.* [7], offers interesting solutions to these issues. Indeed, a policy is embedded inside each user's private key, any user can finely-tune the policy for each of his devices when delegating his keys, for any more restrictive policy. Besides, since keys become different in each device, one could expect to trace and revoke keys independently. However, delegation and tracing capabilities might look contradictory with current approaches, as explained below. But we bridge this gap and we also suggest complementing these features with a certain level of unlinkability between the different keys of a single user in order to better protect the privacy of users.

1.1 Related Work

Attribute-Based Encryption (ABE) has first been proposed in the paper by Goyal *et al.* [7]. In an ABE system, on the one hand, there is a policy $\mathcal{P}$ and, on the other hand, there are some attributes $(A_i)_i$, and one can decrypt a ciphertext with a key if the policy $\mathcal{P}$ is satisfied on the attributes $(A_i)_i$. They formally defined two approaches: Key-Policy Attribute-Based Encryption (KP-ABE), where the policy is specified in the decryption key and the attributes are associated to the ciphertext; Ciphertext-Policy Attribute-Based Encryption (CP-ABE), where the policy is specified in the ciphertext and the attributes are associated to the decryption key.

In their paper, they proposed a concrete construction of KP-ABE, for any monotonous access structure defined by a policy expressed as an access-tree with threshold internal gates and leaves associated to attributes. Attributes in the ciphertext are among a large universe $\mathcal{U}$ (not polynomially bounded). Given an access-tree $\mathcal{T}$ embedded in a private key, and a set of attributes $\Gamma \subset \mathcal{U}$ associated to a ciphertext, one can decrypt if and only if Γ satisfies $\mathcal{T}$. Furthermore, they laid down the bases for delegation of users' private keys: one can delegate a new key, associated with a more restrictive access-tree.

This first paper on KP-ABE allows fine-grained access-control for multiple devices, dealing with delegation of keys for more restrictive policies. However, their approach for delegation of keys is conflictual with traceability. Indeed, on the one hand, for delegation to work properly, users must be given enough information in the public key to be able to produce valid delegated keys. On the other hand, for the tracing process to be effective in a black-box way, attackers must not be able to detect it. From our knowledge, this natural tension between the two features is in all the existing literature.

Predicate Encryption/Inner-Product Encryption (IPE) were used by Okamoto and Takashima [13–15], together with LSSS: the receiver can read the message if a predicate is satisfied on some information in the decryption key and in the ciphertext. Inner-product encryption (where the predicate checks whether the vectors embedded in the key and in the ciphertext are orthogonal) is the major tool. Their technique of Dual Pairing Vector Space (DPVS) provided two major advantages in KP-ABE applications: whereas previous constructions were only secure against selective attacks (the attributes in the challenge ciphertext were known before the publication of the keys), this technique allowed full security (a.k.a. adaptive security, where the attributes in the challenge ciphertext are chosen at the challenge-query time). In addition, it allows the notion of attribute-hiding (from [8]) where no information leaks about the attributes associated to the ciphertext, except for the fact that they are accepted or not by the policies in the keys. It gets closer to our goals, as tracing might become undetectable. However, it does not seem any longer compatible with delegation, as the security proofs require all the key generation material to remain a secret information for the key issuer only.

As follow-up works, Chen *et al.* [3,4] designed multiple systems for IPE, with adaptive security, and explored full attribute-hiding with weaker assumptions and shorter ciphertexts and secret keys than in the previous work of Okamoto-Takashima. However, it does not fit our expectations on delegation, for the same reasons. On the other hand, Attrapadung also proposed new ABE schemes based on Pair Encoding Systems, which allow for all possible predicates and large universes [1], but this deals neither with delegation nor with any kind of attribute-hiding, as we would need.

1.2 Contributions

Since the approach of [14] is close to our goal, with attribute-hiding that seems promising for traceability, we extend the original construction to make it compatible with delegation. We propose and prove, in the full version [6], a simple variant that handles delegation with adaptive security under the SXDH assumption. Then, we target delegatable KP-ABE with some additional attribute-hiding property in the ciphertext to allow undetectable tracing.

To this aim, we first detail one of the main limitation we have to overcome in order to get delegation and traceability: with the original approach of [7], attributes associated to the ciphertext are explicitly stated as elements in the ciphertext. Removing some attributes can thus allow to single out specific private keys, but this is a public process, and thus incompatible with any tracing procedure, that would then be detectable by the adversary. To prevent that, **our first contribution** is the new primitive: Switchable-Attribute Key-Policy Attribute-Based Encryption (SA-KP-ABE), where one can invalidate some attributes in the ciphertext, without removing them. More precisely, we will bring new properties to the attributes in ciphertexts (for undetectable tracing) but also symmetrically to the leaves in keys (for anonymity).

In a SA-KP-ABE scheme, attributes in a ciphertext and leaves in an access-tree $\mathcal{T}$ defining the policy in a key can be switched in two different states: Attributes can be set to valid or invalid in a ciphertext at encryption time, using

Feature	[14]	[11]	[4]	Ours
Security	Adaptive	Adaptive	Adaptive	Adaptive
Assumptions	DLIN	q-type	XDLIN	SXDH
Construction type	CP/KP ABE	CP/KP ABE	IPE	KP ABE
Delegation	✓	×	×	✓
Traceability	×	✓	×	✓

Fig. 1. Comparison with Related Work

a secret encryption key. We then denote $\Gamma = \Gamma_v \uplus \Gamma_i$, the set of attributes for a ciphertext, as the disjoint union of valid and invalid attributes; Leaves can be set to passive or active in the access-tree in a key at key generation time, using the master secret key. We also denote $\mathcal{L} = \mathcal{L}_p \uplus \mathcal{L}_a$, the set of leaves, as the disjoint union of passive and active leaves. A set of valid/invalid attributes $\Gamma = \Gamma_v \uplus \Gamma_i$ is accepted by an access-tree $\mathcal{T}$ with passive/active leaves $\mathcal{L} = \mathcal{L}_p \uplus \mathcal{L}_a$, if the tree $\mathcal{T}$ is accepting when all the leaves in $\mathcal{L}$ associated to an attribute in Γ are set to True, except if the leaf is active (in $\mathcal{L}_a$) and the associated attribute invalid (in Γ_i). As already presented above, passive/active leaves in $\mathcal{L}$ are decided during the Key Generation procedure by the authority, using the master secret key. Then the keys are given to the users. During the Encryption procedure, a ciphertext is generated for attributes in Γ, but one might specify some attributes to be invalid by using a secret tracing key, which virtually and secretly switches some active leaves to False. Passive leaves are not impacted by invalid attributes.

A second contribution is a concrete and efficient instantiation of SA-KP-ABE, with security proofs under the SXDH assumption. We eventually explain how one can deal with delegatable and traceable KP-ABE from such a primitive. As shown on Fig. 1, our scheme is the first one that can combine both delegation and traceability of keys for KP-ABE. Computational assumptions are recalled in the next section and in the full version [6].

Our first simple construction (in the full version [6]) following the initial proof from [14], only allows a polynomial-size universe for the attributes involved in the policy, encoded as a Boolean access-tree. This is due to a limited theorem with static attributes in the change of basis in the DPVS framework (see the next section). The latter construction will allow an unbounded universe for the attributes, with an adaptive variant in the change of basis (see Theorem 3). This result is of **independent interest**.

Discussions. Our setting bears common characteristics with recent KP-ABE approaches, but with major differences. First, Waters [16] introduced the Dual System Encryption (DSE) technique, to improve the security level of KP-ABE, from selective security in [7] to adaptive security. In DSE, keys and ciphertexts can be set *semi-functional*, which is in the same vein as our active leaves in keys and invalid attributes in ciphertexts. However, DSE solely uses semi-functional keys and ciphertexts during the simulation, in the security proof, while our construction exploits them in the real-life construction. The security proof thus needs another layer of tricks.

Second, the attribute-hiding notions are strong properties that have been well studied in different IPE works. However, one does not need to achieve such a strong result for tracing: Our (Distinct) Attribute-Indistinguishability is properly tailored for KP-ABE and tracing.

Finally, we detail the advantage of our solution over a generic KEM approach that would combine a Delegatable KP-ABE and a black-box traitor-tracing scheme. This generic solution works if one is not looking for optimal bounds on collusion-resistance during tracing: The main issue with such a use of two independent schemes is that for each user, the KP-ABE key and the traitor-tracing key are not linked. As a consequence, the encryptions of the ABE part and the tracing part are done independently. The colluding users can all try to defeat the traitor tracing without restriction: the collusion-resistance for tracing in the global scheme will exactly be the collusion-resistance of the traitor tracing scheme. On the other hand, our construction will leverage the collusion-resistance of KP-ABE to improve the collusion-resistance of tracing: only players non-revoked by the KP-ABE part can try to defeat the traitor tracing part. Hence, during tracing, one can revoke arbitrary users thanks to the policy/attributes part. This allows to lower the number of active traitors, possibly keeping them below the collusion-resistance of the traitor tracing scheme, so that tracing remains effective.

2 Preliminaries

We will make use of a pairing-friendly setting $\mathcal{G} = (\mathbb{G}_1, \mathbb{G}_2, \mathbb{G}_t, e, G_1, G_2, q)$, with a bilinear map e from $\mathbb{G}_1 \times \mathbb{G}_2$ into $\mathbb{G}_t$, and G_1 (respectively G_2) is a generator of $\mathbb{G}_1$ (respectively $\mathbb{G}_2$). We will use additive notation for $\mathbb{G}_1$ and $\mathbb{G}_2$, and multiplicative notation in $\mathbb{G}_t$.

Definition 1 (Decisional Diffie-Hellman Assumption). *The DDH assumption in $\mathbb{G}$, of prime order q with generator G, states that no algorithm can efficiently distinguish the two distributions*

$$\mathcal{D}_0 = \{(a \cdot G, b \cdot G, ab \cdot G), a, b \stackrel{\$}{\leftarrow} \mathbb{Z}_q\} \quad \mathcal{D}_1 = \{(a \cdot G, b \cdot G, c \cdot G), a, b, c \stackrel{\$}{\leftarrow} \mathbb{Z}_q\}$$

And we will denote by $\mathsf{Adv}_{\mathbb{G}}^{\mathsf{ddh}}(T)$ the best advantage an algorithm can get in distinguishing the two distributions within time bounded by T. Eventually, we will make the following more general Symmetric eXternal Diffie-Hellman (SXDH) Assumption which makes the DDH assumptions in both $\mathbb{G}_1$ and $\mathbb{G}_2$. Then, we define $\mathsf{Adv}_{\mathcal{G}}^{\mathsf{sxdh}}(T) = \max\{\mathsf{Adv}_{\mathbb{G}_1}^{\mathsf{ddh}}(T), \mathsf{Adv}_{\mathbb{G}_2}^{\mathsf{ddh}}(T)\}$.

2.1 Dual Pairing Vector Spaces

We review the main points on Dual Pairing Vector Spaces (DPVS) to help following the intuition provided in this paper. Though not necessary for the comprehension of the paper, the full details are provided in the full version [6]. DPVS have been used for schemes with adaptive security [9,12,13,15] in the same vein as Dual System Encryption (DSE) [16], in prime-order groups under the DLIN assumption. In [10], and some subsequence works, DSE was defined using pairings on composite-order elliptic curves. Then, prime-order groups have been used, for efficiency reasons, first with the DLIN assumption and then with the SXDH assumption [5]. In all theses situations, one exploited indistinguishability of sub-groups or sub-spaces. While we could have used any of them, the latter prime-order groups with the SXDH assumption lead to much more compact and efficient constructions.

In this paper, we thus use the SXDH assumption in a pairing-friendly setting $\mathcal{G}$, with the additional law between elements $\mathbf{X} \in \mathbb{G}_1^n$ and $\mathbf{Y} \in \mathbb{G}_2^n$: $\mathbf{X} \times \mathbf{Y} \stackrel{\text{def}}{=} \prod_i e(\mathbf{X}_i, \mathbf{Y}_i)$. If $\mathbf{X} = (X_i)_i = \vec{x} \cdot G_1 \in \mathbb{G}_1^n$ and $\mathbf{Y} = (Y_i)_i = \vec{y} \cdot G_2 \in \mathbb{G}_2^n$: $(\vec{x} \cdot G_1) \times (\vec{y} \cdot G_2) = \mathbf{X} \times \mathbf{Y} = \prod_i e(X_i, Y_i) = g_t^{\langle \vec{x}, \vec{y} \rangle}$, where $g_t = e(G_1, G_2)$ and $\langle \vec{x}, \vec{y} \rangle$ is the inner product between vectors $\vec{x}$ and $\vec{y}$.

From any basis $\mathcal{B} = (\vec{b}_i)_i$ of $\mathbb{Z}_q^n$, we can define the basis $\mathbb{B} = (\mathbf{b}_i)_i$ of $\mathbb{G}_1^n$, where $\mathbf{b}_i = \vec{b}_i \cdot G_1$. Such a basis $\mathcal{B}$ is equivalent to a random invertible matrix $B \stackrel{\$}{\leftarrow} \mathrm{GL}_n(\mathbb{Z}_q)$, the matrix with $\vec{b}_i$ as its i-th row. If we additionally use $\mathbb{B}^* = (\mathbf{b}_i^*)_i$, the basis of $\mathbb{G}_2^n$ associated to the matrix $B' = (B^{-1})^\top$, as $B \cdot B'^\top = I_n$, $\mathbf{b}_i \times \mathbf{b}_j^* = (\vec{b}_i \cdot G_1) \times (\vec{b}'_j \cdot G_2) = g_t^{\langle \vec{b}_i, \vec{b}'_j \rangle} = g_t^{\delta_{i,j}}$, where $\delta_{i,j} = 1$ if $i = j$ and $\delta_{i,j} = 0$ otherwise, for $i, j \in \{1, \ldots, n\}$: $\mathbb{B}$ and $\mathbb{B}^*$ are called *Dual Orthogonal Bases.* A pairing-friendly setting $\mathcal{G}$ with such dual orthogonal bases $\mathbb{B}$ and $\mathbb{B}^*$ of size n is called a *Dual Pairing Vector Space.*

2.2 Change of Basis

Let us consider the basis $\mathbb{U} = (\mathbf{u}_i)_i$ of $\mathbb{G}^n$ associated to a random matrix $U \in \mathrm{GL}_n(\mathbb{Z}_q)$, and the basis $\mathbb{B} = (\mathbf{b}_i)_i$ of $\mathbb{G}^n$ associated to the product matrix BU, for any $B \in \mathrm{GL}_n(\mathbb{Z}_q)$. For a vector $\vec{x} \in \mathbb{Z}_q^n$, we denote $(\vec{x})_\mathbb{B} = \sum_i x_i \cdot \mathbf{b}_i$. Then, $(\vec{x})_\mathbb{B} = (\vec{y})_\mathbb{U}$ where $\vec{y} = \vec{x} \cdot B$. Hence, $(\vec{x})_\mathbb{B} = (\vec{x} \cdot B)_\mathbb{U}$ and $(\vec{x} \cdot B^{-1})_\mathbb{B} = (\vec{x})_\mathbb{U}$ where we denote $\mathbb{B} \stackrel{\text{def}}{=} B \cdot \mathbb{U}$. For any invertible matrix B, if $\mathbb{U}$ is a random basis, then $\mathbb{B} = B \cdot \mathbb{U}$ is also a random basis. Furthermore, if we consider the random dual orthogonal bases $\mathbb{U} = (\mathbf{u}_i)_i$ and $\mathbb{U}^* = (\mathbf{u}_i^*)_i$ of $\mathbb{G}_1^n$ and $\mathbb{G}_2^n$ respectively associated to a matrix U (which means that $\mathbb{U}$ is associated to the matrix U and $\mathbb{U}^*$ is associated to the matrix $U' = (U^{-1})^\top$): the bases $\mathbb{B} = B \cdot \mathbb{U}$ and $\mathbb{B}^* = B' \cdot \mathbb{U}^*$, where $B' = (B^{-1})^\top$, are also random dual orthogonal bases:

$$\mathbf{b}_i \times \mathbf{b}_j^* = g_t^{\vec{b}_i \cdot \vec{b'}_j^\top} = g_t^{\vec{u}_i \cdot B \cdot (B^{-1})^\top \cdot \vec{u'}_j^\top} = g_t^{\vec{u}_i \cdot \vec{u'}_j^\top} = g_t^{\delta_{i,j}}.$$

All the security proofs will exploit changes of bases, from one game to another game, with two kinds of changes: formal or computational.

Formal Change of Basis, where we start from two dual orthogonal bases $\mathbb{U}$ and $\mathbb{U}^*$ of dimension 2, and set

$$B = \begin{pmatrix} 1 & 1 \\ 0 & 1 \end{pmatrix} \qquad B' = \begin{pmatrix} 1 & 0 \\ -1 & 1 \end{pmatrix} \qquad \mathbb{B} = B \cdot \mathbb{U} \qquad \mathbb{B}^* = B' \cdot \mathbb{U}^*$$

then,

$$(x_1, x_2)_{\mathbb{U}} = (x_1, x_2 - x_1)_{\mathbb{B}} \qquad (y_1, y_2)_{\mathbb{U}^*} = (y_1 + y_2, y_2)_{\mathbb{B}^*} \tag{1}$$
$$(0, x_2)_{\mathbb{U}} = (0, x_2)_{\mathbb{B}} \qquad (0, y_2)_{\mathbb{U}^*} = (y_2, y_2)_{\mathbb{B}^*} \tag{2}$$

In practice, this change of basis makes $\mathbf{b}_1 = \mathbf{u}_1 + \mathbf{u}_2$, $\mathbf{b}_2 = \mathbf{u}_2$, $\mathbf{b}_1^* = \mathbf{u}_1^*$, $\mathbf{b}_2^* = -\mathbf{u}_1^* + \mathbf{u}_2^*$. If $\mathbf{u}_1/\mathbf{b}_1$ and $\mathbf{u}_2^*/\mathbf{b}_2^*$ are kept private, the adversary cannot know whether we are using $(\mathbb{U}, \mathbb{U}^*)$ or $(\mathbb{B}, \mathbb{B}^*)$. This will be used to duplicate some component, from a game to another game, as shown in the above Example (2).

Computational Change of Basis, where we define vectors in a dual orthogonal basis $(\mathbb{U}, \mathbb{U}^*)$ of dimension 2. From a Diffie-Hellman challenge $(a \cdot G_1, b \cdot G_1, c \cdot G_1)$, where $c = ab + \tau \bmod q$ with either $\tau = 0$ or $\tau \xleftarrow{\$} \mathbb{Z}_q^*$, one can set

$$B = \begin{pmatrix} 1 & a \\ 0 & 1 \end{pmatrix} \qquad B' = \begin{pmatrix} 1 & 0 \\ -a & 1 \end{pmatrix} \qquad \mathbb{B} = B \cdot \mathbb{U} \qquad \mathbb{B}^* = B' \cdot \mathbb{U}^* \tag{3}$$

then, in basis $(\mathbb{B}, \mathbb{B}^*)$, we implicitly define

$$(b, c)_{\mathbb{U}} + (x_1, x_2)_{\mathbb{B}} = (b, c - ab)_{\mathbb{B}} + (x_1, x_2)_{\mathbb{B}} = (x_1 + b, x_2 + \tau)_{\mathbb{B}}$$
$$(y_1, y_2)_{\mathbb{U}^*} = (y_1 + a y_2, y_2)_{\mathbb{B}^*}$$

where τ can be either 0 or random, according to the Diffie-Hellman challenge. And the two situations are indistinguishable. We should however note that in this case, $\mathbf{b}_2^*$ cannot be computed, as $a \cdot G_2$ is not known. This will not be a problem if this element is not provided to the adversary.

Partial Change of Basis: in the constructions, bases will be of higher dimension, but we will often only change a few basis vectors. We will then specify the vectors as indices to the change of basis matrix: in a space of dimension n,

$$B = \begin{pmatrix} 1 & a \\ 0 & 1 \end{pmatrix}_{1,2} \qquad B' = \begin{pmatrix} 1 & 0 \\ -a & 1 \end{pmatrix}_{1,2} \qquad \mathbb{B} = B \cdot \mathbb{U} \qquad \mathbb{B}^* = B' \cdot \mathbb{U}^* \tag{4}$$

means that only the two first coordinates are impacted, and thus $\mathbf{b}_1, \mathbf{b}_2$ and $\mathbf{b}_1^*, \mathbf{b}_2^*$. We complete the matrices B and B' with the identity matrix: $\mathbf{b}_i = \mathbf{u}_i$ and $\mathbf{b}_i^* = \mathbf{u}_i^*$, for $i \geq 3$.

2.3 Particular Changes

The security proofs will rely on specific indistinguishable modifications that we detail here. We will demonstrate the first of them to give the intuition of the methodology to the reader. A full demonstration for the other modifications can be found in the full version [6]. These results hold under the DDH assumption in $\mathbb{G}_1$, (but it can also be applied in $\mathbb{G}_2$), on random dual orthogonal bases $\mathbb{B}$ and $\mathbb{B}^*$.

With the above change of basis provided in Eq. (4), we can compute $\mathbb{B} = (\mathbf{b}_i)_i$, as we know $a \cdot G_1$ and all the scalars in U:

$$\mathbf{b}_i = \sum_k B_{i,k} \cdot \mathbf{u}_k \qquad \mathbf{b}_{i,j} = \sum_k B_{i,k} \cdot \mathbf{u}_{k,j} = \sum_k B_{i,k} U_{k,j} \cdot G_1 = \sum_k U_{k,j} \cdot (B_{i,j} \cdot G_1).$$

Hence, to compute $\mathbf{b}_i$, one needs all the scalars in U, but only the group elements $B_{i,j} \cdot G_1$, and so G_1 and $a \cdot G_1$. This is the same for $\mathbb{B}^*$, except for the vector $\mathbf{b}_2^*$ as $a \cdot G_2$ is missing. One can thus publish $\mathbb{B}$ and $\mathbb{B}^* \backslash \{\mathbf{b}_2^*\}$.

Indistinguishability of Sub-spaces (3). As already remarked, for such a fixed matrix B, if $\mathbb{U}$ is random, so is $\mathbb{B}$ too, and $(\vec{x})_\mathbb{B} = (\vec{x} \cdot B)_\mathbb{U}$, so $(\vec{x})_\mathbb{U} = (\vec{x} \cdot B^{-1})_\mathbb{B}$. Note that $B^{-1} = B'^{\top}$. So, $(b, c, 0, \ldots, 0)_\mathbb{U} = (b, c - ab, 0, \ldots, 0)_\mathbb{B}$, then

$$(b, c, 0, \ldots, 0)_\mathbb{U} + (x_1, x_2, x_3, \ldots, x_n)_\mathbb{B} = (x_1 + b, x_2 + \tau, x_3, \ldots, x_n)_\mathbb{B}$$

where τ can be either 0 or random. Note that whereas we cannot compute $\mathbf{b}_2^*$, this does not exclude this second component in the computed vectors, as we can use $(y_1, \ldots, y_n)_{\mathbb{U}^*} = (y_1 + ay_2, y_2, \ldots, y_n)_{\mathbb{B}^*}$.

Theorem 2. *Under the DDH Assumption in $\mathbb{G}_1$, for random dual orthogonal bases $\mathbb{B}$ and $\mathbb{B}^*$, once having seen $\mathbb{B}$ and $\mathbb{B}^* \backslash \{\mathbf{b}_2^*\}$, and any vector $(y_1, y_2, \ldots, y_n)_{\mathbb{B}^*}$, for any $y_2, \ldots, y_n \in \mathbb{Z}_q$, but unknown random $y_1 \stackrel{\$}{\leftarrow} \mathbb{Z}_q$, one cannot distinguish $(x_1, x_2', x_3, \ldots, x_n)_\mathbb{B}$ and $(x_1, x_2, x_3, \ldots, x_n)_\mathbb{B}$, for any $x_2, \ldots, x_n \in \mathbb{Z}_q$, but unknown random $x_1, x_2' \stackrel{\$}{\leftarrow} \mathbb{Z}_q$.*

Some scalar coordinates can be chosen (and thus definitely known) by the adversary, whereas some other must be random. Eventually the adversary only sees the vectors in $\mathbb{G}_1^n$ and $\mathbb{G}_2^n$. We now directly state two other properties for which the demonstration (which works similarly as the SubSpace-Ind one) can be found in the full version [6].

Swap-Ind Property, on $(\mathbb{B}, \mathbb{B}^*)_{1,2,3}$: from the view of $\mathbb{B}$ and $\mathbb{B}^* \backslash \{\mathbf{b}_1^*, \mathbf{b}_2^*\}$, and the vector $(y_1, y_1, y_3, \ldots, y_n)_{\mathbb{B}^*}$, for any $y_1, y_3, \ldots, y_n \in \mathbb{Z}_q$, one cannot distinguish the vectors $(x_1, 0, x_3, x_4, \ldots, x_n)_\mathbb{B}$ and $(0, x_1, x_3, x_4, \ldots, x_n)_\mathbb{B}$, for any $x_1, x_4, \ldots, x_n \in \mathbb{Z}_q$, but unknown random $x_3 \stackrel{\$}{\leftarrow} \mathbb{Z}_q$.

(Static) Index-Ind Property, on $(\mathbb{B}, \mathbb{B}^*)_{1,2,3}$: from the view of $\mathbb{B}$ and $\mathbb{B}^* \backslash \{\mathbf{b}_3^*\}$, for fixed $t \neq p \in \mathbb{Z}_q$, and the $(\pi \cdot (t, -1), y_3, \ldots, y_n)_{\mathbb{B}^*}$, for any $y_3, \ldots, y_n \in \mathbb{Z}_q$, but unknown random $\pi \stackrel{\$}{\leftarrow} \mathbb{Z}_q$, one cannot distinguish $(\sigma \cdot (1, p), x_3, x_4, \ldots, x_n)_\mathbb{B}$ and $(\sigma \cdot (1, p), x_3', x_4, \ldots, x_n)_\mathbb{B}$, for any $x_3', x_3, x_4, \ldots, x_n \in \mathbb{Z}_q$, but unknown random $\sigma \stackrel{\$}{\leftarrow} \mathbb{Z}_q$.

We stress that, in this static version, t and p must be fixed, and known before the simulation starts in the security analysis, as they will appear in the matrix B. In the Okamoto-Takashima's constructions [13,15], such values t and p were for bounded names of attributes. In the following, we want to consider unbounded attributes, we thus conclude this section with an adaptive version, where t and p do not need to be known in advance, from a large universe:

Theorem 3 (Adaptive Index-Ind Property). *Under the DDH Assumption in $\mathbb{G}_1$, for random dual orthogonal bases $\mathbb{B}$ and $\mathbb{B}^*$, once having seen $\mathbb{B}$ and $\mathbb{B}^*\backslash\{\mathbf{b}_3^*\}$, and $(\pi \cdot (t, -1), y_3, 0, 0, y_6, \ldots, y_n)_{\mathbb{B}^*}$, for any $t, y_3, y_6, \ldots, y_n \in \mathbb{Z}_q$, but unknown random $\pi \stackrel{\$}{\leftarrow} \mathbb{Z}_q$, one cannot distinguish $(\sigma \cdot (1,p), x_3, 0, 0, x_6, \ldots, x_n)_{\mathbb{B}}$ and $(\sigma \cdot (1,p), x_3', 0, 0, x_6, \ldots, x_n)_{\mathbb{B}}$, for any $x_3, x_3', x_6, \ldots, x_n \in \mathbb{Z}_q$, and $p \neq t$, but unknown random $\sigma \stackrel{\$}{\leftarrow} \mathbb{Z}_q$, with an advantage better than $8 \times \mathsf{Adv}_{\mathbb{G}_1}^{\mathsf{ddh}}(T) + 4 \times \mathsf{Adv}_{\mathbb{G}_2}^{\mathsf{ddh}}(T)$, where T is the running time of the adversary.*

Proof. For the sake of simplicity, we will prove indistinguishability between $(\sigma \cdot (1,p), 0, 0, 0)_{\mathbb{B}}$ and $(\sigma \cdot (1,p), x_3, 0, 0)_{\mathbb{B}}$, in dimension 5 only, instead of n. Additional components could be chosen by the adversary. Applied twice, we obtain the above theorem. The proof follows a sequence of games.

Game $\mathbf{G_0}$: The adversary can choose $p \neq t$ and x_3, y_3 in $\mathbb{Z}_q$, but $\pi, \sigma \stackrel{\$}{\leftarrow} \mathbb{Z}_q$ are unknown to it:

$$\mathbf{k}^* = (\pi(t, -1), y_3, 0, 0)_{\mathbb{B}^*} \qquad \mathbf{c}_0 = (\sigma(1,p), 0, 0, 0)_{\mathbb{B}}$$
$$\mathbf{c}_1 = (\sigma(1,p), x_3, 0, 0)_{\mathbb{B}}$$

Vectors $(\mathbf{b}_1, \mathbf{b}_2, \mathbf{b}_3, \mathbf{b}_1^*, \mathbf{b}_2^*)$ and $(\mathbf{c}_b, \mathbf{k}^*)$ are provided to the adversary that must decide on b: Adv_0 is its advantage in correctly guessing b. Only $\mathbf{k}^*$ and $\mathbf{c}_0$ will be modified in the following games, so that eventually $\mathbf{c}_0 = \mathbf{c}_1$ in the last game, which leads to perfect indistinguishability.

Game $\mathbf{G_1}$: We replicate the first sub-vector $(t, -1)$, with $\rho \stackrel{\$}{\leftarrow} \mathbb{Z}_q$, in the hidden components: $\mathbf{k}^* = (\pi(t, -1), y_3, \rho(t, -1))_{\mathbb{B}^*}$. To show the indistinguishability, one applies the $\mathsf{SubSpace\text{-}Ind}$ property on $(\mathbb{B}^*, \mathbb{B})_{1,2,4,5}$. Indeed, we can consider a triple $(a \cdot G_2, b \cdot G_2, c \cdot G_2)$, where $c = ab + \tau \bmod q$ with either $\tau = 0$ or random, which are indistinguishable under the DDH assumption in $\mathbb{G}_2$. Let us assume we start from random dual orthogonal bases $(\mathbb{V}, \mathbb{V}^*)$. We define

$$B' = \begin{pmatrix} 1 & 0 & a & 0 \\ 0 & 1 & 0 & a \\ 0 & 0 & 1 & 0 \\ 0 & 0 & 0 & 1 \end{pmatrix}_{1,2,4,5} \qquad B = \begin{pmatrix} 1 & 0 & 0 & 0 \\ 0 & 1 & 0 & 0 \\ -a & 0 & 1 & 0 \\ 0 & -a & 0 & 1 \end{pmatrix}_{1,2,4,5} \qquad \mathbb{B}^* = B' \cdot \mathbb{V}^* \quad \mathbb{B} = B \cdot \mathbb{V}$$

The vectors $\mathbf{b}_4, \mathbf{b}_5$ can not be computed, but they are hidden from the adversary's view, and are not used in any vector. We compute the new vectors:

$$\begin{aligned} \mathbf{k}^* &= (b(t, -1), y_3, c(t, -1))_{\mathbb{V}^*} \\ &= (b(t, -1), y_3, (c - ab)(t, -1)_{\mathbb{B}^*} \\ &= (b(t, -1), y_3, \tau(t, -1)_{\mathbb{B}^*} \end{aligned} \qquad \mathbf{c}_0 = (\sigma(1,p), 0, 0, 0)_{\mathbb{B}}$$

One can note that when $\tau = 0$, this is the previous game, and when τ random, we are in the new game, with $\pi = b$ and $\rho = \tau$: $\mathsf{Adv}_0 - \mathsf{Adv}_1 \leq \mathsf{Adv}_{\mathbb{G}_2}^{\mathsf{ddh}}(T)$.

Game $\mathbf{G_2}$: We replicate the non-orthogonal sub-vector $(1, p)$, with $\theta \xleftarrow{\$} \mathbb{Z}_q$:

$$\mathbf{k}^* = (\pi(t, -1), y_3, \rho(t, -1))_{\mathbb{B}^*} \qquad \mathbf{c}_0 = (\sigma(1, p), 0, \theta(1, p))_{\mathbb{B}}$$

To show the indistinguishability, one applies the SubSpace-Ind property on $(\mathbb{B}, \mathbb{B}^*)_{1,2,4,5}$. Indeed, we can consider a triple $(a \cdot G_1, b \cdot G_1, c \cdot G_1)$, where $c = ab + \tau \bmod q$ with either $\tau = 0$ or random, which are indistinguishable under the DDH assumption in $\mathbb{G}_1$. Let us assume we start from random dual orthogonal bases $(\mathbb{V}, \mathbb{V}^*)$. Then we define the matrices

$$B = \begin{pmatrix} 1 & 0 & a & 0 \\ 0 & 1 & 0 & a \\ 0 & 0 & 1 & 0 \\ 0 & 0 & 0 & 1 \end{pmatrix}_{1,2,4,5} \qquad B' = \begin{pmatrix} 1 & 0 & 0 & 0 \\ 0 & 1 & 0 & 0 \\ -a & 0 & 1 & 0 \\ 0 & -a & 0 & 1 \end{pmatrix}_{1,2,4,5} \qquad \mathbb{B} = B \cdot \mathbb{V} \quad \mathbb{B}^* = B' \cdot \mathbb{V}^*$$

The vectors $\mathbf{b}_4^*, \mathbf{b}_5^*$ can not be computed, but they are hidden from the adversary's view. We compute the new vectors in $\mathbb{V}$ and $\mathbb{V}^*$:

$$\begin{aligned} \mathbf{c}_0 &= (b(1,p), 0, c(1,p))_{\mathbb{V}} \\ &= (b(1,p), 0, (c - ab)(1,p))_{\mathbb{B}} \\ &= (b(1,p), 0, \tau(1,p))_{\mathbb{B}} \end{aligned} \qquad \begin{aligned} \mathbf{k}^* &= (\pi'(t,-1), y_3, \rho(t,-1))_{\mathbb{V}^*} \\ &= ((\pi' + a\rho)(t,-1), y_3, \rho(t,-1))_{\mathbb{B}^*} \end{aligned}$$

One can note that when $\tau = 0$, this is the previous game, and when τ random, we are in the new game, with $\pi = \pi' + a\rho$, $\sigma = b$, and $\theta = \tau$: $\mathsf{Adv}_1 - \mathsf{Adv}_2 \leq \mathsf{Adv}_{\mathbb{G}_1}^{\mathsf{ddh}}(T)$.

Game $\mathbf{G_3}$: We randomize the two non-orthogonal sub-vectors, with random scalars $u_1, u_2, v_1, v_2 \xleftarrow{\$} \mathbb{Z}_p$:

$$\mathbf{k}^* = (\pi(t, -1), y_3, u_1, u_2)_{\mathbb{B}^*} \qquad \mathbf{c}_0 = (\sigma(1, p), 0, v_1, v_2)_{\mathbb{B}}$$

To show the indistinguishability, one makes a formal change of basis on $(\mathbb{B}^*, \mathbb{B})_{4,5}$, with a random unitary matrix Z, with $z_1 z_4 - z_2 z_3 = 1$:

$$B' = Z = \begin{pmatrix} z_1 & z_2 \\ z_3 & z_4 \end{pmatrix}_{4,5} \qquad B = \begin{pmatrix} z_4 & -z_3 \\ -z_2 & z_1 \end{pmatrix}_{4,5} \qquad \mathbb{B}^* = B' \cdot \mathbb{V}^* \quad \mathbb{B} = B \cdot \mathbb{V}$$

This only impacts the hidden vectors $(\mathbf{b}_4, \mathbf{b}_5)$, $(\mathbf{b}_4^*, \mathbf{b}_5^*)$. If one defines $\mathbf{k}^*$ and $\mathbf{c}_0$ in $(\mathbb{V}^*, \mathbb{V})$, this translates in $(\mathbb{B}^*, \mathbb{B})$:

$$\begin{aligned} \mathbf{k}^* &= (\pi(t,-1), y_3, \rho(t,-1))_{\mathbb{V}^*} = (\pi(t,-1), y_3, \rho(tz_1 - z_3, tz_2 - z_4))_{\mathbb{B}^*} \\ \mathbf{c}_0 &= (\sigma(1,p), 0, \theta(1,p))_{\mathbb{V}} = (\sigma(1,p), 0, \theta(z_4 - pz_2, -z_3 + pz_1))_{\mathbb{B}} \end{aligned}$$

Let us consider random $u_1, u_2, v_1, v_2 \xleftarrow{\$} \mathbb{Z}_p$, and solve the system in z_1, z_2, z_3, z_4. This system admits a unique solution, if and only if $t \neq p$. And with random ρ, θ, and random unitary matrix Z,

$$\mathbf{k}^* = (\pi(t, -1), y_3, u_1, u_2)_{\mathbb{B}^*} \qquad \mathbf{c}_0 = (\sigma(1, p), 0, v_1, v_2)_{\mathbb{B}}$$

with random scalars $u_1, u_2, v_1, v_2 \xleftarrow{\$} \mathbb{Z}_p$. In bases $(\mathbb{V}, \mathbb{V}^*)$, we are in the previous game, and in bases $(\mathbb{B}, \mathbb{B}^*)$, we are in the new game, if $p \neq t$: $\mathsf{Adv}_2 = \mathsf{Adv}_3$.

Game $\mathbf{G}_4$: We now randomize the third component in $\mathbf{c}_0$:

$$\mathbf{k}^* = (\pi(t,-1), y_3, u_1, u_2)_{\mathbb{B}^*} \qquad \mathbf{c}_0 = (\sigma(1,p), x_3, v_1, v_2)_{\mathbb{B}}$$

To show the indistinguishability, one applies the SubSpace-Ind property on $(\mathbb{B},\mathbb{B}^*)_{4,3}$. Indeed, we can consider a triple $(a \cdot G_1, b \cdot G_1, c \cdot G_1)$, where $c = ab + \tau \bmod q$ with either $\tau = 0$ or $\tau = x_3$, which are indistinguishable under the DDH assumption in $\mathbb{G}_1$. Let us assume we start from random dual orthogonal bases $(\mathbb{V},\mathbb{V}^*)$. Then we define the matrices

$$B = \begin{pmatrix} 1 & 0 \\ a & 1 \end{pmatrix}_{3,4} \qquad B' = \begin{pmatrix} 1 & -a \\ 0 & 1 \end{pmatrix}_{3,4} \qquad \mathbb{B} = B \cdot \mathbb{V} \qquad \mathbb{B}^* = B' \cdot \mathbb{V}^*$$

The vectors $\mathbf{b}_3^*$ can not be computed, but it is not into the adversary's view. We compute the new vectors:

$$\begin{aligned} \mathbf{k}^* &= (\pi(t,-1), y_3, u_1', u_2)_{\mathbb{V}^*} & \mathbf{c}_0 &= (\sigma(1,p), c, b, v_2)_{\mathbb{V}} \\ &= (\pi(t,-1), y_3, u_1' + a y_3, u_2)_{\mathbb{B}^*} & &= (\sigma(1,p), c - ab, b, v_2)_{\mathbb{B}} \\ & & &= (\sigma(1,p), \tau, b, v_2)_{\mathbb{B}} \end{aligned}$$

One can note that when $\tau = 0$, this is the previous game, and when $\tau = x_3$, we are in the new game, with $v_1 = b$ and $u_1 = u_1' + a y_3$: $\mathsf{Adv}_3 - \mathsf{Adv}_4 \leq 2 \times \mathsf{Adv}^{\mathsf{ddh}}_{\mathbb{G}_1}(T)$, by applying twice the Diffie-Hellman indistinguishability game.

We can undo successively games $\mathbf{G}_3$, $\mathbf{G}_2$, and $\mathbf{G}_1$ to get, after a gap bounded by $\mathsf{Adv}^{\mathsf{ddh}}_{\mathbb{G}_1}(t) + \mathsf{Adv}^{\mathsf{ddh}}_{\mathbb{G}_2}(t)$: $\mathbf{k}^* = (\pi(t,-1), y_3, 0, 0)_{\mathbb{B}^*}$ and $\mathbf{c}_0 = (\sigma(1,p), x_3, 0, 0)_{\mathbb{B}}$. In this game, the advantage of any adversary is 0. The global difference of advantages is bounded by $4 \cdot \mathsf{Adv}^{\mathsf{ddh}}_{\mathbb{G}_1}(T) + 2 \cdot \mathsf{Adv}^{\mathsf{ddh}}_{\mathbb{G}_2}(T)$, which concludes the proof.

3 Key-Policy ABE with Switchable Attributes

Classical definitions and properties for KP-ABE, and more details about policies, are reviewed in the full version [6], following [7]. We recall here the main notions on labeled access-trees as a secret sharing to embed a policy in keys.

3.1 Policy Definition

Access Trees. As in the seminal paper [7], we will consider an access-tree $\mathcal{T}$ to model the policy on attributes in an unbounded universe $\mathcal{U}$, but with only AND and OR gates instead of more general threshold gates: an AND-gate being an n-out-of-n gate, whereas an OR-gate is a 1-out-of-n gate. This is also a particular case of the more general LSSS technique. Nevertheless, such an access-tree with only AND and OR gates is as expressive as with any threshold gates or LSSS. For any monotonic policy, we define our access-tree in the following way: $\mathcal{T}$ is a rooted labeled tree from the root ρ, with internal nodes associated to AND and OR gates and leaves associated to attributes. More precisely, for each leaf $\lambda \in \mathcal{L}$,

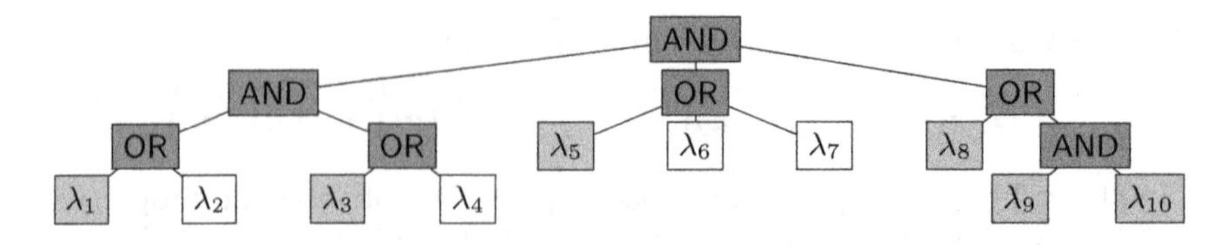

Fig. 2. Example of an access-tree with two different evaluation pruned trees for the leaves colored in green: $\{\lambda_1, \lambda_3, \lambda_5, \lambda_8\}$ or $\{\lambda_1, \lambda_3, \lambda_5, \lambda_9, \lambda_{10}\}$ (Color figure online)

$A(\lambda) \in \mathcal{U}$ is an attribute, and any internal node $\nu \in \mathcal{N}$ is labeled with a gate $G(\nu) \in \{\mathsf{AND}, \mathsf{OR}\}$ as an AND or an OR gate to be satisfied among the children in $\mathsf{children}(\nu)$. We will implicitly consider that any access-tree $\mathcal{T}$ is associated to the attribute-labeling A of the leaves and the gate-labeling G of the nodes. For any leaf $\lambda \in \mathcal{L}$ of $\mathcal{T}$ or internal node $\nu \in \mathcal{N}\backslash\{\rho\}$, the function parent links to the parent node: $\nu \in \mathsf{children}(\mathsf{parent}(\nu))$ and $\lambda \in \mathsf{children}(\mathsf{parent}(\lambda))$.

On a given list $\Gamma \subseteq \mathcal{U}$ of attributes, each leaf $\lambda \in \mathcal{L}$ is either satisfied (considered or set to True), if $A(\lambda) \in \Gamma$, or not (ignored or set to False) otherwise: we will denote $\mathcal{L}_\Gamma$ the restriction of $\mathcal{L}$ to the satisfied leaves in the tree $\mathcal{T}$ (corresponding to an attribute in Γ). Then, for each internal node ν, one checks whether all children (AND-gate) or at least one of the children (OR-gate) are satisfied, from the attributes associated to the leaves, and then ν is itself satisfied or not. By induction, if for each node ν we denote $\mathcal{T}_\nu$ the subtree rooted at the node ν, $\mathcal{T} = \mathcal{T}_\rho$. A leaf $\lambda \in \mathcal{L}$ is satisfied if $\lambda \in \mathcal{L}_\Gamma$ then, recursively, $\mathcal{T}_\nu$ is satisfied if the AND/OR-gate associated to ν via $G(\nu)$ is satisfied with respect to status of the children in $\mathsf{children}(\nu)$: we denote $\mathcal{T}_\nu(\Gamma) = 1$ when the subtree is satisfied, and 0 otherwise:

$$\begin{array}{lll}
\mathcal{T}_\lambda(\Gamma) = 1 & \text{iff } \lambda \in \mathcal{L}_\Gamma & \text{for any leaf } \lambda \in \mathcal{L} \\
\mathcal{T}_\nu(\Gamma) = 1 & \text{iff } \forall \kappa \in \mathsf{children}(\nu), \mathcal{T}_\kappa(\Gamma) = 1 & \text{when } G(\nu) = \mathsf{AND} \\
\mathcal{T}_\nu(\Gamma) = 1 & \text{iff } \exists \kappa \in \mathsf{children}(\nu), \mathcal{T}_\kappa(\Gamma) = 1 & \text{when } G(\nu) = \mathsf{OR}
\end{array}$$

Evaluation Pruned Trees. In the above definition, we considered an access-tree $\mathcal{T}$ on leaves $\mathcal{L}$ and a set Γ of attributes, with the satisfiability $\mathcal{T}(\Gamma) = 1$ where the predicate defined by $\mathcal{T}$ is true when all the leaves $\lambda \in \mathcal{L}_\Gamma$ are set to True. A Γ-evaluation tree $\mathcal{T}' \subset \mathcal{T}$ is a pruned version of $\mathcal{T}$, where one children only is kept to OR-gate nodes, down to the leaves, so that $\mathcal{T}'(\Gamma) = 1$. Basically, we keep a skeleton with only necessary True leaves to evaluate the internal nodes up to the root. We will denote $\mathsf{EPT}(\mathcal{T}, \Gamma)$ the set of all the evaluation pruned trees of $\mathcal{T}$ with respect to Γ. $\mathsf{EPT}(\mathcal{T}, \Gamma)$ is non-empty if and only if $\mathcal{T}(\Gamma) = 1$.

Figure 2 gives an illustration of such an access-tree for a policy: when the colored leaves $\{\lambda_1, \lambda_3, \lambda_5, \lambda_8, \lambda_9, \lambda_{10}\}$ are True, the tree is satisfied, and there are two possible evaluation pruned trees: down to the leaves $\{\lambda_1, \lambda_3, \lambda_5, \lambda_8\}$ or $\{\lambda_1, \lambda_3, \lambda_5, \lambda_9, \lambda_{10}\}$.

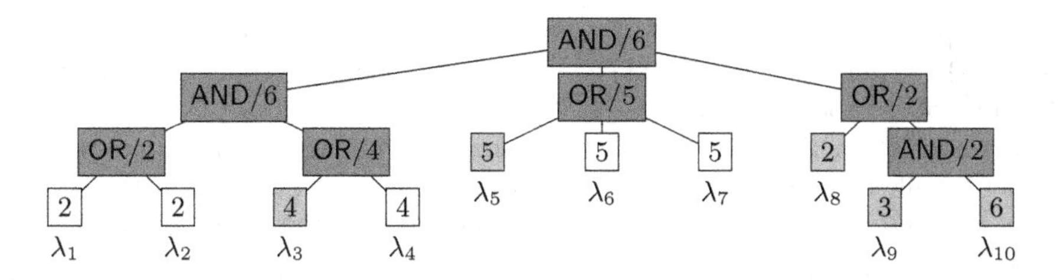

Fig. 3. Example of a 6-labeling in $\mathbb{Z}/7\mathbb{Z}$, with a non-satisfying set of (colored) attributes: leaves λ_8, λ_9 and λ_{10} are not independent (Color figure online)

Partial Order on Policies. Delegation will only be possible for a more restrictive access-tree, or a less accessible tree $\mathcal{T}'$, than $\mathcal{T}$ with the following partial order: $\mathcal{T}' \leq \mathcal{T}$, if and only if for any subset Γ of attributes, $\mathcal{T}'(\Gamma) = 1 \Longrightarrow \mathcal{T}(\Gamma) = 1$. In our case of access-trees, a more restrictive access-tree is, for each node ν: if $G(\nu) = \mathsf{AND}$, one or more children are added (*i.e.*, more constraints); if $G(\nu) = \mathsf{OR}$, one or more children are removed (*i.e.*, less flexibility); the node ν is moved one level below as a child of an AND-gate at node ν', with additional sub-trees as children to this AND-gate (*i.e.*, more constraints).

3.2 Labeling of Access-Trees

Labeled Access-Trees. We will label such trees with integers so that some labels on the leaves will be enough/necessary (according to the policy) to recover the labels above, up to the root, as illustrated on Fig. 3.

Definition 4 (Random y-Labeling). *For an access-tree $\mathcal{T}$ and any $y \in \mathbb{Z}_p$, the probabilistic algorithm $\Lambda_y(\mathcal{T})$ sets $a_\rho \leftarrow y$ for the root, and then in a top-down manner, for each internal node ν, starting from the root: if $G(\nu) = \mathsf{AND}$, with n children, a random n-out-of-n sharing of a_ν is associated to each children; if $G(\nu) = \mathsf{OR}$, with n children, each children is associated to the value a_ν.*

Algorithm $\Lambda_y(\mathcal{T})$ outputs $\Lambda_y = (a_\lambda)_{\lambda \in \mathcal{L}}$, for all the leaves $\lambda \in \mathcal{L}$ of the tree $\mathcal{T}$. Because of the linearity, from any y-labeling $(a_\lambda)_\lambda$ of the tree $\mathcal{T}$, and a random z-labeling $(b_\lambda)_\lambda$ of $\mathcal{T}$, the sum $(a_\lambda + b_\lambda)_\lambda$ is a random $(y+z)$-labeling of $\mathcal{T}$. In particular, from any y-labeling $(a_\lambda)_\lambda$ of $\mathcal{T}$, and a random zero-labeling $(b_\lambda)_\lambda$ of $\mathcal{T}$, the values $c_\lambda \leftarrow a_\lambda + b_\lambda$ provide a random y-labeling of $\mathcal{T}$.

Labels on leaves are a secret sharing of the root that allows reconstruction of the secret if and only if the policy is satisfied, as explained below:

Properties of Labelings. For an acceptable set Γ for $\mathcal{T}$ and a labeling Λ_y of $\mathcal{T}$ for a random y, given only $(a_\lambda)_{\lambda \in \mathcal{L}_\Gamma}$, one can reconstruct $y = a_\rho$. Indeed, as $\mathcal{T}(\Gamma) = 1$, we use an evaluation pruned tree $\mathcal{T}' \in \mathsf{EPT}(\mathcal{T}, \Gamma)$. Then, in a bottom-up way, starting from the leaves, one can compute the labels of all the internal nodes, up to the root.

On the other hand, when $\mathcal{T}(\Gamma) = 0$, with a random labeling Λ_y of $\mathcal{T}$ for a random y, given only $(a_\lambda)_{\lambda \in \mathcal{L}_\Gamma}$, y is unpredictable: for any $y, y' \in \mathbb{Z}_p$, $\mathcal{D}_y$ and

$\mathcal{D}_{y'}$ are perfectly indistinguishable, where $\mathcal{D}_y = \{(a_\lambda)_{\lambda \in \mathcal{L}_\Gamma}, (a_\lambda)_\lambda \xleftarrow{\$} \Lambda_y(\mathcal{T})\}$. Intuitively, given $(a_\lambda)_{\lambda \in \mathcal{L}_\Gamma}$, as $\mathcal{T}(\Gamma) = 0$, one can complete the labeling so that the label of the root is any y.

For our notion of Attribute-Indistinguishability, we need to identify a specific property called *independent leaves*, which describes leaves for which the secret share leaks no information in any of the other leaves in the access-tree.

Definition 5 (Independent Leaves). *Given an access-tree $\mathcal{T}$ and a set Γ so that $\mathcal{T}(\Gamma) = 0$, we call independent leaves, in $\mathcal{L}_\Gamma$ with respect to $\mathcal{T}$, the leaves μ such that, given only $(a_\lambda)_{\lambda \in \mathcal{L}_\Gamma \setminus \{\mu\}}$, a_μ is unpredictable: for any y, the two distributions $\mathcal{D}_y^{\$}(\Gamma) = \{(a_\lambda)_{\lambda \in \mathcal{L}_\Gamma}\}$ and $\mathcal{D}_y(\Gamma, \mu) = \{(b_\mu) \cup (a_\lambda)_{\lambda \in \mathcal{L}_\Gamma \setminus \{\mu\}}\}$ are perfectly indistinguishable, where $(a_\lambda)_\lambda \xleftarrow{\$} \Lambda_y(\mathcal{T})$ and $b_\mu \xleftarrow{\$} \mathbb{Z}_p$.*

With the illustration on Fig. 3, with non-satisfied tree, when only colored leaves are set to True, leaves λ_3 and λ_5 are independent among the True leaves $\{\lambda_3, \lambda_5, \lambda_8, \lambda_9, \lambda_{10}\}$. But leaves λ_8, λ_9 and λ_{10} are not independent as $a_{\lambda_8} = a_{\lambda_9} + a_{\lambda_{10}} \bmod 7$ for any random labeling. Intuitively, given $(a_\lambda)_{\lambda \in \mathcal{L}_\Gamma \setminus \{\mu\}}$ and any a_μ, one can complete it into a valid labeling (with any random root label y as $\mathcal{T}(\Gamma) = 0$), for $\mu \in \{3, 5\}$, but not for $\mu \in \{8, 9, 10\}$.

3.3 Switchable Leaves and Attributes

For a Key-Policy ABE with Switchable Attributes (SA-KP-ABE), leaves in the access-tree can be made active or passive, and attributes in the ciphertext can be made valid or invalid. We thus enhance the access-tree $\mathcal{T}$ into $\tilde{\mathcal{T}} = (\mathcal{T}, \mathcal{L}_a, \mathcal{L}_p)$, where the implicit set of leaves $\mathcal{L} = \mathcal{L}_a \uplus \mathcal{L}_p$ is now the explicit disjoint union of the active-leaf and passive-leaf sets. Similarly, a ciphertext will be associated to the pair (Γ_v, Γ_i), also referred as a disjoint union $\Gamma = \Gamma_v \uplus \Gamma_i$, of the valid-attribute and invalid-attribute sets.

We note $\tilde{\mathcal{T}}(\Gamma_v, \Gamma_i) = 1$ if there is an evaluation pruned tree $\mathcal{T}'$ of $\mathcal{T}$ that is satisfied by $\Gamma = \Gamma_v \uplus \Gamma_i$ (*i.e.*, $\mathcal{T}' \in \mathsf{EPT}(\mathcal{T}, \Gamma)$), with the additional condition that all the active leaves in $\mathcal{T}'$ correspond only to valid attributes in Γ_v: $\exists \mathcal{T}' \in \mathsf{EPT}(\mathcal{T}, \Gamma), \forall \lambda \in \mathcal{T}' \cap \mathcal{L}_a$, $A(\lambda) \in \Gamma_v$. In other words, this means that an invalid attribute in the ciphertext should be considered as inexistent for active leaves, but only for those leaves.

We also have to enhance the partial order on $\mathcal{T}$ to $\tilde{\mathcal{T}}$, so that we can deal with delegation: $\tilde{\mathcal{T}}' = (\mathcal{T}', \mathcal{L}'_a, \mathcal{L}'_p) \leq \tilde{\mathcal{T}} = (\mathcal{T}, \mathcal{L}_a, \mathcal{L}_p)$ if and only if $\mathcal{T}' \leq \mathcal{T}$, $\mathcal{L}'_a \cap \mathcal{L}_p = \mathcal{L}'_p \cap \mathcal{L}_a = \emptyset$ and $\mathcal{L}'_a \subseteq \mathcal{L}_a$. More concretely, $\mathcal{T}'$ must be more restrictive, existing leaves cannot change their passive or active status, and new leaves can only be passive.

3.4 Key-Policy Attribute-Based Encapsulation with Switchable Attributes

We can now define the algorithms of an SA-KP-ABE, with the usual description of Key Encapsulation Mechanism, that consists in generating an ephemeral key K and its encapsulation C. The encryption of the actual message under the key K, using a symmetric encryption scheme is then appended to C. We will however call

C the *ciphertext*, and K the *encapsulated key* in C. In our definitions, there are two secret keys: the master secret key MK for the generation of users' keys, and the secret key SK for running the advanced encapsulation with invalid attributes:

Setup(1^κ). From the security parameter κ, the algorithm defines all the global parameters PK, the secret key SK and the master secret key MK;

KeyGen(MK, $\tilde{\mathcal{T}}$). The algorithm outputs a key $\mathsf{dk}_{\tilde{\mathcal{T}}}$ which enables the user to decapsulate keys generated under a set of attributes $\Gamma = \Gamma_v \uplus \Gamma_i$ if and only if $\tilde{\mathcal{T}}(\Gamma_v, \Gamma_i) = 1$;

Delegate($\mathsf{dk}_{\tilde{\mathcal{T}}}, \tilde{\mathcal{T}}'$). Given a key $\mathsf{dk}_{\tilde{\mathcal{T}}}$, generated from either the KeyGen or the Delegate algorithms, for a policy $\tilde{\mathcal{T}}$ and a more restrictive policy $\tilde{\mathcal{T}}' \leq \tilde{\mathcal{T}}$, the algorithm outputs a decryption key $\mathsf{dk}_{\mathcal{T}'}$;

Encaps(PK, Γ). For a set Γ of (valid only) attributes, the algorithm generates the ciphertext C and an encapsulated key K;

Encaps*(SK, Γ_v, Γ_i). For a pair (Γ_v, Γ_i) of disjoint sets of valid/invalid attributes, the algorithm generates the ciphertext C and an encapsulated key K;

Decaps($\mathsf{dk}_{\tilde{\mathcal{T}}}, C$). Given the key $\mathsf{dk}_{\tilde{\mathcal{T}}}$ from either KeyGen or Delegate, and the ciphertext C, the algorithm outputs the encapsulated key K.

We stress that fresh keys (from the KeyGen algorithm) and delegated keys (from the Delegate algorithm) are of the same form, and can both be used for decryption and can both be delegated. This allows multi-hop delegation.

On the other hand, one can note the difference between Encaps with PK and Encaps* with SK, where the former runs the latter on the pair $(\Gamma, \emptyset)$. And as $\Gamma_i = \emptyset$, the public key is enough. This is thus still a public-key encryption scheme when only valid attributes are in the ciphertext, but the invalidation of some attributes require the secret key SK. For the advanced reader, this will lead to secret-key traceability, as only the owner of SK will be able to invalidate attributes for the tracing procedure (as explained in Sect. 5). For correctness, the Decaps algorithm should output the encapsulated key K if and only if C has been generated for a pair (Γ_v, Γ_i) that satisfies the policy $\tilde{\mathcal{T}}$ of the decryption key $\mathsf{dk}_{\tilde{\mathcal{T}}}$: $\tilde{\mathcal{T}}(\Gamma_v, \Gamma_i) = 1$. The following security notion enforces this property. But some other indistinguishability notions need to be defined in order to be able to exploit these switchable attributes in more complex protocols.

3.5 Security Notions

For the sake of simplicity, we focus on one-challenge definitions (one encapsulation with Real-or-Random encapsulated key, one user key with Real-or-All-Passive leaves, and one encapsulation with Real-or-All-Valid attributes), in the same vein as the Find-then-Guess security game. But the adversary could generate additional values, as they can either be publicly generated or an oracle is available. Then, the definitions can be turned into multi-challenge security games, with an hybrid proof, as explained in [2].

Definition 6 (Delegation-Indistinguishability for SA-KP-ABE). *Del-IND security for SA-KP-ABE is defined by the following game:*

Initialize: *The challenger runs the* Setup *algorithm of SA-KP-ABE and gives the public parameters* PK *to the adversary;*

Oracles: *The following oracles can be called in any order and any number of times, except for* RoREncaps *which can be called only once.*

- OKeyGen($\tilde{\mathcal{T}}$)*: this models a* KeyGen*-query for any access-tree* $\tilde{\mathcal{T}} = (\mathcal{T}, \mathcal{L}_a, \mathcal{L}_p)$*. It generates the decryption key but only outputs the index* k *of the key;*
- ODelegate($k, \tilde{\mathcal{T}}'$)*: this models a* Delegate*-query for any more restrictive access-tree* $\tilde{\mathcal{T}}' \leq \tilde{\mathcal{T}}$*, for the* k*-indexed generated decryption key for* $\tilde{\mathcal{T}}$*. It generates the decryption key but only outputs the index* k' *of the new key;*
- OGetKey(k)*: the adversary gets back the* k*-indexed decryption key generated by* OKeyGen *or* ODelegate *oracles;*
- OEncaps(Γ_v, Γ_i)*: The adversary may be allowed to issue* Encaps**-queries, with* $(K, C) \leftarrow \mathsf{Encaps}^*(\mathsf{SK}, \Gamma_v, \Gamma_i)$*, and* C *is returned;*
- RoREncaps(Γ_v, Γ_i)*: The adversary submits a unique real-or-random encapsulation query on a set of attributes* $\Gamma = \Gamma_v \uplus \Gamma_i$*. The challenger asks for an encapsulation query on* (Γ_v, Γ_i) *and receives* (K_0, C)*. It also generates a random key* K_1*. It eventually flips a random coin* b*, and outputs* (K_b, C) *to the adversary;*

Finalize(b'): *The adversary outputs a guess* b' *for* b*. If for some access-tree* $\tilde{\mathcal{T}}'$ *corresponding to a key asked to the* OGetKey*-oracle,* $\tilde{\mathcal{T}}'(\Gamma_v, \Gamma_i) = 1$*, on the challenge set* (Γ_v, Γ_i)*,* $\beta \stackrel{\$}{\leftarrow} \{0, 1\}$*, otherwise one sets* $\beta = b'$*. One outputs* β*.*

$\mathsf{Adv}^{\mathsf{del\text{-}ind}}(\mathcal{A})$ *denotes the advantage of an adversary* $\mathcal{A}$ *in this game.*

In the basic form of Del-IND-security, where Encaps* encapsulations are not available, the RoREncaps-oracle only allows $\Gamma_i = \emptyset$, and no OEncaps-oracle is available. But as Encaps (with $\Gamma_i = \emptyset$) is a public-key algorithm, the adversary can generate valid ciphertexts by himself. We will call it "Del-IND-security for Encaps". For the more advanced security level, RoREncaps-query will be allowed on any pair (Γ_v, Γ_i), with the additional OEncaps-oracle. We will call it "Del-IND-security for Encaps*".

With these disjoint unions of $\mathcal{L} = \mathcal{L}_a \uplus \mathcal{L}_p$ and $\Gamma = \Gamma_v \uplus \Gamma_i$, we will also consider some indistinguishability notions on $(\mathcal{L}_a, \mathcal{L}_p)$ and (Γ_v, Γ_i), about which leaves are active or passive in $\mathcal{L} = \mathcal{L}_a \uplus \mathcal{L}_p$ for a given key, and which attributes are valid or invalid in $\Gamma = \Gamma_v \uplus \Gamma_i$ for a given ciphertext. The former will be the key-indistinguishability, whereas the latter will be attribute-indistinguishability. Again, as Encaps is public-key, the adversary can generate valid encapsulations by himself. However, we may provide access to an OEncaps-oracle to allow Encaps* queries, but with constraints in the final step, to exclude trivial attacks against key-indistinguishability. Similarly there will be constraints in the final step on the OKeyGen/ODelegate-queries for the attribute-indistinguishability.

Definition 7 (Key-Indistinguishability). *Key-IND security for SA-KP-ABE is defined by the following game:*

Initialize: *The challenger runs the* Setup *algorithm of SA-KP-ABE and gives the public parameters* PK *to the adversary;*

Oracles: $\mathsf{OKeyGen}(\tilde{\mathcal{T}})$, $\mathsf{ODelegate}(k, \tilde{\mathcal{T}}')$, $\mathsf{OGetKey}(k)$, $\mathsf{OEncaps}(\Gamma_v, \Gamma_i)$, *and* $\mathsf{RoAPKeyGen}(\tilde{\mathcal{T}})$: *The adversary submits one Real or All-Passive* KeyGen-*query for any access structure* $\tilde{\mathcal{T}}$ *of its choice, with a list* $\mathcal{L} = \mathcal{L}_a \uplus \mathcal{L}_p$ *of active and passive leaves, and gets* $\mathsf{dk}_0 = \mathsf{KeyGen}(\mathsf{MK}, (\mathcal{T}, \mathcal{L}_a, \mathcal{L}_p))$ *or* $\mathsf{dk}_1 = \mathsf{KeyGen}(\mathsf{MK}, (\mathcal{T}, \emptyset, \mathcal{L}))$. *It eventually flips a random coin* b, *and outputs* dk_b *to the adversary;*

Finalize(b'): *The adversary outputs a guess* b' *for* b. *If for some* (Γ_v, Γ_i) *asked to the* OEncaps-*oracle,* $\mathcal{T}(\Gamma_v \uplus \Gamma_i) = 1$, *for the challenge access-tree* $\mathcal{T}$ *where* $\mathcal{L} = \mathcal{L}_a \uplus \mathcal{L}_p$, $\beta \stackrel{\$}{\leftarrow} \{0, 1\}$, *otherwise one sets* $\beta = b'$. *One outputs* β.

$\mathsf{Adv}^{\mathsf{key\text{-}ind}}(\mathcal{A})$ *denotes the advantage of an adversary* $\mathcal{A}$ *in this game.*

In this first definition, the constraints in the finalize step require the adversary not to ask for an encapsulation on attributes that would be accepted by the policy with all-passive attributes in the leaves.

A second version deals with accepting policies: it allows encapsulations on attributes that would be accepted by the policy with all-passive leaves in the challenge key, until attributes associated to the active leaves in the challenge key and invalid attributes in the ciphertexts are **distinct**. Hence, the **Distinct Key-Indistinguishability** (dKey-IND) where **Finalize**(b') reads: *The adversary outputs a guess* b' *for* b. *If some active leaf* $\lambda \in \mathcal{L}_a$ *from the challenge key corresponds to some invalid attribute* $t \in \Gamma_i$ *in an* OEncaps-*query, then set* $\beta \stackrel{\$}{\leftarrow} \{0, 1\}$, *otherwise set* $\beta = b'$. *One outputs* β.

Definition 8 (Attribute-Indistinguishability). *Att-IND security for SA-KP-ABE is defined by the following game:*

Initialize: *The challenger runs the* Setup *algorithm of SA-KP-ABE and gives the public parameters* PK *to the adversary;*

Oracles: $\mathsf{OKeyGen}(\tilde{\mathcal{T}})$, $\mathsf{ODelegate}(k, \tilde{\mathcal{T}}')$, $\mathsf{OGetKey}(k)$, $\mathsf{OEncaps}(\Gamma_v, \Gamma_i)$, *and* $\mathsf{RoAVEncaps}(\Gamma_v, \Gamma_i)$: *The adversary submits one Real-or-All-Valid encapsulation query on distinct sets of attributes* (Γ_v, Γ_i). *The challenger generates* $(K, C) \leftarrow \mathsf{Encaps}^*(\mathsf{SK}, \Gamma_v, \Gamma_i)$ *as the real case, if* $b = 0$, *or* $(K, C) \leftarrow \mathsf{Encaps}(\mathsf{PK}, \Gamma_v \uplus \Gamma_i)$ *as the all-valid case, if* $b = 1$, *and outputs* C *to the adversary;*

Finalize(b'): *The adversary outputs a guess* b' *for* b. *If for some access-tree* $\tilde{\mathcal{T}}'$ *corresponding to a key asked to the* OGetKey-*oracle,* $\tilde{\mathcal{T}}'(\Gamma_v \uplus \Gamma_i, \emptyset) = 1$, *on the challenge set* (Γ_v, Γ_i), $\beta \stackrel{\$}{\leftarrow} \{0, 1\}$, *else one sets* $\beta = b'$. *One outputs* β.

$\mathsf{Adv}^{\mathsf{att\text{-}ind}}(\mathcal{A})$ *denotes the advantage of an adversary* $\mathcal{A}$ *in this game.*

This definition is a kind of attribute-hiding, where a user with keys for access-trees that are not satisfied by $\Gamma = \Gamma_v \uplus \Gamma_i$ cannot distinguish valid from invalid attributes in the ciphertext.

As above on key-indistinguishability, this first definition excludes accepting policies on the challenge ciphertext. However, for tracing, one also needs to deal with ciphertexts on accepting policies. More precisely, we must allow keys and a challenge ciphertext that would be accepted in the all-valid case, and still have indistinguishability, until attributes associated to the active leaves in the keys and invalid attributes in the challenge ciphertext are **distinct**. Hence, the **Distinct Attribute-Indistinguishability** (dAtt-IND) where **Finalize**(b') reads: *The adversary outputs a guess b' for b. If some attribute $t \in \Gamma_i$ from the challenge query corresponds to some active leaf $\lambda \in \mathcal{L}'_a$ in a* OGetKey*-query, then set $\beta \stackrel{\$}{\leftarrow} \{0,1\}$, otherwise set $\beta = b'$. One outputs β.*

4 Our SA-KP-ABE Scheme

4.1 Description of Our KP-ABE with Switchable Attributes

We extend the basic KP-ABE scheme proven in the full version [6], with leaves that can be made active or passive in a decryption key, and some attributes can be made valid or invalid in a ciphertext, and prove that it still achieves the Del-IND-security. For our construction, we will use two DPVS, of dimensions 3 and 9 respectively, in a pairing-friendly setting $(\mathbb{G}_1, \mathbb{G}_2, \mathbb{G}_t, e, G_1, G_2, q)$, using the notations introduced in Sect. 2.1. Essentially, we introduce a 7-th component to deal with switchable attributes. The two new basis-vectors $\mathbf{d}_7$ and $\mathbf{d}_7^*$ are in the secret key SK and the master secret key MK respectively. The two additional 8-th and 9-th components are to deal with the unbounded universe of attributes, to be able to use the adaptive Index-Ind property (see Theorem 3), instead of the static one. These additional components are hidden, and for the proof only:

Setup(1^κ). The algorithm chooses two random dual orthogonal bases

$$\mathbb{B} = (\mathbf{b}_1, \mathbf{b}_2, \mathbf{b}_3) \quad \mathbb{B}^* = (\mathbf{b}_1^*, \mathbf{b}_2^*, \mathbf{b}_3^*) \quad \mathbb{D} = (\mathbf{d}_1, \ldots, \mathbf{d}_9) \quad \mathbb{D}^* = (\mathbf{d}_1^*, \ldots, \mathbf{d}_9^*).$$

It sets the public parameters $\mathsf{PK} = \{(\mathbf{b}_1, \mathbf{b}_3, \mathbf{b}_1^*), (\mathbf{d}_1, \mathbf{d}_2, \mathbf{d}_3, \mathbf{d}_1^*, \mathbf{d}_2^*, \mathbf{d}_3^*)\}$, whereas the master secret key is $\mathsf{MK} = \{\mathbf{b}_3^*, \mathbf{d}_7^*\}$ and the secret key is $\mathsf{SK} = \{\mathbf{d}_7\}$. Other basis vectors are kept hidden.

KeyGen($\mathsf{MK}, \tilde{\mathcal{T}}$). For an extended access-tree $\tilde{\mathcal{T}} = (\mathcal{T}, \mathcal{L}_a, \mathcal{L}_p)$, the algorithm first chooses a random $a_0 \stackrel{\$}{\leftarrow} \mathbb{Z}_q$, and a random a_0-labeling $(a_\lambda)_\lambda$ of the access-tree $\mathcal{T}$, and builds the key:

$$\mathbf{k}_0^* = (a_0, 0, 1)_{\mathbb{B}^*} \qquad \mathbf{k}_\lambda^* = (\pi_\lambda(1, t_\lambda), a_\lambda, 0, 0, 0, r_\lambda, 0, 0)_{\mathbb{D}^*}$$

for all the leaves λ, where $t_\lambda = A(\lambda)$, $\pi_\lambda \stackrel{\$}{\leftarrow} \mathbb{Z}_q$, and $r_\lambda \stackrel{\$}{\leftarrow} \mathbb{Z}_q^*$ if λ is an active leaf in the key ($\lambda \in \mathcal{L}_a$) or else $r_\lambda = 0$ for a passive leaf ($\lambda \in \mathcal{L}_p$). The decryption key $\mathsf{dk}_{\tilde{\mathcal{T}}}$ is then $(\mathbf{k}_0^*, (\mathbf{k}_\lambda^*)_\lambda)$.

Delegate($\mathsf{dk}_{\tilde{\mathcal{T}}}, \tilde{\mathcal{T}}'$). Given a private key for a tree $\tilde{\mathcal{T}}$ and a more restrictive subtree $\tilde{\mathcal{T}}' \leq \tilde{\mathcal{T}}$, the algorithm creates a delegated key $\mathsf{dk}_{\tilde{\mathcal{T}}'}$. It chooses a random $a'_0 \stackrel{\$}{\leftarrow} \mathbb{Z}_q$ and a random a'_0-labeling $(a'_\lambda)_\lambda$ of $\mathcal{T}'$; Then, it updates $\mathbf{k}_0^* \leftarrow \mathbf{k}_0^* + (a'_0, 0, 0)_{\mathbb{B}^*}$; It sets $\mathbf{k}_\lambda^* \leftarrow (\pi'_\lambda \cdot (1, t_\lambda), a'_\lambda, 0, 0, 0, 0, 0, 0)_{\mathbb{B}^*}$ for a new leaf, or updates $\mathbf{k}_\lambda^* \leftarrow \mathbf{k}_\lambda^* + (\pi'_\lambda \cdot (1, t_\lambda), a'_\lambda, 0, 0, 0, 0, 0, 0)_{\mathbb{B}^*}$ for an old leaf, with $\pi'_\lambda \stackrel{\$}{\leftarrow} \mathbb{Z}_q$.

$\mathsf{Encaps}(\mathsf{PK}, \Gamma)$. For a set Γ of attributes, the algorithm first chooses random scalars $\omega, \xi \xleftarrow{\$} \mathbb{Z}_q$. It then sets $K = g_t^\xi$ and generates the ciphertext $C = (\mathbf{c}_0, (\mathbf{c}_t)_{t\in\Gamma})$ where

$$\mathbf{c}_0 = (\omega, 0, \xi)_\mathbb{B} \qquad\qquad \mathbf{c}_t = (\sigma_t(t, -1), \omega, 0, 0, 0, 0, 0, 0)_\mathbb{D}$$

for all the attributes $t \in \Gamma$, with $\sigma_t \xleftarrow{\$} \mathbb{Z}_q$.

$\mathsf{Encaps}^*(\mathsf{SK}, (\Gamma_v, \Gamma_i))$. For a disjoint union $\Gamma = \Gamma_v \uplus \Gamma_i$ of sets of attributes (Γ_v is the set of valid attributes and Γ_i is the set of invalid attributes), the algorithm first chooses random scalars $\omega, \xi \xleftarrow{\$} \mathbb{Z}_q$. It then sets $K = g_t^\xi$ and generates the ciphertext $C = (\mathbf{c}_0, (\mathbf{c}_t)_{t\in(\Gamma_v \uplus \Gamma_i)})$ where

$$\mathbf{c}_0 = (\omega, 0, \xi)_\mathbb{B} \qquad\qquad \mathbf{c}_t = (\sigma_t(t, -1), \omega, 0, 0, 0, u_t, 0, 0)_\mathbb{D}$$

for all the attributes $t \in \Gamma_v \uplus \Gamma_i$, $\sigma_t \xleftarrow{\$} \mathbb{Z}_q$ and $u_t \xleftarrow{\$} \mathbb{Z}_q^*$ if $t \in \Gamma_i$ or $u_t = 0$ if $t \in \Gamma_v$.

$\mathsf{Decaps}(\mathsf{dk}_{\tilde{\mathcal{T}}}, C)$. The algorithm first selects an evaluation pruned tree $\mathcal{T}'$ of $\mathcal{T}$ that is satisfied by $\Gamma = \Gamma_v \cup \Gamma_i$, such that any leaf λ in $\mathcal{T}'$ is either passive in the key ($\lambda \in \mathcal{L}_p$) or associated to a valid attribute in the ciphertext ($t_\lambda \in \Gamma_v$). This means that the labels a_λ for all the leaves λ in $\mathcal{T}'$ allow to reconstruct a_0 by simple additions, where $t = t_\lambda$:

$$\mathbf{c}_t \times \mathbf{k}_\lambda^* = g_t^{\sigma_t \cdot \pi_\lambda \cdot \langle (t,-1),(1,t_\lambda)\rangle + \omega\cdot a_\lambda + u_t \cdot r_\lambda} = g_t^{\omega\cdot a_\lambda},$$

as $u_t = 0$ or $r_\lambda = 0$. Hence, the algorithm can derive $g_t^{\omega\cdot a_0}$. From $\mathbf{c}_0$ and $\mathbf{k}_0^*$, it can also compute $\mathbf{c}_0 \times \mathbf{k}_0^* = g_t^{\omega\cdot a_0 + \xi}$, which then easily leads to $K = g_t^\xi$.

First, note that the delegation works as $\mathbf{b}_1^*$, $\mathbf{d}_1^*, \mathbf{d}_2^*, \mathbf{d}_3^*$ are public. This allows to create a new key for $\tilde{\mathcal{T}}' \leq \tilde{\mathcal{T}}$. But as $\mathbf{d}_7^*$ is not known, any new leaf is necessarily passive, and an active existing leaf in the original key cannot be converted to passive, and vice-versa. Indeed, all the randomnesses are fresh, except for the last components r_λ that remain unchanged: this is perfectly consistent with the definition of $\tilde{\mathcal{T}}' \leq \tilde{\mathcal{T}}$.

Second, in encapsulation, for invalidating a contribution $\mathbf{c}_t$ in the ciphertext with a non-zero u_t, for $t \in \Gamma_i$, one needs to know $\mathbf{d}_7$, hence the Encaps^* that requires SK, whereas Encaps with $\Gamma_i = \emptyset$ just needs PK.

Eventually, we stress that in the above decryption, one can recover $g_t^{\omega\cdot a_0}$ if and only if there is an evaluation pruned tree $\mathcal{T}'$ of $\mathcal{T}$ that is satisfied by Γ and the active leaves in $\tilde{\mathcal{T}}'$ correspond to valid attributes in Γ_v (used during the encapsulation). And this holds if and only if $\tilde{\mathcal{T}}(\Gamma_v, \Gamma_i) = 1$.

4.2 Del-IND-Security of Our SA-KP-ABE for Encaps

For this security notion, we first consider only valid contributions in the challenge ciphertext, with indistinguishability of the Encaps algorithm. Which means that $\Gamma_i = \emptyset$ in the challenge pair. And the security result holds even if the vector $\mathbf{d}_7$ is made public:

G_0 Real Del-IND-Security game

$$\mathbf{c}_0 = (\ \omega \quad 0 \quad \xi\ ) \quad \mathbf{c}_t = (\ \sigma_t(1,t) \quad \omega \mid 0 \quad 0 \quad 0 \quad u_t \quad 0\ 0\ )$$
$$\mathbf{k}^*_{\ell,0} = (\ a_{\ell,0} \quad 0 \quad 1\ ) \quad \mathbf{k}^*_{\ell,\lambda} = (\ \pi_{\ell,\lambda}(t_{\ell,\lambda},-1) \quad a_{\ell,\lambda} \mid 0 \quad 0 \quad 0 \quad r_{\ell,\lambda} \quad 0\ 0\ )$$

G_1 SubSpace-Ind Property, on $(\mathbb{B},\mathbb{B}^*)_{1,2}$ and $(\mathbb{D},\mathbb{D}^*)_{3,4}$, between 0 and $\tau \xleftarrow{\$} \mathbb{Z}_q$

$$\mathbf{c}_0 = (\ \omega \quad \tau \quad \xi\ ) \quad \mathbf{c}_t = (\ \sigma_t(1,t) \quad \omega \mid \tau \quad 0 \quad 0 \quad u_t \quad 0\ 0\ )$$
$$\mathbf{k}^*_{\ell,0} = (\ a_{\ell,0} \quad 0 \quad 1\ ) \quad \mathbf{k}^*_{\ell,\lambda} = (\ \pi_{\ell,\lambda}(t_{\ell,\lambda},-1) \quad a_{\ell,\lambda} \mid 0 \quad 0 \quad 0 \quad r_{\ell,\lambda} \quad 0\ 0\ )$$

G_2 SubSpace-Ind Property, on $(\mathbb{D},\mathbb{D}^*)_{1,2,6}$, between 0 and τz_t

$$\mathbf{c}_0 = (\ \omega \quad \tau \quad \xi\ ) \quad \mathbf{c}_t = (\ \sigma_t(1,t) \quad \omega \mid \tau \quad 0 \quad \tau z_t \quad u_t \quad 0\ 0\ )$$
$$\mathbf{k}^*_{\ell,0} = (\ a_{\ell,0} \quad 0 \quad 1\ ) \quad \mathbf{k}^*_{\ell,\lambda} = (\ \pi_{\ell,\lambda}(t_{\ell,\lambda},-1) \quad a_{\ell,\lambda} \mid 0 \quad 0 \quad 0 \quad r_{\ell,\lambda} \quad 0\ 0\ )$$

G_3 Introduction of an additional random-labeling.

$$\mathbf{c}_0 = (\ \omega \quad \tau \quad \xi\ ) \quad \mathbf{c}_t = (\ \sigma_t(1,t) \quad \omega \mid \tau \quad 0 \quad \tau z_t \quad u_t \quad 0\ 0\ )$$
$$\mathbf{k}^*_{\ell,0} = (\ a_{\ell,0} \quad r_{\ell,0} \quad 1\ ) \quad \mathbf{k}^*_{\ell,\lambda} = (\ \pi_{\ell,\lambda}(t_{\ell,\lambda},-1) \quad a_{\ell,\lambda} \mid 0 \quad 0 \quad \frac{s_{\ell,\lambda}}{z_{t_{\ell,\lambda}}} \quad r_{\ell,\lambda} \quad 0\ 0\ )$$

G_4 Formal basis change, on $(\mathbb{B},\mathbb{B}^*)_{2,3}$, to randomize ξ

$$\mathbf{c}_0 = (\ \omega \quad \tau \quad \xi''\ ) \quad \mathbf{c}_t = (\ \sigma_t(1,t) \quad \omega \mid \tau \quad 0 \quad \tau z_t \quad u_t \quad 0\ 0\ )$$
$$\mathbf{k}^*_{\ell,0} = (\ a_{\ell,0} \quad r_{\ell,0} \quad 1\ ) \quad \mathbf{k}^*_{\ell,\lambda} = (\ \pi_{\ell,\lambda}(t_{\ell,\lambda},-1) \quad a_{\ell,\lambda} \mid 0 \quad 0 \quad \frac{s_{\ell,\lambda}}{z_{t_{\ell,\lambda}}} \quad r_{\ell,\lambda} \quad 0\ 0\ )$$

Gray cells x mean they have been changed in this game.

Fig. 4. Global sequence for the Del-IND-security proof of our SA-KP-ABE

Theorem 9. *Our SA-KP-ABE scheme is Del-IND for* Encaps *(with only valid attributes in the challenge ciphertext), even if* $\mathbf{d}_7$ *is public.*

The proof essentially reduces to the IND-security result of the KP-ABE scheme, and is available in the full version [6]. We present an overview of the proof, as the structure of the first games is common among most of our proofs. The global sequence of games is described on Fig. 4, where $(\mathbf{c}_0, (\mathbf{c}_t))$ is the challenge ciphertext for all the attributes $t \in \Gamma$, and $(\mathbf{k}^*_{\ell,0}, (\mathbf{k}^*_{\ell,\lambda}))$ are the keys, for $1 \leq \ell \leq K$, and $\lambda \in \mathcal{L}_\ell$ for each ℓ-query, with active and passive leaves.

In the two first games G_1 and G_2, one is preparing the floor with a random τ and random masks z_t in the ciphertexts $\mathbf{c}_t$ (actually, the challenge ciphertext corresponding to the attribute t). Note that until the actual challenge query is asked, one does not exactly know the attributes in Γ (as we are in the adaptive-set setting), thus we will decide on the random mask z_t, where t is virtually associated to the number of the attribute in their order of apparition in the security game. The main step is to get to Game G_3, starting with an additional labeling $(s_{\ell,0}, (s_{\ell,\lambda})_\lambda)$, using hybrid games that begins from Game G_2. To do this, the new labelling is added in each ℓ-th key, then each label is masked by the random z_t for each attribute t. One then exploits the limitations expected from the adversary in the security game: the adversary cannot ask keys on access-trees $\mathcal{T}$ such that $\mathcal{T}(\Gamma) = 1$, for the challenge set Γ. This limitation translates into the value $s_{\ell,0}$ being unpredictable for the adversary with regards to $(s_{\ell,\lambda})_\lambda$, as for each key requested by the adversary, there is at least one $s_{\ell,\lambda}$ by lack of a corresponding ciphertext. Thus, we can replace $s_{\ell,0}$ by a random independent

$r_{\ell,0}$ without giving any advantage to the adversary. To formally mask the shares $s_{\ell,\lambda}$, we need another level of hybrid games: we will change all the keys associated with a specific attribute λ at the same time, by using the Adaptive Index-Ind technique. This allows us to mask the $s_{\ell,\lambda}$ share in each key with z_t, one λ at a time inside the ℓ-th key.

Simulation of delegation can just be done by using the key generation algorithm, making sure we use the same randomness for all the keys delegated from the same one. As the vector $\mathbf{d}_7^*$ is known to the simulator, this is easy. As $\mathbf{d}_7$ is public, the adversary can run by himself both Encaps and Encaps*.

We stress that our construction makes more basis vectors public, than in the schemes from [15], as only $\mathbf{b}_3^*$ is for the key issuer. This makes the proof more tricky, but this is the reason why we can deal with delegation for any user.

4.3 Del-IND-Security of Our SA-KP-ABE for Encaps*

We now study the full indistinguishability of the ciphertext generated by an Encaps* challenge, with delegated keys. The intuition is that when $u_t \cdot r_{\ell,\lambda} \neq 0$, the share $a_{\ell,\lambda}$ in $g_t^{\omega \cdot a_{\ell,\lambda} + u_t \cdot r_{\ell,\lambda}}$ is hidden, but we have to formally prove it.

The main issue in this proof is the need to anticipate whether $u_t \cdot r_{\ell,\lambda} = 0$ or not when simulating the keys, and the challenge ciphertext as well (even before knowing the exact query (Γ_v, Γ_i)). Without being in the selective-set setting where both Γ_v and Γ_i would have to be specified before generating the public parameters PK, we ask to know disjoint super-sets $A_v, A_i \subseteq \mathcal{U}$ of attributes. Then, in the challenge ciphertext query, we will ask that $\Gamma_v \subseteq A_v$ and $\Gamma_i \subseteq A_i$. We will call this setting the *semi-adaptive super-set* setting, where the super-sets have to be specified before the first decryption keys are issued. Furthermore, the set of attributes $\Gamma = \Gamma_v \uplus \Gamma_i$ used in the real challenge query is only specified at the moment of the challenge, as in the adaptive setting.

For this proof, $\mathbf{d}_7$ must be kept secret (cannot be provided to the adversary). We will thus give access to an Encaps* oracle. We then need to simulate it.

Theorem 10. *Our SA-KP-ABE scheme is Del-IND for* Encaps*, *in the semi-adaptive super-set setting (where $A_v, A_i \subseteq \mathcal{U}$ so that $\Gamma_v \subseteq A_v$ and $\Gamma_i \subseteq A_i$ are specified before asking for keys).*

We stress that the semi-adaptive super-set setting is much stronger than the selective-set setting where the adversary would have to specify both Γ_v and Γ_i before the setup. Here, only super-sets have to be specified, and just before the first key-query. The adversary is thus given much more power.

The full proof can be found in the full version [6], we provide some hints, that extend the above sketch: we only consider keys that are really provided to the adversary, and thus delegated keys. They can be generated as fresh keys except for the r_λ's that have to be the same for leaves in keys delegated from the same initial key. However, in order to randomize $s_{\ell,0}$ once all of the shares have been masked, one cannot directly conclude that $s_{\ell,0}$ is independent from the view of the adversary: we only know $\tilde{\mathcal{T}}_\ell(\Gamma_v, \Gamma_i) = 0$, but not necessarily $\mathcal{T}_\ell(\Gamma_v \uplus \Gamma_i) = 0$, as in the previous proof.

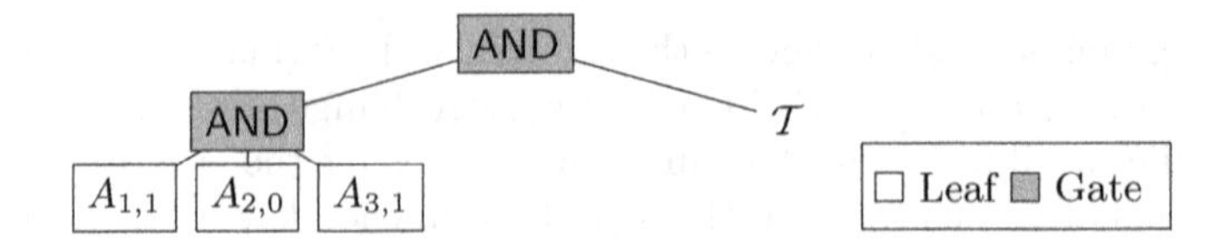

Fig. 5. Tracing sub-tree for the codeword $w = (1, 0, 1)$

To this aim, we revisit this gap with an additional sequence where we focus on the k-th key and the challenge ciphertext. In that sequence, we first prepare with additional random values $y_{\ell,\lambda}$ in all the keys, with the same repetition properties as the $r_{\ell,\lambda}$. Thereafter, in another sub-sequence of games on the attributes, we can use the Swap-Ind property to completely randomize $s_{k,\lambda}$ when $u_{t_{k,\lambda}} \cdot r_{k,\lambda} \neq 0$. Hence, the $s_{k,\lambda}$ are unknown either when $z_{t_{k,\lambda}}$ is not known (the corresponding element is not provided in the challenge ciphertext) or this is a random $s'_{k,\lambda}$ when $u_{t_{k,\lambda}} \cdot r_{k,\lambda} \neq 0$. The property of the access-tree then makes $s_{k,0}$ perfectly unpredictable, which can be replaced by a random independent $r_{k,0}$.

4.4 Distinct Indistinguishability Properties

We first claim easy results, for which the proofs are symmetrical:

Theorem 11. *Our SA-KP-ABE scheme is dKey-IND, even if* $\mathbf{d}_7^*$ *is public.*

Theorem 12. *Our SA-KP-ABE scheme is dAtt-IND, even if* $\mathbf{d}_7$ *is public.*

Both proofs can be found in the full version [6]. In these alternative variants, all the invalid attributes in all the queried ciphertexts do not correspond to any active leaf in the challenge keys (for dKey-IND) or all active leaves in all the queried keys do not correspond to any invalid attribute in the challenge ciphertext (for dAtt-IND). Then, we can gradually replace all the real keys by all-passive in the former proof or all the real ciphertexts by all-valid in the latter proof.

4.5 Attribute-Indistinguishability

Theorem 13. *Our SA-KP-ABE scheme is Att-IND, even if* $\mathbf{d}_7$ *is public, if all the active keys correspond to independent leaves with respect to the set of attributes* $\Gamma = \Gamma_v \uplus \Gamma_i$ *in the challenge ciphertext.*

The proof can be found in the full version [6]. This is an important result with respect to our target application of tracing, combined with possible revocation. Indeed, with such a result, if a user is excluded independently of the tracing procedure (the policy would reject him even if all his passive leaves match valid attributes in the ciphertext), he will not be able to detect whether there are invalid attributes in the ciphertext and thus that the ciphertext is from a tracing procedure. This gives us a strong resistance to collusion.

5 Application to Tracing

In our Traitor-Tracing approach, any user would be given a key associated to a word in a traceable code at key generation time. To embed a word inside a key, the key generation authority only needs to create a new policy for a user with policy $\mathcal{T}$: the new policy will be a root AND gate, that connects the original access-tree $\mathcal{T}$ as one child, and a word-based access-tree composed of active leaves as another child, as illustrated on Fig. 5.

From there, the tracing authority, using the secret key SK, could trace any Pirate Decoder by invalidating attributes associated to the positions in words, one position at a time. Since an adversary cannot know whether attributes are valid or invalid, until it is not impacted by the invalid attributes (thanks to the Distinct Attribute-Indistinguishability), he will answer each queries of the tracer, when it is able to do it, effectively revealing the bits of his word on each position, until the tracer finds his complete word, to eventually trace back the traitors, from the traceable-code properties. Furthermore, thanks to the Attribute-Indistinguishability (not Distinct), a traitor that has been identified by the tracing authority can be removed from the target set at tracing time, and can thus no longer participate in the coalition, as it will be excluded from the policy, whatever the valid/invalid attributes. We stress that the secret key SK is required for invalidating some attributes, and so for the tracing. We thus have secret-key black-box traceability. More details are given in the full version [6].

6 Conclusion

We have designed a $\mathsf{KP\text{-}ABE}$ scheme that allows an authority to generate keys with specific policies for each user, so that these users can thereafter delegate their keys for any more restrictive rights. Thanks to the (Distinct) Attribute-Indistinguishability and Attribute-Indistinguishability, it can also include key material for tracing a compromised key involved in a pirate device while limiting the size of collusions. In addition, with Key-Indistinguishability on active leaves and perfect randomization on passive leaves, one achieves a strong level of anonymity: one cannot detect whether two keys have been delegated by the same original key.

Acknowledgment. This work was supported in part by the French ANR Project ANR-19-CE39-0011 PRESTO.

References

1. Attrapadung, N., Tomida, J.: Unbounded dynamic predicate compositions in ABE from standard assumptions. In: Moriai, S., Wang, H. (eds.) ASIACRYPT 2020. LNCS, vol. 12493, pp. 405–436. Springer, Cham (2020). https://doi.org/10.1007/978-3-030-64840-4_14

2. Bellare, M., Desai, A., Jokipii, E., Rogaway, P.: A concrete security treatment of symmetric encryption. In: 38th FOCS, pp. 394–403. IEEE Computer Society Press, October 1997. https://doi.org/10.1109/SFCS.1997.646128
3. Chen, J., Gay, R., Wee, H.: Improved dual system ABE in prime-order groups via predicate encodings. In: Oswald, E., Fischlin, M. (eds.) EUROCRYPT 2015. LNCS, vol. 9057, pp. 595–624. Springer, Heidelberg (2015). https://doi.org/10.1007/978-3-662-46803-6_20
4. Chen, J., Gong, J., Wee, H.: Improved inner-product encryption with adaptive security and full attribute-hiding. In: Peyrin, T., Galbraith, S. (eds.) ASIACRYPT 2018. LNCS, vol. 11273, pp. 673–702. Springer, Cham (2018). https://doi.org/10.1007/978-3-030-03329-3_23
5. Chen, J., Lim, H.W., Ling, S., Wang, H., Wee, H.: Shorter IBE and signatures via asymmetric pairings. In: Abdalla, M., Lange, T. (eds.) Pairing 2012. LNCS, vol. 7708, pp. 122–140. Springer, Heidelberg (2013). https://doi.org/10.1007/978-3-642-36334-4_8
6. Delerablée, C., Gouriou, L., Pointcheval, D.: Key-policy ABE with delegation of rights. Cryptology ePrint Archive, Report 2021/867 (2021). https://eprint.iacr.org/2021/867
7. Goyal, V., Pandey, O., Sahai, A., Waters, B.: Attribute-based encryption for fine-grained access control of encrypted data. In: Juels, A., Wright, R.N., De Capitani di Vimercati, S. (eds.) ACM CCS 2006, pp. 89–98. ACM Press, October/November 2006. https://doi.org/10.1145/1180405.1180418. Available as Cryptology ePrint Archive Report 2006/309
8. Katz, J., Sahai, A., Waters, B.: Predicate encryption supporting disjunctions, polynomial equations, and inner products. In: Smart, N. (ed.) EUROCRYPT 2008. LNCS, vol. 4965, pp. 146–162. Springer, Heidelberg (2008). https://doi.org/10.1007/978-3-540-78967-3_9
9. Lewko, A., Okamoto, T., Sahai, A., Takashima, K., Waters, B.: Fully secure functional encryption: attribute-based encryption and (hierarchical) inner product encryption. In: Gilbert, H. (ed.) EUROCRYPT 2010. LNCS, vol. 6110, pp. 62–91. Springer, Heidelberg (2010). https://doi.org/10.1007/978-3-642-13190-5_4
10. Lewko, A., Waters, B.: New techniques for dual system encryption and fully secure HIBE with short ciphertexts. In: Micciancio, D. (ed.) TCC 2010. LNCS, vol. 5978, pp. 455–479. Springer, Heidelberg (2010). https://doi.org/10.1007/978-3-642-11799-2_27
11. Liu, Z., Wong, D.S.: Practical ciphertext-policy attribute-based encryption: traitor tracing, revocation, and large universe. In: Malkin, T., Kolesnikov, V., Lewko, A.B., Polychronakis, M. (eds.) ACNS 2015. LNCS, vol. 9092, pp. 127–146. Springer, Cham (2015). https://doi.org/10.1007/978-3-319-28166-7_7
12. Okamoto, T., Takashima, K.: Homomorphic encryption and signatures from vector decomposition. In: Galbraith, S.D., Paterson, K.G. (eds.) Pairing 2008. LNCS, vol. 5209, pp. 57–74. Springer, Heidelberg (2008). https://doi.org/10.1007/978-3-540-85538-5_4
13. Okamoto, T., Takashima, K.: Fully secure functional encryption with general relations from the decisional linear assumption. In: Rabin, T. (ed.) CRYPTO 2010. LNCS, vol. 6223, pp. 191–208. Springer, Heidelberg (2010). https://doi.org/10.1007/978-3-642-14623-7_11
14. Okamoto, T., Takashima, K.: Adaptively attribute-hiding (hierarchical) inner product encryption. In: Pointcheval, D., Johansson, T. (eds.) EUROCRYPT 2012. LNCS, vol. 7237, pp. 591–608. Springer, Heidelberg (2012). https://doi.org/10.1007/978-3-642-29011-4_35

15. Okamoto, T., Takashima, K.: Fully secure unbounded inner-product and attribute-based encryption. In: Wang, X., Sako, K. (eds.) ASIACRYPT 2012. LNCS, vol. 7658, pp. 349–366. Springer, Heidelberg (2012). https://doi.org/10.1007/978-3-642-34961-4_22
16. Waters, B.: Dual system encryption: realizing fully secure IBE and HIBE under simple assumptions. In: Halevi, S. (ed.) CRYPTO 2009. LNCS, vol. 5677, pp. 619–636. Springer, Heidelberg (2009). https://doi.org/10.1007/978-3-642-03356-8_36

Mix-Nets from Re-randomizable and Replayable CCA-Secure Public-Key Encryption

Antonio Faonio and Luigi Russo(✉)

EURECOM, Sophia Antipolis, France
{faonio,russol}@eurecom.fr

Abstract. Mix-nets are protocols that allow a set of senders to send messages anonymously. Faonio *et al.* (ASIACRYPT'19) showed how to instantiate mix-net protocols based on Public-Verifiable Re-randomizable Replayable CCA-secure (Rand-RCCA) PKE schemes. The bottleneck of their approach is that public-verifiable Rand-RCCA PKEs are less efficient than typical CPA-secure re-randomizable PKEs. In this paper, we revisit their mix-net protocol, showing how to get rid of the cumbersome public-verifiability property, and we give a more efficient instantiation for the mix-net protocol based on a (non publicly-verifiable) Rand-RCCA scheme. Additionally, we give a more careful security analysis of their mix-net protocol.

1 Introduction

Mixing Networks (aka mix-nets), originally proposed by Chaum [11], are protocols that allow a set of senders to send messages anonymously. Typically, a mix-net is realized by a chain of mix-servers (aka mixers) that work as follows. Senders encrypt their messages and send the ciphertexts to the first mix-server in the chain; each mix-server applies a transformation to every ciphertext (e.g., partial decryption, or re-encryption), re-orders the ciphertexts according to a secret random permutation, and passes the new list to the next mix-server. The idea is that the list returned by the last mixer contains (either in clear or encrypted form, depending on the mixing approach) the messages sent by the senders in a randomly permuted order.

Mix-net protocols are fundamental building blocks to achieve privacy in a variety of application scenarios, including anonymous e-mail [11], anonymous payments [24], and electronic voting [11]. Informally, the basic security property of mix-nets asks that, when enough mix-servers are honest, the privacy of the senders of the messages (i.e., "who sent what") is preserved. In several applications, it is also desirable to achieve correctness even in the presence of an arbitrary number of dishonest mixers. This is for example fundamental in electronic voting where a dishonest mixer could replace all the ciphertexts with encrypted votes for the desired candidate.

C. Galdi and S. Jarecki (Eds.): SCN 2022, LNCS 13409, pp. 172–196, 2022.
https://doi.org/10.1007/978-3-031-14791-3_8

Realizing Mix-Nets. A popular design paradigm of mixing networks are *re-encryption mix-nets* [27] in which each server decrypts and freshly encrypts every ciphertext. Interestingly, such a transformation can be computed even publicly using re-randomizable encryption schemes (e.g., El Gamal). The process of re-randomizing and randomly permuting ciphertexts is typically called a *shuffle*. Although shuffle-based mix-nets achieve privacy when all the mix-servers behave honestly, they become insecure if one or more mixers do not follow the protocol. An elegant approach proposed to solve this problem is to let each mixer prove the correctness of its shuffle with a zero-knowledge proof. This idea inspired a long series of works on zero-knowledge shuffle arguments, e.g., [5,19,20,22,26,30,32,33]. Notably, some recent works [5,30,33] improved significantly over the early solutions, and they have been implemented and tested in real-world applications (elections) [34]. In spite of the last results, zero-knowledge shuffle arguments are still a major source of inefficiency in mix-nets. This is especially a concern in applications like electronic voting where mix-nets need to be able to scale up to millions of senders (i.e., voters).

Mix-Nets from Replayable CCA Security. Most of the research effort for improving the efficiency of mix-nets has been so far devoted to improving the efficiency of shuffle arguments. A notable exception is the work of Faonio *et al.* [17]. Typical mixing networks based on re-randomizable encryption schemes make use of public-key encryption (PKE) schemes that are secure against chosen-plaintext attack (CPA), thus to obtain security against malicious mixers they leverage on the strong integrity property offered by the zero-knowledge shuffle arguments. The work of Faonio *et al.* instead showed that, by requiring stronger security properties from the re-randomizable encryption scheme, the NP-relation proved by the zero-knowledge shuffle arguments can be relaxed. This design enables faster and more efficient instantiations for the zero-knowledge proof but, on the other hand, requires more complex ciphertexts and thus a re-randomization procedure that is slower in comparison, for example, with the re-randomization procedure for ElGamal ciphertexts. More in detail, Faonio *et al.* propose a secure mixing network in the universal composability model of Canetti [7] based on re-randomizable PKE schemes that are replayable-CCA (RCCA) secure (as defined by Canetti *et al.* [9]) and publicly-verifiable. The first notion, namely RCCA security, is a relaxation of the standard notion of chosen-ciphertext security. This notion offers security against malleability attacks on the encrypted message (i.e. an attacker cannot *transform* a ciphertext of a message $\mathtt{M}$ to a ciphertext of a message $\mathtt{M}'$) but it still allows for malleability on the ciphertext (i.e. we can re-randomize the ciphertexts). The second requirement, namely public verifiability, requires that anyone in possession of the public key can check that a ciphertext decrypts correctly to a valid message, in other words, that the decryption procedure would not output an error message on input such a ciphertext. Unfortunately, this second requirement is the source of the major inefficiency in the mixing networks of Faonio *et al.*. For example, the re-randomization procedure of the state-of-art non publicly-verifiable re-randomizable PKE scheme with RCCA-security (Rand-RCCA PKE, in brief) in the random oracle model of Faonio and Fiore [16] costs 19 exponentiations in a pairing-free cryptographic group, while the re-randomization procedure of the publicly-verifiable Rand-RCCA PKE of [17] costs around 90 exponentiations plus 5 pairing operations.

1.1 Our Contribution

We revisit the mix-net design of Faonio *et al.* [17]. Our contributions are two-fold: we generalize the mix-net protocol of [17] showing how to get rid of the cumbersome public verifiability property, and we give a more efficient instantiation for the mix-net protocol based on the (non publicly-verifiable) Rand-RCCA scheme of [17]. Our generalization of the mix-net protocol is based on two main ideas. The first idea is that, although the verification of the ciphertexts is still necessary, it is not critical for the verification to be public and non-interactive. In particular, we can replace the public verifiability property with a multi-party protocol (that we call a *verify-then-decrypt* protocol) that verifies the ciphertexts before the decryption phase and that decrypts the ciphertexts from the last mixer in the chain only if the verification succeeded. The second idea is that in the design of the *verify-then-decrypt* multiparty protocol we can trade efficiency for security. In particular, we could design a protocol that eventually leaks partial information about the secret key and, if the Rand-RCCA PKE scheme is resilient against this partial leakage of the secret key, we could still obtain a secure mix-net protocol. Along the way, we additionally (1) abstract the necessary properties required by the zero-knowledge proof that the mixers need to attach to their shuffled ciphertexts and (2) give a more careful security analysis of the mixnet protocol. More technically, we define the notion *sumcheck-admissible relation* w.r.t. the Rand-RCCA PKE scheme (see Definition 2) which is a property of an NP-relation that, informally, states that given two lists of ciphertexts if all the ciphertexts in the lists decrypt to valid messages, then the sum of the messages in the first list is equal to the sum of the messages in the second list. For example, a shuffle relation is a sumcheck-admissible relation, however simpler (and easier to realize in zero-knowledge) NP-relations over the lists of ciphertexts can be considered as well.

Our second contribution is a concrete instantiation of the mix-net protocol. The main idea of our concrete protocol is that many (R)CCA PKE schemes can be conceptually divided into two main components: the first *"CPA-secure"* component assures that the messages are kept private, while the second component assures the integrity of the ciphertexts, namely, the component can identify malformed ciphertexts and avoid dangerous decryptions through the CPA-secure component. Typical examples for such PKE schemes are those based on the Cramer-Shoup paradigm [13]. Intuitively, these schemes should be secure even if the adversary gets to see the secret key associated with the second component under the constraint that once such leakage is available the adversary must lose access to the decryption oracle. This suggests a very efficient design for the *verify-then-decrypt* multiparty protocol: the mixers commit to secret shares of the secret key, once all the ciphertexts are available the mixers open to the secret key material for the second component, now any mixer can non-interactively and efficiently verify the validity of the ciphertexts. If all the ciphertexts are valid the mixers can engage a CPA-decryption multiparty protocol for the ciphertexts in the last list. As last contribution, we show that the Rand-RCCA PKE scheme of [17] is leakage resilient (under the aforementioned notion) and we instantiate all the necessary parts.

A final remark, an important property of a mixnet protocol is the so-called *auditability*[1], namely the capability of an external party to verify that a given transcript of a protocol execution has produced an alleged output. Intuitively, mixnets based on non-interactive zero-knowledge proofs of shuffle usually should have this property. However, one must be careful, because not only the shuffling phase, but the full mixnet protocol should be auditable. In particular, for our mixnet protocol to be auditable the verify-then-decrypt protocol should be auditable as well. We show that the latter protocol for our concrete instantiation is indeed auditable.

1.2 Related Work

The notion of mix-net was introduced by Chaum [11]. The use of zero-knowledge arguments to prove the correctness of a shuffle was first suggested by Sako and Kilian [29]. The first proposals used expensive *cut-and-choose*-based zero-knowledge techniques [1,29]. Abe *et al.* removed the need for cut-and-choose by proposing a shuffle based on permutation networks [2,3]. Furukawa and Sako [19] and independently Neff [26] proposed the first zero-knowledge shuffle arguments for ElGamal ciphertexts that achieve a complexity linear in the number of ciphertexts. These results have been improved by Wikström [33], and later Terelius and Wikström [30], who proposed arguments where the proof generation can be split into an offline and online phase (based on an idea of Adida and Wikström [4]). These protocols have been implemented in the Verificatum library [34]. Groth and Ishai [23] proposed the first zero-knowledge shuffle argument with sublinear communication. Bayer and Groth gave a faster argument with sublinear communication in [5]. The notion of Rand-RCCA PKE encryption was introduced by Groth [21]. The work of Prabhakaran and Rosulek [28] showed the first Rand-RCCA PKE in the standard model. The work of Faonio and Fiore [16] presented a practical Rand-RCCA PKE scheme in the random oracle model. Recently, Wang *et al.* [31] introduced the first receiver-anonymous Rand-RCCA PKE, solving the open problem raised by Prabhakaran and Rosulek in [28]. The state-of-art Rand-RCCA PKE scheme can be found in the work of Faonio *et al.* [17]. Other publicly-verifiable Rand-RCCA PKE schemes were presented by Chase *et al.* [10] and Libert *et al.* [25]. As far as we know, our design for the *verify-then-decrypt* protocol cannot be easily instantiated with the schemes in [16,28,31]. The reason is that for all these schemes the decryption procedures have a "verification step" that depends on the encrypted message.

[1] This notion is sometimes called *verifiability*, however, we prefer to use the term "auditability" to avoid confusion with the verifiability of the ciphertexts property.

2 Preliminaries

For space reasons, we give the basic preliminaries and notations in the full version [18]. Calligraphic letters denote the sets, while capital letters denote the lists (they are represented as ordered tuples). Given n lists $L_i, i \in [n]$, and an element x, we define the following operations: (i) $\mathsf{Count}(x, L_i)$ returns the number of times the value x appears in the list L_i, (ii) $\mathsf{Concat}(L_1, \dots, L_n)$ returns a list L as a concatenation of the input lists, and $L_1 \subseteq L_2$ returns 1 if each element of L_1 is contained in the list L_2, or 0 otherwise.

Re-randomizable PKE. A re-randomizable PKE (Rand-PKE) scheme PKE is a tuple of five algorithms $\mathsf{PKE} = (\mathsf{Setup}, \mathsf{KGen}, \mathsf{Enc}, \mathsf{Dec}, \mathsf{Rand})$ where the first four represent a PKE, and the last one allows for re-randomization of the ciphertexts. For space reasons, we formally define Rand-PKE and perfect re-randomizability in the full version [18]. Here we give a short description of the latter notion. The notion of perfect re-randomizability consists of three conditions: (i) the re-randomization of a valid ciphertext and a fresh ciphertext (for the same message) are equivalently distributed; (ii) the re-randomization procedure maintains correctness, i.e. the randomized ciphertext and the original decrypt to the same value, in particular, invalid ciphertexts keep being invalid; (iii) it is hard to find a valid ciphertext that is not in the support of the encryption scheme.

All-But-One Tag-Based NIZK Systems. An ABO Perfect-Hiding tag-based NIZK is a NIZK proof system with tags where there exists an algorithm $\mathsf{ABOInit}$ which on input a tag τ creates a common reference string crs together with a trapdoor such that for any tag $\tau' \neq \tau$ the trapdoor allows for zero-knowledge while for τ the proof system is adaptive sound. In an ABO Perfect-Sound tag-based NIZK, instead, for any tag $\tau' \neq \tau$ the proof system is adaptive sound, while for τ the trapdoor allows for zero-knowledge.

The Universal Composability Model. We review some basic notions of the Universal Composability model of Canetti [7] and defer the definitions in the full version [18]. In a nutshell, a protocol Π *UC-realizes* an ideal functionality $\mathcal{F}_{\mathrm{F}}$ with setup assumption $\mathcal{F}_{\mathrm{G}}$ if there exists a PPT simulator S such that no PT environment Z can distinguish an execution of the protocols Π which can interact with the setup assumption $\mathcal{F}_{\mathrm{G}}$ from a joint execution of the simulator S with the ideal functionality $\mathcal{F}_{\mathrm{F}}$. The environment Z provides the inputs to all the parties of the protocols, decides which party to corrupt (we consider static corruption, where the environment decides the corrupted parties before the protocol starts), and schedules the order of the messages in the networks. When specifying an ideal functionality, we use the "delayed outputs" terminology of Canetti [7]. Namely, when a functionality $\mathcal{F}$ *sends a public delayed output* M *to party* $\mathcal{P}$ we mean that M is first sent to the simulator and then forwarded to $\mathcal{P}$ only after acknowledgment by the simulator.

Experiment $\mathbf{Exp}^{\mathsf{1RCCA}}_{\mathcal{A},\mathsf{PKE},f}(\lambda, b)$	Oracle $\mathsf{ODec}(\mathtt{C})$
$\mathsf{prm} \leftarrow \mathsf{Setup}(1^\lambda)$	$\mathtt{M} \leftarrow \mathsf{Dec}(\mathsf{sk}, \mathtt{C})$
$(\mathsf{pk}, \mathsf{sk}) \leftarrow\!\!\$ \ \mathsf{KGen}(\mathsf{prm})$	**if** $\mathtt{M} \in \{\mathtt{M}_0, \mathtt{M}_1\}$:
$(\mathtt{M}_0, \mathtt{M}_1, z) \leftarrow \mathcal{A}_1^{\mathsf{ODec}}(\mathsf{pk})$	**return** $\diamond$
$\mathtt{C} \leftarrow\!\!\$ \ \mathsf{Enc}(\mathsf{pk}, \mathtt{M}_b)$	**return** $\mathtt{M}$
$z' \leftarrow \mathcal{A}_2^{\mathsf{ODec}}(\mathtt{C}, z)$	
$b' \leftarrow \mathcal{A}_3(f(\mathsf{sk}), z')$	
return $b' \stackrel{?}{=} b$	

Fig. 1. The lRCCA security experiment.

3 Definitions

Replayable CCA with Leakage Security. We rely on the following notion of security for Rand-PKE. Our notion is similar to the RCCA security game, with the difference that here $\mathcal{A}$ is given the additional leakage $f(\mathsf{sk})$ just before returning b'. $\mathcal{A}$ cannot invoke the decryption oracle after the leakage.

Definition 1 (RCCA with leakage Security). *Consider the experiment* $\mathbf{Exp}^{\mathsf{1RCCA}}_{\mathcal{A},\mathsf{PKE},f}$ *in Fig. 1, with parameters* λ*, an adversary* $\mathcal{A} := (\mathcal{A}_1, \mathcal{A}_2, \mathcal{A}_3)$*, a PKE scheme* PKE*, and a leakage function* f*.* PKE *is* leakage-resilient replayable CCA-secure (lRCCA-secure) *w.r.t.* f *if for any PPT adversary* $\mathcal{A}$*:*

$$\mathbf{Adv}^{\mathsf{1RCCA}}_{\mathcal{A},\mathsf{PKE},f}(\lambda) := \left|2\Pr[\mathbf{Exp}^{\mathsf{1RCCA}}_{\mathcal{A},\mathsf{PKE},f}(\lambda, b) = 1, b \leftarrow\!\!\$ \ \{0,1\}] - 1\right| \in \mathsf{negl}(\lambda).$$

The Mix-Net Ideal Functionality. The Mix-Net ideal functionality is described in Fig. 2. We follow the definition of [32]. The Mix-Net accepts input messages from the senders and waits for the acknowledgment from the mixers to run. It outputs the input messages sorted according to a specific order.

The Verify-then-Decrypt Ideal Functionality. We give in Fig. 3 the formal definition of this ideal functionality. Informally, the ideal functionality accepts two lists of ciphertexts, such that the first list includes all the ciphertexts in the second list, it first verifies that all the ciphertexts in the first list decrypt to valid messages (i.e. no decryption error) and releases such output together with the decryption from the second list. The functionality has parameter f that denotes the leakage of secret information allowed to realize such functionality.

4 Mix-Net

We now describe our mixnet protocol that UC-realizes $\mathcal{F}_{\mathsf{Mix}}$ with setup assumptions $\mathcal{F}_{\mathsf{VtDec}}$ and $\mathcal{F}_{\mathsf{crs}}$. We start by giving the definition of Sumcheck-Admissible

Functionality $\mathcal{F}_{\text{Mix}}$

The functionality has n sender parties $\mathcal{P}_{S_i}$, m mixer parties $\mathcal{P}_{M_i}$.

Input. Upon activation on message $(\mathsf{INPUT}, \mathsf{sid}, \mathtt{M})$ from $\mathcal{P}_{S_i}$ (or the adversary if $\mathcal{P}_{S_i}$ is corrupted), if $i \in L_{S,\mathsf{sid}}$ ignore the message else register the index i in the list of the senders $L_{S,\mathsf{sid}}$ and register the message $\mathtt{M}$ in the list $L_{I,\mathsf{sid}}$ of the input messages. Notify the adversary that $\mathcal{P}_{S_i}$ has sent an input.

Mix. Upon activation on message $(\mathsf{MIX}, \mathsf{sid})$ from $\mathcal{P}_{M_i}$ (or the adversary if $\mathcal{P}_{M_i}$ is corrupted), register the index i in the list of the mixers $L_{\mathsf{mix},\mathsf{sid}}$ and notify the adversary.

Delivery. Upon activation on message $(\mathsf{DELIVER}, \mathsf{sid})$ from the adversary $\mathcal{S}$ If $|L_{\mathsf{mix},\mathsf{sid}}| = m$ and $|L_{S,\mathsf{sid}}| = n$ then send a public delayed output $M_{\mathsf{sid}} \leftarrow \mathsf{Sort}(L_{I,\mathsf{sid}})$ to all the mixer parties.

Fig. 2. UC ideal functionality for MixNet.

relation with respect to a PKE. In this definition we abstract the necessary property for the zero-knowledge proof system used by the mixers in the protocol.

Definition 2 (Sumcheck-Admissible Relation w.r.t. PKE). *Let* PKE *be a public-key encryption scheme with public space $\mathcal{PK}$ and the ciphertext space being a subset of $\mathcal{CT}$. For any λ, any* $\mathsf{prm} \in \mathsf{Setup}(1^\lambda)$, *let* $\mathcal{R}_{ck}^{\mathsf{prm}} : (\mathcal{PK} \times \mathcal{CT}^{2n}) \times \{0,1\}^*$ *be an NP-relation. We parse an instance of* $\mathcal{R}_{ck}^{\mathsf{prm}}$ *as* $x = (\mathsf{pk}, L_1, L_2)$ *where* $L_j = (\mathsf{C}_i^j)_{i\in[n]}$ *for* $j \in \{1,2\}$. $\mathcal{R}_{ck}$ *is Sumcheck-Admissible w.r.t.* PKE *if:*

(Sumcheck) *For any* $(\mathsf{pk}, \mathsf{sk}) \leftarrow\$ \mathsf{KGen}(\mathsf{prm})$ *and for any* $x := (\mathsf{pk}, L_1, L_2)$ *we have that if* $x \in \mathcal{L}(\mathcal{R}_{ck})$ *and* $\forall j,i : \mathsf{Dec}(\mathsf{sk}, \mathsf{C}_i^j) \neq \bot$ *then* $\sum_i \mathsf{Dec}(\mathsf{sk}, \mathsf{C}_i^1) - \mathsf{Dec}(\mathsf{sk}, \mathsf{C}_i^2) = 0$.

(Re-Randomization Witness) *For any* $(\mathsf{pk}, \mathsf{sk}) \leftarrow\$ \mathsf{KGen}(\mathsf{prm})$ *and for any* $x := (\mathsf{pk}, L_1, L_2)$ *such that there exists* $(r_i)_{i\in[n]}$ *where* $\forall i \in [n], \exists j \in [n] : \mathsf{C}_i^2 = \mathsf{Rand}(\mathsf{pk}, \mathsf{C}_j^1; r_i)$ *we have that* $(x, (r_i)_{i\in[n]}) \in \mathcal{R}_{ck}$.

Building Blocks. Let PKE be a Rand-PKE scheme, let f be any efficiently-computable function and let $\mathcal{R}_{\mathsf{ck}}$ be any Sumcheck-Admissible relation w.r.t. PKE. The building blocks for our Mix-Net are:

1. A Rand-PKE scheme PKE that is lRCCA-secure w.r.t. f (cfr. Definition 1).
2. An All-but-One Perfect-Sound tag-based NIZK (cfr. Sect. 2) $\mathsf{NIZK}_{\mathsf{mx}} := (\mathsf{Init}_{\mathsf{mx}}, \mathsf{P}_{\mathsf{mx}}, \mathsf{V}_{\mathsf{mx}})$ for proving membership in $\mathcal{R}_{\mathsf{ck}}$, with tag space $[m]$.
3. An All-but-One Perfect-Hiding tag-based NIZK $\mathsf{NIZK}_{\mathsf{sd}} = (\mathsf{Init}_{\mathsf{sd}}, \mathsf{P}_{\mathsf{sd}}, \mathsf{V}_{\mathsf{sd}})$ for knowledge of the plaintext, i.e. a NIZK for the relation $\mathcal{R}_{\mathsf{msg}} := \{(\mathsf{pk}, \mathsf{C}), (\mathtt{M}, r) : \mathsf{C} = \mathsf{Enc}(\mathsf{pk}, \mathtt{M}; r)\}$, with tag space $[n]$. In particular, a weaker notion of extractability that guarantees that the message $\mathtt{M}$ is extracted is sufficient.
4. An ideal functionality $\mathcal{F}_{\mathsf{VtDec}}^{\mathsf{PKE},f}$, as defined in Fig. 3.

Functionality $\mathcal{F}_{\mathsf{VtDec}}^{\mathsf{PKE},f}$

The ideal functionality has as parameters a public-key encryption scheme $\mathsf{PKE} := (\mathsf{Setup}, \mathsf{KGen}, \mathsf{Enc}, \mathsf{Dec})$, an efficiently-computable function f and (implicit) group parameters $\mathsf{prm} \in \mathsf{Setup}(1^\lambda)$. The functionality interacts with m parties $\mathcal{P}_i$ and with an adversary S.

Public Key. Upon message $(\mathsf{KEY}, \mathsf{sid})$ from a party $\mathcal{P}_i$, $i \in [m]$, if $(\mathsf{sid}, \mathsf{pk}, \mathsf{sk})$ is not in the database sample $(\mathsf{pk}, \mathsf{sk}) \leftarrow\!\!\$\ \mathsf{KGen}(\mathsf{prm})$ and store the tuple $(\mathsf{sid}, \mathsf{pk}, \mathsf{sk})$ in the database. Send $(\mathsf{KEY}, \mathsf{sid}, \mathsf{pk})$ to $\mathcal{P}_i$.

Verify then Decrypt. Upon message $(\mathsf{VTDEC}, \mathsf{sid}, C_V, C_D)$ from party $\mathcal{P}_i$:

- If the tuple $(\mathsf{sid}, \mathsf{pk}, \mathsf{sk})$ does not exist in the database, ignore the message.
- Check that a tuple $(\mathsf{sid}, C_V, C_D, \mathcal{I})$ where $\mathcal{I} \subseteq [m]$ exists in the database; if so, update $\mathcal{I}$ including the index i, otherwise create the new entry $(\mathsf{sid}, C_V, C_D, \{i\})$ in the database.

If $|\mathcal{I}| = m$ and $C_D \subseteq C_V$ then:

- Send $(\mathsf{sid}, f(\mathsf{sk}))$ to the adversary S.
- Parse C_V as $(\mathsf{C}_i^V)_{i \in [|C_V|]}$ and C_D as $(\mathsf{C}_i^D)_{i \in [|C_D|]}$
- Compute $\mathbf{b} \in \{0,1\}^{|C_V|}$ such that for any i, $b_i = 1$ iff $\mathsf{Dec}(\mathsf{sk}, \mathsf{C}_i^V) \neq \bot$.
- If $\exists i : b_i = 0$ set $M_o := ()$, else compute $M_o := (\mathsf{Dec}(\mathsf{sk}, \mathsf{C}_i^D))_{i \in [|C_D|]}$, send a public delayed output $(\mathsf{VTDEC}, \mathsf{sid}, \mathbf{b}, M_o)$ to the parties $\mathcal{P}_i$ for $i \in [m]$,

Fig. 3. UC ideal functionality for Verify-then-Decrypt.

5. An ideal functionality for the common reference string (see Fig. 4) of the above NIZKs. In particular, the functionality initializes a CRS $\mathsf{crs}_{\mathsf{mx}}$ for $\mathsf{NIZK}_{\mathsf{mx}}$, and an additional CRS $\mathsf{crs}_{\mathsf{sd}}$ for $\mathsf{NIZK}_{\mathsf{sd}}$.

Finally, we assume parties have access to point-to-point authenticated channels.

Protocol Description. To simplify the exposition, we describe in this section the case of a single invocation, i.e. the protocol is run only once with a single, fixed session identifier sid; in Fig. 5 we describe in detail the protocol for the general case of a multi-session execution. At the first activation of the protocol, both the mixer parties and the sender parties receive from $\mathcal{F}_{\mathsf{VtDec}}$ the public key pk for the scheme PKE and the CRSs from $\mathcal{F}_{\mathrm{CRS}}$. At submission phase, each sender $\mathcal{P}_{S_i}$ encrypts their input message $\mathtt{M}_i$ by computing $\mathtt{C}_i \leftarrow\!\!\$\ \mathsf{Enc}(\mathsf{pk}, \mathtt{M}_i)$, and attaches a NIZK proof of knowledge π_{sd}^i of the plaintext, using i as tag. Finally, the party $\mathcal{P}_{S_i}$ broadcasts their message $(\mathtt{C}_i, \pi_{\mathsf{sd}}^i)$. After all sender parties have produced their ciphertexts, the mixers, one by one, shuffle their input lists and forward to the next mixer their output lists. In particular, the party $\mathcal{P}_{M_i}$ produces a random permutation of the input list of ciphertexts L_{i-1} (L_0 is the list of ciphertexts from the senders) by re-randomizing each ciphertext in the list and then permuting the whole list, thus computing a new list L_i. Additionally, the mixer computes a NIZK proof of membership π_{mx}^i with tag i, for the instance $(\mathsf{pk}, L_{i-1}, L_i)$ being in the sumcheck-admissible relation, because of the re-randomization witness property of Definition 2, the mixer holds a valid

Functionality $\mathcal{F}_{\text{CRS}}^{\mathsf{Init}}$

The functionality interacts with n parties $\mathcal{P}_i$ and an adversary S and has parameters a PPT algorithm Init that outputs obliviously sampleable common-reference string and an (implicit) public parameter prm.

Initialization. Upon activation, sample $\mathsf{crs} \leftarrow\!\$\ \mathsf{Init}(\mathsf{prm})$ and store it.
Public Value. Upon activation on message CRS from $\mathcal{P}_i$, send crs to $\mathcal{P}_i$.

Fig. 4. UC ideal functionality for Common Reference String.

witness for such an instance. After this phase, the mixers are ready for the verification: the mixers invoke the Verify-then-Decrypt functionality $\mathcal{F}_{\mathsf{VtDec}}$ to (i) verify that each list seen so far is made up only of valid ciphertexts and (ii) decrypt the ciphertexts contained in the final list. Finally publishes the list of the messages received by $\mathcal{F}_{\mathsf{VtDec}}$, sorted according to some common deterministic criterion, e.g. the lexicographical order.

Theorem 1. *For any arbitrary leakage function f, if PKE is lRCCA-secure w.r.t. f, $\mathsf{NIZK}_{\mathsf{mx}}$ is ABO Perfect Sound, $\mathsf{NIZK}_{\mathsf{sd}}$ is ABO Perfect Hiding, then the protocol described in Fig. 5 UC-realizes the functionality $\mathcal{F}_{\text{Mix}}$, described in Fig. 2, with setup assumptions $\mathcal{F}_{\mathsf{VtDec}}^{\mathsf{PKE},f}$ and $\mathcal{F}_{\mathsf{crs}}$.*

Proof. We now prove the existence of a simulator S, and we show that no PPT environment Z can distinguish an interaction with the real protocol from an interaction with S and the ideal functionality $\mathcal{F}_{\text{Mix}}$ (the ideal world), i.e. the distribution $(\mathcal{F}_{\mathsf{VtDec}}, \mathcal{F}_{\mathsf{crs}})\text{-}\mathsf{Hybrid}_{Z,\Pi_{\text{Mix}},\mathcal{A}}(\lambda)$ is indistinguishable from $\mathsf{Ideal}_{Z,\mathcal{F}_{\text{Mix}},\mathsf{S}}(\lambda)$. In our proof, we give a sequence of hybrid experiments in which the $(\mathcal{F}_{\mathsf{VtDec}}, \mathcal{F}_{\mathsf{crs}})$-hybrid world is progressively modified until reaching an experiment that is identically distributed to the ideal world. In what follows, we indicate with h^* the index of the first honest mixer. For label $\in \{\text{in}, \text{hide}\}$, we introduce the set Ψ_{label} consisting of tuples (x, y). We define the functions ψ_{label} and ψ_{label}^{-1} associated with the corresponding set:

$$\psi_{\text{label}}(x) := \begin{cases} y & \text{if } (x,y) \in \Psi_{\text{label}} \\ x & \text{otherwise} \end{cases} \qquad \psi_{\text{label}}^{-1}(y) := \begin{cases} x & \text{if } (x,y) \in \Psi_{\text{label}} \\ y & \text{otherwise} \end{cases}$$

Informally, the pair of functions $\psi_{\text{in}}, \psi_{\text{in}}^{-1}$ helps the hybrids to keep track of the ciphertexts sent by the honest senders while they are mixed by the first $h^* - 1$ mixers, while the pair of functions $\psi_{\text{hide}}, \psi_{\text{hide}}^{-1}$ helps to keep track of the ciphertexts output by the first honest mixer while they are mixed by the remaining mixers in the chain. We recall that in the protocol the mixers $\mathcal{P}_{M_i}$, for $i \in [m]$, send a message which includes a list L_i of ciphertexts. Whenever it is convenient we parse L_i as $(\mathsf{C}_{i,j})_{j\in[n]}$. Let `Invalid` be the event that, during the interaction of Z with the simulator/protocol, there exist $i \in [m], j \in [n]$ such

Protocol Π_{Mix}

Input. Upon activation on message $(\mathsf{INPUT}, \mathsf{sid}, \mathtt{M})$, $\mathcal{P}_{S_i}$ computes $\mathsf{C} \leftarrow\$ \mathsf{Enc}(\mathsf{pk}, \mathtt{M})$, and $\pi_{\mathsf{sd}} \leftarrow\$ \mathsf{P}_{\mathsf{sd}}(\mathsf{crs}_{\mathsf{sd}}, i, (\mathsf{pk}, \mathsf{C}), (\mathtt{M}, r))$. Broadcasts $(\mathsf{sid}, i, \mathsf{C}, \pi_{\mathsf{sd}})$.

Mix. Upon activation, the party $\mathcal{P}_{M_i}$, depending on its state, does as follow:

- If it is the first activation with message $(\mathsf{MIX}, \mathsf{sid})$ from the environment sends the message $(\mathsf{KEY}, \mathsf{sid})$ to $\mathcal{F}_{\mathsf{VtDec}}$ and return.
- If the message $(\mathsf{KEY}, \mathsf{sid}, \mathsf{pk})$, the messages $(\mathsf{sid}, i, \mathsf{C}, \pi_{\mathsf{sd}})$ for all senders and the messages $(\mathsf{sid}, L_j, \pi^j_{\mathsf{mx}})$ for all mixers with index $j \leq i-1$ were received:
  1. Samples a permutation ζ_i
  2. Reads the pair message $(L_{i-1}, \pi^i_{\mathsf{mx}})$ sent by the party $\mathcal{P}_{M_{i-1}}$ (or simply reads L_0 if this is the first mixer party)
  3. Shuffles and re-randomizes the list of ciphertexts: produces the new list $L_i = (\mathsf{C}'_{\zeta_i(j)})_{j \in [n]}$ where $\mathsf{C}'_j \leftarrow \mathsf{Rand}(\mathsf{pk}, \mathsf{C}_{i-1}; r_j)$ and r_j uniformly random string.
  4. Computes the sumcheck proof for the two lists of ciphertexts $\pi^i_{\mathsf{mx}} \leftarrow\$ \mathsf{P}_{\mathsf{mx}}(\mathsf{crs}_{\mathsf{mx}}, (\mathsf{pk}, L_1, L_2), (r_j)_{j \in [n]})$
  5. Sends to all the mixers $(\mathsf{sid}, L_i, \pi^i_{\mathsf{mx}})$.
- If the message $(\mathsf{sid}, L_m, \pi^m_{\mathsf{mx}})$ was received, checks that all the mixer proofs π^i_{mx}, for $i \in [m]$ accept, else abort.
- Computes $L := \mathsf{Concat}(L_1, \ldots, L_m)$ and sends $(\mathsf{VtDEC}, \mathsf{sid}, L, L_m)$ to $\mathcal{F}_{\mathsf{VtDec}}$
- If the message $(\mathsf{sid}, \mathbf{b}, M_o)$ from $\mathcal{F}_{\mathsf{VtDec}}$ was received, if $\exists i : b_i = 0$ then returns $\perp$, else computes and returns $L_o := \mathsf{Sort}(M_o)$

Fig. 5. Our protocol Π_{Mix}.

that $\mathsf{Dec}(\mathsf{sk}, \mathsf{C}_{i,j}) = \perp$ or $\mathsf{Vf}(\mathsf{crs}_{\mathsf{mx}}, (\mathsf{pk}, L_{i-1}, L_i), \pi^i_{\mathsf{mx}}) = 0$ (namely, π^i_{mx} does not verify). Clearly, when the event `Invalid` occurs, the protocol aborts.

Hybrid $\mathbf{H}_0$. This first hybrid is equivalent to $(\mathcal{F}_{\mathsf{VtDec}}, \mathcal{F}_{\mathsf{crs}})\text{-}\mathsf{Hybrid}_{\mathcal{Z}, \Pi_{\text{Mix}}, \mathcal{A}}(\lambda)$.

Hybrid $\mathbf{H}_1$. In this hybrid, we change the way $\mathsf{crs}_{\mathsf{mx}}$ is generated. We run $(\mathsf{crs}_{\mathsf{mx}}, \mathsf{tps}) \leftarrow\$ \mathsf{ABOInit}(\mathsf{prm}, h^*)$. Also, the proof $\pi^{h^*}_{\mathsf{mx}}$ of the first honest mixer is simulated. $\mathbf{H}_1$ is indistinguishable from $\mathbf{H}_0$ because of the ABO Composable Perfect Zero-Knowledge property of the NIZK.

Hybrid $\mathbf{H}_2$. The first honest mixer $\mathcal{P}_{M_{h^*}}$, rather than re-randomizing the ciphertexts received in input, decrypts and re-encrypts all the ciphertexts. If the decryption fails for some ciphertext C_i, $\mathcal{P}_{M_{h^*}}$ re-randomizes this "invalid" ciphertext and continues. $\mathbf{H}_2$ is indistinguishable from $\mathbf{H}_1$ because PKE is perfectly re-randomizable: because of the tightness of the decryption property, we have that $\forall j$, if $\mathsf{Dec}(\mathsf{sk}, \mathsf{C}_{h^*-1,j}) = \mathtt{M}_{h^*-1,j} \neq \perp$ then $\mathsf{C}_{h^*,j} \in \mathsf{Enc}(\mathsf{pk}, \mathtt{M}_{h^*-1,j})$ with overwhelming probability; also, by the indistinguishability property, the distribution of the re-randomized ciphertext $\mathsf{Rand}(\mathsf{pk}, \mathsf{C}_{h^*-1,j})$ and a fresh encryption $\mathsf{Enc}(\mathsf{pk}, \mathtt{M}_{h^*-1,j})$ are statistically close.

Hybrid $\mathbf{H}_3$. Here we introduce the set Ψ_{hide} and we populate it with the pairs $(\mathtt{M}_{h^*-1,i}, \mathtt{H}_i)_{i\in[n]}$, where $\mathtt{H}_1, \ldots, \mathtt{H}_n$ are distinct and sampled at random from the message space $\mathcal{M}$. When we simulate the ideal functionality $\mathcal{F}_{\mathsf{VtDec}}$, we output $\psi_{\text{hide}}^{-1}(\mathtt{M})$ for all successfully decrypted messages $\mathtt{M}$. The only event that can distinguish the two hybrids is the event that $\neg\mathtt{Invalid}$ and $\exists j, j' : \mathsf{Dec}(\mathsf{sk}, \mathsf{C}_{m,j}) = \mathtt{H}_{j'}$. However, $\mathtt{H}_1, \ldots, \mathtt{H}_n$ are not in the view of Z, thus the probability of such event is at most $\frac{n^2}{|\mathcal{M}|}$. $\mathbf{H}_3$ and $\mathbf{H}_2$ are statistically indistinguishable.

Hybrid $\mathbf{H}_4$. In this hybrid, rather than re-encrypting the same messages, the first honest mixer re-encrypts the fresh and uncorrelated messages $\mathtt{H}_1, \ldots, \mathtt{H}_n$ (used to populate Ψ_{hide}). Specifically, $\mathcal{P}_{M_{h^*}}$ samples a random permutation ζ_{h^*} and computes the list $L_{h^*} := (\mathsf{C}_{h^*,j})_{j\in[n]}$, with $\mathsf{C}_{h^*,\zeta_{h^*}(j)} \leftarrow\!\!\$ \; \mathsf{Enc}(\mathsf{pk}, \psi_{\text{hide}}(\mathtt{M}_{h^*-1,j}))$.

Lemma 1. *Hybrids $\mathbf{H}_3$ and $\mathbf{H}_4$ are computationally indistinguishable.*

Proof. We use a hybrid argument. Let $\mathbf{H}_{3,i}$ be the hybrid game in which the first honest mixer computes the list $L_{h^*} := (\mathsf{C}_{h^*,j})_{j\in[n]}$ as:

$$\mathsf{C}_{h^*,\zeta_{h^*}(j)} := \begin{cases} \mathsf{Enc}(\mathsf{pk}, \psi_{\text{hide}}(\mathtt{M}_{h^*-1,j})) & \text{if } j \le i \\ \mathsf{Enc}(\mathsf{pk}, \mathtt{M}_{h^*-1,j}) & \text{if } j > i \end{cases}$$

In particular, it holds that $\mathbf{H}_3 \equiv \mathbf{H}_{3,0}$ and $\mathbf{H}_4 \equiv \mathbf{H}_{3,n}$. We prove that $\forall i \in [n]$ the hybrid $\mathbf{H}_{3,i-1}$ is computationally indistinguishable from $\mathbf{H}_{3,i}$, reducing to the lRCCA-security of the scheme PKE. Consider the following adversary against the lRCCA-security experiment.

Adversary $\mathcal{B}(\mathsf{pk})$ with oracle access to $\mathsf{ODec}(\cdot)$.

- Simulate $\mathbf{H}_{3,i-1}$, in particular, when the environment instructs a corrupted mixer to send the message $(\mathsf{KEY}, \mathsf{sid})$ simulate the ideal functionality $\mathcal{F}_{\mathsf{VtDec}}$ sending back the answer $(\mathsf{KEY}, \mathsf{sid}, \mathsf{pk})$.
- When it is time to compute the list of the first honest mixer L_{h^*}, namely, when the mixer $\mathcal{P}_{M_{h^*}}$ is activated by the environment and has received for all $j \in [n]$ the messages $(\mathsf{sid}, j, \mathsf{C}, \pi_{\mathsf{sd}})$ from the senders and the messages $(\mathsf{sid}, L_j, \pi_{\mathsf{mx}}^j)$ from all the mixers with index $j \le h^* - 1$, first decrypt all the ciphertexts received so far using $\mathsf{ODec}(\cdot)$. Let $\mathtt{M}_{h^*-1,i}$ be the decryption of the ciphertext $\mathsf{C}_{h^*-1,i}$. If $\mathtt{M}_{h^*-1,i} = \perp$ then output a random bit, else send the pair of messages $(\mathtt{M}_{h^*-1,i}, \mathtt{H}_i)$ to the lRCCA challenger, thus receiving a challenge ciphertext C^*.
- Populate the list L_{h^*} by setting $\mathsf{C}_{\zeta_{h^*}(i)} \leftarrow \mathsf{C}^*$, and computing all the other ciphertexts as described in $\mathbf{H}_{3,i-1}$. Continue the simulation as the hybrid does.
- When all the mixers have sent the message (VtDEC, L, L_m), to $\mathcal{F}_{\mathsf{VtDec}}$, check that all the mixer proofs accept, otherwise abort the simulation and output a random bit. Then decrypt all the ciphertexts in L by sending queries to the guarded decryption oracle, i,e. send the query $\mathsf{C}_{i',j}$, receiving back the message $\mathtt{M}_{i',j} \in \mathcal{M} \cup \{\diamond, \perp\}$. If $\mathtt{M}_{i',j} = \perp$, abort and output a random bit.

If $\mathtt{M}_{i',j} = \diamond$, then set $\mathtt{M}_{i',j} := \mathtt{M}_{h^*-1,i}$. Simulate the leakage from $\mathcal{F}_{\mathsf{VtDec}}$ through the leakage received by the lRCCA security experiment: in particular, the reduction loses access to the guarded decryption oracle, receives the value $f(\mathsf{sk})$ and sends the message $(\mathsf{sid}, \mathbf{b}, \{\mathtt{M}_{m,j}\}_{j\in[n]})$ as required by the protocol.
- Finally, forward the bit returned by Z.

First we notice that when the guarded decryption oracle returns a message $\mathtt{M}_{i',j} = \diamond$ then the reduction can safely return $\mathtt{M}_{h^*-1,i}$. In fact, the ciphertext would decrypt to either $\mathtt{H}_i$ or to $\mathtt{M}_{h^*-1,i}$, however by the change introduced in $\mathbf{H}_3$, we have that $\mathtt{M}_{h^*-1,i} = \psi_{\text{hide}}^{-1}(\mathtt{H}_i)$ and $\mathtt{M}_{h^*-1,i} = \psi_{\text{hide}}^{-1}(\mathtt{M}_{h^*-1,i})$.

It is easy to see that when the challenge bit b of the experiment is equal to 0, the view of Z is identically distributed to the view in $\mathbf{H}_{3,j-1}$, while if the challenge bit is 1, the view of Z is identically distributed to the one in $\mathbf{H}_{3,j}$. Thus $|\Pr[\mathbf{H}_{3,j-1}(\lambda) = 1] - \Pr[\mathbf{H}_{3,j}(\lambda) = 1]| \leq \mathbf{Adv}^{\mathtt{lRCCA}}_{\mathcal{B},\mathsf{PKE},f}(\lambda)$.

Hybrid $\mathbf{H}_5$. Let $V_m := (\mathtt{M}_{m,j})_{j\in[n]}$ (resp. $V_{h^*} := (\mathtt{M}_{h^*,j})_{j\in[n]}$) be the list of decrypted ciphertexts output by the last mixer $\mathcal{P}_{M_m}$ (resp. by the first honest mixer $\mathcal{P}_{M_{h^*}}$). In the hybrid $\mathbf{H}_5$ the simulation aborts if $\neg\mathtt{Invalid}$ and $V_m \neq V_{h^*}$.

Lemma 2. *Hybrids $\mathbf{H}_4$ and $\mathbf{H}_5$ are computationally indistinguishable.*

Proof. Since $|V_m| = |V_{h^*}|$ and the messages $\mathtt{H}_1, \ldots, \mathtt{H}_n$ are distinct, the event $V_{h^*} \neq V_m$ holds if and only if there exists an index $j \in [n]$ such that $\mathsf{Count}(\mathtt{H}_j, V_m) \neq 1$. Let $\mathbf{H}_{4,i}$ be the same as $\mathbf{H}_4$ but the simulation aborts if $\neg\mathtt{Invalid}$ and $\exists j \in [i] : \mathsf{Count}(\mathtt{H}_j, V_m) \neq 1$. Clearly, $\mathbf{H}_{4,0} \equiv \mathbf{H}_4$ and $\mathbf{H}_{4,n} \equiv \mathbf{H}_5$. Let $\mathtt{Bad}_i$ be the event that $(\neg\mathtt{Invalid} \wedge \mathsf{Count}(\mathtt{H}_i, V_m) \neq 1)$. It is easy to check that:

$$|\Pr[\mathbf{H}_{4,i-1}(\lambda) = 1] - \Pr[\mathbf{H}_{4,i}(\lambda) = 1]| \leq \Pr[\mathtt{Bad}_i].$$

In fact, the two hybrids are equivalent if the event $\mathtt{Bad}_i$ does not happen.

We define an adversary to the lRCCA security of PKE that makes use of the event above.

Adversary $\mathcal{B}(\mathsf{pk})$ with oracle access to $\mathsf{ODec}(\cdot)$.

1. Simulate $\mathbf{H}_5$; in particular, when the environment instructs a corrupted mixer to send the message $(\mathsf{KEY}, \mathsf{sid})$ simulate the ideal functionality $\mathcal{F}_{\mathsf{VtDec}}$ sending back the answer $(\mathsf{KEY}, \mathsf{sid}, \mathsf{pk})$. (Thus embedding the public key from the challenger in the simulation.)
2. When it is time to compute the list of the first honest mixer L_{h^*}, namely, when the mixer $\mathcal{P}_{M_{h^*}}$ is activated by the environment and has received the messages $(\mathsf{sid}, i, \mathtt{C}, \pi_{\mathsf{sd}})$ for all senders and the messages $(\mathsf{sid}, L_j, \pi^j_{\mathsf{mx}})$ for all mixers with index $j \leq h^* - 1$, first decrypt all the ciphertexts received so far using the guarded decryption oracle. If there is a decryption error, output a random bit b'.
3. Sample $\mathtt{H}^{(0)}, \mathtt{H}^{(1)} \leftarrow\!\!\$\; \mathcal{M}$ and send the pair of messages $(\mathtt{H}^{(0)}, \mathtt{H}^{(1)})$ to the lRCCA challenger, receiving back the challenge ciphertext $\mathtt{C}^*$. Set the list $L_{h^*} = (\mathtt{C}_{h^*,j})_{j\in[n]}$ as follow:

$$\mathtt{C}_{h^*,\zeta_{h^*}(j)} := \begin{cases} \mathsf{Enc}(\mathsf{pk}, \mathtt{M}_{h^*-1,j}) & \text{if } j \neq i \\ \mathtt{C}^* & \text{else} \end{cases}$$

where recall that ζ_{h^*} is the random permutation used by the h^*-th mixer. Continue the simulation as the hybrid does.

4. When all the mixer have sent the message (VtDEC, L, L_m), to $\mathcal{F}_{\mathsf{VtDec}}$, decrypt all of the ciphertexts in L by sending queries to the guarded decryption oracle, namely, send the query $\mathtt{C}_{i',j}$ for all $i' > h^*$ and all $j \in [n]$, receiving back as answer $\mathtt{M}_{i',j} \in \mathcal{M} \cup \{\diamond, \perp\}$.
If the event $\mathtt{Invalid}$ holds, then abort the simulation and output a random bit b'.
5. Let $C \leftarrow \mathsf{Count}(\diamond, V_m)$, if $C = 1$ then abort the simulation and output a random bit b'.
6. From now one we can assume that $\neg\mathtt{Invalid}$ and $C \neq 1$; Compute

$$\mathtt{M} \leftarrow (C-1)^{-1} \cdot \left(\sum_{j \in [n], \mathtt{M}_{m,j} \neq \diamond} \mathtt{M}_{m,j} - \sum_{j \neq \zeta_{h^*}(i)} \mathtt{M}_{h^*,j} \right). \tag{1}$$

Output b' s.t. $\mathtt{M} = \mathtt{H}^{(b')}$.

First, we notice that the simulation $\mathcal{B}$ provides to the environment Z is perfect, indeed, independently of the challenge bit, the message $\mathtt{H}^{(b)}$ is distributed identically to $\mathtt{H}_j$. Thus the probability that $\mathtt{Bad}_i$ happens in the reduction is the same as the probability the event happens in the hybrid experiments.

Let $\mathtt{Abort}$ be the event that $\mathcal{B}$ aborts and outputs a random bit. Notice that:

$$\mathtt{Abort} \equiv \mathtt{Invalid} \vee (C = 1).$$

Let $\mathtt{Wrong}$ be the event that $\exists j : \mathsf{Dec}(\mathsf{sk}, \mathtt{C}_{m,j}) = \mathtt{H}^{(1-b)}$; notice that the message $\mathtt{H}^{(1-b)}$ is independent of the view of the environment Z, thus the probability of $\mathtt{Wrong}$ is at most $n/|\mathcal{M}|$. Moreover, we have $\mathtt{Bad}_i \equiv \neg\mathtt{Abort} \wedge \neg\mathtt{Wrong}$ because, by definition of $\neg\mathtt{Wrong}$, all the ciphertexts that decrypt to $\diamond$ in L_m are indeed an encryption of $\mathtt{H}^{(b)}$; thus, assuming the event holds, $C \neq 1$ iff $\mathsf{Count}(\mathtt{H}^{(b)}, V_m) \neq 1$. The probability of guessing the challenge bit when $\mathcal{B}$ aborts is $\frac{1}{2}$, thus we have:

$$\Pr[b = b'] \geq \tfrac{1}{2} \Pr[\neg\mathtt{Bad}_i] + \Pr[b = b' | \mathtt{Bad}_i] \Pr[\mathtt{Bad}_i] - \tfrac{n}{|\mathcal{M}|} \tag{2}$$

We now compute the probability that $b = b'$ conditioned on $\mathtt{Bad}_i$. First notice that $\neg\mathtt{Invalid}$ implies that the ciphertexts in the lists $L_{h^*}, \ldots, L_m$ decrypt correctly and that the proofs π^j_{mx} for $j > h^*$ verify. Thus by applying the sumcheck-admissibility w.r.t. PKE of the relation $\mathcal{R}_{\mathsf{mx}}$ and by the ABO perfect soundness of $\mathsf{NIZK}_{\mathsf{mx}}$ we have:

$$\sum_{j \in [n]} \mathsf{Dec}(\mathsf{sk}, \mathtt{C}_{h^*,j}) - \sum_{j \in [n]} \mathsf{Dec}(\mathsf{sk}, \mathtt{C}_{m,j}) = 0.$$

If we condition on $\neg\mathtt{Wrong}$ then:

$$\left(\mathtt{H}^{(b)} + \sum_{j \neq \zeta_{h^*}(j^*)} \mathtt{M}_{h^*,j} \right) - \left(C \cdot \mathtt{H}^{(b)} + \sum_{j \in [n], \mathtt{M}_{m,j} \neq \diamond} \mathtt{M}_{m,j} \right) = 0.$$

By solving the above equation for $\mathtt{H}^{(b)}$, we obtain $\mathtt{M} = \mathtt{H}^{(b)}$, therefore $\mathcal{B}$ guesses the challenge bit with probability 1 when conditioning on $\neg\mathtt{Abort} \wedge \neg\mathtt{Wrong}$.

Hybrid $\mathbf{H}_6$. Here we modify the decryption phase. When for all $j \in [m]$ the mixer has sent $(\mathsf{VtDEC}, \mathsf{sid}, L, L_m)$ to $\mathcal{F}_{\mathsf{VtDec}}$, the hybrid simulates the answer of the ideal functionality sending the message $(\mathsf{sid}, \mathbf{b}, M'_o)$ where $\mathbf{b}$ is computed as defined by the ideal functionality $\mathcal{F}_{\mathsf{VtDec}}$ and M'_o is the empty list () if $\mathtt{Invalid}$ occurs; else, if all the messages in L correctly decrypt and the mixer proofs are valid, compute $M'_o \leftarrow (\mathtt{M}_{h^*-1,\zeta_o(j)})_{j\in[n]}$, where ζ_o is an uniformly random permutation. Notice that $\mathbf{H}_6$ does not use the map ψ^{-1}_{hide} at decryption phase. We show that this hybrid and the previous one are equivalently distributed. First, by the change introduced in the previous hybrid, if the hybrid does not abort then $V_m = V_{h^*-1}$. Moreover, the two sets below are equivalently distributed:

$$\{(\mathtt{M}_{h^*-1,j}, \mathtt{H}_j) : j \in [n]\} \equiv \{(\mathtt{M}_{h^*-1,j}, \mathtt{H}_{\zeta_o(j)} : j \in [n])\}$$

because the messages $\mathtt{H}_1, \ldots, \mathtt{H}_n$ are uniformly distributed.

Hybrid $\mathbf{H}_7$. Similarly to what done in $\mathbf{H}_3$, in this hybrid we introduce the set Ψ_{in}, and we populate it with the pairs $(\mathtt{M}_i, \tilde{\mathtt{M}}_i)_{i\leq[n]}$, where the messages $\mathtt{M}_i$ are the inputs of the honest senders, and the messages $\tilde{\mathtt{M}}_i$ are distinct and sampled uniformly at random from the message space $\mathcal{M}$. When we simulate the ideal functionality $\mathcal{F}_{\mathsf{VtDec}}$, in case all the ciphertexts decrypts, we output the list $M_o := (\mathtt{M}_{o,i})_i$, where $\mathtt{M}_{o,\zeta_o(i)} \leftarrow \psi^{-1}_{\text{in}}(\mathtt{M}_{h^*-1,i})$. We notice that if $V_{h^*-1} \cap \mathcal{M}_H \neq \emptyset$, the map ψ^{-1}_{in} would modify the returned value; however, since the messages $\tilde{\mathtt{M}}_i$ are not in the view of Z, there is a probability of at most $\frac{n^2}{|\mathcal{M}|}$ that this event happens and that Z distinguishes $\mathbf{H}_6$ from $\mathbf{H}_7$.

Hybrid $\mathbf{H}_8$. In this hybrid, we encrypt the simulated (honest) sender inputs $\tilde{\mathtt{M}}_j$ instead of the (honest) sender inputs $\mathtt{M}_j$ to populate the list L_0. The proof that this hybrid and the previous one are computationally indistinguishable follows by the lRCCA security of PKE and the zero-knowledge of $\mathsf{NIZK}_{\mathsf{sd}}$. The proof follows along the same line of the proof for $\mathbf{H}_5$, the details can be found in the full version [18].

We now introduce the latest two hybrids that ensure that none of the inputs of the honest senders is duplicated or discarded: we start by introducing a check on malicious senders, while in $\mathbf{H}_{10}$ we ensure that no malicious mixer can duplicate or discard the honest inputs.

Hybrid $\mathbf{H}_9$. Let $\mathcal{M}_H$ be the set of simulated messages $\{\tilde{\mathtt{M}}_i\}_{i\leq[n]}$ for the honest sender parties and let V_0 be the decryption of the list of ciphertexts received by the first mixer. If $\neg\mathtt{Invalid}$ and a message $\mathtt{M} \in \mathcal{M}_H$ appears more than once in the list V_0 then the simulation aborts. The analysis of this hybrid is very similar to the analysis in Lemma 2, and we therefore defer it to the full version [18].

Hybrid $\mathbf{H}_{10}$. Recall that $V_{h^*} := (\mathtt{M}_{h^*,j})_{j\in[n]}$ is the list of decrypted ciphertexts output by the first honest mixer $\mathcal{P}_{M_{h^*}}$. In the hybrid $\mathbf{H}_{10}$ the simulation aborts if $\neg\texttt{Invalid}$ and $\exists i \in [n]$ such that $\mathsf{Count}(\tilde{\mathtt{M}}_i, V_{h^*-1}) \neq 1$, i.e., some of the simulated honest inputs do not appear or appear more than once, encrypted, in the list received in input by the first honest mixer. With this check we ensure that none of the inputs of the honest senders has been discarded or duplicated by the (malicious) mixers. The proof is given in the full version [18] since it is similar to the proof of Lemma 1.

Simulator S.

Initialization. Simulate the ideal functionality $\mathcal{F}_{\mathsf{crs}}$ by sampling $\mathsf{crs}_{\mathsf{mx}}$ in ABO Perfect Sound mode on the tag h^*, while $\mathsf{crs}_{\mathsf{sd}}$ is honestly generated with $\mathsf{Init}(1^\lambda)$. Also, simulate $\mathcal{F}_{\mathsf{VtDec}}$ by a sampling key pair $(\mathsf{pk}, \mathsf{sk}) \leftarrow\$ \mathsf{KGen}(\mathsf{prm})$. Populate the set $\mathcal{M}_H$ of the simulated honest inputs, by sampling uniformly random (and distinct) messages from the message space $\mathcal{M}$.

Honest Senders. On activation of the honest sender $\mathcal{P}_{S_i}$, where $i \in [n]$, simulate by executing the code of the honest sender on input the simulated message $\tilde{\mathtt{M}}_j$ chosen uniformly at random, without re-introduction, from $\mathcal{M}_H$.

Extraction of the Inputs. Let L_{h^*-1} be the list produced by the malicious mixer $\mathcal{P}_{M_{h^*-1}}$. For any $j \in [n]$, decrypt $\mathtt{M}_j \leftarrow\$ \mathsf{Dec}(\mathsf{sk}, \mathsf{C}_{h^*-1,j})$ and if a decryption error occurs, or some of the mixer proofs π^j_{mx} is not valid, i.e. the event $\texttt{Invalid}$ occurs, abort the simulation. If $\mathtt{M}_j \notin \mathcal{M}_H$ then submit it as input to the ideal functionality $\mathcal{F}_{\mathrm{Mix}}$.

First Honest Mixer. Simulate by computing L_{h^*} as a list of encryption of random (distinct) messages $\mathtt{H}_1, \ldots, \mathtt{H}_n$, simulating the proof of mixing $\pi^{h^*}_{\mathsf{mx}}$.

Verification Phase. Receive from the ideal mixer functionality $\mathcal{F}_{\mathrm{Mix}}$ the sorted output $(\mathtt{M}_i)_{i\in[n]}$. Sample a random permutation ζ_o and populate the list of outputs $M_o := (\mathtt{M}_{o,i})_{i\in[n]}$ with $\mathtt{M}_{o,\zeta_o(i)} \leftarrow \mathtt{M}_i$.

We notice that there are some differences between $\mathbf{H}_{10}$ and the interaction of S with the ideal functionality $\mathcal{F}_{\mathrm{Mix}}$. In particular, the hybrid defines the function ψ_{in} by setting a mapping between the inputs of the honest senders and the simulated ones, and, during the decryption phase, and uses ψ_{in}^{-1} to revert this change. S cannot explicitly set this mapping, because the inputs of the honest senders are sent directly to the functionality and are unknown to S. However, the simulator is implicitly defining the function ψ_{in} (and ψ_{in}^{-1}) since during the simulation chooses a simulated input $\tilde{\mathtt{M}}_i$ for each honest sender and at decryption phase outputs the messages coming from the sorted list (given in output by the ideal functionality) which contains the inputs of the honest senders.

5 A Concrete Mix-Net Protocol from RCCA-PKE

As already mentioned, to instantiate the blue-print protocol defined in Fig. 2 we need two main components: (1) a Rand lRCCA PKE scheme PKE and (2) a verify-then-decrypt protocol for such PKE.

5.1 Split PKE

We start by introducing the notion of Split Public-Key Encryption scheme. Informally, a Split PKE scheme is a special form of PKE scheme that extends and builds upon another PKE scheme. For example, CCA-secure PKE schemes alá Cramer-Shoup [12] can be seen as an extension of CPA-secure PKE schemes. We give the formal definition in the following.

Definition 3 (Split PKE). *A split PKE scheme* PKE *is a tuple of seven randomized algorithms:*

$\mathsf{Setup}(1^\lambda)$: *upon input the security parameter* 1^λ *produces public parameters* prm, *which include the description of the message* ($\mathcal{M}$) *and two ciphertext spaces* ($\mathcal{C}_1, \mathcal{C}_2$).

$\mathsf{KGen}_A(\mathsf{prm})$: *upon input the parameters* prm, *outputs a key pair* $(\mathsf{pk}_A, \mathsf{sk}_A)$.

$\mathsf{KGen}_B(\mathsf{prm}, \mathsf{pk}_A)$: *upon inputs the parameters* prm *and a previously generated public key* pk_A, *outputs a key pair* $(\mathsf{pk}_B, \mathsf{sk}_B)$.

$\mathsf{Enc}_A(\mathsf{pk}_A, \mathtt{M}; r)$: *upon inputs a public key* pk_A, *a message* $\mathtt{M} \in \mathcal{M}$, *and randomness* r, *outputs a ciphertext* $\mathtt{C}_A \in \mathcal{C}_A$.

$\mathsf{Enc}_B(\mathsf{pk}_A, \mathsf{pk}_B, \mathtt{C}; r)$: *upon inputs a pair of public keys* $(\mathsf{pk}_A, \mathsf{pk}_B)$, *a ciphertext* $\mathtt{C} \in \mathcal{C}_A$, *and some randomness* r, *outputs a ciphertext* $\mathtt{C}_B \in \mathcal{C}_B$.

$\mathsf{Dec}_A(\mathsf{pk}_A, \mathsf{sk}_A, \mathtt{C})$: *upon inputs a secret key* sk_A *and a ciphertext* $\mathtt{C} \in \mathcal{C}_A$, *outputs a message* $\mathtt{M} \in \mathcal{M}$ *or an error symbol* $\perp$.

$\mathsf{Dec}_B(\mathsf{pk}_A, \mathsf{pk}_B, \mathsf{sk}_A, \mathsf{sk}_B, \mathtt{C})$: *upon inputs secret keys* $\mathsf{sk}_A, \mathsf{sk}_B$ *and a ciphertext* $\mathtt{C} \in \mathcal{C}_B$, *outputs a message* $\mathtt{M} \in \mathcal{M}$ *or an error symbol* $\perp$.

Moreover, we say that a split PKE scheme PKE splits on *a PKE scheme* $\mathsf{PKE}_A := (\mathsf{KGen}_A, \mathsf{Enc}_A, \mathsf{Dec}_A)$ *defined over message space* $\mathcal{M}$ *and ciphertext space* $\mathcal{C}_A$ *and we say that a split PKE scheme* PKE forms *a PKE* $\mathsf{PKE} := (\mathsf{KGen}, \mathsf{Enc}, \mathsf{Dec})$ *defined over message space* $\mathcal{M}$ *and ciphertext space* $\mathcal{C}_B$ *where* $\mathsf{KGen}(\mathsf{prm})$ *is the algorithm that first runs* $\mathsf{pk}_A, \mathsf{sk}_A \leftarrow\$ \mathsf{KGen}_A(\mathsf{prm})$, *then runs* $\mathsf{pk}_B, \mathsf{sk}_B \leftarrow\$ \mathsf{KGen}_B(\mathsf{prm}, \mathsf{pk}_A)$ *and sets* $\mathsf{pk} := (\mathsf{pk}_A, \mathsf{pk}_B)$, $\mathsf{sk} := (\mathsf{sk}_A, \mathsf{sk}_B)$, *where* $\mathsf{Enc}(\mathsf{pk}, \mathtt{M})$ *is the algorithm that outputs* $\mathsf{Enc}_B(\mathsf{pk}_A, \mathsf{pk}_B, \mathsf{Enc}_A(\mathsf{pk}_A, \mathtt{M}; r); r)$ *and* $\mathsf{Dec} := \mathsf{Dec}_B$.

The correctness property is straightforward: a split PKE is correct if it forms a PKE that is correct in the standard sense. Our definition is general enough to capture a large class of schemes. We first note that any PKE scheme is trivially split: it suffices that Enc_B on input $\mathtt{C}$ outputs $\mathtt{C}$, and Dec_B runs Dec_A. A more natural (and less trivial) example is the above-cited Cramer-Shoup.

In this paper, we will focus on PKE schemes that are Re-Randomizable and Verifiable. Since, as we noted above, any PKE can be parsed as a Split PKE, Re-Randomizability is captured by an additional algorithm $\mathsf{Rand}(\mathsf{pk}, \mathtt{C}; r)$ that takes as input a ciphertext $\mathtt{C}$ and outputs a new ciphertext $\hat{\mathtt{C}}$.

As for the verifiability property, instead, there are three possible levels: (i) both the secret keys are required to verify a ciphertext, or (ii) only sk_A is needed, or (iii) no secret key is required at all. We refer to the third one as the *public* setting, while the other two are different flavors of a private/designated-verifier setting. We give the definition of (ii) in what follows.

Definition 4 (verifiable split PKE). *A verifiable split PKE is a split PKE, as defined above, with an additional algorithm* $\mathsf{Vf}(\mathsf{pk}, \mathsf{sk}_B, \mathsf{C})$ *that takes as input the public key* pk*, the secret key* sk_B *and a ciphertext* $\mathsf{C} \in \mathcal{C}_B$ *and outputs* 1 *whenever* $\mathsf{Dec}_B(\mathsf{pk}, \mathsf{sk}, \mathsf{C}) \neq \bot$*, otherwise outputs* 0 *for invalid ciphertexts.*

5.2 A Protocol for Verify-then-Decrypt for Verifiable Split PKE

Functionality $\mathcal{F}_{\mathsf{Dec}}^{\mathsf{PKE}}$

The ideal functionality has as parameters a public-key encryption scheme $\mathsf{PKE} := (\mathsf{KGen}, \mathsf{Enc}, \mathsf{Dec})$ and (implicit) public parameters prm. The functionality interacts with m parties $\mathcal{P}_i$ and with an adversary S.

Public Key. Upon activation on message $(\mathsf{KEY}, \mathsf{sid})$ from a party $\mathcal{P}_i$, $i \in [m]$, if $(\mathsf{sid}, \mathsf{pk}, \mathsf{sk})$ is not in the database sample $(\mathsf{pk}, \mathsf{sk}) \leftarrow\!\!\$\ \mathsf{KGen}(\mathsf{prm})$ and store the tuple $(\mathsf{sid}, \mathsf{pk}, \mathsf{sk})$ in the database and send $(\mathsf{KEY}, \mathsf{sid}, \mathsf{pk})$ to $\mathcal{P}_i$.

Decryption. Upon activation on $(\mathsf{DECRYPT}, \mathsf{sid}, C)$ from party $\mathcal{P}_i, i \in [m]$:
- If the tuple $(\mathsf{sid}, \mathsf{pk}, \mathsf{sk})$ does not exist in the database, ignore the message.
- Check that a tuple $(\mathsf{sid}, C, M_o, \mathcal{I})$, where $\mathcal{I} \subseteq [m]$, exists in the database; if so, update $\mathcal{I}$ including the index i. Else, parse C as $(\mathsf{C}_i)_i$ and compute the list $M_o := (\mathsf{Dec}(\mathsf{sk}, \mathsf{C}_i))_{i \in [|C|]}$, and create the new entry $(\mathsf{sid}, C, M_o, \{i\})$ in the database.
- If $|\mathcal{I}|$ equals m, then send a public delayed output $(\mathsf{DECRYPT}, \mathsf{sid}, M_o)$ to the parties $\mathcal{P}_i$ for $i \in [m]$.

Fig. 6. UC ideal functionality for (n-out-n Threshold) Key-Generation and Decryption of PKE

We realize the Verify-then-Decrypt ideal functionality (see Sect. 3) needed to instantiate our Mix-Net protocol. Let PKE be a verifiable split PKE. We define in Fig. 8 the protocol Π_{VtDec} that realizes $\mathcal{F}_{\mathsf{VtDec}}$ in the $\mathcal{F}_{\mathsf{Com}}$-hybrid model. Before doing that, we need to assume an extra property for our verifiable split PKE, so we introduce the notion of linear key-homomorphism for a PKE.

Definition 5 (Linearly Key-Homomorphic PKE). *We say that a PKE* $\mathsf{PKE} := (\mathsf{Setup}, \mathsf{KGen}, \mathsf{Enc}, \mathsf{Dec})$ *is linearly key-homomorphic if there exist PPT algorithms* $\mathsf{GenPK}, \mathsf{CheckPK}$ *and an integer* s *such that:*

- $\mathsf{KGen}(\mathsf{prm})$*, where* prm *contains the description of a group of order* q*, first executes* $\mathsf{sk} \leftarrow\!\!\$\ \mathbb{Z}_q^s$*, and then produces the public key* $\mathsf{pk} \leftarrow\!\!\$\ \mathsf{GenPK}(\mathsf{sk})$.
- GenPK *is linearly homomorphic in the sense that for any* $\mathsf{sk}_1, \mathsf{sk}_2 \in \mathbb{Z}_q^s$ *and* $\alpha \in \mathbb{Z}_q^s$ *we have* $\mathsf{GenPK}(\alpha \cdot \mathsf{sk}_1 + \mathsf{sk}_2) = \alpha \cdot \mathsf{GenPK}(\mathsf{sk}_1) + \mathsf{GenPK}(\mathsf{sk}_2)$.
- $\mathsf{CheckPK}$ *on input the public key* pk *outputs a bit* b *to indicate if the public key belongs on the subgroup of* $\mathcal{PK}$ *spanned by* GenPK*. Namely, for any* pk *we have* $\mathsf{CheckPK}(\mathsf{pk}) = 1$ *iff* $\mathsf{pk} \in Im(\mathsf{GenPK}(\mathsf{prm}, \cdot))$.

Moreover, a split PKE PKE *is linearly key-homomorphic it forms a linearly key-homomorphic PKE and it splits to a key-homomorphic PKE.*

It is not hard to verify that the key generation of a linearly key-homomorphic split PKE can be seen as sampling two secret vectors $\mathsf{sk}_A \in \mathbb{Z}_q^s$ and $\mathsf{sk}_B \in \mathbb{Z}_q^{s'}$ for $s, s' \in \mathbb{N}$ and then applying two distinct homomorphisms $\mathsf{GenPK}_A, \mathsf{GenPK}_B$ to derive the public key.

Building Blocks. Let PKE be a split PKE that splits over PKE_A, consider the following building blocks:

1. An ideal functionality $\mathcal{F}_{\mathsf{Dec}}^{\mathsf{PKE}_A}$ for threshold decryption, as defined in Fig. 6, of PKE_A.
2. A single-sender multiple-receiver commitment ideal functionality $\mathcal{F}_{\mathsf{Com}}$ [8] for strings, as defined in Fig. 7.

We describe the protocol in Fig. 8. At a high level, the protocol works as follows. Each party $\mathcal{P}_i$ interacts with the ideal functionality $\mathcal{F}_{\mathsf{Dec}}$ to get the public key pk_A and, after that, samples the pair of keys $(\mathsf{pk}_B^i, \mathsf{sk}_B^i)$. The secret key is committed through the ideal functionality $\mathcal{F}_{\mathsf{Com}}$. After this step, the parties compute the final key pk_B as the sum of all their input public key shares. To verify the ciphertexts C_V, the parties reveal their secret key shares sk_B^i, verify that all the keys are consistent, and locally verify the ciphertexts. Finally, to decrypt the ciphertexts C_D, the parties invoke $\mathcal{F}_{\mathsf{Dec}}$ after checking that $C_D \subseteq C_V$.

Functionality $\mathcal{F}_{\mathsf{Com}}$

The functionality interacts with n parties $\mathcal{P}_i$ and an adversary S.

Commitment. Upon activation on message $(\mathsf{COMMIT}, \mathsf{sid}, \mathcal{P}_i, s)$ from a party $\mathcal{P}_i$, where $s \in \{0,1\}^*$, record the tuple $(\mathsf{sid}, \mathcal{P}_i, s)$ and send the public delayed output $(\mathsf{RECEIPT}, \mathsf{sid}, \mathcal{P}_i)$ to all the parties $\mathcal{P}_j$, $j \in [n], j \neq i$.

Opening. Upon activation on message $(\mathsf{OPEN}, \mathsf{sid}, \mathcal{P}_i)$ from a party $\mathcal{P}_i$, $i \in [n]$, proceed as follows: if the tuple $(\mathsf{sid}, \mathcal{P}_i, s)$ was previously recoded, then send the public delayed output $(\mathsf{OPEN}, \mathsf{sid}, \mathcal{P}_i, s)$ to all other parties $\mathcal{P}_j, j \in [n], j \neq i$. Otherwise halt.

Fig. 7. UC ideal functionality for (Single) Commitment.

Theorem 2. *Let* PKE *be a verifiable split PKE that is linearly key-homomorphic, let* f *be the leakage function that on input* $\mathsf{sk} := (\mathsf{sk}_A, \mathsf{sk}_B)$ *outputs* sk_B. *The protocol* $\Pi_{\mathsf{VtDec}}^{\mathsf{PKE}}$ *described in Fig. 8 UC-realizes the functionality* $\mathcal{F}_{\mathsf{VtDec}}^{\mathsf{PKE},f}$ *described in Fig. 3 with setup assumptions* $\mathcal{F}_{\mathsf{Dec}}^{\mathsf{PKE}_A}$ *and* $\mathcal{F}_{\mathsf{Com}}$.

Protocol $\Pi^{\mathsf{PKE}}_{\mathsf{VtDec}}$

The party $\mathcal{P}_i$ executes the following commands:

Public Key. Upon activation on message:
- $(\mathsf{KEY}, \mathsf{sid})$ from the environment, forward the message to $\mathcal{F}^{\mathsf{PKE}_A}_{\mathsf{Dec}}$.
- $(\mathsf{KEY}, \mathsf{sid}, \mathsf{pk}_A)$ from $\mathcal{F}^{\mathsf{PKE}_A}_{\mathsf{Dec}}$ proceed as below:
  1. Sample $\mathsf{sk}^i_B \leftarrow\!\!\$\ \mathbb{Z}^s_q$ compute $\mathsf{pk}^i_B \leftarrow \mathsf{GenPK}(\mathsf{sk}^i_B)$.
  2. Commit the secret key sk^i_B through the ideal functionality $\mathcal{F}_{\mathsf{Com}}$, i.e. send the message $(\mathsf{COMMIT}, \mathsf{sid}, \mathsf{sk}^i_B)$ to the functionality $\mathcal{F}_{\mathsf{Com}}$.
- $(\mathsf{RECEIPT}, \mathsf{sid}, \mathcal{P}_j)$ from all $j \in [m]$ broadcast $(\mathsf{KEY}, \mathsf{sid}, i, \mathsf{pk}^i_B)$.

When the parties have sent their public key shares, compute $\mathsf{pk}_B := \sum_i \mathsf{pk}^i_B$ and abort if $\exists i : \mathsf{CheckPK}(\mathsf{pk}_A, \mathsf{pk}^i_B) = 0$ else output $(\mathsf{KEY}, \mathsf{sid}, \mathsf{pk})$.

Verify then Decrypt. Upon activation on message:
- $(\mathsf{VTDEC}, \mathsf{sid}, C_V, C_D)$ send $(\mathsf{OPEN}, \mathsf{sid}, \mathcal{P}_i)$ to $\mathcal{F}_{\mathsf{Com}}$ and broadcast $(\mathsf{VTDEC}, \mathsf{sid}, C_V, C_D)$ to the other parties.
- $(\mathsf{OPEN}, \mathsf{sid}, \mathcal{P}_j, \mathsf{sk}^j_B)$ for all $i \in [m]$ compute $\mathsf{sk}_B := \sum_i \mathsf{sk}^j_B$ and assert that $\mathsf{GenPK}_B(\mathsf{sk}_B) \stackrel{?}{=} \mathsf{pk}_B$ and that all parties broadcast the same lists C_V and C_D. Parse C_V as $(\mathsf{C}^i_V)_{i\in|C_V|}$, compute $\forall j : b_j \leftarrow \mathsf{Vf}(\mathsf{pk}, \mathsf{sk}_B, \mathsf{C}^j_V)$. If $C_D \not\subseteq C_V$ or $\exists i : b_i = 0$ return $(\mathsf{DECRYPT}, \mathsf{sid}, \mathbf{b}, ())$ else send $(\mathsf{DECRYPT}, \mathsf{sid}, C_D)$ to $\mathcal{F}^{\mathsf{PKE}_A}_{\mathsf{Dec}}$ and upon receipt of $(\mathsf{DECRYPT}, \mathsf{sid}, M_o)$, output $(\mathsf{DECRYPT}, \mathsf{sid}, \mathbf{b}, M_o)$

Fig. 8. Our protocol Π_{VtDec}.

Proof. We now prove that there exists a simulator S such that no PPT environment Z can distinguish an interaction with the real protocol from an interaction with S and the ideal functionality $\mathcal{F}_{\mathsf{VtDec}}$.

Simulator S.

Public Key. S receives in input from Z the set of corrupted parties, and receives from $\mathcal{F}_{\mathsf{VtDec}}$ the public key pk that is parsed as the tuple $(\mathsf{pk}_A, \mathsf{pk}_B)$. S gets to see the secret key shares of the corrupted parties when they send the message $(\mathsf{COMMIT}, \mathsf{sid}, \mathsf{sk}^i_B)$. Let h^* be the index of an honest party. S samples at random the secret keys sk^i_B for all honest parties $\mathcal{P}_i$, with $i \neq h^*$, from which can honestly compute the corresponding public keys through GenPK. As for the h^*-th party, S checks if $\forall j \neq h^* : \mathsf{CheckPK}(\mathsf{pk}_A, \mathsf{pk}^j_B) = 1$. If so it computes directly the public key $\mathsf{pk}^{h^*}_B := \mathsf{pk}_B - \sum_{i \neq h^*} \mathsf{pk}^i_B$, else it samples $\mathsf{sk}^{h^*}_B$ and computes the corresponding public key.

Verification. When all the parties have sent the message $(\mathsf{OPEN}, \mathsf{sid}, \mathcal{P}_i)$ to the commitment functionality $\mathcal{F}_{\mathsf{Com}}$, the simulator receives the leakage $(\mathsf{sid}, \mathsf{sk}_B)$ from $\mathcal{F}^{\mathsf{PKE},f}_{\mathsf{VtDec}}$, it computes the secret key for party $\mathcal{P}_{h^*}$, i.e. it computes $\mathsf{sk}^{h^*}_B := \mathsf{sk}_B - \sum_{i \neq h^*} \mathsf{sk}^i_B$. From this point on, the simulation becomes trivial since the simulator follows the protocol, and can easily verify and decrypt all the ciphertexts by interacting with the ideal functionality $\mathcal{F}_{\mathsf{VtDec}}$.

We observe that the inputs simulated for the honest parties $\mathcal{P}_i$, for $i \neq h^*$, are perfectly simulated since S chooses uniformly at random the matrices and the vectors for the secret keys sk_B^i. The public key for the h^*-th party is chosen dependently of the message of the corrupted parties. In particular, if one of the corrupted parties sends an invalid public key the h^*-th mixer follows the specification of the protocol, thus the simulation is perfect; if all the public keys are valid, the public key of h^*-th party is chosen as a function of the previously chosen keys and the public key given in input to the simulator. This is distributed identically to a real execution of the protocol: the only difference is that S computes the random public key, while in the real execution the party $\mathcal{P}_{h^*}$ would choose at random their secret key and then project it to compute the corresponding public key, but this difference is only syntactical. In the next steps, the simulation is perfect since it proceeds exactly as in the real protocol.

5.3 Our Concrete Verifiable Split PKE

In this section, we show that the Rand-PKE in [17] has all the properties needed to instantiate our protocol Π_{Mix}. In particular, in Fig. 9 we parse their PKE as a split PKE, and we prove that the scheme is lRCCA w.r.t. the leakage function f such that $f(\mathsf{sk}) := \mathsf{sk}_B$, and that the scheme is linearly key-homomorphic.

The schemes in [17] are proven secure under a decisional assumption that we briefly introduce here. Let ℓ, k be two positive integers. We call $\mathcal{D}_{\ell,k}$ a matrix distribution if it outputs (in probabilistic polynomial time, with overwhelming probability) matrices in $\mathbb{Z}_q^{\ell \times k}$.

Definition 6 (Matrix Decisional Diffie-Hellman Assumption in $\mathbb{G}_\gamma$, [15]). *The $\mathcal{D}_{\ell,k}$-MDDH assumption holds if for all non-uniform PPT adversaries $\mathcal{A}$,*

$$|\Pr[\mathcal{A}(\mathcal{G}, [\mathbf{A}]_\gamma, [\mathbf{Aw}]_\gamma) = 1] - \Pr[\mathcal{A}(\mathcal{G}, [\mathbf{A}]_\gamma, [\mathbf{z}]_\gamma) = 1]| \in \mathsf{negl}(\lambda),$$

where the probability is taken over $\mathcal{G} := (q, \mathbb{G}_1, \mathbb{G}_2, \mathbb{G}_T, e, \mathcal{P}_1, \mathcal{P}_2) \leftarrow \mathsf{GGen}(1^\lambda)$, $\mathbf{A} \leftarrow\$ \mathcal{D}_{\ell,k}, \mathbf{w} \leftarrow\$ \mathbb{Z}_q^k, [\mathbf{z}]_\gamma \leftarrow\$ \mathbb{G}_\gamma^\ell$ and the coin tosses of adversary $\mathcal{A}$.

Theorem 3. PKE *described in Fig. 9 is linearly key-homomorphic and lRCCA-secure w.r.t. f such that $f(\mathsf{sk}) := \mathsf{sk}_B$ under the $\mathcal{D}_{k+1,k}$-MDDH assumption.*

The proof of Theorem 3 is in the full version of this paper [18].

5.4 Putting All Together

We can instantiate the ABO Perfect Hiding NIZK proof of membership $\mathsf{NIZK}_{\mathsf{mx}}$ using Groth-Sahai proofs [14]. In particular, notice that the necessary tag-space for $\mathsf{NIZK}_{\mathsf{mx}}$ is the set $[m]$ which in typical scenarios is a constant small number (for example 3 mixers). Thus we can instantiate the tag-based ABO Perfect Hiding $\mathsf{NIZK}_{\mathsf{mx}}$ by considering an Init algorithm that samples m different common reference strings $(\mathsf{crs}_i)_{i \in [m]}$, the prover algorithm (resp. the verify algorithm) on tag j invokes the GS prover algorithm (resp. verifier algorithm) with input the

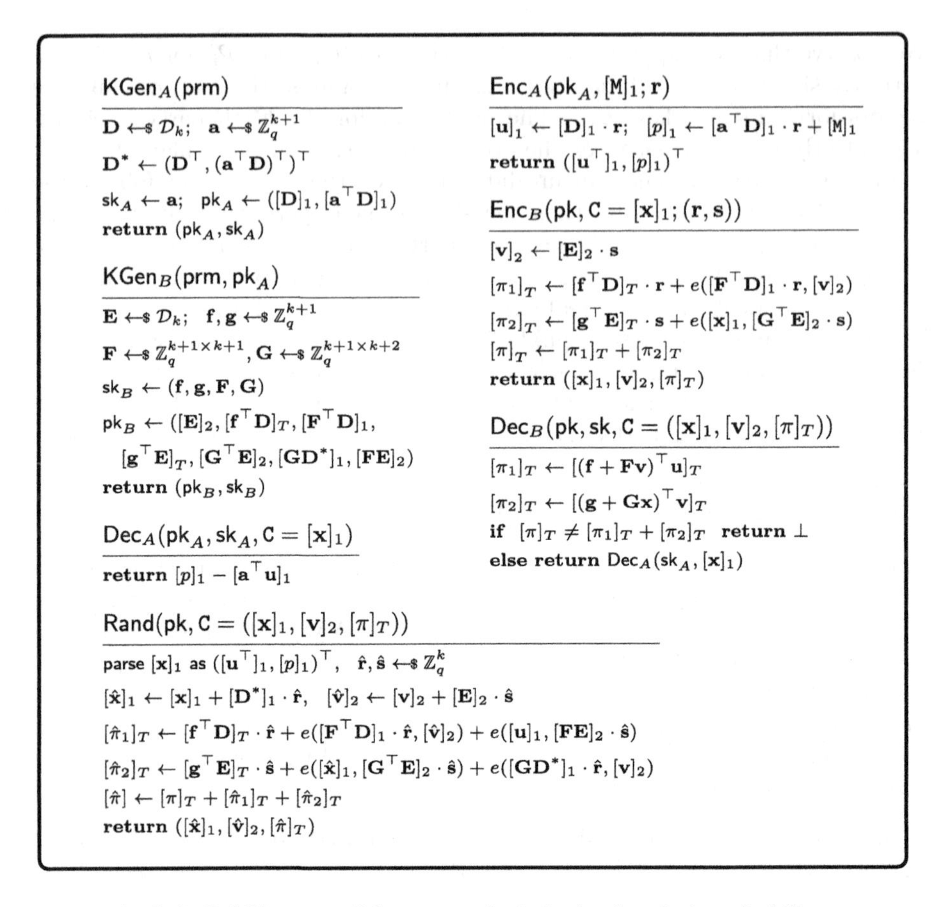

Fig. 9. The Split RCCA-secure Scheme. prm include the description of a bilinear group.

common reference string crs_j. We can instantiate the tag-based ABO Perfect Sound NIZK $\mathsf{NIZK}_{\mathsf{sd}}$ using the technique presented in the full version of [17]. By the universal composability theorem, once we compose the protocol Π_{Mix} from Fig. 5 and Π_{VtDec} from Fig. 8 we obtain a protocol with setup assumption $\mathcal{F}_{\mathsf{Dec}}$, $\mathcal{F}_{\mathsf{Com}}$ and $\mathcal{F}_{\mathrm{CRS}}$. The first ideal functionality can be implemented using classical approaches (for example, see Benaloh [6]). Briefly, the mixers can compute the shares of the public key $[\mathbf{a}^\top \mathbf{D}]_1$ for $\mathsf{KGen}_\mathcal{A}$ as in Fig. 9 and prove the knowledge of the secret key share $\mathbf{a}^{(i)}$ where $\mathbf{a} = \sum_i \mathbf{a}^{(i)}$, to obtain UC security in the malicious setting against static corruptions we can use an ABO Perfect Hiding NIZK proof system for this step. At decryption time, the mixers can compute a batched zero-knowledge proof of knowledge for "*encryption of zero*", they can use a NIZK proof of membership and, for UC security, it is sufficient for such proofs to be adaptive perfect sound.

Auditability. For space reasons, we only sketch the auditability of our protocol. Roughly speaking, a protocol Π is *auditable* if there exists a PT algorithm

Audit that on input a transcript τ and an output y output 1 if and only if the execution of the protocol that produces the transcript τ ends up with the parties outputting y. We focus on the auditability of the protocol obtained composing Π_{Mix} from Fig. 5 and Π_{VtDec} from Fig. 8. The auditing algorithm, given a transcript of Π_{VtDec} can reconstruct the secret key sk_2 and can check that $\mathsf{Vf}(\mathsf{sk}_2, \mathsf{C}_{i,j}) = 1$ for all $i \in [m]$ and $j \in [n]$ moreover it checks that all the NIZK proofs verify. The checks performed guarantee that the protocol execution resulting to the transcript did not abort, moreover, the auditability is guaranteed by the correctness of the protocol. Finally, we notice that the protocol for $\mathcal{F}_{\mathsf{Dec}}$ sketched in the previous section is auditable (see [6]).

Efficiency. We analyze the efficiency of the protocol obtained composing Π_{Mix} and Π_{VtDec}, and we consider the most efficient instantiation of the scheme in [17] based on SXDH assumption, i.e. for $k = 1$. We denote with E_1, E_2 (resp. E_T) the cost of a multiplication in groups $\mathbb{G}_1$ and $\mathbb{G}_2$ (resp. exponentiation in $\mathbb{G}_T$), and with P the cost of computing a bilinear pairing. We give an intuition on how much the protocol scales when a mixer is given N processors and may make use of parallelism. We compare our results with the Mix-Net protocol of [17]. In our protocol Π_{Mix}, each mixer re-randomizes a list of n ciphertexts which requires $n(7E_1 + 7E_2 + 2E_T + 9P)$, and additionally computes a proof π_{mx} for the sumcheck relation $\mathcal{R}_{\mathsf{mx}}$ which requires n additions in $\mathbb{Z}_q$ and $6E_1 + 8E_2$. Re-randomization of a ciphertext in the list does not depend on other ciphertexts in the list, so the parallel cost is $\frac{n}{N}(7E_1 + 7E_2 + 2E_T + 9P)$. Additionally, the mixers verify all the sumcheck NIZK proofs, which requires $3nm$ additions in $\mathbb{G}_1$ and around 8 pairings. The parallel cost is $\frac{8m}{N}$ pairings plus $\log_N(3n)\frac{m}{N}$ additions.

In the protocol Π_{VtDec}, each mixer sends a commitment of their secret key share, which requires a UC-commitment for the elements of the secret key sk, and receives commitments of secret key shares of the other $m - 1$ mixers. Additionally, the mixers derives the public key shares, using GenPK, this corresponds to the cost of generating m times a key pk_B^i and requires $m(4E_T + 6E_1 + 6E_2)$. Finally, each mixer needs to verify the $n \cdot m$ ciphertexts produced in the protocol execution of the last list which requires $n(m - 1)(6E_1 + 4E_2 + 4P)$.

In the protocol of [17] the public key shares pk_B^i (and not the secret ones) are committed using an equivocable commitment and an ABO NIZK proof (which can be seen as a UC-secure commitment against static corruption). The parallel cost of re-randomize their ciphertexts is $\frac{n}{N}36E_1 + 45E_2 + 6E_T + 5P$, while the cost of verifying the ciphertexts and decrypting the last list is equal to $\frac{nm}{N}36P + \frac{m}{N}(2E_1 + 50P)$. In comparison, our approach allows to save at least $\frac{n}{N}(30E_1 + 39E_2 + 36P)$ cryptographic operations, where we recall that n is the number of shuffled ciphertexts.

Acknowledgements. This work has been partially supported by the MESRI-BMBF French-German joint project named PROPOLIS (ANR-20-CYAL-0004-01).

References

1. Abe, M.: Universally verifiable mix-net with verification work independent of the number of mix-servers. In: Nyberg, K. (ed.) EUROCRYPT 1998. LNCS, vol. 1403, pp. 437–447. Springer, Heidelberg (1998). https://doi.org/10.1007/BFb0054144
2. Abe, M.: Mix-networks on permutation networks. In: Lam, K.-Y., Okamoto, E., Xing, C. (eds.) ASIACRYPT 1999. LNCS, vol. 1716, pp. 258–273. Springer, Heidelberg (1999). https://doi.org/10.1007/978-3-540-48000-6_21
3. Abe, M., Hoshino, F.: Remarks on mix-network based on permutation networks. In: Kim, K. (ed.) PKC 2001. LNCS, vol. 1992, pp. 317–324. Springer, Heidelberg (2001). https://doi.org/10.1007/3-540-44586-2_23
4. Adida, B., Wikström, D.: Offline/online mixing. In: Arge, L., Cachin, C., Jurdziński, T., Tarlecki, A. (eds.) ICALP 2007. LNCS, vol. 4596, pp. 484–495. Springer, Heidelberg (2007). https://doi.org/10.1007/978-3-540-73420-8_43
5. Bayer, S., Groth, J.: Efficient zero-knowledge argument for correctness of a shuffle. In: Pointcheval, D., Johansson, T. (eds.) EUROCRYPT 2012. LNCS, vol. 7237, pp. 263–280. Springer, Heidelberg (2012). https://doi.org/10.1007/978-3-642-29011-4_17
6. Benaloh, J.: Simple verifiable elections. In: 2006 USENIX/ACCURATE Electronic Voting Technology Workshop (EVT 06). USENIX Association, Vancouver, B.C., August 2006. https://www.usenix.org/conference/evt-06/simple-verifiable-elections
7. Canetti, R.: Universally composable security: a new paradigm for cryptographic protocols. In: 42nd FOCS, pp. 136–145 (2001)
8. Canetti, R., Fischlin, M.: Universally composable commitments. In: Kilian, J. (ed.) CRYPTO 2001. LNCS, vol. 2139, pp. 19–40. Springer, Heidelberg (2001). https://doi.org/10.1007/3-540-44647-8_2
9. Canetti, R., Krawczyk, H., Nielsen, J.B.: Relaxing chosen-ciphertext security. In: Boneh, D. (ed.) CRYPTO 2003. LNCS, vol. 2729, pp. 565–582. Springer, Heidelberg (2003). https://doi.org/10.1007/978-3-540-45146-4_33
10. Chase, M., Kohlweiss, M., Lysyanskaya, A., Meiklejohn, S.: Malleable proof systems and applications. In: Pointcheval, D., Johansson, T. (eds.) EUROCRYPT 2012. LNCS, vol. 7237, pp. 281–300. Springer, Heidelberg (2012). https://doi.org/10.1007/978-3-642-29011-4_18
11. Chaum, D.L.: Untraceable electronic mail, return addresses, and digital pseudonyms. Commun. ACM **24**(2), 84–90 (1981). https://doi.org/10.1145/358549.358563
12. Cramer, R., Shoup, V.: A practical public key cryptosystem provably secure against adaptive chosen ciphertext attack. In: Krawczyk, H. (ed.) CRYPTO 1998. LNCS, vol. 1462, pp. 13–25. Springer, Heidelberg (1998). https://doi.org/10.1007/BFb0055717
13. Cramer, R., Shoup, V.: Universal hash proofs and a paradigm for adaptive chosen ciphertext secure public-key encryption. In: Knudsen, L.R. (ed.) EUROCRYPT 2002. LNCS, vol. 2332, pp. 45–64. Springer, Heidelberg (2002). https://doi.org/10.1007/3-540-46035-7_4
14. Escala, A., Groth, J.: Fine-tuning Groth-Sahai proofs. In: Krawczyk, H. (ed.) PKC 2014. LNCS, vol. 8383, pp. 630–649. Springer, Heidelberg (2014). https://doi.org/10.1007/978-3-642-54631-0_36
15. Escala, A., Herold, G., Kiltz, E., Ràfols, C., Villar, J.: An algebraic framework for Diffie-Hellman assumptions. In: Canetti, R., Garay, J.A. (eds.) CRYPTO 2013,

Part II. LNCS, vol. 8043, pp. 129–147. Springer, Heidelberg (2013). https://doi.org/10.1007/978-3-642-40084-1_8
16. Faonio, A., Fiore, D.: Improving the efficiency of re-randomizable and replayable CCA secure public key encryption. In: Conti, M., Zhou, J., Casalicchio, E., Spognardi, A. (eds.) ACNS 2020, Part I. LNCS, vol. 12146, pp. 271–291. Springer, Cham (2020). https://doi.org/10.1007/978-3-030-57808-4_14
17. Faonio, A., Fiore, D., Herranz, J., Ràfols, C.: Structure-preserving and re-randomizable RCCA-secure public key encryption and its applications. In: Galbraith, S.D., Moriai, S. (eds.) ASIACRYPT 2019, Part III. LNCS, vol. 11923, pp. 159–190. Springer, Cham (2019). https://doi.org/10.1007/978-3-030-34618-8_6
18. Faonio, A., Russo, L.: Mix-nets from re-randomizable and replayable CCA-secure public-key encryption. Cryptology ePrint Archive, Paper 2022/856 (2022). https://eprint.iacr.org/2022/856
19. Furukawa, J., Sako, K.: An efficient scheme for proving a shuffle. In: Kilian, J. (ed.) CRYPTO 2001. LNCS, vol. 2139, pp. 368–387. Springer, Heidelberg (2001). https://doi.org/10.1007/3-540-44647-8_22
20. Groth, J.: A verifiable secret shuffe of homomorphic encryptions. In: Desmedt, Y.G. (ed.) PKC 2003. LNCS, vol. 2567, pp. 145–160. Springer, Heidelberg (2003). https://doi.org/10.1007/3-540-36288-6_11
21. Groth, J.: Rerandomizable and replayable adaptive chosen ciphertext attack secure cryptosystems. In: Naor, M. (ed.) TCC 2004. LNCS, vol. 2951, pp. 152–170. Springer, Heidelberg (2004). https://doi.org/10.1007/978-3-540-24638-1_9
22. Groth, J.: A verifiable secret shuffle of homomorphic encryptions. J. Cryptol. **23**(4), 546–579 (2010)
23. Groth, J., Ishai, Y.: Sub-linear zero-knowledge argument for correctness of a shuffle. In: Smart, N. (ed.) EUROCRYPT 2008. LNCS, vol. 4965, pp. 379–396. Springer, Heidelberg (2008). https://doi.org/10.1007/978-3-540-78967-3_22
24. Jacobson, M., M'Raïhi, D.: Mix-based electronic payments. In: Tavares, S., Meijer, H. (eds.) SAC 1998. LNCS, vol. 1556, pp. 157–173. Springer, Heidelberg (1999). https://doi.org/10.1007/3-540-48892-8_13
25. Libert, B., Peters, T., Qian, C.: Structure-preserving chosen-ciphertext security with shorter verifiable ciphertexts. In: Fehr, S. (ed.) PKC 2017, Part I. LNCS, vol. 10174, pp. 247–276. Springer, Heidelberg (2017). https://doi.org/10.1007/978-3-662-54365-8_11
26. Neff, C.A.: A verifiable secret shuffle and its application to e-voting. In: ACM CCS 2001, pp. 116–125 (2001)
27. Park, C., Itoh, K., Kurosawa, K.: Efficient anonymous channel and all/nothing election scheme. In: Helleseth, T. (ed.) EUROCRYPT 1993. LNCS, vol. 765, pp. 248–259. Springer, Heidelberg (1994). https://doi.org/10.1007/3-540-48285-7_21
28. Prabhakaran, M., Rosulek, M.: Rerandomizable RCCA encryption. In: Menezes, A. (ed.) CRYPTO 2007. LNCS, vol. 4622, pp. 517–534. Springer, Heidelberg (2007). https://doi.org/10.1007/978-3-540-74143-5_29
29. Sako, K., Kilian, J.: Receipt-free mix-type voting scheme - a practical solution to the implementation of a voting booth. In: Guillou, L.C., Quisquater, J.-J. (eds.) EUROCRYPT 1995. LNCS, vol. 921, pp. 393–403. Springer, Heidelberg (1995). https://doi.org/10.1007/3-540-49264-X_32
30. Terelius, B., Wikström, D.: Proofs of restricted shuffles. In: Bernstein, D.J., Lange, T. (eds.) AFRICACRYPT 2010. LNCS, vol. 6055, pp. 100–113. Springer, Heidelberg (2010). https://doi.org/10.1007/978-3-642-12678-9_7

31. Wang, Y., Chen, R., Yang, G., Huang, X., Wang, B., Yung, M.: Receiver-anonymity in rerandomizable RCCA-secure cryptosystems resolved. In: Malkin, T., Peikert, C. (eds.) CRYPTO 2021. LNCS, vol. 12828, pp. 270–300. Springer, Cham (2021). https://doi.org/10.1007/978-3-030-84259-8_10
32. Wikström, D.: A sender verifiable mix-net and a new proof of a shuffle. In: Roy, B. (ed.) ASIACRYPT 2005. LNCS, vol. 3788, pp. 273–292. Springer, Heidelberg (2005). https://doi.org/10.1007/11593447_15
33. Wikström, D.: A commitment-consistent proof of a shuffle. In: Boyd, C., González Nieto, J. (eds.) ACISP 2009. LNCS, vol. 5594, pp. 407–421. Springer, Heidelberg (2009). https://doi.org/10.1007/978-3-642-02620-1_28
34. Wikström, D.: Verificatum (2010). https://www.verificatum.com

New and Improved Constructions for Partially Equivocable Public Key Encryption

Benoît Libert[1,2(✉)], Alain Passelègue[2,3(✉)], and Mahshid Riahinia[2(✉)]

[1] CNRS, Laboratoire LIP, Lyon, France
[2] ENS de Lyon, Laboratoire LIP (U. Lyon, CNRS, ENSL, Inria, UCBL), Lyon, France
benoit.libert@ens-lyon.fr
[3] Inria, Lyon, France

Abstract. Non-committing encryption (NCE) is an advanced form of public-key encryption which guarantees the security of a Multi-Party Computation (MPC) protocol in the presence of an adaptive adversary. Brakerski et al. (TCC 2020) recently proposed an intermediate notion, termed Packed Encryption with Partial Equivocality (PEPE), which implies NCE and preserves the ciphertext rate (up to a constant factor). In this work, we propose three new constructions of rate-1 PEPE based on standard assumptions. In particular, we obtain the first constant ciphertext-rate NCE construction from the LWE assumption with polynomial modulus, and from the Subgroup Decision assumption. We also propose an alternative DDH-based construction with guaranteed polynomial running time.

Keywords: Non-committing encryption · standard assumptions · ciphertext rate · equivocable encryption

1 Introduction

Non-committing encryption (NCE) was introduced by Canetti et al. [6] as a form of encryption that guarantees the security of an MPC protocol in the presence of an adaptive adversary. Informally, NCE is a form of public-key encryption that allows one to generate "dummy" ciphertexts that can be later opened to an arbitrary message. Intuitively, by using NCE as the encryption tool in an MPC protocol, we can fool the adversary by opening the internal state of a newly corrupted party to an arbitrary message while being able to prove that this arbitrary internal state is consistent with the public transcript of the protocol.

An important property of an NCE scheme that determines its efficiency, like any other public-key encryption scheme, is its ciphertext rate, i.e., the ratio of ciphertext length to message length.

C. Galdi and S. Jarecki (Eds.): SCN 2022, LNCS 13409, pp. 197–219, 2022.
https://doi.org/10.1007/978-3-031-14791-3_9

Prior Works. There is a large literature on NCE and we will mostly focus on NCE constructions achieving optimal round complexity without random oracles.

Canetti et al. [6] presented the first NCE constructions based on the RSA or the computational Diffie-Hellman (CDH) assumptions. Each of their constructions achieves a ciphertext rate of $\mathcal{O}(\lambda^2)$. Beaver [1] proposed 3-round NCE construction with ciphertext rate $\mathcal{O}(\lambda)$ from the DDH assumption. Damgård and Nielsen [10] generalized the work of Beaver and achieved 3-round NCE with the same ciphertext rate based on simulatable public-key encryption and showed an instantiation from the RSA assumption. Nielsen [19] proved that non-interactive NCE is impossible without random oracles. In the following, we mostly discuss 2-round protocols. First improvements were only achieved after thirteen years by Choi et al. [9]. In the latter work, the authors constructed an NCE scheme based on the factoring problem and achieving linear ciphertext rate $\mathcal{O}(\lambda)$. Hemenway et al. [13] achieved sub-linear ciphertext-rate $\mathcal{O}(\log \ell)$ from the Φ-hiding assumption, where ℓ is the length of message. Later, in [12], they improved their result in terms of assumption and public key size, and removed the oblivious sampling requirement that appeared in [13]. The latter construction is based on the (Ring) Learning-with-Errors (LWE) assumption with super-polynomial modulus-to-noise ratio and they achieved a rate of $\mathsf{poly}(\log \lambda)$. Canetti et al. [8] obtained optimal ciphertext-rate using the power of indistinguishability obfuscation (iO) and in the CRS model. Yoshida et al. [21] put forth an approach allowing to construct NCE with ciphertext rate $\mathcal{O}(\log \lambda)$ under the standard Decisional Diffie-Hellman (DDH) assumption. Under standard assumptions, constant ciphertext rate was recently achieved in two concurrent works: Yoshida et al. [22] obtained constructions from DDH or LWE with super-polynomial modulus; Brakerski et al. [3] obtained similar results via a new abstraction which yields a construction from the DDH assumption and a construction from LWE with super-polynomial modulus-to-noise ratio.

1.1 Our Contributions

We follow the approach of Brakerski et al. [3] and obtain constant-rate NCE by constructing an intermediate primitive called *packed encryption with partial equivocality* (PEPE) that the latter authors proved to imply NCE with only a constant factor loss in the ciphertext rate. NCE is obtained by composing any PEPE scheme with a constant-rate error-correcting code (ECC), the latter being implied by the existence of one-way functions: to encrypt a message, first encode it using an ECC, and then encrypt the encoding using the PEPE encryption algorithm (decryption is done via decrypting-then-decoding). We refer the reader to [3] for more details on this generic transform. We thus focus on constructing rate-1 PEPE from various assumptions, and rely on the transformation of [3] to obtain constant-ciphertext-rate NCE. Specifically, we obtain three constructions of rate-1 PEPE, therefore of constant-ciphertext-rate NCE. Our first construction is secure assuming the hardness of the LWE problem with *polynomial* modulus and inverse-error rate, and our second construction is secure under the DDH assumption. Assuming a common reference string (CRS), we then provide a construction of rate-1 PEPE from Subgroup Decision (SD) assumption in pairing-free composite order groups. To our knowledge, this construction is the first rate-1 PEPE based on a factoring-related assumption.[1] Our SD-based construction requires a trusted setup (CRS) in order to generate the composite order group. However, the trusted setup requirement appears to arise in any PEPE construction based on the hardness of factoring as long as no individidual party should learn the factorization. Table 1 provides a comparison between our results and prior ones.

Table 1. Comparison between our NCE schemes and previously proposed NCE schemes. λ denotes the security parameter and ℓ denotes the message length. We only discuss 2-round constructions without random oracle.

	Ciphertext Rate	Assumption	Setup
[6]	$\mathcal{O}(\lambda^2)$	RSA, CDH	-
[9]	$\mathcal{O}(\lambda)$	Factoring Blum integers	-
[13]	$\mathcal{O}(\log \ell)$	Φ-hiding	Oblivious sampling of RSA modulus
[12]	$\mathsf{poly}(\log \lambda)$	LWE, Ring-LWE	superpolynomial LWE modulus-to-noise ratio
[8]	$1 + o(1)$	$i\mathcal{O}$	CRS
[21]	$\mathcal{O}(\log \lambda)$	DDH	-
[3]	$\mathcal{O}(1)$	LWE, DDH	superpolynomial LWE modulus-to-noise ratio
[22]	$\mathcal{O}(1)$	LWE, DDH	superpolynomial LWE modulus-to-noise ratio
This Work	$\mathcal{O}(1)$	LWE, DDH	-
		SD	CRS

LWE Construction. We propose the first constant ciphertext-rate NCE scheme relying on the hardness of LWE with polynomial modulus-to-noise ratio. This result improves the recent works of Brakerski et al. [3] and Yoshida et al. [22], which rely on LWE with super-polynomial modulus-to-noise ratio. Our construction is identical to the one from [3], except that we avoid the use of noise flooding to equivocate the ciphertext randomness. Instead, we convolve discrete Gaussians using a lemma from [17] to properly simulate the noise of simulated ciphertexts.

[1] In the proceedings version of [3], a PEPE candidate based on the quadratic residuostity assumption was proposed. Besides a CRS, this construction required oblivious sampling to avoid assuming erasures. In hidden-order groups, it is not clear how to obliviously sample a group element without knowing the group order and while satisfying the requirements of the security proof. The authors of [3] confirmed this issue and removed the QR-based construction in an updated version of their paper.

DDH Construction. We present a simple DDH-based construction of rate-1 PEPE, which differs from the construction in [3]. The latter uses a ciphertext compression algorithm (which relies on sampling a PRF secret key such that evaluation on some ciphertext-dependent messages satisfies some property) that runs in expected polynomial time. Instead, we apply a universal hash function to the encryption randomness and then encrypt the message using the output of the hash as a one-time pad. Thus, we preserve the constant ciphertext rate while avoiding the disadvantage of the compression algorithm. While our scheme loses the linearly homomorphic property of [3], its encryption algorithm works in strict polynomial time.

SD Construction. We propose the first constant ciphertext-rate NCE (via PEPE) based on the subgroup decision (SD) assumption [2]. This construction uses a CRS, which seems inherent when relying on the hardness of factoring. To our knowledge, it is the first constant ciphertext-rate NCE construction based on a factoring-related assumption.

1.2 Technical Overview

PEPE. As defined in [3], a *Packed Encryption with Partial Equivocality (PEPE)* scheme is a tuple $(\mathsf{KeyGen}, \mathsf{Enc}, \mathsf{Dec}, \mathsf{EquivPK}, \mathsf{EquivCT})$ of efficient (PPT) algorithms such that $\mathsf{KeyGen}(b, I, r_G)$ algorithm takes as input a bit b, a subset $I \subset [\ell]$, where ℓ is the length of the messages that can be encrypted in the scheme, and it uses some randomness r_G to produce a public key pk and a secret key sk. This algorithm runs in two modes: real mode (if $b = 0$), or ideal mode (if $b = 1$). In the real mode, the scheme should satisfy the correctness property of a regular public-key encryption scheme restricted to the subset I. Namely, the output (of length ℓ) of the decryption algorithm on a ciphertext encrypting a message M should be equal to M_i, for $i \in I$.

The two other algorithms $\mathsf{EquivPK}$ and $\mathsf{EquivCT}$ can be used in the following way: $\mathsf{EquivPK}(\mathsf{sk}, b, (I, r_G), I')$ on input $I' \subset I$, and sk, where $(\mathsf{pk}, \mathsf{sk}) \leftarrow \mathsf{KeyGen}(b, I, r_G)$, outputs a new randomness r'_G, such that r'_G is indistinguishable from any honest (real-mode) r'_G that is used in $\mathsf{KeyGen}(0, I', r'_G)$ for set I'. That is, an efficient adversary cannot distinguish between r'_G obtained by equivocating with respect to I' from a larger set $I \supset I'$, and honest r'_G that is used in $\mathsf{KeyGen}(0, I', r'_G)$.

The second equivocation algorithm allows to equivocate ciphertexts in the ideal mode: $\mathsf{EquivCT}(\mathsf{sk}, (M, r_E), \{M'_i\}_{i \notin I})$, on input an encryption randomness r_E, and messages M and M', such that $M_i = M'_i$ for $i \in I$, outputs a new encryption randomness r'_E. No efficient adversary should be able to tell apart whether the distribution (pk, M', r'_E) was obtained by equivocating an encryption of a different message M in the ideal mode or by honestly encrypting in the real mode.

We now dive into the details of our PEPE constructions.

LWE Construction. We recall the LWE-based PEPE scheme of [3] which requires a super-polynomial modulus-to-noise ratio, and then show how we modify their scheme and obtain a rate-1 PEPE scheme from LWE with polynomial modulus. In the real mode, the public key consists of a random integer matrix $\mathbf{A} \xleftarrow{\$} \mathbb{Z}_q^{n\times k}$, and vectors $\{\mathbf{v}_i\}_{i=1}^{\ell}$ that are either LWE samples $\mathbf{v}_i = \mathbf{A}\mathbf{s}_i + \mathbf{e}_i$ if $i \in I$, or random vectors $\mathbf{v}_i \xleftarrow{\$} \mathbb{Z}_q^n$ if $i \notin I$. In the equivocal mode, the public key has the same structure as in the real mode, except that the matrix $\mathbf{A}$ and random vectors $\{\mathbf{v}_i\}_{i\notin I}$ now come from the columns of a random matrix $\mathbf{B} \in \mathbb{Z}_q^{n\times(k+\ell-|I|)}$ for which a lattice trapdoor $\mathsf{td}_\mathbf{B}$ [11,18] is available. Other vectors $\{\mathbf{v}_i\}_{i\in I}$ are chosen as LWE samples as in the real mode. To encrypt a message $M \in \{0,1\}^\ell$, they use the packed Regev encryption scheme [20] together with a masking noise as follows: first, it samples a random vector $\mathbf{r} \xleftarrow{\$} D_\sigma^n$ and computes $\mathbf{c}_1 \leftarrow \mathbf{r}^T\mathbf{A}$, and $w_{2,i} \leftarrow \mathbf{r}^T\mathbf{v}_i + e_i + \lfloor q/2 \rceil M_i \in \mathbb{Z}_q$, where $e_i \xleftarrow{\$} D_{\sigma'}$ for each $i \in [\ell]$. Next, it compresses $(\mathbf{c}_1, \{w_{2,i}\}_{i=1}^{\ell})$ using a technique introduced in [4]. This technique changes a ciphertext of the form $\mathsf{ct} = (\mathbf{c}_0, w_{2,1}, \cdots, w_{2,\ell}) \in \mathbb{Z}_q^n \times \mathbb{Z}_q^\ell$ into a tuple $(\mathbf{c}_0, \{c_i\}_{i\in[\ell]}, z)$, where $c_i \in \{0,1\}$ for each $i \in [\ell]$, and $z \in \mathbb{Z}_q$. Decryption also proceeds using the decryption algorithm of this compression procedure.

The equivocation of public key randomness for a subset $I' \subseteq I$ is done simply by outputting the secret keys for the indices that are in the subset I', and the unmodified public key elements for the rest. Note that here, for indices in $I \setminus I'$, we are claiming that $\mathbf{v}_i$'s which are formed as $\mathbf{A}\mathbf{s}_i + \mathbf{e}_i$ (as the output of $\mathsf{KeyGen}(b = 1, I, r_G)$), are indistinguishable from random vectors of $\mathbb{Z}_q^n$ (as the output of $\mathsf{KeyGen}(b = 0, I', r'_G)$). This holds assuming the hardness of LWE.

We now explain the ciphertext equivocation algorithm of [3]. Recall that $\mathsf{td}_\mathbf{B}$ allows sampling a short vector of the lattice $\Lambda_\mathbf{y}^\perp(\mathbf{B}) = \{\mathbf{r} \in \mathbb{Z}_q^n : \mathbf{B}^T \cdot \mathbf{r} = \mathbf{y}\}$, where $\mathbf{y} \in \mathbb{Z}_q^{k+\ell-|I|}$. Let us assume that $(\mathbf{c}_1, \{w_{2,i}\}_{i=1}^{\ell})$ is a packed Regev encryption of a message M with the encryption randomness $(\mathbf{r}, \{e_i^*\}_{i\in[\ell]})$ and we want to explain it as an encryption of a message M', where $M_i = M'_i$ for $i \in I$. Using the lattice trapdoor $\mathsf{td}_\mathbf{B}$, one can sample a short (in fact, Gaussian) $\bar{\mathbf{r}} \in \mathbb{Z}^n$ such that

$$\bar{\mathbf{r}}^T\mathbf{A} = \mathbf{r}^T\mathbf{A} \quad \text{and} \quad \bar{\mathbf{r}}^T\mathbf{v}_i = w_{2,i} - e'_i - \lfloor q/2 \rceil M'_i \ ,$$

for $i \notin I$, where e'_i is sampled from $D_{\sigma'}$. This gives a Gaussian vector $\bar{\mathbf{r}}$ and encryption noise e'_i, for indices $i \notin I$, that can explain $(\mathbf{c}_1, \{w_{2,i}\}_{i\notin I})$ as a valid encryption of bits $\{M'_i\}_{i\notin I}$. At this point, one still has to craft an encryption noise e'_i for all $i \in I$ such that

$$\begin{aligned}
\bar{\mathbf{r}}^T\mathbf{v}_i + e'_i + \lfloor q/2 \rceil M'_i = \mathbf{r}^T\mathbf{v}_i + e_i^* + \lfloor q/2 \rceil M_i &\xRightarrow[M_i = M'_i]{i\in I} \bar{\mathbf{r}}^T\mathbf{v}_i + e'_i = \mathbf{r}^T\mathbf{v}_i + e_i^* \\
&\xRightarrow[\mathbf{v}_i = \mathbf{A}\mathbf{s}_i + \mathbf{e}_i]{i\in I} \bar{\mathbf{r}}^T\mathbf{e}_i + e'_i = \mathbf{r}^T\mathbf{e}_i + e_i^* \\
&\Longrightarrow e'_i = e_i^* + (\mathbf{r} - \bar{\mathbf{r}})^T\mathbf{e}_i.
\end{aligned}$$

The security proof requires to make sure that the distribution of e'_i which is computed by this equation is indistinguishable from the distribution $D_{\sigma'}$ used in the real mode. To this end, Brakerski et al. [3] use the noise flooding technique, which is based on the property that, if B/σ' is negligible (where B is bound for $|e|$), then $D_{\sigma'} + e$ is statistically close to $D_{\sigma'}$. Thus, if the modulus-to-noise ratio is set to be super-polynomial, the equivocation algorithm of [3] outputs randomnesses within negligible statistical distance from the correct distribution.

We remove this issue by relying on a Lemma from [17] which states that, for matrices $\mathbf{B} \in \mathbb{Z}_q^{n\times k'}$ and $\mathbf{E} \in \mathbb{Z}^{n\times \ell'}$, given a tuple of the form $(\mathbf{r}^T\mathbf{B}, \mathbf{r}^T\mathbf{E} + \mathbf{e}^T)$, where $(\mathbf{r}, \mathbf{e})$ is sampled from $D_\sigma^n \times D_{\sigma'}^{\ell'}$, a trapdoor for $\mathbf{B}$ allows resampling a short vector $\bar{\mathbf{r}}$ such that $\bar{\mathbf{r}}^T\mathbf{B} = \mathbf{r}^T\mathbf{B}$ while obtaining $\bar{\mathbf{e}}$ with the correct distribution such that $\bar{\mathbf{r}}^T\mathbf{E} + \bar{\mathbf{e}}^T = \mathbf{r}^T\mathbf{E} + \mathbf{e}^T$. We then tweak the equivocation algorithm of [3] by resampling the Gaussian vector $\bar{\mathbf{r}}$ with an appropriate covariance matrix, making sure that the output of the equivocation algorithm is statistically indistinguishable from the real encryption randomness, without the super-polynomial modulus-to-noise requirement.

DDH Construction. Under the DDH assumption, we work with a group $\mathbb{G}$ of prime order p and generator g. Denote by $n \in \mathbb{N}$ some integer. In the real mode, the public key is of the form $(\{g_j\}_{j\in[n]}, \{h_{i,j}\}_{i\in[\ell],j\in[n]})$, where each g_j is a random element of the group $\mathbb{G}$, and $h_{i,j}$ is equal to $g_j^{s_i}$, where $s_i \xleftarrow{\$} \mathbb{Z}_p$ if $i \in I$, or it is sampled randomly from $\mathbb{G}$, otherwise. Here, the secret key consists of the subset I, and the secrets $\{s_i\}_{i\in I}$. The public key has the same structure in the ideal mode, except that we set each g_j to be of the form g^{a_j}, where $a_j \xleftarrow{\$} \mathbb{Z}_p$, and each $h_{i,j}$ is equal to $g^{z_{i,j}}$, where $z_{i,j} \xleftarrow{\$} \mathbb{Z}_p$, if $i \notin I$. The secret key in this case is of the form $\mathsf{sk} = (I, \{s_i\}_{i\in I}, \{a_j\}_{j\in[n]}, \{z_{i,j}\}_{i\notin I, j\in[n]})$.

To encrypt a message $M \in \{0,1\}^\ell$, we first sample randomness $r_1, \cdots, r_n \xleftarrow{\$} \mathbb{Z}_p$. We use a universal hash function, $H : \mathbb{G} \to \{0,1\}$, to compute a ciphertext as $(c_0, c_1, \cdots, c_\ell)$, where $c_0 = \prod_j^n g_j^{r_j}$, and $c_i = M_i \oplus H(\prod_{j=1}^n h_{i,j}^{r_j}) \in \{0,1\}$. Note that for each $i \in [\ell]$, we have:

$$\text{(i) If } i \in I : c_i = M_i \oplus H\left(\prod_{j=1}^n h_{i,j}^{r_j}\right) = M_i \oplus H\left((\prod_{j=1}^n g_j^{r_j})^{s_i}\right) = M_i \oplus H(c_0^{s_i})$$

$$\text{(ii) If } i \in [\ell] \setminus I : c_i = M_i \oplus H\left(\prod_{j=1}^n h_{i,j}^{r_j}\right) = M_i \oplus H\left(\prod_{j=1}^n g^{z_{i,j}\cdot r_j}\right) \text{ (when } b = 1)$$

To decrypt, each M_i can be computed as $c_i \oplus H(c_0^{s_i})$ for all $i \in I$.

The equivocation of public key randomness for a subset $I' \subseteq I$ is done simply by outputting the secret keys for the indices that are in the subset I', and the unmodified public key elements for the rest. Here again, for indices in $I \setminus I'$, we are claiming that $h_{i,j}$'s which are formed as $g_j^{s_i} = g^{a_j \cdot s_i}$ (as the output of $\mathsf{KeyGen}(b = 1, I, r_G)$), are indistinguishable from random elements of $\mathbb{G}$ (as the output of $\mathsf{KeyGen}(b = 0, I', r'_G)$). This holds assuming DDH in $\mathbb{G}$.

The idea behind the $\mathsf{EquivCT}$ algorithm is inspired by the construction of sender-equivocable lossy public-key encryption from the Matrix Diffie-Hellman assumptions [14]. Suppose that $\mathsf{ct} = (c_0, c_1, \cdots, c_\ell)$ encrypts the message $M \in \{0,1\}^\ell$ using the encryption randomness $r_1, \cdots, r_n$. Let $M' \in \{0,1\}^\ell$ a targeted message such that $M_i = M'_i$ for all $i \in I$. To equivocate the ciphertext randomness for M', we have to find $\bar{r}_1, \cdots, \bar{r}_n$ such that $c_0 = \prod_j^n g_j^{\bar{r}_j}$, and

$$c_i \oplus M'_i = H\Big(\prod_{j=1}^{n} g^{z_{i,j} \cdot \bar{r}_j}\Big).$$

Note that, since M' agrees with M on indices $i \in I$, keeping c_0 unchanged guarantees that $c_i = M'_i \oplus H(c_0^{s_i})$ for all $i \in I$ (Equation (i)). In order to find such a randomness, we do as follows: we first find a random element t_i of $\mathbb{Z}_p$, for indices $i \notin I$, such that $c_i = M'_i \oplus H(g^{t_i})$. Since H is a universal hash function, due to the Leftover Hash Lemma, the distribution of $H(g^{t_i})$ is statistically close to uniform over $\{0,1\}$. The probability $\Pr[H(g^{t_i}) = c_i \oplus M'_i]$, for a random t_i, is thus $\geq 1/2 - \mathsf{negl}(\lambda)$, where λ is the security parameter. Hence, this task terminates in polynomial time with overwhelming probability if we repeatedly sample t_i until a suitable candidate is found. Then, we solve the following system of equations to find a vector $\bar{\mathbf{r}}$ over $\mathbb{Z}_q$ such that:

$$\begin{aligned} \mathbf{a} \cdot \bar{\mathbf{r}}^T &= \mathbf{a} \cdot \mathbf{r}^T \\ \mathbf{z}_{i_1} \cdot \bar{\mathbf{r}}^T &= t_{i_1} \\ &\vdots \\ \mathbf{z}_{i_\alpha} \cdot \bar{\mathbf{r}}^T &= t_{i_\alpha}, \end{aligned}$$

where $\{i_1, \cdots, i_\alpha\} = [\ell] \setminus I$, $\mathbf{z}_{i_k} = (z_{i_k,1}, \cdots, z_{i_k,n})$, $\mathbf{a} = (a_1, \cdots, a_n)$, and $\mathbf{r} = (r_1, \cdots, r_n)$. Note that, since $\mathbf{a}$ and each $\mathbf{z}_{i_k}$ are chosen uniformly at random, this system of equation is full rank with overwhelming probability. We can thus find suitable encryption randomness $\bar{\mathbf{r}}$ that explains the ciphertext ct as an encryption of the message M'.

On CRS and Oblivious Sampling Requirements. We now recall the importance of oblivious sampling. As illustrated above, public key elements are of 2 types; (1) elements for positions in I, for which we know the underlying secrets (denoted by $\{s_i\}_{i \in I}$) in both modes, and (2) elements outside I for which the underlying secrets are only known in the ideal mode. To avoid relying on erasures, public key elements for indices outside I should be sampled *obliviously* (i.e., without knowing the underlying secrets) in the real mode.

Recall that a PEPE scheme has to satisfy two properties: For indices in I, decryption must be correct while, for indices outside I, ciphertexts must be equivocable in ideal mode. In the ideal mode, the key components for indices in and outside I thus have to satisfy different properties. Elements within I should be associated with some secret information enabling decryption (e.g., their discrete logarithm). At the same time, in order to equivocate public key randomness, it should be possible to equivocate from a set I to a smaller set I' without changing the public key. To this end, one requirement is that the components for indices in $I \setminus I'$, which were originally sampled to enable decryption in either mode (e.g., as DDH tuples with known discrete logarithm), should be indistinguishable from elements that were originally sampled outside I in the real mode (e.g., random group elements). More specifically, they should be indistinguishable even given the randomness used to generate the key components. Since some computational assumption has to underlie the pseudorandomness of key components in $I \setminus I'$, some information should remain hidden about these elements given the randomness (e.g., in the DDH case, it would be easy to know whether they are DDH tuple or random group elements given their discrete log). For this reason, public key elements outside I should be sampled obliviously. Then, when equivocating, it is sufficient to directly include the public key elements for those indices in the key generation randomness, and use the hardness assumption to prove indistinguishability.

However, there should be a way to explain how obliviously sampled elements were chosen and this "explanation" should be compatible with a reduction from the computational assumption that underlies the indistinguishability of public key components. In the DDH case, for instance, there should be an inverse-sampling algorithm that, on input of a group element $h \in \mathbb{G}$ which is part of a DDH instance, samples uniformly from the set of random coins leading the real oblivious sampling algorithm to output h. While oblivious sampling is efficiently doable using standard techniques (see, e.g., [7, Section 4.3.2]), it is more problematic in groups of hidden order where standard inverse-sampling techniques require knowing the group order. In particular, the problem arises if we try to use the Quadratic Residuosity assumption modulo a safe prime product. Letting g be a generator of the subgroup $\mathbb{QR}_N$ of quadratic residues, it is not clear how to sample an element from $\mathbb{QR}_N$ without knowing its discrete logarithm with respect to g and while remaining able to use the Quadratic Residuosity assumption in the security proof. The only obvious way to sample from this group is to pick a random element from $\mathbb{Z}_N^*$ and square it. In this case, the key-generation randomness r_G would have to contain these square roots, which hinders a reduction from the QR assumption when we want to prove the public-key randomness indistinguishablity property. To circumvent this difficulty, our SD-based PEPE uses a group of public (but composite) order.

Regarding the need for a CRS, let us imagine a construction relying on factoring-related assumption where a composite integer $N = pq$ would be sampled during the key generation in real mode (when $b = 0$). According to the definition of PEPE, the randomness used to sample N should be included in the key generation randomness r_G. This randomness would include the factors p and q (or a random seed allowing to recompute them). Then, when equivocating the key generation randomness, it would not be possible to rely on any assumption related to hardness of factoring N since p and q would be part of r_G and thus available to the adversary. As a result, we need to consider a separate Setup algorithm that generates the group order $N = pq$ as part of a common reference string crs, for which a trapdoor (i.e., p and q) can be used by randomness equivocation algorithms.

SD Construction. Our construction from the SD assumption avoids oblivious sampling difficulties (which arise in previous factoring-based constructions) because it only requires to obliviously sample from a public order group. It works over a multiplicative cyclic group $\mathbb{G} \approx \mathbb{G}_q \times \mathbb{G}_p$, where $\mathbb{G}$ is of order $N = pq$, $\mathbb{G}_p = \{x^q \mod N : x \in \mathbb{G}\}$ is the subgroup of $\mathbb{G}$ of order p, and $\mathbb{G}_q = \{x^p \mod N : x \in \mathbb{G}\}$ is the subgroup of $\mathbb{G}$ of order q, and p and q are sufficiently large prime numbers. Since the assumption is implied by the hardness of factoring, we require that there exists a trusted Setup algorithm that generates a group order $N = pq$, and provides the factorization p and q for randomness equivocation algorithms. Let $\hat{g}$ and $\hat{h}$, be generators of $\mathbb{G}_p$, and $\mathbb{G}_q$, respectively. The public key contains $(N, \hat{g}, \hat{h}, \{g_j\}_{j\in[n]}, \{h_{i,j}\}_{i\in[\ell],j\in[n]})$, where each $g_j = g^{a_j}$, for a random element $a_j \xleftarrow{\$} \mathbb{Z}_N$, is sampled during the Setup, and $h_{i,j} = g_j^{s_i}$, where $s_i \xleftarrow{\$} \mathbb{Z}_N$ if $i \in I$, or it is sampled randomly from $\mathbb{G}$, otherwise. Here, the secret key is $\mathsf{sk} = \{I, \{s_i\}_{i\in I}\}$. The public key has the same structure in the ideal mode, except that we set each $h_{i,j}$ to be equal to $h_i^{\delta_{i,j}} \cdot g_j^{s_i}$, where $h_i \xleftarrow{\$} \mathbb{G}_q$, and $s_i \xleftarrow{\$} \mathbb{Z}_N$, if $i \notin I$. The secret key in this case is $\mathsf{sk} = (I, \{s_i\}_{i\in[\ell]}, \{h_i\}_{i\notin I})$. The encryption, decryption and public key randomness equivocation algorithms proceed more or less in the same way as in the DDH-based construction. The equivocation of the ciphertext randomness is achieved regarding the fact that $c_0 = \prod_j g_j^{r_j}$ is an element of the subgroup $\mathbb{G}_p$, so it only determines the randomness $\{r_i\}_{i\in[l]}$ modulo the order of the group, p. So, it is enough to find $r_i' = r_i \mod p$ such that $H(h_i^{r_i'} \cdot c_0^{s_i} \mod N^2) = c_i \oplus M_i'$ for all $i \notin I$. Since H is a universal hash function and r_i' is considered modulo p, a similar argument as in the DDH case shows that this task terminates in polynomial time with all but negligible probability.

2 Preliminaries

We use λ to denote the security parameter. For a natural integer $n \in \mathbb{N}$, the set $\{1, 2, \cdots, n\}$ is denoted by $[n]$. For $q \in \mathbb{N}$, we consider the rounding function $\lfloor \cdot \rceil_2 : \mathbb{Z}_q \rightarrow \mathbb{Z}_2$ to be $\lfloor x \rceil_2 = \lfloor x \cdot 2/q \rceil (\mod 2)$ for $x \in \mathbb{Z}_q$. We use bold lowercase letters (e.g., $\mathbf{v}$) to denote vectors and bold uppercase letters (e.g., $\mathbf{V}$) to denote matrices. For a vector $\mathbf{v} = (v_1, \cdots, v_n)$, the vector $(g^{v_1}. \cdots, g^{v_n})$ is denoted by $g^{\mathbf{v}}$. We write $\mathsf{poly}(\lambda)$ to denote an arbitrary polynomial function. We denote by $\mathsf{negl}(\lambda)$ a negligible function in λ, and PPT stands for probabilistic polynomial-time. Two distributions $\mathcal{D}_1$ and $\mathcal{D}_2$ are computationally (*resp.* statistically) indistinguishable if no PPT (*resp.* unbounded) adversary can distinguish them, and we write $\mathcal{D}_1 \approx_c \mathcal{D}_2$ (*resp.* $\mathcal{D}_1 \approx_s \mathcal{D}_2$). We write $\Delta(\mathcal{D}_1, \mathcal{D}_2)$ to denote the statistical distance between the distributions $\mathcal{D}_1$ and $\mathcal{D}_2$. For a finite set S, we write $x \xleftarrow{\$} S$ to denote that x is sampled uniformly at random from S. If $\mathcal{D}$

is a distribution over the set S, we write $x \leftarrow \mathcal{D}$ to denote that x is sampled from S according to $\mathcal{D}$. For an algorithm $\mathcal{A}$, we denote by $y \leftarrow \mathcal{A}(x)$ the output y after running $\mathcal{A}$ on input x. We use discrete Gaussian distributions, defined as follows.

Definition 1 ((Univariate) Discrete Gaussian Distribution). *For a real $\sigma > 0$, the discrete Gaussian distribution with variance σ is denoted by D_σ that is a probability distribution with support $\mathbb{Z}$ that assigns to each $x \in \mathbb{Z}$ a probability proportional to* $\exp(-\pi x^2/\sigma^2)$.

Definition 2. *Let Λ be a full-rank n-dimensional lattice. Let $\mathbf{\Sigma} \in \mathbb{R}^{n \times n}$ be a symmetric definite positive matrix, and $\mathbf{r}', \mathbf{c} \in \mathbb{R}^n$. $D_{\Lambda+\mathbf{r}',\mathbf{\Sigma},\mathbf{c}}$ denotes the discrete Gaussian distribution with support $\Lambda+\mathbf{r}'$, covariance $\mathbf{\Sigma}$, and mean $\mathbf{c}$ that assigns to each $\mathbf{x} \in \Lambda + \mathbf{r}'$ a probability proportional to* $\exp(-\pi(\mathbf{x} - \mathbf{c})^T\mathbf{\Sigma}^{-1}(\mathbf{x} - \mathbf{c}))$.

We also restate the definition of universal hash functions and the Leftover Hash Lemma:

Definition 3 (Universal Hash Function). *A family of hash functions $\mathcal{H} = \{H : \mathcal{X} \to \{0,1\}^\ell\}$ is universal if for all $x_1, x_2 \in \mathcal{X}$, where $x_1 \neq x_2$, we have* $\Pr[H \xleftarrow{\$} \mathcal{H}, H(x_1) = H(x_2)] \leq 1/2^\ell$.

Lemma 1 (Leftover Hash Lemma, [15]). *Let $\mathcal{H} = \{H : \mathcal{X} \to \{0,1\}^\ell\}$ be a universal family of hash functions. Let $\epsilon > 0$ and $\mathcal{D}$ be a distribution over $\mathcal{X}$ with min-entropy $H_\infty(\mathcal{D}) \geq \ell + 2\log(1/\epsilon)$. Then*

$$\Delta((H, H(x)), (H, U)) = \epsilon \ ,$$

where $H \xleftarrow{\$} \mathcal{H}$, $x \xleftarrow{\$} \mathcal{D}$, and $U \xleftarrow{\$} \{0,1\}^\ell$.

2.1 Reminders on Standard Assumptions

We now provide a brief reminder on standard hardness assumptions and classical lattice results used throughout our work.

Lattices

Definition 4 (Learning With Errors assumption, [20]). *Let λ be the security parameter, $k, q \in \mathbb{Z}$, and let χ be an efficiently samplable distribution over $\mathbb{Z}_q$. The $\mathsf{LWE}_{k,q,\chi}$ assumption holds if for any polynomial $n = n(\lambda)$ we have*

$$(\mathbf{A}, \mathbf{A}\mathbf{s} + \mathbf{e}) \approx_c (\mathbf{A}, \mathbf{u}) \ ,$$

where $\mathbf{A} \xleftarrow{\$} \mathbb{Z}_q^{n \times k}$, $\mathbf{s} \xleftarrow{\$} \mathbb{Z}_q^k$, $\mathbf{e} \xleftarrow{\$} \chi^n$, and $\mathbf{u} \xleftarrow{\$} \mathbb{Z}_q^n$.

In the above definition, if we set the error distribution χ to be a discrete Gaussian distribution $D_{\alpha.q}$, where $\alpha \in (\sqrt{k}/q, 1)$, then LWE is at least as hard as standard worst-case lattice problems [5,20].

We also use the following lemma about lattice trapdoors.

Lemma 2 ([18]). *There exists a pair of PPT algorithms* (TrapGen, SampleD) *such that the* TrapGen *algorithm on receiving the security parameter* λ *and* $n, k', q \in \mathbb{Z}$ *as input, outputs a matrix* $\mathbf{B} \in \mathbb{Z}_q^{n \times k'}$ *and a trapdoor* td, *where* $\mathbf{B}$ *is* $2^{-k'}$ *close to uniform. Also, the* SampleD *algorithm takes as input a trapdoor* td, *a matrix* $\mathbf{B}$ *and a vector* $\mathbf{y} \in \mathbb{Z}_q^{k'}$ *and outputs* $\mathbf{r} \in \mathbb{Z}_q^n$ *such that* $\mathbf{r} \xleftarrow{\$} D_{\Lambda_{\mathbf{y}}^{\perp}(\mathbf{B}^T),\sigma}$.

We also need the following result about sampling from lattice Gaussians.

Lemma 3 ([5], **Lemma 2.3**). *There exists a PPT algorithm that, given a basis* $(b_i)_{i \le k}$ *of a full-rank lattice* Λ, *vectors* $\mathbf{r}', \mathbf{c} \in \mathbb{R}^n$, *and a symmetric positive definite matrix* $\mathbf{\Sigma} \in \mathbb{R}^{n \times n}$ *such that* $\Omega(\sqrt{\log n}). \max_i ||\mathbf{\Sigma}^{-1/2} \cdot b_i|| \le 1$, *returns a sample from* $D_{\Lambda + \mathbf{r}', \mathbf{\Sigma}, \mathbf{c}}$.

We finally recall the following lemma which plays a central role in our LWE-based PEPE construction for resampling randomness and noise.

Lemma 4 ([17], **Lemma 11**). *Let* $\mathbf{B} \in \mathbb{Z}_q^{n \times k'}$ *and* $\mathbf{E} \in \mathbb{Z}^{n \times \ell'}$. *Sample* $(\mathbf{r}, \mathbf{e}) \leftarrow D_\sigma^n \times D_{\sigma'}^{\ell'}$ *and define* $(\mathbf{u}, \mathbf{f}) = (\mathbf{r}^T\mathbf{B}, \mathbf{r}^T\mathbf{E} + \mathbf{e}^T) \in \mathbb{Z}_q^{k'} \times \mathbb{Z}^{\ell'}$. *The conditional distribution of* $\mathbf{r}$ *given* $(\mathbf{u}, \mathbf{f})$ *is* $D^{S_{\mathbf{E},\mathbf{u},\mathbf{f}}}_{\Lambda^{\perp}(\mathbf{B}^T) + \mathbf{r}', \sqrt{\mathbf{\Sigma}}, \mathbf{c}}$ *with support*

$$S_{\mathbf{E},\mathbf{u},\mathbf{f}} = \{\bar{\mathbf{r}} \in \Lambda^{\perp}(\mathbf{B}^T) + \mathbf{r}' : \bar{\mathbf{r}} \in \mathbb{Z}_q^n, (\mathbf{f} - \bar{\mathbf{r}}^T\mathbf{E}) \in \mathbb{Z}_q^{\ell'}\} \ ,$$

where $\mathbf{r}'$ *is any solution to* $\mathbf{r}'^T\mathbf{B} = u$, *and*

$$\mathbf{\Sigma} = \sigma^2\sigma'^2 \cdot (\sigma^2 \cdot \mathbf{E}^T \cdot \mathbf{E} + \sigma'^2 \cdot \mathbf{I}_n)^{-1}, \quad \mathbf{c} = \sigma^2 \cdot (\sigma^2 \cdot \mathbf{E}^T \cdot \mathbf{E} + \sigma'^2 \cdot \mathbf{I}_n)^{-1} \cdot \mathbf{E}^T \cdot \mathbf{f} \ .$$

Decisional Diffie-Hellman

Let $\mathcal{G}$ be polynomial-time a group generator that takes the security parameter λ as input and outputs $(\mathbb{G}, p, g)$, where $\mathbb{G}$ is a multiplicative cyclic group of prime order p and g is a generator of the group.

Definition 5 (Decisional Diffie-Hellman problem). *Let* λ *be the security parameter. We say that the decisional Diffie-Hellman problem is hard relative to* $\mathcal{G}$ *if*

$$(\mathbb{G}, p, g, g^a, g^b, g^{ab}) \approx_c (\mathbb{G}, p, g, g^a, g^b, g^c) \ ,$$

where $(\mathbb{G}, p, g) \xleftarrow{\$} \mathcal{G}(1^\lambda)$ *and* $(a, b, c) \xleftarrow{\$} \mathbb{Z}_p$.

Subgroup Decision Assumption

Here we provide some reminders on the subgroup decision assumption over composite-order groups. The following definition is derived from the one of Boneh et al. [2]. An important difference is that we do *not* require bilinear groups, which allows us to reveal generators of both subgroups.

Let $\mathcal{G}$ be a polynomial-time algorithm that takes the security parameter λ as input and outputs a tuple $(p, q, \mathbb{G}, g)$, where p and q are λ-bit prime numbers, and $\mathbb{G}$ is (multiplicative) cyclic group of order $N = pq$, generated by g. In particular, we have $\mathbb{G} \approx \mathbb{G}_q \times \mathbb{G}_p$ where $\mathbb{G}_p = \{x^q \mod N : x \in \mathbb{G}\}$ is the subgroup of $\mathbb{G}$ of order p and $\mathbb{G}_q = \{x^p \mod N : x \in \mathbb{G}\}$ is the subgroup of $\mathbb{G}$ of order q. Note also that g^p (resp. g^q) is a generator of $\mathbb{G}_q$ (resp. $\mathbb{G}_p$).

Definition 6 (Subgroup Decision, [2]). *Let λ be the security parameter. We say that the subgroup decision assumption is hard relative to $\mathcal{G}$ if*

$$(N, \mathbb{G}, g_p, g_q, x^q) \approx_c (N, \mathbb{G}, g_p, g_q, x) \ ,$$

where $(p, q, \mathbb{G}, g) \overset{\$}{\leftarrow} \mathcal{G}(1^\lambda)$, $N = pq$, g_p (resp. g_q) is a random element of $\mathbb{G}_p$ (resp. $\mathbb{G}_q$), and x is a random element of $\mathbb{G}$.

Note that a cyclic group of composite order N can be obtained by considering the subgroup of a-th residues in $\mathbb{Z}_P^*$, where $a \in \mathbb{N}$ is chosen so that $P = a \cdot N + 1$ is prime. We insist that we use the assumption in groups without a pairing.

2.2 Non-Committing Encryption

Non-committing encryption (NCE) was first introduced in [6] as a central primitive for constructing adaptively-secure multi-party computation. Here we recall the formal definition of an NCE scheme.

Definition 7 (Non-Committing Encryption). *Let a security parameter λ. A Non-Committing Encryption (NCE) scheme consists of five PPT algorithms* $(\mathsf{KeyGen}, \mathsf{Enc}, \mathsf{Dec}, \mathsf{Sim}_1, \mathsf{Sim}_2)$ *such that:*

- $\mathsf{KeyGen}(1^\lambda, r_G) \rightarrow (\mathsf{pk}, \mathsf{sk})$: *On input the security parameter λ and a randomness r_G, the key-generation algorithm outputs a public key* pk *and a secret key* sk.
- $\mathsf{Enc}(\mathsf{pk}, M, r_E) \rightarrow \mathsf{ct}$: *On input the public key* pk, *a message M, and some randomness r_E, the encryption algorithm outputs a ciphertext* ct.
- $\mathsf{Dec}(\mathsf{sk}, \mathsf{ct}) \rightarrow M/\bot$: *On input the secret key* sk *and a ciphertext* ct, *the decryption algorithm outputs a message M or returns $\bot$.*
- $\mathsf{Sim}_1(1^\lambda) \rightarrow (\mathsf{pk}, \mathsf{ct}, \mathsf{st})$: *On input of the security parameter λ, the* Sim_1 *algorithm outputs a simulated public key* pk *and a ciphertext* ct *together with an internal state* st.
- $\mathsf{Sim}_2(M, \mathsf{st}) \rightarrow (r_G, r_E)$: *On input a message M and an internal state* st, *the* Sim_2 *algorithm outputs a key-generation and encryption randomness pair (r_G, r_E).*

We require an NCE scheme to satisfy the following properties:

- ***Correctness.*** *For any message $M \in \{0,1\}^l$,*

$$\Pr\left[M \leftarrow \mathsf{Dec}(\mathsf{sk}, \mathsf{ct}) : \begin{array}{l} (\mathsf{pk}, \mathsf{sk}) \leftarrow \mathsf{KeyGen}(1^\lambda) \\ \mathsf{ct} \leftarrow \mathsf{Enc}(\mathsf{pk}, M) \end{array}\right] \geq 1 - \mathsf{negl}(\lambda) \ .$$

- ***Simulatability.*** *The following two distributions should be computationally indistinguishable:*

$$\mathsf{REAL} = \left\{ (M, \mathsf{pk}, \mathsf{ct}, r_G, r_E) : \begin{array}{l} (\mathsf{pk}, \mathsf{sk}) \leftarrow \mathsf{KeyGen}(1^\lambda, r_G) \\ M \leftarrow \mathcal{A}(\mathsf{pk}) \\ \mathsf{ct} \leftarrow \mathsf{Enc}(\mathsf{pk}, M, r_E) \end{array} \right\} ,$$

and

$$\mathsf{IDEAL} = \left\{ (M, \mathsf{pk}, \mathsf{ct}, r_G, r_E) : \begin{array}{l} (\mathsf{pk}, \mathsf{ct}, \mathsf{st}) \leftarrow \mathsf{Sim}_1(1^\lambda) \\ M \leftarrow \mathcal{A}(\mathsf{pk}) \\ (r_G, r_E) \leftarrow \mathsf{Sim}_2(M, \mathsf{st}) \end{array} \right\},$$

for any PPT adversary $\mathcal{A}$, and any key-generation randomness r_G and encryption randomness r_E in the REAL *distribution.*

Next, we recall the definition of PEPE, introduced in [3] by Brakerski *et al.*, which is proven to imply non-committing encryption.

Definition 8 (PEPE). *Let λ be a security parameter and $\{0,1\}^\lambda$ be the message space. A Packed Encryption with Partial Equivocality scheme consists of five PPT algorithms* ($\mathsf{KeyGen}, \mathsf{Enc}, \mathsf{Dec}, \mathsf{EquivPK}, \mathsf{EquivCT}$) *such that:*

- $\mathsf{KeyGen}(1^\lambda, b \in \{0,1\}, I, r_G) \to (\mathsf{pk}, \mathsf{sk})$: *On input the security parameter λ, a bit b, a subset of indices $I \subset [\ell]$, and a key generation randomness r_G, the key-generation algorithm outputs a public key* pk *and a secret key* sk. *If $b = 0$, we say that the keys are generated in the real mode. Otherwise, we say that the keys are generated in the ideal mode.*
- $\mathsf{Enc}(\mathsf{pk}, M \in \{0,1\}^\ell, r_E) \to \mathsf{ct}$: *On input the public key* pk, *a message $M \in \{0,1\}^\ell$ and an encryption randomness, the encryption algorithm outputs a ciphertext* ct.
- $\mathsf{Dec}(\mathsf{sk}, \mathsf{ct}) \to (M_i)_{i \in I}$: *On input the secret key* sk *and a ciphertext* ct, *the decryption algorithm outputs bits M_i for $i \in I$.*
- $\mathsf{EquivPK}(\mathsf{sk}, b, I, r_G, I') \to r'_G$: *On input the secret key* sk, *a bit b, subsets $I, I' \subset [n]$ and a (key-generation) randomness r_G, the public-key-equivocation algorithm outputs a randomness r'_G.*
- $\mathsf{EquivCT}(\mathsf{sk}, (M, r_E), \{M'_i\}_{i \notin I}) \to r'_E$: *On input the secret key* sk, *a pair of message and randomness (M, r_E), and some bits $\{M'_i\}_{i \notin I}$, the ciphertext-equivocation algorithm outputs a randomness r'_E.*

We require a PEPE scheme to satisfy the following properties:

- ***Correctness.*** *For any message $M \in \{0,1\}^l$ and any subset $I \subset [l]$ we have*

$$\Pr\left[\{M_i\}_{i \in I} = \{M'_i\}_{i \in I} : \begin{array}{l} (\mathsf{pk}, \mathsf{sk}) \leftarrow \mathsf{KeyGen}(1^\lambda, 0, I, r_G) \\ \mathsf{ct} \leftarrow \mathsf{Enc}(\mathsf{pk}, M, r_E) \\ (M'_i)_{i \in I} \leftarrow \mathsf{Dec}(\mathsf{sk}, \mathsf{ct}) \end{array} \right] \geq 1 - \mathsf{negl}(\lambda)$$

- ***Public key randomness indistinguishability.*** *The random coins output by the* EquivPK *algorithm should be computationally indistinguishable from true random coins. Meaning that the two following joint distributions should be computationally indistinguishable:*

$$\mathsf{REAL}_{\mathsf{pk}} = \{r_G : \quad (\mathsf{pk}, \mathsf{sk}) \leftarrow \mathsf{KeyGen}(1^\lambda, 0, I, r_G)\},$$

and

$$\mathsf{IDEAL}_{\mathsf{pk}_b} = \left\{ r_G : \begin{array}{l} (\mathsf{pk}, \mathsf{sk}) \leftarrow \mathsf{KeyGen}(1^\lambda, b, I', r'_G) \\ r_G \leftarrow \mathsf{EquivPK}(\mathsf{sk}, b, (I', r'_G), I) \end{array} \right\},$$

for any subsets $I, I' \subset [\ell]$ such that $I \subset I'$, and for any key-generation randomness r_G in $\mathsf{REAL}_{\mathsf{pk}}$ and r'_G in $\mathsf{IDEAL}_{\mathsf{pk}_b}$, for $b \in \{0,1\}$.

- ***Ciphertext randomness indistinguishability.*** *The random coins output by the* EquivCT *algorithm should be statistically close to true random coins. Meaning that for any subset $I \subset [\ell]$, any r_G, any r'_E, and any message $M' \in \{0,1\}^\ell$, the following two distributions should be statistically indistinguishable:*

$$\mathsf{IDEAL}_{\mathsf{ct}} = \left\{ (\mathsf{pk}, M, r_E) : \begin{array}{l} (\mathsf{pk}, \mathsf{sk}) \leftarrow \mathsf{KeyGen}(1^\lambda, 1, I, r_G) \\ \mathsf{ct} \leftarrow \mathsf{Enc}(\mathsf{pk}, M', r'_E) \\ M \leftarrow \mathcal{A}(\mathsf{pk}) \\ r_E \leftarrow \mathsf{EquivCT}(\mathsf{sk}, (M', r'_E), \{M_i\}_{i \notin I}) \end{array} \right\},$$

and

$$\mathsf{REAL}_{\mathsf{ct}} = \left\{ (\mathsf{pk}, M, r_E) : \begin{array}{l} (\mathsf{pk}, \mathsf{sk}) \leftarrow \mathsf{KeyGen}(1^\lambda, 0, I, r_G) \\ M \leftarrow \mathcal{A}(\mathsf{pk}) \\ \mathsf{ct} \leftarrow \mathsf{Enc}(\mathsf{pk}, M, r_E) \end{array} \right\},$$

where $\mathcal{A}$ is an unbounded adversary which outputs M such that $M_i = M'_i$ for all $i \in I$.

PEPE implies NCE via an efficient transform incurring only a constant loss in the rate, we therefore focus on building more efficient *rate*-1 PEPE schemes.

3 PEPE Constructions

We now present our different rate-1 PEPE constructions. As already mentioned, we propose the first construction from LWE with polynomial modulus, a DDH-based construction with strict polynomial running time, and the first PEPE construction from the subgroup decision assumptions. In all of our constructions, we consider a mapping from the random coins used in the key generation algorithm to the elements that it generates, and for the sake of simplicity, we consider the key generation randomness (r_G) to include those elements. We refer the reader to the full version of the paper for the proof of our DDH-based and SD-based constructions.

3.1 PEPE from LWE

We present a construction for PEPE from the LWE assumption. First, we recall the post-processing technique of ciphertext shrinking introduced in [4] which is used in our scheme.

Ciphertext Shrinking Algorithm for LWE-Based Encryption Schemes.

Construction 1. Consider a public-key encryption scheme with ciphertexts of the form $(\mathbf{c}_1, w_{2,1}. \cdots, w_{2,\ell}) \in \mathbb{Z}_q^k \times \mathbb{Z}_q^\ell$ and secret key $\mathbf{S} \in \mathbb{Z}_q^{k\times\ell}$, where decryption is computed by $\lfloor (w_{2,1}, \cdots, w_{2,\ell}) - \mathbf{c}_1\mathbf{S} \rceil_2 = \lfloor M + e \rceil_2$ where e is sampled from a B-bounded distribution. We describe the shrinking algorithms in detail:

- $\mathsf{Shrink}(\mathsf{pk}, (\mathbf{c}_1, w_{2,1}. \cdots, w_{2,\ell}))$:
  - Choose $z \xleftarrow{\$} \mathbb{Z}_q \setminus U$, where

$$U = \bigcup_{i=1}^{\ell} \left(\left[-\tfrac{q}{4} - w_{2,i} - B, -\tfrac{q}{4} - w_{2,i} + B\right] \cup \left[\tfrac{q}{4} - w_{2,i} - B, \tfrac{q}{4} - w_{2,i} + B\right] \right)$$

  - For all $i \in [\ell]$, compute $c_{2,i} = \lfloor w_{2,i} + z \rceil_2 \in \mathbb{Z}_2$.
  - Output $\mathsf{ct} = (\mathbf{c}_1, c_{2,1}, \cdots, c_{2,\ell}, z)$.
- $\mathsf{ShrinkDec}(\mathsf{sk} = \mathbf{S}, ct)$:
  - Parse ct as $(\mathbf{c}_1, c_{2,1}, \cdots, c_{2,\ell}, z)$.
  - Compute $M_i \leftarrow (c_{2,i} - \lfloor \mathbf{c}_1\mathbf{s}_i + z \rceil_2) \mod 2$ where $\mathbf{s}_i$ is the i-th row of $\mathbf{S}$.
  - Output $M = (M_1, \cdots, M_\ell)$.

  Note that we can give a subset $I \subset [\ell]$ as input to the $\mathsf{ShrinkDec}$ algorithm and only receive $\{M_i\}_{i\in I}$ as output. In [4], the authors prove that if $q > 4\ell B$, then this construction is correct.

We now detail our LWE-based PEPE scheme.

Construction 2. Let $(\mathsf{Shrink}, \mathsf{ShrinkDec})$ be the shrinking pair of algorithms described in Construction 1, and $\mathsf{TrapGen}$ the PPT algorithm for generating lattice trapdoors as proposed in [18].

- $\mathsf{KeyGen}(1^\lambda, b \in \{0,1\}, I, r_G)$:
  - if $b = 0$ do:
    - Choose $\mathbf{A} \xleftarrow{\$} \mathbb{Z}_q^{n\times k}$.
    - For all $i \in I$, set $\mathbf{v}_i = \mathbf{A}\mathbf{s}_i + \mathbf{e}_i$, where $\mathbf{s}_i \xleftarrow{\$} \mathbb{Z}_q^k$, and $\mathbf{e}_i \xleftarrow{\$} D_\sigma^n$.
    - For all $i \notin I$, set $\mathbf{v}_i \xleftarrow{\$} \mathbb{Z}_q^n$.
    - Set $\mathsf{pk} = (\mathbf{A}, \{\mathbf{v}_i\}_{i\in[\ell]})$, and $\mathsf{sk} = (I, \{\mathbf{s}_i\}_{i\in I})$.
    - The key generation randomness is $r_G = (\mathbf{A}, \{\mathbf{s}_i\}_{i\in I}, \{\mathbf{e}_i\}_{i\in I}, \{\mathbf{v}_i\}_{i\notin I})$.
  - if $b = 1$ do:
    - Run $(\mathbf{B}, \mathsf{td}_\mathbf{B}) \leftarrow \mathsf{TrapGen}(1^\lambda, n, k + l - |I|, q)$ and parse $\mathbf{B}$ as $\mathbf{B} = \left[\mathbf{A}\middle|\mathbf{V}\right] \in \mathbb{Z}_q^{n\times(k+\ell-|I|)}$.
    - For all $i \in I$, set $\mathbf{v}_i = \mathbf{A}\mathbf{s}_i + \mathbf{e}_i$, where $\mathbf{s_i} \xleftarrow{\$} \mathbb{Z}_q^k$, and $\mathbf{e}_i \xleftarrow{\$} D_\sigma^n$.
    - For all $i \notin I$, set $\mathbf{v}_i := \mathbf{V}_i$, where $\mathbf{V}_i$ is the i-th column of matrix $\mathbf{V}$.
    - Set $\mathsf{pk} = (\mathbf{A}, \{\mathbf{v}_i\}_{i\in[\ell]})$, and $\mathsf{sk} = (I, \{\mathbf{s}_i\}_{i\in I}, \mathsf{td}_\mathbf{B})$.
    - The key generation randomness r_G is the randomness used in the $\mathsf{TrapGen}$ algorithm together with $\{\mathbf{s}_i, \mathbf{e}_i\}_{i\in I}$.
- $\mathsf{Enc}(\mathsf{pk}, M \in \{0,1\}^\ell, r_E)$:
  - Parse $\mathsf{pk} = (\mathbf{A}, \{\mathbf{v}_i\}_{i\in[\ell]})$.

- Sample $\mathbf{r} \xleftarrow{\$} D_{\sigma}^{n}$.
- Compute $\mathbf{c}_1 \leftarrow \mathbf{r}^T\mathbf{A}$ and $w_{2,i} = \mathbf{r}^T\mathbf{v}_i + e_i + \lfloor q/2 \rceil \cdot M_i \in \mathbb{Z}_q, \forall i \in [\ell]$, where $e_i \xleftarrow{\$} D_{\sigma'}$.
- Compress $(\mathbf{c}_1, w_{2,1}, \cdots, w_{2,\ell})$ into

$$ct = (\mathbf{c}_1, c_{2,1}, \cdots, c_{2,\ell}, z) \leftarrow \mathsf{Shrink}(\mathsf{pk}, (\mathbf{c}_1, w_{2,1}, \cdots, w_{2,\ell})).$$

- Set $r_E = (\mathbf{r}, \{e_i\}_{i\in[\ell]}, z)$.
- Output ct.

• $\mathsf{Dec}(\mathsf{sk}, ct)$:
  - Use sk to run $\mathsf{ShrinkDec}(\mathsf{sk}, ct)$ and recover M.
  - Output $\{M_i\}_{i\in I}$.

• $\mathsf{EquivPK}(\mathsf{sk}, b, I, r_G, I')$:
  - If $I' \not\subseteq I$, abort.
  - Let $\mathsf{pk} = (\mathbf{A}, \{\mathbf{v}_i\}_{i\in[\ell]})$ be the output of KeyGen on input $(1^\lambda, b, I, r_G)$. Parse $\mathsf{sk} = (I, \{\mathbf{s}_i\}_{i\in I})$ if $b = 0$, or $\mathsf{sk} = (I, \{\mathbf{s}_i\}_{i\in I}, \mathsf{td}_{\mathbf{B}})$ if $b = 1$.
  - Compute $\{\mathbf{e}_i = \mathbf{v}_i - \mathbf{A}\mathbf{s}_i\}_{i\in I'}$, and output $r'_G = (\mathbf{A}, \{\mathbf{s}_i\}_{i\in I'}, \{\mathbf{e}_i\}_{i\in I'}, \{\mathbf{v}_i\}_{i\notin I'})$.

• $\mathsf{EquivCT}(\mathsf{sk}, (M, r_E), \{M'_i\}_{i\notin I})$:
  - Parse $\mathsf{sk} = (I, \{\mathbf{s}_i\}_{i\in I}, \mathsf{td}_{\mathbf{B}})$, $\mathsf{pk} = (\mathbf{A}, \{\mathbf{v}_i\}_{i\in[\ell]})$, and compute $(\{\mathbf{e}_i\}_{i\in I}, \{\mathbf{v}_i\}_{i\notin I})$ from sk and pk. Let $(\mathbf{c}_1, w_{2,1}, \cdots, w_{2,\ell})$ be the LWE encryption of M w.r.t pk and $r_E = (\mathbf{r}, \{e_i^*\}_{i\in[\ell]}, z)$.
  - For $i \notin I$, sample $e'_i \xleftarrow{\$} D_{\sigma'}$.
  - Using $\mathsf{td}_{\mathbf{B}}$, sample $\bar{\mathbf{r}} \xleftarrow{\$} D^{S_{\mathbf{E},\mathbf{u},\mathbf{f}}}_{\Lambda^{\perp}(\mathbf{B}^T)+\mathbf{r}', \sqrt{\mathbf{\Sigma}}, \mathbf{c}}$, where

$$\begin{aligned}
\mathbf{E} &= \left[\mathbf{e}_{i_1} | \cdots | \mathbf{e}_{i_{|I|}}\right] \text{ for } i_1, \cdots, i_{|I|} \in I,\\
\mathbf{u} &= (\mathbf{c}_1, \{w_{2,i} - \lfloor q/2 \rceil M'_i - e'_i\}_{i\notin I}),\\
\mathbf{f} &= \mathbf{r}^T\mathbf{E} + \mathbf{e}^*, \text{ where } \mathbf{e}^* = (e^*_{i_1}, \cdots, e^*_{i_{|I|}}) \text{ for } i_1, \cdots, i_{|I|} \in I,\\
\mathbf{\Sigma} &= \sigma^2\sigma'^2 \cdot (\sigma^2 \cdot \mathbf{E}^T \cdot \mathbf{E} + \sigma'^2 \cdot \mathbf{I}_n)^{-1},\\
\mathbf{c} &= \sigma^2 \cdot (\sigma^2 \cdot \mathbf{E}^T \cdot \mathbf{E} + \sigma'^2 \cdot \mathbf{I}_n)^{-1} \cdot \mathbf{E}^T \cdot \mathbf{f}.
\end{aligned}$$

  Regarding Lemma 4 the output of the sampling would be a vector $\bar{\mathbf{r}}$ satisfying $\bar{\mathbf{r}}^T\mathbf{B} = \mathbf{u}$.
  - For $i \in I$, set $e'_i = e^*_i + (\mathbf{r} - \bar{\mathbf{r}})^T\mathbf{e}_i$.
  - Output $r'_E = (\bar{\mathbf{r}}, \{e'_i\}_{i\in[\ell]}, z)$.

Theorem 3. *Assuming LWE, Construction 2 is a rate-*1 *PEPE scheme.*

Proof. We now prove correctness, public key randomness indistinguishability, and ciphertext randomness indistinguishability of the above construction.

Correctness. Correctness follows from the fact that in the ciphertext shrinking technique described in Construction 1 we have:

$$(c_{2,i} - \lfloor \mathbf{c}_1 \mathbf{s}_i + z \rceil_2) \mod 2 = \lfloor w_{2,i} - \mathbf{c}_1 \mathbf{s}_i \rceil_2 \ ,$$

where $i \in I$. Also, similarly to Regev's public-key encryption scheme [20], for all $i \in I$ we have

$$\begin{aligned} \lfloor w_{2,i} - \mathbf{c}_1 \mathbf{s}_i \rceil_2 &= \lfloor \mathbf{r}^T(\mathbf{A}\mathbf{s}_i + \mathbf{e}_i) + e_i + \lfloor q/2 \rceil M_i - \mathbf{r}^T \mathbf{A}\mathbf{s}_i \rceil_2 \\ &= \lfloor \mathbf{r}^T \mathbf{e}_i + e_i + \lfloor q/2 \rceil M_i \rceil_2 = M_i \ . \end{aligned}$$

Thus, the scheme is correct.

Public Key Randomness Indistinguishability. We prove the public key randomness indistinguishability using a sequence of games. Assume that $b = 1$ in the experiment $\mathsf{IDEAL}_{\mathsf{pk}_b}$. We start with $\mathcal{H}_0$ which is the experiment $\mathsf{IDEAL}_{\mathsf{pk}_1}$, and we end up at $\mathcal{H}_2$ which is the experiment $\mathsf{REAL}_{\mathsf{pk}}$. We show that the advantage of an adversary in distinguishing between each two successive games is negligible. Hence, the distribution of the public key randomness is indistinguishable in $\mathsf{IDEAL}_{\mathsf{pk}_1}$ and in $\mathsf{REAL}_{\mathsf{pk}}$.

Hybrid $\mathcal{H}_0$. This is the experiment $\mathsf{IDEAL}_{\mathsf{pk}_1}$:

- $(\mathsf{pk}, \mathsf{sk}) \leftarrow \mathsf{KeyGen}(1^\lambda, 1, I', r'_G)$, where $\mathsf{pk} = (\mathbf{A}, \{\mathbf{v}_i\}_{i \in [\ell]})$ and $\mathsf{sk} = (I', \{\mathbf{s}_i\}_{i \in I'}, \mathsf{td}_{\mathbf{B}})$.
- Run $r_G \leftarrow \mathsf{EquivPK}(\mathsf{sk}, 1, (I', r'_G), I)$.
- $b \leftarrow \mathcal{A}(r_G)$.

Hybrid $\mathcal{H}_1$. Here, we replace the matrix $\mathbf{A}$ and the vectors $\{\mathbf{v}_i\}_{i \notin I'}$ to be uniform.

- Choose $\mathbf{A} \xleftarrow{\$} \mathbb{Z}_q^{n \times k}$ and for all $i \notin I'$, choose $\mathbf{v}_i \xleftarrow{\$} \mathbb{Z}_q^n$. For $i \in I'$, do as before.
- Run $r_G \leftarrow \mathsf{EquivPK}(\mathsf{sk}, 1, (I', r'_G), I)$.
- $b \leftarrow \mathcal{A}(r_G)$.

Indistinguishability of $\mathcal{H}_0$ and $\mathcal{H}_1$ follows from Lemma 2, which guarantees that matrix $\mathbf{B}$ is 2^{-k} close to uniform. Thus, $\mathbf{A}$ and $\{\mathbf{v}_i\}_{i \notin I'}$ are also statistically close to uniform.

Hybrid $\mathcal{H}_2$. Here, we replace each vector $\{\mathbf{v}_i\}_{i \in I' \setminus I}$ by a random vector from $\mathbb{Z}_q^n$.

- Choose $\mathbf{A} \xleftarrow{\$} \mathbb{Z}_q^{n \times k}$ and for all $i \notin I'$ and $i \in I' \setminus I$, choose $\mathbf{v}_i \xleftarrow{\$} \mathbb{Z}_q^n$. For $i \in I$, set $\mathbf{v}_i$ as before.
- Run $r_G \leftarrow \mathsf{EquivPK}(\mathsf{sk}, 1, (I', r'_G), I)$.
- $b \leftarrow \mathcal{A}(r_G)$.

Indistinguishability of $\mathcal{H}_2$ and $\mathcal{H}_1$ immediately follows from the LWE assumption. Since $\mathcal{H}_2$ is identical to experiment $\mathsf{REAL}_{\mathsf{pk}}$, this concludes the proof. Note that hybrid $\mathcal{H}_1$ is identical to experiment $\mathsf{IDEAL}_{\mathsf{pk}_0}$. So, we also proved that $\mathsf{IDEAL}_{\mathsf{pk}_0} \approx_c \mathsf{REAL}_{\mathsf{pk}}$.

Ciphertext Randomness Indistinguishability. For a key pair $(\mathsf{pk}, \mathsf{sk}) \leftarrow \mathsf{KeyGen}(1^\lambda, 1, I, r_G)$, let $ct = (\mathbf{c}_1, (c_{2,1}, \cdots, c_{2,\ell})) \leftarrow \mathsf{Enc}(\mathsf{pk}, M, r_E)$ with $r_E = (\mathbf{r}, \{e_i^*\}_{i\in[\ell]}, z)$, where $\mathsf{pk} = (\mathbf{A}, \{\mathbf{v}_i\}_{i\in[\ell]})$, and $\mathsf{sk} = (I, \{\mathbf{s}_i\}_{i\in I}, \mathsf{td}_\mathbf{B})$. Now, let $M' \in \{0,1\}^\ell$ be such that $M_i = M'_i$ for all $i \in I$, and $M_i \neq M'_i$ otherwise. After running $\mathsf{EquivCT}((\mathsf{sk}, r_G), (M, r_E), \{M'_i\}_{i\notin I})$ we obtain

$$r'_E = (\bar{\mathbf{r}}, \{e'_i\}_{i\in[\ell]}, z).$$

First we show that the result of encrypting M' using r'_E is exactly equal to ct. Let $ct' = (\mathbf{c}'_1, (c'_{2,1}, \cdots, c'_{2,\ell}))$ be the Regev encryption of M' w.r.t pk and r'_E. We have:

- $\mathbf{c}'_1 = \mathbf{c}_1$. In the third step of $\mathsf{EquivCT}$ algorithm, $\bar{\mathbf{r}}$ is sampled such that $\bar{\mathbf{r}}^T\mathbf{B} = \mathbf{u}$, so $\bar{\mathbf{r}}$ satisfies
$$\bar{\mathbf{r}}^T\mathbf{A} = \mathbf{c}_1 = \mathbf{r}^T\mathbf{A}$$
So, $\mathbf{c}_1 = \mathbf{c}'_1$.
- For all $i \notin I$, $c'_{2,i} = c_{2,i}$. Regarding how $\bar{\mathbf{r}}$ is sampled, for all $i \notin I$ we have
$$\bar{\mathbf{r}}^T\mathbf{v}_i = w_{2,i} - \lfloor q/2 \rceil M'_i - e'_i,$$
so,
$$c'_{2,i} = \lfloor \bar{\mathbf{r}}^T\mathbf{v}_i + \lfloor q/2 \rceil M'_i + e'_i \rceil_2 = \lfloor w_{2,i} \rceil_2 = c_{2,i}.$$
- For all $i \in I$, $c'_{2,i} = c_{2,i}$. For $i \in I$ we have
$$\begin{aligned}\mathbf{r}^T\mathbf{v}_i + \lfloor q/2 \rceil M_i + e_i^* &= \mathbf{r}^T\mathbf{v}_i + \lfloor q/2 \rceil M'_i + e_i^* \\ &= \bar{\mathbf{r}}^T\mathbf{v}_i + \lfloor q/2 \rceil M'_i + e'_i.\end{aligned}$$
So, $c'_{2,i} = c_{2,i}$.
Next, we prove that $\{e_i^*\}_{i\in[\ell]} \approx_s \{e'_i\}_{i\in[\ell]}$. For all $i \notin I$, we pick e'_i from the same distribution as e_i^*. Also, for $i \in I$, we sample $\bar{\mathbf{r}}$ from a distribution with parameters according to Lemma 4. It guarantees that the distribution of e'_i is the same as e_i^*. Note that given a sampler for $D_{\Lambda^\perp(\mathbf{A}^T)+\mathbf{r}',\sqrt{\mathbf{\Sigma}},\mathbf{c}}$ we can get independent samples from $D^{S_{\mathbf{E},\mathbf{u},\mathbf{f}}}_{\Lambda^\perp(\mathbf{A}^T)+\mathbf{r}',\sqrt{\mathbf{\Sigma}},\mathbf{c}}$ by rejection sampling. The former exists regarding Lemma 3. Finally, since (pk, ct) remains the same after the equivocation, and $r'_E \approx_s r_E$, the distribution of (pk, M', r_E) in the ideal mode is statistically close to that of the real mode.

This concludes the proof of Theorem 3. □

3.2 PEPE from DDH

In this section, we detail our DDH-based construction that deviates from prior constructions by using a universal hash functions. Doing so, we obtain a simpler construction that additionally features an encryption algorithm running in strict polynomial time. The construction is inspired from the lossy encryption scheme of [14] and the hidden-bit-generator of [16].

Construction 4. Let $n \in \mathbb{N}$ and H be a universal hash function from $\mathbb{G}$ to $\{0,1\}$.

- $\mathsf{KeyGen}(1^\lambda, b \in \{0,1\}, I, r_G)$:
  - Run $(\mathbb{G}, g, p) \leftarrow \mathcal{G}(1^\lambda)$.
  - if $b = 0$ do:
    - For all $j \in [n]$, choose $g_j \xleftarrow{\$} \mathbb{G}$.
    - For all $i \in I$ and $j \in [n]$, set $h_{i,j} = g_j^{s_i}$, for $s_i \xleftarrow{\$} \mathbb{Z}_p$.
    - For all $i \notin I$ and $j \in [n]$, choose $h_{i,j} \xleftarrow{\$} \mathbb{G}$.
    - Set $\mathsf{pk} = (\mathbb{G}, g, p, \{g_j\}_{j\in[n]}, \{h_{i,j}\}_{i\in[\ell],j\in[n]})$, and $\mathsf{sk} = (I, \{s_i\}_{i\in I})$.
    - The key generation randomness is $r_G = (\mathbb{G}, g, p, \{g_j\}_{j\in[n]}, \{s_i\}_{i\in I}, \{h_{i,j}\}_{i\notin I, j\in[n]})$.
  - if $b = 1$ do:
    - For all $j \in [n]$, choose $a_j \xleftarrow{\$} \mathbb{Z}_p$ and set $g_j = g^{a_j}$.
    - For all $i \in I$ and $j \in [n]$, set $h_{i,j} = g_j^{s_i}$, for $s_i \xleftarrow{\$} \mathbb{Z}_p$.
    - For all $i \notin I$ and $j \in [n]$, set $h_{i,j} = g^{z_{i,j}}$, for $z_{i,j} \xleftarrow{\$} \mathbb{Z}_p$.
    - Define the public key as $\mathsf{pk} = \mathbb{G}, g, p, (\{g_j\}_{j\in[n]}, \{h_{i,j}\}_{i\in[\ell],j\in[n]})$, and the secret key as $\mathsf{sk} = (I, \{s_i\}_{i\in I}, \{a_j\}_{j\in[n]}, \{z_{i,j}\}_{i\notin I, j\in[n]})$.
    - The key generation randomness is $r_G = (\mathbb{G}, g, p, \{g_j\}_{j\in[n]}, \{s_i\}_{i\in I}, \{a_j\}_{j\in[n]}, \{z_{i,j}\}_{i\notin I, j\in[n]})$.
- $\mathsf{Enc}(\mathsf{pk}, M \in \{0,1\}^\ell, r_E)$:
  - Parse $\mathsf{pk} = (g, \{g_j\}_{j\in[n]}, \{h_{i,j}\}_{i\in[\ell],j\in[n]})$.
  - Sample $r_1, \cdots, r_n \xleftarrow{\$} \mathbb{Z}_p$.
  - Compute $c_0 = \prod_j^n g_j^{r_j}$, and for all $i \in [\ell]$ compute

$$c_i = M_i \oplus H\Big(\prod_{j=1}^{n} h_{i,j}^{r_j}\Big) \in \{0,1\}.$$

  - Set $r_E = (r_1, \cdots, r_n)$.
  - Output $ct = (c_0, c_1, \cdots, c_\ell)$.
- $\mathsf{Dec}(\mathsf{sk}, ct)$:
  - Parse $\mathsf{sk} = (I, \{s_i\}_{i\in I})$.
  - For all $i \in I$, compute $M_i = c_i \oplus H(c_0^{s_i})$.
  - Output $\{M_i\}_{i\in I}$.
- $\mathsf{EquivPK}(\mathsf{sk}, b, I, r_G, I')$:
  - If $I' \not\subseteq I$ abort.
  - Let $\mathsf{pk} = (\mathbb{G}, g, p, \{g_j\}_{j\in[n]}, \{h_{i,j}\}_{i\in[\ell],j\in[n]})$ be the output of KeyGen on input $(1^\lambda, b, I, r_G)$.
    Parse $\mathsf{sk} = (I, \{s_i\}_{i\in I})$ if $b = 0$, or $\mathsf{sk} = (I, \{s_i\}_{i\in I}, \{a_j\}_{j\in[n]}, \{z_{i,j}\}_{i\notin I, j\in[n]})$ if $b = 1$.
  - Set and output $r'_G = (\mathbb{G}, g, p, \{g_j\}_{j\in[n]}, \{s_i\}_{i\in I'}, \{h_{i,j}\}_{i\notin I', j\in[n]})$.
- $\mathsf{EquivCT}(\mathsf{sk}, (M, r_E), \{M'_i\}_{i\notin I})$:

- Parse $\mathsf{sk} = (I, \{s_i\}_{i \in I}, \{a_j\}_{j \in [n]}, \{z_{i,j}\}_{i \notin I, j \in [n]})$. Let $(c_0, c_1, \cdots, c_\ell)$ be the encryption of M w.r.t pk and $r_E = (r_1, \cdots, r_n)$.
- For all $i \notin I$, repeatedly sample $t_i \xleftarrow{\$} \mathbb{Z}_p$ until $H(g^{t_i}) = c_i \oplus M'_i$. If no such t_i is found after λ attempts, abort and output $\perp$.
- Let $\mathbf{a} = (a_1, \cdots, a_n)$, $\mathbf{r} = (r_1, \cdots, r_n)$, and $\{i_1, \cdots, i_\alpha\} = [\ell] \setminus I$. Also, for all $i \notin I$, let $\mathbf{z}_i = (z_{i,1}, \cdots, z_{i,n})$. Now sample uniformly a solution $\bar{\mathbf{r}} \in \mathbb{Z}_p^n$ for

$$\begin{bmatrix} \mathbf{a} \\ \mathbf{z}_{i_1} \\ \vdots \\ \mathbf{z}_{i_\alpha} \end{bmatrix} \cdot \bar{\mathbf{r}}^T = \begin{bmatrix} \mathbf{a}\mathbf{r}^T \\ t_{i_1} \\ \vdots \\ t_{i_\alpha} \end{bmatrix}. \quad (1)$$

- Output $r'_E = \bar{\mathbf{r}}$.

Due to space limitation, the security proof is deferred to the full version of the paper.

3.3 PEPE from Subgroup Decision

We now present our construction from the SD assumption for which the security proof is also given in the full version of the paper.

Construction 5. Consider a group $\mathbb{G} \approx \mathbb{G}_q \times \mathbb{G}_p$ of order $N = pq$, where $\mathbb{G}_p = \{x^q \bmod N : x \in \mathbb{G}\}$ is the subgroup of $\mathbb{G}$ of order p, and $\mathbb{G}_q = \{x^p \bmod N : x \in \mathbb{G}\}$ is the subgroup of $\mathbb{G}$ of order q. Let $n \in \mathbb{N}$ such that $n > \ell$, and H be a universal hash function from $\mathbb{G}$ to $\{0, 1\}$.

- $\mathsf{Setup}(1^\lambda, 1^n)$:
  - Sample $(p, q, \mathbb{G}, g) \leftarrow \mathcal{G}(1^\lambda)$. Let $N = pq$.
  - Set $\hat{g} \leftarrow u^q$, where $u \xleftarrow{\$} \mathbb{G}$. Note that $\hat{g}$ is a random element (and a generator) of $\mathbb{G}_p$.
  - For all $j \in [n]$, choose $g_j \leftarrow \hat{g}^{a_j}$, where $a_j \xleftarrow{\$} \mathbb{Z}_N$. Note that each g_j is a random element of $\mathbb{G}_p$.
  - Set $\hat{h} \leftarrow v^p$, where $v \xleftarrow{\$} \mathbb{G}$. Note that $\hat{h}$ is a random element (and a generator) of $\mathbb{G}_q$.
  - Output $\mathsf{crs} = (N, \mathbb{G}, \hat{g}, \hat{h}, \{g_j\}_{j \in [n]})$, and $\mathsf{td} = (p, q)$.
- $\mathsf{KeyGen}(\mathsf{crs}, b \in \{0, 1\}, I, r_G)$:
  - Parse $\mathsf{crs} = (N, \mathbb{G}, \hat{g}, \hat{h}, \{g_j\}_{j \in [n]})$.
  - if $b = 0$:
    - For all $i \in I$ and $j \in [n]$, set $h_{i,j} = g_j^{s_i} \in \mathbb{G}$, where $s_i \xleftarrow{\$} \mathbb{Z}_N$.
    - For all $i \notin I$ and $j \in [n]$, sample obliviously $h_{i,j} \xleftarrow{\$} \mathbb{G}$.
    - Set $\mathsf{sk} = (I, \{s_i\}_{i \in I})$. Also, $r_G = (\{s_i\}_{i \in I}, \{h_{i,j}\}_{i \notin I, j \in [n]})$.

- if $b = 1$:
  - For all $i \in I$ and $j \in [n]$, set $h_{i,j} = g_j^{s_i} \in \mathbb{G}$, where $s_i \xleftarrow{\$} \mathbb{Z}_N$.
  - For all $i \notin I$ and $j \in [n]$, choose $h_i \leftarrow \hat{h}^{b_i}$, where $b_i \xleftarrow{\$} \mathbb{Z}_N$, and set $h_{i,j} = h_i^{\delta_{i,j}} \cdot g_j^{s_i} \in \mathbb{G}$, where $s_i \xleftarrow{\$} \mathbb{Z}_N$, and $\delta_{i,j}$ is the Kronecker delta.
  - Set $\mathsf{sk} = (I, \{s_i\}_{i \in [\ell]}, \{h_i\}_{i \notin I})$. Also, $r_G = (\{s_i\}_{i \in [\ell]}, \{b_i\}_{i \notin I})$.
- Set $\mathsf{pk} = (N, \mathbb{G}, \hat{g}, \hat{h}, \{g_j\}_{j \in [n]}, \{h_{i,j}\}_{i \in [\ell], j \in [n]})$.

- $\mathsf{Enc}(\mathsf{pk}, M \in \{0,1\}^\ell, r_E)$:
  - Parse $\mathsf{pk} = (N, \mathbb{G}, \hat{g}, \hat{h}, \{g_j\}_{j \in [n]}, \{h_{i,j}\}_{i \in [\ell], j \in [n]})$.
  - Sample $r_1, \cdots, r_n \xleftarrow{\$} \mathbb{Z}_N$ and compute $c_0 = \prod_{j=1}^{n} g_j^{r_j} \in \mathbb{G}$. Then, for each $i \in [\ell]$, compute $c_i = M_i \oplus H(\prod_{j=1}^{n} h_{i,j}^{r_j}) \in \{0,1\}$.
  - Set $r_E = (r_1, \cdots, r_n)$.
  - Output $ct = (c_0, c_1, \cdots, c_\ell)$.
- $\mathsf{Dec}(\mathsf{sk}, ct)$:
  - Parse $\mathsf{sk} = (I, \{s_i\}_{i \in I})$.
  - For all $i \in I$, compute $M_i = c_i \oplus H(c_0^{s_i})$.
  - Output $\{M_i\}_{i \in I}$.
- $\mathsf{EquivPK}(\mathsf{sk}, \mathsf{td}, b, I, r_G, I')$:
  - If $I' \nsubseteq I$ abort.
  - Parse $\mathsf{td} = (p, q)$.
  - Let $\mathsf{pk} = (N, \mathbb{G}, \hat{g}, \hat{h}, \{g_j\}_{j \in [n]}, \{h_{i,j}\}_{i \in [\ell], j \in [n]})$ be the output of KeyGen on input $(\mathsf{crs}, b, I, r_G)$.
    Parse $\mathsf{sk} = (I, \{s_i\}_{i \in I})$, if $b = 0$, or $\mathsf{sk} = (I, \{s_i\}_{i \in [\ell]}, \{h_i\}_{i \notin I})$, if $b = 1$.
  - Set and output $r'_G = (\{s_i\}_{i \in I'}, \{h_{i,j}\}_{i \notin I', j \in [n]})$.
- $\mathsf{EquivCT}(\mathsf{sk}, \mathsf{td}, (M, r_E), \{M'_i\}_{i \notin I})$:
  - Parse $\mathsf{sk} = (I, \{a_j\}_{j \in [n]}, \{s_i\}_{i \in [\ell]}, \{h_i\}_{i \notin I})$, and $\mathsf{td} = (p, q)$.
    Let $(c_0, c_1, \cdots, c_\ell)$ be the encryption of M w.r.t pk and $r_E = (r_1, \cdots, r_n)$.
  - For all $i \notin I$, repeatedly sample $r'_i \xleftarrow{\$} \mathbb{Z}_N$ such that $r'_i = r_i \mod p$ and $r'_i \neq r_i \mod q$ until

$$H(h_i^{r_i} \cdot c_0^{s_i}) = c_i \oplus M'_i. \quad (2)$$

    If no candidate is found after λ attempts, abort and output $\perp$.
  - For all $i \in I$, set $r'_i \leftarrow r_i$.
  - Output $r'_E = (r'_1, \cdots, r'_n)$.

On Oblivious Sampling in SD Construction. We now explain how oblivious sampling can be done in the above construction. The construction works over the group $\mathbb{G} \approx \mathbb{G}_q \times \mathbb{G}_p$ of order $N = pq$. During the real-mode key generation, we require that some public key elements be obliviously sampled from $\mathbb{G}$. To see why it can be done, we use the sampling technique as done in [7].

Let $P = a \cdot N + 1$ be a prime number, where $\gcd(a, N) = 1$. Since N is public, then such P can be generated by a real-mode party. Now, since $\mathbb{G}$ is isomorphic to the subgroup of order N of $\mathbb{Z}_P^*$, it is enough to be able to obliviously sample from this subgroup. The idea for doing so is to generate a random element in $\mathbb{Z}_P^*$, and then raise it to the a-th power. To generate random elements in $\mathbb{Z}_P^*$, for a prime P, it is enough to pick a random bit string of length $2\log(P)$, and then reduce its decimal value modulo P. It turns out that the distribution of elements sampled in this way, is statistically close to the uniform distribution over $\mathbb{G}$.

Also, as explained in [7], the sampling is invertible, meaning that given a random element h of the subgroup $\mathbb{G}$, we can efficiently recover an underlying random element $h_P \in \mathbb{Z}_P^*$, such that $h_P^a = h(\mod P)$. This should be used in the EquivPK algorithm, and can be done as follows: First, we find the inverse of a modulo N, which exists since $\gcd(a, N) = 1$. Let g_P be a generator of $\mathbb{Z}_P^*$. Now, given an element $h \in \mathbb{G}$, we set $h_p := h^{a^{-1}} \cdot g_P^{iN} \mod P$, where i is a random element from $\mathbb{Z}_a^*$. It is easy to see that $h_p^a = h(\mod P)$. Also, it is a random element among the elements of $\mathbb{Z}_P^*$ whose a-th power is equal to h. Generating a random decimal value (thus a random bit string) who is equal to h_P modulo P is easily done by choosing a random $k \in \mathbb{Z}_p$ and computing $h_P + kP$.

Acknowledgements. We thank the anonymous reviewers for useful comments. This work was supported in part by the French ANR ALAMBIC project (ANR-16-CE39-0006).

References

1. Beaver, D.: Plug and play encryption. In: Kaliski, B.S. (ed.) CRYPTO 1997. LNCS, vol. 1294, pp. 75–89. Springer, Heidelberg (1997). https://doi.org/10.1007/BFb0052228
2. Boneh, D., Goh, E.-J., Nissim, K.: Evaluating 2-DNF formulas on ciphertexts. In: Kilian, J. (ed.) TCC 2005. LNCS, vol. 3378, pp. 325–341. Springer, Heidelberg (2005). https://doi.org/10.1007/978-3-540-30576-7_18
3. Brakerski, Z., Branco, P., Döttling, N., Garg, S., Malavolta, G.: Constant ciphertext-rate non-committing encryption from standard assumptions. In: Pass, R., Pietrzak, K. (eds.) TCC 2020. LNCS, vol. 12550, pp. 58–87. Springer, Cham (2020). https://doi.org/10.1007/978-3-030-64375-1_3
4. Brakerski, Z., Döttling, N., Garg, S., Malavolta, G.: Leveraging linear decryption: rate-1 fully-homomorphic encryption and time-lock puzzles. In: Hofheinz, D., Rosen, A. (eds.) TCC 2019. LNCS, vol. 11892, pp. 407–437. Springer, Cham (2019). https://doi.org/10.1007/978-3-030-36033-7_16
5. Brakerski, Z., Langlois, A., Peikert, C., Regev, O., Stehlé, D.: Classical hardness of learning with errors. In: STOC (2013)
6. Canetti, R., Feige, U., Goldreich, O., Naor, M.: Adaptively secure multi-party computation. In: STOC (1996)
7. Canetti, R., Fischlin, M.: Universally composable commitments. In: Kilian, J. (ed.) CRYPTO 2001. LNCS, vol. 2139, pp. 19–40. Springer, Heidelberg (2001). https://doi.org/10.1007/3-540-44647-8_2
8. Canetti, R., Poburinnaya, O., Raykova, M.: Optimal-rate non-committing encryption. In: Takagi, T., Peyrin, T. (eds.) ASIACRYPT 2017. LNCS, vol. 10626, pp. 212–241. Springer, Cham (2017). https://doi.org/10.1007/978-3-319-70700-6_8

9. Choi, S.G., Dachman-Soled, D., Malkin, T., Wee, H.: Improved non-committing encryption with applications to adaptively secure protocols. In: Matsui, M. (ed.) ASIACRYPT 2009. LNCS, vol. 5912, pp. 287–302. Springer, Heidelberg (2009). https://doi.org/10.1007/978-3-642-10366-7_17
10. Damgård, I., Nielsen, J.B.: Improved non-committing encryption schemes based on a general complexity assumption. In: Bellare, M. (ed.) CRYPTO 2000. LNCS, vol. 1880, pp. 432–450. Springer, Heidelberg (2000). https://doi.org/10.1007/3-540-44598-6_27
11. Gentry, C., Peikert, C., Vaikuntanathan, V.: Trapdoors for hard lattices and new cryptographic constructions. In: STOC (2008)
12. Hemenway, B., Ostrovsky, R., Richelson, S., Rosen, A.: Adaptive security with quasi-optimal rate. In: Kushilevitz, E., Malkin, T. (eds.) TCC 2016. LNCS, vol. 9562, pp. 525–541. Springer, Heidelberg (2016). https://doi.org/10.1007/978-3-662-49096-9_22
13. Hemenway, B., Ostrovsky, R., Rosen, A.: Non-committing encryption from ϕ-hiding. In: Dodis, Y., Nielsen, J.B. (eds.) TCC 2015. LNCS, vol. 9014, pp. 591–608. Springer, Heidelberg (2015). https://doi.org/10.1007/978-3-662-46494-6_24
14. Hofheinz, D., Jager, T., Rupp, A.: Public-key encryption with simulation-based selective-opening security and compact ciphertexts. In: Hirt, M., Smith, A. (eds.) TCC 2016. LNCS, vol. 9986, pp. 146–168. Springer, Heidelberg (2016). https://doi.org/10.1007/978-3-662-53644-5_6
15. Håstad, J., Impagliazzo, R., Levin, L.A., Luby, M.: A pseudorandom generator from any one-way function. SIAM J. Comput. **28**(4), 1364–1396 (1999)
16. Libert, B., Passelègue, A., Wee, H., Wu, D.J.: New constructions of statistical NIZKs: dual-mode DV-NIZKs and more. In: Canteaut, A., Ishai, Y. (eds.) EUROCRYPT 2020. LNCS, vol. 12107, pp. 410–441. Springer, Cham (2020). https://doi.org/10.1007/978-3-030-45727-3_14
17. Libert, B., Sakzad, A., Stehlé, D., Steinfeld, R.: All-but-many lossy trapdoor functions and selective opening chosen-ciphertext security from LWE. In: Katz, J., Shacham, H. (eds.) CRYPTO 2017. LNCS, vol. 10403, pp. 332–364. Springer, Cham (2017). https://doi.org/10.1007/978-3-319-63697-9_12
18. Micciancio, D., Peikert, C.: Trapdoors for lattices: simpler, tighter, faster, smaller. In: Pointcheval, D., Johansson, T. (eds.) EUROCRYPT 2012. LNCS, vol. 7237, pp. 700–718. Springer, Heidelberg (2012). https://doi.org/10.1007/978-3-642-29011-4_41
19. Nielsen, J.B.: Separating random oracle proofs from complexity theoretic proofs: the non-committing encryption case. In: Yung, M. (ed.) CRYPTO 2002. LNCS, vol. 2442, pp. 111–126. Springer, Heidelberg (2002). https://doi.org/10.1007/3-540-45708-9_8
20. Regev, O.: On lattices, learning with errors, random linear codes, and cryptography. In: STOC (2005)
21. Yoshida, Y., Kitagawa, F., Tanaka, K.: Non-committing encryption with quasi-optimal ciphertext-rate based on the DDH problem. In: Galbraith, S.D., Moriai, S. (eds.) ASIACRYPT 2019. LNCS, vol. 11923, pp. 128–158. Springer, Cham (2019). https://doi.org/10.1007/978-3-030-34618-8_5
22. Yoshida, Y., Kitagawa, F., Xagawa, K., Tanaka, K.: Non-committing encryption with constant ciphertext expansion from standard assumptions. In: Moriai, S., Wang, H. (eds.) ASIACRYPT 2020. LNCS, vol. 12492, pp. 36–65. Springer, Cham (2020). https://doi.org/10.1007/978-3-030-64834-3_2

On Access Control Encryption Without Sanitization

Cecilia Boschini[1](✉), Ivan Damgård[2], and Claudio Orlandi[2]

[1] Technion and Reichman University (IDC), Haifa, Herzliya, Israel
cecilia.bo@cs.technion.ac.il
[2] Aarhus University, Aarhus, Denmark
{ivan,orlandi}@cs.au.dk

Abstract. Access Control Encryption (ACE) [4] allows to control information flow between parties by enforcing a policy that specifies which user can send messages to whom. The core of the scheme is a sanitizer, i.e., an entity that "sanitizes" all messages by essentially re-encrypting the ciphertexts under its key. In this work we investigate the natural question of whether it is still possible to achieve some meaningful security properties in scenarios when such a sanitization step is not possible. We answer positively by showing that it is possible to limit corrupted users to communicate only through insecure subliminal channels, under the necessary assumption that parties do not have pre-shared randomness. Moreover, we show that the bandwidth of such channels can be limited to be $O(\log(\lambda))$ by adding public ciphertext verifiability to the scheme under computational assumptions. In particular, we rely on a new security definition for obfuscation, Game Specific Obfuscation (GSO), which is a weaker definition than VBB, as it only requires the obfuscator to obfuscate programs in a specific family of programs, and limited to a fixed security game.

1 Introduction

Designers of practical secure IT systems are often interested in controlling the flow of information in their system. For this purpose one sets up a security policy that contains rules on what operations the entities in the system are allowed to execute. Crucially, such rules must constrain both write and read operations as both types may lead to unwanted transfer of data. This was formalized in the classical Bell-Lapadula security policy as the "no read up" (entities with low security clearance cannot read top-secret data) and "no write-down" rules (entities with a high security clearance cannot write to public files). If entities are not assumed to be honest, such a security policy cannot be enforced unless we assume a trusted party, often known as a *sanitizer*, which will stop and/or modify unwanted communication. Of course, the sanitizer cannot do this unless we assume that parties can only communicate via the sanitizer. In practical systems one usually tries to ensure this by a combination of hardware security and software design, for instance in the kernel of the operating system.

C. Galdi and S. Jarecki (Eds.): SCN 2022, LNCS 13409, pp. 220–243, 2022.
https://doi.org/10.1007/978-3-031-14791-3_10

In [4] Damgård et al. asked whether cryptography can be used to simplify the job of the sanitizer, and reduce the amount of trust we need to place in it. To this end, they introduced the notion of Access Control Encryption (ACE). Using an ACE scheme, the sanitizer does not need to know the security policy or the identities of any parties in the system. It just needs to process every message it receives and pass it on. The processing essentially amounts to re-randomize every message received. Instead of asking the sanitizer to enforce the security policy, an ACE scheme integrates the policy in the key generation algorithm, which gives an encryption key to each sender, a decryption key to each receiver and a sanitizer key for the sanitizer. The keys are designed such that, after sanitization, a receiver can decrypt a message, only if it was encrypted by a sender that is allowed to send to that receiver.

Observe that security requires the physical assumption that a corrupt sender cannot bypass the sanitizer and send directly to any receiver she wants. Indeed, it may seem that nothing non-trivial can be achieved if we drop this assumption. On the other hand, assuming such a communication bottleneck may be hard to justify in practice, and makes the system vulnerable to DDoS attacks (in case the sanitizer is offline). It is then natural to wonder:

Can we achieve any meaningful security without sanitization?

2 Our Results

In this paper, we answer affirmatively to the previous question analyzing two new models, both avoiding the need of preprocessing ciphertexts before delivery. We present formal definitions of ACE in these models, and we instantiate them under various computational assumptions. Along the way we obtain a standard ACE with sender anonymity from standard assumptions, which had been left as an open problem in [6] (deferred to the full version due to lack of space).

2.1 Modeling ACE Without Sanitization

ACE without Sanitizer (ACEnoS). Removing the sanitization bottleneck implies that senders can now post to a bulletin board that receivers can read from. As in standard ACE, parties have no other communication channel available, and key generation assumes a trusted party. However, senders are now free to post whatever they want. What security properties can we hope to achieve in such a model? Clearly, we can do what cryptography "natively" allows us to do, namely what we call the *No Read Rule* (NRR): an honest sender can encrypt a message such that only the designated receiver can extract information about the plaintext from the ciphertext; furthermore we can guarantee that a ciphertext does not reveal the identity of the sender. What we can do about a corrupt sender is more subtle: clearly, we cannot stop a sender from simply posting any message she wants, thus broadcasting confidential data. But, on the other hand, this is often not what a corrupt sender wants to do. If, for instance, the data involved is extremely valuable, it may be more attractive to break the security policy by sending a *secret* message that can only be decrypted by a specific (corrupted) receiver she is not allowed to send to. This attack we can actually hope to stop, through what we call the *No Secret Write Rule* (NSWR)[1]: parties cannot communicate secretly if the policy does not allow it. If parties manage to communicate against policy, then anyone can read their communication.

Communication Restrictions. For this goal to be meaningful, we can allow corrupted senders and receivers to share a common strategy, but not randomness. Without this constraint, any no secret write rule can trivially be broken just using one-time-pad encryption, for instance. Assuming that the parties' initial states are uncorrelated, the rough intuition is that if the key generation does not supply a corrupted sender and receiver with sufficiently correlated key material, the receiver's ability to decrypt a ciphertext cannot depend on the keys she has. But if it does not, then anyone should be able to extract the message the corrupted sender wants to leak, and so the message is effectively publicly available. Observe that the assumption that parties do not have pre-shared randomness is not new: in fact, Alwën et al. [1] already pointed out the need for such an assumption when building collusion-free protocols.

Verifiable ACE (VACE). Our solution above implies that whatever information a corrupt sender embeds in his message can in principle be accessed by anyone. But there is no limit on the *amount* of information she can leak in this way. Is there some way to plausibly limit such leakage? We answer affirmatively, by adding a way to publicly verify the posted ciphertexts. Intuitively, if a ciphertext verifies, it is correctly formed according to the encryption algorithm, not something the sender can choose as he likes (e.g., no unencrypted messages). However, a sender may still try to output a valid ciphertext that equals the encoding of an n-bit subliminal message. The hope is that now the sender's situation becomes somewhat similar to having to generate ciphertexts by calling a random (encryption) oracle. In this scenario embedding a random n-bits string requires a number of queries exponential in n, as the sender can only make a polynomial number of calls and cannot control the (somewhat) random outputs. This limits senders to leak up to a logarithmic number of bits, which is optimal[2].

Finally, as anyone can verify, senders are discouraged from posting invalid ciphertexts (e.g., unencrypted messages) – as in practice, content that does not verify would be taken down and there might be consequences for the sender. With this we obtain fast communication (no need of a sanitization bottleneck), while maintaining some accountability. Observe that public verification yields something different from a standard ACE, albeit very close. The difference is

[1] This is closely related to the notion of subliminal channels [10], where the information sent is hidden in messages that are seemingly created for a different purpose. In that language, NSWR says that, while a corrupt sender may be able to establish a subliminal channel to a receiver he should not send to, any such channel is non-secret.

[2] This reasoning yields a clear lower bound: no ACEnoS can prevent a sender to embed a logarithmic number of bits in a ciphertext (by generating ciphertexts until, say, the first few bits of the string are equal to the message bits she wants to embed).

that not only the sanitization key is public (as in [5]), but the sanitization step (the verification in this case) can be performed by *any* party, after ciphertexts are posted. This was not the case in [5], where the sanitizer does more than just a routine check (in fact, it injects honestly generated randomness in ciphertexts).

2.2 Instantiating ACEnoS and VACE

Constructing ACEnoS. Even assuming parties not to have shared randomness, it is not straightforward to obtain a ACEnoS by simply "removing" the sanitization step from pre-existing ACE constructions: the security of existing ACE schemes strongly relies on some transformation to be applied on a ciphertext *before* its delivery. In our work, we give several constructions under various standard assumptions that match in efficiency the existing ACE constructions (e.g., [4,5]). One of these requires a new primitive, key-indistinguishable predicate encryption. The definition is rather natural, and very useful, as it immediately yields a solution of a problem left open by Kim and Wu [6] (see full version).

Constructing VACE. We give a construction of an ACE scheme with verification and minimal leakage based on a new definition of obfuscation. The need of a new assumption arises from the fact that building a VACE is highly non-trivial. To see why, we can consider what seems at first a promising solution: assume the sender is committed to a PRF key K and is supposed to compute the ciphertext c she posts using randomness generated from K and the encrypted message m, via the PRF, i.e., $c = E_{pk}(m, \mathsf{PRF}_K(m))$. In addition, the sender adds a non-interactive zero-knowledge proof that c was correctly computed. This allows verification. Moreover, it also seems to imply that a malicious sender cannot manipulate the randomness to embed a subliminal message m' in c. However a closer look shows that this is not clear at all: the intuition assumes that the sender chooses a message m to encrypt and the subliminal message m' first, then generates randomness using the PRF key and hopes that the resulting ciphertext will be an encoding m'. In fact, the sender does not have to do this: she might be able to instead compute simultaneously c and m from the subliminal message m', in a way that depends on K, such that $c = E_{pk}(m, \mathsf{PRF}_K(m))$ holds. The security properties of the PRF and the encryption function do not imply that this is infeasible: the PRF is only secure if the key is not known, and the encryption function is only hard to invert on a random ciphertext, and this does not prevent the adversary from generating c and m simultaneously from K. With this approach, it is completely unclear that c could not be an encoding of a subliminal message m' that the adversary wants. One might be able to make these problems go away if one is willing to model the PRF as a random oracle. But now the problem is that the zero-knowledge proof requires access to the code of the instantiation of the oracle. This code is no longer available once we pass to the random oracle model, so it is not clear how to prove security.

In the absence of a solution based on standard assumptions, we rely on a new model for security of obfuscation that we call Game-Specific Obfuscation (GSO). As the name suggests, GSO only requires the obfuscator to obfuscate programs in a specific family of programs $\mathcal{F}$ used in a fixed security game G. Roughly speaking, the security requirement is that the obfuscated program does not help an adversary to win the specific game any more than oracle access to the program would have allowed. Note that while implied by VBB, GSO makes a much weaker demand than VBB: we assume that the obfuscation gives nothing more than oracle access, only as far as winning G is concerned, and the obfuscator only needs to obfuscate programs in $\mathcal{F}$. In particular, the impossibility result for VBB [2] does not apply to GSO. At the same time, GSO and iO are somewhat incomparable: GSO has no specific requirement on the family of programs, while iO needs them to compute the same function; on the other hand, iO still guarantees indistinguishability for every game, while GSO targets a specific one. Nevertheless, assuming GSO is a strong assumption, and our result mainly serves to rule out impossibility results for VACE with minimal leakage.

2.3 Concurrent Work

Recently, Lu et al. [7] explore an analogous question in the context of collusion-preserving MPC [1]: could one get rid of mediation? At a high level, their solution is similar to our VACE construction: parties' messages are encrypted, signed, and sent on an authenticated broadcast channel by a trusted hardware, which thus performs the same task as the obfuscated program in our construction. However, to completely prevent subliminal channels they have to assume that senders cannot run the trusted hardware multiple times and choose which ciphertext to send, which is a stronger assumption than our communication model.

2.4 Future Directions

We believe that the question we study here is a fundamental one that is of interest, also outside the scope of ACE, as it can be phrased in a much more general context: assume a polynomial-time sender who is limited to sending messages that satisfy some verification predicate. The question is to what extent we can use the verification to limit the bandwidth of any subliminal channel that the sender may be able to embed? Given our results, it seems that a logarithmic number of bits per message can be achieved. However, we leave a solution based on standard assumptions as an open problem.

3 Access Control Encryption Without Sanitization

Let $[n] = 0, 1, \ldots, n$ for an integer $n \in \mathbb{N}$, and λ be the security parameter. Denote by $|s|$ the length of a bit string s.

Parties. The protocol is run by n parties P_i. Each party can be *either* a sender *or* a receiver. We denote by n_S (resp., n_R) the number of senders (resp., receivers); thus $n = n_S + n_R$.

Policy. A policy is a function $\mathcal{P} : [n_S] \times [n_R] \to \{0, 1\}$ defined as follows:

- $\mathcal{P}(i,j) = 1$ means that the i-th sender can send messages to the j-th receiver (i.e., R_j can decrypt ciphertexts generated by S_i);
- $\mathcal{P}(i,j) = 0$ means that the i-th sender cannot send messages to the j-th receiver (i.e., R_j cannot decrypt ciphertexts generated by S_i);

Finally, the party identity $i = 0$ represents a sender or receiver with no rights, i.e., for all $j \in [n_R]$, $k \in [n_S]$ it holds $\mathcal{P}(0,j) = \mathcal{P}(k,0) = 0$.

Communication Model. We assume only one-way channels between parties:
- parties cannot share any randomness nor other key setup, and
- parties only communicate through a bulletin board, and do not have private channels, or, in general, communication channels outside the protocol (analogously to ACE). Senders are the only ones allowed to write on the bulletin board, while receivers have read-only access to it.

An Access Control Encryption scheme without sanitizer (denoted by ACEnoS in this work) is composed by four algorithms:

Setup: $(pp, msk) \leftarrow \mathsf{Setup}(1^\lambda, \mathcal{P})$
Takes as input the security parameter λ and the policy $\mathcal{P}$, and outputs the public parameters of the scheme (that include the message space $\mathcal{M}$) and the master secret key.

Key Generation: $k_i \leftarrow \mathsf{KGen}(pp, msk, i, t)$
Takes as input the public parameters of the scheme, the master secret key, the identity of the party, and a type $t \in \{\mathsf{sen}, \mathsf{rec}\}$, and outputs a key k_i, generated depending on t and i as follows:
- $ek_i \leftarrow \mathsf{KGen}(pp, msk, i, \mathsf{sen})$ is the encryption key for $i \in [n_S]$;
- $dk_i \leftarrow \mathsf{KGen}(pp, msk, i, \mathsf{rec})$ is the decryption key for $i \in [n_R]$;
- $ek_0 = dk_0 = pp$.

Encryption: $c \leftarrow \mathsf{Enc}(pp, ek_i, m)$
On input the secret key of S_i and a message $m \in \mathcal{M}$, outputs the ciphertext.

Decryption: $m' \leftarrow \mathsf{Dec}(pp, dk_i, c)$
On input a ciphertext and the secret key of the receiver i, it outputs either a message or $\perp$ (representing a decryption failure).

As in the original scheme, an ACE without sanitizer has to satisfy:

Correctness: a honestly generated ciphertext can always be decrypted by the designated receivers.

No Read Rule: only the designated receiver can extract information about the plaintext from a ciphertext; senders anonymity is guaranteed under natural assumptions.

No *Secret* Write Rule: parties cannot communicate secretly if the policy does not allow it. If parties manage to communicate despite being forbidden by the policy, then anyone can read their communication.

When compared to the security definitions of ACE, only the No write Rule requires major changes, as it is the only property where the sanitizer plays a fundamental role. Correctness and the No Real Rule only need small adjustments.

Definition 3.1 (Correctness). *An ACE without sanitizer is correct if for all $m \in \mathcal{M}$, $i \in [n_S]$, $j \in [n_R]$ such that $\mathcal{P}(i,j) = 1$ it holds*

$$\Pr\left[\mathsf{Dec}(pp, dk_j, \mathsf{Enc}(pp, ek_i, m)) \neq m \;:\; \begin{array}{r} (pp, msk) \leftarrow \mathsf{Setup}(1^\lambda, \mathcal{P}), \\ ek_i \leftarrow \mathsf{KGen}(pp, msk, i, \mathsf{sen}), \\ dk_j \leftarrow \mathsf{KGen}(pp, msk, j, \mathsf{rec}) \end{array}\right] \leq \mathsf{negl}(\lambda),$$

where the probabilities are taken over the random coins of all the algorithms.

The NRR models the case in which a coalition of parties (both senders and receivers) tries to either break the confidentiality of a message (payload privacy) or to break the anonymity of target senders. We consider the most powerful adversary, that has even access to the target senders' encryption keys. This guarantees sender's anonymity (and payload privacy) even for senders whose encryption key was leaked.

Definition 3.2 (No-Read Rule). *Consider the following security experiment, where* A *is a stateful adversary and $b \in \{0,1\}$,*

Experiment $\mathsf{Exp}^{\mathsf{nr}}_{\mathsf{A},b}(\lambda, \mathcal{P})$	*Oracles*	
$(pp, msk) \leftarrow \mathsf{Setup}(1^\lambda, \mathcal{P})$	$\mathcal{O}_G(j, t)$:	$\mathcal{O}_E(j, m)$:
$(m_0, m_1, i_0, i_1, st) \leftarrow \mathsf{A}^{\mathcal{O}_G(\cdot),\, \mathcal{O}_E(\cdot)}(pp)$	If $\exists\ k_j$ s.t. $(k_j, j, t) \in \mathcal{L}$, return k_j	$ek_j \leftarrow \mathcal{O}_G(j, \mathsf{sen})$
$c_b \leftarrow \mathsf{Enc}(pp, \mathcal{O}_G(i_b, \mathsf{sen}), m_b)$	*Else* $k_j \leftarrow \mathsf{KGen}(pp, msk, j, t)$	$c \leftarrow \mathsf{Enc}(pp, ek_j, m)$
$b' \leftarrow \mathsf{A}^{\mathcal{O}_G(\cdot),\, \mathcal{O}_E(\cdot)}(st, c_b)$	$\mathcal{L} \leftarrow \mathcal{L} \cup \{(k_j, j, t)\}$	*Return* c.
Return b'.	*Return* k_j.	

Given the following requirement,

Necessary Condition: $b = b'$, $|m_0| = |m_1|$, $i_0, i_1 \in [n_S]$,

we say that A *wins the experiment if one of the following holds:*

Payload Privacy *(*PP*). The Necessary Condition holds, and for all queries $q = (j, \mathsf{rec})$ to $\mathcal{O}_G$ it holds that: $\mathcal{P}(i_0, j) = \mathcal{P}(i_1, j) = 0$.*
Sender Anonymity *(*SA*). The Necessary Condition holds, and for all queries $q = (j, \mathsf{rec})$ to $\mathcal{O}_G$ it holds that: $\mathcal{P}(i_0, j) = \mathcal{P}(i_1, j)$ and $m_0 = m_1$.*

An ACE without sanitizer satisfies the No-Read rule if for all PPT A*, $b \xleftarrow{\$} \{0,1\}$*

$$2 \cdot \left| \Pr\left[(\mathsf{PP} \ \vee\ \mathsf{SA}) \;:\; b' \leftarrow \mathsf{Exp}^{\mathsf{nr}}_{\mathsf{A},b}(\lambda, \mathcal{P})\right] - \frac{1}{2} \right| \leq \mathsf{negl}(\lambda).$$

NRR vs. Indistinguishability. The NRR corresponds to the indistinguishability properties of the PKE, which in fact can be seen as special cases of the NRR: Payload Privacy when $i_0 = i_1$ guarantees IND-CPA security, while the Sender Anonymity case is analogous of key-indistinguishability [3].

The goal of the No Secret Write Rule is to prevent unauthorized communications. However, as the sanitization step is not present anymore, there is no countermeasure in place to prevent parties to try to establish subliminal channels [10]: parties might try to embed messages in the bits of a valid ciphertext using some shared randomness (for example, bits of their secret keys). As completely preventing subliminal channels without some kind of sanitization step is impossible (cf. Sect. 7.2), we settle for preventing *secure* exfiltration of information: if two parties manage to communicate despite this being against the policy, they can only succeed in establishing an insecure subliminal channel (i.e., they can only send unencrypted messages). This is useful in scenarios where leaking information by broadcasting it in the clear is not an option (e.g., if the information allows to identify the party that leaked it). Thus we need to assume that the corrupted sender and receiver *do not share randomness or private communication channels*. An obvious implication is that they cannot corrupt the same party and they should only communicate through the bulletin board. In fact, this imposes much bigger limitations to their corruption abilities:

- They cannot corrupt parties that have parts of the key in common (e.g., in constructions relying on symmetric key cryptography), as in this case the common bits can be used as shared randomness.
- They cannot corrupt parties whose keys can be recovered from each other (as it is the case for public key cryptography, where usually the public key can be recovered from the secret key).
- Neither of them can have both read and write access to the board, otherwise they would have an (insecure but) two-way communication channel that would then allow for key-exchange. This means that the corrupted sender can only corrupt other senders, and analogously for the receiver. Moreover, corrupted senders should not have access to an encryption oracle, while corrupted receivers do: the first requirement is due to the fact that a corrupt sender could trivially break the property by "replaying" encryptions under keys of (honest) senders who are allowed to communicate to the corrupted receiver, while the latter is due to the fact that we want to model that receivers have access to the entire bulletin board, which may contain encryptions of known messages under keys of known identities.

The definition says that if a corrupted receiver can recover a message, then knowing some decryption keys did not help in the process. This is modeled by imposing that a party B without access to keys can recover the message with a similar success probability[3]. Remark that there is no consistency check on the ciphertext $\bar{s}$ output by the corrupted sender A_1: $\bar{s}$ could even be the entire view of A_1. In Sect. 7.2 we show that adding ciphertext verifiability yields stronger limitation on the communication between unauthorized parties.

Definition 3.3 (No Secret Write (NSW) Rule). *Let $\mathsf{A} = (\mathsf{A}_1, \mathsf{A}_2)$ be an adversary and consider the following game (oracles $\mathcal{O}_G$ and $\mathcal{O}_E$ are the key generation oracle and encryption oracle defined in Definition 3.2):*

[3] Alternatively one could require A_2 (and consequently B) to distinguish whether a ciphertext contains a subliminal message at all. This case is clearly implied by ours.

Experiments	
$\mathsf{Exp}^{\mathsf{nsw}}_{(\mathsf{A}_1,\mathsf{A}_2)}(\lambda, \mathcal{P})$	$\mathsf{Exp}^{\mathsf{nsw}}_{(\mathsf{A}_1,\mathsf{B})}(\lambda, \mathcal{P})$
$(pp, msk) \leftarrow \mathsf{Setup}(1^\lambda, \mathcal{P})$ $(\bar{m}, \bar{s}) \leftarrow \mathsf{A}_1^{\mathcal{O}_G(\cdot,\mathsf{sen})}(pp)$ $m' \leftarrow \mathsf{A}_2^{\mathcal{O}_G(\cdot,\mathsf{rec}),\ \mathcal{O}_E(\cdot)}(pp, \bar{s})$ *Return* 1 *if* $\bar{m} = m'$, 0 *otherwise.*	$(pp, msk) \leftarrow \mathsf{Setup}(1^\lambda, \mathcal{P})$ $(\bar{m}, \bar{s}) \leftarrow \mathsf{A}_1^{\mathcal{O}_G(\cdot,\mathsf{sen})}(pp)$ $m'' \leftarrow \mathsf{B}^{\mathcal{O}_E(\cdot)}(pp, \bar{s})$ *Return* 1 *if* $\bar{m} = m''$, 0 *otherwise.*

Let $\mathcal{Q}_1$ *(resp.,* $\mathcal{Q}_2$*) be the set of all queries* $q = (i, \mathsf{sen})$ *(resp.,* $q = (j, \mathsf{rec})$*) that* A_1 *(resp.,*A_2*) issues to* $\mathcal{O}_G$*. The adversary wins the experiment if* $m' = \bar{m}$ *while the following holds:*

No Communication Rule (NCR). $\forall\ (i, \mathsf{sen}) \in \mathcal{Q}_1,\ (j, \mathsf{rec}) \in \mathcal{Q}_2,\ \mathcal{P}(i, j) = 0.$

Given λ *and a policy* $\mathcal{P}$*, an ACE without sanitizer satisfies the No Secret Write rule if for all PPT* $\mathsf{A} = (\mathsf{A}_1, \mathsf{A}_2)$ *there exists a PPT algorithm* B *and a negligible function* negl *such that*

$$\Pr\left[1 \leftarrow \mathsf{Exp}^{\mathsf{nsw}}_{(\mathsf{A}_1,\mathsf{B})}(\lambda, \mathcal{P})\right] \geq \Pr\left[1 \leftarrow \mathsf{Exp}^{\mathsf{nsw}}_{(\mathsf{A}_1,\mathsf{A}_2)}(\lambda, \mathcal{P}) \ \wedge \ \mathsf{NCR}\right] - \mathsf{negl}(\lambda).$$

Further remarks on defining NSWR security can be found in the full version, alongside the intuition behind the impossibility to instantiate an ACE without sanitization from symmetric key primitives.

4 Linear ACE Without Sanitizer from PKE

The first construction is akin to the original linear ACE from standard assumptions by Damgård et al. [4]. In such scheme, senders are given the public keys of all the receivers they are allowed to communicate with, and "decoy/placeholder" public keys for the receivers they are not allowed to communicated with (to make sure that ciphertexts generated by different senders have the same length). The encryption algorithm then encrypts the message under all the keys. The i-th receiver just decrypts the i-th ciphertext using its secret key. Sender's anonymity requires that ciphertexts do not leak any information about the key used to generate them, i.e., key indistinguishability [3].

Let ($\mathsf{PKE.KeyGen}, \mathsf{PKE.Enc}, \mathsf{PKE.Dec}$) be a public key encryption scheme, that is IND-CPA secure[4] and IK-CPA. An ACE without sanitizer from PKE (denoted $\mathsf{ACE}^{\mathsf{pke}}$) can be instantiated as follow.

[4] It is enough that the PKE is IND-CPA, as whenever the receiver has to distinguish between the encryption of 2 different messages, it is not allowed to get the decryption key (as it would be in the Payload privacy game). In the sender anonymity game, when the adversary can ask for decryption keys, the only requirement is that is should be impossible to identify a sender from the encryption key it uses, which is guaranteed by the key-indistinguishability property.

Communication Model: parties communicate through a bulletin board. Only senders are allowed to write on the board. Receivers can only read from it.
Message Space: $\mathcal{M} := \{0,1\}^\ell$.
Setup: $(pp, msk) \leftarrow \mathsf{Setup}(1^\lambda, \mathcal{P})$
It generates the message set, and the number of parties n, of senders n_S, and of receivers n_R; all are included in pp, along with the policy. The master secret key is a list of $2n_R$ (distinct) pairs of asymmetric keys, i.e.,

$$msk = \left\{ ((pk_j^0, sk_j^0), (pk_j^1, sk_j^1)) \ : \ \begin{array}{l} \text{For } i = 1,2 \\ (pk_j^i, sk_j^i) \leftarrow \mathsf{PKE.KeyGen}(1^\lambda) \end{array} \right\}_{j \in [n_R]}.$$

Key Generation: $k_i \leftarrow \mathsf{KGen}(pp, msk, i, t)$
On input (i, t), the algorithm parses $msk = \{((pk_j^0, sk_j^0), (pk_j^1, sk_j^1))\}_j$, and behaves as it follows.

- If $i \neq 0$ and $t = \mathsf{sen}$, it returns a vector $ek_i = (ek_i[j])_{j \in [n_R]}$ such that $ek_i[j] \leftarrow pk_j^{\mathcal{P}(i,j)}$.
- If $i \neq 0$ and $t = \mathsf{rec}$, it returns $dk_i = sk_i^1$.
- If $i = 0$, returns $ek_0 = dk_0 = pp$.

Encryption: $c \leftarrow \mathsf{Enc}(pp, ek_i, m)$
Run $c_j \leftarrow \mathsf{PKE.Enc}(ek_i[j], m; \rho_j)$ for all $j \in [n_R]$ (ρ_j is a random string). Return $c = (c_j)_{j=1,\dots,n}$.
Decryption: $m' \leftarrow \mathsf{Dec}(pp, dk_j, c)$
Let $c = (c_1, \dots, c_{n_R})$. Return the output of $\mathsf{PKE.Dec}(dk_j, c_j)$ (which could be either a message m or $\perp$).

Theorem 4.1. *The* $\mathsf{ACE}^{\mathsf{pke}}$ *scheme is correct, and satisfies the properties of No-Read and No Secret Write as described in Sect. 3 if the public key encryption scheme is IND-CPA secure and key-indistinguishable.*

Proof. The proof is as follows.

Correctness. Correctness directly follows from the correctness of the PKE scheme.

No Read Rule. The No-Read Rule relies on both the IK-CPA and IND-CPA properties of the PKE scheme. The proof is deferred to the full version, as it closely follows the proof of [4, Theorem 3].

No Secret Write Rule. Given an adversary $\mathsf{A} = (\mathsf{A}_1, \mathsf{A}_2)$ that wins the game $\mathsf{Exp}^{\mathsf{nsw}}_{(\mathsf{A}_1,\mathsf{A}_2)}(\lambda, \mathcal{P})$ with probability ϵ_A, to prove that the scheme satisfies the NSW Rule we need to construct an algorithm B that wins game $\mathsf{Exp}^{\mathsf{nsw}}_{(\mathsf{A}_1,\mathsf{B})}(\lambda, \mathcal{P})$ with essentially the same probability (up to a negligible difference). Upon receiving $\bar{s}$ from A_1, the algorithm B runs A_2 internally on input $(pp, \bar{s})$ simulating the oracles as follows. First, it generates $2n_R$ pairs of PKE keys, and collects them in a fresh master secret key $\bar{msk} = \{((\bar{pk}_j^0, \bar{sk}_j^0), (\bar{pk}_j^1, \bar{sk}_j^1))\}_{j \in [n_R]}$. The oracles are then simulated using msk':

$\mathcal{O}_G$: on input (j, t) from A_2, B generates new keys according to the policy $\mathcal{P}$ using $\bar{msk}$. If $t = \mathsf{sen}$ B sends $ek_j = (\bar{pk}_i^{\mathcal{P}(j,i)})_{i \in [n_R]}$; if $t = \mathsf{rec}$, it sends $dk_j = \bar{sk}_j^1$. It stores the keys in a list $\mathcal{K}$.

$\mathcal{O}_E$: simulates the encryption oracle as specified in the security experiment using the appropriate key from $\mathcal{K}$.

Finally, B outputs the message that A_2 returns. By the definition of conditional probability, the success probability of B is

$$\Pr\left[1 \leftarrow \mathsf{Exp}^{\mathsf{nsw}}_{(\mathsf{A}_1,\mathsf{B})}(\lambda, \mathcal{P})\right] = \Pr\left[1 \leftarrow \mathsf{Exp}^{\mathsf{nsw}}_{(\mathsf{A}_1,\mathsf{A}_2)}(\lambda, \mathcal{P}) \ \wedge \ \mathsf{NCR}\right] \cdot \Pr(\mathbf{E}),$$

where we denote by $\mathbf{E}$ the event "A_2 does not distinguish the simulated oracles from real ones". The only way A_2 could distinguish, is if the answers of the simulated oracles were inconsistent with the challenge ciphertext $\bar{s}$. However, in the real game the encryption keys queried by A_1 are statistically independent of the decryption keys queried by A_2, and they do not share state, thus any information encoded in $\bar{s}$ is statistically independent of the keys A_2 queries. The only way A_2 could get information about the encryption keys owned by A_1 would be by querying the encryption oracle on (i, m) for an i that A_1 has corrupted (such identity could be hardcoded in A_2, so the attack can be performed even in absence of shared state). If A_2 can distinguish that the ciphertext is not generated using the same key that A_1 received, then A can be exploited to break the key indistinguishability property of the PKE. Let q_E be the number of queries by A_2 to the encryption oracle. One can prove this by a sequence of hybrid games:

Game 0. This is the No-Secret-Write experiment.

Hybrid k **for** $0 \leq k \leq 2n_R$**.** In all hybrid games the view of A_1 is generated according to the NSWR experiment, i.e., using the master secret key msk generated at the beginning of the experiment. However, when generating the view of A_2, the challenger in Hybrid k generates the j-th key pairs in $\bar{msk}$ as follows:

Case $j < \lfloor k/2 \rfloor$**:** it generates fresh PKE key pairs $(\bar{pk}_j^0, \bar{sk}_j^0, \bar{pk}_j^1, \bar{sk}_j^1)$.

Case $j = k$**:** it generates a fresh key pair $(\bar{pk}, \bar{sk})$, and sets the j-th PKE pairs to be $(\bar{pk}, \bar{sk}, pk_j^1, sk_j^1)$ if k is odd and $(\bar{pk}_j^0, \bar{sk}_j^0, \bar{pk}, \bar{sk})$ if k is even, where $(pk_j^0, sk_j^0, pk_j^1, sk_j^1)$ is the j-th key pair in msk and $(\bar{pk}_j^0, \bar{sk}_j^0,) \leftarrow$ $\mathsf{PKE.KeyGen}(1^\lambda)$.

Case $j > \lfloor k/2 \rfloor$**:** it uses the same PKE key pairs $(pk_j^0, sk_j^0, pk_j^1, sk_j^1)$ as in msk.

Let E_k be the event that A distinguishes between Hybrid k and Hybrid $k-1$. Lemma 4.2 shows that $\Pr(\mathrm{E}_k) \leq \frac{2}{3} q_E \epsilon_{\mathsf{ik\text{-}cpa}}(\lambda)$.

Game 1. This is the No-Secret-Write experiment as simulated by B. By definition, Hybrid 0 is exactly equal to Game 0, and Hybrid $2n_R$ is the same as Game 1. Therefore:

$$\Pr(\mathbf{E}) \geq 1 - 3 n_R q_E \epsilon_{\mathsf{ik\text{-}cpa}}(\lambda),$$

where $\epsilon_{\text{ik-cpa}}(\lambda)$ is the probability of breaking the IK-CPA property of the PKE scheme and $q_E = poly(\lambda)$ as A is a polynomial-time algorithm. □

Lemma 4.2. $\Pr(E_k) \leq 3\epsilon_{ik\text{-}cpa}(\lambda) q_E$ *for all* $k \in [2n_R]$.

Proof. We split the proof in 3 cases:

Case 1: for all queries (j, sen) by A_1 to $\mathcal{O}_G$, $\mathcal{P}(j,k) = 0$.
Case 2: there are $\bar{i}, \bar{j} \in [n_S]$ such that A_1 queried $(\bar{i}, \mathsf{sen})$ and $(\bar{j}, \mathsf{sen})$ to $\mathcal{O}_G$ and $\mathcal{P}(\bar{i}, k) = 1$, $\mathcal{P}(\bar{j}, k) = 0$.
Case 3: for all queries (j, sen) by A_1 to $\mathcal{O}_G$, $\mathcal{P}(j,k) = 1$.

If $k = 0$ this is exactly the NSW experiment. If $k = 2n_R$ this is the NSW experiment as simulated by B. Assume now $0 < k < 2n_R$.

Let us start from k odd. In Case 1 A_1 sees pk_k^0 but not pk_k^1, while A_2 can query dk_k and receives sk_k^1 both in Hybrid k and in Hybrid $k-1$. The only difference is that in Hybrid k $\mathcal{O}_E$ uses $\bar{pk}_k, pk_k^1$ instead of pk_k^0, pk_k^1 as in Hybrid $k-1$. If A can distinguish in this case, we construct a PPT algorithm C that can win the IK-CPA experiment running A as a subroutine. C receives pk_0 and pk_1 from the IK-CPA experiment and generates msk setting $(pk_k^0, sk_k^0) = (pk_0, \perp)$ and $(\bar{pk}, \bar{sk}) = (pk_1, \perp)$. The rest of the master secret keys msk and $\bar{msk}$ are generated as specified by Hybrid k. Then it answers to $\mathcal{O}_G$ using msk for the queries by A_1 and $\bar{msk}$ for the queries by A_2. To answer queries from A_2 to $\mathcal{O}_E$, C selects a random $q \xleftarrow{\$} [q_E]$ and behaves as follows:

- C answers to the first $q-1$ queries using pk_0, pk_k^1 as the k-th encryption keys.
- When A_2 sends the q-th query (i, m), C returns m to the IK-CPA experiment and receives a challenge ciphertext $\bar{c}$. Then it generates the encryption of m as follows:

$$c_j \leftarrow \mathsf{PKE.Enc}(pk_j^{\mathcal{P}(i,j)}, m) \quad \text{for } j = 1, \ldots, k-1$$
$$c_j \leftarrow \bar{c} \quad \text{for } j = k \text{ if } \mathcal{P}(i,k) = 0$$
$$c_j \leftarrow \mathsf{PKE.Enc}(pk_j^1, m) \quad \text{for } j = k \text{ if } \mathcal{P}(i,k) = 1$$
$$c_j \leftarrow \mathsf{PKE.Enc}(\bar{pk}_j^{\mathcal{P}(i,j)}, m) \quad \text{for } j = k+1, \ldots, n_R$$

- C answers to the remaining $q_E - q + 1$ queries using pk_1, pk_k^1 as the k-th encryption keys.

Thus it follows that for k odd

$$\begin{aligned}
\Pr(\mathrm{E}_k \mid \text{Case 1}) &\leq |\Pr(\mathsf{A} \text{ wins Hybrid } k-1 \mid \text{Case 1}) - \Pr(\mathsf{A} \text{ wins Hybrid } k \mid \text{Case 1})| \\
&\leq |\sum_{Q=1}^{q_E} \Pr(\mathsf{A} \text{ wins the game } \mid q = Q \ \wedge\ \bar{c} \leftarrow \mathsf{PKE.Enc}(pk_0, m)) + \\
&\qquad - \Pr(\mathsf{A} \text{ wins the game } \mid q = Q \ \wedge\ \bar{c} \leftarrow \mathsf{PKE.Enc}(pk_1, m))| \\
&\leq q_E \epsilon_{\text{ik-cpa}}(\lambda).
\end{aligned}$$

In Case 2 A_1 sees both pk_k^0 and pk_k^1, while A_2 cannot query dk_k both in Hybrid k and in Hybrid $k-1$. The difference is that in Hybrid k $\mathcal{O}_E$ uses

$\bar{pk}_k, pk_k^1$ instead of pk_k^0, pk_k^1 as in Hybrid $k-1$. The reduction shown for Case 1 can be replicated without changes in this case. In Case 3 A_1 sees pk_k^1 but not pk_k^0, while A_2 cannot query dk_k both in Hybrid k and in Hybrid $k-1$. Again the only difference is that in Hybrid k $\mathcal{O}_E$ uses $\bar{pk}_k, pk_k^1$ instead of pk_k^0, pk_k^1 as in Hybrid $k-1$. Thus in this case the view of A in Hybrid k is statistically indistinguishable from the view of A in Hybrid $k-1$.

Finally, assume that k is even. In Case 1 A_1 sees pk_k^0 but not pk_k^1, while A_2 can query dk_k and receives $\bar{sk}_k^1$ in Hybrid k and sk_k^1 in Hybrid $k-1$. The encryption oracle $\mathcal{O}_E$ uses $\bar{pk}_k{}^0, \bar{pk}$ in Hybrid k, and $\bar{pk}_k^0, pk_k^1$ in Hybrid $k-1$. As the adversary does not see pk_k^1, the view of A in Hybrid k is statistically indistinguishable by the view of A in Hybrid $k-1$. In Case 3 A_1 sees pk_k^1 but not pk_k^0, while A_2 cannot query dk_k both in Hybrid k and in Hybrid $k-1$. The difference is that in Hybrid k $\mathcal{O}_E$ uses $\bar{pk}_k{}^0, \bar{pk}$ instead of $\bar{pk}_k^0, pk_k^1$ as in Hybrid $k-1$. The previous reduction can be adapted to this case as follows. C receives pk_0 and pk_1 from the IK-CPA experiment and generates msk setting $(pk_k^1, sk_k^1) = (pk_0, \perp)$ and $(\bar{pk}, \bar{sk}) = (pk_1, \perp)$. The rest of the master secret keys msk and $\bar{msk}$ are generated as specified by Hybrid k. Then it answers to $\mathcal{O}_G$ using msk for the queries by A_1 and $\bar{msk}$ for the queries by A_2. To answer queries from A_2 to $\mathcal{O}_E$, C selects a random $q \xleftarrow{\$} [q_E]$ and behaves as follows:

- C answers to the first $q-1$ queries using pk_0, pk_k^1 as the k-th encryption keys.
- When A_2 sends the q-th query (i, m), C returns m to the IK-CPA experiment and receives a challenge ciphertext $\bar{c}$. Then it generates the encryption of m as follows:

$$c_j \leftarrow \mathsf{PKE.Enc}(pk_j^{\mathcal{P}(i,j)}, m) \quad \text{for } j = 1, \ldots, k-1$$
$$c_j \leftarrow \mathsf{PKE.Enc}(\bar{pk}_j^0, m) \quad \text{for } j = k \text{ if } \mathcal{P}(i,k) = 0$$
$$c_j \leftarrow \quad \bar{c} \quad \text{for } j = k \text{ if } \mathcal{P}(i,k) = 1$$
$$c_j \leftarrow \mathsf{PKE.Enc}(\bar{pk}_j^{\mathcal{P}(i,j)}, m) \quad \text{for } j = k+1, \ldots, n_R$$

- C answers to the remaining $q_E - q + 1$ queries using pk_1, pk_k^1 as the k-th encryption keys.

Analogously to the case of k odd, for k even it holds that

$$\Pr(\mathrm{E}_k \mid \text{Case } 3) \le q_E \epsilon_{\mathsf{ik\text{-}cpa}}(\lambda).$$

Finally, in Case 2 A_1 sees both pk_k^0 and pk_k^1, while A_2 cannot query dk_k both in Hybrid k and in Hybrid $k-1$. The difference is again that in Hybrid k $\mathcal{O}_E$ uses $\bar{pk}_k{}^0, \bar{pk}$ instead of $\bar{pk}_k^0, pk_k^1$ as in Hybrid $k-1$. The reduction shown for Case 1 can be replicated without changes in this case. Therefore, for all k it holds that

$$\Pr(\mathrm{E}_k) = \sum_{i=1}^{3} \Pr(\text{Case } i)\Pr(\mathrm{E}_k \mid \text{Case } i) \le 3 q_E \epsilon_{\mathsf{ik\text{-}cpa}}(\lambda).$$

□

5 Compact ACE from Hybrid Encryption

The previous construction has the problem that the length of ciphertexts depends linearly on $\ell \cdot n_R$. This can be improved using a hybrid encryption technique: combining $\mathsf{ACE}^{\mathsf{pke}}$ with a rate-1 symmetric key encryption (SKE) scheme yields a more compact ACE (denoted by $\mathsf{ACE}^{\mathsf{he}}$), which outputs ciphertexts whose size scales with $\ell + n_R$ instead. Interestingly, there is no known analogous hybrid encryption version of the original construction of [4].

Let $(\mathsf{SE.KeyGen}, \mathsf{SE.Enc}, \mathsf{SE.Dec})$ be a rate-1 symmetric encryption scheme that is $\mathsf{lor\text{-}cpa}$ secure, and let $\mathsf{ACEnoS} = (\mathsf{ACE.Setup}, \mathsf{ACE.KGen}, \mathsf{ACE.Enc}, \mathsf{ACE.Dec})$ be an ACE without sanitizer that is NRR and NSWR secure.

Communication Model: parties communicate through a bulletin board; senders and receivers have write-only and read-only access respectively.

Message Space: $\mathcal{M} := \{0,1\}^\ell$.

Setup: $(pp, msk) \leftarrow \mathsf{Setup}(1^\lambda, \mathcal{P})$
Return $(pp, msk) \leftarrow \mathsf{ACE.Setup}(1^\lambda, \mathcal{P})$.

Key Generation: $k_i \leftarrow \mathsf{KGen}(pp, msk, i, t)$
Return $k_i \leftarrow \mathsf{ACE.KGen}(pp, msk, i, t)$.

Encryption: $c \leftarrow \mathsf{Enc}(pp, ek_i, m)$
Generate a one-time secret key $sk \leftarrow \mathsf{SE.KeyGen}(1^\lambda)$, and encrypt the message using it: $c_1 \leftarrow \mathsf{SE.Enc}_{sk}(m)$. Then encrypt the key using the ACEnoS: $c_2 \leftarrow \mathsf{ACE.Enc}(pp, ek_i, sk)$. Return $c = (c_1, c_2)$.

Decryption: $m' \leftarrow \mathsf{Dec}(pp, dk_j, c)$
Parse $c = (c_1, c_2)$. Decrypt the secret key $sk' \leftarrow \mathsf{ACE.Dec}(pp, dk_j, c_2)$. If $sk' = \perp$, return $\perp$. Else return $m' \leftarrow \mathsf{SE.Dec}_{sk'}(c_1)$.

Efficiency, Storage Requirements, and Optimizations. The length of the ciphertext is $\mathrm{O}(n_R + \ell)$ using a rate-1 SKE. The full version contains a construction from predicate encryption that outputs more compact ciphertexts (of length $\mathrm{O}(\log(n_S)+\lambda)$) when instantiated for policies such that $\min_{j\in[n_R]} S_j = \mathrm{O}(\log n_S)$ where S_j is the set of senders allowed to communicate with the receiver j.

Theorem 5.1. *The protocol previously described is correct, and satisfies the properties of No-Read and No Secret Write if the SKE is* $\mathsf{lor\text{-}cpa}$ *secure, and* ACEnoS *satisfies correctness, NRR and NSWR as described in Sect. 3.*

The security proof is akin to that of $\mathsf{ACE}^{\mathsf{pke}}$, and is deferred to the full version.

6 Game-Specific Obfuscation

We suggest a variant of obfuscation that is weaker that Virtual Blackbox (VBB) obfuscation and hence may be possible to implement in general. VBB obfuscation requires that the obfuscated program gives nothing to the receiver, other than oracle access to the original program, and it is well known that no obfuscator can be capable of VBB-obfuscating every program.

Experiment $\mathsf{Exp}^{G^0}_{\mathsf{A},\mathsf{Obf}}(\lambda, \mathcal{F}, q)$	**Experiment** $\mathsf{Exp}^{G^1}_{\mathsf{B},\mathsf{Obf}}(\lambda, \mathcal{F}, q)$
$st \leftarrow (\lambda, \mathcal{F}, q)$ $(pp, k) \leftarrow \mathsf{C}(0; st)$ For $i = 1, \ldots, q$: $\quad z_i^{\mathsf{A}} \leftarrow \mathsf{A}^{\mathsf{C}(1,k,\cdot;st),\mathsf{C}(3,\cdot;st)}(pp)$ $b \leftarrow \mathsf{C}(4, z_1^{\mathsf{A}}, \ldots, z_q^{\mathsf{A}}; st)$ Return b.	$st \leftarrow (\lambda, \mathcal{F}, q)$ $(pp, k) \leftarrow \mathsf{C}(0; st)$ For $i = 1, \ldots, q$: $\quad z_i^{\mathsf{B}} \leftarrow \mathsf{B}^{\mathsf{C}(2,k,\cdot,\cdot;st),\mathsf{C}(3,\cdot;st)}(pp)$ $b \leftarrow \mathsf{C}(4, z_1^{\mathsf{B}}, \ldots, z_q^{\mathsf{B}}; st)$ Return b.

Fig. 1. Security experiment for Game-Specific obfuscation.

Here, we consider instead a security game G (formalized as an experiment in Fig. 1), in which a challenger C plays against an adversary A, using an obfuscator Obf. The game comes with a specification of a family of programs $\mathcal{F} := \{\mathsf{P}_{k,\mathsf{p}}\}_{k \in \{0,1\}^\lambda, \mathsf{p} \in \{0,1\}^m}$, parameterized by k and by a label p of some length m, so we have one member of the family for each pair (k, p). This is meant to cover a wide range of applications where obfuscated programs may be used: very often, an application bakes one or more cryptographic keys into the program, this is modelled by the parameter k. The label p is useful in a multiparty scenario, where parties may be given programs that depend on their identity, for instance.

The game proceeds in rounds, where in each round of the game, A can query C on various labels p to obtain obfuscated programs $\hat{\mathsf{P}}^{\mathsf{p}}_k = \mathsf{Obf}(\mathsf{P}^{\mathsf{p}}_k)$, as well as for other data (such as public parameters). At the end of each round, A returns some final output z_i, which is remembered between rounds. Optionally, the game may allow A to remember additional state information between rounds (not represented in Fig. 1). In the end, C decides if A won the game. Our definition compares this to a similar experiment where, however, the adversary B only gets oracle access to the programs.

Importantly, C can decide not to answer a query, based on the label and its current state. This models conditions one would typically have in a game, such as: the game models a scheme with several parties participating, some of which are corrupt, and the adversary is not allowed to query a program that was given to an honest player. Since the same C plays against both A and B, they are under the same constraints, so B cannot "cheat" and make queries that A could not.

For simplicity, we let C choose a single parameter k initially. We can easily generalize to cases where programs using several different values of k are used.

Definition 6.1 (Game-Specific Obfuscation). *We say that* Obf *is a* game-specific secure obfuscator *(GSO) relative to G and $\mathcal{F}$ if for every PPT adversary* A, *there exists a PPT adversary* B *which plays G using only oracle access to each obfuscated program, and where* $|\Pr[1 \leftarrow \mathsf{Exp}^{G^0}_{\mathsf{A},\mathsf{Obf}}(\lambda, \mathcal{F}, q)] - \Pr[1 \leftarrow \mathsf{Exp}^{G^1}_{\mathsf{B},\mathsf{Obf}}(\lambda, \mathcal{F}, q)]|$ *is negligible, where the challenger behaves as follows:*

Challenge Generation: *on input* $(0; (\lambda, \mathcal{F}, q))$, *it returns* $k \in \{0,1\}^\lambda$ *and some general public parameters pp.*
Program Obfuscation: *on input* $(1, k, \mathsf{p}; st)$, *it returns the obfuscation* $\hat{\mathsf{P}}^{\mathsf{p}}_k \leftarrow \mathsf{Obf}(\mathsf{P}^{\mathsf{p}}_k)$ *of the program, or* $\perp$.
Oracle Access to Programs: *on input* $(2, (k, \mathsf{p}, m); st)$ *it returns the evaluation of the program* $\mathsf{P}^{\mathsf{p}}_k(m)$, *or* $\perp$.
Other Data: *on input* $(3, \cdot; st)$ *it can return additional data.*
Winning Condition Check: *on input* $(4, z_1, \ldots, z_q; st)$ *it returns* 1 *if the adversary won the game, 0 otherwise.*

Every mode of operation can update the state st of the challenger too, if required by the game.

Note that this definition, while implied by VBB, makes a much weaker demand than VBB: we assume that the obfuscation gives nothing more than oracle access, only as far as winning G is concerned, and the obfuscator only needs to obfuscate programs in $\mathcal{F}$. Indeed, the impossibility result for VBB does not apply to game-specific obfuscation in general, it just rules out its existence for a specific game and family of programs. The notion is somewhat incomparable to iO obfuscation: obfuscators secure in the iO sense are usually claimed to be able to obfuscate any program, and can potentially be applied in any security game, but on the other hand, iO only guarantees indistinguishability between programs with the same input/output behavior. Even when restricting to assume the existence of iO/GSO for specific programs (as it happens in constructions relying on iO), still iO and GSO target different aspects: GSO has no specific requirement on the family of programs, while iO needs them to compute the same function; on the other hand, iO still guarantees indistinguishability for every game, while GSO targets a specific one.

As usual, we also require the obfuscators to *preserve functionality* (the input-output behaviour of the obfuscated program is equivalent to the original program) and *polynomial slowdown* (the obfuscated program should can at most be polynomially slower/larger than the original one).

7 ACE with Ciphertext Verifiability

In this section we explore whether it is possible to obtain more than just preventing parties from establishing secure subliminal channels. The intuition is that it should be possible to restrict corrupted parties in the bandwidth of their subliminal channels by adding some form of *ciphertext verifiability* to our model. Ciphertext verifiability allows any party with access to the bulletin board to verify that ciphertexts appended to the public board have been generated honestly and according to policy, *even if the party is not allowed to decrypt them by the policy.* We then show a scheme that allows to restrict the bandwidth of corrupted senders to logarithmic in the security parameter under a novel variant of obfuscation, namely the GSO introduced in the previous section. We find this a promising indication that public verification can help to restrict subliminal communication between corrupted parties. As a byproduct, we get a construction whose complexity only scales polylogarithmically with the number of parties.

7.1 Ciphertext Verifiability

Parties, policies and the communication model are the same as in Sect. 3. The difference is that an ACE with ciphertext verifiability (VACE) is composed by 5 algorithms ($\mathsf{Setup}, \mathsf{KGen}, \mathsf{Enc}, \mathsf{Verify}, \mathsf{Dec}$). The verification algorithm Verify allows receivers to verify that ciphertexts published in the bulletin board are well-formed according to their decryption key:

Verification $b \in \{0,1\} \leftarrow \mathsf{Verify}(dk_j, c)$
On input a ciphertext c and a decryption key, the algorithm outputs 1 if $c \leftarrow \mathsf{Enc}(pp, ek_i, m)$ for some (unknown) honestly generated sender's key ek_i and message $m \in \mathcal{M}$, and 0 otherwise.

Remark that the definition implies that verification can be done using dk_0, i.e., the decryption key of the receiver with identity $j = 0$ which by policy cannot receive messages[5]. Differently from ACEnoS, now dk_0 might not be equal to the public parameters (while ek_0 still is). Moreover, dk_0 is not part of them: it is given only to receivers, not to the senders. This follows quite naturally from the communication model: as senders have write-only access to the public board, they cannot see (thus verify) ciphertexts by other senders than themselves[6].

The introduction of such algorithm requires to modify the properties of security and correctness as well. This new construction of ACE should satisfy both correctness as defined in Sect. 3 and a completeness requirement (i.e., that honestly generated ciphertexts pass verification).

Definition 7.1 (Completeness). *A VACE scheme is complete if for all λ, $m \in \mathcal{M}$, $i \in [n_S]$, $j \in [n_R]$ it holds*

$$\Pr\left[1 \leftarrow \mathsf{Verify}(dk_j, \mathsf{Enc}(pp, ek_i, m)) \;:\; \begin{array}{r} (pp, msk) \leftarrow \mathsf{Setup}(1^\lambda, \mathcal{P}), \\ ek_i \leftarrow \mathsf{KGen}(pp, msk, i, \mathsf{sen}), \\ dk_j \leftarrow \mathsf{KGen}(pp, msk, j, \mathsf{rec}) \end{array}\right] = 1,$$

where the probabilities are taken over the random coins of all the algorithms.

To ensure that verification is meaningful, the outcome of verification should be consistent when done with different keys.

---

[5] The inclusion of the identity 0 for senders and receivers with no rights is standard in normal access control encryption, cf. [4].

[6] In fact, it seems to be necessary for a more technical reason related to the NSWR (as the verification key could be seen as shared randomness between corrupted senders and receivers).

Definition 7.2 (Verification Consistency). *Given a policy $\mathcal{P}$, a* VACE *scheme verifies consistently if, for every PPT adversary* A *there exists a negligible function* negl *such that*

$$\Pr\left[b_0 \neq b_1 \;\middle|\; \begin{array}{l} (pp, msk) \leftarrow \mathsf{Setup}(1^\lambda, \mathcal{P}) \\ (i_0, i_1, c) \leftarrow \mathsf{A}^{\mathcal{O}_G(\cdot,\cdot)}(pp) \\ \textit{For } k = 0, 1 \\ \quad dk_{i_k} \leftarrow \mathsf{KGen}(pp, msk, i_k, \mathsf{rec}) \\ \quad b_k \leftarrow \mathsf{Verify}(dk_{i_k}, c) \end{array} \right] \leq \mathsf{negl}(\lambda),$$

where the $\mathcal{O}_G$ returns ek_j on input (j, sen), and dk_j on input (j, rec).

The No Read Rule remains unchanged as such property is not concerned with enforcing the policy, but with the anonymity and privacy of the scheme. On the other hand, the winning condition of the No Secret Write Rule changes to impose that the challenge ciphertext successfully verifies w.r.t. some fixed receiver key. This, combined with consistency of verification (which we just defined) implies that a successful verification w.r.t. even just the public verification key dk_0 is enough to guarantee it w.r.t. all receiver keys (which could be impossible to check efficiently in the game if the number of receivers is superpolynomial).

The verification key dk_0 is only given to the corrupted receiver A_2 and to the public verifier B but not to the corrupted sender A_1, as the latter cannot read from the public board, but just write on it.

Definition 7.3 (No Secret Write Rule). *Let $\mathsf{A} = (\mathsf{A}_1, \mathsf{A}_2)$ be an adversary and consider the following game:*

Experiments	
$\mathsf{Exp}^{\mathsf{nusw}}_{(\mathsf{A}_1,\mathsf{A}_2)}(\lambda, \mathcal{P})$	$\mathsf{Exp}^{\mathsf{nusw}}_{(\mathsf{A}_1,\mathsf{B})}(\lambda, \mathcal{P})$
$(pp, msk) \leftarrow \mathsf{Setup}(1^\lambda, \mathcal{P})$ $(\bar{m}, c) \leftarrow \mathsf{A}_1^{\mathcal{O}_G(\cdot,\mathsf{sen})}(pp)$ $m' \leftarrow \mathsf{A}_2^{\mathcal{O}_G(\cdot,\mathsf{rec}),\ \mathcal{O}_E(\cdot)}(pp, c)$ *Return* 1 *if* $\bar{m} = m' \wedge 1 \leftarrow \mathsf{Verify}(dk_0, c), dk_0 \leftarrow \mathcal{O}_G(0, \mathsf{rec})$, 0 *otherwise.*	$(pp, msk) \leftarrow \mathsf{Setup}(1^\lambda, \mathcal{P})$ $(\bar{m}, c) \leftarrow \mathsf{A}_1^{\mathcal{O}_G(\cdot,\mathsf{sen})}(pp, \bar{m})$ $m'' \leftarrow \mathsf{B}^{\mathcal{O}_E(\cdot),\mathcal{O}_G(0,\mathsf{rec})}(pp, c)$ *Return* 1 *if* $\bar{m} = m'' \wedge 1 \leftarrow \mathsf{Verify}(dk_0, c), dk_0 \leftarrow \mathcal{O}_G(0, \mathsf{rec})$, 0 *otherwise.*

Oracles	
$\mathcal{O}_G(j, t)$: *If* $\exists\ k_j$ s.t. $(k_j, j, t) \in \mathcal{L}$, *return* k_j *Else* $k_j \leftarrow \mathsf{KGen}(pp, msk, j, t)$ $\quad \mathcal{L} \leftarrow \mathcal{L} \cup \{(k_j, j, t)\}$ *Return* k_j.	$\mathcal{O}_E(j, m)$: $ek_j \leftarrow \mathcal{O}_G(j, \mathsf{sen})$ *Return* $c \leftarrow \mathsf{Enc}(pp, ek_j, m)$.

Let $\mathcal{Q}_1$ (resp., $\mathcal{Q}_2$) be the set of all queries $q = (i, \mathsf{sen})$ (resp., $q = (j, \mathsf{rec})$) that A_1 (resp.,A_2) issues to $\mathcal{O}_G$. The adversary wins the experiment if $m' = \bar{m}$ and the ciphertext verifies while the following holds:

No Communication Rule *(*NCR*).* $\forall\ (i, \mathsf{sen}) \in \mathcal{Q}_1$, $(j, \mathsf{rec}) \in \mathcal{Q}_2$, *it should hold that $\mathcal{P}(i, j) = 0$.*

Given λ and a policy $\mathcal{P}$, a ACE without sanitizer with verifiable ciphertexts satisfies the No Secret Write rule if for all PPT $\mathsf{A} = (\mathsf{A}_1, \mathsf{A}_2)$ there exists a PPT algorithm B and a negligible function negl *such that*

$$\Pr\left[1 \leftarrow \mathsf{Exp}^{\mathsf{nsw}}_{(\mathsf{A}_1,\mathsf{B})}(\lambda, \mathcal{P})\right] \geq \Pr\left[1 \leftarrow \mathsf{Exp}^{\mathsf{nsw}}_{(\mathsf{A}_1,\mathsf{A}_2)}(\lambda, \mathcal{P}) \ \wedge \ \mathsf{NCR}\right] - \mathsf{negl}(\lambda).$$

Ciphertext Verifiability vs. Sanitization. It is fair to wonder whether adding public verifiability yields an ACE with sanitization. This is not the case because: (1) the sanitizer/verification key is public; (2) in the VACE case, behavior of sanitizer/verifier is checkable by other receivers; (3) the access structure to a public board usually requires an authentication layer: verification (and possible identification of dishonest senders) can be enforced in that layer.

7.2 VACE from Game Specific Obfuscation

Verifiability of a ciphertext means that any party can verify that the ciphertext satisfies some relation, i.e., that *has some structure*, which bounds the entropy of the ciphertext. While this is not enough to prevent subliminal channels completely (as this seems to require the injection of true randomness, e.g., cf. [4,8]), in this section we show that this is enough to meaningfully restrict the bandwidth of corrupted senders.

We build a VACE following the IND-CCA PKE construction from iO by Sahai and Waters [9], with the following changes: (1) we impose that every ciphertext encrypts the identity of the sender in addition to the message, and (2) decryption is done by an obfuscated program that checks the policy too. As the original protocol outputs ciphertexts composed by two parts, the encryption of the message and a value used as authentication/integrity check, we easily get a VACE construction that is NRR secure assuming iO with a proof similar to [9]. However, proving NSWR from iO seems impossible, thus we rely on a GSO assumption on the obfuscator (further details in Sect. 7.3).

We now consider messages to be just one bit, i.e., $\mathcal{M} = \{0, 1\}$, and assume that $n_S = \mathsf{poly}(\lambda)$ (as this is needed when using the puncturable PRF in the proof of the NRR rule).

Setup: $(pp, msk) \leftarrow \mathsf{Setup}(1^\lambda, \mathcal{P})$
Generate the keys for the PRFs: $K_k \xleftarrow{\$} \{0,1\}^\lambda$, $k = 1, 2$. The algorithm returns $pp = (\lambda, \mathcal{P}, \mathcal{M})$ and the master secret key $msk = (K_1, K_2)$.
Key Generation: $k_i \leftarrow \mathsf{KGen}(pp, msk, i, t)$
Generate the obfuscated circuits $\hat{\mathsf{P}}^s_i \leftarrow \mathsf{Obf}(\lambda, \mathsf{P}^s_i)$, $i \in [n_S] \setminus \{0\}$, and $\hat{\mathsf{P}}^r_i \leftarrow \mathsf{Obf}(\lambda, \mathsf{P}^r_i)$, $i \in [n_R]$, of the programs P^s_i and P^r_j in Fig. 2, padded so that they are as long as the programs in the reductions (cf. proof of Theorem 7.4 and 7.7).
- If $i \neq 0$ and $t = \mathsf{sen}$, return $ek_i = (\hat{\mathsf{P}}^s_i)$.
- If $i = 0$ and $t = \mathsf{sen}$, return $ek_0 = pp$.
- If $t = \mathsf{rec}$, return $dk_i = (\hat{\mathsf{P}}^r_i)$.

$\mathsf{P}_i^s(m,s)$
$t \leftarrow \mathsf{PRG}(s)$ $cipher \leftarrow \mathsf{PRF}_1(K_1,t) \oplus (m,i)$ $sig \leftarrow \mathsf{PRF}_2(K_2,(t \mid\mid cipher))$ $c \leftarrow (t, cipher, sig))$ Return c.

$\mathsf{P}_j^r(c)$

Parse $c = (t, cipher, sig)$.
$b \leftarrow (sig == \mathsf{PRF}_2(K_2,(t \mid\mid cipher)))$
If $(b == 1)$
  $(m,i) \leftarrow cipher \oplus \mathsf{PRF}_1(K_1,t)$
  If $(\mathcal{P}(i,j) == 1)$
    Return $(1,m)$
  Else return $(1,\perp)$.
Else Return $(0,\perp)$.

Fig. 2. Encryption and decryption programs.

Encryption: $c \leftarrow \mathsf{Enc}(pp, ek_i, m)$
Sample $s \xleftarrow{\$} \{0,1\}^\lambda$. Return $c \leftarrow \hat{\mathsf{P}}_i^s(m,s)$.
Decryption: $m' \leftarrow \mathsf{Dec}(pp, dk_j, c)$
Run $(b, m') \leftarrow \hat{\mathsf{P}}_j^r(c)$ and return m'.
Verification: $b \in \{0,1\} \leftarrow \mathsf{Verify}(dk_j, c)$
Run $(b, m') \leftarrow \hat{\mathsf{P}}_j^r(c)$ and return b.

For ease of exposition we split the security proof of the VACE in two theorems, as the NRR and NSWR require different assumptions on Obf. In particular Theorem 7.4 shows NRR security and only requires the standard notion of iO, whereas Theorem 7.7 uses the novel GSO assumption. Note that one could also have chosen to prove the NRR security of the VACE assuming GSO instead of iO, but we opted for using the minimal assumptions for each theorem.

Theorem 7.4. *The* VACE *previously defined satisfies correctness and completeness, and has consistent verification, assuming the correctness of its building blocks. In addition, if* Obf *is a iO and* PRF_1, PRF_2 *and* PRG *are two puncturable PRF and a PRG respectively, the previous* VACE *and is NRR secure.*

The proof of Theorem 7.4 relies on the standard techniques introduced in [9], and is deferred to the full version. Remark that verification consistency follows easily from the fact that the first bit of the output of $\hat{\mathsf{P}}_j^r$ is independent of the value of j, thus it is the same for all $j \in [n_R]$.

7.3 No Secret Write Rule of VACE

We argue that indistinguishability obfuscation does not seem enough to prove NSWR security for our VACE. A major hint in this direction is that proving that the NSWR holds seems to require to show that A_2 cannot distinguish the real experiment from an experiment where both the encryption oracle and the receiver keys are simulated using only the information available to B (i.e., the encryption oracle and the verification key). However, we do not see a way to simulate the decryption keys that preserves their I/O behavior without knowing the master secret keys. Such a consistency in the I/O behavior of the keys is needed because A_1 could still transmit information to A_2 related to the behavior of the senders' keys queried by A_1, e.g., the output on a particular input (s, m): as B does not know which keys have been queried by A_1, it cannot rely on the encryption oracle to answer these queries consistently. However, simulation can be done assuming Obf to be a secure GSO. In particular, the obfuscator is assumed to be GSO secure for the following family of programs and game.

Definition 7.5 ($\mathcal{F}$). *The family $\mathcal{F} = \{\mathsf{P}_{k,\mathsf{p}}\}_{k,\mathsf{p}}$ contains all the possible keys:*

- $k = msk = (K_1, K_2)$, *and*
- $\mathsf{p} = (j, t)$ *is the identity and type of party, and*
- $\mathsf{P}_{k,(j,t)} = \mathsf{P}_j^t$, $t \in \{s, r\}$ *as defined in Fig. 2.*

Definition 7.6 (G_{nsw}). *The game G_{nsw} runs for $q = 2$ rounds and is played by a challenger $\mathsf{C}_{\mathsf{nsw}}$ that behaves as follows:*

- $\mathsf{C}(0, \ldots; st)$ *returns* $(pp, k) = (pp, msk) \leftarrow \mathsf{Setup}(1^\lambda, \mathcal{P})$ *and stores them in st (alongside a round counter).*
- $\mathsf{C}(1, (k, (j, t)); st)$ *returns the output of* $\mathsf{KGen}(pp, msk, j, t)$ *and stores the query in a list* q_i *for* $i = 1, \ldots, q$ *in st.*
- $\mathsf{C}(2, (k, (j, t), m); st)$ *it returns the evaluation of the program* $\mathsf{P}_j^t(m)$.
- $\mathsf{C}(3, st)$ *returns* $\perp$ *during round 1, and* $\bar{s}$ *in round 2.*
- $\mathsf{C}(4, z_1, z_2; st)$ *parses* $z_1 = (\bar{m}, \bar{s})$ *and returns 1 if the following three conditions hold:*
  1. $z_2 = \bar{m}$
  2. $1 \leftarrow \mathsf{Verify}(dk_0, \bar{s})$
  3. q_1 *(resp.,* q_2*) contains only queries for sender (resp., receiver) keys, and for every* $(i, \mathsf{sen}) \in q_1$ *and* $(j, \mathsf{rec}) \in q_2$ *it holds that* $\mathcal{P}(i, j) = 0$.

Note that we have chosen to only use the GSO assumption where it is necessary, namely the NSWR property. Therefore, since the NRR property is still proven using the iO assumption, the PRFs used in the construction are still puncturable even if this property is not explicitly used in the proof of the NSWR property.

Theorem 7.7. *Assuming* Obf *is a secure GSO for $\mathcal{F}$ and G_{nsw} as in Definition 7.5 and 7.6, and given two puncturable PRF and a PRG, the previous* VACE *is NSWR secure. Moreover, assuming that only ciphertexts that pass the verification are posted, it only allows for subliminal channels of bandwidth at most* $O(\log(\lambda))$.

Proof. Proving the NSWR relies on the hypothesis that Obf is a secure GSO for $(\mathcal{F}, G_{\mathsf{nsw}})$. Indeed, the NSWR experiment in Definition 7.3 is exactly equal to the game in Fig. 1 where $(\mathcal{F}, G_{\mathsf{nsw}})$ are as in Definition 7.5 and 7.6, and the adversary A in the GSO experiment behaves like A_1 in the first round, and like A_2 in the second. This implies that the probability that $(\mathsf{A}_1, \mathsf{A}_2)$ win the NSWR experiment is the same as the probability that A wins the GSO experiment. In fact, from GSO security it follows that for any adversary A there exists a second adversary A' that has only oracle access to all the keys, but wins the game G_{nsw} (i.e., the NSWR experiment) with almost the same probability:

$$\begin{aligned}\mathsf{Pr}\left[1 \leftarrow \mathsf{Exp}^{\mathsf{nsw}}_{(\mathsf{A}_1,\mathsf{A}_2)}(\lambda, \mathcal{P}) \ \wedge \ \mathsf{NCR}\right] &= \mathsf{Pr}\left[1 \leftarrow \mathsf{Exp}^{G^0_{\mathsf{nsw}}}_{\mathsf{A},\mathsf{Obf}}(\lambda, \mathcal{F}, 2)\right] \\ &\leq \mathsf{Pr}\left[1 \leftarrow \mathsf{Exp}^{G^1_{\mathsf{nsw}}}_{\mathsf{A}',\mathsf{Obf}}(\lambda, \mathcal{F}, 2)\right] + \epsilon_{GSO}. \end{aligned} \quad (1)$$

Let us now analyze the winning probability of A'. Denote by $(\mathsf{A}'_1, \mathsf{A}'_2)$ the execution of A' in the first and second round of G^1_{nsw} respectively. This adversary now does not receive the sender (or receiver) keys, but is only given oracle access to them. In fact, the oracle only evaluates the plaintext version of the keys, thus it is possible to substitute the PRF and PRG used in the keys with random functions, without significantly impacting the winning probability of A':

$$\mathsf{Pr}\left[1 \leftarrow \mathsf{Exp}^{G^1_{\mathsf{nsw}}}_{\mathsf{A}',\mathsf{Obf}}(\lambda, \mathcal{F}, 2)\right] = \mathsf{Pr}\left[1 \leftarrow \mathsf{Exp}^{G^2_{\mathsf{nsw}}}_{\mathsf{A}',\mathsf{Obf}}(\lambda, \mathcal{F}, 2)\right] + \epsilon_\rho, \quad (2)$$

where ϵ_ρ is the probability of distinguishing the PRF and PRG from a random function, and the game G^2_{nsw} is a modification of G^1_{nsw} where $\mathsf{C}(2, \cdot)$ answers the queries executing the code of P^t_i where PRF_1, PRF_2 and PRG have been substituted by random functions.

At this point we can already observe that the bandwidth of the subliminal channel (for ciphertexts that pass the verification) has to be at most $\mathrm{O}(\log(\lambda))$. Indeed, in game G^2_{nsw} the components t and *cipher* of the ciphertext are uniformly random while the tag *sig* is deterministically generated from them, thus a corrupted sender is restricted to encode a subliminal message in a ciphertext only through rejection sampling: A'_1 can only try encrypting randomly chosen messages (the ciphertext does not reveal anything about the plaintext, thus it is fair to assume that the subliminal message and the plaintext are independently chosen) until the ciphertext finally encodes the subliminal message. If the sender runtime is restricted to be polynomial-time, this limits the amount of rejection sampling that it can do, restricting the amount of information encoded in the ciphertext (the subliminal message) to $\mathrm{O}(\log(\lambda))$. The GSO assumption allows to conclude the argument: as A_1 cannot do (much) better than A'_1, the adversary can send short subliminal messages in the real experiment too.

Finally, we conclude the proof of the NSWR by showing an algorithm B that can win the NSWR experiment running A'_2 internally, with almost the same probability as the adversary A. Recall that in game G^2_{nsw} the sender keys oracle (i.e., the simulated $\mathsf{C}(2, (\cdot, (\cdot, \mathsf{sen}), m); st)$, which can be called in both rounds) returns a uniformly random bit string. This in particular implies that the view of A'_1 (i.e., A' at round 1) and A'_2 are independent of the master secret key *msk* generated at the beginning of the game. Therefore, a simulator B can win the NSWR experiment running A' at round 2 internally by generating a fresh pp', msk' for the VACE and use them to simulate $\mathsf{C}(2, \cdot)$. As the public parameters of the scheme only contain λ, $\mathcal{M}$ and $\mathcal{P}$, there is no way for A'_2 to distinguish between the real and simulated experiment, and it holds that

$$\mathsf{Pr}\left[1 \leftarrow \mathsf{Exp}^{G^2_{\mathsf{nsw}}}_{\mathsf{A}',\mathsf{Obf}}(\lambda, \mathcal{F}, 2)\right] = \mathsf{Pr}\left[1 \leftarrow \mathsf{Exp}^{G^2_{\mathsf{nsw}}}_{(\mathsf{A}'_1,\mathsf{B}),\mathsf{Obf}}(\lambda, \mathcal{F}, 2)\right] = \mathsf{Pr}\left[1 \leftarrow \mathsf{Exp}^{\mathsf{nsw}}_{(\mathsf{A}_1,\mathsf{B})}(\lambda, \mathcal{P})\right]. \quad (3)$$

Combining Eqs. (1), (2), and (3) yields the claim. □

On the Need of Ciphertext Verifiability. Ciphertext verifiability is crucial for the previous argument to go through: if one cannot verify that the ciphertext has been generated by the obfuscated program, a corrupted sender could just set the ciphertext to be the (subliminal) message it wants to send. So long as the data structure of the ciphertext fits the specifications, the subliminal channel cannot be detected. The next lemma (which is a folklore result) shows that our result is optimal: stricter restrictions on the subliminal channel require sanitization.

Lemma 7.8. *Let λ be the security parameter. An encoding scheme* $(\mathsf{KG}, \mathsf{Enc}, \mathsf{Dec})$ *(either symmetric or asymmetric, deterministic or probabilistic) such that the domain of* Enc_k *has dimension at least* $\mathsf{poly}(\lambda)$ *for every k output by the key generation* KG *always allows for insecure subliminal channels with bandwidth* $O(\log(\lambda))$ *(in absence of a trusted sanitization step) assuming the adversary runs in polynomial-time and has* oracle access *to the encryption algorithm.*

Proof. Consider an encoding $(\mathsf{KG}, \mathsf{Enc}, \mathsf{Dec})$ that satisfies basic correctness (reportend in the following for completeness):

Correctness: $\forall \lambda \in \mathbb{N},\ \forall m \in \mathcal{M},\ \exists \epsilon = \mathsf{negl}(\lambda)\ :\ \mathsf{Pr}(m' \neq m \mid (k_e, k_d) \leftarrow \mathsf{KG}(1^\lambda),\ c \leftarrow \mathsf{Enc}(k_e, m),\ m' \leftarrow \mathsf{Dec}(k_d, c)) \leq \epsilon.$

Then a PPT adversary A_1 that has only *oracle access* to the encryption algorithm can transmit any subliminal message $\bar{m}$ such that $|\bar{m}| \leq O(\log(\lambda))$ to a PPT receiver A_2 by sending a single valid ciphertext, even in the worst case scenario in which A_2 cannot decrypt the ciphertext, nor it shares state with A_1, and independently of the security guarantees of the encoding scheme.

The attack is very simple. Having oracle access to the encoding algorithm means that on input m, the oracle returns its encryption under a key fixed at the beginning of the game (and unknown to A_1). The adversary A_1 can query the encryption oracle to obtain $q = \mathsf{poly}(\lambda)$ *distinct* ciphertexts $\{c_i\}_{i=1,\ldots,q}$ (because it runs in polynomial-time, and the domain of the encryption algorithm is large enough for the ciphertexts to be distinct). As they are all distinct, there exists w.h.p. a ciphertext c_i whose (w.l.o.g.) first $|\bar{m}|$ bits are equal to $\bar{m}$. □

Acknowledgments. Cecilia Boschini is supported by the Università della Svizzera Italiana under the SNSF project number 182452, and by the Postdoc.Mobility grant No. P500PT_203075. Claudio Orlandi is supported by: the Concordium Blockhain Research Center, Aarhus University, Denmark; the Carlsberg Foundation under the Semper Ardens Research Project CF18-112 (BCM); the European Research Council (ERC) under the European Unions's Horizon 2020 research and innovation programme under grant agreement No 803096 (SPEC).

References

1. Alwen, J., Shelat, A., Visconti, I.: Collusion-free protocols in the mediated model. In: Wagner, D. (ed.) CRYPTO 2008. LNCS, vol. 5157, pp. 497–514. Springer, Heidelberg (2008). https://doi.org/10.1007/978-3-540-85174-5_28
2. Barak, B., et al.: On the (im)possibility of obfuscating programs. In: Kilian, J. (ed.) CRYPTO 2001. LNCS, vol. 2139, pp. 1–18. Springer, Heidelberg (2001). https://doi.org/10.1007/3-540-44647-8_1
3. Bellare, M., Boldyreva, A., Desai, A., Pointcheval, D.: Key-privacy in public-key encryption. In: Boyd, C. (ed.) ASIACRYPT 2001. LNCS, vol. 2248, pp. 566–582. Springer, Heidelberg (2001). https://doi.org/10.1007/3-540-45682-1_33
4. Damgård, I., Haagh, H., Orlandi, C.: Access control encryption: enforcing information flow with cryptography. In: Hirt, M., Smith, A. (eds.) TCC 2016. LNCS, vol. 9986, pp. 547–576. Springer, Heidelberg (2016). https://doi.org/10.1007/978-3-662-53644-5_21
5. Fuchsbauer, G., Gay, R., Kowalczyk, L., Orlandi, C.: Access control encryption for equality, comparison, and more. In: Fehr, S. (ed.) PKC 2017. LNCS, vol. 10175, pp. 88–118. Springer, Heidelberg (2017). https://doi.org/10.1007/978-3-662-54388-7_4
6. Kim, S., Wu, D.J.: Access control encryption for general policies from standard assumptions. In: Takagi, T., Peyrin, T. (eds.) ASIACRYPT 2017. LNCS, vol. 10624, pp. 471–501. Springer, Cham (2017). https://doi.org/10.1007/978-3-319-70694-8_17
7. Lu, Y., Ciampi, M., Zikas, V.: Collusion-preserving computation without a mediator. To appear at CSF 2022
8. Mironov, I., Stephens-Davidowitz, N.: Cryptographic reverse firewalls. In: Oswald, E., Fischlin, M. (eds.) EUROCRYPT 2015. LNCS, vol. 9057, pp. 657–686. Springer, Heidelberg (2015). https://doi.org/10.1007/978-3-662-46803-6_22
9. Sahai, A., Waters, B.: How to use indistinguishability obfuscation: deniable encryption, and more. In: STOC (2014)
10. Simmons, G.J.: The prisoners' problem and the subliminal channel. In: Chaum, D. (eds.) Advances in Cryptology. Springer, Boston, MA (1984). https://doi.org/10.1007/978-1-4684-4730-9_5

Watermarkable Public Key Encryption with Efficient Extraction Under Standard Assumptions

Foteini Baldimtsi[1](✉), Aggelos Kiayias[2], and Katerina Samari[3]

[1] George Mason University, Fairfax, VA 22030, USA
foteini@gmu.edu
[2] University of Edinburgh, IOG, Edinburgh EH8 9YL, UK
aggelos.kiayias@ed.ac.uk
[3] Hypertech Energy Labs, Athens, Greece

Abstract. The current state of the art in watermarked public-key encryption schemes under standard cryptographic assumptions suggests that extracting the embedded message requires either linear time in the number of marked keys or the a-priori knowledge of the marked key employed in the decoder. We present the first scheme that obviates these restrictions in the secret-key marking model, i.e., the setting where extraction is performed using a private extraction key. Our construction offers constant time extraction complexity with constant size keys and ciphertexts and is secure under standard assumptions, namely the Decisional Composite Residuosity Assumption [Eurocrypt'99] and the Decisional Diffie Hellman in prime order subgroups of square higher order residues.

Keywords: Watermarking · Public-key encryption

1 Introduction

Watermarking is a mechanism used to secure copyrighted material and counter the unauthorized distribution of digital content. In a high level, a watermarking scheme embeds a "mark" into a digital object and ensures that (a) the watermarked object is functionally equivalent to the original object (*functionality preserving*), and (b) it is difficult for an adversary to remove the mark without damaging the object (*unremovability*).

Recently, there has been an extensive line of research focusing in the special case of software watermarking with software being modeled as a Boolean circuit C. A software watermarking schemes consists of two main algorithms: the Mark algorithm that takes as input a circuit C and optionally a mark τ (for the case of message embedding watermarking) and outputs $\widetilde{C}$, and an Extract algorithm that takes as input a circuit C and outputs marked or not alongside with the mark τ if relevant.

C. Galdi and S. Jarecki (Eds.): SCN 2022, LNCS 13409, pp. 244–267, 2022.
https://doi.org/10.1007/978-3-031-14791-3_11

The first rigorous study and formal definitions of software watermarking dates back to 2001 when Barak et al. [4,5] explored the relation between software watermarking and indistinguishability obfuscation (iO) and provided an impossibility result. In particular, they showed that if a marked circuit $\widetilde{C}$ has *exactly* the same functionality as the original, unmarked circuit C, then under the assumption that iO exists, watermarking is impossible. To overcome this impossibility result, a first line of work proposed schemes that are secure in restricted models where the allowed strategies for the unremovability adversary were limited [25,32]. Later, [14,15] considered a more relaxed, in the statistical sense, variation of the functionality preserving property and propose a watermarking scheme for any family of *puncturable* pseudorandom functions (PRFs). Following the work of Cohen et al. [15], a long line of work has appeared in the literature focusing on watermarking PRFs under different models and assumptions [8,22,23,28,31]. Beyond watermarking schemes for PRFs, a number of works have focused on watermarking primitives such as encryption and signatures [3,15,17,24,30]. This entails the topic of the present work.

Watermarking Public Key Primitives. Cohen et al. [14,15], were the first to consider the notion of watermarking for the case of public-key cryptographic primitives. In particular, they define the notions of "Watermarkable Public-key Encryption" and "Watermarkable Signatures" making the important observation that the marking and key generation algorithms can be fused into one. Such primitives —watermarkable public-key encryption in particular— can be very useful to the enterprise setting, where multiple users belonging to the same organization use personal enterprise keys to access various services, such as a VPN. In such a setting, an organization may want to embed marks on the cryptographic algorithms used by employees and ensure that such marks can be extracted given any functioning decoder of one of the users. Cohen et al. [14,15], proceeded to describe how watermarkable schemes can be constructed by taking advantage of the work of Sahai and Waters [29], where public key encryption schemes and digital signature schemes are constructed based on iO. In the aforementioned constructions, a decryption or a signing algorithm is essentially an evaluation of a puncturable PRF. The idea of relying to the work of Sahai and Waters [29] for constructing watermarkable primitives has subsequently been utilized in [30]. Yang et al. [30] introduce the notion of *collusion-resistant watermarking*, meaning that an adversary is capable of receiving multiple watermarked copies of the same initial circuit embedded with different messages. The authors provide a watermarking scheme for PRFs and based on that and the constructions in [29] propose constructions for primitives like public key encryption, digital signatures, symmetric-key encryption and message-authentication codes.

The crucial question of whether watermarkable public key primitives can be constructed from *standard assumptions* was subsequently addressed by the works [3,17] and [24] where different watermarking models are considered. Baldimtsi et al. [3] mainly focus on watermarking existing public key encryption schemes under minimal hardness assumptions and they achieve this for a more relaxed watermarking framework where a small public shared state is maintained between the marking and extraction algorithms. In their definitions, they follow a general approach in defining watermarking for public key primitives by distinguishing between the notions of watermarking of a given scheme (watermarking the implementation) versus constructing watermarkable instances of a public key primitive in the sense of [14,15].

Goyal et al. [17], revisit the notion of watermarkable public key primitives by considering stronger properties such as *public marking*, meaning that one can mark circuits as a public procedure, and *collusion-resistance*. They provide a construction for watermarkable signatures, as well as watermarkable constructions for more generalized notions for encryption, such as Attribute-based encryption (ABE) and Predicate Encryption (PE), by relying on standard assumptions. Regarding their watermarkable constructions for encryption primitives, even for the case of public key encryption, although they rely on the LWE assumption, they require heavy tools like Mixed Functional Encryption [18] and Hierarhical Functional Encryption [12].

Nishimaki [24] showed how to watermark existing public key cryptographic primitives under the condition that they have a canonical all-but-one (ABO) reduction, which is a standard technique usually employed for proving selective security. Nishimaki presents a general framework which shows how to transform a public key scheme with the above feature to a watermarked public key primitive by utilizing the simulation algorithms that appear in the proofs as the watermarked versions of the algorithms. Based on this novel idea, they provide watermarking constructions for IBE, IPE, ABE which are secure under the same assumptions as the underlying primitives. We note that a selective secure variant for watermarking definitions is employed in [24].

One of the key issues in terms of the efficiency of watermarkable primitives is the complexity of the extraction algorithm, i.e., the steps required to extract (or detect) the embedded mark from a circuit. Ideally, the process of extraction should be independent (or at least polylogarithmic) in the number of marked programs. This is particularly crucial when in the underlying application extraction is time sensitive. For instance, for the application of tracing unauthorized distribution of digital content there is often the need to immediately identify (and potentially revoke) malicious users. Thus, if one assumes that the mark is some identifiable user information, it is important to be able to extract efficiently.

Unfortunately, all previous approaches that provided constructions under standard assumptions require a linear running time for this step. The linear overhead either comes directly, e.g., in [3] where the extraction algorithm has to re-generate one-by-one all the marked public keys in order to decide whether a circuit is marked or not, or indirectly by requiring the marked public-key as separate input to the extraction algorithm (an approach followed by [17, 24]). In the latter case, this is due to the fact that the extraction algorithm needs to traverse *all* marked public keys in order to determine whose associated decryption circuit is being detected (we discuss this in more details in Sect. 1.3). Relying on non-standard assumptions, such as iO, is the only known approach so far to allow for efficient extraction [15] without knowledge of the marked public-key.

Motivated by the above, in this work, we study the following question:

Can we build efficient watermarkable public key encryption schemes under standard assumptions where the extraction algorithm is sublinear or even constant in the number of marked programs, without relying on the knowledge of the key in the given decoder?

We answer this question in the affirmative.

1.1 Our Contribution

We present a concrete watermarkable PKE scheme with the following features: (1) The running time of the extraction algorithm is **independent** of the number of generated marked circuits (decryption circuits in the case of PKE) and does not require knowledge of the marked key, (2) the ciphertexts, the public and secret keys have all **constant size** in all salient parameters exhibiting only a linear dependency in the security parameter.

Our construction is an El-Gamal like scheme that shares features with Paillier encryption and whose security relies on the Decisional Composite Residuosity DCR assumption [27] as well the $\mathsf{DDH}_{\mathsf{SQNR}}$ assumption [20]. The latter assumption is simply the Decisional Diffie Hellman assumption over prime order subgroups of the group of n-th residues modulo n^2, where n is an RSA modulus as in Paillier encryption. We note that residuosity and discrete-logarithm related assumptions over modular arithmetic groups have been studied extensively and are considered standard assumptions compared to more recent cryptographic assumptions such as those needed to obtain iO. We provide a technical overview of our construction in Sect. 1.2.

Our scheme is proven secure in the secret-marking model, under the definitional framework of [3,15] where there exists a single marking algorithm responsible for both key-generation of the public-key encryption scheme and marking at the same time (i.e., a mark is embedded into a circuit when generating public and secret encryption keys). We provide a more detailed discussion of our model and how it compares to related work in Sect. 1.3.

1.2 Technical Overview of Our Construction

Our main goal is to construct a watermarkable PKE scheme with an extraction algorithm that is independent of the number of previously marked decryption circuits. In a typical watermarked PKE scheme, the marked object is a decryption circuit C. As noted above, in all previous works in order to detect whether C is marked or not, the extraction algorithm had to either re-generate and test all marked public keys [3] or require the marked public-key as separate input to the extraction algorithm [17,24]).

To avoid this linear dependency to the number of public keys, we need to take a very different extraction approach. Our starting point is a PKE with the following property: it should be possible to generate a probability distribution in the ciphertext space in a manner independent of the public-key. At the same time, when such ciphertexts are sampled and given as input to a decryption circuit C, it should be possible to extract information about the decryption key hidden inside the decoder. Assume for example that by giving such a ciphertext as input to C, one can reconstruct a public key indicating that the corresponding secret key was used to decrypt the ciphertext. However, deciding whether C is marked or not would still require to check whether the reconstructed public key is one of the keys that had been previously marked by the marking service. Thus, we additionally require the PKE to allow the embedding of some authenticated information as part of the secret and public keys, which can only be recovered by using the private extraction key.

Consider the El-Gamal PKE scheme with public parameters $(\mathbb{G}, q, g)$ where $\mathbb{G}$ is a cyclic group of prime order q and g is a generator of that group. Assume a public-secret key pair (g^x, x) where $x \xleftarrow{\$} \mathbb{Z}_q$. An encrypted plaintext m is of the form $(g^r, g^{rx} \cdot m)$, where $r \xleftarrow{\$} \mathbb{Z}_q$, is indistinguishable from a random pair $(g^r, g^{r'})$, where $r, r' \xleftarrow{\$} \mathbb{Z}_q$. If $(g^r, g^{r'})$ is fed to a decryption algorithm under the secret key $sk = x$ the result would be $\mathsf{Dec}(x, ((g^r, g^{r'})) = g^{r'-rx}$. Given we have chosen r, r', it is possible to apply a simple calculation over $g^{r'-rx}$ to extract the public key g^x. Therefore, assuming a circuit C as black-box, if one runs it on input the pair $(g^r, g^{r'})$ and then performs the computation described above, one can deduce the public key (if the circuit indeed uses a single public key). With respect to our objective however this approach is still too weak: since we bound the extraction algorithm to be independent of the number of marked circuits, having recovered the public-key cannot help us detect whether the key was indeed marked or not. Here comes our second technical observation: we can take advantage of the partial discrete logarithm trapdoor of Paillier's encryption scheme to turn the public-key of a marked scheme to something that the marking algorithm can "decrypt" and identify some internal property of it to assist the extraction algorithm.

To accomplish this plan, the first cryptographic design challenge is to create this hybrid encryption scheme, that behaves like ElGamal from the perspective of the user, while its public-key is akin to ciphertext for a Paillier-like encryption whose secret-key is used during the extraction process. This means that the ElGamal variant has to operate within $\mathbb{Z}_{n^2}^*$ and specifically within a suitable order subgroup $\langle g_1 \rangle$ where DDH is expected to hold, while the public-key will belong to a suitable coset $\langle g_1 \rangle \cdot (1+n)^v$ with v containing the salient features the extraction algorithm can recover via Paillier decryption. The second design challenge, is that the extraction algorithm needs to check the integrity of the recovered public-key; this is done by incorporating into v a message authentication code (actually a PRF) that tags the ElGamal component of the public-key. The third design challenge is to be able to embed robustly an arbitrary mark within the public-key without disturbing the functional properties of the public-key itself. To achieve that we utilize an authenticated symmetric encryption that extends the value v with a ciphertext that contains the mark.

The final challenge is to ensure that decryption from the user side works similarly to ElGamal and all the attributes that were inserted by the above requirements into the public-key do not disturb the decryption operation of the PKE.

1.3 Relations to Prior Work

In the first part of the introduction we covered related work in watermarkable cryptographic primitives as well as watermarking in general. In this section we provide a more extensive discussion on how our work differs from related work in terms of definitional model, security properties and efficiency. We focus our attention on related work for watermarkable public key primitives. Finally, we also discuss the relation to traitor tracing.

Definitional Model. In this work, we adopt a model that is based on the definitional framework proposed by Cohen et al. [15]. Namely, we define a watermarkable PKE scheme where the Mark algorithm is responsible for both generating a key pair instance (pk, sk) for the encryption scheme, as well as marking it at the same time.

Other works [17,24,30] impose a stronger requirement where the key generation and marking algorithms are decoupled: (unmarked) keys can be independently generated and, subsequently, marked. For completeness, we point out some differences between the models considered in the aforementioned works. First of all, in contrast to all other works, the model of Goyal et al. [17] considers both public marking and public extraction. These properties are satisfied by the watermarkable predicate encryption scheme presented in the same paper. The model of [24] considers secret marking and secret extraction while [30] considers public extraction and secret marking.

We note that the model of coupling key generation and marking is natural in certain applications (i.e. watermarking a VPN client). Most importantly though, coupling key generation and marking *does not trivialize the problem*: If one considered a trivial watermarking scheme where the marking authority simply associates every secret key with the identity of the owner, it will have to store one associated key with each identity. This is completely inefficient, since it results in a stateful watermarkable encryption scheme with both linear state and linear extraction time.

Security Properties. We require watermarkable PKE schemes to preserve IND-CPA security and also support unremovability and unforgeability. In our unremovability definition we consider adversaries that have access to Challenge, Corrupt and Extract oracles. This is a stronger definition than the one considered in [15]. An important point when defining unremovability is in respect to when we consider that the adversary successfully removed the mark. Cohen et al. required the adversarial circuit to agree with a decryption circuit on a fraction of inputs. However, as pointed in [17], this can lead to trivial attacks. We follow the definitional approach of [17] who in order to address this issue, they require that an adversary should output a "useful" circuit which is at the same time unmarked (or marked with a different than the original message). We capture the notion of "useful" by defining closeness and farness relations to capture the adversary's ability to create circuits that are close or far to marked ones.

Since we focus on the secret-marking setting we also consider unforgeability which guarantees that an adversary cannot create a marked circuit with sufficiently different functionality from that of given marked circuits without access to a marking key. Similar to unremovability, we define unforgeability for adversaries that have access to Challenge, Corrupt and Extract oracles. The constructions of [14] do not support unforgeability. The more recent work of [24] describes a possible direction to achieve unforgeability. Unforgeability does not make sense as a property in the public marking setting of [17].

In addition, [17,30] consider the notion of collusion-resistance, or else "Collusion-resistance w.r.t. watermarking" (as coined in [24]). A watermarking scheme is collusion-resistant w.r.t. watermarking if it is unremovable even if adversaries are given many watermarked keys for the same original key. We note that the collusion-resistance property cannot be inherently considered in our model since the user does not choose the initial key and request marked versions embedded with different messages. Also, as noted in [24], this property is not crucial for classic applications of watermarking such as ownership identification.

Efficiency. In this paragraph, we present several efficiency parameters of previous watermarkable public key encryption schemes, in particular [24] and [17], and provide a comparison with the construction presented in this work. Starting with [17], a watermarkable predicate encryption scheme can be instantiated from hierarchical functional encryption scheme, which, in turn, according to [1] can be constructed from any PKE scheme. In such a construction, the size of ciphertexts is linear in the number of colluding users. In [24], the efficiency parameters of the initial public key encryption scheme are almost preserved. Specifically, the ciphertext size does not change, while the public and secret keys have also a linear dependence on the size of the embedded message and the security parameter. Regarding the complexity of the extraction algorithm, in both [17,24] we note that the master public key (which is the public key of a user in the case of Watermarkable PKE) is part of the input of the extraction algorithm. This is particularly limiting in applications where one might detect the use of marked circuit in the wild (i.e. a stolen decryption circuit). Excluding the public key from the input of the Extract algorithm, as in our model, implies that Extract would have to search over all the public keys generated so far. The construction presented in this work (cf. Sect. 4) achieves constant size ciphertexts, constant size public-secret keys and the extraction time is independent of the number of generated marked keys.

Relation to Traitor-Tracing. Watermarkable PKE is also related to the notion of traitor tracing, which was put forth by Chor et al. [13] and studied extensively (see e.g. [9–11,16,21] and references therein). Briefly speaking, in traitor tracing, an authority delivers keys to a set of users and encrypts content which is intended to be decrypted by all users, or a subset of them in cases where an authority is capable of revoking decryption keys (i.e. trace and revoke schemes). In the occasion where a number of users collude by constructing an even partially working implementation of the decryption function, the authority can identify at least one of the colluding users.

Previous works [17,24,30], point to the relation between traitor tracing and watermarkable encryption. In particular, Goyal et al. [17] present a generic construction which shows how to obtain a watermarkable PKE scheme (in the sense of Cohen et al. definition [15]) from a traitor tracing scheme with embedded identities and a regular public-key encryption. We note that a traitor tracing scheme with embedded identities (cf. [19,26]) is an extension of the standard traitor tracing where not only the index of a colluding user is traced, but a whole string is extracted, i.e. the identity. Based on this, [17] argue that "in the particular case where we allow a single algorithm that both generates the public/secret keys together with the watermark" the notion of watermarkable PKE would be entirely subsumed by traitor tracing. While valid, this observation sidesteps the serious disadvantage that the generic construction blows up the complexity of the watermarkable PKE to be at least as much as underlying traitor tracing. As a result, the state of the art in traitor tracing cannot yield efficient watermarkable PKE under standard assumptions, to the best of our knowledge (even the most efficient construction in terms of keys and ciphertexts from [19], which is provable under LWE, will require an extraction algorithm linear in the number of users). Moreover, watermarking seems a simpler primitive than traitor tracing since in the latter, users should share the decryption functionality and apply it to the same ciphertext, while in watermarking users' functionalities are entirely decoupled. In our view, this is the key issue in the design of watermarking PKE schemes and we demonstrate that we can obtain constructions where the size of ciphertexts, the size of keys, as well as the extraction complexity is independent of the number of users.

2 Preliminaries

Notation. By λ we denote the security parameter and by $\mathsf{negl}(\lambda)$ we denote a negligible function in λ. By $x||y$, we denote the concatenation of the bitstrings x, y. By $x \xleftarrow{\$} S$ we denote that x is sampled uniformly at random from S. By $\mathsf{poly}(\lambda)$ we denote a polynomial in λ. In addition, we write $\mathcal{D}_1 \overset{c}{\approx} \mathcal{D}_2$ to denote that the distributions $\mathcal{D}_1$, $\mathcal{D}_2$ are computationally indistinguishable.

Assumptions. We first introduce the assumptions which will be necessary for proving the properties of our watermarkable PKE scheme.

Definition 1 (DCR assumption [27]**).** *No PPT adversary can distinguish between: (i) tuples of the form $(n, u^n \mod n^2)$, where n is a composite RSA modulus and $u \xleftarrow{\$} \mathbb{Z}^*_{n^2}$ and (ii) tuples on the form (n, v), where $v \xleftarrow{\$} \mathbb{Z}^*_{n^2}$.*

Definition 2 (DDH for square n-th residues [20]). *Let n be a composite RSA modulus, i.e. $n = pq$, where $p = 2p'+1$, $q = 2q'+1$ and p', q' are also primes. By $\mathcal{X}_{n^2}$ we denote the subgroup of $\mathbb{Z}_{n^2}$ that contains all square n-th residues. The Decisional Diffie Hellman assumption for square n-th residues ($\mathsf{DDH}_{\mathsf{SQNR}}$) is defined as follows: The distribution $\langle n, g_1, y, g_1^r, y^r \rangle$, where g_1 generates $\mathcal{X}_{n^2}$, $y \xleftarrow{\$} \mathcal{X}_{n^2}$ and $r \xleftarrow{\$} [p'q']$, is computationally indistinguishable from the distribution $\langle n, g_1, y, g_1^r, y^{r'} \rangle$, where g_1, y, r defined as above and $r' \xleftarrow{\$} [p'q']$.*

In our construction we use a seemingly stronger variant of the above assumption where the factorization of n is also provided as part of the tuples. While this appears to provide more power to the adversary, it is straightforward to see that it reduces, via the Chinese remainder theorem, to the two DDH assumptions for the underlying subgroups $\langle g_1^{q'} \rangle$ and $\langle g_1^{p'} \rangle$ of prime order p', q' respectively.[1] For simplicity and due to its relation to the DDH assumptions in the underlying groups, we will use the same notation $\mathsf{DDH}_{\mathsf{SQNR}}$ to denote this variant.

Cryptographic Primitives. For completeness we recall the definitions of some cryptographic primitives to be used below.

Definition 3 (Pseudorandom function). *Let $F : \mathcal{K} \times \mathcal{X} \to \mathcal{Y}$ be a keyed function with key space $\mathcal{K}$, input space $\mathcal{X}$ and output space $\mathcal{Y}$. We say that F is a pseudorandom function (PRF) if for any PPT distinguisher D it holds that*

$$\left| \mathsf{Pr}_{k \xleftarrow{\$} \mathcal{K}}[D^{F(k,\cdot)}(1^n) = 1] - \mathsf{Pr}_{f \xleftarrow{\$} \mathcal{F}}[D^{f(\cdot)}(1^n) = 1] \right| \leq \mathsf{negl}(\lambda),$$

where $\mathcal{F}$ is the set of all functions with input space $\mathcal{X}$ and output space $\mathcal{Y}$ and $\mathcal{X} = \{0,1\}^n$.

We consider an authenticated symmetric encryption scheme that satisfies the notion of *integrity of ciphertexts* as defined in [7], i.e. an adversary that only has access to a signing oracle, cannot produce any fresh valid ciphertext.

Definition 4. *A symmetric encryption scheme* (S.Gen, S.Enc, S.Dec) *satisfies integrity of ciphertexts if for any PPT adversary $\mathcal{A}$ it holds that*

$$\mathsf{Pr}[\mathcal{G}_{\mathcal{A}}^{\mathsf{int-ctxt}}(1^\lambda) = 1] = \mathsf{negl}(\lambda).$$

---

[1] To see this, consider A DDH challenge for the two underlying groups $\langle g_1^{q'}, y_\mathsf{l}, G_\mathsf{l}, Y_\mathsf{l} \rangle$ $\langle g_1^{p'}, y_\mathsf{r}, G_\mathsf{r}, Y_\mathsf{r} \rangle$, we can combine them to $\langle g_1, y_\mathsf{l} \cdot y_\mathsf{r}, G_\mathsf{l} \cdot G_\mathsf{r}, Y_\mathsf{l}^{q'} \cdot Y_\mathsf{r}^{p'} \rangle$. Observe that if the challenge pair is DDH distributed then $G_\mathsf{l} \cdot G_\mathsf{r} = g_1^{q' r_\mathsf{l} + p' r_\mathsf{r}}$ and $Y_\mathsf{l}^{q'} \cdot Y_\mathsf{r}^{p'} = y_\mathsf{l}^{q' r_\mathsf{l}} y_\mathsf{r}^{p' r_\mathsf{r}} = g_1^{(q')^2 t_\mathsf{l} r_\mathsf{l} + (p')^2 t_\mathsf{r} r_\mathsf{r}}$. Now observe that $(q' t_\mathsf{l} + p' t_\mathsf{r})(q' r_\mathsf{l} + p' r_\mathsf{r}) = (q')^2 t_\mathsf{l} r_\mathsf{l} + (p')^2 t_\mathsf{r} r_\mathsf{r} \bmod p'q'$. Given that $y_\mathsf{l} \cdot y_\mathsf{r} = g_1^{q' t_\mathsf{l} + p' t_\mathsf{r}}$, this establishes that the combined challenge is DDH distributed. For the other case, when the challenge pair follows the random distribution, then $Y_\mathsf{l}^{q'} \cdot Y_\mathsf{r}^{p'} = y_\mathsf{l}^{q' r'_\mathsf{l}} y_\mathsf{r}^{p' r'_\mathsf{r}} = g_1^{(q')^2 t_\mathsf{l} r'_\mathsf{l} + (p')^2 t_\mathsf{r} r'_\mathsf{r}}$ that can be easily seen to be uniformly distributed over $\mathcal{X}_{n^2}$ and as a result the combined challenge is randomly distributed.

$\mathcal{G}_{\mathcal{A}}^{\mathsf{int-ctxt}}(1^\lambda)$:

1. The Challenger $\mathcal{C}$ generates a key $k_{\mathsf{e}} \leftarrow \mathsf{S.Gen}(1^\lambda)$. Then initializes the set $S \leftarrow \emptyset$, which will include the ciphertexts that will be returned as answers to $\mathcal{A}$'s queries.
2. $\mathcal{A}$ is allowed to issue a number of queries to the encryption oracle $\mathsf{S.Enc}(k_{\mathsf{e}}, \cdot)$. Upon receiving a message m from $\mathcal{A}$, $\mathcal{C}$ computes $c \leftarrow \mathsf{S.Enc}(k_{\mathsf{e}}, m)$, returns c to $\mathcal{A}$ and sets $S \leftarrow S \cup \{c\}$.
3. $\mathcal{A}$ wins, if there is c' issued as a query to the decryption oracle $\mathsf{S.Dec}(k_{\mathsf{e}}, \cdot)$ s.t. $c' \notin S$ and $m' \neq \perp$ where $m' \leftarrow \mathsf{S.Dec}(k_{\mathsf{e}}, c')$. Then the game returns 1.

Fig. 1. The integrity of ciphertexts game.

Next, we state the definition of real-or-random CPA security for symmetric encryption [6]. In a high level, an adversary should not be able to distinguish a ciphertext from a random string from the ciphertext space (Fig. 1).

Definition 5. *A symmetric encryption scheme* $(\mathsf{S.Gen}, \mathsf{S.Enc}, \mathsf{S.Dec})$ *with plaintext space* $\{0,1\}^\nu$ *and ciphertext space* $\{0,1\}^\mu$ *satisfies real-or-random security against chosen plaintext attacks if for any PPT adversary* $\mathcal{A}$ *(Fig. 2),*

$$\Pr[\mathcal{G}_{\mathcal{A}}^{\mathsf{ror-cpa}}(1^\lambda) = 1] = \mathsf{negl}(\lambda).$$

$\mathcal{G}_{\mathcal{A}}^{\mathsf{ror-cpa}}(1^\lambda)$:

1. The Challenger $\mathcal{C}$ generates a key $k_{\mathsf{e}} \leftarrow \mathsf{S.Gen}(1^\lambda)$.
2. $\mathcal{A}$ is allowed to issue queries to the encryption oracle, i.e. $\mathcal{A}$ issues a query m to $\mathcal{C}$, and $\mathcal{C}$ responds to $\mathcal{A}$ with c s.t. $c \leftarrow \mathsf{S.Enc}(k_{\mathsf{e}}, m)$.
3. Challenge phase: $\mathcal{A}$ sends a message m to the challenger. Then $\mathcal{C}$ chooses $b \xleftarrow{\$} \{0,1\}$. If $b = 0$ it computes $c^* \leftarrow \mathsf{S.Enc}(k_{\mathsf{e}}, m)$, otherwise it chooses $c^* \xleftarrow{\$} \{0,1\}^\mu$. $\mathcal{C}$ returns c^* to $\mathcal{A}$.
4. $\mathcal{A}$ outputs b^*. If $b = b^*$ then $\mathcal{A}$ wins and the game returns 1.

Fig. 2. Real or Random CPA Security.

3 Watermarkable Public Key Encryption

We start by introducing the definition for a watermarkable public-key encryption scheme. Our definition follows the framework of [3,15] by considering a single algorithm, PKE.Mark responsible for both key-generation of the public-key encryption scheme and marking at the same time (i.e., a mark is embedded into a circuit when generating public and secret encryption keys).

Definition 6 (Watermarkable PKE). *A watermarkable public key encryption scheme with message space $\mathcal{M}$, tag space $\mathcal{T}$ and ciphertext space $\mathcal{CT}$ is a tuple of algorithms* (WM.Gen, PKE.Mark, Enc, Dec, Extract) *with the following syntax:*

- $\mathsf{WM.Gen}(1^\lambda) \rightarrow (params, mk, xk)$: *On input the security parameter λ, it outputs the public parameters params, a marking key mk, and an extraction key xk. The marking key is private and it is kept by an authority, while the extraction key may be either public or private depending on whether the scheme allows public or private extraction.*
- $\mathsf{PKE.Mark}(params, mk, \tau) \rightarrow (pk, sk)$: *On input the marking key mk, params, and a tag $\tau \in \mathcal{T}$, it outputs a public-secret key pair (pk, sk).*
- $\mathsf{Enc}(pk, m) \rightarrow c$: *On input a public key pk and a plaintext $m \in \mathcal{M}$, it outputs a ciphertext c.*
- $\mathsf{Dec}(sk, c) \rightarrow m$: *On input a secret key sk and ciphertext c, it outputs a plaintext m.*
- $\mathsf{Extract}(params, xk, C) \rightarrow \tau/\bot$: *On input xk, params and a circuit C which maps $\mathcal{CT}$ to $\mathcal{M}$, it outputs a tag $\tau' \in \mathcal{T}$ or returns a special symbol $\bot$, indicating that the circuit is unmarked.*

Remark 1. We say that a watermarkable PKE scheme supports *public marking* if the marking key is equal to the public watermarking parameters are $params = mk$. Otherwise we say that it only supports *private marking*. Similarly, we say that a scheme supports *public extraction* if $params = xk$ and *private extraction* otherwise. In this work we focus in the private setting.

We now define correctness. In the definitions below, Dec_{sk} denotes a decryption circuit with secret key sk embedded.

Definition 7 (Extraction correctness). *We say that a watermarkable PKE scheme satisfies extraction correctness if for any tag $\tau \in \mathcal{T}$, it holds that:*

$$\Pr\left[\mathsf{Extract}(xk, \mathsf{Dec}_{sk}) \neq \tau \,\middle|\, \begin{array}{l}(params, mk, xk) \leftarrow \mathsf{WM.Gen}(1^\lambda)\\(pk, sk) \leftarrow \mathsf{PKE.Mark}(params, mk, \tau)\end{array}\right] = \mathsf{negl}(\lambda),$$

A watermarkable PKE scheme should be functionality-preserving, i.e. maintain encryption correctness and IND-CPA security. We first define encryption correctness:

Definition 8 (Encryption Correctness). *We say that a watermarkable PKE scheme satisfies encryption correctness if for any tag $\tau \in \mathcal{T}$ and any plaintext $m \in \mathcal{M}$, it holds that:*

$$\Pr\left[\mathsf{Dec}(sk, c) \neq m \,\middle|\, \begin{array}{c} (params, mk, xk) \leftarrow \mathsf{WM.Gen}(1^\lambda); \\ (pk, sk) \leftarrow \mathsf{PKE.Mark}(params, mk, \tau); \\ c \leftarrow \mathsf{Enc}(pk, m) \end{array}\right] = \mathsf{negl}(\lambda)$$

We now define IND-CPA security for watermarked PKE. We require that IND-CPA should hold even if the adversary gets to see the marking and extraction keys mk, xk.

Definition 9 (IND-CPA security). *We say that a watermarkable PKE scheme satisfies IND-CPA security if for any tag $\tau \in \mathcal{T}$ and for any PPT adversary $\mathcal{A}$,*

$$\Pr\left[\mathcal{A}(c_b) = b \,\middle|\, \begin{array}{c} (params, mk, xk) \leftarrow \mathsf{WM.Gen}(1^\lambda); \\ (pk, sk) \leftarrow \mathsf{PKE.Mark}(params, mk, \tau); \\ (m_0, m_1) \leftarrow \mathcal{A}(1^\lambda, params, mk, xk, pk); \\ b \xleftarrow{\$} \{0,1\}; c_b \leftarrow \mathsf{Enc}(pk, m_b); \end{array}\right] = \frac{1}{2} + \mathsf{negl}(\lambda)$$

Before defining unremovability and unforgeability, we first define a number of oracles, namely the Challenge, Corrupt and Extract oracles, which are crucial part of the definitions of the security games of unremovability and unforgeability.

The Challenge, Corrupt and Extract Oracles. The Challenge oracle, on input a tag τ calls the PKE.Mark algorithm and returns only the (marked) public key as output, along with an index i which shows how many times PKE.Mark has been invoked so far. We note that in the definitions of unremovability and unforgeability security games the index i will be initialized to 0. The Corrupt oracle, receives an index i as input and outputs the key pair (pk_i, sk_i) generated in the i-th Challenge oracle query by the PKE.Mark algorithm. Finally, the Extract oracle, receives as input a circuit, simply runs Extract algorithm on that input and returns the corresponding output of the algorithm. The formal description of the oracles is given below in Fig. 3.

Furthemore, we define the notions of *closeness* and *farness* (cf. Definitions 10, 11) which are crucial for correctly capturing the unremovability and unforgeability notions respectively since those notions capture the notion of "useful" circuits as discussed in Sect. 1.3. Specifically, in the simpler case of watermarking where circuits are either marked or unmarked, when defining unremovability we have to make sure that an adversary cannot create a circuit which is "close" to a marked circuit but it is unmarked, while, unforgeability requires that it should be difficult for an adversary to come up with a circuit which is "far" from a marked circuit but it remains marked.

Definition 10. *We say that a circuit C is ρ-close to a circuit Dec_{sk}, and we denote $C \sim_\rho \mathsf{Dec}_{sk}$, if $\Pr_{m \xleftarrow{\$} \mathcal{M}}[C(\mathsf{Enc}_{pk}(m)) = m] \geq \rho$.*

ChallengeOracle($\tau, \cdot$):
1. $i \leftarrow i+1$;
2. $(pk_i, sk_i) \leftarrow \mathsf{PKE.Mark}(params, mk, \tau)$;
3. $\mathsf{Marked} \leftarrow \mathsf{Marked} \cup \{(i, pk_i, sk_i, \tau_i)\}$;
5. Return (i, pk_i);

CorruptOracle(i):
1. Retrieve (i, pk_i, sk_i, τ_i) from Marked;
2. $\mathsf{Corrupted} \leftarrow \mathsf{Corrupted} \cup \{(i, pk_i, sk_i, \tau_i)\}$;
3. Return (i, pk_i, sk_i, τ_i);

ExtractOracle(C):
1. $\tau/\bot \leftarrow \mathsf{Extract}(xk, params, C)$;
2. Return τ or $\bot$;

Fig. 3. The Challenge, Corrupt and Extract oracles.

Definition 11. *We say that a circuit C is γ-far from a circuit Dec_{sk}, and we denote $C \not\sim_\gamma \mathsf{Dec}_{sk}$, if $\Pr_{m \xleftarrow{\$} \mathcal{M}}[C(\mathsf{Enc}_{pk}(m)) \neq m] \geq \gamma$.*

We now proceed by defining ρ-unremovability. In plain words, an adversary should not be able to create a circuit which is ρ-close to a marked circuit generated by the Challenge oracle and at the same time the extraction algorithm returns a different tag or unmarked. As discussed in Sect. 1.3, our unremovability definition is stronger than that of [15] as it gives oracle access to the adversary.

Definition 12 (ρ-unremovability). *We say that a watermarking scheme satisfies ρ-unremovability if for any PPT adversary $\mathcal{A}$ participating in the game defined in Fig. 4 it holds that:*

$$\Pr[\mathcal{G}^{\mathsf{unrmv}}_{\rho,\mathcal{A}}(1^\lambda) = 1] = \mathsf{negl}(\lambda).$$

$\mathcal{G}^{\mathsf{unrmv}}_{\rho,\mathcal{A}}(1^\lambda)$:

1. The Challenger $\mathcal{C}$ runs $\mathsf{WM.Gen}(1^\lambda)$ and outputs $(params, mk, xk)$. It gives $params$ to the adversary $\mathcal{A}$. Then, $\mathcal{C}$ sets $\mathsf{Marked} \leftarrow \{\}$, $\mathsf{Corrupted} \leftarrow \{\}$ and $i \leftarrow 0$.
2. $\mathcal{A}$ issues queries to the ChallengeOracle, CorruptOracle, ExtractOracle.
3. $\mathcal{A}$ outputs a circuit C^*.
4. $\mathcal{A}$ wins the game iff
   (a) there exists $(j, pk_i, sk_i, \tau_j) \in \mathsf{Marked}$ such that $C^* \sim_\rho \mathsf{Dec}_{sk_j}$, and
   (b) $\mathsf{Extract}(xk, params, C^*) \neq \tau_j$.

Fig. 4. The ρ-unremovability game.

Finally, we consider the notion of γ-unforgeability. At a high level, this property requires that an adversary cannot create a marked circuit that is γ-far with respect to any of the given marked circuits and at the same is marked.

Definition 13 (γ-unforgeability). *We say that a watermarking scheme satisfies γ-unforgeability if for any PPT adversary $\mathcal{A}$ participating in the game defined in Fig. 5, it holds that:*

$$\Pr[\mathcal{G}^{\mathsf{unforge}}_{\gamma,\mathcal{A}}(1^\lambda) = 1] = \mathsf{negl}(\lambda).$$

$\underline{\mathcal{G}^{\mathsf{unforge}}_{\gamma,\mathcal{A}}(1^\lambda)}$:

1. The Challenger $\mathcal{C}$ runs $\mathsf{WM.Gen}(1^\lambda)$ and outputs $(params, mk, xk)$. It gives $params$ to the adversary $\mathcal{A}$.Then, $\mathcal{C}$ sets $\mathsf{Marked} \leftarrow \{\}$, $\mathsf{Corrupted} \leftarrow \{\}$ and $i \leftarrow 0$.
2. $\mathcal{A}$ issues queries to ExtractOracle, ChallengeOracle and CorruptOracle.
3. $\mathcal{A}$ outputs a circuit C^*.
4. $\mathcal{A}$ wins the game iff
   (a) For all j s.t. $(j, pk_j, sk_j, \tau_j) \in \mathsf{Corrupted}$ it holds that $C^* \not\sim_\gamma \mathsf{Dec}_{sk_j}$, **and**
   (b) $\mathsf{Extract}(params, xk, C^*) \neq \perp$.

Fig. 5. The γ-unforgeability game.

4 Our Watermarkable PKE Scheme

As discussed in the introduction, our construction is based on a hybrid encryption scheme for which the public-key has a similar structure to a Pailler ciphertext, while the rest of the scheme (from the point of view of the user) behaves like an ElGamal encryption scheme. We exploit the structure of $\mathbb{Z}^*_{n^2}$, where $n = pq$ and p, q are primes. In our construction, p, q are *safe primes*, meaning that they are of the form $p = 2p' + 1$, $q = 2q' + 1$ where p', q' are also primes. Wen also require a pseudorandom function F, an authenticated symmetric encryption scheme $(\mathsf{S.Gen}, \mathsf{S.Enc}, \mathsf{S.Dec})$, and a collision resistant hash function H.

The tuple of $(\mathsf{WM.Gen}, \mathsf{PKE.Mark}, \mathsf{Enc}, \mathsf{Dec}, \mathsf{Extract})$ algorithms that comprise our waterkable PKE scheme is presented below.

$\underline{\mathsf{WM.Gen}:}$ On input 1^λ,

- Run $\mathsf{Param}(1^\lambda)$: Choose safe primes $p = 2p' + 1$ and $q = 2q' + 1$, where p, q are of size at least $\lfloor \lambda/2 \rfloor + 1$. Sample $g \xleftarrow{\$} \mathbb{Z}^*_{n^2}$ and compute $g_1 = g^{2n} \mod n^2$. Return $params = (n, g_1)$.
  We denote as $\mathcal{X}_{n^2} = \langle g_1 \rangle$, the subgroup that contains all square n-th residues modulo n^2. Observe that the order of $\mathcal{X}_{n^2}$ is $p'q'$. Note that all elements in

$\mathbb{Z}_{n^2}$ can be written in a unique way as $g_1^r(1+n)^v(-1)^\alpha(p_2p - q_2q)^\beta$, where $r \in [p'q']$, $v \in [n]$, $\alpha, \beta \in \{0,1\}$ and $p_1p^2 \equiv 1 \mod q^2$ and $q_2q^2 \equiv 1 \mod p^2$. With $\mathcal{Q}_{n^2}$ we denote the subgroup of quadratic residues modulo n^2 which can be seen that they contain all elements of the form $g_1^r(1+n)^v$, where $r \in [p'q']$ and $v \in \mathbb{Z}_n$. The order of $\mathcal{Q}_{n^2}$ is $np'q'$, one fourth of the order of $\mathbb{Z}^*_{n^2}$. Recall that the order of $\mathbb{Z}^*_{n^2}$ is $n\phi(n) = 4p'q'n$.

- Let $F : \mathcal{K} \times \mathcal{Y} \rightarrow \{0,1\}^{\lambda/2}$ be a PRF and a key $k_\mathsf{p} \xleftarrow{\$} \mathcal{K}$.
- Let $(\mathsf{S.Gen}, \mathsf{S.Enc}, \mathsf{S.Dec})$ be an authenticated symmetric encryption scheme with security parameter κ_1 and message space $\mathcal{T} = \{0,1\}^{\kappa_2}$ and ciphertext space $\{0,1\}^{\lambda/2}$. Run $k_\mathsf{e} \leftarrow \mathsf{S.Gen}(1^{\kappa_1})$.
- Let $H : \{0,1\}^* \rightarrow \{0,1\}^{\kappa_3}$ be a hash function.
- Set the marking key as $mk = (k_\mathsf{p}, k_\mathsf{e})$, the extraction key as $xk = (k_\mathsf{p}, k_\mathsf{e}, p', q')$ and the public parameters $params = (n, g_1)$.
- Choose $\delta \geq 1/\mathsf{poly}(\lambda)$.

We assume that the parameters $\kappa_1, \kappa_2, \kappa_3$ and λ are compatible.

<u>PKE.Mark :</u> On input $mk = (k_\mathsf{p}, k_\mathsf{e})$, and a tag $\tau \in \mathcal{T}$,

- Choose $x \xleftarrow{\$} [n/4]$.
- Compute $g_1^x \mod n^2$ and $v_1 = F(k_\mathsf{p}, (g_1^x, \tau))$.
- Compute $v_2 = \mathsf{S.Enc}(k_e, H(v_1)||\tau)$.
- Concatenate v_1 and v_2, i.e. compute $v = v_1||v_2$. Compute $h = g_1^x(1+n)^v$.
- Return $pk = h = g_1^x(1+n)^v$, $sk = (x, v)$.

<u>Enc :</u> On input $m \in \mathcal{M}$ and $pk = (n, g_1, h)$, choose $r \xleftarrow{\$} [n^2/4]$ and compute a ciphertext $\psi = \langle g_1^r \mod n^2, (1+n)^r \mod n^2, h^r \cdot m \mod n^2 \rangle$.

<u>Dec :</u> On input $\psi = \langle a, b, c \rangle$ and $sk = (x, v)$, compute $\hat{m} = (a^x b^v)^{-1} c$.

<u>Extract</u>: On input $xk = (k_\mathsf{p}, k_\mathsf{e}, p', q')$ and a (decryption) circuit C,

(D1). $\mathsf{Count} \leftarrow [\,]$
(D2). Set $\ell = \frac{\lambda}{\delta^2}$ and $\ell^* = \frac{\lambda}{2\delta^2}$.
(D3). For $i = 1$ to ℓ:

  (a) Choose $r \xleftarrow{\$} [n/4]$, $r' \xleftarrow{\$} [n/4]$, $s, s' \xleftarrow{\$} \mathbb{Z}_n$.
  Compute $\psi_i = \langle g_1^r, (1+n)^s, g_1^{r'}(1+n)^{s'} \rangle$.
  (b) Run the algorithm G_ext of Fig. 6 with inputs C and ψ_i.
  (c) If $G_\mathsf{ext}(C, \psi_i)$ returns $((y_i, \tau_i), v_{i,1})$
  - if there is record $((y_i, \tau_i), v_{i,1}, \mathsf{count}_i)$ in Count, set $\mathsf{count}_i \leftarrow \mathsf{count}_i + 1$. If no such record exists initialize $\mathsf{count}_i = 1$ and insert to the table Count a record $((y_i, \tau_i), v_{i,1}, \mathsf{count}_i)$.

(D4). If there is a record $((y_i, \tau_i), v_{i,1}, \mathsf{count}_i)$ in Count s.t. $\mathsf{count}_i \geq \ell^*$ then return τ_i, else, return $\mathsf{unmarked}$.

$\underline{G_{\mathsf{ext}}}$: On input xk, C, ψ_i.

1. Run $C(\psi_i)$. On output $\hat{m}_i$ s.t. $(\hat{m}_i \neq \perp \wedge \hat{m}_i \in \mathcal{Q}_{n^2})$ compute $\hat{c} = \hat{m}_i{}^{\phi(n)} \mod n^2$.
2. $\hat{z} = (\hat{c} - 1)/n$.
3. $z = \hat{z} \cdot \phi(n)^{-1} \mod n$.
4. $v_i = -s^{-1}(z - s') \mod n$.
5. $f = g_1^{-nr'} \hat{m}_i^n \mod n^2$.
6. $y_i = \left(f^{[n^{-1} \mod p'q'][r^{-1} \mod p'q']}\right)^{-1} \mod n^2$.
7. Split the bit representation of v into two parts of $\lambda/2$ bits each, i.e. $v_i = v_{i,1}||v_{i,2}$. Run $h_i||\tau_i \leftarrow \mathsf{S.Dec}(k_{\mathsf{e}}, v_{i,2})$
8. If $\left(h_i||\tau_i \neq \perp \ \wedge H(v_{i,1}) = h_i \ \wedge F(k_{\mathsf{p}}, (y_i, \tau_i)) = v_{i,1}\right)$ return $\left((y_i, \tau_i), v_{i,1}\right)$. Otherwise return $\perp$.

Fig. 6. The G_{ext} algorithm.

5 Security Analysis

In this section, we prove that the scheme (WM.Gen, PKE.Mark, Enc, Dec, Extract) presented in Sect. 4 is a watermarkable PKE scheme according to the model presented in Sect. 3.

Theorem 1. *The scheme* (WM.Gen, PKE.Mark, Enc, Dec, Extract) *of Sect. 4 is a watermarkable PKE scheme assuming (1) that the* DCR *assumption holds, (2) the* $\mathsf{DDH_{SQNR}}$ *assumption holds, (3) F is a PRF, (4)* (S.Gen, S.Enc, S.Dec) *is an authenticated encryption scheme that additionally satisfies indistinguishability between real and random ciphertexts and the hash function H is collision resistant.*

Proving Theorem 1 requires to prove that the properties defined in Sect. 3 are satisfied. We start in Subsect. 5.1 by proving that the watermarkable PKE scheme satisfies encryption correctness and IND-CPA security. Then, we proceed in Sects. 5.2 by proving extraction correctness property, and finally, in Sect. 5.3 we prove that ρ-unremovability and γ-unforgeability properties are satisfied, where $\rho \geq 1/2 + 1/\mathsf{poly}(\lambda)$ and $\gamma \leq 1/2 - 1/\mathsf{poly}(\lambda)$. Regarding the ρ-unremovability notion, we note that the lower bound of Cohen et al. [15] applies to our message-embedding construction. In particular, Cohen et al. [15] showed that message-embedding watermarking schemes satisfy ρ-unremovability only if $\rho \geq 1/2 + 1/\mathsf{poly}(\lambda)$.

Before proceeding to the detailed proofs, we present the following well-known propositions which will be required for our analysis, i.e. Propositions 1, 2.

Proposition 1. *Let $\mathcal{X}_{n^2} = \langle g_1 \rangle$, the subgroup that contains all square n-th residues modulo n^2, with order $p'q'$. Let $\mathcal{D}_1, \mathcal{D}_2$ the following distributions. $\mathcal{D}_1 : (n, g_1^r)$ where $r \leftarrow [p'q']$, $\mathcal{D}_2 : (n, g_1^r)$, where $r \leftarrow [n/4]$. $\mathcal{D}_1, \mathcal{D}_2$ are statistically indistinguishable.*

Proposition 2. *Let $\mathcal{X}_{n^2} = \langle g_1 \rangle$, the subgroup that contains all square n-th residues modulo n^2, with order $p'q'$. Let $\mathcal{D}_3, \mathcal{D}_4$ the following distributions. $\mathcal{D}_3 : (n, g_1^r)$ where $r \leftarrow [np'q']$, $\mathcal{D}_4 : (n, g_1^r)$, where $r \leftarrow [n^2/4]$. $\mathcal{D}_3, \mathcal{D}_4$ are statistically indistinguishable.*

5.1 Encryption Correctness and IND-CPA Security

Lemma 1 (Encryption Correctness). *The Watermarkable PKE scheme presented in Sect. 4 satisfies the encryption correctness property.*

Proof. We prove that for any $m \in \mathcal{X}_{n^2}$, and any (pk, sk) generated by the PKE.Mark algorithm, it holds that $\mathsf{Dec}(sk, \mathsf{Enc}(pk, m)) = m$. It can be easily seen that $(g_1^{rx}(1+n)^{rv})^{-1} g_1^{rx}(1+n)^{rv} m = m$. □

Lemma 2 (IND-CPA security). *The Watermarkable PKE scheme of Sect. 4 is IND-CPA secure under the* $\mathsf{DDH}_{\mathsf{SQNR}}$ *assumption.*

Proof. We will prove this lemma by defining a sequence of games. By $\mathcal{G}_0$ we denote the IND-CPA security game for the watermarkable PKE scheme.

Game $\mathcal{G}_0$: On input 1^λ,

1. $(n, g_1) \leftarrow \mathsf{Param}(1^\lambda)$; $k_{\mathsf{p}} \xleftarrow{\$} \mathcal{K}$; $k_{\mathsf{e}} \xleftarrow{\$} \mathsf{S.Gen}(1^{\kappa_1})$; $mk = (k_{\mathsf{p}}, k_{\mathsf{e}})$; $xk = (p', q', k_{\mathsf{p}}, k_{\mathsf{e}})$;
2. $x \xleftarrow{\$} [n/4]$; $v_1 = F(k_{\mathsf{p}}, (g_1^x, \tau))$; $v_2 = \mathsf{S.Enc}(k_{\mathsf{e}}, H(v_1)||\tau)$;$v = v_1||v_2$; $h = g_1^x(1+n)^v$; $pk = (n, g_1, h)$; $sk = (x, v)$;
3. $(m_0, m_1) \leftarrow \mathcal{A}(pk, mk, xk)$;
4. $b \xleftarrow{\$} \{0,1\}$; $r \xleftarrow{\$} [n^2/4]$; $c = \langle g_1^r, (1+n)^r, h^r \cdot m_b \rangle$;
5. $b^* \leftarrow \mathcal{A}(c)$;

In the game $\mathcal{G}_0$, $c = \langle g_1^r, (1+n)^r, g_1^{rx}(1+n)^{rv} \cdot m_b \rangle$.

Game $\mathcal{G}_1$: $\mathcal{G}_1$ is the same as $\mathcal{G}_0$, except the following: At Step 4 of the game, the Challenger samples $r_1 \xleftarrow{\$} [n/4]$, $s_1 \xleftarrow{\$} [n]$ and computes $c = \langle g_1^{r_1}, (1+n)^{s_1}, g_1^{r_1 x}(1+n)^{s_1 v} m_b \rangle$.

Game $\mathcal{G}_2$: The game $\mathcal{G}_2$ is the same as $\mathcal{G}_1$ except the following: At Step 4 of game $\mathcal{G}_2$, the Challenger chooses $r^* \xleftarrow{\$} [n/4]$ and computes $c = \langle g_1^{r_1}, (1+n)^{s_1}, g_1^{r^*}(1+n)^{s_1 v} \rangle$.

We include the analysis in the full version of our paper [2].

5.2 Extraction Correctness

Lemma 3 (Extraction correctness). *The Watermarkable PKE scheme of Sect. 4 satisfies extraction correctness, under the following assumptions: (1) correctness is satisfied (cf. Lemma 1), (2) F is a pseudorandom function and (3) the symmetric encryption scheme* (S.Gen, S.Enc, S.Dec) *is correct.*

Proof. Consider a pair $(pk, sk) \leftarrow \mathsf{PKE.Mark}(params, mk, \tau)$, where $sk = (x, v)$ with $v = v_1||v_2$ s.t. $v_1 = F(k_\mathsf{p}, (g_1^x, \tau))$ and $pk = (n, g_1, h)$ with $h = g_1^x(1+n)^v$. We will prove that if Extract receives as input Dec_{sk}, it always returns τ. Let $\psi_i = \langle g_1^r, (1+n)^s, g_1^{r'}(1+n)^{s'}\rangle$ be a ciphertext generated as described at Step (D3)a of the Extract algorithm. Following the steps 1–8 of the G_ext algorithm of Fig. 6, we prove that Extract on input Dec_{sk} and ψ_i returns $((g_1^x, \tau), v_1)$.

Step 1: $\mathsf{Dec}_{sk}(\psi_i) = g_1^{r'-xr}(1+n)^{s'-sv}$. Since $\hat{m}_i = g_1^{r'-xr}(1+n)^{s'-sv} \in \mathcal{Q}_{n^2}$, we compute $\hat{c} = \hat{m}_i^{\phi(n)} = g_1^{\phi(n)(r'-xr)}(1+n)^{\phi(n)(s'-sv)} = (1+n)^{\phi(n)(s'-sv)} = 1 + n[\phi(n)(s'-sv) \mod n]$.
Step 2: $\hat{z} = \frac{\hat{c}-1}{n} = \phi(n)(s'-sv) \mod n$.
Step 3: $z = \phi(n)^{-1}\hat{z} \mod n = \phi(n)^{-1}\phi(n)(s'-sv) = (s'-sv) \mod n$.
Step 4: $-s^{-1}(z-s') \mod n = -s^{-1}(s'-sv-s') \mod n = v$.
Step 5: $f = g_1^{-nr'}\hat{m}_i^n \mod n^2 = g_1^{-nr'}g_1^{n(r'-xr)}(1+n)^{n(s'-sv)} = g_1^{-nr'}g_1^{n(r'-xr)} = g_1^{-nxr}$.
Step 6: $\left(f^{[n^{-1} \mod p'q'][r^{-1} \mod p'q']}\right)^{-1} \mod n^2 = \left(g_1^{-nxr[n^{-1} \mod p'q'][r^{-1} \mod p'q']}\right)^{-1} = g_1^x$.
Step 7: Split the bit representation of v into two parts of $\lambda/2$ bits each, i.e. $v = v_1||v_2$. Due to the correctness property of the symmetric encryption scheme, it holds that $H(v_1)||\tau \leftarrow \mathsf{S.Dec}(k_\mathsf{e}, v_2)$.
Step 8: It holds that $v_1 = F(k_\mathsf{p}, (g_1^x, \tau))$ and therefore G_ext returns $((g_1^x, \tau), v_1)$.

Since G_ext returns $((g_1^x, \tau), v_1)$ for any of the ciphertexts $\psi_1, \ldots, \psi_\ell$, which are generated by Extract at Step (D3)a , then Extract returns the message τ.

5.3 Proving Unremovability and Unforgeability Properties

As it will become clear in the proofs of unremovability and unforgeability properties in this section, it is crucial that our watermarkable PKE scheme satisfies a property called *ciphertext indistinguishability.* At a high-level, no PPT adversary should be able to distinguish between the ciphertexts constructed as described at Step (D3)a of the Extract algorithm and standard encrypted plaintexts, under any public key *pk*. For the simplicity, we will refer to the ciphertexts computed at Step (D3)a as "extraction ciphertexts". We intuitively explain why this property is essential in proving unremovability and unforgeability by presenting below some simple scenarios where it is assumed that a potential attacker could distinguish between standard ciphertexts and extraction ciphertexts. The examples below refer to the simpler case of watermarking where circuits are either marked or unmarked.

- Assume an attacker $\mathcal{A}$ against the ρ-unremovability game which has obtained a pair (pk_i, sk_i) by issuing a CorruptOracle query. If $\mathcal{A}$ could distinguish "extraction ciphertexts" from valid ciphertexts under pk_i, then it could construct a circuit C^* which runs Dec_{sk_i} when receving as input an encrypted plaintext under the key pk_i and returns $\perp$ when receiving as input a "extraction ciphertext". Therefore, $\mathcal{A}$ wins the ρ-unremovability game since C^* is "close" (specifically 1-close) to Dec_{sk_i} and $\mathsf{Extract}$ on input C^* returns $\perp$, i.e. *unmarked.*

- Assume an attacker $\mathcal{A}'$ against the γ-unforgeability game which has obtained a pair (pk_i, sk_i) through a query to the CorruptOracle. If $\mathcal{A}'$ could distinguish "extraction ciphertexts" from valid ciphertexts under pk_i, then it could construct a circuit C^* which returns $\perp$ when receiving as input a valid ciphertext under pk_i and runs Dec_{sk_i} when receiving as input a "extraction ciphertext". In that case, $\mathcal{A}'$ the attacker managed to break γ-unforgeability since C^* which is "far" (specifically 1-far) from Dec_{sk_i} but $\mathsf{Extract}$ would decide that C^* is *marked* the decryption circuit under the key sk which is at the same time *marked.*

Before proving *unremovability* and *unforgeability*, we present some intermediate lemmas which will be necessary in our proofs. First, we show that for any public key pk, even if the adversary is given the corresponding secret key sk, the adversary is not able to distinguish between ciphertexts encrypted under pk from ciphertexts prepared under Extract algorithm.

Lemma 4. *Let $\tau \in \mathcal{T}$ and $pk = (n, g_1, h)$, $sk = (x, v)$ returned by* PKE.Mark *(mk, τ), where $x \overset{\$}{\leftarrow} [n/4]$, $v = v_1 || v_2$, $v_1 = F(K, (g_1^x, \tau))$, $v_2 = \mathsf{S.Enc}(k_e, H(v_1)||\tau)$ and $h = g_1^x(1+n)^v$. Assuming that the* DCR *assumption holds, F is a PRF and the symmetric encryption scheme* (S.Gen, S.Enc, Dec) *satisfies real-or-random security against chosen plaintext attacks (cf. Definition 5), it holds that*

$$\langle n, g_1, x, v, g_1^r, (1+n)^r, g_1^{xr}(1+n)^{rv} \cdot m \rangle \overset{c}{\approx} \langle n, g_1, x, v, g_1^{r_1}, (1+n)^{s_1}, g_1^{r_2}(1+n)^{s_2} \rangle,$$

where $r \overset{\$}{\leftarrow} [n^2/4]$, $r_1, r_2, x \overset{\$}{\leftarrow} [n/4]$, $s_1, s_2 \overset{\$}{\leftarrow} \mathbb{Z}_n$ and $m \overset{\$}{\leftarrow} \mathcal{X}_{n^2}$.

The proof of the above is included in the full version of our paper [2].

Next, we proceed with the proof of Lemma 5, which shows that if G_{ext} on input dk, C^* and "extraction ciphertext" ψ, at Step 4 outputs a value $v \in \mathbb{Z}_n$ and at Step 6 it outputs $y = g_1^x \mod n^2$, then this implies that C^* has run $\mathsf{Dec}_{sk}(\psi)$, where $sk = (x, v)$.

Lemma 5. *Let $\psi = \langle g_1^r, (1+n)^s, g_1^{r'}(1+n)^{s'} \rangle$ where $r \overset{\$}{\leftarrow} [n/4]$, $r' \overset{\$}{\leftarrow} [n/4]$, $s, s' \overset{\$}{\leftarrow} \mathbb{Z}_n$ and let C^* be a circuit which on input ψ returns $\hat{m}$ s.t. (1) G_{ext} at Step 4 outputs v, and (2) G_{ext} and Step 6 outputs g^x. Then, $\hat{m} = g_1^{r'-xr}(1+n)^{s'-sv} \mod n^2$.*

The proof of the above Lemma is included in in the full version of our paper [2].

Testing Closeness Between Circuits. Below, we include standard bounds which are utilized for testing closeness and farness between circuits.

Proposition 3. *Let* $\delta \geq \frac{1}{\mathsf{poly}(\lambda)}$, $\rho > \frac{1}{2} + \delta$ *and* $\gamma \leq \frac{1}{2} - \delta$ *(Fig. 7).*

Test algorithm
Input: Two circuits C^* and Dec_{sk} and $\mathcal{M}$ the input space of $\mathsf{Enc}_{pk}(\cdot)$.
Parameters: $\delta \geq 1/\mathsf{poly}(\lambda), \rho \geq 1/2 + \delta$.

1. Set $\mathsf{cnt} = 0$ and $\ell = \lambda/\delta^2$.
2. Sample $m_1, \ldots, m_\ell$ independently and uniformly at random from $\mathcal{M}$.
3. For $j = 1, \ldots, \ell$, compute $c_j = \mathsf{Enc}_{pk}(m_j)$.
4. For $j = 1, \ldots, \ell$, do
   (a) Compute $C^*(c_j) = m_j$ set $\mathsf{cnt} = \mathsf{cnt} + 1$.
5. If $\mathsf{cnt} \geq \frac{\lambda}{2\delta^2}$ return 1, otherwise return 0.

Fig. 7. Test algorithm.

- *For any* $\delta \geq 1/\mathsf{poly}(\lambda)$, *if* $C^* \sim_\rho \mathsf{Dec}_{sk}$, *then* $\Pr[\mathsf{cnt} < \frac{\lambda}{2\delta^2}] = \mathsf{negl}(\lambda)$.
- *For any* $\delta \geq 1/\mathsf{poly}(\lambda)$, *if* $C^* \nsim_\gamma \mathsf{Dec}_{sk}$, *then* $\Pr[\mathsf{cnt} < \frac{\lambda}{2\delta^2}] = 1 - \mathsf{negl}(\lambda)$.

Proposition 3 holds by Chernoff bounds.

Lemma 6 (ρ-Unremovability). *The watermarkable PKE scheme* ($\mathsf{WM.Gen}$, $\mathsf{PKE.Mark}$, Enc, Dec, $\mathsf{Extract}$) *satisfies ρ-Unremovability under the following assumptions: (1) correctness property is satisfied (cf. Lemma 1), (2) F is a pseudorandom function and (3) ciphertext indisinguishability holds (cf. Lemma 4), (4) the symmetric encryption scheme* ($\mathsf{S.Gen}, \mathsf{S.Enc}, \mathsf{S.Dec}$) *satisfied integrity of ciphertexts and (5) the hash function H is collision resistant.*

Proof Idea. We now provide the general idea behind our unremovability proof and give the full proof in the full version of our paper [2].

Recall by the definition of the ρ-unremovability game that an adversary is allowed to obtain a number of (watermarked) public-secret key pairs as well as a number of public keys by issuing queries to the Corrupt and Challenge oracles respectively. Given that, our first goal is to prove that an adversary is not able to create a new valid watermarked secret key, e.g. possibly by combining the secret keys that he possesses. In more detail, we prove that if an adversary issues a circuit C as a query to the Extract oracle (or outputs C in the end of the game) and the Extract oracle returns a tag τ, then this means that C implements the decryption algorithm under one of the secret keys generated previously by the challenger. We prove this via a sequence of hybrid games in the detailed proof.

In each of the hybrid games the algorithm G_{ext} is gradually altered so that in an intermediate game, the modified G_{ext} performs as follows: On input a circuit C and a extraction ciphertext ψ, if a value $y = g_1^x$ is computed at Step 6 and a value v is computed at Step 4 it simply checks whether there is a secret key (x, v) generated previously by the Challenge oracle. Recall by the definition of the ρ-unremovability game that the challenger stores every public-secret key pair which is generated together with the corresponding tag (such information is stored at a table called Marked). Therefore, if such secret key $sk = (x, v)$ exists, the tag τ associated with the secret key sk would be returned as the output of the Extract algorithm (assuming that for the *majority* of extraction ciphertexts given as input to G_{ext}, the same (x, v) will be computed). Based on Lemma 5, this implies that the decryption algorithm under the key $sk = (x, v)$ has been run by the circuit C for the majority of ciphertexts. Given that, in one of the hybrid games the computation of the (modified) G_{ext} algorithm, i.e. Steps 1–6, are replaced by an algorithm which pre-computes how the extraction ciphertext which is received as input is decrypted by each secret key that has been generated so far. Then, by running the circuit with input the extraction ciphertext, and matching the output with the previous results, the algorithm infers which secret key has been used for the decryption (assuming there is one).

Then, since the first winning condition of the ρ-unremovability game is that the circuit C^* output by the adversary should be ρ-close to a marked decryption circuit, the challenger can guess such a circuit. Based on that and the *ciphertext indistinguishability* property of the watermarkable PKE scheme (cf. Lemma 4) the challenger can gradually substitute extraction ciphertexts sampled in the Step (D3)a with encrypted plaintexts under the marked public key guessed by the challenger. We note that the plaintexts which are encrypted at this stage are chosen uniformly at random from the plaintext space. The above change is performed in a series of ℓ hybrid games for this step where eventually the adversarial circuit C^* in run on input ℓ encrypted plaintexts under the aforementioned public key and it is checked how which portion of such ciphertexts is decrypted correctly by C^* in order to decide whether C^* is marked or not. Last, by utilizing a Chernoff bound, we prove that if C^* is ρ-close to a decryption circuit then it cannot decrypt correctly less than ℓ ciphertexts except with negligible probability. To put it differently, C^* will be detected as marked with the tag τ which was initially related with this specific public-secret key pair (i.e. was given as input to the Mark algorithm).

Lemma 7 (γ-Unforgeability). *The watermarkable PKE scheme* (WM.Gen, PKE.Mark, Enc, Dec, Extract) *satisfies γ-unforgeability under the following assumptions: (1)ciphertext indistinguishability holds (cf. Lemma 4), (2) IND-CPA security holds , (3) F is a pseudorandom function.*

Proof Sketch. Without loss of generality, we assume that an adversary $\mathcal{A}$ interacting with a Challenger in the unforgeability game $\mathcal{G}^{\mathsf{unforge}}_{\gamma,\mathcal{A}}$ issues q_1 queries to the ChallengeOracle, q_2 queries to the CorruptOracle and q_3 queries to the ExtractOracle. This means that q_1 public-secret key pairs have been generated by PKE.Mark, i.e. $(pk_1, sk_1), \ldots, (pk_{q_1}, sk_{q_1})$, the adversary has obtained all the public keys, but also $\mathcal{A}$ has obtained q_2 public-secret key pairs, i.e. (pk_{j_1}, sk_{j_1}) $\ldots, (pk_{j_{q_2}}, sk_{j_{q_2}})$. Recall that $\mathcal{A}$ wins if (1) for any $\mathsf{Dec}_{sk_i} \in$ Corrupted, C^* is γ-far from Dec_{sk_i}, and (2) $\mathsf{Extract}(params, xk, C^*) = \tau \neq \bot$.

This proof is similar to the unremovability proof. Let us first provide some intuition on a potential scenario where unforgeability is broken. Assume an adversary which holds at least two secret keys could combine their components (i.e. the values $v_{i,1}, v_{i,2}$ of the component $v = v_{i,1}||v_{i,2}$) and obtain a new valid "watermarked" secret key, then the decryption algorithm would be far from any decryption algorithm in the set Corrupted and Extract would return would extract a tag indicating that the circuit is marked. Intuitively, this is prevented due to the fact that the components $v_{i,1}, v_{i,2}$ are related between each other as $v_{i,2}$ encrypts $H(v_{i,1})||\tau$. In addition, by requiring that the symmetric encryption scheme is authenticated, an adversary cannot create new valid ciphertexts on its own. This combination essentially ensures that new valid watermarked secret keys cannot be easily created. We follow the same sequence of games as described in the unremovability game.

In particular, in a series of games we prove that if an adversary issues a circuit C as a query to the Extract oracle (or outputs C in the end of the game) that is *marked* with a tag τ, then this means that C implements the decryption algorithm under one of the secret keys generated previously by the challenger. Due to Lemma 5, in an intermediate hybrid game the computation of the (modified) G_{ext} algorithm, i.e. Steps 1–6, are replaced by an algorithm which pre-computes how the extraction ciphertext which is received as input is decrypted by each secret key that has been generated so far. Then, due to ciphertext indistinguishability "extraction ciphertexts" can be replaced by standard ciphertexts under a chosen public key (chosen uniformly at random by the challenger). Since for any $\mathsf{Dec}_{sk_i} \in \mathsf{Corrupted}$, C^* should be γ-far from Dec_{sk_i}, by Proposition 3, C^* decrypts correctly ℓ^* out of ℓ ciphertexts only with negligible probability. Therefore, the only chance that an adversary wins the unforgeability game is breaking the IND-CPA security of the watermarkable PKE scheme (cf. Lemma 2), as the adversary should decrypt correctly at least ℓ^* out of ℓ ciphertexts under a secret key that it does possess, i.e. it does not belong to the set Corrupted.

References

1. Ananth, P., Vaikuntanathan, V.: Optimal bounded-collusion secure functional encryption. In: Hofheinz, D., Rosen, A. (eds.) TCC 2019. LNCS, vol. 11891, pp. 174–198. Springer, Cham (2019). https://doi.org/10.1007/978-3-030-36030-6_8
2. Baldimtsi, F., Kiayias, A., Samari, K.: Watermarkable public key encryption with efficient extraction under standard assumptions. IACR Cryptology ePrint Archive (2022)
3. Baldimtsi, F., Kiayias, A., Samari, K.: Watermarking public-key cryptographic functionalities and implementations. In: Nguyen, P., Zhou, J. (eds.) ISC 2017. LNCS, vol. 10599, pp. 173–191. Springer, Cham (2017). https://doi.org/10.1007/978-3-319-69659-1_10
4. Barak, B., et al.: On the (im)possibility of obfuscating programs. J. ACM **59**(2), 6 (2012)
5. Barak, B., et al.: On the (im)possibility of obfuscating programs. In: Kilian, J. (ed.) CRYPTO 2001. LNCS, vol. 2139, pp. 1–18. Springer, Heidelberg (2001). https://doi.org/10.1007/3-540-44647-8_1

6. Bellare, M., Desai, A., Jokipii, E., Rogaway, P.: A concrete security treatment of symmetric encryption. In: FOCS 1997, pp. 394–403 (1997)
7. Bellare, M., Namprempre, C.: Authenticated encryption: relations among notions and analysis of the generic composition paradigm. In: Okamoto, T. (ed.) ASIACRYPT 2000. LNCS, vol. 1976, pp. 531–545. Springer, Heidelberg (2000). https://doi.org/10.1007/3-540-44448-3_41
8. Boneh, D., Lewi, K., Wu, D.J.: Constraining pseudorandom functions privately. In: Fehr, S. (ed.) PKC 2017. LNCS, vol. 10175, pp. 494–524. Springer, Heidelberg (2017). https://doi.org/10.1007/978-3-662-54388-7_17
9. Boneh, D., Sahai, A., Waters, B.: Fully collusion resistant traitor tracing with short ciphertexts and private keys. In: Vaudenay, S. (ed.) EUROCRYPT 2006. LNCS, vol. 4004, pp. 573–592. Springer, Heidelberg (2006). https://doi.org/10.1007/11761679_34
10. Boneh, D., Waters, B.: A fully collusion resistant broadcast, trace, and revoke system. In: CCS 2006, pp. 211–220, November 2006
11. Boneh, D., Zhandry, M.: Multiparty key exchange, efficient traitor tracing, and more from indistinguishability obfuscation. In: Garay, J.A., Gennaro, R. (eds.) CRYPTO 2014. LNCS, vol. 8616, pp. 480–499. Springer, Heidelberg (2014). https://doi.org/10.1007/978-3-662-44371-2_27
12. Brakerski, Z., Chandran, N., Goyal, V., Jain, A., Sahai, A., Segev, G.: Hierarchical functional encryption. In: 8th Innovations in Theoretical Computer Science Conference, ITCS, pp. 8:1–8:27 (2017)
13. Chor, B., Fiat, A., Naor, M.: Tracing traitors. In: Desmedt, Y.G. (ed.) CRYPTO 1994. LNCS, vol. 839, pp. 257–270. Springer, Heidelberg (1994). https://doi.org/10.1007/3-540-48658-5_25
14. Cohen, A., Holmgren, J., Nishimaki, R., Vaikuntanathan, V., Wichs, D.: Watermarking cryptographic capabilities. SIAM J. Comput. **47**(6), 2157–2202 (2018)
15. Cohen, A., Holmgren, J., Nishimaki, R., Vaikuntanathan, V., Wichs, D.: Watermarking cryptographic capabilities. In: STOC 2016, pp. 1115–1127, June 2016
16. Dodis, Y., Fazio, N., Kiayias, A., Yung, M.: Scalable public-key tracing and revoking. In: PODC 2003, pp. 190–199, July 2003
17. Goyal, R., Kim, S., Manohar, N., Waters, B., Wu, D.J.: Watermarking public-key cryptographic primitives. In: Boldyreva, A., Micciancio, D. (eds.) CRYPTO 2019. LNCS, vol. 11694, pp. 367–398. Springer, Cham (2019). https://doi.org/10.1007/978-3-030-26954-8_12
18. Goyal, R., Koppula, V., Waters, B.: Collusion resistant traitor tracing from learning with errors. In: STOC, pp. 660–670 (2018)
19. Goyal, R., Koppula, V., Waters, B.: New approaches to traitor tracing with embedded identities. In: Hofheinz, D., Rosen, A. (eds.) TCC 2019. LNCS, vol. 11892, pp. 149–179. Springer, Cham (2019). https://doi.org/10.1007/978-3-030-36033-7_6
20. Kiayias, A., Tsiounis, Y., Yung, M.: Group encryption. In: Kurosawa, K. (ed.) ASIACRYPT 2007. LNCS, vol. 4833, pp. 181–199. Springer, Heidelberg (2007). https://doi.org/10.1007/978-3-540-76900-2_11
21. Kiayias, A., Yung, M.: Traitor tracing with constant transmission rate. In: Knudsen, L.R. (ed.) EUROCRYPT 2002. LNCS, vol. 2332, pp. 450–465. Springer, Heidelberg (2002). https://doi.org/10.1007/3-540-46035-7_30
22. Kim, S., Wu, D.J.: Watermarking PRFs from lattices: stronger security via extractable PRFs. In: Boldyreva, A., Micciancio, D. (eds.) CRYPTO 2019. LNCS, vol. 11694, pp. 335–366. Springer, Cham (2019). https://doi.org/10.1007/978-3-030-26954-8_11

23. Kim, S., Wu, D.J.: Watermarking cryptographic functionalities from standard lattice assumptions. In: Katz, J., Shacham, H. (eds.) CRYPTO 2017. LNCS, vol. 10401, pp. 503–536. Springer, Cham (2017). https://doi.org/10.1007/978-3-319-63688-7_17
24. Nishimaki, R.: Equipping public-key cryptographic primitives with watermarking (or: a hole is to watermark). In: Pass, R., Pietrzak, K. (eds.) TCC 2020. LNCS, vol. 12550, pp. 179–209. Springer, Cham (2020). https://doi.org/10.1007/978-3-030-64375-1_7
25. Nishimaki, R.: How to watermark cryptographic functions. In: Johansson, T., Nguyen, P.Q. (eds.) EUROCRYPT 2013. LNCS, vol. 7881, pp. 111–125. Springer, Heidelberg (2013). https://doi.org/10.1007/978-3-642-38348-9_7
26. Nishimaki, R., Wichs, D., Zhandry, M.: Anonymous traitor tracing: how to embed arbitrary information in a key. In: Fischlin, M., Coron, J.-S. (eds.) EUROCRYPT 2016. LNCS, vol. 9666, pp. 388–419. Springer, Heidelberg (2016). https://doi.org/10.1007/978-3-662-49896-5_14
27. Paillier, P.: Public-key cryptosystems based on composite degree residuosity classes. In: Stern, J. (ed.) EUROCRYPT 1999. LNCS, vol. 1592, pp. 223–238. Springer, Heidelberg (1999). https://doi.org/10.1007/3-540-48910-X_16
28. Quach, W., Wichs, D., Zirdelis, G.: Watermarking PRFs under standard assumptions: public marking and security with extraction queries. In: Beimel, A., Dziembowski, S. (eds.) TCC 2018. LNCS, vol. 11240, pp. 669–698. Springer, Cham (2018). https://doi.org/10.1007/978-3-030-03810-6_24
29. Sahai, A., Waters, B.: How to use indistinguishability obfuscation: deniable encryption, and more. In: STOC 2014, pp. 475–484 (2014)
30. Yang, R., Au, M.H., Lai, J., Xu, Q., Yu, Z.: Collusion resistant watermarking schemes for cryptographic functionalities. In: Galbraith, S.D., Moriai, S. (eds.) ASIACRYPT 2019. LNCS, vol. 11921, pp. 371–398. Springer, Cham (2019). https://doi.org/10.1007/978-3-030-34578-5_14
31. Yang, R., Au, M.H., Yu, Z., Xu, Q.: Collusion resistant watermarkable PRFs from standard assumptions. In: Micciancio, D., Ristenpart, T. (eds.) CRYPTO 2020. LNCS, vol. 12170, pp. 590–620. Springer, Cham (2020). https://doi.org/10.1007/978-3-030-56784-2_20
32. Yoshida, M., Fujiwara, T.: Toward digital watermarking for cryptographic data. IEICE Trans. **94–A**(1), 270–272 (2011)

Authentication and Signatures

A Provably Secure, Lightweight Protocol for Anonymous Authentication

Jonathan Katz(✉)

Department of Computer Science, University of Maryland,
College Park, MD 20902, USA
jkatz2@gmail.com

Abstract. We propose a lightweight, anonymous authentication protocol that can be based on any block cipher and is suitable for use by, e.g., RFID tags. We formally define three security properties that our protocol is intended to satisfy—mutual authentication, anonymity, and desynchronization resilience—and prove concrete bounds on the probability the protocol satisfies these properties in the presence of an active attacker. Our protocol is more efficient than any other protocol we are aware of that achieves these three properties.

1 Introduction

In this work we introduce an authentication protocol suitable for use by resource-constrained devices such as Radio Frequency Identification (RFID) tags. The protocol is intended to be run between a reader $\mathcal{R}$ (that can be viewed as a "server") and a tag $\mathcal{T}$ (that can be thought of as a "client") that have established some shared, secret information in advance. The protocol is primarily intended to provide *mutual authentication*: the tag should be convinced it is communicating with the legitimate reader, and the reader should be convinced it is communicating with a legitimate tag, even in the presence of an active adversary who can arbitrarily interact with both the reader and all the tags in the system. An additional concern—motivated by, but not exclusive to, the setting of RFID—is *tag anonymity*; roughly speaking, this means it should be infeasible for an attacker to track a tag over time. One way anonymity can be achieved, which we pursue here, is to make both the tag and the reader *stateful* (aka *synchronized*) so their shared, secret information is updated each time the protocol is successfully executed. This introduces a new security concern called *desynchronization resilience* [10], which requires that it be infeasible for an attacker to cause a legitimate tag and the reader to get out-of-sync to the point where an honest execution of the authentication protocol between them fails.

There is an extensive literature devoted to designing and analyzing protocols for anonymous RFID authentication [2–4], and it is not our intention to survey it here. However, in order to situate our protocol relative to prior work, we highlight the desiderata that guided our design:

C. Galdi and S. Jarecki (Eds.): SCN 2022, LNCS 13409, pp. 271–288, 2022.
https://doi.org/10.1007/978-3-031-14791-3_12

Security Goals. As stated above, the security goals we targeted were mutual authentication, anonymity, and desynchronization resilience. Some anonymous RFID authentication protocols are designed to provide only *unilateral* authentication of the tag (e.g., [11,15]). Other lightweight authentication protocols are vulnerable to desynchronization attacks [9,10] that can lead to denial of service.

Provable Security Based on Symmetric-Key Primitives. Some anonymous RFID authentication protocols are based on public-key techniques; however, public-key techniques are too expensive for use on extremely low-cost tags. At the other extreme, there have been several suggestions of "ultralightweight" protocols that do not rely on any cryptographic primitives at all. Unfortunately, such protocols have a poor track record, and have generally been broken soon after their publication (see, e.g., surveys of prior such work [3,13]). Since a secure mutual authentication protocol implies the existence of one-way functions, protocols that do not explicitly rely on some cryptographic assumption are unlikely to be secure.

We take a middle ground, seeking to design a protocol based (only) on symmetric-key primitives such as hash functions or block ciphers. The security of our protocol can (provably) be reduced to the security of an underlying block cipher modeled as a pseudorandom function, which lends confidence to our overall design. From a practical perspective, there have been many proposals of lightweight block ciphers, and any of those could be used to instantiate our protocol even on low-cost RFID tags.

Sublinear Complexity at the Reader. It is fairly easy to design anonymous authentication protocols that are efficient for the tag, but require the reader to do (cryptographic) work linear in the number of tags N in the system [12,14]. Since the number of tags in the system may be high, we sought a protocol in which the reader performs only $O(1)$ cryptographic operations.

We are aware of only two existing protocols that satisfy all the criteria outlined above. Burmester and Munilla [7] show a lightweight protocol for anonymous authentication that can be based on any pseudorandom number generator (PRNG). However, although they prove that their protocol achieves mutual authentication, their definition of mutual authentication is weaker than ours and their protocol does not satisfy our definition. (The reader in their protocol is stateful but deterministic, and so it is possible for an attacker to interact with a tag and then impersonate that tag to the reader at a later point in time.) In addition, our protocol is more efficient than theirs; see further discussion in the following section. On the other hand, the Burmester-Munilla protocol satisfies stronger notions of anonymity (namely, forward/backward security) than our protocol; see Sect. 2.4 for further discussion.

Our protocol shares some similarities with the modification of the OSK protocol [11] proposed by Avoine et al. [3, Fig. 5]. They use a cryptographic hash function rather than a block cipher as their underlying primitive, although their protocol could be suitably modified to rely on a block cipher instead. Our protocol is more efficient than theirs; see the following section. Moreover, Avoine et al. do not provide any concrete security analysis or proofs of security.

In concurrent work, Boyd et al. [6] formally define the notion of "synchronization robustness" for key-exchange protocols, analogous to our notion of desynchronization resilience. Our definitions are similar in spirit, though technically different (in part because they consider key exchange while we only consider authentication). We remark that they do not consider anonymity at all, and the key-exchange protocol they design is not particularly lightweight even though it relies on symmetric-key primitives (e.g., it relies on puncturable PRFs).

1.1 Our Contributions

We propose a protocol for lightweight anonymous authentication along with formal definitions of security, and prove that our protocol achieves our definitions. Our protocol is carefully designed to be suitable for implementation on lightweight tags; specifically, we highlight:

- Our protocol has only three rounds, with low communication complexity.
- Our protocol requires only a pseudorandom *function*, not a pseudorandom permutation. This could be realized by an appropriately keyed, lightweight hash function, or by a (truncated version of a) lightweight block cipher. In the latter case inversion of the cipher is not required, which reduces the footprint of an implementation.
- The tag algorithm in our protocol need not maintain a clock, nor does it require access to a source of randomness. On the other hand, in order to ensure anonymity we do require the tag to maintain *state* that can be updated over time. Our protocol is designed so the state stored by the tag is small.
- The algorithm run by the reader is efficient, even as the number of tags in the system grows. In particular, the reader invokes the block cipher only $O(1)$ times per protocol execution, and runs in time sublinear in the number of tags in the system.

Our protocol is more efficient than prior protocols satisfying our requirements [3,7]. An exact comparison is complicated by the fact that the various protocols rely on different cryptographic building blocks and have different concrete security reductions, but for the purposes of our comparison we fix an n-bit security level and assume equal cost for (1) evaluating a block cipher with an n-bit block length, (2) evaluating a PRNG to obtain n bits of output, and (3) evaluating a hash function on an n-bit input, and count each of these as a single cryptographic operation. The Burmester-Munilla protocol runs in three rounds in the normal case but requires five rounds when an attack is detected; in either case, the tag performs five cryptographic operations in an execution of the protocol. The protocol by Avoine et al. [3, Fig. 5] runs in three rounds and requires the tag and reader to each perform four cryptographic operations per execution. Our protocol also runs in three rounds, but requires only three cryptographic operations by the tag and reader.

1.2 Outline of the Paper

In Sect. 2 we provide formal definitions of our three security goals: mutual authentication, tag anonymity, and desynchronization resilience. Our definition of mutual authentication follows the general approach of Bellare and Rogaway [5], though simplified for our intended application scenario (where concurrent executions of the protocol by a tag are not supported) and adapted to the case of stateful protocols. Several definitions of anonymity have been given in the literature (see, e.g., [12,16]); our definition here is inspired by those, though not identical to any of them. Our definition is intended to capture the notion of *unlinkability* [1,7], which informally means that an eavesdropping adversary should be unable to tell whether two interactions correspond to the same tag or to two different tags. (We do not consider the stronger notions of *forward/backward security*, which require that an adversary cannot link sessions of a compromised tag; see Sect. 2.4.) Although desynchronization resilience has been considered informally in many previous works [3,7,8,10,13,17], we are not aware of any prior formal treatment of this problem.

We describe our protocol in Sect. 3. In Sect. 4 we prove that our protocol satisfies our formal definitions. Our theorems specify concrete bounds quantifying the security of the protocol as a function of the resources of an attacker.

2 Model and Definitions

In this section we provide an abstract syntax for stateful authentication protocols, as well as a model and definitions of security.

2.1 Preliminaries

We assume a system with a single reader[1] and multiple tags, where each tag has a unique identity ID of some fixed length. An *authentication protocol* consists of three algorithms $\mathsf{Init}, \mathsf{Tag}$, and Reader. The initialization algorithm Init, run by some central authority, takes as input a tag identity ID and generates (secret) initial state information st that is given to the tag, along with a record corresponding to the tag that is given to the reader. The protocol itself is executed by interactive algorithms Tag and Reader run by a tag and the reader, respectively. Tag begins execution with current state st; algorithm Reader begins execution holding a collection $\mathcal{C}$ of records, one for each tag in the system. Upon termination, Tag either *rejects*, or else it *accepts* and locally outputs a session identifier[2] sid, and updated state st'. Upon termination, Reader either *rejects*, or else it *accepts* and locally outputs a value ID, a session identifier sid, and

[1] In practice, there may be multiple physical readers all communicating with a single back-end server. The server in that case then plays the role of the reader.

[2] A session identifier need not be output in the real-world protocol; we use it to define mutual authentication.

an updated collection $\mathcal{C}'$, where only the record corresponding to the tag with identity ID is updated.

In each of our eventual security definitions, we imagine an attacker running in a given experiment; security is quantified by bounds on the probabilities of certain events in that experiment. The experiments are defined within a common framework, in which we allow the attacker to initialize as many tags as desired with IDs of the attacker's choice (with the restriction that IDs are unique), eavesdrop on executions between tags and the reader, and to interact with tags or the reader in an arbitrary way. To capture this formally, we provide the attacker with access to various *oracles* that affect the global state of the system (namely, the current states of all tags and the reader):

- The Init oracle allows the attacker to register new tags. On input ID, this oracle runs $\mathsf{Init}(ID)$ to generate st and the corresponding record, creates a new tag with identity ID holding state st, and adds the record to the collection of records held by the reader.
  As noted above, we impose the restriction that the attacker cannot query this oracle with the same ID twice. This corresponds to the real-world assumption that all tags are assigned unique identities.
- The $\mathsf{Send}_{\mathcal{R}}$ oracle models the attacker's ability to impersonate a tag and interact with the reader. Given an *instance identifier* inst (see below) and an incoming message from the attacker, this oracle runs the next step of Reader using the incoming message and the current state of the specified instance of the reader, and returns an outgoing message (if any) to the attacker. The oracle also updates the state of the specified instance of the reader. If the specified instance of the reader accepts after receiving the message, this oracle also returns to the attacker the values ID, sid output by that instance of the reader. The attacker may submit a special start message to this oracle that prompts Reader to initiate[3] the protocol; this is a formalism of our framework, but does not correspond to any real protocol message.
  The instance identifier provides a formal way to enable concurrent executions at the reader, and allows the attacker to specify the instance to which a particular message is directed. In practice, separate instances could be defined by separate physical readers connected to a back-end server, or by physical-layer characteristics of the communication.
- The $\mathsf{Send}_{\mathcal{T}}$ oracle models the attacker's ability to spoof the reader and interact with a tag. The first input to this oracle specifies the ID of the tag with which the attacker wishes to interact. The second input specifies a message from the attacker. In response, this oracle runs the next step of Tag using the current state of the tag with identity ID and the specified message, updates the state of the tag accordingly, and returns the response (if any) to the attacker. If Tag terminates after receiving the message, this oracle also returns to the attacker the tag's decision whether to accept or reject and, in the former case, also returns the value sid output by that tag.

[3] For simplicity, we assume the reader sends the first message of the protocol (as is the case for our protocol).

In our formal model, we provide a special abort message the attacker can submit that prompts Tag to terminate the protocol.[4] For simplicity, we assume that each tag supports only one active instance; i.e., concurrent executions at a single tag are disallowed. In practice, it seems unlikely and unnecessary for tags to support concurrent executions.
- The Execute oracle takes as input an ID and runs an honest execution of the protocol between the tag holding ID and the reader, updating their state as specified by the protocol. (If the tag with that ID is in the middle of a session when this oracle is called, that session is first terminated.) The oracle returns the transcript of this execution (i.e., all messages sent by either party) as well as the sids output by both parties. This oracle is used to model passive eavesdropping of protocol executions.

With the above in place, we can formally define correctness in the absence of active interference. In response to a query Execute(ID), let sid be the session identifier output by the tag, and let ID', sid' be the tag identity and session identifier output by the reader. We say this execution *failed* if either the tag or reader rejects, or they both accept but $ID' \neq ID$ or $\mathsf{sid}' \neq \mathsf{sid}$. Let Fail be the event that there is ever a failed execution. A protocol is *correct* if for all efficient attackers $\mathcal{A}$ that *only* query Init and Execute (i.e., that do not carry out an active attack), $\Pr[\mathsf{Fail}] = 0$.

In the following sections, we define our desired security properties against an active attacker (i.e., an attacker who can query the $\mathsf{Send}_{\mathcal{T}}$ and $\mathsf{Send}_{\mathcal{R}}$ oracles).

2.2 Desynchronization Resilience

We consider desynchronization resilience first, since it is the simplest to define. It can be viewed as a strengthening of the correctness requirement, where authentication must succeed in an honest execution of the protocol even if the attacker has previously carried out *active* attacks on tags and/or the reader. Namely, consider an attacker $\mathcal{A}$ who has access to *all* the oracles described previously. We say *desynchronization occurs* if $\mathcal{A}$ ever makes a query Execute(ID) and event Fail (defined above) occurs. A protocol is *desynchronization resilient* if for all efficient attackers $\mathcal{A}$, the probability that desynchronization occurs is small.

2.3 Mutual Authentication

We follow the general approach of [5] in defining mutual authentication; however, because we wish to allow for deterministic tag algorithms, we must weaken their definition to have any hope of satisfying it. (See below.) To simplify things, we assume a 3-message protocol in which the reader sends the first and third messages and the tag sends the second message (as is the case for our protocol).

[4] In the real world the tag might implement a "time-out" mechanism that would have the same effect.

Consider an attacker who can access all the oracles that were described earlier. Fix a query $\mathsf{Send}_{\mathcal{R}}(\mathsf{inst}, \mathsf{msg}_2)$ (i.e., a query to the reader corresponding to the second message of the protocol) made at some time[5] t_2, following which the reader accepts with local output ID, sid. The given instance of the reader can only possibly accept if it had already initiated the protocol at some earlier time in response to a query $\mathsf{Send}_{\mathcal{R}}(\mathsf{inst}, \mathsf{start})$; let t_1 be the time at which that query was made. We say *tag authentication holds for instance* inst if a query $\mathsf{Send}_{\mathcal{T}}(ID, \star)$ or $\mathsf{Execute}(ID)$ was made at some time between t_1 and t_2. (Indeed, in that case the tag with identity ID was involved in running the protocol at some point in time between t_1 and t_2.) We say *tag authentication fails* for that instance (i.e., the attacker has succeeded in falsely impersonating the tag) otherwise.

In a model in which there are multiple readers, one can strengthen the above definition by requiring that each inst as above is associated with a *unique* query $\mathsf{Send}_{\mathcal{T}}(ID, \star)$ or $\mathsf{Execute}(ID)$. This implies that the tag with identity ID ran the protocol (at some appropriate point in time) at least once for every accepting instance of some reader.

From the perspective of the tag, consider a query $\mathsf{Send}_{\mathcal{T}}(ID, \mathsf{msg}_3)$ (i.e., the second query made to some tag, corresponding to the third message of the protocol) after which the tag holding ID accepts, and let sid be the session identifier that is output locally by the tag. We say *reader authentication fails* for that instance (i.e., the attacker has succeeded in falsely impersonating the reader) if either (1) there is no prior (accepting) instance at the reader with output ID, sid, or (2) there was a prior accepting instance of that same tag with the same sid (this rules out trivial protocols in which, e.g., sid is always some fixed value). See below for a discussion as to why the definition for the tag is different from the one for the reader.

A protocol is said to *achieve mutual authentication* if for all efficient attackers $\mathcal{A}$, the probability that either tag authentication or reader authentication ever fails is small.

Notes on the Definition. There is an asymmetry in how we define authentication for the reader and the tag. Roughly, successful impersonation of a tag to the reader occurs if the attacker causes the reader to accept without that tag's executing the protocol *at the same time*, whereas a successful impersonation of the reader to the tag occurs if the attacker causes a tag to accept but *at no time in the past* was there a corresponding accepting session at the reader. Thus, the notion of authentication we achieve is *weaker* with regard to impersonation of the reader to a tag.

The reason for this asymmetry is that the tag algorithm in our protocol is *deterministic* and *does not update its state until successful completion of the protocol.* Any such protocol always admits the following "attack":

[5] "Time" can be quantified by the number of oracle queries made at some point in the experiment.

1. The adversary allows a tag and the reader to execute the protocol honestly but drops the final message of the protocol from the reader to the tag so the tag aborts (and does not accept or update its state).
2. Subsequently, the attacker initiates a second execution of the protocol with the tag and simply replays all previous messages from the reader (including the final message), thus causing the tag to accept.

The above is not considered an attack with respect to our definition. Whether it is a concern depends on the environment in which the protocol is deployed.

We remark that the above "attack" could potentially be prevented by relying on randomness generation at the tag, or synchronized clocks at the tags and the reader. However, we do not wish to assume that lightweight tags have access to a good source of randomness or a clock.

2.4 Tag Anonymity

Tag anonymity is intended to prevent an attacker from tracking a tag over time. (We stress here that we consider anonymity at the *protocol* level; anonymity at the *physical* level must be ensured by physical-layer considerations.) Roughly, our formal definition ensures that an attacker who eavesdrops on executions of the protocol cannot later identify a tag after interacting with it. We present here a clean and simple definition of anonymity in which an attacker is allowed to eavesdrop on known tags before eavesdropping on and/or interacting with an unknown tag. We assume the attacker knows that the unknown tag in question corresponds to one of two possible identities; the attacker violates anonymity if it can determine which is the actual identity with probability better than random guessing. Although one could imagine strengthening our definition in various ways, doing so is cumbersome because of the need to rule out various "trivial" attacks that apply to any protocol in which the tag is deterministic.

In the formal definition, we consider a two-phase experiment. In the first phase, the attacker may initialize tags by querying Init, and passively eavesdrop on tags by querying $\mathsf{Execute}$. The first phase ends when the attacker outputs two distinct identities ID_0, ID_1. In the second phase of the experiment, a uniform bit b is chosen and then the attacker may interact with two new oracles:

- The $\mathsf{Execute}^*$ oracle behaves exactly as $\mathsf{Execute}(ID_b)$. This oracle models passive eavesdropping on the interaction between the reader and the tag holding (unknown) identity ID_b.
- The $\mathsf{Send}^*_{\mathcal{T}}$ oracle models the attacker's interaction with the tag holding ID_b; formally, $\mathsf{Send}^*_{\mathcal{T}}(m)$ is defined to be the same as $\mathsf{Send}_{\mathcal{T}}(ID_b, m)$.

At the end of its execution, $\mathcal{A}$ outputs a guess b', and $\mathcal{A}$ *succeeds* if $b' = b$.

Consider the above experiment, where b is a uniform bit chosen at the outset. The *de-anonymization advantage* of $\mathcal{A}$ is the absolute value of the difference between the probability that $\mathcal{A}$ succeeds and $1/2$. A protocol achieves *tag anonymity* if for all efficient $\mathcal{A}$ the de-anonymization advantage is small.

Forward/Backward Security. Stronger notions of anonymity (namely, forward/backward security [7]) have been considered in other work. Roughly, such definitions ensure that even if the tag's internal state is compromised, past/future executions of that tag are unlinkable. We do not pursue such security guarantees here, though we believe it would be possible to modify our protocol to achieve them at the cost of an additional cryptographic operation by the tag and reader.

3 Protocol Description

We let F denote a block cipher with an n-bit block length, but remark that our protocol does not require F to be invertible. For $x \in \{0,1\}^n$, we let $[x]_{n-1}$ denote the $n-1$ least-significant bits of x.

Overview. A tag's state st includes a key K, a counter ctr, and two pseudorandom values computed using K and ctr: a *pseudonym* IDS and a mask mask. (If memory is constrained, the tag may avoid storing IDS, mask and simply recompute then from K and ctr when needed.) The counter, pseudonym, and mask are updated each time the tag successfully executes the protocol.

For each tag in the system, the reader stores a record that includes that tag's key and what is believed to be the current[6] value of that tag's counter, in addition to both the current and previous versions of the tag's pseudonym and mask; the counter, pseudonyms, and masks are updated whenever the reader successfully executes a protocol with that tag.

Our protocol proceeds in three rounds. In the first two rounds, the reader sends a random challenge and the tag sends a response computed using its key. In addition, the tag sends its current pseudonym, which is used by the reader to identify the tag (and thus find the appropriate key as well as the current value of the tag's counter). The third round authenticates the reader to the tag, effectively using the counter as a challenge. It also serves as a "confirmation" message indicating that the reader has accepted. Upon successful completion of the protocol, both the tag and the reader update their state to reflect new values for the tag's counter, pseudonym, and mask.

Formal Specification. We now formally describe the protocol. The initialization algorithm Init chooses a uniform key K for the block cipher, sets $\mathsf{ctr} = 0^{n-2}$ (importantly, ctr is always treated as a string of length exactly $n-2$), and computes the pseudonym $IDS = F_K(11 \| \mathsf{ctr})$ and the mask $\mathsf{mask} = F_K(10 \| \mathsf{ctr})$. The tag with identity ID is then given $\mathsf{st} = \langle K, \mathsf{ctr}, IDS, \mathsf{mask} \rangle$, and the reader is given the record $(ID, K, \langle \mathsf{ctr}, IDS, \mathsf{mask} \rangle, \langle \mathsf{ctr}, IDS, \mathsf{mask} \rangle)$.[7]

---

[6] Because messages may be dropped, the counter stored at the reader may be greater than the counter stored by the tag. But the protocol ensures that the difference between the counters is at most one.

[7] At initialization time, the two vectors stored by the reader are redundant; following a successful execution of the protocol, however, the first vector will store values associated with the current counter, while the second will store values associated with the previous counter.

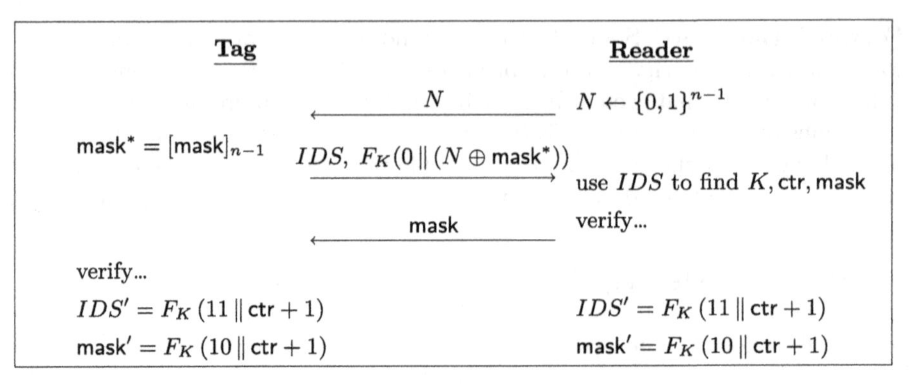

Fig. 1. High-level overview of the protocol. Note that this overview omits important details of the protocol; see the text for a formal specification.

An execution of the protocol between a tag with state $\mathsf{st} = \langle K, \mathsf{ctr}, IDS, \mathsf{mask}\rangle$ and the reader holding a collection $\mathcal{C}$ of records, as described above, proceeds as follows (see Fig. 1):

1. The reader chooses a uniform nonce $N \in \{0,1\}^{n-1}$, and sends it to the tag.
2. Upon receiving the incoming message N, the tag computes $\mathsf{mask}^* = [\mathsf{mask}]_{n-1}$ followed by $C = F_K(0 \,\|\, (N \oplus \mathsf{mask}^*))$, and then sends IDS, C to the reader.
3. Upon receiving IDS, C from a tag, the reader searches $\mathcal{C}$ to find a record corresponding to IDS. This is done in the following way:
   (a) The reader searches $\mathcal{C}$ for a record containing IDS in the third entry. If such a record $r = (ID, K, \langle \mathsf{ctr}, IDS, \mathsf{mask}\rangle, \star)$ exists, the first such record is removed from $\mathcal{C}$ and the reader uses ID, K, ctr, and mask in the rest of the protocol.
   (b) Otherwise, the reader searches $\mathcal{C}$ for a record with IDS in the last entry. If such a record $r = (ID, K, \star, \langle \mathsf{ctr}, IDS, \mathsf{mask}\rangle)$ exists, the first such record is removed from $\mathcal{C}$ and the reader uses ID, K, ctr, and mask in the rest of the protocol.
   (c) If both the above fail, the reader terminates the protocol (without accepting).

   Let $\mathsf{mask}^* = [\mathsf{mask}]_{n-1}$. The reader checks if $F_K(0 \,\|\, (N \oplus \mathsf{mask}^*)) \stackrel{?}{=} C$. If not, it stores the original record r back in $\mathcal{C}$ and terminates (without accepting). Otherwise, it sends $D = \mathsf{mask}$ to the tag. The reader then computes[8] $IDS' = F_K(11 \,\|\, \mathsf{ctr}+1)$ and $\mathsf{mask}' = F_K(10 \,\|\, \mathsf{ctr}+1)$, and stores the (possibly updated) record $(ID, K, \langle \mathsf{ctr}+1, IDS', \mathsf{mask}'\rangle, \langle \mathsf{ctr}, IDS, \mathsf{mask}\rangle)$ in $\mathcal{C}$. Finally, it accepts with local output ID and $\mathsf{sid} = IDS$.
4. Upon receiving D, the tag checks if $\mathsf{mask} \stackrel{?}{=} D$. If not, it terminates (without accepting) and does not update its state. Otherwise, the tag accepts with local output $\mathsf{sid} = IDS$, computes $IDS' = F_K(11 \,\|\, \mathsf{ctr}+1)$ and $\mathsf{mask}' = F_K(10 \,\|\, \mathsf{ctr}+1)$, and updates its state to $\langle K, \mathsf{ctr}+1, IDS', \mathsf{mask}'\rangle$.

[8] If the reader took branch 3(b) then this step is redundant and can be skipped.

It is not hard to verify that the protocol is correct with overwhelming probability, assuming F is a secure block cipher. (A formal proof of correctness follows from the proof of desynchronization resilience given later.)

4 Proofs of Security

We now prove that our protocol satisfies our definitions of security. In our proof, we model F as a pseudorandom function (PRF). Formally, F is (t, q, ϵ)*-secure PRF* if for any attacker $\mathcal{A}$ running in time at most t and making at most q queries to its oracle, it holds that

$$\left|\Pr[\mathcal{A}^{F_K(\cdot)} = 1] - \Pr[\mathcal{A}^{f(\cdot)} = 1]\right| \leq \epsilon,$$

where the first probability is taken over uniform choice of key K, and the second probability is taken over uniform choice of a function f mapping n-bit inputs to n-bit outputs.

For our proofs it will be useful to introduce the following notation. At any given point of the experiment, and for ID the identity of some tag initialized during the experiment, let $\mathsf{ctr}^{\mathcal{T}}_{ID}$ denote the value of ctr held by the tag with identity ID, and let $\mathsf{ctr}^{\mathcal{R}}_{ID}$ be the value of ctr held by the reader in the third entry of the record associated with the tag with identity ID (i.e., the reader stores a record of the form $(ID, \star, \langle \mathsf{ctr}^{\mathcal{R}}_{ID}, \star, \star\rangle, \star)$). We refer to the time period when $\mathsf{ctr}^{\mathcal{T}}_{ID} = i$ as the *ith tag-epoch for the tag with identity* ID; note that these epochs (for some fixed ID) are non-overlapping and contiguous. Finally, for $\mathsf{mask} \in \{0,1\}^n$ we let $\mathsf{mask}^* \stackrel{\text{def}}{=} [\mathsf{mask}]_{n-1}$.

4.1 Mutual Authentication

We begin by considering mutual authentication, arguably the most important property.

Theorem 1. *Fix an attacker $\mathcal{A}$ such that running the mutual authentication experiment with $\mathcal{A}$ takes time t. Let I denote an upper bound on the number of tags initialized by $\mathcal{A}$, and let t_{tag}, $t_{reader} < 2^{n-2}$ be upper bounds on the number of sessions initiated by $\mathcal{A}$ at tags and the reader, respectively. If F is a $(t,\ 2 + 3\cdot(t_{tag} + t_{reader}),\ \epsilon)$-secure PRF, then the probability that mutual authentication fails is at most*

$$\left(2\,t_{tag}^2 + 4\,t_{reader}t_{tag} + t_{tag} + t_{reader}\right) \cdot 2^{-n} + I \cdot \epsilon\,.$$

Proof. We consider a sequence of experiments $\mathsf{Expt}_0, \mathsf{Expt}_1, \mathsf{Expt}_2$, where Expt_0 corresponds to the one described in Sects. 2 and 2.3. We let $\Pr_i[\cdot]$ denote the probability of an event in Expt_i.

Let tFail be the event that tag authentication fails. Let rFail be the event that there is an accepting session at some tag with identity ID having some sid, but there is no accepting instance at the reader with the same values ID, sid. Let rFail' be the event that there are two accepting sessions at some tag that have the same sid; by definition, $\mathsf{rFail} \vee \mathsf{rFail}'$ is the event that reader authentication fails. Since F is a block cipher, and hence $F_K(11\|\mathsf{ctr}) \neq F_K(11\|\mathsf{ctr}')$ when $\mathsf{ctr} \neq \mathsf{ctr}'$, it is immediate that $\Pr_0[\mathsf{rFail}'] = 0$. Defining $\delta_i = \Pr_i[\mathsf{tFail} \vee \mathsf{rFail}]$, we are thus left with bounding δ_0, the probability with which mutual authentication fails in Expt_0. We assume the experiment ends as soon as either tFail or rFail occur.

Expt_1 is the same as Expt_0 except that for each tag with identity ID we replace the block cipher F_K associated with that tag with a function f_{ID} chosen uniformly and independently from the set of all functions with domain and range $\{0,1\}^n$. Since at most I different tags are initialized during the experiment, and the block cipher F_K associated with any particular tag is evaluated on at most $2 + 3 \cdot (t_{tag} + t_{reader})$ different inputs during the course of Expt_0 (in fact, a tighter bound is possible), it follows from security of F that $|\delta_1 - \delta_0| \leq I \cdot \epsilon$.

Let $\mathsf{mask}_{ID,i} \stackrel{\text{def}}{=} f_{ID}(10\|i)$ and $IDS_{ID,i} \stackrel{\text{def}}{=} f_{ID}(11\|i)$ (where i is encoded using $n-2$ bits). In Expt_2 we defer choice of $\mathsf{mask}_{ID,i}$ until the reader accepts with output $ID, IDS_{ID,i}$ and returns $\mathsf{mask}_{ID,i}$ as the final message of the protocol; when that happens we say $\mathsf{mask}_{ID,i}$ becomes *defined.* Thus, $\mathsf{mask}_{ID,i}$ is *undefined* until $\mathsf{ctr}^{\mathcal{R}}_{ID} > i$. For every undefined $\mathsf{mask}_{ID,i}$, we maintain a set $\mathcal{L}_{ID,i}$, initially empty, containing pairs of the form (N, C); see below. It is convenient to also maintain a set $\mathcal{L}_{ID}$, initially empty, containing pairs of the form (x, C). Whenever a query $f_{ID}(0\|x)$ is made, if there is a pair of the form (x, C) in $\mathcal{L}_{ID}$ we return C; otherwise, we choose uniform $C \in \{0,1\}^n$, return C, and add (x, C) to $\mathcal{L}_{ID}$.

We now formally describe how Expt_2 is implemented by describing how the oracles are modified:

- $\mathsf{Init}(ID)$ computes $IDS_{ID,0}$ as before, but now simply lets $\mathsf{mask}_{ID,0}$ be a formal variable.
- Consider an oracle call of the form $\mathsf{Send}_{\mathcal{T}}(ID, \mathsf{msg})$ and say $\mathsf{ctr}^{\mathcal{T}}_{ID} = i$. If $\mathsf{mask}_{ID,i}$ is defined, then the oracle call is answered as before. Otherwise, there are two cases depending on whether the incoming message msg is the first or last message of the protocol:
  - In response to an initial message N, if there is a pair of the form (N, C) in $\mathcal{L}_{ID,i}$ then return C; otherwise, choose a uniform $C \in \{0,1\}^n$, return C, and add (N, C) to $\mathcal{L}_{ID,i}$.
  - If msg is the third message of the protocol, terminate without accepting.
- Oracle calls $\mathsf{Send}_{\mathcal{R}}(\mathsf{inst}, \mathsf{start})$ are answered as before. Oracle calls of the form $\mathsf{Send}_{\mathcal{R}}(\mathsf{inst}, (\mathsf{IDS}, \mathsf{C}))$ are answered in the following way. Let N be the initial message sent by instance inst of the reader. The reader searches $\mathcal{C}$ for a record containing IDS as in Expt_1. If it finds no record, it terminates without accepting. If there is a matching record r, then remove that record from $\mathcal{C}$ and let ID and $\mathsf{ctr} = i$ be the corresponding values that will be used for the rest of the execution. There are two cases:
  - Say $\mathsf{mask}_{ID,i}$ is defined (in which case $\mathsf{ctr}^{\mathcal{R}}_{ID} = i + 1$), and let $x = N \oplus \mathsf{mask}^*_{ID,i}$. If $(x, C) \notin \mathcal{L}_{ID}$, then terminate without accepting. Otherwise,

accept with output ID, IDS and return the final message $\mathsf{mask}_{ID,i}$. In either scenario, store r back in $\mathcal{C}$.

- Say $\mathsf{mask}_{ID,i}$ is undefined (in which case $\mathsf{ctr}_{ID}^{\mathcal{R}} = i$). If $(N, C) \notin \mathcal{L}_{ID,i}$, then terminate without accepting and store r back in $\mathcal{C}$. Otherwise, sample uniform $\mathsf{mask}_{ID,i} \in \{0,1\}^n$ (thus defining $\mathsf{mask}_{ID,i}$), return $\mathsf{mask}_{ID,i}$ as the response to the oracle query, and accept with output ID, IDS. Also compute $IDS' = f_{ID}(11\|i+1)$ and store the updated record $(ID, \langle i+1, IDS', \perp\rangle, \langle i, IDS, \mathsf{mask}_{ID,i}\rangle)$ in $\mathcal{C}$. (Note that $\mathsf{mask}_{ID,i+1}$ is undefined.) Finally, for every pair of the form $(N, C) \in \mathcal{L}_{ID,i}$, if there is no pair of the form $(N \oplus \mathsf{mask}^*_{ID,i}, \star)$ in $\mathcal{L}_{ID}$ then add $(N \oplus \mathsf{mask}^*_{ID,i}, C)$ to $\mathcal{L}_{ID}$. Finally, set $\mathcal{L}_{ID,i} = \emptyset$.

– Execute queries are handled by repeated invocation of $\mathsf{Send}_{\mathcal{R}}$ and $\mathsf{Send}_{\mathcal{T}}$, in the natural way.

At the end of the experiment it is useful to explicitly define any undefined values $\mathsf{mask}_{ID,i}$ and then, for every $(N, C) \in \mathcal{L}_{ID,i}$, if there is no pair of the form $(N \oplus \mathsf{mask}^*_{ID,i}, \star)$ in $\mathcal{L}_{ID}$ then add $(N \oplus \mathsf{mask}^*_{ID,i}, C)$ to $\mathcal{L}_{ID}$. Finally, for each ID, x for which there is no pair of the form $(x, \star)$ in $\mathcal{L}_{ID}$, choose uniform C and add (x, C) to $\mathcal{L}_{ID}$.

The differences between Expt_1 and Expt_2 occur due to the following events:

1. There is an oracle call $\mathsf{Send}_{\mathcal{T}}(ID, N)$ when $\mathsf{ctr}_{ID}^{\mathcal{T}} = i$ and $\mathsf{mask}_{ID,i}$ is undefined, and this represents the first message of the protocol. A pair (N, C) is added to $\mathcal{L}_{ID,i}$ but then, when $\mathsf{mask}_{ID,i}$ becomes defined, there is already a pair of the form $(N \oplus \mathsf{mask}^*_{ID,i}, \star)$ in $\mathcal{L}_{ID}$.

   For each (N, C) in one of the sets $\mathcal{L}_{ID,i}$, the probability (over choice of $\mathsf{mask}_{ID,i}$) that there is a pair of the form $(N \oplus \mathsf{mask}^*_{ID,i}, \star)$ in $\mathcal{L}_{ID}$ is exactly $|\mathcal{L}_{ID}|/2^{n-1}$. Since at most t_{tag} pairs are added to all the sets $\mathcal{L}_{ID,i}$, and there are at most t_{tag} pairs in all the sets $\mathcal{L}_{ID}$, the probability of this event is at most $t_{tag}^2/2^{n-1}$.
2. There is an oracle call $\mathsf{Send}_{\mathcal{T}}(ID, D)$ when $\mathsf{ctr}_{ID}^{\mathcal{T}} = i$ and $\mathsf{mask}_{ID,i}$ is undefined, and this represents the final message of the protocol. Then, when $\mathsf{mask}_{ID,i}$ becomes defined, it holds that $\mathsf{mask}_{ID,i} = D$.

   The probability of this event is easily seen to be at most $t_{tag}/2^n$.
3. There is an oracle call $\mathsf{Send}_{\mathcal{R}}(\mathsf{inst}, (\mathsf{IDS}, \mathsf{C}))$ when $\mathsf{mask}_{ID,i}$ is defined and $(x, C) \notin \mathcal{L}_{ID}$ at that time (so the oracle rejects), but at the end of the experiment $(x, C) \in \mathcal{L}_{ID}$.

   Assuming the first event (above) does not occur, for each x exactly one pair of the form $(x, \star)$ is added to each set $\mathcal{L}_{ID}$. For any oracle call $\mathsf{Send}_{\mathcal{R}}(\mathsf{inst}, (\mathsf{IDS}, \mathsf{C}))$ when $\mathsf{mask}_{ID,i}$ is defined and $(x, C) \notin \mathcal{L}_{ID}$ at that time, the probability that $(x, C) \in \mathcal{L}_{ID}$ at the end of the experiment is maximized if every pair in $\mathcal{L}_{ID,i+1}$ is of the form $(\star, C)$. In that case, $(x, C) \in \mathcal{L}_{ID}$ at the end of the experiment if either (1) for some $(N, C) \in \mathcal{L}_{ID,i+1}$ it holds that $N \oplus \mathsf{mask}^*_{ID,i+1} = x$ (this occurs with probability $|\mathcal{L}_{ID,i+1}|/2^{n-1} \leq t_{tag}/2^{n-1}$ over choice of $\mathsf{mask}_{ID,i+1}$), or (2) when the pair (x, C') is added to $\mathcal{L}_{ID}$ it holds that $C' = C$ (assuming the former does not occur, this occurs with probability $1/2^n$). Taking a union bound over all instances of the reader, the probability of this event is at most $t_{reader} \cdot \left(t_{tag}/2^{n-1} + 1/2^n\right)$.

4. There is an oracle call $\mathsf{Send}_{\mathcal{R}}(\mathsf{inst}, (\mathsf{IDS}, \mathsf{C}))$ when $\mathsf{mask}_{ID,i}$ is undefined and $(N, C) \notin \mathcal{L}_{ID,i}$ at that time (so the oracle rejects), but at the end of the experiment $(N \oplus \mathsf{mask}^*_{ID,i}, C) \in \mathcal{L}_{ID}$.

   This case is like the previous one. In fact, since each Send_R query is relevant to either this case or the previous one, the probability that either occurs (assuming the first event does not occur) is at most $t_{reader} \cdot \left(t_{tag}/2^{n-1} + 1/2^n\right)$.

Summarizing, we have

$$|\delta_2 - \delta_1| \leq \left(2t_{tag}^2 + t_{tag} + 2t_{reader}t_{tag} + t_{reader}\right) \cdot 2^{-n}.$$

It is easily observed that reader authentication cannot fail in Expt_2, and so we turn to consideration of the probability with which tag authentication fails. For an instance inst of the reader that has sent an initial message N at some time t_1 but has not yet received the second message of the protocol, we say that instance is *vulnerable* if for some ID with $\mathsf{ctr}_{ID}^{\mathcal{R}} = i$ either (1) there is a pair of the form (N, C) in $\mathcal{L}_{ID,i}$ or (2) there is a pair of the form $(N \oplus \mathsf{mask}^*_{ID,i-1}, C)$ in $\mathcal{L}_{ID}$. Observe that tag authentication can only possibly fail in Expt_2 for a vulnerable instance. Moreover, the *first* time tag authentication fails—say, for an instance of the reader that accepts with output ID, IDS—must be for an instance that was vulnerable the moment it sent its initial message N. (The only other possibilities are that the instance became vulnerable after sending its initial message due to (1) a change in $\mathcal{L}_{ID}$ or $\mathcal{L}_{ID,i}$, or (2) an update to the collection $\mathcal{C}$ of records the reader holds. But either of those can only occur if the attacker queries $\mathsf{Send}_{\mathcal{T}}(ID, \star)$ or $\mathsf{Execute}(ID)$, in which case tag authentication holds for the instance in question.) It is easy to see that the probability that the N chosen as the initial message by some instance makes that instance vulnerable is at most $(|\mathcal{L}_{ID}| + |\mathcal{L}_{ID,i}|)/2^{n-1} \leq t_{tag}/2^{n-1}$. A union bound over all $\mathsf{Send}_{\mathcal{R}}$ queries shows that the probability that tag authentication fails is at most $t_{reader}t_{tag}/2^{n-1}$. □

4.2 Desynchronization Resilience

The proof of desynchronization resilience uses many of the ideas from the previous proof.

Theorem 2. *Fix an attacker $\mathcal{A}$ such that running the desynchronization experiment with $\mathcal{A}$ takes time t. Let I be an upper bound on the number of tags initialized by $\mathcal{A}$, and let t_{tag}, $t_{reader} < 2^{n-2}$ be upper bounds on the number of sessions initiated by $\mathcal{A}$ at tags and the reader, respectively. If F is a $(t, 2 + 3 \cdot (t_{tag} + t_{reader}), \epsilon)$-secure PRF, the probability that desynchronization occurs is at most*

$$\left(2\,I^2 + 3\,I \cdot t_{reader} + 2t_{tag}^2 + 2t_{reader}t_{tag} + t_{reader} + t_{tag}\right) \cdot 2^{-n} + I \cdot \epsilon.$$

Proof. Let Expt_0 be the experiment defined in Sect. 2, and for an experiment Expt_i let δ_i denote the probability with which desynchronization occurs in Expt_i. As in the proof of Theorem 1, we consider an experiment Expt_1 that is identical to Expt_0 except that, for each tag with identity ID, we replace the block cipher F_K associated with that tag with a function f_{ID} chosen uniformly from the set of all functions with domain and range $\{0,1\}^n$. As previously, we have $|\delta_1 - \delta_0| \leq I \cdot \epsilon$.

Consider an honest execution in Expt_1 between the reader and the tag with identity ID holding state $\mathsf{ctr}, IDS, \mathsf{mask}$. There are two ways desynchronization can occur: either the reader has more than one record containing IDS, or the reader has no records containing IDS.

It is easy to bound the probability of the first event. At any given point in time, the reader stores at most I records, each of which contains at most two IDS values. When the reader accepts, it computes at most one new IDS value; since that value is a uniform n-bit string, the probability that it is equal to any of the existing IDS values stored by the reader is at most $2I/2^n$. Taking a union bound over the IDS values generated during tag initialization as well as the number of sessions initialized at the reader shows that the probability that the reader ever stores two equal IDS values is at most $2I \cdot (I + t_{reader})/2^n$.

The second event occurs if, for some ID, we have $\mathsf{ctr}_{ID}^{\mathcal{R}} > \mathsf{ctr}_{ID}^{\mathcal{T}} + 1$ or $\mathsf{ctr}_{ID}^{\mathcal{T}} > \mathsf{ctr}_{ID}^{\mathcal{R}}$. The only way the first case can occur is if at some point $\mathcal{A}$ sends the reader a message IDS, C such that $IDS = IDS_{ID,i} \stackrel{\text{def}}{=} f_{ID}(11\|i)$ for some ID, even though $\mathsf{ctr}_{ID}^{\mathcal{T}} < i$ and so the tag with identity ID never output a message containing $IDS_{ID,i}$. Since $IDS_{ID,i}$ is a uniform n-bit string, the probability this occurs in any particular interaction with the reader is at most $I/2^n$, and the probability that it occurs at any point is at most $t_{reader}I/2^n$.

On the other hand, if $\mathsf{ctr}_{ID}^{\mathcal{T}} > \mathsf{ctr}_{ID}^{\mathcal{R}}$ then reader authentication has failed. As in the proof of Theorem 1, the probability that this occurs is at most $\left(2t_{tag}^2 + t_{tag} + 2t_{reader}t_{tag} + t_{reader}\right) \cdot 2^{-n}$. This completes the proof. □

4.3 Tag Anonymity

Theorem 3. *Fix an attacker $\mathcal{A}$ such that running the anonymity experiment with $\mathcal{A}$ takes time t. Let I be an upper bound on the number of tags initialized by $\mathcal{A}$, and let $t_{tag}, t_{execute} < 2^{n-2}$ be upper bounds on the number of $\mathsf{Send}_{\mathcal{T}}^*$ and $\mathsf{Execute}/\mathsf{Execute}^*$ queries, respectively, made by $\mathcal{A}$. If F is a $(t, 2 + 3 \cdot (t_{tag} + t_{execute}), \epsilon)$-secure PRF, then the deanonymization advantage of $\mathcal{A}$ is at most*

$$\left(2I^2 + 2I \cdot t_{execute} + 2t_{tag}t_{execute}\right) \cdot 2^{-n} + I \cdot \epsilon.$$

Proof. Let Expt_0 be the experiment defined in Sect. 2.4, and for an experiment Expt_i let δ_i be the probability with which $\mathcal{A}$ succeeds in that experiment. As in the previous proofs, we first consider an experiment Expt_1 that is identical to Expt_0 except that, for each tag with identity ID, we replace the block cipher F_K associated with that tag with a function f_{ID} chosen uniformly from the set of all functions with domain and range $\{0,1\}^n$. As previously, we have $|\delta_1 - \delta_0| \leq I \cdot \epsilon$.

Expt_2 is the same as Expt_1 except that it terminates, and $\mathcal{A}$ does not succeed, if the reader ever stores two equal IDS values. As in the proof of Theorem 2, we have $|\delta_2 - \delta_1| \leq 2I \cdot (I + t_{execute})/2^n$. Note that desynchronization cannot occur during the first phase of Expt_2.

Let ID_0, ID_1 be the two identities output by the attacker at the end of the first phase. For convenience, let f_0, f_1 denote f_{ID_0}, f_{ID_1}, and let $IDS_{0,i} = f_0(11\|i)$, $\mathsf{mask}_{0,i} = f_0(10\|i)$, $IDS_{1,i} = f_1(11\|i)$, and $\mathsf{mask}_{1,i} = f_1(10\|i)$.

Say $\mathsf{ctr}^{\mathcal{T}}_{ID_0} = i_0$ and $\mathsf{ctr}^{\mathcal{T}}_{ID_1} = i_1$ at the end of the first phase. Since desynchronization does not occur, we have $\mathsf{ctr}^{\mathcal{R}}_{ID_0} = i_0$ and $\mathsf{ctr}^{\mathcal{R}}_{ID_1} = i_1$ at that time as well. Observe that the first phase of Expt_2 does not depend on $IDS_{0,j}$ or $\mathsf{mask}_{0,j}$ for $j \geq i_0$, and similarly does not depend on $IDS_{1,j}$ or $\mathsf{mask}_{1,j}$ for $j \geq i_1$. Moreover, the second phase of Expt_2 does not depend on $IDS_{0,j}$ or $\mathsf{mask}_{0,j}$ for $j < i_0$, and similarly does not depend on $IDS_{1,j}$ or $\mathsf{mask}_{1,j}$ for $j < i_0$. (This holds regardless of the value of the uniform bit b.) Thus, the first and second phases of Expt_2 are independent unless there is a query of the form $f_b(0\|x)$ made in the second phase for which either $f_0(0\|x)$ or $f_1(0\|x)$ was made in the first phase. As in the analysis of the transition from Expt_1 to Expt_2 in the proof of Theorem 1 (only the first event is relevant here), the probability with which that occurs is at most $t_{tag} \cdot t_{execute}/2^{n-1}$. This completes the proof. □

For completeness, we describe two attacks that are outside our formal definition, but may nevertheless be a concern in some deployments of the protocol.

First, there is an obvious attack exploiting the fact that the tag repeatedly sends the same IDS value until it successfully completes an execution. Thus, for example, an attacker can interact with an unknown tag by sending an arbitrary nonce N and receiving a response IDS, C; if the attacker later interacts with that tag again, or even passively eavesdrops on an execution between that tag and the reader, it will observe the same IDS value being sent (so long as the tag had not successfully completed an execution in the interim) and thus know—with overwhelming probability—that the same tag is involved in the execution.

There is also a man-in-the-middle attack that can be used to deanonymize tags. Assume the attacker has eavesdropped on an execution of some known tag, and let the transcript of that execution be $N, (IDS, C), \mathsf{mask}$. The attacker thus learns that $C = F_K(0 \,\|\, (N \oplus \mathsf{mask}^*))$, where K is the key held by the tag. Say the attacker then interacts with an unknown tag at a later point in time, and wants to determine if this tag is the same one as before. To do so, it can act as a man-in-the-middle during an execution between that unknown tag and the reader, forwarding all messages except the last. From the final message sent by the reader (but not forwarded to the tag), the attacker learns the value $\overline{\mathsf{mask}}$ currently held by the tag. The attacker can then send initial message $N' = N \oplus \mathsf{mask}^* \oplus \overline{\mathsf{mask}}^*$ to the unknown tag; if the tag is the same one as before, then it will respond with some value IDS' along with

$$C' = F_K(0 \,\|\, (N' \oplus \overline{\mathsf{mask}}^*)) = F_K(0 \,\|\, (N \oplus \mathsf{mask}^*)) = C.$$

On the other hand, a different tag will send an entirely unrelated value C' (which is unlikely to be equal to C). Thus, the attacker can learn—with overwhelming probability—whether it is interacting with the same tag as before.

Acknowledgments. I thank Kelley Burgin for suggesting the problem, and Doug Shors, Laurie Law, and Louis Wingers for their encouragement as well as their helpful comments on earlier drafts. This work was performed under a consultancy agreement with University Technical Services, Inc. on behalf of the National Security Agency.

References

1. Avoine, G.: Adversary model for radio frequency identification. Technical report LASEC-REPORT-2005-001, Swiss Federal Institute of Technology (EPFL), Security and Cryptography Laboratory (LASEC) (2005)
2. Avoine, G.: RFID Security & Privacy Lounge. http://www.avoine.net/rfid
3. Avoine, G., Bingöl, M.A., Carpent, X., Yalcin, S.B.O.: Privacy-friendly authentication in RFID systems: on sublinear protocols based on symmetric-key cryptography. IEEE Trans. Mob. Comput. **12**(10), 2037–2049 (2013)
4. Avoine, G., Carpent, X., Martin, B.: Privacy-friendly synchronized ultralightweight authentication protocols in the storm. J. Netw. Comput. Appl. **35**, 826–843 (2012)
5. Bellare, M., Rogaway, P.: Entity authentication and key distribution. In: Stinson, D.R. (ed.) CRYPTO 1993. LNCS, vol. 773, pp. 232–249. Springer, Heidelberg (1994). https://doi.org/10.1007/3-540-48329-2_21
6. Boyd, C., Davies, G.T., de Kock, B., Gellert, K., Jager, T., Millerjord, L.: Symmetric key exchange with full forward security and robust synchronization. In: Tibouchi, M., Wang, H. (eds.) ASIACRYPT 2021. LNCS, vol. 13093, pp. 681–710. Springer, Cham (2021). https://doi.org/10.1007/978-3-030-92068-5_23
7. Burmester, M., Munilla, J.: Lightweight RFID authentication with forward and backward security. ACM Trans. Inf. Syst. Secur. **14**(1), 11 (2011)
8. Chien, H.-Y.: SASI: a new ultralightweight RFID authentication protocol providing strong authentication and strong integrity. IEEE Trans. Dependable Secure Comput. **4**(4), 337–340 (2007)
9. Hanatanil, Y., Ohkubo, M., Matsuo, S., Sakiyama, K., Ohta, K.: A study on computational formal verification for practical cryptographic protocol: the case of synchronous RFID authentication. In: Danezis, G., Dietrich, S., Sako, K. (eds.) FC 2011. LNCS, vol. 7126, pp. 70–87. Springer, Heidelberg (2012). https://doi.org/10.1007/978-3-642-29889-9_7
10. Juels, A., Weis, S.: Defining strong privacy for RFID. In: International Conference on Pervasive Computing and Communications (PerCom) (2007)
11. hkubo, M., Suzuki, K., Kinoshita, S.: Cryptographic approach to "Privacy-Friendly" tags. In: RFID Privacy Workshop (2003)
12. Paise, R.I., Vaudenay, S.: Mutual authentication in RFID: security and privacy. In: Proceedings of the 2008 ACM Symposium on Information, Computer and Communications Security (ASIACCS), pp. 292–299. ACM (2008)
13. Peris-Lopez, P., Hernandez-Castro, J.C., Tapiador, J.M.E., Ribagorda, A.: Advances in ultralightweight cryptography for low-cost RFID tags: gossamer protocol. In: Chung, K.-I., Sohn, K., Yung, M. (eds.) WISA 2008. LNCS, vol. 5379, pp. 56–68. Springer, Heidelberg (2009). https://doi.org/10.1007/978-3-642-00306-6_5

14. Song, B., Mitchell, C.J.: RFID authentication protocol for low-cost tags. In: Proceedings of the 1st ACM Conference on Wireless Network Security (WISEC), pp. 140–147. ACM (2008)
15. Tsudik, G.: YA-TRAP: yet another trivial RFID authentication protocol. In: International Conference on Pervasive Computing and Communications (PerCom) (2006)
16. Vaudenay, S.: On privacy models for RFID. In: Kurosawa, K. (ed.) ASIACRYPT 2007. LNCS, vol. 4833, pp. 68–87. Springer, Heidelberg (2007). https://doi.org/10.1007/978-3-540-76900-2_5
17. Yeh, K.H., Lo, N.W., Winata, E.: An efficient ultralightweight authentication protocol for RFID systems. In: Workshop in RFID Security—RFIDSec Asia, vol. 4 of Cryptology and Information Security, IOC Press (2010)

Anonymous Authenticated Communication

Fabio Banfi(✉) and Ueli Maurer

Department of Computer Science, ETH Zurich, 8092 Zurich, Switzerland
{fabio.banfi,maurer}@inf.ethz.ch

Abstract. Anonymity and authenticity are apparently conflicting goals. Anonymity means *hiding* a party's identity whereas authenticity means *proving* a party's identity. So how can a set of senders authenticate their messages without revealing their identity? Despite the paradoxical nature of this problem, there exist many cryptographic schemes designed to achieve both goals simultaneously, in some form.

This paper provides a composable treatment of communication channels that achieve different forms of anonymity and authenticity. More specifically, three channel functionalities for many senders and one receiver are introduced which provide some trade-off between authenticity and anonymity (of the senders). For each of them, composably realizing it is proved to corresponds to the use of a certain type of cryptographic scheme, namely (1) a new type of scheme which we call *bilateral signatures* (syntactically related to designated verifier signatures), (2) *partial signatures*, and (3) *ring signatures*. This treatment hence provides composable semantics for (game-based) security definitions for these types of schemes.

The results of this paper can be interpreted as the dual of the work by Kohlweiss et al. (PETS 2013), where composable notions for anonymous confidential communication were introduced and related to the security definitions of certain types of public-key encryption schemes, and where the treatment of anonymous authenticated communication was stated as an open problem.

Keywords: anonymous authenticity · composable security · bilateral signatures · partial signatures · anonymous signatures · ring signatures

1 Introduction

1.1 Background and Motivation

When studying the security of public-key encryption (PKE) it is natural to consider a setting with one sender and many receivers, each generating its own key-pair and authentically transmitting the public key to the sender. Then a reasonable concern is whether ciphertexts subsequently generated by the sender for distinct receivers are (computationally) indistinguishable. This captures the intuitive notion of receiver anonymity from the standpoint of an eavesdropper,

C. Galdi and S. Jarecki (Eds.): SCN 2022, LNCS 13409, pp. 289–312, 2022.
https://doi.org/10.1007/978-3-031-14791-3_13

and is formalized by the security definition of *key-indistinguishability*, first proposed by Bellare et al. [5]. Almost a decade later, Abdalla et al. [1] introduced another related notion for PKE, *robustness*, which intuitively captures the fact that ciphertexts can only be meaningfully decrypted using the correct corresponding private key, meaning that trying to decrypt with a wrong key results in an error.

It turns out that this further property is crucially needed in conjunction with key-indistinguishability in order to provide a "usable" form of anonymous PKE, and this has been highlighted by Kohlweiss et al. [11] by showing that both properties, together with IND-CCA security, are needed in order for a PKE scheme to enhance an anonymous insecure broadcast channel into an anonymous confidential broadcast channel. Importantly, their work also highlights how key-indistinguishability is a security notion that exclusively *preserves* anonymity, rather than "creating" it, whereas IND-CCA *lifts* insecurity to confidentiality, thus "creating" more security along the secrecy axis.

On the other hand, for the security of digital signature schemes (DSS) the natural setting to consider is the dual of the above: Many senders, each authentically publishing their public verification key, send messages to the same party, the receiver. Here too it is reasonable to consider anonymity (preservation), of the sender in this case, from the standpoint of an eavesdropper. But in this setting it is additionally also meaningful to study the stronger notion of anonymity from the standpoint of the receiver, that is, we might want the senders to remain anonymous not only towards an external attacker (the eavesdropper), but towards the receiver as well. We distinguish those two separate notions of anonymity in this setting as *external* and *internal*, respectively, where clearly the latter implies the former (but not vice versa). However, unlike for PKE, the situation is arguably more intricate for DSS; in fact, providing external anonymity alone already appears paradoxical: How can we guarantee (computational) indistinguishability of signatures, when in the usual application of DSS it is assumed that an eavesdropper has access to the corresponding message as well as all possible verification keys, and could therefore easily distinguish signatures generated with different keys by simply verifying the signature on the message against all keys?

A direct consequence of this apparent dilemma is that for the setting discussed above, the standard syntactic definition of a DSS cannot possibly achieve any meaningful form of anonymity, as we prove later within our framework. This is in fact the reason why in the cryptographic literature there exist a multitude of different security notions capturing various forms of anonymity in relation to syntactic modifications of the usual DSS definition. A non-exhaustive list of examples includes: group signatures [8], ring signatures [17], anonymous signatures [9,19,21], and partial signatures [6,18].

In this work we take an alternative approach in order to treat the apparently oxymoronic problem of achieving anonymous authenticity: Instead of creating new syntactic modifications of DSS and ad-hoc game-based security definitions thereof, we begin from a more abstract point of view and identify possible applications where those two goals simultaneously come into play, and directly define security in a composable fashion, using the framework of constructive cryptography of Maurer and Renner [13,15], requiring that a protocol realizes such an application relying on the public-key infrastructure (PKI). More precisely, we introduce three novel composable security notions for generic protocols, and then present concrete protocols satisfying each of those. The first protocol makes use of a novel cryptographic scheme, dubbed *bilateral signatures*, while the other two employ *partial signatures* and *ring signatures*, respectively.

1.2 Related Work

The goal of this work is to fill a blank in the composable treatment of anonymous *communication.*[1] In order to illustrate this, we need to first briefly and informally introduce some key concept that we will elaborate later.

As opposed to game-based security definitions, composable security definitions in constructive cryptography are simulation-based; on an abstract level, they are statements asserting that a cryptographic protocol constructs an ideal resource from a set of real ones, where a resource is a mathematical object capturing a certain functionality, and thus has interfaces through which parties, honest and dishonest, can interact. In more detail, for the simple setting with two honest parties—the sender and the receiver—and a dishonest party—the adversary—we consider a real resource $\mathbf{R}$ and an ideal resource $\mathbf{S}$, both having the same set of interfaces, S for the sender, R for the receiver, and E for the adversary. Then we say that a protocol π executed by the honest parties constructs $\mathbf{S}$ from $\mathbf{R}$, informally denoted as $\mathbf{R} \overset{\pi}{\Longmapsto} \mathbf{S}$, if there exists a simulator sim such that $\pi^{S,R}\mathbf{R}$ (the resource resulting from applying the protocol at the honest interfaces of the real resource) is indistinguishable from $\mathsf{sim}^E\mathbf{S}$ (the resource resulting from applying the simulator at the dishonest interface of the ideal resource).

Typical resources used in this simple setting are the *insecure channel* INS (which leaks everything the sender inputs to the adversary, and allows the latter to inject messages), the *authentic channel* AUT, the *confidential channel* CNF, and the secure (i.e., authentic and confidential) channel SEC, all allowing to send multiple messages. But in order to capture anonymity, we are interested in a setting where there are multiple parties. More concretely, we consider resources with n senders $S_1, \ldots, S_n$ and one receiver R (for which we use the intuitive notation ${}_{n\to 1}$), and resources with one sender and n receivers (for which we use the intuitive notation ${}_{1\to n}$). If one considers the above channels, a natural approach to extend them to this setting would be to simply compose them in parallel, but this would imply that the leakage now includes the identities of the sender S_i or the receiver R_i, since the individual channels are distinguishable by definition by the adversary. In the following table we summarize the guarantees provided by resources combining such channels (which we also denote as channels) in terms of what is leaked to the adversary relative to a message m input by a sender and whether the adversary can inject messages (such that the receiver can not distinguish whether the message was sent by the sender S or the adversary E).

[1] In particular, we are not directly considering (anonymous) *entity* authentication.

Channel Name	Symbol	Leaked	Inject	Symbol	Leaked	Inject
Insecure	$\mathsf{INS}_{n\to 1}$	S_i, m	yes	$\mathsf{INS}_{1\to n}$	R_i, m	yes
Authentic	$\mathsf{AUT}_{n\to 1}$	S_i, m	no	$\mathsf{AUT}_{1\to n}$	R_i, m	no
Confidential	$\mathsf{CNF}_{n\to 1}$	$S_i, \|m\|$	yes	$\mathsf{CNF}_{1\to n}$	$R_i, \|m\|$	yes
Secure	$\mathsf{SEC}_{n\to 1}$	$S_i, \|m\|$	no	$\mathsf{SEC}_{1\to n}$	$R_i, \|m\|$	no

It seems natural that truly *anonymous* versions of these channels, that is, channels capturing sender and receiver anonymity, must *not* leak such identities to the adversary. Therefore we enhance the above channels with these guarantees (adding the prefix A- for *anonymous*), and summarize the new channels in the following table (note that in $\mathsf{A\text{-}AUT}_{n\to 1}$, $\mathsf{A\text{-}CNF}_{n\to 1}$, and $\mathsf{A\text{-}SEC}_{n\to 1}$, the receiver also obtains the identity S_i of the sender, along with the message m).

Channel Name	Symbol		Leaked	Inject
	Sender anon.	Receiver anon.		
Anonymous & Insecure	$\mathsf{A\text{-}INS}_{n\to 1}$	$\mathsf{A\text{-}INS}_{1\to n}$	m	yes
Anonymous & Authentic	$\mathsf{A\text{-}AUT}_{n\to 1}$	$\mathsf{A\text{-}AUT}_{1\to n}$	m	no
Anonymous & Confidential	$\mathsf{A\text{-}CNF}_{n\to 1}$	$\mathsf{A\text{-}CNF}_{1\to n}$	$\|m\|$	yes
Anonymous & Secure	$\mathsf{A\text{-}SEC}_{n\to 1}$	$\mathsf{A\text{-}SEC}_{1\to n}$	$\|m\|$	no

Other (non-anonymous) resources that we need in this setting are: $\mathsf{KEY}_{n\leftrightarrow 1}$, which provides each sender with a (different) *shared secret-key* with the receiver; $\mathsf{KEY}_{1\leftrightarrow n}$, which provides each receiver with a shared secret-key with the sender (in both resources, the adversary's interface is inactive); $\mathsf{1\text{-}AUT}_{n\to 1}$, which provides each sender with a (different) *single-use authentic channel* to the receiver; $\mathsf{1\text{-}AUT}_{1\leftarrow n}$, which provides the receiver with n (different) *single-use authentic channels*, one to each of the senders.

We stress again that we are considering anonymity *preservation*, therefore in the following we summarize the previous results from the literature in terms of constructions among the anonymous channels mentioned above (plus shared secret keys and one-time authentic channels). This means that both real and ideal core resources are anonymous, and hence the enhancement of security provided by a construction happens along a different axis (namely confidentiality, authenticity, or both).

- In the symmetric-key setting, two works provide sender anonymous constructions:
  - In [2], Alwen et al. show that for a simple protocol π_{pMAC} based on key-indistinguishable and unforgeable *probabilistic MAC* schemes,

$$[\mathsf{KEY}_{n\leftrightarrow 1}, \mathsf{A\text{-}INS}_{n\to 1}] \xrightarrow{\pi_{\mathsf{pMAC}}} \mathsf{A\text{-}AUT}_{n\to 1}.$$

- In [3], Banfi and Maurer show that for a simple protocol π_{pE} based on key-indistinguishable and IND-CPA *probabilistic encryption* schemes,

$$[\mathsf{KEY}_{n\leftrightarrow 1}, \mathsf{A\text{-}AUT}_{n\rightarrow 1}] \xmapsto{\pi_{\mathsf{pE}}} \mathsf{A\text{-}SEC}_{n\rightarrow 1},$$

and for a simple protocol π_{pAE} based on key-indistinguishable and IND-CCA3 *probabilistic authenticated encryption* schemes,

$$[\mathsf{KEY}_{n\leftrightarrow 1}, \mathsf{A\text{-}INS}_{n\rightarrow 1}] \xmapsto{\pi_{\mathsf{pAE}}} \mathsf{A\text{-}SEC}_{n\rightarrow 1}.$$

- In the public-key setting, Kohlweiss et al. [11] show that for a simple protocol π_{PKE} based on key-indistinguishable and robust IND-CCA *public-key encryption* schemes,

$$[\mathsf{1\text{-}AUT}_{1\leftarrow n}, \mathsf{A\text{-}INS}_{1\rightarrow n}] \xmapsto{\pi_{\mathsf{PKE}}} \mathsf{A\text{-}CNF}_{1\rightarrow n}.$$

So far, no public-key constructions achieving sender anonymity were given, and we fill precisely this gap here, stated as an open problem in [11].

1.3 Contributions

Referring to the above discussion, it is natural to ask whether it is possible to construct $\mathsf{A\text{-}AUT}_{n\rightarrow 1}$ from $\mathsf{1\text{-}AUT}_{n\rightarrow 1}$ and $\mathsf{A\text{-}INS}_{n\rightarrow 1}$, using a protocol based on signature schemes achieving some form of anonymity. But it is rather easy to see that for regular signature schemes, this is impossible. Using an intuitive notation, the first result that we show is in fact that for any such protocol π,

$$[\mathsf{1\text{-}AUT}_{n\rightarrow 1}, \mathsf{A\text{-}INS}_{n\rightarrow 1}] \not\xmapsto{\pi} \mathsf{A\text{-}AUT}_{n\rightarrow 1}, \tag{1}$$

that is, no protocol can construct $\mathsf{A\text{-}AUT}_{n\rightarrow 1}$ from $\mathsf{1\text{-}AUT}_{n\rightarrow 1}$ and $\mathsf{A\text{-}INS}_{n\rightarrow 1}$ *only*. We prove this in the full version [4].

The main goal of this paper is to show how to get around this impossibility result by rethinking what can actually be achieved in this setting. We still did not discuss the guarantees of the receiver: In $\mathsf{A\text{-}AUT}_{n\rightarrow 1}$, while only the message m is leaked to the adversary, the receiver will see both the message m and the sender's identity S_i. Therefore, we identify two natural ways in which we can modify this resource such that we can then make meaningful statements. We see this systematic approach as a further contribution of this paper.

- We introduce the new resource *de-anonymizable authentic channel* $\mathsf{D\text{-}AUT}_{n\rightarrow 1}$, which is similar to $\mathsf{A\text{-}AUT}_{n\rightarrow 1}$, except that it only guarantees authenticity of a sender once it decides to give up its anonymity. In more detail, a sender S_i can send a message m, and both the adversary and the receiver will only see m, but can decide at a later point to leak its identity to both parties, and this capability is not available to the adversary. This channel could be used for example in an anonymous auction, where bids need to be anonymous but the winner is required to later give up its anonymity in order to (authentically) claim the winning bet.

- We also introduce the new ideal resource *receiver-side anonymous authentic channel* $\textsf{RA-AUT}_{n\to 1}$, which is similar to $\textsf{A-AUT}_{n\to 1}$, except that the anonymity of the sender is guaranteed also towards the receiver, not just the adversary. Therefore, $\textsf{RA-AUT}_{n\to 1}$ also captures *internal* anonymity.

In the following table we summarize the guarantees provided by those resources.

Channel Name	Symbol	Leaked	Inject	Received
Anonymous & Authentic	$\textsf{A-AUT}_{n\to 1}$	m	no	S_i, m
De-Anonymizable & Authentic	$\textsf{D-AUT}_{n\to 1}$	$m/(S_i, m)$	$\tilde{m}/$~~$(S_j, \tilde{m})$~~	$m/(S_i, m)$
Receiver-Side Anon. & Authentic	$\textsf{RA-AUT}_{n\to 1}$	m	no	m

We can now summarize our contribution as providing constructions that, compared to (1), (i) use a different set of assumed resources, (ii) realize a different kind of ideal resource, or (iii) both. For (i) we show that a new scheme that we introduce, *bilateral signatures*, can be used to construct $\textsf{A-AUT}_{n\to 1}$ if we further assume a (single-use) authentic channel from the receiver to the senders, $\textsf{1-AUT}_{n\leftarrow 1}$. Informally, we show that

$$[\textsf{1-AUT}_{n\to 1}, \textsf{1-AUT}_{n\leftarrow 1}, \textsf{A-INS}_{n\to 1}] \xmapsto{\pi_{\textsf{BS}}} \textsf{A-AUT}_{n\to 1},$$

which amounts to giving composable semantics to bilateral signatures. For (ii) we show that $\textsf{D-AUT}_{n\to 1}$ can be constructed from the original set of assumed resources from (1) using *partial signatures* from [6,18]. Informally, we show that

$$[\textsf{1-AUT}_{n\to 1}, \textsf{A-INS}_{n\to 1}] \xmapsto{\pi_{\textsf{PS}}} \textsf{D-AUT}_{n\to 1},$$

which amounts to giving composable semantics to partial signatures. Finally, for (iii) we show that $\textsf{RA-AUT}_{n\to 1}$ can be constructed using *ring signatures* [7,17] if instead of $\textsf{1-AUT}_{n\to 1}$, we assume a (single-use) *broadcast authentic channel*, $\textsf{1-AUT}_{n\circlearrowleft 1}$, which from each sender authentically transmits a message to the receiver, as well as all other senders. Informally, we show that

$$[\textsf{1-AUT}_{n\circlearrowleft 1}, \textsf{A-INS}_{n\to 1}] \xmapsto{\pi_{\textsf{RS}}} \textsf{RA-AUT}_{n\to 1},$$

which amounts to giving composable semantics to ring signatures.

1.4 Outline

In Sect. 2 we introduce our notation and the specific version of constructive cryptography used to present our results. We present and relate game-based and composable security notions for *bilateral signatures* in Sect. 3, for *partial signatures* in Sect. 4, and for *ring signatures* in Sect. 5.

2 Preliminaries

2.1 Notation

We write $x, \ldots \leftarrow y$ to assign the value y to variables $x, \ldots$, and $z, \ldots \leftarrow \mathcal{D}$ to assign independently and identically distributed values to variables $z, \ldots$ according to distribution $\mathcal{D}$, where we usually describe $\mathcal{D}$ as a probabilistic function. $\varnothing$ denotes the empty set, $\mathbb{N} \doteq \{0, 1, 2, \ldots\}$ denotes the set of natural numbers, and for $n \in \mathbb{N}$, we use the convention $[n] \doteq \{1, \ldots, n\}$. For a random variable X over a set $\mathcal{X}$, we define $\operatorname{supp} X \doteq \{x \in \mathcal{X} \mid \Pr[X = x] > 0\}$. For a logical statement S, $\mathbb{1}\{S\}$ is 1 if S is true, and 0 otherwise. Finally, for tuples we sometimes abuse notation in the following way: $(x, (y, z)) = (x, y, z)$.

2.2 Constructive Cryptography

In this work we use the composable framework of *constructive cryptography* (CC), originally introduced by Maurer and Renner [13,15], incorporating ideas later exposed in [16] and [10]. At the most abstract level, CC is a theory that allows to define security of cryptographic protocols as statements about *constructions* transforming a number of resources satisfying some real (easier to achieve) *specification* $\mathcal{R}$ into a resource satisfying an ideal (simple and abstract) specification $\mathcal{S}$. In this work we use the version of CC in which a specification $\mathcal{S}$ is simply modeled as a subset of the set of all resources Φ, therefore, $\mathcal{S} \subseteq \Phi$. For a resource $\mathsf{R} \in \Phi$ we will often abuse notation and use the expression R in order to refer to the singleton specification $\{\mathsf{R}\}$.

On this abstract level, we define a *constructor* γ simply as a function $\Phi \to \Phi$, which given a resource $\mathsf{R} \in \Phi$, returns the constructed resource $\gamma(\mathsf{R}) \in \Phi$, and we also consider the natural lift-up $\gamma : 2^{\Phi} \to 2^{\Phi}$ of constructor γ to specifications by extending the definitions to include $\gamma(\mathcal{S}) \doteq \{\gamma(\mathsf{R}) \mid \mathsf{R} \in \mathcal{S}\} \subseteq \Phi$. Therefore, we formalize the concept of *construction* via the subset relation.

Definition 1. *Given specifications* $\mathcal{R}, \mathcal{S} \subseteq \Phi$ *and constructor* $\gamma : \Phi \to \Phi$, γ constructs $\mathcal{R}$ from $\mathcal{S}$, *denoted* $\mathcal{R} \xrightarrow{\gamma} \mathcal{S}$, *if and only if* $\gamma(\mathcal{R}) \subseteq \mathcal{S}$.

Since this implies that $\mathcal{S}$, as a set, is potentially larger than $\gamma(\mathcal{R})$, it also highlights the fact that the guarantees given by the specification $\mathcal{S}$ are generally weaker than those given by $\mathcal{R}$. This results in $\mathcal{S}$ having simpler and easier to analyze guarantees, and therefore the statement can be interpreted as a distillation of the relevant properties.

Another important ingredient of CC is the concept of a *relaxation*. Given a resource $\mathsf{R} \in \Phi$, a relaxation $\rho : \Phi \to 2^{\Phi}$ maps R into a specification $\rho(\mathsf{R}) \subseteq \Phi$ and is such that $\mathsf{R} \in \rho(\mathsf{R})$. We use the shorthand notation $\mathsf{R}^{\rho} \doteq \rho(\mathsf{R})$. As we did for constructors, we also consider the natural lift-up $\rho : 2^{\Phi} \to 2^{\Phi}$ of a relaxation ρ to a specification $\mathcal{S} \subseteq \Phi$ by extending the definitions to include $\mathcal{S}^{\rho} \doteq \rho(\mathcal{S}) \doteq \bigcup_{\mathsf{R} \in \mathcal{S}} \mathsf{R}^{\rho} \subseteq \Phi$.

Systems, Resources, Converters, and Protocols. So far we defined CC on an abstract level, now we specify more concretely what kind of resources we consider, and how constructors are concretely instantiated for such objects. We model resources and constructors as random systems, just *systems* for short, as introduced in [12] and later refined in [14]. Simplistically, such mathematical objects can be considered as probabilistic discrete reactive systems, that can be queried with labeled inputs in a sequential fashion, where each distinct label corresponds to a distinct interface, and for each such input generate (possibly probabilistically) an equally labeled output depending on the input and the current state (formally defined by the sequence of all previous inputs and the associated outputs). Systems can be composed in parallel: given two (or more) systems $\mathbf{S}$ and $\mathbf{T}$, we denote $[\mathbf{S}, \mathbf{T}]$ as the system which can be independently queried at the interfaces of both $\mathbf{S}$ and $\mathbf{T}$. Following [3], we also use *correlated* parallel composition, where $\mathbf{S}$ and $\mathbf{T}$ are *not* independent (they might for example share a state, or depend on the same random variable), denoted $\langle \mathbf{S}, \mathbf{T} \rangle$. Such a system can be modeled by introducing another system $\mathbf{C}$ that has access to $[\mathbf{S}, \mathbf{T}]$, that is, $\langle \mathbf{S}, \mathbf{T} \rangle = \mathbf{C}[\mathbf{S}, \mathbf{T}]$.

In the following we consider only resources relevant to our setting for convenience, but of course everything can be phrased at a more abstract level for any kind of resource modeled as a system. Following [3], in this work all resources are parameterized by an integer $n \geq 2$, and each defines $n + 2$ interfaces: n for the senders, denoted S_i, for $i \in [n]$, one for the adversary, denoted E, one for the receiver, denoted R, and we define $\mathcal{I}_n \doteq \{S_1, \ldots, S_n, R, E\}$. In the following we use the expression n-resource to make explicit such parameter, and denote the set of all such resources as Φ_n. To any interface $I \in \mathcal{I}_n$ of an n-resource $\mathbf{R} \in \Phi_n$, we can attach a *converter* α (also formally modeled as a random system) which we assume results in a new n-resource, denoted as $\alpha^I \mathbf{R} \in \Phi_n$. We denote the set of all converters as Σ, and assume that they naturally compose, that is, for converters $\alpha, \beta \in \Sigma$, $\alpha\beta \in \Sigma$ is also a converter. Moreover, we assume commutativity of converters attached at different interfaces, that is, considering converters $\alpha, \beta \in \Sigma$ and interfaces $I, J \in \mathcal{I}_n$, with $I \neq J$, then $\alpha^I \beta^J \mathbf{R} = \beta^J \alpha^I \mathbf{R}$. Finally, we define the special converter $id \in \Sigma$ as the *identity converter* such that $id^I \mathbf{R} = \mathbf{R}$, for any $\mathbf{R} \in \Phi_n$ and $I \in \mathcal{I}_n$.

In order to make security statements using CC, we still need to define constructors for this specific type of resources. To do so, we first model a protocol π executed by n senders and one receiver (an n-protocol) as a list of $n + 1$ converters $(\alpha_1, \ldots, \alpha_{n+1})$, where the adopted convention is that α_i is attached to sender interface S_i, for $i \in [n]$, while α_{n+1} is attached to the receiver interface R. In the following, we use the short-hand notation $\pi\mathbf{R}$ for the n-resource $\alpha_1^{S_1} \cdots \alpha_n^{S_n} \alpha_{n+1}^R \mathbf{R}$. This way, we can now instantiate the concept of a constructor γ simply as attachment of a n-protocol, that is, for each n-protocol π, we consider the associated constructor γ_π, and define $\gamma_\pi(\mathbf{R}) \doteq \pi\mathbf{R}$. Moreover, for a second n-protocol $\pi' \doteq (\beta_1, \ldots, \beta_{n+1})$, we define the composition of π' with π as $\pi'\pi \doteq (\beta_1\alpha_1, \ldots, \beta_{n+1}\alpha_{n+1})$, and therefore $\pi'\pi\mathbf{R}$ is the n-resource $(\beta_1\alpha_1)^{S_1} \cdots (\beta_n\alpha_n)^{S_n} (\beta_{n+1}\alpha_{n+1})^R \mathbf{R}$. Therefore composition of the constructors corresponding to π and π', that is, $\gamma_{\pi'} \circ \gamma_\pi$, is simply modeled as $\pi'\pi$. In the following, we will just use the concept of protocol attachment rather than the more abstract concept of a constructor.

Finally, for n-resources $\mathbf{R}_1, \ldots, \mathbf{R}_\ell \in \Phi_n$, we overload notation and define their parallel composition $[\mathbf{R}_1, \ldots, \mathbf{R}_\ell]$ also as an n-resource, but where each interface $I \in \mathcal{I}_n$ exports ℓ sub-interfaces I_j, for $j \in [\ell]$, with the convention that I_j provides direct access to the interface I of $\mathbf{R}_j$.

Indistinguishability of Systems. In order to define security, we also need to formalize the notion of indistinguishability of n-resources, and more in general of systems. For that, we formally define a *distinguisher* $\mathbf{D}$, also as a system but with the exception that it initially produces an output with no need for an input, and finally produces a binary output (which depends on the probabilistic interaction with another system). We always tacitly assume that a distinguisher $\mathbf{D}$ interacting with any system $\mathbf{S}$ has *matching interfaces* with $\mathbf{S}$; for n-resources we denote the set of all such distinguishers as Θ_n. We can attach a converter $\alpha \in \Sigma$ also to any distinguisher $\mathbf{D}$, at any of its interfaces, say I, which we assume results in a new distinguisher, denoted as $\mathbf{D}^I\alpha$, and in the case of an n-protocol π (and $\mathbf{D}$ being an appropriate distinguisher for an n-resource) we can naturally consider $\mathbf{D}\pi$. For a distinguisher $\mathbf{D}$ and systems $\mathbf{S}, \mathbf{T}$, we denote $\mathbf{D}$'s output after interacting with $\mathbf{S}$ as $\mathbf{DS} \in \{0,1\}$, and define $\mathbf{D}$'s advantage in $\mathbf{S}$ from $\mathbf{T}$ as

$$\Delta^{\mathbf{D}}(\mathbf{S}, \mathbf{T}) \doteq |\Pr[\mathbf{DS} = 0] - \Pr[\mathbf{DT} = 0]| .$$

Considering a converter $\alpha \in \Sigma$ and an interface I, note that $\mathbf{D}^I\alpha\mathbf{S} = \mathbf{D}\alpha^I\mathbf{S}$, and therefore $\Delta^{\mathbf{D}}(\alpha^I\mathbf{S}, \alpha^I\mathbf{T}) = \Delta^{\mathbf{D}^I\alpha}(\mathbf{S}, \mathbf{T})$. Finally, given a function ε that maps distinguishers to $[0,1]$, we can define the ε-indistinguishability relation between systems $\mathbf{S}$ and $\mathbf{T}$, called *ε-closeness*, as

$$\mathbf{S} \approx_\varepsilon \mathbf{T} \quad :\Longleftrightarrow \quad \forall \mathbf{D}: \ \Delta^{\mathbf{D}}(\mathbf{S}, \mathbf{T}) \leq \varepsilon(\mathbf{D}).$$

For a distinguisher $\mathbf{D}$, $\varepsilon(\mathbf{D})$ might be a negligible value (depending on some security parameter, which we do not make explicit in this work). More generally, ε maps a distinguisher $\mathbf{D}$ for systems $\mathbf{S}$ and $\mathbf{T}$ to the advantage that a new distinguisher $\tilde{\mathbf{D}}$ has in distinguishing two different systems $\tilde{\mathbf{S}}$ and $\tilde{\mathbf{T}}$, where $\tilde{\mathbf{D}}$ uses $\mathbf{D}$ as a black-box. For this we need to define a *reduction* system $\mathbf{C}$ that on one side exports all the interfaces of $\mathbf{D}$ (which has the same interface set as $\mathbf{S}$ and $\mathbf{T}$), and on the other side exports all interfaces of $\tilde{\mathbf{S}}$ (which has the same interface set as $\tilde{\mathbf{T}}$). Then if $\mathbf{C}$ is composed with $\tilde{\mathbf{S}}$ or $\tilde{\mathbf{T}}$, denoted $\mathbf{C}\tilde{\mathbf{S}}$ or $\mathbf{C}\tilde{\mathbf{T}}$, respectively, we usually show that $\mathbf{S} = \mathbf{C}\tilde{\mathbf{S}}$ and $\mathbf{T} = \mathbf{C}\tilde{\mathbf{T}}$. Just as we did for converters, we can assume more generally that such a system $\mathbf{C}$ can be attached to $\mathbf{D}$ resulting in a distinguisher system $\tilde{\mathbf{D}} \doteq \mathbf{DC}$ for $\tilde{\mathbf{S}}$ and $\tilde{\mathbf{T}}$. Then if we know (or assume) that $\tilde{\mathbf{S}} \approx_{\tilde{\varepsilon}} \tilde{\mathbf{T}}$, we have

$$\varepsilon(\mathbf{D}) = \Delta^{\mathbf{D}}(\mathbf{S}, \mathbf{T}) = \Delta^{\mathbf{D}}(\mathbf{C}\tilde{\mathbf{S}}, \mathbf{C}\tilde{\mathbf{T}}) = \Delta^{\mathbf{DC}}(\tilde{\mathbf{S}}, \tilde{\mathbf{T}}) \leq \tilde{\varepsilon}(\mathbf{DC}),$$

and by defining $\tilde{\varepsilon}^{\mathbf{C}}(\mathbf{D}) \doteq \tilde{\varepsilon}(\mathbf{DC})$, we establish the (function) inequality $\varepsilon \leq \tilde{\varepsilon}^{\mathbf{C}}$ which entails that by showing (or just assuming) that $\tilde{\varepsilon}$ is negligible (for all distinguishers), then so is ε.

Relevant Resource Specification Relaxations. Recall that for our specific instantiation of CC, a specification $\mathcal{S} \subseteq \Phi_n$ is a set of n-resources. Then for a converter $\alpha \in \Sigma$ and an interface $I \in \mathcal{I}_n$, we define $\alpha^I \mathcal{S} \doteq \{\alpha^I \mathbf{R} \,|\, \mathbf{R} \in \mathcal{S}\}$, and for an n-protocol π, we analogously define $\pi\mathcal{S} \doteq \{\pi\mathbf{R} \,|\, \mathbf{R} \in \mathcal{S}\}$. Next we define two important relaxations, as introduced in [16].

First, we define the *ε-relaxation* of $\mathbf{R}$ as the set of all resources which are ε-close to $\mathbf{R}$, for some function $\varepsilon : \Theta_n \to [0,1]$, that is,

$$\mathbf{R}^{\varepsilon} \doteq \{\mathbf{S} \in \Phi_n \,|\, \mathbf{S} \approx_{\varepsilon} \mathbf{R}\}.$$

We can naturally extend this notion to a specification $\mathcal{S} \subseteq \Phi_n$, that is, we define

$$\mathcal{S}^{\varepsilon} \doteq \bigcup_{\mathbf{R} \in \mathcal{S}} \mathbf{R}^{\varepsilon} = \{\mathbf{S} \in \Phi_n \,|\, \exists \mathbf{R} \in \mathcal{S} : \mathbf{S} \approx_{\varepsilon} \mathbf{R}\}.$$

Secondly, we define the *$*$-relaxation* (spelled "star relaxation") of $\mathbf{R}$, relative to a set of interfaces $\mathcal{C} \subseteq \mathcal{I}_n$, with $t \doteq |\mathcal{C}|$ and $\mathcal{C} \doteq \{I_1, \ldots, I_t\}$, as the set of all resources which behave arbitrarily at those interfaces, that is,

$$\mathbf{R}^{*\mathcal{C}} \doteq \{\alpha_1^{I_1} \cdots \alpha_t^{I_t} \mathbf{R} \,|\, \alpha_1, \ldots, \alpha_t \in \Sigma\}.$$

We can again extend this notion to a specification $\mathcal{S} \subseteq \Phi_n$, that is, we define

$$\mathcal{S}^{*\mathcal{C}} \doteq \bigcup_{\mathbf{R} \in \mathcal{S}} \mathbf{R}^{*\mathcal{C}} = \{\alpha_1^{I_1} \cdots \alpha_t^{I_t} \mathbf{R} \,|\, \alpha_1, \ldots, \alpha_t \in \Sigma, \mathbf{R} \in \mathcal{S}\}.$$

This relaxation intuitively captures a scenario in which a set of parties is dishonest, namely those which are assigned to the interfaces in $\mathcal{C}$. We often consider the singleton $\mathcal{C} = \{E\}$ for which we write $\mathbf{R}^{*E}$ and $\mathcal{S}^{*E}$ instead of $\mathbf{R}^{*\{E\}}$ and $\mathcal{S}^{*\{E\}}$, respectively.

Constructions Capturing Anonymity. Using the specifications introduced above, we can now illustrate the specific type of construction statements that we will show in this work. Intuitively, we want to say that a weaker (that is, "smaller") specification $\mathcal{S}$ can be constructed from a stronger (that is, "larger") specification $\mathcal{R}$ by an n-protocol π if applying π to any n-resource $\mathbf{R} \in \mathcal{R}$ satisfying the specification $\mathcal{R}$, results in an n-resource $\pi\mathbf{R} \in \Phi_n$ not too far from an n-resource $\mathbf{S} \in \mathcal{S}$ satisfying the specification $\mathcal{S}$. As usual in cryptography, we also require that such n-resource $\mathbf{S}$ can exhibit arbitrary behavior at the adversarial interface E, reflecting the fact that whatever the adversary can do in the real-world, modeled by $\pi\mathbf{R}$, it can also do in the ideal-world. This is conventionally modeled by considering a special converter $\mathsf{sim} \in \Sigma$ (a *simulator*) that is attached to $\mathbf{S}$'s adversarial interface E, resulting in the resource $\mathsf{sim}^E \mathbf{S} \in \Phi_n$. Therefore, on a high level the statement that one need to prove is $\mathcal{R} \xrightarrow{\pi} \mathcal{S}^{*E}$, if we would consider perfect closeness, that is, information theoretic security. But more in general, we formalize the concept of "not too far" by means of the ε-relaxation, hence a more frequent kind of statement to prove in cryptography is $\mathcal{R} \xrightarrow{\pi} (\mathcal{S}^{*E})^{\varepsilon}$, which essentially allows us to rely on cryptographic assumptions.

But this specific type of construction still does not allow us to appropriately model anonymity in our setting; in order to capture anonymity, we exploit the power of the $*$-relaxation once more. Concretely, as pointed out earlier, we want to make statements about the *preservation* of anonymity: We want to capture that a protocol neither increases, nor degrades anonymity, and we do so by modeling the "level" of anonymity by a corruption set $\mathcal{C} \subseteq \{S_i\}_{i=1}^n$. Then we show that for any such corruption set $\mathcal{C}$, if the senders which are *not* part of such set execute the protocol, they still obtain the desired properties. To formalize this for a protocol $\pi \doteq (\alpha_1, \ldots, \alpha_{n+1})$, we use the notation $\pi^{\overline{\mathcal{C}}}$, by which we mean the list of protocols $(\alpha_1, \ldots, \alpha_{n+1})$, but where for any $S_i \in \mathcal{C}$, for some $i \in [n]$, α_i is replaced by the identity converter *id*. We now formalize the specific type of construction statements that we will make (and in the full version [4] we show they compose).

Definition 2. *For an n-protocol π, a function ε, and n-resources* $\mathbf{R}, \mathbf{S}$, *π anonymously constructs* $\mathbf{S}$ *from* $\mathbf{R}$ *within ε, denoted* $\mathbf{R} \xmapsto{\pi,\varepsilon} \mathbf{S}$, *if for all $\mathcal{C} \subseteq \{S_i\}_{i=1}^n$,* $\mathbf{R}^{*\mathcal{C}} \xrightarrow{\pi^{\overline{\mathcal{C}}}} (\mathbf{S}^{*\mathcal{C}\cup\{E\}})^\varepsilon$, *that is,* $\pi^{\overline{\mathcal{C}}}\mathbf{R}^{*\mathcal{C}} \subseteq (\mathbf{S}^{*\mathcal{C}\cup\{E\}})^\varepsilon$.

2.3 Anonymous and Authentic Resources

In this section we present the n-resources that we need later in order to make our security statements (we provide more formal descriptions in the full version [4]). Instead of bold-face letters, for such resources we will use suggestive sans-serif abbreviations. We describe all resources first on an intuitive level, and then formally following the model introduced in [3], in which communication is modeled by a sender buffer $\mathfrak{S}$ and a receiver buffer $\mathfrak{R}$, both allowing to insert single elements and to read in chunks. Note that all our resources are parameterized by a set, either $\mathcal{K}$ (ideally for public keys), $\mathcal{M}$ (ideally for messages), or $\mathcal{X}$ (for anything), but we will make the instantiation of such set implicit when showing constructions.

We begin by describing the three single-use authentic channels needed as assumed resources in order to authentically exchange public keys. The first such resource is $\textsf{1-AUT}_{n\to 1}$, which allows to input a value once at every sender interface S_i, for $i \in [n]$, and allows to read these values at the receiver and adversary interfaces, R and E, respectively. Based on this resource, we then simply define $\textsf{1-AUT}_{n\leftarrow 1}$ as somewhat the dual of this, namely, the resource that allows to input a value once at the receiver interface R, and that allows to read this value at every sender and adversary interface, S_i, for $i \in [n]$, and E, respectively. Finally, we also need the resource $\textsf{1-AUT}_{n\circlearrowleft 1}$, which similarly to $\textsf{1-AUT}_{n\to 1}$ allows to input a value once at every sender interface S_i, for $i \in [n]$, but additionally allows to read these values at all the sender interfaces S_i as well. We tacitly assume that protocols first use those resources to exchange public-keys, and only once all keys have been exchanged, they use the channel resources. We also point out that our results are in a model in which public keys are therefore assumed to always be honestly generated. We leave open the problem of strengthening the model by replacing these resources by a *certificate authority*, which would allow the adversary to also register keys.

We next describe the assumed channel resource $\textsf{A-INS}_{n\to 1}$ as well as the three different ideal anonymous channel resources $\textsf{A-AUT}_{n\to 1}$, $\textsf{D-AUT}_{n\to 1}$, and $\textsf{RA-AUT}_{n\to 1}$ (all depicted in Fig. 1).

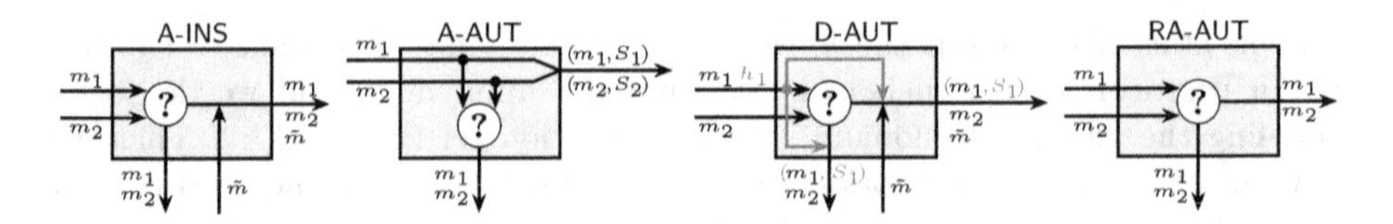

Fig. 1. Sketches of the anonymous channel resources for $n = 2$ senders (S_1 sending m_1 and S_2 sending m_2). For D-AUT, only S_1 de-anonymizes its message.

- The *anonymous insecure channel* $\textsf{A-INS}_{n\to1}$ allows to input multiple values at every sender interface S_i, for $i \in [n]$. Those values are stored in the sender buffer $\mathfrak{S}$, from which they can be read at the adversary interface E. Moreover, at this interface $\textsf{A-INS}_{n\to1}$ also allows the adversary to inject multiple arbitrary values. Those values are stored in the receiver buffer $\mathfrak{R}$, from which they can be read at the receiver interface R.
- In the *anonymous authentic channel* $\textsf{A-AUT}_{n\to1}$, the sender buffer $\mathfrak{S}$ is used exactly as in $\textsf{A-INS}_{n\to1}$, except that for every message sent, information about the sender is also stored, but not leaked to the adversary. Unlike $\textsf{A-INS}_{n\to1}$, at the interface E, $\textsf{A-AUT}_{n\to1}$ only allows the adversary to select which messages previously input by a sender will be transmitted to the receiver. Those messages, along with the sender information, will be transferred from the sender buffer $\mathfrak{S}$ to the receiver buffer $\mathfrak{R}$, from which they can be read at the receiver interface R.
- The *de-anonymizable authentic channel* $\textsf{D-AUT}_{n\to1}$ allows to input two type of values at every sender interface S_i, for $i \in [n]$: one to commit a message m, $(\underline{\texttt{cmt}}, m)$, and the other to authenticate a previously committed message m', $(\underline{\texttt{aut}}, h_{m'})$, where $h_{m'}$ is a handle for m' generated by $\textsf{D-AUT}_{n\to1}$. Those values are stored in the sender buffer $\mathfrak{S}$, from which they can be read at the adversary interface E. Information about the sender is also stored, but is only leaked to the adversary along with $\underline{\texttt{aut}}$ values. At the interface E, $\textsf{D-AUT}_{n\to1}$ allows the adversary to select which values (of both types) previously input by a sender will be transmitted to the receiver, as well as to inject additional $\underline{\texttt{cmt}}$ values. Those values, including sender information only in case of $\underline{\texttt{aut}}$ values, will be transferred from the sender buffer $\mathfrak{S}$ to the receiver buffer $\mathfrak{R}$, from which they can be read at the receiver interface R.
- The *receiver-side anonymous authentic channel* $\textsf{RA-AUT}_{n\to1}$ works exactly as $\textsf{A-AUT}_{n\to1}$, except that sender information is concealed from the receiver as well (and therefore never stored in the buffers $\mathfrak{S}$ and $\mathfrak{R}$).

3 Achieving Anonymous Authenticity

We start by introducing a new flavor of a signature scheme with some anonymity property, dubbed *bilateral signatures.* This scheme shares the syntax of designated verifier signatures (DVS): both sender and receiver have a key-pair; signing a message requires the secret key of the sender and the public key of the receiver, and verifying a signature requires the secret key of the receiver and the public key of the sender. The receiver's key-pair is essentially what allows to circumvent the impossibility result, by introducing one-time authenticated information from the receiver to the senders: it enables indistinguishability of signatures by making verification exclusive to the receiver, as opposed to public.

Definition 3 (Bilateral Signature Scheme). *A* bilateral signature scheme (BSS) $\Sigma_{\mathsf{BS}} \doteq (\mathtt{Gen}_S, \mathtt{Gen}_R, \mathtt{Sgn}, \mathtt{Vrf})$ *over message-space* $\mathcal{M}$ *and signature-space* $\mathcal{S}$ *(with* $\perp \notin \mathcal{M} \cup \mathcal{S}$*), is such that*

- $\mathtt{Gen}_S$ *is a distribution over the sender key-spaces* $\mathcal{SK}_S \times \mathcal{PK}_S$*;*
- $\mathtt{Gen}_R$ *is a distribution over the receiver key-spaces* $\mathcal{SK}_R \times \mathcal{PK}_R$*;*
- $\mathtt{Sgn} : \mathcal{SK}_S \times \mathcal{PK}_R \times \mathcal{M} \to \mathcal{S}$ *is a probabilistic function;*
- $\mathtt{Vrf} : \mathcal{SK}_R \times \mathcal{PK}_S \times \mathcal{M} \times \mathcal{S} \to \{0,1\}$ *is a deterministic function.*

We require the above to be efficiently samplable/computable. For sender key-pair $(ssk, spk) \in \mathcal{SK}_S \times \mathcal{PK}_S$ *and receiver key-pair* $(rsk, rpk) \in \mathcal{SK}_R \times \mathcal{PK}_R$ *we use the short-hand notation* $\mathtt{Sgn}_{ssk,rpk}(\cdot)$ *for* $\mathtt{Sgn}(ssk, rpk, \cdot)$ *and* $\mathtt{Vrf}_{rsk,spk}(\cdot,\cdot)$ *for* $\mathtt{Vrf}(rsk, spk, \cdot, \cdot)$*. Moreover, we assume* correctness *of* Σ_{BS}*, that is, for all key-pairs* (ssk, spk) *and* (rsk, rpk) *distributed according to* $\mathtt{Gen}_S$ *and* $\mathtt{Gen}_R$*, respectively, all messages* $m \in \mathcal{M}$*, and all signatures* $\sigma \in \mathcal{S}$*,* $\mathtt{Vrf}_{rsk,spk}(m, \sigma) = \mathbb{1}\left\{\sigma \in \operatorname{supp}\left(\mathtt{Sgn}_{ssk,rpk}(m)\right)\right\}$.

Note that we only introduce bilateral signatures as an abstract syntactic object. As we discuss in the full version [4], there exist concrete schemes satisfying such syntax, as well as the semantics we define later. Nevertheless, such schemes provide additional security guarantees that are not required in our setting. We leave the problem of finding a bilateral signature scheme which is *minimal*.

3.1 Game-Based Security of Bilateral Signatures

We begin our study of the semantics of bilateral signatures by defining their game-base security. In order to define the security of a fixed scheme Σ_{BS}, we define the following systems (where the dependency on Σ_{BS} is implicit), parameterized by keys $(ssk, spk) \in \mathcal{SK}_S \times \mathcal{PK}_S$, $\boldsymbol{spk} \doteq (spk_1, \ldots, spk_n) \in \mathcal{PK}_S^n$, for any $n \in \mathbb{N}$, and $(rsk, rpk) \in \mathcal{SK}_R \times \mathcal{PK}_R$.

- $\langle \mathbf{S}_{ssk,rpk}, \mathbf{V}_{rsk,spk} \rangle$:
  - On input $m \in \mathcal{M}$, return $(m, \sigma) \in \mathcal{M} \times \mathcal{S}$, for $\sigma \leftarrow \mathtt{Sgn}_{ssk,rpk}(m)$.
  - On input $(m, \sigma) \in \mathcal{M} \times \mathcal{S}$, return m if $\mathtt{Vrf}_{rsk,spk}(m, \sigma) = 1$ and $\perp$ otherwise.
- $\langle \mathbf{S}_{ssk,rpk}, \mathbf{V}^{\perp} \rangle$: Set $\mathcal{Q} \subseteq \mathcal{M} \times \mathcal{S}$ to $\varnothing$ and then:
  - On input $m \in \mathcal{M}$, return $(m, \sigma) \in \mathcal{M} \times \mathcal{S}$, for $\sigma \leftarrow \mathtt{Sgn}_{ssk,rpk}(m)$, and set $\mathcal{Q}$ to $\mathcal{Q} \cup \{(m, \sigma)\}$.
  - On input $(m, \sigma) \in \mathcal{M} \times \mathcal{S}$, return m if $(m, \sigma) \in \mathcal{Q}$ and $\perp$ otherwise.
- $\mathbf{K}_{\boldsymbol{spk},rpk}$: On input $\diamond$, output $(\boldsymbol{spk}, rpk)$.

In our definitions, all keys will *always* be random variables distributed (as key-pairs) according to Σ_{BS}'s $\mathtt{Gen}_S$ and $\mathtt{Gen}_R$.

We define a combined notion for bilateral signatures capturing both authenticity and anonymity at once. For this, we define a distinction problem between a real system that correctly generates and verifies signatures, via signing and verification oracles for n (different) senders and one receiver, and an ideal system that also correctly generates signatures and only correctly verifies signatures previously signed, but via n copies of signing and verification oracles for the *same* (randomly selected) sender and one receiver.

Definition 4 (UF-IK-Secure Bilateral Signature). *A bilateral signature scheme* Σ_{BS} *is* (n, ε)-unforgeable-and-anonymous *(or* (n, ε)-UF-IK -secure*) if*

$$[\langle \mathbf{S}_{ssk_1,rpk}, \mathbf{V}_{rsk,spk_1}\rangle, \ldots, \langle \mathbf{S}_{ssk_n,rpk}, \mathbf{V}_{rsk,spk_n}\rangle, \mathbf{K}_{\boldsymbol{spk},rpk}]$$
$$\approx_\varepsilon$$
$$[\underbrace{\langle \mathbf{S}_{ssk_I,rpk}, \mathbf{V}^\perp\rangle, \ldots, \langle \mathbf{S}_{ssk_I,rpk}, \mathbf{V}^\perp\rangle}_{n \text{ times}}, \mathbf{K}_{\boldsymbol{spk},rpk}]$$

for key-pairs $(ssk_1, spk_1), \ldots, (ssk_n, spk_n) \leftarrow \mathtt{Gen}_S$*,* $(rsk, rpk) \leftarrow \mathtt{Gen}_R$*,* $\boldsymbol{spk} \doteq (spk_1, \ldots, spk_n)$*, and random variable* $I \overset{\$}{\leftarrow} [n]$*.*

As we formally show in the full version [4], it is easy to see that if a bilateral signature scheme is ε-UF-secure *and* (n, ε')-IK-secure (as defined there), then it is $(n, \varepsilon^{\mathbf{C}} + \varepsilon')$-UF-IK-secure, for a specific reduction $\mathbf{C}$.

3.2 Composable Security of Bilateral Signatures

We continue our study of the semantics of bilateral signatures by defining their composable security in the constructive cryptography framework. Recall that we want to define composable security of a bilateral signature scheme Σ_{BS} as the construction of the resource $\mathsf{A\text{-}AUT}_{n\to 1}$ from the resources $\mathsf{1\text{-}AUT}_{n\to 1}$, $\mathsf{1\text{-}AUT}_{n\leftarrow 1}$, and $\mathsf{A\text{-}INS}_{n\to 1}$. In order to make this statement formal, we need to define how a protocol π_{BS}, attached to the resource $[\mathsf{1\text{-}AUT}_{n\to 1}, \mathsf{1\text{-}AUT}_{n\leftarrow 1}, \mathsf{A\text{-}INS}_{n\to 1}]$, naturally makes use of Σ_{BS}. First, π_{BS} runs $\mathtt{Gen}_S$ for every sender S_i, for $i \in [n]$, generating key-pairs $(ssk_1, spk_1), \ldots, (ssk_n, spk_n)$, as well as $\mathtt{Gen}_R$ for the receiver R, generating the key-pair (rsk, rpk). Then it transmits the sender public keys $spk_1, \ldots, spk_n$ to the receiver through $\mathsf{1\text{-}AUT}_{n\to 1}$ and the receiver public key rpk to each of the senders through $\mathsf{1\text{-}AUT}_{n\leftarrow 1}$. After that, once a sender S_i inputs a message m on its interface, π_{BS} uses ssk_i and rpk to generate $\sigma \leftarrow \mathtt{Sgn}_{ssk_i,rpk}(m)$, and inputs (m, σ) to the interface S_i of $\mathsf{A\text{-}INS}_{n\to 1}$. Once the receiver R inputs $\diamond$ on its interface, π_{BS} also inputs $\diamond$ to the interface R of $\mathsf{A\text{-}INS}_{n\to 1}$, obtaining a set $\mathfrak{D} \subseteq \mathbb{N} \times \mathcal{M} \times \mathcal{S}$, and outputs the set $\{(j, m, i) \mid \exists\, (j, m, \sigma) \in \mathfrak{D}, i \in [n] : \mathtt{Vrf}_{rsk,spk_i}(m, \sigma) = 1\}$ to R. We call π_{BS} the protocol using Σ_{BS} in the *natural way*.

Definition 5. *A bilateral signature scheme* Σ_{BS} *is* (n, ε)-composably secure *if*

$$[\text{1-AUT}_{n\to 1}, \text{1-AUT}_{n\leftarrow 1}, \text{A-INS}_{n\to 1}] \xmapsto{\pi_{\mathsf{BS}}, \varepsilon} \text{A-AUT}_{n\to 1},$$

where π_{BS} *is the protocol using* Σ_{BS} *in the natural way.*

Finally, we show that game-based security of bilateral signatures implies their composable security (we defer the proof to the full version [4]).

Theorem 1. *There exists a reduction system* $\mathbf{C}$ *such that, if a bilateral signature scheme* Σ_{BS} *is* (n, ε)-UF-IK*-secure, then it is* $(n, \varepsilon^{\mathbf{C}})$*-composably secure.*

4 Achieving De-anonymizable Authenticity

In the previous section we studied a way to achieve the anonymous resource $\text{A-AUT}_{n\to 1}$, at the cost of assuming additional one-time authenticated information from the receiver to all senders. In this section we tackle what can be interpreted as the dual problem, that is, we study what can at most be achieved by only assuming one-time authenticated information from the receivers to the sender (in addition to an insecure channel). Considering to our impossibility result, we know that the constructed resource will need to be weaker than $\text{A-AUT}_{n\to 1}$.

Considering the constraint on the assumed resources, intuitively we need a scheme that, on the sender side, requires the same input as regular signatures, that is, just a secret key and a message. But since anonymity is unachievable if both the message and the signature are disclosed, one either needs to relax the security definition of digital signatures, or to slightly change their syntax.

A first workaround to this impossibility was initially studied by Yang et al. [19], and subsequently refined independently by Fischlin [9] and Zhang and Imai [21], where the first approach is taken and essentially the anonymity of the signature alone is considered. Modeling such a security definition composably, makes it apparent how, from an application point of view, this approach is moot: it requires to assume that an adversary only sees signatures in transit, but not messages. Clearly, a different kind of assumed resources is needed; ideally, the message should be transmitted over a confidential channel. Composably, this hints to the fact that anonymous signatures might only be appropriate in a context where one wants to combine signatures with public-key encryption. This can be interpreted as the study of anonymity preservation of signcryption, and we briefly discuss this in the full version [4].

A different workaround, following the second approach, was independently taken later by Saraswat and Yun [18] and by Bellare and Duan [6]. There, the syntax of regular DSS was slightly modified to allow the signature to bear some form of anonymity. More precisely, the security definitions are changed to capture anonymity when the message and only a portion of the signature are disclosed, and authenticity only once the full signature is disclosed. We remark that the two works essentially introduce the same syntax and security notions, but [18] uses the term anonymous signatures introduced earlier in [19], whereas [6] adopts the new term *partial signatures*, which we will adopt here as well. More precisely, in such a scheme the signing function returns a signature that is defined as a tuple (σ, τ), where σ is called the *stub*, τ the *tag*, and (σ, τ) the *full signature*. Then the stub σ alone guarantees anonymity of the sender on a message m (but not its authenticity), whereas authenticity of m (but not anonymity anymore) is guaranteed once the tag τ is subsequently disclosed.

Definition 6 (Partial Signature Scheme). *A partial signature scheme (PSS)* $\Sigma_{\mathsf{PS}} \doteq (\mathtt{Gen}, \mathtt{Sgn}, \mathtt{Vrf})$ *over message-space* $\mathcal{M}$*, stub-space* $\mathcal{S}$*, and tag-space* $\mathcal{T}$ *(with* $\bot \notin \mathcal{M} \cup \mathcal{S} \cup \mathcal{T}$*), is such that*

- $\mathtt{Gen}$ *is a distribution over the key-spaces* $\mathcal{SK} \times \mathcal{PK}$*;*
- $\mathtt{Sgn} : \mathcal{SK} \times \mathcal{M} \to \mathcal{S} \times \mathcal{T}$ *is a probabilistic function;*
- $\mathtt{Vrf} : \mathcal{PK} \times \mathcal{M} \times \mathcal{S} \times \mathcal{T} \to \{0, 1\}$ *is a deterministic function.*

We require the above to be efficiently samplable/computable. For key-pair $(sk, pk) \in \mathcal{SK} \times \mathcal{PK}$ *we use the short-hand notation* $\mathtt{Sgn}_{sk}(\cdot)$ *for* $\mathtt{Sgn}(sk, \cdot)$ *and* $\mathtt{Vrf}_{pk}(\cdot, \cdot, \cdot)$ *for* $\mathtt{Vrf}(pk, \cdot, \cdot, \cdot)$*. Moreover, we assume* correctness *of* Σ_{PS}*, that is, for all key-pairs* (sk, pk) *distributed according to* $\mathtt{Gen}$*, all messages* $m \in \mathcal{M}$*, and all signatures* $(\sigma, \tau) \in \mathcal{S} \times \mathcal{T}$*,* $\mathtt{Vrf}_{pk}(m, \sigma, \tau) = \mathbb{1}\{(\sigma, \tau) \in \operatorname{supp}(\mathtt{Sgn}_{sk}(m))\}$*.*

4.1 Game-Based Security of Partial Signatures

We begin our study of the semantics of partial signatures by defining their game-base security. Originally, in [19] anonymous signatures (the precursors of partial signatures), were only defined to be unforgeable and anonymous, by requiring that no adversary can forge valid signatures and distinguish signatures when messages are withheld, respectively. In [18] and [6], for the succeeding partial signatures, the unforgeability notion is essentially unchanged, whereas anonymity is defined with a game where the adversary sees only a part of the signatures, but also the whole associated messages. Additionally, both works realize that a crucial third security guarantee is also necessary: *unambiguouity* (named unpretendability in [18]). This notion ensures that only the original creator of a signature is able to later show that it indeed generated it. This security guarantee is modeled via a game where an adversary tries to come up with two messages m_0, m_1, a stub σ, and two tags τ_0, τ_1, such that $\mathtt{Vrf}_{pk_0}(m_0, \sigma, \tau_0) = \mathtt{Vrf}_{pk_1}(m_1, \sigma, \tau_1) = 1$, for two different public keys pk_0, pk_1, which in our setting must be two of the n known (and fixed) sender public keys. In the full version [4] we relate those notions from the literature to the new definitions we introduce next.

In order to define the security of a fixed scheme Σ_{PS}, we define the following systems (where the dependency on Σ_{PS} is implicit), parameterized by keys $sk \in \mathcal{SK}$, $pk \in \mathcal{PK}$, $\boldsymbol{pk} \doteq (pk_1, \ldots, pk_n) \in \mathcal{PK}^n$, for any $n \in \mathbb{N}$.

- $\langle \mathbf{S}_{sk}, \mathbf{V}_{pk} \rangle$:
  - On input $m \in \mathcal{M}$, return $(m, \sigma, \tau) \in \mathcal{M} \times \mathcal{S} \times \mathcal{T}$, for $(\sigma, \tau) \leftarrow \mathtt{Sgn}_{sk}(m)$.
  - On input $(m, \sigma, \tau) \in \mathcal{M} \times \mathcal{S} \times \mathcal{T}$, return m if $\mathtt{Vrf}_{pk}(m, \sigma, \tau) = 1$ and $\bot$ otherwise.

- $\langle \mathbf{S}_{sk}, \mathbf{V}^{\perp} \rangle$: Set the (potentially) *shared* set $\mathcal{Q} \subseteq \mathcal{M} \times \mathcal{S} \times \mathcal{T}$ to $\varnothing$ and then:
  - On input $m \in \mathcal{M}$, return $(m, \sigma, \tau) \in \mathcal{M} \times \mathcal{S} \times \mathcal{T}$, for $(\sigma, \tau) \leftarrow \mathtt{Sgn}_{sk}(m)$, and set $\mathcal{Q}$ to $\mathcal{Q} \cup \{(m, \sigma, \tau)\}$.
  - On input $(m, \sigma, \tau) \in \mathcal{M} \times \mathcal{S} \times \mathcal{T}$, return m if $(m, \sigma, \tau) \in \mathcal{Q}$ and $\perp$ otherwise.
- $\mathbf{S}^{-}_{sk}$: On input $m \in \mathcal{M}$, return $(m, \sigma) \in \mathcal{M} \times \mathcal{S}$, for $(\sigma, \cdot) \leftarrow \mathtt{Sgn}_{sk}(m)$.
- $\mathbf{K}_{\boldsymbol{pk}}$: On input $\diamond$, output $\boldsymbol{pk}$.

In our definitions, all keys will *always* be random variables distributed (as key-pairs) according to Σ_{PS}'s $\mathtt{Gen}$.

We begin by defining a combined notion for bilateral signatures capturing both authenticity and unambiguity at once. For this, we define a distinction problem between a real system that correctly generates and verifies signatures, via signing and verification oracles for n (different) senders, and an ideal system that also correctly generates signatures for n (different) senders, but only correctly verifies signatures previously signed by *any* signing oracle.

Definition 7 (UF-UA-Secure Partial Signature). *A partial signature scheme Σ_{PS} is (n, ε)-unforgeable-and-unambiguous (or (n, ε)-UF-UA -secure) if*

$$[\langle \mathbf{S}_{sk_1}, \mathbf{V}_{pk_1} \rangle, \ldots, \langle \mathbf{S}_{sk_n}, \mathbf{V}_{pk_n} \rangle, \mathbf{K}_{\boldsymbol{pk}}] \approx_{\varepsilon} [\langle \mathbf{S}_{sk_1}, \mathbf{V}^{\perp} \rangle, \ldots, \langle \mathbf{S}_{sk_n}, \mathbf{V}^{\perp} \rangle, \mathbf{K}_{\boldsymbol{pk}}],$$

for key-pairs $(sk_1, pk_1), \ldots, (sk_n, pk_n) \leftarrow \mathtt{Gen}$ and $\boldsymbol{pk} \doteq (pk_1, \ldots, pk_n)$.

As we formally show in the full version [4], it is easy to see that if a partial signature scheme is ε-UF-secure *and* (n, ε')-UA-secure (as defined there), then it is $(n, n \cdot \varepsilon^{\mathbf{C}} + \varepsilon')$-UF-UA-secure, for a specific reduction $\mathbf{C}$.

We next define anonymity of partial signatures. For this, we define a distinction problem between a real system that correctly generates *only* stubs, via (reduced) signing oracles for n (different) senders, and an ideal system that also correctly generates only stubs, but via n copies of (reduced) signing oracles for the *same* (randomly selected) sender.

Definition 8 (IK-Secure Partial Signature). *A partial signature scheme Σ_{PS} is (n, ε)-anonymous (or (n, ε)-IK -secure) if*

$$[\mathbf{S}^{-}_{sk_1}, \ldots, \mathbf{S}^{-}_{sk_n}, \mathbf{K}_{\boldsymbol{pk}}] \approx_{\varepsilon} [\mathbf{S}^{-}_{sk_I}, \ldots, \mathbf{S}^{-}_{sk_I}, \mathbf{K}_{\boldsymbol{pk}}]$$

for key-pairs $(sk_1, pk_1), \ldots, (sk_n, pk_n) \leftarrow \mathtt{Gen}$, $\boldsymbol{pk} \doteq (pk_1, \ldots, pk_n)$, and random variable $I \stackrel{\$}{\leftarrow} [n]$.

Unlike what we did for bilateral signatures (and will later do for ring signatures as well), it is not possible to define a combined security notion for partial signatures capturing both UF-UA-security and IK-security at once. This is because a unified distinction problem would necessarily require a full signing oracle, in order to model unforgeability, thus making it possible to trivially distinguish signatures generated by different senders, that is, making the modeling of anonymity impossible.

4.2 Composable Security of Partial Signatures

As it is made clear by the concrete construction given in [6], partial signature schemes inherently involve a special form of commitment. In fact, such straightforward construction from a regular signature scheme and a commitment scheme involves generating a normal signature on the message, and committing to it and the verification key. The resulting commitment bitstring will then be the stub σ (the one ensuring anonymity, but not authenticity), and the opening (or "decommital key") will correspond to the tag τ (the one ensuring authenticity, but not anonymity).

From this, it becomes immediately apparent that trying to capture security of partial signatures in a composable fashion, would necessarily incur the so-called *simulator commitment problem.* In this specific case, the issue is as follows: Intuitively, in the real world a sender S_i, for $i \in [n]$, generates a full signature (σ, τ) on a message m, and in a first phase sends only (m, σ) to the receiver R, while in a second phase it sends (m, σ, τ), which must satisfy $\texttt{Vrf}_{pk_i}(m, \sigma, \tau) = 1$. But in the ideal world, during the first phase the simulator only receives the message m from $\mathsf{D\text{-}AUT}_{n \to 1}$, and does not know who the sender is (in particular, it does not know the value $i \in [n]$). Even though it emulates all n secret/public keys sk_i, pk_i of the senders, it must output a partial signature σ by producing a full signature (σ, τ) for m using a *different* random secret key sk (this difference in the real and ideal worlds is what exactly captures anonymity of the stub σ). In the second phase, once it obtains the identity i of the sender S_i who sent m, the simulator must be able to output, along with the previously defined stub σ, a valid tag τ that satisfies $\texttt{Vrf}_{pk_i}(m, \sigma, \tau) = 1$. But because upon generation of σ from m, the simulator did not use sk_i, it is infeasible for it to correctly generate such a valid τ.

Recently, a generic workaround to this problem was put forth by Jost and Maurer [10], where the use of a new type of relaxation, the so-called *interval-wise relaxation*, allows to make formal statements capturing security notions that in regular composability frameworks would incur in the commitment problem. The interval-wise relaxation builds upon the combination of two other relaxations, the from-relaxation and the until-relaxation. Informally, given a resource $\mathbf{R}$ and two monotone[2] predicates P_1, P_2 (on the history of events happening globally in an experiment involving $\mathbf{R}$), the from-relaxation $\mathbf{R}^{[P_1}$ consists of all resources behaving arbitrarily until P_2 is true and exactly as $\mathbf{R}$ afterwards, whereas the until-relaxation $\mathbf{R}^{P_2]}$ consists of all resources behaving exactly as $\mathbf{R}$ until P_1 is true and arbitrarily afterwards. Hence, intuitively the combined relaxation $\mathbf{R}^{[P_1,P_2]}$ consist of all resources behaving exactly as $\mathbf{R}$ from when P_1 is true and until P_2 is true, and arbitrarily otherwise (technically, it actually corresponds to the transitive closure of taking the from- and until-relaxation in alternating order). Finally, for a function $\varepsilon : \Theta_n \to [0, 1]$, the interval-wise relaxation $\mathbf{R}^{[P_1,P_2]:\varepsilon}$ informally corresponds to all resources in $\mathbf{R}^{[P_1,P_2]}$ that are also ε-close to $\mathbf{R}$. Formally, this is defined using the ε-relaxation introduced in Sect. 2.2 as $\mathbf{R}^{[P_1,P_2]:\varepsilon} \doteq ((\mathbf{R}^{[P_1,P_2]})^{\varepsilon})^{[P_1,P_2]}$ (see [10] for more details).

[2] A monotone predicate is a predicate that once becomes true cannot be false anymore.

Recall that we want to define composable security of a partial signature scheme Σ_{PS} as the construction of the resource $\mathsf{D\text{-}AUT}_{n \to 1}$ from the resources $\mathsf{1\text{-}AUT}_{n \to 1}$, and $\mathsf{A\text{-}INS}_{n \to 1}$. In order to make this statement formal, we need to define how a protocol π_{PS}, attached to the resource $[\mathsf{1\text{-}AUT}_{n \to 1}, \mathsf{A\text{-}INS}_{n \to 1}]$, naturally makes use of Σ_{PS}. First, π_{PS} runs $\mathtt{Gen}$ for every sender S_i, for $i \in [n]$, generating key-pairs $(sk_1, pk_1), \ldots, (sk_n, pk_n)$. Then it transmits the public keys $pk_1, \ldots, pk_n$ to the receiver through $\mathsf{1\text{-}AUT}_{n \to 1}$. After that, for each sender S_i it sets up two look-up tables, modeled here as sets $\mathfrak{H}_i \subseteq \mathbb{N} \times \mathcal{M} \times \mathcal{S} \times \mathcal{T}$ and $\mathfrak{H}'_i \subseteq \mathbb{N} \times \mathcal{M} \times \mathcal{S}$, as well as a handle value $h_i \in \mathbb{N}$, initially set to 0. Then sender S_i might input messages of two different types on its interface:

- $(\underline{\mathtt{cmt}}, m)$, for some $m \in \mathcal{M}$: in this case, π_{PS} uses sk_i to generate $(\sigma, \tau) \leftarrow \mathtt{Sgn}_{sk_i}(m)$, and inputs $(\underline{\mathtt{cmt}}, m, \sigma)$ to the interface S_i of $\mathsf{A\text{-}INS}_{n \to 1}$. Then it sets $h_i \leftarrow h_i + 1$ and $\mathfrak{H}_i \leftarrow \mathfrak{H}_i \cup \{(h_i, m, \sigma, \tau)\}$.
- $(\underline{\mathtt{aut}}, h)$, for some $h \in \mathbb{N}$: in this case, π_{PS} first checks whether $(h, m, \sigma, \tau) \in \mathfrak{H}_i$, for some m, σ, τ. If that is the case, then π_{PS} inputs $(\underline{\mathtt{aut}}, m, \sigma, \tau)$ to the interface S_i of $\mathsf{A\text{-}INS}_{n \to 1}$.

Once the receiver R inputs $\diamond$ on its interface, π_{PS} also inputs $\diamond$ to the interface R of $\mathsf{A\text{-}INS}_{n \to 1}$, obtaining a set $\mathfrak{D} \subseteq (\mathbb{N} \times \{\underline{\mathtt{cmt}}\} \times \mathcal{M} \times \mathcal{S}) \cup (\mathbb{N} \times \{\underline{\mathtt{aut}}\} \times \mathcal{M} \times \mathcal{S} \times \mathcal{T})$. Then it sets $\mathfrak{H}' \leftarrow \mathfrak{H}' \cup \{(j, m, \sigma) \mid (j, (\underline{\mathtt{cmt}}, m, \sigma)) \in \mathfrak{D}\}$, computes the sets $\mathfrak{D}' \doteq \{(\underline{\mathtt{cmt}}, j, m) \mid \exists \sigma \in \mathcal{S} : (j, (\underline{\mathtt{cmt}}, m, \sigma)) \in \mathfrak{D}\}$, $\mathfrak{D}'' \doteq \{(\underline{\mathtt{aut}}, j', j, i) \mid \exists m \in \mathcal{M}, \sigma \in \mathcal{S}, \tau \in \mathcal{T} : (j', \underline{\mathtt{aut}}, m, \sigma, \tau) \in \mathfrak{D}, (j, m, \sigma) \in \mathfrak{H}', \mathtt{Vrf}_{pk_i}(m, \sigma, \tau) = 1\}$, and outputs the set $\mathfrak{D}' \cup \mathfrak{D}''$ to R. We call π_{PS} the protocol using Σ_{PS} in the *natural way.*

Intuitively, we model composable security of a partial signature scheme by making a statement for each interval defined by a sequence of inputs at the sender interfaces $\{S_i\}_{i=1}^n$ that are of the same type, that is, either all are of the form $(\underline{\mathtt{cmt}}, \cdot)$ (*messages*), or all are of the form $(\underline{\mathtt{aut}}, \cdot)$ (*handles*). This way, we make sure that the individual security statement is within an interval in which the simulator cannot incur the commitment problem. For this we define the following predicates:

- $P_{\mathsf{msg}(j)}$: true if j-th sender input is a *message* m (E would obtain (m, σ));
- $P_{\mathsf{hnd}(j)}$: true if j-th sender input is a *handle* h (E would obtain (m, σ, τ));
- $P_{\mathsf{fst}(j)}$: true at *first* consecutive sender input of *same type as the j-th;*
- $P_{\mathsf{lst}(j)}$: true at *last* consecutive sender input of *same type as the j-th.*

Definition 9. *A partial signature scheme Σ_{PS} is $(n, t, \varepsilon_{\mathsf{m}}, \varepsilon_{\mathsf{h}})$-composably secure if for all $\mathcal{C} \subseteq \{S_i\}_{i=1}^n$,*

$$\pi_{\mathsf{PS}}^{\overline{\mathcal{C}}}[\mathsf{1\text{-}AUT}_{n \to 1}, \mathsf{A\text{-}INS}_{n \to 1}]^{*\mathcal{C}} \subseteq \bigcap\nolimits_{(P_1, P_2, \varepsilon) \in \Omega} (\mathsf{D\text{-}AUT}_{n \to 1}^{*\mathcal{C} \cup \{E\}})^{[P_1, P_2] : \varepsilon},$$

for $\Omega = \{(P_{\mathsf{fst}(j)}, P_{\mathsf{lst}(j)}, \varepsilon_{\mathsf{m}})\}_{j \in [t] : P_{\mathsf{msg}(j)}} \cup \{(P_{\mathsf{fst}(j)}, P_{\mathsf{lst}(j)}, \varepsilon_{\mathsf{h}})\}_{j \in [t] : P_{\mathsf{hnd}(j)}}$, where $t \in \mathbb{N}$ is an upper-bound on the number of transmitted messages and π_{PS} is the protocol using Σ_{PS} in the natural way.

Finally, we show that game-based security of partial signatures implies their composable security (we defer the proof to the full version [4]).

Theorem 2. *There exist reduction systems* $\mathbf{C}_{\mathsf{m}}$ *and* $\mathbf{C}_{\mathsf{h}}$ *such that, if a partial signature scheme* Σ_{PS} *is* $(n, \varepsilon_{\mathsf{m}})$*-*$\mathsf{IK}$*-secure and* $(n, \varepsilon_{\mathsf{h}})$*-*$\mathsf{UF\text{-}UA}$*-secure, then it is* $(n, t, \varepsilon_{\mathsf{m}}^{\mathbf{C}_{\mathsf{m}}}, \varepsilon_{\mathsf{h}}^{\mathbf{C}_{\mathsf{h}}})$*-composably secure, for any* $t \in \mathbb{N}$.

Remark 1. It is natural to ask whether regular signatures would also achieve the notion of Definition 9. This would correspond to asking whether a partial signature scheme with empty strings as stubs would still satisfy Theorem 2. The short answer is no, because it is easy to see that such a scheme does not necessarily achieve unambiguity. Nevertheless, we point out that in principle it should be possible to construct unambiguous regular signature schemes, but still we chose to use partial signatures instead because they offer more: If the adversary also publishes its public-key, then non-empty stubs and unambiguity ensure that it cannot falsely claim any message of the honest senders. This would follow trivially by appropriately extending our definitions, but it would not if a regular signature scheme was used instead. We leave the problem of formalizing this variant open for future work.

5 Achieving Receiver-Side Anonymous Authenticity

One of the first alternative signature schemes providing some form of anonymity were *group signatures*, introduced by Chaum and Van Heyst [8]. The main idea is that members of a group share a public verification key, which can be used to verify a message-signature pair generated by any of the group members using their own (different) secret keys. Anonymity is enforced by ensuring that the verification process does not reveal any partial information about the secret key used to generate the signature, hence effectively allowing a member to anonymously sign a message on behalf of the group. Technically, this is achieved by assigning the role of group manager to a selected member, which is responsible for generating all members' secret keys as well as the group's public verification key. Therefore, the group manager also has the ability to reveal the original signer.

This drawback of group signatures was later circumvented by Rivest, Shamir, and Tauman [17], who introduced *ring signature.* In this new scheme, a signature is generated by using not only the sender secret key, but also all the public keys of the group's members, called a ring in this context. Therefore, a signature must be transmitted along with the list of all public keys used, and anonymity is again enforced by requiring that the verification process does not reveal any partial information about the secret key used to generate the signature. Another advantage of ring signatures, compared to group signatures, is that the ring can be dynamically chosen by the sender, and does not require any cooperation.

The syntax of a ring signature scheme, for a fixed ring size of $n \in \mathbb{N}$, extends that of a regular DSS as follows: each sender generates its key-pair (sk_i, pk_i), for $i \in [n]$, but in order to generate a signature σ on a message m, in addition to sk_i, the list $\boldsymbol{pk} \doteq (pk_1, \ldots, pk_n)$ of all other senders public keys is needed. Moreover, also the index i itself is required by the signing function, in order to link the given secret key to the public key of the sender. Then, the receiver can verify that σ is a valid signature for m by using $\boldsymbol{pk}$, and be assured that the message was authentically transmitted by one of the known senders, and no external adversary.

Definition 10 (Ring Signature Scheme). *A ring signature scheme (RSS) $\Sigma_{\mathsf{RS}} \doteq (\mathtt{Gen}, \mathtt{Sgn}, \mathtt{Vrf})$ for $n \geq 2$ users over message-space $\mathcal{M}$ and signature-space $\mathcal{S}$ (with $\perp \notin \mathcal{M} \cup \mathcal{S}$), is such that*

- $\mathtt{Gen}$ *is a distribution over the key-space $\mathcal{SK} \times \mathcal{PK}$;*
- $\mathtt{Sgn} : [n] \times \mathcal{SK} \times \mathcal{PK}^n \times \mathcal{M} \to \mathcal{S}$ *is a probabilistic function;*
- $\mathtt{Vrf} : \mathcal{PK}^n \times \mathcal{M} \times \mathcal{S} \to \{0, 1\}$ *is a deterministic function.*

We require the above to be efficiently samplable/computable. For index $i \in [n]$ and keys $sk \in \mathcal{SK}$, $\boldsymbol{pk} \doteq (pk_1, \ldots, pk_n) \in \mathcal{PK}^n$, for any $n \in \mathbb{N}$, we use the shorthand notation $\mathtt{Sgn}_{i,sk,\boldsymbol{pk}}(\cdot)$ for $\mathtt{Sgn}(i, sk, \boldsymbol{pk}, \cdot)$ and $\mathtt{Vrf}_{\boldsymbol{pk}}(\cdot, \cdot)$ for $\mathtt{Vrf}(\boldsymbol{pk}, \cdot, \cdot)$. Moreover, we assume correctness *of Σ_{RS}, that is, for all $n \geq 2$, all $i \in [n]$, all possible lists of n key-pairs $(sk_1, pk_1), \ldots, (sk_n, pk_n)$ distributed according to* $\mathtt{Gen}$*, with $\boldsymbol{pk} \doteq (pk_1, \ldots, pk_n)$, all messages $m \in \mathcal{M}$, and all signatures $\sigma \in \mathcal{S}$, $\mathtt{Vrf}_{\boldsymbol{pk}}(m, \sigma) = \mathbb{1}\left\{\sigma \in \bigcup_{i=1}^{n} \operatorname{supp}\left(\mathtt{Sgn}_{i,sk_i,\boldsymbol{pk}}(m)\right)\right\}$.*

5.1 Game-Based Security of Ring Signatures

When ring signatures were introduced in [17], no formal game-based security definitions were given, this was only done later in [7]. There, a stronger model than the one considered here was introduced, namely one where the adversary can generate and publish its own public key, which, as discussed in Sect. 2.3, would require a certificate authority. Therefore, here we use adapted versions of the weaker security notions of *unforgeability against fixed-ring attacks* and *basic anonymity* from [7]. In the full version [4] we relate those notions from the literature to the new combined definition we introduce next.

In order to define the security of a fixed scheme Σ_{RS}, we define the following systems (where the dependency on Σ_{RS} is implicit), parameterized by index $i \in [n]$ and keys $sk \in \mathcal{SK}$, $\boldsymbol{pk} \doteq (pk_1, \ldots, pk_n) \in \mathcal{PK}^n$, for any $n \in \mathbb{N}$.

- $\langle \mathbf{S}_{i,sk,\boldsymbol{pk}}, \mathbf{V}_{\boldsymbol{pk}} \rangle$:
  - On input $m \in \mathcal{M}$, return $(m, \sigma) \in \mathcal{M} \times \mathcal{S}$, for $\sigma \leftarrow \mathtt{Sgn}_{i,sk,\boldsymbol{pk}}(m)$.
  - On input $(m, \sigma) \in \mathcal{M} \times \mathcal{S}$, return m if $\mathtt{Vrf}_{\boldsymbol{pk}}(m, \sigma) = 1$ and $\perp$ otherwise.
- $\langle \mathbf{S}_{i,sk,\boldsymbol{pk}}, \mathbf{V}^{\perp} \rangle$: Set $\mathcal{Q} \subseteq \mathcal{M} \times \mathcal{S}$ to $\varnothing$, and then:
  - On input $m \in \mathcal{M}$, return $(m, \sigma) \in \mathcal{M} \times \mathcal{S}$, for $\sigma \leftarrow \mathtt{Sgn}_{i,sk,\boldsymbol{pk}}(m)$, and set $\mathcal{Q}$ to $\mathcal{Q} \cup \{(m, \sigma)\}$.
  - On input $(m, \sigma) \in \mathcal{M} \times \mathcal{S}$, return m if $(m, \sigma) \in \mathcal{Q}$ and $\perp$ otherwise.
- $\mathbf{K}_{\boldsymbol{pk}}$: On input $\diamond$, output $\boldsymbol{pk}$.

In our definitions, all keys will *always* be random variables distributed (as key-pairs) according to Σ_{RS}'s $\mathtt{Gen}$.

We define a combined notion for ring signatures capturing both authenticity and anonymity at once. For this, we define a distinction problem between a real system that correctly generates and verifies signatures, via signing and verification oracles for n (different) senders, and an ideal system that also correctly generates signatures and only correctly verifies signatures previously signed, but via n copies of signing and verification oracles for the *same* (randomly selected) sender.

Definition 11 (UF-IK-Secure Ring Signature). *A ring signature scheme* Σ_{RS} *is* (n, ε)-unforgeable-and-anonymous *(or* (n, ε)-UF-IK -secure*) if*

$$[\langle \mathbf{S}_{1,sk_1,\boldsymbol{pk}}, \mathbf{V}_{\boldsymbol{pk}} \rangle, \ldots, \langle \mathbf{S}_{n,sk_n,\boldsymbol{pk}}, \mathbf{V}_{\boldsymbol{pk}} \rangle, \mathbf{K}_{\boldsymbol{pk}}]$$
$$\approx_\varepsilon$$
$$[\underbrace{\langle \mathbf{S}_{I,sk_I,\boldsymbol{pk}}, \mathbf{V}^\perp \rangle, \ldots, \langle \mathbf{S}_{I,sk_I,\boldsymbol{pk}}, \mathbf{V}^\perp \rangle}_{n \text{ times}}, \mathbf{K}_{\boldsymbol{pk}}],$$

for key-pairs $(sk_1, pk_1), \ldots, (sk_n, pk_n) \leftarrow \texttt{Gen}$*,* $\boldsymbol{pk} \doteq (pk_1, \ldots, pk_n)$*, and random variable* $I \xleftarrow{\$} [n]$.

As we formally show in the full version [4], it is easy to see that if a ring signature scheme is (n, ε)-UF-secure *and* (n, ε')-IK-secure (as defined there), then it is $(n, \varepsilon^{\mathbf{C}} + \varepsilon')$-UF-IK-secure, for a specific reduction $\mathbf{C}$.

5.2 Composable Security of Ring Signatures

We continue our study of the semantics of ring signatures by defining their composable security in the constructive cryptography framework. Composable security notions for ring signatures have been previously studied in [20] within the universal composability (UC) framework. There, an ideal functionality was introduced, and it was shown to be securely realized by a protocol employing ring signatures. Unlike with our approach, such functionality was completely tailored to the ring signature scheme used by the protocol, that is, it exported operations such as signing and verifying, it did not model a communication channel between senders and receiver. Here we define an ideal resource, independent of any cryptographic scheme, and show that (among other possible ones), a protocol employing ring signatures indeed realizes such a resource.

Recall that we want to define composable security of a ring signature scheme Σ_{RS} as the construction of the resource $\mathsf{RA\text{-}AUT}_{n \to 1}$ from the resources $\mathsf{1\text{-}AUT}_{n \circlearrowleft 1}$ and $\mathsf{A\text{-}INS}_{n \to 1}$. In order to make this statement formal, we need to define how a protocol π_{RS}, attached to the resource $[\mathsf{1\text{-}AUT}_{n \circlearrowleft 1}, \mathsf{A\text{-}INS}_{n \to 1}]$, naturally makes use of Σ_{RS}. First, π_{RS} runs $\texttt{Gen}$ for every sender S_i, for $i \in [n]$, generating key-pairs $(sk_1, pk_1), \ldots, (sk_n, pk_n)$. Then it transmits the public keys $\boldsymbol{pk} \doteq (pk_1, \ldots, pk_n)$ to the receiver and all senders through $\mathsf{1\text{-}AUT}_{n \circlearrowleft 1}$. After that, once a sender S_i inputs a message m on its interface, π_{RS} uses sk_i and $\boldsymbol{pk}$ to generate $\sigma \leftarrow \texttt{Sgn}_{i,sk_i,\boldsymbol{pk}}(m)$, and inputs (m, σ) to the interface S_i of $\mathsf{A\text{-}INS}_{n \to 1}$. Once the receiver R inputs $\diamond$ on its interface, π_{RS} also inputs $\diamond$ to the interface R of $\mathsf{A\text{-}INS}_{n \to 1}$, obtaining a set $\mathfrak{D} \subseteq \mathbb{N} \times \mathcal{M} \times \mathcal{S}$, and outputs the set $\{(j, m) \mid \exists\, (j, m, \sigma) \in \mathfrak{D} : \texttt{Vrf}_{\boldsymbol{pk}}(m, \sigma) = 1\}$ to R. We call π_{RS} the protocol using Σ_{RS} in the *natural way*.

Definition 12. *A ring signature scheme* Σ_{RS} *is* (n, ε)-composably secure *if*

$$[\mathsf{1\text{-}AUT}_{n\circlearrowleft 1}, \mathsf{A\text{-}INS}_{n\to 1}] \xrightarrow{\pi_{\mathsf{RS}}, \varepsilon} \mathsf{RA\text{-}AUT}_{n\to 1},$$

where π_{RS} *is the protocol using* Σ_{RS} *in the natural way.*

Finally, we show that game-based security of ring signatures implies their composable security (we defer the proof to the full version [4]).

Theorem 3. *There exists a reduction system* **C** *such that, if a ring signature scheme* Σ_{RS} *is* (n, ε)-$\mathsf{UF\text{-}IK}$*-secure, then it is* $(n, \varepsilon^{\mathbf{C}})$*-composably secure.*

6 Concluding Remarks and Future Work

This work focused on filling a gap in the composable treatment of anonymity preservation in the public-key setting. Being of definitional nature, it was centered around providing clear composable semantics of existing schemes, as well as showing how existing and new game-based security notions for such schemes imply composable statements. This is very desirable in order to understand how such schemes should be used in practice.

Still, since the scope of this work was very ample, we see it as merely paving the way. For example, additional alternative solutions circumventing our impossibility result, employing different schemes, might be interesting to analyze. Moreover, all of our results hold under static corruptions, therefore a natural extension would be to consider a stronger security model capturing adaptive corruptions. This would allow to rely on stronger game-based notions from the literature for partial signatures and ring signatures.

References

1. Abdalla, M., Bellare, M., Neven, G.: Robust encryption. In: Micciancio, D. (ed.) TCC 2010. LNCS, vol. 5978, pp. 480–497. Springer, Heidelberg (2010). https://doi.org/10.1007/978-3-642-11799-2_28
2. Alwen, J., Hirt, M., Maurer, U., Patra, A., Raykov, P.: Anonymous authentication with shared secrets. In: Aranha, D.F., Menezes, A. (eds.) LATINCRYPT 2014. LNCS, vol. 8895, pp. 219–236. Springer, Cham (2015). https://doi.org/10.1007/978-3-319-16295-9_12
3. Banfi, F., Maurer, U.: Anonymous symmetric-key communication. In: Galdi, C., Kolesnikov, V. (eds.) SCN 2020. LNCS, vol. 12238, pp. 471–491. Springer, Cham (2020). https://doi.org/10.1007/978-3-030-57990-6_23
4. Banfi, F., Maurer, U.: Anonymous authenticated communication. Cryptology ePrint Archive, Report 2021/1581 (2021). https://eprint.iacr.org/2021/1581
5. Bellare, M., Boldyreva, A., Desai, A., Pointcheval, D.: Key-privacy in public-key encryption. In: Boyd, C. (ed.) ASIACRYPT 2001. LNCS, vol. 2248, pp. 566–582. Springer, Heidelberg (2001). https://doi.org/10.1007/3-540-45682-1_33
6. Bellare, M., Duan, S.: Partial signatures and their applications. Cryptology ePrint Archive, Report 2009/336 (2009). https://eprint.iacr.org/2009/336

7. Bender, A., Katz, J., Morselli, R.: Ring signatures: stronger definitions, and constructions without random oracles. In: Halevi, S., Rabin, T. (eds.) TCC 2006. LNCS, vol. 3876, pp. 60–79. Springer, Heidelberg (2006). https://doi.org/10.1007/11681878_4
8. Chaum, D., van Heyst, E.: Group signatures. In: Davies, D.W. (ed.) EUROCRYPT 1991. LNCS, vol. 547, pp. 257–265. Springer, Heidelberg (1991). https://doi.org/10.1007/3-540-46416-6_22
9. Fischlin, M.: Anonymous signatures made easy. In: Okamoto, T., Wang, X. (eds.) PKC 2007. LNCS, vol. 4450, pp. 31–42. Springer, Heidelberg (2007). https://doi.org/10.1007/978-3-540-71677-8_3
10. Jost, D., Maurer, U.: Overcoming impossibility results in composable security using interval-wise guarantees. In: Micciancio, D., Ristenpart, T. (eds.) CRYPTO 2020. LNCS, vol. 12170, pp. 33–62. Springer, Cham (2020). https://doi.org/10.1007/978-3-030-56784-2_2
11. Kohlweiss, M., Maurer, U., Onete, C., Tackmann, B., Venturi, D.: Anonymity-preserving public-key encryption: a constructive approach. In: De Cristofaro, E., Wright, M. (eds.) PETS 2013. LNCS, vol. 7981, pp. 19–39. Springer, Heidelberg (2013). https://doi.org/10.1007/978-3-642-39077-7_2
12. Maurer, U.: Indistinguishability of random systems. In: Knudsen, L.R. (ed.) EUROCRYPT 2002. LNCS, vol. 2332, pp. 110–132. Springer, Heidelberg (2002). https://doi.org/10.1007/3-540-46035-7_8
13. Maurer, U.: Constructive cryptography – a new paradigm for security definitions and proofs. In: Mödersheim, S., Palamidessi, C. (eds.) TOSCA 2011. LNCS, vol. 6993, pp. 33–56. Springer, Heidelberg (2012). https://doi.org/10.1007/978-3-642-27375-9_3
14. Maurer, U., Pietrzak, K., Renner, R.: Indistinguishability amplification. In: Menezes, A. (ed.) CRYPTO 2007. LNCS, vol. 4622, pp. 130–149. Springer, Heidelberg (2007). https://doi.org/10.1007/978-3-540-74143-5_8
15. Maurer, U., Renner, R.: Abstract cryptography. In: ICS 2011, pp. 1–21. Tsinghua University Press, Beijing (2011)
16. Maurer, U., Renner, R.: From indifferentiability to constructive cryptography (and Back). In: Hirt, M., Smith, A. (eds.) TCC 2016. LNCS, vol. 9985, pp. 3–24. Springer, Heidelberg (2016). https://doi.org/10.1007/978-3-662-53641-4_1
17. Rivest, R.L., Shamir, A., Tauman, Y.: How to leak a secret. In: Boyd, C. (ed.) ASIACRYPT 2001. LNCS, vol. 2248, pp. 552–565. Springer, Heidelberg (2001). https://doi.org/10.1007/3-540-45682-1_32
18. Saraswat, V., Yun, A.: Anonymous signatures revisited. In: Pieprzyk, J., Zhang, F. (eds.) ProvSec 2009. LNCS, vol. 5848, pp. 140–153. Springer, Heidelberg (2009). https://doi.org/10.1007/978-3-642-04642-1_13
19. Yang, G., Wong, D.S., Deng, X., Wang, H.: Anonymous signature schemes. In: Yung, M., Dodis, Y., Kiayias, A., Malkin, T. (eds.) PKC 2006. LNCS, vol. 3958, pp. 347–363. Springer, Heidelberg (2006). https://doi.org/10.1007/11745853_23
20. Yoneyama, K., Ohta, K.: Ring signatures: universally composable definitions and constructions. IPSJ Digit. Courier **3**, 571–584 (2007). https://doi.org/10.2197/ipsjdc.3.571
21. Zhang, R., Imai, H.: Strong anonymous signatures. In: Yung, M., Liu, P., Lin, D. (eds.) Inscrypt 2008. LNCS, vol. 5487, pp. 60–71. Springer, Heidelberg (2009). https://doi.org/10.1007/978-3-642-01440-6_7

Credential Transparency System

Melissa Chase[1], Georg Fuchsbauer[2], Esha Ghosh[1(✉)], and Antoine Plouviez[3]

[1] Microsoft Research, Redmond, USA
Esha.Ghosh@microsoft.com
[2] TU Wien, Vienna, Austria
Georg.Fuchsbauer@ens.fr
[3] ENS INRIA, Paris, France

Abstract. A major component of the entire digital identity ecosystem are verifiable credentials. However, for users to have complete control and privacy of their digital credentials, they need to be able to store and manage these credentials and associated cryptographic key material on their devices. This approach has severe usability challenges including portability across devises. A more practical solution is for the users to trust a more reliable and available service to manage credentials on their behalf, such as in the case of Single Sign-On (SSO) systems and identity hubs. But the obvious downside of this design is the immense trust that the users need to place on these service providers.

In this work, we introduce and formalize a *credential transparency system (CTS)* framework that adds strong transparency guarantees to a credential management system while preserving privacy and usability features of the system. CTS ensures that if a service provider presents any credential to an *honest* verifier on behalf of a user, and the user's device tries to audit all the shows presented on the user's behalf, the service provider will not be able to drop or modify any show information without getting caught. We define CTS to be a general framework that is compatible with a wide range of credential management systems including SSO and anonymous credential systems. We also provide a CTS instantiation and prove its security formally.

Keywords: Credential transparency · SSO · anonymous credentials · zero-knowledge sets · accumulators · zero-knowledge proofs

1 Introduction

A major component of the entire digital identity ecosystem are verifiable credentials. These credentials can range from simple ones such as email id's to more sophisticated ones such as government issued IDs [1,3]. Due to their wide-spread use in the web, a W3C working group [5] is trying to standardize the mechanism for expressing and exchanging different types of credentials on the web.

On the more academic research side, there has been a long line of work on anonymous credentials that built privacy-preserving technology for presenting

C. Galdi and S. Jarecki (Eds.): SCN 2022, LNCS 13409, pp. 313–335, 2022.
https://doi.org/10.1007/978-3-031-14791-3_14

credentials in a flexible way while disclosing minimal information [6–10,13–15, 18,19,22].

However, for users to have complete control and privacy of their credential presentations, they need to be able to store and manage these credentials and associated cryptographic key material on their devices. This is notoriously hard for an average user and has severe usability limitations. For example, it is difficult to port these credentials across devices; these are not readily available in case the primary device gets lost or stolen or when the user is traveling and using a different device but she still needs to access her credentials. Yet another security risk with user-device bound credentials is the threat of malware on the device: the credentials can be stolen by malware and either exported or used without the user's knowledge.

The most practical solution is therefore that the users trust a more reliable and available (possibly cloud-based) service to manage credentials on their behalf. For example, single sign-on (SSO) is a widely popular authentication mechanism on the web that lets a user securely authenticate to multiple websites using the same credential [4]. At a high level, SSO systems leverage the trust relationship between the websites and the identity providers (such as Google, Microsoft etc.) directly, rather than passing the credentials through the user. The identity provider signs certain credentials of the user (e.g., the user's email address or a username) and passes this signature along with the signed identity information to the website. The website can thus be convinced about the authenticity of these credentials.

While services to manage user credentials are great for usability, the obvious downside of this approach is the immense trust that the users need to place on these service providers. The users have to trust the service provider completely, with no recourse, and do not even have any visibility into how their credentials are used. For example, in case the service provider gets compromised, the users' credentials could be used to open accounts on other services, completely without the user's knowledge. This begs the question of whether this complete trust is inherent. In other words, is there any way we could reduce trust on the service providers, while still maintaining the usability guarantees.

Trusting the service provider with the privacy of the users' information (such as their credentials and information necessary to present it on their behalf) seems inherent in this setting. Similarly, if users can't store local secrets (due to usability and portability issues), the server will always be able to present the user's credential and claim to act on her behalf, without her permission. But can we make the credential management *transparent* to the users, so that their devices can monitor all the credential presentations on their behalf? We would like to add strong transparency guarantees as in other transparency log applications such as auditable public-key directories (CONIKS [20], SEEMless [11], Google Key Transparency [2]) or software [17,21] or key recovery transparency [16]. This means, we want to ensure that if a service provider presents any credential to an *honest* verifier on behalf of a user, and the user's device tries to monitor for all the shows presented on the user's behalf, the service provider will not be able to drop or modify any show information without an overwhelming probability of getting caught. Note that we emphasize *honest* verifier here, since it seems impossible to provide such strong detectability guarantees if both the service provider and the verifier are malicious and colluding to share user information.

In this work, we aim to define a general *credential transparency system (CTS)* framework that adds strong transparency guarantees to a credential management system. CTS is compatible with a wide range of credential systems, ranging from SSO systems to more sophisticated anonymous credential management systems. This means we must define the framework carefully, so as not to introduce any additional leakage in the underlying credential system. For example, in a classical anonymous credential system multiple verifiers verifying a certain user's credentials do not learn when/where else this user's credentials were presented. We retain this privacy guarantee in CTS. In addition, we preserve privacy of the credential presentation mechanism of the underlying system (such as unlinkability in case of anonymous credentials) in CTS. We discuss this in detail in Sect. 1.1.

CONTRIBUTIONS

- To the best of our knowledge, this is the first work to introduce and formalize a credential transparency framework (CTS). CTS adds strong transparency guarantees to a credential management system, thereby reducing the trust assumption on the service provider of a credential management system. The guiding principle of CTS is retaining usability features for users, while providing strong (in a cryptographic sense) transparency guarantees. This means we avoided any unrealistic assumption from the user (such as they can maintain a long-term cryptographic secret) in our design. We believe taking such usability features into consideration from the very beginning is important in building realistic security systems.
- We designed CTS to be compatible with a wide range of credential management systems: from SSO systems to more sophisticated, unlinkable anonymous credentials. This means we had to be careful in preserving the privacy requirements of the underlying credential management systems themselves. For example, if the credential presentation system is such that every show of the credential to a verifier is unlinkable from each other, we have to ensure that CTS retains that feature. However, such strong unlinkability is not a requirement in every application (e.g., SSO). So, we do not want CTS to enforce such a feature if the application does not require it. Instead, we took the approach of *preserving the privacy requirement* of the underlying credential management application in our formal definitions.
- Finally, we provide a CTS instantiation and prove its security formally. At a high level, the construction works as follows. The service provider in CTS (also called the cloud) manages the credentials on the users' behalf. The provider maintains a log internally, in which it stores all the credential shows for each user's credentials. Each verifier will ensure that every time the provider shows it a credential on behalf of a user (potentially anonymously), that credential is logged. The service provider also publishes privacy-preserving snapshots

of this log periodically, which are audited for consistency. When devices of a user monitor her credential show history, the service provider produces proofs of the history, which are verified against these public snapshots.

Note that this requires that we can guarantee that all parties in the system (in this case the users and verifiers and auditors) see the same snapshots. This requirement is shared by all previous transparency works, including (CONIKS [20], SEEMless [11], Google Key Transparency [2]) software transparency [17,21], and key recovery transparency [16]. There have been several proposals for how to achieve this, including posting snapshots to a blockchain, having parties or their representatives engage in a gossip protocol, or merely posting the snapshot signed by the service provider/cloud to many honest websites. Here we remain agnostic to the technique used and just assume that we have some way of guaranteeing that all parties see the same snapshots or detect misbehaviour.

In our instantiation, each snapshot contains two snapshots internally: one append-only strong accumulator snapshot (SA) and one append-only zero-knowledge set (ZKS) snapshot (for formal descriptions of these primitives, please refer to the Appendix). The SA accumulates all the shows of all users and the ZKS accumulates some special markers that count the number of shows performed on a particular user's behalf. Each user has a counter associated with her (which starts from 1 for the first show that the cloud performs for this user). If the counter reaches n for a some user such that $n = 2^\alpha$ for some $\alpha \in \mathbb{N}$, then the cloud adds α to the ZKS. The concept of using these α's to speed up verifier's work was introduced in SEEMless [11]; following the notation of SEEMless we call these "α"s *markers*.

Finally, as in SEEMless [11], we assume a set of auditors who audit the snapshots for consistency; these auditors can be users or third parties - they do not see any private information and we only need that at least one honest auditor audits each pair of snapshots. Each time a credential is presented, an (honest) verifier verifies that the show is correctly included in the log by checking that it has been added to the SA and ZKS (if the count reached a marker). However, we do not want to leak the counter and the marker of each show to the verifier. So we prove validity of this statement using a zero-knowledge proof.

The cloud also needs to prove validity of a user's history (when the user device checks it) with respect to the latest snapshots. While learning counters and markers for one's own credential shows is not a leakage, we need to be careful not to leak any information about other shows belonging to other users in the log. This is guaranteed by the simulatability of proofs in SA and ZKS.

Difference with SEEMless [11]: SEEMless [11] is a privacy-preserving key transparency system that enables a service provider to maintain an auditable PKI for client certificates; auditable PKI which has strong application in end-to-end encrypted messaging systems. Our CTS design is inspired from SEEMless, but CTS has significant technical differences with SEEMless as we discuss below.

Definitional Framework. We need to accommodate the diversity of the credential management system, to which we are adding transparency guarantee, within our definitional framework. To do this, we depart from the privacy definition of SEEMless completely and introduce two new concepts in our definition: user secret keys and pseudonyms. We discuss the details of our privacy formalization in Sect. 1.1.

Construction. While the data structures we use in CTS have some similarities with the data structures used in SEEMless [11], there are some significant technical differences since CTS requires more privacy than SEEMless. SEEMless data structures is composed of two ZKS. In the CTS instantiation we use one ZKS and one SA instead: SA for storing the user show information and ZKS for storing the markers for each user. In SEEMless, someone who communicates with the user can search for user's key inside the log and get access to the version number (equivalent of the counter) to verify if the key is up to date. While this leakage could be benign in case of a verifiable key directory such as SEEMless, leaking the counter and marker to a verifier seems like a significant leakage as it will leak how many shows for a user has been done to different verifiers. In case the underlying credential system provides unlinkability we need to hide the user identity from the verifier as well. This is why deviate from the SEEMless design (which only used ZKS proofs) and use ZKS and SA proofs + a ZK proof as described above.

1.1 Definitional Framework for Diverse Credential Systems

As discussed above, the techniques we use in our CTS proposal are compatible with many different types of credential systems, from privacy-preserving anonymous credentials to more common single sign-on systems. To capture this diversity within one definitional framework we focus on two concepts: user secret keys (usk) and pseudonyms.

The user secret key defines what is unique to the user, so that the basic goal of CTS is to ensure that all credential presentations that use a given user secret key must be listed when that user queries the log for her history[1]. In an SSO system, this might simply be the user's email or login ID. In a privacy-preserving credential system, this would often be a random secret selected by the user (or the user's device together with the issuer) and known only to the user. This type of secret is often used to tie together many credentials issued to the same user.

However, in these privacy-preserving schemes, the user secret key is obviously not presented directly to the verifier. On the other hand, it is essential that the credential presentation is in some way directly tied to the user secret key in

[1] Note that, in cases where usk is not a human-memorable, we want the service provider to commit to the mapping from a username (or equivalent user memorable string) to usk. Then service provider would first show which usk corresponds to the username, and then use CTS to show the presentations linked to that usk. This additional mapping is just a straightforward append only ZKS, so we don't describe it here.

question, so that there is a well defined user in whose history this presentation should appear. To capture this, we use the notion of a pseudonym – a value which encapsulates the user secret key and which will be given to the verifier as part of the presentation. We require that the pseudonym be binding, in that there is at most one usk which can be consistent with the pseudonym – so that there is a unique user corresponding to each presentation. Depending on the credential scheme, the pseudonym may provide varying degrees of privacy by hiding the usk, in which case we guarantee that the CTS will not reveal more about the usk than is directly revealed by the pseudonym. In a anonymous credential scheme, the user will present the pseudonym and then prove possession of a credential with appropriate attributes that has been issued to the usk represented by the given pseudonym.

Our pseudonym will be allowed to depend on both the context of the presentation and the usk. This allows for credential schemes in which the user has a different unlinkable pseudonym for every context, as well as those where the user's pseudonym is required to be consistent across different presentations to the same verifier. If the context also includes a timestamp, nonce, or other value that is guaranteed to be different for each presentation, then this can give full unlinkability, in which every presentation looks like it could have come from a different user.

Finally, we will require that the pseudonym be computed via a deterministic function of the context and the usk. This is not strictly essential, but it simplifies our definitions, construction, and analysis. This is trivial in non-privacy preserving contexts, where the function can be defined to directly output the usk (for example the user login) as a pseudonym. Technically, it is also not hard to achieve in most credential schemes. For example, in the random oracle model, there is a simple construction for any credential that supports discrete-log representation proofs. (This includes RSA-based [9], prime-order group [6,8,13] and pairing-based constructions [7,10,22].) This construction hashes some portion of the context (depending on the privacy goals as described above) into the group, and then raises the resulting group element to the usk. The base will thus be computable by the verifier, and DDH will guarantee that when the context changes appropriately the pseudonym will be unlinkable. If the credential supports discrete-log representation proofs, then it is straightforward to prove that the usk in the pseudonym matches that encoded in the credential.

2 Credential Transparency System (CTS)

In this section we will introduce a primitive called *Credential Transparency System (CTS)*. A CTS consists of four types of parties: the **users**; the **verifiers**; the **cloud**; and external **auditors**. The cloud manages the user's credentials on their behalf. In CTS, we want to guarantee that every credential show that the cloud performs on behalf of the user is logged (in a tamper proof and privacy-preserving manner), so that the cloud cannot lie about it later.

The verifiers (sometimes also referred to as Relying Parties or RPs) are the consumers of the credentials. When they consume a credential show, they also check that the show is logged by the cloud service. When some user asks the cloud service to show her credentials, the cloud issues a credential show that the verifier checks. This show can be unlinkable and privacy preserving (as in anonymous credentials), should the application require it to be so, or not privacy-preserving such as in SSO [4]. This choice depends on the application and CTS does not take any position on it. CTS captures both private and non-private credential presentations by abstracting the presentation as a *show* and ensures that adding logging guarantees does not introduce any significant additional leakage over what the credential presentation system already leaks. This means, if the credential presentation is unlinkable, CTS logging preserves this property. We discuss this in more details in Sect. 1.1.

The cloud service provider maintains an internal log of all credential presentations of all users that it performs. After presenting some credential to a verifier, the cloud will update its log by appending this show information and, at regular intervals of time, it will publish snapshots ($\mathsf{CTS.Publish}$) of its log and prove to the verifiers that the updated log has correctly registered all the shows that occurred in the interval ($\mathsf{CTS.InclProof}$). It also maintains a data structure of all the published snapshots so far.

The auditors in the system ensure global consistency of the published snapshots by checking update proofs ($\mathsf{CTS.PublishVer}$), so that the cloud won't be able to equivocate. Auditing can be performed by Users or Verifiers, but also by some third party as audit proofs do not reveal any sensitive information.

We do assume that there is some way of ensuring that all parties have consistent views of the current snapshot or at least that they periodically compare these values to make sure that their views have not forked. One way of doing this would be for the cloud to publish the snapshots periodically to a blockchain. Alternatively, this could be implemented using a gossip protocol. For further discussion on this, please see SEEMless [11].

The users' devices query the cloud in the background to monitor the history of shows presented on her behalf (using $\mathsf{CTS.Hist}$).

Definition 1. *A Credential Transparency Log consists of the Algorithms: CTS.ParamSetup, CTS.ServerSetup, CTS.GetNym, CTS.Publish, CTS.PublishVer, CTS.InclProof, CTS.InclVer, CTS.Hist, CTS.HistVer.*

System Setup

$\triangleright$ $\widehat{\mathsf{pp}} \leftarrow \mathsf{CTS.ParamSetup}(1^\lambda)$: This algorithm takes the security parameter as input and outputs some public parameters pp for the scheme. We include this algorithm mainly for compatibility with standard definitions. In reality we will want to instantiate our protocols with schemes that don't require trusted setup or, if a common random string is required, we will generate it with a random oracle so that we do not need any trusted party.

$\triangleright$ $(\mathsf{pp}, \mathsf{st}_0) \leftarrow \mathsf{CTS.ServerSetup}(\widehat{\mathsf{pp}})$: This algorithm is run by the **cloud** and takes as input the public parameters $\widehat{\mathsf{pp}}$, it generates the public parameters pp, it outputs pp and initializes the state of the cloud server: st_0. We consider pp and $\widehat{\mathsf{pp}}$ to be implicit inputs to all the following algorithms.

Credential Presentation
$\triangleright$ $\mathsf{nym} \leftarrow \mathsf{CTS.GetNym}(\mathsf{usk}, \mathsf{ctext})$: This algorithm is run by the **cloud**. It takes as input the user's secret key usk and context information ctext. It outputs a pseudonym called nym, which is used for the credential presentation. ctext contains information about context in which the credential will be presented. For example, this can be the verifier's URL/identity information + timestamp of presentation.

The pseudonym should be **binding**, meaning that for all ctext and $(\mathsf{usk}_1, \mathsf{usk}_2)$, $\mathsf{usk}_1 \neq \mathsf{usk}_2$ implies that $\mathsf{CTS.GetNym}(\mathsf{usk}_1, \mathsf{ctext}) \neq \mathsf{CTS.GetNym}(\mathsf{usk}_2, \mathsf{ctext})$. We also assume the pseudonym is **deterministic**. Note that for unlinkable presentations, additional privacy properties will be required of nym. But, as explained above, CTS leaves it up to the application and minimally requires the pseudonym to be binding. See Sect. 1.1 for more discussion.

Snapshot Publications
$\triangleright$ $(\pi_t^{\mathsf{Upd}}, \mathsf{snap}_t, \mathsf{st}_t) \leftarrow \mathsf{CTS.Publish}(\mathsf{st}_{t-1}, \mathsf{Show}_t)$: This algorithm is run by the **cloud**. It takes as input the current state of the Cloud st_{t-1} and a list Show_t of show information to register in the log. Each show corresponds to presented credential information and includes the corresponding context ctext. It outputs the updated state st_t, a public snapshot snap_t and a proof π_t^{Upd} that nothing was removed from the log. Note that, in case the usk's used by the system are not human-memorable strings, the Cloud is also required to maintain an auditable mapping from a username (or equivalent user memorable string) to usk and publish the mapping as a part of snap. This is a straight-forward addition to make, so we do not make it explicit in CTS.

$\triangleright$ $0/1 \leftarrow \mathsf{CTS.PublishVer}(\mathsf{snap}_t, \mathsf{snap}_{t-1}, \pi_t^{\mathsf{Upd}})$: This algorithm is run by the external **auditors**. It takes in input the new snapshot snap_t, the previous one snap_{t-1} and a proof π_t^{Upd}. It verifies consistency of the new snapshot with respect to the last one. This outputs a bit indicating success or failure of this verification.

Verification of Inclusion in the New Snapshot
$\triangleright$ $\pi^{\mathsf{Inc}} \leftarrow \mathsf{CTS.InclProof}(\mathsf{st}_T, \mathsf{usk}, \mathsf{ctext})$: This algorithm is run by the **cloud**. It takes as input the state of the Cloud corresponding to the last published snapshot st_T, the user's secret key usk and the context information of the show ctext Note that **the context information should be unique for every show** because it is used by the verifier to identify the show in order to verify its inclusion later. It outputs a proof π^{Inc} of inclusion of the context information in the log. In case, usk is not a human-memorable string, π^{Inc} will also include the human-memorable *username* and the proof of mapping between the *username* and usk. As we explain above, this is straight-forward to add to a CTS system. We do not make it explicit to keep the description simple.

$\triangleright$ $0/1 \leftarrow \mathsf{CTS.InclVer}(\mathsf{snap}_T, \mathsf{nym}, \mathsf{ctext}, \pi^{\mathsf{Inc}})$: This algorithm is used by the **verifier**. It takes as input the last published snapshot snap_T, the pseudonym of the user nym, the context information of the show ctext and a proof π^{Inc}. It outputs a bit that indicates if the verification of π^{Inc} is correct or not.

User Verification of History

▷ $((\mathsf{ctext}_i)_{i=1}^n, \pi^{\mathsf{Hist}}) \leftarrow \mathsf{CTS.Hist}(\mathsf{st}_T, \mathsf{usk})$: This algorithm is run by the **cloud**. It takes as input the state of the Cloud st_T corresponding to the last published snapshot snap_T and the user's secret key usk. It outputs a list of contexts $(\mathsf{ctext}_i)_{i=1}^n$ about the shows of the User's credential and a proof π^{Hist} that those contexts are correct and nothing is omitting with respect to the committed log.

▷ $0/1 \leftarrow \mathsf{CTS.HistVer}(\mathsf{snap}_T, \mathsf{usk}, (\mathsf{ctext}_i)_{i=1}^n, \pi^{\mathsf{Hist}})$: This algorithm is used by the **user**. It takes as input the last published snapshot snap_T, the user's secret key usk, a proof π^{Hist} and a list of contexts $(\mathsf{ctext}_i)_{i=1}^n$ about all the shows of the user's credential. It outputs a bit that indicates if the verification of π^{Hist} is correct or not.

2.1 Security Properties

In this section we state the security properties of a CTS.

Completeness: The Completeness property is satisfied if all the verifications of the proofs accept with overwhelming probability when all the parties behave honestly. We define a completeness game in which the stateful adversary wins if it finds an input for a proof algorithm that is rejected in the protocol; we let the adversary choose all the shows that will be included in the log. Then the snapshots are produced for every set of show, using $\mathsf{CTS.Publish}$. Once all the snapshots have been published, the adversary tries to find one proof that is not valid to win the game.

Definition. The game $G_{compl}^{\mathcal{A}}(\lambda)$ is defined in Fig. 1.

CTS is *complete* if for all $n \in \mathbb{N}$, and all PPT stateful adversary $\mathcal{A}$, there exists a negligible function ν such that for all $\lambda > 0$, we have $\Pr[0 \leftarrow \mathrm{G}_{compl}(\lambda, n)] < \nu(\lambda)$.

Soundness: The Soundness property holds if the Cloud cannot cheat about inclusion of show information in the Log. That is to say: the Cloud should not be able to prove to the verifier that ctext information about a show under some nym has been included while proving to the user under the nym that ctext is not in the log.

In the soundness game, the adversary is the Cloud and will compute snapshots and proofs of updates of the log. Then it will output a proof π_{Inc} of inclusion of $\mathsf{ctext}_{\mathsf{Inc}}$ under the identity of $\mathsf{nym}_{\mathsf{Inc}}$ at epoch i_{Inc}. It will also output a list of $(\mathsf{ctext}_{\mathsf{Hist},i})_i$ corresponding to $\mathsf{usk}_{\mathsf{Hist}}$ and a proof π^{Hist} of inclusion of those at epoch $i_{\mathsf{Hist}} > i_{\mathsf{Inc}}$ The adversary wins if all the proofs are valid, if $\mathsf{nym}_{\mathsf{Inc}}$ corresponds to $\mathsf{usk}_{\mathsf{Hist}}$ and if $\mathsf{ctext}_{\mathsf{Inc}} \notin (\mathsf{ctext}_{\mathsf{Hist},i})_i$

Definition. The game $G_{sound}^{\mathcal{A}}(\lambda)$ is defined in Fig. 2.

CTS is *sound* if for all PPT adversary $\mathcal{A}$ there exists a negligible function ν such that for all $\lambda > 0$, we have $\Pr[1 \leftarrow G_{sound}^{\mathcal{A}}(\lambda)] < \nu(\lambda)$.

Game $\mathrm{G}_{compl}(\lambda, n)$

$\widehat{\mathsf{pp}} \leftarrow \mathsf{CTS.ParamSetup}(1^\lambda)$
$(\mathsf{pp}, \mathsf{st}_0, \mathsf{snap}_0) \leftarrow \mathsf{CTS.ServerSetup}(\widehat{\mathsf{pp}})$
$\mathsf{st}_0 := \emptyset;\ \pi_0^{\mathsf{Upd}} := \varepsilon$ // The initial proof is an empty string
for $i = 1 \ldots n$
  $\mathsf{Show}_i \leftarrow \mathcal{A}(\mathsf{pp}, \mathsf{st}_{i-1}, \pi_{i-1}^{\mathsf{Upd}})$
  $(\pi_i^{\mathsf{Upd}}, \mathsf{snap}_i, \mathsf{st}_i) \leftarrow \mathsf{CTS.Publish}(\mathsf{st}_{i-1}, \mathsf{Show}_i)$
$i \leftarrow \mathcal{A}(\mathsf{st}_n, \pi_n^{\mathsf{Upd}})$
$b \leftarrow \mathsf{CTS.PublishVer}(\mathsf{pp}, \mathsf{snap}_i, \mathsf{snap}_{i-1}, \pi_i^{\mathsf{Upd}})$
$(i, j) \leftarrow \mathcal{A}(\cdot)$; **Parse** $(\mathsf{usk}_l, \mathsf{ctext}_l) := \mathsf{Show}_i$
$\pi^{\mathsf{Inc}} \leftarrow \mathsf{CTS.InclProof}(\mathsf{pp}, \mathsf{snap}_i, \mathsf{usk}_j, \mathsf{ctext}_j)$
$\mathsf{nym} \leftarrow \mathsf{CTS.GetNym}(\mathsf{pp}, \mathsf{usk}_j, \mathsf{ctext}_j)$
$b' \leftarrow \mathsf{CTS.InclVer}(\mathsf{pp}, \mathsf{snap}_i, \mathsf{nym}, \mathsf{ctext}_j, \pi_i^{\mathsf{Upd}})$
$(i, \mathsf{usk}) \leftarrow \mathcal{A}(\cdot)$
$\mathsf{L}' := ()$
for $k = 1 \cdots n$
  Parse $\mathsf{Show}_k = (\mathsf{usk}_l, \mathsf{ctext}_l)_{l=1}^r$
  for $l = 1 \cdots r$
    if $\mathsf{usk}_l = \mathsf{usk}$ **then**
      $\mathsf{L}' = \mathsf{L}' \cup \{\mathsf{ctext}_l\}$
$(\pi^{\mathsf{Hist}}, (\mathsf{ctext}_l)_l) \leftarrow \mathsf{CTS.Hist}(\mathsf{st}_i, \mathsf{usk})$; $\mathsf{L} := (\mathsf{ctext}_l)_l$
$b'' \leftarrow \mathsf{CTS.HistVer}(\mathsf{pp}, \mathsf{snap}_i, \mathsf{usk}, \pi^{\mathsf{Hist}}, \mathsf{L})$
return $b \wedge b' \wedge b'' \wedge (\mathsf{L} = \mathsf{L}')$

Fig. 1. CTS Completeness game

Game $\mathrm{G}_{sound}^{\mathcal{A}}(\lambda)$

$\widehat{\mathsf{pp}} \leftarrow \mathsf{CTS.ParamSetup}(1^\lambda)$
$(\mathsf{pp}, (\mathsf{snap}_i, \pi_i^{\mathsf{Upd}})_{i=1}^n, (\mathsf{ctext}_{\mathsf{Inc}}, \mathsf{nym}_{\mathsf{Inc}}, \pi^{\mathsf{Inc}}, i_{\mathsf{Inc}}),$
$(\mathsf{usk}_{\mathsf{Hist}}, (\mathsf{ctext}_{\mathsf{Hist},j})_j, \pi^{\mathsf{Hist}}, i_{\mathsf{Hist}})) \leftarrow \mathcal{A}(\widehat{\mathsf{pp}})$
$b := \wedge_{i=1}^n \mathsf{CTS.PublishVer}(\mathsf{snap}_{i-1}, \mathsf{snap}_i, \pi_i^{\mathsf{Upd}})$
$b' \leftarrow \mathsf{CTS.InclVer}(\mathsf{snap}_{i_{\mathsf{Inc}}}, \mathsf{nym}_{\mathsf{Inc}}, \mathsf{ctext}_{\mathsf{Inc}}, \pi^{\mathsf{Inc}})$
$b'' \leftarrow \mathsf{CTS.HistVer}(\mathsf{snap}_{i_{\mathsf{Hist}}}, \mathsf{usk}_{\mathsf{Hist}}, \pi^{\mathsf{Hist}}, \mathsf{ctext}_{\mathsf{Hist},j})_j)$
$b''' := (\mathsf{nym}_{\mathsf{Inc}} = \mathsf{CTL.GetNym}(\mathsf{usk}_{\mathsf{Hist}}, \mathsf{ctext}_{i}nc))$
return $b \wedge b' \wedge b'' \wedge b''' \wedge (1 \leqslant i_{\mathsf{Inc}} \leqslant i_{\mathsf{Hist}} \leqslant n) \wedge (\mathsf{ctext}_{\mathsf{Inc}} \notin (\mathsf{ctext}_{\mathsf{Hist},j})_j)$

Fig. 2. CTS Soundness game

Privacy: At a high level, the privacy guarantee of a CTS is that the outputs of CTS.InclProof, CTS.Hist, or CTS.Publish should not reveal anything beyond the answer and a well defined leakage function on the cloud's log state. So, the proofs for each of these queries should be simulatable given the output of the leakage function and the response.

For the privacy definition, we assume that the verifier can collude with other users; we call these corrupted users and record them in the set CU. There is also a set for honest users HU. CTS should protect the privacy of users registered in HU. We assume for this property that the Cloud is honest, otherwise he can clearly reveal whatever information he chooses and guaranteeing any privacy is impossible.

The adversary will play a game in which it has access to some Oracles. We want to be able to replace all the oracles by simulators that will be constructed without using any honest user secret information. We want the adversary not to be able to distinguish if it interacts with the oracles or with the simulators. This way, we can be sure that the protocol does not leak any information about honest users (beyond a well defined leakage function).

Definition. The game $G^{\mathcal{A}}_{b,privacy}(\lambda)$ for $b \in \{0,1\}$ is defined in Fig. 3.

CTS is *private* if for all PPT adversary $\mathcal{A}$, there exists a negligeable function ν such that for all $\lambda > 0$, we have $|\Pr[1 \leftarrow G^{\mathcal{A}}_{1,privacy}(\lambda)] - \Pr[1 \leftarrow G^{\mathcal{A}}_{0,privacy}(\lambda)]| < \nu(\lambda)$.

3 CTS Construction

3.1 Overview of Our Construction

Here we give an overview of our construction and defer the pseudocode to the full version. In the CTS construction, the Cloud maintains an append only Strong Accumulator (SA) of (label, com) pairs. The label label is evaluated from the user secret key usk and a counter count[usk] (which enumerates the shows of this user) by applying a VRF on usk, count[usk]. com is a commitment to the context information of the show. Each usk is being attributed a counter which is incremented each time a show occurs.

In addition, the cloud maintains an append only Zero-Knowledge Set (ZKS). The ZKS is used to store the number of uses of the user's credential. For each user, the cloud maintains a list of markers, which is the logarithms of the counters. When the counter of one user reaches a new level: $\mathsf{count[usk]} = 2^\alpha$, then the Cloud will add $\mathsf{marker} := \alpha = \log_2(\mathsf{count})$ together with usk to ZKS. This way all the markers in $[1, \log_2(\mathsf{count[usk]})]$ are stored in ZKS as usk||marker.

To prove inclusion of an element in the log, the cloud will produce a proof of inclusion in the SA of a label pair (label, com) and a proof of inclusion of usk||marker in the ZKS. When the proof of inclusion is made for the user in CTS.Hist, the Cloud will also reveal the context ctext that has been used to compute the commitment. Every time one user asks the cloud for its history, the

Game $\mathrm{G}^{\mathcal{A}}_{0,privacy}(\lambda)$

$\widehat{\mathsf{pp}} \leftarrow \mathsf{CTS.ParamSetup}(1^\lambda)$
$(\mathsf{pp}, \mathsf{st}_0) \leftarrow \mathsf{CTS.ServerSetup}(\widehat{\mathsf{pp}})$
$\mathtt{HU} := \emptyset;\ \mathtt{CU} := \emptyset;\ \ell = 0;\ T = 0$
$b \leftarrow \mathcal{A}^{\mathsf{O}_R}(\mathsf{pp})$
return b

Oracle $\mathsf{O}_{R,\mathsf{nym}}(i, \mathsf{ctext})$

if $i \notin \mathtt{HU}$ **then return** $\perp$
$\mathsf{nym} = \mathsf{CTS.GetNym}(\mathsf{usk}_i, \mathsf{ctext})$
return nym

Oracle $\mathsf{O}_{R,\mathsf{Inc}}(i, \mathsf{ctext})$

$\pi_{\mathsf{Inc}} = \mathsf{CTS.InclProof}(\mathsf{st}_T, \mathsf{usk}_i, \mathsf{ctext})$
return π^{Inc}

Oracle $\mathsf{O}_{\mathtt{HU}}(\cdot)$

$\mathtt{HU} = \mathtt{HU} \cup \{\ell\}$
Pick $\mathsf{usk}_\ell;\ \ell = \ell + 1$

Oracle $\mathsf{O}_{\mathtt{CU}}(\mathsf{usk})$

$\mathtt{CU} = \mathtt{CU} \cup \{\ell\}$
$\mathsf{usk}_\ell = \mathsf{usk};\ \ell = \ell + 1$

Oracle $\mathsf{O}_{R,\mathsf{Publish}}((i_j, \mathsf{ctext}_j)_{j=1}^k)$

$\mathsf{Show} = \{(\mathsf{usk}_{i_j}, \mathsf{ctext}_j)_{j=1}^k)\}$
$(\pi_T^{\mathsf{Upd}}, \mathsf{snap}_T, \mathsf{st}_T) \leftarrow \mathsf{CTS.Publish}(\mathsf{st}_{T-1}, \mathsf{Show})$
$T = T + 1$
return $(\pi_T^{\mathsf{Upd}}, \mathsf{snap}_T)$

Oracle $\mathsf{O}_{R,\mathsf{Hist}}(i)$

if $i \notin \mathtt{CU}$ **then return** $\perp$
$(\pi_{\mathsf{Hist}}, (\mathsf{ctext}_j)_{j=1}^k) = \mathsf{CTS.Hist}(\mathsf{st}_T, \mathsf{usk}_i)$
return $(\pi^{\mathsf{Hist}}, (\mathsf{ctext}_j)_{j=1}^k)$

Game $\mathrm{G}^{\mathcal{A}}_{1,privacy}(\lambda)$

$\widehat{\mathsf{pp}} \leftarrow \mathsf{CTS.ParamSetup}(1^\lambda)$
$(\mathsf{pp}, \mathsf{st}) \leftarrow \mathsf{CTS.ServerSetup}(\widehat{\mathsf{pp}})$
$\mathtt{HU} := \emptyset;\ \mathtt{CU} := \emptyset;\ \ell = 0;\ T = 0$
$\mathsf{ShowList} := \emptyset$
$b \leftarrow \mathcal{A}^{\mathsf{O}_I}(\mathsf{pp})$
return b

Oracle $\mathsf{O}_{I,\mathsf{nym}}(i, \mathsf{ctext})$

if $i \notin \mathtt{HU}$ **then return** $\perp$
$\mathsf{nym} \leftarrow \mathsf{CTS.GetNym}(\mathsf{usk}_i, \mathsf{ctext})$
return nym

Oracle $\mathsf{O}_{I,\mathsf{Inc}}(i, \mathsf{ctext})$

if $(i, \mathsf{ctext}) \notin \mathsf{ShowList}$ **then**
  return $\perp$
$\mathsf{nym} \leftarrow \mathsf{O}_{I,\mathsf{nym}}(i, \mathsf{ctext})$
$T = \mathsf{L}_2(i, \mathsf{ctext}_j, \mathsf{ShowList})$
if $i \in \mathtt{CU}$ **then**
  $\pi \leftarrow \mathsf{Sim.Incl}_1(\mathsf{st}, \mathsf{usk}_i, \mathsf{ctext}, T)$
else
  $\pi \leftarrow \mathsf{Sim.Incl}_2(\mathsf{st}, \mathsf{nym}, \mathsf{ctext}, T)$
return π

Oracle $\mathsf{O}_{\mathtt{HU}}(\cdot)$

$\mathtt{HU} = \mathtt{HU} \cup \{\ell\}$
Pick $\mathsf{usk}_\ell;\ \ell = \ell + 1$

Oracle $\mathsf{O}_{\mathtt{CU}}(\mathsf{usk})$

$\mathtt{CU} = \mathtt{CU} \cup \{\ell\}$
$\mathsf{usk}_\ell = \mathsf{usk};\ \ell = \ell + 1$

Oracle $\mathsf{O}_{I,\mathsf{Publish}}((i_j, \mathsf{ctext}_j)_{j=1}^k)$

$T = T + 1$
$(\pi, \mathsf{snap}) \leftarrow \mathsf{SimPublish}(\mathsf{st}, k, \mathsf{L}_1((i_j, \mathsf{ctext}_j)_{j=1}^k, \mathtt{CU}))$
Append $((i_j, \mathsf{ctext}_j; T)_{j=1}^k)$ **to** $\mathsf{ShowList}$
  return (π, snap)

Oracle $\mathsf{O}_{I,\mathsf{Hist}}(i)$

if $i \notin \mathtt{CU}$ **then return** $\perp$
$L = \emptyset;\ L' = \emptyset$
for $(i_j, \mathsf{ctext}_j) \in \mathsf{ShowList}$
  if $i_j = i$ **then**
    Append ctext_j **to** L.
    Append $\mathsf{L}_2(i, \mathsf{ctext}_j, \mathsf{ShowList})$ **to** L'
$\pi = \mathsf{Sim.Hist}(\mathsf{st}, \mathsf{usk}_i, L, L')$
return (π, L)

Fig. 3. CTS Privacy game

cloud gives the proofs of inclusion of all the shows that concern this user. The user can verify that the proofs are correct, and also that the shows are stored at the right position inside the SA.

The cloud also needs to build proofs of inclusion of show information for the verifier: it computes a proof that a $(\mathsf{label}, \mathsf{com})$ pair is included in the SA, with com corresponding to ctext. The cloud computes a Zero Knowledge proof of knowledge of the witness $\mathsf{witness} := (\mathsf{usk}, \mathsf{count}, \mathsf{marker}, \pi_{\mathsf{VRF}}, \pi_{\mathsf{ZKS}})$ for the statement $\mathsf{statement} = (\mathsf{nym}, \mathsf{ctext}, \mathsf{snap}_{T,\mathsf{ZKS}})$ such that:

- $\mathsf{VRF.Verif}(\mathsf{pp}, (\mathsf{usk}||\mathsf{count}), \mathsf{label}, \pi_{\mathsf{VRF}}) = 1$, which proves that the label computed corresponds to the user secret usk (thus the user will have access to it via the algorithm CTS.Hist.
- $\mathsf{nym} = \mathsf{CTS.GetNym}(\mathsf{usk}, \mathsf{ctext})$ which proves that the pseudonym nym was computed correctly.
- $\mathsf{ZKS.Verif}(\mathsf{pp}, \mathsf{snap}_{T,\mathsf{ZKS}}, (\mathsf{usk}||\mathsf{marker}), 1, \pi_{\mathsf{ZKS}})$ which proves that the marker marker is correctly included inside the ZKS
- $2^{\mathsf{marker}} \leqslant \mathsf{count} < 2^{\mathsf{marker}+1}$ which proves that the marker marker corresponds to the counter count.

We want the verifier not to be able to link multiple credential shows by a user (if the underlying pseudonym is unlinkable), or learn the count or the marker. That's why we need the ZK proof described above. All the algorithms are described more precisely in the next section.

In case usk is not a human memorable string, the Cloud will need to maintain an additions ZKS that maps a human-memorable username to usk. Since this can be easily implemented using a separate ZKS, we will not explicitly describe this in our construction.

3.2 Construction Description

In this section we explain how the different algorithms of CTS are instantiated. The algorithmic pseudocode is deferred to the full version [12].

We introduce an example to make the instantiation more concrete. We have two users, Alice and Bob whose credentials are managed by the Cloud, and one Verifier. On the first update, Alice requests two shows of her credential to the verifier and Bob one.

CTS.ParamSetup: This algorithm is run by a trusted authority which generates the parameters for most of the schemes. It generates the public parameters of the ZKS scheme, the VRF scheme, the commitment scheme and the ZK protocol. those parameters are grouped in $\widehat{\mathsf{pp}}$ which is outputed. We include this mainly for compatability with the definitions of the building blocks. In reality we will want to use random oracle based schemes for all of these building blocks, so the setup will only include specifying the hash function.

CTS.ServerSetup: This algorithm takes as input the parameters $\widehat{\mathsf{pp}}$. It generates lists and parameters for the server (cloud). First it initialises the snapshot and states of the ZKS and the SA, after that it generates the keys $(\mathsf{cpk}, \mathsf{csk})$ for the VRF. Then it initialises the list List, the counter table count[] and the maximum marker $\mathsf{markerM} = 2^\lambda$. It then groups those elements inside pp, snap_0 and st_0 and outputs pp and st_0 (which contains snap_0).

CTS.Publish: This algorithm takes as input a list of the public parameters pp, the actual state st_{T-1} and a list of shows Show_T.

- It shuffles the set of Shows, so that it is not ordered (this operation is useful for privacy).
- It initialises two lists, S_T and C_T which gather respectively the elements that should be included inside the SA and the ZKS during the update.
- For every tuple $(\mathsf{usk}, \mathsf{ctext})$ in the set of shows :
  - It increments the counter $\mathsf{count}[\mathsf{usk}]$ (which counts the shows of usk) or initialises the counter to 1 if it's the first show for usk.
  - It computes a label label using the VRF on $\mathsf{usk}||\mathsf{count}[\mathsf{usk}]$.
  - It generates a random opening value open and uses it to build a commitment com on ctext.
  - It updates S_T with the $(\mathsf{label}, \mathsf{com})$ pair and the list List with $(\mathsf{usk}, \mathsf{count}[\mathsf{usk}], \mathsf{label}, \mathsf{ctext}, \mathsf{open})$.
  - It verifies if the counter $\mathsf{count}[\mathsf{usk}]$ reached a marker. If $\mathsf{count}[\mathsf{usk}] := 2^{\mathsf{marker}}$ for some $\mathsf{marker} \in [0, \mathsf{markerM}]$, then it adds $\mathsf{usk}||\mathsf{marker}$ in the list C_T.
- Then the algorithm updates the SA with the elements in S_T and the ZKS with the elements in C_T. This generates a proof of update and a snapshot for both the SA and the ZKS.
- The algorithm updates the state and outputs it with the proofs of update and the snapshot of the SA and ZKS.

In our example, Alice made two shows, and Bob one. The shows are shuffled so their initial order is not important. Alice's counter is incremented two times: $\mathsf{count}[\mathsf{usk}_{\mathsf{Alice}}] = 2$ and Bob, one time : $\mathsf{count}[\mathsf{usk}_{\mathsf{Bob}}] = 1$. It computes two labels for Alice $\mathsf{label}_{\mathsf{Alice},i}$ and one for Bob $\mathsf{label}_{\mathsf{Bob},1}$ using the VRF. It also builds two commitments on the context information of Alice's show and same for Bob. Thus the SA is updated with the set S_T which is equal to $\{(\mathsf{label}_{\mathsf{Alice},1}, \mathsf{com}_{\mathsf{Alice},1}), (\mathsf{label}_{\mathsf{Alice},2}, \mathsf{com}_{\mathsf{Alice},2}), (\mathsf{label}_{\mathsf{Bob},1}, \mathsf{com}_{\mathsf{Bob},1})\}$. The list List stores the following information:

$$\begin{aligned} \mathsf{List} := \{&(\mathsf{usk}_{\mathsf{Alice}}, 1, \mathsf{label}_{\mathsf{Alice},1}, \mathsf{ctext}_{\mathsf{Alice},1}, \mathsf{open}_{\mathsf{Alice},1}) \\ &(\mathsf{usk}_{\mathsf{Alice}}, 2, \mathsf{label}_{\mathsf{Alice},2}, \mathsf{ctext}_{\mathsf{Alice},2}, \mathsf{open}_{\mathsf{Alice},2}) \\ &(\mathsf{usk}_{\mathsf{Bob}}, 1, \mathsf{label}_{\mathsf{Bob},1}, \mathsf{ctext}_{\mathsf{Bob},1}, \mathsf{open}_{\mathsf{Bob},1})\} \end{aligned} \quad (1)$$

Alice's counter reached two markers: $1 = 2^0$ and $2 = 2^1$, and the counter of Bob reached the marker $1 = 2^0$. Thus the ZKS is updated with the set $C_T = \{0||\mathsf{usk}_{\mathsf{Alice}}, 1||\mathsf{usk}_{\mathsf{Alice}}, 0||\mathsf{usk}_{\mathsf{Bob}}\}$ containing the markers.

CTS.PublishVer: This algorithm verifies the proofs of update and the snapshot provided by the algorithm $\mathsf{CTS.Publish}$ and outputs 1 if they are both correct, 0 otherwise.

CTS.Hist: This algorithm takes as input the public parameters pp, the state st_T and the user secret key usk. It works as follows:

- First it computes the last marker $\mathsf{marker} := \log_2(\mathsf{count}[\mathsf{usk}])$ reached by the user. It also builds the maximum counter $\mathsf{countM} := 2^{\mathsf{marker}+1} - 1$ for which corresponding labels needs to be verified in the SA.
- The algorithm uses the list List to obtain all the informations on shows related to usk. The algorithm gets $(\mathsf{usk}, i, \mathsf{label}_i, \mathsf{ctext}_i, \mathsf{open}_i)_{i=1}^{\mathsf{count}[\mathsf{usk}]}$ from List.
- For every counter i from 1 to countM, the algorithm:
  - Computes the label label_i on the value $\mathsf{usk}||i$ (note that for $i \leqslant \mathsf{count}[\mathsf{usk}]$, those have already been computed and stored in List. But this is not the case for $i > \mathsf{count}[\mathsf{usk}]$).
  - Obtain the commitment com_i stored at the position label_i in the SA and a proof of inclusion (if $i > \mathsf{count}[\mathsf{usk}]$, we get $\mathsf{com}_i = \bot$ and a proof of emptiness).
  - Proves that the label label_i is computed correctly from $\mathsf{usk}||i$ using the VRF.
- Then, for every marker i from $\mathsf{marker}+1$ to $\mathsf{markerM}$, the algorithm builds a non membership proof for $\mathsf{usk}||i$ in the ZKS.
- The algorithm outputs all the proofs, but also the labels computed, the commitments, opening values and contexts which correspond to usk.

In our example, if Alice wants to check her history, then the algorithm computes the marker $\mathsf{marker} = \log(\mathsf{count}[\mathsf{usk}_{\mathsf{Alice}}]) = \log(2) = 1$ and deduces the maximum counter that it must check : $\mathsf{countM} := 2^{\mathsf{marker}+1} - 1 = 2^2 - 1 = 3$. The algorithm produces membership proofs to prove the inclusion of the pairs $(\mathsf{label}_{\mathsf{Alice},1}, \mathsf{com}_{\mathsf{Alice},1}), ((\mathsf{label}_{\mathsf{Alice},2}, \mathsf{com}_{\mathsf{Alice},2})$ in the SA. Then, it computes the label for Alice associated with counter 3 using the VRF and produces a non membership proof for this label. Finally, it produces non membership proofs in the ZKS for all the markers from 2 to $\mathsf{markerM} := \lambda$.

CTS.HistVer: This algorithm takes as input the public parameters pp, the last snapshot snap_T, the user secret key usk and all the proofs and the context obtained from the algorithm $\mathsf{CTS.Hist}$. It then verifies that all the proofs are correct, but also that all the commitments are correctly computed from the corresponding contexts. It outputs 1 if all the proofs verify and 0 otherwise.

CTS.InclProof: This algorithm takes as input the public parameters pp, the state st_T, the user secret key usk, the context ctext and the domain ctext. It works as follows:

- Computes the pseudonym nym of the user using the usk and ctext information.
- Search for the show corresponding to the usk and ctext given as input inside the list List. It thus gets the tuple $(\mathsf{usk}, \mathsf{count}, \mathsf{ctext}, \mathsf{open})$ from List.
- Get the commitment com stored in the SA at the position label.
- Compute the marker $\mathsf{marker} := \log_2(\mathsf{count})$ corresponding to the counter of this show.
- Compute a proof that the label was computed correctly by using the VRF on $\mathsf{usk}||\mathsf{count}$.
- Build a membership proof for the marker marker inside the ZKS.
- Build the statement and the witness for the zero knowledge proof that follows. The statement is composed of $(\mathsf{nym}, \mathsf{ctext}, \mathsf{snap}_{T,\mathsf{ZKS}})$ and the witness is composed of $(\mathsf{usk}, \mathsf{count}, \mathsf{marker}, \pi_{\mathsf{VRF}}, \pi_{\mathsf{ZKS}})$.
- Compute the ZK proof, using the statement and witness. This should prove the following properties:
  - The VRF proof π_{VRF} from the witness verifies.
  - nym is a pseudonym for usk using the domain information.
  - the ZKS proof π_{ZKS} from the witness verifies.
  - $2^{\mathsf{marker}} \leqslant \mathsf{count} < 2^{\mathsf{marker}+1}$
- Output the ZK proof and the SA proof of inclusion, together with the label, the opening open and the commitment com.

In our example, the verifier would have to check the inclusion of all the three shows he received to check that they are included in the log. If the verifier wants to check the first show of Alice, it means the algorithm uses $\mathsf{ctext}_{\mathsf{Alice},1}$ as input. It gets $(\mathsf{usk}_{\mathsf{Alice}}, 1, \mathsf{label}_{\mathsf{Alice},1}, \mathsf{ctext}_{\mathsf{Alice},1}, \mathsf{open}_{\mathsf{Alice},1})$ from the list List then, it gets the commitment $\mathsf{com}_{\mathsf{Alice},1}$ from the SA. It computes the marker : $\mathsf{marker} = \log(1) = 0$ and a membership proof for this marker inside the ZKS.

CTS.InclVer: This algorithm verifies the two proofs of the ZK and the SA and also verifies that the commitment com is correctly computed from ctext.

3.3 Simulation Algorithms

In this section we describe the instantiation of the simulated algorithms introduced in the privacy game in Fig. 3.

We start by describing the leakage functions. The first leakage function is used for $\mathsf{Sim.Publish}$ and leaks the number of updates of the ZKS, the secret key of corrupted users involved in the shows and the set $C \cap S'$ which is the intersection between the set C of update in the ZKS and the set S' of values for which non membership proofs have been produced (thus values that belong only to corrupted users). The second leakage function is used for $\mathsf{Sim.Hist}$ and $\mathsf{Sim.Inc}$. It takes as input a show and outputs the epoch at which the show was included inside the log.

Leakage L_1 : This leakage function takes as input a list of shows $(i_j, \mathsf{ctext}_j)_{j=1}^k$ and the list of corrupted users CU. It does the following:

- Initialises the table $\mathsf{U} := []$ which remembers usk for all the shows of corrupted users and the list C which stores the markers reached with the shows.
- For every index j from 1 to k, the algorithm:
  - Updates the user's counter $\mathsf{count}[i_j]$: if $\mathsf{count}[i_j]$ is $\perp$ then it initialises it to 1, else it increments it.
  - If $\mathsf{count}[i_j] \in \{1, 2, 2^2, \ldots, 2^{\mathsf{markerM}}\}$, then the counter reaches a new marker $\mathsf{marker} := \log_2(\mathsf{count}[i_j])$ and C is updated with usk||marker.
  - If i_j is corrupted then, $\mathsf{U}[j] = \mathsf{usk}$ else, $\mathsf{U}[j] = \perp$.
- The game outputs the size of C, the table U and the intersection $C \cap S'$ (S' is the set of all the usk||marker for which non-inclusion proofs were produced during the game. This set is built in algorithm Sim.Hist and thus contains only information for corrupted users.)

Leakage L_2: This leakage function takes as input a show (i, ctext) and the global show list ShowList. It outputs the epoch T at which the show was included inside the SA.

Sim.ParamSetup: This algorithm is the simulation for the algorithm CTS.ParamSetup. It uses the Simset algorithms for all the simulatable schemes, to produce the public parameters together with a trapdoor which will be used as input the simulation algorithms. It outputs all the public parameters and trapdoors.

Sim.ServerSetup: This algorithm is the simulation for the algorithm CTS.ServerSetup. It works as follows:

- Generates the public parameters for the SA and initial state and snapshot for both the SA and the ZKS.
- Initializes the counter table $\mathsf{count} := []$, the maximal marker $\mathsf{markerM} := 2^\lambda$.
- Initializes the lists and table:
  - $S' := ()$ which will contain the usk||marker which have been proved non-inclusion of during the game.
  - LabList $:= ()$ which matches the label to the usk and the epoch T.
  - HistList $:= ()$ which matches the com, ctext and open.
  - UserList $:= ()$ which is used to recall which corrupted users have been attributed some unused labels.
  - LabTable $:= []$ which stores the unused labels of corrupted users.
- Defines simList which regroups all those lists, pp which regroups the public parameters, snap which regroups the snapshots and the state st (which contains simList and snap).
- Outputs pp and st.

Sim.Publish: This algorithm is the simulation for the algorithm CTS.Publish. It takes as input the state st, the number of updates k and a leakage L_1 over the shows. It does the following:

- Get the output $(c, \mathsf{U}, C_T \cap S')$ from L_1 .
- Initialize $S_T = ()$ which contains the elements to put inside the SA.
- For index i from 1 to k:
  - Define $\mathsf{usk} = \mathsf{U}[i]$ (thus $\mathsf{usk} = \mathsf{usk}_i$ if the user is corrupted, else $\mathsf{usk} = \bot$).
  - If $\mathsf{usk} \in \mathsf{UserList}$, it means that some labels have been defined for usk, thus we search in LabTable (which stores the labels) for the lowest counter j such that $\mathsf{LabTable}[\mathsf{usk}, j]$ is a label. We define $\mathsf{label} := \mathsf{LabTable}[\mathsf{usk}, j]$ and we remove this label from $\mathsf{LabTable}[\mathsf{usk}, j]$ so that we never use it again. If there is no other labels for usk inside LabTable we remove usk from UserList.
  - Else sample label randomly.
  - Use Com.Sim to generate a commitment (com, aux) and add (label, com) to S_T.
  - Add $(\mathsf{label}, \mathsf{aux}, \mathsf{usk}, T)$ to LabList.
- Update the SA with S_T and update the ZKS using the simulation algorithm ZKS.SimUpd with the number of updates c, the trapdoor and the intersection $C_T \cap S'$ given as input. Update the state.
- Output the proofs and snapshots generated by the updates.

Sim.Hist: This algorithm is the simulation for the algorithm CTS.Hist. It takes as input the state st, the user secret key usk, the list of contexts $(\mathsf{ctext}_i)_{i=1}^{\mathsf{count}}$ and a corresponding list of leakage of the L_2 function. It works as follows:

- Compute the marker corresponding to the counter $\mathsf{marker} := \log_2(\mathsf{count})$ and $\mathsf{countM} := 2^{\mathsf{marker}+1} - 1$.
- For index j from 1 to count:
  - Use the $\mathsf{Sim.Inc}_1$ algorithm on ctext_j (because a commitment of the SA need to be attributed to ctext_j).
  - From ctext_j, get the tuple $(\mathsf{label}_j, \mathsf{com}_j, \mathsf{open}_j, \mathsf{usk}, \mathsf{ctext}_j)$ in HistList.
  - Generate a proof of inclusion for the commitment com_j inside the SA at position label_j.
  - Simulate a VRF proof that the label label_j was computed correctly.
- If $\mathsf{count} < \mathsf{countM}$, it means that the user will check more labels than the labels already used for the context it checks. so we add usk to the list UserList of user which have labels already.
- For index j from $\mathsf{count} + 1$ to countM:
  - Check in LabTable if the label is already defined for this user and counter j. If $\mathsf{LabTable}[\mathsf{usk}, j] = \bot$ then sample a random label an put it inside $\mathsf{LabTable}[\mathsf{usk}, j]$.
  - Define the label $\mathsf{label} := \mathsf{LabTable}[\mathsf{usk}, j]$.
  - Generate a proof that the SA is empty at position label_j.
  - Simulate a VRF proof that the label label_j was computed correctly.
- For index j from $\mathsf{marker} + 1$ to markerM, simulate ZKS non membership proof of $\mathsf{usk}||j$ and add $\mathsf{usk}||j$ to the list S'.
- Output all the proofs, labels, commitments, openings and contexts used in the algorithm.

Sim.Inc$_1$: This algorithm is the simulation for the algorithm CTS.InclProof for corrupted users. It takes as input the state st, the (corrupted) user secret key usk, the context ctext and a leakage of L_2 on the show. It works as follows:

- compute the pseudonym nym of the user using the usk and the ctext information.
- Verify if (usk, ctext) $\in$ HistList. If yes, it means that the *open* and commitment com have already been attributed to ctext so:
  - Get the corresponding tuple (label, open, com, usk, ctext) from HistList.
  - Build the SA proof of inclusion of the commitment com at position label.
  - Compute the ZK simulation proof using the same statement as in the algorithm CTS.InclProof (statement := (label, nym, ctext, $\mathsf{snap}_{T,\mathsf{ZKS}}$)).
- Else define T as the output of L_2.
- Search for usk, T in LabList and get a corresponding tuple (label, aux, usk, T) (If there are more than one tuple working, then pick one randomly).
- Get the commitment com from the SA using the SA.Incl algorithm and label.
- Compute a valid opening value using Com.SimOpen on com and ctext.
- Simulate a ZK proof using the same statement as in the algorithm CTS.InclProof.
- Add the tuple (label, open, com, usk, ctext) to the list HistList to remember the commitment and opening associated to ctext.
- Remove (label, aux, usk, T) from the list LabList so that we do not reuse it.
- Output the proofs and the label, commitment, context.

Sim.Inc$_2$: This algorithm is the simulation for the algorithm CTS.InclProof for honest users. It is similar to Sim.Inc$_1$, the differences are:

- It takes as input the pseudonym nym of the user instead of the usk and ctext.
- It stores the pseudonym nym in HistList instead of usk.
- It searches for $\perp, T$ in LabList and gets a corresponding tuple (label, aux, $\perp, T$).

4 Security Proof

Theorem 1. *The protocol CTS consisting of the algorithms CTS.ParamSetup, CTS.ServerSetup, CTS.GetNym, CTS.Publish, CTS.PublishVer, CTS.InclProof, CTS.InclVer, CTS.Hist, CTS.HistVer satisfies* ***completeness, soundness*** *and* ***privacy****.*

4.1 Intuition for the Proof of Soundness

The soundness of CTS is mainly based on the security properties of the building blocks, namely, we use the extractability property of the Zero-Knowledge scheme, the Append only properties of both the SA and the ZKS schemes, and the binding properties of both the Commitment scheme and the VRF.

Since in this security game, the adversary has the role of the Cloud, it means that as a challenger, we only get access to the verification algorithms of CTS.

In the proof, we aim to build hybrids for those verification algorithms that will make the game impossible to win for the adversary in the last hybrid. In the last hybrid, the context $\mathsf{ctext}^{\mathsf{Inc}}$ given as input to $\mathsf{CTS.InclVer}$ is necessarily one of the contexts $(\mathsf{ctext}^{\mathsf{Hist}})_{i=1}^{\mathsf{count}}$ given as input to $\mathsf{CTS.HistVer}$.

The first hybrid consists in modifying the $\mathsf{CTS.InclVer}$ algorithm which verifies the zero knowledge proof by using the extractability property of the ZK scheme. By doing this, we enforce the adversary to reveal the witness $\mathsf{witness} = (\mathsf{usk}^{\mathsf{Inc}}, \mathsf{count}^{\mathsf{Inc}}, \mathsf{marker}^{\mathsf{Inc}}, \pi_{\mathsf{VRF}}, \pi_{\mathsf{ZKS}})$ it used to build the zero knowledge proof.

The following hybrids match a lot of binding properties together to get the result:

- First, the Append-Only property of the SA binds the commitments com_i to the labels label_i such that for some π we have $1 \leftarrow \mathsf{SA.Verif}(\mathsf{pp}, \mathsf{snap}_T, \mathsf{label}_i, \mathsf{com}_i, \pi)$. We get $\mathsf{label}_i = \mathsf{label}^{\mathsf{Inc}} \implies \mathsf{com}_i = \mathsf{com}^{\mathsf{Inc}}$.
- Second, the Binding property of the commitment scheme binds the commitments com_i to the contexts ctext_i such that $1 \leftarrow \mathsf{Com.Verif}(\mathsf{pp}, \mathsf{ctext}_i, \mathsf{open}, \mathsf{com}_i)$. We get $\mathsf{com}_i = \mathsf{com}^{\mathsf{Inc}} \implies \mathsf{ctext}_i = \mathsf{ctext}^{\mathsf{Inc}}$.
- Third, the Append-Only property of the ZKS scheme matches the marker marker computed in the history proof to the marker $\mathsf{marker}^{\mathsf{Inc}}$. It proves that since the inclusion of $\mathsf{marker}^{\mathsf{Inc}}$ was verified by getting $1 \leftarrow \mathsf{ZKS.Verif}(\mathsf{pp}, \mathsf{snap}_T, \mathsf{marker}^{\mathsf{Inc}}, 1, \pi^{\mathsf{Inc}})$ with the apprnd-only property of the ZK scheme, we get that $\mathsf{marker}^{\mathsf{Inc}} \leqslant \mathsf{marker}$, thus $\mathsf{count}^{\mathsf{Inc}} \leqslant 2^{\mathsf{marker}^{\mathsf{Inc}}+1} - 1 \leqslant 2^{\mathsf{marker}+1} - 1 = \mathsf{countM}$. It means that $\exists i \in [1, \mathsf{countM}]$ such that $i = \mathsf{count}^{\mathsf{Inc}}$. We have matched one of the counters in the $\mathsf{CTS.HistVer}$ algorithm to $\mathsf{count}^{\mathsf{Inc}}$.
- Finally, we use the VRF binding property to bind the $\mathsf{usk}||i$ value to the label label_i such that $1 \leftarrow \mathsf{VRF.Verif}(\mathsf{pp}, \mathsf{usk}||i, \mathsf{label}_i, \pi)$. We get that $\mathsf{usk}||i = \mathsf{usk}^{\mathsf{Inc}}||\mathsf{count}^{\mathsf{Inc}} \implies \mathsf{label}_i = \mathsf{label}^{\mathsf{Inc}}$.

In the end, we also need to use the binding property of the $\mathsf{CTS.GetNym}$ algorithm to have $\mathsf{nym}_{\mathsf{Inc}} = \mathsf{CTL.GetNym}(\mathsf{usk}^{\mathsf{Hist}}, \mathsf{domain})$ imply $\mathsf{usk}^{\mathsf{Hist}} = \mathsf{usk}^{\mathsf{Inc}}$. From this and the implications described above we get, for $i = \mathsf{count}^{\mathsf{Inc}}$:

$$\mathsf{usk}^{\mathsf{Hist}}||i = \mathsf{usk}^{\mathsf{Inc}}||\mathsf{count}^{\mathsf{Inc}} \implies \mathsf{label}_i = \mathsf{label}^{\mathsf{Inc}} \implies \mathsf{com}_i = \mathsf{com}^{\mathsf{Inc}} \implies \mathsf{ctext}_i = \mathsf{ctext}^{\mathsf{Inc}}.$$

Note that this also implies that $\mathsf{count}^{\mathsf{Inc}} \leqslant \mathsf{count}$ since otherwise we get $\mathsf{label}_i = \mathsf{label}^{\mathsf{Inc}}$ which implies $\mathsf{com}^{\mathsf{Inc}} = \mathsf{com}_i = \perp$, which is impossible because $\mathsf{com}^{\mathsf{Inc}}$ is a valid commitment over the context $\mathsf{ctext}^{\mathsf{Inc}}$ and thus $\mathsf{com}^{\mathsf{Inc}} \neq \perp$.

So in the end, we get that $\mathsf{ctext}^{\mathsf{Inc}}$ belongs to the list of contexts $(\mathsf{ctext}^{\mathsf{Hist}})_{i=1}^{\mathsf{count}}$ given as input to $\mathsf{CTS.HistVer}$ which concludes the proof.

4.2 Intuition for the Proof of Privacy

To prove the privacy of CTS, we rely mainly on the Simulatable property of the building blocks. Namely we use the simulatable property of the ZK scheme, of the ZKS scheme, of the Commitment scheme and of the VRF scheme.

The aim is to move from $\mathsf{Game}_{0,privacy}$ to $\mathsf{Game}_{1,privacy}$ defined in Fig. 3 by building intermediate hybrids. In this game, the adversary represents a collusion of the corrupted users and verifiers. Thus the challenger performs the Cloud algorithms for the adversary as oracle requests.

The hybrids consist in modifying the algorithms CTS.Publish,CTS.Hist, CTS.InclProof, CTS.ParamSetup, CTS.ServerSetup by their simulation equivalent and also in modifying the oracles and introducing some leakage functions.

The first step consists in simulating the ZK scheme. This allows us to not define the witness witness in the CTS.InclProof algorithm and thus, not produce for example a membership proof for the inclusion of marker inside the ZKS.

After this, we can easily replace the ZKS algorithms by their simulations in both the algorithm CTS.Publish (in which the ZKS is updated) and the algorithm CTS.Hist (in which we produce non-membership proofs).

The next step consists in replacing the commitment algorithms by their simulation. In CTS.Publish, instead of picking a random open and use it to create a regular commitment com on the context ctext, we use the simulation algorithm Com.Sim to produce an empty commitment, and after that we create an opening value open using the algorithm Com.SimOpen to match the commitment com and the context ctext. This modification allows us to separate the definition of the commitment and the moment at which the commitment is attributed to a context. While we leave the commitment creation command Com.Sim inside the algorithm CTS.Publish, we can move the command Com.SimOpen (which links com to some context ctext) to the algorithm CTS.InclProof (in which the verifier checks that some context has a commitment corresponding to it inside the SA). Thus we can remove all the uses of contexts inside the CTS.Publish algorithm.

To make this consistent, we need to give more information to the algorithm CTS.InclProof on the show which it proves inclusion of: we introduce the leakage function L_2 which reveals the epoch at which the show was included inside the log. This is important because from the perspective of a corrupted user, the shows included inside the log follow some order related to the different epochs T. The user can check that this order is respected by using the CTS.Hist algorithm.

Then, we replace the VRF algorithms by their simulation. In order to do that, we need to identify the moment at which the VRF of some value $\mathsf{usk}||i$ is defined for the first time in the game, and store it in a table so that we don't redefine it again during the game. This is important because a simulation of the VRF consists in replacing the VRF evaluation by a random sample which must not change if the input is the same. We use a table (called LabTable in the instantiation), to replace the VRF by its simulation. This modification allows to remove all the use of usk (user identity) and count[usk] inside the CTS.Publish algorithm. We still need a leakage function given as input of CTS.Publish to leak the usk for the corrupted users concerned by the update (so that we can get their labels if they were already defined by using CTS.Hist). We also need to give as leakage the number of counters of users that reach a marker (number of elements to add into the ZKS) during the update and the intersection $C_T \cap S'$, which contains only information about corrupted users: C_T are the markers that should be added to the ZKS with the update and S' are the markers which have been proved non membership of during the game (this happens only for corrupted users in the algorithm CTS.Hist).

After all those modifications, we obtain the game $\mathsf{Game}_{1,privacy}$ which does not use any secret information from the honest users as input of the algorithms (beyond the leakage).

Acknowledgements. This work was partly funded by the MSR–Inria Joint Centre. The second author is supported by the Vienna Science and Technology Fund (WWTF) through project VRG18-002. Thanks also to Markulf Kohlweiss and Sarah Meiklejohn for early discussions on the problem.

References

1. e-identity. https://e-estonia.com/solutions/e-identity/smart-id/. Accessed 15 Sept 2021
2. Google key transparency. https://github.com/google/keytransparency. Accessed 16 Sept 2021
3. GOV.UK verify. https://www.gov.uk/government/publications/introducing-govuk-verify/introducing-govuk-verify. Accessed 15 Sept 2021
4. How does single sign-on work. https://www.onelogin.com/learn/how-single-sign-on-works. Accessed 15 Sept 2021
5. Verifiable credentials working group. https://www.w3.org/2017/vc/WG/. Accessed 15 Sept 2021
6. Baldimtsi, F., Lysyanskaya, A.: Anonymous credentials light. In: Sadeghi, A.-R., Gligor, V.D., Yung, M. (eds.) 2013 ACM SIGSAC Conference on Computer and Communications Security, CCS 2013, Berlin, Germany, 4–8 November 2013, pp. 1087–1098. ACM (2013)
7. Belenkiy, M., Chase, M., Kohlweiss, M., Lysyanskaya, A.: P-signatures and non-interactive anonymous credentials. In: Canetti, R. (ed.) TCC 2008. LNCS, vol. 4948, pp. 356–374. Springer, Heidelberg (2008). https://doi.org/10.1007/978-3-540-78524-8_20
8. Brands, S.A.: Rethinking Public Key Infrastructures and Digital Certificates: Building in Privacy. MIT Press, Cambridge (2000)
9. Camenisch, J., Lysyanskaya, A.: A signature scheme with efficient protocols. In: Cimato, S., Persiano, G., Galdi, C. (eds.) SCN 2002. LNCS, vol. 2576, pp. 268–289. Springer, Heidelberg (2003). https://doi.org/10.1007/3-540-36413-7_20
10. Camenisch, J., Lysyanskaya, A.: Signature schemes and anonymous credentials from bilinear maps. In: Franklin, M. (ed.) CRYPTO 2004. LNCS, vol. 3152, pp. 56–72. Springer, Heidelberg (2004). https://doi.org/10.1007/978-3-540-28628-8_4
11. Chase, M., Deshpande, A., Ghosh, E., Malvai, H.: SEEMless: secure end-to-end encrypted messaging with less trust. In: Proceedings of the 2019 ACM SIGSAC Conference on Computer and Communications Security (2019)
12. Chase, M., Fuchsbauer, G., Ghosh, E., Plouviez, A.: Credential transparency system. Cryptology ePrint Archive (2022). https://eprint.iacr.org/
13. Chase, M., Meiklejohn, S., Zaverucha, G.: Algebraic macs and keyed-verification anonymous credentials. In: Ahn, G-J., Yung, M., Li, N. (eds.) Proceedings of the 2014 ACM SIGSAC Conference on Computer and Communications Security, Scottsdale, AZ, USA, 3–7 November 2014, pp. 1205–1216. ACM (2014)

14. Chaum, D.: Security without identification: transaction systems to make big brother obsolete. Commun. ACM **28**(10), 1030–1044 (1985)
15. Damgård, I.B.: Payment systems and credential mechanisms with provable security against abuse by individuals. In: Goldwasser, S. (ed.) CRYPTO 1988. LNCS, vol. 403, pp. 328–335. Springer, New York (1990). https://doi.org/10.1007/0-387-34799-2_26
16. Dauterman, E., Corrigan-Gibbs, H., Mazières, D.: SafetyPin: encrypted backups with human-memorable secrets. In: 14th USENIX Symposium on Operating Systems Design and Implementation, OSDI 2020, Virtual Event, 4–6 November 2020, pp. 1121–1138. USENIX Association (2020)
17. Fahl, S., Dechand, S., Perl, H., Fischer, F., Smrcek, J., Smith, M.: Hey, NSA: stay away from my market! future proofing app markets against powerful attackers. In: Ahn, G.-J., Yung, M., Li, N. (eds.) Proceedings of the 2014 ACM SIGSAC Conference on Computer and Communications Security, Scottsdale, AZ, USA, 3–7 November 2014, pp. 1143–1155. ACM (2014)
18. Fuchsbauer, G.: Commuting signatures and verifiable encryption. In: Paterson, K.G. (ed.) EUROCRYPT 2011. LNCS, vol. 6632, pp. 224–245. Springer, Heidelberg (2011). https://doi.org/10.1007/978-3-642-20465-4_14
19. Fuchsbauer, G., Hanser, C., Slamanig, D.: Structure-preserving signatures on equivalence classes and constant-size anonymous credentials. J. Cryptol. **32**(2), 498–546 (2019)
20. Melara, M.S., Blankstein, A., Bonneau, J., Felten, E.W., Freedman, M.J.: CONIKS: bringing key transparency to end users. In: 24th USENIX Security Symposium (USENIX Security 15), pp. 383–398. USENIX Association, Washington, D.C. (2015)
21. Nikitin, K., et al.: CHAINIAC: proactive software-update transparency via collectively signed skipchains and verified builds. In: 26th USENIX Security Symposium (USENIX Security 17), pp. 1271–1287, Vancouver, BC, USENIX Association (2017)
22. Pointcheval, D., Sanders, O.: Short randomizable signatures. In: Sako, K. (ed.) CT-RSA 2016. LNCS, vol. 9610, pp. 111–126. Springer, Cham (2016). https://doi.org/10.1007/978-3-319-29485-8_7

Cumulatively All-Lossy-But-One Trapdoor Functions from Standard Assumptions

Benoît Libert[1,2], Ky Nguyen[3,4](✉), and Alain Passelègue[2,4]

[1] CNRS, Laboratoire LIP, Lyon, France
[2] ENS de Lyon, Laboratoire LIP (U. Lyon, CNRS, ENSL, Inria, UCBL), Lyon, France
benoit.libert@ens-lyon.fr
[3] DIENS, École normale supérieure, CNRS, PSL University, Paris, France
ky.nguyen@ens.psl.eu
[4] Inria, Paris, France
alain.passelegue@inria.fr

Abstract. Chakraborty, Prabhakaran, and Wichs (PKC'20) recently introduced a new tag-based variant of lossy trapdoor functions, termed cumulatively all-lossy-but-one trapdoor functions (CALBO-TDFs). Informally, CALBO-TDFs allow defining a public tag-based function with a (computationally hidden) special tag, such that the function is lossy for all tags except when the special secret tag is used. In the latter case, the function becomes injective and efficiently invertible using a secret trapdoor. This notion has been used to obtain advanced constructions of signatures with strong guarantees against leakage and tampering, and also by Dodis, Vaikunthanathan, and Wichs (EUROCRYPT'20) to obtain constructions of randomness extractors with extractor-dependent sources. While these applications are motivated by practical considerations, the only known instantiation of CALBO-TDFs so far relies on the existence of indistinguishability obfuscation.

In this paper, we propose the first two instantiations of CALBO-TDFs based on standard assumptions. Our constructions are based on the LWE assumption with a sub-exponential approximation factor and on the DCR assumption, respectively, and circumvent the use of indistinguishability obfuscation by relying on lossy modes and trapdoor mechanisms enabled by these assumptions.

Keyword: Lossy trapdoor functions, cumulative lossiness, standard assumptions

1 Introduction

As introduced by Peikert and Waters [48], *lossy trapdoor functions* (LTDFs) are function families where evaluation keys can be sampled in two modes: In the

C. Galdi and S. Jarecki (Eds.): SCN 2022, LNCS 13409, pp. 336–361, 2022.
https://doi.org/10.1007/978-3-031-14791-3_15

injective mode, a function $F_{\mathsf{ek}}(\cdot)$ is injective and can be inverted using a trapdoor tk that comes with the evaluation key ek; In the *lossy mode*, a function $F_{\mathsf{ek}}(\cdot)$ has a much smaller image size and thus loses a certain amount of information about its input. The standard security of an LTDF requires that the two modes be indistinguishable. That is, no efficient distinguisher can tell apart lossy evaluation keys from injective ones.

Lossy trapdoor functions have been built from a variety of standard cryptographic assumptions, such as the Decisional Diffie-Hellman (DDH) [25,29,48] and Learning with Errors (LWE) assumptions [2,8,48], the Quadratic Residuosity (QR) [24,25,37] and Composite Residuosity (DCR) assumptions [25], the Phi-hiding assumption [3,41] and more [46,53]. They have found numerous applications in cryptography, including chosen-ciphertext security, trapdoor functions with many hard-core bits, collision-resistant hash functions, oblivious transfer [48], deterministic [9,50] and hedged public-key encryption [6,52] in the standard model, instantiability of RSA-OAEP [41], computational extractors [23,27], pseudo-entropy functions [18], selective-opening security [7], and more.

Several generalizations of LTDFs have been considered. Of particular interest are the tag-based variants, where algorithms take an additional tag as input. In all-but-one LTDFs [48] for instance, the evaluation key obtained by running the sampling algorithm with a special tag tag^* is such that the function $F_{\mathsf{ek}}(\cdot, \mathsf{tag})$ is injective for all tags $\mathsf{tag} \neq \mathsf{tag}^*$, but the function $F_{\mathsf{ek}}(\cdot, \mathsf{tag}^*)$ is lossy. All-but-one LTDFs have been generalized to all-but-N LTDFs [36] (which admit $N > 1$ lossy tags) or all-but-many lossy trapdoor functions (where arbitrarily many lossy tags can be adaptively created). The latter notion notably found applications to selective-opening chosen-ciphertext security with compact ciphertexts [14,39,43].

In a setting where multiple lossy evaluations are provided (e.g., for multiple lossy evaluation keys in the context of standard LTDFs or for multiple lossy tags in the context of tag-based LTDFs), one may want to guarantee that multiple lossy evaluations on the same input x do not reveal more information about x than a single evaluation. This additional property was termed *cumulative lossiness* in [19] where it was formalized by requiring the existence of a (possibly inefficient) algorithm that starts with some fixed, partial information about x and recovers the entire information provided by the multiple lossy evaluations. The fact that all these evaluations can be recovered (even inefficiently) from the same amount of partial information on x then guarantees that multiple lossy evaluations on the same input x preserve the entropy of x. In particular, they do not end up leaking x entirely.

In this paper, we investigate the notion of *cumulatively all-lossy-but-one trapdoor functions*, suggested by Chakraborty, Prabharkaran and Wichs [19], which considers the case where *all tags are lossy, except one*. This notion has been used to obtain advanced constructions of randomness extractors [23] and signatures in the leakage and tampering model [19].

Cumulatively All-Lossy-But-One Lossy Trapdoor Functions. A *cumulatively all-lossy-but-one trapdoor functions* (CALBO-TDFs) is a tag-based LTDFs where the function $F_{\mathsf{ek}}(\cdot, \mathsf{tag})$ is lossy for any tag tag except one special injective tag tag^*, for which $F_{\mathsf{ek}}(\cdot, \mathsf{tag}^*)$ is invertible using a trapdoor td associated with ek. In addition, the lossiness is required to be *cumulative* in the sense that multiple evaluations $F_{\mathsf{ek}}(x, \mathsf{tag}_i)$ for lossy tags $\mathsf{tag}_i \neq \mathsf{tag}^*$ always leak the same information about x. Finally, the evaluation key should computationally hide the special injective tag and evaluation keys generated with distinct injective tags are required to be (computationally) indistinguishable.

In [23], the notion of CALBO-TDFs was relaxed by not requiring the existence of a trapdoor for the injective tag tag^*. This relaxed notion, termed CALBO functions (or CALBOs for short), is also implicit in [18,26]. By dropping the trapdoor requirement, these works obtained CALBOs from standard lossy functions (without trapdoor). Therefore it has been possible to construct CALBOs from many standard assumptions such as DDH, LWE, or DCR.

The design of CALBO-TDFs, for which a trapdoor is required in injective mode, is much harder. Indeed, the only known instantiation so far [19] relies on the existence of *indistinguishability obfuscation* [28] (iO) besides the DDH (or LWE) assumption. At a high level, the construction of [19] starts with *cumulative* LTDFs (C-LTDFs), which can be built from LWE or DDH, and combines it with iO and puncturable PRFs [13,15,40]. The idea of [19] is to generate a CALBO-TDF evaluation key as an obfuscated program in which the special injective tag tag^* is hard-wired together with an injective evaluation key for the underlying C-LTDF. This program, on input tag, outputs the hard-wired injective evaluation key if $\mathsf{tag} = \mathsf{tag}^*$; Otherwise, it samples a lossy evaluation key using randomness derived from a puncturable PRF (of which the key is also hard-wired in the program) evaluated on the input tag, and finally returns the resulting evaluation key. When it comes to evaluating a function for an input x and a tag tag, [19] evaluates the underlying C-LTDF on input x using the evaluation key obtained by running the obfuscated program on input tag. The injectivity on the special tag tag^* and the cumulative lossiness property immediately follow from the same properties in the underlying C-LTDF. Indistinguishability of evaluation keys simply follows from the security of iO, the pseudorandomness of the puncturable PRF when puncturing the tags, and the indistinguishability of lossy and injective keys in the underlying C-LTDF.

In [19], CALBO-TDFs served as a building block to construct *leakage and tamper resilient* signature schemes with a *deterministic* signing algorithm, a notion that provides a natural solution to protect signature schemes against leakage, e.g. physical analysis and timing measurements, or tampering attacks, where the adversary deliberately targets the randomness used by the algorithms. The complexity of the CALBO-TDF candidate of [19] motivates the search for simpler, more efficient instantiations of CALBO-TDFs that avoid the use of heavy hammers like obfuscation and rely on more standard assumptions.

1.1 Our Contributions

We present two constructions of CALBO-TDFs based solely on standard assumptions. Our first construction relies on the LWE assumption [51] with *sub-*

exponential approximation factor in reducing LWE to a worst-case lattice problem[1], while our second construction relies on Paillier's Composite Residuosity assumption [47] (DCR).

We thus avoid the use of indistinguishability obfuscation (which was used to hide the hard-wired values including the special tag and the injective evaluation key) by relying on lossy modes and trapdoor mechanisms enabled by LWE and DCR. The first construction uses the lossy mode and trapdoor mechanism of LWE in a similar way to [2,32,45]. By exploiting ideas from [44], it achieves a mildly relaxed notion of cumulative lossiness, where cumulative lossiness only holds with overwhelming probability over the choice of (non-injective) tags. The same relaxed notion was used in the LWE+iO-based construction of [19]. This relaxation does not hurt any of the applications, as shown [19]. Our second construction relies on the lossiness and trapdoor mechanism of the Decision Composite Residuosity (DCR) assumption. In particular, it uses the Damgård-Jurik cryptosystem [20] in a similar way to the LTDF of Freeman *et al.* [25].

1.2 Technical Overview

RELAXED CALBO-TDFS FROM LWE. We start from the observation that CALBOs (without a trapdoor) can be viewed as selectively secure unpredictable functions when the key of the function is the CALBO's input and the input of the function serves as the CALBO's tag. We then upgrade the LWE-based PRF of Libert, Stehlé and Titiu [44] whose security proof precisely relies on the cumulative lossiness of the LWE function (in its derandomized version based on the rounding technique of [4]) for an appropriate choice of parameters. The LWE function (which maps a pair of short integer column-vectors $(\mathbf{s}, \mathbf{e}) \in \mathbb{Z}^n \times \mathbb{Z}^m$ to $\mathbf{s}^\top \mathbf{A} + \mathbf{e}^\top$, for a random matrix $\mathbf{A} \in \mathbb{Z}_q^{n \times m}$) is known [32] to provide a lossy function, and even a lossy trapdoor function for an appropriate choice of parameters [2,8]. The PRF of [44] interprets a variant of the key-homomorphic PRF of [11] as a lossy function in its security proof. More specifically, letting $\lfloor \cdot \rfloor_p : \mathbb{Z}_q \to \mathbb{Z}_p$ denote the rounding function of [4] for moduli $p < q$ defined as $\lfloor \mathbf{x} \rfloor_p = \lfloor (p/q) \cdot \mathbf{x} \rfloor$, the function mapping $\mathbf{x} \in \mathbb{Z}_q^n$ to $\lfloor \mathbf{x}^\top \cdot \mathbf{A} \rfloor_p$ is injective when $\mathbf{A} \in \mathbb{Z}_q^{n \times m}$ is uniformly random and lossy (as shown in [2]) when $\mathbf{A}$ is of the form $\mathbf{D}^\top \cdot \mathbf{B} + \mathbf{E}$ for some random $\mathbf{B} \in \mathbb{Z}_q^{\ell \times m}, \mathbf{D} \in \mathbb{Z}_q^{\ell \times n}$, $\ell \ll n$, and some small-norm matrix $\mathbf{E}$. The PRF of [44] maps an input x to $\lfloor \mathbf{s}^\top \mathbf{A}(x) \rfloor_p$, where $\mathbf{s} \in \mathbb{Z}^n$ is the secret key and $\mathbf{A}(x) \in \mathbb{Z}_q^{n \times m}$ is an input-dependent matrix derived from public matrices. The latter matrix is actually obtained using fully homomorphic encryption techniques, by multiplying Gentry-Sahai-Waters (GSW) ciphertexts [31] indexed by the bits of x. The security proof of [44] "programs" $\mathbf{A}(x)$ in such a way that all evaluation queries reveal a lossy function of the secret key $\mathbf{s}$ while the challenge evaluation reveals a non-lossy function $\lfloor \mathbf{s}^\top \mathbf{A}(x^\star) \rfloor_p$ of $\mathbf{s}$. By choosing a large

[1] The approximation factor is closely related to the modulus-to-noise ratio q/σ if the LWE problem is defined over the ring of integers modulo q and the errors are sampled from a discrete Gaussian distribution D_σ.

enough ratio q/p, they show that all evaluation queries reveal the same information about the secret key $\mathbf{s}$, which is exactly what we need to prove cumulative lossiness in the CALBO setting. At the same time, [44] shows that $\lfloor \mathbf{s}^\top \mathbf{A}(x^\star) \rfloor_p$ retains a large amount of entropy conditionally on the information revealed by all evaluation queries.

We introduce two modifications in the function of [44]. First, we only need a selectively secure version of their PRF since the injective tag tag^* is known ahead of time in the security experiment whereas [44] has to prove adaptive security using an admissible hash function [10]. We thus remove the admissible hash function and directly compute $\mathbf{A}(x)$ as a product of public GSW ciphertexts indexed by the tag bits without encoding them first. As a second modification w.r.t [44], we need to extend the tag-dependent matrix $\mathbf{A}(x)$ so as to ensure invertibility in injective mode.

Our CALBO construction can be outlined as follows. Given the injective tag $\mathsf{tag}^* \in \{0,1\}^t$, the setup algorithm first generates $\mathbf{A} = \mathbf{D}^\top \cdot \mathbf{B} + \mathbf{E} \in \mathbb{Z}_q^{n \times m}$ as a lossy matrix, where $\mathbf{B} \in \mathbb{Z}_q^{\ell \times m}$, $\mathbf{D} \in \mathbb{Z}_q^{\ell \times n}$ and $\mathbf{E} \in \mathbb{Z}^{n \times m}$, with $\ell \ll n < m$. Then, the setup algorithm embeds $(\mathbf{A}, \mathbf{B})$ in the evaluation key ek via a set of GSW ciphertexts [31]

$$\mathbf{A}_{i,b} = \mathbf{A} \cdot \mathbf{R}_{i,b} + \delta_{b,\mathsf{tag}_i^*} \cdot \mathbf{G} \qquad \forall i \in [t],\, b \in \{0,1\} \tag{1}$$

where tag_i^* denotes the i-th bit of tag^*, $\delta_{b,\mathsf{tag}_i^*} = (b \stackrel{?}{=} \mathsf{tag}_i^*)$, $\mathbf{G} \in \mathbb{Z}_q^{n \times \lceil n \cdot \log q \rceil}$ is the gadget matrix of Micciancio and Peikert [45], and $\mathbf{R}_{i,b} \in \{0,1\}^{m \times \lceil n \cdot \log q \rceil}$ for each $i \in [t]$. The trapdoor tk (which allows inverting in injective mode) contains $\{\mathbf{R}_{i,b}\}_{i \in [t], b \in \{0,1\}}$. The computational indistinguishability of keys for different injective tags follows from the LWE assumption. The latter implies that the lossy matrix $\mathbf{A} = \mathbf{D}^\top \cdot \mathbf{B} + \mathbf{E}$ is indistinguishable from a uniform matrix in $\mathbb{Z}_q^{n \times m}$. When $\mathbf{A}$ is uniform, the Leftover Hash Lemma implies that each product $\mathbf{A} \cdot \mathbf{R}_{i,b}$ is statistically close to the uniform distribution $U(\mathbb{Z}_q^{n \times m})$. This ensures that matrices (1) statistically hide tag^* as they are statistically indistinguishable from i.i.d. random matrices over $\mathbb{Z}_q$.

In order to evaluate the function on an input $\mathbf{x}$ for a tag tag, the evaluation algorithm computes a product of GSW ciphertexts $\{\mathbf{A}_{i,\mathsf{tag}_i}\}_{i=1}^t$ chosen among $\{(\mathbf{A}_{i,0}, \mathbf{A}_{i,1})\}_{i=1}^t$ and then obtains a ciphertext $\mathbf{A}(\mathsf{tag})$ encrypting the logical AND $C_{\mathsf{tag}}(\mathsf{tag}^*) \triangleq \bigwedge_{i=1}^t (\mathsf{tag}_i = \mathsf{tag}_i^*)$, where $\{\mathsf{tag}_i\}_{i=1}^t$ are the bits of tag. Said otherwise, the tag-dependent matrix $\mathbf{A}(\mathsf{tag}) = \mathbf{A} \cdot \mathbf{R}_{\mathsf{tag}} + C_{\mathsf{tag}^*}(\mathsf{tag}) \cdot \mathbf{G}$ is an encryption of $C_{\mathsf{tag}}(\mathsf{tag}^*) = \prod_{i=1}^t \delta_{\mathsf{tag}_i,\mathsf{tag}_i^*}$, where the circuit $C_{\mathsf{tag}}(\cdot)$ is homomorphically evaluated by computing a subset product of GSW ciphertexts in the most sequential way (according to the terminology in [5]) so as to minimize the noise growth. This is done by making sure that each multiplication always involves a fresh GSW ciphertext.

Finally, the output of the evaluation is $\lfloor \mathbf{x}^\top \cdot [\mathbf{A} \mid \mathbf{A}(\mathsf{tag})] \rfloor_p$. Here, we slightly modify [44] where the challenge evaluation is of the form $\lfloor \mathbf{x}^\top \mathbf{A}(\mathsf{tag}) \rfloor_p$. The reason is that, in order to ensure invertibility for the injective tag tag^*, we need to exploit the fact that $\mathbf{A}(\mathsf{tag}^*)$ depends on $\mathbf{G}$. To this end, we need an injective evaluation of $\mathbf{x}$ to be of the form

$$\lfloor \mathbf{x}^\top \cdot [\mathbf{A} \mid \mathbf{A}(\mathsf{tag}^*)] \rfloor_p = \lfloor \mathbf{x}^\top \cdot [\mathbf{A} \mid \mathbf{A} \cdot \mathbf{R}_{\mathsf{tag}^*} + \mathbf{G}] \rfloor_p$$

for some small-norm matrix $\mathbf{R}_{\mathsf{tag}^*} \in \mathbb{Z}^{n \times \lceil n \cdot \log q \rceil}$. In this case, the binary matrices $\mathbf{R}_{i,b}$ contained in tk can be used to compute $\mathbf{R}_{\mathsf{tag}^*}$, which is a Micciancio-Peikert trapdoor [45] for the matrix $[\mathbf{A} \mid \mathbf{A}(\mathsf{tag}^*)]$ and allows inverting the function $\mathbf{x} \rightarrow \lfloor \mathbf{x}^\top \cdot [\mathbf{A} \mid \mathbf{A}(\mathsf{tag}^*)] \rfloor_p$ in the same way as in the LTDF of [2].

In lossy mode (when tag differs from tag^* in at least one bit), we can achieve cumulative lossiness only for a fixed input, due to the error introduced by the rounding operation. The argument is essentially the same as that in [44]: We exploit the lossy form of $\mathbf{A}$ and the fact that, for any lossy tag $\mathsf{tag} \neq \mathsf{tag}^*$, the matrix $[\mathbf{A} \mid \mathbf{A}(\mathsf{tag})] = [\mathbf{A} \mid \mathbf{A} \cdot \mathbf{R}_{\mathsf{tag}}]$ does not depend on $\mathbf{G}$. Then, with overwhelming probability, evaluations $\lfloor \mathbf{x}^\top \cdot [\mathbf{A} \mid \mathbf{A} \cdot \mathbf{R}_{\mathsf{tag}}] \rfloor_p$ always reveal the same information about $\mathbf{x} \in \mathbb{Z}^n$ since w.h.p. we have

$$\lfloor \mathbf{x}^\top \cdot [\mathbf{A} \mid \mathbf{A} \cdot \mathbf{R}_{\mathsf{tag}}] \rfloor_p = \lfloor \mathbf{x}^\top \cdot \mathbf{D}^\top \cdot \mathbf{B} \mid (\mathbf{x}^\top \cdot \mathbf{D}^\top \cdot \mathbf{B}) \cdot \mathbf{R}_{\mathsf{tag}} \rfloor_p$$

when q/p is sufficiently large. Hence, evaluations $\left\{ \lfloor \mathbf{x}^\top \cdot [\mathbf{A} \mid \mathbf{A}(\mathsf{tag})] \rfloor_p \right\}_{\mathsf{tag} \neq \mathsf{tag}^*}$ do not reveal any more information than $\mathbf{D} \cdot \mathbf{x} \in \mathbb{Z}_q^\ell$. Concerning the relaxation of cumulative lossiness, Chakraborty *et al.* [19] have the same restriction in their use of the LWE assumption. However, as discussed in [19, Apppendix A], this relaxed notion is not a problem in their applications of CALBO-TDFs.

CALBO-TDFs FROM DCR. We give a construction of CALBO-TDFs based on the Damgård-Jurik homomorphic encryption scheme [20] with additional insights from [21,22]. The construction is obtained by composing together multiple instances of the DCR-based lossy trapdoor *permutation* of Freeman *et al.* [25], which is index-dependent as its domain depends on the evaluation key. Recall that the Damgård-Jurik cryptosystem uses the group $\mathbb{Z}_{N^{\zeta+1}}^*$, where $N = pq$ is an RSA modulus and $\zeta \geq 1$ is some natural number. Given an injective tag $\mathsf{tag}^* \in \{0,1\}^t$, the evaluation key ek of our CALBO-TDFs includes (N, ζ) and the following Damgård-Jurik ciphertexts

$$g_{i,b} = (1+N)^{\delta_{b,\mathsf{tag}_i^*}} \cdot \alpha_{i,b}^{N^\zeta} \bmod N^{\zeta+1} \qquad \forall (i,b) \in [t] \times \{0,1\} ,$$

where $\alpha_{i,b} \hookleftarrow U(\mathbb{Z}_N^*)$ for each $i \in [t]$, $b \in \{0,1\}$, $\delta_{b,\mathsf{tag}_i^*} = (b \stackrel{?}{=} \mathsf{tag}_i^*)$ and tag_i^* denotes the i-th bit of tag^*. The trapdoor tk consists of the Damgård-Jurik decryption key.

For an evaluation of an input $x \in \mathbb{Z}_{N^{\zeta+1}}$ given a tag tag, we first write $x_0 := x = y_0 \cdot N + z_0$ for $(y_0, z_0) \in \mathbb{Z}_{N^\zeta} \times \mathbb{Z}_N$. Then, we iterate for $i \in [t]$ and, at each iteration, we compute a Damgård-Jurik ciphertext x_i of y_{i-1}:

$$x_i = g_{i,\mathsf{tag}_i}^{y_{i-1}} \cdot z_{i-1}^{N^\zeta} \bmod N^{\zeta+1} .$$

The output of the function consists of x_t.

In the injective mode (where $\mathsf{tag} = \mathsf{tag}^*$), we have that g_{i,tag_i^*} is an encryption of 1 for each $i \in [t]$. Then, each x_i is an encryption of y_{i-1}. Using tk, the inverter can thus recover (y_{i-1}, z_{i-1}) from x_i and eventually recover (y_0, z_0) and $x = x_0$ as long as $z_{i-1} \in \mathbb{Z}_N^*$ at each iteration. For any input x such that $z_{i-1} \notin \mathbb{Z}_N^*$ at some iteration, the evaluation algorithm outputs 0 (analogously to an index-dependent DCR-based LTDF proposed by Auerbach *et al.* [3, Sect. 6.1]). We note that our DCR-based construction is not perfectly invertible injective mode, the fraction of inputs for which the function is not invertible is overwhelming. Moreover, finding such inputs is as hard as factoring N and thus contradicts the DCR assumption.

In the lossy mode (where $\mathsf{tag} \neq \mathsf{tag}^*$), let the smallest index $i \in [t]$ such that $\mathsf{tag}_i \neq \mathsf{tag}^*$. For this index i, g_{i,tag_i} is a Damgård-Jurik encryption of 0, and so is x_i at the i-th evaluation step. This implies that x_i loses information about y_{i-1} as it can take at most $\varphi(N)$ values.

We then observe that injectivity and indistinguishability follow from the correctness and semantic security of Damgård-Jurik. Cumulative lossiness can be argued using the same arguments as in the CALBO function of [23, Sect. 5.3.1]. At each evaluation step, the information $(y_{i-1}, z_{i-1}) \in \mathbb{Z}_{N^\varsigma} \times \mathbb{Z}_N$ about x is fully carried over to the next step of the evaluation if $\mathsf{tag}_i = \mathsf{tag}_i^*$ and $z_{i-1} \in \mathbb{Z}_N^*$. As soon as tag_i differs from tag_i^*, the information about y_{i-1} is lost and subsequent evaluation steps (and therefore the final output of the evaluation) only depend on at most $\log \varphi(N) < \log N$ bits of x. Since there are t positions where a lossy tag can differ from tag^* for the first time, the function $\{F_{\mathsf{ek}}(\cdot, \mathsf{tag})\}_{\mathsf{tag} \neq \mathsf{tag}^*}$ has image size $\leq \varphi(N)^t$. So, the union of all lossy evaluations $\{F_{\mathsf{ek}}(x, \mathsf{tag})\}_{\mathsf{tag} \neq \mathsf{tag}^*}$ on some input x reveals at most $\log(\varphi(N)^t) < t \cdot \log N$ bits about x.

1.3 Related Work

Dodis, Vaikuntanathan and Wichs [23, Sect. 5.3.1] considered a notion of cumulatively all-lossy-but-one (CALBO) functions without trapdoor, which they used to extract randomness from extractor-dependent sources. They showed that CALBOs can be generically realized from standard lossy functions by relaxing the injectivity property. Due to their relaxed notion of injectivity, their construction is not invertible in injective mode. Our DCR-based CALBO-TDF is inspired by their construction (which is itself similar to the pseudo-entropy function of Braverman *et al.* [18]) with the difference that we do not need to compose a standard lossy function with a compressing d-wise independent function at each iterative evaluation step. This is the reason why our injective mode is invertible.

In a recent work, Quach, Waters, and Wichs [49] introduced a new notion of *targeted lossy functions* (TLFs), where lossy evaluations only lose information on some targeted inputs and no trapdoor allows efficiently inverting in the injective mode. Quach *et al.* [49] also extended TLFs to *targeted all-lossy-but-one* (T-ALBOs) and *targeted all-injective-but-one* (T-AIBOs) variants. Interestingly, it was shown in [49] that, in contrast with lossy *trapdoor* functions, TLFs, T-ALBOs, and T-AIBOs can be realized in Minicrypt. We can also consider the relaxation of targeted lossiness alone, while still asking for a trapdoor in the injective mode. This notion was discussed in [29] where a construction based on the Computational Diffie-Hellman assumption was given.

Lossy algebraic filters (LAFs) [38,42] are tag-based lossy functions that were used to construct public-key encryption schemes with circular chosen-ciphertext security [38]. They provide similar functionalities to CALBO in that they explicitly require multiple evaluations $\{F_{\mathsf{ek}}(x, \mathsf{tag}_i)\}_i$ on distinct lossy tags to always leak the same information about x. One difference is that LAFs admit arbitrarily many injective tags and arbitrarily many lossy tags. The requirement is that lossy tags should be hard to find without a trapdoor key. In contrast with CALBO-TDF, LAFs do not support efficient inversion on injective tags.

2 Background

We write $[n]$ to denote the set $\{1, 2, \ldots, n\}$ for an integer n. For any $q \geq 2$, we let $\mathbb{Z}_q$ denote the ring of integers with addition and multiplication modulo q, containing the representatives in the interval $(-q/2, q/2)$. We always set q as a prime integer. For $2 \leq p < q$ and $x \in \mathbb{Z}_q$, we define $\lfloor x \rfloor_p := \lfloor (p/q) \cdot x \rfloor \in \mathbb{Z}_p$ where the operator $\lfloor y \rfloor$ means taking the largest integer less than or equal to y. This notation is readily extended to vectors over $\mathbb{Z}_q$. Given a distribution D, we write $x \sim D$ to denote a random variable x distributed according to D. For a finite set S, we let $U(S)$ denote the uniform distribution over S. If X and Y are distributions over the same domain $\mathcal{D}$, then $\Delta(X, Y)$ denotes their statistical distance. We write ppt as a shorthand for "probabilistic polynomial-time" when considering the complexity of algorithms. We use a generalized version of the *Leftover Hash Lemma* [35].

Lemma 1 ([1], Lemma 14). *Let $\mathcal{H} = \{h : X \to Y\}_{h \in \mathcal{H}}$ be a family of universal hash functions. Let $f : X \to Z$ be some function. Let $T_1, \ldots, T_k$ be k independent random variables over X and we define $\gamma := \max_k \gamma(T_i)$ where $\gamma(T_i) := \max_{t \in X} \Pr[T_i = t]$. Then, we have*

$$\Delta\Big((h, h(T_1), f(T_1), \ldots, h(T_k), f(T_k)) \,;\, \Big(h, U_Y^{(1)}, f(T_1), \ldots, U_Y^{(k)}, f(T_k)\Big) \Big) \leq \frac{k}{2}\sqrt{\gamma \cdot |Y| \cdot |Z|}$$

where $U_Y^{(1)}, \ldots, U_Y^{(k)}$ denote k uniformly random variables over Y.

2.1 Cumulatively All-Lossy-But-One Trapdoor Functions

We now recall the definition of *cumulatively all-lossy-but-one trapdoor functions (CALBO-TDFs)*, a notion recently introduced in [19,23] as an extension of lossy trapdoor functions. We also recall its variant with relaxed cumulative lossiness that we achieve assuming LWE. We refer the reader to the introduction for an overview of these notions in the general context of lossy trapdoor functions.

Definition 1 (CALBO-TDF). *Let $\lambda \in \mathbb{N}$ be a security parameter and $\ell, \alpha : \mathbb{N} \to \mathbb{N}$ be functions. Let $\mathcal{T} = \{\mathcal{T}_\lambda\}_{\lambda \in \mathbb{N}}$ be a family of sets of tags. An*

(ℓ, α)-cumulatively-all-lossy-but-one trapdoor function family (CALBO-TDF) *with respect to the tag family* $\mathcal{T}$ *is a triple of algorithms* $(\mathsf{Sample}, \mathsf{Eval}, \mathsf{Invert})$, *where the first is probabilistic and the latter two are deterministic:*

- $\mathsf{Sample}(1^\lambda, \mathsf{tag}^*)$*: on inputs* 1^λ *and* $\mathsf{tag}^* \in \mathcal{T}_\lambda$*, sample and output* $(\mathsf{ek}, \mathsf{tk})$.
- $\mathsf{Eval}(\mathsf{ek}, \mathsf{tag}, x)$*: on inputs* $x \in \{0,1\}^{\ell(\lambda)}$*, an evaluation key* ek *and* tag*, output an element* y *in some set* $\mathcal{R}$ *of images.*
- $\mathsf{Invert}(\mathsf{tk}, \mathsf{tag}, y)$*: on inputs* $y \in \mathcal{R}$*, a trapdoor key* tk*, and* tag*, output* $x' \in \{0,1\}^{\ell(\lambda)}$.

We require the following properties:

- *(Injectivity) There exists a negligible function* $\mathsf{negl} : \mathbb{N} \to \mathbb{N}$ *such that for all* $\lambda \in \mathbb{N}$*,* $\mathsf{tag}^* \in \mathcal{T}_\lambda$*,* $(\mathsf{ek}, \mathsf{tk}) \leftarrow \mathsf{Sample}(1^\lambda, \mathsf{tag}^*)$ *we have*

$$\frac{|\{x \in \{0,1\}^{\ell(\lambda)} : \mathsf{Invert}(\mathsf{tk}, \mathsf{tag}^*, \mathsf{Eval}(\mathsf{ek}, \mathsf{tag}^*, x)) = x\}|}{2^{\ell(\lambda)}} \geq 1 - \mathsf{negl}(\lambda) .$$

- *(α-cumulative lossiness) For all* $\lambda \in \mathbb{N}$*, all tags* $\mathsf{tag}^* \in \mathcal{T}_\lambda$*, and all* $(\mathsf{ek}, \mathsf{tk}) \leftarrow \mathsf{Sample}(1^\lambda, \mathsf{tag}^*)$*, there exists a (possibly inefficient) function* $\mathsf{compress}_{\mathsf{ek}} : \{0,1\}^{\ell(\lambda)} \to \mathcal{R}_{\mathsf{ek}}$ *where* $|\mathcal{R}_{\mathsf{ek}}| \leq 2^{\ell(\lambda) - \alpha(\lambda)}$ *such that for all* $\mathsf{tag} \neq \mathsf{tag}^*$ *and* $x \in \{0,1\}^{\ell(\lambda)}$*, there exists a (possibly inefficient) function* $\mathsf{expand}_{\mathsf{ek},\mathsf{tag}} : \mathcal{R}_{\mathsf{ek}} \to \mathcal{R}$ *satisfying*

$$\mathsf{Eval}(\mathsf{ek}, \mathsf{tag}, x) = \mathsf{expand}_{\mathsf{ek},\mathsf{tag}}(\mathsf{compress}_{\mathsf{ek}}(x)) . \quad (2)$$

- *(Indistinguishability) For all* $\mathsf{tag}_0^*, \mathsf{tag}_1^* \in \mathcal{T}_\lambda$*, the two ensembles*

$$\{\mathsf{ek}_0 : (\mathsf{ek}_0, \mathsf{tk}_0) \leftarrow \mathsf{Sample}(1^\lambda, \mathsf{tag}_0^*)\}_{\lambda \in \mathbb{N}}$$
$$\{\mathsf{ek}_1 : (\mathsf{ek}_1, \mathsf{tk}_1) \leftarrow \mathsf{Sample}(1^\lambda, \mathsf{tag}_1^*)\}_{\lambda \in \mathbb{N}}$$

  are computationally indistinguishable.

An alternative, relaxed notion of CALBO-TDFs was also proposed in [19,23]. In this relaxed variant, cumulative lossiness is slightly simplified by requiring Equation (2) to only hold with overwhelming probability over the choice of tags. This minor relaxation does not impact applications, as the relaxed notion was proven sufficient for all known applications of CALBO-TDFs in [19, Appendix A]. We use this relaxation in our LWE-based construction in Sect. 3.1, and recall it below. We refer to this notion as relaxed CALBO-TDFs.

(relaxed α-cumulative lossiness) There exists a negligible function $\mathsf{negl} : \mathbb{N} \to (0,1)$ and for sufficiently large $\lambda \in \mathbb{N}$, for any $\mathsf{tag}^* \in \mathcal{T}_\lambda$, for all $(\mathsf{ek}, \mathsf{tk}) \leftarrow \mathsf{Sample}(1^\lambda, \mathsf{tag}^*)$, there exists a (possibly inefficient) function $\mathsf{compress}_{\mathsf{ek}} : \{0,1\}^{\ell(\lambda)} \to \mathcal{R}_{\mathsf{ek}}$ where $|\mathcal{R}_{\mathsf{ek}}| \leq 2^{\ell(\lambda) - \alpha(\lambda)}$ such that for any fixed randomly chosen $x \in \{0,1\}^{\ell(\lambda)}$, there exists a (possibly inefficient) function $\mathsf{expand}_{\mathsf{ek},\mathsf{tag}} : \mathcal{R}_{\mathsf{ek}} \to \mathcal{R}$ satisfying

$$\Pr[\mathsf{Eval}(\mathsf{ek}, \mathsf{tag}, x) = \mathsf{expand}_{\mathsf{ek},\mathsf{tag}}(\mathsf{compress}_{\mathsf{ek}}(x))] \geq 1 - \mathsf{negl}(\lambda) ,$$

where the probability is taken over the choices of $\mathsf{tag} \neq \mathsf{tag}^*$. We call $\mathsf{negl}(\lambda)$ the *lossiness error* of the CALBO-TDF.

Lossiness Rate. We define the *lossiness rate* of an (ℓ, α)-CALBO-TDF by the rate of bits lost on lossy tags, namely $1 - (\ell - \alpha)/\ell = \alpha/\ell$. This is similar to the notion of lossiness rate used in [29,48]. Ideally, we want this rate to be as close to 1 as possible, for example $1 - o(1)$.

2.2 Lattices

Unless stated otherwise, we write vectors as column vectors. For a full-row rank matrix $\mathbf{A} \in \mathbb{Z}_q^{n\times m}$, we define the lattice $\Lambda(\mathbf{A})$ admitting $\mathbf{A}$ as a basis by $\Lambda(\mathbf{A}) = \{\mathbf{s}^\top \cdot \mathbf{A} : \mathbf{s} \in \mathbb{Z}_q^n\}$. We also define the lattice $\Lambda^\perp(\mathbf{A}) = \{\mathbf{x} \in \mathbb{Z}^m : \mathbf{A}\mathbf{x} = \mathbf{0} \bmod q\}$. Given a vector $\mathbf{x} \in \mathbb{Z}_q^n$, we define its ℓ_∞-norm as $\|\mathbf{x}\|_\infty = \max_{i\in[n]} |\mathbf{x}[i]|$ where $\mathbf{x}[i]$ denotes the i-th coordinate of $\mathbf{x}$. We let $\|\mathbf{x}\|_2 = \sqrt{\mathbf{x}[1]^2 + \cdots + \mathbf{x}[n]^2}$ denote the Euclidean norm of $\mathbf{x}$. The *minimum distance* measured in ℓ_∞-norm of a lattice Λ is given by $\lambda_1^\infty(\Lambda) := \min_{\mathbf{x}\neq\mathbf{0}} \|\mathbf{x}\|_\infty$. For a basis $\mathbf{B}$ of $\mathbb{R}^n$, the origin-centered parallelepiped is defined as $\mathcal{P}_{1/2}(\mathbf{B}) := \mathbf{B} \cdot [-1/2, 1/2)^n$. We also use the following infinity norm for matrices $\mathbf{B} \in \mathbb{Z}^{n\times m}$:

$$\|\mathbf{B}\|_\infty = \max_{i\in[n]} \left(\sum_{j=1}^{m} |\mathbf{B}_{i,j}| \right) .$$

Let $\mathbf{\Sigma} \in \mathbb{R}^{n\times n}$ be a symmetric positive definite matrix and $\mathbf{c} \in \mathbb{R}^n$ be a vector. We define the *Gaussian function* over $\mathbb{R}^n$ by $\rho_{\mathbf{\Sigma},\mathbf{c}}(\mathbf{x}) = \exp(-\pi(\mathbf{x}-\mathbf{c})^\top \mathbf{\Sigma}^{-1}(\mathbf{x}-\mathbf{c}))$ and if $\mathbf{\Sigma} = \sigma^2 \cdot \mathbf{I}_n$ and $\mathbf{c} = \mathbf{0}$, we write ρ_σ for $\rho_{\mathbf{\Sigma},\mathbf{c}}$. For any discrete set $\Lambda \subset \mathbb{R}^n$, the *discrete Gaussian distribution* $D_{\Lambda,\mathbf{\Sigma},\mathbf{c}}$ has probability mass $\Pr_{X\sim D_{\Lambda,\mathbf{\Sigma},\mathbf{c}}}[X = \mathbf{x}] = \frac{\rho_{\mathbf{\Sigma},\mathbf{c}}(\mathbf{x})}{\rho_{\mathbf{\Sigma},\mathbf{c}}(\Lambda)}$, for any $\mathbf{x} \in \Lambda$. When $\mathbf{c} = \mathbf{0}$ and $\mathbf{\Sigma} = \sigma^2 \cdot \mathbf{I}_n$ we denote $D_{\Lambda,\mathbf{\Sigma},\mathbf{c}}$ by $D_{\Lambda,\sigma}$.

Learning-with-Errors Assumption. Our first CALBO-TDF relies on the LWE assumption.

Definition 2. *Let $\alpha : \mathbb{N} \to (0,1)$ and $m \geq n \geq 1$, $q \geq 2$ be functions of a security parameter $\lambda \in \mathbb{N}$. The* **Learning with Errors** *(LWE) problem consists in distinguishing between the distributions $(\mathbf{A}, \mathbf{s}^\top\mathbf{A} + \mathbf{e}^\top)$ and $U(\mathbb{Z}_q^{n\times m} \times \mathbb{Z}_q^m)$, where $\mathbf{A} \sim U(\mathbb{Z}_q^{n\times m})$, $\mathbf{s} \sim U(\mathbb{Z}_q^n)$ and $\mathbf{e} \sim D_{\mathbb{Z}^m,\alpha q}$. For an algorithm $\mathcal{A} : \mathbb{Z}_q^{n\times m} \times \mathbb{Z}_q^m \to \{0,1\}$, we define*

$$\mathbf{Adv}^{\mathsf{LWE}}_{q,m,n,\alpha}(\mathcal{A}) = \left|\Pr[\mathcal{A}\left(\mathbf{A}, \mathbf{s}^\top\mathbf{A} + \mathbf{e}^\top\right) = 1] - \Pr[\mathcal{A}\left(\mathbf{A}, \mathbf{u}\right) = 1\right|,$$

where the probabilities are over $\mathbf{A} \sim U(\mathbb{Z}_q^{n\times m})$, $\mathbf{s} \sim U(\mathbb{Z}_q^n)$, $\mathbf{u} \sim U(\mathbb{Z}_q^m)$ and $\mathbf{e} \sim D_{\mathbb{Z}^m,\alpha q}$ and the internal randomness of $\mathcal{A}$. We say that $\mathsf{LWE}_{q,m,n,\alpha}$ is hard if for all ppt *algorithm $\mathcal{A}$, the advantage $\mathbf{Adv}^{\mathsf{LWE}}_{q,m,n,\alpha}(\mathcal{A})$ is negligible in λ.*

We require that $\alpha \geq 2\sqrt{n}/q$ for the reduction from worst-case lattice problems and refer the readers to, e.g., [17] for more details.

We will need the techniques for *homomorphic encryption (HE)* [31] in order to build CALBO-TDFs from LWE. In this paper, we consider only binary circuits with fan-in-2 gates for homomorphic evaluation. We use the terms *size* and *depth* of a circuit to refer to the number of its gates and the length of its longest input-to-output path, respectively. We note that in our construction from LWE, we do not need the general fully homomorphic encryption thanks to the fact that all evaluated circuits have bounded depths, for the sole purpose of comparing tags. Hence, *leveled* homomorphic encryption suffices for our purposes.

Gadget Matrix. We recall the "gadget matrix" from [45] and their homomorphic properties. The technique is later developed further in [12,33,34]. For an integer modulus q, the gadget vector over $\mathbb{Z}_q$ is defined as $\mathbf{g} = (1, 2, 4, \ldots, 2^{\lceil \log q \rceil - 1})$. The gadget matrix $\mathbf{G}_n$ is the tensor (or Kronecker) product $\mathbf{I}_n \otimes \mathbf{g} \in \mathbb{Z}_q^{n \times n'}$ where $n' = \lceil n \log q \rceil$. There exists an efficiently computable function $\mathbf{G}_n^{-1} : \mathbb{Z}_q^{n \times n'} \to \{0,1\}^{n' \times n'}$ such that $\mathbf{G}_n \cdot \mathbf{G}_n^{-1}(\mathbf{A}) = \mathbf{A}$ for all $\mathbf{A} \in \mathbb{Z}_q^{n \times n'}$. In particular, we can define $\mathbf{G}_n^{-1}$ to be the entry-wise binary decomposition of matrices in $\mathbb{Z}_q^{n \times n'}$. In the following, we omit the subscript n and write $\mathbf{G}$ when it is clear from context. Lemma 2 helps bound the noise of the output ciphertext after homomorphically evaluating a depth-τ circuit C containing only AND gates. This will affect our parameter choices for the LWE-based CALBO-TDFs as well as our later argument for its relaxed cumulative lossiness.

Lemma 2 (Adapted from [12,16,31]). *Let $\lambda \in \mathbb{N}$ and $m = m(\lambda), n = n(\lambda)$. We define $n' := \lceil n \log q \rceil$. Let $C : \{0,1\}^t \to \{0,1\}$ be a AND Boolean circuit of depth τ. Let $\mathbf{A}_i = \mathbf{A} \cdot \mathbf{R}_i + b_i \cdot \mathbf{G} \in \mathbb{Z}_q^{n \times m}$ with $\mathbf{A} \in \mathbb{Z}_q^{n \times m}$, $\mathbf{R}_i \in \{-1,1\}^{m \times n'}$ and $b_i \in \{0,1\}$, for $i \le t$. There exist deterministic algorithms* FHEval *and* EvalPriv *with running time* $\mathsf{poly}(4^\tau, t, m, n, \log q)$ *that satisfy:*

$$\mathsf{FHEval}(C, (\mathbf{A}_i)_i) = \mathbf{A} \cdot \mathbf{R}_C + C(b_1, \ldots, b_t) \cdot \mathbf{G} = \mathbf{A} \cdot \mathbf{R}_C + \bigwedge_{i=1}^{t} b_i \cdot \mathbf{G},$$

where $\mathbf{R}_C = \mathsf{EvalPriv}\big(C, ((\mathbf{R}_i, b_i))_i\big)$ *and* $\|\mathbf{R}_C\|_\infty \le \max_i\{\|\mathbf{R}_i\|_\infty\} \cdot (n'+1)^\tau$.

Lossy mode of LWE. We recall the Lossy sampler for LWE that is introduced by Goldwasser *et al.* in [32] and later developed by Alwen *et al.* in [2].

Definition 3. *Let $\chi = \chi(\lambda)$ be an efficiently sampleable distribution over $\mathbb{Z}$. We define an efficient* lossy sampler $(\mathbf{A}, \mathbf{B}) \leftarrow \mathsf{Lossy}(1^m, 1^n, 1^\ell, q, \chi)$ *via:*

> $\mathsf{Lossy}(1^m, 1^n, 1^\ell, q, \chi)$: *Sample* $\mathbf{B} \hookleftarrow U(\mathbb{Z}_q^{\ell \times m}), \mathbf{D} \hookleftarrow U(\mathbb{Z}_q^{\ell \times n}), \mathbf{E} \hookleftarrow \chi^{n \times m}$, *where $\ell \ll n$, and output* $\mathbf{A} = \mathbf{D}^\top \cdot \mathbf{B} + \mathbf{E} \in \mathbb{Z}_q^{n \times m}$ *together with* $\mathbf{B}$.

We remark that the lossy sampler reveals the coefficient matrix $\mathbf{B}$ along with $\mathbf{A}$ but as long as the secret matrix $\mathbf{D}$ is not leaked, this does not compromise the pseudorandomness of $\mathbf{A}$. Indeed, it can be shown that under the $\mathsf{LWE}_{q,m,\ell,\alpha}$ assumption, $\mathbf{A}$ is computationally indistinguishable from a uniformly random matrix. Intuitively, the dimension of the secret is now ℓ and we view each row of $\mathbf{D}^\top$ as a secret vector, $\mathbf{B}$ as the uniform coefficients and each row of $\mathbf{A}$ as the resulting LWE vector. Formally, we have the following lemma:

Lemma 3 ([32]). *Let a random matrix $\tilde{\mathbf{A}} \hookleftarrow U(\mathbb{Z}_q^{n\times m})$ and let a pair $(\mathbf{A}, \mathbf{B}) \leftarrow \mathsf{Lossy}(1^m, 1^n, 1^\ell, q, \chi)$, where $\chi = D_{\mathbb{Z},\alpha q}$ is an error distribution. Then, under the $\mathsf{LWE}_{q,m,\ell,\alpha}$ assumption, the following two distributions are computationally indistinguishable: $\mathbf{A} \overset{\text{comp}}{\approx} \tilde{\mathbf{A}}$.*

Trapdoor Mechanisms for LWE. Micciancio and Peikert [45] introduced a trapdoor mechanism for LWE. Their technique makes use of the "gadget matrix" $\mathbf{G} \in \mathbb{Z}_q^{n\times n'}$, where $n' = \lceil n \log q \rceil$, and for $\mathbf{A}' \in \mathbb{Z}_q^{n\times(m+n')}$, they call a short matrix $\mathbf{R} \in \mathbb{Z}^{m\times n'}$ a $\mathbf{G}$-trapdoor of $\mathbf{A}'$ if $\mathbf{A}' \cdot [\mathbf{R}^\top \mid \mathbf{I}_m]^\top = \mathbf{H}\mathbf{G}$ for some invertible $\mathbf{H} \in \mathbb{Z}_q^{n\times n}$. Micciancio and Peikert also showed that using a $\mathbf{G}$-trapdoor allows one to invert the LWE function $(\mathbf{s}, \mathbf{e}) \mapsto \mathbf{s}^\top\mathbf{A}' + \mathbf{e}^\top$ for any $\mathbf{s} \in \mathbb{Z}_q^n$ and any error $\mathbf{e} \in \mathbb{Z}^{m+n'}$ such that $\|\mathbf{e}\|_2 \leq q/O(\sqrt{n \log q})$. More specifically, we have the following lemma:

Lemma 4 ([45], **Theorem 4.1 and Sect. 5**). *Let $n' = \lceil n \log q \rceil$ and $\delta = \mathsf{negl}(n)$. Assume that $m \geq n \log q + 2 \log \frac{n'}{2\delta}$. Then there exists a* ppt *algorithm* GenTrap *that takes as inputs matrices $\mathbf{A} \in \mathbb{Z}_q^{n\times m}, \mathbf{H} \in \mathbb{Z}_q^{n\times n}$, outputs a short matrix $\mathbf{R} \in \{-1, 0, 1\}^{m\times n'}$ and $\mathbf{A}' = [\mathbf{A} \mid -\mathbf{A} \cdot \mathbf{R} + \mathbf{H} \cdot \mathbf{G}] \in \mathbb{Z}_q^{n\times(m+n')}$ such that if $\mathbf{H}$ is invertible, then $\mathbf{R}$ is a $\mathbf{G}$-trapdoor of $\mathbf{A}'$ and we call $\mathbf{H}$ the* invert tag *of $\mathbf{A}'$.*

In particular, inverting the function $g_{\mathbf{G}}(\mathbf{s}, \mathbf{e}) := \mathbf{s}^\top \cdot \mathbf{G} + \mathbf{e}^\top$ can be done in quasi-linear time $O(n \cdot \log^c n)$ for any $\mathbf{s} \in \mathbb{Z}_q^n$ and any $\mathbf{e} \in \mathcal{P}_{1/2}(q \cdot (\mathbf{B}^{-1})^\top)$, where $\mathbf{B}$ is a basis of the lattice $\Lambda^\perp(\mathbf{G}) = \{\mathbf{z} \in \mathbb{Z}^{n'} : \mathbf{G} \cdot \mathbf{z} = 0 \ (mod\ q)\}$.

In a follow-up work, Alwen *et al.* [2] used GenTrap to construct trapdoors for inverting *Learning with Rounding* (LWR) instances $\lfloor \mathbf{s}^\top \mathbf{A} \rfloor_p$. Their main observation is that one can convert $\lfloor \mathbf{s}^\top \mathbf{A} \rfloor_p$ to $\mathbf{s}^\top\mathbf{A} + \mathbf{e}^\top$ where $\|\mathbf{e}\|_2 \leq \sqrt{m}q/p$, by first multiplying with q/p then taking the ceiling value. Afterwards, using a $\mathbf{G}$-trapdoor of $\mathbf{A}$, e.g. a sample from GenTrap, allows one to compute back $\mathbf{s}$. Formally, we have the following lemma:

Lemma 5 ([2], **Lemma 6.3**). *Let $n' = \lceil n \log q \rceil$ and $\delta = \mathsf{negl}(n)$. Assume that $m \geq n \log q + 2 \log \frac{n'}{2\delta}$ and $p \geq O(\sqrt{(m + n')n'})$. Then there exists a* ppt *algorithm* LWRInvert *that takes as inputs $(\mathbf{A}', \mathbf{R})$ with $\mathbf{R}$ being a $\mathbf{G}$-trapdoor of $\mathbf{A}'$, together with some $\mathbf{c} \in \mathbb{Z}_p^{m+n'}$ such that $\mathbf{c} = \lfloor \mathbf{s}^\top \mathbf{A}' \rfloor_p$ for some $\mathbf{s} \in \mathbb{Z}_q^n$, then outputs $\mathbf{s}$.*

We will also need the following technical lemmas. Lemma 6 comes from a work by Gentry, Peikert, and Vaikuntanathan [30].

Lemma 6 ([30], **Lemma 5.3**). *Let ℓ and q be positive integers and q be prime. Let $n \geq 2\ell \log q$. Then for all but an at most q^{-n} fraction of $\mathbf{D} \in \mathbb{Z}_q^{\ell\times n}$, we have $\lambda_1^\infty(\Lambda(\mathbf{D})) \geq q/4$, where $\Lambda(\mathbf{D}) = \{\mathbf{s}^\top\mathbf{D} : \mathbf{s} \in \mathbb{Z}_q^\ell\}$ and $\lambda_1^\infty(\Lambda(\mathbf{D}))$ is the* minimum distance *of $\Lambda(\mathbf{D})$ measured in the ℓ_∞-norm.*

Lemma 7 **([2], Lemma 2.7).** *Let p, q be positive integers and $p < q$. Let $R > 0$ be an integer. Then, the probability that there exists $e \in [-R, R]$ such that $\lfloor y \rfloor_p \neq \lfloor y + e \rfloor_p$, where $y \hookleftarrow U(\mathbb{Z}_q)$, is at most $2pR/q$.*

The following lemma is well-known, e.g. a simple proof can be found in [44, Lemma 2.3].

Lemma 8. *Let q be a prime a $D_{m,n,q}$ be a distribution over $\mathbb{Z}_q^{n\times m}$ such that $\Delta(D_{m,n,q}, U(\mathbb{Z}_q^{n\times m})) \leq \epsilon$. Then, let $V_{n,q}$ be any distribution over $\mathbb{Z}_q^n$, we have $\Delta(V_{n,q}^\top \cdot D_{m,n,q}, U(\mathbb{Z}_q^m)) \leq \epsilon + \alpha \cdot \left(1 - \frac{1}{q^m}\right)$ where $\alpha := \Pr[\mathbf{v} \hookleftarrow V_{n,q} : \mathbf{v} = \mathbf{0}]$.*

2.3 Composite Residuosity

Our second construction of CALBO-TDFs relies on Paillier's composite residuosity assumption.

Definition 4 **([20,47]).** *Let a composite $N = pq$, for primes p, q, and let an integer $\zeta \geq 1$. The* **Decision Composite Residuosity** *(ζ-DCR) problem is to distinguish between the distributions $D_0 := \{z = z_0^{N^\zeta} \bmod N^{\zeta+1} \mid z_0 \hookleftarrow U(\mathbb{Z}_N^*)\}$ and $D_1 := \{z \hookleftarrow U(\mathbb{Z}_{N^{\zeta+1}}^*)\}$.*

For each $\zeta > 0$, the ζ-DCR assumption was shown to be equivalent to the original 1-DCR assumption [20]. Damgård and Jurik [20] initially gave their security proof using a recursive argument (rather than a sequence of hybrid experiments) that loses a factor 2 at each step, thus incurring an apparent security loss 2^ζ. However, the semantic security of their scheme under the 1-DCR assumption for any polynomial ζ is a well-known result. The proof of Lemma 9 is perhaps folklore but for completeness we will include it in the full version of this paper.

Lemma 9 (Adapted from [20]). *Let $\zeta = \mathsf{poly}(\lambda)$. Then ζ-DCR is equivalent to 1-DCR with a security loss at most ζ.*

3 Cumulatively All-Lossy-But-One Trapdoor Functions

We now describe two constructions of CALBO-TDFs from standard assumptions. So far, the only known CALBO-TDFs construction was proposed by Chakraborty *et al.* [19] and relies on puncturable PRFs, cumulatively-lossy-trapdoor functions (C-LTDFs) and indistinguishability obfuscation (iO). This construction relies on iO to obfuscate a program, which first compares a given input tag with the hardcoded injective tag and outputs the hardcoded injective evaluation key if the comparison goes through. Otherwise, it generates a fresh lossy key. All auxiliary key generations in the program are realized using the algorithms from the underlying C-LTDF. The obfuscated program is described in the evaluation key for the CALBO-TDF. An evaluation on a pair of tag and input proceeds by first calling the obfuscated program on the given tag to get a C-LTDF key, then use the evaluation of the C-LTDF on the received key and the given input. The obfuscated program uses a puncturable PRF, which receives the given tag as input, to generate randomness needed for producing a fresh lossy key. Our constructions are much simpler and require neither CPRFs nor iO. They thus drastically improve the efficiency compared to [19].

We construct CALBO-TDFs from the LWE and DCR assumptions. Our LWE-based CALBO-TDFs only achieves the relaxed variant of cumulative lossiness while our DCR-based construction achieves the full notion. The fact that we have to relax the cumulative lossiness in the LWE case seems intrinsic due to the noise that appears in the LWE samples. We remark that Chakraborty *et al.* faced a similar problem when constructing C-LTDFs from LWE as well as when boostrapping C-LTDFs to CALBO-TDFs using iO in [19].

3.1 Relaxed CALBO-TDFs from LWE

In this section, we describe our construction of CALBO-TDFs from LWE. It is inspired from the PRF from [44], which can be seen as a CALBO-TDFs without inversion. We extend ideas from [44] to achieve inversion via trapdoors.

Let λ be a security parameter and let $\ell = \ell(\lambda), n = n(\lambda), m = m(\lambda), q = q(\lambda), p = p(\lambda), t = t(\lambda), \beta = \beta(\lambda)$ be natural numbers and $\chi = \chi(\lambda) = D_{\mathbb{Z},\alpha q}$ be an LWE error distribution. We denote $n' = \lceil n \log q \rceil$. The tag space is $\mathcal{T}_\lambda = \{0,1\}^t$. Our construction now goes as follows:

Sample$(1^\lambda, \mathsf{tag}^*)$**:** Sample $(\mathbf{A}, \mathbf{B}) \leftarrow \mathsf{Lossy}(1^m, 1^n, 1^\ell, q, \chi)$, then set the evaluation key$\mathsf{ek} := \left(\mathbf{A} \in \mathbb{Z}_q^{n \times m},\ \mathbf{B} \in \mathbb{Z}_q^{\ell \times m},\ \{\mathbf{A}_{i,0}, \mathbf{A}_{i,1}\}_{i=1}^t\right)$ where

$$\mathbf{A}_{i,b} = \mathbf{A} \cdot \mathbf{R}_{i,b} + \delta_{b,\mathsf{tag}_i^*} \cdot \mathbf{G} \in \mathbb{Z}_q^{n \times n'} \quad \forall i \in [t], b \in \{0,1\}$$

for $\mathbf{R}_{i,b} \leftarrow U(\{0,1\}^{m \times n'})$, tag_i^* denotes the i-th bit of tag^*, and $\delta_{b,\mathsf{tag}_i^*} = (b \stackrel{?}{=} \mathsf{tag}_i^*)$. Afterwards, set the trapdoor key $\mathsf{tk} := \{\mathbf{R}_{i,b}\}_{i \in [t], b \in \{0,1\}}$ and output $(\mathsf{ek}, \mathsf{tk})$.

Eval$(\mathsf{ek}, \mathsf{tag}, \mathbf{x} \in [0,\beta]^n)$**:** Let $C_{\mathsf{tag}} : \{0,1\}^t \to \{0,1\}$ be the circuit $C_{\mathsf{tag}}(\mathsf{tag}') = \prod_{i=1}^t \delta_{\mathsf{tag}_i,\mathsf{tag}'_i}$ and $\delta_{\mathsf{tag}_i,\mathsf{tag}'_i} = 1$ if and only if $\mathsf{tag}_i = \mathsf{tag}'_i$. Parse the evaluation key $\mathsf{ek} = (\mathbf{A}, \mathbf{B}, \{\mathbf{A}_{i,0}, \mathbf{A}_{i,1}\}_{i=1}^t)$ and perform the homomorphic evaluation

$$\mathbf{A}(\mathsf{tag}) := \mathsf{FHEval}\left(C_{\mathsf{tag}}, \left(\mathbf{A}_{i,\mathsf{tag}_i}\right)_{i=1}^t\right) = \mathbf{A} \cdot \mathbf{R}_{\mathsf{tag}} + C_{\mathsf{tag}}(\mathsf{tag}^*) \cdot \mathbf{G}$$
$$= \left\{ \begin{array}{l} \mathbf{A} \cdot \mathbf{R}_{\mathsf{tag}} + \mathbf{G} \text{ if } \mathsf{tag} = \mathsf{tag}^* \\ \mathbf{A} \cdot \mathbf{R}_{\mathsf{tag}} \text{ otherwise} \end{array} \right. \in \mathbb{Z}_q^{n \times n'} \qquad (3)$$

where the procedure FHEval is specified by:

$$\mathsf{FHEval}\left(C_{\mathsf{tag}}, \left(\mathbf{A}_{i,\mathsf{tag}_i}\right)_{i=1}^t\right) := \mathbf{A}_{1,\mathsf{tag}_1} \cdot \mathbf{G}^{-1}\left(\mathbf{A}_{2,\mathsf{tag}_2} \cdot \mathbf{G}^{-1}\left(\cdots \mathbf{G}^{-1}(\mathbf{A}_{t,\mathsf{tag}_t}) \cdots\right)\right)$$

and $\mathbf{R}_{\mathsf{tag}} \in \mathbb{Z}^{m \times n'}$. Finally, compute and output $\left\lfloor \mathbf{x}^\top \cdot [\mathbf{A} \mid \mathbf{A}(\mathsf{tag})] \right\rceil_p$.

Invert$(\mathsf{tk}, \mathsf{tag}^*, \mathbf{y} \in \mathbb{Z}_p^{m+n'})$**:** Parse the trapdoor key $\mathsf{tk} = \{\mathbf{R}_{i,b}\}_{i\in[t],b\in\{0,1\}}$ then compute $\mathsf{FHEval}\left(C_{\mathsf{tag}^*}, \left(\mathbf{A}_{i,\mathsf{tag}_i^*}\right)_{i=1}^{t}\right) = \mathbf{A} \cdot \mathbf{R}_{\mathsf{tag}^*} + \mathbf{G}$, and following Lemma 2, obtain $\mathsf{EvalPriv}\big(C_{\mathsf{tag}^*}, ((\mathbf{R}_{i,\mathsf{tag}_i^*}, \mathsf{tag}_i^*))_{i\in[t]}\big) = \mathbf{R}_{\mathsf{tag}^*}$. Afterwards, compute $\mathbf{x} \leftarrow \mathsf{LWRInvert}([\mathbf{A} \mid \mathbf{A} \cdot \mathbf{R}_{\mathsf{tag}^*} + \mathbf{G}], -\mathbf{R}_{\mathsf{tag}^*}, \mathbf{y})$ as per Lemma 5 and output $\mathbf{x}$.

The way we carry out the homomorphic computation FHEval involved in equation (3) is not unique. Roughly speaking, at each step of the homomorphic evaluation of C_{tag}, we "decompose" the result from the previous step using $\mathbf{G}^{-1}$ (the decomposed entries become binary) before multiplying so as to obtain a ciphertext for the AND gate's output. This gives the smallest possible increase in the error term of the resulting homomorphic ciphertext, following Lemma 2. Different approaches for computing FHEval will lead to different error increases. Indeed, we homomorphically evaluate the circuit C_{tag} in the most possible "sequential" way, which is inspired by [5], and always multiply ciphertexts whose noise terms are not too large. A less sequential computation will work, but at the cost of a larger modulus, which then becomes exponential not only in the security paramter but also in the depth of C_{tag}.

Parameter Selection. Let λ be the security parameter. First of all, we set the bound $\beta = 1$ for the entries of inputs, which gives a domain $\{0,1\}^n$. We set the tag length $t = \log\lambda$, which means the circuits to be homomorphically evaluated have depths bounded by $t - 1 \leq \log\lambda$. By Lemma 6, we must choose ℓ such that $n \geq 2\ell \log q$. In addition, for the trapdoor mechanism to work, Lemma 5 requires that $m \geq n \log q + 2 \log \frac{n'}{2\delta}$ and $p \geq O(\sqrt{(m+n')n'})$, where $n' = \lceil n \log q \rceil$ and $\delta = \mathsf{negl}(n)$.

We will need $m \geq n \log q + \omega(\log n)$ in order to apply Lemma 3. Moreover, for the $\mathsf{LWE}_{q,m,n-1,\alpha}$ problem to be hard, it is necessary that $q \leq 2^{n^\epsilon} < 2^n$ and $2\sqrt{n}/q \leq \alpha \leq n \cdot 2^{-n^\epsilon}$, for some $0 < \epsilon < 1$. We refer to [17, Corollary 3.2] for more details on these bounds for q and α. Similarly, we also need to ensure that the $\mathsf{LWE}_{q,m,\ell,\alpha}$ problem is hard. Last but not least, we need $q/p > 2^\lambda$ for the rounding operation to anihilate the noise term, following Lemma 7. Concretely, let $0 < \epsilon < 1$ be a constant and $d \geq 1$, we set up the parameters as follows:

$$n = \Theta(\lambda^d);\quad n' = n\log q = \Theta\left(\lambda^{d+d\epsilon}\right);\quad \beta = 1;\quad t = \log\lambda;\quad q = 2^{n^\epsilon} = \Theta\left(2^{\lambda^{d\epsilon}}\right);$$

$$\alpha = n \cdot 2^{-n^\epsilon} = \Theta\left(\lambda^d \cdot 2^{-\lambda^{d\epsilon}}\right);\qquad m = 2\lambda + \lceil n \log q \rceil = \Theta\left(\lambda^{d+d\epsilon}\right);$$

$$\ell = \frac{n}{2\log q} = \Theta\left(\lambda^{d-d\epsilon}\right);\qquad p = \Theta\left(\sqrt{(m+n')n'}\right) = \Theta\left(\lambda^{d+d\epsilon}\right).$$

Theorem 1. *Let $\lambda \in \mathbb{N}$ be a security parameter. Under the $\mathsf{LWE}_{q,m,\ell,\alpha}$ and $\mathsf{LWE}_{q,m,n-1,\alpha}$ assumptions, the above construction* (Sample, Eval, Invert) *is a relaxed $(n, n - \ell \log q)$-cumulatively-all-lossy-but-one trapdoor function family with tag space $\mathcal{T}_t = \{0,1\}^t$.*

Proof. We now prove each of the required properties.

Injectivity. The correctness of FHEval and EvalPriv in Invert follows Lemma 2. It is straightforward to see that $-\mathbf{R}_{\mathsf{tag}^*}$ is a $\mathbf{G}$-trapdoor for the matrix $\mathbf{A}' := [\mathbf{A} \mid \mathbf{A} \cdot \mathbf{R}_{\mathsf{tag}^*} + \mathbf{G}]$. Hence, given as inputs $\mathbf{y} = \mathsf{Eval}(\mathsf{ek}, \mathsf{tag}^*, \mathbf{x}) = \lfloor \mathbf{x}^\top \cdot \mathbf{A}' \rfloor_p$ and the pair $(\mathbf{A}', -\mathbf{R}_{\mathsf{tag}^*})$, the algorithm LWRInvert will be able to compute back $\mathbf{x}$ as per Lemma 5.

Indistinguishability. Let $\mathsf{tag}_0^*, \mathsf{tag}_1^* \in \{0,1\}^t$ and $(\mathsf{ek}_b, \mathsf{tk}_b) \leftarrow \mathsf{Sample}(1^\lambda, \mathsf{tag}_b^*)$ for $b \in \{0,1\}$. We want to prove that ek_0 and ek_1 are indistinguishable. Let $b \in \{0,1\}$. The evaluation key ek_b is parsed as

$$\mathsf{ek}_b = \left(\mathbf{A}^{(b)} \in \mathbb{Z}_q^{n \times m}, \mathbf{B}^{(b)} \in \mathbb{Z}_q^{\ell \times m}, \{\mathbf{A}_{i,0}^{(b)}, \mathbf{A}_{i,1}^{(b)}\}_{i=1}^t\right)$$

where $(\mathbf{A}^{(b)}, \mathbf{B}^{(b)}) \leftarrow \mathsf{Lossy}(1^m, 1^n, 1^\ell, q, \chi)$ and $\mathbf{B}^{(b)} \sim U(\mathbb{Z}_q^{\ell \times m})$, $\mathbf{A}_{i,b'}^{(b)}$ are encryptions of $\delta_{b', \mathsf{tag}_{b,i}^*} \in \{0,1\}$ for $i \in [t]$ and $\mathsf{tag}_{b,i}^*$ is the i-th bit of tag_b^*, respectively. Similarly to the proof of semantic security for the GSW encryption scheme [31], we first notice that $\mathbf{A}^{(b)}$ is indistinguishable from a uniformly random matrix $\tilde{\mathbf{A}}^{(b)}$ in $\mathbb{Z}_q^{n \times m}$ thanks to Lemma 3 and the parameter choice $m \geq n \log q + 2\lambda$. Hence, changing $\mathbf{A}^{(b)}$ to $\tilde{\mathbf{A}}^{(b)}$ is computationally indistinguishable under LWE.

We then apply Lemma 1 for the family of universal hash functions $\mathcal{H} = \{h_{\mathbf{A}} : \mathbb{Z}_q^n \to \mathbb{Z}_q^m\}$ where $h_{\mathbf{A}}(\mathbf{x}) := \mathbf{x}^\top \cdot \mathbf{A}$ is indexed by $\mathbf{A} \in \mathbb{Z}_q^{n \times m}$ and q is prime. Therefore, it holds that $\left(\tilde{\mathbf{A}}^{(b)} \mathbf{R}_{i, \mathsf{tag}_{b,i}^*}^{(b)}\right)_{i \in [t]}$ is statistically close to a t-tuple of independent uniformly random matrices. As a result, for all i, the pair $(\tilde{\mathbf{A}}_{i,0}^{(b)}, \tilde{\mathbf{A}}_{i,1}^{(b)})$, where $\tilde{\mathbf{A}}_{i,b'}^{(b)} := \tilde{\mathbf{A}}^{(b)} \mathbf{R}_{i, \mathsf{tag}_{b,i}^*}^{(b)} + \delta_{b', \mathsf{tag}_{b,i}^*} \cdot \mathbf{G}$ for $b' \in \{0,1\}$, is statistically close to a pair of uniformly random matrices. In the end, for $b \in \{0,1\}$, ek_b is computationally indistinguishable from $\tilde{\mathsf{ek}}_b$ whose components are sampled uniformly at random in the corresponding domain and the indistinguishability is concluded.

Relaxed Cumulative Lossiness. Let $\mathsf{tag}^* \in \mathcal{T}_t$, $(\mathsf{ek}, \mathsf{tk}) \leftarrow \mathsf{Sample}(1^\lambda, \mathsf{tag}^*)$, and fix an input $\mathbf{x} \in [0, \beta]^n = \{0,1\}^n$ by the parameter choice $\beta = 1$. For every $\mathsf{tag} \in \mathcal{T}_t$ such that $\mathsf{tag} \neq \mathsf{tag}^*$, we need to describe two functions $\mathsf{compress}_{\mathsf{ek}}$ and $\mathsf{expand}_{\mathsf{ek},\mathsf{tag}}$ such that$\mathsf{Eval}(\mathsf{ek}, \mathsf{tag}, \mathbf{x}) = \mathsf{expand}_{\mathsf{ek},\mathsf{tag}}(\mathsf{compress}_{\mathsf{ek}}(\mathbf{x}))$ except for a negligible probability over the choices of $\mathsf{tag} \neq \mathsf{tag}^*$.

The function $\mathsf{compress}_{\mathsf{ek}}(\mathbf{x} \in \{0,1\}^n)$ is described as follows:

1. Parse ek as $\mathsf{ek} := (\mathbf{A}, \mathbf{B}, \{\mathbf{A}_{i,0}, \mathbf{A}_{i,1}\}_{i=1}^t)$ then use $\mathbf{A} \in \mathbb{Z}_q^{n \times m}$ and $\mathbf{B} \in \mathbb{Z}_q^{\ell \times m}$ to recover (inefficiently) $\mathbf{D} \in \mathbb{Z}_q^{\ell \times n}$ and $\mathbf{E} \in \mathbb{Z}^{n \times m}$. This is essentially inverting an LWE function $(\mathbf{D}, \mathbf{E}) \to \mathbf{D}^\top \mathbf{B} + \mathbf{E}$ for the matrix $\mathbf{B}$.
2. Compute and output $\mathbf{D} \cdot \mathbf{x} \in \mathbb{Z}_q^\ell$.

Let $\mathbf{y} \in \mathbb{Z}_q^\ell$ and $\mathsf{tag} \in \mathcal{T}_t$ such that $\mathsf{tag} \neq \mathsf{tag}^*$. The function $\mathsf{expand}_{\mathsf{ek},\mathsf{tag}}(\mathbf{y})$ is described as follows:

1. Parse the ek as $\mathsf{ek} := (\mathbf{A}, \mathbf{B}, \{\mathbf{A}_{i,0}, \mathbf{A}_{i,1}\}_{i=1}^t)$ then use $(\mathbf{A}, \mathbf{B})$ to (inefficiently) recover $\mathbf{D} \in \mathbb{Z}_q^{\ell \times n}$ and $\mathbf{E} \in \mathbb{Z}_q^{n \times m}$. Using $\mathbf{A}$ and $\{\mathbf{A}_{i,0}, \mathbf{A}_{i,1}\}_{i=1}^t$, compute $\mathbf{A}(\mathsf{tag})$ as in the Eval algorithm, i.e.

$$\mathbf{A}(\mathsf{tag}) := \mathsf{FHEval}\left(C_{\mathsf{tag}}, \left(\mathbf{A}_{i,\mathsf{tag}_i}\right)_{i=1}^t\right) = \mathbf{A} \cdot \mathbf{R}_{\mathsf{tag}} + C_{\mathsf{tag}}(\mathsf{tag}^*) \cdot \mathbf{G} \stackrel{(*)}{=} \mathbf{A} \cdot \mathbf{R}_{\mathsf{tag}} \in \mathbb{Z}_q^{n \times n'}$$

where the $(*)$ equality comes from the fact that $\mathsf{tag} \neq \mathsf{tag}^*$. We will denote $\mathbf{A}' := [\mathbf{A} \mid \mathbf{A}(\mathsf{tag})] = [\mathbf{A} \mid \left(\mathbf{D}^\top \cdot \mathbf{B} + \mathbf{E}\right) \cdot \mathbf{R}_{\mathsf{tag}}] \in \mathbb{Z}_q^{n \times (m+n')}$.
2. Compute (inefficiently) a matrix $\mathbf{F} \in \mathbb{Z}_q^{\ell \times n'}$ such that $\mathbf{F}$ is an LWE secret for $(\mathbf{D}, \mathbf{A}(\mathsf{tag}))$. Specifically, the matrix $\mathbf{F}$ statisfies that $\mathbf{A}(\mathsf{tag}) = \mathbf{D}^\top \cdot \mathbf{F} + \mathbf{E}_{\mathsf{tag}}$ where $\mathbf{E}_{\mathsf{tag}} \in \mathbb{Z}^{n \times n'}$ has bounded entries. The bound will be analyzed below.
3. Compute (inefficiently) an arbitrary but small matrix $\mathbf{R}' \in \mathbb{Z}^{m \times n'}$ such that $\mathbf{B} \cdot \mathbf{R}' = \mathbf{F}$.
4. Compute and return $\lfloor [\mathbf{y}^\top \cdot \mathbf{B} \mid \mathbf{y}^\top \cdot \mathbf{F}] \rfloor_p \in \mathbb{Z}_p^{m+n'}$.

Given a fixed input $\mathbf{x} \in \{0,1\}^n$, for $\mathsf{tag} \in \mathcal{T}_t$ and $\mathsf{tag} \neq \mathsf{tag}^*$, we consider

$$\mathsf{expand}_{\mathsf{ek},\mathsf{tag}}(\mathsf{compress}_{\mathsf{ek}}(\mathbf{x})) = \mathsf{expand}_{\mathsf{ek},\mathsf{tag}}(\mathbf{D} \cdot \mathbf{x}) = \lfloor [(\mathbf{D}\mathbf{x})^\top \cdot \mathbf{B} | (\mathbf{D}\mathbf{x})^\top \cdot \mathbf{B}\mathbf{R}'] \rfloor_p$$

where $\mathbf{B}, \mathbf{D}, \mathbf{R}', \mathbf{F}$ are computed as specified in $\mathsf{compress}_{\mathsf{ek}}$ and $\mathsf{expand}_{\mathsf{ek},\mathsf{tag}}$.

To begin with, we analyze the bound of the entries in the error matrix $\mathbf{E}_{\mathsf{tag}}$ so that the matrix $\mathbf{F}$ computed in step 2 of $\mathsf{expand}_{\mathsf{ek},\mathsf{tag}}$ is uniquely determined. It suffices to bound the infinity norm of $\mathbf{E} \cdot \mathbf{R}_{\mathsf{tag}}$. We evaluate homomorphically the ciphertexts $\mathbf{A}_{i,b}$ on a circuit C_{tag} defined as a sequential AND-ing of t bits in tag and has depth $t-1$. Moreover, the matrices $\mathbf{A}_{i,b}$ are obtained using binary $\mathbf{R}_i \in \{0,1\}^{m \times n'}$, for all $i \in [t]$ and $b \in \{0,1\}$. As a corollary of Lemma 2, we have $\|\mathbf{R}_{\mathsf{tag}}\|_\infty \leq n'(n'+1)^t$. With $\mathbf{E} \in \mathbb{Z}_q^{n \times m}$, we also have $\|\mathbf{E}\|_\infty = \max_{i \in [n]} \left(\sum_{j=1}^m |\mathbf{E}_{i,j}|\right) \leq m\alpha q$. This implies that $\|\mathbf{E} \cdot \mathbf{R}_{\mathsf{tag}}\|_\infty \leq \|\mathbf{E}\|_\infty \cdot \|\mathbf{R}_{\mathsf{tag}}\|_\infty \leq n'(n'+1)^t \cdot m \cdot \alpha q$. We choose the parameters for $n'(n'+1)^t \cdot m \cdot \alpha q$ to be small enough, for example smaller than $q/4$ given a sufficiently large λ. Thus $\left(\mathbf{D}^\top \cdot \mathbf{B} + \mathbf{E}\right) \cdot \mathbf{R}_{\mathsf{tag}}$ uniquely determines $\mathbf{B} \cdot \mathbf{R}_{\mathsf{tag}}$ as a corollary of Lemma 6. Consequently, the (inefficient) step 2 of $\mathsf{expand}_{\mathsf{ek},\mathsf{tag}}$ will be able to find the unique $\mathbf{F} = \mathbf{B} \cdot \mathbf{R}_{\mathsf{tag}}$. Then, we have $\mathbf{B} \cdot \mathbf{R}' = \mathbf{B} \cdot \mathbf{R}_{\mathsf{tag}}$ and $\lfloor [(\mathbf{D}\mathbf{x})^\top \cdot \mathbf{B} \mid (\mathbf{D}\mathbf{x})^\top \cdot \mathbf{B} \cdot \mathbf{R}'] \rfloor_p = \lfloor [(\mathbf{D}\mathbf{x})^\top \cdot \mathbf{B} \mid (\mathbf{D}\mathbf{x})^\top \cdot \mathbf{B} \cdot \mathbf{R}_{\mathsf{tag}}] \rfloor_p$. Let us define an event BAD as

$$\lfloor [(\mathbf{D}\mathbf{x})^\top \cdot \mathbf{B} \mid (\mathbf{D}\mathbf{x})^\top \cdot \mathbf{B} \cdot \mathbf{R}_{\mathsf{tag}}] \rfloor_p \neq \lfloor [(\mathbf{D}\mathbf{x})^\top \cdot \mathbf{B} + \mathbf{x}^\top \mathbf{E} \mid (\mathbf{D}\mathbf{x})^\top \cdot \mathbf{B} \cdot \mathbf{R}_{\mathsf{tag}} + \mathbf{x}^\top \cdot \mathbf{E} \cdot \mathbf{R}_{\mathsf{tag}}] \rfloor_p$$

and we observe that the right-hand side is actually $\mathsf{Eval}(\mathsf{ek}, \mathsf{tag}, \mathbf{x})$. A simple computation gives us $\Pr[\mathsf{Eval}(\mathsf{ek}, \mathsf{tag}, \mathbf{x}) = \mathsf{expand}_{\mathsf{ek},\mathsf{tag}}(\mathsf{compress}_{\mathsf{ek}}(\mathbf{x}))] \geq 1 - \Pr[\mathsf{BAD}]$ where the probabilities are taken over the choices of $\mathsf{tag} \in \mathcal{T}_t$ such that $\mathsf{tag} \neq \mathsf{tag}^*$, for the fixed input $\mathbf{x} \in \{0,1\}^n$. The following lemma proves that $\Pr[\mathsf{BAD}]$ is negligible under current parameter and completes the proof.

Lemma 10. *We have the following bound:*

$$\Pr[\mathsf{BAD}] \leq 2^{t+1} \cdot p \cdot m\alpha \cdot \left(1 + n'(n'+1)^t\right) \ .$$

A proof for Lemma 10 can be found in the full version of this paper. □

3.2 CALBO-TDFs from DCR

In this section we give a construction of CALBO-TDF achieving non-relaxed cumulative lossiness from the DCR assumption. We start by recalling the Damgård-Jurik encryption scheme, whose decryption algorithm along with other useful properties are used in our CALBO-TDFs.

Damgård-Jurik Encryption. Damgård and Jurik introduced in [20] a generalization of Paillier's cryptosystem based on the ζ-DCR assumption. Given a modulus $N = pq$ such that $\gcd(N, \varphi(N)) = 1$, where p and q are primes, Damgård and Jurik proved that the multiplicative group $\mathbb{Z}^*_{N^{\zeta+1}}$ is isomorphic to the direct product of $\mathbb{Z}_{N^\zeta}$ and $\mathbb{Z}^*_N$:

Theorem 2 ([20], **Theorem 1**). *For any N satisfying $\gcd(N, \varphi(N)) = 1$ and for $\zeta < \min(p, q)$, the map $\psi_\zeta : \mathbb{Z}_{N^\zeta} \times \mathbb{Z}^*_N \to \mathbb{Z}^*_{N^{\zeta+1}}$ given by $(m, r) \mapsto (1 + N)^m r^{N^\zeta} \pmod{N^{\zeta+1}}$ is invertible in polynomial time using $\mathrm{lcm}(p-1, q-1)$.*

The Damgård-Jurik encryption exploits this isomorphic property: a public key is a pair (N, ζ) associated with secret key (p, q) and ψ_ζ is the encryption function (where r plays the role of randomness), that can be inverted (decryption) given (p, q). Semantic security is easily proven under the ζ-DCR assumption [20, Theorem 2]. We are now ready to describe our construction of CALBO-TDFs from the ζ-DCR assumption. We remark that the domain is currently index-dependent, i.e. inputs are taken in $\mathbb{Z}^*_{N^{\zeta+1}}$ where N and ζ are specified in the evaluation key. The domain can be made index-independent by using $\{0,1\}^n$ for some bitlength n in the same way Freeman et al. have done in [25], e.g. we can choose any $n \in \mathbb{N}$ such that $n < \min(\log p, \log q)$.

Sample$(1^\lambda, \mathsf{tag}^*)$: Given $\mathsf{tag}^* \in \mathcal{T}_t = \{0,1\}^t$, generate an evaluation key $\mathsf{ek} := \left(N,\ \zeta,\ \{g_{i,0}, g_{i,1}\ \in \mathbb{Z}^*_{N^{\zeta+1}}\ \}_{i=1}^t\right)$, consisting of the following components:

- A modulus $N = pq$ such that $p, q > 2^{l(\lambda)}$ and $\gcd(N, \varphi(N)) = 1$, where $l : \mathbb{N} \to \mathbb{N}$ is a polynomial dictating the bitlength of p and q as a function of λ, and an integer $\zeta > t$.
- Elements $g_{i,0}, g_{i,1} \in \mathbb{Z}^*_{N^{\zeta+1}}$ which are generated as

$$g_{i,b} = (1+N)^{\delta_{b,\mathsf{tag}^*_i}} \cdot \alpha_{i,b}^{N^\zeta} \bmod N^{\zeta+1} \qquad \forall (i,b) \in [t] \times \{0,1\},$$

where $\alpha_{i,b} \hookleftarrow U(\mathbb{Z}^*_N)$ for each $i \in [t]$, $b \in \{0,1\}$, tag^*_i denotes the i-th bit of tag^*, and $\delta_{b,\mathsf{tag}^*_i} = (b \stackrel{?}{=} \mathsf{tag}^*_i)$. We note that $g_{i,b}$ is a Damgård-Jurik ciphertext of $\delta_{b,\mathsf{tag}^*_i}$.

Output ek and $\mathsf{tk} = (p, q)$.

Eval$(\mathsf{ek}, \mathsf{tag}, x)$**:** Given an input $x \in \mathbb{Z}_{N^{\zeta+1}}$ and $\mathsf{tag} \in \mathcal{T}_t = \{0,1\}^t$, let $x_0 = x$. Find $(y_0, z_0) \in \mathbb{Z}_{N^\zeta} \times \mathbb{Z}_N$ such that $x_0 = y_0 \cdot N + z_0$. If $\gcd(z_0, N) > 1$, output 0. Otherwise, for $i = 1$ to t, do the following:

1. Parse $x_{i-1} \in \mathbb{Z}_{N^{\zeta+1}}$ as a pair of integers $(y_{i-1}, z_{i-1}) \in \mathbb{Z}_{N^\zeta} \times \mathbb{Z}_N^*$ such that $x_{i-1} = y_{i-1} \cdot N + z_{i-1}$.
2. Compute $x_i = g_{i,\mathsf{tag}_i}^{y_{i-1}} \cdot z_{i-1}^{N^\zeta} \bmod N^{\zeta+1}$.

In the end, output $z = x_t \in \mathbb{Z}_{N^{\zeta+1}}^*$.

Invert$(\mathsf{tk}, \mathsf{tag}, z)$**:** Set $x_t = z$ and find $(y_t, z_t) \in \mathbb{Z}_{N^\zeta} \times \mathbb{Z}_N$ such that $x_t = y_t \cdot N + z_t$. If $\gcd(z_t, N) > 1$, output 0. Otherwise, for $i = t$ down to $i = 1$, conduct the following steps:

1. Using $\mathsf{tk} = (p, q)$, compute the unique pair $(y_{i-1}, z_{i-1}) \in \mathbb{Z}_{N^\zeta} \times \mathbb{Z}_N^*$ such that $x_i = g_{i,\mathsf{tag}_i}^{y_{i-1}} \cdot z_{i-1}^{N^\zeta} \bmod N^{\zeta+1}$. This is done by first recovering $y_{i-1} = \mathsf{Dec}((p,q), x_i) \in \mathbb{Z}_{N^\zeta}$ using the Damgård-Jurik decryption algorithm for obtaining $z_{i-1} = \left(x_i \cdot g_{i,\mathsf{tag}_i}^{-y_{i-1}} \bmod N^{\zeta+1}\right)^{N^{-\zeta}} \bmod N$. Note that $z_{i-1} \in \mathbb{Z}_N^*$ is well-defined thanks to the isomorphism ψ_ζ^{-1} used in Damgård-Jurik decryption.
2. Let $x_{i-1} = y_{i-1} \cdot N + z_{i-1}$. Output x_0 when $i = 1$.

The check $\gcd(z_0, N) = 1$ in **Eval** implies that, as long as factoring is hard, it is infeasible to find non-invertible inputs, i.e. $x = y_0 \cdot N + z_0 \in \mathbb{Z}_{N^{\zeta+1}}$ such that $\gcd(z_0, N) > 1$ for $(y_0, z_0) \in \mathbb{Z}_{N^\zeta} \times \mathbb{Z}_N$. Moreover, the fraction of non-invertible inputs is bounded by $N^\zeta \cdot (p+q)/N^{\zeta+1} = (p+q)/N$, which is negligible. We now prove that the above construction is a CALBO-TDF assuming $\zeta-\mathsf{DCR}$ holds.

Theorem 3. *Let $\lambda \in \mathbb{N}$ is a security parameter. Let $\zeta = \zeta(\lambda), l = l(\lambda), t = t(\lambda)$ be functions in λ such that $\zeta > t$. Assuming the ζ-DCR assumption, the triplet* $(\mathsf{Sample}, \mathsf{Eval}, \mathsf{Invert})$ *is a $((\zeta+1)\log N, (\zeta+1)\log N - t\log N - 1)$-cumulatively-all-lossy-but-one trapdoor function family with tag space $\mathcal{T}_t = \{0,1\}^t$.*

Proof. We prove injectivity, indistinguishability and cumulative lossiness properties as defined in Sect. 2.1. Let $\lambda \in \mathbb{N}$ be a security parameter and $\zeta = \zeta(\lambda), l = l(\lambda), t = t(\lambda)$ be polynomials in λ such that $\zeta > t$. Let $\mathsf{tag}^* \in \mathcal{T}_t$ be the injective tag and $(\mathsf{ek}, \mathsf{tk}) \leftarrow \mathsf{Sample}(1^\lambda, \mathsf{tag}^*)$.

We first justify why we only need to check $\gcd(z_0, N) = 1$ and can be sure that if it holds, $\gcd(z_i, N) = 1$ for all $i \geq 1$. Indeed, let $i \in [t]$. By construction $x_i = y_i \cdot N + z_i$ for $(y_i, z_i) \in \mathbb{Z}_{N^\zeta} \times \mathbb{Z}_N$. Suppose $z_0 \in \mathbb{Z}_N^*$, we verify the claim by induction. Indeed $x_1 = \psi_\zeta(y_0, z_0) \in \mathbb{Z}_{N^{\zeta+1}}^*$. Hence $\gcd(z_1, N) = \gcd(z_1 + y_1 \cdot N, N) = \gcd(x_1, N) = 1$. For the inductive step, suppose $z_{i-1} \in \mathbb{Z}_N^*$, then $x_i = \psi_\zeta(y_{i-1}, z_{i-1}) \in \mathbb{Z}_{N^{\zeta+1}}^*$. By the same argument, we have $\gcd(z_i, N) = \gcd(z_i + y_i \cdot N, N) = \gcd(x_i, N) = 1$.

Injectivity. Let $\mathsf{tag}^* \in \{0,1\}^t$ be an injective tag. We consider two cases for invertibility of $\mathsf{Eval}(\mathsf{ek}, \mathsf{tag}^*, x)$ given the trapdoor tk of tag^*. If $x \in \mathbb{Z}_{N^{\zeta+1}} \setminus \mathbb{Z}^*_{N^{\zeta+1}}$, equivalently by Theorem 2 it holds that $x = y_0 \cdot N + z_0$ and $\gcd(z_0, N) > 1$, then $\mathsf{Eval}(\mathsf{ek}, \mathsf{tag}^*, x) = 0$ by construction and cannot be inverted using tk. The fraction of such inputs in $\mathbb{Z}_{N^{\zeta+1}}$ is $N^{\zeta} \cdot (N - \varphi(N))/N^{\zeta+1} = (p+q-1)/N$, which is negligible in λ.

Otherwise, suppose that $x \in \mathbb{Z}^*_{N^{\zeta+1}}$. By the correctness of Damgård-Jurik decryption algorithm and Theorem 2, for each $i = t$ down to 1, step 1 in Invert correctly recovers $y_{i-1} \in \mathbb{Z}_{N^{\zeta}}$ and $z_{i-1} \in \mathbb{Z}^*_N$ such that $x_{i-1} = y_{i-1} \cdot N + z_{i-1}$, where x_{i-1} is used at step $i-1$ in $\mathsf{Eval}(\mathsf{ek}, \mathsf{tag}^*, x)$. Inductively, $x_0 = y_0 \cdot N + z_0$ is recovered correctly. In summary, $\mathsf{Invert}(\mathsf{tk}, \mathsf{tag}^*, \mathsf{Eval}(\mathsf{ek}, \mathsf{tag}^*, x)) = x$ for an overwhelming fraction of the domain $\mathbb{Z}_{N^{\zeta+1}}$ and the injectivity is concluded.

Indistinguishability. Let $\mathsf{tag}^*_0, \mathsf{tag}^*_1 \in \{0,1\}^t$ and $(\mathsf{ek}_b, \mathsf{tk}_b) \leftarrow \mathsf{Sample}(1^\lambda, \mathsf{tag}^*_b)$ for $b \in \{0,1\}$. We want to prove that ek_0 and ek_1 are indistinguishable. Let $b \in \{0,1\}$. The evaluation key ek_b is parsed as

$$\mathsf{ek}_b = \Big(N,\ \zeta,\ \{g^{(b)}_{i,0}, g^{(b)}_{i,1}\ \in \mathbb{Z}^*_{N^{\zeta+1}}\ \}^t_{i=1}\Big)$$

where $g^{(b)}_{i,b'}$ is a Damgård-Jurik encryption of $\delta_{b',\mathsf{tag}^*_{b,i}}$ for $i \in [t]$ and $b' \in \{0,1\}$, respectively and $\mathsf{tag}^*_{b,i}$ is the i-th bit of tag^*_b. The indistinguishability readily follows the semantic security of the Damgård-Jurik encryption scheme under a standard hybrid argument.

Cumulative Lossiness. For $(\mathsf{ek}, \mathsf{tk}) \leftarrow \mathsf{Sample}(1^\lambda, \mathsf{tag}^*)$ and $\mathsf{tag} \in \{0,1\}^t$ such that $\mathsf{tag} \neq \mathsf{tag}^*$, we want to describe two (possibly inefficient) functions $\mathsf{compress}_{\mathsf{ek}}$ and $\mathsf{expand}_{\mathsf{ek},\mathsf{tag}}$ satisfying $\mathsf{Eval}(\mathsf{ek}, \mathsf{tag}, x) = \mathsf{expand}_{\mathsf{ek},\mathsf{tag}}(\mathsf{compress}_{\mathsf{ek}}(x))$ for all $x \in \mathbb{Z}_{N^{\zeta+1}}$.

Given $x \in \mathbb{Z}_{N^{\zeta+1}}$, the function $\mathsf{compress}_{\mathsf{ek}}(x)$ is described as follows:

1. Parse the evaluation key as $\mathsf{ek}_b = \big(N,\ \zeta,\ \{g_{i,0}, g_{i,1}\ \in \mathbb{Z}^*_{N^{\zeta+1}}\ \}^t_{i=1}\big)$ and (inefficiently) factor $N = pq$.
2. Initialize a list List to empty. Compute $(y, z) \in \mathbb{Z}_{N^{\zeta}} \times \mathbb{Z}_N$ such that $x = y \cdot N + z$. If $\gcd(z, N) > 1$ then add 0 to List and output List.
3. Otherwise, having p, q, for all $(i, b) \in [t] \times \{0,1\}$, use the Damgård-Jurik decryption $\mathsf{Dec}((p,q), g_{i,b}) = \delta_{b,\mathsf{tag}^*_i}$ and in the end obtain $\mathsf{tag}^* \in \{0,1\}^t$. Moreover, use the isomorphism ψ^{-1}_{ζ} from Theorem 2 to also recover all the $\alpha_{i,b} \in \mathbb{Z}^*_N$ while knowing $g_{i,b} \in \mathbb{Z}^*_{N^{\zeta+1}}$ and $\delta_{b,\mathsf{tag}^*_i} \in \mathbb{Z}_{N^{\zeta}}$.
4. For $i = 1$ to t, define

$$\mathsf{sibling}_i := \mathsf{tag}^*_{[1..(i-1)]} \,\|\, (1 - \mathsf{tag}^*_i)$$

   where $\mathsf{tag}^*_{[1..(i-1)]}$ denotes the first $i-1$ bits of tag^*.
5. For $j = 1$ to t, perform the following:
   - Let $x_0 = x$ and find (y_0, z_0) such that $x_0 = y_0 \cdot N + z_0$.

- For $k = 1$ to $j - 1$, compute

$$x_k = g_{k,\mathsf{sibling}_j[k]}^{y_{k-1}} \cdot z_{k-1}^{N^\zeta} \pmod{N^{\zeta+1}}$$

where $\mathsf{sibling}_j[k]$ is the k-th bit of $\mathsf{sibling}_j$.
- Let $b = \mathsf{sibling}_j[j]$. Compute (y_{j-1}, z_{j-1}) such that $x_{j-1} = y_{j-1} \cdot N + z_{j-1}$ and add

$$(\alpha_{j-1,b}^{y_{j-1}} \cdot z_{j-1})^{N^\zeta} \pmod{N^{\zeta+1}} \in \mathbb{Z}_N$$

to List.

6. Output $\mathsf{List} \in \mathbb{Z}_N^t$.

Given $\mathsf{tag} \neq \mathsf{tag}^*$ and a $\mathsf{List} \in \mathbb{Z}_N^t$, the function $\mathsf{expand}_{\mathsf{ek},\mathsf{tag}}(\mathsf{List})$ is given below:

1. Parse the evaluation key as $\mathsf{ek}_b = \big(N,\ \zeta,\ \{g_{i,0}, g_{i,1}\ \in \mathbb{Z}_{N^{\zeta+1}}^*\ \}_{i=1}^t\big)$ and (inefficiently) factor $N = pq$.
2. If List contains only one element 0, output 0.
3. Otherwise, having p, q, for all $(i, b) \in [t] \times \{0, 1\}$, use the Damgård-Jurik decryption $\mathsf{Dec}((p, q), g_{i,b}) = \delta_{b,\mathsf{tag}_i^*}$ and in the end obtain $\mathsf{tag}^* \in \{0, 1\}^t$.
4. Compute $i = \min_{j \in [t]}(\mathsf{tag}_j \neq \mathsf{tag}_j^*)$. It holds that $1 \leq i \leq t$ is well-defined because $\mathsf{tag} \neq \mathsf{tag}^*$.
5. Let $x_i = \mathsf{List}[i]$. For $k = i + 1$ to t, conduct the following:
   - Compute (y_{k-1}, z_{k-1}) satisfying $x_{k-1} = y_{k-1} \cdot N + z_{k-1}$.
   - Compute

$$x_k = g_{k,\mathsf{tag}_k}^{y_{k-1}} \cdot z_{k-1}^{N^\zeta} \pmod{N^{\zeta+1}}\ .$$

6. Output $x_t \in \mathbb{Z}_{N^{\zeta+1}}^*$.

Relating to cumulative lossiness, we evaluate $|\{\mathsf{compress}_{\mathsf{ek}}(x) : x \in \mathbb{Z}_{N^{\zeta+1}}\}|$. By construction, for $x \in \mathbb{Z}_{N^{\zeta+1}}^*$, the output of $\mathsf{compress}_{\mathsf{ek}}(x)$ is a list of t elements in $\mathbb{Z}_N$. If $x \in \mathbb{Z}_{N^{\zeta+1}} \setminus \mathbb{Z}_{N^{\zeta+1}}^*$, $\mathsf{compress}_{\mathsf{ek}}(x)$ outputs a list of one single element, namely 0. We then have the bound

$$|\{\mathsf{compress}_{\mathsf{ek}}(x) : x \in \mathbb{Z}_{N^{\zeta+1}}\}| = N^t + 1 \leq 2 \cdot N^t\ .$$

We want to prove that $\mathsf{Eval}(\mathsf{ek}, \mathsf{tag}, x) = \mathsf{expand}_{\mathsf{ek},\mathsf{tag}}(\mathsf{compress}_{\mathsf{ek}}(x))$ for all $x \in \mathbb{Z}_{N^{\zeta+1}}$ and $\mathsf{tag} \neq \mathsf{tag}^*$. If $x \in \mathbb{Z}_{N^{\zeta+1}} \setminus \mathbb{Z}_{N^{\zeta+1}}^*$, then $\mathsf{Eval}(\mathsf{ek}, \mathsf{tag}, x) = 0$ by construction. Moreover, we have $x = y \cdot N + z$ for $(y, z) \in \mathbb{Z}_{N^\zeta} \times \mathbb{Z}_N$ such that $\gcd(z, N) > 1$. Thus, $\mathsf{compress}_{\mathsf{ek}}(x)$ outputs List containing only 0 and step 2 in $\mathsf{expand}_{\mathsf{ek},\mathsf{tag}}(\mathsf{List})$ recovers exactly 0. Otherwise, suppose $x \in \mathbb{Z}_{N^{\zeta+1}}^*$. Our main observation is that for $i = \min_{j \in [t]}(\mathsf{tag}_j \neq \mathsf{tag}_j^*)$, the value x_i will uniquely determine x_t, by the fact that ψ_ζ is an isomorphism from Theorem 2. Moreover, because $\mathsf{tag}_i \neq \mathsf{tag}_i^*$ and $\mathsf{tag}_k = \mathsf{tag}_k^*$ for all $k < i$, we have

$$x_i = (\alpha_{i-1,b}^{y_{i-1}} \cdot z_{i-1})^{N^\zeta} \pmod{N^{\zeta+1}}$$

and the sequence $(x_0, \ldots, x_{i-1} = y_{i-1} \cdot N + z_{i-1})$ stays the same as if the input tag is tag^*. By definition of $\mathsf{sibling}_i$, it is easily verified that the loop 5 in

$\mathsf{compress_{ek}}$ constructs List such that $\mathsf{List}[i] = x_i$ and $i = \min_{j\in[t]}(\mathsf{tag}_j \neq \mathsf{tag}^*_j)$. Finally, the loop 5 in $\mathsf{expand_{ek,tag}}(\mathsf{List})$ performs exactly the same computation as $\mathsf{Eval}(\mathsf{ek}, \mathsf{tag}, x)$ would do, starting from i. Hence, the equality $\mathsf{Eval}(\mathsf{ek}, \mathsf{tag}, x) = \mathsf{expand_{ek,tag}}(\mathsf{compress_{ek}}(x))$ is justified. □

Remark 1. The domain is $\mathbb{Z}_{N^{\zeta+1}}$ and its size is $\log(N^{\zeta+1}) = (\zeta+1)\log N$. Moreover, by setting the tag length $t = O(\lambda)$ and the exponent $\zeta = \omega(\lambda)$ so that our CALBO-TDFs can be used for the applications to randomness extractors in [23, Corollary 5.12], the lossiness rate of the above construction becomes

$$\frac{(\zeta+1)\log N - \log(2\cdot N^t)}{(\zeta+1)\log N} = 1 - \frac{t}{\zeta+1} - \frac{1}{(\zeta+1)\log N} = 1 - o(1)$$

and is indeed better than what the LWE-based CALBO-TDF achieves, which is $1 - \Theta(1)$ by the parameter choices.

Acknowledgements. This work was supported in part by the French ANR Project ANR-19-CE39-0011 PRESTO and in part by the French ANR ALAMBIC project (ANR-16-CE39-0006).

References

1. Agrawal, S., Boneh, D., Boyen, X.: Efficient lattice (H) IBE in the standard model. In: Gilbert, H. (ed.) EUROCRYPT 2010. LNCS, vol. 6110, pp. 553–572. Springer, Heidelberg (2010). https://doi.org/10.1007/978-3-642-13190-5_28
2. Alwen, J., Krenn, S., Pietrzak, K., Wichs, D.: Learning with rounding, revisited. In: Canetti, R., Garay, J.A. (eds.) CRYPTO 2013. LNCS, vol. 8042, pp. 57–74. Springer, Heidelberg (2013). https://doi.org/10.1007/978-3-642-40041-4_4
3. Auerbach, B., Kiltz, E., Poettering, B., Schoenen, S.: Lossy trapdoor permutations with improved lossiness. In: Matsui, M. (ed.) CT-RSA 2019. LNCS, vol. 11405, pp. 230–250. Springer, Cham (2019). https://doi.org/10.1007/978-3-030-12612-4_12
4. Banerjee, A., Peikert, C., Rosen, A.: Pseudorandom functions and lattices. In: Pointcheval, D., Johansson, T. (eds.) EUROCRYPT 2012. LNCS, vol. 7237, pp. 719–737. Springer, Heidelberg (2012). https://doi.org/10.1007/978-3-642-29011-4_42
5. Banerjee, A., Peikert, C.: New and improved key-homomorphic pseudorandom functions. In: Garay, J.A., Gennaro, R. (eds.) CRYPTO 2014. LNCS, vol. 8616, pp. 353–370. Springer, Heidelberg (2014). https://doi.org/10.1007/978-3-662-44371-2_20
6. Bellare, M., et al.: Hedged public-key encryption: how to protect against bad randomness. In: Matsui, M. (ed.) ASIACRYPT 2009. LNCS, vol. 5912, pp. 232–249. Springer, Heidelberg (2009). https://doi.org/10.1007/978-3-642-10366-7_14
7. Bellare, M., Hofheinz, D., Yilek, S.: Possibility and impossibility results for encryption and commitment secure under selective opening. In: Joux, A. (ed.) EUROCRYPT 2009. LNCS, vol. 5479, pp. 1–35. Springer, Heidelberg (2009). https://doi.org/10.1007/978-3-642-01001-9_1
8. Bellare, M., Kiltz, E., Peikert, C., Waters, B.: Identity-lased (lossy) trapdoor functions and applications. In: Pointcheval, D., Johansson, T. (eds.) EUROCRYPT 2012. LNCS, vol. 7237, pp. 228–245. Springer, Heidelberg (2012). https://doi.org/10.1007/978-3-642-29011-4_15

9. Boldyreva, A., Fehr, S., O'Neill, A.: On notions of security for deterministic encryption, and efficient constructions without random oracles. In: Wagner, D. (ed.) CRYPTO 2008. LNCS, vol. 5157, pp. 335–359. Springer, Heidelberg (2008). https://doi.org/10.1007/978-3-540-85174-5_19
10. Boneh, D., Boyen, X.: Secure identity based encryption without random oracles. In: Franklin, M. (ed.) CRYPTO 2004. LNCS, vol. 3152, pp. 443–459. Springer, Heidelberg (2004). https://doi.org/10.1007/978-3-540-28628-8_27
11. Boneh, D., Lewi, K., Montgomery, H., Raghunathan, A.: Key homomorphic PRFs and their applications. In: Canetti, R., Garay, J.A. (eds.) CRYPTO 2013. LNCS, vol. 8042, pp. 410–428. Springer, Heidelberg (2013). https://doi.org/10.1007/978-3-642-40041-4_23
12. Boneh, D., et al.: Fully key-homomorphic encryption, arithmetic circuit ABE and compact garbled circuits. In: Nguyen, P.Q., Oswald, E. (eds.) EUROCRYPT 2014. LNCS, vol. 8441, pp. 533–556. Springer, Heidelberg (2014). https://doi.org/10.1007/978-3-642-55220-5_30
13. Boneh, D., Waters, B.: Constrained pseudorandom functions and their applications. In: Sako, K., Sarkar, P. (eds.) ASIACRYPT 2013. LNCS, vol. 8270, pp. 280–300. Springer, Heidelberg (2013). https://doi.org/10.1007/978-3-642-42045-0_15
14. Boyen, X., Li, Q.: All-but-many lossy trapdoor functions from lattices and applications. In: Katz, J., Shacham, H. (eds.) CRYPTO 2017. LNCS, vol. 10403, pp. 298–331. Springer, Cham (2017). https://doi.org/10.1007/978-3-319-63697-9_11
15. Boyle, E., Goldwasser, S., Ivan, I.: Functional signatures and pseudorandom functions. In: Krawczyk, H. (ed.) PKC 2014. LNCS, vol. 8383, pp. 501–519. Springer, Heidelberg (2014). https://doi.org/10.1007/978-3-642-54631-0_29
16. Brakerski, Z., Vaikuntanathan, V.: Lattice-based FHE as secure as PKE. In: Naor, M. (ed.) ITCS 2014, pp. 1–12. ACM, January 2014. https://doi.org/10.1145/2554797.2554799
17. Brakerski, Z., Vaikuntanathan, V.: Circuit-Abe from LWE: unbounded attributes and semi-adaptive security. In: Robshaw, M., Katz, J. (eds.) CRYPTO 2016. LNCS, vol. 9816, pp. 363–384. Springer, Heidelberg (2016). https://doi.org/10.1007/978-3-662-53015-3_13
18. Braverman, M., Hassidim, A., Kalai, Y.T.: Leaky pseudo-entropy functions. In: Chazelle, B. (ed.) ICS 2011, pp. 353–366. Tsinghua University Press, January 2011
19. Chakraborty, S., Prabhakaran, M., Wichs, D.: Witness maps and applications. In: Kiayias, A., Kohlweiss, M., Wallden, P., Zikas, V. (eds.) PKC 2020. LNCS, vol. 12110, pp. 220–246. Springer, Cham (2020). https://doi.org/10.1007/978-3-030-45374-9_8
20. Damgård, I., Jurik, M.: A generalisation, a simplification and some applications of paillier's probabilistic public-key system. In: Kim, K. (ed.) PKC 2001. LNCS, vol. 1992, pp. 119–136. Springer, Heidelberg (2001). https://doi.org/10.1007/3-540-44586-2_9
21. Damgård, I., Nielsen, J.B.: Perfect hiding and perfect binding universally composable commitment schemes with constant expansion factor. In: Yung, M. (ed.) CRYPTO 2002. LNCS, vol. 2442, pp. 581–596. Springer, Heidelberg (2002). https://doi.org/10.1007/3-540-45708-9_37
22. Damgård, I., Nielsen, J.B.: Universally composable efficient multiparty computation from threshold homomorphic encryption. In: Boneh, D. (ed.) CRYPTO 2003. LNCS, vol. 2729, pp. 247–264. Springer, Heidelberg (2003). https://doi.org/10.1007/978-3-540-45146-4_15

23. Dodis, Y., Vaikuntanathan, V., Wichs, D.: Extracting randomness from extractor-dependent sources. In: Canteaut, A., Ishai, Y. (eds.) EUROCRYPT 2020. LNCS, vol. 12105, pp. 313–342. Springer, Cham (2020). https://doi.org/10.1007/978-3-030-45721-1_12
24. Döttling, N., Garg, S., Ishai, Y., Malavolta, G., Mour, T., Ostrovsky, R.: Trapdoor hash functions and their applications. In: Boldyreva, A., Micciancio, D. (eds.) CRYPTO 2019. LNCS, vol. 11694, pp. 3–32. Springer, Cham (2019). https://doi.org/10.1007/978-3-030-26954-8_1
25. Freeman, D.M., Goldreich, O., Kiltz, E., Rosen, A., Segev, G.: More constructions of lossy and correlation-secure trapdoor functions. In: Nguyen, P.Q., Pointcheval, D. (eds.) PKC 2010. LNCS, vol. 6056, pp. 279–295. Springer, Heidelberg (2010). https://doi.org/10.1007/978-3-642-13013-7_17
26. Garg, A., Kalai, Y.T., Khurana, D.: Computational extractors with negligible error in the CRS model. Cryptology ePrint Archive, Report 2019/1116. https://eprint.iacr.org/2019/1116
27. Garg, A., Kalai, Y.T., Khurana, D.: Low error efficient computational extractors in the CRS model. In: Canteaut, A., Ishai, Y. (eds.) EUROCRYPT 2020. LNCS, vol. 12105, pp. 373–402. Springer, Cham (2020). https://doi.org/10.1007/978-3-030-45721-1_14
28. Garg, S., Gentry, C., Halevi, S., Raykova, M., Sahai, A., Waters, B.: Candidate indistinguishability obfuscation and functional encryption for all circuits. In: 54th FOCS, pp. 40–49. IEEE Computer Society Press, October 2013. https://doi.org/10.1109/FOCS.2013.13
29. Garg, S., Gay, R., Hajiabadi, M.: New techniques for efficient trapdoor functions and applications. In: Ishai, Y., Rijmen, V. (eds.) EUROCRYPT 2019. LNCS, vol. 11478, pp. 33–63. Springer, Cham (2019). https://doi.org/10.1007/978-3-030-17659-4_2
30. Gentry, C., Peikert, C., Vaikuntanathan, V.: Trapdoors for hard lattices and new cryptographic constructions. In: 40th ACM STOC (2008). https://doi.org/10.1145/1374376.1374407
31. Gentry, C., Sahai, A., Waters, B.: Homomorphic encryption from learning with errors: conceptually-simpler, asymptotically-faster, attribute-based. In: Canetti, R., Garay, J.A. (eds.) CRYPTO 2013. LNCS, vol. 8042, pp. 75–92. Springer, Heidelberg (2013). https://doi.org/10.1007/978-3-642-40041-4_5
32. Goldwasser, S., Kalai, Y.T., Peikert, C., Vaikuntanathan, V.: Robustness of the learning with errors assumption. In: Yao, A.C.C. (ed.) ICS 2010, pp. 230–240. Tsinghua University Press, January 2010
33. Gorbunov, S., Vaikuntanathan, V., Wee, H.: Predicate encryption for circuits from LWE. In: Gennaro, R., Robshaw, M. (eds.) CRYPTO 2015. LNCS, vol. 9216, pp. 503–523. Springer, Heidelberg (2015). https://doi.org/10.1007/978-3-662-48000-7_25
34. Gorbunov, S., Vaikuntanathan, V., Wichs, D.: Leveled fully homomorphic signatures from standard lattices. In: 47th ACM STOC (2015). https://doi.org/10.1145/2746539.2746576
35. Håstad, J., Impagliazzo, R., Levin, L.A., Luby, M.: A pseudorandom generator from any one-way function. SIAM J. Comput. **28**(4), 1364–1396 (1999)
36. Hemenway, B., Libert, B., Ostrovsky, R., Vergnaud, D.: Lossy encryption: constructions from general assumptions and efficient selective opening chosen ciphertext security. In: Lee, D.H., Wang, X. (eds.) ASIACRYPT 2011. LNCS, vol. 7073, pp. 70–88. Springer, Heidelberg (2011). https://doi.org/10.1007/978-3-642-25385-0_4

37. Hemenway, B., Ostrovsky, R.: Extended-DDH and lossy trapdoor functions. In: Fischlin, M., Buchmann, J., Manulis, M. (eds.) PKC 2012. LNCS, vol. 7293, pp. 627–643. Springer, Heidelberg (2012). https://doi.org/10.1007/978-3-642-30057-8_37
38. Hofheinz, D.: Circular chosen-ciphertext security with compact ciphertexts. In: Johansson, T., Nguyen, P.Q. (eds.) EUROCRYPT 2013. LNCS, vol. 7881, pp. 520–536. Springer, Heidelberg (2013). https://doi.org/10.1007/978-3-642-38348-9_31
39. Hofheinz, D.: All-but-many lossy trapdoor functions. In: Pointcheval, D., Johansson, T. (eds.) EUROCRYPT 2012. LNCS, vol. 7237, pp. 209–227. Springer, Heidelberg (2012). https://doi.org/10.1007/978-3-642-29011-4_14
40. Kiayias, A., Papadopoulos, S., Triandopoulos, N., Zacharias, T.: Delegatable pseudorandom functions and applications. In: ACM CCS 2013. https://doi.org/10.1145/2508859.2516668
41. Kiltz, E., O'Neill, A., Smith, A.: Instantiability of RSA-OAEP under chosen-plaintext attack. In: Rabin, T. (ed.) CRYPTO 2010. LNCS, vol. 6223, pp. 295–313. Springer, Heidelberg (2010). https://doi.org/10.1007/978-3-642-14623-7_16
42. Libert, B., Qian, C.: Lossy algebraic filters with short tags. In: Lin, D., Sako, K. (eds.) PKC 2019. LNCS, vol. 11442, pp. 34–65. Springer, Cham (2019). https://doi.org/10.1007/978-3-030-17253-4_2
43. Libert, B., Sakzad, A., Stehlé, D., Steinfeld, R.: All-but-many lossy trapdoor functions and selective opening chosen-ciphertext security from LWE. In: Katz, J., Shacham, H. (eds.) CRYPTO 2017. LNCS, vol. 10403, pp. 332–364. Springer, Cham (2017). https://doi.org/10.1007/978-3-319-63697-9_12
44. Libert, B., Stehlé, D., Titiu, R.: Adaptively secure distributed PRFs from LWE. In: Beimel, A., Dziembowski, S. (eds.) TCC 2018. LNCS, vol. 11240, pp. 391–421. Springer, Cham (2018). https://doi.org/10.1007/978-3-030-03810-6_15
45. Micciancio, D., Peikert, C.: Trapdoors for lattices: simpler, tighter, faster, smaller. In: Pointcheval, D., Johansson, T. (eds.) EUROCRYPT 2012. LNCS, vol. 7237, pp. 700–718. Springer, Heidelberg (2012). https://doi.org/10.1007/978-3-642-29011-4_41
46. Mol, P., Yilek, S.: Chosen-ciphertext security from slightly lossy trapdoor functions. In: Nguyen, P.Q., Pointcheval, D. (eds.) PKC 2010. LNCS, vol. 6056, pp. 296–311. Springer, Heidelberg (2010). https://doi.org/10.1007/978-3-642-13013-7_18
47. Paillier, P.: Public-key cryptosystems based on composite degree residuosity classes. In: Stern, J. (ed.) EUROCRYPT 1999. LNCS, vol. 1592, pp. 223–238. Springer, Heidelberg (1999). https://doi.org/10.1007/3-540-48910-X_16
48. Peikert, C., Waters, B.: Lossy trapdoor functions and their applications. In: 40th ACM STOC (2008). https://doi.org/10.1145/1374376.1374406
49. Quach, W., Waters, B., Wichs, D.: Targeted lossy functions and applications. In: Malkin, T., Peikert, C. (eds.) CRYPTO 2021. LNCS, vol. 12828, pp. 424–453. Springer, Cham (2021). https://doi.org/10.1007/978-3-030-84259-8_15
50. Raghunathan, A., Segev, G., Vadhan, S.: Deterministic public-key encryption for adaptively chosen plaintext distributions. In: Johansson, T., Nguyen, P.Q. (eds.) EUROCRYPT 2013. LNCS, vol. 7881, pp. 93–110. Springer, Heidelberg (2013). https://doi.org/10.1007/978-3-642-38348-9_6
51. Regev, O.: On lattices, learning with errors, random linear codes, and cryptography. J. ACM **56**(6), 1–40 (2009)

52. Vergnaud, D., Xiao, D.: Public-key encryption with weak randomness: security against strong chosen distribution attacks. Cryptology ePrint Archive: Report 2013/681 (2013)
53. Wee, Hoeteck: Dual projective hashing and its applications — lossy trapdoor functions and more. In: Pointcheval, David, Johansson, Thomas (eds.) EUROCRYPT 2012. LNCS, vol. 7237, pp. 246–262. Springer, Heidelberg (2012). https://doi.org/10.1007/978-3-642-29011-4_16

On the Related-Key Attack Security of Authenticated Encryption Schemes

Sebastian Faust[1], Juliane Krämer[2], Maximilian Orlt[1](✉), and Patrick Struck[2]

[1] Technische Universität Darmstadt, Darmstadt, Germany
{sebastian.faust,maximilian.orlt}@tu-darmstadt.de
[2] Universität Regensburg, Regensburg, Germany
{juliane.kraemer,patrick.struck}@ur.de

Abstract. Related-key attacks (RKA) are powerful cryptanalytic attacks, where the adversary can tamper with the secret key of a cryptographic scheme. Since their invention, RKA security has been an important design goal in cryptography, and various works aim at designing cryptographic primitives that offer protection against related-key attacks. At EUROCRYPT'03, Bellare and Kohno introduced the first formal treatment of related-key attacks focusing on pseudorandom functions and permutations. This was later extended to cover other primitives such as signatures and public key encryption schemes, but until now, a comprehensive formal security analysis of authenticated encryption schemes with associated data (AEAD) in the RKA setting has been missing. The main contribution of our work is to close this gap for the relevant class of nonce-based AEAD schemes.

To this end, we revisit the common approach to construct AEAD from encryption and message authentication. We extend the traditional security notion of AEAD to the RKA setting and consider an adversary that can tamper with the key K_e and K_m of the underlying encryption and MAC, respectively. We study two security models. In our weak setting, we require that tampering will change both K_e and K_m, while in our strong setting, tampering can be arbitrary, i.e., only one key might be affected. We then study the security of the standard composition methods by analysing the nonce-based AEAD schemes N1 (Encrypt-and-MAC), N2 (Encrypt-then-MAC), and N3 (MAC-then-Encrypt) due to Namprempre, Rogaway, and Shrimpton (EUROCRYPT'14). We show that these schemes are weakly RKA secure, while they can be broken under a strong related-key attack. Finally, based on the N3 construction, we give a novel AEAD scheme that achieves our stronger notion.

1 Introduction

The security of cryptographic schemes fundamentally relies on the secrecy of its keys. In particular, the secret key used by cryptographic algorithms must neither be revealed to the adversary nor must the adversary be able to change it. Unfortunately, countless advanced cryptanalytical attacks illustrate that the

C. Galdi and S. Jarecki (Eds.): SCN 2022, LNCS 13409, pp. 362–386, 2022.
https://doi.org/10.1007/978-3-031-14791-3_16

assumption on the secrecy of a key ceases to hold in practice. Prominent examples include side-channel attacks such as power analysis or timing attacks that partially reveal the secret key [26,27]; or tampering and fault attacks [17], where the adversary can change the secret key and observe the effect of this change via the outputs. The latter type of attack often is referred to as a *related-key attack (RKA)*, and has been intensively studied by the research community over the last years [1,4–6,8,12,13,16,19,21,23,24,28,29,37]. But related keys may not only appear when the adversary actively tampers with the key. Another important setting where we have to deal with related keys is key updates. In this setting related-key cryptanalysis may exploit the relation of keys caused by bad key updates [14–16,25]. Another scenario are devices with related keys. As a simple example consider a manufacturer that has some master key K. Rather than generating a fresh key for each device, it derives the key from the master key and some device id – for instance XORing the two.

The first work that provided a formal model for related-key attacks is the seminal work of Bellare and Kohno [8]. In this model, the related-key attacker can specify a related-key-deriving (RKD) function φ (from some set Φ) together with each black-box query to the cryptographic primitive, and observe the input/output behaviour for the primitive under the related key $\varphi(K)$. For instance, consider a PRF $\mathtt{F}(K, \cdot)$, that the adversary can query on some input X. As a result of a related-key attack the adversary receives $\mathtt{F}(\varphi(K), X)$, where φ is the RKD function. Starting with [8], several works extend the notion of RKA security to a wide range of cryptographic primitives. This includes pseudorandom functions [1,6], pseudorandom permutations [5], encryption schemes [4], and MACs [12,37].

Somewhat surprisingly, RKA security has not been considered for the important case of authenticated encryption schemes with associated data[1] (AEAD). AEAD is a fundamental cryptographic primitive used, e.g., to secure communication in the Internet and is therefore ubiquitously deployed, especially in TLS 1.3 [32]. Lately, AEAD has received a lot of attention, for instance through the CAESAR competition [11] and the ongoing NIST standardization process on lightweight cryptography [31]. An important type of AEAD schemes, and simultaneously the focus of the NIST standardization process [31], are so-called nonce-based schemes [33]. These schemes have the advantage that they are deterministic, and hence their security does not rely on good quality randomness during encryption. Instead, they use nonces (e.g., a simple counter) and require that these nonces are never repeated to guarantee security [33].

1.1 Our Contribution

The main contribution of our work is to extend the notion of RKA security to nonce-based AEAD schemes. We study the common generic composition paradigms to construct AEAD from encryption schemes and MACs, and explore

[1] Associated data corresponds to header information that has to be authenticated but does not need to be confidential.

if RKA security of the underlying primitives carries over to the AEAD scheme. More concretely, let K_e and K_m be the keys of the encryption and MAC, respectively. Assuming that the encryption scheme is secure against the class Φ_e of related-key deriving functions and the MAC is secure against Φ_m, then we ask if the AEAD scheme is secure with respect to related-key derivation functions from the Cartesian product $\Phi_e \times \Phi_m$.[2] In particular, we show that under certain restrictions of $\Phi_e \times \Phi_m$ the schemes N1, N2, and N3 by Namprempre et al. [30], falling into the composition paradigms E&M, EtM, and MtE, respectively, are secure under related-key attacks. By giving concrete attacks against all schemes in case the restrictions are dropped, we show further that these restrictions are necessary. Finally, on the positive side, we give a new construction for AEAD that is secure for the general case of functions from $\Phi_e \times \Phi_m$, i.e., without the aforementioned restrictions. We provide more details on our contribution below.

RKA Security Notions for Nonce-Based AEAD Schemes. We give two RKA security notions s-RKA-AE and RKA-AE for nonce-based AEAD schemes. In our weaker notion (RKA-AE), we assume that the key is updated such that each underlying primitive never uses the same key twice.[3] This is modelled by imposing an additional restriction on the adversary, where the adversary is not allowed to make queries with RKD functions that would result in keys that have already appeared during earlier RKA queries. More precisely, let K_e^i and K_m^i the result of the i-th RKA query. We require that for all i, j, we have $K_e^i = K_e^j$ if and only if $K_m^i = K_m^j$. In our stronger notion (s-RKA-AE), the above restriction is not imposed on the adversary, i.e., it is allowed to make queries i, j such that $K_e^i = K_e^j$ and $K_m^i \neq K_m^j$. Note that any adversary can trivially make such queries by repeating the RKD function for key K_e while using two different RKD functions for K_m. One may object that our weaker security notion looks rather artificial for modelling tampering attacks. We believe however that it is interesting to study for what key relations state-of-the-art AEAD constructions that are widely deployed remain secure under related-key attacks. Moreover, we emphasize another setting where such weak key relations may occur naturally – so-called bad key updates. In this setting the RKA adversary may observe ciphertexts for different related keys, where the relation stems from the key updates described by the RKD functions. Since the users update the keys, the relation between the keys is in fact not chosen by the adversary. Hence, the weaker notion guarantees security if the users ensure that, after each update, both keys K_e and K_m are fresh. In contrast, the stronger notion guarantees security even in the case when the users might only update one of the keys. Further details on these two notions are given in Sect. 3.

RKA Security of the N1, N2, and N3 Construction. We study the security of the N1, N2, and N3 constructions for nonce-based AEAD schemes [30],

[2] A similar question using the Cartesian product of the related-key deriving functions from the underlying primitives is answered in [5] for Feistel constructions.

[3] Note that the adversary can still ask for several encryptions under each key.

which follow the Encrypt-and-MAC (E&M), Encrypt-then-MAC (EtM), and MAC-then-Encrypt (MtE) paradigm [9], respectively. These constructions build a nonce-based AEAD scheme from a nonce-based encryption scheme and a MAC. We show that all schemes achieve our weaker security notion, i.e., when it is ensured that both keys are updated properly. The overall proof approach is similar to the classical setting. The challenge lies in the analysis that all queries by the reduction are permitted due to the related keys. Regarding our stronger security notion, we show that all schemes have limitations. We show that N1 and N2 are insecure, irrespective of the underlying primitive, by giving concrete attacks. For N3, we show that the security crucially depends on the underlying encryption scheme, by giving an attack against any instantiation using a stream cipher. These results appear in Sect. 4.

RKA-Secure AEAD Scheme. Finally, we give a new construction, called N*, of an AEAD scheme which is based on the N3 construction, and follows the MAC-then-Encrypt (MtE) paradigm. The underlying encryption scheme relies on an RKA-secure block cipher and a MAC. The resulting AEAD scheme achieves our stronger security notion s-RKA-AE, in fact, even in the case of nonce misuse. For simplicity we omit details regarding the nonce here, and discuss this setting more detail in Sect. 3. The construction and the proof is shown in Sect. 5.

RKA-Secure Encryption and MAC from Pseudorandom Functions. We show that RKA-secure nonce-based encryption schemes and MACs can be built from RKA-secure pseudorandom functions. Combined with the results for the N1, N2, and N3 constructions, this reduces the task of constructing RKA-secure nonce-based AEAD schemes to the task of constructing RKA-secure pseudorandom functions which is a general goal in the RKA literature. More precisely, we show that the nonce-based encryption scheme and the MAC proposed by Degabriele et al. [18] in the setting of leakage-resilient cryptography achieve RKA security if the underlying pseudorandom function is RKA-secure. This is shown in the extended version of the paper [20].

1.2 Related Work

Based on the initial work by Biham [13] and Knudsen [24], the first formalisation of RKA security has been given by Bellare and Kohno [8]. They studied pseudorandom functions as well as pseudorandom permutations and showed an inherent limitation on the set of allowed RKD functions. Bellare and Cash [6] proposed RKA-secure pseudorandom functions based on the DDH assumption, which allowed a large class of RKD functions. Abdalla et al. [1] further increased the allowed class of RKD functions. Several other works study the RKA security for various primitives, e.g., pseudorandom permutations from Feistel networks [5], encryption schemes [4], and MACs [12,37]. Harris [22], and later Albrecht et al. [3], showed inherent limitations of the Bellare-Kohno formalism by giving a generic attack against encryption schemes if the set of related-key deriving functions can depend on the primitive in question. The practical relevance of the alternative model by Harris has been questioned by Vaudenay [36].

Closer to our setting is the work by Lu et al. [29], who also study RKA security for authenticated encryption schemes. However, instead of nonce-based authenticated encryption schemes, they analyse probabilistic authenticated encryption schemes and only for the specific case of affine functions. Moreover, Han et al. [21] found their proof to be flawed, invalidating the results. To the best of our knowledge, these are the only works that consider RKA security for authenticated encryption schemes.

The practical relevance of RKA security has been shown by a number of works [16,19,23,28] which present attacks against concrete primitives.

2 Preliminaries

In Sect. 2.1 we recall the used notation. The syntax of the cryptographic primitives and existing RKA security notions are given in Sect. 2.2 and Sect. 2.3, respectively. Additional background on security notions in the classical setting is given in the extended version of the paper [20].

2.1 Notation

By $\{0,1\}^*$ and $\{0,1\}^x$ we denote the set of bit strings with arbitrary length and length x, respectively. We refer to probabilistic polynomial-time algorithms as adversaries if not otherwise specified, and use the code-based game-playing framework by Bellare and Rogaway [10]. For a game G and adversary $\mathcal{A}$, we write $\mathsf{G}^{\mathcal{A}} \Rightarrow y$ to indicate that the output of the game, when played by $\mathcal{A}$, is y. Likewise, $\mathcal{A}^{\mathsf{G}} \Rightarrow y$ indicates that $\mathcal{A}$ outputs y when playing game G. In case $\mathcal{A}$ has access to an oracle $\mathcal{O}$ we write $\mathcal{A}^{\mathcal{O}}$. We only use distinguishing games in which an adversary $\mathcal{A}$ tries to guess a secret bit b. The advantage of $\mathcal{A}$ in such a distinguishing game G is defined as $\mathbf{Adv}^{\mathsf{G}}(\mathcal{A}) := |2\Pr[\mathsf{G}^{\mathcal{A}} \Rightarrow \text{true}] - 1|$. Equivalent notions using adversarial advantages are $|\Pr[\mathcal{A}^{\mathsf{G}} \Rightarrow 0 \,|\, b = 0] - \Pr[\mathcal{A}^{\mathsf{G}} \Rightarrow 0 \,|\, b = 1]|$ and $|\Pr[\mathcal{A}^{\mathsf{G}} \Rightarrow 1 \,|\, b = 1] - \Pr[\mathcal{A}^{\mathsf{G}} \Rightarrow 1 \,|\, b = 0]|$. For sets $\mathcal{X}$ and $\mathcal{Y}$, the set of all functions mapping from $\mathcal{X}$ to $\mathcal{Y}$ is denoted by $\mathsf{Func}(\mathcal{X},\mathcal{Y})$ and the set of permutations over $\mathcal{X}$ by $\mathsf{Perm}(\mathcal{X})$. We write $\mathsf{Func}(\mathcal{K},\mathcal{X},\mathcal{Y})$ and $\mathsf{Perm}(\mathcal{K},\mathcal{X})$ for keyed functions in $\mathsf{Func}(\mathcal{X},\mathcal{Y})$ and $\mathsf{Perm}(\mathcal{X})$, respectively, where $\mathcal{K}$ denotes the key space. Tables f are initialised with $\perp$ if not mentioned differently. For sets $\mathcal{S}$ and $\mathcal{T}$, we write $\mathcal{S} \leftarrow_{\cup} \mathcal{T}$ instead of $\mathcal{S} \leftarrow \mathcal{S} \cup \mathcal{T}$. Our main focus lies in the RKA setting and we use the term *classical setting* whenever we refer to the setting which does not consider related-key attacks.

2.2 Primitives

A nonce-based authenticated encryption scheme with associated data (AEAD), is a tuple of two deterministic algorithms $(\mathtt{Enc}, \mathtt{Dec})$. The encryption algorithm

$\texttt{Enc}\colon \mathcal{K} \times \mathcal{N} \times \mathcal{A} \times \mathcal{M} \to \mathcal{C}$ maps a key K, a nonce N, associated data A, and a message M, to a ciphertext C. The decryption algorithm $\texttt{Dec}\colon \mathcal{K} \times \mathcal{N} \times \mathcal{A} \times \mathcal{C} \to \mathcal{M} \cup \{\perp\}$ maps a key K, a nonce N, associated data A, and a ciphertext C, to either a message or $\perp$ indicating an invalid ciphertext. The sets $\mathcal{K}$, $\mathcal{N}$, $\mathcal{A}$, $\mathcal{M}$, and $\mathcal{C}$, denote the key space, nonce space, associated data space, message space, and ciphertext space, respectively. An AEAD scheme is called *correct* if for any $K \in \mathcal{K}$, any $N \in \mathcal{N}$, any associated data $A \in \mathcal{A}$, and any $M \in \mathcal{M}$, it holds that $\texttt{Dec}(K, N, A, \texttt{Enc}(K, N, M, A)) = M$. It is called *tidy* if for any $K \in \mathcal{K}$, any $N \in \mathcal{N}$, any associated data $A \in \mathcal{A}$, any $M \in \mathcal{M}$, and any $C \in \mathcal{C}$ with $\texttt{Dec}(K, N, A, C) = M$, it holds that $\texttt{Enc}(K, N, A, M) = C$.

A nonce-based symmetric key encryption is similarly defined. The difference is that neither algorithm permits associated data as an input and only rejects ciphertext, i.e., outputs $\perp$, if computed on values outside the corresponding sets. For both primitives, we let c denote the length of a ciphertext.

A message authentication code (MAC) is a tuple of two deterministic algorithms $(\texttt{Tag}, \texttt{Ver})$. The tagging algorithm $\texttt{Tag}\colon \mathcal{K} \times \mathcal{X} \to \{0,1\}^t$ maps a key K and message X to a tag T. The verification algorithm $\texttt{Ver}\colon \mathcal{K} \times \mathcal{X} \times \{0,1\}^t \to \{\top, \perp\}$ takes as input a key K, a message M, and a tag T, and outputs either $\top$, indicating a valid tag, or $\perp$, indicating an invalid tag. Correctness requires that $\texttt{Ver}(K, X, \texttt{Tag}(K, X)) = \top$, for any $K \in \mathcal{K}$ and $X \in \mathcal{X}$. We denote the length of tags by t.

2.3 Security Notions Against Related-Key Attacks

We recall some of the existing RKA security notions. All notions follow the style introduced by Bellare and Kohno [8]. That is, the set of admissible RKD functions is fixed at the start of the game. All our results, however, also apply to the alternative definition given by Harris [22], where the adversary first picks the set of RKD functions before the concrete scheme (from a family of primitives) is chosen by the game. This prevents an inherent limitation of the Bellare-Kohno formalism as the RKD function can not depend on the primitive.[4]

Φ-Restricted Adversaries. For RKA security notions, the adversary is typically restricted to a set of functions that it can query to its oracles. This restriction is necessary, as Bellare and Kohno [8] showed that RKA security is unachievable without such restrictions. Let $\mathcal{K}$ be the key space of some primitive, then the set of permitted RKD functions is $\Phi \subset \mathsf{Func}(\mathcal{K}, \mathcal{K})$. We call an adversary that only queries functions from the set Φ to its oracles, a *Φ-restricted adversary.*

Repeating Queries. To avoid trivial wins certain queries must be excluded from the security games. In case of a MAC, we must forbid the adversary to query its challenge verification oracle on a tag it obtained from its tagging oracle. To do this, one can either adapt the game by keeping a list of such queries and let the

[4] It is questionable whether RKD functions that depend on the actual primitive are relevant in practice.

verification oracle check for such forbidden queries. The other option, would be to simply exclude adversaries that do such queries in the security definition. For ease of exposition, we use the latter approach.

Game rkaSUF	$\mathsf{Ver}(M, T, \varphi)$	$\mathsf{Tag}(M, \varphi)$
$b \leftarrow_\$ \{0,1\}$	**if** $b = 0$	$T \leftarrow \mathtt{Tag}(\varphi(K), M)$
$K \leftarrow_\$ \mathcal{K}$	**return** $\mathtt{Ver}(\varphi(K), M, T)$	**return** T
$b' \leftarrow \mathcal{A}^{\mathsf{Ver},\mathsf{Tag}}()$	**else**	
return $(b' = b)$	**return** $\bot$	

Fig. 1. Security game rkaSUF.

RKA Security for MACs and Pseudorandom Functions/Permutations. We give the definition of related-key attack security of MACs. Existing notions define it as an unforgeability game where the adversary finally outputs a forgery attempt [12,37]. In this work, we define unforgeability of a MAC against RKA as a distinguishing game. Here the adversary aims to distinguish whether its challenge oracle implements the real verification algorithm or simply rejects any queried tag.

Definition 1 (RKA-SUF **Security).** *Let* $\Gamma = (\mathtt{Tag}, \mathtt{Ver})$ *be a MAC and* $\Phi \subset \mathsf{Func}(\mathcal{K}, \mathcal{K})$. *Let the game* rkaSUF *be defined as in Fig. 1. For a* Φ*-restricted RKA adversary* $\mathcal{A}$, *that never forwards a query from its oracle* Tag, *we define its* RKA-SUF *advantage as*

$$\mathbf{Adv}_{\Gamma}^{\mathsf{rkaSUF}}(\mathcal{A}, \Phi) = 2 \Pr[\mathsf{rkaSUF}^{\mathcal{A}} \Rightarrow \text{true}] - 1.$$

Games rkaPRF, rkaPRP	$\mathsf{F}(X, \varphi)$ in rkaPRF	$\mathsf{F}(X, \varphi)$ in rkaPRP
$b \leftarrow_\$ \{0,1\}$	**if** $b = 0$	**if** $b = 0$
$K \leftarrow_\$ \mathcal{K}$	$y \leftarrow F(\varphi(K), X)$	$y \leftarrow F(\varphi(K), X)$
$\mathtt{F}' \leftarrow_\$ \mathsf{Func}(\mathcal{K}, \mathcal{X}, \mathcal{Y})$	**else**	**else**
$\mathtt{P}' \leftarrow_\$ \mathsf{Perm}(\mathcal{K}, \mathcal{X})$	$y \leftarrow_\$ \mathtt{F}'(\varphi(K), X)$	$y \leftarrow \mathtt{P}'(\varphi(K), X)$
$b' \leftarrow \mathcal{A}^{\mathsf{F}}()$	**return** y	**return** y
return $(b' = b)$		

Fig. 2. Security games rkaPRF and rkaPRP.

RKA-Security for pseudorandom functions (PRFs) and pseudorandom permutations (PRPs) have been studied in many works, e.g., [3,6–8], and are defined as the advantage in distinguishing the real function/permutation from a random function/permutation when having access to an oracle implementing either of these.

Definition 2 (RKA-PRF **Security**). *Let* $\mathsf{F}\colon \mathcal{K} \times \mathcal{X} \rightarrow \mathcal{Y}$ *and* $\Phi \subset \mathsf{Func}(\mathcal{K}, \mathcal{K})$. *Let the game* rkaPRF *be defined as in Fig. 2. For a* Φ*-restricted RKA adversary* $\mathcal{A}$*, that never repeats a query, we define its* RKA-PRF *advantage as*

$$\mathbf{Adv}_{\mathsf{F}}^{\mathsf{rkaPRF}}(\mathcal{A}, \Phi) = 2 \Pr[\mathsf{rkaPRF}^{\mathcal{A}} \Rightarrow \mathsf{true}] - 1.$$

Definition 3 (RKA-PRP **Security**). *Let* $\mathsf{F}\colon \mathcal{K} \times \mathcal{X} \rightarrow \mathcal{X}$ *and* $\Phi \subset \mathsf{Func}(\mathcal{K}, \mathcal{K})$. *Let the game* rkaPRP *be defined as in Fig. 2. For a* Φ*-restricted RKA adversary* $\mathcal{A}$*, that never repeats a query, we define its* RKA-PRP *advantage as*

$$\mathbf{Adv}_{\mathsf{F}}^{\mathsf{rkaPRP}}(\mathcal{A}, \Phi) = 2 \Pr[\mathsf{rkaPRP}^{\mathcal{A}} \Rightarrow \mathsf{true}] - 1.$$

3 RKA Security Notions for Nonce-Based AEAD

In this section, we define security for nonce-based encryption schemes and nonce-based AEAD schemes under related-key attacks. RKA security notions for encryption and authenticated encryption schemes have been proposed by Bellare et al. [7] and Lu et al. [29], respectively. However, neither notion considers nonce-based primitives and instead considers the case of probabilistic primitives. Furthermore, both works define indistinguishability in a left-or-right sense, while we follow the stronger IND$ (indistinguishability from random bits) approach put forth by Rogaway [34]. For this notion, the adversary has to distinguish the encryption of a message from randomly chosen bits. We discuss how the classical property of nonce-respecting adversaries is extended to the RKA setting in Sect. 3.1 and provide two RKA security notions for nonce-based AEAD schemes in Sect. 3.2. In Sect. 3.3, we extend the notion to the nonce misuse case and Sect. 3.4 provides the RKA security notion for nonce-based encryption schemes.

3.1 Nonce Selection

Security notions in the classical setting are often restricted to adversaries which are *nonce-respecting*. These are adversaries that never repeat a nonce across their encryption queries. Hence, security proven against nonce-respecting adversaries guarantees security as long as the encrypting party never repeats a nonce. Below we argue why this adversarial restriction needs to be updated in the RKA setting.

Consider the following scenario. Alice and Bob communicate using an AEAD scheme across several sessions. In each session, Alice will send several encrypted messages to Bob, each time using a fresh nonce implemented as a counter. Instead of exchanging a fresh secret key for each session, they exchange a key for the first session and between two consecutive sessions, they update the key using some update function F. There is no guarantee that Alice does not reuse a nonce in different sessions. In fact, due to using a simple counter which might be reset between the sessions, this is likely to happen. This means that an adversary can observe encryptions using the same nonce under related keys, where the relation is given by the update function F.

The same applies to the scenario where different devices have related keys. Every user would only ensure unique nonces for the own device while there will be colliding nonces across related devices.

If we declare an RKA adversary to be nonce-respecting if and only if it never repeats a nonce, then a proof of security does not tell us anything for the scenarios depicted above. Instead, we define an RKA adversary to be *RKA-nonce-respecting* if it never repeats *the pair* of nonce and RKD function. An interpretation of this definition is that nonce-respecting is defined with respect to individual keys. Since in the classical setting there is only ever one key, this interpretation reflects this.

3.2 RKA-Security Notions for AEAD Schemes

We extend security for AEAD schemes to the RKA setting. Instead of the approach used in [29], which defines two separate RKA security notions for confidentiality and authenticity, we follow the unified security notion by Rogaway and Shrimpton [35]. That is, the adversary has access to two oracles Enc and Dec. The goal of the adversary is to distinguish the real world, in which the oracles implement the encryption and decryption algorithm, from the ideal world, where the first oracle returns random bits while the latter rejects any ciphertext. The adversary wins the game if it can distinguish in which world it is. To make our new RKA security notion achievable, we impose standard restrictions on the adversary. That is, first, the adversary is not allowed to forward the response of an encryption query to the decryption query and, second, the adversary must not repeat a query to its encryption oracle.[5] More precisely, we say that an adversary forwards a query from its encryption oracle, if it queries its decryption oracle on a ciphertext C that it has obtained as a response from its encryption oracle, while the other queried values N, A, φ are the same for both queries. We call the resulting notion s-RKA-AE, the "s" indicating strong. The reason for that is that we introduce a weaker notion below.

Definition 4 (s-RKA-AE **Security).** *Let* $\Sigma = (\texttt{Enc}, \texttt{Dec})$ *be an AEAD scheme and* $\Phi \subset \mathsf{Func}(\mathcal{K}, \mathcal{K})$. *Let the game* s-rka-AE *be defined as in Fig. 3. For an RKA-nonce-respecting and* Φ*-restricted RKA adversary* $\mathcal{A}$*, that never repeats/forwards a query to/from* Enc*, we define its* RKA-AE *advantage as*

$$\mathbf{Adv}_{\Sigma}^{\mathsf{s\text{-}rka\text{-}AE}}(\mathcal{A}, \Phi) = 2 \Pr[\mathsf{s\text{-}rka\text{-}AE}^{\mathcal{A}} \Rightarrow \text{true}] - 1.$$

The above definition treats the AEAD scheme to have a single key K. Such schemes, however, are often constructed from smaller building blocks which have

[5] The latter restriction can also be handled by letting the encryption oracle return the same response as it did when the query was made the first time. For ease of exposition, we simply forbid such queries to avoid additional bookkeeping in the security games.

Game s-rka-AE	$\mathsf{Enc}(N, A, M, \varphi)$	$\mathsf{Dec}(N, A, C, \varphi)$
$b \leftarrow_\$ \{0,1\}$	**if** $b = 0$	**if** $b = 0$
$K \leftarrow_\$ \mathcal{K}$	$C \leftarrow \mathtt{Enc}(\varphi(K), N, A, M)$	$M \leftarrow \mathtt{Dec}(\varphi(K), N, A, C)$
$b' \leftarrow \mathcal{A}^{\mathsf{Enc},\mathsf{Dec}}()$	**else**	**else**
return $(b' = b)$	$C \leftarrow_\$ \{0,1\}^c$	$M \leftarrow \bot$
	return C	**return** M

Fig. 3. Security game s-rka-AE.

individual keys. This encompasses the N constructions [30], on which we focus in the next section, but also all other constructions combining an encryption scheme and a MAC into an AEAD schemes. In this case, the set of RKD functions of the AEAD scheme is the Cartesian product of the set of RKD functions for the individual primitives. More precisely, let E and M be the underlying primitives and Φ_e and Φ_m be the respective sets of RKD functions. Then for the combined primitive AE, the set of RKD functions is $\Phi_{ae} = \Phi_e \times \Phi_m$. Thus the s-RKA-AE security game above allows the adversary to query the encryption oracle on $(N, \varphi_e, \varphi_m) \in \mathcal{N} \times \Phi_e \times \Phi_m$ and later querying it on $(N, \varphi_e, \varphi'_m) \in \mathcal{N} \times \Phi_e \times \Phi_m$, where $\varphi_m \neq \varphi'_m$. This essentially allows the adversary to bypass the nonce-respecting property of the underlying primitive.

Recall the key-update scenario described above. Allowing the adversary to query the same nonce while the queried RKD functions agree in exactly one part, models a scenario in which the key update either does not update one of the keys or later updates a key to a previously used key. We introduce a weaker security notion, in which these queries are forbidden. Security according to this notion then reflects security as long as *the pair of keys* is updated appropriately.

Definition 5 (RKA-AE **Security**). *Let* $\Sigma = (\mathtt{Enc}, \mathtt{Dec})$ *be an AEAD scheme and* $\Phi = \Phi_e \times \Phi_m \subset \mathsf{Func}(\mathcal{K}, \mathcal{K})$. *Let the game* rka-AE *be defined as in Fig. 4. For an RKA-nonce-respecting and Φ-restricted RKA adversary $\mathcal{A}$, that never repeats/forwards a query to/from* Enc, *we define its* RKA-AE *advantage as*

$$\mathbf{Adv}_{\Sigma}^{\mathsf{rka\text{-}AE}}(\mathcal{A}, \Phi) = 2 \Pr[\mathsf{rka\text{-}AE}^{\mathcal{A}} \Rightarrow \mathrm{true}] - 1.$$

The weaker security notion bears similarities to split-state non-malleable codes [2]. Here, the secret is encoded in such a way that it is secure against fault attacks as long as the left and right half of the code are tampered independently. In more detail, the decoding of such tampered codes is independent from the original secret and might be invalid. However, if we consider key-related devices or bad-key updates, non-malleable codes are not helpful any more since they are used for faults and not bad randomised keys. The reason for this is that after each key update we need to take care that the resulting key is still valid. Further, we do not want to update the keys independently but simultaneously such that all keys are fresh after the key update. So the requirement to the

```
Game rka-AE
  b ←$ {0,1}
  (K_e || K_m) ←$ 𝒦
  𝒮 ← ∅
  b' ← 𝒜^{Enc,Dec}()
  return (b' = b)

Enc(N, A, M, φ_e, φ_m)
  if ∃φ'_e ≠ φ_e st (N, φ'_e, φ_m) ∈ 𝒮
    return ⊥
  if ∃φ'_m ≠ φ_m st (N, φ_e, φ'_m) ∈ 𝒮
    return ⊥
  𝒮 ←∪ {(N, φ_e, φ_m)}
  if b = 0
    C ← Enc(φ_e(K_e) || φ_m(K_m), N, A, M)
  else
    C ←$ {0,1}^c
  return C

Dec(N, A, C, φ_e, φ_m)
  if ∃φ'_e ≠ φ_e st (N, φ'_e, φ_m) ∈ 𝒮
    return ⊥
  if ∃φ'_m ≠ φ_m st (N, φ_e, φ'_m) ∈ 𝒮
    return ⊥
  𝒮 ←∪ {(N, φ_e, φ_m)}
  if b = 0
    M ← Dec(φ_e(K_e) || φ_m(K_m), N, A, M)
  else
    M ← ⊥
  return M
```

Fig. 4. Security game rka-AE. The set $\mathcal{S}$ is used to detect forbidden queries, that is, queries where the triple of nonce and the two RKD functions differ in exactly one of the functions. Both oracles reject such queries by returning $\perp$.

weaker notion is the opposite of that of non malleable codes. For key updates, it is a reasonable assumption to say that all underlying keys have to be updated for a new session.

3.3 RKA-Security Against Nonce Misuse

Similar to the classical setting, we extend security to nonce-misuse resistance. In this case, the adversary is allowed to repeat nonces to the encryption oracle. Below we define security in this stronger sense for s-RKA-AE security. Note that the game is the same as in Definition 4 (cf. Fig. 3), the sole difference is that the adversary is no longer restricted to be RKA-nonce-respecting.

Definition 6 (mr-s-RKA-AE **Security).** *Let* $\Sigma = (\mathsf{Enc}, \mathsf{Dec})$ *be an AEAD scheme and* $\Phi \subset \mathsf{Func}(\mathcal{K}, \mathcal{K})$. *Let the game* s-rka-AE *be defined as in Fig. 3. For an RKA-respecting and* Φ*-restricted RKA adversary* $\mathcal{A}$, *that never repeats/forwards a query to/from* Enc, *we define its* mr-s-RKA-AE *advantage as*

$$\mathbf{Adv}_{\Sigma}^{\mathsf{mr\text{-}s\text{-}rka\text{-}AE}}(\mathcal{A}, \Phi) = 2 \Pr[\mathsf{s\text{-}rka\text{-}AE}^{\mathcal{A}} \Rightarrow \mathsf{true}] - 1.$$

In the same way, we can extend RKA-AE security to the nonce misuse scenario. However, we believe this notion not to be meaningful. The RKA-AE security notion already requires that keys are updated properly, i.e., they do not repeat.

Since this task is way more complex than ensuring that nonces do not repeat, it seems strange to require this one while simultaneously dropping the simple requirement of unique nonces.

3.4 RKA-Security Notions for Encryption

The following definition extends the classical IND-CPA security notion for nonce-based encryption schemes to the RKA setting. The adversary has to tell apart the real encryption oracle from an idealised encryption oracle which returns random bits. The main distinction lies in the nonce selection of the adversary as it is allowed to repeat a nonce if the RKD functions are different.

Game rkaIND	$\mathsf{Enc}(N, M, \varphi)$
$b \leftarrow_{\$} \{0,1\}$	**if** $b = 0$
$K \leftarrow_{\$} \mathcal{K}$	$\quad C \leftarrow \mathtt{Enc}(\varphi(K), N, M)$
$b' \leftarrow \mathcal{A}^{\mathsf{Enc}}()$	**else**
return $(b' = b)$	$\quad C \leftarrow_{\$} \{0,1\}^c$
	return C

Fig. 5. Security game rkaIND.

Definition 7 (RKA-IND **Security).** *Let* $\Sigma = (\mathtt{Enc}, \mathtt{Dec})$ *be an encryption scheme and* $\Phi \subset \mathsf{Func}(\mathcal{K}, \mathcal{K})$. *Let the game* rkaIND *be defined as in Fig. 5. For an RKA-nonce-respecting and* Φ*-restricted RKA adversary* $\mathcal{A}$, *that never repeats a query, we define its* RKA-IND *advantage as*

$$\mathbf{Adv}_{\Sigma}^{\mathsf{rkaIND}}(\mathcal{A}, \Phi) = 2\ \Pr[\mathsf{rkaIND}^{\mathcal{A}} \Rightarrow \mathrm{true}] - 1.$$

4 RKA Security of the N1, N2, and N3 Constructions

In this section we study the security of the nonce-based AEAD schemes N1, N2, and N3 [30], which fall into the generic composition paradigms Encrypt-and-MAC (E&M), Encrypt-then-MAC (EtM), MAC-then-Encrypt (MtE) [9]. We analyse each scheme with respect to the two security notions RKA-AE and s-RKA-AE defined above. The analysis reveals that all schemes achieve RKA-AE security if the underlying primitives are RKA-secure. Regarding the stronger s-RKA-AE security, the situation is more involved. We show that both N1 and N2 are insecure irrespective of the underlying primitives. For N3, we provide a concrete attack exploiting any instantiation using a stream cipher for the underlying encryption scheme.

Section 4.1 covers the analysis of the N1 construction. The N2 construction is analysed in Sect. 4.2 while we analyse the N3 construction in Sect. 4.3.

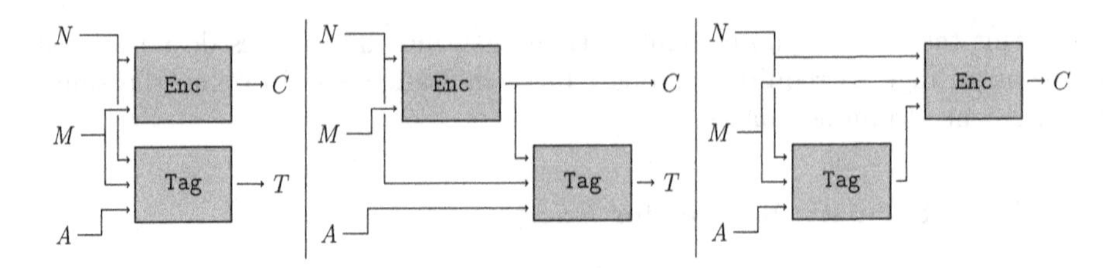

Fig. 6. The AEAD schemes N1 (left), N2 (middle), and N3 (right) [30].

4.1 N1 - Instantiation of Encrypt-and-MAC

The N1 construction composes a nonce-based encryption scheme and a MAC into an AEAD scheme. It follows the E&M paradigm. The encryption algorithm is used to encrypt the message as is the MAC to compute a tag for the message. The ciphertext of the AEAD scheme consists of the ciphertext and the tag.

The following theorem shows that the N1 construction achieves RKA-AE security if the underlying primitives are RKA-secure. The overall proof approach is similar to the classical setting but needs some extra treatment when analysing that all queries of the reductions are permitted. The full proof is given in the extended version of the paper [20].

Theorem 8. *Let* $\Sigma = (\mathtt{Enc}, \mathtt{Dec})$ *be an encryption scheme and* $\Gamma = (\mathtt{Tag}, \mathtt{Ver})$ *be a MAC with RKA function sets* Φ_e *and* Φ_m*, respectively. Further, let* N1 *be the AEAD scheme built from* Σ *and* Γ *using the N1 construction with RKA function set* $\Phi_{ae} = \Phi_e \times \Phi_m$*. Then for any RKA-nonce-respecting and* Φ_{ae}*-restricted RKA adversary* $\mathcal{A}$ *against* N1*, that never repeats/forwards a query to/from* Enc*, there exists an RKA-nonce-respecting and* Φ_e*-restricted RKA adversary* $\mathcal{A}_{se}$*, a* Φ_m*-restricted RKA adversary* $\mathcal{A}_{mac}$*, and a* Φ_m*-restricted RKA adversary* $\mathcal{A}_{prf}$ *such that*

$$\mathbf{Adv}^{\mathsf{rka\text{-}AE}}_{\mathrm{N1}}(\mathcal{A}, \Phi_{ae}) \leq \mathbf{Adv}^{\mathsf{rkaIND}}_{\Sigma}(\mathcal{A}_{se}, \Phi_e) + \mathbf{Adv}^{\mathsf{rkaSUF}}_{\Gamma}(\mathcal{A}_{mac}, \Phi_m) + \mathbf{Adv}^{\mathsf{rkaPRF}}_{\mathtt{Tag}}(\mathcal{A}_{prf}, \Phi_m).$$

□

Proof (Sketch). The proof consists of multiple game hops. In the first game hop, the decryption oracle is replaced by $\perp$ which is bound by the RKA security of Γ. In the subsequent game hops, first the tag and then the ciphertext are replaced by random values which is bound by the RKA security of Tag and Σ, respectively.

The following theorem shows that the N1 construction does not achieve the stronger s-RKA-AE security. The reason is that a ciphertext is the concatenation of a ciphertext from the underlying encryption scheme and tag from the underlying MAC. By making two queries which solely differ in one of the RKD functions, the adversary can easily distinguishing between the real and the ideal case. The proof appears in the extended version of the paper [20].

Theorem 9. *Let $\Sigma = (\mathtt{Enc}, \mathtt{Dec})$ be an encryption scheme and $\Gamma = (\mathtt{Tag}, \mathtt{Ver})$ be a MAC with RKA function sets Φ_e and Φ_m, respectively. Further, let* N1 *be the AEAD scheme built from Σ and Γ using the N1 construction with RKA function set $\Phi_{ae} = \Phi_e \times \Phi_m$. Then* N1 *is not* s-RKA-AE*-secure. There exists an RKA-nonce-respecting and Φ_{ae}-restricted RKA adversary $\mathcal{A}$ such that*

$$\mathbf{Adv}_{\mathrm{N1}}^{\mathsf{s\text{-}rka\text{-}AE}}(\mathcal{A}) = 1.$$

4.2 N2 - Instantiation of Encrypt-then-MAC

The N2 construction composes a nonce-based encryption scheme and a MAC into an AEAD scheme. It follows the EtM paradigm and is displayed in Fig. 6. The scheme first encrypts the message using the encryption scheme. Subsequently, the MAC is used to compute a tag for the ciphertext. The ciphertext of the AEAD scheme consists of both the ciphertext and the tag.

The theorem below shows that the N2 construction achieves RKA-AE security if the underlying primitives are sound. The overall proof follows the classical one, except for a more complex analysis regarding the permitted queries. The full proof is given in the extended version of the paper [20].

Theorem 10. *Let $\Sigma = (\mathtt{Enc}, \mathtt{Dec})$ be an encryption scheme and $\Gamma = (\mathtt{Tag}, \mathtt{Ver})$ be a MAC with RKA function sets Φ_e and Φ_m, respectively. Further, let* N2 *be the AEAD scheme built from Σ and Γ using the N2 construction with RKA function set $\Phi_{ae} = \Phi_e \times \Phi_m$. Then for any RKA-nonce-respecting and Φ_{ae}-restricted RKA adversary $\mathcal{A}$ against* N2*, that never repeats/forwards a query to/from* Enc*, there exists an RKA-nonce-respecting and Φ_e-restricted RKA adversary $\mathcal{A}_{se}$, a Φ_m-restricted RKA adversary $\mathcal{A}_{mac}$, and a Φ_m-restricted RKA adversary $\mathcal{A}_{prf}$ such that*

$$\mathbf{Adv}_{\mathrm{N2}}^{\mathsf{rka\text{-}AE}}(\mathcal{A}, \Phi_{ae}) \leq \mathbf{Adv}_{\Sigma}^{\mathsf{rkaIND}}(\mathcal{A}_{se}, \Phi_e) + \mathbf{Adv}_{\Gamma}^{\mathsf{rkaSUF}}(\mathcal{A}_{mac}, \Phi_m) + \mathbf{Adv}_{\mathsf{Tag}}^{\mathsf{rkaPRF}}(\mathcal{A}_{prf}, \Phi_m).$$

Proof (Sketch). In the first game hop, the decryption oracle is replaced by $\perp$ which is bound by the RKA security of Γ. In the subsequent game hops, first the tag and then the ciphertext are replaced by random values which is bound by the RKA security of $\mathtt{Tag}$ and Σ, respectively. □

Below we show that the N2 construction does not achieve s-RKA-AE security. It exhibits the same structure as the N1 construction, that is, a concatenation of a ciphertext and a tag from the underlying primitives. The difference is the tag is computed on the ciphertext rather than the message. While we give two attacks against the N1 construction, only one attack also applies against the N2 construction. The proof is given in the extended version of the paper [20].

Theorem 11. *Let $\Sigma = (\mathtt{Enc}, \mathtt{Dec})$ be an encryption scheme and $\Gamma = (\mathtt{Tag}, \mathtt{Ver})$ be a MAC with RKA function sets Φ_e and Φ_m, respectively. Further, let* N2 *be the AEAD scheme built from Σ and Γ using the N2 construction with RKA* *function set* $\Phi_{ae} = \Phi_e \times \Phi_m$. *Then* N2 *is not* s-RKA-AE*-secure. There exists an RKA-nonce-respecting and* Φ_{ae}*-restricted RKA adversary* $\mathcal{A}$ *such that*

$$\mathbf{Adv}_{\mathrm{N2}}^{\text{s-rka-AE}}(\mathcal{A}) = 1.$$

4.3 N3 - Instantiation of MAC-then-Encrypt

The N3 construction composes a nonce-based encryption scheme and a MAC into an AEAD scheme. It follows the MtE paradigm and is displayed in Fig. 6. The message is first used as an input to the MAC and then both the message and the tag are encrypted. In contrast to the other compositions, the ciphertext of the AEAD scheme consists only of the ciphertext from the underlying encryption scheme.

In the theorem below, we show that the N3 construction is RKA-AE secure if both of the underlying primitives are secure. The overall proof follows the classical setting, except for the analysis that all queries by the reductions are indeed valid queries.

Theorem 12. *Let* $\Sigma = (\texttt{Enc}, \texttt{Dec})$ *be an encryption scheme and* $\Gamma = (\texttt{Tag}, \texttt{Ver})$ *be a MAC with RKA function sets* Φ_e *and* Φ_m*, respectively. Further, let* N3 *be the AEAD scheme built from* Σ *and* Γ *using the N3 construction with RKA function set* $\Phi_{ae} = \Phi_e \times \Phi_m$. *Then for any RKA-nonce-respecting and* Φ_{ae}*-restricted RKA adversary* $\mathcal{A}$ *against* N3*, that never repeats/forwards a query to/from* Enc*, there exists an RKA-nonce-respecting and* Φ_e*-restricted RKA adversary* $\mathcal{A}_{se}$*, a* Φ_m*-restricted RKA adversary* $\mathcal{A}_{mac}$*, and a* Φ_m*-restricted RKA adversary* $\mathcal{A}_{prf}$ *such that*

$$\begin{aligned}\mathbf{Adv}_{\mathrm{N3}}^{\text{rka-AE}}(\mathcal{A}, \Phi_{ae}) \leq \mathbf{Adv}_{\Sigma}^{\text{rkaIND}}(\mathcal{A}_{se}, \Phi_e) + \mathbf{Adv}_{\Gamma}^{\text{rkaSUF}}(\mathcal{A}_{mac}, \Phi_m) \\ + \mathbf{Adv}_{\text{Tag}}^{\text{rkaPRF}}(\mathcal{A}_{prf}, \Phi_m).\end{aligned}$$

Proof. We prove the theorem using the hybrid games G_0, G_1, G_2, and G_3 displayed in Fig. 7. For sake of simplicity, the games do not contain the set $\mathcal{S}$ to detect invalid queries. Instead, we assume that the adversary does not make such queries, which the reduction can simply answer with $\perp$. Game G_0 is rka-AE instantiated with N3 and secret bit b fixed to 0. In G_1, the decryption oracle is modified to reject any ciphertext. In G_2, encryption oracle computes a random tag which is then encrypted along with the message. Game G_3 equals rka-AE with secret bit b fixed to 1, where the encryption oracle outputs random ciphertexts and the decryption oracle rejects any ciphertext. We have

$$\begin{aligned}\mathbf{Adv}_{\mathrm{N3}}^{\text{rka-AE}}(\mathcal{A}) &= \Pr[\mathcal{A}^{\text{rka-AE}} \Rightarrow 0 \mid b = 0] - \Pr[\mathcal{A}^{\text{rka-AE}} \Rightarrow 0 \mid b = 1] \\ &= \Pr[\mathcal{A}^{\mathsf{G}_0} \Rightarrow 0] - \Pr[\mathcal{A}^{\mathsf{G}_3} \Rightarrow 0] \\ &= \sum_{i=1}^{3} \Pr[\mathcal{A}^{\mathsf{G}_{i-1}} \Rightarrow 0] - \Pr[\mathcal{A}^{\mathsf{G}_i} \Rightarrow 0].\end{aligned}$$

Game G_i	$\mathsf{Enc}(N, A, M, (\varphi_e, \varphi_m))$ in G_0, G_1
$(K_e, K_m) \leftarrow_\$ \mathcal{K}$ $b' \leftarrow \mathcal{A}^{\mathsf{Enc},\mathsf{Dec}}()$	$T \leftarrow \mathtt{Tag}(\varphi_m(K_m), N, A, M)$ $C \leftarrow \mathtt{Enc}(\varphi_e(K_e), N, M \parallel T)$ **return** C
$\mathsf{Dec}(N, A, C, (\varphi_e, \varphi_m))$ in G_0	$\mathsf{Enc}(N, A, M, (\varphi_e, \varphi_m))$ in G_2
$M \parallel T \leftarrow \mathtt{Dec}(\varphi_e(K_e), N, C)$ **if** $\mathtt{Ver}(\varphi_m(K_m), N, A, M, T) = \top$ **return** M **return** $\perp$	$T \leftarrow_\$ \{0,1\}^t$ $C \leftarrow \mathtt{Enc}(\varphi_e(K_e), N, M \parallel T)$ **return** C
$\mathsf{Dec}(N, A, C, (\varphi_e, \varphi_m))$ in G_1, G_2, G_3	$\mathsf{Enc}(N, A, M, (\varphi_e, \varphi_m))$ in G_3
return $\perp$	$C \leftarrow_\$ \{0,1\}^c$ **return** C

Fig. 7. Hybrid games G_i used to prove Theorem 12 (RKA-AE security of N3).

To bound the term $\Pr[\mathcal{A}^{\mathsf{G}_0} \Rightarrow 0] - \Pr[\mathcal{A}^{\mathsf{G}_1} \Rightarrow 0]$ we construct the following adversary $\mathcal{A}_{mac}$ against the RKA-SUF security of Γ. It chooses a random key K_e for the encryption scheme Σ and then runs $\mathcal{A}$. When $\mathcal{A}$ makes a query $(N, A, M, (\varphi_e, \varphi_m))$ to Enc, $\mathcal{A}_{mac}$ proceeds as follows. It queries its oracle Tag on (N, A, M, φ_m) to obtain a tag T. Then it locally computes $C \leftarrow \mathtt{Enc}(\varphi_e(K_e), N, M \parallel T)$ and sends C back to $\mathcal{A}$. For queries $(N, A, C, (\varphi_e, \varphi_m))$ to Dec by $\mathcal{A}$, $\mathcal{A}_{mac}$ locally computes $M \parallel T \leftarrow \mathtt{Dec}(\varphi_e(K_e), N, C)$ and queries (N, A, M, T, φ_m) to its challenge oracle Ver. If the response is $\perp$, it forwards it to $\mathcal{A}$, otherwise, it sends M to $\mathcal{A}$. When $\mathcal{A}$ outputs a bit b', $\mathcal{A}_{mac}$ outputs the same bit.

Ir remains to argue that $\mathcal{A}_{mac}$ never makes a forbidden query (forwarding from Tag to Ver) conditioned on $\mathcal{A}$ making only permitted queries. Assume, for sake of contradiction, that $\mathcal{A}$ makes a valid query $(N, A, C, \varphi_e, \varphi_m)$ to Dec for which $\mathcal{A}_{mac}$ makes a forbidden query. By construction $\mathcal{A}_{mac}$ computes $M \parallel T \leftarrow \mathtt{Dec}(\varphi_e(K_e), N, C)$ and queries Ver on (N, A, M, T, φ_m). This query is forbidden if $\mathcal{A}_{mac}$ has queried (N, A, M, φ_m) to Tag which resulted in T. This happens if $\mathcal{A}$ has made a query $(N, A, M, \varphi'_e, \varphi_m)$ to Enc. We need to distinguish between the case $\varphi'_e = \varphi_e$ and $\varphi'_e \neq \varphi_e$. The former is forbidden as this means that $\mathcal{A}$ forwards a query from Enc to Dec. The latter is forbidden since game $\mathsf{rka\text{-}AE}$ forbids queries that agree on the nonce and exactly one of the RKD functions while disagreeing on the other RKD function. Hence $\mathcal{A}_{mac}$ only makes permitted queries.

By construction, $\mathcal{A}_{mac}$ simulates either G_0 or G_1 for $\mathcal{A}$, depending on its secret bit b from game rkaSUF. More precisely, it simulates G_0 and G_1 if its own challenge is 0 and 1, respectively. This gives us

$$\begin{aligned}\Pr[\mathcal{A}^{\mathsf{G}_0} \Rightarrow 0] - \Pr[\mathcal{A}^{\mathsf{G}_1} \Rightarrow 0] \leq & \Pr[\mathcal{A}_{mac}^{\mathsf{rkaSUF}} \Rightarrow 0 \mid b = 0] - \Pr[\mathcal{A}_{mac}^{\mathsf{rkaSUF}} \Rightarrow 0 \mid b = 1] \\ \leq & \mathbf{Adv}_{\Gamma}^{\mathsf{rkaSUF}}(\mathcal{A}_{mac}, \Phi_m).\end{aligned}$$

For the term $\Pr[\mathcal{A}^{\mathsf{G}_1} \Rightarrow 0] - \Pr[\mathcal{A}^{\mathsf{G}_2} \Rightarrow 0]$, we construct an adversary $\mathcal{A}_{prf}$ against the RKA-PRF security of the tagging algorithm Tag. First, $\mathcal{A}_{prf}$ chooses a random key K_e to simulate all encryption related functionalities. Queries to Dec by $\mathcal{A}$ are answered with $\perp$. Queries $(N, A, M, (\varphi_e, \varphi_m))$ to Enc, are processed as follows. The reduction $\mathcal{A}_{prf}$ invokes its own oracle F on (N, A, M, φ_m) to obtain T, locally computes $C \leftarrow \mathtt{Enc}(\varphi_e(K_e), N, M \parallel T)$, and sends C back to $\mathcal{A}$. When $\mathcal{A}$ terminates, $\mathcal{A}_{prf}$ also terminates and outputs whatever $\mathcal{A}$ does.

We briefly argue that $\mathcal{A}_{prf}$ never repeats a query to F. By construction, every query (N, A, M, φ_m) by $\mathcal{A}_{prf}$ stems from a query $(N, A, M, \varphi_e, \varphi_m)$ by $\mathcal{A}$. The only cases that result in a repeating query are (1) $\mathcal{A}$ repeats a query and (2) $\mathcal{A}$ makes two queries which only differ in φ_e. However, both cases are forbidden queries for $\mathcal{A}$. This yields that every output of Tag is a random value.

The adversary $\mathcal{A}_{prf}$ simulates game G_1 for $\mathcal{A}$ if its own challenge bit b equals 0, while it simulates G_2 for $\mathcal{A}$ if b equals 1. Thus it holds that

$$\begin{aligned}\Pr[\mathcal{A}^{\mathsf{G}_1} \Rightarrow 0] - \Pr[\mathcal{A}^{\mathsf{G}_2} \Rightarrow 0] &\leq \Pr[\mathcal{A}_{prf}^{\mathsf{rkaPRF}} \Rightarrow 0 \mid b = 0] - \Pr[\mathcal{A}_{prf}^{\mathsf{rkaPRF}} \Rightarrow 0 \mid b = 1] \\ &\leq \mathbf{Adv}_{\Gamma}^{\mathsf{rkaPRF}}(\mathcal{A}_{prf}, \Phi_m).\end{aligned}$$

We bound the final term $\Pr[\mathcal{A}^{\mathsf{G}_2} \Rightarrow 0] - \Pr[\mathcal{A}^{\mathsf{G}_3} \Rightarrow 0]$ by constructing an adversary $\mathcal{A}_{se}$ against the RKA-IND security of the underlying encryption scheme Σ. At the start, $\mathcal{A}_{se}$ chooses a random key K_m. Any query to Dec is answered with $\perp$. When $\mathcal{A}$ queries its oracle Enc on $(N, A, M, (\varphi_e, \varphi_m))$, $\mathcal{A}_{se}$ chooses a random tag T of length t, invokes its oracle Enc on $(N, M \parallel T, \varphi_e)$ to obtain C, and sends C to $\mathcal{A}$. At the end, $\mathcal{A}_{se}$ outputs whatever $\mathcal{A}$ outputs.

It holds that $\mathcal{A}_{se}$ is RKA-nonce-respecting as any query $(N, M \parallel T, \varphi_e)$ stems from a query $(N, A, M, \varphi_e, \varphi_m)$ by $\mathcal{A}$. This means that $\mathcal{A}_{se}$ repeats a pair of nonce N and RKD function φ_e if $\mathcal{A}$ makes two queries using $(N, \varphi_e, \varphi_m)$ and $(N, \varphi_e, \varphi'_m)$. We can distinguish between the cases (1) $\varphi_m = \varphi'_m$ and (2) $\varphi_m \neq \varphi'_m$. Case (1) does not occur, as $\mathcal{A}$ is RKA-nonce-respecting and case (2) is forbidden in game $\mathsf{rka\text{-}AE}$. The other option would be that $\mathcal{A}$ makes two queries differing only in the associated data A. This turns out not to be an issue, as the tag T that $\mathcal{A}_{se}$ queries along with the message depends on A, i.e., different A results in a different message queries by $\mathcal{A}_{se}$.

The adversary $\mathcal{A}_{se}$ perfectly simulates games G_2 or G_3 for $\mathcal{A}$ depending on its own challenge from rkaIND. Hence we have

$$\begin{aligned}\Pr[\mathcal{A}^{\mathsf{G}_2} \Rightarrow 0] - \Pr[\mathcal{A}^{\mathsf{G}_3} \Rightarrow 0] &\leq \Pr[\mathcal{A}_{se}^{\mathsf{rkaIND}} \Rightarrow 0 \mid b = 0] - \Pr[\mathcal{A}_{se}^{\mathsf{rkaIND}} \Rightarrow 0 \mid b = 1] \\ &\leq \mathbf{Adv}_{\Gamma}^{\mathsf{rkaIND}}(\mathcal{A}_{se}, \Phi_e).\end{aligned}$$

Collecting the bounds above proves the claim. □

Unlike for the N1 and N2 construction, the s-RKA-AE security of the N3 construction is more subtle. The difference is that the tag is appended to the ciphertext for both the N1 and N2 construction while it is encrypted alongside the message for the N3 construction. The attacks against the N1 and N2 construction rely on the property that the ciphertext consists of two parts which can be manipulated separately. Due to the construction such attacks do not work against the N3 construction.

It turns out that the s-RKA-AE security of the N3 construction crucially depend on the used encryption scheme. Namely, if the underlying encryption scheme is a stream cipher, then the N3 construction is s-RKA-AE insecure. Below we show an attack against any instantiation using a stream cipher. For such ciphers the ciphertext is the XOR of the message and a keystream derived from the key and the nonce.

Theorem 13. *Let* $\Sigma = (\texttt{Enc}, \texttt{Dec})$ *be a stream cipher and* $\Gamma = (\texttt{Tag}, \texttt{Ver})$ *be a MAC with RKA function sets* Φ_e *and* Φ_m*, respectively. Further, let* N3 *be the AEAD scheme built from* Σ *and* Γ *using the N2 construction with RKA function set* $\Phi_{ae} = \Phi_e \times \Phi_m$*. Then* N3 *is not* s-RKA-AE*-secure. There exists an RKA-nonce-respecting and* Φ_{ae}*-restricted RKA adversary* $\mathcal{A}$ *such that*

$$\mathbf{Adv}_{\mathrm{N3}}^{\mathsf{s\text{-}rka\text{-}AE}}(\mathcal{A}) = 1.$$

Proof. Adversary $\mathcal{A}$ chooses a nonce N, associated data A, a message M, RKD functions φ_e, φ_m, and φ'_m from the respective sets such that $\varphi_m \neq \varphi'_m$. Then it queries its encryption oracle Enc on $(N, A, M, (\varphi_e, \varphi_m))$ and $(N, A, M, (\varphi_e, \varphi'_m))$ to obtain ciphertext C_1 and C_2. If the first $|M|$ bits of C_1 and C_2 are equal, $\mathcal{A}$ outputs 0, otherwise, it outputs 1.

In case $b = 0$, we have $C_1 = \texttt{Enc}(\varphi_e(K_e), N, M \parallel \texttt{Tag}(\varphi_m(K_m), N, A, M))$ and $C_2 = \texttt{Enc}(\varphi_e(K_e), N, M \parallel \texttt{Tag}(\varphi'_m(K_m), N, A, M))$. Since the encryption uses the same nonce and the same key, the same keystream for the stream cipher will be used. Together with the fact that the first $|M|$ bits are identical as the same message is encrypted, this yields that C_1 and C_2 agree on the first bits. In case $b = 1$, both C_1 and C_2 are chosen at random, hence they will not agree on the first $|M|$ bits.[6] $\square$

In the attack above, the RKA-nonce-respecting adversary essentially bypasses the nonce-respecting property of the underlying encryption scheme by repeating the nonce N and the RKD function φ_e for the encryption scheme. Then it exploits the fact that the underlying stream cipher is secure only against nonce-respecting adversaries. We conjecture that any instantiation using an encryption scheme that can be broken in the nonce-misuse case results in an s-RKA-AE insecure instantiation of the N3 construction. The problematic part is that both the message and the tag are encrypted. While the adversary has full control over the former, it can not choose the latter at will. This seems to thwart a simple proof showing that any nonce-misuse adversary against the underlying encryption scheme can be turned into an s-RKA-AE adversary against N3.

[6] Note that there is a negligible chance that the ciphertexts will agree on their first $|M|$ bits which we drop here for simplicity.

5 RKA Nonce-Misuse-Resistant AEAD

As described in Sect. 4, N1, N2, and N3 are not secure in the strong RKA setting.[7] In this section we give a new AE scheme, N*, that achieves mr-s-RKA-AE security and hence also s-RKA-AE security. The construction, following the N3 construction, is displayed in Fig. 8. The message, nonce, and associated data are first used as an input to the MAC, and then both the message and the tag are encrypted. The difference to the N3 construction is that the encryption scheme no longer takes the nonce as input. Instead, the (pseudorandom) tag ensures that the encryption is randomised.

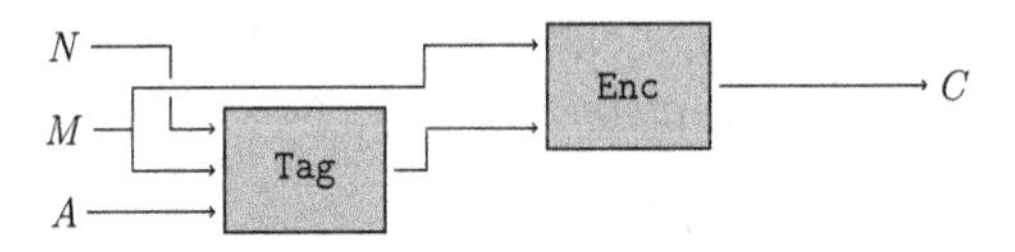

Fig. 8. The AEAD scheme N* [This work].

The theorem below shows that the new construction achieves our strong RKA security notion conditioned on the encryption scheme being an RKA-secure block cipher (pseudorandom permutation).

Theorem 14. *Let* $\Sigma = (\texttt{Enc}, \texttt{Dec})$ *be an encryption scheme and* $\Gamma = (\texttt{Tag}, \texttt{Ver})$ *be a MAC with RKA function sets* Φ_e *and* Φ_m*, respectively. Further, let* N* *be the AEAD scheme built from* Σ *and* Γ *using the* N* *construction with RKA function set* $\Phi_{ae} = \Phi_e \times \Phi_m$*. Then for any* Φ_{ae}*-restricted RKA adversary* $\mathcal{A}$ *against* N* *with* q *queries to the encryption and decryption oracle, that never repeats/forwards a query to/from* Enc*, there exists* Φ_e*-restricted RKA adversaries* $\mathcal{A}_{prp}$*, and* Φ_m*-restricted RKA adversaries* $\mathcal{A}_{mac}$ *and* $\mathcal{A}_{prf}$ *such that*

$$\mathbf{Adv}_{\mathrm{N}^*}^{\text{mr-s-rka-AE}}(\mathcal{A}, \Phi_{ae}) \leq \mathbf{Adv}_{\Gamma}^{\text{rkaSUF}}(\mathcal{A}_{mac}, \Phi_m) + \mathbf{Adv}_{\Sigma}^{\text{rkaPRP}}(\mathcal{A}_{prp}, \Phi_e) + \mathbf{Adv}_{\text{Tag}}^{\text{rkaPRF}}(\mathcal{A}_{prf}, \Phi_m) + \frac{2q^2}{2^c}.$$

Proof. Game G_0 in Fig. 9 is the mr-s-rka-AE security game instantiated with N* and secret bit $b = 0$ and game G_5 is the mr-s-rka-AE security game with $b = 1$. To estimate the security of N*, four additional games G_1, G_2, G_3, and G_4 are needed. Starting with mr-s-rka-AE with $b = 0$ (G_0), we modify the intermediate games as follows: In game G_1 the decryption always outputs $\perp$ except if the resulting message was sent to the encryption oracle with the same N, A, and φ_m before. In G_2, the underlying encryption scheme is replaced by a random permutation. In G_3, the decryption oracle always outputs $\perp$. In G_4, the Tag

[7] One solution would be to use the key derivation technique proposed in [7]. However, this requires the usage of an additional PRF on top of the existing AE scheme.

algorithm is replaced by a random function. Finally, in game G_5, the encryption oracle ignores the input, and outputs a uniform random cipher C as in mr-s-rka-AE with $b = 1$. With $\mathbf{Adv}^{\text{mr-s-rka-AE}}_{\text{N*}}(\mathcal{A}, \Phi_{ae}) \leq \mathbf{Adv}(\mathcal{A}^{\mathsf{G}_0}, \mathcal{A}^{\mathsf{G}_5})$ and $\mathbf{Adv}(\mathcal{A}^{\mathsf{G}_0}, \mathcal{A}^{\mathsf{G}_5}) \leq \sum_{i=0}^{4} \mathbf{Adv}(\mathcal{A}^{\mathsf{G}_i}, \mathcal{A}^{\mathsf{G}_{i+1}})$, Claim 15–19 conclude the proof. □

```
Game G_i
  (K_e, K_m) <-$ K
  T <- ∅
  F <-$ Func(K_m, N × A × M, {0,1}^t)
  P <-$ Perm(K_e, {0,1}^c)
  b' <- A^{Enc,Dec}()

Enc(N, A, M, (φ_e, φ_m)) in G0, G1
  T <- Tag(φ_m(K_m), N, A, M)
  C <- Enc(φ_e(K_e), M || T)
  T <-∪ {(N, A, C, (φ_e, φ_m))}
  return C

Enc(N, A, M, (φ_e, φ_m)) in G2, G3
  T <- Tag(φ_m(K_m), N, A, M)
  f[N, A, φ_m] <-∪ {(M, T)}
  C <- P(φ_e(K_e), M || T)
  T <-∪ {(N, A, C, (φ_e, φ_m))}
  return C

Enc(N, A, M, (φ_e, φ_m)) in G4
  T <- F(φ_m(K_m), N, A, M)
  return C <- P(φ_e(K_e), M || T)

Enc(N, A, M, (φ_e, φ_m)) in G5
  return C <-$ {0,1}^c

Dec(N, A, C, (φ_e, φ_m)) in G0
  if (N, A, C, (φ_e, φ_m)) ∈ T
    return ⊥
  M || T <- Dec(φ_e(K_e), C)
  V <- Ver(φ_m(K_m), N, A, M, T)
  if V = ⊥
    return ⊥
  return M

Dec(N, A, C, (φ_e, φ_m)) in G1
  if (N, A, C', (φ'_e, φ_m)) ∈ T with φ_e ≠ φ'_e
    if Dec(φ_e(K_e), C) = Dec(φ'_e(K_e), C')
      (M || T) <- Dec(φ'_e(K_e), C')
      return M
  return ⊥

Dec(N, A, C, (φ_e, φ_m)) in G2
  if (N, A, C', (φ'_e, φ_m)) ∈ T with φ_e ≠ φ'_e
    for (M, T) ∈ f[N, A, φ_m]
      if C = P(φ_e(K_e), M || T))
      return M
  return ⊥

Dec(N, A, C, (φ_e, φ_m)) in G3, G4, G5
  return ⊥
```

Fig. 9. Hybrid games G_i used to prove Theorem 14.

Claim 15. *For any Φ_{ae}-restricted RKA distinguisher $\mathcal{A}$ between game G_0 and G_1 defined in Fig. 9, there exists a Φ_m-restricted RKA adversary $\mathcal{A}_{mac}$ such that*

$$\mathbf{Adv}(\mathcal{A}^{\mathsf{G}_0}, \mathcal{A}^{\mathsf{G}_1}) \leq \mathbf{Adv}^{\mathsf{rkaSUF}}_{\Gamma}(\mathcal{A}_{mac}, \Phi_m).$$

Proof. In the following, an adversary $\mathcal{A}_{mac}$ is given that wins the game with the advantage of $\mathcal{A}$. $\mathcal{A}_{mac}$ simulates the game by using the oracles of the security game rkaSUF to get the tags T for the encryption and to verify T

for the decryption of the N* scheme. Further, $\mathcal{A}_{mac}$ computes the encryption scheme Σ locally with a key K_e chosen uniform at random to simulate the encryption oracle of game G_0 and G_1. $\mathcal{A}_{mac}$ simulates both games perfectly and $\mathcal{A}$ can only distinguish both games if it requests a decryption of a valid ciphertext $(N, A, C, (\varphi_e, \varphi_m))$ with $(M \parallel T) = \mathsf{Dec}(\varphi_e(K_e), N, C)$, such that (N, A, M, T, φ_m) is new and the Tag T is valid. Hence, (N, A, M, φ_m) was not forwarded to the Tag oracle of rkaSUF and $\mathcal{A}_{mac}$ can use this request to win the game rkaSUF by forwarding (N, A, M, T, φ_m) to the verification oracle Ver of rkaSUF, since it was not sent to the oracle Tag of rkaSUF before. Hence, $\mathcal{A}_{mac}$ is a Φ_m-restricted RKA adversary because $\mathcal{A}$ is Φ_{ae}-restricted, and it holds $\Pr[\mathcal{A}^{\mathsf{G}_0} \Rightarrow 0] - \Pr[\mathcal{A}^{\mathsf{G}_1} \Rightarrow 0] \leq \Pr[\mathcal{A}_{mac}^{\mathsf{rkaSUF}} \Rightarrow 0 \,|\, b = 0] - \Pr[\mathcal{A}_{mac}^{\mathsf{rkaSUF}} \Rightarrow 0 \,|\, b = 1]$, and therefore $\mathbf{Adv}(\mathcal{A}^{\mathsf{G}_0}, \mathcal{A}^{\mathsf{G}_1}) \leq \mathbf{Adv}_{\Gamma}^{\mathsf{rkaSUF}}(\mathcal{A}_{mac}, \Phi_m)$. □

Claim 16. *For any Φ_{ae}-restricted RKA distinguisher $\mathcal{A}$ between game G_1 and G_2 defined in Fig. 9, there exists an Φ_e-restricted RKA adversary $\mathcal{A}_{prp}$ such that*

$$\mathbf{Adv}(\mathcal{A}^{\mathsf{G}_1}, \mathcal{A}^{\mathsf{G}_2}) \leq \mathbf{Adv}_{\Sigma}^{\mathsf{rkaPRP}}(\mathcal{A}_{prp}, \Phi_e).$$

Proof. Before we describe the simulator, we transform G_1 to G_1' to avoid that we need to query the inverse of the oracle F in rkaPRP. In G_1'[8] we replace the underling decryption function with the encryption function in such a way that the input/output behaviour of G_1 and G_1' is still the same.

$\mathsf{Dec}(N, A, C, (\varphi_e, \varphi_m))$ in G_1'	$\mathsf{Enc}(N, A, M, (\varphi_e, \varphi_m))$ in G_1'
if $(N, A, C', (\varphi_e', \varphi_m)) \in \mathcal{T}$ *with* $\varphi_e \neq \varphi_e'$	$T \leftarrow \mathsf{Tag}(\varphi_m(K_m), N, A, M)$
for $(M, T) \in f[N, A, \varphi_m]$	$C \leftarrow \mathsf{Enc}(\varphi_e(K_e), N, M \parallel T)$
if $C = \mathsf{Enc}(\varphi_e'(K_e), N, M \parallel T)$	$f[N, A, \varphi_m] \leftarrow_{\cup} \{(M, T)\}$
return M	$\mathcal{T} \leftarrow_{\cup} \{(N, A, C, (\varphi_e, \varphi_m))\}$
return $\perp$	**return** C

In G_1 the decryption oracle only returns the decrypted message M if M was sent to the encryption oracle before. Since the underlying **Enc** is deterministic, we can also save the queries to the encryption oracles in f and test if it encrypts to C as we do in the decryption oracle of G_1'. Hence, it holds that the games are identical and it is enough to show that $\mathbf{Adv}(\mathcal{A}^{\mathsf{G}_1'}, \mathcal{A}^{\mathsf{G}_2}) \leq \mathbf{Adv}_{\Sigma}^{\mathsf{rkaPRP}}(\mathcal{A}_{prp}, \Phi_e)$. We construct an adversary $\mathcal{A}_{prp}$ simulating G_1' and G_2 by computing the MAC locally with a uniform random key K_m and using oracle F of rkaPRP for the encryption. $\mathcal{A}_{prp}$ is Φ_e-restricted because $\mathcal{A}$ is Φ_{ae}-restricted. Hence, $\mathcal{A}_{prp}$ perfectly simulates G_1' if the challenge bit of rkaPRP is 0, and G_2 if the challenge bit is 1. It holds $\mathbf{Adv}(\mathcal{A}^{\mathsf{G}_1}, \mathcal{A}^{\mathsf{G}_2}) = \mathbf{Adv}(\mathcal{A}^{\mathsf{G}_1'}, \mathcal{A}^{\mathsf{G}_2}) \leq \mathbf{Adv}_{\Sigma}^{\mathsf{rkaPRP}}(\mathcal{A}_{prp}, \Phi_e)$. □

Claim 17. *For any Φ_{ae}-restricted RKA distinguisher $\mathcal{A}$ with q queries between game G_2 and G_3 defined in Fig. 9, it holds*

$$\mathbf{Adv}(\mathcal{A}^{\mathsf{G}_2}, \mathcal{A}^{\mathsf{G}_3}) \leq \frac{q^2}{2^c}.$$

[8] This transformation allows us to use a normal PRP for the simulation, and not a strong PRP.

Proof. Both games only differ if $\mathcal{A}$ asks for a decryption of a cipher text C which maps to a message which was already encrypted with the same (N, A, φ_m). Since the underlying encryption is a random permutation this collision happens with probability less then $\frac{q^2-q}{2^c}$. In detail $\mathcal{A}$ makes q_e queries to the encryption oracle, and q_d queries to the decryption oracle with $q_e + q_d = q$. The collision probability is less then $\frac{q_e}{2^c}$ for each query to the decryption oracle. Hence, the probability to get at least one collision is less then $\frac{q_e q_d}{2^c}$ with q_d queries to the decryption oracle. Hence, $\mathbf{Adv}(\mathcal{A}^{\mathsf{G}_1}, \mathcal{A}^{\mathsf{G}_2}) \leq \frac{q^2}{2^c}$. □

Claim 18. *For any Φ_{ae}-restricted RKA distinguisher $\mathcal{A}$ between game G_3 and G_4 defined in Fig. 9, there exists a Φ_m-restricted RKA adversary $\mathcal{A}_{prf}$ such that*

$$\mathbf{Adv}(\mathcal{A}^{\mathsf{G}_3}, \mathcal{A}^{\mathsf{G}_4}) \leq \mathbf{Adv}^{\mathsf{rkaPRF}}_{\mathsf{Tag}}(\mathcal{A}_{prf}, \Phi_m).$$

Proof. $\mathcal{A}_{prf}$ simulates G_3 and G_4 for $\mathcal{A}$ with the oracles of the security game rkaPRF. For any request $(N, M, A, (\varphi_e, \varphi_m))$ to the oracle Enc, $\mathcal{A}_{prf}$ forwards (N, A, M, φ_m) to the rkaPRF game's oracle F to get the tag T, computes the ciphertext $C \leftarrow \mathtt{Enc}(\varphi_e(K_e), N, M \parallel T)$ locally with a random key K_e, and sends the ciphertext C to $\mathcal{A}$. Since $\mathcal{A}$ is Φ_{ae}-restricted, $\mathcal{A}_{prf}$ is Φ_m-restricted and $\mathcal{A}_{prf}$ perfectly simulates G_{b+3} where b is the challenge bit of game rkaPRF and outputs b' if $\mathcal{A}$ does. It holds that $\Pr[\mathcal{A}^{\mathsf{G}_3} \Rightarrow 0] - \Pr[\mathcal{A}^{\mathsf{G}_4} \Rightarrow 0] \leq \Pr[\mathcal{A}_{prf}^{\mathsf{rkaPRF}} \Rightarrow 0 \,|\, b = 0] - \Pr[\mathcal{A}_{prf}^{\mathsf{rkaPRF}} \Rightarrow 0 \,|\, b = 1]$. Hence, $\mathbf{Adv}(\mathcal{A}^{\mathsf{G}_3}, \mathcal{A}^{\mathsf{G}_4}) \leq \mathbf{Adv}^{\mathsf{rkaPRF}}_{\mathsf{Tag}}(\mathcal{A}_{prf}, \Phi_m)$. □

Claim 19. *For any Φ_{ae}-restricted RKA distinguisher $\mathcal{A}$ between game G_4 and G_5 with q queries to the encryption oracle defined in Fig. 9, it holds*

$$\mathbf{Adv}(\mathcal{A}^{\mathsf{G}_4}, \mathcal{A}^{\mathsf{G}_5}) \leq \frac{q^2}{2^c}.$$

Proof. Both games only differ from the choice of the underlying encryption. Game G_4 uses a random permutation and G_5 generates randomly chosen ciphertexts. Since the adversary is not allowed to query the same tuple $(N, A, M, (\varphi_e, \varphi_m))$ and $\mathtt{F}$ is a real random function, it follows T is fresh and uniform distributed or φ_e is fresh. In case of a fresh φ_e, it follows directly that C is chosen uniformly at random. If φ_e was already used, an adversary can only distinguish both games if it finds a collision in G_5 since G_4 uses a permutation it is not possible to get the same C twice with the same φ_e. The probability for such a collision is less then $\frac{q^2-q}{2^c}$. In detail we know that the probability to get a collision for the ith query is less then $\frac{i-1}{2^c}$ and hence $\mathbf{Adv}(\mathcal{A}^{\mathsf{G}_4}, \mathcal{A}^{\mathsf{G}_5}) \leq \sum_{i=1}^{q} \frac{i-1}{2^c} \leq \frac{q^2}{2^c}$. This proves the claim. □

Similar to the N* construction, we can also use a block cipher (PRP) in the N3 construction to achieve security in the stronger security model. As discussed in the previous section this only works for N3 since the attack on N1 and N2 work independent of the underlying encryption scheme. Further, the security proof for N3 is similar to the proof of Theorem 14, we only have to adapt the block cipher that it also takes the nonce as input. We emphasize that the new construction N* is more efficient then N3, since the block cipher does not receive the nonce as an input. For the instantiation of the block cipher we refer to [5], where the authors construct an RKA-secure PRP using a three-round Feistel construction. The construction contains three RKA-secure PRFs, where the last two PRFs are initialized with the same key. Hence, with Theorem 14, we can build an mr-s-RKA-AE-secure AE scheme out of four RKA-secure PRFs, three to instantiate the block cipher and one for the MAC.

Acknowledgements. This work was funded by the German Research Foundation (DFG) – SFB 1119 – 236615297 and the Emmy Noether Program FA 1320/1-1 of the German Research Foundation (DFG).

References

1. Abdalla, M., Benhamouda, F., Passelègue, A., Paterson, K.G.: Related-key security for pseudorandom functions beyond the linear barrier. J. Cryptol. **31**(4), 917–964 (2018)
2. Aggarwal, D., Agrawal, S., Gupta, D., Maji, H.K., Pandey, O., Prabhakaran, M.: Optimal computational split-state non-malleable codes. In: Kushilevitz, E., Malkin, T. (eds.) TCC 2016, Part II. LNCS, vol. 9563, pp. 393–417. Springer, Heidelberg (2016). https://doi.org/10.1007/978-3-662-49099-0_15
3. Albrecht, M.R., Farshim, P., Paterson, K.G., Watson, G.J.: On cipher-dependent related-key attacks in the ideal-cipher model. In: Joux, A. (ed.) FSE 2011. LNCS, vol. 6733, pp. 128–145. Springer, Heidelberg (2011). https://doi.org/10.1007/978-3-642-21702-9_8
4. Applebaum, B., Harnik, D., Ishai, Y.: Semantic security under related-key attacks and applications. In: ICS (2011)
5. Barbosa, M., Farshim, P.: The related-key analysis of Feistel constructions. In: Cid, C., Rechberger, C. (eds.) FSE 2014. LNCS, vol. 8540, pp. 265–284. Springer, Heidelberg (2015). https://doi.org/10.1007/978-3-662-46706-0_14
6. Bellare, M., Cash, D.: Pseudorandom functions and permutations provably secure against related-key attacks. In: Rabin, T. (ed.) CRYPTO 2010. LNCS, vol. 6223, pp. 666–684. Springer, Heidelberg (2010). https://doi.org/10.1007/978-3-642-14623-7_36
7. Bellare, M., Cash, D., Miller, R.: Cryptography secure against related-key attacks and tampering. In: Lee, D.H., Wang, X. (eds.) ASIACRYPT 2011. LNCS, vol. 7073, pp. 486–503. Springer, Heidelberg (2011). https://doi.org/10.1007/978-3-642-25385-0_26
8. Bellare, M., Kohno, T.: A theoretical treatment of related-key attacks: RKA-PRPs, RKA-PRFs, and applications. In: Biham, E. (ed.) EUROCRYPT 2003. LNCS, vol. 2656, pp. 491–506. Springer, Heidelberg (2003). https://doi.org/10.1007/3-540-39200-9_31
9. Bellare, M., Namprempre, C.: Authenticated encryption: relations among notions and analysis of the generic composition paradigm. In: Okamoto, T. (ed.) ASIACRYPT 2000. LNCS, vol. 1976, pp. 531–545. Springer, Heidelberg (2000). https://doi.org/10.1007/3-540-44448-3_41

10. Bellare, M., Rogaway, P.: The security of triple encryption and a framework for code-based game-playing proofs. In: Vaudenay, S. (ed.) EUROCRYPT 2006. LNCS, vol. 4004, pp. 409–426. Springer, Heidelberg (2006). https://doi.org/10.1007/11761679_25
11. Bernstein, D.J.: CAESAR: competition for authenticated encryption: security, applicability, and robustness (2014)
12. Bhattacharyya, R., Roy, A.: Secure message authentication against related-key attack. In: Moriai, S. (ed.) FSE 2013. LNCS, vol. 8424, pp. 305–324. Springer, Heidelberg (2014). https://doi.org/10.1007/978-3-662-43933-3_16
13. Biham, E.: New types of cryptanalytic attacks using related keys (extended abstract). In: Helleseth, T. (ed.) EUROCRYPT 1993. LNCS, vol. 765, pp. 398–409. Springer, Heidelberg (1994). https://doi.org/10.1007/3-540-48285-7_34
14. Biham, E., Dunkelman, O., Keller, N.: Related-key boomerang and rectangle attacks. In: Cramer, R. (ed.) EUROCRYPT 2005. LNCS, vol. 3494, pp. 507–525. Springer, Heidelberg (2005). https://doi.org/10.1007/11426639_30
15. Biryukov, A., Khovratovich, D.: Related-key cryptanalysis of the full AES-192 and AES-256. In: Matsui, M. (ed.) ASIACRYPT 2009. LNCS, vol. 5912, pp. 1–18. Springer, Heidelberg (2009). https://doi.org/10.1007/978-3-642-10366-7_1
16. Biryukov, A., Khovratovich, D., Nikolić, I.: Distinguisher and related-key attack on the full AES-256. In: Halevi, S. (ed.) CRYPTO 2009. LNCS, vol. 5677, pp. 231–249. Springer, Heidelberg (2009). https://doi.org/10.1007/978-3-642-03356-8_14
17. Boneh, D., DeMillo, R.A., Lipton, R.J.: On the importance of checking cryptographic protocols for faults (extended abstract). In: Fumy, W. (ed.) EUROCRYPT 1997. LNCS, vol. 1233, pp. 37–51. Springer, Heidelberg (1997). https://doi.org/10.1007/3-540-69053-0_4
18. Degabriele, J.P., Janson, C., Struck, P.: Sponges resist leakage: the case of authenticated encryption. In: Galbraith, S.D., Moriai, S. (eds.) ASIACRYPT 2019, Part II. LNCS, vol. 11922, pp. 209–240. Springer, Cham (2019). https://doi.org/10.1007/978-3-030-34621-8_8
19. Dunkelman, O., Keller, N., Kim, J.: Related-key rectangle attack on the full SHACAL-1. In: Biham, E., Youssef, A.M. (eds.) SAC 2006. LNCS, vol. 4356, pp. 28–44. Springer, Heidelberg (2007). https://doi.org/10.1007/978-3-540-74462-7_3
20. Faust, S., Krämer, J., Orlt, M., Struck, P.: On the related-key attack security of authenticated encryption schemes. Cryptology ePrint Archive, Paper 2022/140 (2022)
21. Han, S., Liu, S., Lyu, L.: Efficient KDM-CCA secure public-key encryption for polynomial functions. In: Cheon, J.H., Takagi, T. (eds.) ASIACRYPT 2016, Part II. LNCS, vol. 10032, pp. 307–338. Springer, Heidelberg (2016). https://doi.org/10.1007/978-3-662-53890-6_11
22. Harris, D.G.: Critique of the related-key attack concept. Des. Codes Cryptogr. **59**, 159–168 (2011)
23. Isobe, T.: A single-key attack on the full GOST block cipher. In: Joux, A. (ed.) FSE 2011. LNCS, vol. 6733, pp. 290–305. Springer, Heidelberg (2011). https://doi.org/10.1007/978-3-642-21702-9_17
24. Knudsen, L.R.: Cryptanalysis of LOKI 91. In: Seberry, J., Zheng, Y. (eds.) AUSCRYPT 1992. LNCS, vol. 718, pp. 196–208. Springer, Heidelberg (1993). https://doi.org/10.1007/3-540-57220-1_62
25. Knudsen, L.R., Kohno, T.: Analysis of RMAC. In: Johansson, T. (ed.) FSE 2003. LNCS, vol. 2887, pp. 182–191. Springer, Heidelberg (2003). https://doi.org/10.1007/978-3-540-39887-5_14

26. Kocher, P.C.: Timing attacks on implementations of Diffie-Hellman, RSA, DSS, and other systems. In: Koblitz, N. (ed.) CRYPTO 1996. LNCS, vol. 1109, pp. 104–113. Springer, Heidelberg (1996). https://doi.org/10.1007/3-540-68697-5_9
27. Kocher, P., Jaffe, J., Jun, B.: Differential power analysis. In: Wiener, M. (ed.) CRYPTO 1999. LNCS, vol. 1666, pp. 388–397. Springer, Heidelberg (1999). https://doi.org/10.1007/3-540-48405-1_25
28. Koo, B., Hong, D., Kwon, D.: Related-key attack on the full HIGHT. In: Rhee, K.-H., Nyang, D.H. (eds.) ICISC 2010. LNCS, vol. 6829, pp. 49–67. Springer, Heidelberg (2011). https://doi.org/10.1007/978-3-642-24209-0_4
29. Lu, X., Li, B., Jia, D.: KDM-CCA security from RKA secure authenticated encryption. In: Oswald, E., Fischlin, M. (eds.) EUROCRYPT 2015, Part I. LNCS, vol. 9056, pp. 559–583. Springer, Heidelberg (2015). https://doi.org/10.1007/978-3-662-46800-5_22
30. Namprempre, C., Rogaway, P., Shrimpton, T.: Reconsidering generic composition. In: Nguyen, P.Q., Oswald, E. (eds.) EUROCRYPT 2014. LNCS, vol. 8441, pp. 257–274. Springer, Heidelberg (2014). https://doi.org/10.1007/978-3-642-55220-5_15
31. National Institute of Standards and Technology. Lightweight cryptography standardization process (2015)
32. Rescorla, E.: the transport layer security (TLS) protocol version 1.3. RFC 8446 (2018)
33. Rogaway, P.: Authenticated-encryption with associated-data. In: ACM CCS 2002 (2002)
34. Rogaway, P.: Nonce-based symmetric encryption. In: Roy, B., Meier, W. (eds.) FSE 2004. LNCS, vol. 3017, pp. 348–358. Springer, Heidelberg (2004). https://doi.org/10.1007/978-3-540-25937-4_22
35. Rogaway, P., Shrimpton, T.: A provable-security treatment of the key-wrap problem. In: Vaudenay, S. (ed.) EUROCRYPT 2006. LNCS, vol. 4004, pp. 373–390. Springer, Heidelberg (2006). https://doi.org/10.1007/11761679_23
36. Vaudenay, S.: Clever arbiters versus malicious adversaries - on the gap between known-input security and chosen-input security. In: Ryan, P.Y.A., Naccache, D., Quisquater, J.-J. (eds.) The New Codebreakers. LNCS, vol. 9100, pp. 497–517. Springer, Heidelberg (2016). https://doi.org/10.1007/978-3-662-49301-4_31
37. Xagawa, K.: Message authentication codes secure against additively related-key attacks. Cryptology ePrint Archive, Report 2013/111 (2013)

The State of the Union: Union-Only Signatures for Data Aggregation

Diego F. Aranha[1], Felix Engelmann[2](✉), Sebastian Kolby[1], and Sophia Yakoubov[1]

[1] Department of Computer Science, Aarhus University, Aarhus, Denmark
{dfaranha,sk,sophia.yakoubov}@cs.au.dk
[2] IT University of Copenhagen, Copenhagen, Denmark
fe-research@nlogn.org

Abstract. A *union-only signature (UOS) scheme* (informally introduced by Johnson *et al.* at CT-RSA 2002) allows signers to sign sets of messages in such a way that (1) any third party can merge two signatures to derive a signature on the union of the message sets, and (2) no adversary, given a signature on some set, can derive a valid signature on any strict subset of that set (unless it has seen such a signature already).

Johnson *et al.* originally posed building a UOS as an open problem. In this paper, we make two contributions: we give the first formal definition of a UOS scheme, and we give the first UOS constructions. Our main construction uses hashing, regular digital signatures, Pedersen commitments and signatures of knowledge. We provide an implementation that demonstrates its practicality. Our main construction also relies on the hardness of the short integer solution (SIS) problem; we show how that this assumption can be replaced with the use of groups of unknown order. Finally, we sketch a UOS construction using SNARKs; this additionally gives the property that the size of the signature does not grow with the number of merges. (A full version of this paper, with all proofs and preliminaries, is available on the ePrint Archive).

Keywords: homomorphic signatures · union-only signature schemes · history-hiding · software implementation

1 Introduction

A set-homomorphic digital signature is a signature scheme which supports the computation of set operations—for example union and difference—over signed messages. Let $\mathsf{Sign}(\mathsf{sk}, M)$ be the signing operation for such a signature scheme, for some private signing key sk and a set of messages M.

For sets of messages $X = \{x_1, \ldots, x_k\}$ and $Y = \{y_1, \ldots, y_n\}$ which were signed as $\mathsf{Sign}(\mathsf{sk}, X)$ and $\mathsf{Sign}(\mathsf{sk}, Y)$, any third party can compute the signature on their union as $\mathsf{Sign}(\mathsf{sk}, X) \times \mathsf{Sign}(\mathsf{sk}, Y)$ (we use $\times$ to denote the homomorphic union operation). If the homomorphic operation $\times$ is invertible, and $X \subseteq Y$, one

C. Galdi and S. Jarecki (Eds.): SCN 2022, LNCS 13409, pp. 387–410, 2022.
https://doi.org/10.1007/978-3-031-14791-3_17

can also compute the signature on their difference $\mathsf{Sign}(\mathsf{sk}, X \setminus Y) = \mathsf{Sign}(\mathsf{sk}, X) \times \mathsf{Sign}(\mathsf{sk}, Y)^{-1}$. The notion was initially introduced by Johnson *et al.* [15], together with a practical construction based on RSA accumulators, but there are instantiations based on hardness assumptions other than integer factorization [1,16].

A union-only signature (UOS) scheme is a special case of a set-homomorphic signature scheme where the homomorphic operation is *not* invertible (that is, it is one-way). In a UOS scheme, computing a signature on a set of messages is *easy* given signatures on subsets of those messages, but computing the signature on the difference of two sets (the inverse operation) is *hard*. Constructing union-only signatures was first posed as an open problem in the seminal work of Johnson *et al.* [15]. Because previous set-homomorphic constructions represent signatures as multiplicative structures (rings and multiplicative groups), computing the difference operation amounts to inverting elements in such structures, which can be done efficiently. For this reason, building a UOS based on those constructions is challenging, and implies the existence of groups with infeasible inversion (GIIs) [19], a powerful algebraic structure that further implies strong associative one-way functions [22], efficient two-party secret key agreement protocols, and direct transitive signatures [14]. In a GII, computing the inverse of a group element is required to be *hard*, while performing the group operation is computationally efficient. While GIIs are not known to exist, there are recent candidate constructions based on self-bilinear maps assuming indistinguishability obfuscation [24] and isogeny graphs [5].

Contributions. In this paper, we make two contributions. First, we take the opportunity to formalize the definition of a secure UOS scheme. Second, we present two constructions which circumvent the roadblock described above by choosing the signature format to *not* have a multiplicative structure. Our first construction is based on hashing, Schnorr signatures, Pedersen commitments and signatures of knowledge instantiated with elliptic curves. It also relies on the hardness of the short integer solution (SIS) problem [3,18]. We show how to replace this assumption with the use of groups of unknown order in a variant. A second construction based on SNARKs appears in the full version of this paper.

All of our constructions support multiple signers and offer a notion of *privacy* which precludes an adversary from learning how the signatures were derived (i.e., which subsets were actually signed by the signer, and which order the signatures were merged in). The first construction performs much better, so we explore it in detail; the SNARK-based construction produces constant-size signatures, offering a trade-off between performance and compactness.

In our first construction, we employ *multisets*; we design a scheme that preserves duplicates in the intersection of the merged sets instead of removing them, which technically makes it homomorphic with respect to multiset *sum*. However, this naturally coincides with the union operation for disjoint input sets and satisfies the original intuition of UOS given by Johnson *et al.* [15]. From this point on, we abstract this technicality away in the scheme's interface and refer only to the set union operation for simplicity. We provide a proof-of-concept implementation in `Rust` that shows that the construction is indeed *efficient and scalable*.

Applications. To the best of our knowledge, the literature does not contain concrete applications specific to UOS schemes. We devise application scenarios considering a minimum of 4 parties:

Signer(s): Assumed to be *honest*, one or more **Signers** sign(s) sets of messages with their signing keys, and make them available to a **Merger**. Importantly, signatures over sets containing individual messages should not be publicly available; otherwise, a third party (e.g. **Prover**) can remove them from a merged signature simply by re-executing the merge on all the *other* signatures.

Merger: A **Merger** merges signatures following a public procedure and forwards the resulting signature to a **Prover**. The merger must be independent of the signer(s), and is trusted only to discard the merge history (when hiding the history is desirable for privacy reasons).

Prover: A **Prover** trusts the public key(s) belonging to the **Signer(s)**, and therefore can be convinced that signatures are valid. It attempts to convince a **Verifier** that all relevant messages are included in the merged signature provided by the **Merger**.

Verifier: A **Verifier** verifies the signature and wants to check that the prover did not exclude any messages from the set.

Figure 1 illustrates the workflow. In terms of incentives, signers want to publish their signed messages for credibility or to achieve some common goal. They do not trust each other unconditionally (e.g. they still want privacy against one another) and thus have their own key pairs. Signatures are merged by the merger, and used by the prover to convince external parties (verifiers) that uncomfortable messages or data points were not omitted on purpose.

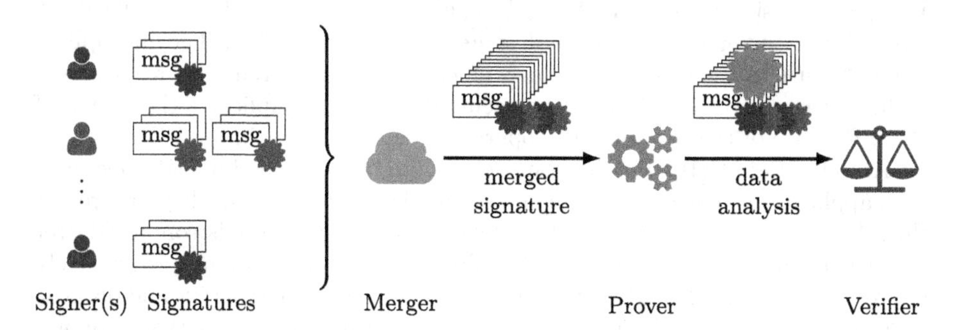

Fig. 1. Application scenario illustrating how authenticated data flows from Signer(s) to the interaction between Prover and Verifier, after being merged by the Merger.

The general framework motivates a few scenarios. In epidemiology studies, healthcare providers sign patient medical records (e.g. containing vaccination or infection information) that are of interest to researchers. An independent government entity merges the medical records from multiple providers, with an incentive to have as many as possible for credibility, even if specific data points are not desirable. In this case, the government does not have a trusted signing key to include new authenticated records (otherwise, we could imagine the government using this key to inflate the number of records). Researchers can then perform statistical analysis of the records and verifiably convince the public that all data points available were taken into consideration to reach the conclusions. Privacy guarantees are important to prevent the public from matching certain patient data to a given healthcare provider, increasing their chances of de-anonymizing the patient in question.

In a biodiversity setting, databases are jointly built[1] by multiple curators contributing data points (e.g. wildlife sightings for species in danger of extinction). The database infrastructure merges the individual datasets with an incentive to have as much data as possible available to researchers, who can then analyse records and provide guarantees to the public that all data was considered. We argue that privacy guarantees are important to collect data and perform impactful research in these domains, as to prevent the public from being able to track down and further jeopardize endangered species.

Related Work. Homomorphic signatures were initially proposed by Johnson *et al.* [15]. Many possibilities for the homomorphic operation were developed in the literature [7,10,11,23], but the original paper already gave constructions for redactable and set-homomorphic signatures. For the latter, assume that N is an RSA modulus for which only the signer knows the factorization $\mathsf{sk} = (p, q)$. For $X = \{x_1, \ldots, x_k\}$, define $\mathsf{Sign}(\mathsf{sk}, X) = v^{1/d} \bmod N$ for random $v \in \mathbb{Z}_N^*$ and a hash function $h(\cdot)$ that maps elements to a set of primes and $d = \prod_{i=0}^{k} h(x_i)$. Given a signature σ on X, one can compute a signature on a subset $X \backslash \{x_i\}$ by computing $\sigma^{h(x_i)} \bmod N$. For d, X as above and $Y = \{y_1, \ldots, y_n\}$, $e = \prod_{j=0}^{n} h(y_j)$, a signature on $X \cup Y$ can be computed as $v^{1/lcm(d,e)} = (v^{1/d})^a (v^{1/e})^b \bmod N$ with integers (a, b) such that $ae + bd = GCD(d, e)$. The multiplicative structure of the signatures allows efficient union/difference by respectively adding/removing elements from the accumulator, but complicates the design of UOS. Because of the set difference operation, this does *not* imply UOS.

Abiteboul *et al.* [1] study homomorphic signatures for modifiable collections, with applications to access control and secure data aggregation. They first recast the scheme above as *delete-only*, for which an initial signature is computed over the entire universe of elements and individual elements can be progressively removed. They also give privacy definitions in a single-signer context and propose an *insert-only* signature scheme satisfying computational privacy that supports both insertion of individual elements and computation of a set intersection. The scheme is constructed from a cryptographically-enforced "write-only" memory and the delete-only scheme as building blocks, and imposes an upper bound on the collection size, forcing a key refresh when the limit is reached. Additional constructions based on zero-knowledge proofs are given for both delete- and insert-only schemes, but without privacy claims.

[1] Global Biodiversity Information Facility: https://www.gbif.org/.

Kaaniche *et al.* [16] propose pairing-based set-homomorphic signatures supporting union, difference and intersection for secure data aggregation within the Internet of Things. The construction builds on efficient accumulators from bilinear maps instead of RSA accumulators. Privacy is informally defined as the adversary not being able to link signatures to signers or to detect removed content. In terms of performance, pairing-based schemes rely on rather special pairing-friendly curves, which are known to be less efficient than plain elliptic curves due to their larger parameters [8].

A generalized notion introduced by Ahn et al. in [2] is *P-homomorphic* signatures, in which anyone can derive a signature for a message m' from the signatures of a set of messages M as long as the predicate $P(M, m')$ holds. The paper puts forward not only the abstract notion, but also a few concrete constructions for fixed predicates, including string subset. Many homomorphic, transitive and redactable signature schemes can be recast under this notion, but it is not clear how to extend such constructions for the union-only predicate efficiently. Another related notion is *mergeable* signatures [20,21], which are defined for redactable signature schemes which allow a subset operation by design. A construction based on signed RSA accumulators is also given, together with applications such as merging databases while redacting specific entries.

A last related notion is that of extendable threshold ring signatures [6], where signatures can be thought of as homomorphic with respect to the set of signers (i.e., given a message signed by an anonymous subset of a set of signers, new signers can contribute their support and potentially expand the anonymity set). However, extendable threshold ring signatures do not offer any homomorphism when it comes to the message in question. They also offer a very different notion of privacy: they protect the identities of the signers, while our history-hiding property protects the history and origins of the message set.

The schemes discussed previously do not satisfy the UOS requirement of allowing union of messages as the only homomorphic operation, since they support deletion and/or set intersection, or operate over the set of signers.

Organization. The paper is organized as follows. Section 2 defines the syntax for UOS, and Sect. 3 defines the desired security notions. Section 4 presents our main and most efficient construction. The experimental results supporting our efficiency claims are discussed in Sect. 5, followed by the conclusion. An interested reader can find our SNARK-based construction in the full version of this paper.

2 Syntax

As described above, in a UOS scheme, signers sign *sets* of messages, and any third party can merge signatures on such sets.

Definition 1 (Union-only Signature Scheme). *A* $\mathsf{UOS} = (\mathsf{Setup}, \mathsf{KeyGen}, \mathsf{Sign}, \mathsf{Merge}, \mathsf{Verify})$ *consists of five algorithms with the following syntax:*

$\mathsf{Setup}(1^\lambda) \rightarrow \mathsf{p}$ *takes the security parameter* λ *and outputs public parameters* p *which are implicitly given to all algorithms.*

$\mathsf{KeyGen}() \rightarrow (\mathsf{pk}, \mathsf{sk})$ *generates a public-secret key pair.*
$\mathsf{Sign}(\mathsf{sk}, M) \rightarrow \sigma$ *takes a secret key* sk *and a set of messages* M*. Outputs a signature* σ*.*
$\mathsf{Merge}(\{(\sigma_i, M_i, PK_i)\}_{i=1}^{\mu}) \rightarrow \sigma$ *takes a set of* μ *tuples, where each tuple consists of a set of messages* M_i*, a signature* σ_i *and a set public keys* PK_i*. Outputs a new signature* σ *(which should verify for the message set* $M = \cup_{i=1}^{\mu} M_i$ *under the public key set* $PK = \cup_{i=1}^{\mu} PK_i$*).*
$\mathsf{Verify}(\sigma, M, PK) \rightarrow \{\texttt{accept}, \texttt{reject}\}$ *takes a signature* σ*, a set of messages* M *and a set of public keys* PK*, and outputs either* `accept` *or* `reject`*.*

These algorithms should satisfy the natural notion of correctness; that is, the output of any sequence of honestly executed Sign *and* Merge *operations should be a verifying signature. They should also satisfy Definition 4 and Definition 3, described in Sect. 3.*

3 Security Definitions

We require two properties of a UOS: *unforgeability* and *history-hiding*. Informally, unforgeability demands that an adversary not be able to sign on behalf of a set of signers none of whom are corrupt. History-hiding demands that an adversary not be able to determine how a given signature was derived.

3.1 Notation

We formalise the power of the adversary through four oracles, with access to some common state, described in Fig. 4. The first three oracles provide bookkeeping of identities: $\mathsf{KeyGen}\mathcal{O}$ adds a new honest party to the system, while $\mathsf{Corrupt}\mathcal{O}$ corrupts an existing party, and $\mathsf{RegKey}\mathcal{O}$ registers a new corrupt party. The keys in the system are stored by the oracles in a list L_K; the indices corresponding to honest and corrupt parties in the key list are tracked in the sets H and C respectively.

The final oracle we define is the signing oracle, denoted $\mathsf{Merge}\mathcal{O}$. It takes a sequence of sign and merge operations described by the adversary, and outputs the resulting signature. The oracle maintains a set of past queries L_T, and a counter q_s for the number of queries made. For ease of notation, we define a *query tree* T representing the kind of query an adversary can submit to a signing oracle in our security games. (Since a signature can be derived by merging other signatures, our signing oracle takes queries that are more complex than a single message set and the signer the adversary wishes to see a signature from).

In a query tree T, each leaf l represents a signature on a set of messages $l.M$ by signers in $l.PK$. If a leaf does not contain a signature provided by the adversary and $l.PK$ is a singleton containing the public key $\mathsf{pk}_{l.i}$ of an honest signer $l.i$, we call this an honest leaf. The leaves of T may be partitioned into the set of honest leaves $hl(T)$ and the set of corrupt leaves $cl(T)$. Corrupt leaves may have an arbitrary $l.PK$ and can contain a signature provided by the adversary.

The signing oracle $\mathsf{Merge}\mathcal{O}$ only answers queries where corrupt leaves contain verifying signatures. To enforce this we introduce the VerifyLeaves procedure, which checks that all corrupt leaves verify (Fig. 2).

```
VerifyLeaves(T):
  for l ∈ cl(T) do
    if Verify(l.σ, l.M, l.PK) = ⊥ then
      return ⊥
```

Fig. 2. VerifyLeaves. This algorithm checks that all signatures included in a query tree by the adversary verify. It is used in Fig. 4. The set of public keys PK contains all public keys pk_i associated with the tree. Note that. if $l.\sigma$ is not provided, verification will always return $\perp$.

Each internal node n of T represents the signature derived by merging its children. So, each node n has associated message and signer sets $n.M$ and $n.PK$ respectively. These are defined as the union of the corresponding sets across the children of n. We denote the set of signers at the root of the tree as $T.PK$.

When given a query tree T, the challenger signs the appropriate leaves on behalf of the honest signers, and merges the nodes as specified by the tree structure, until it derives the signature associated with the tree root. That signature will be the query answer. The $\mathsf{Merge}\mathcal{O}$ oracle produces signatures following the SignAndMerge procedure, described in Fig. 3. It uses a depth first approach to signing and merging following the structure of the tree T. During the traversal signatures are produced for each honest leaf, while corrupt leaves already contain a signature provided by the adversary. The signatures at leaves are progressively merged towards the root, such that each node contains the signature produced by merging the signatures of its children.

3.2 Unforgeability

We define unforgeability with respect to the security game described in Fig. 6. Informally, we don't want an adversary to be able to forge a signature on behalf of a set of honest signers, as long as that signature is on a set of messages that could not have been obtained through taking unions of message sets on which the signing oracle was queried. To formalize this, we define an *outside span* algorithm (Definition 2, Fig. 5) that determines whether a given set of messages and honest signer identities are outside the span of the set of signing oracle queries.

Definition 2 (Outside span). *We define the predicate*

$$\mathsf{OutsideSpan}(M^*, PK^*, \{(M_i^h, PK_i^h)\}_{i\in[n]})$$

```
SignAndMerge(T, SK):
  Q := {T.root}                                          ▷ new stack
  while ¬Q.isEmpty do
    n := Q.pop()
    if n.isLeaf ∧ n.σ = ∅ then
      n.σ := Sign(sk_{n.i}, n.M)
    else if n.childrenQueued then
      n.σ := Merge({(c.σ, c.M, c.PK)}_{c∈n.children})
    else
      Q.push(n)
      for c ∈ n.children do
        c.childrenQueued := ⊥
        Q.push(c)
      n.childrenQueued := ⊤
  return n.σ
```

Fig. 3. SignAndMerge. The set of secret keys SK contains all honest parties' secret keys sk_i.

for sets of messages and public keys M_i^h, PK_i^h *as*

$$\nexists S \subseteq [n] : \left(M^* = \bigcup_{i \in S} M_i^h\right) \wedge \left(PK^* = \bigcup_{i \in S} PK_i^h\right).$$

This can be efficiently checked as described in the algorithm in Fig. 5.

For instance, imagine that we asked the signing oracle the set of queries $S = \{(\{m_1\}, \{\mathsf{pk}_1\}), (\{m_2\}, \{\mathsf{pk}_2\})\}$; in other words, we requested a signature on m_1 under pk_1, and a signature m_2 under pk_2 from the signing oracle. Then, a signature on $\{m_1, m_2\}$ under $\{\mathsf{pk}_1, \mathsf{pk}_2\}$ should be computable in a UOS scheme; so, it is within the span (in other words, $\mathsf{OutsideSpan}(\{m_1, m_2\}, \{\mathsf{pk}_1, \mathsf{pk}_2\}, S) = \bot$). However, anything which is not computable via union operations is outside the span. As an example, a signature on $\{m_1, m_2\}$ under pk_1 alone should not be computable (so, $\mathsf{OutsideSpan}(\{m_1, m_2\}, \{\mathsf{pk}_1\}, S) = \top$). A signature on $\{m_1, m_2, m_3\}$ under $\{\mathsf{pk}_1, \mathsf{pk}_2\}$ should also not be computable (so, $\mathsf{OutsideSpan}(\{m_1, m_2, m_3\}, \{\mathsf{pk}_1, \mathsf{pk}_2\}, S) = \top$).

Definition 3 (Unforgeability). *A UOS scheme is* unforgeable *if for all PPT adversaries* $\mathcal{A}$ *it holds that*

$$|\Pr[\mathcal{A} \textit{ wins } \mathrm{EUF}(\lambda)]| \leq \mathsf{negl}(\lambda)$$

with the game EUF defined in Fig. 6.

3.3 History Hiding

We define history-hiding for UOS schemes to require that no adversary can tell the difference between signatures on trees which are "similar enough". We leave

$\mathsf{KeyGen}\mathcal{O}(i)$	$\mathsf{RegKey}\mathcal{O}(i, \mathsf{pk}_i)$
1 : **if** $(i, \cdot, \cdot) \in \mathsf{L}_K$: **return** $\perp$	1 : **if** $(i, \cdot, \cdot) \in \mathsf{L}_K$: **return** $\perp$
2 : $(\mathsf{pk}_i, \mathsf{sk}_i) \leftarrow \mathsf{KeyGen}()$	2 : $\mathsf{L}_K \leftarrow \mathsf{L}_K \cup \{(i, \mathsf{pk}_i, \perp)\}$
3 : $\mathsf{L}_K \leftarrow \mathsf{L}_K \cup \{(i, \mathsf{pk}_i, \mathsf{sk}_i)\}$	3 : $C \leftarrow C \cup \{i\}$
4 : $H \leftarrow H \cup \{i\}$	$\mathsf{Merge}\mathcal{O}(T_j)$
5 : **return** pk_i	1 : $q_s \leftarrow q_s + 1$
$\mathsf{Corrupt}\mathcal{O}(i)$	2 : $\mathsf{L}_T \leftarrow \mathsf{L}_T \cup \{(q_s, T_j)\}$
1 : **if** $(i, \cdot, \cdot) \notin \mathsf{L}_K$: **return** $\perp$	3 : **if** $(T_j.PK \not\subset \{\mathsf{pk}_i \mid i \in H \cup C\}) \vee$
2 : **retrieve** $(i, \mathsf{pk}_i, \mathsf{sk}_i)$ **from** L_K	$(\mathsf{VerifyLeaves}(T_j) = \perp)$:
3 : $H \leftarrow H \setminus \{i\}$	4 : **return** $\perp$
4 : $C \leftarrow C \cup \{i\}$	5 : $\sigma_j \leftarrow \mathsf{SignAndMerge}(T_j, \{\mathsf{sk}_i \mid i \in H\})$
5 : **return** sk_i	6 : **return** σ_j

Fig. 4. Oracles for key generation, signing and corruption, used in the Unforgeability and History Hiding games.

$\mathsf{OutsideSpan}(M^*, PK^*, \{(M_i, PK_i)\}_{i=1}^{\mu})$

$S := \{i \in [n] \mid (M_i \setminus M^* = \emptyset) \wedge (PK_i \setminus PK^* = \emptyset)\}$

$M := \bigcup_{i \in S} M_i$

$PK := \bigcup_{i \in S} PK_i$

return $\neg((M^* = M) \wedge (PK^* = PK))$

Fig. 5. OutsideSpan

the definition of "similar enough" as a parameter of the history-hiding property, formalized as an equivalence relation $\equiv_T$. We describe two options for $\equiv_T$ here.

$\equiv_{strong}$: This equivalence relation deems two trees T_0 and T_1 equivalent if the union of their leaf message sets, and the union of their leaf identities, are the same.

$\equiv_{weak}$: This equivalence relation deems two trees T_0 and T_1 equivalent if:
1. The set of corrupt leaves on the two trees are the same.
2. The number of leaves per honest signer is equal.
3. The multiset union of the *honest* leaf message sets are equal.

The use of both these relations within the history-hiding definition demands that honest signers who contribute signatures to a merged signature cannot be linked to a specific subset of the signed messages, even in the presence of malicious signers. The use of $\equiv_{strong}$ additionally demands that even corrupt parties cannot be linked to a specific subset of messages.

$\text{EUF}(\lambda)$

1: $H \leftarrow \emptyset;\ C \leftarrow \emptyset;\ \mathsf{L}_K \leftarrow \emptyset;\ \mathsf{L}_T \leftarrow \emptyset; q_s \leftarrow 0$
2: $\mathsf{p} \leftarrow \mathsf{Setup}(1^\lambda)$
3: $\mathcal{O} \leftarrow \{\mathsf{KeyGen}\mathcal{O}, \mathsf{Corrupt}\mathcal{O}, \mathsf{RegKey}\mathcal{O}, \mathsf{Merge}\mathcal{O}\}$
4: $(\sigma^*, M^*, PK^*) \leftarrow \mathcal{A}^{\mathcal{O}}(\mathsf{p})$
5: **for** $(\cdot, T_j) \in \mathsf{L}_T$:
6: $\quad PK_j^h := \{\mathsf{pk}_{l.i}\}_{l \in hl(T_j)}$
7: $\quad M_j^h := \bigcup_{l \in hl(T_j)} l.M$
8: **if** $\mathsf{Verify}(\sigma^*, M^*, PK^*) = \bot : \mathcal{A}$ *loses*
9: **if** $\mathsf{OutsideSpan}(M^*, PK^*, \{(M_j^h, PK_j^h)\}_{j=1}^{q_s}) = \bot$:
10: $\quad \mathcal{A}$ *loses*
11: **if** $PK^* \setminus \{\mathsf{pk}_i\}_{i \in H} \neq \emptyset : \mathcal{A}$ *loses*
12: **else** $\mathcal{A}$ *wins*

Fig. 6. The Unforgeability Game

$\text{HH}_b(\lambda)$

1: $H \leftarrow \emptyset;\ C \leftarrow \emptyset;\ \mathsf{L}_K \leftarrow \emptyset;\ \mathsf{L}_T \leftarrow \emptyset; q_s \leftarrow 0$
2: $\mathsf{p} \leftarrow \mathsf{Setup}(1^\lambda)$
3: $\mathcal{O} \leftarrow \{\mathsf{KeyGen}\mathcal{O}, \mathsf{Corrupt}\mathcal{O}, \mathsf{RegKey}\mathcal{O}, \mathsf{Merge}\mathcal{O}\}$
4: $(T_0, T_1, \mathsf{aux}) \leftarrow \mathcal{A}_1^{\mathcal{O}}(\mathsf{p})$
5: **if** $\mathsf{VerifyLeaves}(T_0, T_0.PK) = \bot : \mathcal{A}$ *loses*
6: **if** $\mathsf{VerifyLeaves}(T_1, T_1.PK) = \bot : \mathcal{A}$ *loses*
7: $\sigma_b \leftarrow \mathsf{SignAndMerge}(T_b)$
8: $b' \leftarrow \mathcal{A}_2^{\mathcal{O}}(\sigma_b, \mathsf{aux})$
9: **if** $\neg(T_0 \equiv_T T_1) : \mathcal{A}$ *loses*
10: **if** $b \neq b' : \mathcal{A}$ *loses*
11: **else** $\mathcal{A}$ *wins*

Fig. 7. The History-Hiding Game

Definition 4 (History Hiding). *A UOS scheme is* history-hiding *with respect to equivalence relation* $\equiv_T$ *if for all PPT adversaries* $\mathcal{A} = \{\mathcal{A}_1, \mathcal{A}_2\}$ *it holds that*

$$|\Pr[\mathcal{A} \text{ wins } \text{HH}_0(\lambda)] - \Pr[\mathcal{A} \text{ wins } \text{HH}_1(\lambda)]| \leq \frac{1}{2} + \mathsf{negl}(\lambda)$$

with the game HH_b *defined in Fig. 7.*

Remark 1. Note that the equivalence of the trees ($T_0 \equiv_T T_1$) depends on which signers are corrupt; for that reason, the equivalence check is performed after the adversary (possibly using access to the corruption oracle) produces the bit b'.

4 A UOS Scheme

In this section, we present a concrete UOS scheme. The construction uses signatures, Pedersen commitments and signatures of knowledge. The proof of security additionally uses additive and multiplicative secret sharing, the discrete logarithm assumption, and either the short integer solution (SIS) assumption or groups of unknown order. Formal preliminaries are presented in the full version of this paper; here, we go directly to the construction. We first describe an intuitive construction similar the anonymously aggregatable signature of SwapCT [13] which doesn't quite give us the unforgeability guarantees we would like. We then describe the two ways to obtain those guarantees.

4.1 Initial Construction

When signing a set of messages $\{m_j\}_{j=1}^{\mu}$, the signer assigns each message m_j a random proxy $s_j \in \mathbb{G}$.[2] The signer commits to the proxy as $C_j = G^{s_j} H^{r_j}$, using a freshly chosen random witness r_j. To ensure that the signer knows the commitment opening (i.e. to ensure that she didn't simply copy someone else's commitment without knowing its contents), and to bind the commitment to the message m_j, the signer creates a signature of knowledge π_j of m_j, using s_j and r_j as the witness.

To complete the signature, the signer adds up all of the proxies as $s := \sum_{j=1}^{\mu} s_j$, and commits to s as $D := G^s$. She then signs D using a regular signature scheme Sig, resulting in σ'.

The resulting UOS signature σ contains three parts:

1. The value D and the associated signature σ' (together with the public signature verification key of the signer, for ease of notation). We denote this part of the signature as
$$L = \{(\sigma', D, \mathsf{pk})\}.$$
(We write this as a set to facilitate notation for merging later).
2. The set of messages m_j, commitments C_j and associated signatures of knowledge π_j. We denote this part of the signature as
$$R = \{(\pi_j, C_j, m_j)\}_{j=1}^{\mu}.$$
3. The *sum* $r := \sum_{j=1}^{\mu} r_j$ of all the values r_j used in the commitments.[3]

[2] A signer might want to sign an empty message set, if she is contributing the signature solely for the purposes of expanding the others' anonymity set. If this is the case, and the message set is empty, a placeholder message $\perp$ outside of the message space is added.

[3] If the order of the group $\mathbb{G}$ is known, the sum can be computed modulo that order.

To merge two signatures $\sigma_1 = (L_1, R_1, r_1)$ and $\sigma_2 = (L_2, R_2, r_2)$, any third party can simply compute $\sigma = (L_1 \cup L_2, R_1 \cup R_2, r = r_1 + r_2)$.

Note that the public verification key pk is included in L, and the messages m_j are included in R, even though the public keys and the messages are independently given to verification algorithm. This is done to make clear that a given public key should be used to verify σ' on D, and that a given message corresponds to commitment C_j. This mapping is necessary for verification of $\sigma = (L, R, r)$, during which the verifier checks the following three things:

1. For $(\sigma', D, \mathsf{pk}) \in L$, the signature σ' on D verifies under the key pk.
2. For $(\pi, C, m) \in R$, the signature of knowledge π verifies on the message m for the corresponding statement C.
3. Let $D' = \prod_{(\cdot,D,\cdot)\in L} D$, and $C' = \prod_{(\cdot,C,\cdot)\in R} C$. Then, $H^r D' = C'$.

Informally, we get the weak history hiding property because the items in L correspond to signers and the items in R correspond to messages, but there is nothing to link a given item in L to a given item in R. Unforgeability is a bit trickier to argue. There are several kinds of forgeries we would like to prevent:

1. One where the attacker adds a new value D.
2. One where the attacker uses a subset of D's produced by the honest signers, but changes the set of corresponding C's.

We can rule out the first kind of forgery simply by relying on the unforgeability of the underlying digital signature scheme: the attacker cannot sign a new value D on behalf of any of the honest signers. Within the second kind of forgery, we must consider the case where the attacker uses a strict subset of the honestly produced C's, and the case where the attacker adds new values of C. In the first case, we can use the attacker to find the discrete logarithm relationship between G and H.

However, in the second case, there is a trivial attack—the attacker can add the message m to any signature $\sigma = (L, R, r)$ by (1) choosing r' randomly, (2) choosing $s = 0$ modulo the order of the group $\mathbb{G}$, (3) computing (π, C, m) using those values of s and r', and (4) setting the new signature to be

$$\sigma' = (L, R \cup \{(\pi, C, m)\}, r + r').$$

This new signature will verify, since we have not changed the exponent of G on either side, and have made sure that the exponents of H change consistently on the two sides (by adding r' to r).

We can preclude this kind of attack in one of two ways: by relying on groups of unknown order, or by relying on the hardness of the short integer solution problem. We describe our construction formally in Fig. 8, and informally below.

4.2 Secure Variant from Groups of Unknown Order

If we require that every signature of knowledge π additionally prove that the s contained in the witness is positive, then to carry out the above attack, the

---

Setup(1^λ):

$(\mathbb{G}, q, G) \leftarrow$ GroupGen(1^κ), where κ is the bit-length of the group order q, and G is a generator of $\mathbb{G}$.
Pick a second generator H of $\mathbb{G}$.
for all $k \in [w]$ **do**
    $G_k \xleftarrow{\$} \mathbb{G}, \mathsf{H}_k \xleftarrow{\$} \mathcal{H}$
$\mathbf{crs} \leftarrow \mathsf{SoK}[\mathcal{L}^{\mathsf{ped}}].\mathsf{Setup}(1^\lambda)$
return $\mathsf{p} := (H, G, (G_1, \ldots, G_w), (\mathsf{H}_1, \ldots, \mathsf{H}_w), \mathbf{crs})$

KeyGen():

$(\mathsf{pk}, \mathsf{sk}) \leftarrow \mathsf{Sig.KeyGen}(1^\lambda)$
return $(\mathsf{pk}, \mathsf{sk})$

Sign(sk, $M = \{m_j\}_{j=1}^{\mu}$):

if $\mu = 0$ **then** $\mu := 1$; $m_1 := \perp$
for all $j \in [\mu]$ **do**
    ▷ Let q be the order of $\mathbb{G}$ or $2^{2\kappa}$ chosen such that 2^κ is bigger than the order of $\mathbb{G}$
    $s_j, r_j \xleftarrow{\$} \mathbb{Z}_q$
    $C_j := H^{r_j} G^{s_j}$
    $\pi_j \leftarrow \mathsf{SoK}[\mathcal{L}^{\mathsf{ped}}$ or $\mathcal{L}^{\mathsf{ped}'}].\mathsf{Sign}(\mathsf{x} := C_j, \mathsf{w} := (s_j, r_j), m_j)$
    for all $k \in [w]$ **do** $h_{k,j} := \mathsf{H}_k(C_j)$
$s := \sum_{j=1}^{\mu} s_j \pmod q$
for all $k \in [w]$ **do** $h_k = \sum_{j=1}^{\mu} h_{k,j} \pmod q$
$D := G^s \prod_{k=1}^{w} G_k^{h_k}$
$\sigma' \leftarrow \mathsf{Sig.Sign}(\mathsf{sk}, D)$
$r := \sum_{j=1}^{\mu} r_j \pmod q$
return $\sigma := (\{(\sigma', D, \mathsf{pk})\}, \{(\pi_j, C_j, m_j)\}_{j \in [\mu]}, r)$, where pk is the public key corresponding to sk.

Merge($\{\sigma_i, M_i, PK_i\}_{i=1}^{n}$):

parse σ_i as (L_i, R_i, r_i)
$L := \bigcup_{i \in [n]} L_i, R := \bigcup_{i \in [n]} R_i$
$r := \sum_{i=1}^{n} r_i \pmod q$
return $\sigma := (L, R, r)$ (where sets are represented in lexicographic order to hide how they were formed).

Verify(σ, M, PK):

parse σ as (L, R, r), with $L := \{(\sigma_i', D_i, \mathsf{pk}_i)\}_{i \in [n]}$ and $R := \{(\pi_j, C_j, m_j)\}_{j \in [\mu]}$
if $\{m_j\}_{j \in [\mu]} \neq M$ **then return** 0
if $\{\mathsf{pk}_i\}_{i \in [n]} \neq PK$ **then return** 0
if $C_j = C_{j'}$ for $j \neq j'$ **then return** 0
for all $j \in [\mu]$ **do**
    if $\mathsf{SoK}[\mathcal{L}^{\mathsf{ped}}$ or $\mathcal{L}^{\mathsf{ped}'}].\mathsf{Verify}(\mathsf{x} = C_j, \pi_j, m_j) = 0$ **then return** 0
for all $i \in [n]$ **do**
    if $\mathsf{Sig.Verify}(\sigma_i', D_i, \mathsf{pk}_i) = 0$ **then return** 0
    for all $k \in [w]$ **do** $h_{k,j} := \mathsf{H}_k(C_j)$
return $H^r \prod_{i=1}^{n} D_i = \prod_{j=1}^{\mu} (C_j \prod_{k=1}^{w} G_k^{h_{k,j}})$

Fig. 8. Constructions for UOS. We mark steps only present in the variant based on a group of unknown order in blue; and steps only present in the lattice variant in teal. (Color figure online)

adversary would need to find a (set of) value(s) s whose sum is positive, but *is zero modulo the order of* $\mathbb{G}$. Then, we can use any adversary who can carry out the attack described above to take roots in the group $\mathbb{G}$, which should be hard to do in a group of unknown order. However, using groups of unknown order is very costly in terms of modulus size, since the parameters scale closer to RSA than to elliptic curves [12].

4.3 Secure Variant from Lattices

We could instead make sure that we can use any adversary who carries out the attack described above to solve the *short integer solution* (SIS) problem. We can embed a SIS instance by using several additional generators $G_1, \ldots, G_w$ and several hash functions $\mathsf{H}_1, \ldots, \mathsf{H}_w$, and by modeling each hash function as a random oracle.

During signing, the signer does almost everything as before. However, she additionally computes $h_{k,j} = \mathsf{H}_k(C_j)$ for each $k \in [1, \ldots, w]$ and $j \in [1, \ldots, \mu]$, sets $h_k = \sum_{j=1}^{\mu} h_{k,j}$, and changes D to be $D = G^s \prod_{k=1}^{w} G_k^{h_k}$. The third step of the verification algorithm now consists of checking that

$$H^r \prod_{i=1}^{n} D_i = \prod_{j=1}^{\mu} (C_j G_1^{\mathsf{H}_1(C_j)} \ldots G_w^{\mathsf{H}_w(C_j)}).$$

If an adversary now succeeds in adding new commitments, either we can use her to solve for the discrete logarithm relationship of some of the generators, or we can use her to solve an instance of the SIS problem which we can embed into the hash values (by means of the random oracle assumption).

4.4 Security Analysis

In Fig. 8, we describe our constructions formally.

Theorem 1. *The construction based on lattices described in Fig. 8, including teal steps, is unforgeable (Definition 3) assuming that (a) the* $\mathsf{SIS}(w, m, q, \sqrt{m})$ *problem is hard (where the parameters are* w *hash functions,* m *random oracle queries, and group order* q*), (b) the discrete logarithm problem is hard in for group generation algorithm* GroupGen, *(c) the signature scheme* Sig *is secure, and (d) the signature of knowledge scheme* SoK *is secure.*

We prove Theorem 1 in Sect. 4.4.1.

Theorem 2. *Both variants of the construction described in Fig. 8 are history-hiding (Definition 4) with respect to equivalence relation* $\equiv_{weak}$ *assuming that the signature of knowledge scheme* SoK *is secure.*

We prove Theorem 2 in Sect. 4.4.2.

Theorem 3. *The construction based on groups of unknown order described in Fig. 8, including blue steps, is unforgeable (Definition 3) assuming that (a) the discrete logarithm problem is hard in group* $\mathbb{G}$*, (b) finding roots is hard for group generation algorithm* GroupGen *(as it produces groups off unknown order), (c) the signature scheme* Sig *is secure, and (d) the signature of knowledge scheme* SoK *is secure.*

The proof of Theorem 3 may be found in the full version of this paper.

4.4.1 Proof of Theorem 1

To prove this theorem we rely on reducing to discrete log in the final step. Achieving a tight reduction proves difficult, since if the reduction included the discrete log challenge in any single commitment the adversary would have to exclude that specific commitment while keeping the corresponding left side fixed for it to be possible to solve the challenge. Similarly, trying to embed the challenge in any one leaf of the tree when producing a signature does not yield a tight reduction. To avoid this we must instead take special care to embed the challenge throughout an entire signature.

Lemma 1 shows how a discrete log challenge P may be embedded throughout the values produced by signing while maintaining the same distribution as honestly produced signatures. Given this lemma, we can exploit the properties of additive secret sharing to construct the values we will need for our reduction.

Lemma 1. *Consider the distribution*

$$((D'_1, \ldots, D'_n), ((C_1^1, \ldots C_1^{\mu_1}), \ldots, (C_n^1, \ldots C_n^{\mu_n})), r)$$

where

- P, G *and* H *are generators in a group of prime order* q*,*
- s, t, r *are independent uniformly random values modulo* q*,*
- $D'_i = G^{s_i^{\mathsf{left}}} P^{t_i^{\mathsf{left}}}$ *for additive secret sharings* $\langle s \rangle = (s_i^{\mathsf{left}})_{i \in [n]}$ *and* $\langle t \rangle = (t_i^{\mathsf{left}})_{i \in [n]}$*,*
- $C_i^j = G^{s_{i,j}^{\mathsf{right}}} P^{t_{i,j}^{\mathsf{right}}} H^{r_{i,j}}$ *for fresh additive secret sharings* $(s_i^{\mathsf{right}})_{i \in [n]}$*,* $(t_i^{\mathsf{right}})_{i \in [n]}$ *and* $(r_i)_{i \in [n]}$ *of* s, t *and* r*, with secondary sharings* $\langle s_i^{\mathsf{right}} \rangle = (s_{i,j}^{\mathsf{right}})_{j \in [\mu_j]}$*,* $\langle t_i^{\mathsf{right}} \rangle = (t_{i,j}^{\mathsf{right}})_{j \in [\mu_j]}$ *and* $\langle r_i \rangle = (r_{i,j})_{j \in [\mu_j]}$*.*

Then, the following properties hold:

1. *For any strict subset* $I \subset [n]$*,* $\{t_i^{\mathsf{left}}\}_{i \in I}$ *is independent of* $\{t_{i,j}^{\mathsf{right}}\}_{i \in [n], j \in [\mu_i]}$*.*
2. *For any strict subset* $I \subset \{(i,j) | i \in [n], j \in [\mu_i]\}$*,* $\{t_{i,j}^{\mathsf{right}}\}_{(i,j) \in I}$ *is independent of* $\{t_i^{\mathsf{left}}\}_{i \in [n]}$*.*
3. *The distribution is independent of* t *and the subsequent choices of* $\{t_i^{\mathsf{left}}\}_{i \in [n]}$ *and* $\{t_{i,j}^{\mathsf{right}}\}_{i \in [n], j \in [\mu_i]}$*.*
4. *The distribution conditioned on* t*,* s *and subsequent choices of* $\{t_i^{\mathsf{left}}\}_{i \in [n]}$*,* $\{t_{i,j}^{\mathsf{right}}\}_{i \in [n], j \in [\mu_i]}$ *is independent of the choices of* $\{s_i^{\mathsf{right}}\}_{i \in [n]}$*.*

Note that (3) and (4) imply that the described values would be indistinguishable to those produced by the construction in Fig. 8 (where each D_i *is set to* $D'_i \prod_{j=1}^{\mu_i} G^{\mathsf{H}(C_i^j)}$*). The construction fits the case where all* t_i^{left} *and* $t_{i,j}^{\mathsf{right}}$ *are* 0 *and* $\{s_i^{\mathsf{right}}\}_{i\in[n]} = \{s_i^{\mathsf{left}}\}_{i\in[n]}$.

Proof. We prove the four parts of the lemma separately. First, we note that (1) and (2) follow directly from the properties of additive secret sharing.

(3) follows from the fact that for every fixed value $((D'_1, \ldots, D'_n), ((C_1^1, \ldots C_1^{\mu_1}), \ldots, (C_n^1, \ldots C_n^{\mu_n})), r)$ in the distribution and for every choice of values $\{t_i^{\mathsf{left}}\}_{i\in[n]}$, $\{t_{i,j}^{\mathsf{right}}\}_{i\in[n],j\in[\mu_i]}$ and $\{r_{i,j}\}_{i\in[n],j\in[\mu_i]}$ (consistent with r), there exists a unique choice of values $\{s_i^{\mathsf{left}}\}_{i\in[n]}$ and $\{s_{i,j}^{\mathsf{right}}\}_{i\in[n],j\in[\mu_i]}$ that explains $((D'_1, \ldots, D'_n), ((C_1^1, \ldots C_1^{\mu_1}), \ldots, (C_n^1, \ldots C_n^{\mu_n})), r)$.

(4) follows from the fact that for every fixed t, s, r and subsequent choice of $\{t_{i,j}^{\mathsf{right}}\}_{i\in[n],j\in[\mu_i]}$, for every choice of $\{s_{i,j}^{\mathsf{right}}\}_{i\in[n],j\in[\mu_i]}$ and every set $\{C_i^j\}_{i\in[n],j\in[\mu_i]}$ such that $G^s P^t H^r = \prod_{i\in[n],j\in[\mu_i]} C_i^j$, there exists a unique choice of $\{r_{i,j}\}_{i\in[n],j\in[\mu_i]}$ such that $G^{s_{i,j}^{\mathsf{right}}} P^{t_{i,j}^{\mathsf{right}}} H^{r_{i,j}} = C_i^j$.

Now, we move on to prove Theorem 1.

Proof (of Theorem 1). We reduce the unforgeability of our lattice-based construction to the assumptions enumerated in the theorem. The construction relies on the hardness of the SIS and discrete log problems, as well as the security of the underlying signature scheme and the signature of knowledge scheme.

In the following hybrids we will consider an adversary producing a verifying forgery σ^*, M^*, PK^*, where σ^* is of the form $(L^*, R^*, r^*) = (\{(\sigma_z, D_z, \mathsf{pk}_z)\}_{z=1}^{n^*}, \{(\pi_j, C_j, m_j)\}_{j=1}^{\mu^*}, r^*)$. We define a reduction R in a sequence of hybrids:

1. In this hybrid, the reduction runs the challenger according to the instructions in Fig. 6.
2. In this hybrid, the reduction aborts if it gets a forged (underlying) signature. This hybrid is indistinguishable from the previous one by the unforgeability of the underlying signature scheme.
   At this point, since PK^* must all belong to honest parties, all signatures must be generated by the challenger, allowing us to only consider honestly generated D_z.
3. In this hybrid, the reduction uses a trapdoor to simulate the SoKs.
   This hybrid is indistinguishable from the previous one by the zero knowledge property of the SoK scheme.
4. In this hybrid, the reduction aborts if it cannot extract a witness from any signature of knowledge.
   This hybrid is indistinguishable from the previous one by the simulation extractability of the SoK scheme. At this point the reduction knows a witness for each commitment which is part of a verifying forgery.
5. In the following hybrid the reduction aborts if the adversary provides a verifying forgery where $C_j = G^{s_j} H^{r_j}$ for each $j \in [\mu^*]$, but $r^* \neq \sum_{j=1}^{\mu^*} r_j$.

That is, the reduction aborts if the provided r^* does not correspond appropriately to the witnesses extracted from the sigantures of knowledge.
This is indistinguishable from the previous hybrid as an adversary providing a forgery where this is the case may be used to solve a discrete log challenge H base G.
Each G_k for $k \in [w]$ may be chosen at setup by the reduction as a uniform power of G. Since the forgery is valid, $H^{r^*} \prod_{z=1}^{n^*} D_z = \prod_{j=1}^{\mu^*}(C_j \prod_{k=1}^{w} G_k^{\mathsf{H}_k(C_j)})$ must hold. The reduction knows a witness for each commitment, and the exponents for D_z, which it itself must have produced in response to signing queries. It can then find the discrete logarithm of H, since $r^* - \sum_{j=1}^{\mu^*} r_j \neq 0$.
6. In the following two hybrids we will address the case where the forgery is a valid merging of the outputs of the signing oracle queries, with some extra commitments $C_1, \ldots, C_v$ on the right-hand side. As all other commitments are part of a verifying signature and $r^* = \sum_{j=1}^{\mu^*} r_j$ the extra commitments must not affect the product in the verification formula, i.e. $\prod_{j=1}^{v}(G^{s_j} \prod_{k=1}^{w} G_k^{\mathsf{H}_k(C_j)}) = 1$.
In this hybrid, the reduction will abort if either $\prod_{j=1}^{v} G^{s_j} \neq 1$ or $\prod_{k=1}^{v} G_k^{\mathsf{H}_k(C_j)} \neq 1$ for any $k \in [w]$. In the next hybrid we will exploit the separation of these generators to embed an instance of the SIS problem, where each generator G_k may be used for a separate dimension of the problem. This hybrid is indistinguishable from the previous by a reduction to a discrete log challenge.
For notational convenience, throughout the rest of this hybrid, we will denote G as G_0 and define $s_{0,j} = s_j$ and $s_{k,j} = \mathsf{H}_k(C_j)$. Note the reduction knows both the powers s_j and $\mathsf{H}_k(C_j)$. To find the discrete log of a challenge Y base X the reduction proceeds by first choosing G_k for $k \in [w] \cup \{0\}$ as $X^{a_k} Y^{b_k}$ where a_k and b_k are uniformly random integers modulo q.
For an adversary successfully producing a forgery where $(\prod_{k \in [w] \cup \{0\}} \prod_{j=1}^{v} G_k^{s_{k,j}}) = 1$ but there is an i such that:

$$\prod_{j=1}^{v} G_i^{s_{i,j}} = Z \neq 1, \quad \prod_{\substack{k \in [w] \cup \{0\} \\ k \neq i}} (\prod_{j=1}^{v} G_k^{s_{k,j}}) = Z^{-1} \neq 1,$$

the reduction may find the discrete log with probability at least $1 - 1/\mathrm{q}$. The only case where a discrete log cannot be found is when

$$a_i(\sum_{j=1}^{v} s_{i,j}) = \sum_{\substack{k \in [w] \cup \{0\} \\ k \neq i}} a_k(\sum_{j=1}^{v} s_{k,j}).$$

Consider the distribution of $G_0, \ldots, G_k$ provided to the adversary by the reduction. A fixed G_i may have been produced by any choice of $a_i \in \mathbb{Z}_q$ along with the one possible corresponding b_i, where each of these cases is indistinguishable to the adversary. When all other values are fixed the above equality may only hold for exactly one value of a_i, thus the reduction will only fail to find a discrete log of Y with probability $1/q$.

7. In this hybrid, the reduction embeds an instance of the $\mathsf{SIS}(w, m, q, \sqrt{m})$ problem by programming the random oracle. Recall we are still focusing on the case where the forgery is a valid merge of the outputs of the signing oracle queries, with some extra commitments $C_1, \ldots, C_v$ on the right-hand side. This hybrid now aborts if this is the case.
The indistinguishability of this hybrid from the previous will follow from the hardness of the $\mathsf{SIS}(w, m, q, \sqrt{m})$ problem. For a bound m on the number of random oracle queries made by the adversary, we may consider a uniformly random matrix $\mathbf{A} \in \mathbb{Z}_q^{w \times m}$ provided by an $\mathsf{SIS}(w, m, q, \sqrt{m})$ challenger. We let $\mathbf{A}_{i,j}$ denote the jth entry of the ith row of $\mathbf{A}$.
For each distinct query to the random oracle we may embed one column of the matrix $\mathbf{A}$ in the oracle responses. Specifically, for the ith unique commitment C queried to the random oracle we define $\mathsf{H}_k(C) = \mathbf{A}_{k,i}$ for each $k \in [w]$. The output distribuition of the random oracle is unchanged by this as each entry $\mathbf{A}_{i,j}$ is uniform and independent.
Due to the previous hybrid we know that verification with only extra commitments $C_1, \ldots, C_v$ implies $\prod_{k=1}^{v} G_k^{\mathsf{H}_k(C_j)} = 1$ for all $k \in [w]$. Thus the adversary has provided commitments such that $\sum_{j=1}^{v} \mathsf{H}_k(C_j) = 0 \mod q$ for each $k \in [w]$.
Let $t(j)$ be the index of the first query of C_j to the oracle. The adversary will then have found indices $t(j)$, such that $\sum_{j=1}^{\mu} \mathbf{A}_{k,t(j)} = 0$ for each $k \in [w]$. This provides a solution to the $\mathsf{SIS}(w, m, q, \sqrt{m})$ instance defined by $\mathbf{A}$, as the vector $\mathbf{v}$ which is one exactly for each index in $\{t(j)\}_{j \in [v]}$ and zero otherwise satisfies $\mathbf{A} \cdot \mathbf{v} = \mathbf{0}$. Note $\mathbf{v}$ satisfies the length requirements as each commitment must be unique and the ℓ_2-norm of a zero-one vector of dimension m is bounded by $\sqrt{m}$.
8. In this hybrid, the reduction embeds a discrete log challenge P base G. An adversary breaking the unforgeability of our UOS may be used to find the discrete log with high probability. In this hybrid the H and G_k for $k \in [w]$ are chosen as uniform powers of G. The reduction proceeds as follows:
   (a) For each query to the oracle $\mathsf{Merge}\mathcal{O}(T_i)$, instead of using the $\mathsf{SignAndMerge}$ procedure in Fig. 3 the challenger generates values for the honest leaves following the structure of Lemma 1. This produces $((D_1', \ldots, D_n'), ((C_1^1, \ldots, C_1^{\mu_1}), \ldots, (C_n^1, \ldots, C_n^{\mu_n})), r)$, and the reduction sets $D_i := D_i' \prod_{j=1}^{\mu_i} \prod_{k=1}^{w} G_k^{\mathsf{H}_k(C_i^j)}$. Now, D_i and $(C_i^1, \ldots C_i^{\mu_i})$ correspond to the values of the ith honest leaf. The reduction produces the necessary signatures and simulates each required SoK.
   From properties (3) and (4) of Lemma 1, it follows that this is indistinguishable from the original distribution. The distribution produced by the $\mathsf{SignAndMerge}$ procedure corresponds to the case where all t_i^{left} and $t_{i,j}^{\mathsf{right}}$ are 0, and $(s_i^{\mathsf{left}})_{i \in [n]} = (s_i^{\mathsf{right}})_{i \in [n]}$.

(b) Say the adversary produces some forgery σ^*, M^*, PK^* winning the EUF game, where σ^* is of the form $(L^*, R^*, r^*) = (\{(\sigma_z, D_z, \mathsf{pk}_z)\}_{z=1}^{n^*}, \{(\pi_j, C_j, m_j)\}_{j=1}^{\mu^*}, r^*)$. We may start by removing elements from L^* and R^* where the adversary has used the entire content of a signature σ_i produced by the reduction on $M_i^h \subseteq M^*$, such that $L_i^h \subseteq L^*$ and $R_i^h \subseteq R^*$. The forged signature σ^* is updated to $(L^* \backslash L_i^h, R^* \backslash R_i^h, r^* - r_i^h)$. Messages which no longer appear in R^* are removed from M^*, and public keys which no longer appear in L^* are removed from PK^*. This must leave R^* non-empty, as a winning forgery must satisfy $\mathsf{OutsideSpan}(M^*, PK^*, \{(PK_i^h, M_i^h)\}_{i=1}^{q_s})$, i.e. M^* cannot be produced as the union of honestly signed message sets. Importantly, if the original forgery verified, then $H^{r^*} \prod_{D \in L^*} D = \prod_{C \in R^*} C \prod_{k=1}^{w} G_k^{\mathsf{H}_k(C)}$ is maintained. We update $n^* := |L^*|$ and $\mu^* := |R^*|$.

There are three cases for the contents of L^* and R^*; we state them now and analyze them below.

i. L^* is empty and R^* contains only fresh C's (not produced by the reduction).
ii. At least one C was produced by the reduction (in response to a signing oracle query), but is now linked to a new message via a new signature of knowledge.
iii. The above don't hold, and for at least one signing oracle query, either a D is missing from L^* or a C is missing from R^*.

We consider these cases separately.

(i) This option is excluded, as the reduction did not abort in hybrid (7).

(ii) The adversary reuses a commitment $C_j = G^{s_j^{\mathsf{right}}} P^{t_j^{\mathsf{right}}} H^{r_j}$ with a new signature of knowledge (on a new message) separately. Extracting the witness from the SoK would give s, r such that $C_j = G^s H^r$. This clearly allows finding the discrete log of P base G when $t_j^{\mathsf{right}} \neq 0$ which is the case except with probability $1/q$. The distribution seen by the adversary is independent of t_j^{right} by property (3) of Lemma 1

(iii) Now, we move on to consider the case where the adversary *did not* reuse a commitment with a new signature of knowledge. Verification requires $H^{r^*} \prod_{z=1}^{n^*} D_z = \prod_{j=1}^{\mu^*} (C_j \prod_{k=1}^{w} G_k^{\mathsf{H}_k(C_j)})$. The commitments C_j were either produced earlier by the challenger (such that $C_j = G^{s_j^{\mathsf{right}}} P^{t_j^{\mathsf{right}}} H^{r_j}$ for known s_j^{right}, t_j^{right} and r_j) or constructed by the adversary with an accompanying signature of knowledge π (such that $s_j^{\mathsf{right}}, r_j$ satisfying $C_j = G^{s_j^{\mathsf{right}}} H^{r_j}$ can be extracted; this may be regarded as a special case where $t_j^{\mathsf{right}} = 0$).

Since we did not abort in hybrid (2), and the forgery may not contain any corrupt signer public keys, we may be certain all $D_z \in L^*$ were signed by the reduction. Therefore the reduction knows s_z^{left}, t_z^{left} such that $D_z = G^{s_z^{\mathsf{left}}} P^{t_z^{\mathsf{left}}}$ for each $z \in [n^*]$.

The reduction may find the discrete log of P as long as $\sum_{j\in[n^*]} t_j^{\mathsf{left}} \neq \sum_{j\in[\mu^*]} t_j^{\mathsf{right}}$, we argue that the adversary cannot avoid this with non-negligible probability.
For any $L_i^h \subset L^*$ at least one element of R_i^h must not be in R^*. We denote the included subset as $R' \subset R_i^h$. Due to property (2) from Lemma 1, the difference in powers of P between L_i^h and R', $\sum_{D_z\in L_i^h} t_z^{\mathsf{left}} - \sum_{C_j\in R'} t_j^{\mathsf{right}}$ will be uniformly random and independent. Therefore even if the adversary knew all remaining t_z^{left}, t_j^{right} they would not be able to make $\sum_{j\in[n^*]} t_j^{\mathsf{left}} = \sum_{j\in[\mu^*]} t_j^{\mathsf{right}}$ with probability better than chance, $1/q$.
The case where $R_i^h \subset R^*$ and $L_i^h \not\subset L^*$ is largely analogous, but using property (1). If both L_i^h and R_i^h are partially included the difference in powers of P will also be uniform and independent following both properties (1) and (2).

4.4.2 Proof of Theorem 2

Proof (of Theorem 2). We reduce the history hiding of our UOS construction to the simulatability property of the signature of knowledge scheme or the hiding property of the commitment scheme. (Since the Pedersen commitment scheme used in our construction is perfectly hiding, this does not require an additional assumption.) We define a reduction R in a sequence of hybrids as follows:

1. In this hybrid, the reduction runs the challenger according to the instructions in Fig. 7.
2. In this hybrid, when answering a SignAndMerge query, the reduction uses a trapdoor to simulate SoKs.
   This hybrid is indistinguishable from the previous one by the simulatability of the SoK scheme.
3. In this hybrid, when answering a SignAndMerge query, for each honest leaf $i \in H$ containing μ_i messages, the reduction computes the right side R of the signature as follows:
   - For $j \in [\mu_i]$, it picks the commitment $C_{i,j}$ as a random element of $\mathbb{G}$.

   It then independently computes r_i as follows:
   - For $j \in [\mu_i]$, it picks $r_{i,j}$ at random (from the appropriate space; either at random modulo q, or as a random 2κ-bit integer).
   - It computes r_i as the modular or integer sum of the $r_{i,j}$'s. (Note that when the modular sum is used, this is the same as choosing r_i at random directly, without going through the step of choosing the $r_{i,j}$'s).

   It computes the final R and r as per the merge algorithm (including the values from the corrupt leaves). Finally, the reduction produces the left side L of the signature as follows, to ensure a total lack of coupling between elements of R and elements of L:
   - It computes D as $(\prod_{C\in R} C \prod_{k=1}^{w} G_k^{\mathsf{H}_k(C)})/H^r$, and computes the individual D_i's (for honest leaves) as a random factoring of D (divided by

corrupt leaf D_i's). That is, it produces all but the last honest D_i as random elements of $\mathbb{G}$; it picks the last honest D_i as D divided by all other D_i's (including the corrupt ones).
- It signs the honest D_i's on behalf of the honest parties.

This hybrid is indistinguishable from the previous one because the responses to the challenge SignAndMerge query are indistinguishable (identical) in the two hybrids, by the perfect hiding property of the commitment scheme; for each choice of factoring of D, there exists a unique consistent multiplicative decomposition of H^r.

Observe that now, there is no link at all between the D_i's (linked to party identities) and the C_j's (linked to messages). So, the outputs of SignAndMerge on T_0 and T_1 are identically distributed as long as $T_0 \equiv_{weak} T_1$.

5 Performance

To evaluate the performance of our signature scheme, we provide an implementation in `Rust` based on the `curve25519-dalek` crate implementing the `edwards25519` elliptic curve [9] and the Ristretto encoding for points. The signature scheme used is a Schnorr signature. As hash function, we use SHA256 which is hardware accelerated on modern processors. Most of the signature generation and verification is independent of each other. This allows parallel execution on multi-core processors. As our benchmarking system, we use an Intel Core i7-6820HQ CPU at 2.70 GHz for a total of 8 threads.

Figure 9 shows the signing and verification time for an increasing number of messages and different number of hash functions. There are clearly visible and linear steps at multiples of 8 messages, supporting our claim of efficient parallelization. To achieve a difficulty for the SIS problem similar to the discrete logarithm in `edwards25519`, we require 478 dimensions. We used the approach described in [17] with the model put forward by Albrecht *et al.* [4] to estimate the bit-security of $\mathsf{SIS}(w, m, q, \sqrt{m})$. In this case $m = 2^{128}$ is a bound on the number of oracle queries, and q is the order of the `edwards25519` curve, allowing us to find the smallest dimension w providing the necessary difficulty. This results in signatures which require 1 group element and the size of the Schnorr signature (1 group element and 1 scalar) for each merged leaf plus an additional 2 group elements and 2 scalars for each message. Concretely, 100 merged signatures, over 100 messages each for a total of 10,000 messages, requires 1.2 MB.

The merging of signatures consists of adding the randomness, which is independent of the messages and linear in the number of parts. To maintain history hiding, the inputs and outputs need to be sorted, which is possible in $\mathcal{O}(n \log k)$ where n is the total number of messages and k is the number of already ordered signatures to be merged. There are always less or equal signatures to be sorted.

Figure 10 shows the time required for merging signatures. The two dependencies are the number of signatures on the x-axis and we measured this for different numbers of messages per signature. For all experiments with more than one message per signature, we notice that the majority of time is required copying memory and sorting the messages and adding the randomness is marginal.

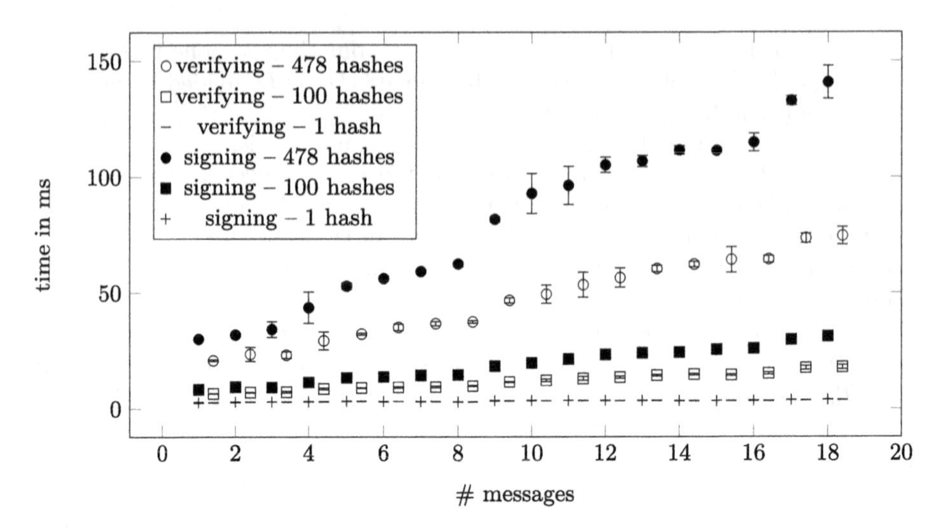

Fig. 9. Signing and verification time depending on number of messages with 8 threads.

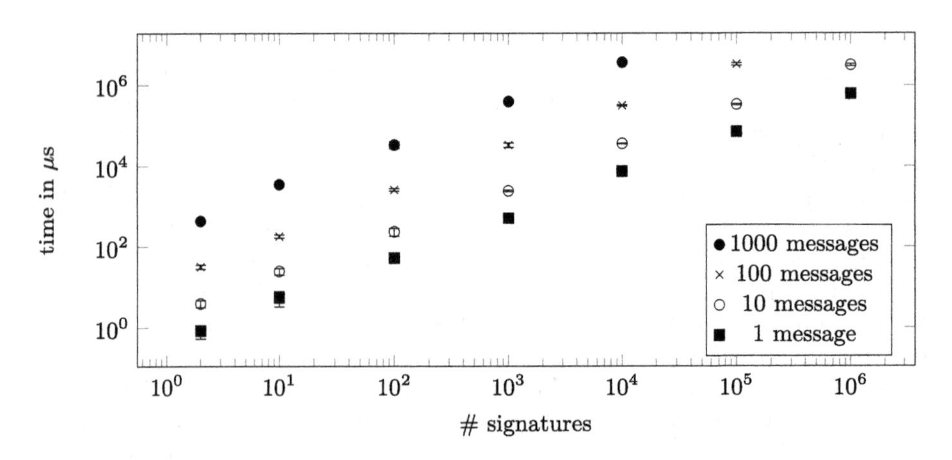

Fig. 10. Merging of signatures with n messages in each signature. The operation is mostly memory bound and depends on the amount of signatures copied. It is independent on the security parameter of the number of hash functions

This observation is derived from the fact, that merging with an equal number of messages have the same timings. Each step right are 10 times more signatures but a 10th of the messages per signature, resulting in the same total number. For single message signatures, adding the randomness is noticeable and they are a bit slower than the experiment with an equal number of messages distributed in a 10th of the signatures.

In absolute terms, our implementation handles merging a million messages in less than half a second, making it usable for large datasets.

6 Conclusion

We presented two constructions for UOS schemes, closing the open problem posed by Johnson *et al.* [15]. This is made possible by the fact that our signatures do not have a multiplicative structure. Our first construction is experimentally evaluated as computationally efficient when instantiated with a state-of-the-art elliptic curve implementation, but not compact in terms of signature size. Our second construction is based in SNARKs and produces constant-size signatures, but with a significant performance penalty due to the inherent cost of SNARKs. We finish by pointing out that our first step may lead to more efficient UOS constructions, and hope that it provides techniques useful to close the other open problem of *concatenable* signatures posed in the same paper.

Acknowledgements. This work was partially funded by the Carlsberg Foundation under the Semper Ardens Research Project CF18-112 (BCM), the Sapere Aude: DFF-Starting Grant number 0165-00079B "Foundations of Privacy Preserving and Accountable Decentralized Protocols" and by the European Research Council (ERC) under the European Unions's Horizon 2020 research and innovation programme under grant agreement No. 669255 (MPCPRO) and No. 803096 (SPEC). The first author acknowledges support from the Concordium Blockchain Research Center (COBRA) and the DIGIT Centre for Digitalisation, Big Data and Data Analytics at Aarhus University.

References

1. Abiteboul, S., Cautis, B., Fiat, A., Milo, T.: Digital signatures for modifiable collections. In: ARES, pp. 390–399. IEEE Computer Society (2006)
2. Ahn, J.H., Boneh, D., Camenisch, J., Hohenberger, S., shelat, A., Waters, B.: Computing on authenticated data. In: Cramer, R. (ed.) TCC 2012. LNCS, vol. 7194, pp. 1–20. Springer, Heidelberg (2012). https://doi.org/10.1007/978-3-642-28914-9_1
3. Ajtai, M.: Generating hard instances of lattice problems (extended abstract). In: 28th ACM STOC, pp. 99–108. ACM Press, May 1996. https://doi.org/10.1145/237814.237838
4. Albrecht, M.R., Cid, C., Faugère, J.-C., Fitzpatrick, R., Perret, L.: On the complexity of the BKW algorithm on LWE. Cryptology ePrint Archive, Report 2012/636(2012). https://eprint.iacr.org/2012/636
5. Altuğ, S.A., Chen, Y.: Hard isogeny problems over RSA moduli and groups with infeasible inversion. In: Galbraith, S.D., Moriai, S. (eds.) ASIACRYPT 2019. LNCS, vol. 11922, pp. 293–322. Springer, Cham (2019). https://doi.org/10.1007/978-3-030-34621-8_11
6. Aranha, D.F., Hall-Andersen, M., Nitulescu, A., Pagnin, E., Yakoubov, S.: Count me in! extendability for threshold ring signatures. Cryptology ePrint Archive, Report 2021/1240 (2021). https://ia.cr/2021/1240
7. Aranha, D.F., Pagnin, E.: The simplest multi-key linearly homomorphic signature scheme. In: Schwabe, P., Thériault, N. (eds.) LATINCRYPT 2019. LNCS, vol. 11774, pp. 280–300. Springer, Cham (2019). https://doi.org/10.1007/978-3-030-30530-7_14

8. Barbulescu, R., Duquesne, S.: Updating key size estimations for pairings. J. Cryptol. **32**(4), 1298–1336 (2018). https://doi.org/10.1007/s00145-018-9280-5
9. Bernstein, D.J., Duif, N., Lange, T., Schwabe, P., Yang, B.-Y.: High-speed high-security signatures. In: Preneel, B., Takagi, T. (eds.) CHES 2011. LNCS, vol. 6917, pp. 124–142. Springer, Heidelberg (2011). https://doi.org/10.1007/978-3-642-23951-9_9
10. Boneh, D., Freeman, D., Katz, J., Waters, B.: Signing a linear subspace: signature schemes for network coding. In: Jarecki, S., Tsudik, G. (eds.) PKC 2009. LNCS, vol. 5443, pp. 68–87. Springer, Heidelberg (2009). https://doi.org/10.1007/978-3-642-00468-1_5
11. Catalano, D., Fiore, D.: Using linearly-homomorphic encryption to evaluate degree-2 functions on encrypted data. In: Ray, I., Li, N., Kruegel, C. (eds.) ACM CCS 2015, pp. 1518–1529. ACM Press, October 2015. https://doi.org/10.1145/2810103.2813624
12. Dobson, S., Galbraith, S.D., Smith, B.: Trustless unknown-order groups. Math. Cryptol. **1**(2), 25–39 (2021). https://journals.flvc.org/mathcryptology/issue/view/6013
13. Engelmann, F., Müller, L., Peter, A., Kargl, F., Bösch, C.: SwapCT: swap confidential transactions for privacy-preserving multi-token exchanges. PoPETs **2021**(4), 270–290 (2021). https://doi.org/10.2478/popets-2021-0070
14. Hohenberger, S.R.: The cryptographic impact of groups with infeasible inversion. Master's thesis, Massachusetts Institute of Technology (2003). http://hdl.handle.net/1721.1/87357
15. Johnson, R., Molnar, D., Song, D., Wagner, D.: Homomorphic signature schemes. In: Preneel, B. (ed.) CT-RSA 2002. LNCS, vol. 2271, pp. 244–262. Springer, Heidelberg (2002). https://doi.org/10.1007/3-540-45760-7_17
16. Kaaniche, N., Jung, E., Gehani, A.: Efficiently validating aggregated IoT data integrity. In: BigDataService, pp. 260–265. IEEE Computer Society (2018)
17. Kosba, A., et al.: C $\emptyset$ c $\emptyset$: a framework for building composable zero-knowledge proofs. Cryptology ePrint Archive (2015)
18. Micciancio, D., Regev, O.: Worst-case to average-case reductions based on Gaussian measures. In: 45th FOCS, pp. 372–381. IEEE Computer Society Press, October 2004. https://doi.org/10.1109/FOCS.2004.72
19. Molnar, D.: Homomorphic signature schemes (2003). BSc. Senior thesis. Harvard College. https://www.dmolnar.com/papers/papers.html
20. Pöhls, H.C., Samelin, K., Posegga, J., de Meer, H.: Transparent mergeable redactable signatures with signer commitment and applications. Inst. IT-Security Security-Law, Univ. Passau, Passau, Germany (2012)
21. Pöhls, H.C., Samelin, K.: On updatable redactable signatures. In: Boureanu, I., Owesarski, P., Vaudenay, S. (eds.) ACNS 2014. LNCS, vol. 8479, pp. 457–475. Springer, Cham (2014). https://doi.org/10.1007/978-3-319-07536-5_27
22. Rabi, M., Sherman, A.T.: Associative one-way functions: a new paradigm for secret-key agreement and digital signatures. Technical report, University of Maryland Institute for Advanced Studies (1993). cS-TR-3183/UMIACS-/R-93-124
23. Traverso, G., Demirel, D., Buchmann, J.: Homomorphic Signature Schemes - A Survey. Springer Briefs in Computer Science, Springer, Cham (2016). https://doi.org/10.1007/978-3-319-32115-8
24. Yamakawa, T., Yamada, S., Hanaoka, G., Kunihiro, N.: Self-bilinear map on unknown order groups from indistinguishability obfuscation and its applications. In: Garay, J.A., Gennaro, R. (eds.) CRYPTO 2014, Part II. LNCS, vol. 8617, pp. 90–107. Springer, Heidelberg (2014). https://doi.org/10.1007/978-3-662-44381-1_6

Traceable Constant-Size Multi-authority Credentials

Chloé Hébant[1(✉)] and David Pointcheval[2]

[1] Cosmian, Paris, France
chloe.hebant@cosmian.com
[2] DIENS, École normale supérieure, CNRS, Inria, PSL University, Paris, France

Abstract. Many attribute-based anonymous credential (ABC) schemes have been proposed allowing a user to prove the possession of some attributes, anonymously. They became more and more practical with, for the most recent papers, a constant-size credential to show a subset of attributes issued by a unique credential issuer. However, proving possession of attributes coming from K different credential issuers usually requires K independent credentials to be shown. Only attribute-based credential schemes from aggregate signatures can overcome this issue.

In this paper, we propose new ABC schemes from aggregate signatures with randomizable tags. We consider malicious credential issuers, with adaptive corruptions and collusions with malicious users. Whereas our constructions only support selective disclosures of attributes, to remain compact, our approach significantly improves the complexity in both time and memory of the showing of multiple attributes: for the first time, the cost for the prover is (almost) independent of the number of attributes *and* the number of credential issuers. Whereas anonymous credentials require privacy of the user, we also propose the first schemes allowing traceability by a specific tracing authority.

1 Introduction

In an anonymous credential scheme, a user asks to an organization (a credential issuer) a credential on an attribute, so that he can later claim its possession, even multiple times, but in an anonymous and unlinkable way.

Usually, a credential on one attribute is not enough and the user needs credentials on multiple attributes. Hence, the interest of an attribute-based anonymous credential scheme (ABC in short): depending on the construction, the user receives one credential per attribute or directly for a set of attributes. One goal is to be able to express relations between attributes (or at least selective disclosure), with *one showing*. As different attributes may have different meanings (e.g. a university delivers a diploma while a city hall delivers a birth certification), there should be several credential issuers. Besides multiple credential issuers, it can be useful to have a multi-show credential system to allow a user to prove an arbitrary number of times one credential still without loosing anonymity. For that, the showings are required to be unlinkable to each other.

C. Galdi and S. Jarecki (Eds.): SCN 2022, LNCS 13409, pp. 411–434, 2022.
https://doi.org/10.1007/978-3-031-14791-3_18

Classically, a credential is a signature by the credential issuer of the attribute with the public key of the user. The latter is thus the only one able to prove the ownership with an interactive zero-knowledge (ZK) proof of knowledge of the secret key. Anonymity is provided by the probabilistic encryption of the signature. As many signature schemes with various interesting properties have been proposed, many ABC schemes have been designed with quite different approaches. We can gather them into two families: the ABC schemes where a credential is obtained on a set of attributes and then, according to the properties of the signature, it is possible either to prove the knowledge of a subset of the attributes (CL-signatures [7,8], blind signatures [1,11]), or to modify some of the attributes to default values (sanitizable signatures [10]), or simply to remove them (unlinkable redactable signatures [6,17], SPS-EQ with set commitments [12]); and the ABC schemes where the user receives one credential per attribute and then combines them (aggregate signatures [9]). In the former family, whereas it is possible to efficiently show a subset of attributes issued in a unique credential, showing attributes coming from K different credential issuers requires K independent credentials to be proven. On the other hand, with aggregate signatures, credentials on different attributes can be combined together even if they have been issued by different credential issuers. This leads to more compact schemes and this paper follows this latter approach.

Moreover, except some constructions based on blind signatures where the credentials can be shown only once, all ABC schemes allow multi-shows. To this aim, they exploit advanced properties of the signature scheme, with randomizability for anonymity and unlinkability of the showings. Before these properties, one had to use encryption for anonymity and complex zero-knowledge proofs for unforgeability.

1.1 Our Contributions

Our goal is to obtain a compact ABC system with a compact-size credential allowing different credential issuers. Our first contribution is then the formal definition of the scheme which supports possibly malicious credential issuers.

Following the path of anonymous credentials from aggregate signatures [9] and inspired by the definition of linearly homomorphic signatures, our second contribution is the formalization of an (aggregate) signature scheme with randomizable tags (ART-Sign). It comes with a practical construction based on a signature scheme of Hébant *et al.* [14, Appendix C.5]. With such a primitive, two signatures of different messages under different keys can be aggregated only if they are associated to the same tag. In our case, tags will eventually be like pseudonyms, but with some properties which make them ephemeral (hence EphemerId scheme) and randomizable. After randomization, while they are still associated to the same user, they will be unlinkable. This will provide anonymity.

The EphemerId scheme provides ephemeral keys to users, that will allow anonymous authentication. Public keys being randomizable, still for a same secret key, multiple authentications will remain unlinkable. In addition, these public keys will be used as (randomizable) tags with the above ART-Sign scheme when the credential issuer signs an attribute. Thanks to aggregation, multiple credentials for multiple attributes and from multiple credential issuers but under the same tag, and thus for the same user, can be combined into a unique compact (constant-size) credential.

We achieve the optimal goal of constant-size multi-show credentials even for multiple attributes from multiple credential issuers and we stress that aggregation can be done on-the-fly, for any selection of attributes issued by multiple credential issuers: our scheme allows multi-show of any selective disclosure of attributes. About security, whereas there exists a scheme proven in the universal composability (UC) framework [6], for our constructions, we consider a game-based security model for ABC inspired from [12]. As we support different credentials issuers, we additionally consider adaptive corruptions of both credential issuers and users. However, the keys need to be honestly generated, thus our proofs hold in the certified key setting. This is quite realistic, as this is enough to wait for a valid proof of knowledge of the secret key before certifying the public key. As most of the recent ABC schemes, our constructions rely on signature schemes proven in the bilinear generic group model.

Our last contribution is traceability, in the same vein as group signatures: whereas showings are anonymous, a tracing authority owns a tracing key for being able to link a credential to its owner. In such a case, we also consider malicious tracing authorities, with the non-frameability guarantee. As in [10] we thus define trace and judge algorithms to trace the defrauder and prove its identity to a judge. This excludes malicious behavior of the tracing authority. Very few papers deal with traceability: the first one [10] exploits sanitizable signatures, where the sanitizer can be traced back, but a closer look shows privacy weaknesses (see the full version [15]) and a more recent one [16] that has thereafter been broken [19]. Our scheme is thus the first traceable attribute-based anonymous credential scheme.

1.2 Related Work

The most recent papers on attribute-based anonymous credential schemes are [12,17]. The former proposes the first constant-size credential to prove k-of-N attributes, with computational complexity in $O(N-k)$ for the prover and in $O(k)$ for the verifier. However, it only works for one credential issuer ($K=1$). The latter one improves this result enabling multiple showings of relations (r) of attributes. All the other known constructions allow, at best, selective (s) disclosures of attributes.

In [9], Canard and Lescuyer use aggregate signatures to construct an ABC system. It is thus the closest to our approach. Instead of having *tags*, their signatures take *indices* as input. We follow a similar path but, we completely formalize this notion of tag/index with an EphemerId scheme. To our knowledge, aggregate signatures are the only way to deal with multiple credential issuers but still showing a unique compact credential for the proof of possession of attributes coming from different credential issuers. However, the time-complexity of a prover during a verification depends on the number k of shown attributes.

Scheme	P	T	k-of-N attributes from $K = 1$ credential issuer			
			|CI key| $\mathbb{G}_1, \mathbb{G}_2$	|Show| $\mathbb{G}_1, \mathbb{G}_2, (\mathbb{G}_T), \mathbb{Z}_p$	Prover exp., pairings	Verifier exp., pairings
[9]	s	✗	$\mathbf{1, 1}$	$16, 2, (4), 7$	$16\mathbb{G}_1 + 2\mathbb{G}_2 + 10\mathbb{G}_T$, $18 + k$	$12\mathbb{G}_1 + 20\mathbb{G}_T$, $18 + k$
[12]	s	✗	$0, N$	$8, 1, 2$	$9\mathbb{G}_1 + 1\mathbb{G}_2, 0$	$4\mathbb{G}_1, k + 4$
[17]	r	✗	$0, 2N + 1$	$2, 2, (1), 2$	$(2(N-k)+2)\mathbb{G}_1 + 2\mathbb{G}_2, 1$	$(k+1)\mathbb{G}_1 + 1\mathbb{G}_T, 5$
Sec. 5.2	s	✓	$0, 2k + 3$	$\mathbf{3, 0, 1}$	$\mathbf{6\mathbb{G}_1, 0}$	$\mathbf{4\mathbb{G}_1 + k\mathbb{G}_2, 3}$
App. D	s	✓	$0, 2N + 2$	$\mathbf{3, 0, 1}$	$\mathbf{6\mathbb{G}_1, 0}$	$\mathbf{4\mathbb{G}_1 + 2N\mathbb{G}_2, 3}$

Scheme	k = 1-of-N attribute from K credential issuers			
	|CI key| $\mathbb{G}_1, \mathbb{G}_2$	|Show| $\mathbb{G}_1, \mathbb{G}_2, (\mathbb{G}_T), \mathbb{Z}_p$	Prover exp., pairings	Verifier exp., pairings
[9]	$\mathbf{K \times (1, 1)}$	$16, 2, (4), 7$	$16\mathbb{G}_1 + 2\mathbb{G}_2 + 10\mathbb{G}_T$, $18 + k$	$12\mathbb{G}_1 + 20\mathbb{G}_T$, $18 + k$
[12]	$K \times (0, N)$	$K \times (8, 1, 2)$	$K \times (9\mathbb{G}_1 + 1\mathbb{G}_2, 0)$	$K \times (4\mathbb{G}_1, k + 4)$
[17]	$K \times (0, 2N + 1)$	$K \times (2, 2, (1), 2)$	$K \times ((2(N-k)+2)\mathbb{G}_1$ $+2\mathbb{G}_2, 1)$	$K \times ((k+1)\mathbb{G}_1+$ $1\mathbb{G}_T, 5)$
Sec. 5.2	$K \times (0, 2k + 3)$	$\mathbf{3, 0, 1}$	$\mathbf{6\mathbb{G}_1, 0}$	$\mathbf{4\mathbb{G}_1 + k\mathbb{G}_2, 3}$
App. D	$K \times (0, 2N + 2)$	$\mathbf{3, 0, 1}$	$\mathbf{6\mathbb{G}_1, 0}$	$\mathbf{4\mathbb{G}_1 + 2KN\mathbb{G}_2, 3}$

Fig. 1. Comparison of different ABC systems.

We solve this issue at the cost of a larger key for the credential issuers (but still in the same order as [12,17]) and a significantly better showing cost for the prover (also better than [12,17]).

1.3 Comparison of Different ABC Systems

In Fig. 1, we provide some comparisons with the most efficient ABC schemes, where the column "P" (for policy) specifies whether the scheme just allows selective disclosure of attributes (s) or relations between attributes (r). The column "T" (for traceability) indicates whether traceability is possible or not. Then, "|CI key|" gives the size of the keys (public keys of the credential issuers) required to verify the credentials, "|Show|" is the communication bandwidth during a show, while "Prover" and "Verifier" are the computational cost during a show, for the prover and the verifier respectively. Bandwidths are in number of elements $\mathbb{G}_1$, $\mathbb{G}_2$, $\mathbb{G}_T$ and $\mathbb{Z}_p$. Computations are in number of exponentiations in $\mathbb{G}_1$, $\mathbb{G}_2$ and $\mathbb{G}_T$, and of pairings. Due to their negligible impact on performance, we ignore multiplications. We denote N the global number of attributes owned by a user, k the number of attributes he wants to show and K the number of credential issuers involved in the issuing of the credentials. In the first table, we focus on the particular case of proving a credential with k attributes, among N attributes issued from 1 credential issuer. Our first scheme, from Sect. 5.2, is already the most efficient, but this is even better for a larger K, as shown in the second table. However this is for a limited number of attributes. Our second scheme, in the full version [15], has similar efficiency, but with less limitations on the attributes.

Note that both schemes have a constant-size communication for the showing of any number of attributes, and the computation cost for the prover is almost constant too (as we ignore multiplications). Our two instantiations are derived from the second linearly-homomorphic signature scheme of [14, Appendix C.5]. As already said, our scheme is the first traceable attribute-based anonymous credential scheme, hence the only one in the tables.

2 Preliminaries

A reminder on the classical notations and assumptions (namely DL and DDH) used in this paper is given in the full version [15]. In an asymmetric bilinear setting $(\mathbb{G}_1, \mathbb{G}_2, \mathbb{G}_T, p, g, \mathfrak{g}, e)$, or just in a simple group $\mathbb{G}$, we can define the following assumptions:

Definition 1 (Square Discrete Logarithm (SDL) Assumption). *In a group $\mathbb{G}$ of prime order p, it states that for any generator g, given $y = g^x$ and $z = g^{x^2}$, it is computationally hard to recover x.*

Definition 2 (Decisional Square Diffie-Hellman (DSqDH) Assumption). *In a group $\mathbb{G}$ of prime order p, it states that the two following distributions are computationally indistinguishable:*

$$\mathcal{D}_{\mathsf{sqdh}} = \{(g, g^x, g^{x^2}); g \stackrel{\$}{\leftarrow} \mathbb{G}, x \stackrel{\$}{\leftarrow} \mathbb{Z}_p\} \quad \mathbb{G}_\$^3 = \{(g, g^x, g^y); g \stackrel{\$}{\leftarrow} \mathbb{G}, x, y \stackrel{\$}{\leftarrow} \mathbb{Z}_p\}.$$

It is worth noticing that the DSqDH Assumption implies the SDL Assumption: if one can break SDL, from g, g^x, g^{x^2}, one can compute x and thus break DSqDH. Such Square Diffie-Hellman triples will be our tags, or ephemeral public keys. For anonymity, we will use the following theorem:

Theorem 3. *The DDH and DSqDH assumptions imply the indistinguishability between the two distributions, for $g_0, g_1 \stackrel{\$}{\leftarrow} \mathbb{G}$ and $x, y \stackrel{\$}{\leftarrow} \mathbb{Z}_p$*

$$\mathcal{D}_0 = \{(g_0, g_0^x, g_0^{x^2}, g_1, g_1^x, g_1^{x^2})\} \qquad \mathcal{D}_1 = \{(g_0, g_0^x, g_0^{x^2}, g_1, g_1^y, g_1^{y^2})\}.$$

Proof. For this indistinguishability, one can show they are both indistinguishable from random independent 6-tuples (the distribution $\mathbb{G}_\$^6$):

$$\begin{aligned} \mathcal{D}_0 &\approx \{(g_0, g_0^x, g_0^y, g_1, g_1^x, g_1^y), g_0, g_1 \stackrel{\$}{\leftarrow} \mathbb{G}, x, y \stackrel{\$}{\leftarrow} \mathbb{Z}_p\} && \text{under DSqDH} \\ &\approx \{(g_0, g_0^x, g_0^y, g_1, g_1^u, g_1^v), g_0, g_1 \stackrel{\$}{\leftarrow} \mathbb{G}, x, y, u, v \stackrel{\$}{\leftarrow} \mathbb{Z}_p\} = \mathbb{G}_\$^6 && \text{under DDH} \\ &\approx \{(g_0, g_0^x, g_0^{x^2}, g_1, g_1^u, g_1^{u^2}), g_0, g_1 \stackrel{\$}{\leftarrow} \mathbb{G}, x, u \stackrel{\$}{\leftarrow} \mathbb{Z}_p\} = \mathcal{D}_1 && \text{under DSqDH} \end{aligned}$$

For unforgeability in our construction, we will use the following theorem on Square Diffie-Hellman tuples, stated and proven in [14, Appendix C.5]:

Theorem 4. *Given n valid Square Diffie-Hellman tuples $(g_i, a_i = g_i^{w_i}, b_i = a_i^{w_i})$, together with w_i, for random $g_i \stackrel{\$}{\leftarrow} \mathbb{G}^*$ and $w_i \stackrel{\$}{\leftarrow} \mathbb{Z}_p^*$, outputting $(\alpha_i)_{i=1,\dots,n}$ such that $(G = \prod g_i^{\alpha_i}, A = \prod a_i^{\alpha_i}, B = \prod b_i^{\alpha_i})$ is a valid Square Diffie-Hellman tuple, with at least two non-zero coefficients α_i, is computationally hard under the DL assumption.*

Intuitively, from Square Diffie-Hellman tuples where the exponents are known but random (and so distinct with overwhelming probability) and the bases are also known and random, it is impossible to construct a new Square Diffie-Hellman tuple melting the exponents (with linear combinations).

3 Multi-authority Anonymous Credentials

In this section, we define a *multi-authority* anonymous attribute-based credential scheme by adapting the model of [12,17] to the multiple credential issuers, and then, provide the associated security definitions.

3.1 Definition

Throughout the paper, we will consider the certified key setting. Indeed, we assume a Certification Authority (CA) first checks the knowledge of the secret keys before certifying public keys and then, that the keys are always checked before being used by any players in the system. Moreover, we assume that an identity id is associated (and included) to any verification key vk, which is in turn included in the secret key sk.

Our general definition of anonymous credential scheme supports multiple users $(\mathcal{U}_i)_i$ and multiple credential issuers $(\mathsf{CI}_j)_j$:

Definition 5 (Anonymous Credential). *An anonymous credential system is defined by the following algorithms:*

$\mathsf{Setup}(1^\kappa)$: *It takes as input a security parameter and outputs the public parameters* param*;*

$\mathsf{CIKeyGen}(\mathsf{ID})$: *It generates the key pair* $(\mathsf{sk}, \mathsf{vk})$ *for the credential issuer with identity* ID*;*

$\mathsf{UKeyGen}(\mathsf{id})$: *It generates the key pair* $(\mathsf{usk}, \mathsf{uvk})$ *for the user with identity* id*;*

$(\mathsf{CredObtain}(\mathsf{usk}, \mathsf{vk}, a), \mathsf{CredIssue}(\mathsf{uvk}, \mathsf{sk}, a))$: *A user with identity* id *(associated to* $(\mathsf{usk}, \mathsf{uvk})$*) runs* $\mathsf{CredObtain}$ *to obtain a credential on the attribute a from the credential issuer* ID *(associated to* $(\mathsf{sk}, \mathsf{vk})$*) running* $\mathsf{CredIssue}$*. At the end of the protocol, the user receives a credential* σ*;*

$(\mathsf{CredShow}(\mathsf{usk}, (\mathsf{vk}_j, a_j, \sigma_j)_j), \mathsf{CredVerify}((\mathsf{vk}_j, a_j)_j))$: *In this two-party protocol, a user with identity* id *(associated to* $(\mathsf{usk}, \mathsf{uvk})$*) runs* $\mathsf{CredShow}$ *and interacts with a verifier running* $\mathsf{CredVerify}$ *to prove that he owns valid credentials* $(\sigma_j)_j$ *on* $(a_j)_j$ *issued respectively by credential issuers* ID_j *(associated to* $(\mathsf{sk}_j, \mathsf{vk}_j)$*). At the end of the protocol, the verifier receives* 1 *if the proof is correct and* 0 *otherwise;*

3.2 Security Model

As for the definition, we follow [12,17] for the security model, with multi-show unlinkable credentials, but considering multiple credential issuers. Informally, the scheme needs to have the three properties:

- Correctness: the verifier must accept any set of credentials honestly obtained;
- Unforgeability: the verifier should not accept a set of credentials if one of them has not been legitimately obtained by this user;
- Anonymity: credentials shown multiple times by a user should be unlinkable, even for the possibly malicious credential issuers. This furthermore implies that credentials cannot be linked to their owners.

Definition 6 (Correctness). *An anonymous credential scheme is said correct if, for any user* id, *any set of honest credential issuers* HCI, *and any set* A *of attributes:*

$$\begin{aligned} \mathsf{param} &\leftarrow \mathsf{Setup}(1^\kappa), \\ (\mathsf{usk}, \mathsf{uvk}) &\leftarrow \mathsf{UKeyGen}(\mathsf{id}), \\ (\mathsf{sk}_j, \mathsf{vk}_j) &\leftarrow \mathsf{CIKeyGen}(\mathsf{ID}_j) \text{ for } \mathsf{ID}_j \in \mathsf{HCI}, \\ \sigma_j &\leftarrow (\mathsf{CredObtain}(\mathsf{usk}, \mathsf{vk}_j, a_j), \mathsf{CredIssue}(\mathsf{uvk}, \mathsf{sk}_j, a_j)) \text{ for } a_j \in A, \end{aligned}$$

then, $1 \leftarrow (\mathsf{CredShow}(\mathsf{usk}, (\mathsf{vk}_j, a_j, \sigma_j)_j), \mathsf{CredVerify}((\mathsf{vk}_j, a_j)_j))$.

For the two security notions of unforgeability and anonymity, one can consider malicious adversaries able to corrupt some parties. We thus define the following lists: HU the list of honest user identities, CU the list of corrupted user identities, similarly we define HCI and CCI for the honest/corrupted credential issuers. For a user identity id, we define $\mathsf{Att}[\mathsf{id}]$ the list of the attributes of id and $\mathsf{Cred}[\mathsf{id}]$ the list of his individual credentials obtained from the credential issuers. All these lists are initialized to the empty set. For both unforgeability and anonymity, the adversary has unlimited access to the oracles (in any order, but queries are assumed to be atomic):

- $\mathcal{O}\mathsf{HCI}(\mathsf{ID})$ corresponds to the creation of an honest credential issuer with identity ID. If he already exists (i.e. $\mathsf{ID} \in \mathsf{HCI} \cup \mathsf{CCI}$), it outputs $\perp$. Otherwise, it adds $\mathsf{ID} \in \mathsf{HCI}$ and runs $(\mathsf{sk}, \mathsf{vk}) \leftarrow \mathsf{CIKeyGen}(\mathsf{ID})$ and returns vk;
- $\mathcal{O}\mathsf{CCI}(\mathsf{ID}, \mathsf{vk})$ corresponds to the corruption of a credential issuer with identity ID and optionally public key vk. If he does not exist yet (i.e. $\mathsf{ID} \notin \mathsf{HCI} \cup \mathsf{CCI}$), it creates a new corrupted credential issuer with public key vk by adding ID to CCI. Otherwise, if $\mathsf{ID} \in \mathsf{HCI}$, it removes ID from HCI and adds it to CCI and outputs sk;
- $\mathcal{O}\mathsf{HU}(\mathsf{id})$ corresponds to the creation of an honest user with identity id. If the user already exists (i.e. $\mathsf{id} \in \mathsf{HU} \cup \mathsf{CU}$), it outputs $\perp$. Otherwise, it creates a new user by adding $\mathsf{id} \in \mathsf{HU}$ and running $(\mathsf{usk}, \mathsf{uvk}) \leftarrow \mathsf{UKeyGen}(\mathsf{id})$. It initializes $\mathsf{Att}[\mathsf{id}] = \{\}$ and $\mathsf{Cred}[\mathsf{id}] = \{\}$ and returns uvk;
- $\mathcal{O}\mathsf{CU}(\mathsf{id}, \mathsf{uvk})$ corresponds to the corruption of a user with identity id and optionally public key uvk. If the user does not exist yet (i.e. $\mathsf{id} \notin \mathsf{HU} \cup \mathsf{CU}$), it creates a new corrupted user with public key uvk by adding id to CU. Otherwise, if $\mathsf{id} \in \mathsf{HU}$, it removes id from HU and adds it to CU and outputs usk and all the associated credentials $\mathsf{Cred}[\mathsf{id}]$;

- $\mathcal{O}$ObtIss(id, ID, a) corresponds to the issuing of a credential from an honest credential issuer with identity ID (associated to (sk, vk)) to an honest user with identity id (associated to (usk, uvk)) on the attribute a. If id $\notin$ HU or ID $\notin$ HCI, it outputs $\perp$. Otherwise, it runs $\sigma \leftarrow$ (CredObtain(usk, vk, id), CredIssue(uvk, sk, a)) and adds (ID, a) to Att[id] and (ID, a, σ) to Cred[id]. The adversary receives the full transcript;
- $\mathcal{O}$Obtain(id, ID, a) corresponds to the issuing of a credential from the adversary playing the role of a malicious credential issuer with identity ID (associated to vk) to an honest user with identity id (associated to (usk, uvk)) on the attribute a. If id $\notin$ HU or ID $\notin$ CCI, it outputs $\perp$. Otherwise, it runs CredObtain(usk, a) and adds (ID, a) to Att[id] and (ID, a, σ) to Cred[id];
- $\mathcal{O}$Issue(id, ID, a) corresponds to the issuing of a credential from an honest credential issuer with identity ID (associated to (sk, vk)) to the adversary playing the role of a malicious user with identity id (associated to uvk) on the attribute a. If id $\notin$ CU or ID $\notin$ HCI, it outputs $\perp$. Otherwise, it runs CredIssue(uvk, sk, a) and adds (ID, a) to Att[id] and (ID, a, σ) to Cred[id];
- $\mathcal{O}$Show(id, $(\mathsf{ID}_j, a_j)_j$) corresponds to the showing by an honest user with identity id (associated to (usk, uvk)) of credentials on the set $(\mathsf{ID}_j, a_j)_j \subset$ Att[id] (with ID_j associated to vk_j). If id $\notin$ HU or $\exists j, (\mathsf{ID}_j, a_j) \notin$ Att[id], it outputs $\perp$. Otherwise, it runs CredShow(usk, $(\mathsf{vk}_j, a_j, \sigma_j)_j$) with the adversary playing the role of a malicious verifier.

Let $\mathcal{O}$ be the list of all the above oracles: $\mathcal{O}$ = {$\mathcal{O}$HCI, $\mathcal{O}$CCI, $\mathcal{O}$HU, $\mathcal{O}$CU, $\mathcal{O}$ObtIss, $\mathcal{O}$Obtain, $\mathcal{O}$Issue, $\mathcal{O}$Show}.

Definition 7 (Unforgeability). *An anonymous credential scheme is said unforgeable if, for any polynomial time adversary $\mathcal{A}$ having access to oracles listed in $\mathcal{O}$, the advantage* $\mathsf{Adv}^{unf}(\mathcal{A}) = \Pr[\mathsf{Exp}^{unf}_{\mathcal{A}}(1^\kappa) = 1]$ *is negligible with* $\mathsf{Exp}^{unf}_{\mathcal{A}}(1^\kappa)$ *defined in Fig. 2.*

Intuitively, the unforgeability notion guarantees it is impossible to make accepted a *bad* credential to a verifier. To be able to interact with the verifier, the adversary needs to corrupt at least one user and can corrupt credential issuer(s). Hence, in the security experiment in Fig. 2, the adversary chooses the honest and malicious credential issuers: for the honest ones, the adversary provides their identities and the attributes in which they have authority for; while for the malicious ones, the adversary directly gives public keys and attributes. Attributes from the corrupted credential issuers can be generated by the adversary itself, using the secret keys.

Thus, the adversary wins the security game if it manages to prove its ownership of a credential, on behalf of a corrupted user id $\in$ CU whereas this user did not ask the attributes to the honest credential issuers. In other words, if among the corrupted users there is one (id $\in$ CU) having credentials on all the proposed attributes for a forgery issued by either:

$\mathsf{Exp}_{\mathcal{A}}^{\mathrm{unf}}(1^\kappa)$:
 $\mathsf{param} \leftarrow \mathsf{Setup}(1^\kappa)$
 $((\mathsf{ID}_j, a_j)_{j\in J}, (\mathsf{vk}_j, a_j)_{j\in J^*}) \leftarrow \mathcal{A}^{\mathcal{O}}(\mathsf{param})$
 $\forall j \in J, (\mathsf{sk}_j, \mathsf{vk}_j) \leftarrow \mathsf{CIKeyGen}(\mathsf{ID}_j)$
 $b \leftarrow (\mathcal{A}^{\mathcal{O}}((\mathsf{vk}_j)_{j\in J}), \mathsf{CredVerify}((\mathsf{vk}_j, a_j)_{j\in J\cup J^*}))$
 If $\exists \mathsf{id} \in \mathsf{CU}$, $\forall j$, either $\mathsf{ID}_j \in \mathsf{CCI}$, or ($\mathsf{ID}_j \in \mathsf{HCI}$ and $(\mathsf{ID}_j, a_j) \in \mathsf{Att}[\mathsf{id}]$),
 then return 0
 Return b

$\mathsf{Exp}_{\mathcal{A}}^{\mathrm{ano}-b}(1^\kappa)$:
 $\mathsf{param} \leftarrow \mathsf{Setup}(1^\kappa)$
 $(\mathsf{id}_0, \mathsf{id}_1, (\mathsf{ID}_j, a_j)_{j\in J}, (\mathsf{vk}_j, a_j)_{j\in J^*}) \leftarrow \mathcal{A}^{\mathcal{O}}(\mathsf{param})$
 If for some $\mathsf{ID}_j \in \mathsf{CCI} \cup \mathsf{HCI}$, $(\mathsf{ID}_j, a_j) \notin \mathsf{Att}[\mathsf{id}_0] \cap \mathsf{Att}[\mathsf{id}_1]$, then return 0
 $\forall j \in J$,
 $(\mathsf{sk}_j, \mathsf{vk}_j) \leftarrow \mathsf{CIKeyGen}(\mathsf{ID}_j)$
 $\sigma_{0,j} \leftarrow (\mathsf{CredObtain}(\mathsf{usk}_0, \mathsf{vk}_j, a_j), \mathsf{CredIssue}(\mathsf{uvk}_0, \mathsf{sk}_j, a_j))$
 $\sigma_{1,j} \leftarrow (\mathsf{CredObtain}(\mathsf{usk}_1, \mathsf{vk}_j, a_j), \mathsf{CredIssue}(\mathsf{uvk}_1, \mathsf{sk}_j, a_j))$
 $(\mathsf{CredShow}(\mathsf{usk}_b, (a_j, \sigma_{b,j})_j), \mathcal{A}^{\mathcal{O}}((\mathsf{vk}_j, \sigma_{0,j}, \sigma_{1,j})_{j\in J}, \mathsf{uvk}_0, \mathsf{uvk}_1))$
 $b^* \leftarrow \mathcal{A}^{\mathcal{O}}()$
 If $\mathsf{id}_0 \in \mathsf{CU}$ or $\mathsf{id}_1 \in \mathsf{CU}$, then return 0
 Return b^*

In both experiments, the adversary $\mathcal{A}^{\mathcal{O}}$ has unlimited access to the oracles $\mathcal{O} = \{\mathcal{O}\mathsf{HCI}, \mathcal{O}\mathsf{CCI}, \mathcal{O}\mathsf{HU}, \mathcal{O}\mathsf{CU}, \mathcal{O}\mathsf{ObtIss}, \mathcal{O}\mathsf{Obtain}, \mathcal{O}\mathsf{Issue}, \mathcal{O}\mathsf{Show}\}$. It is also supposed to maintain an internal state all along the games.

Fig. 2. Unforgeability and anonymity experiments

- corrupted credential issuers,
- honest credential issuers (in that case, for ID_j honest, (ID_j, a_j) is in $\mathsf{Att}[\mathsf{id}]$),

then, the forgery is a trivial one and excluded by definition. This is not a legitimate attack.

Definition 8 (Anonymity). *An anonymous credential scheme is said anonymous if, for any polynomial time adversary $\mathcal{A}$ having access to oracles listed in $\mathcal{O}$, the advantage $\mathsf{Adv}^{ano}(\mathcal{A}) = |\Pr[\mathsf{Exp}_{\mathcal{A}}^{ano-1}(1^\kappa) = 1] - \Pr[\mathsf{Exp}_{\mathcal{A}}^{ano-0}(1^\kappa) = 1]|$ is negligible with $\mathsf{Exp}_{\mathcal{A}}^{ano-b}(1^\kappa)$ defined in Fig. 2.*

The anonymity is defined by an unlinkability notion: the adversary tries to distinguish if two showings come from the same user or not. More precisely, the adversary wins the security game if it can distinguish showings from (honest) users id_0 and id_1 of its choice, on the same set of attributes $\{(\mathsf{ID}_j, a_j)\}_j$, even after having seen/verified credentials from the two identities, as it has access to the oracle $\mathcal{O}\mathsf{Show}$ to interact with them. Note that we do not hide the attributes nor the issuers during the showings: uvk_0 and uvk_1 are given to the adversary.

As for the unforgeability, the adversary is authorized to corrupt as many credential issuers as it wants (possibly all of them) and at any time thanks to the oracle $\mathcal{O}$CCI. For the honest ones, the adversary provides their identities and the attributes in which they have authority for; while for the malicious ones, the adversary directly gives their public keys and their attributes.

Contrarily to [17], unless the attributes contain explicit ordering (as it will be the case with our first construction), we are dealing with unlinkability as soon as the sets of attributes are the same for the two players (with the second construction).

4 Anonymous Credentials from New Primitives

Before we present our credential scheme, let us formally define the way users will be identified.

4.1 Anonymous Ephemeral Identities

In attribute-based authentication, a credential usually consists of a signature on some attributes together with the public key of a user. The identity of the user is then ensured by the correctness of its key provided by a Certification Authority (CA). Hence, one can represent the identity of a user in an anonymous credential scheme by a pair $(\tilde{\tau}, \tau)$, where $\tilde{\tau}$ is a secret tag and τ the associated public tag, that requires to be randomizable for anonymity.

Formally, one defines this tag pair as an ephemeral identity provided by an EphemerId scheme:

Definition 9 (EphemerId). *An EphemerId scheme consists of the algorithms:*

Setup(1^κ): *Given a security parameter κ, it outputs the global parameter* param, *which includes the tag space $\mathcal{T}$;*

GenTag(param): *Given a public parameter* param, *it outputs a secret tag $\tilde{\tau}$ and an associated public tag τ;*

RandTag(τ): *Given a public tag τ as input, it outputs a new tag τ' and the randomization link $\rho_{\tau \to \tau'}$ between τ and τ';*

DerivWitness$(\tilde{\tau}, \rho_{\tau \to \tau'})$: *Given a witness $\tilde{\tau}$ (associated to the tag τ) and a link between the tags τ and τ' as input, it outputs a witness $\tilde{\tau}'$ for τ';*

(ProveVTag$(\tilde{\tau})$, VerifVTag(τ)): *This (possibly interactive) protocol corresponds to the verification of the tag τ. At the end of the protocol, the verifier outputs* 1 *if it accepts τ as a valid tag and* 0 *otherwise;*

(ProveKTag$(s, \tilde{\tau})$, VerifKTag(s, τ)): *This (possibly interactive) protocol corresponds to a fresh proof of knowledge of $\tilde{\tau}$ using the state s. At the end of the protocol, the verifier outputs* 1 *if it accepts the proof and* 0 *otherwise.*

With the above algorithms, one can define the sets:

$$\mathcal{L}_{\tilde{\tau}} = \{\tau \in \mathcal{T}, \tau \text{ public tag associated to } \tilde{\tau}\} \qquad \mathcal{L} = \cup_{x \in \mathbb{Z}_p^*} \mathcal{L}_x$$

and, as the set of all the $\mathcal{L}_{\tilde{\tau}}$ is a partition of $\mathcal{L}$, an equivalence relation $\sim$ between tags: $\tau \sim \tau' \Leftrightarrow \exists \tilde{\tau}, (\tau, \tau' \in \mathcal{L}_{\tilde{\tau}})$. Hence, each authorized user will be associated to a secret tag $\tilde{\tau}$, and represented by the class generated by the public tag τ. One may have to prove the actual membership $\tau \in \mathcal{L}$ to prove the user is authorized. On the other hand, one may also have to prove the knowledge of the witness $\tilde{\tau}$, in a zero-knowledge way, for authentication.

The latter proof of knowledge can be performed, using the (interactive) protocol $(\mathsf{ProveKTag}(\tilde{\tau}), \mathsf{VerifKTag}(\tau))$. Interactive protocol or signature of knowledge on a fresh message will be useful for the freshness in the authentication process, and to avoid replay attacks. The former proof of validity can also be proven using an (interactive) protocol $(\mathsf{ProveVTag}(\tilde{\tau}), \mathsf{VerifVTag}(\tau))$. However this verification can also be non-interactive or even public, without needing any private witness. The only requirement is that this proof or verification of membership should not reveal the private witness involved in the proof of knowledge, whose soundness will guarantee the authentication of the user.

Security. The security notions are the usual ones for zero-knowledge proofs for the protocols $(\mathsf{ProveKTag}(\tilde{\tau}), \mathsf{VerifKTag}(\tau))$ and $(\mathsf{ProveVTag}(\tilde{\tau}), \mathsf{VerifVTag}(\tau))$:

- Soundness: the verification process for the validity of the tag should not accept an invalid tag (not in the language);
- Knowledge-Soundness: if the verification process for the proof of knowledge of the witness accepts with good probability, a simulator can extract it;
- Zero-knowledge: the proof of validity and the proof of knowledge should not reveal any information about the witness.

When the two protocols output 1, the witness-word pair is said to be valid.

Correctness. For an honestly generated pair $(\tilde{\tau}, \tau) \leftarrow \mathsf{GenTag}(\mathsf{param})$, the witness-word pair must be valid (i.e. both protocols $(\mathsf{ProveVTag}(\tilde{\tau}), \mathsf{VerifVTag}(\tau))$ and $(\mathsf{ProveKTag}(s, \tilde{\tau}), \mathsf{VerifKTag}(s, \tau))$ must output 1).

From an honestly generated witness-word pair $(\tilde{\tau}, \tau) \leftarrow \mathsf{GenTag}(\mathsf{param})$, if $(\tau', \rho) \leftarrow \mathsf{RandTag}(\tau)$ and $\tilde{\tau}' \leftarrow \mathsf{DerivWitness}(\tilde{\tau}, \rho)$ then $(\tilde{\tau}', \tau')$ must also be a valid witness-word pair.

Unlinkability. The algorithm $\mathsf{RandTag}$ must randomize the tag τ within the equivalence class in an unlinkable way: for any pair $((\tilde{\tau}_1, \tau_1), (\tilde{\tau}_2, \tau_2))$ issued from GenTag, the two distributions $\{(\tau_1, \tau_2, \tau_1', \tau_2')\}$ and $\{(\tau_1, \tau_2, \tau_2', \tau_1')\}$, where $\tau_1' \leftarrow \mathsf{RandTag}(\tau_1)$ and $\tau_2' \leftarrow \mathsf{RandTag}(\tau_2)$, must be (computationally) indistinguishable.

4.2 Tag-Based Signatures

For a pair $(\tilde{\tau}, \tau)$, where $\tilde{\tau}$ is a secret tag and τ the associated public tag, one can define a new primitive called *tag-based signature*:

Definition 10 (Tag-Based Signature).

$\mathsf{Setup}(1^\kappa)$: *Given a security parameter κ, it outputs the global parameter* param, *which includes the message space $\mathcal{M}$ and the tag space $\mathcal{T}$;*

$\mathsf{Keygen}(\mathsf{param})$: *Given a public parameter* param, *it outputs a key pair* $(\mathsf{sk}, \mathsf{vk})$*;*

$\mathsf{GenTag}(\mathsf{param})$: *Given a public parameter* param, *it generates a witness-word pair $(\tilde{\tau}, \tau)$;*

$\mathsf{Sign}(\mathsf{sk}, \tau, m)$: *Given a signing key* sk, *a tag τ, and a message m, it outputs the signature σ under the tag τ;*

$\mathsf{VerifSign}(\mathsf{vk}, \tau, m, \sigma)$: *Given a verification key* vk, *a tag τ, a message m and a signature σ, it outputs* 1 *if σ is valid relative to* vk *and τ, and* 0 *otherwise.*

The security notion would expect no adversary able to forge, for any honest pair $(\mathsf{sk}, \mathsf{vk})$, a new signature for a pair (τ, m), for a valid tag τ, if the signature has not been generated using sk and the tag τ on the message m.

Two classical cases are: $(\tilde{\tau} = \mathsf{sk}, \tau = \mathsf{vk})$, which corresponds to a classical signature of m; $\tilde{\tau} = \tau$, with no secret witness, this is just a classical signature of (τ, m). In fact, more subtle situations can be handled, as shown below.

Signatures with Randomizable Tags. When randomizing τ into τ', one must be able to keep track of the change to update $\tilde{\tau}$ to $\tilde{\tau}'$ and the signatures. Formally, we will require to have the algorithm:

$\mathsf{DerivSign}(\mathsf{vk}, \tau, m, \sigma, \rho_{\tau \to \tau'})$: Given a valid signature σ on tag τ and message m, and $\rho_{\tau \to \tau'}$ the randomization link between τ and another tag τ', it outputs a new signature σ' on the message m and the new tag τ'. Both signatures are under the same key vk.

For compatibility with the tag and correctness of the signature scheme, we require that for all honestly generated keys $(\mathsf{sk}, \mathsf{vk}) \leftarrow \mathsf{Keygen}(\mathsf{param})$, all tags $(\tilde{\tau}, \tau) \leftarrow \mathsf{GenTag}(\mathsf{param})$, and all messages m, if $\sigma \leftarrow \mathsf{Sign}(\mathsf{sk}, \tau, m)$, $(\tau', \rho) \leftarrow \mathsf{RandTag}(\tau)$ and $\sigma' \leftarrow \mathsf{DerivSign}(\mathsf{vk}, \tau, m, \sigma, \rho)$, then $\mathsf{VerifSign}(\mathsf{vk}, \tau', m, \sigma')$ should output 1.

For privacy reasons, in case of probabilistic signatures, it will not be enough to just randomize the tag, but the random coins of the signing algorithm too:

$\mathsf{RandSign}(\mathsf{vk}, \tau, m, \sigma)$: Given a valid signature σ on tag τ and message m, it outputs a new signature σ' on the same message m and tag τ.

Correctness extends the above one, where the algorithm $\mathsf{VerifSign}(\mathsf{vk}, \tau', m, \sigma'')$ should output 1 with $\sigma'' \leftarrow \mathsf{RandSign}(\mathsf{vk}, \tau', m, \sigma')$. One additionally expects unlinkability: the distributions $\mathcal{D}_0$ and $\mathcal{D}_1$ are (computationally) indistinguishable, for any vk and m (possibly chosen by the adversary), where for $i = 0, 1$, $(\tilde{\tau}_i, \tau_i) \leftarrow \mathsf{GenTag}(1^\kappa)$, $\sigma_i \leftarrow \mathsf{Sign}(\mathsf{sk}, \tau_i, m)$, $(\tau'_i, \rho_i) \leftarrow \mathsf{RandTag}(\tau_i)$, $\sigma'_i \leftarrow \mathsf{DerivSign}(\mathsf{vk}, \tau_i, m, \sigma_i, \rho_i)$ and $\sigma''_i \leftarrow \mathsf{RandSign}(\mathsf{vk}, \tau'_i, m, \sigma'_i)$, and for $b = 0, 1$, we set $\mathcal{D}_b = \{(m, \mathsf{vk}, \tau_0, \sigma_0, \tau'_b, \sigma''_b, \tau_1, \sigma_1, \tau'_{1-b}, \sigma''_{1-b})\}$. We stress that this indistinguishability should also hold with respect to the signer, who knows the signing key, after randomization of the signature (and not just of the tag) in case of probabilistic signature.

Signatures with Randomizable Tags on Vectors. We will extend the above algorithms to vectors of keys $\vec{\mathsf{sk}}$, $\vec{\mathsf{pk}}$, messages $\vec{m}$, and signatures $\vec{\sigma}$, of the same length, but for a common tag τ, by applying the algorithms on the component-wise elements:

$\mathsf{Sign}(\vec{\mathsf{sk}}, \tau, \vec{m})$ outputs $\vec{\sigma}$ where each component $\sigma_i \leftarrow \mathsf{Sign}(\mathsf{sk}_i, \tau, m_i)$, for the common tag τ;

$\mathsf{VerifSign}(\vec{\mathsf{vk}}, \tau, \vec{m}, \vec{\sigma})$ outputs the conjunction of the Boolean output by all the verifications $\mathsf{VerifSign}(\mathsf{vk}_i, \tau, m_i, \sigma_i)$ on each component, under the common tag τ (whether all the verifications accept or not);

$\mathsf{DerivSign}(\vec{\mathsf{vk}}, \tau, \vec{m}, \vec{\sigma}, \rho_{\tau \to \tau'})$ outputs $\vec{\sigma'}$ where each component is derived as $\sigma'_i \leftarrow \mathsf{DerivSign}(\mathsf{vk}_i, \tau, m_i, \sigma_i, \rho_{\tau \to \tau'})$;

$\mathsf{RandSign}(\vec{\mathsf{vk}}, \tau, \vec{m}, \vec{\sigma})$ outputs $\vec{\sigma'}$ where each component is randomized as $\sigma'_i \leftarrow \mathsf{RandSign}(\mathsf{vk}_i, \tau, m_i, \sigma_i)$, for the common tag τ.

This is a preliminary step towards aggregate signatures that will allow a compact representation of $\vec{\sigma}$, independent of the length of the vector, when the tag τ is the same for all the components. This will be the core of our compact anonymous credentials. In both cases, with vectors of any length or of length 1, some properties will be required.

Correctness. From any valid tag-pair $(\tilde{\tau}, \tau)$ and honestly generated pairs of keys $(\mathsf{sk}_j, \mathsf{vk}_j) \leftarrow \mathsf{Keygen}(\mathsf{param})$, if $\sigma_j = \mathsf{Sign}(\mathsf{sk}_j, \tau, m_j)$ are valid signatures on message $m_j \in \mathcal{M}$, for $j = 1, \cdots, \ell$, if $(\tau', \rho) \leftarrow \mathsf{RandTag}(\tau)$:

- either after the derivation for the tag, $\vec{\sigma'} \leftarrow \mathsf{DerivSign}(\vec{\mathsf{vk}}, \tau, \vec{m}, \vec{\sigma}, \rho)$, and the randomization of the signature, $\vec{\sigma''} \leftarrow \mathsf{RandSign}(\vec{\mathsf{vk}}, \tau', \vec{m}, \vec{\sigma'})$
- or after the randomization of the signature $\vec{\sigma'} \leftarrow \mathsf{RandSign}(\vec{\mathsf{vk}}, \tau, \vec{m}, \vec{\sigma})$, and the derivation for the tag, $\vec{\sigma''} \leftarrow \mathsf{DerivSign}(\vec{\mathsf{vk}}, \tau, \vec{m}, \vec{\sigma'}, \rho)$

then the verification $\mathsf{VerifSign}(\vec{\mathsf{vk}}, \tau', \vec{m}, \vec{\sigma''})$ should output 1.

Unforgeability. In the Chosen-Message Unforgeability security game, the adversary has unlimited access to the following oracles, with lists KList and TList initially empty:

- $\mathcal{O}\mathsf{GenTag}()$ outputs the tag τ and keeps track of the associated witness $\tilde{\tau}$, with $(\tilde{\tau}, \tau)$ appended to TList;
- $\mathcal{O}\mathsf{Keygen}()$ outputs the verification key vk and keeps track of the associated signing key sk, with $(\mathsf{sk}, \mathsf{vk})$ appended to KList;
- $\mathcal{O}\mathsf{Sign}(\tau, \mathsf{vk}, m)$, for $(\tilde{\tau}, \tau) \in \mathsf{TList}$ and $(\mathsf{sk}, \mathsf{vk}) \in \mathsf{KList}$, outputs $\mathsf{Sign}(\mathsf{sk}, \tau, m)$.

It should not be possible to generate a signature that falls outside the range of $\mathsf{DerivSign}$ or $\mathsf{RandSign}$:

Definition 11 (Unforgeability for RT-Sign). *An RT-Sign scheme is said unforgeable if, for any adversary $\mathcal{A}$ that, given signatures σ_i for tuples $(\tau_i, \mathsf{vk}_i, m_i)$ of its choice but for τ_i and vk_i issued from the* GenTag *and* Keygen *algorithms respectively (for Chosen-Message Attacks), outputs a tuple $(\vec{\mathsf{vk}}, \tau, \vec{m}, \vec{\sigma})$ where both τ is a valid tag and $\vec{\sigma}$ is a valid signature w.r.t. $(\vec{\mathsf{vk}}, \tau, \vec{m})$, there exists a subset J of the signing queries with a common tag $\tau' \in \{\tau_i\}_i$ such that $\tau \sim \tau'$, $\forall j \in J, \tau_j = \tau'$, $\vec{\mathsf{vk}} = (\mathsf{vk}_j)_{j \in J}$, and $\vec{m} = (m_j)_{j \in J}$, with overwhelming probability.*

Since there are multiple secrets, we can consider corruptions of some of them:

- $\mathcal{O}\mathsf{CorruptTag}(\tau)$, for $(\tilde{\tau}, \tau) \in \mathsf{TList}$, outputs $\tilde{\tau}$;
- $\mathcal{O}\mathsf{Corrupt}(\mathsf{vk})$, for $(\mathsf{sk}, \mathsf{vk}) \in \mathsf{KList}$, outputs sk.

The forgery should not involve a corrupted key (but corrupted tags are allowed). Note again that all the tags are valid (either issued from GenTag or verified). In the unforgeability security notion, some limitations might be applied to the signing queries: one-time queries (for a given tag-key pair) or a bounded number of queries.

Unlinkability. Randomizability of both the tag and the signature are expected to provide anonymity, with some unlinkability property:

Definition 12 (Unlinkability for RT-Sign). *An RT-Sign scheme is said unlinkable if, for any $\vec{\mathsf{vk}}$ and $\vec{m}$, no adversary $\mathcal{A}$ can distinguish the distributions $\mathcal{D}_0$ and $\mathcal{D}_1$, where for $i = 0, 1$, we have $(\tilde{\tau}_i, \tau_i) \leftarrow \mathsf{GenTag}(1^\kappa)$, $(\tau'_i, \rho_i) \leftarrow \mathsf{RandTag}(\tau_i)$, $\vec{\sigma_i}$ is any valid signature of $\vec{m}$ under τ_i and $\vec{\mathsf{vk}}$, and eventually $\vec{\sigma'_i} \leftarrow \mathsf{DerivSign}(\vec{\mathsf{vk}}, \tau_i, \vec{m}, \vec{\sigma_i}, \rho_i)$ and $\vec{\sigma''_i} \leftarrow \mathsf{RandSign}(\vec{\mathsf{vk}}, \tau'_i, \vec{m}, \vec{\sigma'_i})$, and for $b = 0, 1$ we set $\mathcal{D}_b = \{(\vec{m}, \vec{\mathsf{vk}}, \tau_0, \vec{\sigma_0}, \tau'_b, \vec{\sigma''_B}, \tau_1, \vec{\sigma_1}, \tau'_{1-b}, \vec{\sigma''_{1-b}})\}$.*

We stress that this indistinguishability should also hold with respect to the signer, who might have generated the initial signatures $\vec{\sigma_0}$ and $\vec{\sigma_1}$, but then after randomization of the signature (and not just of the tag, with derivation) in case of probabilistic signature.

4.3 Anonymous Credential from EphemerId and RT-Sign

We first explain how EphemerId and RT-Sign can lead to anonymous credentials, in a black-box way. Our concrete constructions will thereafter exploit aggregate RT-Sign, to achieve compactness, independently of the number of credentials and authorities (credential issuers).

Let $\mathcal{E}$ be an EphemerId scheme and S^{rt} an RT-Sign scheme, one can construct an anonymous attribute-based credential scheme. The user's keys will be tag pairs and the credentials will be RT-Sign signatures on both the tags and the attributes. Since the tag is randomizable, the user can anonymously show any set of credentials: multiple showings will use unlinkable tags.

Furthermore, as the signature scheme tolerates corruptions of users and signers, we will be able to consider corruptions of users and credential issuers, and even possible collusions:

$\mathsf{Setup}(1^\kappa)$: Given a security parameter κ, it runs $\mathsf{S}^{\mathrm{rt}}.\mathsf{Setup}$ and outputs the public parameters param which includes all the parameters;

$\mathsf{CIKeyGen}(\mathsf{ID})$: Credential issuer CI with identity ID, runs $\mathsf{S}^{\mathrm{rt}}.\mathsf{Keygen}(\mathsf{param})$ to obtain his key pair $(\mathsf{sk}, \mathsf{vk})$;

$\mathsf{UKeyGen}(\mathsf{id})$: User $\mathcal{U}$ with identity id, runs $\mathcal{E}.\mathsf{GenTag}(\mathsf{param})$ to obtain his key pair $(\mathsf{usk}, \mathsf{uvk})$;

$(\mathsf{CredObtain}(\mathsf{usk}, \mathsf{vk}, a), \mathsf{CredIssue}(\mathsf{uvk}, \mathsf{sk}, a))$: User $\mathcal{U}$ with identity id and key-pair $(\mathsf{usk}, \mathsf{uvk})$ asks the credential issuer CI for a credential on attribute a: $\sigma = \mathsf{S}^{\mathrm{rt}}.\mathsf{Sign}(\mathsf{sk}, \mathsf{uvk}, a)$, which can be checked by the user;

$(\mathsf{CredShow}(\mathsf{usk}, (\mathsf{vk}_j, a_j, \sigma_j)_j), \mathsf{CredVerify}((\mathsf{vk}_j, a_j)_j))$: User $\mathcal{U}$ randomizes his public key $(\mathsf{uvk}', \rho) = \mathcal{E}.\mathsf{RandTag}(\mathsf{uvk})$. Then, it adapts the secret key $\mathsf{usk}' = \mathcal{E}.\mathsf{DerivWitness}(\mathsf{usk}, \rho)$, thanks to ρ, as well as the signatures $(\sigma'_j)_j = \mathsf{S}^{\mathrm{rt}}.\mathsf{DerivSign}((\mathsf{vk}_j)_j, \mathsf{uvk}, (a_j, \sigma_j)_j, \rho)$, using the above algorithm on vectors. It then randomizes them: $(\sigma''_j)_j = \mathsf{S}^{\mathrm{rt}}.\mathsf{RandSign}((\mathsf{vk}_j)_j, \mathsf{uvk}', (a_j, \sigma'_j)_j)$. It eventually sends the anonymous credentials $((\mathsf{vk}_j, a_j, \sigma''_j)_j, \mathsf{uvk}')$ to the verifier $\mathcal{V}$. The verifier first checks the freshness of the credentials with a proof of ownership of uvk'. This is performed using the interactive protocol $(\mathcal{E}.\mathsf{ProveKTag}(\mathsf{usk}'), \mathcal{E}.\mathsf{VerifKTag}(\mathsf{uvk}'))$. It then verifies the validity of the credentials with $\mathsf{S}^{\mathrm{rt}}.\mathsf{VerifSign}((\mathsf{vk}_j)_j, \mathsf{uvk}', (a_j, \sigma''_j)_j)$.

We stress that for all the above notations $(u_j)_j$, we use the algorithms on vectors, that apply the initial algorithms component-wise. This does not lead to compact credentials, as they are vectors $(\sigma_j)_j$, but we only consider security in this section. Efficiency will be dealt in the next section, with aggregate signatures.

If one considers corruptions, when one corrupts a user or a credential issuer, the corresponding secret key is provided.

With secure EphemerId and RT-Sign schemes, the above construction is an anonymous attribute-based credential scheme, with security results stated below and proven in the full version [15].

Theorem 13. *Assuming EphemerId achieves knowledge-soundness and RT-Sign is unforgeable, the generic construction is an unforgeable attribute-based credential scheme, in the certified key model.*

Theorem 14. *Assuming EphemerId is zero-knowledge and RT-Sign is unlinkable, the generic construction is an anonymous attribute-based credential scheme, in the certified key model.*

5 Constructions

Our concrete constructions will provide compact credentials. To this aim, we need more compact signatures on vectors than vectors of signatures. We thus recall the notion of aggregate signatures, and define the aggregate signatures with randomizable tags.

5.1 Aggregate Signatures with Randomizable Tags

Aggregate Signatures. Boneh et al. [4] remarked it was possible to aggregate the BLS signature [5], we will follow this path, but for tag-based signatures, with possible aggregation only between signatures with the same tag, in a similar way as the indexed aggregated signatures [9]. We will even consider aggregation of public keys, which can either still be a simple concatenation or a more evolved combination as in [3]. Hence, an aggregate (tag-based) signature scheme ($\mathsf{AggrSign}$) is a signature scheme with the algorithms:

$\mathsf{AggrKey}((\mathsf{vk}_j)_{j=1}^{\ell})$: Given ℓ verification keys vk_j, it outputs an aggregated verification key avk;
$\mathsf{AggrSign}(\tau, (\mathsf{vk}_j, m_j, \sigma_j)_{j=1}^{\ell})$: Given ℓ signed messages m_j in σ_j under vk_j and the same tag τ, it outputs a signature σ on the message vector $\vec{m} = (m_j)_{j=1}^{\ell}$ under the tag τ and aggregated verification key avk.

One can note that avk can be $\vec{\mathsf{vk}}$ or a more compact encoding. Similarly, the aggregate signature σ from $\vec{\sigma} = (\sigma_j)_j$ can remain this concatenation or a more compact representation.

While we will still focus on signing algorithm of a single message with a single key, we have to consider verification algorithm on vectors of keys and message, but on a compact signature.

Correctness of an aggregate (tag-based) signature scheme requires that for any valid tag-pair $(\tilde{\tau}, \tau)$ and honestly generated keys $(\mathsf{sk}_j, \mathsf{vk}_j) \leftarrow \mathsf{Keygen}(\mathsf{param})$, if $\sigma_j = \mathsf{Sign}(\mathsf{sk}_j, \tau, m_j)$ are valid signatures for $j = 1, \cdots, \ell$, then for both key $\mathsf{avk} \leftarrow \mathsf{AggrKey}((\mathsf{vk}_j)_{j=1}^{\ell})$ and signature $\sigma = \mathsf{AggrSign}(\tau, (\mathsf{vk}_j, m_j, \sigma_j)_{j=1}^{\ell})$, the verification $\mathsf{VerifSign}(\mathsf{avk}, \tau, (m_j)_{j=1}^{\ell}, \sigma)$ should output 1.

Aggregate Signatures with Randomizable Tags. We can now provide the formal definition of an aggregate signature scheme with randomizable tags, where some algorithms exploit compatibility between the $\mathsf{EphemerId}$ scheme and the signature scheme:

Definition 15 (Aggregate Signatures with Randomizable Tags (ART-Sign)). *An ART-Sign scheme, associated to an* $\mathsf{EphemerId}$ *scheme* $\mathcal{E} = (\mathsf{Setup}, \mathsf{GenTag}, \mathsf{RandTag}, \mathsf{DerivWitness}, (\mathsf{ProveVTag}, \mathsf{VerifVTag}))$ *consists of the algorithms* $(\mathsf{Setup}, \mathsf{Keygen}, \mathsf{Sign}, \mathsf{AggrKey}, \mathsf{AggrSign}, \mathsf{DerivSign}, \mathsf{RandSign}, \mathsf{VerifSign})$*:*

$\mathsf{Setup}(1^{\kappa})$*: Given a security parameter* κ*, it runs* $\mathcal{E}.\mathsf{Setup}$ *and outputs the global parameter* param*, which includes* $\mathcal{E}.\mathsf{param}$ *with the tag space* $\mathcal{T}$*, and extends it with the message space* $\mathcal{M}$*;*
$\mathsf{Keygen}(\mathsf{param})$*: Given a public parameter* param*, it outputs a key-pair* $(\mathsf{sk},\mathsf{vk})$*;*
$\mathsf{Sign}(\mathsf{sk}, \tau, m)$*: Given a signing key, a valid tag* τ*, and a message* $m \in \mathcal{M}$*, it outputs the signature* σ*;*
$\mathsf{AggrKey}((\mathsf{vk}_j)_{j=1}^{\ell})$*: Given* ℓ *verification keys* vk_j*, it outputs an aggregated verification key* avk*;*

$\mathsf{AggrSign}(\tau, (\mathsf{vk}_j, m_j, \sigma_j)_{j=1}^{\ell})$: *Given* ℓ *signed messages* m_j *in* σ_j *under* vk_j *and the same valid tag* τ, *it outputs a signature* σ *on the vector* $\vec{m} = (m_j)_{j=1}^{\ell}$ *under the tag* τ *and aggregated verification key* avk;

$\mathsf{VerifSign}(\mathsf{avk}, \tau, \vec{m}, \sigma)$: *Given a verification key* avk, *a valid tag* τ, *a vector* $\vec{m}$ *and a signature* σ, *it outputs* 1 *if* σ *is valid relative to* avk *and* τ, *and* 0 *otherwise;*

$\mathsf{DerivSign}(\mathsf{avk}, \tau, \vec{m}, \sigma, \rho_{\tau \to \tau'})$: *Given a signature* σ *on a vector* $\vec{m}$ *under a valid tag* τ *and aggregated verification key* avk, *and the randomization link* $\rho_{\tau \to \tau'}$ *between* τ *and another tag* τ', *it outputs a signature* σ' *on the vector* $\vec{m}$ *under the new tag* τ' *and the same key* avk;

$\mathsf{RandSign}(\mathsf{avk}, \tau, \vec{m}, \sigma)$: *Given a signature* σ *on a vector* $\vec{m}$ *under a valid tag* τ *and aggregated verification key* avk, *it outputs a new signature* σ' *on the vector* $\vec{m}$ *and the same tag* τ.

We stress that all the tags must be valid: their verification must be performed before the verification of the signatures.

Note that using algorithms from $\mathcal{E}$, tags are randomizable at any time, and signatures adapted and randomized, even after an aggregation: avk and $\vec{m}$ can either be single key and message or aggregations of keys and messages. Note that only protocol ($\mathsf{ProveVTag}$, $\mathsf{VerifVTag}$) from $\mathcal{E}$ is involved in the ART-Sign scheme, as one just needs to check the validity of the tag, not the ownership. The latter will be useful in anonymous credentials with fresh proof of ownership.

Correctness, unforgeability, and unlinkability are the same as above, where the compact aggregate signature σ replaces the vector $\vec{\sigma}$.

5.2 Constructions

We can now instantiate the different primitives. More precisely, we provide two constructions of a multi-authority anonymous credential scheme each one based on a construction of an ART-Sign scheme: a one-time version and a bounded version. In the first construction, we consider attributes where the index i determines the attribute type (age, city, diploma) and the exact value is encoded in $a_i \in \mathbb{Z}_p^*$ (possibly $\mathcal{H}(m) \in \mathbb{Z}_p^*$ if the value is a large bitstring), or 0 when empty. The second construction (see the full version [15]) does not require any such ordering on the attributes. Arbitrary bit strings are supported. However, the construction of the EphemerId scheme is in common.

SqDH-based EphemerId Scheme. With tags in $\mathcal{T} = \mathbb{G}_1^3$, in an asymmetric bilinear setting $(\mathbb{G}_1, \mathbb{G}_2, \mathbb{G}_T, p, g, \mathfrak{g}, e)$, and $\tau = (h, h^{\tilde{\tau}}, h^{\tilde{\tau}^2})$ a Square Diffie-Hellman tuple, one can define the SqDH EphemerId scheme:

$\mathsf{Setup}(1^\kappa)$: Given a security parameter κ, let $(\mathbb{G}_1, \mathbb{G}_2, \mathbb{G}_T, p, g, \mathfrak{g}, e)$ be an asymmetric bilinear setting, where g and $\mathfrak{g}$ are random generators of $\mathbb{G}_1$ and $\mathbb{G}_2$ respectively. The set of (valid and invalid) tags is $\mathcal{T} = \mathbb{G}_1^3$. We then define $\mathsf{param} = (\mathbb{G}_1, \mathbb{G}_2, \mathbb{G}_T, p, g, \mathfrak{g}, e; \mathcal{T})$;

$\mathsf{GenTag}(\mathsf{param})$: Given a public parameter param, it randomly chooses a generator $h \overset{\$}{\leftarrow} \mathbb{G}_1^*$ and outputs $\tilde{\tau} \overset{\$}{\leftarrow} \mathbb{Z}_p^*$ and $\tau = (h, h^{\tilde{\tau}}, h^{\tilde{\tau}^2}) \in \mathbb{G}_1^3$.

$\mathsf{RandTag}(\tau)$: Given a tag τ as input, it chooses $\rho_{\tau\to\tau'} \xleftarrow{\$} \mathbb{Z}_p$ and constructs $\tau' = \tau^{\rho_{\tau\to\tau'}}$ the derived tag. It outputs $(\tau', \rho_{\tau\to\tau'})$.

$\mathsf{DerivWitness}(\tilde{\tau}, \rho_{\tau\to\tau'})$: The derived witness remains unchanged: $\tilde{\tau}' = \tilde{\tau}$.

$\mathsf{ProveVTag}(\tilde{\tau}), \mathsf{VerifVTag}(\tau)$: The prover constructs the proof $\pi = \mathsf{proof}(\tilde{\tau} : \tau = (h, h^{\tilde{\tau}}, h^{\tilde{\tau}^2}))$ (see the full version [15] for a non-interactive proof using the Groth-Sahai [13] framework). The verifier outputs 1 if it accepts the proof and 0 otherwise.

Valid tags are Square Diffie-Hellman pairs in $\mathbb{G}_1$:

$$\mathcal{L} = \{(h, h^x, h^{x^2}), h \in \mathbb{G}_1^*, x \in \mathbb{Z}_p^*\} = \cup_{x\in\mathbb{Z}_p^*}\mathcal{L}_x \quad \mathcal{L}_x = \{(h, h^x, h^{x^2}), h \in \mathbb{G}_1^*\}$$

The randomization does not affect the exponents, hence there are $p-1$ different equivalence classes $\mathcal{L}_x$, for all the non-zero exponents $x \in \mathbb{Z}_p^*$, and correctness is clearly satisfied within equivalence classes. The validity check (see the full version [15]) is sound as the Groth-Sahai commitment is in the perfectly binding setting. Such tags also admit an interactive Schnorr-like zero-knowledge proof of knowledge of the exponent $\tilde{\tau}$ for $(\mathsf{ProveKTag}(\tilde{\tau}), \mathsf{VerifKTag}(\tau))$ which also provides extractability (knowledge-soundness). With the Fiat-Shamir heuristic and the random oracle, this proof of knowledge can be transformed into a non-interactive one, also called a signature of knowledge. Under the DSqDH and DL assumptions, given the tag τ, it is hard to recover the exponent $\tilde{\tau} = x$. The tags, after randomization, are uniformly distributed in the equivalence class, and under the DSqDH-assumption, each class is indistinguishable from $\mathbb{G}_1^3$, and thus one has unlinkability: see Theorem 3.

One-Time SqDH-based ART-Sign Scheme. The above EphemerId scheme can be extended into an ART-Sign scheme where implicit vector messages are signed. As the aggregation can be made on signatures of messages under the same tag but from various signers, the description is given for multiple and independent signers, each indexed by j, and any signed message by the j-signer for coordinate i is indexed by (j, i).

We stress that this *one-time* scheme needs to be state-full as there is the limitation for a signer j not to sign more than one message with index (j, i) for a given tag: a signer must use two different indices to sign two messages for one tag. This is due to the linearly-homomorphic signature scheme: each coordinate a is signed, as a pair (g, g^a), in a subspace of dimension 2. The linearity limits to Diffie-Hellman pairs with constant ratio a. But with two independent 2-dimension vectors, one can generate the full subspace $\mathbb{G}_1 \times \mathbb{G}_1$.

Our construction of aggregate signature with randomizable tags is based on the second linearly-homomorphic signature scheme of [14, Appendix C.5]:

$\mathsf{Setup}(1^\kappa)$: It extends the above setup with the set of messages $\mathcal{M} = \mathbb{Z}_p$;

$\mathsf{Keygen}(\mathsf{param})$: Given the public parameters param, it outputs the signing and verification keys

$$\begin{aligned}\mathsf{sk}_{j,i} &= (\ \mathsf{SK}_j = [\ t_j,\ u_j,\ v_j\ ],\ \mathsf{SK}'_{j,i} = [\ r_{j,i},\ s_{j,i}\ ]\ ) \xleftarrow{\$} \mathbb{Z}_p^5,\\ \mathsf{vk}_{j,i} &= (\ \mathsf{VK}_j = [\ \mathfrak{g}^{t_j},\ \mathfrak{g}^{u_j},\ \mathfrak{g}^{v_j}\ ],\ \mathsf{VK}'_{j,i} = [\ \mathfrak{g}^{r_{j,i}},\ \mathfrak{g}^{s_{j,i}}\ ]\ ) \in \mathbb{G}_2^5.\end{aligned}$$

Note that one could dynamically add new $\mathsf{SK}'_{j,i}$ and $\mathsf{VK}'_{j,i}$ to sign implicit vector messages: $\mathsf{sk}_j = \mathsf{SK}_j \cup [\mathsf{SK}'_{j,i}]_i$, $\mathsf{vk}_j = \mathsf{VK}_j \cup [\mathsf{VK}'_{j,i}]_i$;

$\mathsf{Sign}(\mathsf{sk}_{j,i}, \tau, m)$: Given a signing key $\mathsf{sk}_{j,i} = [t, u, v, r, s]$, a message $m \in \mathbb{Z}_p$ and a public tag $\tau = (\tau_1, \tau_2, \tau_3)$, it outputs the signature (of m, by the j-th signer on the index (j,i)): $\sigma = \tau_1^{t+r+ms} \times \tau_2^u \times \tau_3^v \in \mathbb{G}_1$.

$\mathsf{AggrKey}((\mathsf{vk}_{j,i})_{j,i})$: Given verification keys $\mathsf{vk}_{j,i}$, it outputs the aggregated verification key $\mathsf{avk} = [\mathsf{avk}_j]_j$, with $\mathsf{avk}_j = \mathsf{VK}_j \cup [\mathsf{VK}'_{j,i}]_i$ for each j;

$\mathsf{AggrSign}(\tau, (\mathsf{vk}_{j,i}, m_{j,i}, \sigma_{j,i})_{j,i})$: Given tuples of verification key $\mathsf{vk}_{j,i}$, message $m_{j,i}$ and signature $\sigma_{j,i}$ all under the same tag τ, it outputs the signature $\sigma = \prod_{j,i} \sigma_{j,i} \in \mathbb{G}_1$ of the concatenation of the messages verifiable with $\mathsf{avk} \leftarrow \mathsf{AggrKey}((\mathsf{vk}_{j,i})_{j,i})$. Note that one needs to keep track of the indices of the $m_{j,i}$ in the concatenation;

$\mathsf{DerivSign}(\mathsf{avk}, \tau, \vec{M}, \sigma, \rho_{\tau\to\tau'})$: Given a signature σ on tag τ and a vector $\vec{M}$ (of tuples), and $\rho_{\tau\to\tau'}$ the randomization link between τ and another tag τ', it outputs $\sigma' = \sigma^{\rho_{\tau\to\tau'}}$;

$\mathsf{RandSign}(\mathsf{avk}, \tau, \vec{M}, \sigma)$: The scheme being deterministic, it returns σ;

$\mathsf{VerifSign}(\mathsf{avk}, \tau, \vec{M}, \sigma)$: Given a valid tag $\tau = (\tau_1, \tau_2, \tau_3)$, an aggregated verification key $\mathsf{avk} = [\mathsf{avk}_j]$ and a vector $\vec{M} = [\mathsf{m}_j]$, with both for each j, $\mathsf{avk}_j = \mathsf{VK}_j \cup [\mathsf{VK}'_{j,i}]_i$ and $\mathsf{m}_j = [m_{j,i}]_i$, and a signature σ, one checks if the following equality holds or not, where $n_j = \#\{\mathsf{VK}'_{j,i}\}$:

$$e(\sigma, \mathfrak{g}) = e\left(\tau_1, \prod_j \mathsf{VK}_{j,1}{}^{n_j} \times \prod_i \mathsf{VK}'_{j,i,1} \cdot \mathsf{VK}'_{j,i,2}{}^{m_{j,i}}\right)$$
$$\times\, e\left(\tau_2, \prod_j \mathsf{VK}_{j,2}{}^{n_j}\right) \times e\left(\tau_3, \prod_j \mathsf{VK}_{j,3}{}^{n_j}\right).$$

In case of similar public keys in the aggregation (a unique index j), $\mathsf{avk} = \mathsf{VK} \cup [\mathsf{VK}'_i]_i$ and verification becomes, where $n = \#\{\mathsf{VK}'_i\}$,

$$e(\sigma, \mathfrak{g}) = e\left(\tau_1, \mathsf{VK}_1{}^n \times \prod_{i=1}^n \mathsf{VK}'_{i,1} \cdot \mathsf{VK}'_{i,2}{}^{m_i}\right) \times e(\tau_2, \mathsf{VK}_2{}^n) \times e(\tau_3, \mathsf{VK}_3{}^n).$$

Recall that the validity of the tag has to be verified, either with a proof of knowledge of the witness (as it will be the case in the ABC scheme, or with the proof $\pi = \mathsf{proof}(\tilde{\tau} : \tau = (h, h^{\tilde{\tau}}, h^{\tilde{\tau}^2}))$ (such as the one given in the full version [15]).

Security of the One-Time SqDH-based ART-Sign Scheme. As argued in the article [14, Appendix C.5], the signature scheme defined above is unforgeable in the generic group model [18], if signing queries are asked at most once per tag-index pair. About unlinkability, it relies on the DSqDH assumption, but between signatures that contain the same messages at the same shown indices (the same vector $\vec{M}$). Both security properties are stated below and proven in the full version [15]:

Theorem 16. *The One-Time SqDH-based ART-Sign is unforgeable with one signature only per index, for a given tag, even with adaptive corruptions of keys and tags, in the generic group model.*

Theorem 17. *The One-Time SqDH-based ART-Sign is unlinkable under the* DSqDH *and* DDH *assumptions.*

The Basic SqDH-based Anonymous Credential Scheme. The basic construction directly follows the instantiation of the above construction with the SqDH-based ART-Sign:

$\mathsf{Setup}(1^\kappa)$: Given a security parameter κ, let $(\mathbb{G}_1, \mathbb{G}_2, \mathbb{G}_T, p, g, \mathfrak{g}, e)$ be an asymmetric bilinear setting, where g and $\mathfrak{g}$ are random generators of $\mathbb{G}_1$ and $\mathbb{G}_2$ respectively. We then define $\mathsf{param} = (\mathbb{G}_1, \mathbb{G}_2, \mathbb{G}_T, p, g, \mathfrak{g}, e, \mathcal{H})$, where $\mathcal{H}$ is an hash function in $\mathbb{G}_1$;

$\mathsf{CIKeyGen}(\mathsf{ID})$: Credential issuer CI with identity ID, generates its keys for n kinds of attributes

$$\begin{aligned}\mathsf{sk}_j &= (\ \mathsf{SK}_j = [\ t_j,\ u_j,\ v_j\ ], \mathsf{SK}'_{j,i} = [\ r_{j,i},\ s_{j,i}\ ]_i\ ) \xleftarrow{\$} \mathbb{Z}_p^{3+2n},\\ \mathsf{vk}_j &= (\ \mathsf{VK}_j = [\ \mathfrak{g}^{t_j}, \mathfrak{g}^{u_j}, \mathfrak{g}^{v_j}\ ], \mathsf{VK}'_{j,i} = [\ \mathfrak{g}^{r_{j,i}}, \mathfrak{g}^{s_{j,i}}\ ]_i\ ) \in \mathbb{G}_2^{3+2n}.\end{aligned}$$

More keys for new attributes can be generated on-demand: by adding the pair $[r_{j,i}, s_{j,i}] \xleftarrow{\$} \mathbb{Z}_p^2$ to the secret key and $[\mathfrak{g}^{r_{j,i}}, \mathfrak{g}^{s_{j,i}}]$ to the verification key, the keys can works on $n+1$ kinds of attributes;

$\mathsf{UKeyGen}(\mathsf{id})$: User $\mathcal{U}$ with identity id, sets $h = \mathcal{H}(\mathsf{id}) \in \mathbb{G}_1^*$, generates its secret tag $\tilde{\tau} \xleftarrow{\$} \mathbb{Z}_p^*$ jointly with CA (to guarantee randomness) and computes $\tau = (h, h^{\tilde{\tau}}, h^{\tilde{\tau}^2}) \in \mathbb{G}_1^3$: $\mathsf{usk} = \tilde{\tau}$ and $\mathsf{uvk} = \tau = (h, h^{\tilde{\tau}}, h^{\tilde{\tau}^2})$;

$(\mathsf{CredObtain}(\mathsf{usk}, \mathsf{vk}, a_i), \mathsf{CredIssue}(\mathsf{uvk}, \mathsf{sk}, a_i))$: User $\mathcal{U}$ with identity id and $\mathsf{uvk} = (\tau_1, \tau_2, \tau_3)$ asks to the credential issuer CI for a credential on the attribute a_i: $\sigma = \tau_1^{t+r_i+a_i s_i} \times \tau_2^u \times \tau_3^v \in \mathbb{G}_1$. The credential issuer uses the appropriate index i, making sure this is the first signature for this index;

$(\mathsf{CredShow}(\mathsf{usk}, (\mathsf{VK}_j, \mathsf{VK}'_{j,i}, a_{j,i}, \sigma_{j,i})_{j,i}), \mathsf{CredVerify}((\mathsf{VK}_j, \mathsf{VK}'_{j,i}, a_{j,i})_{j,i}))$:
First, user $\mathcal{U}$ randomizes his public key with a random $\rho \xleftarrow{\$} \mathbb{Z}_p^*$ into $\mathsf{uvk}' = (\tau_1^\rho, \tau_2^\rho, \tau_3^\rho)$, concatenates the keys $\mathsf{avk} = \cup_j([\mathsf{VK}_j] \cup [\mathsf{VK}'_{j,i}]_i)$, agregates $\sigma = \prod_{j,i} \sigma_{j,i} \in \mathbb{G}_1$, and adapts the signature $\sigma' = \sigma^\rho$. Then it sends the anonymous credential $(\mathsf{avk}, (a_{j,i})_{j,i}, \mathsf{uvk}', \sigma')$ to the verifier. The latter first checks the freshness of the credential with a proof of both ownership and validity of uvk' using a Schnorr-like interactive proof and then verifies the validity of the credential, with $n_j = \#\{\mathsf{VK}'_{j,i}\}$:

$$\begin{aligned}e(\sigma', \mathfrak{g}) = e&\left(\tau_1, \prod_j {\mathsf{VK}_{j,1}}^{n_j} \times \prod_i \mathsf{VK}'_{j,i,1} \cdot {\mathsf{VK}'_{j,i,2}}^{a_{j,i}}\right)\\ &\times e\left(\tau_2, \prod_j {\mathsf{VK}_{j,2}}^{n_j}\right) \times e\left(\tau_3, \prod_j {\mathsf{VK}_{j,3}}^{n_j}\right).\end{aligned}$$

We stress that for the unforgeability of the signature, generator h for each tag must be random, and so it is generated as $\mathcal{H}(\mathsf{id})$, with a hash function $\mathcal{H}$ in $\mathbb{G}_1$. This way, the credential issuers will automatically know the basis for each user. There is no privacy issue as this basis is randomized when used in an anonymous credential. Moreover, the user needs his secret key $\tilde{\tau}$ to be random. Therefore, he jointly generates $\tilde{\tau}$ with the Certification Authority (see the full version [15]). During the showing of a credential, the user has to make a fresh proof of knowledge of the witness for the validity of the tag. Again, in the security proof of unforgeability, one may need a rewinding, but only for the target alleged forgery.

In this construction, we can consider a polynomial number n of attributes per credential issuer, where a_i is associated to key $\mathsf{vk}_{j,i}$ of the Credential Issuer CI_j. Again, to keep the unforgeability of the signature, the credential issuer should provide at most one attribute per key $\mathsf{vk}_{j,i}$ for a given tag. At the showing time, for proving the ownership of k attributes (possibly from K different credential issuers), the users has to perform $k - 1$ multiplications in $\mathbb{G}_1$ to aggregate the credentials into one, and 4 exponentiations in $\mathbb{G}_1$ for randomization, but just one element from $\mathbb{G}_1$ is sent, as anonymous credential, plus an interactive Schnorr-like proof of SqDH-tuple with knowledge of usk (see the full version [15]: 2 exponentiations in $\mathbb{G}_1$, 2 group elements from $\mathbb{G}_1$, and a scalar in $\mathbb{Z}_p$); whereas the verifier first has to perform 4 exponentiations and 2 multiplications in $\mathbb{G}_1$ for the proof of validity/knowledge of usk, and less than $3k$ multiplications and k exponentiations in $\mathbb{G}_2$, and 3 pairings to check the credential. While this is already better than [9], we can get a better construction (see the full version [15]).

We additionally remark that the aggregation σ is deterministic and can thus be kept for another showing of the same credentials. Only a new randomization of uvk into uvk' with the adaptation of σ into σ' is required for anonymity.

6 Traceable Anonymous Credentials

As the SqDH-based ART-Sign schemes provide computational unlinkability only, it opens the door of possible traceability in case of abuse, with anonymous but traceable tags.

The idea is that one can extend an EphemerId scheme with a modified GenTag algorithm and additional TraceId and JudgeId ones and use this traceable EphemerId to construct a traceable anonymous credentials, with similar properties as the ones defined for group signatures [2]: an opener or a tracing authority can revoke anonymity (traceability), and publish the identity of the guilty, without being able to accuse an innocent (non-frameability or exculpability).

6.1 Traceable EphemerId

To help the reader, we extend the notations used in the anonymous credential to define the traceable EphemerId scheme:

Definition 18 (Traceable EphemerId). *Based on an EphemerId scheme:*

GenTag(param)*: Given a public parameter* param*, it outputs the user-key pair* (usk,uvk) *and the tracing key* utk*;*
TraceId(utk, uvk′)*: Given the tracing key* utk *associated to* uvk *and a public key* uvk′*, it outputs a proof* π *of whether* uvk $\sim$ uvk′ *or not;*
JudgeId(uvk, uvk′, π)*: Given two public keys and a proof, the judge checks the proof* π *and outputs* 1 *if it is correct.*

Construction. One can enhance our SqDH-based EphemerId scheme:

GenTag(param): Given a public parameter param, it randomly chooses a generator $h \stackrel{\$}{\leftarrow} \mathbb{G}_1^*$ and outputs $\mathsf{usk} = \tilde{\tau} \stackrel{\$}{\leftarrow} \mathbb{Z}_p^*$, $\mathsf{uvk} = \tau = (h, h^{\tilde{\tau}}, h^{\tilde{\tau}^2}) \in \mathbb{G}_1^3$ and $\mathsf{utk} = \mathfrak{g}^{\tilde{\tau}}$;
TraceId(utk, uvk′): Given the tracing key utk associated to $\mathsf{uvk} = (\tau_1, \tau_2, \tau_3)$ and a public key uvk′, it outputs a Groth-Sahai proof π (as shown in the full version [15]) that proves, in a zero-knowledge way, the existence of utk such that

$$e(\tau_1, \mathsf{utk}) = e(\tau_2, \mathfrak{g}) \qquad e(\tau_2, \mathsf{utk}) = e(\tau_3, \mathfrak{g}) \tag{1}$$
$$e(\tau_1', \mathsf{utk}) = e(\tau_2', \mathfrak{g}) \qquad e(\tau_2', \mathsf{utk}) = e(\tau_3', \mathfrak{g}); \tag{2}$$

JudgeId(uvk, uvk′, π): Given two public keys and a proof, the judge checks the proof π and outputs 1 if it is correct.

Correctness. The tracing key allows to check whether $\tau' \sim \tau$ or not: $e(\tau_1', \mathsf{utk}) = e(\tau_2', \mathfrak{g})$ and $e(\tau_2', \mathsf{utk}) = e(\tau_3', \mathfrak{g})$. If one already knows the tags are valid (SqDH tuples), this is enough to verify whether $e(\tau_1', \mathsf{utk}) = e(\tau_2', \mathfrak{g})$ holds or not. However we provide the complete proof in the full version [15], as it is already quite efficient. The first Eq. (1) proves that utk is the good tracing key for $\mathsf{uvk} = \tau$, and the second line (2) shows it applies to $\mathsf{uvk}' = \tau'$ too. It can be observed this can also be a proof of innocence of id with key uvk if the first Eq. (1) is satisfied while the second one is not.

The trapdoor allows traceability, and the soundness of the proof guarantees non-frameability or exculpability, as one cannot wrongly accuse a user.

6.2 Traceable Anonymous Credentials

For traceability in an anonymous credential scheme, we need an additional player: the *tracing authority*. During the user's key generation, this tracing authority will either be the certification authority, or a second authority, that also has to certify user's key uvk once it has received the tracing key utk.

We consider a non-interactive proof of tracing, produced by the TraceId algorithm and verified by anybody using the JudgeId algorithm. This proof could be interactive.

Non-frameability. In case of abuse of a credential σ under anonymous key uvk', a tracing algorithm outputs the initial uvk and id, with a proof a correct tracing. A new security notion is quite important: *non-frameability*, which means that the tracing authority should not be able to declare guilty a wrong user: only correct proofs are accepted by the judge.

A successful adversary $\mathcal{A}$ against non-frameability is able to forge a valid credential σ^* under the key uvk^* and a valid proof $\pi = \mathsf{TraceId}(\mathsf{utk}^*, \mathsf{uvk})$ for some honest user with identity id and key uvk which is not possible without breaking the unforgeability of the credential or the soundness of the proof. Hence, the tracing authority cannot frame a user and we obtain the first secure traceable anonymous credential scheme.

Acknowledgments. We warmly thank Olivier Sanders for fruitful discussions. This work was supported in part by the European Community's Seventh Framework Programme (FP7/2007-2013 Grant Agreement no. 339563 – CryptoCloud).

References

1. Baldimtsi, F., Lysyanskaya, A.: Anonymous credentials light. In: Sadeghi, A.R., Gligor, V.D., Yung, M. (eds.) ACM CCS 2013, pp. 1087–1098. ACM Press, November 2013. https://doi.org/10.1145/2508859.2516687
2. Bellare, M., Micciancio, D., Warinschi, B.: Foundations of group signatures: formal definitions, simplified requirements, and a construction based on general assumptions. In: Biham, E. (ed.) EUROCRYPT 2003. LNCS, vol. 2656, pp. 614–629. Springer, Heidelberg (2003). https://doi.org/10.1007/3-540-39200-9_38
3. Boneh, D., Drijvers, M., Neven, G.: Compact multi-signatures for smaller blockchains. In: Peyrin, T., Galbraith, S. (eds.) ASIACRYPT 2018. LNCS, vol. 11273, pp. 435–464. Springer, Cham (2018). https://doi.org/10.1007/978-3-030-03329-3_15
4. Boneh, D., Gentry, C., Lynn, B., Shacham, H.: Aggregate and verifiably encrypted signatures from bilinear maps. In: Biham, E. (ed.) EUROCRYPT 2003. LNCS, vol. 2656, pp. 416–432. Springer, Heidelberg (2003). https://doi.org/10.1007/3-540-39200-9_26
5. Boneh, D., Lynn, B., Shacham, H.: Short signatures from the Weil pairing. In: Boyd, C. (ed.) ASIACRYPT 2001. LNCS, vol. 2248, pp. 514–532. Springer, Heidelberg (2001). https://doi.org/10.1007/3-540-45682-1_30
6. Camenisch, J., Dubovitskaya, M., Haralambiev, K., Kohlweiss, M.: Composable and modular anonymous credentials: definitions and practical constructions. In: Iwata, T., Cheon, J.H. (eds.) ASIACRYPT 2015. LNCS, vol. 9453, pp. 262–288. Springer, Heidelberg (2015). https://doi.org/10.1007/978-3-662-48800-3_11
7. Camenisch, J., Lysyanskaya, A.: A signature scheme with efficient protocols. In: Cimato, S., Persiano, G., Galdi, C. (eds.) SCN 2002. LNCS, vol. 2576, pp. 268–289. Springer, Heidelberg (2003). https://doi.org/10.1007/3-540-36413-7_20
8. Camenisch, J., Lysyanskaya, A.: Signature schemes and anonymous credentials from bilinear maps. In: Franklin, M. (ed.) CRYPTO 2004. LNCS, vol. 3152, pp. 56–72. Springer, Heidelberg (2004). https://doi.org/10.1007/978-3-540-28628-8_4

9. Canard, S., Lescuyer, R.: Anonymous credentials from (indexed) aggregate signatures. In: Bhargav-Spantzel, A., Groß, T. (eds.) DIM 2011, Proceedings of the 2013 ACM Workshop on Digital Identity., pp. 53–62. ACM (2011). https://doi.org/10.1145/2046642.2046655
10. Canard, S., Lescuyer, R.: Protecting privacy by sanitizing personal data: a new approach to anonymous credentials. In: Chen, K., Xie, Q., Qiu, W., Li, N., Tzeng, W.G. (eds.) ASIACCS 13, pp. 381–392. ACM Press, May 2013
11. Fuchsbauer, G., Hanser, C., Slamanig, D.: Practical round-optimal blind signatures in the standard model. In: Gennaro, R., Robshaw, M. (eds.) CRYPTO 2015. LNCS, vol. 9216, pp. 233–253. Springer, Heidelberg (2015). https://doi.org/10.1007/978-3-662-48000-7_12
12. Fuchsbauer, G., Hanser, C., Slamanig, D.: Structure-preserving signatures on equivalence classes and constant-size anonymous credentials. J. Cryptol. **32**(2), 498–546 (2018). https://doi.org/10.1007/s00145-018-9281-4
13. Groth, J., Sahai, A.: Efficient Non-interactive proof systems for bilinear groups. In: Smart, N. (ed.) EUROCRYPT 2008. LNCS, vol. 4965, pp. 415–432. Springer, Heidelberg (2008). https://doi.org/10.1007/978-3-540-78967-3_24
14. Hébant, C., Phan, D.H., Pointcheval, D.: Linearly-homomorphic signatures and scalable mix-nets. Cryptology ePrint Archive, Report 2019/547 (2019). https://eprint.iacr.org/2019/547
15. Hébant, C., Pointcheval, D.: Traceable constant-size multi-authority credentials. Cryptology ePrint Archive, Report 2020/657 (2020). https://eprint.iacr.org/2020/657
16. Kaaniche, N., Laurent, M.: Attribute-based signatures for supporting anonymous certification. In: Askoxylakis, I., Ioannidis, S., Katsikas, S., Meadows, C. (eds.) ESORICS 2016. LNCS, vol. 9878, pp. 279–300. Springer, Cham (2016). https://doi.org/10.1007/978-3-319-45744-4_14
17. Sanders, O.: Efficient redactable signature and application to anonymous credentials. In: Kiayias, A., Kohlweiss, M., Wallden, P., Zikas, V. (eds.) PKC 2020. LNCS, vol. 12111, pp. 628–656. Springer, Cham (2020). https://doi.org/10.1007/978-3-030-45388-6_22
18. Shoup, V.: Lower bounds for discrete logarithms and related problems. In: Fumy, W. (ed.) EUROCRYPT 1997. LNCS, vol. 1233, pp. 256–266. Springer, Heidelberg (1997). https://doi.org/10.1007/3-540-69053-0_18
19. Vergnaud, D.: Comment on 'Attribute-Based Signatures for Supporting Anonymous Certification' by N. Kaaniche and M. Laurent (ESORICS 2016). Comput. J. **60**(12), 1801–1808 (2017)

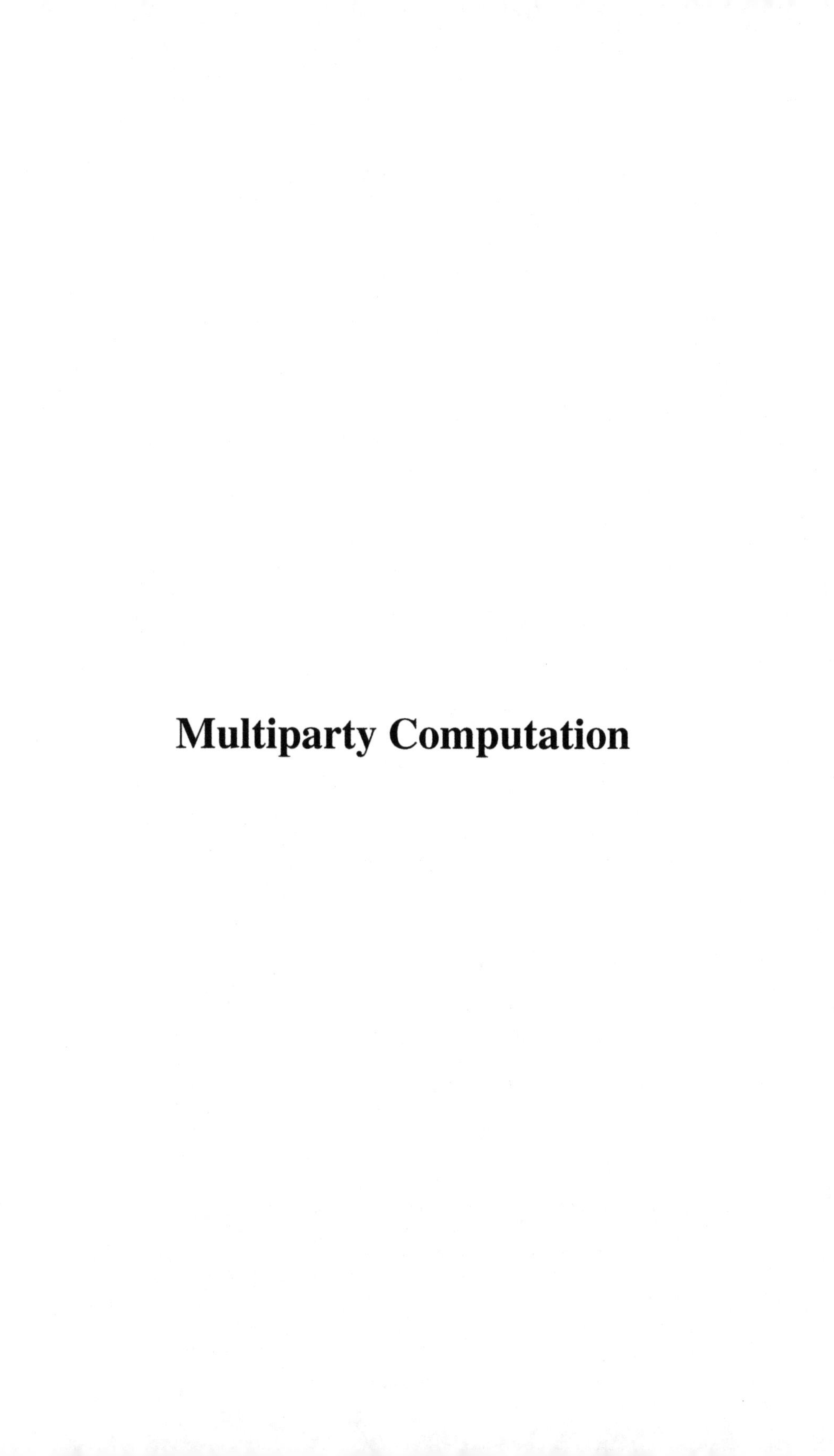

Multiparty Computation

3-Party Distributed ORAM from Oblivious Set Membership

Brett Hemenway Falk[1(✉)], Daniel Noble[1], and Rafail Ostrovsky[2]

[1] University of Pennsylvania, Philadelphia, USA
{fbrett,dgnoble}@cis.upenn.edu
[2] UCLA, Los Angeles, USA
rafail@cs.ucla.edu

Abstract. Distributed Oblivious RAM (DORAM) protocols allow a group of participants to obliviously access a secret-shared array at a secret-shared index, and DORAM is the key tool for secure multiparty computation (MPC) in the RAM model.

In this work we present an efficient DORAM protocol with $O((\kappa + D)\log N)$ communication per access, where N is the size of the memory, κ is a security parameter and D is the block size.

Our DORAM protocol is secure in the 3-party honest-majority setting, and is built from two novel, efficient components.

The first is a novel data structure for answering set membership queries. This data structure has asymptotically optimal (with tiny constants) memory usage, lookup cost and negligible failure probability. We show how this data structure can also be efficiently instantiated under MPC. The second is a Distributed Oblivious Hash Table protocol (in the 3-party honesty-majority setting) with asymptotically optimal memory usage and $O(\kappa + D)$ communication per access. To our knowledge, this is the first Distributed Oblivious Hash Table with this efficiency that does not use homomorphic encryption.

Finally, we use this to build the aforementioned DORAM protocol. Our protocol performs polylogarithmic computation and does not require homomorphic encryption. Under natural parameter choices, it is the most communication-efficient DORAM with these properties.

1 Introduction

Oblivious RAM (ORAM) [23,43] provides a method for a trusted processor to execute a program that reads from and writes to an untrusted memory array such that the *access pattern* is independent of the (private) inputs to the program itself. Although traditional encryption algorithms can protect the *content* of the data, protecting data *access patterns* is critical for security.

The original application of ORAM was for *software protection*, where a tamper-resistant CPU had to maintain program security while making use of an untrusted external memory. This problem is exemplified in systems that make use of "secure enclaves" like Intel's SGX [2,13,29,38] and AMD's SEV

C. Galdi and S. Jarecki (Eds.): SCN 2022, LNCS 13409, pp. 437–461, 2022.
https://doi.org/10.1007/978-3-031-14791-3_19

[31] that read and write to untrusted system memory. Indeed, several types of "cache-attacks" (e.g. [27,53]) have shown that access pattern leakage can be used to extract secret key material, and that even trusted enclaves like SGX are vulnerable [9,41].

A similar application of ORAM arises in the setting of cloud storage, where a client wants to outsource its data storage needs to an (untrusted) cloud provider. Encryption can hide the *contents* of the data, but not the access pattern. This setting is similar to the setting of trusted CPU, but the data sizes are larger, and the bandwidth is reduced. On the other hand, in the cloud-storage setting, it may be reasonable to assume the cloud provider is willing to perform some amount of computation in order to respond to a user's request, and the efficiency requirements may be relaxed somewhat compared to the CPU setting.

Most ORAM protocols aim to minimize the amount of communication between the client and the server, and the efficiency of an ORAM protocol is measured by the (multiplicative) communication increase incurred by executing the ORAM protocol. In other words, the *overhead* of an ORAM protocol is the communication cost of accessing t blocks (of size D) under the ORAM protocol divided by tD (as the number of database accesses, t, tends towards infinity). Sometimes, the asymptotic overhead depends on the relationship between D and other parameters. In this case it is often simpler to explicitly state the amortized communication cost, which we often refer to just as the communication cost, which is the cost of t accesses divided by t.

Early ORAM protocols were designed to allow a single, trusted processor to make a series of reads and writes to a single untrusted memory store. The application we target, however, is *secure multiparty computation* (MPC).

The goal of MPC is to allow a group of data owners to securely compute a function of their joint data without revealing any information beyond the output of the computation. This notion of security requires that MPC protocols be *data oblivious*, in particular the running time, memory accesses and communication patterns of the participants cannot depend on other private data. To achieve data obliviousness, most MPC protocols work in the circuit-model. Circuits are inherently data-oblivious, and the MPC protocol securely computes the target circuit gate by gate. Although any computation can be expressed as a circuit, this representation may not be compact. Thus for efficiency reasons, it would be highly desirable to securely compute *RAM programs*. (A time-bounded RAM program of size $O(N)$ can be converted to a circuit of size $O\left(N^3 \log N\right)$ [12,48], but in most situations this efficiency loss is unacceptable.) Combining ORAM with a traditional, circuit-based MPC protocol provides a method for securely computing RAM programs, and can drastically increase the efficiency of certain types of secure computations.

This type of MPC-compatible ORAM protocol is called *Distributed ORAM* (DORAM). One of the challenges of building a DORAM protocol is that there is no longer a trusted client who is allowed to learn the indices being queried. Note that this is different from multi-server ORAM protocols (e.g. [25,26,34,37,45]) which aim to increase efficiency by using multiple, non-colluding servers, but still require a trusted client.

Our main construction is a novel 3-party DORAM protocol that has $\mathcal{O}((\kappa + D)\log N)$ communication and is extremely efficient in theory and in practice.

Theorem 1 ((3, 1)-DORAM (informal)). *There exists a 3-server DORAM protocol with amortized communication complexity $\mathcal{O}((\kappa + D)\log N)$ bits. The protocol provides security in the semi-honest model against one corruption.*

Our construction builds on the "hierarchical ORAM" solution of [23]. In principle a hierarchical ORAM is built by constructing several *Oblivious Hash Tables*, protocols which provide oblivious memory accesses provided the same item is not queried twice. However, Oblivious Hash Tables are hard to implement efficiently. Thus, most hierarchical ORAMs instead use variants of Oblivious Hash Tables which cannot store all of the desired elements, and reinsert the leftover elements back into the ORAM. These ORAMs therefore break the abstraction of a hierarchical ORAM being composed of Oblivious Hash Tables. Breaking this abstraction is unsatisfactory from a theoretical standpoint, and has led to widespread errors [18].

In this paper we present the first Distributed Oblivious Hash Table construction with $\mathcal{O}(\kappa + D)$ communication per access (without requiring of Homomorphic Encryption).

Theorem 2 (Distributed Oblivious Hash Table). *Protocol $\Pi_{OHTable}$ (Fig. 6) implements a 3-party Distributed Oblivious Hash Table with amortized communication complexity $\mathcal{O}(\kappa + D)$ bits. The protocol provides security in the semi-honest model against one corruption.*

This is made possible by our novel set-membership data structure that has negligible failure probability, and only reads $\mathcal{O}(\log N)$ *bits* per access.

Theorem 3 (Set-Membership Data structure). *The data structure outlined in Sect. 6 can store $n = \omega(\log N)$ elements, from a universe of size N, with linear storage overhead ($\mathcal{O}(n \log N)$-bits), negligible false-positive rate (in N), zero false-negative rate, negligible probability of build failure (in N) and logarithmic lookup cost ($\mathcal{O}(\log N)$ bits).*

Note that these properties are *not* simultaneously satisfied by existing data structures like Cuckoo Hash Tables and Bloom Filters. Cuckoo hashing has a non-negligible probability of build failure, cuckoo-hashing with a stash has $\mathcal{O}(\log^2 N)$ lookup cost, and Bloom Filters cannot simultaneously achieve logarithmic lookup cost and negligible false-positive rates. See Sect. 6 for a more detailed discussion.

2 Prior Work

It is possible to convert any ORAM protocol into a DORAM protocol by emulating the client using an MPC protocol, and allowing the MPC participants to play the role of the untrusted server(s). This is a common approach to building DORAMs, and thus a cursory overview of ORAM is in order.

Early ORAM protocols had an overhead of $O\left(\log^3 N\right)$ [23], while later works improved this to $O\left(\log N\right)$ [6,52,55] which is known to be optimal [23,35]. These early works considered a model with a single, trusted client, and a single, server that could *only store and retrieve data.*

Several other models have been developed in an attempt to improve performance. These include adding multiple (non-colluding) servers, or allowing the server(s) to perform computation.

Active ORAM: If the ORAM server(s) are allowed to *compute* on data, rather than just store and retrieve data, the $\mathcal{O}\left(\log N\right)$ lower-bound of [23,35] can be avoided, and several *active ORAM* protocols achieve *constant* client-server overhead [4,14,20,49,50].

Multi-server ORAM: The communication complexity of ORAM protocols can also be improved by allowing multiple (non-colluding) servers. Multi-server ORAM protocols include [11,25,26,34,37,45,50]. Although multi-server ORAM and DORAM both involve multiple servers, the models are fairly different. Multi-server ORAM assumes a single, trusted client (who can perform operations locally), whereas in DORAM, there is no "client."

It is worth noting that any k-server DORAM protocol trivially yields a k-server active ORAM with $\mathcal{O}(\log N)$ client-server communication, since you can always add a fully-trusted, lightweight, client whose queries consist of secret-sharing an index without compromising security.[1]

More relevant for this work, it is also possible to go in the opposite direction, that is, to convert ORAM protocols to DORAM protocols by simulating the client under MPC. Since MPC requires a significant computational overhead, simulating the ORAM client under MPC is only practical if the ORAM client uses minimal computational and storage resources. Circuit ORAM [55] is an ORAM protocol particularly amenable to secure multiparty computation, since its client can be efficiently represented as a circuit. Instantiating Circuit ORAM with a generic MPC protocol (e.g. garbled circuits or BGW [7]) yields a DORAM scheme with $\mathcal{O}\left(\log^3 N + D\log N\right)$ communication. The $(3,1)$-DORAM protocol of [30] also builds on Circuit ORAM, and achieves communication complexity $O\left(\kappa\log^3 N + D\log N\right)$, where D is the record size. Although the asymptotic *communication* complexity of the [30] protocol is κ times larger than that of a generic 3PC implementation of Circuit ORAM, the *round* complexity is improved from $\mathcal{O}\left(\log^2 N\log\log N\right)$ to $\mathcal{O}\left(\log N\right)$.

Since DORAM protocols already require multiple, computing servers, it is natural to create DORAM protocols by using MPC to emulate the trusted client in a multi-server or active ORAM protocol. This is a promising approach

[1] Note that a k-server DORAM protocol does not immediately yield a $(k-1)$-server active ORAM by allowing one of the DORAM servers to play role of the trusted client, because in active ORAM the client must use sublinear storage, and there is no such restriction for DORAM servers.

since several efficient multi-server ORAM protocols exist [25,26,34,37,45,50] and some have even been implemented [15,25,56,58]. Unfortunately, most of these *multi-server* ORAM protocols are not suited for secure multiparty computation, because their clients often perform complex computations that cannot be efficiently executed inside an MPC. For instance, [34]'s PIR solutions require that the client generate a key for a Distributed Point Function.

[37] is an exception, in that the [37] client can be (asymptotically) efficiently instantiated using a generic MPC protocol. [37] builds on the (single-server) "hierarchical solution" [23,43,44], but uses two (non-colluding) servers, each holding alternate levels of the hierarchy. Each level holds an Oblivious Hash Table, storing encryptions of the elements on that level. To construct a level, one server passes all the (encrypted and shuffled) elements for that level to the client, who then decrypts and re-encrypts them, and passes them to the other server. The client also provides PRF outputs to the other server, which allows the server to build the Oblivious Hash Table in the clear since it knows which location each item should be placed, even though the items are encrypted. This server then passes the level back to the client, who decrypts it, re-encrypts it, and passes the encrypted Oblivious Hash Table back to the original server. This process means that the Oblivious Hash Table build, which is usually a bottleneck, can be performed in the clear, but requires the client to perform a linear number of (symmetric-key) encryptions. In the traditional ORAM setting, this is cheap, since the client can perform symmetric-key encryption extremely efficiently (e.g. using AES with hardware acceleration). Unfortunately, when using the ORAM protocol within a secure computation, the client is *simulated* by the MPC protocol, and thus all the client operations (including the encryptions) need to be performed under MPC. Although encryptions can be performed under MPC, this cost dominates the cost of the overall protocol, and makes the entire scheme inefficient in practice.

Nevertheless, this scheme is in fact efficient asymptotically. Assuming executing a symmetric cipher on D bits with security parameter κ under MPC requires $\mathcal{O}(\kappa + D)$ communication (see the full version of this work [17] for a justification of this claim) the communication cost of [37] is $\mathcal{O}\left((\kappa + D)\log N\right)$. This is *better* than that achieved by subsequent DORAM protocols [10,16,30,55,56]. This was observed in [16], but seems to have been largely ignored in later works (e.g. [10,30]). Our scheme has the same asymptotic behavior as [37], but dramatically better constants. An encryption under MPC can be performed by a Shared-Input, Shared-Output PRP (SISO-PRP), which are explained in Sect. 4. In the full version of this work, [17], we calculate the concrete number of SISO-PRP calls, and show that our construction achieves the same asymptotics, but reduces the concrete number of SISO-PRP calls by a factor of 50.

Bunn et al. use an alternative approach based on Function Secret-Sharing (FSS) [8,22] to build a (3, 1)-DORAM [10]. Although FSS-based protocols have bad asymptotics ([10] has $\mathcal{O}\left(\sqrt{N}\right)$ communication, and $\mathcal{O}\left(N\right)$ server-side computation), they are extremely efficient in practice (note that $\sqrt{N} < \log^3 N$ for

$N < 6 \cdot 10^8$). The FSS-based DORAM of [10] is also the only known DORAM protocol with *constant* round complexity.

Asymptotically, the best communication efficiency is achieved by instantiating the 2-server hierarchical ORAM of [37] using a generic MPC, but in practice schemes with suboptimal asymptotics, e.g. the BGW-instantiated Circuit ORAM with a cost of $\mathcal{O}\left(\log^3 N + D \log N\right)$ are superior. See Table 1.

Our work achieves amortized communication cost $\mathcal{O}\left((\kappa + D)\log N\right)$, but with dramatically better concrete cost than the only other DORAM protocol with this asymptotic cost.

Table 1. Communication complexity of DORAM protocols. N denotes the number of records, κ is a cryptographic security parameter, σ is a statistical security parameter, and D is the record size. Although instantiating the [37] 2-party ORAM using generic MPC has the same asymptotic complexity as our protocol, concretely, we reduce the number of SISO-PRP calls by a factor of more than 50 (see the full version, [17], for a detailed accounting).

Protocol	Complexity
GC Circuit ORAM [55]	$\mathcal{O}\left(\kappa \log^3 N + \kappa D \log N\right)$
2PC Sqrt-ORAM [58]	$\mathcal{O}\left(\kappa D \sqrt{N \log^3 N}\right)$
2PC FLORAM [15]	$\mathcal{O}\left(\sqrt{\kappa D N \log N}\right)$
2PC ORAM [28]	$\mathcal{O}\left(\sqrt{\kappa D N \log N}\right)$
BGW Circuit ORAM [55]	$\mathcal{O}\left(\log^3 N + D \log N\right)$
BGW 2-server hierarchical [37]	$\mathcal{O}\left((\kappa + D)\log N\right)$
3PC ORAM [16]	$\mathcal{O}\left(\kappa\sigma \log^3 N + \sigma D \log N\right)$
3PC ORAM [30]	$\mathcal{O}\left(\kappa \log^3 N + D \log N\right)$
3PC ORAM [10]	$\mathcal{O}\left(D\sqrt{N}\right)$
Our protocol	$\mathcal{O}\left((\kappa + D)\log N\right)$

Implementations: Several works have implemented DORAM protocols. [25] implements the [51] ORAM using garbled circuits, SCORAM [56] uses the ObliVM [54] MPC framework. [58] uses the Obliv-C MPC framework to implement the original square-root ORAM solution [23]. FLORAM [15] uses the Obliv-C framework to implement function-secret-sharing-based ORAM.

Hierarchical ORAM: Our work builds on the "hierarchical ORAM," which was explored in the single-server setting [23,33] and the multi-server setting [34,37].

In the hierarchical model, the server stores a hierarchy of Oblivious Hash Tables of geometrically increasing sizes. An Oblivious Hash Table has the property that physical memory accesses leak no information about virtual accesses *provided* each item is only queried once. Hierarchical ORAMs satisfy this condition by building smaller tables that act as memory caches for the larger tables.

Then, when an item is found in a smaller table, the protocol searches for a nonce instead of the real value in all larger tables. See the full version of this work [17] for a more detailed explanation of hierarchical ORAM.

In the original "hierarchical ORAM" scheme [23], each oblivious hash table required accessing $\mathcal{O}(\log N)$ elements. It was realized [47] that using Cuckoo Hashing, oblivious hash tables could be constructed that only required accessing $\mathcal{O}(1)$ elements. However, when a cuckoo hash table is built, there is a non-negligible probability that some items cannot be stored in the main table. Because of this, the initial cuckoo-based ORAM [47] had a flaw (identified in [33]) so subsequent works [6,24,33,34,37,46], instead of creating true Oblivious Hash Tables, took items that could not be stored in the cuckoo table and reinserted them into the top level. Doing this naïvely results in a subtle flaw [18]. Even though this flaw can be remedied for the ORAM setting, these works still do not create true Oblivious Hash Tables. This work instead presents a method of efficiently implementing true Distributed Oblivious Hash Tables in the $(3, 1)$ semi-honest setting.

3 Preliminaries

Let P_1, P_2 and P_3 be the three parties in the protocol. For a positive integer B, we use single square brackets, $[B]$, to represent the set $\{1, \ldots, B\}$.

We assume the parties have access to an Arithmetic Black Box (ABB) functionality $\mathcal{F}_{ABB}$ (Fig. 1). This is a reactive functionality that provides input, retention and output of secret-shared data. It also provides basic arithmetic operations and some advanced operations which we explain further below.

We use standard secret-sharing notation to represent variables stored in the ABB. Each variable in the ABB has a public identifier and $[\![x]\!]$ denotes the public identifier for a variable x that is stored in the ABB. We use notation from [5] that a $\binom{n}{t+1}$-sharing is a secret sharing where $t+1$ of the n shares are sufficient and necessary to learn the secret.

For notational convenience, we use normal assignment notation to show a new variable being stored in the ABB and drop its variable name from the function declaration. For instance, $\mathcal{F}_{ABB}$.AND($[\![x]\!]$, $[\![y]\!]$, z) will alternatively be written as $[\![z]\!] = \mathcal{F}_{ABB}$.AND($[\![x]\!]$, $[\![y]\!]$). Assignment notation is similarly used to show a new local variable being assigned based on a call to Output. We also use the notation $[\![z]\!] = [\![x]\!]$ to show that the value of $[\![x]\!]$, stored in the ABB, was copied to a new location, $[\![z]\!]$. Lastly, we occasionally place constants in the secret-sharing notation (e.g. $[\![true]\!]$). In this case, the constant is implicitly first input as a secret variable from any party.

The ABB abstracts away the details of the secret-sharing implementation and underlying MPC framework. Our efficiency results are based on instantiating $\mathcal{F}_{ABB}$ with the generic MPC protocol of Araki et al. [5]. We use this protocol because it is designed for our setting ($(3, 1)$ semi-honest) and is extremely

Functionality $\mathcal{F}_{ABB}$

Input(x, pId, varName): Receive x from party pId and store it as $[\![varName]\!]$.
ReshareTo2Sharing($[\![x]\!]$, sharing, varName): Share x as $[\![varName]\!]$, accessible by qualified set $sharing$, where $|sharing| = 2$.
ReshareFrom2Sharing($[\![x]\!]_{sharing}$, sharing, varName): Receive shares of x from the qualified set $sharing$, where $|sharing| = 2$ and store it as $[\![varName]\!]$.
AND($[\![x]\!]$, $[\![y]\!]$, outName): Compute $z = x \wedge y$ and store z in $[\![outName]\!]$.
OR($[\![x]\!]$, $[\![y]\!]$, outName): Compute $z = x \vee y$ and store z in $[\![outName]\!]$.
Equal($[\![x]\!]$, $[\![y]\!]$, outName): If $x \stackrel{?}{=} y$ set z to $true$, otherwise to $false$. Store z in $[\![outName]\!]$.
IfThenElse($[\![b]\!]$, $[\![x]\!]$, $[\![y]\!]$, outName): If $b \stackrel{?}{=} true$, set z to x, otherwise to y. Store z in $[\![outName]\!]$.
PRP_keygen(N, keyName): Generate a new random key, k, for a PRP $f_k : [N] \rightarrow [N]$. Store k in $[\![keyName]\!]$.
PRP_eval($[\![x]\!]$, $[\![k]\!]$, outName): Compute $z = f_k(x)$ and store z in $[\![outName]\!]$.
Shuffle($[\![X]\!]$, outName): Given an array $[\![X]\!] = [\![X_1]\!], \ldots, [\![X_n]\!]$, generate a random permutation of the contents of $[\![X]\!]$ and store the result in $[\![outName]\!]$. If multiple arrays are given as inputs/outputs, they are all shuffled using the same permutation.
Output($[\![z]\!]$, pIds, localVarName): Send z to every party in set $pIds$, who store it in the local variable $localVarName$.

Fig. 1. Arithmetic Black Box functionality

communication-efficient at Boolean operations. XORs are free and AND gates require only 3 bits of communication, total. However, the number of rounds of communication is equal to the AND-depth of the circuit.[2]

In addition to basic arithmetic and IO functionalities, our ABB also has the ability to convert between $\binom{2}{2}$-sharings and $\binom{3}{2}$-sharings. Our protocol never *computes* on $\binom{2}{2}$ shares, so the functionality does not define any calculations that occur on $\binom{2}{2}$-shared data. A detailed explanation of the resharing protocol can be found in the full version [17].

One way to implement the functionality $\mathcal{F}_{ABB}$. Shuffle is to use the 3-party shuffle of [36]. This shuffle has concrete communication cost of $24nD$ bits to shuffle n bits, each of size D. See the full version of this paper, [17], for a detailed accounting of the communication cost.

[2] Our protocol could also be executed using garbled circuits. This would increase the communication cost by a factor of κ, since 2 ciphertexts would need to be sent per AND gate [57]. However the round complexity would be reduced to linear in the "openings" depth of the protocol, rather than the AND depth of the circuit.

Table 2. Communication costs of $\mathcal{F}_{ABB}$. Costs ignore a setup phase in which each pair of parties pick a PRG key for generating identical randomness. This set-up phase occurs only once for $\mathcal{F}_{ABB}$ and requires 3κ bits of communication. $\mathcal{F}_{ABB}$.Equal, $\mathcal{F}_{ABB}$.IfThenElse, $\mathcal{F}_{ABB}$.PRP_keygen and $\mathcal{F}_{ABB}$. PRP_eval are executed as boolean circuits using the aforementioned operations from [5].

Functionality	Communication (bits, total)	Source
$\mathcal{F}_{ABB}$.Input	4 (per input bit)	[5] §2.1
$\mathcal{F}_{ABB}$.ReshareTo2Sharing	0	[17]
$\mathcal{F}_{ABB}$.ReshareFrom2Sharing	8 (per input bit)	[17]
$\mathcal{F}_{ABB}$.XOR	0	[5] §2.1
$\mathcal{F}_{ABB}$.AND	3	[5] §2.1
$\mathcal{F}_{ABB}$.OR	3	Using 1 AND and NOTs
$\mathcal{F}_{ABB}$.Equal (n bits)	3(n-1)	Standard, e.g. [3]
$\mathcal{F}_{ABB}$.IfThenElse (n bits)	3n	Mux $z = (b \wedge (x \oplus y)) \oplus y$
$\mathcal{F}_{ABB}$.PRP_keygen	0	[5] §3.4
$\mathcal{F}_{ABB}$.PRP_eval (D bits)	$21(\kappa + D)$	[1], [17]
$\mathcal{F}_{ABB}$.Shuffle (n each D bits)	$24nD$	[36], [17]
$\mathcal{F}_{ABB}$.Output	3	[5], send x_i to P_{i+1}

We will be looking at an ORAM of size N, *i.e.*, it represents a RAM of size N. We assume N is a power of 2, so that indices are representable by $\log N$ bits where all logs are base-2. We will seek to achieve statistical failure that is negligible in N. Each data block will be of size D, where $D = \Omega(\log N)$.

Our protocol achieves κ-bit security, by which we mean the protocol achieves symmetric security roughly equivalent to AES-κ. We assume a PRP exists with κ-bit security that can be represented as a circuit with $\mathcal{O}(\kappa)$ AND gates. We suggest instantiating this with LowMCv3 which requires about 7κ AND gates to achieve κ-bit security (see Sect. 4). Throughout this work, as is standard, we assume $\kappa = \omega(\log N)$.

4 SISO-PRPs

A pseudo-random function (PRF) is a keyed deterministic function such that the output appears random to any polynomially bounded adversary.

A *Shared-Input, Shared-Output PRF* (SISO-PRF) is a multiparty protocol to securely evaluate a PRF when the input, outputs and keys are secret-shared between the participants. Note that this is slightly different from the notion of an *Oblivious Pseudo-Random Function* (OPRF) [21]. Most OPRF protocols have focused on a 2-party evaluation of a PRF, where one party holds a key, k, and the other holds an input, x, and the output, $F_k(x)$ is delivered to one party.

In our applications, however, it is critical that the inputs to the PRF are secret-shared, thus most existing OPRF protocols are not applicable. In principle, it is possible to evaluate any PRF with secret-shared keys, inputs and outputs, using generic MPC protocols, but this is often fairly inefficient.

In this work, we will focus on *Shared-Input Shared-Output PRPs* (SISO-PRPs) where the pseudorandom function is actually a permutation.

Concretely, we imagine implementing our SISO-PRP using the "MPC-friendly" LowMC block cipher, which is highly optimized for evaluation as a SISO-PRP [1]. In addition to being MPC-friendly, LowMC has two additional features that make it useful in our setting. (1) LowMC has configurable block sizes, allowing us to reduce the communication and computational costs when the index space is small, and (2) when the maximum number of queries to the PRP is bounded (as is the case in our construction), LowMC can be instantiated with more aggressive parameters, increasing efficiency.

In Table 3, we compare the efficiency of LowMC, vs AES for 128-bit security. We present various parameter choices for LowMC using the LowMCv3 security estimator.[3] In Table 3, "Data" represents the log of the number of PRP evaluations the adversary will ever learn.

Table 3. Block cipher costs for 128-bit Security (AES-128 from [1][Table 2], LowMC from LowMCv3 security estimator)

Cipher	Blocksize	Data	rounds	AND gates
AES	128	128	40	5120
LowMC	128	128	19	1824
LowMC	128	128	252	861
LowMC	10	10	32	288
LowMC	10	10	94	282

5 Construction Overview

Our main construction is a (3, 1)-DORAM protocol with amortized $\mathcal{O}((\kappa + D) \log N)$ communication cost.

Our construction builds on the "hierarchical solution" which is essentially a tool for converting an oblivious hash table that only provides obliviousness on *distinct* queries into an oblivious data structure that provides obliviousness on *repeated* queries. We describe the hierarchical solution in more detail in Sect. 9.

[3] https://github.com/LowMC/lowmc/blob/master/determine_rounds.py.

Informally, an oblivious hash table is a data structure that provides obliviousness on distinct queries, thus the hierarchical solution reduces the problem of designing a DORAM protocol to building an oblivious hash table that can be *built* and *queried* efficiently in a distributed manner.

Starting with [47], Cuckoo Hash Tables have been widely used in ORAM protocols [6,24,33,34,37,46]. The key property of Cuckoo Hash Tables is that in a series of *distinct* queries, the physical access pattern is independent of the underlying queries.

However, it is tricky to correctly incorporate Cuckoo Hash Tables into a hierarchical ORAM protocol. Cuckoo Hash Tables have a non-trivial probability of build failure (and a failure would leak information). Thus Cuckoo Hash Tables are instantiated with a "stash" of size $\omega(1)$ to hold elements that cannot be stored in the main Cuckoo Hash Table [32]. In the hierarchical solution, adding a separate stash at every level of the hierarchy increases the asymptotic query complexity, thus most hierarchical ORAM protocols sought to combine the stashes across different levels of the hierarchy. This breaks the abstraction of each level of the hierarchy being an Oblivious Hash Table and was often done in a way that led to flaws in the ORAM protocol [18]. In short, while Cuckoo Hash Tables with combined stashes can be used to implement hierarchical ORAM protocols efficiently, this makes the protocol and its analysis undesirably complicated.

Rather than instantiating the hierarchical solution with Cuckoo Hash Tables, we design a novel Oblivious Hash Table that requires $\Theta(\kappa + D)$ bits of communication per access (amortized). Our starting point is the observation [39] that once it is known whether an element is stored in a table, Distributed, Oblivious Hash Tables can be constructed using any non-oblivious, but secret-shared, hash table structure by searching for distinct pre-inserted dummy elements when an element is not in the set.

This essentially reduces the problem to that of designing an efficient data structure for *set membership.* We do this by building a Cuckoo Hash Table with a stash, but instantiating the stash with a Bloom Filter. Surprisingly, this simple combination increases the asymptotic efficiency of the data structure beyond what can be achieved by Cuckoo Hash Tables or Bloom Filters alone.

The main technical challenge is then to construct the Oblivious Set Membership structure and Oblivious Hash Tables in the distributed setting efficiently, and *without leaking any sensitive data.*

We solve this in the $(3, 1)$-security setting by using a shared-input PRP, where one party learns the outputs in the clear during builds and the other two parties to learn the PRP outputs during accesses. We show that a single party can construct the Bloom Filter and Cuckoo Table objects in the clear based on the PRP evaluations alone, but without any shares of the actual indexes or data. The Bloom Filter and Cuckoo Table data structures can then be secret-shared between the remaining two parties who can then evaluate lookups without revealing any PRP outputs to the third party.

We present our Oblivious Set Membership protocol in Sect. 7 followed by our full Oblivious Hash Table protocol in Sect. 8. Finally, we use our novel Oblivious Hash Table protocol together with the hierarchical solution to construct a $(3,1)$-DORAM protocol (Sect. 9).

The formal definitions of hashing, oblivious hashing, Bloom Filters and Cuckoo Hash Tables can be found in the full version of this paper [17].

6 Set Membership

Let there be some set of n elements from a universe of size N, each represented by $\log N \geq \log n$ bits. In this section we outline a novel data structure that supports *set membership queries* that simultaneously achieves the following properties:

1. Linear storage overhead ($\mathcal{O}(n \log N)$)
2. Negligible false-positive rate in N
3. Zero false-negative rate
4. Negligible probability of build failure in N
5. Logarithmic lookup cost ($\mathcal{O}(\log N)$)

Bloom filters and Cuckoo hash tables are widely used data structures that provide efficient storage and retrieval, but they do not satisfy all of the above design criteria simultaneously.

Example 1 (Cuckoo Hashing). Standard Cuckoo Hash Tables have linear storage overhead, zero false-positive rate, and logarithmic[4] lookup cost. Unfortunately, Cuckoo Hash Tables (without a stash) have a non-negligible probability of build failure.

Example 2 (Cuckoo Hashing with a stash). Modifying a standard Cuckoo Hash Table to include a "stash" of size $s = \Theta(\log N)$, for any $n = \omega(\log N)$ makes the failure probability negligible in N [42]. Unfortunately, every lookup query scans the entire stash, which requires reading s locations, which means lookups require accessing $\Theta(\log^2 N)$ bits of memory.

Example 3 (Bloom filters). The false-positive rate for a Bloom filter of size m storing n elements (using k hash functions) is about $\left(1 - e^{-\frac{kn}{m}}\right)^k$. A standard analysis (e.g. [40] [Chapter 5]) shows that the false-positive rate is minimized when $k = \log(2) \cdot (m/n)$, which makes the false-positive probability approximately $(\log 2)^{-m/n}$. Thus to make the false-positive probability negligible in N, we need $m = \omega(n \log N)$, which means that the storage overhead is super-linear.

---

[4] Note that lookups require looking in a constant number of locations, but each location stores an identifier which must be at least $\log n$ bits, so the total lookup cost requires transmitting (at least) a logarithmic number of bits. Even Cuckoo filters [19] requires storing keys that are at least $\log n$ bits.

Although Cuckoo Hashing, and Bloom filters alone cannot achieve our five goals (linear storage overhead, negligible false-positive rate, zero false-negative rate, negligible probability of build failure and logarithmic lookup cost), *combining* the Cuckoo Hashing with Bloom filters allows us to simultaneously achieve all these goals. This is achieved simply by creating a Cuckoo Hash table with a stash, but storing the stash in a Bloom filter.

Build Given a set $\{X_1, \ldots, X_n\}$

1. Create a Cuckoo Hash table with a stash as follows:
   (a) Pick 2 hash functions h_1, h_2 which map $[N] \rightarrow [m]$ for $m = \epsilon n$ for some constant $\epsilon > 1$.
   (b) Create 2 empty tables, T_1 and T_2, each of size m.
   (c) Try to store each X_i in either $T_1[h_1(X_i)]$ or $T_2[h_2(X_i)]$. Find a maximal allocation (e.g., through a matching algorithm). Let S be the set of elements that were not able to be stored in either T_1 or T_2. If $|S| > \log N$, the build fails.
2. Store the stash in a Bloom Filter as follows:
   (a) Create an array, B of length $n \log N$ of all zeros.
   (b) Pick $k = \log N$ hash functions, $g_1, \ldots, g_k$, which map $[N] \rightarrow [n \log N]$.
   (c) For each element $x \in S$, and for $1 \leq i \leq k$ set $B[g_i(x)] = 1$.

Query Given an index x

1. Check if x is stored in the Cuckoo hash table by checking locations $T_1[h_1(x)] = x$ or $T_2[h_2(x)] = x$. If so, return true.
2. Check if x is stored in the Bloom filter, by checking whether $B[g_i(x)] = 1$ for all $1 \leq i \leq k$. If so, return true. Otherwise return false.

Fig. 2. Set Membership

Theorem 4. *When $n = \omega(\log N)$, the Set Membership protocol of Fig. 2 provides a data structure with linear storage overhead, negligible false-positive rate (in N), zero false-negative rate, negligible probability of failure (in N) and logarithmic lookup cost (in bits).*

The proof of Theorem 4 is straightforward and can be found in the full version of this work [17].

7 3-Party Oblivious Set Membership Protocol

We now show how we can securely build and access the set-membership data structure presented in Sect. 6. This will be fundamental to our efficient Oblivious Hash Table construction.

The core idea is that a single party, say P_1, can locally construct the Cuckoo Hash table and Bloom Filter objects. Since the indices must remain secret shared, the Cuckoo Hash table and Bloom Filter are constructed not from the indices X_i, but on PRP evaluations of the indices $q_i = \mathrm{PRP}_k(X_i)$. This PRP is evaluated in a secure computation, and the output revealed to P_1, who constructs the Cuckoo Hash Table and Bloom Filter and secret-share these between P_2 and P_3. The hash functions for the Cuckoo Hash Table and Bloom Filter can be public, since the data structures are secret-shared.

If an index x is queried, the parties securely evaluate $q = \mathrm{PRP}_k(x)$ and reveal this to P_2 and P_3. The locations to be accessed in the secret-shared Cuckoo Hash table and the secret-shared Bloom Filter depend only on q and public hash functions. P_2 and P_3 can therefore access the required locations of the secret-shared Cuckoo Hash Table and Bloom Filter and securely calculate the result of the set membership query.

Our protocol works in the $\mathcal{F}_{ABB}$-hybrid model, where $\mathcal{F}_{ABB}$ is defined in Fig. 1. The Oblivious Set functionality is defined below. Note that it reveals any repetitions in the array of inputs, or in the array of queries (but does not reveal publicly relationships between queries and inputs). This is necessary since certain parties will learn the PRP evaluations of the inputs, or the queries (but no parties will learn both). This will allow these parties to learn of any duplicates.

Functionality $\mathcal{F}_{OSet}$

Build($[\![X]\!]$, N):
Build an Oblivious Set data structure consisting of the elements in array $[\![X]\!] = [\![X_1]\!], \ldots, [\![X_n]\!]$ of variables stored in the ABB, where $X_i \in [N]$ for all $i \in [n]$ (no outputs).
Set $first_i = \min(j : X_j = X_i)$ Reveal $first$ to all parties.
Query($[\![x]\!]$, res):
If $x \in X$ set $z = true$, else set $z = false$. Store z in $[\![res]\!]$ in the ABB (no outputs).
The functionality maintains a counter of the number of times Query is called, $nQueries$. Set $queries_{nQueries} = x$. Set $firstFound = \min\{j : queries_j = x\}$. Reveal $firstFound$ to all parties.

Fig. 3. Oblivious Set functionality

Protocol Π_{OSet}

Build($[\![X]\!]$, N)

1. Set $[\![k]\!] = \mathcal{F}_{ABB}$.PRP_keygen($N$)
2. P_1 generates and shares with P_2 and P_3:
   (a) Public Cuckoo Hash functions $h_1, h_2 : [N] \rightarrow [m]$
   (b) Public Bloom Filter hash functions $g_1, \ldots, g_{\log N} : [N] \rightarrow [n \log N]$.
3. For $i \in [n]$
   (a) Securely evaluate the PRP on X_i: $[\![Q_i]\!] = \mathcal{F}_{ABB}$.PRP_eval($[\![X_i]\!], [\![k]\!]$).
   (b) Reveal to P_1: $qLocal_i = \mathcal{F}_{ABB}$.Output($[\![Q_i]\!], P_1$).
4. For $i \in [n]$, P_1 sets $first_i = j$ where Q_j, $j \leq i$ is the first occurrence of Q_i in Q. P_1 outputs $first$.
5. P_1 constructs a Cuckoo Hash table with a stash for the outputs $qLocal_i$ *i.e.*, P_1 stores $qLocal_i$ in $T_1[h_1(qLocal_i)]$ or $T_2[h_2(qLocal_i)]$ for as many encodings as possible, and stores the remaining random encodings in stash S. If $|S| > \log N$ the build fails and P_1 sends **abort** to all parties, who then abort. In all empty locations in the table, P_1 stores $\perp$ (where $\perp \notin [N]$). Let C be the appended tables of T_1 and T_2. P_1 secret-shares C between P_2 and P_3, i.e. for $i \in [2m]$ call $\mathcal{F}_{ABB}$.InputToSharing($C_i, P_1, cuckoo_i, \{P_2, P_3\}$)
6. P_1 constructs a Bloom Filter B of length $n \log N$, using inputs S and hash functions $g_1, \ldots, g_{\log N}$. P_1 then secret-shares B to P_2 and P_3 as follows: for $i \in [n \log N]$ call $\mathcal{F}_{ABB}$.InputToSharing($B_i, P_1, bloom_i, \{P_2, P_3\}$)
7. P_2 and P_3 create empty local dictionary *queries* for storing *PRP* query results they learn. Set $nQueries = 0$.

Query($[\![x]\!]$, res)

1. Securely evaluate the PRP on the query and reveal the output to P_2 and P_3.
   $[\![qShared]\!] = \mathcal{F}_{ABB}.PRP\_eval([\![x]\!], [\![k]\!])$.
   $q = \mathcal{F}_{ABB}.Output([\![qShared]\!], P_2)$
   $q = \mathcal{F}_{ABB}.Output([\![qShared]\!], P_3)$
2. P_2 and P_3 see if q is already stored in *queries*. If so, set $firstFound = queries[q]$.
   Else set $firstFound = nQueries$ and set $queries[q] = nQueries$. Reveal $firstFound$ to all players. Increment $nQueries$.
3. Securely query q in the Cuckoo Table as follows. For $i \in \{1, 2\}$,
   (a) P_2 and P_3 locally calculate $cLocal_i = h_i(q) + (i-1) * m$.
   (b) $[\![c_i]\!] = \mathcal{F}_{ABB}$.InputFromSharing($[\![cuckoo_{cLocal_i}]\!], \{P_2, P_3\}$)
   (c) $[\![eq_i]\!] = \mathcal{F}_{ABB}$.Equal($[\![c_i]\!], [\![qShared]\!]$)
   Call $[\![inCuckoo]\!] = \mathcal{F}_{ABB}$.OR($[\![eq_1]\!], [\![eq_2]\!]$).
4. Securely query q in the Bloom Filter i.e., call $[\![inBloom]\!] = [\![true]\!]$. For $i \in [\log N]$:
   (a) P_2 and P_3 locally calculate $bLocal_i = g_i(q)$ for $1 \leq i \leq k$.
   (b) $[\![b_i]\!] = \mathcal{F}_{ABB}$.InputFromSharing($[\![bloom_{bLocal_i}]\!], \{P_2, P_3\}$)
   (c) $[\![inBloom]\!] = \mathcal{F}_{ABB}$.AND($[\![inBloom]\!], [\![b_i]\!]$).
5. Securely determine whether it is in either the Cuckoo Table or the Bloom Filter: $[\![res]\!] = \mathcal{F}_{ABB}$.OR($[\![inCuckoo]\!], [\![inBloom]\!]$)

Fig. 4. 3 Party Secure Set Membership

Theorem 5. *Protocol Π_{OSet} (Fig. 4) securely implements $\mathcal{F}_{OSet}$ (Fig. 3) in the $\mathcal{F}_{ABB}$-hybrid model, in the* $(3, 1)$ *semi-honest setting*

Proof. **Build:** Observe that Π_{OSet}.Build has a probability of failure, whereas $\mathcal{F}_{OSet}$.Build does not. However the failure probability is negligible (Theorem 4), so cannot be used to distinguish the real and ideal executions.

Let $S_{BUILD,1}$ be the simulator for P_1 for Π_{OSet}.Build. It is provided with P_1's input and output, and only needs to produce the messages P_1 received from $\mathcal{F}_{ABB}$, namely $qLocal_1, \ldots, qLocal_n$. It proceeds as follows:

1. $S_{BUILD,1}$ is given $first$.
2. Let $unused = \{1, \ldots, N\}$
3. For $i \in \{1, \ldots, n\}$
   (a) If $first_i = i$ select an element r of $unused$ uniformly at random, remove r from $unused$, and set $qLocal_i = r$.
   (b) Otherwise let $j = first_i$. Set $qLocal_i = qLocal_j$.

Firstly, observe that if $qLocal_i = qLocal_j$ in the program execution, then $first_i = first_j$, so $qLocal_i = qLocal_j$ in the simulator's transcript. The unique values in $qLocal_1, \ldots, qLocal_n$ are results of a *truly* random permutation. Therefore, distinguishing the values of $qLocal$ from the real and simulated executions amounts to distinguishing the pseudo-random permutation from a truly random permutation. Since $view_1^{\pi}(x, y, z)$ is indistinguishable from $S_1(1^n, x, f_1(x, y, z))$, and $f(x, y, z)$ and $output^{\pi}(x, y, z, n)$ are deterministic functions of $S_1(1^n, x, f_1(x, y, z))$ and $view_1^{\pi}(x, y, z)$ respectively, the combined distributions $(S_1(1^n, x, f_1(x, y, z)), f(x, y, z))$ and $(view_1^{\pi}(x, y, z, n), output^{\pi}(x, y, z, n))$ are computationally indistinguishable. P_2 and P_3 receive no messages during a build.

Query: There is a negligible probability of a false positive and zero probability of a false negative (Theorem 4). Therefore, the event of a false result does not allow the true and simulated executions to become computationally distinguishable. The simulator for P_2 during a query is almost identical to that of P_1 during a build, except that rather than receiving an entire list of pseudo-random permutations to simulate, it receives one at a time. The simulator has to generate a single value that is consistent with a PRP evaluation. It is given a value $firstFound$ for the current query call. It keeps track of all previous values of $firstFound$, as well as all views generated for previous calls to the query. If $firstFound < nQueries$, $S_{QUERY,2}$ sets the message q to the same one that was generated in the $firstFound^{th}$ query. Otherwise it generates a new, unused message from $[N]$ and sets this to be the message q for the current round. Since P_2 and P_3 have symmetric roles in the protocol, their simulators for the query are identical. P_1 receives no messages during a query.

The communication costs of Π_{OSet} are stated below as Theorems 6 and 7. Their proofs follow from a straightforward accounting of the cost of each step, and can be found in the full version [17].

Theorem 6. *Protocol $\Pi_{OSet.Build}$ (Fig. 4) requires $\mathcal{O}(\kappa n)$ communication. In particular it requires n calls to $\mathcal{F}_{ABB}$PRP_eval.*

Theorem 7. *Protocol $\Pi_{OSet.Query}$ (Fig. 4) requires $\mathcal{O}(\kappa)$ communication. In particular it requires 1 call to $\mathcal{F}_{ABB}$PRP_eval.*

7.1 3 Party Oblivious Set Membership for Small n

Our hierarchical ORAM protocol will need Oblivious Hash Tables, and Oblivious Sets, where n is not $\omega(\log N)$. In this case, the data structure presented above will have non-negligible failure probability.

To solve this, when n is small we use a modified set membership protocol $\Pi_{OSetSmall}$, which uses larger Bloom filters and no Cuckoo Hash Tables. We have some security parameter κ, where $\kappa = \omega(\log N)$. If $n < \kappa$, the Cuckoo Hash Table is not used, and P_1 places all n PRP evaluations in the Bloom Filter, and makes the Bloom filter of size $B = n\kappa$. As before the number of hash functions is $\log N$. This makes the probability of a false positive
$\left(1 - e^{-\frac{\log Nn}{n\kappa}}\right)^{\log N} = \left(1 - e^{-\frac{\log N}{\kappa}}\right)^{\log N}$
which is negligible in N. The proof of security is identical to that of the Π_{OSet}, since the only messages revealed are the PRP evaluations, so $\Pi_{OSetSmall}$ securely implements $\mathcal{F}_{OSet}$ for $n < \omega(\log N)$.

The communication complexity of a build remains $\mathcal{O}(\kappa n)$ with n secure PRP evaluations and the communication complexity of a query remains $\mathcal{O}(\kappa)$ with 1 secure PRP evaluation.

Therefore, in terms of security and communication cost, other protocols can call $\Pi_{OSetSmall}$ in place of Π_{OSet} when n is small and the behavior will be the same. One small difference, however, is that $\Pi_{OSetSmall}$ needs superlinear storage ($\Theta(\kappa n)$ rather than $\Theta(n \log N)$). Nevertheless, in the ORAM data structure, only the smaller levels will be instantiated with this data structure, so it will not increase the asymptotic memory usage.

8 (3, 1)-Secure Oblivious Hash Table

We will now present how an Oblivious Set can be used to construct an efficient Oblivious Hash Table. The essential realization is that once it is known whether an item is in the Hash Table, the protocol can choose whether to search for the item itself or to search for a pre-inserted dummy element. This means that the protocol need not hide where in the data structure data is stored, nor need it hide the location that is accessed. All that needs to be hidden is whether an item is a dummy element or not, and if not, to avoid revealing any information about which element it is. As such, Oblivious Sets turn out to handle the hardest part of the problem, and any regular hash table may be used to store the data.

Like the Oblivious Set, the Oblivious Hash Table will reveal which indices in the input are duplicates of each other, and will also reveal which queries are repetitions of each other. (In our final ORAM protocol, it will be ensured that there are no duplicates, so this will leak no information.)

The Oblivious Hash Table contains a fixed number of pre-inserted dummy items, and since each distinct non-member query needs to access a distinct dummy, the Oblivious Hash Table will only support a limited number of queries. (The table can be rebuilt with new dummies if need be, but this will not be needed for the Oblivious RAM application.) These pre-inserted dummy items are searched for also using a PRP. This increases the size of the inputs space of the PRP to $\log(2N)$.

The Oblivious Hash Table is parameterized by the set of keys and values, $(X_1, Y_1), \ldots, (X_n, Y_n)$, the size of the domain of the indices, N, and the maximum number of distinct queries allowed, T. (By definition $T \leq N$.)

Functionality $\mathcal{F}_{OHTable}$

Build(($[\![X_1]\!]$,$[\![Y_1]\!]$), ..., ($[\![X_n]\!]$, $[\![Y_n]\!]$), N, T):
Let $first_i = \min\{j : X_j = X_i\}$. For all i such that $first_i = i$, store Y_i in a dictionary *dict* under index X_i. (No outputs.)
Reveal $first$ to all parties.
Set $t = 0$ (unique query counter) and $nQueries = 0$ (query counter)
Query($[\![X]\!]$, res):
If $t \geq T$ do nothing. Otherwise, if $X \in \{X_1, \ldots, X_n\}$, set $Y = dict[\![X_i]\!]$, otherwise set $Y = \perp$. Store Y in $[\![res]\!]$ (no outputs).
Set $queries_{nQueries} = x$. Set $firstFound = \min\{j : queries_j = x\}$. If $firstFound = t$ increment t. Increment $nQueries$. Reveal $firstFound$ to all parties.
Extract(res):
Returns $n + T - t$ elements, containing all pairs (X_i, Y_i) where $first_i = i$ and X_i was never queried. The remaining items are set to $(\perp, \perp)$. This array is stored in the ABB in $[\![res]\!]$.

Fig. 5. Oblivious Hash Table functionality

Theorem 8. *$\Pi_{OHTable}$ (Fig. 6) securely implements $\mathcal{F}_{OHTable}$ in the $\mathcal{F}_{ABB}$-$\mathcal{F}_{OSet}$-hybrid model in the* $(3, 1)$ *semi-honest security setting.*

Proof. **Build:** $\mathcal{F}_{OSet}$ generates $first$ exactly according to the requirement for $\mathcal{F}_{OHTable}$. Furthermore this output is a deterministic function of the inputs. It follows that we only need to show that simulators exist for each party whose generated messages are computationally indistinguishable from the real messages.

P_1 receives no messages. P_2 receives $\hat{Q}_1, \ldots, \hat{Q}_{n+T}$. S_2 generates $n + T$ random distinct $\log(4N)$-bit messages in place of these. Since these are the result of PRP evaluations on distinct inputs, any entity that could distinguish these from random distinct messages would be able to distinguish the PRP from a random permutation. Hence, by the security of the PRP, the output of S_2 is indistinguishable from the view of P_2. P_3's role is symmetric to P_2.

Protocol $\Pi_{OHTable}$

Build(($[\![X_1]\!]$, $[\![Y_1]\!]$), ..., ($[\![X_n]\!]$, $[\![Y_n]\!]$), N, T)

1. Call $\mathcal{F}_{OSet}$.Build($[\![X_1]\!], \ldots, [\![X_n]\!], N$). This reveals the value $first$ to all parties.
2. P_1 locally chooses k, a key for the PRP $f_k : [4N] \to [4N]$. Securely input k: $[\![k]\!] = \mathcal{F}_{ABB}$.Input(k, P_1).
3. For $i = 1, \ldots, n$
   (a) If $first_i \neq i$, X_i is a duplicate, set $[\![X_i]\!] = [\![N + i]\!]$ and $[\![Y_i]\!] = [\![\perp]\!]$.
   (b) Set $[\![Q_i]\!] = \mathcal{F}_{ABB}$.PRP_eval($[\![X_i]\!]$, $[\![k]\!]$).
4. P_1 creates and uploads dummies indexed from $2N+1$ to $2N+T$, to be queried when an item is not in the Oblivious Hash Table. For $i = 1, \ldots, T$
   (a) P_1 locally evaluates $Q_{n+i} = f_k(2N + i)$
   (b) $[\![Q_{n+i}]\!] = \mathcal{F}_{ABB}$.Input($Q_{n+i}, P_1$)
   (c) Set $[\![X_{n+i}]\!] = [\![2N + i]\!]$ and $[\![Y_{n+i}]\!] = [\![\perp]\!]$
5. Shuffle the tuples. Set $[\![\hat{Q}]\!], [\![\hat{X}]\!], [\![\hat{Y}]\!] = \mathcal{F}_{ABB}$.Shuffle($[\![Q]\!], [\![X]\!], [\![Y]\!]$)
6. Reveal $\hat{Q}_1, \ldots, \hat{Q}_{n+T}$ to P_2 and P_3. This will allow P_2 and P_3 to find an item's index in the shuffled array, based on its PRP evaluation.
7. Initialize $t = 0$ (counter for unique accesses to data structure).

Query($[\![x]\!]$, res)

1. Check whether the index is stored in the table: $[\![in]\!] = \mathcal{F}_{OSet}$.Query($[\![x]\!]$).
2. The previous function will also reveal to all parties the value $firstQuery$, which shows the first time x was queried to the Oblivious Hash Table. Let $nQueries$ be the number of times the Query function has been called before. If $firstQuery < nQueries$, this item has been queried before. If so, set $[\![res]\!]$ to the same query result that was provided the previous time $[\![x]\!]$ was queried and return. Otherwise increment t.
3. If the index is not in the table, an index of a pre-inserted dummy is used instead. $[\![x_{dummy}]\!] = \mathcal{F}_{ABB}$.Input($2N + t, P_1$).
   $[\![x_{used}]\!] = \mathcal{F}_{ABB}$.IfThenElse($[\![in]\!], [\![x]\!], [\![x_{dummy}]\!]$)
4. The PRP evaluation identifying the real/dummy element is calculated and revealed to P_2 and P_3:
   $[\![q]\!] = \mathcal{F}_{ABB}$.PRP_eval($[\![x_{used}]\!]$, $[\![k]\!]$)
   $q = \mathcal{F}_{ABB}$.Output($[\![q]\!], \{P_2, P_3\}$)
5. P_2 and P_3 find the PRP tag in the permuted PRP array, which allows them to find the value corresponding to that tag. I.e. P_2 and P_3 find j such that $q = \hat{Q}_j$ and reveal j to P_1. The parties set $[\![res]\!] = [\![\hat{Y}_j]\!]$.

Extract(res)

1. It is publicly known which t of the $n + T$ $(\hat{X}, \hat{Y})$ pairs were visited. For $j = 1, \ldots, n + T - t$, let i be the jth unvisited index and set:
   (a) $[\![isDummy]\!] = \mathcal{F}_{ABB}$.Equal($[\![Y_i]\!], [\![\perp]\!]$)
   (b) $[\![X_i]\!] = \mathcal{F}_{ABB}$.IfThenElse($[\![isDummy]\!], [\![\perp]\!], [\![X_i]\!]$)
   (c) $[\![res_j]\!] = ([\![X_i]\!], [\![Y_i]\!])$

Fig. 6. Oblivious Hash Table

Query: We need to show both that the correct value $firstFound$ is returned and that $[\![res]\!]$ is set to the correct value. Based on the definition of $firstFound$ in $\mathcal{F}_{OSet}$, and the fact that every query to $\Pi_{OHTable}$ results in exactly 1 query to $\mathcal{F}_{OSet}$, the value $firstFound$ that $\mathcal{F}_{OSet}$ reveals will satisfy exactly $\mathcal{F}_{OHTable}$. If x has been queried before, the protocol stores in $[\![res]\!]$ the same value as it stored last time, so if x is correct on all new queries it will also be correct on all repeated queries. If x has not been queried before, then there are two cases. Either $[\![x]\!] \in [\![X]\!]$, in which case x is queried, or $[\![x]\!] \notin [\![X]\!]$, in which case $2N+j$ is queried. If $[\![x]\!] \in [\![X]\!]$, then $q = f_k(x)$. Let ρ be the permutation of the shuffle, and let i represent the indices prior to the shuffle and $j = \rho(i)$ represent the indices following the shuffle. Since $x = X_i$ for some $i \in [n]$, and $Q_i = f_k(X_i)$, then $q = \hat{Q}_j$ for some j such that $\hat{Y}_j = Y_i$, so $[\![res]\!]$ is set to the correct value. If $[\![x]\!] \notin [\![X]\!]$ then $q = f_k(2N+t)$. Since $1 \leq t \leq T$, $q = Q_{n+t}$. As such, there is some j such that $\hat{Q}_j = q$ and $[\![\hat{Y}_j]\!] = [\![Y_{n+t}]\!] = [\![\perp]\!]$. Therefore $[\![res]\!]$ is set to $[\![\perp]\!]$ as required.

This shows that the query protocol is correct, but it remains to show that it is secure. If the index was queried before, no messages are sent to any player and the protocol is trivially secure. If the index was not queried before, then P_1 learns the index of the accessed item in the shuffled array. $S_{QUERY,1}$ will generate a random index in $[n+T]$ that has not been accessed before. By the definition of $\mathcal{F}_{ABB}$.Shuffle, the accessed items after the shuffle will be truly random distinct values. As such the distribution of the view of P_1 is identical to the distribution generated by $S_{QUERY,1}$. P_2 receives, in each query, the message $q = \hat{Q}_j$. The simulator $S_{QUERY,2}$, simulates this by selecting an element of $\hat{Q}_j$ uniformly at random from among the elements that have not previously been selected. Again, from the security of the shuffle, each accessed element in the real protocol will also be selected uniformly at random from among the unaccessed elements. Therefore the real and simulated views are identical. Since P_3 is symmetric to P_2 its proof of security is the same.

Extract: $[\![res]\!]$ will contain $n+T-t$ elements as required. If $x = X_i$ for $i \in [n]$, and x was queried, then, from above, the index of x will be visited, so X_i and its data Y_i will not be stored in $[\![res]\!]$. If $x = X_i$ for $i \in [n]$, but x was not queried, then $Q_i = f_k(X_i)$ was never revealed as a result of query, so index $\rho(i)$ was never visited in the permuted array. Since Y_i is a real data element $Y_i \neq \perp$, so $[\![X_i]\!], [\![Y_i]\!]$ will be stored in $[\![res]\!]$. All remaining elements stored in $[\![res]\!]$ will be for some $X_i \notin X$, *i.e.*, $i > N$. In these cases $Y_i = \perp$, $([\![\perp]\!], [\![\perp]\!])$ will be stored in $[\![res]\!]$ as required. The security of Extract is trivial since no parties receive messages.

The communication costs of $\Pi_{OHTable}$ are stated below as Theorems 9–11. The Theorems below follow from a straightforward accounting of the cost of each step, and their proofs can be found in the full version [17].

Theorem 9. *$\Pi_{OHTable}$.Build (Fig. 6) requires $\mathcal{O}(\kappa n + Dn + DT)$ communication. In particular, it requires $2n$ calls to $\mathcal{F}_{ABB}$.PRP_eval.*

Theorem 10. *$\Pi_{OHTable}$.Query (Fig. 6) requires $\mathcal{O}(\kappa)$ communication and, in particular, at most 2 calls to $\mathcal{F}_{ABB}$.PRP_eval.*

Theorem 11. *$\Pi_{OHTable}$.Extract (Fig. 6) requires $\mathcal{O}((n+T-t)D)$ communication and no calls to $\mathcal{F}_{ABB}$.PRP_eval.*

9 Hierarchical ORAM

In order to convert our Oblivious Hash Table functionality into a full-fledged ORAM protocol, we make use of the Hierarchical ORAM construction.

Oblivious Hash Tables (Fig. 5) have several limitations: they only allow writes during the build, they leak duplicated items in the build and they leak query repetitions.

By contrast, the Oblivious RAM functionality (presented formally in Fig. 7) allows a client to read and write into an array, *without* revealing the sequence of indices being accessed, *without* these limitations.

Functionality $\mathcal{F}_{ORAM}$

Init($[\![Y]\!]$, N, D) Initialize the ORAM to initially have stored $([\![i]\!], [\![Y_i]\!])$ for $1 \leq i \leq N$, where $|[\![Y_i]\!]|$ is D bits (no output).
ReadAndWrite($[\![x]\!]$, $[\![y]\!]$, res): (Where $x \in \{1, \ldots, N\}$ and y is D bits.) Set $[\![res]\!]$ to the value that was most recently written to $[\![x]\!]$ and set the new value of index $[\![x]\!]$ to $[\![y]\!]$ (no output).

Fig. 7. Oblivious RAM functionality

The Hierarchical ORAM technique can transform any Oblivious Hash Table to an Oblivious RAM and incurs $\mathcal{O}(\log N)$ overhead [23, 43, 44]. It does this by caching results obtained from a larger hash-table in smaller hash-tables, ensuring that an item is only searched for once in each hash-table before that table is rebuilt. This technique is well-known and oft-used in ORAM solutions (e.g. [18, 24, 33, 37, 47] [Theorem 1]). It applies both in the original client-server setting and the distributed multi-party setting.

Appling the Hierarchical ORAM technique to our novel Oblivious Hash Table (Fig. 6) yields our main result (Theorem 1) The proof is standard, but for completeness, it can be found in the full version of this work [17].

Acknowledgements. This research was sponsored in part by ONR grant (N00014-15-1-2750) "SynCrypt: Automated Synthesis of Cryptographic Constructions". Supported in part by DARPA under Cooperative Agreement HR0011-20-2-0025, NSF grant CNS-2001096, US-Israel BSF grant 2015782, Google Faculty Award, JP Morgan Faculty Award, IBM Faculty Research Award, Xerox Faculty Research Award, OKAWA Foundation Research Award, B. John Garrick Foundation Award, Teradata

Research Award, Lockheed-Martin Research Award, and Sunday Group. The views and conclusions contained herein are those of the authors and should not be interpreted as necessarily representing the official policies, either expressed or implied, of DARPA, the Department of Defense, or the U.S. Government. The U.S. Government is authorized to reproduce and distribute reprints for governmental purposes not withstanding any copyright annotation therein.

References

1. Albrecht, M.R., Rechberger, C., Schneider, T., Tiessen, T., Zohner, M.: Ciphers for MPC and FHE. In: Oswald, E., Fischlin, M. (eds.) EUROCRYPT 2015. LNCS, vol. 9056, pp. 430–454. Springer, Heidelberg (2015). https://doi.org/10.1007/978-3-662-46800-5_17
2. Anati, I., Gueron, S., Johnson, S., Scarlata, V.: Innovative technology for CPU based attestation and sealing. In: HASP (2013)
3. Angluin, D.: Circuits to test equality. https://zoo.cs.yale.edu/classes/cs201/topics/topic-compare-equality.pdf
4. Apon, D., Katz, J., Shi, E., Thiruvengadam, A.: Verifiable oblivious storage. In: Krawczyk, H. (ed.) PKC 2014. LNCS, vol. 8383, pp. 131–148. Springer, Heidelberg (2014). https://doi.org/10.1007/978-3-642-54631-0_8
5. Araki, T., Furakawa, J., Lindell, Y., Nof, A., Ohara, K.: High-throughput semi-honest secure three-party computation with an honest majority. In: CCS (2016)
6. Asharov, G., Komargodski, I., Lin, W.-K., Nayak, K., Peserico, E., Shi, E.: OptORAMa: optimal oblivious RAM. In: Canteaut, A., Ishai, Y. (eds.) EUROCRYPT 2020. LNCS, vol. 12106, pp. 403–432. Springer, Cham (2020). https://doi.org/10.1007/978-3-030-45724-2_14
7. Ben-Or, M., Goldwasser, S., Wigderson, A.: Completeness theorems for non-cryptographic fault-tolerant distributed computation. In: STOC. ACM, New York (1988). https://doi.org/10.1145/62212.62213
8. Boyle, E., Gilboa, N., Ishai, Y.: Function secret sharing. In: Oswald, E., Fischlin, M. (eds.) EUROCRYPT 2015. LNCS, vol. 9057, pp. 337–367. Springer, Heidelberg (2015). https://doi.org/10.1007/978-3-662-46803-6_12
9. Brasser, F., Müller, U., Dmitrienko, A., Kostiainen, K., Capkun, S., Sadeghi, A.R.: Software grand exposure: SGX cache attacks are practical. In: WOOT (2017)
10. Bunn, P., Katz, J., Kushilevitz, E., Ostrovsky, R.: Efficient 3-party distributed ORAM. In: Galdi, C., Kolesnikov, V. (eds.) SCN 2020. LNCS, vol. 12238, pp. 215–232. Springer, Cham (2020). https://doi.org/10.1007/978-3-030-57990-6_11
11. Chan, T.-H.H., Katz, J., Nayak, K., Polychroniadou, A., Shi, E.: More is less: perfectly secure oblivious algorithms in the multi-server setting. In: Peyrin, T., Galbraith, S. (eds.) ASIACRYPT 2018. LNCS, vol. 11274, pp. 158–188. Springer, Cham (2018). https://doi.org/10.1007/978-3-030-03332-3_7
12. Cook, S.A., Reckhow, R.A.: Time bounded random access machines. J. Comp. Syst. Sci. **7**(4), 354–375 (1973)
13. Costan, V., Devadas, S.: Intel SGX explained. IACR ePrint 2017/086 (2016)
14. Devadas, S., van Dijk, M., Fletcher, C.W., Ren, L., Shi, E., Wichs, D.: Onion ORAM: a constant bandwidth blowup oblivious RAM. In: Kushilevitz, E., Malkin, T. (eds.) TCC 2016. LNCS, vol. 9563, pp. 145–174. Springer, Heidelberg (2016). https://doi.org/10.1007/978-3-662-49099-0_6
15. Doerner, J., Shelat, A.: Scaling ORAM for secure computation. In: CCS (2017)

16. Faber, S., Jarecki, S., Kentros, S., Wei, B.: Three-party ORAM for secure computation. In: Iwata, T., Cheon, J.H. (eds.) ASIACRYPT 2015. LNCS, vol. 9452, pp. 360–385. Springer, Heidelberg (2015). https://doi.org/10.1007/978-3-662-48797-6_16
17. Falk, B.H., Noble, D., Ostrovsky, R.: 3-party distributed oram from oblivious set membership. Cryptology ePrint Archive, Paper 2021/1463 (2021). https://eprint.iacr.org/2021/1463
18. Hemenway Falk, B., Noble, D., Ostrovsky, R.: Alibi: a flaw in cuckoo-hashing based hierarchical ORAM schemes and a solution. In: Canteaut, A., Standaert, F.-X. (eds.) EUROCRYPT 2021. LNCS, vol. 12698, pp. 338–369. Springer, Cham (2021). https://doi.org/10.1007/978-3-030-77883-5_12
19. Fan, B., Andersen, D.G., Kaminsky, M., Mitzenmacher, M.D.: Cuckoo filter: Practically better than bloom. In: CoNEXT (2014)
20. Fletcher, C.W., Naveed, M., Ren, L., Shi, E., Stefanov, E.: Bucket ORAM: single online roundtrip, constant bandwidth oblivious RAM (2015)
21. Freedman, M.J., Ishai, Y., Pinkas, B., Reingold, O.: Keyword search and oblivious pseudorandom functions. In: Kilian, J. (ed.) TCC 2005. LNCS, vol. 3378, pp. 303–324. Springer, Heidelberg (2005). https://doi.org/10.1007/978-3-540-30576-7_17
22. Gilboa, N., Ishai, Y.: Distributed point functions and their applications. In: Nguyen, P.Q., Oswald, E. (eds.) EUROCRYPT 2014. LNCS, vol. 8441, pp. 640–658. Springer, Heidelberg (2014). https://doi.org/10.1007/978-3-642-55220-5_35
23. Goldreich, O., Ostrovsky, R.: Software protection and simulation on oblivious RAMs. JACM **43**(3), 431–473 (1996)
24. Goodrich, M.T., Mitzenmacher, M., Ohrimenko, O., Tamassia, R.: Privacy-preserving group data access via stateless oblivious RAM simulation. In: SODA (2012)
25. Gordon, S.D., et al.: Secure two-party computation in sublinear (amortized) time. In: CCS (2012)
26. Gordon, S.D., Katz, J., Wang, X.: Simple and efficient two-server ORAM. In: Peyrin, T., Galbraith, S. (eds.) ASIACRYPT 2018. LNCS, vol. 11274, pp. 141–157. Springer, Cham (2018). https://doi.org/10.1007/978-3-030-03332-3_6
27. Gullasch, D., Bangerter, E., Krenn, S.: Cache games-bringing access-based cache attacks on AES to practice. In: S&P (2011)
28. Hamlin, A., Varia, M.: Two-server distributed ORAM with sublinear computation and constant rounds. IACR ePrint 2020/1547 (2020)
29. Hoekstra, M., Lal, R., Pappachan, P., Phegade, V., Del Cuvillo, J.: Using innovative instructions to create trustworthy software solutions. In: HASP (2013)
30. Jarecki, S., Wei, B.: 3PC ORAM with low latency, low bandwidth, and fast batch retrieval. In: Preneel, B., Vercauteren, F. (eds.) ACNS 2018. LNCS, vol. 10892, pp. 360–378. Springer, Cham (2018). https://doi.org/10.1007/978-3-319-93387-0_19
31. Kaplan, D., Powell, J., Woller, T.: AMD memory encryption. Technical report, AMD (2016)
32. Kirsch, A., Mitzenmacher, M., Wieder, U.: More robust hashing: Cuckoo hashing with a stash. SIAM J. Comput. (2009)
33. Kushilevitz, E., Lu, S., Ostrovsky, R.: On the (in) security of hash-based oblivious RAM and a new balancing scheme. In: SODA (2012)
34. Kushilevitz, E., Mour, T.: Sub-logarithmic distributed oblivious RAM with small block size. In: Lin, D., Sako, K. (eds.) PKC 2019. LNCS, vol. 11442, pp. 3–33. Springer, Cham (2019). https://doi.org/10.1007/978-3-030-17253-4_1

35. Larsen, K.G., Nielsen, J.B.: Yes, there is an oblivious RAM lower bound! In: Shacham, H., Boldyreva, A. (eds.) CRYPTO 2018. LNCS, vol. 10992, pp. 523–542. Springer, Cham (2018). https://doi.org/10.1007/978-3-319-96881-0_18
36. Laur, S., Willemson, J., Zhang, B.: Round-efficient oblivious database manipulation. In: Lai, X., Zhou, J., Li, H. (eds.) ISC 2011. LNCS, vol. 7001, pp. 262–277. Springer, Heidelberg (2011). https://doi.org/10.1007/978-3-642-24861-0_18
37. Lu, S., Ostrovsky, R.: Distributed oblivious RAM for secure two-party computation. In: Sahai, A. (ed.) TCC 2013. LNCS, vol. 7785, pp. 377–396. Springer, Heidelberg (2013). https://doi.org/10.1007/978-3-642-36594-2_22
38. McKeen, F., et al.: Innovative instructions and software model for isolated execution. In: HASP (2013)
39. Mitchell, J.C., Zimmerman, J.: Data-oblivious data structures. In: STACS. Schloss Dagstuhl-Leibniz-Zentrum fuer Informatik (2014)
40. Mitzenmacher, M., Upfal, E.: Probability and Computing: Randomization and Probabilistic Techniques in Algorithms and Data Analysis. Cambridge University Press, Cambridge (2017)
41. Moghimi, A., Irazoqui, G., Eisenbarth, T.: CacheZoom: how SGX amplifies the power of cache attacks. In: Fischer, W., Homma, N. (eds.) CHES 2017. LNCS, vol. 10529, pp. 69–90. Springer, Cham (2017). https://doi.org/10.1007/978-3-319-66787-4_4
42. Noble, D.: An intimate analysis of cuckoo hashing with a stash. IACR ePrint 2021/447 (2021)
43. Ostrovsky, R.: Efficient computation on oblivious RAMs. In: STOC (1990)
44. Ostrovsky, R.: Software protection and simulation on oblivious RAMs. Ph.D. thesis (1992)
45. Ostrovsky, R., Shoup, V.: Private information storage. In: STOC, vol. 97 (1997)
46. Patel, S., Persiano, G., Raykova, M., Yeo, K.: PanORAMa: oblivious RAM with logarithmic overhead. In: FOCS (2018)
47. Pinkas, B., Reinman, T.: Oblivious RAM revisited. In: Rabin, T. (ed.) CRYPTO 2010. LNCS, vol. 6223, pp. 502–519. Springer, Heidelberg (2010). https://doi.org/10.1007/978-3-642-14623-7_27
48. Pippenger, N., Fischer, M.J.: Relations among complexity measures. JACM **26**(2), 361–381 (1979)
49. Ren, L., et al.: Ring ORAM: closing the gap between small and large client storage oblivious RAM. IACR ePrint 2014/997 (2014)
50. Roy, L., Singh, J.: Large message homomorphic secret sharing from DCR and applications. IACR ePrint 2021/274 (2021)
51. Shi, E., Chan, T.-H.H., Stefanov, E., Li, M.: Oblivious RAM with $O((\log N)^3)$ worst-case cost. In: Lee, D.H., Wang, X. (eds.) ASIACRYPT 2011. LNCS, vol. 7073, pp. 197–214. Springer, Heidelberg (2011). https://doi.org/10.1007/978-3-642-25385-0_11
52. Stefanov, E., e tal.: Path ORAM: an extremely simple oblivious RAM protocol. In: CCS (2013)
53. Tromer, E., Osvik, D.A., Shamir, A.: Efficient cache attacks on AES, and countermeasures. J. Cryptology **23**(1), 37–71 (2009). https://doi.org/10.1007/s00145-009-9049-y
54. Wang, X.S., Liu, C., Nayak, K., Huang, Y., Shi, E.: ObliVM: a programming framework for secure computation. In: S & P (2015). http://www.cs.umd.edu/~elaine/docs/oblivm.pdf
55. Wang, X., Chan, H., Shi, E.: Circuit ORAM: on tightness of the goldreich-ostrovsky lower bound. In: CCS (2015)

56. Wang, X.S., Huang, Y., Chan, T.H.H., shelat, a., Shi, E.: SCORAM: oblivious RAM for secure computation. In: CCS (2014)
57. Zahur, S., Rosulek, M., Evans, D.: Two halves make a whole. In: Oswald, E., Fischlin, M. (eds.) EUROCRYPT 2015. LNCS, vol. 9057, pp. 220–250. Springer, Heidelberg (2015). https://doi.org/10.1007/978-3-662-46803-6_8
58. Zahur, S., et al.: Revisiting square-root ORAM: efficient random access in multiparty computation. In: S & P (2016)

Finding One Common Item, Privately

Tyler Beauregard[1], Janabel Xia[2], and Mike Rosulek[3](✉)

[1] Truman State University, Kirksville, MO, USA
trb4137@truman.edu
[2] Massachussetts Institute of Technology, Cambridge, MA, USA
janabel@mit.edu
[3] Oregon State University, Corvallis, OR, USA
rosulekm@eecs.oregonstate.edu

Abstract. Private set intersection (PSI) allows two parties, who each hold a set of items, to learn which items they have in common, without revealing anything about their other items. Some applications of PSI would be better served by revealing only one common item, rather than the entire set of all common items. In this work we develop simple special-purpose protocols for privately finding one common item (FOCI) from the intersection of two sets. The protocols differ in how that item is chosen—*e.g.*, uniformly at random from the intersection; the "best" item in the intersection according to one party's ranking; or the "best" item in the intersection according to the sum of both party's scores. All of our protocols are proven secure against semi-honest adversaries, under the Decisional Diffie-Hellman (DDH) assumption and assuming a random oracle. All of our protocols leak a small amount of information (*e.g.*, the cardinality of the intersection), which we precisely quantify.

1 Introduction

Suppose Alice and Bob want to schedule a meeting, without sharing their entire calendars with each other. One method they might use is **private set intersection (PSI)**. If they run a PSI protocol, with each party using the set of available time slots as their input, then they will learn only the set of common available times—*i.e.*, the intersection of those sets—and nothing else about their calendars.

However, for the application of scheduling a meeting, it is not necessary for them to learn the *entire intersection* of their availabilities. Instead, it is enough that they learn just *a single item* from the intersection. We refer to this problem as (privately) **finding one common item (FOCI)**. We may consider different ways that single item may be chosen. The parties may want to simply learn a random common item. Alternatively, one or both parties may have preferences about the items (*e.g.*, "I am free at these times but prefer Tuesdays/Thursdays and prefer mornings.") and they want to learn the "best" item in the intersection according to those preferences.

C. Galdi and S. Jarecki (Eds.): SCN 2022, LNCS 13409, pp. 462–480, 2022.
https://doi.org/10.1007/978-3-031-14791-3_20

1.1 Related Work

To the best of our knowledge, there has not been work studying this particular variant of PSI. We briefly recall the state of the art for plain PSI, and also discuss secure multi-party computation methods that could be used to achieve FOCI.

Plain PSI. The first PSI protocols date back to the classic Diffie-Hellman-based PSI of Huberman, Franklin, and Hogg [10]. Their protocol has roots dating back to Meadows [16]. Our protocols take inspiration from the protocol of Huberman, Franklin, and Hogg; we elaborate on this connection later. Many other protocols have built on this paradigm, improving its efficiency [12,25] and extending it to achieve security against malicious adversaries [4,5,25]. Besides the Diffie-Hellman paradigm, there are other approaches for PSI—most notably, oblivious polynomial evaluation [6,8,13] and oblivious transfer [3,14,17–19,22–24].

PSI based on oblivious transfer is the most efficient for large sets, and the fastest PSI protocol in that paradigm is due to Rindal and Raghuraman [23]. For small sets, PSI based on the Diffie-Hellman approach is more efficient, and the fastest protocol in that paradigm is due to Rosulek and Trieu [25]. In their work, they found that the Diffie-Hellman approach was faster for sets of around 500 items or fewer.

Computing on the Intersection. Finding one common item is a special case of *computing arbitrary functions of the intersection.* There is a line of work on this problem, where some PSI techniques are used but the intersection is fed into a generic secure multi-party computation protocol [7,9,19–21].

1.2 Our Results

It is possible to privately find one common item, using the approaches just listed above (for computing arbitrary functions of the intersection).[1] However, we point out two issues with these approaches:

1. They all use techniques from oblivious-transfer-based PSI. These techniques are the most scalable for large sets, but they have certain inherent fixed costs (base OTs). In the case of plain PSI, these fixed costs are a significant fraction of the entire protocol cost for small sets. For this reason, Diffie-Hellman techniques are more efficient on small sets (in practice, several hundred items for each party).
   Our motivating application to calendar scheduling is indeed in this regime of set sizes, with ∼360 half-hour time slots in one month of business hours.
2. They all use general-purpose MPC (*e.g.*, garbled circuits or GMW protocol) to compute the function of the intersection. This adds an inherent level of complexity to the protocol. On the other hand, Diffie-Hellman PSI techniques are relatively simple. While describing a real-world and large-scale deployment

[1] All protocols for computing functions of the intersection can be readily augmented to support data associated with the items, *e.g.*, scores/ranks.

of PSI, Ion *et al.* [11] explicitly listed *protocol simplicity* as a major design constraint, motivating simplicity as follows:

> *It is difficult to overstate the importance of simplicity in a practical deployment, especially one involving multiple businesses. A simple protocol is easier to explain to the multiple stakeholders involved, and greatly eases the decision to use a new technology. It is also easier to implement without errors, test, audit for correctness, and modify. It is also often easier to optimize by parallelizing or performing in a distributed manner. Simplicity further helps long-term maintenance, since, as time passes, a constantly increasing group of people needs to understand the details of how a solution works.*

We propose simple protocols for the following variants of privately finding one common item:

- Alice learns the cardinality of the intersection and Bob learns one item chosen uniformly from the intersection. This variant is a simple (and likely folklore) modification of the classic Diffie-Hellman-based PSI protocol of [10].
- Bob has assigned ranks to each of his items, and he learns the item in the intersection with the highest rank. Alice learns the cardinality of the intersection, but nothing about the contents of the intersection, and nothing about Bob's ranks. For example, Alice would not learn whether item x was in the intersection, and she would not learn whether Bob's favorite or least favorite item is in the intersection.
- Both parties have assigned scores to each of the items, and for every item in the intersection we define its *combined score* as the sum of Alice's and Bob's scores for that item. Bob learns the item in the intersection with the highest combined score. Alice learns the cardinality of the intersection and the (unordered) set of combined scores for items in the intersection—*i.e.*, she does not learn which scores are associated with specific items, and she does not learn the individual contributions of Alice's/Bob's scores to the combined scores. For example, if Alice ranks the item x with score 3 and Bob ranks it with score 7, then Alice will learn that there is *some* item of combined rank 10 in the intersection.[2]

All of our protocols are conceptually simple and practical. Each is proven secure against *semi-honest* adversaries, under the standard DDH assumption, and in the random oracle model. The second protocol (with only Bob ranking the items) requires an order-revealing encryption [2], but there exist compact ORE schemes based only the minimal assumption of a PRF [15].

[2] There are some situations where Alice could use this leakage to deduce some information about the intersection and about Bob's ranks. For example, suppose Alice assigns ranks $r_1 < r_2 < \cdots$ to her items $x_1, x_2, \ldots$, respectively, and then she later learns that the intersection contains an item with combined rank r^*. If $r^* < r_2$ (and all ranks are nonnegative), she can deduce that item x_1 is in the intersection, and that Bob must have assigned rank $r^* - r_1$ to that item.

Our protocols reveal more than the minimum amount of information—*i.e.*, more than just the identity of one common item. All three protocols leak the cardinality of the intersection to Alice, for example. However, each protocol hides non-trivial information about the sets; each protocol reveals nothing about items not in the intersection; and leakage about the intersection is disassociated from specific items.

2 Preliminaries

2.1 Decisional Diffie-Hellman Assumption

Definition 1. *Let $\mathbb{G}$ be a cyclic group with generator g and order q. The* ***decisional Diffie-Hellman (DDH) assumption*** *is that the following two distributions are indistinguishable:*

$\mathsf{DH}_{1,\mathbb{G}}$:	$\mathsf{Rand}_{1,\mathbb{G}}$:
$a, b \leftarrow \mathbb{Z}_q$ return (g^a, g^b, g^{ab})	$a, b, c \leftarrow \mathbb{Z}_q$ return (g^a, g^b, g^c)

Using a standard and straight-forward rerandomization technique [1], the DDH assumption is equivalent to the following:

Proposition 2. *Let $\mathbb{G}$ be a cyclic group with generator g and order q. The DDH assumption is equivalent to the assumption that, for all n (polynomially bounded by the security parameter), the following two distributions are indistinguishable:*

$\mathsf{DH}_{n,\mathbb{G}}$:	$\mathsf{Rand}_{n,\mathbb{G}}$:
$a_1, \ldots, a_n, b \leftarrow \mathbb{Z}_q$ return $(g^{a_1}, \ldots, g^{a_n}, g^b, g^{a_1 b}, \ldots, g^{a_n b})$	$a_1, \ldots, a_n, b, c_1, \ldots, c_n \leftarrow \mathbb{Z}_q$ return $(g^{a_1}, \ldots, g^{a_n}, g^b, g^{c_1}, \ldots, g^{c_n})$

2.2 Secure Two-Party Computation

In this work we consider secure two-party computation in the presence of semi-honest adversaries. Let the two parties be denoted P_1 and P_2, and let their private inputs be x_1 and x_2, respectively. Let $f(x_1, x_2) = (f_1(x_1, x_2), f_2(x_1, x_2))$ denote an ideal functionality, which receives x_1, x_2 from the parties and gives output $f_i(x_1, x_2)$ to party P_i.

Let $view_i^\pi(x_1, x_2)$ denote the view of party P_i (consisting of internal randomness and protocol messages received) when the parties run protocol π honestly, on respective inputs x_1 and x_2.

Definition 3. *A protocol π securely realizes a functionality $f = (f_1, f_2)$ if, for $i \in \{1, 2\}$ there exists a simulator $\mathcal{S}_i$ such that for all x_1, x_2, the distributions $view_i^\pi(x_1, x_2)$ and $\mathcal{S}_i(x_i, f_i(x_1, x_2))$ are indistinguishable.*

In other words, the view of party P_i can be simulated given only their input x_i and ideal output $f_i(x_1, x_2)$.

2.3 Symmetric-Key Encryption

We require a simple one-time, symmetric-key encryption scheme, where decryption fails if the wrong (independently random) key is used. Let $\mathcal{K}$ be the set of keys and let $\mathcal{M}$ be the set of plaintexts. Specifically, we require the following properties:

- Correctness: $\mathsf{Dec}(k, \mathsf{Enc}(k, m)) = m$ with probability 1 for all $k \in \mathcal{K}$ and $m \in \mathcal{M}$.
- One-time security: For all $m_0, m_1 \in \mathcal{M}$, the distributions $\mathcal{E}_0$ and $\mathcal{E}_1$ are indistinguishable, where:

$\mathcal{E}_b$:
$k \leftarrow \mathcal{K}$ return $\mathsf{Enc}(k, m_b)$

- Robust decryption: For all $m \in \mathcal{M}$, the following process outputs TRUE with negligible probability:

```
k, k' ← K
c ← Enc(k, m)
return ⊥ ≠ Dec(k', m)
```

2.4 Order-Revealing Encryption

Order-revealing encryption (ORE) is a symmetric-key encryption scheme that reveals no more than the ordering of the plaintexts. See [2,15] for example constructions.

We specialize the notation of ORE for later convenience.

- Syntax: An ORE consists of algorithms $\mathsf{Enc}, \mathsf{Dec}, \mathsf{Argmax}$. The set of keys is $\mathcal{K}$ and the set of plaintexts is $\mathcal{M}$. Without loss of generality, $\mathcal{M} = \mathbb{Z}_N$ for some integer N, and we use the natural total ordering of $\mathbb{Z}_N$.
- Correctness: $\mathsf{Dec}(k, \mathsf{Enc}(k, m)) = m$ with probability 1 for all $k \in \mathcal{K}$ and $m \in \mathcal{M}$.
- Order-revealing: $\mathsf{Argmax}(\mathsf{Enc}(k, m_1), \ldots, \mathsf{Enc}(k, m_n)) = \arg\max_j m_j$, with probability 1 for all $k \in \mathcal{K}$ and $m_1, \ldots, m_n \in \mathcal{M}$.
- Security: for all **distinct** $m_1, \ldots, m_n \in \mathcal{M}$, the following distributions are indistinguishable:

$\mathcal{D}_0$:	$\mathcal{D}_1$:

$k \leftarrow \mathcal{K}$
for $i = 1$ to n:
  $c_i = \mathsf{Enc}(k, \boxed{m_i})$
return shuffle($\{c_1, \ldots, c_n\}$)
	$k \leftarrow \mathcal{K}$
	for $i = 1$ to n:
	  $c_i = \mathsf{Enc}(k, \boxed{i})$
	return shuffle($\{c_1, \ldots, c_n\}$)

In other words, encryptions of distinct plaintexts are indistinguishable from encryptions of the sequence $1, \ldots, n$.

3 Finding a Random Item of the Intersection

Our first simple protocol allows Bob to learn a single, randomly chosen, item from the intersection, while Alice learns only the cardinality of the intersection. For simplicity, we present our protocols for the case where both parties have n items, but all of the protocols are easily generalized for the case where the parties have sets of different sizes.

3.1 Warmup: Cardinality-Only Protocol and Blind Exponentiation

We start by recalling the classic protocol of Huberman, Franklin, and Hogg [10], which allows Alice & Bob to learn the cardinality of their intersection. The heart of the protocol is a *blind exponentiation* subprotocol, in which Alice has a set of items that get raised to a secret exponent known to Bob. Alice learns only the *unordered set* of resulting values. The subprotocol is shown in Fig. 1.

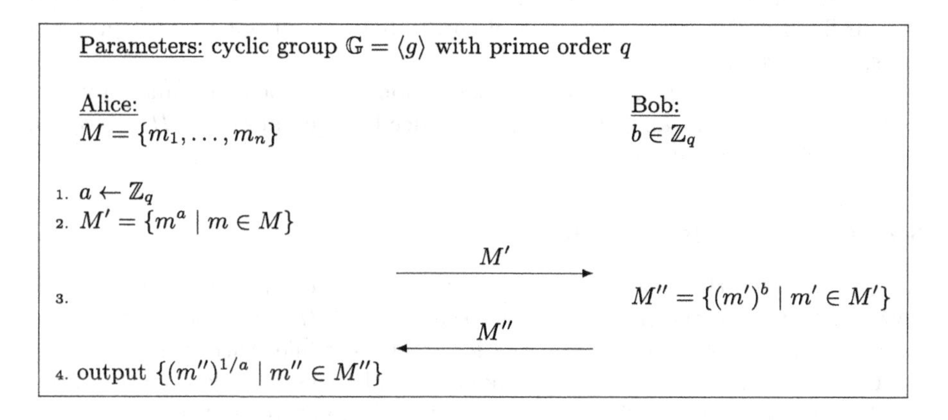

Fig. 1. Blind Exponentiation subprotocol.

Our convention when writing protocols and proving security is that **sets are unordered.** So when Alice/Bob send each other a set during the protocol, that set is assumed to be randomly permuted (equivalently, the set can be sorted).

Lemma 4. *Alice's output is (the unordered set) $\{m^b \mid m \in M\}$. Furthermore, if Alice is semi-honest, then her view in Fig. 1 can be simulated given only this output.*

Proof. Correctness follows from the fact that

$$\{(m'')^{1/a} \mid m'' \in M''\} = \{((m')^b)^{1/a} \mid m' \in M'\} = \{((m^a)^b)^{1/a} \mid m \in M\}.$$

Alice's view consists of M'' and random exponent a. This can be simulated by a simulator choosing random a and then raising every item of the output to the a power.

Lemma 5. *If Bob is semi-honest, and Alice's inputs have the form $m_i = H(x_i)$, for distinct x_i values (chosen by the adversary), then Bob's view in Fig. 1 is indistinguishable from random (assuming the DDH assumption, and with H a random oracle).*

Proof. Consider the following reduction algorithm. Given $\alpha_1, \ldots, \alpha_n, \beta_1, \ldots, \beta_n$: Simulate a random oracle while programming it as $H(x_i) = \alpha_i$—this is possible since the x_i's are distinct. Then simulate Alice's message M' as $M' = \{\beta_1, \ldots, \beta_n\}$. If each $\beta_i = \alpha_i^a$ then Bob's view is exactly as in the protocol. If the β_i values are independently random, then Bob's view is of a random set M'. The two cases are indistinguishable from the DDH assumption (Sect. 2.1).

Cardinality-Only Protocol. In the cardinality protocol of [10], the parties first perform blind exponentiation. If Alice's input set is X, then her input to blind exponentiation subprotocol is $\{H(x_i) \mid x_i \in X\}$. She learns $X' = \{H(x_i)^b \mid x_i \in X\}$ where b is a random exponent chosen by Bob. Bob also sends $Y' = \{H(y_i)^b \mid y_i \in Y\}$, where Y is his input set. The cardinality $|X' \cap Y'|$ corresponds to the cardinality $|X \cap Y|$. The protocol corresponds to all but the last protocol message of Fig. 3.

Since the outputs of the blind exponentiation subprotocol are randomly permuted, Alice does not know the correspondence between matching $H(z)^b$ values and her original x_i values.

3.2 Choosing a Random Item

After performing the basic cardinality protocol, Alice can simply identify a random element from the intersection according to its $H(z)^b$ value. In this way, Bob will learn a single item from the intersection, while Alice learns only the cardinality of intersection. For the sake of completeness, we describe the ideal functionality for this FOCI variant in Fig. 2, and the protocol in Fig. 3.

1. receive input X from Alice and Y from Bob.
2. give $|X \cap Y|$ to Alice.
3. sample $z^* \leftarrow X \cap Y$ uniformly; set $z^* = \perp$ if $X \cap Y = \emptyset$.
4. give z^* to Bob.

Fig. 2. Ideal functionality for sampling a random item from the intersection.

Lemma 6. *The protocol in Fig. 3 is correct.*

Proof. If $z \in X \cap Y$ then $H(z)^b$ will surely be included in A' and also as one of the K_i values. For all other items $x \neq y$, $\Pr[H(x)^b = H(y)^b] = \Pr[H(x) = H(y)]$—*i.e.*, these items contribute to the intersection only in the case of a collision under the random oracle.

Lemma 7. *The protocol in Fig. 3 securely realizes Fig. 2 against a semi-honest Bob.*

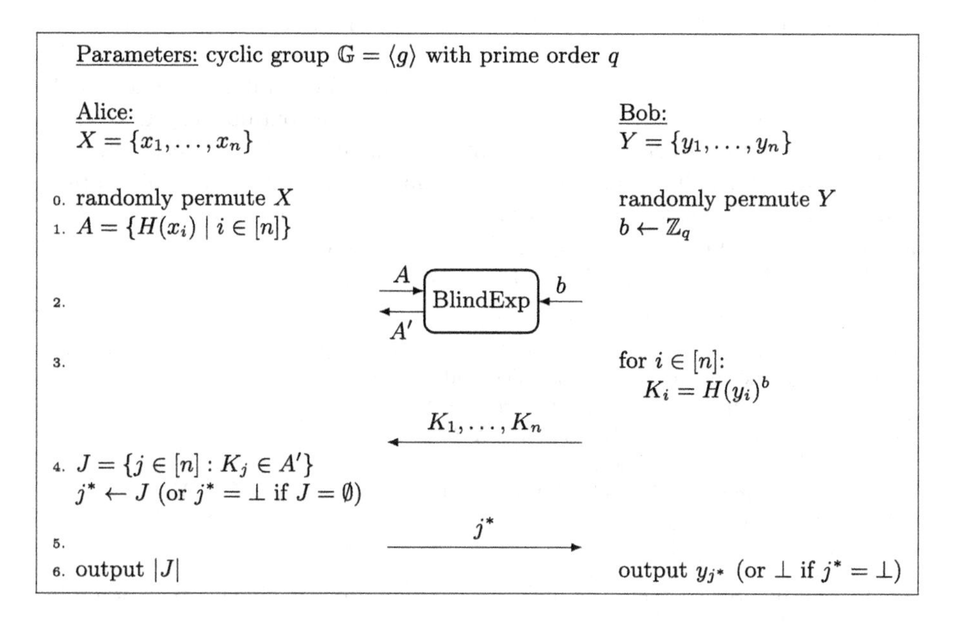

Fig. 3. Protocol for identifying a random item from the intersection.

Proof. Simulation for Bob is trivial. Bob's view consists only of his view from BlindExp (which is indistinguishable from random), and the final protocol message j^*, which is trivially computable from his ideal output.

Lemma 8. *The protocol in Fig. 3 securely realizes Fig. 2 against a semi-honest Alice.*

Proof. Alice's view consists mainly of her output A' from the blind exponentiation subprotocol and the K_i values from Bob. Using a standard reduction from DDH (which programs the $H(x_i)$ and $H(y_i)$ values in the random oracle), all values of the form $H(z)^b$ are indistinguishable from random. For $z \in X \cap Y$, such $H(z)^b$ value appears in A' and as one of the K_i values. For $y \in Y \setminus X$, the corresponding $H(y)^b$ appears only as one of the K_i values. Since the A' set is unordered, and Bob's set is randomly permuted, then Alice's view can be simulated knowing only $|X \cap Y|$—*i.e.*, knowing how many values repeat between A' and the set of K_i values.

4 Finding the Best Item According to a Unilateral Rank

In this section we consider the following variant. Alice holds a set of x_i values, and Bob holds a set of (y_i, v_i) pairs. The value v_i denotes Bob's *rank* of the item

y_i—*i.e.*, a number between 1 and n. We consider the problem of identifying the common item with highest rank. We assume that Bob has assigned **distinct ranks** to each of the items in his set.

In this variant, Alice learns only how many common items they have (*i.e.*, the cardinality of the intersection). In particular, she does not learn anything about the relative rankings of items in the intersection vs items outside of the intersection (e.g., she cannot learn that the intersection contains only Bob's least favorite items). Bob learns only the identity of the item with highest rank.

In Fig. 4 we formally define the ideal functionality for this variant of sampling from the intersection. In the case that there are no common items, V will be empty. We use the following notational conventions for that case: if $V = \emptyset$ then $\max(V) = \bot$; if the value of $j^* = \bot$ then $y_{j^*} = \bot$.

1. receive input X from Alice and Y from Bob.
2. define $K(Y) = \{y \mid \exists v : (y, v) \in Y\}$
3. compute $V = \{v \mid \exists y : y \in X \wedge (y, v) \in Y\}$
4. give $|V|$ to Alice.
5. compute $v^* = \max(V)$ and find y^* such that $(y^*, v^*) \in Y$
6. give y^* to Bob.

Fig. 4. Ideal functionality for sampling the best item from the intersection, according to a unilateral rank.

4.1 Intersection Protocol

The high-level idea behind the protocol is as follows. The parties can first perform the basic PSI-cardinality protocol from Sect. 3. This protocol computes a key $K_z = H(z)^b$ associated to each item z. Alice learns the key corresponding to every item in her set, but all other keys appear random to her.

Hence, Bob can use these keys to encrypt some information about his items' ranks. What should be the payload/associated data that Bob encrypts with each key? It should be enough to allow Alice to determine the highest ranked item in the intersection, without revealing that rank, and without revealing anything also about the relative ranks of items in the intersection.

The appropriate tool for the job is order-revealing encryption (ORE; Sect. 2.4). If Bob has item y with rank v, then he can use the PSI key K_v to *encrypt an ORE encryption of* v. Alice can therefore decrypt the outer ciphertexts to obtain ORE encryptions of the ranks of all items in the intersection. These ORE ciphertexts allow Alice to identify the item with highest rank, but they leak nothing else about the ranks.

Lemma 9. *The protocol in Fig. 5 is correct.*

Proof. If $(y_i, v_i) \in Y$ and $y_i \in X$ then A' will contain $H(y_i)^b$, and we will also have $E_i = \mathsf{Enc}(H(y_i)^b, O_i)$. As such, Alice will eventually decrypt this E_i to

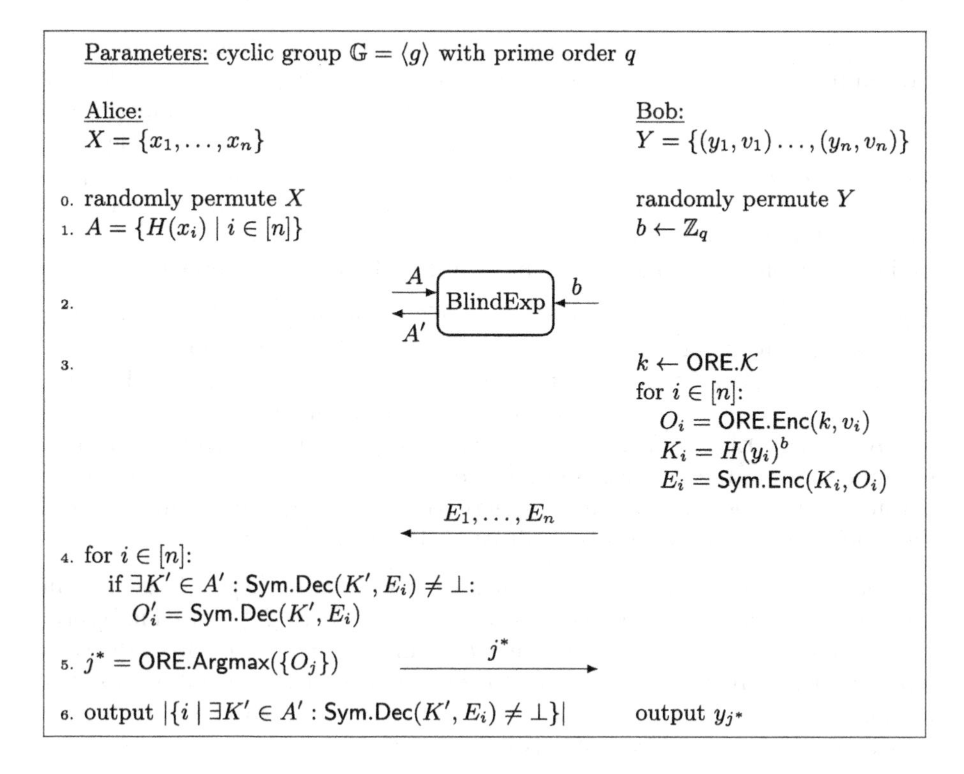

Fig. 5. Protocol for identifying the best item according to a unilateral rank.

obtain O_i, an ORE encryption of v_i. If $y_i \notin X$ then Alice will decrypt E_i with only independently generated keys, which will fail with overwhelming probability (cf. robust decryption Sect. 2.3). She will later compute $\mathsf{Argmax}(\{O_j\})$ which by the ORE correctness is the index j^* of the maximum v_j rank in the intersection.

Lemma 10. *The protocol in Fig. 5 securely realizes Fig. 4 against a semi-honest Bob.*

Proof. Simulation for Bob is trivial. Bob's view consists only of his view from BlindExp (which is indistinguishable from random), and the final protocol message j^*, which can be easily computed from his ideal output.

Lemma 11. *The protocol in Fig. 5 securely realizes Fig. 4 against a semi-honest Alice (assuming the DDH assumption).*

Proof. Alice's view consists of received protocol messages $A', E_1, \ldots, E_n$, and her view of the random oracle. These values are computed as in Hybrid 0 in Fig. 6. Here $\mathcal{A}$ denotes the adversary that receives Alice's view along with oracle access to the random oracle H. For convenience in Hybrid 0 we have named values $H(z)^b$ as K_z^*—if both Alice and Bob have a common element z then they will both refer to the same K_z^*.

In Hybrid 3 we present a simulator for Alice's view. Although this hybrid is written to take both parties' sets as input, it uses these inputs only to calculate the size m of the intersection. It then uses m to compute the remainder of the view. The hybrid also uses permutations μ, π—μ is used to index into elements of A', and π is used to randomly choose which m values are simulated as part of the intersection. Note that A' is given to Alice only as an unordered set—*i.e.*, indices of these items are not meaningful.

It suffices show that adjacent hybrids in Fig. 6 are indistinguishable.

Hybrids 0 & 1: The only difference is that K_z^* values are chosen uniformly. The hybrids are indistinguishable via a reduction to the DDH problem. Specifically, consider a reduction algorithm that receives $(\alpha_1, \ldots, \alpha_m, B, \beta_1, \ldots, \beta_m)$. For each $z_i \in \{x_1, \ldots, x_n, y_1, \ldots, y_n\}$, the reduction algorithm programs $H(z_i) = \alpha_i$ and sets $K_{z_i}^* = \beta_i$. Otherwise, the reduction algorithm runs the code of Hybrid 1. If the input is from the DH distribution—*i.e.*, if $B = g^b$ and $\beta_i = \alpha_i^b$—then the output of the reduction algorithm is exactly that of Hybrid 0. If the input is from the random distribution, then the reduction algorithm is exactly as Hybrid 1.

Hybrids 1 & 2: Consider a value y_i that is distinct from all $\{x_j\}$ values—*i.e.*, an item not in common to the two parties. Then the only place $K_{y_i}^*$ is used in Hybrid 1 is as the value K_i, when the ciphertext $E_i = \mathsf{Enc}(K_i, S_i)$ is generated. Hence, a straight-forward reduction to the one-time security of Enc (Sect. 2.3) shows that E_i is indistinguishable from an encryption of a dummy value 0. Performing such a reduction for each such y_i yields Hybrid 2.

Hybrids 2 & 3: Instead of sampling all K_i^* values upfront, they are sampled later, as needed. In the second for-loop of Hybrid 2, m of the ciphertexts (m = the cardinality of the intersection) are encrypted with keys appearing in A'. Furthermore, since the y_i values are randomly shuffled (and the ordering of A' is not meaningful), the choice of m common keys is random. The same is true of Hybrid 3, which uses the random permutations μ and π to select which m keys are common.

The only other difference is that the O_i values in Hybrid 2 are encryptions of v_i plaintexts, whereas in Hybrid 3 they are encryptions of $\{1, \ldots, m\}$ plaintexts. By a straightforward reduction to the ORE security property (Sect. 2.4), the two hybrids are indistinguishable.

5 Finding the Best Item According to a Combined Score

In this section we consider the following variant. Alice holds a set of (x_i, u_i) pairs, and Bob holds a set of (y_i, v_i) pairs. If Alice and Bob hold a common item, say $z = x_i = y_j$, then define that item's *score* as $u_i + v_j$. In other words, an item's score is the sum of its scores from both parties. We consider the problem of identifying the common item with highest score.

In this variant, Alice will learn (1) how many common items they have (*i.e.*, the cardinality of the intersection), and (2) the set of *combined* scores for all

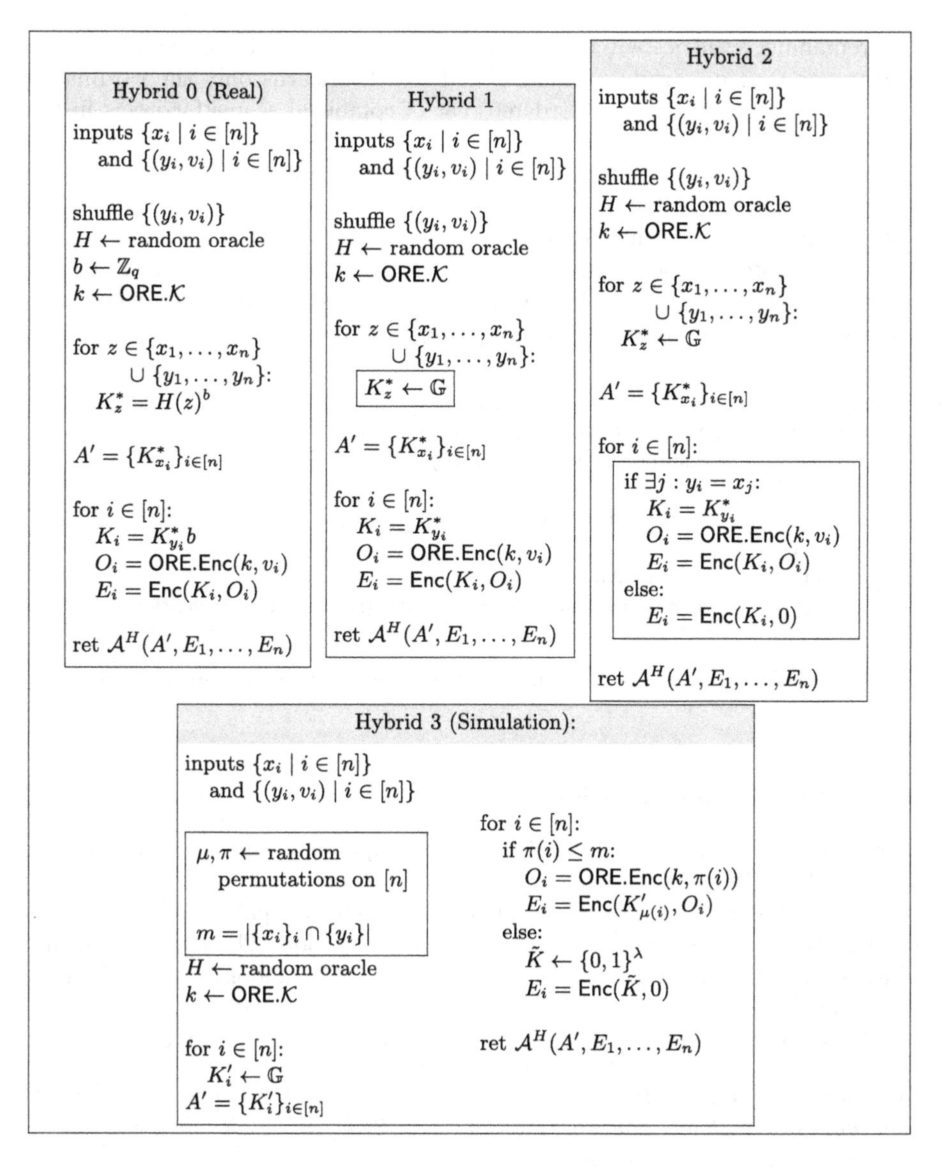

Fig. 6. Hybrids in the security proof for the protocol in Fig. 5

common items. Alice does not learn the individual contributions of the parties (*i.e.*, the u_i and v_j value that are added to give an item's score), nor does she learn which scores correspond to which items, or which items are in the intersection. Bob learns only the identity of the item with highest combined score.

In Fig. 7 we formally define the ideal functionality for this variant of sampling from the intersection. Alice receives a vector $(w_1, \dots, w_n)$, such that if k items are common to the parties, then all but k entries in the vector will be $\perp$.

The remaining k entries will contain the combined scores of the common items. The vector w is uniformly permuted, and so Alice learns only the cardinality of the intersection and the (unordered) set of combined scores for items in the intersection.

In the case that there are no common items, all w_i values will be $\bot$. We use the following notational conventions for that case: if every $w_i = \bot$ then $\arg\max_i w_i = \bot$; if the value of $j^* = \bot$ then $y_{j^*} = \bot$.

In our protocol Alice will learn a value of the form D^{w_i} and will need to compute $\mathrm{dlog}_D(D^{w_i}) = w_i$. Our protocol therefore supports inputs where **the scores (w_i values) have polynomial magnitude.**

1. receive input X from Alice and Y from Bob.
2. assign a random ordering to Y as $\{(y_1, v_1), \ldots, (y_n, v_n)\}$
2. for $i \in [n]$:
3. if $\exists(x, u) \in X$ with $x = y_i$: $w_i := u + v_i$
5. else: $w_i := \bot$
6. give $w_1, \ldots, w_n$ to Alice
7. set $j^* := \arg\max_i w_i$, and give y_{j^*} to Bob (see text for conventions)

Fig. 7. Ideal functionality for sampling the best item from the intersection, according to a combined score.

5.1 2-Blind Exponentiation

Our protocol requires a variant of the blind exponentiation subprotocol from Sect. 3.1. See Fig. 8.

In this variant, Alice has a set of pairs. For each such pair (ℓ, r) Alice wants to learn (ℓ^b, r^d) where b, d are exponents chosen by Bob. The two components of each pair are kept together, but the set of pairs is randomly shuffled. Alice learns only the *unordered set* of (ℓ^b, r^d) values.

The following lemmas are proven analogously to those in Sect. 3.1:

Lemma 12. *Alice's output is $\{(\ell^b, r^d) \mid (\ell, r) \in M\}$. Furthermore, if Alice is semi-honest and Bob's inputs b, d are uniform, then Alice's view in Fig. 8 can be simulated given only this output.*

Lemma 13. *If Bob is semi-honest, and Alice's inputs have the form $(\ell_i, r_i) = (H(x_i), t_i H(x_i))$ for distinct x_i values (x_i and t_i values chosen by the adversary), then Bob's view in Fig. 8 is indistinguishable from random (assuming the DDH assumption).*

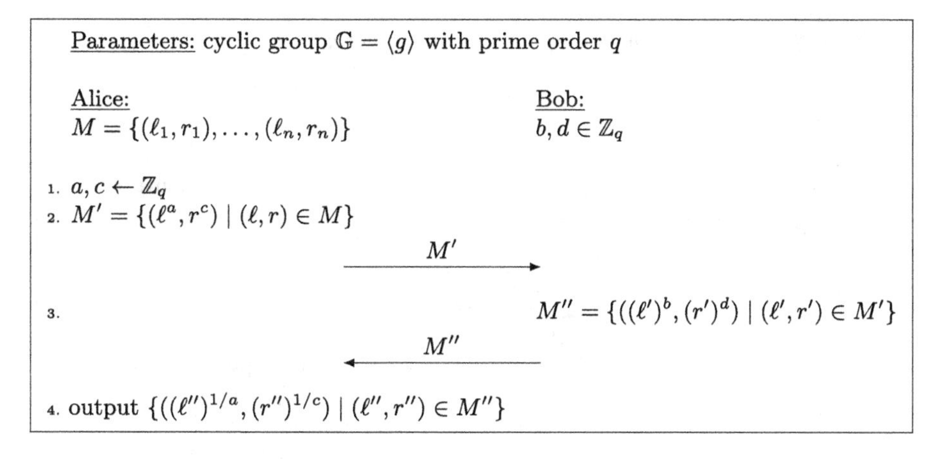

Fig. 8. 2-Blind-Exp subprotocol.

5.2 Intersection Protocol

We first present the high-level intuition behind the protocol. The challenge is to allow Alice to learn the combined score $u_i + v_j$ for a common item $x_i = y_j$, without revealing the individual u_i and v_j terms.

The main idea is to blind Alice's value u_i with some random mask, and blind Bob's value v_j with a complementary mask, so that the two masks can cancel out revealing only $u_i + v_j$. The main question is: *what random value shall serve as the mask?* Alice and Bob must apply the same mask if they have a common item ($x_i = y_j$), so the mask must be derived from the identity of the item. Our approach is as follows.

- For each (x_i, u_i) in Alice's set, she computes $g^{u_i} \cdot H(x_i)$.
- Using a blind exponentiation protocol, Alice obtains $[g^{u_i} \cdot H(x_i)]^d$ where d is a random exponent chosen by Bob. Here the value $H(x_i)^d$ is pseudorandom from Alice's view, so it serves as a blinding mask to the score g^{u_i}.
- For each item (y_j, v_j) in Bob's set, he can compute $[g^{v_j} \cdot H(y_j)^{-1}]^d$. He can encrypt these values (similar to the previous protocol), so that Alice learns them only if she has the matching item in her set.

Given her blinded value and the blinded value obtained from Bob, she can compute:

$$[g^{u_i} \cdot H(x_i)]^d \cdot [g^{v_j} \cdot H(y_j)^{-1}]^d = (g^d)^{u_i + v_j}$$

If Bob also sends g^d then Alice can compute the discrete log with respect to base g^d to obtain $u_i + v_j$. As mentioned above, computing the discrete log requires the combined ranks to be polynomial in magnitude.

Lemma 14. *The protocol in Fig. 9 is correct.*

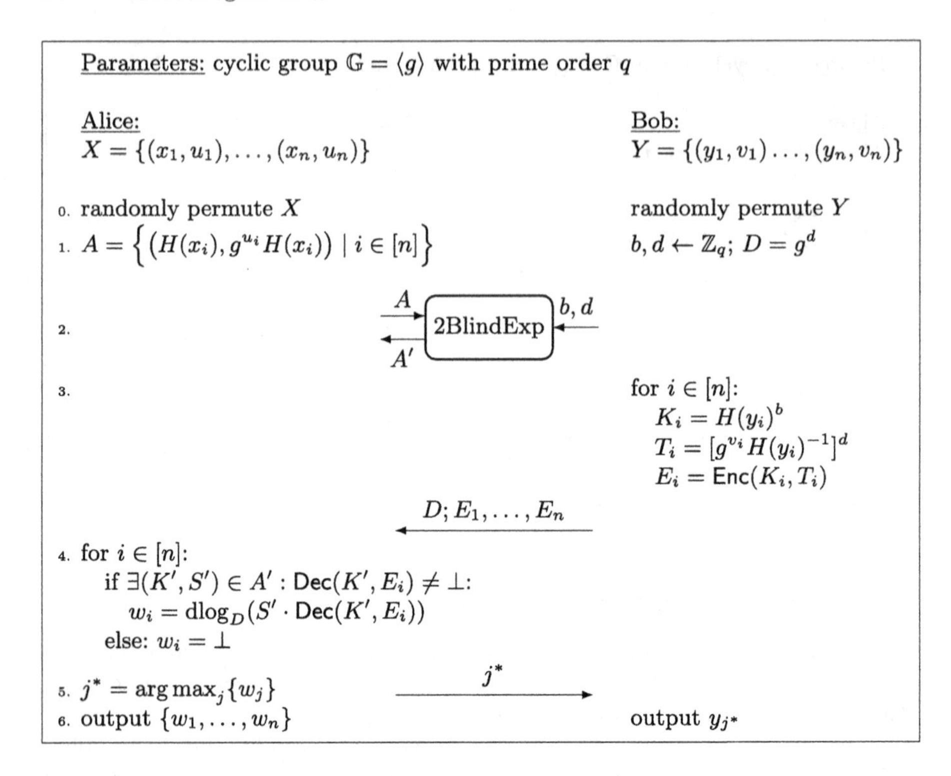

Fig. 9. Protocol for identifying the best item according to a combined score.

Proof. If $z = x_j = y_i$ for some i, j then A' will contain a tuple $\left(H(z)^b, [g^{u_j} H(z)]^d\right)$ and we will also have $E_i = \mathsf{Enc}\left(H(z)^b, [g^{v_i} H(z)^{-1}]^d\right)$. As such, Alice will eventually decrypt this E_i and compute

$$w_i = \operatorname*{dlog}_D\left([g^{u_j} H(z)]^d \cdot [g^{v_i} H(z)^{-1}]^d\right) = \operatorname*{dlog}_D\left(D^{u_j+v_i}\right) = u_j + v_i$$

If $y_i \notin \{x_1, \ldots, x_n\}$ then Alice will decrypt E_i with only independently generated keys, which will fail with overwhelming probability (cf. robust decryption Sect. 2.3). Hence, she sets $w_i = \perp$.

Overall, Alice's vector w contains exactly the combined scores of all items in the intersection. From this, the correctness of the last protocol message follows easily.

Lemma 15. *The protocol in Fig. 9 securely realizes Fig. 7 against a semi-honest Bob.*

Proof. Simulation for Bob is trivial. Bob's view consists only of his view from 2BlindExp (which is indistinguishable from random), and the final protocol message j^*, which can be easily computed from his ideal output.

Lemma 16. *The protocol in Fig. 9 securely realizes Fig. 7 against a semi-honest Alice.*

Proof. Alice's view consists of received protocol messages $A', D, E_1, \ldots, E_n$, and her view of the random oracle. These values are computed as in Hybrid 0 in Fig. 10. Here $\mathcal{A}$ denotes the adversary that receives Alice's view along with oracle access to the random oracle H. For convenience in Hybrid 0 we have given values $H(z)^b$ and $H(z)^d$ names K_z^* and T_z^*, respectively—if both Alice and Bob have a common element z then they will both refer to the same K_z^* and T_z^*.

In Hybrid 3 we present a simulator for Alice's view. Although this hybrid is written to take both parties' sets as input, it uses these inputs only to first compute a vector w that is Alice's output from the ideal functionality. It then uses w to compute the remainder of the view. The hybrid also uses a partial permutation μ that is used to index into the elements of the set A'. This is for notational simplicity, as A' is given to Alice only as an unordered set—*i.e.*, indices of these items are not meaningful.

It suffices show that adjacent hybrids in Fig. 10 are indistinguishable.

Hybrids 0 & 1: The only difference is that K_z^* and T_z^* are chosen uniformly. The hybrids are indistinguishable via two separate reductions to the DDH problem. Specifically, consider a reduction algorithm that receives $(\alpha_1, \ldots, \alpha_m, B, \beta_1, \ldots, \beta_m)$. For each $z_i \in \{x_1, \ldots, x_n, y_1, \ldots, y_n\}$, the reduction algorithm programs $H(z_i) = \alpha_i$ and sets $K_{z_i}^* = \beta_i$. Otherwise, the reduction algorithm runs the code of Hybrid 1. If the input is from the DH distribution—*i.e.*, if $B = g^b$ and $\beta_i = \alpha_i^b$—then the output of the reduction algorithm is exactly that of Hybrid 0. If the input is from the random distribution, then the reduction algorithm is like that of Hybrid 0 except that K_i^* values are chosen as in Hybrid 1.

With another reduction to the DDH assumption (setting $D = B$ and $T_{z_i}^* = \beta_i$), the output of the reduction algorithm becomes exactly that of Hybrid 1.

Hybrids 1 & 2: Consider a value y_i that is distinct from all $\{x_j\}$ values—*i.e.*, an item not in common to the two parties. Then the only place $K_{y_i}^*$ is used in Hybrid 1 is as the value K_i, when the ciphertext $E_i = \mathsf{Enc}(K_i, S_i)$ is generated. Hence, a straight-forward reduction to the one-time security of Enc (Sect. 2.3) shows that E_i is indistinguishable from an encryption of a dummy value 0. Performing such a reduction for each such y_i yields Hybrid 2.

Hybrids 2 & 3: Instead of sampling all K_i^* and T_i^* values upfront, they are sampled later, as needed. If $z = y_i = x_j$ for some i, j, then Hybrid 2 would first sample $S_j' = D^{u_j} T_z^*$ and then $S_i = D^{v_i} (T_z^*)^{-1}$. Since these are the only two places where T_z^* is used, and T_z^* is uniform, this is equivalent to Hybrid 3's behavior of setting $S_j' \leftarrow \mathbb{G}$ and then $S_i = D^{u_j + v_i} (S_j')^{-1}$. If $z = y_i \notin \{x_1, \ldots, x_n\}$ then Hybrid 2 uses K_z^* *only* as encryption to a single ciphertext.

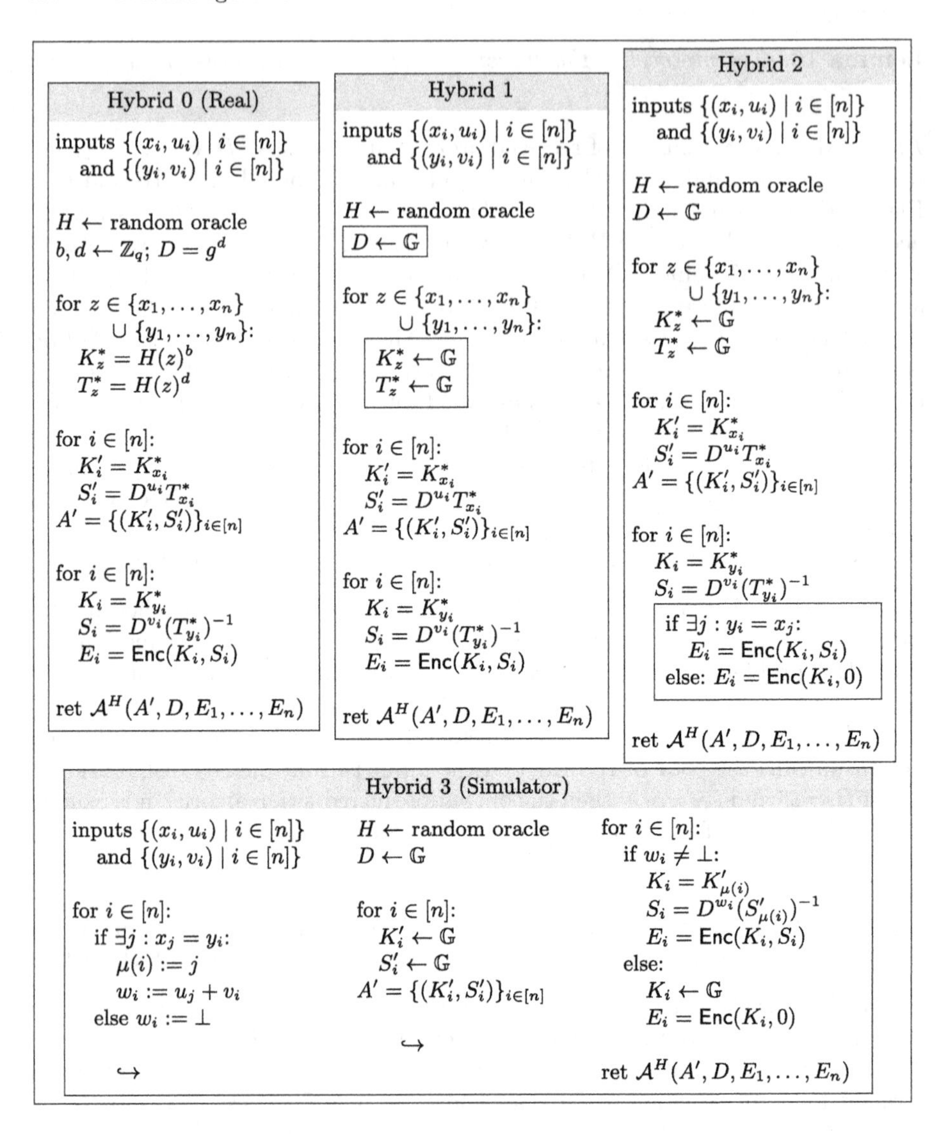

Fig. 10. Hybrids in the security proof for the protocol in Fig. 9

Acknowledgements. The first two authors are supported by NSF award DMS-1757995. We are grateful to anonymous SCN referees for the improvements they suggested to the manuscript.

References

1. Boneh, D.: The decision Diffie-Hellman problem. In: Buhler, J.P. (ed.) ANTS 1998. LNCS, vol. 1423, pp. 48–63. Springer, Heidelberg (1998). https://doi.org/10.1007/BFb0054851. Invited paper

2. Boneh, D., Lewi, K., Raykova, M., Sahai, A., Zhandry, M., Zimmerman, J.: Semantically secure order-revealing encryption: multi-input functional encryption without obfuscation. In: Oswald, E., Fischlin, M. (eds.) EUROCRYPT 2015, Part II. LNCS, vol. 9057, pp. 563–594. Springer, Heidelberg (2015). https://doi.org/10.1007/978-3-662-46803-6_19
3. Chase, M., Miao, P.: Private set intersection in the internet setting from lightweight oblivious PRF. In: Micciancio, D., Ristenpart, T. (eds.) CRYPTO 2020, Part III. LNCS, vol. 12172, pp. 34–63. Springer, Cham (2020). https://doi.org/10.1007/978-3-030-56877-1_2
4. Dachman-Soled, D., Malkin, T., Raykova, M., Yung, M.: Efficient robust private set intersection. In: Abdalla, M., Pointcheval, D., Fouque, P.-A., Vergnaud, D. (eds.) ACNS 2009. LNCS, vol. 5536, pp. 125–142. Springer, Heidelberg (2009). https://doi.org/10.1007/978-3-642-01957-9_8
5. De Cristofaro, E., Kim, J., Tsudik, G.: Linear-complexity private set intersection protocols secure in malicious model. In: Abe, M. (ed.) ASIACRYPT 2010. LNCS, vol. 6477, pp. 213–231. Springer, Heidelberg (2010). https://doi.org/10.1007/978-3-642-17373-8_13
6. Freedman, M.J., Nissim, K., Pinkas, B.: Efficient private matching and set intersection. In: Cachin, C., Camenisch, J.L. (eds.) EUROCRYPT 2004. LNCS, vol. 3027, pp. 1–19. Springer, Heidelberg (2004). https://doi.org/10.1007/978-3-540-24676-3_1
7. Garimella, G., Mohassel, P., Rosulek, M., Sadeghian, S., Singh, J.: Private set operations from oblivious switching. In: Garay, J.A. (ed.) PKC 2021, Part II. LNCS, vol. 12711, pp. 591–617. Springer, Cham (2021). https://doi.org/10.1007/978-3-030-75248-4_21
8. Hazay, C.: Oblivious polynomial evaluation and secure set-intersection from algebraic PRFs. In: Dodis, Y., Nielsen, J.B. (eds.) TCC 2015, Part II. LNCS, vol. 9015, pp. 90–120. Springer, Heidelberg (2015). https://doi.org/10.1007/978-3-662-46497-7_4
9. Huang, Y., Evans, D., Katz, J.: Private set intersection: are garbled circuits better than custom protocols? In: NDSS 2012. The Internet Society (2012)
10. Huberman, B.A., Franklin, M., Hogg, T.: Enhancing privacy and trust in electronic communities. In: ACM Conference on Electronic Commerce. ACM (1999)
11. Ion, M., et al.: On deploying secure computing commercially: private intersection-sum protocols and their business applications. Cryptology ePrint Archive, Report 2019/723 (2019). https://eprint.iacr.org/2019/723
12. Jarecki, S., Liu, X.: Fast secure computation of set intersection. In: Garay, J.A., De Prisco, R. (eds.) SCN 2010. LNCS, vol. 6280, pp. 418–435. Springer, Heidelberg (2010). https://doi.org/10.1007/978-3-642-15317-4_26
13. Kissner, L., Song, D.: Privacy-preserving set operations. In: Shoup, V. (ed.) CRYPTO 2005. LNCS, vol. 3621, pp. 241–257. Springer, Heidelberg (2005). https://doi.org/10.1007/11535218_15
14. Kolesnikov, V., Kumaresan, R., Rosulek, M., Trieu, N.: Efficient batched oblivious PRF with applications to private set intersection. In: Weippl, E.R., Katzenbeisser, S., Kruegel, C., Myers, A.C., Halevi, S. (eds.) ACM CCS 2016, pp. 818–829. ACM Press (2016). https://doi.org/10.1145/2976749.2978381
15. Lewi, K., Wu, D.J.: Order-revealing encryption: new constructions, applications, and lower bounds. In: Weippl, E.R., Katzenbeisser, S., Kruegel, C., Myers, A.C., Halevi, S. (eds.) ACM CCS 2016, pp. 1167–1178. ACM Press (2016). https://doi.org/10.1145/2976749.2978376

16. Meadows, C.: A more efficient cryptographic matchmaking protocol for use in the absence of a continuously available third party. In: 1986 IEEE Symposium on Security and Privacy, pp. 134–134 (1986). https://doi.org/10.1109/SP.1986.10022
17. Pinkas, B., Rosulek, M., Trieu, N., Yanai, A.: SpOT-light: lightweight private set intersection from sparse OT extension. In: Boldyreva, A., Micciancio, D. (eds.) CRYPTO 2019, Part III. LNCS, vol. 11694, pp. 401–431. Springer, Cham (2019). https://doi.org/10.1007/978-3-030-26954-8_13
18. Pinkas, B., Rosulek, M., Trieu, N., Yanai, A.: PSI from PaXoS: fast, malicious private set intersection. In: Canteaut, A., Ishai, Y. (eds.) EUROCRYPT 2020, Part II. LNCS, vol. 12106, pp. 739–767. Springer, Cham (2020). https://doi.org/10.1007/978-3-030-45724-2_25
19. Pinkas, B., Schneider, T., Segev, G., Zohner, M.: Phasing: private set intersection using permutation-based hashing. In: Jung, J., Holz, T. (eds.) USENIX Security 2015, pp. 515–530. USENIX Association (2015)
20. Pinkas, B., Schneider, T., Tkachenko, O., Yanai, A.: Efficient circuit-based PSI with linear communication. In: Ishai, Y., Rijmen, V. (eds.) EUROCRYPT 2019, Part III. LNCS, vol. 11478, pp. 122–153. Springer, Cham (2019). https://doi.org/10.1007/978-3-030-17659-4_5
21. Pinkas, B., Schneider, T., Weinert, C., Wieder, U.: Efficient circuit-based PSI via cuckoo hashing. In: Nielsen, J.B., Rijmen, V. (eds.) EUROCRYPT 2018, Part III. LNCS, vol. 10822, pp. 125–157. Springer, Cham (2018). https://doi.org/10.1007/978-3-319-78372-7_5
22. Pinkas, B., Schneider, T., Zohner, M.: Faster private set intersection based on OT extension. In: Fu, K., Jung, J. (eds.) USENIX Security 2014, pp. 797–812. USENIX Association (2014)
23. Rindal, P., Raghuraman, S.: Blazing fast psi from improved OKVS and subfield vole. Cryptology ePrint Archive, Report 2022/320 (2022). https://ia.cr/2022/320
24. Rindal, P., Rosulek, M.: Malicious-secure private set intersection via dual execution. In: Thuraisingham, B.M., Evans, D., Malkin, T., Xu, D. (eds.) ACM CCS 2017, pp. 1229–1242. ACM Press (2017). https://doi.org/10.1145/3133956.3134044
25. Rosulek, M., Trieu, N.: Compact and malicious private set intersection for small sets. In: Vigna, G., Shi, E. (eds.) ACM CCS 2021, pp. 1166–1181. ACM Press (2021). https://doi.org/10.1145/3460120.3484778

mrNISC from LWE with Polynomial Modulus

Sina Shiehian(✉)

Snap Inc., Berkeley, CA, USA
shiayan@umich.edu

Abstract. Introduced by Benhamouda and Lin [TCC'20], a multi-party reusable non-interactive secure computation protocol (mrNISC) consists of a commitment phase and an unbounded number of computation phases. In the commitment phase, a number of parties first commit to their input in a single broadcast round. Later in a computation phase, any subset of the parties can compute a function on their joint input by each sending a single broadcast message.

Benhamouda and Lin [TCC'20] constructed the first mrNISC for all functions based on standard hardness assumptions in pairing groups. Soon after their work, two concurrent papers by Benhamouda *et al.* [EUROCRYPT'21] and Ananth *et al.* [EUROCRYPT'21] constructed mrNISC for all functions based on the hardness of LWE with *super-polynomial modulus-to-noise ratio.*

In this work we build the first mrNISC for all functions based solely on LWE with polynomial modulus-to-noise ratio. We thus place mrNISC in the same category as public-key encryption and leveled fully homomorphic encryption in terms of the required LWE hardness assumption. We achieve our result by carefully introducing a bootstrapping step in the construction of Behamouda *et al.*.

1 Introduction

Secure multi-party computation (MPC) is one of the most investigated, if not the most investigated, topics in cryptography. An MPC protocol allows potentially dishonest parties to compute a function on their joint input without learning anything beyond what the output of the function reveals naturally.

An extensively studied direction in MPC research is to reduce the number of rounds of the protocol. Minimizing the round complexity is important in settings where the protocol is deployed in WANs and communication can potentially become the bottleneck. Recent works have constructed MPC protocols having as low as 2 rounds under various assumptions and in different models [1,3,6,11, 13,14,21].

A natural question to ask is what can be done in a single round. While it is well known that any single round MPC protocol is vulnerable to residual function attack, Benhamouda and Lin [7] introduced the notion of *multi-party reusable non-interactive secure computation (mrNISC).* In a mrNISC protocol each party

C. Galdi and S. Jarecki (Eds.): SCN 2022, LNCS 13409, pp. 481–493, 2022.
https://doi.org/10.1007/978-3-031-14791-3_21

commits to its input in an initial first round and broadcasts this commitment to other parties. These initial commitments allow *any subset of parties* to securely compute a function on their joint input by each one just sending one additional message. In particular, the initial commitments are reusable across any number of computations.

Benhamouda and Lin [7] built the first mrNISC. Their work is based on a standard hardness assumption in pairing groups and supports evaluation of all polynomial sized functions. Furthermore, it provides semi-malicious adaptive security in the plain model. Soon after [7], two concurrent works [2,5] constructed mrNISC for all polynomial sized functions based on the hardness of the learning with errors (LWE) problem.

A caveat of the constructions in [2,5] is that, when basing their hardness solely on LWE, they both rely on the hardness of LWE with *super-polynomial modulus-to-noise ratio* (in fact sub-exponential modulus-to-noise ratio for achieving λ bits of security). The modulus-to-noise ratio is an important parameter in the LWE problem which is related to its concrete hardness and its connection to lattice problems [23,25]. In more detail, for a fixed noise width parameter, a smaller modulus results in a stronger security guarantee and a smaller lattice dimension. Therefore, while LWE with a super-polynomial modulus is still supported by worst-case to average-case hardness reductions [23,25] and is presumed to be quantum-resistant, we strongly prefer using hardness of the *plain* LWE problem, which is hardness of LWE with polynomial modulus-to-noise ratio against polynomial sized adversaries. This brings us to the main question we investigate in this paper:

Can we build mrNISC for all functions based on polynomial hardness of LWE with polynomial modulus?

1.1 Our Contribution

We answer this question positively and build the first mrNISC for all functions based solely on LWE with polynomial modulus.

Theorem 1 (Main Theorem). *Assuming polynomial hardness of LWE with polynomial modulus, there exists a mrNISC for all functions.*

As shown by [5], such a mrNISC protocol can be used to construct a threshold leveled multi-key FHE scheme [20,21] for bounded number of participants based on LWE with polynomial modulus. Previous constructions needed super-polynomial hardness of LWE.

Corollary 1. *Assuming hardness of LWE with polynomial modulus, there exists a leveled multi-key FHE scheme for any polynomially bounded number of participants.*

1.2 Technical Overview

We start by giving a very high-level overview of the mrNISC construction of Benhamouda *et al.* in [5]. Benhamouda *et al.* construct a mrNISC for all functions via a three step process. In the first step, they consider mrNISC protocols for two parties supporting a class of functionalities called *functional OT* which is an extension of OT. A functional OT consists of two public functions f_S and f_R corresponding to the sender and receiver respectively. The function f_S takes the sender's hidden input x_S and outputs a pair of sender messages m_0, m_1. The receiver's function f_R acts on its hidden input x_R and outputs the receiver's choice bit b. The final output of the functional OT on input (x_S, x_R) is defined as m_b. Benhamouda *et al.* build a functional OT by providing an intriguing interplay between LWE-based homomorphic commitments [16,18] and LWE-based two-round statistical sender private OT [8]. Furthermore, for OT functionalities where the receiver function f_R has bounded logarithmic depth (and there is no restriction on f_S), they are able to base their construction on LWE with just a polynomial modulus by using the evaluation techniques in [10].

Next, in the second step, they upgrade the mrNISC constructed in the first step to support receiver functions of *all* depth. Roughly speaking, at this step, they transform any mrNISC for functional OT where the receiver function f_R can support evaluation of a PRF, to a mrNISC without any restrictions on f_R. The high-level idea here is using randomized encodings [4] to defer the full depth computation of the receiver function to the sender function which is not depth-limited.

In the final step, Benhamouda *et al.* build a compiler based on mrNISC for functional OT, 2-round MPC (in fact constant round MPC), and garbled circuits to construct a mrNISC for all functions (supporting any number of parties) (Fig. 1).

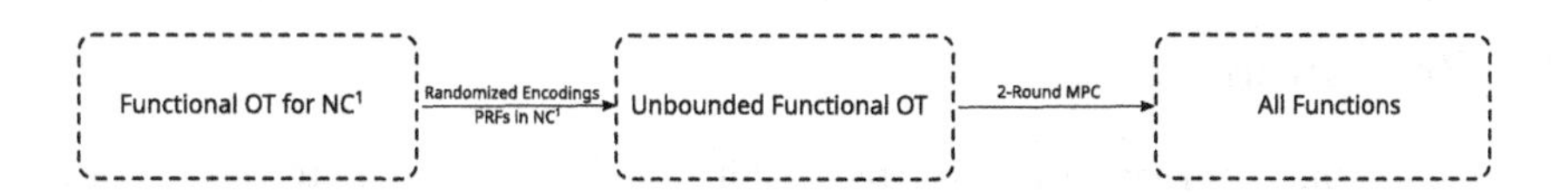

Fig. 1. The three steps of building mrNISC for all functions in [5]

Based on this description of [5], the main obstacle that prevents this construction from being based on LWE with polynomial modulus is the second step. As we already stated, this step needs a PRF with evaluation circuit in NC^1. Unfortunately, building a PRF which (i)is based on LWE (or RLWE) with polynomial modulus, and, (ii)can be evaluated by an NC^1 circuit, and, (iii)provides λ bits of security, is an open problem.

Our main idea is to circumvent this reliance on PRFs in NC^1 by bootstrapping mrNISC for functional OT. More specifically we bootstrap any mrNISC for functional OT where f_R is in NC^1 to a mrNISC for functional OT where f_R can be any polynomially-bounded-depth circuit. We call the latter a mrNISC for leveled functional OT. Fortunately, a standard instantiation of the GGM paradigm [17] with any one way function from LWE with polynomial modulus, gives a PRF that can be evaluated in bounded polynomial depth. In particular such a PRF along with the mrNISC for leveled functional OT can be used in the second step of [5] to obtain mrNISC for unbounded functional OT from LWE with polynomial modulus and consequently mrNISC for all functions from the same assumption.

Our bootstrapping is rather simple and follows the general blueprint of bootstrapping using FHE which has been applied in various contexts such as obfuscation [12,19,26] and correlation intractable hash functions [24] to name a few. In more detail, in our transformation, each one of the parties encrypts its private input x under FHE to obtain a ciphertext ct. It then commits to the message x along with the FHE secret key sk using the underlying mrNISC and publishes the commitment along with ct. Now, to generate second messages corresponding to a public function $f = (f_S, f_R)$ where f_R possibly has polynomially bounded depth, each party first computes ct^R_{eval} by homomorphically evaluating f_R on the receiver's ciphertext ct_R and then replaces f_R with FHE decryption function with ct^R_{eval} hardwired, that is, using the underlying mrNISC, each party generates a second message corresponding to the function $\widetilde{f} = (f_S, \mathsf{FHE.Dec}(\cdot, ct^R_{eval}))$. The key observation here is that, by using a proper FHE scheme [10,16] the decryption function FHE.Dec can be implemented in NC^1 while keeping the LWE modulus polynomially bounded (Fig. 2).

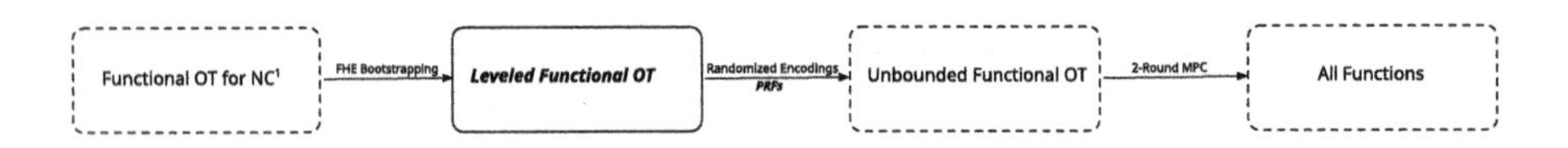

Fig. 2. The [5] process after introducing our bootstrapping step.

2 Preliminaries

We denote the security parameter by λ. For any $\ell \in \mathbb{N}$, we denote the set of the first ℓ positive integers by $[\ell]$. For a set S, $x \leftarrow S$ denotes sampling a uniformly random element x from S.

2.1 Learning with Errors

For a positive integer dimension n and modulus q, and an error distribution χ over $\mathbb{Z}$, the LWE distribution and decision problem are defined as follows. For an $\mathbf{s} \in \mathbb{Z}^n$, the LWE distribution $A_{\mathbf{s},\chi}$ is sampled by choosing a uniformly random $\mathbf{a} \leftarrow \mathbb{Z}_q^n$ and an error term $e \leftarrow \chi$, and outputting $(\mathbf{a}, b = \langle \mathbf{s}, \mathbf{a} \rangle + e) \in \mathbb{Z}_q^{n+1}$.

Definition 1. *The decision-LWE$_{n,q,\chi}$ problem is to distinguish, with non-negligible advantage, between any desired (but polynomially bounded) number of independent samples drawn from $A_{\mathbf{s},\chi}$ for a single $\mathbf{s} \leftarrow \mathbb{Z}_q^n$, and the same number of* uniformly random *and independent samples over $\mathbb{Z}_q^{n+1}$.*

A standard instantiation of LWE is to let χ be a *discrete Gaussian* distribution (over $\mathbb{Z}$) with parameter $r = 2\sqrt{n}$. A sample drawn from this distribution has magnitude bounded by, say, $r\sqrt{n} = \Theta(n)$ except with probability at most 2^{-n}. For this parameterization, it is known that LWE is at least as hard as *quantumly* approximating certain "short vector" problems on n-dimensional lattices, in the worst case, to within $\tilde{O}(q\sqrt{n})$ factors [23,25]. Classical reductions are also known for different parameterizations [9,22].

2.2 (Leveled) Fully Homomorphic Encryption

We recall the notion of leveled FHE from [15]. In this work, we consider leveled FHE schemes with low-depth decryption.

Definition 2. *A* leveled fully homomorphic encryption *scheme is a tuple of algorithms* FHE=$(\mathsf{Gen}, \mathsf{Enc}, \mathsf{Dec}, \mathsf{Eval})$ *with the following interfaces (we use only a symmetric-key version, which is sufficient for our purposes):*

- $\mathsf{Gen}(1^\lambda, 1^d)$ *outputs a secret key* sk.
- $\mathsf{Enc}(sk, m \in \{0,1\}^*)$, *where* m *is a message, outputs a ciphertext* $c \in \mathsf{CT}_{\lambda,d}$, *where,* $\mathsf{CT}_{\lambda,d}$ *denotes the ciphertext space of* FHE *for security parameter* λ *and depth parameter* d. *We also assume that* $\mathsf{CT}_{\lambda,d}$ *is efficiently sampleable.*
- $\mathsf{Eval}(C, c)$, *where* C *is a boolean circuit of depth (at most)* d, *deterministically outputs a ciphertext* c'.
- $\mathsf{Dec}(sk, c)$ *outputs a message (deterministically).*

It should satisfy the following properties:

1. Completeness*: For any circuit* C *of depth at most* d *and message* m, $\mathsf{Dec}(sk, \mathsf{Eval}(C, c)) = C(m)$ *with probability 1, over the random choice of* $sk \leftarrow \mathsf{Gen}(1^\lambda, 1^d)$ *and* $c \leftarrow \mathsf{Enc}(sk, m)$.
2. Pseudorandomness of ciphertexts*: for any sequence of messages* $\{m_\lambda\}_\lambda$, *and any sequence* $\{d_\lambda\}$, *the distribution ensembles*

$$\{\mathsf{Enc}(sk, m_\lambda) : sk \leftarrow \mathsf{Gen}(1^\lambda, 1^{d_\lambda})\}_\lambda \tag{1}$$

and

$$\{ct \leftarrow \mathsf{CT}_{\lambda,d_\lambda}\}_\lambda \tag{2}$$

are computationally indistinguishable.

3. Compactness and low-depth decryption*: the complexity of* Dec *is a fixed polynomial in* λ *alone. Furthermore,* Dec *can be implemented by a circuit in* NC^1.

In this work we use the GSW [16] leveled FHE scheme and the techniques in [10] which keep the modulus size polynomially bounded.

Theorem 2 ([10,16])**.** *Assuming hardness of LWE with polynomial modulus to noise ratio, there exists a leveled FHE scheme with* NC^1 *decryption.*

2.3 Multiparty Reusable Non-interactive Secure Computation

We recall the definition of mrNISC [2,5,7].

Definition 3. *A mrNISC scheme for a class of functions $\mathcal{F} = \{\mathcal{F}_\lambda\}_{\lambda \in \mathbb{N}}$ is a tuple of PPT algorithms $\Pi = (\mathsf{Com}, \mathsf{Encode}, \mathsf{Eval})$ with the following interface:*

- $\mathsf{Com}(1^\lambda, x)$, *on input a security parameter and a bitstring $x \in \{0,1\}^*$ outputs an input encoding $\hat{x}$ and an internal state st.*
- $\mathsf{Encode}(f, \{\hat{x}_j\}_{j \in [k]}, i, st_i)$, *on input a function $f : (\{0,1\}^*)^k \to \{0,1\}^* \in \mathcal{F}_\lambda$, k encoded inputs $\{\hat{x}_j\}_{j \in [k]}$, index $i \in [k]$, and the internal state for the ith input st_i, outputs a computation encoding α_i.*
- $\mathsf{Eval}(f, \{\hat{x}_j\}_{j \in [k]}, \{\alpha_j\}_{j \in [k]})$, *on input a function $f : (\{0,1\}^*)^k \to \{0,1\}^* \in \mathcal{F}_\lambda$, k encoded inputs $\{\hat{x}_j\}_{j \in [k]}$, and k computation encodings $\{\alpha_j\}_{j \in [k]}$, produces an output y.*

We consider the following two properties for mrNISC"

1. Completeness*: For any $\lambda \in \mathbb{N}$, any function $f \in \mathcal{F}_\lambda$, and any k input strings $\{x_j\}_{j \in [k]}$ that are compatible with the input domain of f:*

$$\mathsf{Eval}(f, \{\hat{x}_j\}_{j \in [k]}, \{\alpha_j\}_{j \in [k]}) = f(\{x_j\}_{j \in [k]}).$$

   where, for each $i \in [k]$, $(\hat{x}_i, st_i) \leftarrow \mathsf{Com}(1^\lambda, x_i)$ and $\alpha_i \leftarrow \mathsf{Encode}(f, \{\hat{x}_j\}_{j \in [k]}, i, st_i)$.
2. Adaptive semi-malicious security*: There exists a PPT simulator algorithm $\mathcal{S}$, such that, for any PPT adversary $\mathcal{A}$, the distribution ensembles*

$$\{\mathsf{Real}^{\Pi}_{\mathcal{A}}(1^\lambda)\}_{\lambda \in \mathbb{N}}$$

   and

$$\{\mathsf{Ideal}^{\Pi}_{\mathcal{A},\mathcal{S}}(1^\lambda)\}_{\lambda \in \mathbb{N}}$$

   are computationally indistinguishable, where, the experiments $\mathsf{Real}^{\Pi}_{\mathcal{A}}(1^\lambda)$ and $\mathsf{Ideal}^{\Pi}_{\mathcal{A},\mathcal{S}}(1^\lambda)$ are defined as follows:

   Experiment $\mathsf{Real}^{\Pi}_{\mathcal{A}}(1^\lambda)$: *The experiment is run by a challenger which interacts with the adversary $\mathcal{A}$. The adversary starts by specifying the number of the parties n and a honest subset of the parties $H \subseteq [n]$. The adversary then, submits an arbitrary number of input and computation encoding queries in arbitrary order. The only restriction is that $\mathcal{A}$ submits at most one input encoding per party. The challenger answers these queries as follows:*
   - Corrupt input encoding.
     - *Parse the input as (i, x_i, ρ_i), where, $i \in [k]$ is the party index, x_i is the input string, and ρ_i is the encoding randomness.*
     - *Compute $(\hat{x}_i, st_i) := \mathsf{Com}(1^\lambda, x_i; \rho_i)$.*
     - *Save $(\hat{x}_i, st_i)$.*
   - Honest input encoding.

- *Parse the input as (i, x_i), where, $i \in H$ is the party index, and x_i is the input string.*
- *Compute $(\hat{x}_i, st_i) \leftarrow \mathsf{Com}(1^\lambda, x_i)$.*
- *Send $\hat{x}_i$ to $\mathcal{A}$ and save $(\hat{x}_i, st_i)$.*

– Honest computation encoding.
- *Parse the input as (i, I, f), where, $i \in H$ is the party index, $i \in I \subseteq [k]$ is the participating subset of parties, and $f \in \mathcal{F}_\lambda$ is the function.*
- *If there is an index $j \in I$ for which $\mathcal{A}$ hasn't submitted an input encoding query yet, output $\perp$.*
- *Compute $\alpha_i \leftarrow \mathsf{Encode}(f, \{\hat{x}_j\}_{j \in I}, i, st_i)$.*
- *Send α_i to $\mathcal{A}$.*

The experiment ends when $\mathcal{A}$ terminates, outputting whatever $\mathcal{A}$ outputs.

Experiment $\mathsf{Ideal}^{\Pi}_{\mathcal{A},\mathcal{S}}(1^\lambda)$: *The setting here is exactly the same as $\mathsf{Real}^{\Pi}_{\mathcal{A}}(1^\lambda)$, except that the challenger has access to the simulator $\mathcal{S}$ and answers the queries as follows*

– Corrupt input encoding.
- *Parse the input as (i, x_i, ρ_i) .*
- *Save x_i.*

– Honest input encoding.
- *Parse the input as (i, x_i).*
- *Send i to $\mathcal{S}$ to receive the simulated encoded input $\hat{x}_i$.*
- *Forward $\hat{x}_i$ to $\mathcal{A}$ and save x_i.*

– Honest computation encoding.
- *Parse the input as (i, I, f).*
- *If there is an index $j \in I$ for which $\mathcal{A}$ hasn't submitted an input encoding query yet, output $\perp$.*
- *If for all $j \in (I \cap H) \backslash \{i\}$, $\mathcal{A}$ has submitted an honest computation encoding query corresponding to function f, set $y := f(\{x_j\}_{j \in I})$. Otherwise, set $y := \perp$.*
- *Forward (i, I, f, y) to $\mathcal{S}$ and receive α_i from it.*
- *Send α_i to $\mathcal{A}$.*

The experiment ends when $\mathcal{A}$ terminates, and, outputting whatever $\mathcal{A}$ outputs.

We refer to a mrNISC for 2 parties by the term *2rNISC*. For 2rNISC we are interested in a special class of functionalities called *functional OT* [5] which we denote by $\mathcal{F}^{OT}$.

Definition 4 (Bounded-depth Functional OT). *A* depth-d functional OT *is a function $f : \{0,1\}^* \times \{0,1\}* \to \{0,1\}^*$ that can be represented by two subfunctions $f_S : \{0,1\}^* \to \{0,1\}^* \times \{0,1\}^*$ and $f_R : \{0,1\}^* \to \{0,1\}$ such that, f_R can be implemented by a circuit of depth at most $d(\lambda)$, and evaluation of f on an input (x_S, x_R) proceeds as follows,*

- *First, compute $(m_0, m_1) := f_S(x_S)$.*
- *Next, compute $b := f_R(x_R)$.*
- *Output m_b.*

For a depth parameter $d = d(\lambda)$, *and a positive integer* $\lambda \in \mathbb{N}$, *let* $\mathcal{F}^{OT}_{\lambda,d}$ *be the set of all depth-d functional OTs. Then,* $\mathcal{F}^{OT}_{d}$ *is defined as* $\mathcal{F}^{OT}_{d} = \{\mathcal{F}^{OT}_{\lambda,d}\}_{\lambda \in N}$.

As shown in [5], 2rNISC for log-depth functional OT can be built based on the hardness of LWE with polynomial modulus.

Theorem 3 (Imported from [5]). *Assuming hardness of LWE with polynomial modulus, for every* $d = d(\lambda) = O(\log \lambda)$, *there exists a 2rNISC for* $\mathcal{F}^{OT}_{d}$.

When describing 2rNISC protocols for functional OT, instead of indexing the parties by integers, we use the letters S and R to refer to the sender and the receiver respectively.

3 Our Transformation

In this section we describe our 2rNISC for bounded-logarithmic-depth functional OT to 2rNISC for leveled functional OT transformation. Fix a depth parameter $d = d(\lambda)$. Our transformation uses the following ingredients:

- A leveled FHE scheme FHE, where the depth of FHE.Dec is $\widetilde{d} = \widetilde{d}(\lambda)$.
- A 2rNISC $\widetilde{\Pi}$ for depth $\widetilde{d}$ functional OT.

Construction 1 (2rNISC for leveled functional OT). We describe the three algorithms.

- $\mathsf{Com}(1^\lambda, x)$
  - Sample an FHE key $sk \leftarrow \mathsf{FHE.Gen}(1^\lambda, 1^{\mathsf{d}})$.
  - Using $\widetilde{\Pi}$, commit to (x, sk) to get $(\widetilde{x}, \widetilde{st}) \leftarrow \widetilde{\Pi}.\mathsf{Com}(1^\lambda, (x, sk))$.
  - Encrypt x using sk to get $ct \leftarrow \mathsf{FHE.Enc}(sk, x)$.
  - Output $(\hat{x} := (ct, \widetilde{x}), st := \widetilde{st})$.
- $\mathsf{Encode}(f, \hat{x}_S, \hat{x}_R, i, st_i)$
  - Parse $f = (f_S, f_R)$, $i \in \{S, R\}$, $\hat{x}_S = (ct_S, \widetilde{x}_S)$, and $\hat{x}_R = (ct_R, \widetilde{x}_R)$.
  - Compute $ct^{\mathsf{eval}}_R := \mathsf{FHE.Eval}(ct_R, f_R)$.
  - Define $\widetilde{f} := (\widetilde{f}_S, \widetilde{f}_R)$ as $\widetilde{f}_S(x, sk) := f_S(x)$ and $\widetilde{f}_R(x, sk) := \mathsf{FHE.Dec}(sk, ct^{\mathsf{eval}}_R)$.
  - Output $\alpha_i \leftarrow \widetilde{\Pi}.\mathsf{Encode}(\widetilde{f}, \widetilde{x}_S, \widetilde{x}_R, i, st_i)$.
- $\mathsf{Eval}(f = (f_S, f_R), \hat{x}_S, \hat{x}_R, \alpha_S, \alpha_R)$.
  - Define $\widetilde{f}$ exactly as in Encode.
  - Output $\widetilde{\Pi}.\mathsf{Eval}(\widetilde{f}, \widetilde{x}_S, \widetilde{x}_R, \alpha_S, \alpha_R)$.

The correctness of Construction 1 follows from the correctness of FHE and the correctness of $\widetilde{\Pi}$. Now we prove its security. The proof proceeds by first switching to a hybrid where the input and computation encoding made through $\widetilde{\Pi}$ are simulated instead of being generated honestly. This implies that these queries can be answered without knowing the FHE secret keys used to generate the honest input encodings. Consequently, due to the semantic security of FHE we can switch to a final hybrid where FHE ciphertexts are sample uniformly at random an in particular without knowing the honest inputs. Therefore, this final hybrid is identical to the ideal experiment.

Theorem 4 (Adaptive semi-malicious security). *Assuming $\widetilde{\Pi}$ satisfies adaptive semi-malicious security and* FHE *has pseudorandom ciphertexts, Construction 1 satisfies adaptive semi-malicious security.*

Proof. Let $\widetilde{\mathcal{S}}$ be the simulator for $\widetilde{\Pi}$. We define a simulator $\mathcal{S}$ as follows. The simulator $\mathcal{S}$ runs an instance of $\widetilde{\mathcal{S}}$ and responds to queries as follows:

- *Corrupt input encoding.*
  - Parse the input as $(i,\ x_i,\ \rho_i)$, where, $i \in \{S, R\}$.
  - Parse ρ_i as $\rho_i := (\rho_{i,gen}, \rho_{i,enc}, \rho_{i,\widetilde{\Pi}})$.
  - Compute $sk_i := \mathsf{FHE.Gen}(1^\lambda, 1^d; \rho_{i,gen})$ and $ct_i := \mathsf{FHE.Enc}(sk_i, x_i; \rho_{i,enc})$.
  - Send $(i,\ (x_i, sk_i),\ \rho_{i,\widetilde{\Pi}})$ to $\widetilde{\mathcal{S}}$ and save ct_i internally.
- *Honest input encoding.*
  - Parse the input as $i \in \{S, R\}$.
  - Send i to $\widetilde{\mathcal{S}}$ to obtain $\widetilde{x}_i$.
  - Sample a uniformly random ciphertext ct_i from the ciphertext space of FHE.
  - Output $(ct_i, \widetilde{x}_i)$ and save ct_i.
- *Honest computation encoding.*
  - Parse the input as $(i,\ f = (f_S, f_R),\ y)$.
  - If either of ct_S or ct_R have not been generated yet, output $\perp$ and abort this query.
  - Compute $ct_R^{\mathsf{eval}} := \mathsf{FHE.Eval}(ct_R, f_R)$.
  - Define $\widetilde{f} := (\widetilde{f}_S, \widetilde{f}_R)$ as $\widetilde{f}_S(x, sk) := f_S(x)$ and $\widetilde{f}_R(x, sk) := \mathsf{FHE.Dec}(sk, ct_R^{\mathsf{eval}})$.
  - Send $(i,\ \widetilde{f},\ y)$ to $\widetilde{\mathcal{S}}$ and receive the response $\widetilde{\alpha}$. Output $\widetilde{\alpha}$.

We now show via a series of hybrids that for any PPT adversary $\mathcal{A}$, the experiments $\mathsf{Real}_{\mathcal{A}}^{\Pi}$ and $\mathsf{Ideal}_{\mathcal{A},\mathcal{S}}^{\Pi}$ are computationally indistinguishable.

Hybrid H_0: This is the real experiment. In particular the queries are answered as follows:

- *Corrupt input encoding.*
  - Parse the input as $(i,\ x_i,\ \rho_i)$, where, $i \in \{S, R\}$.
  - Parse ρ_i as $\rho_i = (\rho_{i,gen}, \rho_{i,enc}, \rho_{i,\widetilde{\Pi}})$.
  - Using $\widetilde{\Pi}$, commit to sk_i to get $(\widetilde{sk}_i, \widetilde{st}_i) = \widetilde{\Pi}.\mathsf{Com}(1^\lambda, sk_i; \rho_{i,\widetilde{\Pi}})$.
  - Compute $sk_i := \mathsf{FHE.Gen}(1^\lambda, 1^d; \rho_{i,gen})$ and $ct_i := \mathsf{FHE.Enc}(sk_i, x_i; \rho_{i,enc})$.
  - Output $\hat{x}_i := (ct_i, \widetilde{sk}_i)$ to $\mathcal{A}$ and save $(\hat{x}_i, \widetilde{st}_i)$.
- *Honest input encoding.*
  - Parse the input as (i, x_i), where, $i \in \{S, R\}$.
  - Sample an FHE key $sk_i \leftarrow \mathsf{FHE.Gen}(1^\lambda, 1^\mathsf{d})$.
  - Using $\widetilde{\Pi}$, commit to (x_i, sk_i) to get $(\widetilde{x}_i, \widetilde{st}_i) \leftarrow \widetilde{\Pi}.\mathsf{Com}(1^\lambda, sk_i)$.
  - Encrypt x_i using sk_i to get $ct \leftarrow \mathsf{FHE.Enc}(sk, x)$.
  - Output $\hat{x}_i := (ct_i, \widetilde{x}_i)$ to $\mathcal{A}$ and save $(\hat{x}_i, \widetilde{st}_i)$.

- *Honest computation encoding.*
  - Parse the input as $(i,\, f = (f_S, f_R))$, where, $i \in \{S, R\}$.
  - If either of $\hat{x}_S$ or $\hat{x}_R$ has not been generated yet, abort query and output $\bot$.
  - Compute $ct_R^{\mathsf{eval}} := \mathsf{FHE.Eval}(ct_R, f_R)$.
  - Define $\widetilde{f} := (\widetilde{f}_S, \widetilde{f}_R)$ as $\widetilde{f}_S(x, sk) := f_S(x)$ and $\widetilde{f}_R(x, sk) := \mathsf{FHE.Dec}(sk, ct_R^{\mathsf{eval}})$.
  - Compute $\alpha_i \leftarrow \widetilde{\Pi}.\mathsf{Encode}(\widetilde{f}, \widetilde{x}_S, \widetilde{x}_R, \widetilde{st}_i)$. Output α_i.

Hybrid H_1: The difference between this hybrid and H_0 is how the honest computation and input encoding queries are answered. Specifically, these queries are answered by using $\widetilde{S}$ as follows:

- *Honest input encoding.*
  - Parse the input as (i, x_i).
  - Sample an FHE key $sk \leftarrow \mathsf{FHE.Gen}(1^\lambda, 1^\mathsf{d})$.
  - **Send i to $\widetilde{S}$ to obtain $\widetilde{x}_i$.**
  - Encrypt x_i using sk to get $ct_i \leftarrow \mathsf{FHE.Enc}(sk, x)$.
  - Output $\hat{x}_i := (ct_i, \widetilde{x}_i)$ to $\mathcal{A}$ and save ct_i.
- *Honest computation encoding.*
  - Parse the input as $(i,\, f = (f_S, f_R))$.
  - If either of $\hat{x}_S$ or $\hat{x}_R$ has not been generated yet, abort query and output $\bot$.
  - Compute $ct_R^{\mathsf{eval}} := \mathsf{FHE.Eval}(ct_R, f_R)$.
  - Define $\widetilde{f} := (\widetilde{f}_S, \widetilde{f}_R)$ as $\widetilde{f}_S(x, sk) := f_S(x)$ and $\widetilde{f}_R(x, sk) := \mathsf{FHE.Dec}(sk, ct_R^{\mathsf{eval}})$.
  - If this is the last query corresponding to f, let $y := f(x_S, x_R)$. Otherwise, let $y := \bot$.
  - **Send $(i,\, \widetilde{f},\, y)$ to $\widetilde{S}$ and receive the response $\widetilde{\alpha}_i$. Output $\widetilde{\alpha}_i$.**

Hybrid H_2: The only modification in this hybrid is the way honest input encoding queries are answered. Here, the honest inputs are no longer encrypted under FHE and instead, randomly sampled FHE ciphertext is used. In more detail, honest input queries are answered as follows:

- *Honest input encoding.*
  - Parse the input as (i, x_i).
  - Send i to $\widetilde{S}$ to obtain $\widetilde{x}_i$.
  - **Sample a uniformly random ciphertext ct_i from the ciphertext space of FHE.**
  - Output $\hat{x}_i := (ct_i, \widetilde{x}_i)$ to $\mathcal{A}$ and save ct_i.

Observe that H_2 is identical to $\mathsf{Ideal}^{\Pi}_{\mathcal{A},\mathcal{S}}$.

Lemma 1. *Assuming $\widetilde{\Pi}$ is adaptively semi-malicious secure, $H_0 \overset{c}{\approx} H_1$.*

Proof. Let $\mathcal{A}$ be an adversary trying to distinguish between H_0 and H_1. Using $\mathcal{A}$ we build an adversary $\mathcal{B}$ against the adaptive semi-malicious security of $\widetilde{\Pi}$ with the same advantage. The algorithm $\mathcal{B}$ runs $\mathcal{A}$ and whenever $\mathcal{A}$ makes a query it answers them as follows:

- *Corrupt input encoding.* These queries are answered exactly as in H_0.
- *Honest input encoding.*
  - Parse the input as (i, x_i).
  - Sample an FHE key $sk_i \leftarrow \mathsf{FHE.Gen}(1^\lambda, 1^\mathsf{d})$.
  - Forward $(i, (x_i, sk_i))$ to the challenger and receive $\widetilde{x}_i$ as response.
  - Encrypt x_i using sk_i to get $ct_i \leftarrow \mathsf{FHE.Enc}(sk_i, x_i)$.
  - Output $\hat{x}_i := (ct_i, \widetilde{x}_i)$ to $\mathcal{A}$ and save $(\hat{x}_i, \widetilde{st}_i)$.
- *Honest computation encoding.*
  - Parse the input as $(i, f = (f_S, f_R))$.
  - If either of $\hat{x}_S$ or $\hat{x}_R$ has not been generated yet, abort query and output $\perp$.
  - Compute $ct_R^{\mathsf{eval}} := \mathsf{FHE.Eval}(ct_R, f_R)$.
  - Define $\widetilde{f} := (\widetilde{f}_S, \widetilde{f}_R)$ as $\widetilde{f}_S(x, sk) := f_S(x)$ and $\widetilde{f}_R(x, sk) := \mathsf{FHE.Dec}(sk, ct_R^{\mathsf{eval}})$.
  - Forward $(i, \widetilde{f})$ to the challenger and receive $\widetilde{\alpha}_i$ as response. Output $\widetilde{\alpha}_i$ to $\mathcal{A}$.

Finally, when $\mathcal{A}$ terminates, $\mathcal{B}$ outputs $\mathcal{A}$'s output. Observe that when $\mathcal{B}$ is in the real experiment $\mathsf{Real}_{\mathcal{B}}^{\widetilde{\Pi}}$, then $\mathcal{A}$'s view is identical to its view in H_0. On the other hand, when $\mathcal{B}$ is in the ideal experiment $\mathsf{Ideal}_{\mathcal{B},\widetilde{\mathcal{S}}}^{\widetilde{\Pi}}$, the view of $\mathcal{A}$ is identical to its view in H_1. This completes the proof.

Lemma 2. *Assuming* FHE *has pseudorandom ciphertexts,* $H_1 \overset{c}{\approx} H_2$.

Proof. This is a direct consequence of the pseudorandomness of FHE ciphertexts.

This completes the proof.

Given Theorem 2 and Theorem 3, we thus have proved the following theorem.

Theorem 5. *Assuming hardness of LWE with polynomial modulus, there exists a 2rNISC for leveled functional OT.*

3.1 Putting Everything Together

In this section, we prove the main theorem of this paper. First, we stated the following theorem which is implicitly proved in [5].

Theorem 6 (implied in [5]). *Assuming the existence of a PRF whose evaluation function can be implemented by a circuit of depth* $d = d(\lambda)$, *and the existence of a 2rNISC for* $\{\mathcal{F}_{\mathsf{d}(\lambda)}^{OT}\}_{\lambda \in \mathbb{N}}$, *there exists a mrNISC for all functions.*

We defer the complete proof of Theorem 6 to the full version of this paper. We conclude by proving our main theorem.

Proof (of Theorem 1). We can build a PRF from LWE with polynomial modulus (and with polynomial-depth evaluation circuit) by instantiating the GGM [17] transformation with any LWE-based one-way function. Therefore, the proof follows from Theorem 6 and Theorem 5.

References

1. Ananth, P., Choudhuri, A.R., Goel, A., Jain, A.: Two round information-theoretic MPC with malicious security. In: Ishai, Y., Rijmen, V. (eds.) EUROCRYPT 2019. LNCS, vol. 11477, pp. 532–561. Springer, Cham (2019). https://doi.org/10.1007/978-3-030-17656-3_19
2. Ananth, P., Jain, A., Jin, Z., Malavolta, G.: Unbounded multi-party computation from learning with errors. In: Canteaut, A., Standaert, F.-X. (eds.) EUROCRYPT 2021. LNCS, vol. 12697, pp. 754–781. Springer, Cham (2021). https://doi.org/10.1007/978-3-030-77886-6_26
3. Applebaum, B., Brakerski, Z., Tsabary, R.: Degree 2 is complete for the round-complexity of malicious MPC. In: Ishai, Y., Rijmen, V. (eds.) EUROCRYPT 2019. LNCS, vol. 11477, pp. 504–531. Springer, Cham (2019). https://doi.org/10.1007/978-3-030-17656-3_18
4. Applebaum, B., Ishai, Y., Kushilevitz, E.: Computationally private randomizing polynomials and their applications. Comput. Complex. **15**(2), 115–162 (2006)
5. Benhamouda, F., Jain, A., Komargodski, I., Lin, H.: Multiparty reusable non-interactive secure computation from LWE. In: Canteaut, A., Standaert, F.-X. (eds.) EUROCRYPT 2021. LNCS, vol. 12697, pp. 724–753. Springer, Cham (2021). https://doi.org/10.1007/978-3-030-77886-6_25
6. Benhamouda, F., Lin, H.: k-round multiparty computation from k-round oblivious transfer via garbled interactive circuits. In: Nielsen, J.B., Rijmen, V. (eds.) EUROCRYPT 2018. LNCS, vol. 10821, pp. 500–532. Springer, Cham (2018). https://doi.org/10.1007/978-3-319-78375-8_17
7. Benhamouda, F., Lin, H.: Mr NISC: multiparty reusable non-interactive secure computation. In: Pass, R., Pietrzak, K. (eds.) TCC 2020. LNCS, vol. 12551, pp. 349–378. Springer, Cham (2020). https://doi.org/10.1007/978-3-030-64378-2_13
8. Brakerski, Z., Döttling, N.: Two-message statistically sender-private OT from LWE. In: Beimel, A., Dziembowski, S. (eds.) TCC 2018. LNCS, vol. 11240, pp. 370–390. Springer, Cham (2018). https://doi.org/10.1007/978-3-030-03810-6_14
9. Brakerski, Z., Langlois, A., Peikert, C., Regev, O., Stehlé, D.: Classical hardness of learning with errors. In: STOC, pp. 575–584 (2013)
10. Brakerski, Z., Vaikuntanathan, V.: Lattice-based FHE as secure as PKE. In: ITCS, pp. 1–12 (2014)
11. Garg, S., Gentry, C., Halevi, S., Raykova, M.: Two-round secure MPC from indistinguishability obfuscation. In: Lindell, Y. (ed.) TCC 2014. LNCS, vol. 8349, pp. 74–94. Springer, Heidelberg (2014). https://doi.org/10.1007/978-3-642-54242-8_4
12. Garg, S., Gentry, C., Halevi, S., Raykova, M., Sahai, A., Waters, B.: Candidate indistinguishability obfuscation and functional encryption for all circuits. In: FOCS, pp. 40–49 (2013)
13. Garg, S., Srinivasan, A.: Garbled protocols and two-round MPC from bilinear maps. In: FOCS (2017)

14. Garg, S., Srinivasan, A.: Two-round multiparty secure computation from minimal assumptions. In: Nielsen, J.B., Rijmen, V. (eds.) EUROCRYPT 2018. LNCS, vol. 10821, pp. 468–499. Springer, Cham (2018). https://doi.org/10.1007/978-3-319-78375-8_16
15. Gentry, C.: A fully homomorphic encryption scheme. Ph.D. thesis, Stanford University (2009). http://crypto.stanford.edu/craig
16. Gentry, C., Sahai, A., Waters, B.: Homomorphic encryption from learning with errors: conceptually-simpler, asymptotically-faster, attribute-based. In: Canetti, R., Garay, J.A. (eds.) CRYPTO 2013. LNCS, vol. 8042, pp. 75–92. Springer, Heidelberg (2013). https://doi.org/10.1007/978-3-642-40041-4_5
17. Goldreich, O., Goldwasser, S., Micali, S.: How to construct random functions. J. ACM **33**(4), 792–807 (1986). Preliminary version in FOCS 1984
18. Gorbunov, S., Vaikuntanathan, V., Wichs, D.: Leveled fully homomorphic signatures from standard lattices. In: STOC, pp. 469–477 (2015)
19. Goyal, R., Koppula, V., Waters, B.: Lockable obfuscation. In: FOCS, pp. 612–621 (2017)
20. López-Alt, A., Tromer, E., Vaikuntanathan, V.: On-the-fly multiparty computation on the cloud via multikey fully homomorphic encryption. In: STOC, pp. 1219–1234 (2012)
21. Mukherjee, P., Wichs, D.: Two round multiparty computation via multi-key FHE. In: Fischlin, M., Coron, J.-S. (eds.) EUROCRYPT 2016. LNCS, vol. 9666, pp. 735–763. Springer, Heidelberg (2016). https://doi.org/10.1007/978-3-662-49896-5_26
22. Peikert, C.: Public-key cryptosystems from the worst-case shortest vector problem. In: STOC, pp. 333–342 (2009)
23. Peikert, C., Regev, O., Stephens-Davidowitz, N.: Pseudorandomness of Ring-LWE for any ring and modulus. In: STOC, pp. 461–473 (2017)
24. Peikert, C., Shiehian, S.: Noninteractive zero knowledge for NP from (Plain) learning with errors. In: Boldyreva, A., Micciancio, D. (eds.) CRYPTO 2019. LNCS, vol. 11692, pp. 89–114. Springer, Cham (2019). https://doi.org/10.1007/978-3-030-26948-7_4
25. Regev, O.: On lattices, learning with errors, random linear codes, and cryptography. J. ACM **56**(6), 1–40 (2009). Preliminary version in STOC 2005
26. Wichs, D., Zirdelis, G.: Obfuscating compute-and-compare programs under LWE. In: FOCS, pp. 600–611 (2017)

On Sufficient Oracles for Secure Computation with Identifiable Abort

Mark Simkin[1(✉)], Luisa Siniscalchi[2,3(✉)], and Sophia Yakoubov[2(✉)]

[1] Ethereum Foundation, Zug, Switzerland
mark.simkin@ethereum.org
[2] Aarhus University, Aarhus, Denmark
{lsiniscalchi,sophia.yakoubov}@cs.au.dk
[3] Concordium Blockchain Research Center, Aarhus, Denmark

Abstract. Identifiable abort is the strongest security guarantee that is achievable for secure multi-party computation in the dishonest majority setting. Protocols that achieve this level of security ensure that, in case of an abort, all honest parties agree on the identity of at least one corrupt party who can be held accountable for the abort. It is important to understand what computational primitives must be used to obtain secure computation with identifiable abort. This can be approached by asking which oracles can be used to build perfectly secure computation with identifiable abort. Ishai, Ostrovsky, and Zikas (Crypto 2014) show that an oracle that returns correlated randomness to all n parties is sufficient; however, they leave open the question of whether oracles that return output to fewer than n parties can be used.

In this work, we show that for $t \leq n-2$ corruptions, oracles that return output to $n-1$ parties are sufficient to obtain information-theoretically secure computation with identifiable abort. Using our construction recursively, we see that for $t \leq n - \ell - 2$ and $\ell \in \mathcal{O}(1)$, oracles that return output to $n - \ell - 1$ parties are sufficient.

For our construction, we introduce a new kind of secret sharing scheme which we call unanimously identifiable secret sharing with public and private shares (UISSwPPS). In a UISSwPPS scheme, each share holder is given a public and a private share. Only the public shares are necessary for reconstruction, and the knowledge of a private share additionally enables the identification of at least one party who provided an incorrect share in case reconstruction fails. The important new property of UISSwPPS is that, even given all the public shares, an adversary should not be able to come up with a different public share that causes reconstruction of an incorrect message, or that avoids the identification of a cheater if reconstruction fails.

Keywords: secure computation · identifiable abort

M. Simkin—Supported by a DFF Sapere Aude Grant 9064-00068B.
S. Yakoubov—Supported by the European Research Council (ERC) under the European Unions's Horizon 2020 research and innovation programme under grant agreement No 669255 (MPCPRO).

C. Galdi and S. Jarecki (Eds.): SCN 2022, LNCS 13409, pp. 494–515, 2022.
https://doi.org/10.1007/978-3-031-14791-3_22

1 Introduction

In the setting of secure multiparty computation we have n parties, each with their own private input x_i, that would like to compute an arbitrary function $f(\mathsf{x}_1, \ldots, \mathsf{x}_n)$ of their inputs in the presence of an adversary, who may actively corrupt up to t of the parties. In particular, the parties would like to compute the function in a way that prevents the adversary from learning any unnecessary information, i.e. the corrupted parties should learn no more than what they can deduce from their own inputs and outputs. From a correctness point of view, we would ideally like to guarantee that the honest parties always obtain the output no matter what the corrupted parties do, but unfortunately, such strong guarantees are unattainable when $t \geq n/2$ parties are corrupt, as was shown by Cleve [4].

For this reason, protocols tolerating this many corruptions usually aim for the weaker notion of *active security with unanimous abort (UA)*, where the honest parties either all obtain the correct output or all unanimously output abort. The drawback of such protocols, however, is that they do not provide the honest parties with a mechanism for determining *who* caused the abort in a failed execution, thus potentially allowing an adversary to perform a denial-of-service attack on the whole computation by only corrupting a single party. To overcome this issue, Ishai, Ostrovsky, and Zikas [9] introduced the notion of *active security with identifiable abort (IA)*, which enables the honest parties to always unanimously agree on at least one corrupted party that will be held responsible for an abort.

To eventually construct efficient protocols for either notion, it is important to understand the minimal computationally secure building blocks necessary. Towards this goal, it is convenient to study the task of constructing information-theoretically secure protocols in a world where the parties have access to oracles that compute certain sub-functions correctly and securely on their behalf. In such a world, the question of finding the minimal building blocks reduces to finding the "simplest" oracles. The hope of this approach is that simpler oracles lead to computationally less expensive solutions in an oracle-free world, where the oracles are replaced by computationally secure protocols that often represent the main efficiency bottleneck of the overall protocol.

Fitzi et al. [6] characterize the oracles necessary for secure n-party computation that guarantees output delivery when no broadcast is available. When broadcast is available, for secure computation with UA or IA in the presence of an adversary that corrupts less than half of the parties, i.e. $t < n/2$, no oracles are needed [1,12].[1] For UA and any $t \geq n/2$, oracles are necessary and oracles that realize two-party oblivious transfer [11] are sufficient [5,10]. In contrast to this, an impossibility result by Ishai, Ostrovsky, and Seyalioglu [8] rules out secure computation with IA from *any* two-party oracle for $t \geq 2n/3$. The authors of [9], on the other hand, show that *blackbox* access to adaptively-secure

[1] We assume that parties have access to point-to-point and broadcast channels, and we do not consider those as explicit oracles in this paper.

two-party oblivious transfer is sufficient for constructing protocols with IA for $t > n/2$. (We note that assuming blackbox access to a primitive is a stronger assumption than assuming oracle access, which is the focus of this work. Given blackbox access to a primitive or protocol, independent parties can, for instance, rerun it on the same random tapes and compare protocol transcripts. This is not an option when only given oracle access.) Furthermore, the authors of [9] show that an n-party oracle for setting up correlated randomness is sufficient for secure computation with IA for any t. For $t \geq n/2$ and oracles that realize k-party functionalities for $2 < k < n$, very little is known about the feasibility of IA. The only known (upper) bounds are due to Brandt et al. [3], who show that IA with security against t corruptions can be realized from certain $(t+2)$-party oracles, when $n \in \mathcal{O}(\log \lambda / \log \log \lambda)$, where λ is the security parameter. The authors conjecture that analogous results for larger n are not possible unless $P = NP$.[2]

1.1 Our Contribution

In this work, we make the first progress towards constructing n-party protocols with IA for any $n \in \mathsf{poly}(\lambda)$ from k-party oracles for $k < n$. In particular, we show the following theorem.

Theorem 1 (Informal). *Any number of parties n can securely compute any function f in the presence of t corruptions with IA and information-theoretic security, when given access to oracles that compute arbitrary k-party functions with IA for $t \leq n - \ell - 1$ and $k = n - \ell$ for any constant $\ell > 0$.*

Our result refutes the conjecture of Brandt et al. mentioned above. As a technical tool, which may be of independent interest, we introduce the notion of *unanimously identifiable secret sharing with public and private shares* (UISSw-PPS), which is inspired by the notion of unanimously identifiable secret sharing (UISS) of Ishai, Ostrovsky, and Seyalioglu [8].

Lastly, we remark that in our work, we only focus on oracles that provide us with IA, since oracles that realize k-party functionalities with UA are of no help. To see this, observe that in our parameter settings every call to an oracle necessarily includes a corrupted party, thus the adversary can guarantee that all those calls abort without the honest parties learning anything.

1.2 Subsequent Work

In a work subsequent to ours, Brandt [2] shows that our upper bound can be slightly improved by constructing an n-party protocol that is secure against $t \leq n - 2$ corruptions from an oracle that computes arbitrary k-party functionalities for $k = n - 2$.

[2] After our work appeared online, the authors have removed the conjecture from their work.

1.3 Technical Overview

The starting point of our work is a result of Ishai, Ostrovsky, and Zikas [9], which shows that an n-party oracle with IA for distributing correlated randomness is sufficient for general n-party computation with IA. An n-party oracle generating correlated randomness takes no private inputs from the parties, computes $(\mathsf{r}_1, \ldots, \mathsf{r}_n)$ using some setup function $\texttt{Setup}$, and returns r_i to party i. To solve the general secure computation problem with IA, we can thus focus on the problem of realizing those oracles specifically from k-party oracles for $k < n$. We will require that the number of corruptions t is at most $k-1$ to ensure that every oracle call includes at least one honest party, which we need for our construction. Let us focus on the case of $k = n-1$ for now, which can then be easily extended to any $k = n - \ell$ for any constant ℓ via recursion.

From a high-level perspective, we proceed to construct functionalities of gradually increasing security and expressiveness starting from a functionality that we have oracle access to as depicted in Fig. 1.

$$\mathcal{F}_{\texttt{Setup}',n-1,x,O} \xrightarrow{\text{Thm. 2}} \mathcal{F}_{\texttt{Setup}',n,x} \xrightarrow{\text{Thm. 3}} \mathcal{F}_{\texttt{Setup},n} \xrightarrow{\text{Thm. 4 + [9]}} \mathcal{F}_n$$

Fig. 1. High-level overview of our approach. On the very left, we have an $(n-1)$-party functionality $\mathcal{F}_{\texttt{Setup}',n-1,x,O}$, which we have oracle access to. On the very right, we have $\mathcal{F}_n$ for computing arbitrary functions among n parties with IA.

The basic idea of our approach is to pick a party $x \in [n]$ and exclude it from the computation. The remaining $n-1$ parties use their oracle access to compute a function $\mathcal{F}_{\texttt{Setup}',n-1,x,O}$, which uses $\texttt{Setup}$ to generate correlated randomness, provides every party with its output and additionally secret shares the output r_x belonging to party x among the $n-1$ parties. After calling the oracle, all parties send their share of r_x to party x, who reconstructs its correlated randomness. If all parties behave honestly, then everybody receives the correct output. Privacy of the value r_x is guaranteed, since at least one honest party participated in the oracle call.

To make this approach work in the presence of an active adversary, we need to deal with malicious parties sending incorrect shares to party x or that party itself being malicious and falsely claiming that some received share was bad or not received at all. Through the use of an appropriate secret sharing scheme, we ensure that any tampering of the shares is detectable during reconstruction by party x. If tampering is detected, the excluded party x proceeds to a complain phase, which *does not* unanimously identify a malicious party, but establishes conflicts between the n parties participating in the computation. After establishing those conflicts, the parties again try to use oracle $\mathcal{F}_{\texttt{Setup}',n-1,x,O}$ to generate correlated randomness. The new oracle invocation will also get a set O as input, which contains the (publicly known) indices of parties that party x has a conflict with. Parties in the set O will not receive a share of the output of party x.

To ensure that our protocol can establish "good" conflicts during the complain phase, we rely on our new secret sharing notion of UISSwPPS. In a nutshell, this secret sharing scheme provides every participant with a public and a private share. The public shares are used for reconstructing the secret and allow the excluded party to detect if some share is malformed. The private shares allow honest share holders to agree on a set of public shares they believe to be malformed; even if the adversary outputs its public shares after seeing *all* other public shares.

Now if $\mathcal{F}_{\texttt{Setup}',n-1,x,O}$ aborts too many times, then the parties decide to switch to a different excluded party and start over. All those executions corresponding to one excluded party x realize a functionality $\mathcal{F}_{\texttt{Setup}',n,x}$, which does not achieve IA, but a much more relaxed version thereof. Using a combinatorial argument, we show that the honest parties can agree on at least one malicious party, if too many invocations of $\mathcal{F}_{\texttt{Setup}',n,x}$ (for different x) have not produced the output.

The approach outlined above realizes our desired functionality $\mathcal{F}_{\texttt{Setup},n}$ with IA for generating correlated randomness, albeit with a still slightly weaker security notion, where the adversary can choose one of several possible outputs or abort[3]. We prove that such a functionality is secure enough to be used in combination with the approach of Ishai, Ostrovsky, and Zikas [9] for realizing secure n-party computation with IA of arbitrary functions, i.e. functionality $\mathcal{F}_n$.

1.4 Notation

We write $[n]$ to denote the set $\{1, \ldots, n\}$ and we write $\equiv_s$ to denote statistical indistinguishability.

2 Secure Multiparty Computation (MPC) Definitions

We follow the real/ideal world simulation paradigm.

An n-party protocol $\Pi = (P_1, \ldots, P_n)$ is an n-tuple of probabilistic polynomial-time (PPT) interactive Turing machines (ITMs), where each party P_i is initialized with input $\mathsf{x}_i \in \{0,1\}^*$ and random coins $\mathsf{r}_i \in \{0,1\}^*$. We let $\mathcal{A}$ denote a special ITM that represents the adversary and that is initialized with input that contains the identities of the corrupt parties, their respective private inputs, and an auxiliary input. The protocol is executed in rounds (i.e., the protocol is synchronous), where each round consists of the send phase and the receive phase, where parties can respectively send the messages from this round to other parties and receive messages from other parties. In every round parties can communicate either over a broadcast channel or a fully connected point-to-point (P2P) network, where we additionally assume all communication to be private and ideally authenticated.

[3] Note that in regular security with IA, the adversary gets to see *one* output and then has to decide, whether to accept it or to abort.

During the execution of the protocol, the corrupt parties receive arbitrary instructions from the adversary $\mathcal{A}$, while the honest parties faithfully follow the instructions of the protocol. We consider the adversary $\mathcal{A}$ to be rushing, i.e., during every round the adversary can see the messages the honest parties sent before producing messages from corrupt parties.

At the end of the protocol execution, the honest parties produce output, the corrupt parties produce no output, and the adversary outputs an arbitrary function of its view. The view of a party during the execution consists of its input, random coins and the messages it sees during the execution.

Definition 1 (Real-world execution). *Let $\Pi = (P_1, \ldots, P_n)$ be an n-party protocol and let $C \subseteq [n]$, of size at most t, denote the set of indices of the parties corrupted by $\mathcal{A}$. The joint execution of Π under $(\mathcal{A}, C)$ in the real world, on input vector $\mathsf{x} = (\mathsf{x}_1, \ldots, \mathsf{x}_n)$, auxiliary input aux to $\mathcal{A}$ and security parameter λ, denoted $\mathsf{REAL}_{\Pi,C,\mathcal{A}(\mathsf{aux})}(\mathsf{x}, \lambda)$, is defined as the output vector of $P_1, \ldots, P_n$ and $\mathcal{A}(\mathsf{aux})$ resulting from the protocol interaction.*

Definition 2 (Ideal Computation). *Let $f : (\{0,1\}^*)^n \rightarrow (\{0,1\}^*)^n$ be an n-party function and let $C \subseteq [n]$, of size at most t, be the set of indices of the corrupt parties. Then, the joint ideal execution of f under $(\mathcal{S}, C)$ on input vector $\mathsf{x} = (\mathsf{x}_1, \ldots, \mathsf{x}_n)$, auxiliary input aux to $\mathcal{S}$ and security parameter λ, denoted $\mathsf{IDEAL}_{f,C,\mathcal{S}(\mathsf{aux})}(\mathsf{x}, \lambda)$, is defined as the output vector of $P_1, \ldots, P_n$ and $\mathcal{S}(\mathsf{aux})$ resulting from the interaction to the ideal functionality $\mathcal{F}$ (Fig. 2) with the simulator $\mathcal{S}$ and the honest parties. After interacting with $\mathcal{F}$, the hones parties output the message received from $\mathcal{F}$. The corrupt parties output nothing. The simulator $\mathcal{S}$ outputs an arbitrary function of the initial inputs $\{\mathsf{x}_i\}_{i \in C}$, the messages received by the corrupt parties from the trusted party and its auxiliary input.*

Functionality $\mathcal{F}_{f,n}$

1. For $i \in [n] \backslash C$ receive x_i from party P_i;
2. For $i \in C$ receive x_i from $\mathcal{S}$;
3. Compute $y = f(\mathsf{x}_1, \ldots, \mathsf{x}_n)$;
4. Send y to $\mathcal{S}$;
5. Receive either $\mathsf{continue}$ or $(\mathsf{abort}, \bar{i})$ (for some $\bar{i} \in C$) from $\mathcal{S}$;
6. If $\mathcal{S}$ sent $\mathsf{continue}$: send y to each party $i \in [n] \backslash C$;
7. If $\mathcal{S}$ sent $(\mathsf{abort}, \bar{i})$: send $(\mathsf{abort}, \bar{i})$ to each party $i \in [n] \backslash C$.

Fig. 2. Functionality $\mathcal{F}_{f,n}$ for secure computation of function f among n parties with identifiable abort.

Definition 3. *Let $f : (\{0,1\}^*)^n \to (\{0,1\}^*)^n$ be an n-party function. A protocol Π t-securely computes the function f if for every real-world adversary $\mathcal{A}$ there exists a simulator $\mathcal{S}$ whose running time is polynomial in the running time of $\mathcal{A}$ such that for every $C \subseteq [n]$ of size at most t, it holds that*

$$\{\mathsf{REAL}_{\Pi,C,\mathcal{A}(\mathsf{aux})}(\mathsf{x},\lambda)\}_{\mathsf{x}\in(\{0,1\}^*)^n,\lambda\in\mathsf{N}} \equiv_s \{\mathsf{IDEAL}_{f,C,\mathcal{S}(\mathsf{aux})}(\mathsf{x},\lambda)\}_{\mathsf{x}\in(\{0,1\}^*)^n,\lambda\in\mathsf{N}}.$$

3 Unanimously Identifiable Secret Sharing with Public and Private Shares

A secret sharing schemes allows a dealer to split a message into shares such that certain authorized subsets of those shares can be used to reconstruct the message, whereas unauthorized subsets reveal no information about the message whatsoever.

Definition 4 (Secret Sharing Scheme). *A* secret sharing scheme *for message space $\{0,1\}^*$ consists of a probabilistic polynomial-time algorithm* Share *and a deterministic polynomial-time algorithm* LRec *with the following syntax:*

$\mathtt{Share}(\mathsf{msg}) \to (\mathsf{s}_1,\ldots,\mathsf{s}_n)$: *takes as input a message* $\mathsf{msg} \in \{0,1\}^*$ *and outputs shares* $\mathsf{s}_1,\ldots,\mathsf{s}_n$.

$\mathtt{LRec}(\mathsf{s}_i,\{\mathsf{s}_j\}_{j\in S}) \to (\mathsf{msg},\mathsf{L})$: *takes as input a share* s_i *and a subset of shares* $\{\mathsf{s}_j\}_{j\in S}$*, where $i \in S \subset [n]$, and outputs a reconstructed message in $\{0,1\}^* \cup \{\bot\}$ and a set of accusations* $\mathsf{L} \subset [n]$.

Furthermore, (Share, LRec) *should satisfy* correctness *(Definition 8, with appropriate syntactic modifications and ignoring the requirements on* Rec*, which we do not have in a regular secret sharing scheme) and* privacy *(Definition 9, with appropriate syntactic modifications).*

We introduce the notion of unanimously identifiable secret sharing with public and private shares (UISSwPPS). In such a scheme, each share holder will receive one private and one public share. On an intuitive level, the public shares will correspond to a secret sharing of the message shared by the dealer. The private shares, on the other hand, will be used by the share holders to detect any tampering with public shares. In particular, having additional private shares for each share holder allows us to satisfy a stronger notion of local identifiability, which we define below. We show a construction of UISSwPPS in Sect. 5.

Definition 5 (Secret Sharing Scheme with Public and Private Shares). *A secret sharing scheme with public and private shares for message space $\{0,1\}^*$ consists of a probabilistic polynomial-time algorithm* Share *and deterministic polynomial-time algorithms* Rec *and* LRec *with the following syntax:*

$\mathtt{Share}(\mathsf{msg}) \to (\mathsf{s}_1^{\mathsf{pub}},\ldots,\mathsf{s}_n^{\mathsf{pub}},\mathsf{s}_1^{\mathsf{priv}},\ldots,\mathsf{s}_n^{\mathsf{priv}})$: *takes as input a message* $\mathsf{msg} \in \{0,1\}^*$ *and outputs public shares* $\mathsf{s}_1^{\mathsf{pub}},\ldots,\mathsf{s}_n^{\mathsf{pub}}$ *and private shares* $\mathsf{s}_1^{\mathsf{priv}},\ldots,\mathsf{s}_n^{\mathsf{priv}}$.

$\mathsf{Rec}(\{\mathsf{s}_i^{\mathsf{pub}}\}_{i\in S}) \rightarrow \mathsf{msg}/\bot$: *takes as input a subset of public shares* $\{\mathsf{s}_i^{\mathsf{pub}}\}_{i\in S}$ *(where* $S \subset [n]$*) and outputs a value in* $\{0,1\}^* \cup \{\bot\}$.

$\mathsf{LRec}(\mathsf{s}_i^{\mathsf{priv}}, \{\mathsf{s}_j^{\mathsf{pub}}\}_{j\in S}) \rightarrow (\mathsf{msg}, \mathsf{L})$: *takes as input a private share* $\mathsf{s}_i^{\mathsf{priv}}$ *and a subset of public shares* $\{\mathsf{s}_j^{\mathsf{pub}}\}_{j\in S}$ *(where* $S \subset [n]$*) and outputs a reconstructed message in* $\{0,1\}^* \cup \{\bot\}$ *and a list of accusations* $\mathsf{L} \subset [n]$.

We will use our new secret sharing scheme in combination with a new access structure that effectively corresponds to a threshold access structure with additional observers that hold no information about the dealer's message. Even though these observers are not helpful for reconstructing the message, they will still be able to verify whether other published shares are valid or not.

Definition 6 (Threshold Access Structure). *For an arbitrary but fixed threshold* $t \in [n]$*, the* t*-threshold access structure is defined as* $\mathbb{A}_{n,t} = \{S \subset [n] \mid |S| \geq t\}$.

Definition 7 (Threshold Access Structure with Observers). *For an arbitrary but fixed threshold* $t \in [n]$ *and set* $O \subset \{1,\ldots,n\}$*, the* t*-threshold access structure with observers* O *is defined as* $\mathbb{A}_{n,t}^O = \{S \subset \{1,\ldots,n\} \mid |S \setminus O| \geq t\}$.

Definition 8 (Correctness). *A secret sharing scheme with public and private shares* (Share, Rec, LRec) *for access structure* $\mathbb{A}$ *is* correct *if for any* $S \in \mathbb{A}$*, for any* $i \in S$*, for any message* $\mathsf{msg} \in \{0,1\}^*$*, there exists a negligible function* $\mathsf{negl}(\cdot)$ *such that*

$$\Pr\left[\begin{bmatrix}\mathsf{s}_1^{\mathsf{pub}},\ldots,\mathsf{s}_n^{\mathsf{pub}}\\ \mathsf{s}_1^{\mathsf{priv}},\ldots,\mathsf{s}_n^{\mathsf{priv}}\end{bmatrix} \leftarrow \mathtt{Share}(\mathsf{msg}), (\overline{\mathsf{msg}}, \bot) \leftarrow \mathtt{LRec}\left(\mathsf{s}_i^{\mathsf{priv}}, \{\mathsf{s}_j^{\mathsf{pub}}\}_{j\in S}\right) : \overline{\mathsf{msg}} = \mathsf{msg}\right] = 1 - \mathsf{negl}(\lambda)$$

and

$$\Pr\left[\begin{bmatrix}\mathsf{s}_1^{\mathsf{pub}},\ldots,\mathsf{s}_n^{\mathsf{pub}}\\ \mathsf{s}_1^{\mathsf{priv}},\ldots,\mathsf{s}_n^{\mathsf{priv}}\end{bmatrix} \leftarrow \mathtt{Share}(\mathsf{msg}), \overline{\mathsf{msg}} \leftarrow \mathtt{Rec}\left(\{\mathsf{s}_j^{\mathsf{pub}}\}_{j\in S}\right) : \overline{\mathsf{msg}} = \mathsf{msg}\right] = 1 - \mathsf{negl}(\lambda)$$

where the probability is taken over the random coins of the Share *algorithm.*

Definition 9 (Privacy). *A secret sharing scheme* (Share, LRec) *for access structure* $\mathbb{A}$ *is* private *if for any unbounded adversary* $\mathcal{A}$*, for any* $S \notin \mathbb{A}$*, for any two messages* $\mathsf{msg}, \mathsf{msg}' \in \{0,1\}^*$ *with* $|\mathsf{msg}| = |\mathsf{msg}'|$*, it holds that*

$$\Pr\left[\mathcal{A}(\{(\mathsf{s}_i^{\mathsf{pub}}, \mathsf{s}_i^{\mathsf{priv}})\}_{i\in S}) = 1 \middle| \begin{bmatrix}\mathsf{s}_1^{\mathsf{pub}},\ldots,\mathsf{s}_n^{\mathsf{pub}}\\ \mathsf{s}_1^{\mathsf{priv}},\ldots,\mathsf{s}_n^{\mathsf{priv}}\end{bmatrix} \leftarrow \mathtt{Share}(\mathsf{msg})\right]$$
$$-\Pr\left[\mathcal{A}(\{(\mathsf{s}_i^{\mathsf{pub}}, \mathsf{s}_i^{\mathsf{priv}})\}_{i\in S}) = 1 \middle| \begin{bmatrix}\mathsf{s}_1^{\mathsf{pub}},\ldots,\mathsf{s}_n^{\mathsf{pub}}\\ \mathsf{s}_1^{\mathsf{priv}},\ldots,\mathsf{s}_n^{\mathsf{priv}}\end{bmatrix} \leftarrow \mathtt{Share}(\mathsf{msg}')\right] \leq \mathsf{negl}(\lambda).$$

where the probability is taken over the random coins of Share *and* $\mathcal{A}$.

For our new notion of (adaptive) local identifiability, we consider an adversary that can see *all* public shares before outputting any tampered shares.

Definition 10 (Adaptive Local Identifiability). *Consider the game described in Fig. 3. A secret sharing scheme with public and private shares* (Share, Rec, LRec) *for access structure* $\mathbb{A}$ *has* adaptive local identifiability *if for any message* $\mathsf{msg} \in \{0,1\}^*$ *and adversary* $\mathcal{A}$, *there exists a negligible function* $\mathsf{negl}(\cdot)$ *such that*

$$\Pr[\mathcal{A} \text{ wins } \mathsf{game}_{\mathsf{ali}}(\mathcal{A})] \leq \mathsf{negl}(\lambda)$$

where the probability is taken over the random coins of $\mathcal{C}$ *and* $\mathcal{A}$.

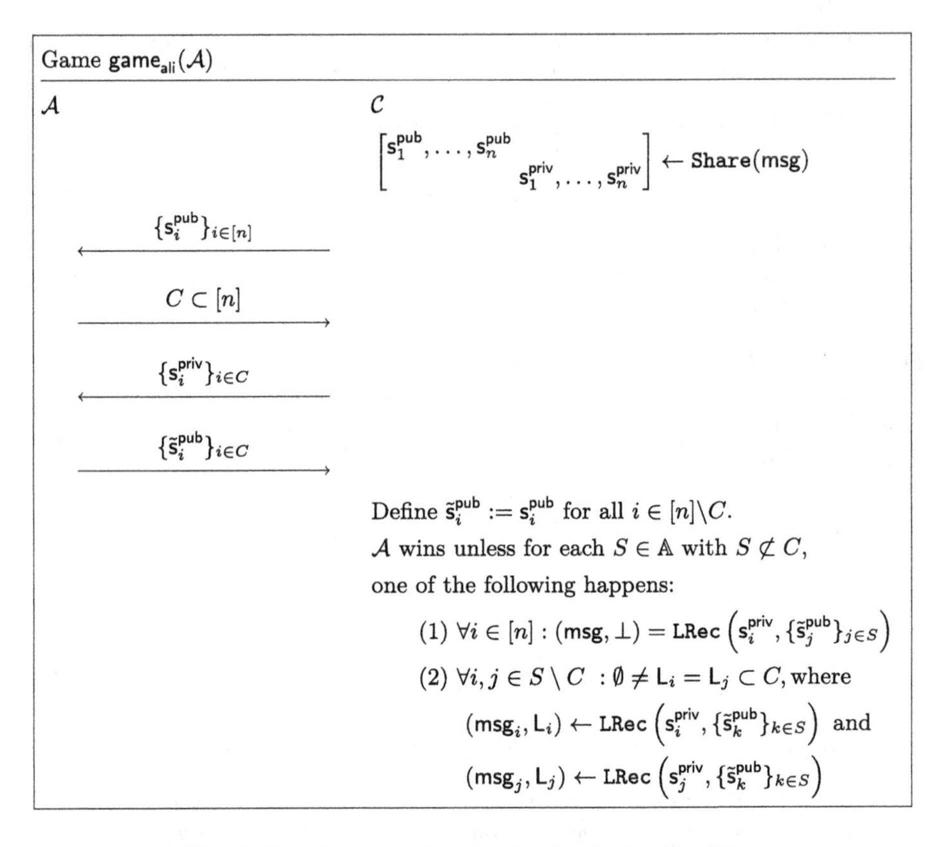

Fig. 3. Security game for adaptive local identifiability.

Remark 1. We will assume that local reconstruction outputs message $\bot$ whenever the list of accusations is not empty.

We require a UISSwPSS to satisfy a mild notion of error detection for outside parties that receive a set of potentially tampered shares and attempt to reconstruct the secret.

Definition 11 (Publicly Detectable Failures). *Consider the game described in Fig. 4. A secret sharing scheme with public and private shares* (Share, Rec, LRec) *has* publicly detectable failures *if for any message* msg $\in \{0,1\}^*$ *and adversary* $\mathcal{A}$, *there exists a negligible function* $\mathsf{negl}(\cdot)$ *such that*

$$\Pr[\mathcal{A} \text{ wins } \mathsf{game}_{\mathsf{pdf}}(\mathcal{A})] \leq \mathsf{negl}(\lambda)$$

where the probability is taken over the random coins of Share *and* $\mathcal{A}$.

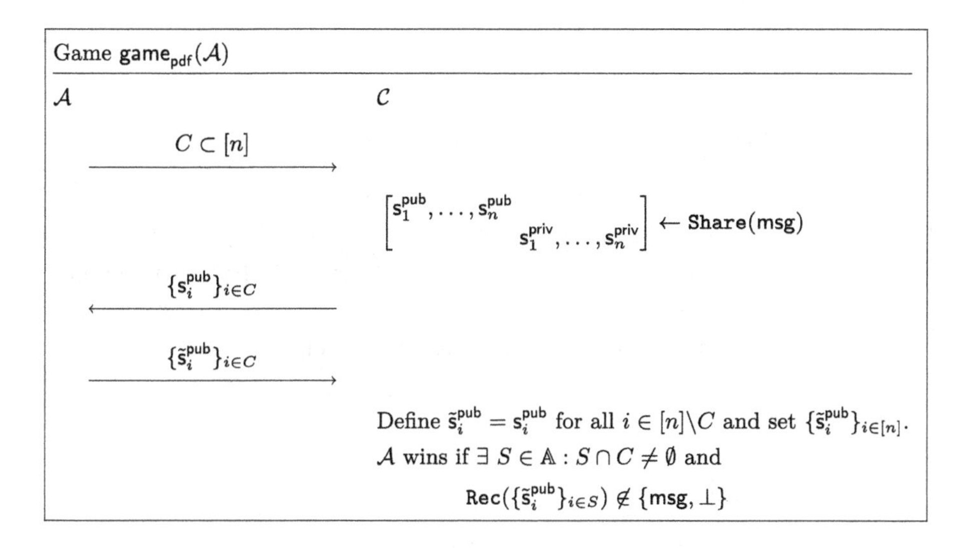

Fig. 4. Security game for publicly detectable failures.

Finally, we require that Rec fails whenever LRec fails.

Definition 12 (Consistent Failures). *Consider the game described in Fig. 5. A secret sharing scheme with public and private shares* (Share, Rec, LRec) *for access structure* $\mathbb{A}$ *has* consistent failures *if for any message* msg $\in \{0,1\}^*$ *and adversary* $\mathcal{A}$, *there exists a negligible function* $\mathsf{negl}(\cdot)$ *such that*

$$\Pr[\mathcal{A} \text{ wins } \mathsf{game}_{\mathsf{cf}}(\mathcal{A})] \leq \mathsf{negl}(\lambda)$$

where the probability is taken over the random coins of $\mathcal{C}$ *and* $\mathcal{A}$.

Definition 13 (Predictable Failures with respect to LRec). *Consider the game described in Fig. 6. A secret sharing scheme* (Share, LRec) *for access structure* $\mathbb{A}$ *has* predictable failures *if there exists a probabilistic polynomial-time algorithm* SLRec *such that for any message* msg $\in \{0,1\}^*$ *and adversary* $\mathcal{A}$, *there exists a negligible function* $\mathsf{negl}(\cdot)$ *such that*

$$\Pr[\mathcal{A} \text{ wins } \mathsf{game}_{\mathsf{pflrec}}(\mathcal{A})] \leq \mathsf{negl}(\lambda)$$

where the probability is taken over the random coins of $\mathcal{C}$ *and* $\mathcal{A}$.

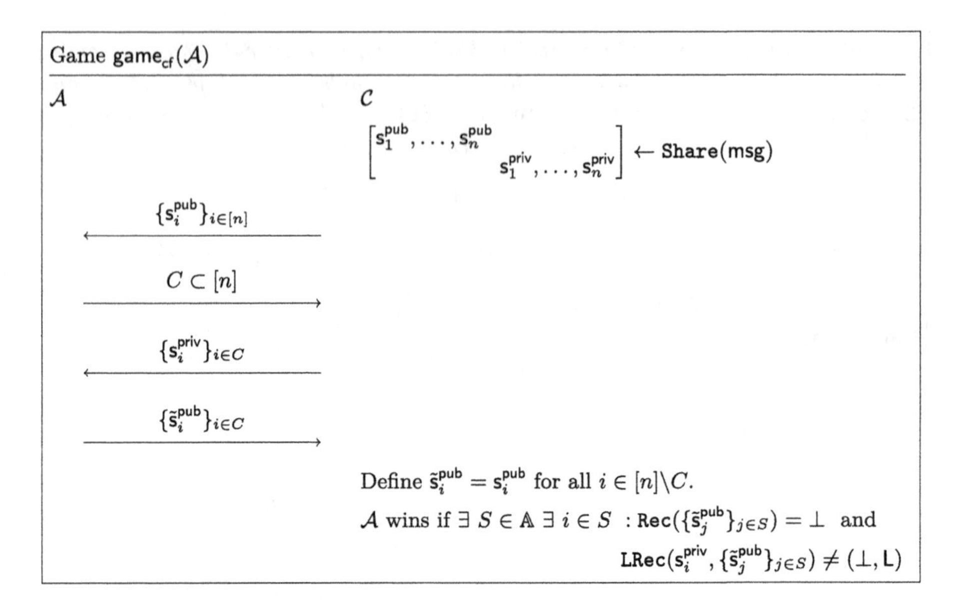

Fig. 5. Security game for consistent failures.

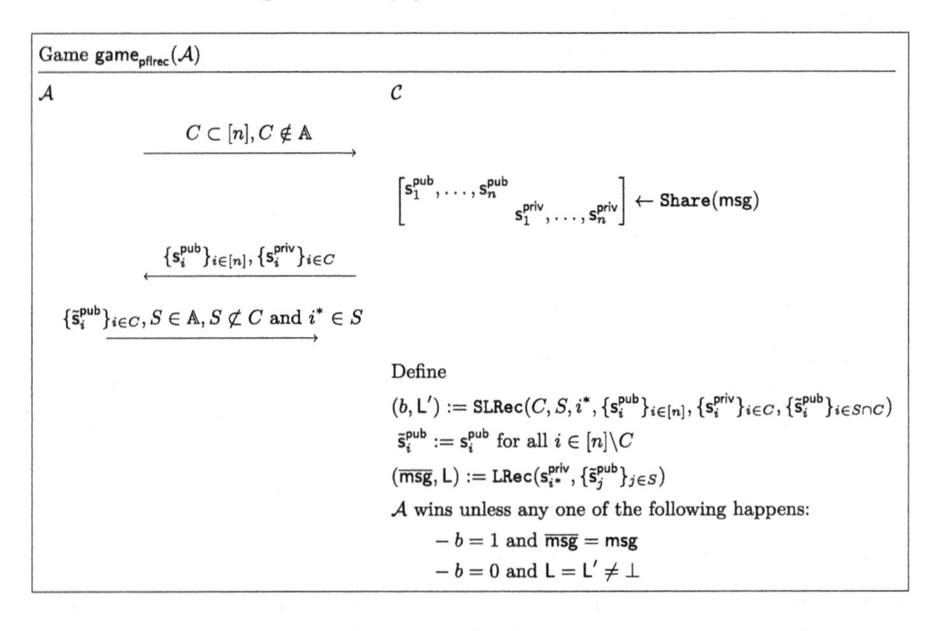

Fig. 6. Security game for predictable failures with respect to $\mathtt{LRec}$.

Definition 14 (Predictable Failures with respect to $\mathtt{Rec}$). *Consider the game described in Fig. 7. A secret sharing scheme with public and private shares* ($\mathtt{Share}, \mathtt{Rec}, \mathtt{LRec}$) *for access structure* $\mathbb{A}$ *has* predictable failures with respect to$\mathtt{Rec}$ *if there exists a probabilistic polynomial-time algorithm* $\mathtt{SRec}$ *such that for* *any message* $\mathsf{msg} \in \{0,1\}^*$ *and adversary* $\mathcal{A}$*, there exists a negligible function* $\mathsf{negl}(\cdot)$ *such that*

$$\Pr[\mathcal{A} \textit{ wins } \mathsf{game}_{\mathsf{pfrec}}(\mathcal{A})] \leq \mathsf{negl}(\lambda)$$

where the probability is taken over the random coins of $\mathcal{C}$ *and* $\mathcal{A}$.

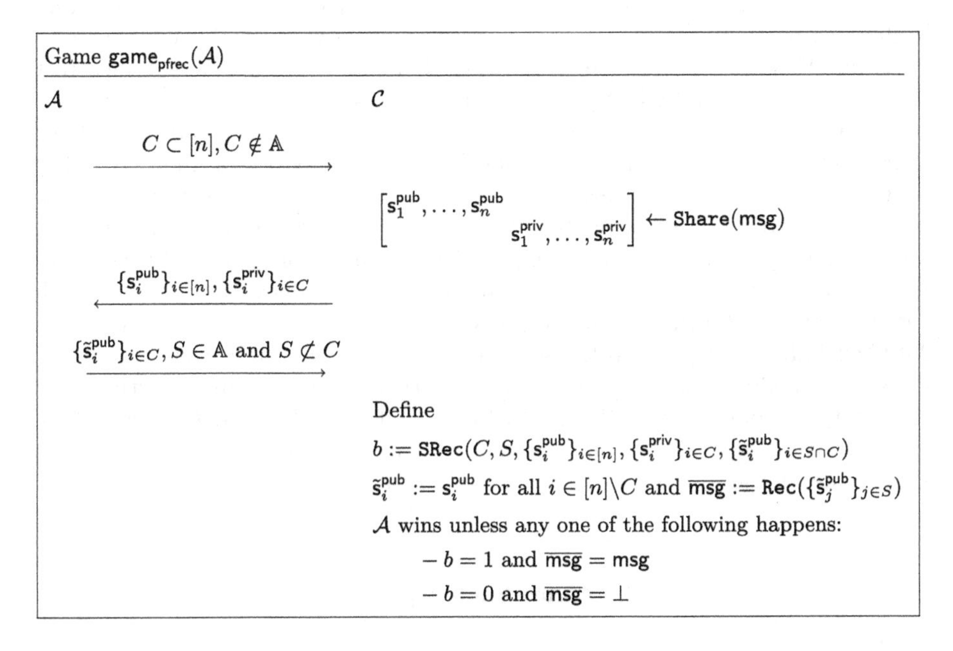

Fig. 7. Security game for predictable failures with respect to Rec.

We say that a secret sharing scheme with public and private shares (Share, Rec, LRec) is a UISSwPPS, if it simultaneously satisfies Definition 8, 9, 10, 11, 12, 13 and 14.

4 Bootstrapping MPC with Identifiable Abort

In this section, we describe how to instantiate MPC with identifiable abort for n parties and $t \leq n-2$ given MPC with identifiable abort for $n-1$ parties and $t \leq n-2$. In Sect. 4.1, we describe the protocol. In the full version of this paper, we prove its security.

4.1 Protocol

Ishai et al. [9] show that given correlated randomness, it is possible to securely compute any function with any threshold t, with identifiable abort and with information-theoretic security. Let $\mathtt{Setup}() \rightarrow (\mathsf{r}_1, \ldots, \mathsf{r}_n)$ be the randomized function that produces the appropriate correlated randomness. $\mathtt{Setup}$ takes no inputs (since correlated randomness is independent of the parties' inputs), and outputs n correlated objects, one for each party.

We would like to make use of the availability of MPC with identifiable abort for $n-1$ parties to run $\mathtt{Setup}$ (for n parties). In order to do this, we define $\mathtt{Setup}'_x$ to be $\mathtt{Setup}$ augmented to return shares of r_x to parties $i \in [n]\backslash\{x\}$, and nothing to party x. We then expect parties $i \in [n]\backslash\{x\}$ to send those shares to party x. Of course, we need to make sure that party x won't accept incorrect shares; so, we use UISSwPPS to authenticate the shares.

If party x is dissatisfied with the shares she receives, she broadcasts all the shares. Then, one of two things happens. Either (1) all parties acknowledge that they sent the broadcast shares to party x, in which case, because of the adaptive local identifiability (Definition 10) of the secret sharing, we obtain identifiable abort among the parties who participated in the MPC; or (2) one of the parties (say, party i) claims that party x misrepresented the share she sent, in which case we have established a conflict between parties i and x, and can repeat the MPC excluding party i from the set of parties who hold public shares of r_x.

We define $\mathtt{Setup}'_{x,O}$ to be the augmented correlated randomness setup function that distributes shares of r_x to parties $i \in [n]$ with observers $O \subseteq [n]$ (where $x \in O$). (We only create an observer share for party x for ease of notation; this share is never used.) $\mathtt{Setup}'_{x,O}$ is described in Fig. 8.

Algorithm $\mathtt{Setup}'_{x,O}$

$(\mathsf{r}_1, \ldots, \mathsf{r}_n) \leftarrow \mathtt{Setup}()$
$\{\mathsf{s}_i^{\mathsf{pub}}, \mathsf{s}_i^{\mathsf{priv}}\}_{i\in[n]} \leftarrow \mathtt{Share}(\mathbb{A}^O_{n,t}, \mathsf{r}_x)$
return $\{(\mathsf{r}_i, \mathsf{s}_i^{\mathsf{pub}}, \mathsf{s}_i^{\mathsf{priv}})\}_{i\in[n]\backslash\{x\}}$

Fig. 8. Algorithm $\mathtt{Setup}'_{x,O}$

Figure 10 describes the functionality $\mathcal{F}_{RS(k),\mathtt{Setup},n}$ that computes $\mathtt{Setup}$ with identifiable abort; the subscript $RS(k)$ signifies that we allow *rejection sampling* by the adversary, who is able to request fresh outputs of $\mathtt{Setup}$ up to k times. Figure 14 describes the protocol $\Pi_{RS(k=n^2),\mathtt{Setup},n}$ that realizes $\mathcal{F}_{RS(k),\mathtt{Setup},n}$ for $k = n^2$. This protocol calls upon a weaker ideal functionality $\mathcal{F}_{RS(k=n),\mathtt{Setup},n,x}$, which is described in Fig. 11; this ideal functionality only has identifiable abort among $n-1$ of the parties (party x cannot necessarily identify a cheater). $\mathcal{F}_{RS(k=n),\mathtt{Setup},n,x}$ either (1) distributes the correlated randomness successfully, (2) identifiably aborts, or (3) identifiably aborts only among $[n]\backslash\{x\}$, in which case $\Pi_{RS(k=n^2),\mathtt{Setup},n}$ calls $\mathcal{F}_{RS(k=n),\mathtt{Setup},n,x}$ again with a different x. Figure 13 describes the protocol $\Pi_{RS(k=n),\mathtt{Setup},n,x}$ that realizes $\mathcal{F}_{RS(k=n),\mathtt{Setup},n,x}$. $\Pi_{RS(k=n),\mathtt{Setup},n,x}$ in turn calls upon an ideal functionality $\mathcal{F}_{\mathtt{Setup}',n,x,O}$; this ideal functionality computes $\mathtt{Setup}'$ among $n-1$ parties with identifiable abort (without rejection sampling). We do not give a protocol realizing $\mathcal{F}_{\texttt{Setup}',n,x,O}$, as we assume that secure protocols with identifiable abort exist for any $(n-1)$-party function.

The flow of $\Pi_{RS(k=n^2),\texttt{Setup},n}$ is described in Fig. 9.

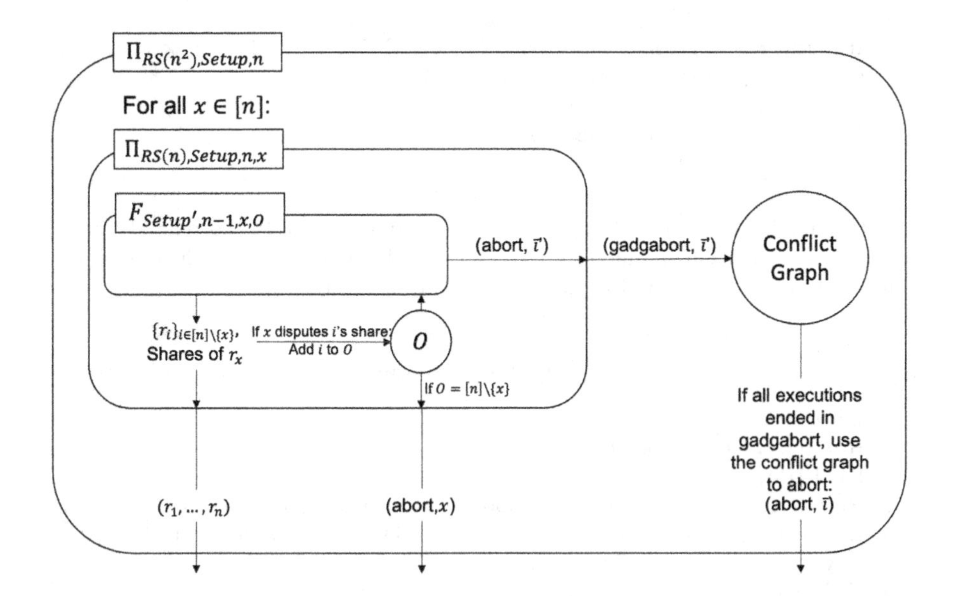

Fig. 9. A diagram of $\Pi_{RS(k=n^2),\texttt{Setup},n}$

Theorem 2. *Protocol* $\Pi^{\mathcal{F}_{\texttt{Setup}',n-1,x,O}}_{RS(k=n),\texttt{Setup},n,x}$ *(Fig. 13) securely realizes the functionality* $\mathcal{F}_{RS(k=n),\texttt{Setup},n,x}$ *(Fig. 11) against* $t \leq n-2$ *corruptions, assuming the availability of a broadcast channel and oracle access to* $\mathcal{F}_{\texttt{Setup}',n-1,x,O}$.

Theorem 3. *Protocol* $\Pi^{\mathcal{F}_{RS(k=n),\texttt{Setup},n,x}}_{RS(k=n^2),\texttt{Setup},n}$ *(Fig. 14) securely realizes the functionality* $\mathcal{F}_{RS(k=n^2),\texttt{Setup},n}$ *(Fig. 10) against* $t \leq n-2$ *corruptions, assuming the availability of a broadcast channel and oracle access to* $\mathcal{F}_{RS(k=n),\texttt{Setup},n,x}$.

Theorem 4. *If a protocol* Π *securely realizes* $\mathcal{F}_{f,n}$ *given a single oracle access to* $\mathcal{F}_{\texttt{Setup},n}$ *as a first action (which can be thought of as a single output of the oracle given as setup), then* Π *also securely realizes* $\mathcal{F}_{f,n}$ *given a single oracle access to* $\mathcal{F}_{RS(k=n^2),\texttt{Setup},n}$ *as a first action (where* $\mathcal{F}_{RS(k=n^2),\texttt{Setup},n}$ *replaces* $\mathcal{F}_{\texttt{Setup},n}$*).*

Given these three theorems, if we have a protocol $\Pi^{\mathcal{F}_{(k=n),\texttt{Setup},n,x}}_{(k=n^2),\texttt{Setup},n}$ realizing $\mathcal{F}_{RS(k=n^2),\texttt{Setup},n}$, we can use that setup to achieve secure computation with identifiable abort of any function f using the approach of Ishai et al. Since $\Pi^{\mathcal{F}_{(k=n),\texttt{Setup},n,x}}_{(k=n^2),\texttt{Setup},n}$ only requires oracle access to $\mathcal{F}_{RS(k=n),\texttt{Setup},n,x}$—which in turn can be realized given only oracle access to $\mathcal{F}_{\texttt{Setup}',n-1,x,O}$—we can claim the following corollary.

Functionality $\mathcal{F}_{RS(k),\mathsf{Setup},n}$

1. Let $\ell := 1$;
2. Run $(\mathsf{r}_1^\ell, \dots, \mathsf{r}_n^\ell) \leftarrow \mathsf{Setup}()$;
3. Send $\{\mathsf{r}_i^\ell\}_{i \in C}$ to $\mathcal{S}$;
4. Receive either retry, continue or $(\mathsf{abort}, \bar{i})$ (for some $\bar{i} \in C$) from $\mathcal{S}$;
5. If $\mathcal{S}$ sent retry: increment ℓ by one ($\ell := \ell + 1$). We only allow up to k retries, so we never get $\ell > k$. Restart from step 2.
6. If $\mathcal{S}$ sent continue: send r_i to each party $i \in [n] \backslash C$;
7. If $\mathcal{S}$ sent $(\mathsf{abort}, \bar{i})$: send $(\mathsf{abort}, \bar{i})$ to each party $i \in [n] \backslash C$.

Fig. 10. Functionality $\mathcal{F}_{RS(k),\mathsf{Setup},n}$ for secure computation of the correlated randomness setup function Setup among n parties with identifiable abort, which allows the simulator to reject the output (requesting a redo) at most k times.

Functionality $\mathcal{F}_{RS(k),\mathsf{Setup},n,x}$

1. Let $\ell := 1$;
2. Run $(\mathsf{r}_1^\ell, \dots, \mathsf{r}_n^\ell) \leftarrow \mathsf{Setup}()$;
3. Send $\{\mathsf{r}_i^\ell\}_{i \in C}$ to $\mathcal{S}$;
4. Receive either retry, continue or $(\mathsf{abort}, \bar{i})$ (for some $\bar{i} \in C$) from $\mathcal{S}$;
5. If $\mathcal{S}$ sent retry: increment ℓ by one ($\ell := \ell + 1$). We only allow up to k retries, so we never get $\ell > k$. Restart from step 2.
6. If $\mathcal{S}$ sent continue: send r_i to each party $i \in [n] \backslash C$;
7. If $\mathcal{S}$ sent $(\mathsf{abort}, \bar{i})$:
   (a) If $\bar{i} = x$: send (abort, x) to each party $i \in [n] \backslash C$;
   (b) If $\bar{i} \neq x$:
      i. Send $(\mathsf{gadgabort}, \bar{i})$ to each party $i \in [n] \backslash (\{x\} \cup C)$
      ii. Send gadgabort to party x if $x \notin C$.

Fig. 11. Functionality $\mathcal{F}_{RS(k),\mathsf{Setup},n,x}$ for secure computation of the correlated randomness setup function Setup among n parties with identifiable abort among all the parties except for x which allows the simulator to reject the output (requesting a redo) at most k times. The functionality uses the gadgabort output flag if party x is unable to identify a cheater; it uses the abort output flag if all honest parties are able to identify a cheater (which happens only when party x is the cheater identified).

Corollary 5. *For any function f, there exists a protocol that securely realizes the functionality $\mathcal{F}_{f,n}$ (with identifiable abort) against $t \leq n - 2$ corruptions, given oracle access to $\mathcal{F}_{\mathsf{Setup}',n-1,x,O}$.*

By using our construction recursively to realize $\mathcal{F}_{\mathsf{Setup}',n-1,x,O}$ given oracle access to a $(n-2)$-party ideal functionality, and so on, we can claim the following corollary.

Functionality $\mathcal{F}_{\mathsf{Setup}',n-1,x,O}$

1. Compute $\{(\mathsf{r}_i, \mathsf{s}_i^{\mathsf{pub}}, \mathsf{s}_i^{\mathsf{priv}})\}_{i\in[n]} \leftarrow \mathsf{Setup}'_{x,O}()$;
2. Send $\{(\mathsf{r}_i, \mathsf{s}_i^{\mathsf{pub}}, \mathsf{s}_i^{\mathsf{priv}})\}_{i\in C}$ to $\mathcal{S}$;
3. Receive either $\mathsf{continue}$ or $(\mathsf{abort}, \bar{i})$ (for some $\bar{i} \in C$) from $\mathcal{S}$;
4. If $\mathcal{S}$ sent $\mathsf{continue}$: send $(\mathsf{r}_i, \mathsf{s}_i^{\mathsf{pub}}, \mathsf{s}_i^{\mathsf{priv}})$ to each party $i \in [n]\backslash(\{x\} \cup C)$;
5. Otherwise: send $(\mathsf{abort}, \bar{i})$ to each party $i \in [n]\backslash(\{x\} \cup C)$.

Fig. 12. Functionality $\mathcal{F}_{\mathsf{Setup}',n-1,x,O}$ for secure computation of function $\mathsf{Setup}'_{x,O}$ with identifiable abort among $n-1$ parties (parties $i \in [n]\backslash\{x\}$).

Corollary 6. *For any function f, for any constant ℓ, there exists a protocol that securely realizes the functionality $\mathcal{F}_{f,n}$ (with identifiable abort) against $t \leq n - \ell - 2$ corruptions, given oracle access to $(n-\ell)$-party ideal functionalities (with identifiable abort).*

We require that the recursion depth l be constant because every $(n-\ell)$-party instance calls at most $n - \ell$ $(n - \ell - 1)$-party instances, and additionally may require $p'(n - \ell, \lambda) = p(\lambda)$ work for some polynomials p', p. Thus, we can only guarantee that the protocol is polynomial time if $p^{\ell}(\lambda) \in \mathsf{poly}(\lambda)$, which is only true when ℓ is constant.

Conflict Graphs. Before presenting our protocol $\Pi^{\mathcal{F}_{(k=n),\mathsf{Setup},n,x}}_{(k=n^2),\mathsf{Setup},n}$, which requires keeping track of conflict graphs (that is similar to the notion of inconsistent graphs described in [7]), we introduce some notation that we use for such graphs. We let S_x be the set of conflicts (denoted as tuples (i, j)) occurring among parties $[n] \setminus \{x\}$. These conflicts result from a call to a functionality with identifiable abort among these $n-1$ parties. Parties i and j are considered to be in conflict if they accuse different parties of aborting the functionality. Since we do not allow a party to accuse itself, this includes the case when one of them accuses the other. For simplicity, we let S_x^i denote the set of parties that party i is in conflict with within S_x.

The proofs of Theorem 2, Theorem 3 and Theorem 4 can be found in the full version of this paper.

5 Building UISSwPPS

In this section, we build a unanimously identifiable secret sharing scheme with public and private shares. In Sect. 5.1, we describe two building blocks: unanimously identifiable commitments and unanimously identifiable secret sharing. In Sect. 5.2, we describe our construction and prove its security.

Protocol $\Pi^{\mathcal{F}_{\mathsf{Setup}',n-1,x,O}}_{RS(k=n),\mathsf{Setup},n,x}$

Let $\mathsf{GS} = [n] \setminus \{x\}$. Let $O = \{x\}$. (GS denotes the fixed set of parties calling the ideal functionality; O denotes the set of parties who do not get a share of r_x, which might change over time.)
The parties repeat the three phases described below until one of the following termination conditions occurs:

1. The parties $i \in \mathsf{GS}$ receive a special broadcast message **done** from party x. When this happens, each party $i \in [n]$ outputs r_i.
2. All of the parties $i \in \mathsf{GS}$ identify party x as a cheater. When this happens, the parties $i \in \mathsf{GS}$ output (abort, x).
3. One of the calls to $\mathcal{F}_{\mathsf{Setup}',n-1,x,O}$ results in an (identifiable) abort blaming party $\bar{i}$. When this happens, the parties $i \in \mathsf{GS}$ output $(\mathsf{gadgabort}, \bar{i})$.
4. Though $\mathcal{F}_{\mathsf{Setup}',n-1,x,O}$ did not abort, the honest parties among the $n-1$ parties who called the functionality unanimously identify (a) cheater(s). When this happens, the parties $i \in \mathsf{GS}$ output $(\mathsf{gadgabort}, \bar{i})$ (where $\bar{i} = \min(\mathsf{L}_i)$ and L_i is the list of parties identified by party i).

Call the Ideal Functionality:

1. The parties $i \in \mathsf{GS}$ invoke the ideal functionality $\mathcal{F}_{\mathsf{Setup}',n-1,x,O}$ to compute $\mathsf{Setup}'_{x,O}$, so that each party $i \in \mathsf{GS}$ learns $(\mathsf{r}_i, \mathsf{s}_i^{\mathsf{pub}}, \mathsf{s}_i^{\mathsf{priv}})$.
2. If $\mathcal{F}_{\mathsf{Setup}',n-1,x,O}$ aborts, we are in termination condition 3; otherwise the parties proceed to the reconstruct phase.

Reconstruct:

3. Each party $i \in \mathsf{GS} \setminus O$ sends $\mathsf{s}_i^{\mathsf{pub}}$ to party x.
4. Party x runs $\mathsf{r}_x \leftarrow \mathsf{Rec}(\{\mathsf{s}_i^{\mathsf{pub}}\}_{i \in \mathsf{GS} \setminus O})$. If $\mathsf{r}_x \neq \bot$, party x broadcasts **done**. (We are now in termination condition 1; the parties all output r_i.) If $\mathsf{r}_x = \bot$, party x broadcasts **complain** and the parties proceed to the complain phase.

Complain:

1. Party x broadcasts the shares it received as $\{\tilde{\mathsf{s}}_i^{\mathsf{pub}}\}_{i \in \mathsf{GS} \setminus O}$.
2. Each party $i \in \mathsf{GS} \setminus O$ broadcasts $\mathsf{s}_i^{\mathsf{pub}}$.
3. If there is an i such that $\tilde{\mathsf{s}}_i^{\mathsf{pub}} \neq \mathsf{s}_i^{\mathsf{pub}}$:
   (a) All parties set $O = O \cup \{i\}_{i \in \mathsf{GS} \text{ s.t. } \tilde{\mathsf{s}}_i^{\mathsf{pub}} \neq \mathsf{s}_i^{\mathsf{pub}}}$.
   (b) If $O = \mathsf{GS}$ (that is, all parties have had conflicting claims with party x), all parties identify party x as a cheater. (We are now in termination condition 2; the parties broadcast and output (abort, x).)
4. Otherwise:
   (a) If $\mathsf{Rec}(\{\tilde{\mathsf{s}}_i^{\mathsf{pub}}\}_{i \in [n] \setminus O}) \neq \bot$: all parties $i \in \mathsf{GS}$ identify party x as a cheater. (We are now in termination condition 2; the parties broadcast and output (abort, x).)
   (b) Otherwise: all parties $i \in \mathsf{GS}$ compute $(\bot, \mathsf{L}_i) \leftarrow \mathsf{LRec}(\mathsf{s}_i^{\mathsf{priv}}, \{\mathsf{s}_j^{\mathsf{pub}}\}_{j \in \mathsf{GS}})$, and broadcast and output $(\mathsf{gadgabort}, \bar{i})$ where $\bar{i} = \min(\mathsf{L}_i)$. (We are now in termination condition 4.)

Fig. 13. Protocol $\Pi^{\mathcal{F}_{\mathsf{Setup}',n-1,x,O}}_{RS(k=n),\mathsf{Setup},n,x}$ for secure computation of the correlated randomness setup function Setup among n parties (with identifiable abort among all of the parties except for x, with threshold $t = n-2$) given access to an ideal functionality $\mathcal{F}_{\mathsf{Setup}',n-1,x,O}$ that distributes the output of Setup' to $n-1$ parties (with identifiable abort, with threshold $t = n-2$).

Protocol $\Pi^{\mathcal{F}_{RS(k=n),\mathtt{Setup},n,x}}_{RS(k=n^2),\mathtt{Setup},n}$

1. For $x \in [n]$: the parties $i \in [n]$ invoke the ideal functionality $\mathcal{F}_{RS(k=n),\mathtt{Setup},n,x}$ to compute $\mathtt{Setup}$. One of the following occurs:
   (a) Each party $i \in [n]$ receives and outputs r_i.
   (b) Each party $i \in [n]$ receives and outputs (abort, x).
   (c) Each party $i \in [n] \setminus \{x\}$ receives $(\mathsf{gadgabort}, \bar{i})$ (for $\bar{i} \neq x$), and party x receives $\mathsf{gadgabort}$. In this case, each party $i \in [n] \setminus \{x\}$ broadcasts $\bar{i}$ as $\bar{i}_i$.
      i. A. If there exists a party $i \in [n] \setminus \{x\}$ such that $\bar{i}_i = i$: all parties output (abort, i).
         B. Otherwise: the parties record the obtained conflict graph S_x: (i, j) is added to S_x if $\bar{i}_i \neq \bar{i}_j$. Each party k then executes step 2.
2. For $i \in [n]$:
   (a) For $j \in [n]$:
      i. If $S_i^j \cap S_j^i \neq \emptyset$: let $\bar{i} := \min(S_i^j \cap S_j^i)$.
         A. If $i \in S_j^k$ and $j \in S_i^k$: party k outputs $(\mathsf{abort}, \min(\{i, j\}))$.
         B. Otherwise: party k outputs $(\mathsf{abort}, \bar{i})$.

Fig. 14. Protocol $\Pi_{RS(k=n^2),\mathtt{Setup},n}$ for secure computation of the correlated randomness setup function $\mathtt{Setup}$ among n parties (with identifiable abort, with threshold $t = n - 2$) given access to an ideal functionality $\mathcal{F}_{RS(k=n),\mathtt{Setup},n,x}$ that distributes the output of $\mathtt{Setup}$ to n parties (with identifiable abort amongall the parties except for x, with threshold $t = n - 2$).

5.1 Building Blocks

Unanimously Identifiable Commitments. Unanimously identifiable commitments (UIC) have been introduced by Ishai, Ostrovsky, and Seyalioglu [8]. Such commitments allow a trusted dealer to commit to a message msg by distributing $\mathsf{com}_1, \ldots, \mathsf{com}_n$ among n recipients and providing a sender with decommitment information dec. From a security point of view, we require that the joint view of all recipients should contain no information about msg and that any decommitment information dec' published by the sender either causes all honest parties to reconstruct msg or all parties to unanimously abort. Ishai, Ostrovsky, and Seyalioglu have shown how to construct such commitments with information-theoretic security.

Definition 15 (Unanimously Identifiable Commitments). *A UIC scheme consists of a probabilistic polynomial-time algorithm* $\mathtt{Commit}$ *and a deterministic polynomial-time algorithm* $\mathtt{Open}$ *with the following syntax:*

$\mathtt{Commit}(s) \rightarrow (\mathsf{com}_1, \ldots, \mathsf{com}_n, \mathsf{dec})$*: takes as input a message* $\mathsf{msg} \in \{0,1\}^*$*, and outputs* n *commitments* $\mathsf{com}_1, \mathsf{com}_2, \ldots, \mathsf{com}_n$*, and decommitment information* dec.

$\mathtt{Open}(\mathsf{com}_i, \mathsf{dec}) \rightarrow \mathsf{msg}/\bot$*: takes as input* com_i *and the decommitment information* dec*, and outputs a value in* $\{0,1\}^* \cup \{\bot\}$.

Furthermore, (Commit, Open) *should satisfy* correctness *(Definition 16),* privacy *(Definition 17), and* binding with agreement on abort *(Definition 18).*

Definition 16 (Correctness). *A UIC* (Commit, Open) *is* correct *if for any* $\mathsf{msg} \in \{0,1\}^*$ *and any* $i \in [n]$,

$$\Pr[(\mathsf{com}_1, \mathsf{com}_2, \ldots, \mathsf{com}_n, \mathsf{dec}) \leftarrow \mathtt{Commit}(\mathsf{msg}) : \mathtt{Open}(\mathsf{com}_i, \mathsf{dec}) = \mathsf{msg}] = 1.$$

Definition 17 (Privacy). *A UIC* (Commit, Open) *is* private *if for any* $\mathsf{msg}, \mathsf{msg}' \in \{0,1\}^*$ *with* $|\mathsf{msg}| = |\mathsf{msg}'|$

$$\begin{aligned} &\{(\mathsf{com}_1, \ldots, \mathsf{com}_n) \mid (\mathsf{com}_1, \mathsf{com}_2, \ldots, \mathsf{com}_n, \mathsf{dec}) \leftarrow \mathtt{Commit}(\mathsf{msg})\} \\ \equiv &\{(\mathsf{com}_1, \ldots, \mathsf{com}_n) \mid (\mathsf{com}_1, \mathsf{com}_2, \ldots, \mathsf{com}_n, \mathsf{dec}) \leftarrow \mathtt{Commit}(\mathsf{msg}')\}. \end{aligned}$$

Definition 18 (Binding with Agreement on Abort). *Consider the security game described in Fig. 15. A UIC* (Commit, Open) *is* binding with agreement on abort *if for any message* $\mathsf{msg} \in \{0,1\}^*$ *and adversary* $\mathcal{A}$*, there exists a negligible function* $\mathsf{negl}(\cdot)$ *such that*

$$\Pr[\mathcal{A} \textit{ wins } \mathsf{game_{baa}}(\mathcal{A})] \leq \mathsf{negl}(\lambda)$$

where the probability is taken over the random coins of $\mathcal{C}$ *and* $\mathcal{A}$.

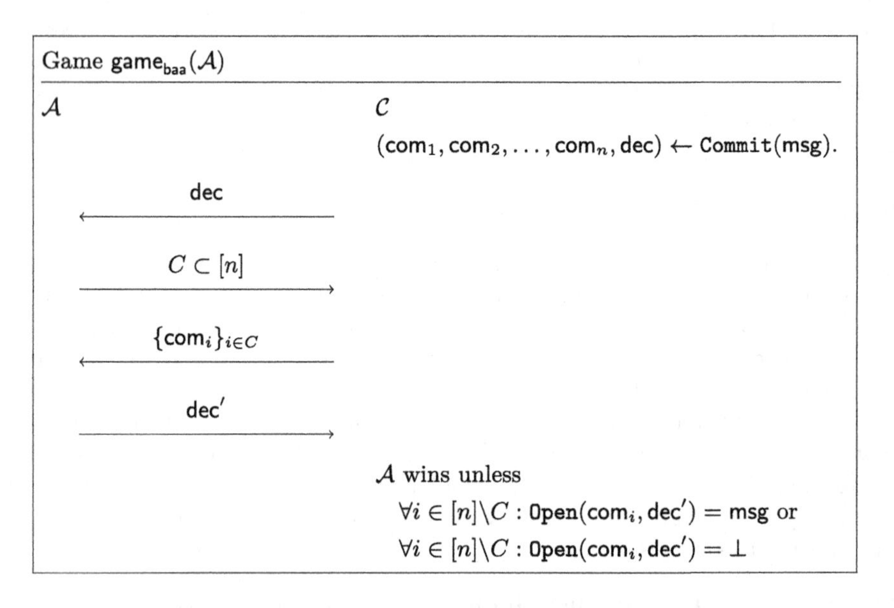

Fig. 15. Security game for binding with agreement on abort.

Remark 2. For technical convenience, we slightly modified the security game $\mathsf{game_{baa}}(\mathcal{A})$ by allowing the adversary to first obtain dec and then query the set C. The original UIC construction of Ishai, Ostrovsky, and Seyalioglu [8] directly satisfies our new notion and if necessary all of our proofs can also be done with the original security definition; albeit with a slightly larger security loss.

Unanimously Identifiable Secret Sharing. Unanimously identifiable secret sharing (UISS) is another primitive that has been introduced and constructed with information-theoretic security by Ishai, Ostrovsky, and Seyalioglu [8].

Definition 19 (Unanimously Identifiable Secret Sharing Scheme). *A* unanimously identifiable secret sharing scheme *for message space* $\{0,1\}^*$ *is a secret sharing scheme (Definition 4) that additionally satisfies* local identifiability *(Definition 20) and* predictable failures *(Definition 14 with the appropriate syntactic modifications).*

A secret sharing scheme is said to be unanimously identifiable if all share holders either reconstruct the correct message, or unanimously agree on some subset of shares which they consider to be invalid.

Definition 20 (Local Identifiability). *Consider the game described in Fig. 16. A secret sharing scheme* $(\mathtt{Share}, \mathtt{LRec})$ *for access structure* $\mathbb{A}$ *is* locally identifiable *if for any message* $\mathsf{msg} \in \{0,1\}^*$ *and adversary* $\mathcal{A}$*, there exists negligible function* $\mathsf{negl}(\cdot)$ *such that*

$$\Pr[\mathcal{A} \text{ wins } \mathsf{game}_{\mathsf{li}}(\mathcal{A})] \leq \mathsf{negl}(\lambda)$$

where the probability is taken over the random coin of $\mathcal{C}$ *and* $\mathcal{A}$*.*

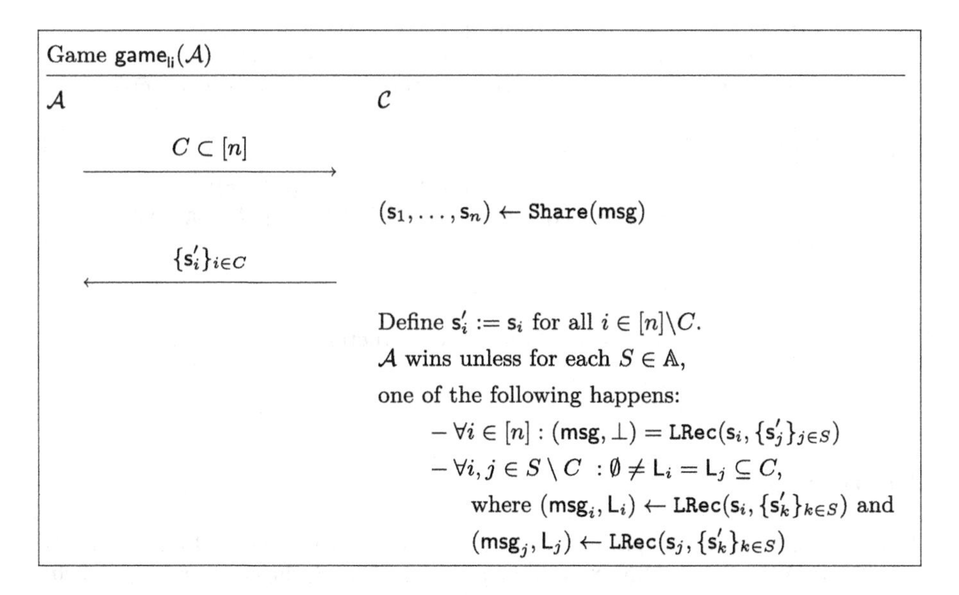

Fig. 16. Security game for local identifiability.

5.2 Construction

Theorem 7. *Let $\mathbb{A}^{O}_{n,t}$ be a threshold access structure with k observers, where $k < n$. Let* (UISS.Share, UISS.Rec) *be a UISS for $\mathbb{A}_{m,t}$, where $m = n - k$. Let* (Commit, Open) *be a n-party UIC. Then, the construction in Fig. 17 is a UISSwPPS for $\mathbb{A}^{O}_{n,t}$.*

The proofs of Theorem 7 can be found in the full version of this paper.

UISSwPPS

$\underline{\mathtt{Share}(\mathsf{msg})}$:

1. Compute $\{\mathsf{s}_i\}_{i\in[n]\setminus O} \leftarrow \mathtt{UISS.Share}(\mathsf{msg})$;
2. For each $i \in [n] \setminus O$, compute $(\mathsf{com}_i^1, \ldots, \mathsf{com}_i^n, \mathsf{dec}_i) \leftarrow \mathtt{Commit}(\mathsf{s}_i)$;
3. If $i \in O$, then $\mathsf{s}_i^{\mathsf{pub}} := \bot$; otherwise, $\mathsf{s}_i^{\mathsf{pub}} := (\mathsf{s}_i, \mathsf{dec}_i)$;
4. Set $\mathsf{s}_i^{\mathsf{priv}} := (\{\mathsf{com}_j^i\}_{j\in[n]\setminus O}, \mathsf{s}_i^{\mathsf{pub}})$.

$\underline{\mathtt{LRec}(\mathsf{s}_i^{\mathsf{priv}}, \{\mathsf{s}_j^{\mathsf{pub}}\}_{j\in S})}$:

1. Let $\mathsf{L}_i := \emptyset$;
2. For each $j \in S \setminus O$, if $\mathtt{Open}(\mathsf{com}_j^i, \mathsf{dec}_j) \neq \mathsf{s}_j$, then $\mathsf{L}_i = \mathsf{L}_i \cup \{j\}$;
3. If $\mathsf{L}_i \neq \emptyset$, then return $(\bot, \mathsf{L}_i)$;
4. If $i \in O$, then
   (a) Set $\mathsf{s}' := \mathsf{s}_j$ where $j = \min(S)$;
   (b) Return $(\overline{\mathsf{msg}}, \bot)$, where $\overline{\mathsf{msg}} = \mathtt{UISS.Rec}(\mathsf{s}', \{\mathsf{s}_j\}_{j\in S})$.
5. Otherwise, if $i \notin O$, then return $(\overline{\mathsf{msg}}, \bot)$, where $\overline{\mathsf{msg}} = \mathtt{UISS.Rec}(\mathsf{s}_i, \{\mathsf{s}_j\}_{j\in S})$.

$\underline{\mathtt{Rec}(\{\mathsf{s}_j^{\mathsf{pub}}\}_{j\in S})}$:

1. For each $i \in S$, compute $(\mathsf{msg}_i, \mathsf{L}_i) = \mathtt{UISS.Rec}(\mathsf{s}_i, \{\mathsf{s}_j\}_{j\in S})$;
2. If $\exists\ i, j$ s.t. $\mathsf{msg}_i \neq \mathsf{msg}_j$ output $\bot$, otherwise output msg_k with $k = \min(S)$.

Fig. 17. UISSwPPS construction.

References

1. Beaver, D.: Multiparty protocols tolerating half faulty processors. In: Brassard, G. (ed.) CRYPTO 1989. LNCS, vol. 435, pp. 560–572. Springer, New York (1990). https://doi.org/10.1007/0-387-34805-0_49
2. Brandt, N.: Tight setup bounds for identifiable abort. Cryptology ePrint Archive, Report 2021/684 (2021). https://ia.cr/2021/684
3. Brandt, N.-P., Maier, S., Müller, T., Müller-Quade, J.: Constructing secure multi-party computation with identifiable abort. IACR Cryptology ePrint Archive, 2020:153 (2020)

4. Cleve, R.: Limits on the security of coin flips when half the processors are faulty (extended abstract). In: Proceedings of the 18th ACM STOC, pp. 364–369. ACM Press (1986)
5. Crépeau, C., van de Graaf, J., Tapp, A.: Committed oblivious transfer and private multi-party computation. In: Coppersmith, D. (ed.) CRYPTO 1995. LNCS, vol. 963, pp. 110–123. Springer, Heidelberg (1995). https://doi.org/10.1007/3-540-44750-4_9
6. Fitzi, M., Garay, J.A., Maurer, U., Ostrovsky, R.: Minimal complete primitives for secure multi-party computation. In: Kilian, J. (ed.) CRYPTO 2001. LNCS, vol. 2139, pp. 80–100. Springer, Heidelberg (2001). https://doi.org/10.1007/3-540-44647-8_5
7. Ishai, Y., Kushilevitz, E., Ostrovsky, R., Sahai, A.: Zero-knowledge from secure multiparty computation. In: Johnson, D.S., Feige, U. (eds.) 39th ACM STOC, pp. 21–30. ACM Press (2007)
8. Ishai, Y., Ostrovsky, R., Seyalioglu, H.: Identifying cheaters without an honest majority. In: Cramer, R. (ed.) TCC 2012. LNCS, vol. 7194, pp. 21–38. Springer, Heidelberg (2012). https://doi.org/10.1007/978-3-642-28914-9_2
9. Ishai, Y., Ostrovsky, R., Zikas, V.: Secure multi-party computation with identifiable abort. In: Garay, J.A., Gennaro, R. (eds.) CRYPTO 2014, Part II. LNCS, vol. 8617, pp. 369–386. Springer, Heidelberg (2014). https://doi.org/10.1007/978-3-662-44381-1_21
10. Kilian, J.: Founding cryptography on oblivious transfer. In: Proceedings of the 20th ACM STOC, pp. 20–31. ACM Press (1988)
11. Rabin, M.O.: How to exchange secrets with oblivious transfer. Technical Memo (1981). https://www.iacr.org/museum/rabin-obt/obtrans-eprint187.pdf
12. Rabin, T., Ben-Or, M.: Verifiable secret sharing and multiparty protocols with honest majority (extended abstract). In: Proceedings of the 21st ACM STOC, pp. 73–85. ACM Press (1989)

Prio+: Privacy Preserving Aggregate Statistics via Boolean Shares

Surya Addanki[1], Kevin Garbe[1], Eli Jaffe[1(✉)], Rafail Ostrovsky[1], and Antigoni Polychroniadou[2]

[1] UCLA, Los Angeles, CA 90095, USA
kgarbe@cs.ucla.edu, jaffe.eli96@gmail.com
[2] J.P. Morgan AI Research, New York, NY 10017, USA

Abstract. This paper introduces Prio+, a privacy-preserving system for the collection of aggregate statistics, with the same model and goals in mind as the original and highly influential Prio paper by Henry Corrigan-Gibbs and Dan Boneh (NSDI 2017). As in the original Prio, each client holds a private data value (e.g. number of visits to a particular website) and a small set of servers privately compute statistical functions over the set of client values (e.g. the average number of visits). To achieve security against faulty or malicious clients, unlike Prio, Prio+ clients use Boolean secret-sharing instead of zero-knowledge proofs to convince servers that their data is of the correct form and Prio+ servers execute a share conversion protocol as needed in order to properly compute over client data. This allows us to ensure that clients' data is properly formatted essentially for free, and the work shifts to novel share-conversion protocols between servers, where some care is needed to make it efficient. Our overall approach is simpler than Prio and our Prio+ strategy reduces the client's computational burden by at least two orders of magnitude (or more depending on the statistic) while keeping server costs comparable to Prio. Prio+ permits computation of exactly the same wide range of complex statistics as the original Prio protocol, including high-dimensional linear regression over private values held by clients.

We report detailed benchmarks of our Prio+ implementation and compare these to both the original Go implementation of Prio and the Mozilla implementation of Prio. Our Prio+ software is open-source and released with the same license as Prio.

1 Introduction

Modern society has exploded with a wave of internet-enabled devices. Smartwatches, cell-phones, cars, and ATMs constantly collect data on their surroundings to improve performance. For many cloud services controlling such devices, collecting and computing statistics over such a large pool of data has become a hugely profitable endeavor. Navigation apps detect congestion with user location data [16], fitness trackers collect average data for user comparison [15]. Aggregate statistics are one of the principal currencies in the modern data-driven economy.

C. Galdi and S. Jarecki (Eds.): SCN 2022, LNCS 13409, pp. 516–539, 2022.
https://doi.org/10.1007/978-3-031-14791-3_23

These services usually want only to compute aggregate statistics, not collect individual data. However, their methods often involve storing users' personal data in the clear. A centralized cache of sensitive user data presents clear security risks. A motivated attacker may steal and disclose this sensitive information [18,27], cloud services could misuse or sell this information for profit [26], and intelligence agencies may acquire the data for targeting or mass surveillance [14].

Our problem in its simplest form is as follows: each client P_i for $i \in [n]$ holds a private value $x_i \in \{0, 1\}$, and they wish to learn the sum $\sum_i x_i$. As described in the original Prio paper [4], several previous systems have also attempted to solve this problem. One such attempt involves using a randomized response system to provide differential privacy [11,13]. That is, some user data is replaced with random data according to some fixed probability $p < 0.5$. By aggregating this "noisy" data, data collectors can get a somewhat accurate estimate of overall statistics. This technique scales well and provides robustness (each malicious client can at most affect the sum by ± 1), but the privacy guarantees are relatively weak. There is an inherent trade-off between the privacy guarantee to the client and the accuracy of the overall statistic. Another option is to have clients submit encryptions of their data to the servers. Then, servers can sum up the ciphertexts and only decrypt the final sum [7,9,17,19–21]. This achieves stronger privacy guarantees but sacrifices robustness: a malicious client can affect the final sum arbitrarily because servers cannot tell the difference between an encryption of 0/1 and an encryption of some large integer. If used for a voting scheme, this would allow any client to submit as many votes as they like. These attacks can be mitigated using zero-knowledge proofs [10], but this heavily impacts scalability. Servers require expensive public-key operations to verify these proofs, and clients are burdened with the computationally difficult task of generating the proofs.

Prio is a brilliant and highly influential private aggregation system which successfully resolves this discrepancy between privacy, robustness, and scalability. Prio works within the client-server model in which the n clients rely on a small number of computationally powerful servers in order to compute aggregate statistics. Prio provides strong privacy guarantees: it guarantees privacy so long as at least one of the computation servers is honest. It also provides robustness: a malicious client cannot affect the protocol beyond misreporting their private data value. For example, if the client is supposed to submit a value in the range $[0, 64]$, Prio servers can syntactically reject submissions of any value outside that range, but not learn anything else about where it is in the range. To achieve this, Prio utilizes a new technique called SNIPs (secret-shared non-interactive proofs), which allow servers to collaboratively check a shared proof of correctness with little communication. In particular, the bandwidth used by servers during verification remains constant as the size of user inputs increases. The Prio protocol has been widely adopted, and has even been re-implemented by Mozilla for use in privately collecting web usage statistics. It is being run as a service for other web-based organizations by the Internet Services Research Group (ISRG), a non-profit focused on reducing barriers to secure communication over the internet. Google has also begun using it to perform analytics in their exposure notifications express (ENX) system for measuring health data.

Prio achieves highly desirable security guarantees, and their solution is significantly more efficient than comparably secure data-collection systems. One drawback, however, is that the client-side computation and client-to-server communication of their solution increases at a superlinear rate as the size of user data increases (see Table 1). Client computation and communication costs are most often the bottlenecks for overall efficiency since clients are on low-power devices and high-latency connections whereas servers are usually collocated high-power machines. For example, clients usually run on either web browsers or cell phones when using the Mozilla Firefox browser. Requiring clients to use SNIPs to verify simple properties like input size places a computational burden on these devices.

In this paper, we present Prio+, a new and improved version of Prio that aims to reduce this burden on the client. Prio+ uses Boolean secret-sharing to let clients prove the size of their input at essentially zero computational cost. Servers then execute a Boolean-to-arithmetic share conversion protocol (if necessary) and compute the output as in the original Prio protocol. For some statistics, Prio+ still uses SNIPs, as they are well-suited for verifying multiplicative relationships. We do not, however, use them to verify everything about client inputs (as is done in Prio). For most statistics, Prio+ uses no SNIPs at all. Furthermore, for some statistics (AND/OR, MAX/MIN) Prio+ does not even use share conversion, and for these statistics, we achieve monumental improvements to both client and server efficiency compared to Prio.

Our strategy significantly reduces both client computation and client-to-server communication, the two most expensive computational resources in our efficiency model. Even for the few statistics where SNIPs are still necessary (variance and linear regression), the size of the SNIPs and work to generate them decreases dramatically. The result is a system which computes the same set of complex statistics as Prio with identical privacy and robustness guarantees but with reduced client computation and client-to-server communication. For example, when collecting the distribution of tens of thousands of client responses to a true/false question, Prio+ clients encode their data over 350x faster than Prio clients, and the client's message size is nearly 5x smaller. Prio+ also often improves server efficiency: for the example given above, once servers have received all client inputs, Prio+ servers compute the output 85x faster with essentially the same server-to-server communication. As input size increases, Prio+ server communication increases whereas Prio's server communication stays constant. But, for practically sized inputs, Prio+ servers still communicate only a few hundred bytes per client submission.

Both Prio and Prio+ compute complex statistics beyond just summation. While Prio applies a general SNIP-based solution, Prio+ applies a specialized approach for each complex statistic and uses SNIPs for lighter relations as needed (the Prio+ protocol for sum, the main statistic used by Mozilla, does not require any SNIPs). This means that the efficiency of Prio+ varies depending on the statistic being computed. For some statistics, Prio+ dramatically improves performance across the board. E.g., when computing the maximum of client data in the range $[0, 128]$, Prio+ servers communicate a constant 16 bytes per client,

Table 1. Table of asymptotic comparisons between Prio and the protocols Π comprising Prio+. M is the number of multiplication gates required to check if an input is properly encoded for the relevant statistic. λ is the bit-length of each client's input, $M' := M - \lambda$ is the number of multiplication gates not used for checking bit-length, and n is the total number of clients. Note $M \geq \lambda$ because λ multiplication gates are always used for checking bit-length in Prio. 'Serv Comm.' is the communication between servers in bits. Note that Prio and the Linear PCP extension implement a general protocol for all statistics, whereas Prio+ uses different protocols for each statistic. Thus the entries in the first two rows represent all statistics computed by Prio, where the value M varies depending on the particular statistic. Note that $\Pi_{\mathsf{sum}}, \Pi_{\mathsf{var/linReg}}, \Pi_{\mathsf{frq}}$ also use λ symmetric key operations (oblivious transfers) during pre-computation. $\Theta(\cdot)$ notation suppressed to improve readability.

	Client Mults	Proof Size	Server Mults	Serv Comm.
Prio [4]	$M \log M$	M	$(M \log M)n$	n
Linear PCPs [3]	$M \log M$	$\log M$	$(M \log M)n$	n
Π_{sum}	None	None	λ	$n + \lambda^2$
$\Pi_{\mathsf{and/or/max/min}}$	None	None	None	n
$\Pi_{\mathsf{var/linReg}}$	$M' \log M'$	M'	$(M' \log M' + \lambda)n$	$n + \lambda^2$
Π_{frq}	None	None	$n\lambda$	$(n + \lambda) \log n$

compared to a constant 740 bytes for Prio servers. This is in addition to a nearly 750x faster client encode time, 5x smaller client message size, and a 43x improvement in server computation time. Even for the few statistics where Prio+ still utilizes SNIPs, we see significant improvements in client encode time, client message size, and server compute time at little-to-no server bandwidth cost.

Contributions: We summarize our contributions below:

- Provide a detailed daBit-based semi-honest Boolean-to-arithmetic share conversion protocol with output in a field $\mathbf{Z}_p$, which was not explicit in [23],
- demonstrate how to use Boolean-to-arithmetic share conversion with Boolean secret-sharing and smaller-scope SNIPs for particular relations in order to provide robustness and privacy in a large-scale data collection system,
- demonstrate that client usage of Boolean representation avoids expensive zero-knowledge proofs leading to dramatic speed-ups of the system, and
- exhibit the effectiveness of our protocols with a full-scale and publicly available implementation allowing private and robust computation of a wide range of complex statistics.

Below we state our results for a single protocol (Π_{sum}). We establish similar results for the remaining protocols according to the asymptotics given in Table 1. Although we state our results in the two-server case, all results generalize trivially to the case of k servers and provide identical security guarantees to those of Prio. Informally, a protocol is private if it leaks nothing to any client/server besides the output, and is robust if no client can affect the output beyond misreporting their private data. Note that the number of multiplications required by servers when computing some are independent of the number of clients, and depend only on the length of their inputs.

Theorem 1 *(Informal). Suppose n players $P_1, \ldots, P_n$ each hold a private λ-bit integer x_i, and they wish to rely on two servers S_L and S_R to compute the sum $f(x_1, \ldots, x_n) = \sum_i x_i$. There exists a protocol Π_{sum}, returning the sum $f(\cdot)$ to each client and returning no output to either server, which is both private and robust against a coalition of up to n malicious clients and one semi-honest server and requires zero client multiplications, no zero-knowledge proofs, $O(\lambda)$ multiplications per server, and $O(n)$ bits of communication between servers.*

With Prio+, we aim to provide the same benefits as Prio to systems and organizations whose clients cannot withstand the burden of generating and sending expensive zero-knowledge proofs.

2 Technical Overview

Arithmetic vs. Boolean Secret-Sharing: Additive secret-sharing is a cryptographic tool which allows a user to "share" a private value x into a set of values such that any strict subset of these values reveals nothing about x, but all values together can be used to reconstruct x. Prio is built around arithmetic secret-sharing: shares are random values in a ring $\mathbf{Z}_M$ (often this is a field and $M = p$) such that they sum to x. Clients share their private inputs and send one share to each server. Servers then sum shares locally and return the summed shares to clients who add them together and learn the output. Servers restrict the size of client data by requiring clients to also submit zero-knowledge proofs.

Boolean secret-sharing is an alternative secret-sharing scheme in which a client holding x secret-shares each bit x_i of x as two random bits such that their XOR is x_i. Similar to arithmetic secret-sharing, each Boolean share appears random except when combined with all other shares. The crucial difference is this: if each Boolean share consists of λ bits, then the private value x is always a λ-bit integer. This allows servers to verify the bit-length of a client's submitted private value via simple local checks on the shares themselves, without zero-knowledge proofs. Note: to distinguish Boolean shares from arithmetic shares, arithmetic shares will be denoted $[x]^A$, and Boolean shares will be denoted $[x]^B$.

Boolean-to-Arithmetic Share Conversion: Using Boolean shares presents an issue: how do servers compute the sum over Boolean shares of client inputs? Prio's method of summing shares locally and then returning those aggregated values to clients only works with arithmetic shares, not Boolean shares. Prio+ servers use Boolean-to-arithmetic share conversion, which converts Boolean shares of x to arithmetic shares of the same x. Such protocols have been studied extensively [5,8,12,23], and the most efficient method based on oblivious transfer (OT) is due to [8] and outputs arithmetic shares in a ring $\mathbf{Z}_M$. For use with SNIPs, M should be a prime.

Semi-Honest Boolean-to-arithmetic Share Conversion into $\mathbf{Z}_p$ via daBits: For more efficient share conversion in this case, we use an offline phase to generate pre-computed daBits (double-authenticated bits) from [23], which allow share conversion with less communication and only use one OT to generate each beforehand. This cheap offline phase makes the resulting online protocol much more efficient than Prio. A daBit is a known primitive used for various functionalities, including share conversion. A daBit is a secret-shared pair $([b]^A, [b]^B)$ where $b \in \{0, 1\}$ is a random secret bit. It is known how to convert Boolean shares of an λ-bit integer to arithmetic shares using λ daBits [23] in the malicious setting, so we present an efficient semi-honest version of this protocol for quick parallelizable share conversion. Malicious security is not necessary since all servers are semi-honest (following the threat model of Prio), and they perform the conversion. Details of the generation and share conversion, as well as measures of the complexity of these procedures, are in Sect. 8. Although we would like to provide an analytical comparison between the efficiency of resulting protocol with Prio, the Prio paper does not give analytic measures of their complexity to enable such a comparison. Thus we rely on a practical comparison of the two systems.

Complex Statistics: Prio+ computes the same statistics as Prio. In addition to SUM, clients can compute Boolean AND/OR (where a client holds a single bit), MAX/MIN, frequency count FRQ (where a client holds a value in some small range $[0, K]$), variance VAR and standard deviation STDDEV (where a client holds an λ-bit integer), and linear regression linReg (where a client holds a degree d feature vector of λ-bit integers). Many of these statistics (AND, OR, MAX, MIN) are even simpler than SUM, requiring no share conversion, no zero-knowledge proofs, and virtually no communication between servers. FRQ, similar to SUM, requires share conversion to allow aggregation, but does not require any zero-knowledge proofs. Instead, servers use simple logical mechanisms on the Boolean shares to detect improperly encoded inputs, details of which can be found in the full paper [1]. The only statistics which do require zero-knowledge proofs are VAR, STDDEV, and linReg. In these cases, clients encode their private values in such a way that SNIPs are the most efficient method for verifying that encoding. The key difference is that SNIPs in this case are only being used to verify one small part of the encoding, whereas in Prio they are used to verify every property of the encoded value. At a high level, we have removed the need for SNIPs to verify the length of client inputs, reducing the overall complexity. Since SNIPs operate on arithmetic shares of the input, we first apply daBit-based Boolean-to-arithmetic share conversion on the clients' submitted Boolean shares, which we need to do anyway to perform aggregation after the validation.

Practical Comparison: We compared Prio+ to both the original Go implementation of Prio (Prio (Go)) as well as another implementation by Mozilla (Prio (Mozilla)) which only computes SUM, no complex statistics. We would have preferred to simply compare against the more efficient of the two implementations, but since some statistics are only supported by the Go implementation, we chose to provide both comparisons. We did not benchmark against the updated Prio construction given in [3] because it has not yet been implemented and in the case of practically-sized inputs, large constant terms overshadow its asymptotically smaller client message sizes. All implementations were executed using a two-server setup. Although the original Prio paper included an evaluation for a large number of servers, the purpose of that evaluation was to show that Prio's server bandwidth remained constant, even as the number of servers and size of data increased. Since our focus is on client efficiency, our evaluation focuses on the two-server case for simplicity. First, we compared all three implementations in evaluating SUM for tens of thousands of clients each with 1-bit, 8-bit, 16-bit, and 32-bit integers. We measured encode time, client message size, server compute time, and server communication. Prio+ clients encoded inputs up to 3000x faster than Prio clients. Client messages in Prio+ were up to 23x smaller than in Prio. Prio+ servers also processed client submissions up to 300x faster than Prio servers online. Even accounting for precomputation time of daBits, Prio+ is still up to 120x faster. Prio+ also requires significantly less bytes, 44x less than Prio (Go) and half as many as Prio (Mozilla). Accounting for precomputation of daBits, the end-to-end time does increase compared to the online time of Prio as the size of the user inputs increases. For 1-bit integers, end-to-end is comparable to Prio (Mozilla) and 18x less than Prio (Go). For 32-bit inputs, the full end-to-end run still communicates 3x less than Prio (Go), and just 7x more than Prio (Mozilla). This improvement is made even more significant by the fact that daBits can be pre-computed during off-hours.

We ran similar experiments between Prio+ and Prio (Go) for MAX and linReg. Since MAX requires no SNIPs and no share conversion in Prio+, we saw improvements across the board: for client values in the range [0, 128], Prio+ client encode time was 750x less, client message size was 5x smaller, server compute time was 43x less, and server communication was 46x less than Prio (Go). Even though linReg still requires some SNIPs (with reduced scope), we saw up to 30x reduced client encode time, and up to 4x smaller client message size. Server computation (online) is between 2.5x to 14x faster, and communication is 5x to 10x lower depending on input size. When including pre-computation, linReg in Prio+ ranges from equal time to 7x faster, but takes between 1.7x to 20x more bytes to generate and run.

3 Preliminaries

Here we describe our ideal functionality, the client/server setup, our efficiency model, the set of adversaries we defend against, and the assumptions we rely upon to build our protocol.

"Two-Party" Setting: Prio+ securely computes a wide range of aggregate statistics in the client-server model. That is, n clients with private data wish to compute statistics on that data with the help of two honest-but-curious servers. The basis of our system is a secure two-party protocol between these servers. Each client with an input, secret-shares his/her input between the two computation servers (which are assumed to not collude). Then, the two servers run the secure two-party computation (2PC) protocol on the input shares which reveals no information about client inputs. Finally, they send the output shares back to the clients who reconstruct the output. This technique of using 2PC in the client-server setting was first described in the ABY framework of [8] and has found many applications since, including [4].

Formally, a Prio+ deployment consists of n clients $\{P_1, \ldots, P_n\}$ and 2 servers S_L and S_R. Each client P_i holds some private input x_i. Each client can communicate with each server (but not with other clients) and servers can communicate with both clients and the other server via private channels. Although Prio+ is described as a two-server protocol, it can be generalized to a k server protocol for any positive integer k by using k-wise instances of all primitives (secret-sharing, share conversion, and SNIPs when needed).

Efficiency Model: We assume clients have low computational power and servers have high computational power. Similarly, we assume a low-bandwidth connection from clients to servers, and a high-bandwidth connection between servers. Thus we seek to minimize client computation and communication as our highest priority, and server costs as an afterthought. In general, we assume network latency is the greatest computational bottleneck and are concerned more with optimizing communication than computation for both clients and servers.

Security Against Semi-honest Servers, Malicious Clients: Prio+ protects client *privacy* as long as at most one server is passively/semi-honest corrupted (regardless of malicious client misbehavior). Our system cannot tolerate malicious, misbehaving servers as this comes at a direct cost of performance, as discussed in [4]. Our deployment always provides *robustness* (correctness) so long as neither server maliciously misbehaves. We summarize our security definitions here and defer formal definitions to the full version of the paper [1].

Privacy: Intuitively, our deployment provides f-privacy for an aggregation function (statistic) f if an adversary controlling any number of clients and one server learns nothing about the honest clients' inputs besides what is revealed by the output of f. More formally, any such adversary can simulate its view of the protocol run given the output of f. For some aggregation functions, we weaken our protocol to provide $\hat{f}$-privacy where $\hat{f}$ leaks slightly more information to the clients than the statistic itself (for example, execution may require clients to learn the number of clients who provided invalid inputs).

Robustness: A protocol is t-robust if a coalition of t malicious clients cannot affect the output of the protocol beyond misreporting their private data values. This is the strictest notion of correctness in the malicious security model, since a client's private input is known to nobody but themselves, meaning we cannot prevent them from misreporting it. If this data value is meant to come from a specific domain, however, malicious clients should *not* be able to submit data from outside of that domain. This is particularly relevant in our setting, where client data must be encoded in specific formats. Clients should not be able to submit improperly encoded data as this would affect the protocol output. Prio+ is robust against malicious clients, but not against malicious servers. Though robustness against malicious servers seems desirable, it comes at a direct cost to performance, as argued in [4].

Analogously to [4], we assume cryptographic primitives for the establishment of pairwise authenticated channels (CCA-secure public key encryption [6], digital signatures [24,25], etc.). We make no synchronicity assumptions about our network and do not rely on external systems to provide users anonymity.

Notation: We write $x \oplus y$ to denote the XOR operation (addition modulo 2). All addition is interpreted as integer addition unless otherwise clear from context. When $\vec{x}, \vec{y} \in \mathbf{Z}_{2^\lambda}$ are vectors of bits, we will write $\vec{z} = \vec{x} \oplus \vec{y}$ to denote the bitwise-XOR operation. That is, $(\vec{z})_i = (\vec{x})_i \oplus (\vec{y})_i$ for each $0 \leq i < \lambda$. We assume a maximum bit-length λ on all integer data and thus treat all integer-valued data as elements of the ring $\mathbf{Z}_{2^\lambda}$ unless otherwise specified that the data should be interpreted within a field $\mathbf{Z}_p$. $[x]^A$ denotes an arithmetic secret-sharing of x, $[x]^B$ denotes a Boolean secret-sharing of x. We exclusively use two-party secret-sharing, and thus shares held by server S_L will be written $[x]^t_L$, $t \in \{A, B\}$, and similarly $[x]^t_R$ for shares held by S_R. For an integer x, we refer to the i'th least significant bit of the binary representation of x as $(x)_i$. We will say that a function $f : \mathbf{N} \rightarrow \mathbf{R}$ is negligible if for every positive polynomial poly there exists an integer N_{poly} such that for $x > N_{\mathsf{poly}}$, $|f(x)| < \frac{1}{\mathsf{poly}(x)}$.

4 Necessary Primitives

For our purposes, we focus on having $N = 2$ servers with secrets shared between them. Clients hold a secret value x, and want to split it into two shares $\mathsf{Share}(x) = [x]_L, [x]_R$ for servers L and R. This can also be reversed, where $\mathsf{Rec}([x]_L, [x]_R) = x$. Privacy here is straightforward, where any one server can't recover the secret, but both together can. Correctness means that Rec succeeds in the presence of both shares.

Definition 1 ***Arithmetic Secret-Sharing:*** *Given an integer $x \in \mathbf{Z}_M$, an arithmetic secret-sharing of x is a random pair $a, b \in \mathbf{Z}_M$ subject to the condition $a + b = x \pmod{M}$.*

Semantics*: The two-party arithmetic secret-sharing scheme consists of the following pair of functions:*

- $\mathsf{Share}_{+,M} : \mathbf{Z}_M \longrightarrow (\mathbf{Z}_M)^2$, $\mathsf{Share}_{+,M}(x) = ([x]^A_L, [x]^A_R)$, *which are random elements of $\mathbf{Z}_M$ subject to the constraint $[x]^A_L + [x]^A_R = x \pmod{M}$.*
- $\mathsf{Rec}_{+,M} : (\mathbf{Z}_M)^2 \longrightarrow \mathbf{Z}_M$, $\mathsf{Rec}_{+,M}([x]^A_L, [x]^A_R) = [x]^A_L + [x]^A_R \pmod{M}$.

Addition/Scalar Multiplication: *Addition and scalar multiplication over arithmetic secret shares are trivial. To compute a share of $z = x + y$ given shares $[x]^A$ and $[y]^A$, each server $i \in \{L, R\}$ locally computes $[z]^A_i = [x]^A_i + [y]^A_i$. Similarly, to compute scalar multiplication $[w]^A = c \cdot [x]^A$ for public $c \in \mathbf{Z}_M$, each server locally computes $[w]^A_i = c \cdot [x]^A_i$.*

Definition 2 ***Boolean Secret-Sharing.*** *Given an integer* $x \in \mathbf{Z}_2$, *a Boolean secret-sharing of* x *is a random pair* $c, d \in \mathbf{Z}_{2^\lambda}$ *subject to the condition* $c \oplus d = x$.

Semantics: *The two-party* λ*-bit Boolean secret-sharing scheme consists of the following pair of functions:*

- $\mathsf{Share}_{\oplus,\lambda} : \mathbf{Z}_{2^\lambda} \longrightarrow (\mathbf{Z}_{2^\lambda})^2$, $\mathsf{Share}_{\oplus,\lambda}(x) = ([x]^B_L, [x]^B_R)$, *which are random elements of* $\mathbf{Z}_{2^\lambda}$ *subject to the constraint* $[x]^A_L \oplus [x]^A_R = x$.
- $\mathsf{Rec}_{\oplus,\lambda} : (\mathbf{Z}_{2^\lambda})^2 \longrightarrow \mathbf{Z}_{2^\lambda}$, $\mathsf{Rec}_{\oplus,\lambda}([x]^A_L, [x]^A_R) = [x]^A_L \oplus [x]^A_R$.

XOR: *Computing XOR over Boolean shares is trivial.* $[z]^B = [x]^B \oplus [y]^B$. *Each server* $s \in \{L, R\}$ *locally computes* $[z]^B_s = [x]^B_s \oplus [y]^B_s$.

These two schemes each have strengths and weaknesses. If client data is arithmetically secret-shared under a large modulus M, servers can efficiently compute the sum of shared values via associativity of addition by locally summing their shares modulo M, as in Prio [4]. This is not efficient with Boolean shares as they are built using bitwise XOR instead. On the other hand, Boolean shares of x are the same bit-length as x itself, meaning servers can trivially verify the size of client inputs. Prio+ leverages both of these advantages to privately compute complex aggregate statistics efficiently. Prio+ clients submit their data in the Boolean scheme (so that servers can verify the bit-length efficiently) and then servers convert these shares back to the arithmetic scheme in order to sum the data together and compute the given statistic.

Boolean to arithmetic share conversion is a well-studied technique. The current most efficient protocol in the semi-honest two-party setting is due to [8] and is based on Oblivious Transfer (OT). In particular, to convert a pair of λ-bit Boolean shares to arithmetic shares in $\mathbf{Z}_{2^\lambda}$, they use λ independent instances of OT where each OT transfers on average a string of length $(\lambda+1)/2$. The total communication cost is $\lambda(\kappa + (\lambda+1)/2) = O(\lambda^2)$ [8].

To achieve share conversion with more efficient online work, we utilize precomputed pairs called daBits (doubly-authenticated bits), discussed in [23]. Although they are primarily used in the malicious setting, we are able to use them very efficiently in the semi-honest setting, which to our knowledge hasn't been detailed explicitly. Compared to OT share conversion above, for the same number of bits converted this uses the same number of OTs for generating the precomputed daBits, and then only communicates a single bit between servers, per bit converted using daBits. They require the same OTs to generate as the share conversion protocol in [8], and only require a single bit communicated per converted bit to perform the computation. See Sect. 8 for further details.

The final piece of Prio+, used only for a few statistics, is the secret-shared non-interactive zero-knowledge proof (SNIP) which underpins the Prio protocol of [4]. Although we claim that Prio overuses SNIPs in unnecessary situations, SNIPs are an incredibly efficient method for verifying multiplicative relationships on secret-shared inputs. Below we review how SNIPs allow servers to efficiently verify that some client input x is valid without learning any additional information. The following description comes directly from [4].

A secret-shared non-interactive proof (SNIP) protocol consists of an interaction between a client (the prover) and multiple servers (the verifiers). At the start of the protocol:

- Each server i holds a share $[x]_i^A \in \mathbf{F}^\lambda$ for some field $\mathbf{F}$.
- The client holds the secret input (vector) $x = \sum_i [x]_i^A \in \mathbf{F}^\lambda$.
- All parties hold an arithmetic circuit representing $\mathsf{Valid} : \mathbf{F}^\lambda \longrightarrow \mathbf{F}$.

The client's goal is to convince the servers that $\mathsf{Valid}(x) = 1$ without revealing any additional information about x. To do so, the client sends a proof string to each server. After receiving these proof strings, the servers gossip amongst themselves and then conclude either that $\mathsf{Valid}(x) = 1$ (accept x) or $\mathsf{Valid}(x) \neq 1$ (reject x).

A valid SNIP must satisfy correctness, soundness, and zero-knowledge.

- **Correctness.** If all parties are honest, the servers will accept x.
- **Soundness.** If all servers are honest, and if $\mathsf{Valid}(x) \neq 1$, then for all malicious clients, even ones running in super-polynomial time, the servers will reject x with overwhelming probability. In other words, no matter how the client cheats, the servers will almost always reject.
- **Zero-knowledge.** If the client and at least one server are honest, then the servers learn nothing about x, except that $\mathsf{Valid}(x) = 1$. More precisely, there exists a simulator (that does not take x as input) that accurately reproduces the view of any proper subset of malicious servers executing the SNIP protocol.

The construction in [4], based on a generalized version of the polynomial-based batched multiplication verification technique of Ben-Sasson et al. [2], satisfies each of these properties as proven in their Appendix D.

5 The Non-robust SUM Scheme

The following simple scheme for computing the sum of clients' private bits is the basis of both Prio and Prio+, and is described further in [4]. Each client P_i, $i \in \{1, \ldots, n\}$, holds a private bit $x_i \in \{0, 1\}$. They wish to learn the sum $f(x_1, \ldots, x_n) = \sum_{i=1}^n x_i$. Consider the following flawed protocol.

1. **Upload:** Each P_i computes $\mathsf{Share}_{+,M}(x_i) = ([x_i]_L^A, [x_i]_R^A)$. The client then sends one additive share to each server over secure pairwise-authenticated channels. Note: although x_i is a single bit, we treat it here as an element of $\mathbf{Z}_M$ for $M > n$.
2. **Aggregate:** S_L and S_R hold accumulator values $A_L, A_R \in \mathbf{Z}_p$ respectively, initially set to zero. For each i, when S_L receives $[x_i]_L^A$ from P_i, computes $A_L \leftarrow A_L + [x_i]_L^A \pmod M$. S_R does the same with its accumulator A_R upon receiving $[x_i]_R^A$ from P_i.
3. **Publish:** Once data is collected, servers publish their accumulator values A_L, A_R to every client.
4. **Client Computation:** Clients compute the sum of the accumulator values $A_L + A_R \pmod M$.

Note that if all players behave, each client's output is $A_L + A_R = \sum_i [x_i]_L^A + \sum_i [x_i]_R^A \pmod{M} = \sum_i x_i \pmod{M}$, as long as $M > n$. The authors of [4] make two crucial observations about this simple scheme. First, it provides privacy as long as one server is honest. The adversary's view includes a single share, say $[x]_L^A$, of an honest client's input, which appears totally random without $[x]_R^A$. Second, the scheme does *not* provide robustness against malicious clients. A single malicious client can corrupt the protocol output by submitting (for example) shares of a random integer $r \in \mathbf{Z}_M$.

6 Protecting Correctness

The reason a malicious client can cheat and submit $x_i \notin \{0, 1\}$ in the non-robust scheme is that a single arithmetic share of x_i reveals nothing about the size of x_i. Prio [4] solves the robustness issue by forcing clients to construct and submit SNIPs proving $x_i \in \{0, 1\}$. This is effective, but requires expensive computation on the clients' part to construct and send these SNIPs to the servers. Since clients are computationally weak compared to servers in our model and latency is high between clients and servers, this is not ideal.

Instead, suppose that P_i shares x_i via the 1-bit Boolean scheme as $x_i = [x_i]_L^B \oplus [x_i]_R^B$. If $[x_i]_L^B \in \{0, 1\}$ and $[x_i]_R^B \in \{0, 1\}$, this implies $x_i \in \{0, 1\}$. Using Boolean-to-arithmetic share conversion, servers can then compute corresponding arithmetic shares $[x_i]^A$ in some large ring $\mathbf{Z}_M$ and continue computation via the simple scheme. As long as conversion is secure, the x_i remains private. Thus, to make the simple scheme robust against malicious clients we need a Boolean-to-arithmetic share conversion protocol achieving the following ideal functionality $\mathcal{F}_{B2A}$.

Definition 3 *The two-player λ-bit ideal functionality $\mathcal{F}_{B2A}$ (with output in $\mathbf{Z}_M$) behaves as follows:*

- *$\mathcal{F}_{B2A}$ receives $[x]_L^B, [x]_R^B \in \mathbf{Z}_{2^\lambda}$ as inputs from S_L, S_R respectively.*
- *$\mathcal{F}_{B2A}$ computes $x = [x]_L^B \oplus [x]_R^B$*
- *$\mathcal{F}_{B2A}$ computes $\mathsf{Share}_{+,M}(x) = ([x]_L^A, [x]_R^A)$ where $[x]_L^A + [x]_R^A = x \pmod{M}$.*
- *$\mathcal{F}_{B2A}$ returns $[x]_L^A, [x]_R^A$ to S_L, S_R respectively as outputs.*

Share conversion is well-studied in both theoretical limitations [5] and practical performance [8]. In this case we use a daBit (double-authenticated bit) based Boolean-to-arithmetic share conversion (see [23] for discussion of daBits). Share conversion is further detailed in Sect. 8.

We can now strengthen the simple scheme from Sect. 5 to prevent malicious clients from corrupting the output as previously described. A formal description of this strengthened protocol Π_{bitSum} is below. For detailed proofs of its privacy and robustness, we defer to the full version of the paper [1].

Π_{bitSum}

Inputs: $x_i \in \{0,1\}$ for $i \in [n]$.
Output: $\sum_{i=1}^{n} x_i$.

1. **Upload:**
   (a) Each client P_i computes $\mathsf{Share}_{\oplus,1}(x_i) \longrightarrow [x_i]_L^B, [x_i]_R^B$ via Definition 2
   (b) Each P_i sends $[x_i]_L, [x_i]_R$ to S_L, S_R respectively.
2. **Verify Bit-Length:** Initially, $n' = n$. If a server receives a share which is not 1 bit in length from P_i (assume S_L w.l.o.g.):
   (a) S_L sends the index i to S_R.
   (b) Both servers discard $[x_i]^B$.
   (c) Both servers set $n' \leftarrow n' - 1$
3. **Convert Shares:** S_L and S_R jointly evaluate $\mathsf{B2A}_{1,2^\lambda}(\{[x_i]_L^B, [x_i]_R^B\})$ on each of the n' valid pairs of Boolean shares. S_L receives as output $\{[x_i]_L^A\}_i$ and S_R receives as output $\{[x_i]_R^A\}_i$.
4. **Aggregate:** S_L locally adds all arithmetic shares into an accumulator A_L, initially zero. That is: $A_L \longleftarrow A_L + \sum_i [x_i]_L^A$. S_R analogously accumulates its arithmetic shares into $A_R \longleftarrow A_R + \sum_i [x_i]_R^A$.
5. **Publish:** Once all n' shares have been accumulated, S_L and S_R publish A_L and A_R to every client.
6. **Client Computation:** Clients output $A_L + A_R$.

This minor modification of the simple scheme guarantees both privacy and robustness without any heavy client-side computation. It easily generalizes to summing λ-bit integers, by sharing data in the λ-bit Boolean scheme. This protocol for computing the sum is sufficient for computing the arithmetic mean as well as long as servers reveal the number of inputs included in the sum. In addition, Prio [4] also computes a wide variety of aggregation functions, which Prio+ replicates as described below in Sect. 7.

7 Complex Statistics

Here we describe the statistics which Prio+ computes. For each statistic, we describe the encoding which enables its computation. That is, the encoding of x_i (written $\mathsf{en}(x_i)$) such that the statistic f we wish to compute is given by $f(x_1, \ldots, x_n) = \sum_i \mathsf{en}(x_i)$ (or some locally computable function of this sum). These encodings are referred to as "affine aggregatable encodings," or AFEs. Note that we use the same AFEs as in the original Prio paper [4], these are not novel to our construction. We omit a detailed discussion of AFEs and instead refer readers to [4] for more information. We also include formal protocols for computing AND. Formal protocols for most remaining statistics can be found in the full paper [1].

Each client P_i holds input x_i from some secret-space $\mathcal{D}$ which will be encoded as $\mathsf{en}(x_i)$. They wish to compute $f(x_1, \ldots, x_n)$ using servers S_L, S_R. The servers must verify that $\mathsf{en}(x_i)$ is a proper encoding of some $x_i \in \mathcal{D}$, sum the encodings, and return them to clients for reconstruction of the value $f(x_1, \ldots, x_n)$. For each statistic f, we give the domain $\mathcal{D}$ of the input x_i (also referred to as the "secret-space"), the necessary encoding, and a brief intuition of why this encoding is sufficient and how the servers will use it to compute f.

$\mathsf{SUM}(x_1, \ldots, x_n) = \sum_{i=1}^{n} x_i$
$\mathsf{MEAN}(x_1, \ldots, x_n) = \frac{1}{n} \cdot \mathsf{SUM}(x_1, \ldots, x_n)$
Secret-Space: $\mathcal{D} = \mathbf{Z}_{2^\lambda}$
Encoding: $\mathsf{en_{int}}(x_i) = x_i$
Intuition: Clients submit their data secret-shared via the λ-bit Boolean scheme. Servers use B2A to convert valid λ-bit Boolean shares to arithmetic shares of the same secret x_i in $\mathbf{Z}_M$ for $M > n$ and then locally sum the resulting arithmetic shares. In order to compute the mean, we allow the servers to modestly leak the number of players $n - c$ whose valid shares are included in the aggregate. Then clients can locally compute the mean. Note: this means our integer mean protocol achieves only $\hat{f}$-privacy, where $\hat{f}$ leaks $n - c$.

$\mathsf{AND}(x_1, \ldots, x_n) = 1 \iff \forall i, x_i = 1$
$\mathsf{OR}(x_1, \ldots, x_n) = 0 \iff \forall i, x_i = 0$
Secret Space: $\mathcal{D} = \{0, 1\}$
Encoding: $\mathsf{en_{and}}(x_i) = (1 - x_i)\vec{r} \in \mathbf{F}_2^\lambda$ for some parameter λ and random $\vec{r} \in \mathbf{F}_2^\lambda$. That is, if $x_i = 1$, $\mathsf{en_{and}}(x_i) = \vec{0}$, and if $x_i = 0$, $\mathsf{en_{and}}(x_i) = \vec{r}$.
$\mathsf{en_{or}}(x_i) = x_i \cdot \vec{r} \in \mathbf{F}_2^\lambda$ for some parameter λ and random $\vec{r} \in \mathbf{F}_2^\lambda$. That is, if $x_i = 0, \mathsf{en_{or}}(x_i) = \vec{0}$, and if $x_i = 1, \mathsf{en_{or}}(x_i) = \vec{r}$.

Intuition: Here, share conversion is unnecessary because the aggregation operator and the reconstruction operator for the Boolean secret-sharing scheme are both XOR. Thus, servers can simply locally XOR their valid shares and publish these aggregated values to clients, who will then XOR the aggregated values together to produce the output. When computing AND, if every client has $x_i = 1$, then every $\mathsf{en}(x_i) = \vec{0}$, and so the XOR of these encodings will certainly be $\vec{0}$. In this case, clients can conclude $\mathsf{AND}(x_1, \ldots, x_n) = 1$. Otherwise, if some client has $x_i = 0$, then $\mathsf{en}(x_i) = \vec{r}$ and the XOR of the encodings will be non-zero with probability $1 - \frac{1}{2^\lambda}$. In this case, they conclude that $\mathsf{AND}(x_1, \ldots, x_n) = 0$. The argument is analogous in the case of OR.

$\mathsf{MAX}(x_1, \ldots, x_n) = \max_i x_i$
$\mathsf{MIN}(x_1, \ldots, x_n) = \min_i x_i$
Secret Space: $\mathcal{D} = \{0, \ldots, M\}$ for small $M \in \mathbf{Z}$
Encoding: $\mathsf{en_{max}}(i) = (\vec{r}_1, \ldots, \vec{r}_i, \vec{0}, \ldots, \vec{0}) \in \mathbf{F}_2^{\lambda \times M}$, for random $\vec{r}_j \in \mathbf{F}_2^\lambda$. This is equivalent to applying the $\mathsf{en_{or}}()$ function to each component of the vector $(1, \ldots, 1, 0, \ldots, 0) \in \mathbf{F}_2^M$ where the first i components are 1.
Intuition: To compute the maximum, servers run the OR protocol M times in parallel on each component of the encoded input. That is, they analogously XOR their shares locally, and return them to clients to XOR and reconstruct the output. The clients parse this $(\lambda \times M)$-bit string in λ-bit chunks, reading

each chunk as a 0 if and only if every bit of that chunk is 0. The clients compute the largest index k for which the corresponding OR protocol gave output 1, and conclude the maximum is k. That is, they compute the largest value k such that the k'th substring of λ consecutive bits contains a 1. This is certainly bounded above by the maximum, and the probability that it undershoots the maximum by Δ is $\frac{1}{2^{\lambda \times \Delta}}$, which is negligible in the security parameter λ.

To compute the minimum, clients first represent their input x_i as $\chi_i = M - x_i$, and compute the maximum of these χ_i values, $y_i = \mathsf{MAX}(\chi_1, \ldots, \chi_n)$, as above. The desired minimum will be precisely $\mathsf{MIN}(x_1, \ldots, x_n) = M - y_i$, with the same error bounds as the MAX protocol.

$\mathsf{VAR}(x_1, \ldots, x_n) = \frac{1}{n} \sum_{i=1}^{n} (x_i - \mathsf{MEAN}(x_1, \ldots, x_n))^2$
$\mathsf{STDDEV}(x_1, \ldots, x_n) = \sqrt{\mathsf{VAR}(x_1, \ldots, x_n)}$
Secret Space: $\mathcal{D} = \mathbf{Z}_{2^\lambda}$
Encoding: $\mathsf{en}_{\mathsf{var}}(x_i) = (x_i, x_i^2)$
Intuition: Servers parse the encoded input into its two parts and compute shares of $(\sum_i x_i, \sum_i x_i^2)$ using two parallel instances of our protocol for SUM, which they return to clients. The clients divide these values by n, which is a public parameter, to compute $\mathbf{E}[X]$ and $\mathbf{E}[X^2]$, where X is a random variable taking on each value x_i with equal probability. From this, clients can locally compute $\mathsf{VAR}(x_1, \ldots, x_n) = \mathbf{E}[X^2] - (\mathbf{E}[X])^2$. Note: in the case where clients may misbehave, this protocol is only $\hat{f}$-private, where $\hat{f}$ leaks $\mathbf{E}[X]$ and the remaining number of behaving players n' in addition to the output. Clients who wish to compute the standard deviation simply add a local square root operation to the end of the protocol.

$\mathsf{linReg}((x_1, y_1), \ldots, (x_n, y_n)) = (c_0, c_1)$, where $\hat{y}(x) = c_0 + c_1 x$ is the line which minimizes the sum of squares loss $\sum_i (y_i - \hat{y}(x_i))^2$.
Secret Space: $\mathcal{D} = \mathbf{Z}_{2^\lambda} \times \mathbf{Z}_{2^\lambda}$
Encoding: $\mathsf{en}_{\mathsf{reg}}(x_i, y_i) = (x_i, x_i^2, y_i, x_i y_i)$
Intuition: Analogously to VAR, servers compute the sum of the various parts of the encoding in parallel and return shares of $(\sum_i x_i, \sum_i x_i^2, \sum_i y_i, \sum_i x_i y_i)$ to all clients. The clients can solve for the desired real regression coefficients c_0 and c_1 locally using the following linear system:

$$\begin{pmatrix} n & \sum x_i \\ \sum x_i & \sum x_i^2 \end{pmatrix} \cdot \begin{pmatrix} c_0 \\ c_1 \end{pmatrix} = \begin{pmatrix} \sum y_i \\ \sum x_i y_i \end{pmatrix} \tag{1}$$

Note that again, in the case of misbehaving clients, this implies servers must also reveal the number of aggregated values n', introducing a modest leakage. Thus this protocol will also be $\hat{f}$-private, where $\hat{f}$ leaks n' in addition to the output. This technique trivially generalizes to d-dimensional client inputs $(x^{(0)}, x^{(1)}, \ldots, x^{(d)})$ for $d > 2$ as described by [4].

$\mathsf{FRQ}(x_1, \ldots, x_n) = \vec{h} = (f_1, \ldots, f_k) \in \mathbf{Z}_{n+1}^k$, where $f_j = |\{x_i : x_i = j\}| \leq n$ is the frequency of input $j \in \mathbf{Z}_k$

Secret Space: $\mathcal{D} = \{0, \ldots, k-1\}$ for small $k \in \mathbf{Z}$
Encoding: $\mathsf{en_{frq}}(x_i) = (\delta_{x_i}) \in \mathbf{Z}_{2^k}$, where the x_i'th component of (δ_{x_i}) is 1 and all other components are 0. That is, (δ_{x_i}) is an impulse at x_i.
Intuition: If all players behave, taking the sum of these encodings yields the desired vector $\vec{h}$. Thus, servers evaluate k independent instances of B2A on each vector (one for each component) and then locally sum the resulting vectors of arithmetic shares. They then publish these aggregated vectors to clients who add them together to get $\vec{h}$ in the same manner as our SUM protocol.

The above details how the servers can efficiently and privately compute these desired statistics. For validation, Boolean Shares provide quick length validation, as the length of the secret cannot be greater than the length of a share, so servers simply expect shares of the right length and discard any others. This is sufficient for SUM, AND, and MAX, and used in linReg, Var, and FRQ. For linReg and Var, servers must verify multiplicative relationships among different parts of the secret-shared encoded inputs, done using SNIPs similarly to [4] described in Sect. 2. For FRQ, servers can efficiently validate that the vector is an impulse with a single 1, with details in the full paper [1].

Below, we provide the formal protocol for computing AND. It is the simplest type of protocol, requiring no share conversion or SNIPs, and is the most efficient type of protocol in Prio+. bitSum is an example of a protocol requiring share conversion but no SNIPs in Prio+, and Var is an example of a protocol requiring both. Full descriptions and detailed breakdowns of all protocols can be found in the full paper [1].

Π_{and}

Inputs: $x_i \in \{0,1\}$ for $i \in [n]$.
Output: 1 if and only if $x_i = 1$ for all $i \in \{1, \ldots, n\}$.

1. **Upload:** Each P_i encodes their as input as:
   $\hat{x}_i = 0 \in \mathbf{Z}_{2^\lambda}$ if $x_i = 1$
   $\hat{x}_i = r \in \mathbf{Z}_{2^\lambda}$ if $x_i = 0$, where r is uniformly random
   P_i then computes $\mathsf{Share}_{\oplus,\lambda}(\hat{x}_i) = ([\hat{x}_i]^B_{L,\lambda}, [\hat{x}_i]^B_{R,\lambda})$ as in Definition 2 and sends one share to each server.
2. **Verify Bit-Length:** Initially, $n' = n$. If some server, say S_L, receives from P_i $[x_i]^B_{L,\lambda}$ which is an λ'-bit integer, $\lambda' \neq \lambda$:
   (a) S_L sends the index i to S_R.
   (b) Both servers discard $[x_i]^B_\lambda$ (removing from accumulator if necessary).
   (c) Both servers set $n' \leftarrow n' - 1$
3. **Aggregate:** S_L and S_R hold accumulator values $A_L, A_R \in \mathbf{Z}_{2^\lambda}$, initially set to 0. Once a λ-bit share is sent to S_L by P_i, S_L *immediately* XORs it with A_L: $A_L \leftarrow A_L \oplus [\hat{x}_i]_L$. S_R does the same with its accumulator A_R upon receiving a valid share. If either server learns that a share already accumulated should be discarded, they simply XOR it with their accumulator again.
4. **Publish:** S_L publishes A_L to all clients, S_R publishes A_R to all clients.
5. **Client Computation:** Clients compute $A = A_L \oplus A_R \in \mathbf{Z}_{2^\lambda}$. If $A = 0$, clients output 1. Otherwise, they output 0.

8 Share Conversion

The core of the semi-honest share conversion is to efficiently convert Boolean shares of a single bit $[b]^B$ to arithmetic shares $[b]^A$, i.e. $b = [b]_L^B \oplus [b]_R^B = [b]_L^A + [b]_R^A$ for secret bit b. Then for an arbitrary λ-bit value x shared using Boolean shares, we can convert the shares to arithmetic in parallel and combine them. Namely, given $[x]^B = ([x_0]^B, \ldots, [x_{\lambda-1}]^B)$ where $x_i \in \{0, 1\}$ is the ith bit of x, we have $[x]^A = \sum_{i=0}^{\lambda-1} 2^i [x_i]^A$, noting that $x = \sum_{i=0}^{\lambda-1} 2^i([x_i]_L^B \oplus [x_i]_R^B) = \sum_{i=0}^{\lambda-1} 2^i([x_i]_L^A + [x_i]_R^A)$. This means that converting a λ-bit Boolean share requires L parallel conversions of a single bit, which requires the same number of rounds. This fact is used by both the OT-based protocol of [8], and the daBit based protocol here in Prio+. Recall that the OT-based protocol of [8] uses OT in the online phase to accomplish the same goal of semi-honest Boolean to arithmetic share conversion.

A daBit is merely a shared correlated pair $([b]^B, [b]^A)$ for some random bit b, where the Boolean share is a single bit, and each server has one share of $[b]^B$ and one share of $[b]^A$. To convert some single bit Boolean share $[x_i]^B$ to $[x_i]^A$, the servers compute their respective shares of $[x_i]^B \oplus [b]^B$ and swap them to get $v = x_i \oplus b$ in the clear. Then, they locally compute $[x_i]_L^A = v + [b]_L^A - 2v[b]_L^A$ and $[x_i]_R^A = [b]_R^A - 2v[b]_R^A$. This requires communication of only a single Boolean value v. If both players behave honestly, we get $[x_i]_L^A + [x_i]_R^A = v + b - 2vb = v \oplus b$ since v and b are single bits, and $v \oplus b = x_i$ by definition of v. To convert a λ-bit integer x, servers convert each bit x_i in parallel and then locally compute $[x]^A = \sum_{i=0}^{\lambda-1} 2^i [x_i]^A \pmod p$ to get arithmetic shares of x. Because we are working in the semi-honest case, as these are used only by the semi-honest servers, this is more efficient than in [23], where they needed to use an arithmetic Beaver triple to generate each daBit in the malicious setting.

The servers are able to generate each daBit in parallel offline using a single OT each. To convert a single bit, the daBit B2A share conversion only needs to communicate a single bit in the online phase (and consume a daBit), while OT share conversion in [8] requires an online OT (OT where inputs depend on client data). Hence, our daBits share conversion is much faster in the online phase. End to end, daBits B2A requires an OT to generate a daBit in the offline phase to precompute the correlated daBit, so end-to-end daBit share conversion including the offline phase only requires a single bit more than the OT protocol in [8]. Formal protocols for daBit generation and share conversion are given below.

$\mathsf{daBitGen}_p$

Inputs: one OT
Output: A random daBit $([b]^A, [b]^B)$ per server.

1. **Sample** Both servers $i \in \{L, R\}$ samples a random bit $b_i \in \{0, 1\}$. S_L also samples a random integer x mod p.
2. **Use OT**
   - S_L acts as the OT sender, sending $(x, x + b_L)$. S_L also sets $y_L = -x \pmod p$.

  - S_R acts as the OT receiver, using b_R as the choice bit. S_R receives $y_R = x + b_L b_R \pmod p$)
3. **Compute**
   (a) Both servers set $[b]_i^A = b_i - 2y_i \pmod p$.
   (b) They also set $[b]_i^B = b_i$.
4. **Output** Server S_i outputs $([b]_i^A, [b]_i^B)$.

$\mathsf{B2A}_p$

Inputs: Boolean shares of a single bit $[x]_L^B, [x]_R^B \in \mathbf{Z}_2$. A single dabit $([b]^A, [b]^B)$
Output: Arithmetic shares of the same bit $[x]_L^A, [x]_R^A \in \mathbf{Z}_p$.

1. **Compute** $v = x \oplus b$
   (a) Both servers $i \in \{L, R\}$ compute $[v]_i^B = [x]_i^B \oplus [v]_i^B$.
   (b) Servers send their share $[v]_i^B$ to each other.
   (c) Servers now have $v = x \oplus b = [v]_L^B \oplus [v]_R^B$ in the clear.
2. **Convert**
   (a) Both servers locally compute $[x]_i^A = v + [b]_i^B - 2v[b]_i^B \pmod p$.
   (b) Since v is in the clear, specifically server λ computes $[x]_L^A = v + [b]_L^B - 2v[b]_L^B \pmod p$, and server R computes $[x]_R^A = [b]_R^B - 2v[b]_R^B \pmod p$.
3. **Output** Server S_i outputs $[x]_i^A$.

9 Security

Here we briefly describe the security properties of Prio+, deferring formal statements and proofs of security to the full version of the paper [1]. Let $0 \leq c^* \leq n$ be the number of corrupted clients who submit invalid input shares. For every protocol, up to n malicious players colluding with one semi-honest server learn nothing but the output except with negligible probability. Clients may learn a modest leakage in some cases based on the specific AFE construction. E.g., to compute MEAN servers must reveal the number of players $n - c^*$ whose inputs were included in the aggregate. Servers must also give this value when computing linReg. Due to the AFE construction for VAR, the output necessarily leaks the expected value in addition to the variance. All of these modest leakages are analogous to the results of [4]. All protocols are robust against malicious clients.

10 Practical Evaluation

We implemented our scheme in 10,000 lines of C/C++. We utilized the libOTe toolkit [22] for OT and silent OT-extension. Silent OT is a variant of OT which we use to speed up our offline pre-computation phase. Our scheme uses semi-honest OTs, since our servers are assumed to be semi-honest. Our implementation supports secure computation of SUM, AND, OR, MAX, MIN, VAR, STDDEV, FRQ and linReg. Two implementations of the original Prio protocol exist which we benchmarked against: the original implementation Prio (Go), written in Go, supports secure computation of SUM, AND, OR, MAX, MIN, and linReg. Since the original paper's publication, another implementation Prio (Mozilla) was written by Mozilla in C. The Mozilla implementation only supports SUM.

We provide comparison data for three statistics: SUM, MAX, and linReg. These represent our three categories of protocols: SUM requires share conversion but no SNIPs, MAX requires neither share conversion nor SNIPs, and linReg requires both share conversion and SNIPs. We collected four types of data for comparison: client encode time (microseconds per client), client message size (bytes per client per server), server compute time (microseconds per server per client), and server communication (bytes per server per client). Most metrics are linear in the total number of clients, and so we ran multiple trials with 10k, 50k, and 100k clients and then averaged the result. The one exception is server compute time for linReg, which increases sub-linearly with number of clients, in which case we used a constant 50k clients for each trial. In our end-to-end implementation we used the exact same servers as the original Prio paper, two c4.2x large AWS servers. All protocols were implemented using just two servers located in the us-east-1f zone as to mimic a low-latency, high bandwidth connection. The client code was run from a separate instance of the same c4.2x large AWS server, and all client data was randomly generated. All three implementations (Go, Mozilla, Prio+) use this same 2-server setup. For some measurements, particularly client encode times, measurements were gathered for a large batch of clients and then averaged to get encode time per client. Since Prio+ has such fast encode time, we chose to represent these times in microseconds rather than milliseconds, simply for ease of comparison with Prio. The original measurements were made in milliseconds, ensuring stability of the resulting data. For more comparison charts, see the full paper [1].

10.1 Data: SUM

For SUM, we compared Prio+ to both Prio implementations. We ran four separate experiments with clients holding 1-bit, 8-bit, 16-bit, and 32-bit integers. We also measured end-to-end runtime of our system including the offline phase. In total, our Prio+ implementation computes the sum of 100,000 16-bit integers in 0.23 s. Also accounting for pre-computing the necessary 800,000 daBits, this becomes 0.63 s in total.

Analysis: Prio+ overwhelmingly outperforms Prio in terms of client encode time and client message size (Figs. 1 and 2). Prio+ also heavily outperforms Prio both in terms of server compute time and communication. Also including precomputation, end-to-end Prio+ servers still heavily outspeed Prio's online time. Prio+ has comparable end-to-end server communication to the online Prio (Mozilla) when summing single-bit integers, but as the size of the integers increases, Prio+ servers communicate more. End-to-end Prio+ servers communicate less than Prio (Go) servers except in the 32-bit case.

10.2 Data: MAX

Since Prio (Mozilla) does not support MAX, we compared Prio+ only to Prio (Go). Clients held integers in the range $[0, x]$ for $x \in \{16, 32, 64, 128\}$. In total, our Prio+ implementation computes the maximum of 100,000 4-bit integers in 5.25 s.

Analysis: Prio+ MAX requires no share conversion and no SNIPs, resulting in dramatic performance benefits for both clients and servers. Most relevant is a nearly 1,000x improvement in client encode time (Fig. 3). Without share conversion, we get an added benefit of sharply decreased server costs.

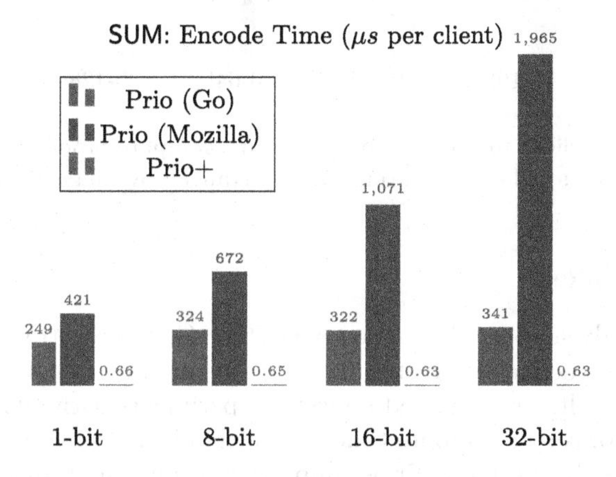

Fig. 1. Time necessary for a client to encode a private value, construct proof(s), and compute shares of the encoding and proof(s) when computing SUM (Prio+ has no proofs)).

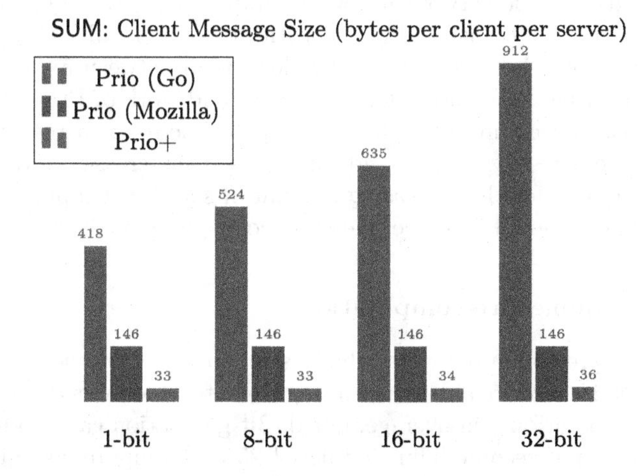

Fig. 2. Size of the message that P_i (holding private value x_i) sends to each server when executing a protocol to compute SUM$(x_1, \ldots, x_n)$. Data is arranged according to the number of bits in x_i.

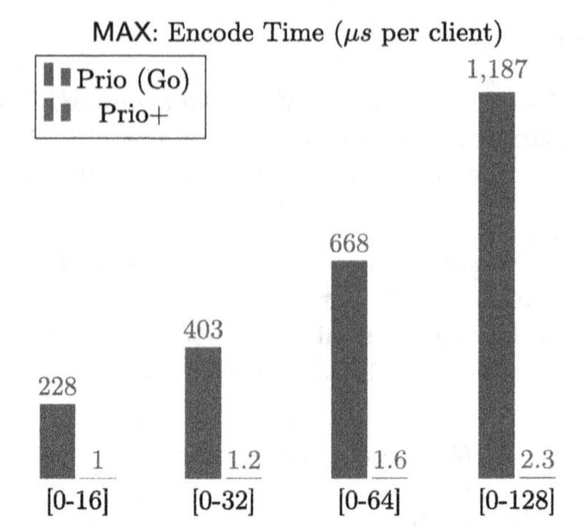

Fig. 3. Time for a client to encode a private value, compute proof(s), and secret-share the encoding/proof(s) when computing MAX. Arranged by range of client values.

10.3 Data: linReg

linReg is also only supported by Prio+ and Prio (Go). We performed four experiments in which the feature vectors held by clients are of degree 2, 4, 6, and 8 respectively. Results are averaged between experiments with 10k, 50k and 100k clients except for server compute time for which all experiments were performed with 50k clients. In total, our Prio+ implementation computes a line-of-best-fit over 100,000 ordered pairs of 8-bit integers in 7.41 s.

Analysis: Prio+ significantly reduces client costs to compute linReg, also significantly reduces online server time with comparable end-to-end time. Client encode time is up to 30x faster (Fig. 4), with up to 4x smaller client messages. Online server work is between 2.5x to 14x less, with between 5x and 10x fewer bytes communicated. Accounting for full end-to-end work of Prio+ to also generate daBits, the server runtime is between equal time to 7x faster, and between 1.7x to 20x more bytes to generate and run. As degree increases, additional share conversion is needed for the increasing amount of shares per input, while SNIPs take up the same amount of space, meaning costs go up as degree increases.

10.4 Data: Offline Pre-computation

Prio+ requires pre-computed data which is independent of client data. In our semi-honest setting, we are able to use a single OT to generate a daBit, leading to very efficient generation. On average, our daBit generation can produce around 4,000,000 daBits per second. Thus it takes 1.25 s to compute enough daBits to perform 8-bit degree 2 linear regression of 100,000 submissions.

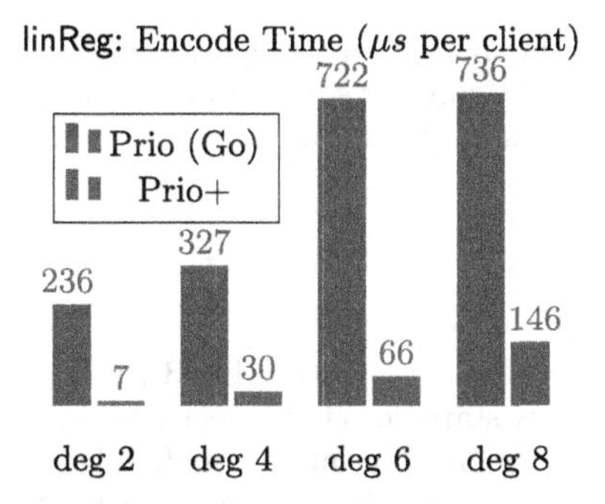

Fig. 4. Time for a client to encode a private value, compute proof(s), and secret-share the encoding and proof(s) when computing linReg. Each input is a degree d vector of 8-bit integers. Data arranged by degree d.

11 Conclusions and Future Work

Prio+ privately computes aggregate statistics with minimal burden on the client, often also reducing server costs. For SUM, client performance and server compute time dramatically improve with slightly increased server communication for large inputs. For MAX, Prio+ significantly reduces the burden on both clients and servers. Using precomputed daBits, Prio+ beats Prio in all examined metrics.

Prio+ requires an offline pre-computation phase, but this is relatively efficient and can be done during otherwise idle times. Even adding in the pre-computation timing for the dabits generation, Prio+ is still faster in all metrics, and requires slightly more server bandwith for large linReg inputs but still requires less for simpler inputs. We hope to expand Prio+ to compute additional aggregate statistics, especially those which require no SNIPs or share conversion.

Acknowledgments. Supported in part by DARPA under Cooperative Agreement HR0011-20-2-0025, NSF grant CNS-2001096, NSF NRT grant DGE-1829071, US-Israel BSF grant 2015782, Cisco Research Award, Google Faculty Award, JP Morgan Faculty Award, IBM Faculty Research Award, Xerox Faculty Research Award, OKAWA Foundation Research Award, B. John Garrick Foundation Award, Teradata Research Award, Lockheed-Martin Research Award and Sunday Group. The views and conclusions contained herein are those of the authors and should not be interpreted as necessarily representing the official policies, either expressed or implied, of DARPA, the Department of Defense, the U.S. Government, or the National Science Foundation. The U.S. Government is authorized to reproduce and distribute reprints for governmental purposes not withstanding any copyright annotation therein. Prepared in part for information purposes by the Artificial Intelligence Research group of JPMorgan Chase & Co and its affiliates ("JP Morgan"), and is not a product of the Research Department of JP Morgan. JP Morgan makes no representation and warranty whatsoever and disclaims all liability, for the completeness, accuracy or reliability of the information contained herein. This document is not intended as investment research or investment advice, or a recommendation, offer or solicitation for the purchase or sale of any security, financial instrument, financial product or service, or to be used

References

1. Addanki, S., Garbe, K., Jaffe, E., Ostrovsky, R., Polychroniadou, A.: Prio+: privacy preserving aggregate statistics via Boolean shares. Cryptology ePrint Archive, Paper 2021/576 (2021). https://eprint.iacr.org/2021/576
2. Ben-Sasson, E., Fehr, S., Ostrovsky, R.: Near-linear unconditionally-secure multiparty computation with a dishonest minority. In: Safavi-Naini, R., Canetti, R. (eds.) CRYPTO 2012. LNCS, vol. 7417, pp. 663–680. Springer, Heidelberg (2012). https://doi.org/10.1007/978-3-642-32009-5_39
3. Boneh, D., Boyle, E., Corrigan-Gibbs, H., Gilboa, N., Ishai, Y.: Zero-knowledge proofs on secret-shared data via fully linear PCPs. Cryptology ePrint Archive, Report 2019/188 (2019). https://eprint.iacr.org/2019/188
4. Corrigan-Gibbs, H., Boneh, D.: Prio: private, robust, and scalable computation of aggregate statistics. In: 14th {USENIX} Symposium on Networked Systems Design and Implementation ({NSDI} 17), pp. 259–282 (2017). https://crypto.stanford.edu/prio/paper.pdf
5. Cramer, R., Damgård, I., Ishai, Y.: Share conversion, pseudorandom secret-sharing and applications to secure computation. In: Kilian, J. (ed.) TCC 2005. LNCS, vol. 3378, pp. 342–362. Springer, Heidelberg (2005). https://doi.org/10.1007/978-3-540-30576-7_19
6. Cramer, R., Shoup, V.: A practical public key cryptosystem provably secure against adaptive chosen ciphertext attack. In: Krawczyk, H. (ed.) CRYPTO 1998. LNCS, vol. 1462, pp. 13–25. Springer, Heidelberg (1998). https://doi.org/10.1007/BFb0055717
7. Danezis, G., Fournet, C., Kohlweiss, M., Zanella-Béguelin, S.: Smart meter aggregation via secret-sharing. In: Proceedings of the First ACM Workshop on Smart Energy Grid Security, SEGS 2013, pp. 75–80. Association for Computing Machinery, New York (2013). https://doi.org/10.1145/2516930.2516944
8. Demmler, D., Schneider, T., Zohner, M.: ABY-a framework for efficient mixed-protocol secure two-party computation. In: NDSS (2015)
9. Elahi, T., Danezis, G., Goldberg, I.: Privex: private collection of traffic statistics for anonymous communication networks. In: Proceedings of the 2014 ACM SIGSAC Conference on Computer and Communications Security, CCS 2014, pp. 1068–1079. Association for Computing Machinery, New York (2014). https://doi.org/10.1145/2660267.2660280
10. Emura, K., Kimura, H., Ohigashi, T., Suzuki, T., Chen, L.: Privacy-preserving aggregation of time-series data with public verifiability from simple assumptions and its implementations. Comput. J. **62**(4), 614–630 (2019). https://doi.org/10.1093/comjnl/bxy135
11. Erlingsson, Ú., Korolova, A., Pihur, V.: RAPPOR: randomized aggregatable privacy-preserving ordinal response. CoRR abs/1407.6981 (2014). http://arxiv.org/abs/1407.6981
12. Escudero, D., Ghosh, S., Keller, M., Rachuri, R., Scholl, P.: Improved primitives for MPC over mixed arithmetic-binary circuits. Cryptology ePrint Archive, Paper 2020/338 (2020). https://eprint.iacr.org/2020/338

13. Fanti, G.C., Pihur, V., Erlingsson, Ú.: Building a RAPPOR with the unknown: privacy-preserving learning of associations and data dictionaries. CoRR abs/1503.01214 (2015). http://arxiv.org/abs/1503.01214
14. Glanz, J., Larson, J., Lehren, A.W.: Spy agencies tap data streaming from phone apps. New York Times (2014)
15. Hilts, A., Parsons, C., Knockel, J.: Every step you fake: a comparative analysis of fitness tracker privacy and security. Open Effect Rep. **76**(24), 31–33 (2016)
16. Jeske, T.: Floating car data from smartphones: what google and waze know about you and how hackers can control traffic. In: Proceedings of the BlackHat Europe, pp. 1–12 (2013)
17. Joye, M., Libert, B.: A scalable scheme for privacy-preserving aggregation of time-series data. In: Sadeghi, A.-R. (ed.) FC 2013. LNCS, vol. 7859, pp. 111–125. Springer, Heidelberg (2013). https://doi.org/10.1007/978-3-642-39884-1_10
18. Keller, J., Lai, K., Perlroth, N.: How many times has your personal information been exposed to hackers. New York Times, 29 July 2015 (2015)
19. Melis, L., Danezis, G., Cristofaro, E.D.: Efficient private statistics with succinct sketches. CoRR abs/1508.06110 (2015). http://arxiv.org/abs/1508.06110
20. Popa, R.A., Balakrishnan, H.: VPriv: protecting privacy in location-based vehicular services. In: 18th USENIX Security Symposium (USENIX Security 2009). USENIX Association, Montreal (2009). https://www.usenix.org/conference/usenixsecurity09/technical-sessions/presentation/vpriv-protecting-privacy-location-based
21. Popa, R.A., Blumberg, A.J., Balakrishnan, H., Li, F.H.: Privacy and accountability for location-based aggregate statistics. In: Proceedings of the 18th ACM Conference on Computer and Communications Security, CCS 2011, pp. 653–666. Association for Computing Machinery, USA (2011). https://doi.org/10.1145/2046707.2046781
22. Rindal, P.: libOTe: an efficient, portable, and easy to use Oblivious Transfer Library. https://github.com/osu-crypto/libOTe
23. Rotaru, D., Wood, T.: Marbled circuits: mixing arithmetic and Boolean circuits with active security. Cryptology ePrint Archive, Report 2019/207 (2019). https://ia.cr/2019/207
24. Shoup, V.: OAEP reconsidered. In: Kilian, J. (ed.) CRYPTO 2001. LNCS, vol. 2139, pp. 239–259. Springer, Heidelberg (2001). https://doi.org/10.1007/3-540-44647-8_15
25. Shoup, V.: A proposal for an ISO standard for public key encryption. IACR Cryptology ePrint Archive 2001, 112 (2001)
26. Smith, B.: Uber executive suggests digging up dirt on journalists. BuzzFeed News 18 (2014)
27. Wang, G., Wang, B., Wang, T., Nika, A., Zheng, H., Zhao, B.Y.: Defending against sybil devices in crowdsourced mapping services. In: Proceedings of the 14th Annual International Conference on Mobile Systems, Applications, and Services, pp. 179–191 (2016)

Scooby: Improved Multi-party Homomorphic Secret Sharing Based on FHE

Ilaria Chillotti[1], Emmanuela Orsini[2], Peter Scholl[3], Nigel Paul Smart[1,2](✉), and Barry Van Leeuwen[2]

[1] Zama, Paris, France
ilaria.chillotti@zama.ai
[2] imec-COSIC, KU Leuven, Leuven, Belgium
{emmanuela.orsini,nigel.smart,barry.vanleeuwen}@kuleuven.be
[3] University of Aarhus, Aarhus, Denmark
peter.scholl@cs.au.dk

Abstract. We present new constructions of multi-party homomorphic secret sharing (HSS) based on a new primitive that we call *homomorphic encryption with decryption to shares* (HEDS). Our first construction, which we call Scooby, is based on many popular fully homomorphic encryption (FHE) schemes with a linear decryption property. Scooby achieves an n-party HSS for general circuits with complexity $O(|F| + \log n)$, as opposed to $O(n^2 \cdot |F|)$ for the prior best construction based on multi-key FHE. Scooby can be based on (ring)-LWE with a super-polynomial modulus-to-noise ratio. In our second construction, Scrappy, assuming any generic FHE plus HSS for NC1-circuits, we obtain a HEDS scheme which does not require a super-polynomial modulus. While these schemes all require FHE, in another instantiation, Shaggy, we show how in some cases it is possible to obtain multi-party HSS without FHE, for a small number of parties and constant-degree polynomials. Finally, we show that our Scooby scheme can be adapted to use multi-key fully homomorphic encryption, giving more efficient spooky encryption and setup-free HSS. This latter scheme, Casper, if concretely instantiated with a B/FV-style multi-key FHE scheme, for functions F which do not require bootstrapping, gives an HSS complexity of $O(n \cdot |F| + n^2 \cdot \log n)$.

1 Introduction

One of the more interesting cryptographic constructions to be developed in recent years has been homomorphic secret sharing (HSS). This concept, which can be seen as a distributed analogue of homomorphic encryption, was introduced in [6], where a two party construction for branching programs was presented based on the decisional Diffie-Hellman assumption. The idea of HSS starts from the concept of a (traditional) secret sharing scheme, where an input x to some function is split into n shares, $(\mathbf{x}_1, \ldots, \mathbf{x}_n)$. This sharing, that in this work we always assume to be a full threshold sharing, is created via an algorithm

C. Galdi and S. Jarecki (Eds.): SCN 2022, LNCS 13409, pp. 540–563, 2022.
https://doi.org/10.1007/978-3-031-14791-3_24

$(\mathbf{x}_1, \ldots, \mathbf{x}_n) \leftarrow \mathsf{Share}^{\mathsf{HSS}}(x)$. An HSS scheme has two additional algorithms, the first $y_i \leftarrow \mathsf{Eval}^{\mathsf{HSS}}(F; \mathbf{x}_i)$ takes a function description F and a share $\mathbf{x}_i$ and produces a corresponding output share y_i. The second $\mathsf{Rec}^{\mathsf{HSS}}(y_1, \ldots, y_n)$ takes the output shares and reconstructs the result $F(x)$. To avoid trivial solutions one requires that the length of the y_j's should be *compact*, i.e. it only depends on the output length of the function F and the security parameter. An important class of HSS schemes are those with *additive reconstruction*, where the function $\mathsf{Rec}^{\mathsf{HSS}}$ simply computes $y_1 + \ldots + y_n$. We refer to these as *additive HSS schemes.* It is such additive HSS schemes that we focus on in this work.

Motivation for HSS. The main application of HSS is towards secure two-party or multi-party computation with succinct communication. Indeed, the breakthrough work of [6] showed that for a large class of circuits, it's possible to achieve secure computation with sublinear communication in the circuit size under DDH, which was previously only known using fully homomorphic encryption. Since then, HSS has proven useful in various other applications, and is closely related to pseudorandom correlation generators [3] and pseudorandom correlation functions [4], which allow generation of correlated randomness with a minimal amount of interaction. HSS for simple classes of functions, particularly the case of distributed point functions [21], has also proven useful for applications including private information retrieval [7] and secure RAM computation [17]. On a more theoretical side, HSS has also been used to build 2-round secure computation and nearly optimal worst-case to average-case reductions [8].

Additive reconstruction is an important feature of HSS in many secure computation settings, where it may be desirable for the output shares to be re-used in another secure computation based on secret sharing. This is the case, for instance, when using HSS to generate preprocessing material for multi-party computation protocols in the dishonest majority setting [3]. It can also be a useful feature in scenarios where a client reconstructing the output is constrained to perform only lightweight computations.

Current State of HSS and Related Primitives. Related to HSS is the dual concept of function secret sharing (FSS) [5,7]. In FSS, the shared data is a secret function F (from some publicly known class of functions), such that the parties can locally obtain secret shares of $F(x)$, for any public input x. For general function classes such as polynomially-sized circuits, function secret sharing and homomorphic secret sharing are equivalent.

Obtaining efficient n-party HSS and FSS is complex for general functions. The most efficient known scheme is that based on an LWE-construction from spooky encryption. Spooky encryption, introduced by Dodis et al. [16], is a rather complex construction based on a multi-key variant of FHE [15,23], and for our purposes we are only interested in *additive-function-sharing* spooky encryption (or AFS-spooky encryption). Spooky encryption is a semantically secure public-key encryption scheme consisting of the usual three algorithms $(\mathsf{KeyGen}^{\mathsf{Spooky}}, \mathsf{Enc}^{\mathsf{Spooky}}_{\mathsf{pk}}, \mathsf{Dec}^{\mathsf{Spooky}}_{\mathsf{sk}})$ as well as an additional algorithm $\mathsf{Eval}^{\mathsf{Spooky}}_{\mathsf{pk}_1,\ldots,\mathsf{pk}_n}(F, \mathsf{ct}_1, \ldots, \mathsf{ct}_n)$. The $\mathsf{Eval}^{\mathsf{Spooky}}$ algorithm, given a function F on n

arguments from a given class, and n ciphertexts ct_i, encrypting x_i under pk_i, produces n new ciphertexts $\mathsf{ct}'_1, \ldots, \mathsf{ct}'_n$ such that, computing $y_i \leftarrow \mathsf{Dec}^{\mathsf{Spooky}}_{\mathsf{sk}_i}(\mathsf{ct}_i)$, we have that $y_1 + \ldots + y_n = F(x_1, \ldots, x_n)$.

In [16], it is shown that it is possible to build FSS from AFS-spooky encryption. Roughly, to *share* an input function F the dealer first generates n AFS-spooky key pairs $(\mathsf{pk}_i, \mathsf{sk}_i) \leftarrow \mathsf{KeyGen}^{\mathsf{Spooky}}(1^\lambda)$. The dealer also generates an n-out-of-n description of the function F, i.e. functions $F_i(x)$ such that $F(x) = F_1(x) + \ldots + F_n(x)$. Finally, the function secret sharing of the input function F is defined to be the tuple $F_i = (\mathsf{sk}_i, \mathsf{pk}_1, \ldots, \mathsf{pk}_n, \mathsf{Enc}^{\mathsf{Spooky}}_{\mathsf{pk}_1}(F_1), \ldots, \mathsf{Enc}^{\mathsf{Spooky}}_{\mathsf{pk}_n}(F_n))$.

To define the FSS evaluation we create a function C_x which takes as input the n additive shares of a function F, and evaluates it on the input x, which is hard-coded into C_x. By applying

$$\mathsf{Eval}^{\mathsf{Spooky}}_{\mathsf{pk}_1,\ldots,\mathsf{pk}_n}\left(C_x, \mathsf{Enc}^{\mathsf{Spooky}}_{\mathsf{pk}_1}(F_1), \ldots, \mathsf{Enc}^{\mathsf{Spooky}}_{\mathsf{pk}_n}(F_n)\right),$$

we obtain ciphertexts $\mathsf{ct}'_1, \ldots, \mathsf{ct}'_n$, where ct'_i can be decrypted (using sk_i) to obtain y_i such that $y_1 + \ldots + y_n = F(x)$.

In [8], Boyle et al. showed how the FSS construction from spooky encryption can be modified to enable an additive HSS scheme. The $\mathsf{Share}^{\mathsf{HSS}}(x)$ operation additively shares x into $x = x_1 + \ldots + x_n$, generates n spooky key pairs $(\mathsf{pk}_1, \mathsf{sk}_1) \leftarrow \mathsf{KeyGen}^{\mathsf{Spooky}}(1^\lambda)$, and then encrypts x_i via $\mathsf{ct}_i \leftarrow \mathsf{Enc}^{\mathsf{Spooky}}_{\mathsf{pk}_i}(x_i)$. The share values $\mathbf{x}_i$ output by $\mathsf{Share}^{\mathsf{HSS}}(x)$ being $\mathbf{x}_i = (\{\mathsf{pk}_i\}_{i=1}^n, \{\mathsf{ct}_i\}_{i=1}^n, \mathsf{sk}_i)$. The $\mathsf{Eval}^{\mathsf{HSS}}(F, \mathbf{x}_i)$ function executes $\mathsf{Eval}^{\mathsf{Spooky}}_{\mathsf{pk}_1,\ldots,\mathsf{pk}_n}$ on the function F and the ciphertext $(\mathsf{ct}_1, \ldots, \mathsf{ct}_n)$ so as to obtain n ciphertexts $\mathsf{ct}'_1, \ldots, \mathsf{ct}'_n$. The output of $\mathsf{Eval}^{\mathsf{HSS}}(F, \mathbf{x}_i)$ then being $\mathsf{Dec}^{\mathsf{Spooky}}_{\mathsf{sk}_i}(\mathsf{ct}'_i)$.

Thus, there is a strong connection between HSS, FSS and spooky constructions, and, as mentioned above, the prior most efficient n-party HSS and FSS constructions for circuits arise from AFS-spooky based on LWE (and a circular security assumption). The best current construction for AFS-spooky encryption of Dodis et al. [16] has a complexity of $O(n^2 \cdot |F|)$. In particular, each gate of the underlying arithmetic circuit F requires a bootstrapping operation which in the multi-key FHE setting has complexity $O(n^2)$.

1.1 Our Contribution

We present new constructions of homomorphic secret sharing in the multi-party setting, supporting up to $n-1$ out of n corruptions. Our constructions improve upon the only previous general construction, based on AFS-spooky encryption [16], either by being more efficient, or in some cases, relying on different assumptions.

HSS from Homomorphic Encryption with Decryption Shares. We present our constructions as a new primitive called *homomorphic encryption with decryption to shares (HEDS)*, which can be seen as a homomorphic encryption scheme with a special decryption algorithm that (non-interactively) outputs an n-party secret share of the encrypted message. HEDS is closely related to both spooky encryption and homomorphic secret sharing (HSS): the major difference compared to spooky is that HEDS needs to set up private decryption keys under a common public key with either a trusted setup algorithm or a secure multiparty computation protocol, while the difference with HSS is that the homomorphic evaluation algorithm is public. As is the case for spooky, HEDS immediately implies additive HSS for the same class of functions.

Scooby Construction: HEDS from Linear Decryption FHE. We show that HEDS can be built using any FHE scheme with a special decryption property, which we call *linear decryption based fully homomorphic encryption* (LD-based FHE) schemes. Examples of such LD-based FHE schemes are LWE-based constructions like BGV [11], BFV [18], GSW [20] and TFHE [13,14]. Notice this special property of almost all FHE schemes, where the decryption function is a linear function of the secret key, has been exploited previously, including for HSS in the two-party setting [9,16] and other applications [10,19].

Any of these schemes can be used to instantiate our Scooby construction, giving additive HSS for circuits. Recall in AFS-spooky the key generation is run independently by the n-parties, in our variation the keys are instead generated by a trusted third party.[1]

Since this construction only requires single-key FHE and not multi-key FHE, we obtain n-party HSS that is simpler and more efficient than the AFS-spooky-based construction. In particular, the computational complexity grows as $O(|F|+\log n)$, whereas AFS-spooky has complexity $O(n^2 \cdot |F|)$ for n parties. In addition, when instantiated with BGV we show that the standard parameter sets for bootstrapping are sufficient for our construction.

At a high level, at the core of Scooby is a well-known 2-party distributed decryption procedure, which non-interactively decrypts an LWE-based ciphertext into two shares, assuming the ciphertext modulus has super-polynomial size. This trick has been used previously, including in the construction of AFS-spooky. Our main contribution is to bootstrap this 2-party non-interactive algorithm into an n-party non-interactive algorithm. We do this by placing the n parties on the leaves of a binary tree, and then homomorphically evaluating the two party protocol at each internal node of the tree. Each party only needs to evaluate the 2-party protocol at each node on the path from the root to its leaf. Each homomorphic evaluation at the internal nodes is exactly equivalent to a bootstrapping operation, namely a homomorphic evaluation of the decryption circuit for some key. Thus, decryption into shares costs $O(\log n)$ operations per party.

Removing the Super-polynomial Modulus. The problem with Scooby, as well as all LWE-based additive HSS schemes, is that we require a super-polynomial modulus-to-noise ratio in the underlying LD-based FHE scheme.

[1] In some sense the "spooky" behaviour exhibited by spooky encryption cannot really be explained, whereas our "spooky" behaviour can be explained by the setup procedure. This setup procedure in some sense acts like the janitor in Scooby-Doo, who has set up the spooky goings-on.

This is a stronger form of LWE assumption that usually requires larger parameters to compensate. We give a variant of the construction where we only need standard FHE, together with an HSS scheme for NC1 circuits. Using recent constructions of HSS [1,25,27] based on either Paillier encryption or class groups, we obtain the first additive HSS schemes for circuits that do not require LWE with a super-polynomial modulus. The complexity of the HSS is also $O(|F| + \log n)$, however, it is likely to be less efficient in practice than Scooby. We call this construction Scrappy. We summarize our results in Table 1.

Table 1. Summary of n-party HSS Constructions. All FHE-based constructions allow arbitrary functions F, and assume circular security to avoid blow-up in the key sizes (this assumption can be removed by relaxing to bounded-depth circuits). The asymptotic complexities ignore potential factors in λ that are independent of n and F.

Construction	Assumptions	Setup	Complexity
DHRW [16] (AFS-Spooky)	LWE with super-polynomial modulus	Uniform CRS	$O(n^2 \cdot \|F\|)$
Scooby: §5 (HEDS)	LD-based FHE with super-polynomial modulus	Trusted	$O(\|F\| + \log n)$
Scrappy: §6.1 (HEDS)	Generic FHE + 2-party HSS for NC1	Trusted	$O(\|F\| + \log n)$
Shaggy: §6.2 (HEDS)	2-party HSS for NC1	Trusted	$O(\|F\|)$ ($n = 4$, constant-deg F)
Casper: (Full Version) (AFS-Spooky)	Specific MK-FHE with super-polynomial modulus	Uniform CRS	$O(n \cdot \|F\| + n^2 \cdot \log n)$ or $O(n^2 \cdot \|F\| + n^2 \cdot \log n)$

Avoiding FHE Entirely. We also show that in certain cases, we can obtain multi-party HSS without using any form of FHE whatsoever. We do this through a variant of the previous construction, where we bootstrap a HEDS scheme to handle more parties by homomorphically evaluating its own decryption circuit. This transformation is more challenging to apply without resorting to FHE, and we are only able to obtain a 4-party HEDS scheme for constant-degree polynomials, based on Paillier encryption. Nevertheless, as far as we are aware, this is the first instance of $>$ 2-party, dishonest majority HSS for constant-degree polynomials, without relying on FHE. We call this construction Shaggy.

Spooky from HEDS. In addition, in the full version, we show how our Scooby scheme can be adapted to give a true AFS-spooky encryption, i.e. with no trusted setup and independent keys, if we base our construction on *specific* multi-key FHE (MK-FHE). This instantiation can have a simpler complexity than that given in [16], in particular, assuming the function F can be evaluated without bootstrapping, our complexity is $O(n \cdot |F| + n^2 \cdot \log n)$. If F requires a bootstrapping for all the operations, it is $O(n^2 \cdot |F| + n^2 \cdot \log n)$. We call this construction Casper.

In the full version we give two variants of Casper, based on two different underlying FHE schemes. We note that being MK-FHE schemes, the construction will be less efficient than our Scooby scheme, which works over most (practical) FHE schemes. It is interesting to note that the spooky construction from [16] also goes via MK-FHE. In particular, they make use of the MK-FHE scheme of [15,23].

The route though is more complex than our tree-based construction, leading to an increased complexity.

2 Preliminaries

For a set S, we denote by $a \leftarrow S$ the process of drawing a from S with a uniform distribution on the set S. If D is a probability distribution, we denote by $a \leftarrow D$ the process of drawing a with the given probability distribution. For a probabilistic algorithm A, we denote by $a \leftarrow A$ the process of assigning a the output of algorithm A; with the underlying probability distribution being determined by the random coins of A.

All reductions modulo an integer p will be assumed to be centered, i.e. in the interval $(-p/2, \ldots, p/2)$.

We let $R = \mathbb{Z}[X]/(X^N + 1)$ and R_p denote the localisation of R at p, i.e. $(\mathbb{Z}/p\mathbb{Z})[X]/(X^N + 1)$. For a real interval I we let R_I denote the restriction of the *set* R to have coefficients in the support of I. Thus as sets (but not as rings) we have $R_q = R_{(-q/2,\ldots,q/2)}$.

2.1 Homomorphic Secret Sharing

The following definition of public-key HSS is adapted from [9]. Note that, as we are only interested in schemes with additive reconstruction, we can disregard the decoding algorithm, $\mathsf{Dec}^{\mathsf{HSS}}_{\mathsf{sk}}$, that is given in the more general definition of HSS [8]. Concretely, in additive HSS the decoding algorithm simply adds up all the shares.

Definition 2.1 (Additive Public Key Homomorphic Secret Sharing). *An n-party, public-key* homomorphic secret sharing (HSS) *scheme for a class of functions $\mathcal{F}$ over a ring $\mathcal{R}$ with input space $\mathcal{I} \subseteq R$ consists of PPT algorithms* $(\mathsf{KeyGen}^{\mathsf{HSS}}, \mathsf{Share}^{\mathsf{HSS}}_{\mathsf{pk}}, \mathsf{Eval}^{\mathsf{HSS}}_{\mathsf{pk}})$ *with the following syntax:*

- $\mathsf{KeyGen}^{\mathsf{HSS}}(1^\lambda, n) \to (\mathsf{pk}, (\mathsf{ek}_1, \ldots, \mathsf{ek}_n))$*: Given a security parameter 1^λ, the setup algorithm outputs a public key* pk *and n evaluation keys* $(\mathsf{ek}_1, \ldots, \mathsf{ek}_n)$.
- $\mathsf{Share}^{\mathsf{HSS}}_{\mathsf{pk}}(\mathsf{pk}, x) \to (\mathbf{x}_1, \ldots, \mathbf{x}_n)$*: Given public key* pk *and private input value $x \in \mathcal{I}$, the share algorithm outputs shares $(\mathbf{x}_1, \ldots, \mathbf{x}_n)$.*
- $\mathsf{Eval}^{\mathsf{HSS}}_{\mathsf{pk}}(F; \mathbf{x}_i, \mathsf{ek}_i) \to y_i$*: On input a function $F \in \mathcal{F}$, the parties share $\mathbf{x}_i$, and it's evaluation key* ek_i*, the homomorphic evaluation algorithm outputs $y_i \in R$, which is party i's share of an output $y \in R$.*

This definition is in the multi-input setting, meaning that it supports a compact evaluation of a function F on shares of inputs $x^{(1)}, \ldots, x^{(\rho)}$ given by ρ parties that are usually referred to as *clients*. More concretely, each client inputs $x^{(i)}$ to the Share algorithm which returns shares $\mathbf{x}_j^{(i)}, j \in [n]$, to n parties (the *servers*). Each server can then locally run Eval on input $(\mathbf{x}_j^{(1)}, \ldots, \mathbf{x}_j^{(\rho)})$ obtaining a share y_j such that $F(x^{(1)}, \ldots, x^{(\rho)}) = \sum_{j \in [n]} y_j$. Note that the $\mathsf{KeyGen}^{\mathsf{HSS}}$

algorithm cannot be run by any single party, so can be seen as a form of correlated randomness generated by a trusted dealer. We describe the required security properties for the algorithms (KeyGen, Share, Eval) according to this more general formulation.

Security Experiment $\mathsf{Exp}^{\mathsf{HSS,sec}}_{\mathcal{A},j}(\lambda)$

Let $I \subset [n]$ be the set of corrupt servers.

1. $(\mathsf{pk}, (\mathsf{ek}_1, \ldots, \mathsf{ek}_n)) \leftarrow \mathsf{KeyGen}^{\mathsf{HSS}}(1^\lambda)$.
2. $(x_0, x_1, \mathsf{state}) \leftarrow \mathcal{A}(1^\lambda)$.
3. $b \leftarrow \{0, 1\}$.
4. $(\mathbf{x}_{b,1}, \ldots, \mathbf{x}_{b,n}) \leftarrow \mathsf{Share}^{\mathsf{HSS}}_{\mathsf{pk}}(\mathsf{pk}, x_b)$.
5. $b' \leftarrow \mathcal{A}(\mathsf{state}, \mathsf{pk}, \{\mathsf{ek}_j, \mathbf{x}_{b,j}\}_{j \in I})$.
6. Return $b' = b$.

Fig. 1. Security Experiment $\mathsf{Exp}^{\mathsf{HSS,sec}}_{\mathcal{A},j}(\lambda)$

Definition 2.2 (HSS (Statistical) Correctness). *We say that an n-party public-key HSS scheme* $(\mathsf{KeyGen}^{\mathsf{HSS}}, \mathsf{Share}^{\mathsf{HSS}}_{\mathsf{pk}}, \mathsf{Eval}^{\mathsf{HSS}}_{\mathsf{pk}})$ *is correct for a class of functions* $\mathcal{F}$ *if, for all security parameters* $\lambda \in \mathbb{N}$*, for all functions* $F \in \mathcal{F}$*, for all* $x^{(1)}, \ldots, x^{(\rho)} \in \mathcal{I}$ *(where* $\mathcal{I}$ *is the input space of* F*), for all* $(\mathsf{pk}, \mathsf{ek}_1, \ldots, \mathsf{ek}_n) \leftarrow \mathsf{KeyGen}^{\mathsf{HSS}}(1^\lambda)$ *and for all* $(\mathbf{x}^{(i)}_1, \ldots, \mathbf{x}^{(i)}_n) \leftarrow \mathsf{Share}^{\mathsf{HSS}}_{\mathsf{pk}}(\mathsf{pk}, x^{(i)}), i \in [\rho]$*, we have*

$$\Pr\left[y_1 + \cdots + y_n = F(x^{(1)}, \ldots, x^{(\rho)})\right] \geq 1 - \mathsf{negl}(\lambda),$$

where

$$y_j \leftarrow \mathsf{Eval}^{\mathsf{HSS}}_{\mathsf{pk}}(F; (\mathbf{x}^{(1)}_j, \ldots, \mathbf{x}^{(\rho)}_j), \mathsf{ek}_j),\ j \in [n],$$

where the probability is taken over the random coins of $\mathsf{KeyGen}^{\mathsf{HSS}}$, $\mathsf{Share}^{\mathsf{HSS}}_{\mathsf{pk}}$ *and* $\mathsf{Eval}^{\mathsf{HSS}}_{\mathsf{pk}}$.

Definition 2.3 (HSS Security). *Let* I *be the set of corrupt servers. For each* $j \in I$ *and non-uniform adversary* $\mathcal{A}$ *(of size polynomial in the security parameter* λ*), it holds that*

$$\left|\Pr[\mathsf{Exp}^{\mathsf{HSS,sec}}_{\mathcal{A},j}(\lambda) = 1]\right| \leq \frac{1}{2} + \mathsf{negl}(\lambda),$$

where $\mathsf{Exp}^{\mathsf{HSS,sec}}_{\mathcal{A},j}(\lambda)$ *is the experiment defined in Fig. 1.*

Remark 2.1 (Private-key HSS). HSS can also be defined in the single-input, private key setting, which is weaker than the public-key flavour above. Here, there is no KeyGen algorithm, and Share is run only once on all inputs together, so can be seen as a trusted dealer algorithm that distributes the shares.

2.2 Spooky Encryption

"Spooky" encryption is a type of public key encryption scheme which exhibits a form of limited malleability, so called "spooky action at a distance" [16]. The particular form of spooky encryption we will use is so called *additive-function-sharing* spooky encryption (or AFS-spooky encryption). We present a definition which works for any finite ring $\mathcal{R}$, and arithmetic circuit C, and not just for the case of $\mathbb{F}_2$ as originally presented.

Definition 2.4 (AFS-spooky Encryption). *An* AFS-spooky *encryption scheme, over a finite field* $\mathbb{F}_p$*, is a public-key encryption scheme given by a tuple of four algorithms* ($\mathsf{KeyGen}^{\mathsf{Spooky}}, \mathsf{Enc}^{\mathsf{Spooky}}_{\mathsf{pk}}, \mathsf{Dec}^{\mathsf{Spooky}}_{\mathsf{sk}}, \mathsf{Eval}^{\mathsf{Spooky}}_{\mathsf{pk}_1,\dots,\mathsf{pk}_n}$) *with the following syntax:*

- $\mathsf{KeyGen}^{\mathsf{Spooky}}(1^\lambda)$*: This is a probabilistic polynomial time algorithm which on input of a security parameter* λ *outputs a public/private key pair* $(\mathsf{pk}, \mathsf{sk})$.
- $\mathsf{Enc}^{\mathsf{Spooky}}_{\mathsf{pk}}(m)$*: This probabilistic polynomial time algorithm takes a message* $m \in \mathcal{R}$ *and generates a ciphertext* ct *encrypting that message under the public key* pk.
- $\mathsf{Dec}^{\mathsf{Spooky}}_{\mathsf{sk}}(\mathsf{ct})$*: Given a ciphertext* ct *encrypted under the public key associated to* sk*, this algorithm produces the underlying plaintext.*
- $\mathsf{Eval}^{\mathsf{Spooky}}_{\mathsf{pk}_1,\dots,\mathsf{pk}_n}(C, \mathsf{ct}_1, \dots, \mathsf{ct}_n)$*: Given an arithmetic circuit description* $C : \mathcal{R}^n \longrightarrow \mathcal{R}$*,* n *public keys* $\mathsf{pk}_1, \dots, \mathsf{pk}_n$*, and* n *of ciphertexts* $\mathsf{ct}_1, \dots, \mathsf{ct}_n$*, this produces* n *ciphertexts* $\mathsf{ct}'_1, \dots, \mathsf{ct}'_n$

An AFS-spooky encryption scheme must be correct, as an encryption scheme, i.e. we must have

$$\forall (\mathsf{pk}, \mathsf{sk}) \leftarrow \mathsf{KeyGen}^{\mathsf{Spooky}}(1^\lambda),\ \forall m \in \mathcal{R} \ :\ \mathsf{Dec}^{\mathsf{Spooky}}_{\mathsf{sk}}(\ \mathsf{Enc}^{\mathsf{Spooky}}_{\mathsf{pk}}(m)\ ) = m.$$

It must also be IND-CPA as an encryption scheme and satisfy the following form of limited malleability called AFS-spooky correctness.

Definition 2.5 (AFS-spooky Correctness). *There exists a negligible function* ν *such that for all* $\lambda \in \mathbb{N}$*, every arithmetic circuit* C *computing a* n*-argument function* $f : \mathcal{R}^n \longrightarrow \mathcal{R}$*, and all inputs* $x_1, \dots, x_n$ *of* C*, we have*

$$\Pr\left[\sum_{i \in [n]} y_i = C(x_1, \dots, x_n) : \begin{array}{c} \forall i \in [n], (\mathsf{pk}_i, \mathsf{sk}_i) \leftarrow \mathsf{KeyGen}^{\mathsf{Spooky}}(1^\lambda), \\ \forall i \in [n], \mathsf{ct}_i \leftarrow \mathsf{Enc}^{\mathsf{Spooky}}_{\mathsf{pk}}(x_i), \\ (\mathsf{ct}'_1, \dots, \mathsf{ct}'_n) \leftarrow \mathsf{Eval}^{\mathsf{Spooky}}_{\mathsf{pk}_1,\dots,\mathsf{pk}_n}(C, \mathsf{ct}_1, \dots, \mathsf{ct}_n), \\ \forall i \in [n], y_i \leftarrow \mathsf{Dec}^{\mathsf{Spooky}}_{\mathsf{sk}_i}(\mathsf{ct}'_i) \end{array}\right] \geq 1 - \nu(\lambda)$$

In [16], it is shown how to construct an AFS-spooky encryption scheme in the CRS model using an LWE-based multi-key FHE [15,23] and assuming a circular security assumption. The common reference string (output by a separate generation algorithm), necessary in the multi-key FHE construction, is assumed as input to the key generation algorithm, and correctness and security hold for all outputs of the common reference string generator.

In their work, Dodis et al. [16] show that AFS-spooky encryption implies FSS for general circuit; in [8], Boyle et al. show that AFS-spooky also enables HSS for multiple inputs; in fact, it implies HSS without any setup, where the key generation algorithm is simply run locally by each client providing input.

3 Homomorphic Encryption with Decryption to Shares (HEDS)

In this section we formally introduce the notion of a scheme which implements Homomorphic Encryption with Decryption to Shares (HEDS) and relate it with other concepts described in previous sections. Loosely speaking, a HEDS encryption scheme is similar to public-key HSS, except with a public evaluation algorithm that outputs a ciphertext, more akin to evaluation in homomorphic encryption. The ciphertext is then convert into shares in the decryption algorithm, which uses one party's private key. In addition, similarly to HSS, but unlike in spooky encryption, the parties need to engage in a protocol, or assume a trusted third party, to set up the associated public and secret keys. Thus the action from the outside seems spooky, but this can be explained away as an effect of the setup protocol.

We start by giving the definition of HEDS, and then we show that it enables both homomorphic and function secret sharing.

Definition 3.1 (HEDS Encryption). *A* HEDS encryption scheme *for a class of functions $\mathcal{F} : \mathcal{R}^* \rightarrow \mathcal{R}$, over a ring $\mathcal{R}$, is given by a tuple of PPT algorithms* $(\mathsf{SetUp}^{\mathsf{HEDS}}, \mathsf{Enc}^{\mathsf{HEDS}}_{\mathsf{pk}}, \mathsf{Dec}^{\mathsf{HEDS}}_{\mathsf{sk}}, \mathsf{Eval}^{\mathsf{HEDS}}_{\mathsf{pk}})$*, with the following syntax:*

- $\mathsf{SetUp}^{\mathsf{HEDS}}(1^\lambda, n)$*: This randomized algorithm takes as input a security parameter λ, a number of parties n. It outputs the tuple* $(\mathsf{pk}, \mathsf{sk}_1, \ldots, \mathsf{sk}_n)$.
- $\mathsf{Enc}^{\mathsf{HEDS}}_{\mathsf{pk}}(m)$*: This takes as input the public key and a message $m \in \mathcal{R}$, and outputs a ciphertext* ct.
- $\mathsf{Dec}^{\mathsf{HEDS}}_{\mathsf{sk}_i}(\mathsf{ct})$*: Given a ciphertext* ct *encrypted under the public key this outputs a value y_i for each $i \in [n]$.*
- $\mathsf{Eval}^{\mathsf{HEDS}}_{\mathsf{pk}}(C, (\mathsf{ct}_1, \ldots, \mathsf{ct}_\rho))$*: On input of the public key* pk*, a set of n ciphertexts, and an arithmetic circuit description $C : \mathcal{R}^\rho \longrightarrow \mathcal{R}$ of a function from the specified class, this produces a ciphertext* ct.

The algorithms $\left(\mathsf{SetUp}^{\mathsf{HEDS}}, \mathsf{Enc}^{\mathsf{HEDS}}_{\mathsf{pk}}, \mathsf{Dec}^{\mathsf{HEDS}}_{\mathsf{sk}}, \mathsf{Eval}^{\mathsf{HEDS}}_{\mathsf{pk}}\right)$ should satisfy the following correctness and security requirements.

Definition 3.2 (HEDS Correctness). *There exists a negligible function ν such that for all $\lambda \in \mathbb{N}$, every arithmetic circuit C computing a ρ-argument function $f : \mathcal{R}^\rho \longrightarrow \mathcal{R}$ in $\mathcal{F}$, and all inputs $x_1, \ldots, x_\rho$ of C, we have*

$$\Pr\left[\sum_{i\in[n]} y_i = C(x_1, \ldots, x_\rho) : \begin{array}{l} (\mathsf{pk}, \mathsf{sk}_1, \ldots, \mathsf{sk}_n) \leftarrow \mathsf{SetUp}^{\mathsf{HEDS}}(1^\lambda, n), \\ \forall i \in [\rho], \mathsf{ct}_i \leftarrow \mathsf{Enc}^{\mathsf{HEDS}}_{\mathsf{pk}}(x_i), \\ \mathsf{ct} \leftarrow \mathsf{Eval}^{\mathsf{HEDS}}_{\mathsf{pk}}(C, (\mathsf{ct}_1, \ldots, \mathsf{ct}_\rho)), \\ \forall i \in [n], y_i \leftarrow \mathsf{Dec}^{\mathsf{HEDS}}_{\mathsf{sk}_i}(\mathsf{ct}) \end{array}\right] \geq 1 - \nu(\lambda).$$

Definition 3.3 (HEDS Security). *For all subsets $A \subset [n]$ of size $< n$, and all probabilistic polynomial time adversaries $(\mathcal{A}_1, \mathcal{A}_2)$ we have*

$$\Pr\left[b = b' : \begin{array}{l} (\mathsf{pk}, \mathsf{sk}_1, \ldots, \mathsf{sk}_n) \leftarrow \mathsf{SetUp}^{\mathsf{HEDS}}(1^\lambda, n), b \in \{0,1\}, \\ (m_0, m_1, \mathsf{state}) \leftarrow \mathcal{A}_1(\mathsf{pk}, \{\mathsf{sk}_i\}_{i\in A}), \\ \mathsf{ct} \leftarrow \mathsf{Enc}^{\mathsf{HEDS}}_{\mathsf{pk}}(m_b), \\ b' \leftarrow \mathcal{A}_2(\mathsf{ct}, \mathsf{state}) \end{array}\right] \leq \mathsf{negl}(\lambda),$$

i.e. the encryption scheme is IND-CPA, even when up to $n-1$ secret keys are given to the adversary.

Compactness. Just as with fully homomorphic encryption, we say that HEDS is *compact* if the share decryption algorithm is independent of the evaluated function.

3.1 Multi-input HSS from HEDS Encryption

Here we relate HEDS encryption and HSS showing that HEDS encryption implies HSS with multiple inputs. Let $\mathcal{P}$ be a set of n servers and $\mathcal{C}$ be a set of m clients. Let C be a circuit representing a function $F : \mathcal{R}^m \to \mathcal{R}$ in a class function $\mathcal{F}$. To build an HSS-scheme, we need to define three algorithms $\mathsf{KeyGen}^{\mathsf{HSS}}$, $\mathsf{Share}^{\mathsf{HSS}}$, $\mathsf{Eval}^{\mathsf{HSS}}$ as in Definition 2.1. Let $(\mathsf{SetUp}^{\mathsf{HEDS}}, \mathsf{Enc}^{\mathsf{HEDS}}_{\mathsf{pk}}, \mathsf{Dec}^{\mathsf{HEDS}}_{\mathsf{sk}}, \mathsf{Eval}^{\mathsf{HEDS}}_{\mathsf{pk}})$ be a HEDS encryption scheme for $\mathcal{F}$, as defined in the previous section, we proceed as follows.

- $\mathsf{KeyGen}^{\mathsf{HSS}}(1^\lambda, n)$:
  1. Run $(\mathsf{pk}, \mathsf{sk}_1, \ldots, \mathsf{sk}_n) \leftarrow \mathsf{SetUp}^{\mathsf{HEDS}}(1^\lambda, n)$
  2. For each $i \in [n]$, set $\mathsf{ek}_i := \mathsf{sk}_i$
  3. Return pk and $(\mathsf{ek}_1, \ldots, \mathsf{ek}_n)$
- $\mathsf{Share}^{\mathsf{HSS}}_{\mathsf{pk}}(x^{(j)})$: Each client $P_j \in \mathcal{P}$, on input $x^{(j)}$ performs the following steps. We recall that the goal is to obtain shares $(\mathbf{x}_1, \ldots, \mathbf{x}_n)$ of $(x^1, \ldots, x^m)$.
  1. For $i \in [n]$ and $j \in [m]$, generate $x_i^{(j)}$ such that $x^{(j)} = x_1^{(j)} + \ldots + x_n^{(j)}$.
  2. For each $x_i^{(j)}$, compute $\mathsf{ct}_i^{(j)} = \mathsf{Enc}^{\mathsf{HEDS}}_{\mathsf{pk}}(x_i^{(j)})$.
  3. Set $\mathbf{x}_i = \{\mathsf{ct}_i^{(j)}\}_{j \in [m]}$, for $i \in [n]$.
- $\mathsf{Eval}^{\mathsf{HSS}}_{\mathsf{pk}}(F; \mathbf{x}_i, \mathsf{ek}_i)$: Given a function $F : \mathcal{R}^m \to \mathcal{R}$, each server $i \in [n]$ computes circuit description C of F and proceeds as follows.
  1. Compute $\mathsf{ct}_i = \mathsf{Eval}^{\mathsf{HEDS}}_{\mathsf{pk}}\left(C, (\mathsf{ct}_i^{(1)}, \ldots, \mathsf{ct}_i^{(m)})\right)$
  2. Compute $y_i = \mathsf{Dec}^{\mathsf{HEDS}}_{\mathsf{ek}_i}(\mathsf{ct}_i)$

By Definition 3.2, we know that the evaluation algorithm outputs to the servers the shares $y_1, \ldots, y_n$ such that $\sum_{i \in [n]} y_i = y = F(x^{(1)}, \ldots, x^{(m)})$.

Proposition 3.1. *Assuming the existence of a HEDS encryption scheme for a class of functions $\mathcal{F}$, there exists a public-key multi-input HSS scheme for $\mathcal{F}$.*

Proof. Correctness follows by inspection of the scheme described above and by correctness of the underlying HEDS construction. Security also follows from the security of HEDS. □

In the other direction, we observe that a public-key HSS scheme implies HEDS for the same class of functions, however, the resulting HEDS scheme may not be compact. This is because the HSS evaluation algorithm will have to be carried out in the HEDS decryption step, since HSS uses a private key for evaluation.

4 Linear-Decryption Based FHE

Our main constructions are based on a form of FHE which comes from LWE-style systems. We abstract much of the details of the specific construction away in what follows, for example the specific key generation and encryption algorithms. This allows us to capture schemes as diverse as BGV [11], BFV [18], GSW [20] and TFHE [13,14]. These schemes all have the same form of decryption equation, namely one based on a linear inner product combination of the ciphertext with the secret key, modulo the ciphertext modulus. The result of this inner product is then processed to produce the plaintext (which is an element of R_p for some prime p) in one of two distinct ways, depending on whether the message is embedded at the top of the range modulo q (as in FV), or the bottom of the range modulo q (as in BGV). We refer to these two types of decryption as FHE as being of type msb and type lsb respectively. We call the whole class of such FHE systems Linear Decryption based, or LD-based FHE. Similar definitions have been considered previously [9,10,19].

Let sec denote some statistical security parameter and λ denote a computational security parameter. We define such a scheme as follows, the precise encryption and evaluation algorithms are not important for our discussion.

Definition 4.1 (LD-based FHE). *An* LD-based FHE *scheme is given by a tuple of algorithms* $(\mathsf{KeyGen}^{\mathsf{FHE}}, \mathsf{Enc}^{\mathsf{FHE}}_{\mathsf{pk}}, \mathsf{Dec}^{\mathsf{FHE}}_{\mathsf{sk}}, \mathsf{Eval}^{\mathsf{FHE}}_{\mathsf{pk}})$, *as follows:*

- $\mathsf{KeyGen}^{\mathsf{FHE}}(1^\lambda, p)$: *This randomized algorithm takes as input the security parameter* λ *and a plaintext modulus space* p. *It outputs a tuple* $(q, N, B, d, \Delta, S, \mathsf{pk}, \mathsf{sk})$. *The value* q *will correspond to the ciphertext modulus*[2], *the value* N *will be the LWE-ring dimension (which for convenience we assume is a power of two), the value* B *will be a "noise bound", the value* d *is one less than the dimension of the ciphertext space, the value* Δ *is set to be* $\lfloor q/p \rfloor$, *the value* S *is a bound on the secret key size* S, *and* pk *(resp.* sk*) will be the public (resp. private) keys.*
  The private key $\mathsf{sk} = (s_1, \ldots, s_d)$ *is assumed to be a random element in* R_q^d *sampled such that* $\|\mathsf{sk}\|_\infty \leq S$. *Note, this is not necessarily sampled uniformly at random subject to this constraint.*
  All subsequent algorithms are assumed to take the tuple (N, q, d, B, Δ) *implicitly as input parameters.*
- $\mathsf{Enc}^{\mathsf{FHE}}_{\mathsf{pk}}(m, \mathsf{type})$: *On input of* $m \in R_p$ *this will output a ciphertext* $\mathsf{ct} \in R_q^{d+1}$ *such that*

$$\mathsf{ct} \cdot (1, -\mathsf{sk}) = \begin{cases} m + p \cdot \epsilon \pmod{q} & \textit{If } \mathsf{type} = \mathsf{lsb}, \\ \Delta \cdot m + \epsilon \pmod{q} & \textit{If } \mathsf{type} = \mathsf{msb}. \end{cases}$$

  A ciphertext such that $\|\epsilon\|_\infty \leq B$ *will be called* valid. *The encryption algorithm produces such a valid ciphertext. The precise algorithm use for encryp-*

[2] In practice there may be many ciphertext moduli depending on which level a ciphertext is sitting at, at a high level this can be ignored. Although it can be important in practice.

tion will depend on the public key, and the specific scheme. All that concerns us is the form of the ciphertext.

- $\mathsf{Eval}^{\mathsf{FHE}}_{\mathsf{pk}}(F(x_1, \ldots, x_\ell), \{\mathsf{ct}_1, \ldots, \mathsf{ct}_\ell\})$: *On input of ℓ valid ciphertexts ct_i and an arithmetic function $F(x_1, \ldots, x_\ell)$ this function will homomorphically evaluate the function F over the ciphertexts, producing a valid ciphertext as output.*
- $\mathsf{Dec}^{\mathsf{FHE}}_{\mathsf{sk}}(\mathsf{ct})$: *On input of a valid ciphertext and a secret key this will compute the message as*

$$m = \begin{cases} (\mathsf{ct} \cdot (1, -\mathsf{sk}) \pmod{q}) \pmod{p} & \text{If } \mathsf{type} = \mathsf{lsb}, \\ \left\lfloor (\mathsf{ct} \cdot (1, -\mathsf{sk}) \pmod{q}) \cdot p/q \right\rceil & \text{If } \mathsf{type} = \mathsf{msb}. \end{cases}$$

The correctness requirement simply says that $\mathsf{Eval}^{\mathsf{FHE}}$, when given ℓ valid ciphertexts, outputs a valid encryption of the correct result. The security requirement is the standard notion of IND-CPA security.

For example: In the case of the BGV scheme [11] from ring-LWE we will have that $\mathsf{ct} = (c_0, c_1)$, so that decryption is given by $\mathsf{ct} \cdot (1, -\mathsf{sk}) = c_0 - s_1 \cdot c_1$, and, hence, for this scheme we have $n = 1$ and $\mathsf{sk} = s_1$. The BFV scheme [18] has the same structure, the main difference being that BFV uses the msb decryption, while BGV uses lsb.

In the case of Ring-GSW, a ciphertext is in $R_q^{(d+1)\times(d+1)\ell}$, with $d = 1$ and $\mathsf{sk} = s_1$. In practice it is composed by $2 \cdot \ell$ FV-like ciphertext (i.e., with the message encrypted in the msb). To decrypt a Ring-GSW ciphertext, we only decrypt one of these ciphertexts: the others contain redundant information. Another way of seeing a Ring-GSW ciphertext, is with a very sparse secret key $\mathsf{sk} = (\mathsf{sk}_1, \ldots, \mathsf{sk}_{2\ell})$, where all the keys corresponding to the FV-like ciphertext that we are not going to decrypt are set to zero. The TFHE scheme [13,14] uses a combination of FV-like ciphertexts (with message encrypted in the msb, called LWE and RLWE ciphertexts) and Ring-GSW ones.

Parameters for Decryption to Shares. For such LD-based FHE schemes we have a special form of non-interactive two party distributed decryption, which we shall now outline in the lsb and the msb cases. We will require the parameters are selected so that

$$q > 2 \cdot p \cdot (B + 1) \cdot 2^{\mathsf{sec}}, \tag{1}$$

where sec is the statistical security parameter. This two-party distributed decryption, which is essentially the same technique as in [9,16], will form the basis of our first multi-party HEDS construction in Sect. 5.

4.1 Two-Party Distributed Decryption: Type lsb

Suppose sk is split into two keys sk_1 and sk_2 with $\mathsf{sk} = \mathsf{sk}_1 + \mathsf{sk}_2 \pmod{q}$, with sk_1 held by party P_1 and sk_2 held by party P_2. Now we can, without interaction, given a valid ciphertext ct encrypting a message m, compute an additive sharing of $m = m_1 + m_2 \pmod{p}$ between P_1 and P_2 as follows. We require that the parties have agreed upon a public random value for each decryption, but later will remove this using a PRF.

2-party DistDec^{lsb}: Let $R \leftarrow \mathbb{Z}_q$ be a public random nonce.

1. P_1 computes $d_1 \leftarrow \mathsf{ct} \cdot (1, -\mathsf{sk}_1) + R \pmod{q}$ and then $m_1 \leftarrow d_1 \pmod{p}$.
2. P_2 computes $d_2 \leftarrow \mathsf{ct} \cdot (0, -\mathsf{sk}_2) - R \pmod{q}$ and then $m_2 \leftarrow d_2 \pmod{p}$.

We prove that this leads to a correct result with overwhelming probability.

Proposition 4.1. *Given an LD-based FHE scheme of type* msb *(Definition 4.1), where* $(q, N, B, d, \Delta, S, \mathsf{pk}, \mathsf{sk}) \leftarrow \mathsf{KeyGen}^{\mathsf{FHE}}(1^\lambda, p)$*, with* $q > 2 \cdot p \cdot (B+1) \cdot 2^{\mathsf{sec}}$ *and* $\mathsf{sk}_1 + \mathsf{sk}_2 = \mathsf{sk}$. *Let* (ct, m) *be a pair of ciphertext/plaintext messages and* m_1 *and* m_2 *values obtained with the 2-party distributed decryption procedure described above. Then, it holds that*

$$m = m_1 + m_2 \pmod{p},$$

with probability at least $1 - N \cdot 2^{\mathsf{sec}}$.

Proof. First we notice that

$$m = ((d_1 + d_2) \pmod{q}) \pmod{p},$$

and that we will always have $m = m_1 + m_2 \pmod{p}$ if the internal reduction modulo q in the decryption equation for m does not need to compensate for a wrap around. However, since we know ct is valid (i.e., $\mathsf{ct} \cdot (1, -\mathsf{sk}) = m + p \cdot \epsilon \pmod{q}$ with $\|\epsilon\|_\infty \leq B$) we also know that the coefficients of $d_1 + d_2 \pmod{q}$ will lie in the range $(-p \cdot (B+1), \ldots, p \cdot (B+1))$. Thus, the distributed decryption will potentially result in an error if and only if the coefficients of d_1 lie in one of the two ranges $(-q/2, -q/2+p \cdot (B+1))$ or $(q/2-p \cdot (B+1), q/2)$. Since each party added or subtracted the random R, it holds that d_1 is uniformly distributed in the range $(-q/2, \ldots, q/2)$. Therefore, the probability there is a wraparound in a single coefficient is bounded by $2 \cdot p \cdot (B+1)/q < 2^{-\mathsf{sec}}$. However, we also known that, if there is a wrap around, it will definitely result in an invalid distributed decryption, as the error only consists of the addition of a single value of $q \pmod{p} \neq 0$. Thus, a single coefficient will be correct with probability $1 - 2^{-\mathsf{sec}}$. To obtain a correct decryption we need all coefficients to be correct, which will happen with probability

$$\left(1 - 2^{-\mathsf{sec}}\right)^N \approx 1 - N \cdot 2^{-\mathsf{sec}}.$$

□

We report details on the two party distributed decryption for the type msb in the full version.

5 Scooby: Multi-party HEDS from LD-Based FHE

In this section we detail how to construct a HEDS encryption scheme for the underlying ring R_p, from generic LD-based FHE. We call our construction Scooby, as it is similar to a spooky encryption but with a trusted setup. To denote the specific nature of this construction we refer to $\mathsf{SetUp}^{\mathsf{Scooby}}$, $\mathsf{Enc}_{\mathsf{pk}}^{\mathsf{Scooby}}$, etc., instead of $\mathsf{SetUp}^{\mathsf{HEDS}}$, $\mathsf{Enc}_{\mathsf{pk}}^{\mathsf{HEDS}}$, etc.

At the core of Scooby is the 2-party distributed decryption procedure described in the previous section. We show that, assuming an LD-based FHE scheme, this directly yields a 2-party Scooby. We then show how to bootstrap the 2-party scheme to the multi-party setting.

5.1 HEDS Key Generation

First, we need to slightly modify the KeyGen algorithm for the underlying FHE scheme to take a "special" form that is common to all standard FHE constructions. More concretely, the algorithm $\mathsf{KeyGen}^{\mathsf{FHE}}(1^\lambda, p)$ proceeds as follows, using two sub-procedures ParamGen() and PubKeyGen():

1. $\mathsf{params} \leftarrow \mathsf{ParamGen}(1^\lambda, p)$: This algorithm takes as input a security parameter λ, a plaintext modulo p and produces the scheme parameters $\mathsf{params} = (q, N, B, d, \Delta, S)$.
2. $\mathsf{sk} \leftarrow R_q^n$ such that $\|\mathsf{sk}\|_\infty \leq S$.
3. $\mathsf{pk} \leftarrow \mathsf{PubKeyGen}(1^\lambda, \mathsf{sk}, \mathsf{params})$: This algorithm, on input the secret key and scheme parameters, samples and outputs an associated public key pk.

5.2 Security Assumption

In our construction, we generate an FHE public key based on a secret-key $\mathsf{sk} = \mathsf{sk}_0 + \mathsf{sk}_1$, where $\mathsf{sk}_0, \mathsf{sk}_1$ are both sampled uniformly with coefficients bounded by the parameter S. For security, we require that the scheme defined by $(\mathsf{pk}, \mathsf{sk})$ satisfies the standard IND-CPA security notion, even when the adversary is given one of the original secret keys sk_i. This is formalized as follows.

Definition 5.1 (Bounded secret key IND-CPA security). *Let* $\mathsf{FHE} = (\mathsf{KeyGen}^{\mathsf{FHE}}, \mathsf{Enc}_{\mathsf{pk}}^{\mathsf{FHE}}, \mathsf{Dec}_{\mathsf{sk}}^{\mathsf{FHE}}, \mathsf{Eval}_{\mathsf{pk}}^{\mathsf{FHE}})$ *be a linear decryption-based FHE scheme, where* $\mathsf{KeyGen}^{\mathsf{FHE}}$ *is split into two sub-routines* ParamGen, PubKeyGen *as above.*

We require that for $(q, N, B, d, \Delta, S) \leftarrow \mathsf{ParamGen}(1^\lambda, p)$, *and* $\mathsf{sk}_0, \mathsf{sk}_1 \leftarrow R_q^d$ *with* $\|\mathsf{sk}_i\| \leq S$, $\mathsf{sk} = \mathsf{sk}_0 + \mathsf{sk}_1$ *and* $\mathsf{pk} \leftarrow \mathsf{PubKeyGen}(\mathsf{sk})$, *it holds that for any PPT algorithm* $\mathcal{A}$, *for any* $\sigma \in \{0, 1\}$, *messages* m_0, m_1 *and bit* $b \leftarrow \{0, 1\}$:

$$\Pr[\mathcal{A}(1^\lambda, \mathsf{pk}, \mathsf{sk}_\sigma, \mathsf{Enc}_{\mathsf{pk}}^{\mathsf{FHE}}(m_b)) = b] \leq 1/2 + \mathsf{negl}(\lambda).$$

It is straightforward to verify that, given a linear decryption-based FHE scheme that satisfies the bounded secret-key IND-CPA security, we obtain a 2-party Scooby encryption scheme using the prior algorithms for 2-party distributed decryption into shares described in the previous section. Indeed, this

2-party distributed decryption forms the basis of the 2-party spooky construction in [16] and HSS construction in [9]. However, to obtain an n-party generalization is not immediate. A direct application of the trick used for 2-party to, say, 3-parties results in decryption errors due to unaccounted for wrap-arounds in the reduction modulo q of the local decryption. Coping with these wrap-arounds, without resorting to interaction, thus seems a challenge. A challenge which we solve in the next section.

5.3 From 2-party to n-party HEDS

Here we give the details of our construction Scooby, for n-party HEDS. The encryption and evaluation algorithms of Scooby are identical to that of the underlying linear decryption FHE scheme, so here we only describe the setup and share decryption procedures. We give two different variants of the construction, depending on whether the FHE scheme encodes the message in the lsb or msb of the ciphertext. In this section, we focus on a linear decryption FHE scheme that encodes the message in the lsb of the ciphertext; in the full version, we give a variant for the msb type.

Scooby Setup. Recall that the setup algorithm in HEDS takes as input a security parameter and outputs a global public key pk, as well as secret keys $\mathsf{sk}_1, \ldots, \mathsf{sk}_n$ to each of the n parties. For Scooby, in both the lsb and msb variants of LD-based FHE scheme, the underlying $\mathsf{SetUp}^{\mathsf{Scooby}}$ algorithm is the same. Note that in the following, the $\mathsf{SetUp}^{\mathsf{Scooby}}$ algorithm should be seen as a trusted setup procedure that is either run by a trusted third party, or executed via an MPC protocol, which can be done, for instance, based on the techniques from [26].

The $\mathsf{SetUp}^{\mathsf{Scooby}}$ algorithm is described in Fig. 2. Recall that the main challenge is to setup up some key material which allows n parties to convert an FHE ciphertext into shares of the message, while using the 2-party distributed decryption method from the previous section. We build a binary tree with n leaves, where the original FHE ciphertext lives at the root node. We split the FHE secret key $\mathsf{sk}^{\mathsf{FHE}}$ into two shares $\widetilde{\mathsf{sk}}_0$, $\widetilde{\mathsf{sk}}_1$, and then generate a fresh FHE key pair for each of the two child nodes, and encrypt each $\widetilde{\mathsf{sk}}_b$, for $b \in \{0, 1\}$, under the corresponding public key. This process is repeated with the FHE secret keys generated for the children, and so on throughout the tree. Note that we abuse notation by writing $\mathsf{ct}_v = \mathsf{Enc}^{\mathsf{FHE}}_{\mathsf{pk}_v}(\widetilde{\mathsf{sk}}_v)$, even though $\widetilde{\mathsf{sk}}_v$ may not lie in the plaintext space; we implicitly assume here that $\widetilde{\mathsf{sk}}_v$ is broken up into bits (or possibly larger chunks), so ct_v is actually a vector of ciphertexts encrypting each bit separately.

The idea is that, during the decryption phase, the parties can homomorphically evaluate the 2-party distributed decryption function at each node of the tree, obtaining a share of the message, now encrypted under a child node's public key. The i-th party repeats this for each node on the path to leaf i, where it finally obtains a ciphertext encrypting an n-party sharing of the original message, which it can decrypt.

Algorithm $\mathsf{SetUp}^{\mathsf{Scooby}}(\lambda, p, n)$

The algorithm takes as input the security parameter λ, plaintext modulus p, and number of parties n. It outputs a public key pk and secret keys $(\mathsf{sk}_1, \ldots, \mathsf{sk}_n)$.

1. Let $\mathsf{params} = (q, N, B, d, \Delta, S) \leftarrow \mathsf{ParamGen}(1^\lambda, p)$.
2. Sample a key $K^{\mathsf{prf}} \leftarrow \{0,1\}^\lambda$.
3. We construct a complete (but not necessarily full at the last layer) binary tree with n leaves and height $h = \lceil \log(n) \rceil$, and index the levels from 0 up to h. Each node in level i of the tree is labelled with a string of i bits, so the root is the empty string $\perp$, and the children of node v are $v\|0$ and $v\|1$.
4. Sample $\widetilde{\mathsf{sk}}_0, \widetilde{\mathsf{sk}}_1 \leftarrow R_q^d$ such that $\|\widetilde{\mathsf{sk}}_j\|_\infty \leq S$.
5. Let $\mathsf{sk}_\perp^{\mathsf{FHE}} = \widetilde{\mathsf{sk}}_0 + \widetilde{\mathsf{sk}}_1$ and sample $\mathsf{pk}_\perp^{\mathsf{FHE}} = \mathsf{PubKeyGen}(1^\lambda, \mathsf{sk}_\perp^{\mathsf{FHE}}, \mathsf{params})$.
6. For each internal node v (excluding the root and leaves) with children $v\|0$ and $v\|1$:
   (a) Sample $\widetilde{\mathsf{sk}}_{v\|0}, \widetilde{\mathsf{sk}}_{v\|1} \leftarrow R_q^d$ such that $\|\widetilde{\mathsf{sk}}_j\|_\infty \leq S$.
   (b) Let $\mathsf{sk}_v^{\mathsf{FHE}} = \widetilde{\mathsf{sk}}_{v\|0} + \widetilde{\mathsf{sk}}_{v\|1}$, sample $\mathsf{pk}_v^{\mathsf{FHE}} = \mathsf{PubKeyGen}(1^\lambda, \mathsf{sk}_v^{\mathsf{FHE}}, \mathsf{params})$.
   (c) Let $\mathsf{ct}_v = \mathsf{Enc}^{\mathsf{FHE}}_{\mathsf{pk}_v}(\widetilde{\mathsf{sk}}_v)$.
7. Let sk_i contain the leaf secret key $\widetilde{\mathsf{sk}}_i$, together with K^{prf} and the public keys and ciphertexts on the path from the root to leaf i.
8. Output $\mathsf{pk} := \mathsf{pk}_\perp^{\mathsf{FHE}}$ and the secret keys $(\mathsf{sk}_1, \ldots, \mathsf{sk}_n)$.

Fig. 2. Trusted setup algorithm for the Scooby construction

Given this setup procedure we define $\mathsf{Enc}^{\mathsf{Scooby}}_{\mathsf{pk}}$ and $\mathsf{Eval}^{\mathsf{Scooby}}_{\mathsf{pk}}$ exactly as is the case in the underlying LD-based FHE scheme. Next, we detail the $\mathsf{Dec}^{\mathsf{Scooby}}_{\mathsf{sk}_i}$ procedure in the lsb case.

Scooby Decryption. The decryption algorithms for Scooby in the lsb/msb-mode are described in Fig. 3 and the full version, respectively. The decryption algorithm requires $\lceil \log n \rceil - 1$ evaluations of the $\mathsf{Eval}^{\mathsf{FHE}}$ function for the underlying LD-based FHE scheme, each for a different public key. Note that the circuit used in $\mathsf{Eval}^{\mathsf{FHE}}$ is almost exactly the decryption circuit, so the complexity of each of these homomorphic operations is the same as a bootstrapping operation in the underlying FHE scheme.

It is also clear that, due to the fact that at each internal branch we are homomorphically evaluating the two-party distributed decryption method from either Sect. 4.1 (for the lsb case) or the method for the msb case given in the full version, the final n messages m_i will sum up to the decryption of the ciphertext ct. The only difference is that instead of adding or subtracting a random nonce R, the parties are using the PRF F to randomize their shares in distributed decryption; thus, the correctness property of the scheme relies on the security of F.

Algorithm $\mathsf{Dec}^{\mathsf{Scooby}}_{\mathsf{sk}_i}(\mathsf{ct})$ (for lsb-based construction)

Let $F : \{0,1\}^\lambda \times [n] \to R_q$ be a pseudorandom function.

$\mathsf{Dec}^{\mathsf{Scooby}}_{\mathsf{sk}_i}(\mathsf{ct})$:

1. Parse sk_i as $\widetilde{\mathsf{sk}}_i$, K^{prf} and $(\mathsf{pk}^{\mathsf{FHE}}_v, \mathsf{ct}_v)$, for every node v from the root to leaf i.
2. Let $\widetilde{\mathsf{ct}}_\perp := \mathsf{ct}$.
3. For each internal node v on the path from the root to leaf i (excluding the root and leaf):
   (a) Write $v = u\|b$, where u is the parent of v (so $b = 0$ if v is a left child and $b = 1$ otherwise).
   (b) Define the function:
   $$f^b_{\widetilde{\mathsf{ct}}_u} : \mathsf{sk} \mapsto \left(\widetilde{\mathsf{ct}}_u \cdot (b, -\mathsf{sk}) + (-1)^b \cdot F(K^{\mathsf{prf}}, u) \pmod q\right) \pmod p$$
   (c) Compute $\widetilde{\mathsf{ct}}_v := \mathsf{Eval}^{\mathsf{FHE}}_{\mathsf{pk}_v}(f^b_{\widetilde{\mathsf{ct}}_u}, \mathsf{ct}_v)$.
4. Write $i = u\|b$, then take the leaf ciphertext $\widetilde{\mathsf{ct}}_i$ and output the share
$$m_i = \left(\widetilde{\mathsf{ct}}_i \cdot (b, -\widetilde{\mathsf{sk}}_i) + (-1)^b \cdot F(K^{\mathsf{prf}}, u) \pmod q\right) \pmod p$$

Fig. 3. Decryption to shares for lsb-based Scooby

Theorem 5.1. *Let F be a pseudorandom function, and suppose there is an LD-like FHE scheme which satisfies the hardness assumption from Definition 5.1, such that $(q, N, B, d, \Delta, S) \leftarrow \mathsf{ParamGen}(1^\lambda, p)$ with $q > 2 \cdot p \cdot (B+1) \cdot 2^{\mathsf{sec}}$. Then the Scooby construction in Fig. 2–3 is a secure n-party homomorphic encryption scheme with decryption to shares.*

The proof is given in the full version.

Remark 5.1. Note that for correctness to hold it is not sufficient that for a single party the path from the root to the node is correctly split. We need this to happen for *all* parties simultaneously. This means that the obtained probability is in fact $1 - n \cdot N \cdot 2^{-\mathsf{sec}}$ and not, as initially might be believed, $1 - \log(n) \cdot N \cdot 2^{-\mathsf{sec}}$.

A Simpler Variant Relying on Circular Security. The previous construction avoids relying on a circular security assumption by switching to a freshly sampled FHE key at each node of the tree. We could instead simplify this slightly, with a variant of the construction where only one set of FHE secret keys is used. Here, we would start by sampling an independent secret key $\widetilde{\mathsf{sk}}_i$ for each leaf i. The public key associated with node v is then defined as $\mathsf{pk}_v = \mathsf{PubKeyGen}(1^\lambda, \mathsf{sk}_v, \mathsf{params})$, where sk_v is the sum of all the leaf secret keys that are descendants of v. We additionally encrypt sk under pk_v and give this out to the relevant parties. This introduces a circular security assumption, however, it does not seem to offer any significant efficiency benefits except for a slightly simpler setup algorithm.

5.4 BGV Parameters Supporting Scooby

It would appear that at first sight the parameters needed for Scooby are larger than those needed for standard FHE bootstrapping, due to the increase in q required by Eq. (1). However, this is not necessarily the case, as we now explain in the case of the BGV encryption scheme.

Standard BGV decryption simply requires the bound $q > 2 \cdot p \cdot (B + 1)$ for valid decryption, so we appear to have boosted the size of q by a factor of 2^{sec}. However, bootstrappable BGV as implemented in (say) HELib [22] utilizes an underlying leveled SHE scheme. At level zero, where no further homomorphic operations may take place without bootstrapping, we have a ciphertext modulus q_0 which satisfies $q_0 > 2 \cdot p \cdot (B + 1)$. At level L, i.e., the initial encryption level, we have a ciphertext modulus q_L which satisfies $q_L > 2 \cdot p \cdot (B + 1) \cdot 2^{b_p \cdot L}$, where b_p is the (average) bits-per-level of the chain of ciphertext moduli. On passing from each level from L down to zero, the size of the ciphertext modulus drops by (on average) 2^{b_p}. Note that, when bootstrapping a ciphertext from level zero, we do not end up with a ciphertext at level L, instead we obtain a ciphertext at level U (which denotes the so-called "usable" number of levels).

To see how this affects Scooby, we need to remember that at the end of the $\mathsf{Eval}_{\mathsf{pk}}^{\mathsf{Scooby}}$ procedure we will have a ciphertext at level U. This will satisfy our bound in Eq. (1) if $2^{b_p \cdot U} \geq 2^{\mathsf{sec}}$. Then, in executing $\mathsf{Dec}_{\mathsf{sk}_i}^{\mathsf{Scooby}}$, at each level of the tree we notice that we are actually executing an operation equivalent to bootstrapping. This is because at each node $v = u\|b$, where u is the parent node and $b \in \{0, 1\}$, we are essentially either performing a homomorphic decryption with the key $(1, -\widetilde{\mathsf{sk}}_{u\|1}^{\mathsf{FHE}})$, or a homomorphic decryption with the key $(0, -\widetilde{\mathsf{sk}}_{u\|0}^{\mathsf{FHE}})$. Thus, at each stage of the execution of $\mathsf{Dec}_{\mathsf{sk}_i}^{\mathsf{Scooby}}$ we have a ciphertext ct which is at level U.

Examining the bootstrappable BGV parameters proposed in [22] we see that in all cases we have $2^{b_p \cdot U} \geq 2^{128}$. Thus the Eq. (1) does not actually result in any increase in parameters, at least in the case of the BGV scheme.

6 Multi-party HEDS from Weaker Assumptions

We now present alternative constructions to the previous section, without relying on FHE with linear decryption and a super-polynomial modulus. In the first construction, in Sect. 6.1, we use any generic FHE scheme and a 2-party HSS scheme that supports homomorphic evaluation of the FHE decryption circuit. This means we no longer need the local decryption trick from Sect. 4.1, so can use FHE based on LWE with a polynomial modulus [12]. All LWE-based FHE constructions have decryption in NC1, so the 2-party HSS can be instantiated based on the Paillier assumption [25] or on class groups [1], which support HSS for all of NC1.

In Sect. 6.2, we also give a variant of the construction that *only* requires 2-party HSS, and not FHE. This gives a way to bootstrap two-party HSS constructions to the multi-party setting. We show how it can be used to transform two-party HSS for branching programs, based on Paillier encryption, into 4-party HSS for homomorphic evaluation of constant-degree polynomials.

6.1 Scrappy: HEDS from Standard FHE + HSS for NC1

This construction, shown in Fig. 4, follows the tree-based structure of Scooby from the previous section. Previously, though, at each node of the tree, an FHE ciphertext was split into two ciphertexts encrypting shares of the message, by doing a special homomorphic decryption procedure tailored to the linear decryption property of the FHE scheme. In Scrappy, we instead do the homomorphic decryption procedure inside a 2-party HSS scheme. Since most FHE schemes have decryption in NC1, it suffices to rely on HSS for NC1, which can be built from non-LWE-based assumptions. Of course, if done naively, this means we no longer get encrypted shares of the previous message, but would actually obtain the shares directly due to use of HSS. To avoid leaking all intermediate shares, we use an additional FHE scheme on each level of the tree, and use this to homomorphically evaluate the HSS evaluation procedure. The HSS evaluation keys are then only given out at the leaves of the tree, while at higher levels they are encrypted under FHE. Note that we only need the weaker, private-key form HSS, from Remark 2.1, where the sharing algorithm can be seen as done by a trusted dealer.

Theorem 6.1. *Suppose there exists fully homomorphic encryption, and a 2-party HSS scheme that supports homomorphic evaluation of the FHE scheme's decryption circuit. Then, there exists an n-party homomorphic encryption scheme with decryption to shares, for any $n = \mathsf{poly}(\lambda)$.*

The proof of the theorem is given in the full version. The above theorem implies n-party HEDS assuming (1) LWE with a polynomial modulus [12], (2) circular security, and (3) HSS for NC1 circuits, which can be based on decisional composite residuosity [25] or a DDH-like assumption in class groups [1]. If we only require n-party HEDS for bounded-depth circuits, we can remove the circular security assumption, since we only required leveled FHE.

6.2 Shaggy: Bootstrapping HEDS to More Parties

We now give a separate transformation that increases the number of parties in HEDS, *without* relying on fully homomorphic encryption. The construction, in Fig. 5, essentially applies one layer of the previous, tree-based construction, with a branching factor of n instead of 2. Additionally, instead of alternating between FHE and HSS evaluation, we always evaluate within an n-party HEDS scheme. This allows bootstrapping any sufficiently powerful n-party HEDS to support n^2 parties.

Scrappy: n-party HEDS from FHE + HSS

Let $(\mathsf{KeyGen}^{\mathsf{FHE}}, \mathsf{Enc}^{\mathsf{FHE}}, \mathsf{Eval}^{\mathsf{FHE}}, \mathsf{Dec}^{\mathsf{FHE}})$ be an FHE scheme and $(\mathsf{Share}^{\mathsf{HSS}}, \mathsf{Eval}^{\mathsf{HSS}})$ be a 2-party HSS scheme for the FHE decryption circuit.

- $\mathsf{SetUp}^{\mathsf{Scrappy}}(1^\lambda, n)$: Construct a complete binary tree of height $h = \lceil \log n \rceil$ and n leaves, and index the levels from 0 (at the root) up to h. Each node in level i of the tree is labelled with a string of i bits, so the root is labelled with the empty string $\perp$, and the children of node v are labelled $v\|0$ and $v\|1$.
  1. Sample a root key pair $(\mathsf{pk}_\perp, \mathsf{sk}_\perp) = \mathsf{KeyGen}^{\mathsf{FHE}}(1^\lambda)$.
  2. Sample HSS shares $(s_0, s_1) = \mathsf{Share}^{\mathsf{HSS}}(\mathsf{sk}_\perp)$.
  3. For each internal node v (excluding the root and leaf nodes), with parent node u and children $v\|0, v\|1$, compute the following values:
     (a) $(\mathsf{pk}_v, \mathsf{sk}_v) = \mathsf{KeyGen}^{\mathsf{FHE}}(1^\lambda)$.
     (b) $\mathsf{ct}_v^s = \mathsf{Enc}_{\mathsf{pk}_v}^{\mathsf{FHE}}(s_v)$
     (c) $(s_{v\|0}, s_{v\|1}) = \mathsf{Share}^{\mathsf{HSS}}(\mathsf{sk}_v)$.
  4. Output $\mathsf{pk} := \mathsf{pk}_\perp$ and the secret keys $\mathsf{sk}_i := \big(s_i, \{\mathsf{pk}_v, \mathsf{ct}_v^s\}_{v \in \mathsf{pathTo}(i)}\big)$, for $i = 0, \ldots, n-1$.
- $\mathsf{Enc}_{\mathsf{pk}}^{\mathsf{Scrappy}}(m)$: Output $\mathsf{ct} = \mathsf{Enc}_{\mathsf{pk}}^{\mathsf{FHE}}(m)$.
- $\mathsf{Eval}_{\mathsf{pk}}^{\mathsf{Scrappy}}(C, (\mathsf{ct}_1, \ldots, \mathsf{ct}_m))$: Output $\widetilde{\mathsf{ct}} = \mathsf{Eval}_{\mathsf{pk}}^{\mathsf{FHE}}(C, \mathsf{ct}_1, \ldots, \mathsf{ct}_m)$.
- $\mathsf{Dec}_{s_i}^{\mathsf{Scrappy}}(\widetilde{\mathsf{ct}})$:
  1. Let $\widetilde{\mathsf{ct}}_\perp := \widetilde{\mathsf{ct}}$.
  2. For each internal node v on the path from the root to leaf i (excluding the root and leaf), with parent node u:
     (a) Define the pair of functions:

$$f_{\widetilde{\mathsf{ct}}_u} : \mathsf{sk} \mapsto \mathsf{Dec}_{\mathsf{sk}}^{\mathsf{FHE}}(\widetilde{\mathsf{ct}}_u)$$
$$g_{\widetilde{\mathsf{ct}}_u} : s_v \mapsto \mathsf{Eval}^{\mathsf{HSS}}(f_{\widetilde{\mathsf{ct}}_u}, s_v)$$

     (b) Compute $\widetilde{\mathsf{ct}}_v := \mathsf{Eval}_{\mathsf{pk}_v}^{\mathsf{FHE}}(g_{\widetilde{\mathsf{ct}}_u}, \mathsf{ct}_v^s)$.
  3. Output $y_i = \mathsf{Eval}^{\mathsf{HSS}}(f_{\mathsf{ct}}, s_i)$.

Fig. 4. Constructing n-party HEDS using standard FHE and 2-party HSS

Theorem 6.2. *Let n-HEDS be an n-party HEDS for a class of circuits $\mathcal{C}$, whose decryption algorithm, when viewed as a function of sk_i, can be written as a circuit in $\mathcal{C}$. Then, n^2-HEDS (in Fig. 5) is an n^2-party HEDS for $\mathcal{C}$. Its encryption and evaluation algorithms are the same as in n-Scooby, while the complexity of decryption increases by a polynomial factor.*

The proof is given in the full version. Note that the decryption complexity of the bootstrapped construction n^2-HEDS is increased by a polynomial factor. Depending on the original n-party scheme, then, it may not be possible to apply the transformation more than once, if the new decryption algorithm is no longer in the class $\mathcal{C}$.

Construction n^2-HEDS

Let n-HEDS be an n-party HEDS. We build n^2-party HEDS, and label the parties $P_{i,j}$, for $i, j \in [n]$

- $\mathsf{SetUp}^{\mathsf{n^2\text{-}HEDS}}(1^\lambda, n^2)$:
  1. Let $(\mathsf{pk}, \mathsf{sk}_1, \ldots, \mathsf{sk}_n) = \mathsf{SetUp}^{\mathsf{n\text{-}HEDS}}(1^\lambda, n)$.
  2. For $i \in [n]$:
     (a) Sample $(\mathsf{pk}_i, \mathsf{sk}_{i,1}, \ldots, \mathsf{sk}_{i,n}) = \mathsf{SetUp}^{\mathsf{n\text{-}HEDS}}(1^\lambda, n)$.
     (b) Sample $\mathsf{ct}_i^s = \mathsf{Enc}_{\mathsf{pk}_i}^{\mathsf{n\text{-}HEDS}}(\mathsf{sk}_i)$.
  3. Output pk and the n^2 secret keys $\mathsf{sk}_{i,j} := (\mathsf{ct}_i, \mathsf{sk}_{i,j}, \mathsf{pk}_i)$, for $i, j \in [n]$.
- $\mathsf{Enc}_{\mathsf{pk}}^{\mathsf{n^2\text{-}HEDS}}(m)$: Output $\mathsf{ct} = \mathsf{Enc}_{\mathsf{pk}}^{\mathsf{n\text{-}HEDS}}(m)$.
- $\mathsf{Eval}_{\mathsf{pk}}^{\mathsf{n^2\text{-}HEDS}}(C, (\mathsf{ct}_1, \ldots, \mathsf{ct}_\rho))$:
  1. Compute $\mathsf{ct} = \mathsf{Eval}_{\mathsf{pk}}^{\mathsf{n\text{-}HEDS}}(C, \mathsf{ct}_1, \ldots, \mathsf{ct}_\rho)$.
  2. Let f_{ct} be the function that takes as input sk_i and outputs $\mathsf{Dec}_{\mathsf{sk}_i}^{\mathsf{n\text{-}HEDS}}(\mathsf{ct})$.
  3. Compute $\widetilde{\mathsf{ct}}_i = \mathsf{Eval}_{\mathsf{pk}_i}^{\mathsf{n\text{-}HEDS}}(f_{\mathsf{ct}}, \mathsf{ct}_i^s)$, for $i = 1, \ldots, n$.
  4. Output $(\widetilde{\mathsf{ct}}_1, \ldots, \widetilde{\mathsf{ct}}_n)$.
- $\mathsf{Dec}_{\mathsf{sk}_{i,j}}^{\mathsf{n^2\text{-}HEDS}}(\widetilde{\mathsf{ct}}_i)$: Output $y_{i,j} = \mathsf{Dec}_{\mathsf{sk}_{i,j}}^{\mathsf{n\text{-}HEDS}}(\widetilde{\mathsf{ct}}_i)$.

Fig. 5. Bootstrapping n-party HEDS to n^2 parties

Instantiation with HSS from Paillier. We show how to apply the above transformation to two-party HSS based on the decisional composite residuosity assumption used in Paillier encryption. We can only apply the transformation once, so we obtain a 4-party HEDS/HSS scheme, which can support homomorphic evaluation of constant-degree polynomials. As the underlying two-party scheme n-HEDS, we can use the HSS construction from [25] or [27].

First, we need to frame the 2-party HSS constructions of [25,27] in our HEDS framework. The constructions are given in a "public-key" flavour of HSS, with $\mathsf{SetUp}^{\mathsf{HSS}}$ and $\mathsf{Enc}^{\mathsf{HSS}}$ algorithms which are the same as in HEDS. The $\mathsf{Eval}^{\mathsf{HSS}}$ algorithm, however, requires knowing a secret key, unlike the syntax for $\mathsf{Eval}^{\mathsf{HEDS}}$. To make this fit our HEDS framework, we define $\mathsf{Eval}^{\mathsf{HEDS}}$ in the scheme to simply be the identity function, and move homomorphic evaluation into $\mathsf{Dec}_{\mathsf{sk}_i}^{\mathsf{HEDS}}$. This makes the resulting HEDS non-compact, but it can still be used for the construction in Fig. 5.

Complexity of Evaluation in Paillier-based HEDS. We now analyze the circuit complexity of the resulting $\mathsf{Dec}^{\mathsf{HEDS}}$ algorithm, which performs HSS evaluation of constant-degree polynomials. We can assume the polynomial is a simple monomial $f(x_1, \ldots, x_c) = x_1 x_2 \cdots x_c$ for a constant number of inputs (since to handle sums of monomials, it's enough to evaluate each monomial separately and add the shares).

With the methods of [25,27], each input x_i is given as a Paillier encryption of x_i, together with encryptions of x_i multiplied with each bit of the secret key. In homomorphic evaluation, the parties perform $c-1$ sequential multiplications, where in each of these, the core operation is a step that computes:

$$z = \mathsf{DDLog}(C^d \mod N^2) + F_k(\mathsf{id}) \mod N$$

Here, $N = pq$ is a public modulus, $C \in \mathbb{Z}_{N^2}^*$ is a ciphertext, d is a secret share that is known only to one party, and F is a pseudorandom function with key k known to both parties. The distributed discrete log function $\mathsf{DDLog}(X)$ computes $\lfloor X/N \rfloor \cdot (X \bmod N)^{-1} \bmod N$.

In general, modular exponentiation and inversion are not known to be in NC1. However, it turns out that $\mathsf{DDLog}(C^d)$, when viewed as a function of d for fixed C, does lie in NC1. The idea is that since C is public, we can consider the powers $C^{2^j} \bmod N^2$ as hard-coded into the description of the function. Similarly, we hardcode $C^{-2^j} \bmod N$, for $j = 1, \ldots, \ell$, where ℓ is the bit length of d. This allows computing

$$C^d = \prod_{j=1}^{\ell} (C^{2^j})^{d_j} \bmod N^2, \quad (C^d \bmod N)^{-1} = \prod_{j=1}^{\ell} (C^{-2^j})^{d_j} \bmod N$$

Since iterated product, modular reduction, addition/subtraction and integer division are all in NC1 [2], $\mathsf{DDLog}(C^d)$ can be computed as an NC1 circuit. Furthermore, evaluation of a PRF based on factoring can be done in NC1 [24].

In the complete multiplication algorithm, the above step is repeated $O(\lambda)$ times in parallel, which does not affect the circuit depth. The multiplication algorithm is run c times sequentially, where the outputs of one multiplication are used as the private d shares input to the next. If c is a constant, it follows that the entire evaluation procedure is in NC1.

Plugging in two-party HSS for poly-sized branching programs (which includes NC1), we obtain the following.

Corollary 6.1. *Assume the decisional composite residuosity assumption holds. Then, there exists a 4-party (non-compact) homomorphic encryption scheme with decryption to shares for constant-degree polynomials.*

Acknowledgements. The work of authors from KU Leuven was supported by Cyber-Security Research Flanders with reference number VR20192203 and by the FWO under an Odysseus project GOH9718N. Peter Scholl was supported by the Independent Research Fund Denmark (DFF) under project number 0165-00107B (C3PO) and the Aarhus University Research Foundation (AUFF).

Any opinions, findings and conclusions or recommendations expressed in this material are those of the author(s) and do not necessarily reflect the views of Cyber Security Research Flanders, the FWO, DFF or AUFF.

References

1. Abram, D., Damgård, I., Orlandi, C., Scholl, P.: An algebraic framework for silent preprocessing with trustless setup and active security. Cryptology ePrint Archive, Report 2022/363 (2022). https://ia.cr/2022/363
2. Beame, P., Cook, S., Hoover, H.: Log depth circuits for division and related problems. In: 25th Annual Symposium on Foundations of Computer Science, pp. 1–6 (1984). https://doi.org/10.1109/SFCS.1984.715894
3. Boyle, E., Couteau, G., Gilboa, N., Ishai, Y., Kohl, L., Scholl, P.: Efficient pseudorandom correlation generators: silent OT extension and more. In: Boldyreva, A., Micciancio, D. (eds.) CRYPTO 2019. LNCS, vol. 11694, pp. 489–518. Springer, Cham (2019). https://doi.org/10.1007/978-3-030-26954-8_16
4. Boyle, E., Couteau, G., Gilboa, N., Ishai, Y., Kohl, L., Scholl, P.: Correlated pseudorandom functions from variable-density LPN. In: 61st FOCS, pp. 1069–1080. IEEE Computer Society Press, November 2020. https://doi.org/10.1109/FOCS46700.2020.00103
5. Boyle, E., Gilboa, N., Ishai, Y.: Function secret sharing. In: Oswald, E., Fischlin, M. (eds.) EUROCRYPT 2015. LNCS, vol. 9057, pp. 337–367. Springer, Heidelberg (2015). https://doi.org/10.1007/978-3-662-46803-6_12
6. Boyle, E., Gilboa, N., Ishai, Y.: Breaking the circuit size barrier for secure computation under DDH. In: Robshaw, M., Katz, J. (eds.) CRYPTO 2016. LNCS, vol. 9814, pp. 509–539. Springer, Heidelberg (2016). https://doi.org/10.1007/978-3-662-53018-4_19
7. Boyle, E., Gilboa, N., Ishai, Y.: Function secret sharing: improvements and extensions. In: Weippl, E.R., Katzenbeisser, S., Kruegel, C., Myers, A.C., Halevi, S. (eds.) ACM CCS 2016, pp. 1292–1303. ACM Press, October 2016. https://doi.org/10.1145/2976749.2978429
8. Boyle, E., Gilboa, N., Ishai, Y., Lin, H., Tessaro, S.: Foundations of homomorphic secret sharing. In: Karlin, A.R. (ed.) ITCS 2018, vol. 94, pp. 21:1–21:21. LIPIcs, January 2018. https://doi.org/10.4230/LIPIcs.ITCS.2018.21
9. Boyle, E., Kohl, L., Scholl, P.: Homomorphic secret sharing from lattices without FHE. In: Ishai, Y., Rijmen, V. (eds.) EUROCRYPT 2019. LNCS, vol. 11477, pp. 3–33. Springer, Cham (2019). https://doi.org/10.1007/978-3-030-17656-3_1
10. Brakerski, Z., Döttling, N., Garg, S., Malavolta, G.: Leveraging linear decryption: rate-1 fully-homomorphic encryption and time-lock puzzles. In: Hofheinz, D., Rosen, A. (eds.) TCC 2019. LNCS, vol. 11892, pp. 407–437. Springer, Cham (2019). https://doi.org/10.1007/978-3-030-36033-7_16
11. Brakerski, Z., Gentry, C., Vaikuntanathan, V.: (Leveled) fully homomorphic encryption without bootstrapping. In: Goldwasser, S. (ed.) ITCS 2012, pp. 309–325. ACM, January 2012. https://doi.org/10.1145/2090236.2090262
12. Brakerski, Z., Vaikuntanathan, V.: Lattice-based FHE as secure as PKE. In: Naor, M. (ed.) ITCS 2014, pp. 1–12. ACM, January 2014. https://doi.org/10.1145/2554797.2554799
13. Chillotti, I., Gama, N., Georgieva, M., Izabachène, M.: Faster fully homomorphic encryption: bootstrapping in less than 0.1 seconds. In: Cheon, J.H., Takagi, T. (eds.) ASIACRYPT 2016. LNCS, vol. 10031, pp. 3–33. Springer, Heidelberg (2016). https://doi.org/10.1007/978-3-662-53887-6_1
14. Chillotti, I., Gama, N., Georgieva, M., Izabachène, M.: TFHE: fast fully homomorphic encryption over the torus. J. Cryptol. **33**(1), 34–91 (2019). https://doi.org/10.1007/s00145-019-09319-x

15. Clear, M., McGoldrick, C.: Multi-identity and multi-key leveled FHE from learning with errors. In: Gennaro, R., Robshaw, M. (eds.) CRYPTO 2015. LNCS, vol. 9216, pp. 630–656. Springer, Heidelberg (2015). https://doi.org/10.1007/978-3-662-48000-7_31
16. Dodis, Y., Halevi, S., Rothblum, R.D., Wichs, D.: Spooky encryption and its applications. In: Robshaw, M., Katz, J. (eds.) CRYPTO 2016. LNCS, vol. 9816, pp. 93–122. Springer, Heidelberg (2016). https://doi.org/10.1007/978-3-662-53015-3_4
17. Doerner, J., Shelat, A.: Scaling ORAM for secure computation. In: Thuraisingham, B.M., Evans, D., Malkin, T., Xu, D. (eds.) ACM CCS 2017, pp. 523–535. ACM Press, October/November 2017. https://doi.org/10.1145/3133956.3133967
18. Fan, J., Vercauteren, F.: Somewhat practical fully homomorphic encryption. Cryptology ePrint Archive, Report 2012/144 (2012). https://eprint.iacr.org/2012/144
19. Gentry, C., Halevi, S.: Compressible FHE with applications to PIR. In: Hofheinz, D., Rosen, A. (eds.) TCC 2019. LNCS, vol. 11892, pp. 438–464. Springer, Cham (2019). https://doi.org/10.1007/978-3-030-36033-7_17
20. Gentry, C., Sahai, A., Waters, B.: Homomorphic encryption from learning with errors: conceptually-simpler, asymptotically-faster, attribute-based. In: Canetti, R., Garay, J.A. (eds.) CRYPTO 2013. LNCS, vol. 8042, pp. 75–92. Springer, Heidelberg (2013). https://doi.org/10.1007/978-3-642-40041-4_5
21. Gilboa, N., Ishai, Y.: Distributed point functions and their applications. In: Nguyen, P.Q., Oswald, E. (eds.) EUROCRYPT 2014. LNCS, vol. 8441, pp. 640–658. Springer, Heidelberg (2014). https://doi.org/10.1007/978-3-642-55220-5_35
22. Halevi, S., Shoup, V.: Bootstrapping for `HElib`. J. Cryptol. **34**(1), 1–44 (2021). https://doi.org/10.1007/s00145-020-09368-7
23. Mukherjee, P., Wichs, D.: Two round multiparty computation via multi-key FHE. In: Fischlin, M., Coron, J.-S. (eds.) EUROCRYPT 2016. LNCS, vol. 9666, pp. 735–763. Springer, Heidelberg (2016). https://doi.org/10.1007/978-3-662-49896-5_26
24. Naor, M., Reingold, O.: Number-theoretic constructions of efficient pseudo-random functions. J. ACM **51**(2), 231–262 (2004)
25. Orlandi, C., Scholl, P., Yakoubov, S.: The rise of Paillier: homomorphic secret sharing and public-key silent OT. In: Canteaut, A., Standaert, F.-X. (eds.) EUROCRYPT 2021. LNCS, vol. 12696, pp. 678–708. Springer, Cham (2021). https://doi.org/10.1007/978-3-030-77870-5_24
26. Rotaru, D., Smart, N.P., Tanguy, T., Vercauteren, F., Wood, T.: Actively secure setup for SPDZ. J. Cryptol. **35**(1), 1–32 (2021). https://doi.org/10.1007/s00145-021-09416-w
27. Roy, L., Singh, J.: Large message homomorphic secret sharing from DCR and applications. In: Malkin, T., Peikert, C. (eds.) CRYPTO 2021. LNCS, vol. 12827, pp. 687–717. Springer, Cham (2021). https://doi.org/10.1007/978-3-030-84252-9_23

Streaming and Unbalanced PSI from Function Secret Sharing

Samuel Dittmer[1(✉)], Yuval Ishai[2], Steve Lu[1], Rafail Ostrovsky[1,3], Mohamed Elsabagh[4], Nikolaos Kiourtis[4], Brian Schulte[4], and Angelos Stavrou[4]

[1] Stealth Software Technologies, Inc., Los Angeles, CA 90025, USA
{samdittmer,steve,rafail}@stealthsoftwareinc.com

[2] Technion - Israel Institute of Technology, Haifa, Israel
yuval@cs.technion.ac.il

[3] University of California, Los Angeles, Los Angeles, CA 90025, USA
rafail@cs.ucla.edu

[4] Kryptowire, LLC, Fairfax, VA 22102, USA
{melsabagh,nkiourtis,bschulte,angelos}@kryptowire.com

Abstract. Private Set Intersection (PSI) is one of the most useful and well-studied instances of secure computation, with many variants and applications. In this work, we present new solutions to PSI and a weighted variant in which the output is the sum of the weights of keywords in the intersection. Our protocols apply to the semi-honest, two-server model and are optimized for the unbalanced case, where one of the sets is much larger than the other, and for a dynamic streaming setting, in which sets can evolve over time.

Our protocols make use of Function Secret Sharing (FSS) to aggregate numerical payloads associated with the intersection while minimizing interaction and computational overhead. They avoid the use of public-key cryptography, giving simple and concretely efficient protocols for unbalanced PSI. In the dynamic setting, we use queuing theory to eliminate leakage with minimal overhead while ensuring low wait times, giving efficient streaming unbalanced PSI.

1 Introduction

In this work, we describe a new lightweight approach to the Private Set Intersection (PSI) problem, which is geared towards the streaming and unbalanced PSI variants. We focus on the two-server model, where the bigger data set is owned by a pair of non-colluding servers. Unlike the traditional two-party setting, the two-server model allows for solutions that avoid the use of public-key cryptography. Such a two-server model is commonly used in the context of practical solutions for private information retrieval and related problems; see, e.g., [6,15,40,41] and references therein.

C. Galdi and S. Jarecki (Eds.): SCN 2022, LNCS 13409, pp. 564–587, 2022.
https://doi.org/10.1007/978-3-031-14791-3_25

Our technical approach makes a novel use of a Distributed Point Function (DPF) [25], an instance of Function Secret Sharing (FSS) [8], to minimize communication and computation costs and to support dynamic data sets. One key feature of FSS is that it natively supports secure keyword search on raw sets of keywords without a need for processing the keywords via a data structure for set membership. Furthermore, the FSS functionality enables adding up numerical payloads associated with multiple matches without additional interaction. These features make FSS an attractive tool for lightweight PSI solutions for a variety of applications, including private contact discovery, aggregated ads analytics, tracking breached passwords, monitoring data feeds for target keywords, and contact tracing.

The bulk of PSI research focuses on the balanced case, where the parties hold sets of roughly equal size. Recently there has been new interest paid to *unbalanced* PSI, where one set has length n and the other has length N, with $n \ll N$, and we desire total communication of $\tilde{O}(n)$.

Additionally, although PSI generally is treated as a one-shot protocol, the concept of updateable PSI was recently formalized [4] for a PSI that is executed in a dynamic *streaming* setting. In many applications it is desirable to run the PSI repeatedly over a period of time, where only a small number of elements from each set changes each epoch, and the amortized work per epoch is proportional to the size of the change. The protocols we present here offer improvements in asymptotic complexity and concrete efficiency over previous protocols in these settings, especially in the case of unbalanced streaming PSI. To further enhance their efficiency without introducing extra information leakage, we also consider a relaxation of the correctness requirement that enables answers to be slightly delayed.

1.1 Our Contribution

Focusing on the setting of a single (semi-honest) client and two non-colluding servers, we present efficient protocols for a generalized variant of PSI referred to as *PSI with weighted cardinality* (PSI-WCA). In PSI-WCA, for each keyword held by the client, there is an associated secret weight. The client learns the weight sum of the keywords in the intersection. This is targeted towards applications where the client wants to obtain a weighted score for the quality of the match between the two sets (e.g., weights can represent the importance of different keywords in a search query).[1] Determining the (unweighted) size of the intersection is a simple special case.

We present 4 protocols for PSI-WCA, two in the one-shot setting and two in the streaming setting. Our one-shot protocols include a baseline protocol for PSI-WCA and our queueing PSI-WCA, and our streaming protocols are a baseline

[1] Note that while PSI-WCA does not return to the client the actual set of keywords in the intersection, it can be used to achieve this by letting each weight include a suitable encoding of the associated keyword (e.g., consecutive powers of this keyword, cf. [15]).

streaming PSI-WCA protocol and a streaming PSI-WCA protocol with greedy scheduling. These solutions have the following features:

- **One round.** Our solutions use minimal interaction. In the one-shot case, the client sends one message to each server and receives a message from each server in return. In a streaming setting, only the servers need to send a message in each epoch when the client's input stays the same.
- **Minimal cryptographic assumptions.** Our solutions rely only on the minimal cryptographic assumption of the existence a secure PRG, which can be instantiated with AES in practice. This gives rise to fast and simple implementations using standard hardware under conservative security assumptions. All single server solutions necessarily require public-key cryptography.
- **Weighted cardinality.** Our protocols natively realize the generalized *PSI with Weighted Cardinality* functionality that enables a fine-grained specification of a matching score.
- **Optimal server response size.** The servers only need to respond to a client query with a single element from the payload group. This is particularly useful in a streaming setting where the same client query is reused for multiple responses. In the case where the client only needs to learn the (unweighted) cardinality of the intersection, each server can send just $\lceil \log_2(n+1) \rceil$ bits to the client, where n is the client set's size.
- **Linear client query size.** In our streaming and baseline solution, the client's queries depend linearly on the client's set size n and the security parameter. In a formal analysis, the security parameter is superlogarithmic in the server set size N, but the query size otherwise does not depend (even logarithmically) on N.
- **Hashing without leakage via queueing.** Hashing can be used to greatly decreases the amount of server work at the expense of leaking information about the client's queries. We use queueing theory to delay certain responses to prevent this leakage, and show that the improvement in efficiency comes with only a small increase in expected wait time for queries to be processed.
- **Nearly linear client query size with nearly linear server computation.** We use our queueing solution to obtain a one-shot protocol with client communication $O(n \log \log n)$ and server computation $O(N \log \log n)$ (ignoring dependence on the security parameter), where n, N are the size of the set of the client and server respectively.

We compare the concrete and asymptotic efficiency to existing protocols in Tables 2 and 3 in Sect. 2.1, along with a more thorough discussion of related work. But first, we give a brief overview of the distinguishing features of each of our four protocols.

Baseline One-Shot Protocol. The baseline variant of our solution already offers several attractive efficiency features. It employs only symmetric cryptography. It involves a single round of interaction consisting of a query from the client to each server followed by a response from each server to the client. The size of the query is comparable to the size of the client's small set Y; concretely, in an

AES-based implementation the client sends roughly 128 bits for each bit of a keyword in Y. The answers are even shorter, and are comparable to the output size.

In terms of computation cost, our basic solution is very fast on the client side: in an AES-based implementation, the client performs roughly 4 AES calls for each bit of each keyword in Y. On the server side, with server set X, the number of AES calls scales linearly with $|X| \cdot |Y|$. While this is acceptable in settings where Y is small or when the client work is the bottleneck, e.g., when using massive parallelism on the server side (as in the recent FSS-based encrypted search system from [16]), this basic solution does not scale well when the size of Y grows.

Traditional approaches for improving server computation and making it comparable to $|X|$ employ batching techniques based on hashing or "batch codes" [1,27,40]. While these techniques offer a significant improvement in server computation, this comes at the cost of higher communication and setup requirements. Moreover, some of these techniques, such as those used in the related context of FSS for multi-point functions [7,11,37], can only efficiently apply to keywords taken from a polynomial domain size, and hence do not apply to most of our motivating applications.

Baseline Streaming Protocol. The minimal interaction pattern of our baseline protocol is particularly useful when the same query is reused for computing intersection with different sets X. We call this the *server streaming* setting. Our baseline streaming solution makes a more fine-grained use of this feature in a setting where both X and Y incrementally change with time, giving both server streaming and full streaming solutions.

This streaming solution is noteworthy for its efficiency. The total client communication and server computation cost of evaluating the intersection $X \cap Y$ over a series of t' time steps in which X and Y pick up some fixed number of new elements N' and n', respectively, in each time step, is almost equal (in fact, asymptotic) to the cost of performing only the last step of this computation in the one-shot setting.

This efficiency is possible because, unlike other one-server PSI protocols, there is no preprocessing or setup required for the server's set X, and so the server can use a different set X_t at each time step with no additional preprocessing cost.

Streaming PSI-WCA with Greedy Scheduling. Instead of the traditional techniques for reducing computational cost, we take the following leaner approach. Our starting point is the standard technique of partitioning the keyword domain into buckets, so that *on average* only a small number of keywords in Y fall in each bucket. This reduces the PSI task to roughly $|Y|$ instances of secure keyword search, each applying to a single bucket that contains roughly $|X|/|Y|$ elements from X. Because FSS outputs are *additively* secret-shared between the servers, the outputs for different buckets can be non-interactively summed up. However, a direct use of this approach requires the client either to reveal the number of keywords in Y that are mapped to each bucket, or alternatively to "flatten the histogram" by using dummy queries. The former results in leaking a small amount of information about Y, whereas the latter has a significant toll on performance. To maximize performance while avoiding leakage, our solution flattens the histogram by deferring keywords from over-populated buckets to be processed with high priority in the next batch of queries, using a technique we call *greedy scheduling.* We use ideas from queueing theory to show that this approach can indeed give superior performance with no leakage, at the price of a very small expected latency in processing queries.

Queueing One-Shot Protocol. As an additional consequence of our streaming protocol with greedy scheduling, we obtain a one-shot protocol by having the client simulate the streaming protocol locally with dummy messages at every message except the first. The client runs this process until they have no deferred keywords, at which point they send the entire batch of queries as their message to the servers.

Using the queueing results of Sect. 5, we show in Sect. 4.4 that the number of iterations required for this simulated process leaks no information, and that, under an appropriate choice of parameters, the expected number of iterations is $O(\log\log n)$. Therefore the average client communication is $O(n\log\log n)$ and the server computation is $O(N\log\log n)$. This represents an improvement over the state-of-the-art unbalanced PSI protocols, which previously could achieve at best $O(N\log n)$ server computation with quasi-linear client communication.

1.2 Notation and PSI Models

The notation we use is comparable to that of existing PSI works, see e.g. [12,40]. There are two servers, who each hold a large set of keywords X, and a client who holds a small set of keywords Y. In the basic version of the problem, the client learns the *cardinality* of the intersection of X and Y without revealing to any *single* server any information about Y (except an upper bound on its size) and without learning any additional information about X. (We assume clients to be semi-honest; lightweight protection against malicious clients can be obtained using techniques from [6,9], and is out of scope for this work.) Following [40], we refer to this as *PSI cardinality* (PSI-CA). We also consider a generalization of PSI-CA in which the client associates to each keyword in Y an integer weight. Here the goal is for the client to obtain the sum of the weights of tokens in the intersection of X and Y. We refer to this extended variant as *PSI with weighted cardinality* (PSI-WCA).[2]

We then consider PSI-WCA in the *streaming* setting, where the sets change over time, presenting optimized solutions for this case. To simplify the presentation, we generally restrict our attention to the case where the client and server sets at time t are denoted by X_t and Y_t, and the parties desire to compute the

[2] This is similar to *private intersection-sum* [26], except that in typical use cases of the latter it is the server who holds the weights. Here both the weights and the output are owned by the client.

intersection of $X := (\cup_{i=1}^{t} X_i)$ and $Y := (\cup_{i=1}^{t} Y_i)$, or equivalently, the difference between the set $X \cap Y$ and the set computed in the previous epoch. However, we also show how a streaming variant appropriate for contact tracing, where tokens expire after T epochs, can also be efficiently implemented using our approach.

One of our variants of streaming PSI-WCA allows for *greedy scheduling* of tokens, where a stash of unmatched tokens is preserved from round to round, with guarantees that the stash size is bounded, and the distribution of which tokens are assigned to the stash from round to round reveals nothing about the tokens' values.

We also mention the simple decision version of PSI that returns a single bit representing whether or the intersection is empty. For this variant of PSI, our protocol requires only $\log_2(M+1)$ bits of communication from each server, where M is an upper bound on the intersection size. This is particularly useful in a setting where the set X changes rapidly while the set Y is unchanged, such as searching an internet feed for a set of targeted keywords.

Finally, we remark that both standard PSI, returning a bit vector, or PSI with payload, returning the payloads of items in the intersection, can be recovered from PSI-WCA by aggregating power sums, as done in [15].

1.3 Outline

In Sect. 2 we give background and related works. In Sect. 3 we provide our baseline PSI-WCA protocol, and show its extension to the server-streaming case. In Sect. 4, we give our streaming PSI-WCA with greedy scheduling protocol, and analyze the expected wait times of the underlying queues in Sect. 5. In Sect. 6 we discuss the implementation of our baseline protocol and associated benchmarks.

2 Background

2.1 Private Set Intersection

A Private Set Intersection (PSI) protocol [23] enables two parties to learn the intersection of their secret input sets X and Y, or some partial information about this intersection, without revealing additional information about the sets. Many variants of this problem have been considered in the literature. We will be interested in *unbalanced* PSI, where $|X| \gg |Y|$ and the output should be received by the party holding Y, to whom we refer as the *client*. We will further restrict the client to learn the *size* of the intersection or, more generally, a weighted sum over the intersection, while revealing no other information to the client.

PSI-Cardinality. The two functional variants of PSI we consider are PSI-Cardinality and PSI-Sum (or referred to as Weighted Cardinality in this work to distinguish the recipient). These variants are not trivially obtainable from PSI: cardinality reveals strictly less than the intersection so a PSI-CA protocol must hide the actual intersection, and PSI-Sum further requires the ability to handle a "payload" which is summed on top of hiding the intersection.

In the early work of De Cristofaro, Gasti, and Tsudik [17], the technique used to achieve PSI-CA was an extension of the DH-based PSI but with appropriate shuffling to hide which elements actually matched. The setting was meant for a balanced PSI in the sense that the communication was proportional to the sizes of both sets. The follow-up work by Ion et al. [26] was able to achieve PSI-Sum by using homomorphic encryption on the payload and expending another round to compute the sum of the matching payloads. Recent work [2,21,40] have focused on the unbalanced case of PSI-CA where one party has much fewer elements and therefore the communication should be proportional to the smaller set size only. Our result is the first to achieve this in 1 round in the 2-server model (with streaming) under the minimal assumption of one-way functions. We summarize our main PSI contribution in comparison to related PSI-CA works in Table 1.

Table 1. Comparison to state-of-the-art PSI-CA results. n = client set size, N = server set size, m = number of parties for multiparty solutions, DH = Diffie-Hellman style assumptions, OWF = minimal assumption of one-way functions, HE = homomorphic encryption. Security parameter factors omitted in O notation. * Bloom filter of size B. † Requires half round input-independent setup which is included. ‡ Delegation requires additional communication between servers which is omitted.

Result	Rounds	Comm.	Assumption	Servers	Flavor
[17]	1	$O(n+N)$	DH	1 server	PSI-CA
[26]	2	$O(n+N)$	DH+HE	1 server	PSI-CA/SUM
[18]	2	$O(mN)$	DH	m-party	PSI-CA
[2]	1.5	$O(n+B)^*$	DH	1 server	PSI-CA
[21]	$1.5^\dagger$	$O(n)^\ddagger$	OPRF	delegated	PSI-CA
[40] 1 server	2	$O(n)$	DH+HE	1 server	PSI-CA
[40] 2 server	2	$O(n)$	DH	2 server	PSI-CA
Ours	1	$O(n)$	OWF	2 server	PSI-CA/SUM

Unbalanced PSI. Most existing PSI protocols from the literature, including protocols based on linearly-homomorphic public-key encryption [26,33], oblivious transfer [30,35], or oblivious linear-function evaluation [24], are unsuitable for the highly unbalanced case because their communication costs scale linearly with the size of the bigger set X. This can be circumvented by PSI protocols that use simple forms of fully homomorphic encryption (FHE) [12,13]. However, FHE-based solutions incur a high computational cost and their concrete communication overhead is large when the set Y is relatively small.

For example, when $|Y| = 128$ and $|X| = 2^{24}$, the FHE approach of [12] would require 3.1 MB of communication from the client and a response of 5.1 MB, while our approach requires a 0.26 MB message from the client in the baseline solution, and only $\log_2(M+1)$ bits of a response from each server in the decision version of PSI. Even the most efficient lattice based homomorphic encryption schemes require a query of at least 14 KB of communication and a response of at least 21 KB, see e.g. Table 2 of [34].

Another family of solutions, which includes [5], later extended by [36], and [29], are optimized for the online-offline model, requiring an expensive one-time setup message by the server that is linear in N, the size of the server's message (although the constant in front of N has been improved by various compression techniques over the years, including Bloom filters and Cuckoo filters). Once the setup is complete, queries require a small amount of client communication and little to no server computation, but a larger amount of *client* computation than the other approaches discussed here. This approach is not compatible with server-side streaming because any changes to the server's database require repeating the preprocessing to maintain security.

Recent works on contact tracing by Trieu et al. [40] and on private contact discovery by Demmler et al. [19], following a more general approach of Chor et al. [14], employ a Cuckoo hashing data structure to reduce the keyword search problem (of matching a single client token y_i with all N tokens x_j) to two invocations of PIR on a $2N$-bit database. This work, like ours, makes use of two non-colluding servers; its main advantage over our baseline solution is that, using the efficient DPF EvalAll procedure from [9], these approaches reduce the number of AES invocations on the server side by a $O(\lambda)$ factor.

However, compared to our direct approach, this makes the solution much more complex. In particular, it requires an additional round of interaction and a bigger answer size and, perhaps most significantly, is not compatible with our streaming server mode of operation, because each time the server set changes another round of preprocessing is required. Additionally, these approaches require $O(n \log N)$ client communication, while our solutions require $O(n)$ or $O(n \log \log n)$ communication.

Table 2. Concrete efficiency features for unbalanced PSI protocols running on a server list X of size $N = 2^{24}$ and a client list Y of size $n = 128$, with client C and server S. Items marked with an asterisk are estimated from other parameter choices combined with an analysis of the theoretical dependence of those protocols on the parameter.

One-shot PSI-CA	Runtime and memory for $n = 128$, $N = 2^{24}$			
	Preprocessing (s)	Online (s)	Comm $C \to S$	Comm $S \to C$
[19]	2.69	0.49	2.4* MB	0
[12]	1368	9.1	3.1 MB	5.1 MB
[36]	333.62	0.42*	0.065 MB online	3.0 MB offline
Ours (baseline)	0	763.5*	0.26 MB	2 bytes
Ours (queueing)	0	4.5*	0.63 MB	2 bytes

Table 3. Asymptotic complexity measures for unbalanced PSI protocols with client C and server S. The parameters m and α in the second line are parameters associated with constructing a cuckoo hash table, and $m\alpha \approx n$.

One-shot PSI-CA	Asymptotic complexity of unbalanced PSI		
	Preprocessing	Online	Comm $C \rightarrow S$
[19]	λ exps	$O(N \log n/\lambda)$ AES calls	$O(\lambda n \log(N \log n/\lambda n))$
[12]	$O(N^2/(m\alpha))$	$O(nN/(m\alpha))$	$n\lambda \log N$
[36]	$O(N)$ exps	$O(n)$ exps	$O(kn)$ online $O(kN)$ offline
Ours (baseline)	0	$O(\lambda knN)$ AES calls	λkn bits
Ours (queueing)	0	$O(\lambda kN \log\log n)$ AES calls	$O(\lambda kn \log\log n)$

Streaming PSI. Many of the common applications of PSI such as private contact discovery, password breach monitoring, and contact tracing are naturally suited to a *streaming* mode of operation, where relatively small changes to the database are made at each time step, and the client only needs to learn the changes in their intersection set. In spite of this, so far little direct attention has been paid to designing PSI protocols for the streaming setting.

The online-offline PIR-based protocols [29,36] do have some advantages in the streaming setting when only the client values are being streamed, since the one-time setup cost no longer has to be paid in subsequent runs. However the $O(N)$ setup cost is large enough that it requires a large time window for streaming before the amortized cost is reasonable, and, critically, if the server set ever changes, the preprocessing step has to be repeated entirely.

The recently introduced notion of *incremental offline/online PIR* [32], which allows updates to the preprocessing for PIR schemes, may also be applicable to PIR-based PSI schemes, as long as the resulting protocol is still secure and the concrete metrics are good enough, but this avenue remains to be explored.

This streaming mode of operation has been formalized recently as *Updatable* PSI by Badrinarayanan et al., [4] which focuses on the case of balanced PSI, in contrast to this work. In the terminology of that paper, our streaming PSI protocol is capable of implementing both the *Addition-Only* and *Weak Deletion* variants. The first variant is where only new elements are added to the sets X, Y, and is the primary version we discuss, for ease of presentation, but we also treat the weak deletion variant, where tokens expire after some set time interval T, which has applications to contact tracing.

2.2 Function Secret Sharing

Our solution heavily builds on the tool of *function secret sharing* (FSS) [8]. A (2-party) FSS scheme for a function family $\mathcal{F}$ splits a function $f \in \mathcal{F}$ into two additive shares, where each share is a function that hides f and is described by a short key. More concretely, a function $f : \{0,1\}^n \rightarrow \mathbb{G}$ for some finite Abelian group $\mathbb{G}$ is split into two functions f_0, f_1, succinctly described by keys k_0, k_1 respectively, such that: (1) each key k_b hides f, and (2) for every $x \in \{0,1\}^n$ we have $f(x) = f_0(x) + f_1(x)$.

We will use FSS for the family $\mathcal{F}$ of *point functions*, where a point function $f_{\alpha,\beta}$ evaluates to β on the special input α and to 0 on all other inputs. An FSS scheme for point functions is referred to as a *distributed point function* (DPF) [25]. We will let $\mathsf{DPF.Gen}(1^\lambda, \alpha, \beta)$ denote the DPF key generation algorithm, which given security parameter λ and the description of a point function $f_{\alpha,\beta}$ outputs a pair of keys (k_0, k_1) (where here we assume for simplicity that the group $\mathbb{G}$ is fixed). We use $\mathsf{DPF.Eval}$ to denote the evaluation algorithm that on input (k_b, x) returns an output share y_b such that $y_0 + y_1 = f_{\alpha,\beta}(x)$.

We rely on the best known DPF construction from [9], which has the following performance features with an AES-based implementation: The length of each key is roughly $128n$ bits (some savings are possible when the group $\mathbb{G}$ is small). The cost of $\mathsf{DPF.Gen}$ is roughly $4n$ AES calls, whereas the cost of $\mathsf{DPF.Eval}$ is roughly n AES calls, where both can be implemented using fixed-key AES.

A direct application of DPF for secure keyword search in a 2-server setting was suggested in [8,25]. Secure keyword search can be viewed as an extreme instance of unbalanced PSI where $|Y| = 1$. Here we generalize this in two dimensions: first, we allow a client to have multiple keywords, thus supporting a standard PSI functionality. We propose different methods for improving the cost of independently repeating the basic keyword search solution for each keyword in the client set Y. Second, we exploit the ability to use a general group $\mathbb{G}$ for implementing a *weighted* variant of PSI where each of the client's secret keywords has an associated secret weight. In fact, we use a product group for revealing multiple weighted sums.

3 Baseline Solution

3.1 The One-Shot Case

The functionality we realize is an extended "weighted" version of PSI Cardinality that attaches a weight to each client item.

Functionality PSI-WCA:

- Inputs:
  - Each of the two servers S_0, S_1 holds the same *tokens* set $X = \{x_1, \ldots, x_N\}$ of k-bit strings.
  - Client holds a set Y of pairs of the form $Y = \{(y_1, w_1), \ldots, (y_n, w_n)\}$, where each y_i is a k-bit token and each w_i is an element of an Abelian group G (typically we choose to work over the integers with large enough modulus to prevent wraparound, but using an arbitrary group allows for the ability even to support product groups with multiple slots encoding different pieces of information). If the cardinality of Y is less than n, it is padded with an additional $n - |Y|$ dummy elements.
- Outputs: Client outputs the sum of the weights of the tokens in the intersection; namely, the output is $w = \sum_{i:y_i \in X} w_i$ where summation is in the group G. Servers have no output.
- Leakage: The size parameters leaked to the adversary are k, n, G.

The Baseline Solution. We follow the approach of Boyle et al. for secure keyword search via a direct use of distributed point functions (DPFs) [9,25]. This departs from the approach of Chor et al. [14] and Trieu et al. [40], which uses a data structure (Cuckoo Hashing in [40]) for reducing keyword search to private information retrieval (PIR). The direct DPF-based approach requires one round of interaction and accommodates the weighted case with almost no extra overhead.

While we describe the protocol using direct interaction of the client with the two servers S_0, S_1, in practice it may be preferable to have the client interact only with S_0 and have (encrypted) communication to and from S_1 routed via S_0. In the following we use λ to denote a security parameter, and we consider security against a *passive* (aka semi-honest) adversary corrupting either one of the two servers or the client.

Protocol PSI-WCA:

- CLIENT-TO-SERVERS COMMUNICATION:
  1. For each client input pair (y_i, w_i), Client generates a pair of DPF keys $(k_i^0, k_i^1) \leftarrow \mathsf{DPF.Gen}(1^\lambda, y_i, w_i)$.
  2. Client sends the n keys k_i^b to server S_b.
- SERVERS-TO-CLIENT COMMUNICATION:
  1. Each server S_b computes $a'_b := \sum_{j=1}^{N} \sum_{i=1}^{n} \mathsf{DPF.Eval}(k_i^b, x_j)$, where summation is in G. (Each such invocation of $\mathsf{DPF.Eval}$ can be implemented with roughly k invocations of fixed-key AES and does not require any communication between servers.)
  2. Letting $r \in_R G$ be a fresh secret random group element shared by the two servers, S_0 sends to Client $a_0 := a'_0 + r$ and S_1 sends $a_1 := a'_1 - r$, where addition and subtraction are in G. This can be generated using a shared pseudorandom sequence known only to the servers (e.g., a common PRF seed).
- CLIENT OUTPUT: Client outputs $w = a_0 + a_1$, where summation is in G.

The correctness of the above protocol is easy to verify. Security against a single server follows directly from the security of the DPF. Security against the Client follows from the blinding by r, which makes the pair of answers received by Client random subject to the restriction that they add to the output. We now discuss the protocol's efficiency.

Performance. Using an AES-based implementation of the DPF from [9], the above protocol has the following performance characteristics:

- ROUNDS: The protocol requires a single round of interaction, where Client sends a query to each server S_b and gets an answer in return. Client's query can be reused when the client's input Y does not change, even when the server input X changes.
- COMMUNICATION: Client sends each server $\approx 128 \cdot kn$ bits and gets back a single element of G from each server.

- COMPUTATION: Client performs $\approx 2kn$ (fixed-key) AES calls to generate the queries. The cost of reconstructing the answer is negligible. The computation performed by each server is dominated by $\approx knN$ AES calls. For modern processors (see Footnote 12 of [40]), each AES call requires 10 machine cycles, which enables $360 \cdot 10^6$ AES calls per second on a 3.6 GHz machine. This can be further sped up via parallelization.

3.2 Baseline Streaming Unbalanced PSI

This baseline solution can be extended directly into an incremental mode that captures a dynamic "streaming" version of the problem where the sets X and Y held by the servers and the client change in each time epoch (say, each day) by N' and n' respectively. We typically consider $N' \ll N$ and $n' \ll n$. For simplicity, we consider the case where at time step t, sets X_t and Y_t are appended to X and Y respectively, so that the set $X = \cup_{i=1}^{t} X_i$ is the union of all sets input by the server so far, and similarly $Y = \cup_{i=1}^{t} Y_i$. Then the client receives the sum of the weights of the terms in $X \cap Y$ minus the sum computed in the previous round.

More formally, we define the functionality below:

Functionality: Streaming PSI-WCA:

- INPUTS:
  - At each time step t, each of the two servers S_0, S_1 holds the same *tokens* $X_t = \{x_1, \ldots, x_N\}$ of k-bit strings.
  - At each time step t, client holds a set Y_t of pairs of the form $Y = \{(y_1, w_1), \ldots, (y_n, w_n)\}$, where each y_i is a k-bit token and each w_i is an element of an Abelian group G. If the cardinality of Y_t is less than n', it is padded with an additional $n' - |Y_t|$ dummy elements.
- OUTPUTS: For each t, define $S_t := (\cup_{i=1}^{t} X_i) \cap (\cup_{i=1}^{t} Y_i)$. Then at time step t, the client outputs the sum of the weights w_i of the tokens in $S_t \setminus S_{t-1}$. Servers have no output.
- LEAKAGE: The size parameters leaked to the adversary are k, n, G.

The protocol to realize this functionality is a straightforward extension of the baseline functionality. The client in time step t generates and communicates new queries only for the n' tokens of Y_t introduced in that epoch. Then servers compute DPF.EVAL only to match the new n' client tokens with all tN' server tokens and the new N' server tokens with all tn' client tokens. Correctness follows from the fact that $S_t \setminus S_{t-1} = X_t \cap (\cup_{i=1}^{t} Y_i) \cup Y_t \cap (\cup_{i=1}^{t} X_i)$, and security follows immediately from the security of the PSI-WCA protocol.

This streaming solution reduces the number of AES calls per epoch on the client side from tkn' to kn', and on the server side from $knN = t^2kn'N'$ to roughly $k \cdot (n'N + nN') \approx 2ktn'N'$. The client communication and server computation per epoch are reduced by a factor of t and $t/2$, respectively, compared to the one-shot solution. If the protocol runs for a total of t' epochs, summing from $t = 1$ to $t = t'$ we see that the total client communication is equal to $t'kn'$

and the total server computation is equal to $k(t'^2+t')n'N'$, so that the streaming functionality can be added with no asymptotic increase in cost.

We remark that the requirement that $|X_i| = N'$ and $|Y_i| = n'$ be constant across all time steps is unnecessary to the functionality and protocol definitions given above, and only the efficiency analysis changes. In particular, we note that if $X_1 = N$ and $X_i = \emptyset$ for $i > 1$, we require zero communication from the client in subsequent epochs and $kn'N$ work per epoch. This is the *server-streaming* PSI solution discussed in Sect. 1.1.

In some applications, such as contact tracing, we instead desire tokens to expire after T epochs, and the goal is to compute the PSI-WCA functionality in the sliding window corresponding to each epoch, where the inputs consist of the $N = TN'$ and $n = Tn'$ tokens collected during the last T epochs by the servers and client, respectively. The protocol above can be modified to realize this alternate functionality by having the servers discard their client and server tokens after T epochs. The rest of the protocol is identical. This reduces the client communication and server work by a factor of T throughout the course of the protocol.

4 Unbalanced PSI-WCA with Greedy Scheduling

4.1 Overview

Similarly to the simple use of hash functions and batch codes for amortizing the server computation of multi-query PIR [1,27], and similar techniques for standard PSI, one can use a similar approach for amortizing the server computation in PSI-WCA. The idea is to randomly partition the token domain into a small number of buckets m via a public hash function $H : \{0,1\}^k \rightarrow [m]$ (typically $m \approx n$), and let the client match each token y_i only with the tokens in bucket $H(y_i)$. To make this possible, we need the client either to reveal the number of tokens y_i mapped to each bucket (which leaks a small amount of information about Y to the servers) or to add dummy tokens y_j^* to ensure all buckets have a fixed size except with small failure probability. Compared to more sophisticated data structures such as Cuckoo hashing, discussed in Sect. 2.1, this approach does not require additional interaction and is well-suited to the incremental mode in which new server tokens are added on the fly.

When buckets are overfilled, we can repeat the process until all tokens are processed, which gives our $O(n \log\log n)$ communication $O(N \log\log n)$ server work solution which we describe in Sect. 4.4. In our streaming solution with greedy scheduling, the protocol instead deals flexibly with overfull buckets: after hashing all tokens, if the client holds any buckets with more than b tokens, the extra tokens are stashed and added to the next day's batch.

The hashing solution increases communication to $m \cdot b$ tokens compared to n for the baseline solution, so we would like to keep $\frac{m \cdot b}{n}$ as small as possible. The incremental mode is therefore well-suited to the hashing solution. However, decreasing b increases the number of tokens that need to be stashed each day. This is the fundamental trade-off explored in Sect. 5.

To keep the buckets more evenly balanced, the protocol can instead choose $c > 1$ public hash functions. The client then inserts their n tokens into the m buckets one by one, hashing each token c times and using a greedy algorithm to determine which of the c candidate buckets to place the token into. The servers then check each of their tokens y against $H_1(y), \ldots, H_c(y)$. This increases server work to $O(bcN)$, but shrinks the stash size, and hence the expected wait time.

Another consequential design choice, in both the $c = 1$ and $c > 1$ cases, is whether to fix the hash functions H_i throughout the procedure, or to choose new hash functions each day. Which choice is optimal depends on the choice of parameters, as we see in Sect. 5.3.

4.2 The Greedy Scheduling Approach

In this section, we describe our solution using *greedy scheduling* and explore optimizations and tradeoffs. The greedy scheduling protocol is a procedure for improving the efficiency of the hashing-based solution by scheduling some client tokens each epoch to be processed in a later epoch.

Other hashing-based solutions either leak some information about queries or use hashing to maintain a permanent data structure on the server side (such as a Cuckoo hash table), which requires a costly initial setup and is ill-suited for server-side streaming. Our approach uses hashing on the client side and fixes the bin size at a small constant (usually $b = 3$). The scheduling is *greedy* in that we schedule only those client tokens which can be most efficiently processed for the current epoch, and transfer the remaining tokens to a stash where they will be scheduled later. We show in Sect. 5.3 that this causes very little delay in processing in exchange for a large improvement in efficiency.

We begin with a formal definition of the streaming functionality for greedy scheduling. This definition requires a distribution ω on functions from $\{1, \ldots, n+s\} \to \{0, 1\}$, where n is the size of the client's list and s is the stash size. This distribution should be thought of as a representation of the queueing process; after sampling a function $f \in \omega$, then the set $f^{-1}(1)$ corresponds to elements which are not processed in that round of the queueing process, and are instead scheduled for a future round, and transferred to the stash.

To simplify the presentation, we formally define a PSI-WCA functionality with greedy scheduling that is streaming with respect to the client, with the server's set X held constant. The baseline streaming approach described in Sect. 3.2 can be applied on top of the approach described here, and, as in Sect. 3.2, this can be done without any increase in asymptotic client communication or server computation.

Functionality: Streaming PSI-WCA with greedy scheduling:

- INPUTS:
  - At each time step t, each of the two servers S_0, S_1 holds the same *tokens* $X = \{x_1, \ldots, x_N\}$ of k-bit strings.

- At each time step t, client holds a set Y_t of pairs of the form $Y = \{(y_1, w_1), \ldots, (y_n, w_n)\}$, where each y_i is a k-bit token and each w_i is an element of an Abelian group G. If the cardinality of Y_t is less than n, it is padded with an additional $n - |Y_t|$ dummy elements.
- As additional inputs, a stash size s and a distribution ω on functions from $\{1, \ldots, n+s\} \to \{0,1\}$ are given, with the property that if f has nonzero probability under ω, then $\sum_{i=1}^{n+s} f(i) \leq s$.

– OUTPUTS: For each time step t, sample a function $f_t \in \omega$. Set $\overline{Y}_1 := Y_1$, append s "dummy" elements, and assign some arbitrary bijection τ_1 from $\{1, \ldots, n+s\}$ to the elements of $\overline{Y}_1$. Then recursively define the set $\overline{Y}_{t+1} = Y_{t+1} \cup \tau_t(f_t^{-1}(1))$ and τ_{t+1} to be some arbitrary bijection from $\{1, \ldots, n+s\}$ to the elements of $\overline{Y}_{t+1}$. Now define $S_t := X \cap (\cup_{i=1}^{t} \overline{Y}_i)$, and at time step t, the client outputs the sum of the weights w_i of the tokens in $S_t \setminus S_{t-1}$. Servers have no output.

– LEAKAGE: The size parameters leaked to the adversary are k, n, G, along with the distribution ω and the stash size s.

We do not give the distribution ω explicitly; it is instead inferred from our description of the protocol.

4.3 Protocol Description

For our streaming protocol with greedy scheduling, we introduce the following notation. For a client with n tokens and a server with N tokens, with each token k bits, the client will hash their tokens into $m = \alpha n$ bins of size b, for some constant $\alpha < 1$. Thus will be done using c hash functions, choosing the bin with the smallest size if $c > 1$. Additionally, we use the bit R to distinguish between two variants of the protocol, where the hash function used is rerandomized after each epoch ($R =$ TRUE) and where the hash function is kept constant ($R =$ FALSE). The protocol then is close to our original PSI-WCA protocol, but with the work of DPF.Eval only done on bins where the client and server tokens could match. We give the protocol below.

Protocol Streaming PSI-WCA with greedy scheduling:

– CLIENT-TO-SERVERS COMMUNICATION:
  1. The client hashes their inputs, along with any elements in the stash, into m bins of size b, applying c hash functions to obtain c candidate bins and greedily assigning the element to the bin with the fewest elements. Any elements that overflow their bins are placed back into the stash. Then, for each client input pair $(y_{i,j}, w_{i,j})$, and the dummy elements, the client generates a pair of DPF keys $(k_{i,j}^0, k_{i,j}^1) \leftarrow \mathsf{DPF.Gen}(1^\lambda, y_{i,j}, w_{i,j})$.
  2. Client sends the mb keys $k_{i,j}^d$ to server S_b.

– SERVERS-TO-CLIENT COMMUNICATION:
  1. Each server S_d, for each element x_k, hashes x_k by each of the c hash functions to obtain a list of indices $I_k = \{i_1, \ldots, i_c\}$, and computes $a_{k,d} := \sum_{i \in I_k} \sum_{j=1}^{b} \mathsf{DPF.Eval}(k_{i,j}^d, x_k)$, where summation is in G. They then compute $a'_d = \sum_k a_{k,d}$.

2. Letting $r \in_R G$ be a fresh secret random group element shared by the two servers, S_0 sends to Client $a_0 := a'_0 + r$ and S_1 sends $a_1 := a'_1 - r$, where addition and subtraction are in G. This can be generated using a shared pseudorandom sequence known only to the servers (e.g., a common PRF seed).

- CLIENT OUTPUT: Client outputs $w = a_0 + a_1$, where summation is in G.

This is a realization of the streaming PSI with greedy scheduling functionality described above, where the stash size s and the distribution ω are determined by the queueing processes described in Sect. 5. In particular, we show in those sections that $s = O(n)$, and, when $Y_i = \emptyset$ for $i > 1$, $c = 2$, and R (the rerandomization bit) is equal to FALSE, all tokens will be processed in expected time $O(\log \log n)$.

Correctness follows because each client token is guaranteed to be processed eventually, and will match a server token x_k only if the client token lies in one of the queues $H_i(x_k)$, for $i \in \{1, \ldots, c\}$. Security against a single server and against a client follows from an identical argument to that in Sect. 3.1. We analyze performance when the client's set size is n per epoch, and the server's set size is a constant N.

Performance. Using an AES-based implementation of the DPF from [9], the above protocol has the following performance characteristics:

- ROUNDS: The protocol requires a single round of interaction per epoch, where Client sends a query to each server S_b and gets an answer in return.
- COMMUNICATION: Client sends each server $\approx 128 \cdot k\alpha bn = O(kn)$ bits per epoch and gets back a single element of G from each server.
- COMPUTATION: Client performs $\approx 2k\alpha bn = O(kn)$ (fixed-key) AES calls to generate the queries. The cost of reconstructing the answer is negligible. The computation performed by each server is dominated by $\approx kbcN$ AES calls.

4.4 Queueing One-Shot PSI Protocol

Our one-shot PSI protocol can be constructed as a corollary of this protocol, setting $Y_i = \emptyset$ for $i > 1$ and $|Y_1| = n$. By the proof of Proposition 4, given in the full version of this paper, we have some value $\kappa = O(\log \log n)$ such that all elements in Y_1 have wait time less than κ except with probability $\exp(O(-n))$. The client re-samples a key for the hash function until this holds, and then runs their half of the protocol for κ rounds and sends the resulting κmb keys to the server.

The server proceeds as if in the streaming with greedy scheduling case, performing $\kappa \cdot bcN$ total work, adding the outputs from each round, and sending the result to the client. We take $b = 3$ and $c = 2$. Since $\kappa = O(\log \log n)$, the client communication is $O(n \log \log n)$ and the server computation is $O(N \log \log n)$, as desired.

5 Analyzing Expected Wait Times Under Greedy Scheduling

5.1 Streaming and Bucketing

The greedy scheduling streaming protocol can be expressed in purely combinatorial terms, so that questions about average wait time and longest wait time become questions in queueing theory, allowing us to abstract away all the mechanics of PSI and FSS. We explain this in more detail in the full version of this paper [20].

The fundamental complication introduced by greedy scheduling is that some tokens will take longer than one day to be processed. Additionally, as time passes, the backlog of unprocessed tokens builds up, and the wait time increases. To understand the tradeoffs involved, we analyze the expected average and worst case wait times. When we choose parameters appropriately, the backlog in the stash reaches a steady state of reasonable size, the average wait time is small, and very large wait times are extraordinarily rare.

The results in Sect. 5.3 are a mixture of calculations using known results and extensions of existing results. We give the proofs of these results in the full version of this paper [20], and refer the interested reader to [22,31] for some of the background in queueing theory and probability, [3] for the crucial $O(\log\log n)$ bound for queues using multiple hash functions, [10] for the derivation of the steady state of the discrete time GI-D-c queue needed for Proposition 2, and [28] for a survey of prior work and additional analytical tools.

5.2 Setting

In our analysis, we consider two metrics under four scenarios. We measure *expected wait time* and *expected worst-case wait time*, both once a steady state has been reached. Formally, the random scheduling process induces some probability distribution $W_{t,n}$ on the n-length vector of wait times of the tokens inserted at time t. If $W_{t,n}$ converges to a limiting distribution W_n as $t \to \infty$, we call W_n the steady state. We then define by an abuse of notation the expected wait time $\mathbb{E}[W] := \lim_{n\to\infty} \mathbb{E}[\frac{1}{n}\sum_{w\in W_n} w]$, and the expected worst case wait time $\mathbb{E}[\max W] := \mathbb{E}[\max_{w\in W_n} w]$.

The four scenarios we consider are (i) Fixing $c = 1$ hash function to distribute tokens, (ii) Refreshing the $c = 1$ hash function each day, (iii) fixing $c > 1$ hash functions and (iv) refreshing $c > 1$ hash functions each day.

For each scenario, we consider parameters n, the number of tokens, m the number of buckets, b the bin size, and the occupancy ratio $\alpha := n/(bm)$. Additionally we have c, the number of hash functions, and R, a single bit representing whether or not we re-randomize each day.

We performed Monte Carlo simulations of this procedure to estimate the expected wait time for fixed values of n. Using integral approximations and a computer algebra package, we can also compute estimates for the expected wait time as $n \to \infty$ for various choices of parameters. We give the results of both kinds of experiments in Table 4, and in Table 5 we present the results given below for the expected and expected worst-case wait times.

5.3 Results

Summary of Results. The bounds on expected wait times and expected worst-case wait times we give here are primarily calculations using existing work. Proposition 3 is an extension of work by Azar et al. ([3]).

- The expected wait time decreases exponentially with b for $c = 1$ hash function, and doubly exponentially with b for $c > 1$ hash functions.
- The expected worst-case wait time is $\Theta(\log n)$ for each scenario except $c > 1$ fixed hash functions, where it is $\Theta(\log \log n)$.

Rerandomization of hash function, c = 1

Proposition 1. *When $c = 1$ and the rerandomization bit $R =$ TRUE, and $e\alpha < 1$,*

$$\mathbb{E}[W] \leq (e\alpha)^b$$

and

$$\mathbb{E}[\max W] \leq -\frac{1 + \log n}{b \log \alpha + b} + 1.$$

Fixed hash function, c = 1

Proposition 2. *Fix $\alpha < 1$. When $c = 1$ and the rerandomization bit $R =$ FALSE,*

$$\mathbb{E}[W] \leq \frac{C(\alpha, b)}{\sqrt{2\pi b}} \mathrm{Li}_{\frac{1}{2}}\left(\alpha^b e^{(1-\alpha)b}\right),$$

where $\mathrm{Li}_{\frac{1}{2}}$ is the polylogarithm of order $\frac{1}{2}$ and $C(\alpha, b) := 1 + (\alpha - 1)\frac{b}{b+1} < 1$. In particular, we have:

- (Estimate for α bounded away from 1.) *For $0 < \alpha < 1 - \delta$,*

$$\mathbb{E}[W] \leq \frac{C(\alpha, b)}{\sqrt{2\pi b}} \left(\alpha^b e^{(1-\alpha)b}\right) + O_{\delta,b}\left(\alpha^b e^{(1-\alpha)b}\right)^2$$

  for any fixed $0 < \delta < 1$.
- (Growth rate as $\alpha \to 1^-$.) *For $1 - (2b)^{-\frac{1}{2}} < \alpha < 1$,*

$$\mathbb{E}[W] = O\left(\frac{1}{b(1-\alpha)}\right).$$

  For any positive constant $C < 1$,

$$\mathbb{E}[\max W] \leq -\frac{\log n}{C \log \alpha} + O(1),$$

where the implied constant depends on $C, \alpha,$ and b.

Rerandomization of hash function, $c > 1$

Proposition 3. *When $c > 1$ and the rerandomization bit $R =$ TRUE, and α and b are chosen such that $0 < \alpha b < \left(ec^b\right)^{-1/(c^b-1)}$, then*

$$\mathbb{E}[W] \leq e(\alpha b)^{c^b-1}$$

and

$$\mathbb{E}[\max W] \leq -\frac{1+\log n}{(c^b-1)\log(\alpha b)+1} + 1.$$

Fixed hash function, $c > 1$

Proposition 4. *When $c > 1$ and the rerandomization bit $R =$ FALSE, and α and b are chosen such that $0 < \alpha b < 1 - \frac{1}{b \cdot 2^{c-2}}$, then*

$$\mathbb{E}[W] \leq \frac{(\alpha b)^{c^b}}{1-(\alpha b)^{c^b/2}}$$

and

$$\mathbb{E}[\max W] \leq \frac{b \log\log n}{\log c} + O(1).$$

Remark 1. The upper bounds on α in Proposition 1 and on αb in Propositions 3 and 4 were chosen to emphasize reasonable parameter choices and to increase the readability of the statements of results and proofs.

The full picture is messier; for example, it is possible to show that, in the $c > 1$ and $R =$ FALSE regime, as $\alpha \to 1$, and b and c are fixed, we have $\mathbb{E}[W] \approx \alpha^{bc}$, rather than α^{c^b}. Describing the transitions in behavior of $\mathbb{E}[W]$ on this parameter space is regrettably outside the scope of this paper.

Table 4. Experimental wait times

Wait time for (α, b, n)	$(0.313, 2, 25000)$	$\lim_{n\to\infty}(0.313, 2, n)$	$(0.417, 3, 25000)$	$\lim_{n\to\infty}(0.417, 3, n)$
$c = 1, R =$ TRUE	0.05319	0.05567	0.04512	0.04604
$c = 1, R =$ FALSE	0.05904	0.06022	0.04961	0.05063
$c = 2, R =$ TRUE	0.00073	0.00075	0.00009	0.00008
$c = 2, R =$ FALSE	0.00076	0.00074	0.00007	0.00008

Table 5. Upper bounds on asymptotic wait times, as a function of (α, b, c)

Wait time	Average	Worst-case
$c = 1, R = \text{TRUE}$	$(\alpha e)^{-b}$	$-\frac{1+\log n}{b \log \alpha} + 1$
$c = 1, R = \text{FALSE}$	$\frac{1}{\sqrt{2\pi b}} \text{Li}_{\frac{1}{2}}\left(\alpha^b e^{(1-\alpha)b}\right)$	$-\frac{\log n}{C \log \alpha} + O(1)$
$c > 1, R = \text{TRUE}$	$(\alpha b)^{c^b - 1}$	$-\frac{1+\log n}{(c^b-1)\log(\alpha b)+1} + 1$
$c > 1, R = \text{FALSE}$	$\frac{(\alpha b)^{c^b}}{1-(\alpha b)^{c^b}/2}$	$\frac{b \log \log n}{\log c} + O(1)$

6 Implementation and Benchmarks

In this section we will present our PSI-WCA implementation for the isolated back end servers. We are using PostgreSQL as our database engine for storing the tokens that are transmitted from the infected users and our test instances are configured as follows:

- CPU: Intel Xeon E5-2680 v3 @ 2.50 GHz with 16 MB L2 cache - 10 logical cores.
- RAM & Storage: 30 GB RAM, 60 GB SSD hard disk.
- OS: PostgreSQL 12 running on Debian 10.

Each of these test instances are virtual machines that are hosted in an OpenStack cloud platform provided by the Texas Advanced Computing Center (TACC) ([38,39]). The operations defined by PSI-WCA are built as a custom extension that is loaded directly by the Postgres database engine. More specifically, the extension defines a custom aggregate function that accepts a key split k and the tokens database table T as input and operates directly in T in order to calculate $\sum_{u_i \in T} \mathsf{DPF.Eval}(k, u_i) \mod G$.

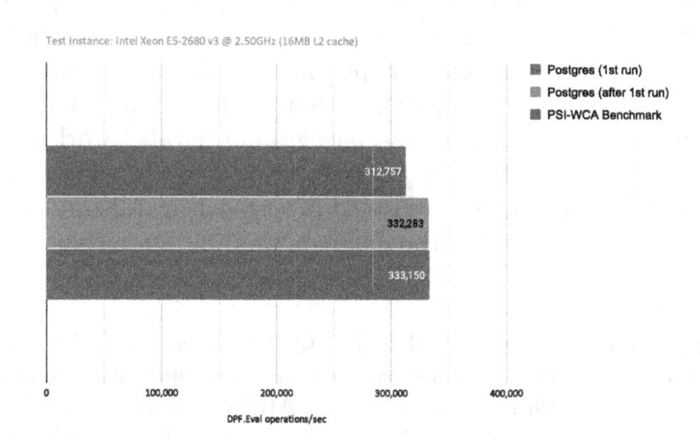

Fig. 1. PSI-WCA PostgreSQL extension performance

Each logical core in our test instance is capable of achieving a theoretical maximum of 333,150 DPF.Eval operations per second when running a simple benchmark that operates on 1000 tokens and 1000 key splits that have been preloaded in RAM. For evaluating our PostgreSQL extension we generated a test data set of 100,000,000 infected tokens that has a total size of 8056 MB. In Fig. 1 it is shown that the first run of DPF.Eval on this test data set results in 312, 757 operations per second which is 6.12% lower than the theoretical maximum. However, for any subsequent run our PostgreSQL extension utilizes memory caching and additional optimizations in the query execution plan which allows it to reach 332, 283 DPF.Eval operations per second, thus decreasing the overhead to 0.26%.

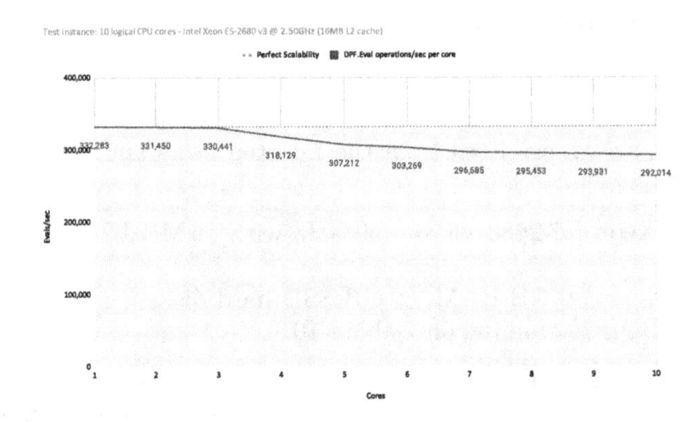

Fig. 2. PSI-WCA PostgreSQL extension DPF.Eval operations/sec per core

We have also evaluated how the DPF.Eval operations per second are affected when utilizing multiple cores in our test instance. For this benchmark we utilized the native functionality provided by PostgreSQL that spawns multiple worker processes for calculating the query results and is defined using the `max_parallel_workers_per_gather` parameter. This introduces some additional small overhead since PostgreSQL reserves a portion of CPU time in the main query process for managing the background parallel workers. As seen in Fig. 2, the DPF.Eval operations per second scale linearly when utilizing more than one core with a maximum overhead of 12% when utilizing all 10 cores in the test instance. For simplicity, the numbers in Table 2 are computed based on using a single core.

Acknowledgments. We thank Paul Bunn, Quinn Grier, and Will Yang for helpful and insightful conversations. This research was developed with funding from the Defense Advanced Research Projects Agency (DARPA) and NIWC Pacific under contract N66001-15-C-4065 and by DARPA, AFRL/RIKD, USAF, and AFMC under contract FA8750-18-C-0054. Y. Ishai was supported in part by ERC Project NTSC (742754), BSF grant 2018393, and ISF grant 2774/20. The U.S. Government is authorized to reproduce and distribute reprints for Governmental purposes not withstanding any copyright notation thereon. The views, opinions and/or findings expressed are those of the author and should not be interpreted as representing the official views or policies of the Department of Defense or the U.S. Government.

References

1. Angel, S., Chen, H., Laine, K., Setty, S.T.V.: PIR with compressed queries and amortized query processing. In: Proceedings of the 2018 IEEE Symposium on Security and Privacy, SP 2018, 21–23 May 2018, San Francisco, California, USA, pp. 962–979. IEEE Computer Society (2018). https://doi.org/10.1109/SP.2018.00062
2. Angelou, N.: Asymmetric private set intersection with applications to contact tracing and private vertical federated machine learning. CoRR abs/2011.09350 (2020). https://arxiv.org/abs/2011.09350
3. Azar, Y., Broder, A.Z., Karlin, A.R., Upfal, E.: Balanced allocations. In: Proceedings of the Twenty-Sixth Annual ACM Symposium on Theory of Computing, pp. 593–602 (1994)
4. Badrinarayanan, S., Miao, P., Xie, T.: Updatable private set intersection. Proc. Priv. Enhanc. Technol. **2022**(2), 378–406 (2022). https://doi.org/10.2478/popets-2022-0051
5. Baldi, P., Baronio, R., Cristofaro, E.D., Gasti, P., Tsudik, G.: Countering GATTACA: efficient and secure testing of fully-sequenced human genomes. In: Chen, Y., Danezis, G., Shmatikov, V. (eds.) Proceedings of the 18th ACM Conference on Computer and Communications Security, CCS 2011, Chicago, Illinois, USA, 17–21 October 2011, pp. 691–702. ACM (2011). https://doi.org/10.1145/2046707.2046785
6. Boneh, D., Boyle, E., Corrigan-Gibbs, H., Gilboa, N., Ishai, Y.: Lightweight techniques for private heavy hitters. IACR Cryptol. ePrint Arch. 2021, 17 (2021). Conference version: IEEE S&P 2021
7. Boyle, E., Couteau, G., Gilboa, N., Ishai, Y.: Compressing vector OLE. In: CCS 2018, pp. 896–912 (2018)
8. Boyle, E., Gilboa, N., Ishai, Y.: Function secret sharing. In: Oswald, E., Fischlin, M. (eds.) EUROCRYPT 2015. LNCS, vol. 9057, pp. 337–367. Springer, Heidelberg (2015). https://doi.org/10.1007/978-3-662-46803-6_12
9. Boyle, E., Gilboa, N., Ishai, Y.: Function secret sharing: improvements and extensions. In: Weippl, E.R., Katzenbeisser, S., Kruegel, C., Myers, A.C., Halevi, S. (eds.) ACM CCS 2016: 23rd Conference on Computer and Communications Security, Vienna, Austria, 24–28 October 2016, pp. 1292–1303. ACM Press (2016). https://doi.org/10.1145/2976749.2978429
10. Bruneel, H., Wuyts, I.: Analysis of discrete-time multiserver queueing models with constant service times. Oper. Res. Lett. **15**(5), 231–236 (1994)
11. de Castro, L., Polychroniadou, A.: Lightweight, maliciously secure verifiable function secret sharing. In: Dunkelman, O., Dziembowski, S. (eds.) EUROCRYPT 2022. LNCS, vol. 13275, pp. 150–179. Springer, Cham (2022). https://doi.org/10.1007/978-3-031-06944-4_6
12. Chen, H., Huang, Z., Laine, K., Rindal, P.: Labeled PSI from fully homomorphic encryption with malicious security. In: ACM CCS 2018, pp. 1223–1237 (2018)
13. Chen, H., Laine, K., Rindal, P.: Fast private set intersection from homomorphic encryption. In: ACM CCS 2017, pp. 1243–1255 (2017)
14. Chor, B., Gilboa, N., Naor, M.: Private information retrieval by keywords. IACR Cryptol. ePrint Arch. **1998**, 3 (1998). http://eprint.iacr.org/1998/003

15. Corrigan-Gibbs, H., Boneh, D., Mazières, D.: Riposte: an anonymous messaging system handling millions of users. In: 2015 IEEE Symposium on Security and Privacy, SP 2015, pp. 321–338 (2015)
16. Dauterman, E., Feng, E., Luo, E., Popa, R.A., Stoica, I.: Dory: an encrypted search system with distributed trust. Cryptology ePrint Archive, Report 2020/1280 (2020). https://eprint.iacr.org/2020/1280
17. De Cristofaro, E., Gasti, P., Tsudik, G.: Fast and private computation of cardinality of set intersection and union. In: Pieprzyk, J., Sadeghi, A.-R., Manulis, M. (eds.) CANS 2012. LNCS, vol. 7712, pp. 218–231. Springer, Heidelberg (2012). https://doi.org/10.1007/978-3-642-35404-5_17
18. Debnath, S.K., Stanica, P., Kundu, N., Choudhury, T.: Secure and efficient multiparty private set intersection cardinality. Adv. Math. Commun. **15**(2), 365–386 (2021)
19. Demmler, D., Rindal, P., Rosulek, M., Trieu, N.: PIR-PSI: scaling private contact discovery. Proc. Priv. Enhanc. Technol. **2018**(4), 159–178 (2018). https://doi.org/10.1515/popets-2018-0037
20. Dittmer, S., et al.: Authenticated garbling from simple correlations. Cryptology ePrint Archive (2022)
21. Duong, T., Phan, D.H., Trieu, N.: Catalic: delegated PSI cardinality with applications to contact tracing. In: Moriai, S., Wang, H. (eds.) ASIACRYPT 2020. LNCS, vol. 12493, pp. 870–899. Springer, Cham (2020). https://doi.org/10.1007/978-3-030-64840-4_29
22. Eisenberg, B.: On the expectation of the maximum of IID geometric random variables. Stat. Probab. Lett. **78**(2), 135–143 (2008)
23. Freedman, M.J., Nissim, K., Pinkas, B.: Efficient private matching and set intersection. In: Cachin, C., Camenisch, J.L. (eds.) EUROCRYPT 2004. LNCS, vol. 3027, pp. 1–19. Springer, Heidelberg (2004). https://doi.org/10.1007/978-3-540-24676-3_1
24. Ghosh, S., Nilges, T.: An algebraic approach to maliciously secure private set intersection. In: Ishai, Y., Rijmen, V. (eds.) EUROCRYPT 2019. LNCS, vol. 11478, pp. 154–185. Springer, Cham (2019). https://doi.org/10.1007/978-3-030-17659-4_6
25. Gilboa, N., Ishai, Y.: Distributed point functions and their applications. In: Nguyen, P.Q., Oswald, E. (eds.) EUROCRYPT 2014. LNCS, vol. 8441, pp. 640–658. Springer, Heidelberg (2014). https://doi.org/10.1007/978-3-642-55220-5_35
26. Ion, M., et al.: Private intersection-sum protocol with applications to attributing aggregate ad conversions. IACR Cryptol. ePrint Arch. **2017**, 738 (2017). http://eprint.iacr.org/2017/738
27. Ishai, Y., Kushilevitz, E., Ostrovsky, R., Sahai, A.: Batch codes and their applications. In: Babai, L. (ed.) Proceedings of the 36th Annual ACM Symposium on Theory of Computing, Chicago, IL, USA, 13–16 June 2004, pp. 262–271. ACM (2004). https://doi.org/10.1145/1007352.1007396
28. Janssen, A.J., Van Leeuwaarden, J.: Analytic computation schemes for the discrete-time bulk service queue. Queueing Syst. **50**(2–3), 141–163 (2005)
29. Kiss, Á., Liu, J., Schneider, T., Asokan, N., Pinkas, B.: Private set intersection for unequal set sizes with mobile applications. Proc. Priv. Enhanc. Technol. **2017**(4), 177–197 (2017). https://doi.org/10.1515/popets-2017-0044
30. Kolesnikov, V., Kumaresan, R., Rosulek, M., Trieu, N.: Efficient batched oblivious PRF with applications to private set intersection. In: Weippl, E.R., Katzenbeisser, S., Kruegel, C., Myers, A.C., Halevi, S. (eds.) Proceedings of the 2016 ACM SIGSAC Conference on Computer and Communications Security, Vienna,

Austria, 24–28 October 2016, pp. 818–829. ACM (2016). https://doi.org/10.1145/2976749.2978381
31. Little, J.D.: A proof for the queuing formula: L= λ w. Oper. Res. **9**(3), 383–387 (1961)
32. Ma, Y., Zhong, K., Rabin, T., Angel, S.: Incremental offline/online PIR (extended version). IACR Cryptol. ePrint Arch., p. 1438 (2021). https://eprint.iacr.org/2021/1438
33. Meadows, C.A.: A more efficient cryptographic matchmaking protocol for use in the absence of a continuously available third party. In: Proceedings of the 1986 IEEE Symposium on Security and Privacy, pp. 134–137 (1986)
34. Menon, S.J., Wu, D.J.: Spiral: fast, high-rate single-server PIR via FHE composition. IACR Cryptol. ePrint Arch., p. 368 (2022). https://eprint.iacr.org/2022/368
35. Pinkas, B., Rosulek, M., Trieu, N., Yanai, A.: SpOT-Light: lightweight private set intersection from sparse OT extension. In: Boldyreva, A., Micciancio, D. (eds.) CRYPTO 2019. LNCS, vol. 11694, pp. 401–431. Springer, Cham (2019). https://doi.org/10.1007/978-3-030-26954-8_13
36. Resende, A.C.D., de Freitas Aranha, D.: Faster unbalanced private set intersection in the semi-honest setting. J. Cryptogr. Eng. **11**(1), 21–38 (2021). https://doi.org/10.1007/s13389-020-00242-7
37. Schoppmann, P., Gascón, A., Reichert, L., Raykova, M.: Distributed vector-OLE: improved constructions and implementation. In: ACM CCS 2019: 26th Conference on Computer and Communications Security, pp. 1055–1072. ACM Press (2019). https://doi.org/10.1145/3319535.3363228
38. Stewart, C.A., et al.: Jetstream: a self-provisioned, scalable science and engineering cloud environment. In: Proceedings of the 2015 XSEDE Conference: Scientific Advancements Enabled by Enhanced Cyberinfrastructure, pp. 1–8 (2015)
39. Towns, J., et al.: XSEDE: accelerating scientific discovery. Comput. Sci. Eng. **16**(5), 62–74 (2014). https://doi.org/10.1109/MCSE.2014.80
40. Trieu, N., Shehata, K., Saxena, P., Shokri, R., Song, D.: Epione: lightweight contact tracing with strong privacy. IEEE Data Eng. Bull. **43**(2), 95–107 (2020). http://sites.computer.org/debull/A20june/p95.pdf
41. Wang, F., Yun, C., Goldwasser, S., Vaikuntanathan, V., Zaharia, M.: Splinter: practical private queries on public data. In: NSDI 2017 (2017)

Zero-Knowledge Proofs and Applications

Black-Box Anonymous Commit-and-Prove

Alessandra Scafuro(✉)

North Carolina State University, Raleigh, NC 27695, USA
ascafur@ncsu.edu

Abstract. Commit-and-prove is a building block that allows a party to commit to a secret input and then later prove something about it. This is a pillar of many cryptographic protocols and especially the ones underlying anonymous systems. In anonymous systems, often there is *a set of public commitments*, and a prover wants to prove a property about *one* of the inputs committed in the set, while hiding which one. This latter property gives the prover anonymity within the set.

Currently, there are numerous commit-and-prove protocols in the *anonymous* setting from various computational and setup assumptions. However, all such approaches are *non-black-box* in the cryptographic primitive. In fact, there exists no anonymous *black-box* construction of commit-and-prove protocols, under any computational or setup assumption. This is despite the fact that, when anonymity is not required, black-box commit-and-prove protocols are well known.

Is this inherent in the anonymous setting?

In this paper we provide a partial answer to the above question by constructing the first (one-time) black-box commit-and-prove protocol in the anonymous setting. We do so by first introducing a new primitive that we call Partially Openable Commitment (POC), and instantiating it in a black-box way from a Random Oracle. Next we show a black-box commit-and-prove protocol based on POC. From a theoretical standpoint, our result reduces the gap between known black-box feasibility results in the non-anonymous setting and the anonymous setting. From a practical standpoint, we show that our protocol can be very efficient for certain relations of interest.

1 Introduction

Commit-and-Prove. Commit-and-prove is a fundamental building block underlying many cryptographic protocols. In this building block, a party first commits to an input x, and at a later point proves some predicate about x, without revealing x. Computing a proof about a committed value typically is done by leveraging the implementation details of the commitment scheme. For instance, one can commit to x using Pedersen's Commitment [19] which is based on group exponentiations (i.e., $g^x h^r$) and then use Sigma protocols that leverage linear properties over the exponents to prove relations about x. More generally, one can use a commitment scheme that use any cryptographic function f,

Supported by NSF grants #1718074, #1764025.

C. Galdi and S. Jarecki (Eds.): SCN 2022, LNCS 13409, pp. 591–614, 2022.
https://doi.org/10.1007/978-3-031-14791-3_26

and a general-purpose zero-knowledge proof system that operates on the *circuit description* of f. Such approaches are said to be *non-black-box* because the computation of the zero-knowledge proof *depends* on the specific implementation of the cryptographic primitive they use. In contrast we say that a construction is *black-box* when it uses only the input/output interface of a cryptographic primitive. Besides providing a higher level of abstraction, the advantages of black-box usage are that the underlying cryptographic primitive can be instantiated in hardware, or modeled an oracle, and the complexity of the black-box protocol is *independent* on the complexity of the cryptographic primitive.

Black-Box Commit-and-Prove. It might seem that in order to prove something about a committed value, one must necessarily use the description (the circuit) of the function used to compute the commitment. However, it turns out that it is not necessary. Indeed, starting from the seminal work by Kilian [13], who showed how to prove equality relation of two committed values in a black-box manner, many follow-up works have shown how to prove arbitrary relations on a committed value, using cryptographic primitives in a black-box manner (e.g., [10–12,14,17,18]).

Anonymous Commit-and-Prove. With the term *anonymous* commit-and-prove we refer to the setting where many *independent* parties compute their own commitments, e.g., N users post commitments $\mathbf{C}^1, \mathbf{C}^2, \ldots$ on some platform, and then at a later point any of the parties can prove a relation $\mathcal{R}$ about *one* of the commitment inputs, but without even revealing *which one*. In other words, in the anonymous setting, additionally to hiding the value she committed to, the prover wants to hide which of the N commitments she "knows" something about. Importantly, the prover should be able to compute the proof by only knowing information about her own commitment and without knowing anything about the commitments computed by other users. Anonymous commit-and-prove are building blocks for various anonymous systems (e.g., anonymous credentials [6], anonymous bitcoin transactions [16]). Notice that the critical difference between commit-and-prove and *anonymous* commit-and-prove is that in the latter the N commitments are computed by arbitrary parties, and an honest prover, who knows the opening of a single commitment, must include all the *other* $N-1$ commitments in order to craft her proof (if she wants to preserve anonymity).

The Unknown Commitments. How to compute a valid proof on behalf of $N-1$ commitments for which you don't know the opening of? If one can leverage the specific structure of the commitment function, then computing a proof over unknown commitments is not more challenging than computing on known commitments. Indeed, one can still leverage the circuit of the commitment scheme and then use any general-purpose zero-knowledge protocol (e.g. ZKboo [9], Ligero [1], SNARKs [4], STARKS [3]) to prove that "one of the commitments" is computed in a certain way and has certain properties. This approach is used in Zcash [21] for instance. In fact, one can even still leverage the algebraic structure of Pedersen's commitment and craft a special Sigma protocols that works even if the prover does not know the randomness used to compute the other commitments. This approach is used in Bulletproofs [5] for example.

Black-Box Anonymous Commit-and-Prove. What about *black-box* commit-and-prove protocols in the anonymous setting? Currently, no construction is known, from any cryptographic primitive. Even ignoring any efficiency requirements (e.g., succinctness, reusability), computational assumptions or even setup assumptions, no black-box construction for commit-and-prove is known. In this work we pose a natural question:

Do commit-and-prove protocols, that treat their underlying cryptographic primitive as a black-box, exist in the anonymous setting?

1.1 Our Contribution

We provide a positive answer to the above question. We construct the first anonymous commit-and-prove system from a random oracle, which has one-time security. In the anonymous setting, the one-time security is well motivated by practical scenarios where tally is required, such as voting, sealed-bid auctions or payments (as we discussed later). More specifically, we provide several contributions:

- **A new primitive called Partially Openable Commitment (POC)** (Sect. 4.1) This is a commitment scheme with new binding properties that allows to overcome the problem of opening unknown commitments (we describe this new primitive in Sect. 2). We also provide a formal definition of linkable anonymous black-box commit-and-prove.
- **A black-box anonymous commit-and-prove protocol** (Sect. 5) for arbitrary relations based on Partially Openable Commitment and the zero-knowledge protocol provided by Giacomelli, Madsen and Orlandi [9], known as ZKBoo. We call our protocol BlackBoo.
- **A concrete instantiation** (Sect. 6) of our commit-and-prove protocol for the equality relation that we use to showcase efficiency of our approach (Table 1). From a practical perspective, our construction requires exclusively symmetric key operations that can be parallelized. Furthermore, it has a communication complexity that is practical in settings where the number of participants is in the thousands, and very competitive if it is in the hundreds.

In the next section we will walk the reader through the main ideas and new techniques behind our constructions.

2 Our Techniques

State-of-the-Art Approach for Black-Box Commit-and-Prove. In a commit-and-prove protocol the goal is to prove a property about the *opening* of a commitment, but without revealing any information about the opening. To design a black-box commit-and-prove scheme the key idea used in the literature (e.g., [11–13,18]) is to open commitments *directly* instead of proving something about the opening. The technique can be abstracted as follows: the commitment

$\mathbf{C}$ of a value x is replaced with κ correlated sub-commitments $\mathbf{C} := (\mathbf{c}_1, \ldots, \mathbf{c}_\kappa)$, where each $\mathbf{c}_i$ is a commitment to a share x_i of x (according to some secret sharing scheme $(\mathsf{Share}, \mathsf{Recon})$). Due to the security of the secret sharing scheme, the prover could safely open t of the κ commitments, thereby revealing t shares, without leaking any information about the committed value x. The prover then proceeds using the shares $(x_1, \ldots, x_\kappa)$ as input of a (t, κ)-secure MPC protocol to securely compute a function that outputs 1 iff the value reconstructed from those shares, x satisfies $\mathcal{R}$, that is, if $\mathcal{R}(x) = 1$, resulting in κ MPC views. This approach is well known as the MPC-in-the-head approach, since the prover runs an MPC protocol imagining κ players. The actual proof that is sent to the verifier consists of: (1) κ commitments of the MPC views; (2) the openings of t such views, (3) the openings of t out of the κ commitments $(\mathbf{c}_1, \ldots, \mathbf{c}_\kappa)$. In order to verify a proof, the verifier checks that the opening of the t views and the opening of t committed shares are **consistent** with each other (this check involves cryptographic material) and with the MPC protocol (this check leverages the information-theoretic security properties of the MPC protocol).

Technical Challenge: The Unknown Commitments. The MPC-in-the-head approach relies on the ability of the prover P^i to *open* t-out-of-κ commitments in $\mathbf{C}^i = (\mathbf{c}_1^i, \ldots, \mathbf{c}_\kappa^i)$. While this is the key idea to ensure a black-box use of the underlying commitment scheme, this strategy is not applicable to the setting where the proof must be computed over N *arbitrary* commitments ($\mathbf{C}^1$, $\mathbf{C}^2$, ..., $\mathbf{C}^N$) that were published by other unknown parties $P^1, P^2, \ldots, P^N$, since in this set, $N-1$ commitments are *unknown* to the prover. The problem is that since the commitments were not computed by P^i, she simply can't provide a valid opening for them (this follows from binding). There is no prior work tackling this problem, since none of the previous work considered black-box constructions in the anonymous setting, where the statement to be proven contains commitments that are *not* computed by the prover.

Our New Tool: Partially Openable Commitments (POC). We introduce a new primitive called Partially Openable Commitment (POC). A POC commitment has the format $\mathbf{C}^i = (\mathbf{c}_1^i, \ldots, \mathbf{c}_\kappa^i)$ and satisfies the following property: it can be *partially* opened by *anyone in the world.* That is, anyone can successfully open t out of κ subcommitments. However, it still holds that the commitment can be correctly *fully* opened only by its legitimate creator[1]. The main challenge for POC is to identify the security properties that it must satisfy in order to be useful as a building block for a secure proof system, in a completely black-box way. In order to build intuition on the abstract properties that we want for POC, we proceed by first describing the ideas behind the construction.

To construct POC we leverage the unstructured nature of hash-based commitments to allow anyone to "explain" a commitment using a random value. At

[1] We remark that partially openable commitment are different from trapdoor or UC-secure [7] commitments. In the latter, the commitments can be opened by anyone who *has a trapdoor*, and the equivocation property is used in the security proof, not the protocol. They are also different from Mercurial Commitments [8] where the prover has the ability to "tease" only commitments *she* created.

high-level our construction works as follows. Assume we commit to a plaintext value x as follows $\mathbf{c} := \mathcal{H}(k) \oplus x$, where k is a random string and is part of the cryptographic material, $\mathcal{H}$ is a random oracle [2]. This commitment is not binding: for a given commitment $\mathbf{c}$, anyone can open it as some plaintext x', by choosing a key k' and sending $x' = \mathbf{c} \oplus \mathcal{H}(k')$ (later on we call these "fake openings"). Nevertheless, note that when $\mathcal{H}$ is a random oracle, one has no control on the value x', which will be distributed uniformly at random. With this idea in mind, recall the approach we have highlighted above, where a commitment for a party i is represented as a vector of correlated sub-commitments: $\mathbf{C}^i = (\mathbf{c}^i_1, \dots, \mathbf{c}^i_\kappa)$, and notice the following. Anyone who is not actually the creator of $\mathbf{C}^i = (\mathbf{c}^i_1, \dots, \mathbf{c}^i_\kappa)$ can only open each $\mathbf{c}^i_j$ to a random value x'_j. Consequently, a *full* plaintext opening $(x'_1, \dots, x'_\kappa)$ obtained by someone who is not the creator of the commitment very luckily will not satisfy any meaningful relation. In the construction, the full plaintext $(x_1, \dots, x_\kappa)$ is a vector of shares computed using a secret sharing scheme on input the actual message m that the committer meant to commit to. That is, POC is parameterized by a sharing scheme $(\mathsf{Share}, \mathsf{Recon})$ and $(x_1, \dots, x_\kappa)$ is the result of $\mathsf{Share}(m)$. A partial opening, is a subset of shares x_j (plaintext openings) and the respective keys k_j (crypto openings). The protocol is formally described in Fig. 2.

We are now ready to describe the choices we made for the formal definition of POC. We choose to explicitly define Partially Openable Commitment so that it supports the decoupling of the *plaintext* openings (which is the secret sharing of the message to commit) and the *cryptographic* openings and emphasize that parties are only given oracle access to a primitive. This formulation is extremely useful when POC is used as a building block for protocols that work on the plaintext openings of a commitment, but want to use the crypto primitives as oracles. For instance, POC can be used in combination with the MPC-in-the-head paradigm, having the plaintext being the input of the MPC players. In this case, the sharing scheme $(\mathsf{Share}, \mathsf{Recon})$ could be the glue between POC and the underlying MPC. For the security properties, privacy of the commitment is captured by the notion of *hiding in presence of partial openings* which means that anyone can open t out of κ sub-commitments of $\mathbf{C}^i = (\mathbf{c}_1, \dots, \mathbf{c}_\kappa)$ by providing t crypto keys $k_{j_1}, \dots, k_{j_t}$, and these so called *fake* openings will be distributed identically to the *real* openings of the original commitments, where t is a parameter related to the secret sharing scheme (See Definition 3). The definition of binding is more nuanced since by design *anyone* should be able to compute (and publish) partial openings for any commitment. Hence, when defining binding we need to provide a concept of binding w.r.t. a "meaningful" plaintext openings. One could define as *meaningful* a plaintext opening for which the reconstruction algorithm Recon is successful. For example, if Recon is a robust version of Shamir's Secret Sharing [20] where reconstruction demands that all points lie on the same polynomial, then passing Recon would be very hard with an adversary who cannot control the opening of all commitments. Hence, while the adversary can give valid openings to random points, put together, these random points will not interpolate the same polynomial. However, this definition of "meaningful full opening" would work only for secret sharing schemes that have such a robust reconstruction property, but not in general. For example, it would not work with the simple sharing scheme based on xor where $t = \kappa - 1$ since every set of shares would pass the reconstruction algorithm. Hence, since we want to be very general and make no assumptions on the properties of the underlying secret sharing scheme (besides t-privacy and correctness), we provide a definition of binding of the full opening w.r.t. a relation $\mathcal{R}$, which can be later tied to the proof system (See Definition 5). Another crucial difference with the usual binding requirement is that in POC we need binding to hold w.r.t. a partial opening. Namely, an adversary should not be able to provide a commitment and partial opening that can be later explained by two different (and meaningful) full openings. This property is necessary when POC is combined with a zero-knowledge proof system to argue about soundness, since in the proof system the full opening is never provided in the clear. Hence, we define binding properties that must holds even when only partial openings are provided (Definition 4). Lastly, another binding concern which is unique to the partial opening setting that we are introducing, is that an adversary could craft her commitment adaptively *after* she has observed the *real* partial openings for some honest commitment that was published before. To capture security against this attack, we define the notion of Unforgeability of Partial Openings w.r.t. Relation $\mathcal{R}$ (Definition 6). This property asks that an adversary who copies commitments and/or partial openings from other parties should not be able to successfully open her own commitments in full.

Black-Box Anonymous Commit-and-Prove from POC. With the POC definition in place, we now have the crypto tool that allows honest parties to open *unknown* commitments, and we are able to finally leverage the MPC-in-the-head paradigm used in literature for black-box commit-and-prove. Given N POC public commitments $(\mathbf{C}^1, \ldots, \mathbf{C}^N)$, a prover $\mathcal{U}^l$, knowing the κ valid full openings committed in $\mathbf{C}^l$, will generate *fake* full openings for the remaining $N-1$ commitments (leveraging partial openability) and use such values as input of an MPC-in-the-head protocol for a specific functionality $\mathcal{F}^{\mathsf{OR}}_{\mathcal{R}}$. This functionality takes in input N full plaintext openings, and outputs 1 if there exists at least one set of κ plaintext openings that reconstruct to a secret s_l such that $\mathcal{R}(s_l) = 1$. Anonymity relies on the indistinguishability between fake openings and real openings, and the t security of the underlying MPC. To prove soundness we will leverage the various binding properties guaranteed by the definition of *POC*. (Hence, our proof works with any implementation of POC). The commit-and-prove protocol is depicted in Fig. 3. A graphic representation is also provided in Fig. 5.

Concrete Instantiation of Anonymous Commit-and-Proof for Tailored OR Circuit (Blackboo). While the generic POC + MPC-in-the-head approach described above works, it does not allow to leverage the concrete practicality of some MPC-in-the-head implementation such as ZKBoo [9]. ZKBoo explicitly defines the MPC-in-the-head computation via a function decomposition (described in Sect. 4) that yields to very efficient implementations. Our key idea is to match the secret sharing scheme used for POC with the secret sharing function used in the (2,3)-Decomposition of ZKboo – which is the simple 3-out-3 xor scheme, so that we can inherit the same proof efficiency. Unfortunately, however, the (2,3)-Decomposition of ZKBoo is tailored for the following type of relations: $\mathcal{R}(y, w) = 1$ if " I know w such that $y = F(w)$", while, in our proof, we will need to prove the OR of N statements. If we were to use ZKBoo as-is we would need to generically compile $\mathcal{R}^{\mathsf{OR}}$ into a circuit bigger than the one required for $\mathcal{R}$, which introduces additional complexity. We take another approach, and we provide a decomposition that is ad-hoc for the relation $\mathcal{R}^{\mathsf{OR}}$. The benefit of this approach is that any improvement in the circuit computation of $\mathcal{R}$ can be used directly in our composition (and it would not require to redesign the circuit for $\mathcal{R}^{OR}$). The final construction will consist in κ parallel repetitions of (2,3)-POCpaired with κ repetition of the (2,3) Function Decomposition. See Sect. 6 for more details of this construction.

On the One-Time Setting. Our one-time anonymous commit-and-prove scheme BlackBoo is suitable for governance applications in *decentralized* settings, such as blockchains. A common task in blockchain environment is to build a community controlled and decentralized collaborative decision-making mechanism for blockchain development and maintenance. In [22] for example, the goal is to provide a mechanism to vote on projects that should be funded with the blockchain treasury. BlackBoo can be used to build a such a voting mechanism by having parties publish commitments to their votes on the blockchain (the commitment can be signed using a permanent valid key, e.g. their wallet) and then claim one vote by proving the opening of one of the commitments. The tally is done transparently by looking at the openings. The tally is correct since proofs are linkable (so one person cannot vote multiple times). Votes are anonymous, since an opening is not linked to any single commitment – but to the entire set of published commitments. BlackBoo can also be used to easily implement a decentralized sealed-bit auction where the winner remains anonymous to the others. Each party P_i commits to their bid b_i and an ephemeral public key epk_i (this commitment could be signed with a permanent key). Once all commitments are published, each party will send the opening (b_i, epk_i) and prove that it is the opening of one of the commitments (the public key will be used for further communication with the winner). From the openings, everyone can determine the winner. We note that this sealed-bid auction will not require any facilitator (as opposed to solutions such as [15]) and can be done in a completely decentralized manner, by simply posting transactions on the blockchain.

3 Definitions

Notation. We use **bold** notation $\mathbf{c}$ to denote a vector of commitments, i.e., $\mathbf{c} = (c_1, \ldots, c_\lambda)$. If $\mathbf{d} = (d_1, \ldots, d_n)$ is a vector of commitments and $\mathcal{I} \subset \{1, \ldots, n\}$ is a set of indexes, we use notation $\mathbf{d}_\mathcal{I}$ as a shorthand for the set $\{d_j\}_{j \in \mathcal{I}}$. Notation $[N]$ means the set $\{1, \ldots, N\}$, $\mathsf{negl}(n)$ denotes a negligible function of n. When $\mathbf{C}$ is a vector of vectors, notation $\mathbf{C}[e, j]$ means, take the e-th vector of $\mathbf{C}$, let $\mathbf{C}^e$ such vector, take the j-th coordinate $\mathbf{C}^e[j]$. When x_i is a bit string we use notation $x_i[j]$ to denote the j-th bit of x. We will sometimes omit obvious checks in the attempt to reduce the burden on the reader.

3.1 Partially Openable Commitment Scheme

A *Partially Openable Commitment* scheme (for short, POC) is a commitment scheme that in addition to hiding and binding provides a "partial opening" property. Partial opening means that anyone can *partially* open a public commitment generated by some unknown party. A POC is parameterized by a secret-sharing scheme $(\mathsf{Share}, \mathsf{Recon})$ with parameters (t, n). A commitment is a vector of n sub commitments $\mathbf{C} = [\mathbf{c}_1, \ldots, \mathbf{c}_n]$, one for each share generated by Share. A partial opening consists in the opening of only t sub-commitments. We explicitly decouple the openings as plaintext openings – the shares of the plaintext value, that we denote by $x_1, \ldots, x_n$ from the cryptographic (crypto) openings that consist of the keys used to evaluate the underlying crypto primitive. We use a field, called tag tag, that is shared by all sub-commitments and uniquely binds a sub-commitment $\mathbf{c}_j$ to the full commitment $\mathbf{C}$.

Definition 1. *A Partially Openable Commitment (POC) parameterized with algorithms* $(\mathsf{Share}, \mathsf{Recon})$, *statistical security parameters* (t, n) *and security parameter* λ, *and with oracle access to cryptographic primitive(s)* $\mathcal{O}$, *is a tuple of algorithms* $(\mathsf{PCom}^{\mathcal{O}}, \mathsf{VerifyCrypto}^{\mathcal{O}}, \mathsf{VerifyPlaintext}, \mathsf{FakeOpen}^{\mathcal{O}}, \mathsf{ValidTag}, \mathsf{IsValid})$ *where:*

- $\mathsf{ValidTag}(1^\lambda)$: *on input the security parameter outputs a tag* $\mathsf{tag} \in \{0,1\}^\lambda$.
- $\mathsf{PCom}^{\mathcal{O}}_{\mathsf{Share}}(v, \mathsf{tag})$: *on input a string* $v \in \{0,1\}^\lambda$ *and a tag* tag, *outputs:*
  - *Commitment:* $\mathbf{C} = [\mathbf{c}_1, \ldots, \mathbf{c}_n]$
  - *Plaintext Vector:* $X = [x_1, \ldots, x_n]$
  - *Cryptographic Vector:* $K = [k_1, \ldots, k_n]$.
- $\mathsf{VerifyPlaintext}_{\mathsf{Recon}}(X)$: *On input a plaintext vector* $\mathbf{d}$, *it outputs* $y \in \{0,1\}^\lambda$ *or* $\bot$.
- $\mathsf{VerifyCrypto}^{\mathcal{O}}(\mathbf{C}, \mathsf{tag}, \mathcal{I}, \{K\}_{|\mathcal{I}})$: *On input a commitment* $\mathbf{C} = [\mathbf{c}_1, \ldots, \mathbf{c}_n]$, *a set* $\mathcal{I} \subset [N]$ *with* $|\mathcal{I}| \leq t$, *a tag* tag *and a subset of crypto openings* $\{K\}_{|\mathcal{I}} = (k_j)_{J \in \mathcal{I}}$, *and having oracle access to* $\mathcal{O}$, *it outputs: either* $y_j \in \{0,1\}^\lambda \forall j \in \mathcal{I}$ *or* $\bot$.
- $\mathsf{FakeOpen}^{\mathcal{O}}(\mathsf{tag}', \mathbf{C})$ *on input a commitment* $\mathbf{C}$ *and having oracle access to* $\mathcal{O}$ *returns:*
  - *Fake plaintext vector:* $FX = [x'_1, \ldots, x'_n]$ *and*
  - *Fake cryptographic vector:* $FK = [k'_1, \ldots, k'_n]$.
- $\mathsf{IsValid}(\mathbf{C})$: *on input a commitments, it outputs* 1 *if it has a valid format.*

A POC has the following properties:

Completeness. For every $v \in \{0,1\}^\lambda$, for all $\mathsf{tag} \leftarrow \mathsf{ValidTag}(1^\lambda)$, $(\mathbf{C}, X, K, \mathsf{tag}) \leftarrow \mathsf{PCom}^{\mathcal{O}}(v, \mathsf{tag})$, for all $\mathsf{tag}' \leftarrow \mathsf{ValidTag}(1^\lambda)$ it holds that:

$$Pr[\mathsf{VerifyPlaintext}(X) \rightarrow v] = 1 \tag{1}$$

$$\forall \mathcal{I} \subset [n], Pr\left[\mathsf{VerifyCrypto}^{\mathcal{O}}(\mathbf{C}, \mathsf{tag}, \mathcal{I}, \{K\}_{|\mathcal{I}}) \rightarrow \{Y_j\}_{j \in \mathcal{I}}\right] = 1 \tag{2}$$

$$\forall \mathcal{I} \subset [n], (FX, FK) \leftarrow \mathsf{FakeOpen}^{\mathcal{O}}(\mathsf{tag}', \mathbf{C}), \tag{3}$$

$$Pr\left[\mathsf{VerifyCrypto}^{\mathcal{O}}(\mathbf{C}, \mathsf{tag}, \mathcal{I}, \{FK\}_{|\mathcal{I}}) \rightarrow \{Y_j\}_{j \in \mathcal{I}})\right] = 1 \tag{4}$$

Openability. The following property says that any commitment (even if computed maliciously) is partially openable, as long it has the expected "format" (i.e., it satisfies predicate $\mathsf{IsValid}$.)

Definition 2 (Partial Openability). *A POC is partially openable if for all* $\mathbf{C}$ *s.t.* $\mathsf{IsValid}(\mathbf{C}) = 1$, *for all* tag' *and* $(FK, FX) \leftarrow \mathsf{FakeOpen}^{\mathcal{O}}(\mathsf{tag}', \mathbf{C})$, *for all* $\mathcal{I}$ *s.t.* $|\mathcal{I}| \leq t$ *it follows that*

$$Pr\left[\mathsf{VerifyCrypto}^{\mathcal{O}}(\mathbf{C}, \mathsf{tag}', \mathcal{I}, \{FK\}_{|\mathcal{I}}) \neq \bot)\right] \geq 1 - \mathsf{negl}(\lambda)$$

Hiding in Presence of Partial Openings. This property states the following: any honest commitment can be partially opened in such a way that the fake partial openings are indistinguishable form the real partial opening.

Definition 3 (Hiding in presence of Partial Openings). *A POC is hiding in presence of partial openings w.r.t a* secret sharing scheme $(\mathsf{Share}, \mathsf{Recon})$ *if the following holds. For all* $v \leftarrow \{0,1\}^\lambda$, *for all* $\mathsf{tag} \leftarrow \mathsf{ValidTag}$, $(\mathbf{C}, X, K,) \leftarrow \mathsf{PCom}(v, \mathsf{tag})$, $\mathcal{I} \subset \{1, \ldots, n\}$ *s.t.* $|\mathcal{I}| \leq t$, *for all* $\mathsf{tag}' \leftarrow \mathsf{ValidTag}(1^\lambda)$, $(FK, FX) \leftarrow \mathsf{FakeOpen}^{\mathcal{O}}(\mathsf{tag}', \mathbf{C})$ *and* $\mathsf{VerifyCrypto}^{\mathcal{O}}(\mathbf{C}, \mathsf{tag}', \mathcal{I}, \{FK\}_{|\mathcal{I}}) \neq \bot$ *the following distributions are perfectly (resp., computational) indistinguishable*

$$\{\mathbf{C}, \mathsf{tag}, K[j]\}_{j \in \mathcal{I}} \approx \{\mathbf{C}, \mathsf{tag}', FK[j]\}_{j \in \mathcal{I}}$$

Binding of Partial Openings. This definition captures the following property. Fixed a commitment $\mathbf{C} = (\mathbf{c}_1, \ldots, \mathbf{c}_n)$, it should be infeasible for an adversary to provide two distinct partial crypto openings that are consistent with the *same* full plaintext openings $(x_1, \ldots, x_n)$.

Definition 4 (Binding of Partial Openings). *A POC satisfies Binding of Partial Openings if for all PPT adversaries* $\mathcal{A}$, *the following holds.*

$$Pr\begin{bmatrix} \mathbf{C}; X = (x_j)_{j \in \mathcal{I}}, (\mathsf{tag}, K) \neq (\tilde{\mathsf{tag}}, \tilde{K}) \\ \forall \mathcal{I}, \mathsf{VerifyCrypto}(\mathbf{C}, \mathsf{tag}, \mathcal{I}, \{k_j\}_{j \in \mathcal{I}}) = (x_j)_{j \in \mathcal{I}} \\ \forall \mathcal{I}, \mathsf{VerifyCrypto}(\mathbf{C}, \tilde{\mathsf{tag}}, \mathcal{I}, \{\tilde{k}_j\}_{j \in \mathcal{I}}) = (x_j)_{j \in \mathcal{I}} \end{bmatrix} \leq \mathsf{negl}(\lambda) \tag{5}$$

Binding of Plaintexts w.r.t. a Relation $\mathcal{R}$. Note that the partial openability property allow anyone to partially open a commitment $\mathbf{C}$. This naturally means that there are many ways $\mathbf{C}$ can be opened, and thus many plaintexts. This property establishes that fixed a commitment $\mathbf{C}$, it is infeasible for an adversary to provide two partial crypto openings that are consistent with two *distinct* full plaintext openings that *satisfy* a relation $\mathcal{R}$.

Definition 5 (Binding of Plaintexts w.r.t. a Relation $\mathcal{R}$). *A POC satisfies binding of Plaintexts w.r.t. a Relation $\mathcal{R}$ if for all PPT adversaries $\mathcal{A}$ the following holds.*

$$Pr\begin{bmatrix} (\mathbf{C}, \mathsf{O}_1, \mathsf{O}_2) \leftarrow \mathcal{A}(1^\lambda) & \mathsf{O}_1 = (\mathsf{tag}, X, K) \neq \mathsf{O}_2 = (\tilde{\mathsf{tag}}, \tilde{X}, \tilde{K}) \\ \tilde{X} = [x_1, \ldots, x_n] & \mathcal{R}(\mathsf{Recon}(x_1, \ldots, x_n)) = 1 \\ \tilde{X} = [\tilde{x}_1, \ldots, \tilde{x}_n] & \mathcal{R}(\mathsf{Recon}(\tilde{x}_1, \ldots, \tilde{x}_n)) = 1 \\ \forall \mathcal{I} & \mathsf{VerifyCrypto}(\mathbf{C}, \mathsf{tag}, \mathcal{I}, \{k_j\}_{j \in \mathcal{I}}) = (x_j)_{j \in \mathcal{I}} \\ \forall \mathcal{I} & \mathsf{VerifyCrypto}(\mathbf{C}, \tilde{\mathsf{tag}}, \mathcal{I}, \{\tilde{k}_j\}_{j \in \mathcal{I}}) = (\tilde{x}_j)_{j \in \mathcal{I}} \end{bmatrix} \leq \mathsf{negl}(\lambda) \tag{6}$$

Unforgeability of Partial Openings w.r.t. Relation $\mathcal{R}$. The following definition captures the fact that valid partial openings should be unforgeable, when the plaintext must satisfy a certain relation $\mathcal{R}$. Namely, while the adversary can always copy the partial openings that she observed from other parties, it should be infeasible to re-use partial openings of others, while still being able to open to a meaningful plaintext. This property holds with probability $1 - \frac{1}{\exp(n,t)}$ since if the adversary guesses the set $\mathcal{I}$ on which she will need to provide the openings, she can simply create commitments that do not open to a meaningful plaintext.

Definition 6 (Unforgeability of Partial Openings w.r.t. Relation $\mathcal{R}$). *A POC satisfies unforgeability of partial openings w.r.t. relation $\mathcal{R}$ if for all PPT adversaries $\mathcal{A}$ there exist function $exp(t,n)$ and a negligible function* $\mathsf{negl}(\lambda)$ *such that:*

$$Pr[\mathsf{Exp}^{\mathsf{Forge-Partial}}_{\mathsf{POC},\mathcal{R}}(\mathcal{A}, 1^\lambda) \rightarrow 1] \leq \frac{1}{exp(t,n)} + \mathsf{negl}(\lambda)$$

where $\mathsf{Exp}^{\mathsf{Forge-Partial}}_{\mathsf{POC},\mathcal{R}}$ is the game described below.

Game 1 *[Unforgeability of Partial Opening w.r.t. $\mathcal{R}$]*
$\mathsf{Exp}^{\mathsf{Forge-Partial}}_{\mathsf{POC},\mathcal{R}}(\mathcal{A}, 1^\lambda)$

1. *$\mathcal{A}$ sends input v, s.t. $\mathcal{R}(v) = 1$ to the challenger .*
2. *Challenger runs $\mathsf{tag} \leftarrow \mathsf{ValidTag}(1^\lambda)$ and $(\mathbf{C}, K, X) \leftarrow \mathsf{PCom}(v, \mathsf{tag})$ and sends $\mathbf{C}$ and X to the adversary.*
3. *$\mathcal{A}$ sends commitment $\mathbf{M}$ (it could be equal to $\mathbf{C}$).*
4. *Challenger picks set $\mathcal{I}$ uniformly at random and send partial crypto openings tag, $K = (k_J)_{j\in\mathcal{I}}$ to $\mathcal{A}$.*
5. *$\mathcal{A}$ sends plaintext openings $\tilde{X} = [\tilde{x}_1, \ldots, \tilde{x}_n]$ s.t. $\mathcal{R}(\mathsf{Recon}(\tilde{X}))= 1$.*
6. *Challenger picks set $\tilde{\mathcal{I}}$ and send it to $\mathcal{A}$.*
7. *When $\mathcal{A}$ responds with $\tilde{K} = (\tilde{k}_j)_{j\in\tilde{\mathcal{I}}}$, if $(X, \mathsf{tag}, K, \mathcal{I}) \neq (\tilde{X}, \tilde{\mathsf{tag}}, \tilde{K}, \tilde{\mathcal{I}})$ (i.e., $\mathcal{A}$ is not simply copying) proceed as follows:*
   - If $(\mathbf{M} = \mathbf{C})$ and $\mathsf{VerifyCrypto}(\mathbf{C}, \mathsf{tag}, \{\tilde{k}_\ell\}_{\ell\in\tilde{\mathcal{I}}}))= (\tilde{x}_\ell)_{\ell\in\tilde{\mathcal{I}}}$ output 1 (honest commitment is forged)
   - Else, if $\mathsf{VerifyCrypto}(\mathbf{M}, \mathsf{tag}, \{\tilde{k}_\ell\}_{\ell\in\tilde{\mathcal{I}}}))= (\tilde{x}_\ell)_{\ell\in\tilde{\mathcal{I}}}$ output 1 (partial opening of honest commitment is forged).
   -Else, output 0.

3.2 Linkable Anonymous Commit-and-Prove System

An anonymous 1-out-of-N Commit-and-Prove System allows a prover to convince a verifier that *the opening* of one out of N commitments satisfies a certain relation $\mathcal{R}$, without revealing which one. The word anonymous is used to emphasize that the opening $N - 1$ commitments are unknown to the honest prover. For simplicity, the definition below assumes that all proofs are performed w.r.t. the same set of commitments $\mathbb{C}$. The same definition can be generalized to the case where a proof can be computed to any subset of $\mathbb{C}$.

Definition 7 (Linkable Anonymous Commit-and-Prove). *A 1-out-of-N Linkable Anonymous Commit-and-Prove scheme for a relation $\mathcal{R}$ is a tuple of PPT algorithms $(\mathsf{ComWitness}, \mathsf{IsValid}, \mathsf{Prove}, \mathsf{Verify}, \mathsf{PLink})$ that have oracle access to cryptographic primitive(s) $\mathcal{O}$ and implement the following functionalities:*

- *$(\mathbf{C}, \mathbf{d}) \leftarrow \mathsf{ComWitness}^{\mathcal{O}}(x^l||w^l)$ is a randomized algorithm run by a party $\mathcal{P}^l$. It takes in input a string $x^l||w^l$ and outputs a commitment $\mathbf{C}$ and opening $\mathbf{d}$. The commitment $\mathbf{C}$ is published and added to a vector of public commitments $\mathbb{C}$, $\mathbf{d}$ is the secret output for $\mathcal{P}^l$.*
- *$b := \mathsf{IsValid}(\mathbf{C})$ is a boolean predicate that on input a commitment outputs 1 if it satisfies a valid format.*
- *$\pi \leftarrow \mathsf{Prove}^{\mathcal{O}}(\mathbf{C}^1, \ldots, \mathbf{C}^N, \mathbf{d}^l)$ is run by a party $\mathcal{P}^l$. It takes in input the list of public commitments $(\mathbf{C}^1, \ldots, \mathbf{C}^N)$ published by parties $\mathcal{P}^1, \ldots, \mathcal{P}^N$, and a private input $\mathbf{d}^l$ of $\mathcal{P}^l$. The output is a proof π.*
- *$b := \mathsf{Verify}^{\mathcal{O}}(\mathbb{C}, \pi)$ is a deterministic algorithm that on input a set of commitments $\mathbb{C} = (\mathbf{C}^1, \ldots, \mathbf{C}^N)$ and a proof π, outputs 0/1.*

– $b := \mathsf{PLink}^{\mathcal{O}}(\mathbb{C}, \pi_1, \pi_2)$ *is a deterministic algorithm that on input set* $\mathbb{C} = (\mathbf{C}^1, \ldots, \mathbf{C}^N)$ *of commitments and two proofs* π_1, π_2 *outputs a bit denoting whether* π_1 *and* π_2 *were computed using the same witness* w.

Definition 8 (Completeness). *For all* $\mathbb{C} = [\mathbf{C}^1, \ldots, \mathbf{C}^N]$, $\mathbf{C}^i \leftarrow \mathsf{ComWitness}(x^i \,||\, w^i)$, $\forall\, l \in [N]$, *s.t.* $\pi \leftarrow \mathsf{Prove}^{\mathcal{O}}(\mathbf{C}^1, \ldots, \mathbf{C}^N, \mathbf{d}^l)$, $\Pr\left[\mathsf{Verify}^{\mathcal{O}}(\mathbb{C}, \pi) \rightarrow 1\right] = 1$.

Definition 9 (Proof of Knowledge). *For every PPT prover strategy* $\mathcal{P}^\star$, *there exists an oracle PPT machine* Ext *called extractor such that for all* $\mathbb{C}^*, \pi^*$ *generated by* $\mathcal{P}^\star$ *it holds that:*

$$\Pr\left[\mathsf{Verify}(\mathbb{C}^*, \pi^*) = 1 \wedge \mathsf{Ext}^{\mathcal{A}^*}(\mathbb{C}, \pi^*) \rightarrow (x, w) \wedge \mathcal{R}(x, w) = 1\right] = 1 - \mathsf{negl}(\lambda)$$

Definition 10 (One-time Prover Anonymity.). *For all* $\lambda \in \mathbb{N}$, *for any PPT adversarial verifier* $\mathcal{A}$, *there exists a PPT simulator* $\mathsf{SimProve} = (\mathsf{SimCom}, \mathsf{SimProve})$ *and a negligible function* negl *such that:*

$$Pr[\mathsf{Exp}^{\mathsf{AnonyLink}}{}_{\mathcal{A},\Pi,\mathsf{SimProve}}(1^\lambda) = 1] = \frac{1}{2} + \mathsf{negl}(\lambda)$$

where $\mathsf{Exp}^{\mathsf{AnonyLink}}$ is the following game.

Game 2 (One-time Anonymity Game) $\mathsf{Exp}^{\mathsf{AnonyLink}}{}_{\mathcal{A},\Pi,\mathsf{SimProve}}(1^\lambda)$.

Game Initialization. *The challenger picks* $b \xleftarrow{\$} \{0,1\}$ *and sets* $\mathcal{L} \leftarrow \emptyset$.
Commitment Stage. $\mathcal{A}$ *outputs a set* IdxHon *of indexes for honest players and a set of theorems/witnesses* $\{x^l, w^l\}_{l \in \mathsf{IdxHon}}$.
– *For* $l \in \mathsf{IdxHon}$: *if* $b = 0$ *the challenger runs* $(\mathbf{C}^l, \mathbf{d}_l) \leftarrow \mathsf{ComWitness}(x^l||w^l)$, *and sets* $\mathbb{H} = \{\mathbf{C}^l\}_{l \in \mathsf{IdxHon}}$. *if* $b = 1$ *it runs* $(\mathsf{state}, \mathbb{H}) \leftarrow \mathsf{SimCom}(\mathsf{IdxHon})$. *The set* $\mathbb{H}$ *is given to* $\mathcal{A}$.
–Malicious Commitments. $\mathcal{A}$ *outputs commitments* $\mathbb{M} = \mathbf{M}_1, \mathbf{M}_2, \ldots$. – *Public Commitment List:* $\mathbb{C} = \mathbb{H} \cup \mathbb{M}$. **Proof Stage.** $\mathcal{A}$ *has access to oracle* $\mathsf{Prove}(\mathbb{C}, l)$ *that behaves as follows.*
If $l \in \mathsf{IdxHon} \wedge\, l \notin \mathcal{L}$: *add* l *into* $\mathcal{L}$ *and*
- *If* $b = 0$ *output* $\pi^l \leftarrow \mathsf{Prove}(\mathbb{C}, \mathbf{d}^l)$ *to* $\mathcal{A}$.
- *If* $b = 1$ *output* $\pi^l \leftarrow \mathsf{SimProve}(\mathsf{state}, \mathbb{C})$.
Else, output $\perp$.
Decision. *When* $\mathcal{A}$ *outputs* b', *output* 1 *iff* $b = b'$.

Definition 11 (Proof Linkability). *This property captures the fact that any two proofs computed using the same openings should be linked. Let* $\mathcal{A}$ *be a PPT algorithm. A commitment and prove scheme is linkable if:*

$$Pr\begin{bmatrix} \mathbb{C}^*, \pi_1^*, \ldots, \pi_{N+1}^* \leftarrow \mathcal{A}(1^\lambda): & |\mathbb{C}^*| = N \\ \forall i \in [N+1]: & \mathsf{Verify}(\mathbb{C}^*, \pi_i) = 1 \\ \forall i, j \in [N+1] i \neq j: & \mathsf{PLink}(\mathbb{C}^*, \pi_i, \pi_j) = 0 \end{bmatrix} \leq \mathsf{negl}(\lambda) \qquad (7)$$

Definition 12 (Proof Non-Frameability). *This property captures the fact that an adversary should not be able to craft a proof that is linkable to an honest proof. This is captured via the following experiment. We say that Π satisfies proof frameability if for all PPT adversaries $\mathcal{A}$, there exists a negligible function* negl *such that:*

$$Pr[\mathsf{Exp}_{\mathcal{A},\Pi}^{\mathsf{ProofFrame}}(1^\lambda) = 1] \leq \mathsf{negl}(\lambda)$$

where $\mathsf{Exp}_{\mathcal{A},\Pi}^{\mathsf{ProofFrame}}(1^\lambda$ *is the following experiment:*

Game 3 (Proof-Framing Game) **Experiment** $\mathsf{Exp}_{\mathcal{A},\Pi}^{\mathsf{ProofFrame}}(1^\lambda)$

1. *The adversary $\mathcal{A}$ on input 1^λ outputs the pair of $(x||w)$.*
2. *The challenger runs* $(\mathbf{C}, \mathbf{d}) \leftarrow \mathsf{ComWitness}(x||w)$ *and send* $\mathbf{C}$ *to the* $\mathcal{A}$.
3. $\mathcal{A}$ *outputs commitments* $\mathbb{M} = \mathbf{M}_1, \mathbf{M}_2, \ldots$. *Set* $\mathbb{C} = \{\mathbb{M} \cup \mathbf{C}\}$.
4. *The challenger compute* $\pi \leftarrow \mathsf{Prove}(\mathbb{C}, \mathbf{d})$ *and send it to* $\mathcal{A}$.
5. $\mathcal{A}$ *outputs* π'.
6. *Decision. Output* 1 *iff:* $\mathsf{Verify}(\mathbb{C}, \pi') = 1 \wedge \mathsf{PLink}(\mathbb{C}, \pi, \pi') = 1$.

4 Ingredients

4.1 Ingredient 1. Partially Openable Commitment Scheme

The high-level description of the protocol was provided in the Introduction. In Fig. 1 we provide the formal description of a POC scheme, instantiated with the secret sharing scheme (ShareD, RecD) described below.

Protocol 1 (Sharing Scheme) *(*ShareD, RecD*)*

- $\mathsf{ShareD}(\mathbf{x}, \psi_1, \psi_2, \psi_3)$: *Output* $\mathbf{x}_1, \mathbf{x}_2, \mathbf{x}_3$ *such that* $\mathbf{x} = \mathbf{x}_1 \oplus \mathbf{x}_2 \oplus \mathbf{x}_3$. *These strings are picked using random tapes* ψ_1, ψ_2, ψ_3. *All strings are in* $\{0,1\}^\lambda$.
- $\mathsf{RecD}(\mathbf{x}'_1, \mathbf{x}'_2, \mathbf{x}'_3)$: *Output* $\mathbf{x}'_1 \oplus \mathbf{x}'_2 \oplus \mathbf{x}'_3$.

Theorem 1 (Protocol 2 **is a Partially Openable Commitment scheme).** *If $\mathcal{H}$ is a random oracle,* (ShareD, RecD) *is* $(2,3)$ *private (Definition 13), then Protocol 1 satisfies Definition 1 with parameters* $(2,3)$.

[Informal]. Informally, security follows directly from the properties of $\mathcal{H}$. Hiding in presence of partial openings follows from the (2,3) privacy of ShareD and the hiding of the remaining unopened commitment. $\mathbf{c}_e$. Binding of partial opening – which means that no sender should be able to open a commitment $\mathbf{C} = (\mathbf{c}_1, \mathbf{c}_2, \mathbf{c}_3)$ to a fixed plaintext (x_1, x_2, x_3) with two *distinct* crypto partial openings (tag, k_a, k_b), $(\tilde{\mathsf{tag}}, \tilde{k_a}, \tilde{k_b})$ – follows from the second-preimage resistance property $\mathcal{H}$. Indeed, for any δ, finding *distinct keys* that decipher the same plaintext x_δ for

Protocol 2 (A Partially Openable Commitment from $\mathcal{O} = \mathcal{H}$)
Parameters: $t = 2, n = 3$.

$\mathsf{POC}^{\mathcal{H}}(\mathsf{ShareD}, \mathsf{RecD})$.

$\mathsf{ValidTag}^{\mathcal{H}}(1^\lambda)$: *Pick a random string* r. *Output* $\mathsf{tag} \leftarrow \mathcal{H}(r)$.
$\mathsf{PCom}^{\mathcal{H}}_{\mathsf{ShareD}}(v, \mathsf{tag})$:
- *Plaintext:* $(x_1, x_2, x_3) \leftarrow \mathsf{ShareD}(v, \mathbf{r}_1, \mathbf{r}_2, \mathbf{r}_3)$ *with* $\mathbf{r}_j \xleftarrow{\$} \{0,1\}^\lambda$.
- *Crypto Material:* $\mathbf{c}_a = \mathcal{H}(\mathsf{tag}||k_a) \oplus x_a$ *with* $k_a \xleftarrow{\$} \{0,1\}^\lambda$, $\forall a \in \{1,2,3\}$
- *Output. Commitment:* $\mathbf{C} := (\mathbf{c}_1, \mathbf{c}_2, \mathbf{c}_3)$.
  Plaintext Vector $X = [x_1, x_2, x_3]$; *Crypto Vector* $K = [k_1, k_2, k_3]$; tag.

$\mathsf{VerifyPlaintext}(X)$: *Output* $v = \mathsf{RecD}(x_1, x_2, x_3)$.
$\mathsf{VerifyCrypto}^{\mathcal{H}}(\mathbf{C}, \mathsf{tag}, \mathcal{I}, \{K\}_{|\mathcal{I}})$:
- If $\mathsf{IsValid}(\mathbf{C}) = 0$ output $\perp$.
- Let $\mathbf{C} = (\mathbf{c}_1, \mathbf{c}_2, \mathbf{c}_3)$. Let $\mathcal{I} = \{a, b\}$.
- Output (x_a, x_b) where $x_a = \mathbf{c}_a \oplus \mathcal{H}(\mathsf{tag}||k_a)$ and $x_b = \mathbf{c}_b \oplus \mathcal{H}(\mathsf{tag}||k_b)$.

$\mathsf{FakeOpen}^{\mathcal{H}}(\mathsf{tag}', \mathbf{C})$:
- Crypto Part: Pick random $fk_a \xleftarrow{\$} \{0,1\}^\lambda$, for $a = 1, 2, 3$.
- Plaintext Part: $fx_a \leftarrow \mathcal{H}(\mathsf{tag}'||fk_a) \oplus \mathbf{c}_a$.
- Output: Plaintext Vector $FX = [fx_1, fx_2, fx_3]$; Crypto Vector $FK = [fk_1, fk_2, fk_3]$; tag tag'.

$\mathsf{IsValid}(\mathbf{C})$: *Output 1 iff* $|\mathbf{C}| = 3\lambda$ *bits.*

Fig. 1. Partially Openable Commitment Scheme POC

commitment $\mathbf{c}_\delta$ corresponds to finding two pre-images of $y = \mathbf{c}_\delta \oplus x_\delta$. Binding of Plaintext wrt a Relation $\mathcal{R}$ – which means that it should be infeasible to open the same commitment $\mathbf{C} = (\mathbf{c}_1, \mathbf{c}_2, \mathbf{c}_3)$ with two partial crypto openings and two *distinct* plaintext openings $X = (x_1, x_2, x_3)$ and $\tilde{X} = (\tilde{x_1}, \tilde{x_2}, \tilde{x_3})$ that satisfy a relation $\mathcal{R}$–, holds with probability 2/3. To see why, first notice that once the adversary $\mathcal{A}$ has fixed $(\mathbf{c}_1, \mathbf{c}_2, \mathbf{c}_3)$ and declared openings $X = (x_1, x_2, x_3)$ and $\tilde{X} = (\tilde{x_1}, \tilde{x_2}, \tilde{x_3})$, in order to provide two crypto openings (tag, k_a, k_b), $(\tilde{\mathsf{tag}}, \tilde{k_a}, \tilde{k_b})$ that are both consistent with the declared plaintext openings, $\mathcal{A}$ should either guess the challenge $e \notin \mathcal{I}$, or should find a pre-image of the value $y = \mathbf{c}_e \oplus x_e$ (resp. $y = \mathbf{c}_e \oplus \tilde{x_e}$). Unforgeability of Partial Openings wrt Relation $\mathcal{R}$ is proved for our relation of interest $\mathcal{R}_{\mathsf{equal}}$ (but the same proof works for any non trivial relation). This property captures the inability of the adversary to forge the crypto openings provided by other users on their own commitment. It follows from similar arguments of binding of plaintext wrt $\mathcal{R}$, since, by copying other user's crypto openings, the adversary is not able to open his own commitment with plaintexts that satisfy $\mathcal{R}$. The formal proof is provided in the full version.

4.2 Ingredient 2. MPC-in-the-Head for or Relation

We will use the 3-party MPC-in-the-head protocol proposed in [9] (see also [9], Sec. 14) presented as a (2,3)-Function Decomposition. The computation is divided in 3 parallel threads such that revealing two threads does not reveal any information about the inputs to the function. In the following we report the definition of linear decomposition as provided in [9].

Definition 13 ((2,3) Linear Decomposition [9]**).** *Let $\Phi : X \to Y$ be a function that can be divided in 3 computation branches $\{\Phi_1, \Phi_2, \Phi_3\}$ performed in steps by gates and let $\mathcal{G}^{\Phi} = \bigcup_{c=1}^{N} \{\Phi_1^{(c)}, \Phi_2^{(c)}, \Phi_3^{(c)}\}$ be the set of gates. A Decomposition (see [9], Sec. 14) for a function Φ is the set of functions*

$$\mathcal{D} = \{\mathsf{ShareD}, \mathsf{Output}_1, \mathsf{Output}_2, \mathsf{Output}_3, \mathsf{RecD}\} \cup \mathcal{G}^{\Phi}$$

such that ShareD *is surjective and satisfies the properties of Correctness (the output of* RecD *is the correct evaluation of Φ) and (2,3)-Privacy (i.e., any two branches do no reveal any information about the input).*

Our Ad-hoc Execution of Decomposition of OR Relation $\mathcal{R}^{\mathsf{OR}}$. We are interested in computing relation $\mathcal{R}^{\mathsf{OR}} : (\{0,1\}^{\lambda})^N \to \{0,1\}$ that takes in input N values $(X^1, \ldots, X^N)$ and outputs 1 if there exists one i such that $\mathcal{R}(X^i) = 1$, for any relation $\mathcal{R}$. We split this task in two functions: (1) $\Phi^{\mathcal{R}} : \{0,1\}^{\lambda} \to \{0,1\}$ is defined as the boolean function computing $\mathcal{R}(X) = 1$ with gates $\mathcal{G}^{\mathcal{R}}$ and (2) $\mathcal{R}^{\mathsf{OR}} : \{0,1\}^N \to \{0,1\}$ is the OR function that computes the OR of N bits, and we denote by $\mathcal{G}^{\mathsf{OR}}$ the gates for $\mathcal{R}^{\mathsf{OR}}$. We present our ad-hoc decomposition for $\mathcal{R}^{\mathsf{OR}}$ in Protocol 3.

Protocol 3 (Ad-hoc Execution of Decomposition for $\mathcal{R}^{\mathsf{OR}}$) *(this work)*

$\Pi^{\mathcal{R}^{\mathsf{OR}}}(X^1, \ldots, X^N)$

Output: $b = \mathcal{R}^{\mathsf{OR}}(X^1 || W^1, \ldots, X^N || W^N) = \mathcal{R}(X^1, W^1) \vee \ldots \mathcal{R}(X^N, W^N)$.

1. Secret Sharing Step:

$\mathbf{x}_1^i, \mathbf{x}_2^i, \mathbf{x}_3^i \leftarrow \mathsf{ShareD}(W^i, \psi_1^i, \psi_2^i, \psi_3^i)$; *for* $i \in [N]$ *(Prot. 1)*

2. Computation Step: $\mathsf{Compute}(\mathcal{G}^{\mathcal{R}^{\mathsf{OR}}}, \mathbf{x}_1^i, \mathbf{x}_2^i, \mathbf{x}_3^i)_{i \in [N]}$

(i) **Secure Computation of $\mathcal{R}(X^i, W^i)$ for each** i:
$(\mathbf{w}_1^i, \mathbf{w}_2^i, \mathbf{w}_3^i) \leftarrow \mathsf{Compute}(\mathcal{G}^{\mathcal{R}}, \mathbf{x}_1^i, \mathbf{x}_2^i, \mathbf{x}_3^i, \mathbf{r}_1^i, \mathbf{r}_2^i, \mathbf{r}_3^i)$; *for* $i \in [N]$.
Let $\mathbf{o}_j^i \leftarrow \mathsf{Output}_j(\mathbf{w}_j^i)$ $j = 1, 2, 3$. *(Note that the output is not reconstructed)*

(ii) **Secure Computation of** OR:
Input shares: $\mathbf{orx}_j := (\mathbf{o}_j^1, \ldots, \mathbf{o}_j^N)$, *for* $j \in [3]$. $(\mathbf{orw}_1, \mathbf{orw}_2, \mathbf{orw}_3) \leftarrow \mathsf{Compute}(\mathcal{G}^{\mathsf{OR}}, \mathbf{orx}_1, \mathbf{orx}_2, \mathbf{orx}_3, \mathbf{r}_1, \mathbf{r}_2, \mathbf{r}_3)$.

3. Outputs.

1. *Let* $\mathbf{or}_j \leftarrow \mathsf{Output}(\mathbf{orw}_j)$
2. **Output Reconstruction:** $b = \mathsf{RecD}(\mathbf{or}_1, \mathbf{or}_2, \mathbf{or}_3)$ *(Prot. 1)*

Fig. 2. Our decomposition $\Pi_{\Phi^{\mathsf{OR}}}$

Protocol 4 (View consistency) TestViewConsistency$^{\Phi^{\mathsf{OR}}}(\mathbf{w}_a, \mathbf{w}_b)$

1. Computation: Check that $\mathbf{w}_a$ is a correct execution of Φ^{OR} (Prot. 3) wrt the inputs contained $\mathbf{w}_a[0]$.
2. Communication. Check that any incoming/outgoing message from player P_a and player P_b are consistent with the messages that appear in the respective views $\mathbf{w}_a, \mathbf{w}_b$.

The security of our decomposition $\Pi_{\Phi^{\mathsf{OR}}}$ follows directly from the security of the (2,3)-decomposition of [9]. This is because $\Pi_{\Phi^{\mathsf{OR}}}$ is a sequential composition of two secure decompositions, where the output of the first decomposition is not reconstructed but instead is left in secret sharing form and fed as input shares of the second execution of the decomposition.

5 Black-Box Anonymous Commit-and-Prove

The protocol consists of two stages: the **POC Commitment Stage** (Protocol 5) and the **Proof stage** (Protocol 6). At high-level the proof stage consists of 4 steps. In the first step the prover must obtain the shares for all the commitments. A prover P^l, who knows the real openings tag^l, X^l, K^l, will first compute the "fake openings" for the other $N-1$ commitments $\mathbf{C}^i \neq \mathbf{C}^l$, using tag tag^l. Namely, P^l obtains a fakes shares $FX^{i,j} = [fx_1^{i,j}, fx_2^{i,j}, fx_3^{i,j}]$ for the remaining $N-1$ inputs. In the second step, the prover must compute the MPC views, on input the shares obtained in step 1. Namely, each tuple of share $(fx_1^{i,j}, fx_2^{i,j}, fx_3^{i,j})$ is used as input of the j-th execution of protocol $\Pi_{\Phi^{\mathsf{OR}}}$, thereby obtaining views $\mathbf{w}_1^j, \mathbf{w}_2^j, \mathbf{w}_3^j$. In the third step, the prover commits to the views above and obtains $(\mathbf{Cview}_1^j, \mathbf{Cview}_2^j, \mathbf{Cview}_3^j)$. Finally, the prover obtains the positions that must be opened by querying the random oracle $\mathcal{H}$ and obtains the challenge sets $\mathcal{I}^1, \ldots, \mathcal{I}^\kappa$. The final proof consists of the commitments $(\mathbf{Cview}_1^j, \mathbf{Cview}_2^j, \mathbf{Cview}_3^j)$, the openings of the commitments in position $(a^j, b^j) \in \mathcal{I}^j$ and the partial openings for each of $\mathbf{C}^{I,j}$. The verifier accepts the proofs if the opened MPC-views use inputs that are consistent with the partial openings of $\mathbf{C}^{i,j}$ and if they are correct according to $\Pi_{\Phi^{\mathsf{OR}}}$. In Fig. 5 we attempted to provide a visual representation of the protocol that we hope will help to visualize the prover's steps, how the keys are used and what is the final view of the verifier. Figure 5 depicts an optimized version of the protocol where the commitments of the views are compressed using a Merkle Tree (hence the gray triangle).

Notation. $\mathbf{w}_1$ denotes the complete view of MPC player 1, $\mathbf{w}_1[0]$ denotes the input in the view of player 1, $\mathbf{w}_1[i, 0]$ denotes the i-th input in view of player 1. Index $i \in [N]$ are used for parties/commitments, $j \in [\kappa]$ is used for sub-proofs.

Protocol 5 (BlackBoo: Commitment Stage)
Let $\mathsf{POC} = (\mathsf{PCom}^{\mathcal{O}}, \mathsf{VerifyCrypto}^{\mathcal{O}}, \mathsf{VerifyPlaintext}, \mathsf{FakeOpen}^{\mathcal{O}}, \mathsf{ValidTag}, \mathsf{IsValid})$ *as in Protocol 2.*

$\underline{\mathsf{ComWitness}(x||w)}$. *On input* (x, w) *for* $\mathcal{R}$, $\mathcal{P}^l$ *computes* $\mathsf{tag}^l \xleftarrow{\$} \mathsf{ValidTag}(1^\lambda)$.
Run $(\mathbf{C}^{l,j}, X^{l,j}, X^{l,j}) \leftarrow \mathsf{PCom}(x||w, \mathsf{tag}^l)$ $\forall j \in [\kappa]$ *where:*
- *Commitment:* $\mathbf{C}^{l,j} = (\mathbf{c}_1^{l,j}, \mathbf{c}_2^{l,j}, \mathbf{c}_3^{l,j})$.
- *Plaintext Vector:* $X^{l,j} = (x_1^{l,j}, x_2^{l,j}, x_3^{l,j})$.
- *Cryptographic Vector:* $X^{l,j} = (k_1^{l,j}, k_2^{l,j}, k_3^{l,j})$.

Publish $\mathbf{C}^{l,j}$. *The witness is* $(\mathsf{tag}^l, X^{l,j}, K^{l,j})$.

6 A Concrete Instantiation for Proof of Equality: $\mathcal{R}_{\mathsf{equal}}^{\mathsf{OR}}$

In this section we focus on specific relation, the equality relation $\mathcal{R}_{\mathsf{equal}}$, and its 1-out-$N$ extension $\mathcal{R}_{\mathsf{equal}}^{\mathsf{OR}}$. Our goal is to show that our black-box approach can lead to very efficient proofs (more efficient than the non-black-box counterpart). Relation $\mathcal{R}_{\mathsf{equal}}^{\mathsf{OR}}$ is defined as follow. $\mathcal{R}_{\mathsf{equal}}^{\mathsf{OR}}(sn, v_1, \ldots, v_n) = 1$ iff there exists an i such that $v_i = sn$. In order to make explicit claims about the concrete complexity of the proof we explicitly design a circuit $\mathsf{C}_{\mathsf{EqOR}}$ for relation $\mathcal{R}_{\mathsf{equal}}^{\mathsf{OR}}$ (and we prove its correctness), in order to be able to count the gates that need to be evaluated. Each gate is then securely evaluated using the secure decomposition of [9] (described in Sect. 4 of [9]). We are then able to identify the precise concrete complexity.

Boolean Circuit Optimized for $\mathcal{R}_{\mathsf{equal}}^{\mathsf{OR}}$. We design a circuit for $\mathcal{R}_{\mathsf{equal}}^{\mathsf{OR}}$ performs the following task. On input a public value sn and N strings $v_1, \ldots, v_N$, outputs 1 if there is an i such that $v_i = sn$. Wlog, we assume that N is even (if not, it can be enforced via padding). The circuit $\mathsf{C}_{\mathsf{EqOR}} : \left(\{0,1\}^\ell\right)^N \rightarrow \{0,1\}^\ell$ is described in Fig. 4.

Claim (Circuit $\mathsf{C}_{\mathsf{EqOR}}$ *correctly implements* $\mathcal{R}_{\mathsf{equal}}^{\mathsf{OR}}$*).* Let N be a positive **even** integer. The circuit $\mathsf{C}_{\mathsf{EqOR}}$, hardwired with value sn, on inputs $sn, v_1, \ldots, v_N$ outputs 0 when for all i all $v_i \neq sn$ and outputs 1 when for an index i (or an even number of i), $v_i = sn$.

It can be checked by inspection, but a formal proof is provided in the full version. *Concrete Efficiency of* $\Pi_{\Phi^{\mathsf{OR}}}$ *with circuit* $\mathsf{C}_{\mathsf{EqOR}}$ In this section we discuss the concrete complexity of $\Pi_{\Phi^{\mathsf{OR}}}$ when: (1) Π_{Pcom} is instantiated with Protocol 1; (2) $\mathsf{Compute}(\mathcal{G}^{\mathcal{R}^{\mathsf{OR}}}, \cdot)$ is instantiated as in [9], (3) $(\mathsf{ExtCom}, \mathsf{ExtVrfy})$ is instantiated as: $\mathsf{ExtCom}(m)$: Pick a random r. Output $c = \mathcal{H}(m||r)$. $\mathsf{ExtVrfy}(c, m, r)$: Output 1 iff $c = \mathcal{H}(m||r)$.

Size of Partial Openings. The final proof consists of the partial opening of *all* N commitments in $\mathbb{C}$, that is $\forall i \in [N], j \in [\kappa], k_{a^j}^{i,j}, k_{b^j}^{i,j}$, $a^j, b^j \in \mathcal{I}^J$. This requires communication of $2\lambda\kappa N$ strings. We can shave off the parameter N, by using PRF keys $\mathsf{prfkey}_1^j, \mathsf{prfkey}_2^j, \mathsf{prfkey}_3^j$ to generate the randomness required to

Protocol 6 (BlackBoo: Proof Stage Π_{CP}) *Let $\Pi^{\mathcal{R}^{\mathsf{OR}}}$ be the (2,3) decomposition (Protocol 3). Let* (ExtCom, ExtVrfy) *be a non-interactive extractable commitment scheme.*

Published Commitments : $\boxed{\mathbb{C} = [(\mathbf{C}^{1,j}), \ldots, (\mathbf{C}^{N,j})]_{j \in \kappa}}$ *(Protocol 5)*

Proof Stage $\mathsf{Prove}^{\mathcal{H}}((\mathbb{C} = [\mathbf{C}^{1,j}, \ldots, \mathbf{C}^{N,j}], (\mathsf{tag}^l, K^{l,j}, X^{l,j}))\ \forall j \in [\kappa]$.

1. **First message:**
   (a) *Open* $N-1$ unknown *commitments:*
   - *Run* $\mathsf{FakeOpen}(\mathsf{tag}^l, \mathbf{C}^{i,j})$ $(\forall i \neq l,\ j \in [\kappa])$ *and obtain: fake plaintext openings:* $FX^{i,j} = [fx_1^{i,j}, fx_2^{i,j}, fx_3^{i,j}]$ *and fake cryptographic openings:* $FK^{i,j} = [fk_1^{i,j}, fk_2^{i,j}, fk_3^{i,j}]$.

   (b) *MPC-in-the-head. Pick random tapes:* $\mathbf{r}_1, \mathbf{r}_2, \mathbf{r}_3$.
   - *Compute MPC Views for the j-th execution: (see Protocol 3, Step 2) : (1) Derive randomness* $\mathbf{r}_a^j$ *from* $\mathbf{r}_a$ *for* $a \in \{1,2,3\}$. *(2) Run* $\mathsf{Compute}(\mathcal{G}^{\mathcal{R}^{\mathsf{OR}}}, (fx_1^{i,j}, fx_2^{i,j}, fx_3^{i,j}, x_1^{l,j}, x_2^{l,j}, x_3^{l,j},), \mathbf{r}_1^j, \mathbf{r}_2^j, \mathbf{r}_3^j)$ *with* $i \neq l \in [N], j \in [\kappa]$ *and obtain the view of the j-th execution:* $(\mathbf{w}_1^j||\mathbf{r}_1^j, \mathbf{w}_2^j||\mathbf{r}_2^j, \mathbf{w}_3^j||\mathbf{r}_3^j)$.
   - *Commit MPC Views for the j-th execution:* $(\mathbf{Cview}_a^j, \mathsf{OpView}_a^j) \leftarrow \mathsf{ExtCom}(\mathbf{w}_a^j||\mathbf{r}_a^j, rand)$, *for* $a = 1,2,3$.
2. **Challenge.** $(\mathcal{I}^1, \ldots, \mathcal{I}^\kappa) = \mathcal{H}(\mathtt{CH}, \mathbb{C}, [\mathbf{Cview}_1^j, \mathbf{Cview}_2^j, \mathbf{Cview}_3^j]_{j \in \kappa})$.
3. **Response.** *For* $a^j, b^j \in \mathcal{I}^j$ *send:*
   (a) *MPC-views:* $(\mathsf{OpView}_{a^j}^j, \mathsf{OpView}_{b^j}^j)$.
   (b) *Crypto Openings:* $(fk_{a^j}^{i,j}, fk_{b^j}^{i,j})$, $(k_{a^j}^{l,j}, k_{b^j}^{l,j})$ *for* $i \in [N], j \in [\kappa]$.
4. **Proof:**
   $\pi := [\mathsf{tag}, \mathbf{Cview}_1^j, \mathbf{Cview}_2^j, \mathbf{Cview}_3^j,\ \mathsf{OpView}_{a^j}^j,\ \mathsf{OpView}_{b^j}^j, k_{a^j}^{i,j}, k_{b^j}^{i,j}],\ \forall i \in [N], j \in [\kappa]$

Verification: $\mathsf{Verify}^{\mathcal{H}}(\mathbb{C}, \pi)$. *(0) Compute* $\mathcal{I}^j$, *for* $j \in [\kappa]$ *from* $\mathcal{H}$.

1. **MPC View Consistency (Soundness of the proof)**. *For all* $j \in [\kappa]$. *(1) Let* $\mathbf{w}_{\delta^j}^j, \mathbf{r}_{\delta^j}^j = \mathsf{ExtVrfy}(\mathbf{Cview}_{\delta^j}^j, \mathsf{OpView}_{\delta^j}^j))$ *for* $\delta^j \in \mathcal{I}^j$. *Run* $\mathsf{TestViewConsistency}(\mathbf{w}_{a^j}^j, \mathbf{w}_{b^j}^j)$ *(Test 4). If any check fails, reject the proof.*
2. **Input Commitment Consistency.** *For all* $i \in [N], \delta^j \in \mathcal{I}^j$*: let* $x_{\delta^j}^{I,j} \leftarrow \mathsf{VerifyCrypto}(\mathsf{tag}, \mathbf{C}_{\delta^j}^{i,j}, k_{\delta^j}^{i,j})$ *check* $\mathbf{w}_{\delta^j}^j[i,0] = x_{\delta^j}^{i,j}$. *If any check fails, output 0.*

Protocol 7 (Proof Link) $\mathsf{PLink}^{\mathcal{H}}(\mathbb{C}, \pi_1, \pi_2)$:
Let $\pi\text{-}\mathsf{com}^l = [\mathbf{Cview}_1^{l,j}, \mathbf{Cview}_2^{l,j}, \mathbf{Cview}_3^{l,j}]$ *for* $j \in \kappa$.
- If $\pi\text{-}\mathsf{com}^1 \neq \pi\text{-}\mathsf{com}^2$ *(no copy) and* $\mathsf{Verify}(\mathbb{C}, \pi_1) = \mathsf{Verify}(\mathbb{C}, \pi_2) = 1$ *proceed.*
Parse $\pi_\delta = (\mathsf{tag}_\delta, \mathbf{Cview}_1^{\delta,j}, \mathbf{Cview}_2^{\delta,j}, \mathbf{Cview}_3^{\delta,j},\ \mathsf{OpView}_{|\mathcal{I}^{\delta,j}}^{\delta,j}, K_{|\mathcal{I}^{\delta,j}}^{\delta,i,j})$ *for* $\delta = (1,2)$.
If $\mathsf{tag}_1 \neq \mathsf{tag}_2$ *output 0. Else output* 1.

Fig. 3. One-time Anonymous 1-out-of-N Commit-and-ZKBoo

Circuit 1 (Boolean Circuit for $\mathsf{C}_{\mathsf{EqOR}}$ computing $\mathcal{R}^{\mathsf{OR}}_{\mathsf{equal}}$.) $\mathsf{C}_{\mathsf{EqOR}}$: $(\{0,1\}^{\ell})^N \to \{0,1\}^{\ell}$.
Inputs: *N strings of* ℓ *bits:* $A_1, \ldots, A_N$. *# Input wires:* $\ell \cdot N$.
Output: *A bit b.*
Computation Gates

- **Step 1.** *XOR with sn.*
  For each $i \in [N]$*:* $A_i = sn \oplus v_i$. *(Rationale: If* $v_i = sn$ *then* A_i *is* 0^{ℓ}*.)*
  # Gates $\ell \cdot N$ *XOR gates added to* $\mathcal{G}^{\mathsf{C}_{\mathsf{EqOR}}}$.
- **Step 2.** *Identify the (unique) equal string: For each i, compute bit* $a_i = A_i[1] \vee A_i[2] \vee A_i[\ell]$. *(Rationale. The OR bit is 0 for the string that is equal to sn, 1 for all the other strings) OR is implemented using NOT and AND gates (using De Morgan's law) as follows:*
  1. *NOT: For each i, negate each bit of* A_i. *Let* $Z_i = \bar{A}_i$.
  2. *Inner AND. For each i computes* $a_i = \wedge_{k=1}^{\ell}(Z_i[k])$ *This step can be performed with* $\log \ell$ *AND gates.*
  3. *NOT. Compute* $a_i = \bar{a}_i$.

  # Gates: $\log \ell \cdot N$ *AND* + $2\ell \cdot N$ *NOT added to* $\mathcal{G}^{\mathsf{C}_{\mathsf{EqOR}}}$.
- **Step 3.** *Final XOR. Let* $a_1, \ldots, a_N$ *the bits obtained. Output* $b = \bigoplus_i a_i$. *(Rationale: If exactly one string is equal, then exactly one* $a_i = 0$*, hence the* $\oplus$ *of* $N-1$ *1s, give* 1 *when N is even).*
  # Gates: $\log N$ *XOR gates added to* $\mathcal{G}^{\mathsf{C}_{\mathsf{EqOR}}}$.

Fig. 4. Circuit for $\mathcal{R}^{\mathsf{OR}}_{\mathsf{equal}}$ relation.

open position $(j,1), (j,2), (j,3)$ for all N commitments. Hence, the number of bits required for the partial opening is $2\kappa\lambda$, which *is independent of the number of commitments* (i.e., the size of the ring) N.

Size of Views for $\mathsf{C}_{\mathsf{EqOR}}$. As shown in Fig. 5 (right side), the proof consists of the commitments of the MPC players views and partial openings: $[\mathbf{Cview}_1^j, \mathbf{Cview}_2^j, \mathbf{Cview}_3^j, \mathsf{OpView}_{a^j}^j, k_{a^j}^{i,j}], \forall a^j \in \mathcal{I}^j$. The first observation is that instead of committing to the entire view, one can commit to a much shorter prf key used to derive the randomness used to run the MPC players, and to the communication channels with other parties. Recall that in the decomposition of [9] communication is required only to compute AND, and only 6 bits are required. Observe that one evaluation of $\mathsf{C}_{\mathsf{EqOR}}$ requires $\log \ell \cdot N$ AND evaluations. For κ parallel evaluations of $\mathsf{C}_{\mathsf{EqOR}}$ the total AND complexity is $(\log \ell \cdot N \cdot \kappa)$. Hence, the **total number of bits** that need to be added to $view_a$ is $6(\log \ell \cdot N \cdot \kappa)$.

Table 1 reports the communication complexity for different choices of N and κ, with a fixed security parameter $\lambda = \ell = 128$.

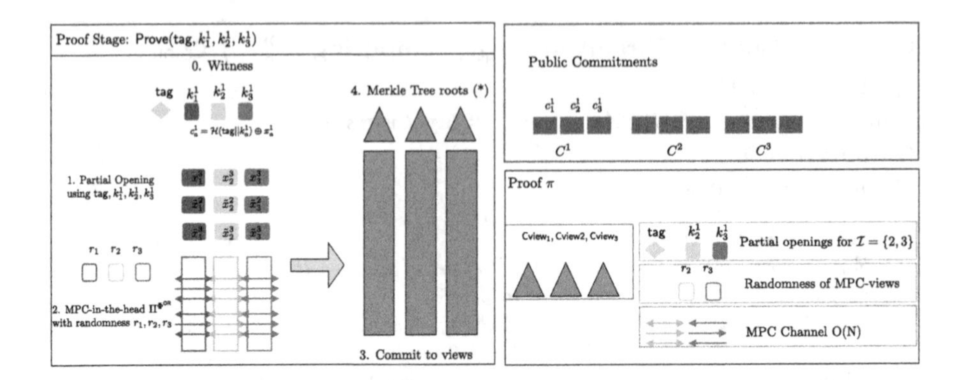

Fig. 5. (Left) $\mathsf{Prove}(\cdot)$ algorithm. (Right) Public Commitments and Proof.

Table 1. Proof size for equality relation $\mathcal{R}_{\mathsf{equal}}^{\mathsf{OR}}$ wrt security parameter $\lambda = 128$.

N Coms	Proof size for κ=80	Proof size for κ=100	Proof size for κ=128
2^7	54 KB	67 KB	86 KB
2^8	107 KB	134 KB	172 KB
2^9	215 KB	268 KB	344 KB

6.1 Security Proof

Theorem 2. *If protocol $\Pi^{\mathcal{R}^{\mathsf{OR}}}$ (Protocol 3) is a secure (2,3) decomposition for $\mathcal{R}^{\mathsf{OR}}$ instantiated with algorithms* $\{\mathsf{ShareD}, \mathsf{Output}_1, \mathsf{Output}_2, \mathsf{Output}_3, \mathsf{RecD}\}$. *If $\mathsf{POC}^{\mathcal{O}}$ (Fig. 1) is a partially openable commitment scheme (Definition 1), instantiated with* (ShareD, RecD) *and with parameters (2, 3)* (ExtCom, $\mathsf{ExtVrfy}$) *is a black-box straight-line extractable commitment scheme, then (multi-branches) Protocol 6 is a linkable anonymous proof system (Definition 7), assuming random oracle $\mathcal{H}$.*

Proof Strategy. The proof is conducted as follows. First, we show that Protocol 3 with $\kappa = 1$ which we call *single branch version* of the protocol satisfies the following properties:

1. Lemma 1 Completeness (Definition 8). It naturally extends to the multi-branch case.
2. Lemma 2 Proof of knowledge with 1/3 error (Definition 7). We then show that soundness naturally amplifies in the κ-branches version to $1 - (\frac{1}{3})^{\kappa}$.
3. Lemma 5 One-time Anonymity (Definition 10) with all but negligible probability. It naturally extends to the multi-branch case.
4. Lemma 3. Proof Non-Frameability(Definition 12) with 1/3 error. We then show that non-frameability naturally amplifies in the κ-branches version to $1 - (\frac{1}{3})^{\kappa}$.

To prove Proof Linkability (Definition 11) we consider directly the multi-branch version of the protocol (see Lemma 4).

We prove Theorem 2 for the specific relation $\mathcal{R}_{\mathsf{equal}}$, but we stress that the same proof works for any relation $\mathcal{R} : \{0,1\}^\lambda \times \{0,1\}^\lambda \rightarrow \{0,1\}$ that outputs 0 on at least some inputs.

Lemma 1 (Completeness). *If* POC *instantiated with* (ShareD, RecD) *and parameters (2,3) satisfies completeness and Partial Openability (Definition 2),* $\Pi_{\Phi\mathsf{OR}}$ *and* (ExtCom, ExtVrfy) *are complete, Protocol 3 satisfies completeness.*

It can be checked by inspection.

Lemma 2 (Proof of Knowledge). *If* $\Pi_{\Phi\mathsf{OR}}$ *is a (2,3) decomposition for* $\mathcal{R}^{\mathsf{OR}}$*, with algorithms:* $\{\mathsf{ShareD}, \mathsf{Output}_1,\ \mathsf{Output}_2,\ \mathsf{Output}_3,\ \mathsf{RecD}\}$*,* $\mathsf{POC}^{\mathcal{O}}$ *satisfies Binding of Partial Openings (Definition 4) and* (ExtCom, ExtVrfy) *is straight-line extractable, then Protocol 6 satisfies the proof of knowledge property as per Definition 9.*

Proof Intuition. We first prove that Protocol 6 with $\kappa = 1$ (one branch) satisfies proof of knowledge property with probability $\left(1 - \frac{1}{3} - \mathsf{negl}(\lambda)\right)$. Let $\mathcal{P}^\star$ be a PPT prover that outputs a set of commitments $\mathbb{C}^* = (\mathbf{C}^1, \ldots, \mathbf{C}^N)$ and an accepting proof $(\mathbb{C}^*, \pi^*)$ with non-negligible probability p. We show that there exists an extractor Ext that on input $(\mathbb{C}^*, \pi^*)$ extracts a witness (x_l, w_l) for $\mathcal{R}$ with probability $\frac{2}{3} - \mathsf{negl}$ and runs in expected polynomial in p. The goal of the extractor is to derive the witness that was used in the proof $(\mathbb{C}^*, \pi^*)$. Toward this, the Ext first extracts the views of the MPC-the-heads committed in $\mathbf{Cview}_1, \mathbf{Cview}_2, \mathbf{Cview}_3$. This is possible since the views are committed using an extractable commitment. By observing the MPC-views, Ext derives the shares in input of the MPC-players, $\mathbf{x}_1^i, \mathbf{x}_2^i, \mathbf{x}_3^i$ and attempts to reconstruct at least one witness $x^i || w^i = \mathsf{RecD}(\mathbf{x}_1^i, \mathbf{x}_2^i, \mathbf{x}_3^i)$. If the extractor finds an l such that $\mathcal{R}(x^l, w^l) = 1$, before giving it in output, it needs to ascertain that it is consistent with the plaintext commitment $\mathbf{C}^l$. In order to do so, Ext needs to observe a full crypto opening. To do so, Ext rewinds $\mathcal{P}^\star$ and uses different challenges with the purpose of obtaining a full crypto opening that is consistent with the plaintext $(\mathbf{x}_1^l, \mathbf{x}_2^l, \mathbf{x}_3^l)$. The extractor will fail in outputting a valid witness from the proof $(\mathbb{C}^*, \pi^*)$ in the following events. (1) It is unable to extract all views from commitments $\mathbf{Cview}_1, \mathbf{Cview}_2, \mathbf{Cview}_3$ or the extracted views are inconsistent with the actual openings. This event must happen with negligible probability due to the extractability property of ComExt. (2) The extracted views are inconsistent with a correct executions of the (2,3)-function decomposition or they plaintext used in the views is inconsistent with the partial openings provided in the proof. This case can happen with probability 1/3 of guessing the challenge, or to the case where the adversary is able to providing distinct *valid* plaintext openings for the same commitment, hence violating partial opening binding (Definition 4). Putting the above claims together, it follows that Ext fails with probability $1/3 + \mathsf{negl}$.

Soundness Amplification. For κ parallel executions it follows that the probability of an extractor to fail κ times in parallel is $\left(\frac{1}{3}\right)^\kappa + \mathsf{negl}(\lambda)$.

Lemma 3 (Non Frameability). *If* POC *satisfies Binding of Partial Openings(Definition 4) then Protocol 6 satisfies Non-Frameability (Definition 12).*

Proof Intuition. First, consider the one-branch version Protocol 6 with $\kappa = 1$. Let $\mathcal{A}^{\mathsf{frame}}$ be an adversary participating in Game $\mathsf{Exp}^{\mathsf{ProofFrame}}$ (Game 3) and winning with non-negligible probability ϵ. Such successful adversary can be used to violate Binding of Partial Openings with probability $(\frac{1}{3}) + p$.

Winning Game $\mathsf{Exp}^{\mathsf{ProofFrame}}$ means to provide a malicious proof π' that is valid, such the partial openings $(\mathsf{tag}, \tilde{k}_2^i, \ldots)$ it contains match the partial openings $(\mathsf{tag}, \ldots)$ contained in an honestly generated proof π, making the two proofs linkable. First, observe the following: *with probability* $\frac{1}{3}$ *the adversary can always link the two proofs.* This follows from the following two facts: first, given any honest commitment $\mathbf{C}$, after observing a partial opening tag, k_a, k_b it is easy to generate another distinct partial openings that is linkable (e.g., one can use tag, k_1, k_2, with latter being random strings). But, the underlying full plaintext openings would not be matching and would not generate an accepting proof. Second, if the adversary can guess the challenge, then consistency of all the MPC views is not required. Instead the adversary can craft the proof so that only the MPC views that are opened are correct and consistent with the partial openings (tag, k_1, k_2), while the remaining unopened view is wrong. It follows then that with probability 1/3, the adversary can always win Game $\mathsf{Exp}^{\mathsf{ProofFrame}}$ while not violating any binding property.

In this proof we are interested in an adversary that is able to win with a better probability $\epsilon(\lambda)= \frac{1}{3}+\mathsf{negl}(\lambda) + p^{\mathsf{frame}}(\lambda)$. Indeed, in such case the adversary is doing something clever in $\mathsf{Exp}^{\mathsf{ProofFrame}}$ besides guessing the challenge. Specifically, he is able to *adjust* the partial openings of its proofs π' so that they match the tag tag used in π. Since π is honest, the tag tag is associated to the l-th honest partial opening of $\mathbf{C}^l$. An adversary that is able to successfully generated π' using tag, either was able to find other keys of the partial opening of $\mathbf{C}^l$ or was able to open one of its own crafted commitments $\mathbf{M}^*$ with tag while still having the full plaintext opening to be a sharing of a valid witness. Thus, $\mathcal{A}^{\mathsf{frame}}$ is able to *forge* a partial opening of an honest commitment $\mathbf{C}^l$, and can be used to break the Unforgeability of Partial Opening Property (see Game 1) with probability greater that $\frac{1}{3} + \mathsf{negl}(\lambda)$.

Lemma 4 (Proof Linkability). *If* $\mathsf{POC}^{\mathcal{O}}$ *satisfies Binding of Plaintexts w.r.t. a Relation* $\mathcal{R}$ $\Pi^{\mathcal{R}^{\mathsf{OR}}}$ *(Protocol 3) is a secure (2,3) decomposition for* $\mathcal{R}^{\mathsf{OR}}$ *instantiated with algorithms* $\{\mathsf{ShareD}, \mathsf{Output}_1, \mathsf{Output}_2, \mathsf{Output}_3, \mathsf{RecD}\}$ *and* ExtCom *is straight-line extractable, then Protocol 6 satisfies proof linkability (Definition 11).*

Proof Intuition. Proof linkability is proved for the κ branches directly. The reason we work directly with the extension is the following. If the proofs are unlinkable, each must use a different tag for the partial opening. We would like to argue if all $N + 1$ proofs are accepting, and if there are N possible plaintexts that are valid witnesses, there must be at least one witness that repeats, unless the POC commitments are not binding and thus one can provide different openings for the same commitment. In order to reach the conclusion, we need to start with the assumption that each if a proof is accepting then the proof of knowledge property holds with all but negligible probability. Indeed if we started with a weaker guarantee (i.e., that each proof is sound with probability 2/3), then we could not claim that a witness must have been used in each proof (since some proofs would go through without witness with probability $\approx 1/3$) and thus we could not claim that $N+1$ proof must have used $N+1$ valid witnesses.

Lemma 5 (One-time Anonymity). *If* POC *instantiated with* $(\mathsf{ShareD}, \mathsf{RecD})$ *satisfies hiding in presence of partial opening (Definition 1), the (2,3) decomposition implemented* $\Pi_{\Phi\mathsf{OR}}$ *satisfies privacy* $(2,3)$ *privacy and* $(\mathsf{ExtCom}, \mathsf{ExtVrfy})$ *is computationally hiding, then protocol in Fig. 3 satisfies Linkable Anonymity (Definition 10.)*

Proof Intuition. A honest verifier zero-knowledge (HVZK) simulator SimProve can be easily provided by using the simulator associated to the (2,3) Function Decomposition, to pass all proofs without knowing any witness (here we are crucially using the fact that the simulator can choose the challenge). The indistinguishability of the simulated proof then follows directly from the hiding of the commitment ExtCom, used to commit to the MPC views, and the hiding in presence of partial opening that is enjoyed by POC.

References

1. Ames, S., Hazay, C., Ishai, Y., Venkitasubramaniam, M.: Ligero: lightweight sublinear arguments without a trusted setup. In: Proceedings of the 2017 ACM SIGSAC, pp. 2087–2104 (2017)
2. Bellare, M., Rogaway, P.: Random oracles are practical: a paradigm for designing efficient protocols. In: Denning, D.E., Pyle, R., Ganesan, R., Sandhu, R.S., Ashby, V. (ed.) ACM CCS 93, pp. 62–73. ACM Press, November 1993
3. Ben-Sasson, E., Bentov, I., Horesh, Y., Riabzev, M.: Scalable, transparent, and post-quantum secure computational integrity. IACR Cryptology ePrint Archive **2018**, 46 (2018)
4. Ben-Sasson, E.: Zerocash: decentralized anonymous payments from bitcoin. In: 2014 IEEE Symposium on Security and Privacy, pp. 459–474 (2014)
5. Bünz, B., Bootle, J., Boneh, D., Poelstra, A., Wuille, P., Maxwell, G.: Bulletproofs: short proofs for confidential transactions and more. In: 2018 IEEE Symposium on Security and Privacy, SP, pp. 315–334 (2018)
6. Camenisch, J., Lysyanskaya, A.: Dynamic accumulators and application to efficient revocation of anonymous credentials. In: Yung, M. (ed.) CRYPTO 2002. LNCS, vol. 2442, pp. 61–76. Springer, Heidelberg (2002). https://doi.org/10.1007/3-540-45708-9_5
7. Canetti, R., Fischlin, M.: Universally composable commitments. In: Kilian, J. (ed.) CRYPTO 2001. LNCS, vol. 2139, pp. 19–40. Springer, Heidelberg (2001). https://doi.org/10.1007/3-540-44647-8_2

8. Chase, M., Healy, A., Lysyanskaya, A., Malkin, T., Reyzin, L.: Mercurial commitments with applications to zero-knowledge sets. In: Cramer, R. (ed.) EUROCRYPT 2005. LNCS, vol. 3494, pp. 422–439. Springer, Heidelberg (2005). https://doi.org/10.1007/11426639_25
9. Giacomelli, I., Madsen, J., Orlandi, C.: ZKBoo: faster zero-knowledge for Boolean circuits. In: 25th USENIX Security Symposium, USENIX Security 16, Austin, TX, USA, 10–12 August 2016, pp. 1069–1083 (2016)
10. Goyal, V., Lee, C.-K., Ostrovsky, R., Visconti, I.: Constructing non-malleable commitments: a black-box approach. In: 53rd FOCS, pp. 51–60. IEEE Computer Society Press, October 2012
11. Ishai, Y., Kushilevitz, E., Ostrovsky, R., Sahai, A.: Zero-knowledge from secure multiparty computation. In: Johnson, D.S., Feige, U. (eds.) 39th ACM STOC, pp. 21–30. ACM Press, June 2007
12. Ishai, Y., Weiss, M.: Probabilistically checkable proofs of proximity with zero-knowledge. In: Lindell, Y. (ed.) TCC 2014. LNCS, vol. 8349, pp. 121–145. Springer, Heidelberg (2014). https://doi.org/10.1007/978-3-642-54242-8_6
13. Kilian, J.: A general completeness theorem for two-party games. In: 23rd ACM STOC, pp. 553–560. ACM Press, May 1991
14. Kiyoshima, S.: Round-optimal black-box commit-and-prove with succinct communication. In: Micciancio, D., Ristenpart, T. (eds.) CRYPTO 2020. LNCS, vol. 12171, pp. 533–561. Springer, Cham (2020). https://doi.org/10.1007/978-3-030-56880-1_19
15. Kosba, A.E., Miller, A., Shi, E., Wen, Z., Papamanthou, C.: Hawk: the blockchain model of cryptography and privacy-preserving smart contracts. In: IEEE Symposium on Security and Privacy, pp. 839–858 (2016)
16. Miers, I., Garman, C., Green, M., Rubin, A.D.: Zerocoin: anonymous distributed e-cash from bitcoin. In: 2013 IEEE Symposium on Security and Privacy, pp. 397–411 (2013)
17. Ostrovsky, R., Richelson, S., Scafuro, A.: Round-optimal black-box two-party computation. In: Gennaro, R., Robshaw, M. (eds.) CRYPTO 2015. LNCS, vol. 9216, pp. 339–358. Springer, Heidelberg (2015). https://doi.org/10.1007/978-3-662-48000-7_17
18. Pass, R., Wee, H.: Black-box constructions of two-party protocols from one-way functions. In: Reingold, O. (ed.) TCC 2009. LNCS, vol. 5444, pp. 403–418. Springer, Heidelberg (2009). https://doi.org/10.1007/978-3-642-00457-5_24
19. Pedersen, T.P.: Non-interactive and information-theoretic secure verifiable secret sharing. In: Feigenbaum, J. (ed.) CRYPTO 1991. LNCS, vol. 576, pp. 129–140. Springer, Heidelberg (1992). https://doi.org/10.1007/3-540-46766-1_9
20. Shamir, A.: How to share a secret. Commun. ACM **22**(11), 612–613 (1979)
21. Z. Zcash project (2013). https://z.cash/
22. Zhang, B., Oliynykov, R., Balogun, H.: A treasury system for cryptocurrencies: enabling better collaborative intelligence. In: Network and Distributed System Security Symposium, NDSS (2019)

Efficient Proof of RAM Programs from Any Public-Coin Zero-Knowledge System

Cyprien Delpech de Saint Guilhem(✉), Emmanuela Orsini, Titouan Tanguy, and Michiel Verbauwhede

imec-COSIC, KU Leuven, Leuven, Belgium
{cyprien.delpechdesaintguilhem,emmanuela.orsini,titouan.tanguy, michiel.verbauwhede}@kuleuven.be

Abstract. We show a compiler that allows to prove the correct execution of RAM programs using any zero-knowledge system for circuit satisfiability. At the core of this work is an arithmetic circuit which verifies the consistency of a list of memory access tuples in zero-knowledge.

Using such a circuit, we obtain the first constant-round and concretely efficient zero-knowledge proof protocol for RAM programs using any *stateless* zero-knowledge proof system for Boolean or arithmetic circuits. Both the communication complexity and the prover and verifier run times asymptotically scale linearly in the size of the memory and the run time of the RAM program; we demonstrate concrete efficiency with performance results of our C++ implementation.

We concretely instantiate our construction with an efficient MPC-in-the-Head proof system, Limbo (ACM CCS 2021). The C++ implementation of our access protocol extends that of Limbo and provides interactive proofs with 40 bits of statistical security with an amortized cost of 0.42 ms of prover time and 2.8 KB of communication per memory access, independently of the size of the memory; with multi-threading, this cost is reduced to 0.12 ms and 1.8 KB respectively. This performance of our *public-coin* protocol approaches that of *private-coin* protocol BubbleRAM (ACM CCS 2020, 0.15 ms and 1.5 KB per access).

1 Introduction

A zero-knowledge (ZK) proof is a fundamental cryptographic tool which proves that a statement is true without revealing any other information. Since their introduction by Goldwasser, Micali and Rackoff [12], ZK proofs have had a significant impact on cryptography and have been the object of intense research work due to their theoretical importance and varied applicability.

Many types of ZK proof systems exist, each presenting different trade-offs between several efficiency measures. While in blockchain applications, the main focus is on succinct proofs of small statements [10,15,25], another line of research

C. Galdi and S. Jarecki (Eds.): SCN 2022, LNCS 13409, pp. 615–638, 2022.
https://doi.org/10.1007/978-3-031-14791-3_27

has focused on prover efficiency [1,4,7,8,21,22], while other works have successfully constructed ZK proof systems for very large statements with good concrete efficiency [2,26–28].

Unfortunately, these works focus mostly on statements represented as circuits, either Boolean or arithmetic, which can incur a significant overhead to prove properties of large statements that are more naturally represented as random-access machine (RAM) programs. Many interesting functions and applications, such as private database search or verification of program execution, greatly benefit from RAM-based expression where their running time can be sublinear in the data size.

Several recent works [6,9,16–19,23] have initiated the study of ZK proof systems for RAM programs, but they have the disadvantage of being in the private-coin setting. In particular, this means that there are no systematic techniques to make those proof publicly verifiable. On the contrary, proofs using public coins can be made non-interactive and therefore publicly verifiable using the Fiat-Shamir heuristic. This raises the following natural question:

Can we design a RAM-based ZK proof system with concrete efficiency in the public-coin setting?

1.1 Contribution

In this work, we answer the above question in the affirmative and describe a generic transformation that enables program verification with any *stateless* zero-knowledge proof system for circuits. In this way, we obtain the first *public-coin, constant-round and constant-overhead*, in both running time and communication complexity, ZK proof system for RAM programs over a field of *any characteristic.*

Our starting point is the recent works by Franzese et al. [9] and Bootle et al. [6] which propose a different approach to RAM-based ZK protocols compared to previous works. In particular, they replace the need for a sorting network—used for example in the TinyRAM framework to avoid the use of oblivious RAM (ORAM) [3,5]—by a polynomial-based permutation check to ensure consistency of memory access.

Public-Coin Constant-Overhead Zero-Knowledge in the RAM Model of Computation over Fields of any Characteristic. Our protocols take inspiration from the work of Franzese et al. which achieves concretely-efficient linear communication complexity and running time for both prover and verifier and that of Bootle et al. which achieves asymptotically superconstant prover computation and sublinear communication and verifier running time. The core of Franzese et al.'s construction is a protocol Π_{ZKArray} for private read and write access that uses a *stateful* circuit-based ZK functionality which can reactively re-use inputs for different proofs in the private-coin setting.

First, we modify Π_{ZKArray} to provide *stateless* ZK proofs. This allows for instantiations with prover-efficient public-coin systems, like those based on the MPC-in-the-Head framework [20]. Secondly, we generalize the protocol to fields of any characteristic, binary or prime. Note that both of these modifications lead to non-trivial changes in Π_{ZKArray} to achieve a final protocol with constant overhead.

More precisely, to realize a stateless ZK functionality we present a 'new circuit compilation' approach which, given a list of array accesses, creates a circuit C_{check} which verifies the list's consistency. The final C_{check} circuit is composed only of standard arithmetic gates and can be given as input to a generic circuit-based ZK functionality $\mathcal{F}_{\mathsf{ZK}}$. However, since the execution of C_{check} requires new inputs from the prover to perform the checks on the accesses, we adapt $\mathcal{F}_{\mathsf{ZK}}$ to accept circuits evaluated on inputs both fresh and previously stored.

When we generalise Π_{ZKArray} to also work with prime fields, the naïve approach of performing equality and comparison tests leads to a non-constant overhead. To avoid this issue, we describe a new ZK protocol for equality testing which, for prime fields, could be of independent interest; we also describe a bound-checking protocol reminiscent of the range relation proof of [6]. These two protocols take advantage of both the new inputs given to C_{check} and of a permutation check similar to the one of Franzese et al. [9]—which dates back to [24]. We also extend this permutation check to handle permutations of tuples, and not only of elements, by using an inner-product compression technique, similarly to Bootle et al.'s [6]. This is different to the packing technique used by Franzese et al. which works efficiently for binary fields but is too costly for prime fields of large characteristic.

Finally, we show how to extend our $\mathcal{F}_{\mathsf{ZKArray}}$ functionality to accept richer circuits and implement ZK protocols for RAM-based computation. We stress that our construction is not only public-coin but also constant-round, unlike that of Bootle et al. [6], and can be made fully non-interactive using standard techniques.

Instantiation with MPC-in-the-Head Protocols. We give a concrete instantiation of our general construction using the MPC-in-the-Head-based ZK protocol, Limbo [7]. We chose this framework since, among other public-coin systems, it offers concrete overall efficiency, which makes such schemes competitive even for relatively large statements. Moreover, they offer linear prover and communication complexity, great flexibility in the choice of parameters and post-quantum security.

We stress that the choice of Limbo was due to its efficient prover running time, but other protocols such as KKW [22] or Ligero [1] can also realize our required ZK functionality, with only minor modifications. Instead of favouring running time, we could improve the communication complexity of our construction by using Ligero instead which achieves sub-linear proof size, and is tailored towards very large circuits. Any improvement in the design of the underlying public-coin zero-knowledge protocol for circuits will reflect in a performance improvement of our construction.

Implementation and Efficiency Results. Finally, we implement our protocols, and compare our results with related work. Our implementation shows that we can indeed achieve a RAM-based ZK system with both concrete and asymptotic efficiency in the public-coin setting. We observe that each RAM access we make is equivalent to proving 8 multiplication gates. In practice, when working over the prime field $GF(2^{61}-1)$ we achieve an amortized cost of 0.12 ms and

1.82 KB for each RAM access. As far as we know this is the best result to date in the public-coin setting, and is comparable to the BubbleRAM protocol [16] which heavily relies on the private-coin nature of the underlying ZK protocol. However, more recent ZK proof for RAM programs, also in the private coin setting, have already superseded BubbleRAM; most notably its direct successor PrORAM [17] as well as the work by Franzese et al. [9] that greatly outperforms BubbleRAM in both communication and running time.

In the light of the rapid development of this line of work, we believe that our construction can be an important step forward in order to bridge the gap between private and public coin ZK protocols in the RAM model of computation. The details of our implementation and further comparison with other works can be found in Sect. 6.

1.2 Additional Related Work

We mainly compare our results with the work of Franzese et al. [9], which instantiate their construction with the VOLE-based ZK protocol QuickSilver [28], with the advantage of having a very efficient underlying ZK protocol in the private-coin setting which naturally supports conversion between Boolean and arithmetic authenticated values with no extra costs, and can rely on stateful zero-knowledge functionalities.

To the best of our knowledge, all known concretely efficient protocols on ZK for RAM programs are in the private-coin setting and use different techniques compared to our construction. In particular, the line of work started with BubbleRAM [16–18] relies on the use of garbled circuit ZK protocols, in the JKO-framework [21], and achieves a non-constant overhead cost per memory access either due the use of ORAM or routing network. The work of Bootle et al. [6] does not appear to have been implemented, and despite its sublinear asymptotic performance, is not recommended for implementation by its authors due to large constants in the big-O notation. We therefore do not take it into account for our performance comparisons.

Concurrently to this work, the Cairo architecture was proposed as a practically efficient, Turing-complete and STARK-friendly architecture [11]. The high-level approach taken in that work is similar to ours: the authors propose an architecture which can provide proofs of execution for any compatible program. However, their work is directed at proof systems based on sets of polynomial equation constraints and not at systems based on arithmetic circuits. Therefore their architecture is best applied with STARK-like proof systems which offer very different efficiency balances from our objective in this work.

1.3 Technical Overview

Our main contribution is a generic construction, tailored to MPC-in-the-Head protocols, to check the consistency of a series of T read or write accesses to an initial array M of size N, using an arithmetic *checking circuit* C_{check} over a sufficiently large field $\mathbb{F}$ of arbitrary characteristic. By using specially designed sub-circuits for equality checks, bound checks and permutation checks, this circuit removes the need for any bit-decomposition, which is expensive in prime fields, to perform these operations. These sub-circuits are arranged to verify the consistency of a list $\mathcal{L}$ of access tuples which contains both the initial array, encoded as N tuples, and the accesses performed as T additional tuples.

We denote by $[x]$ wire values in C_{check} that are sensitive and should not be revealed when C_{check} is proven in zero-knowledge. The initial array M is encoded as a list $\mathcal{M} = (i, i, \mathsf{write}, [M_i])_{i \in [N]}$. Each access then is encoded as a tuple of the form $([l], t, [\mathsf{op}], [d])$, where l denotes the index of the memory being accessed; t is a global timestamp unique to this access, initialized at N; $\mathsf{op} \in \{\mathsf{read}, \mathsf{write}\}$ denotes the type of access, which we identify $\mathsf{read} = 0 \in \mathbb{F}$ and $\mathsf{write} = 1 \in \mathbb{F}$; and d denotes the value being accessed. Given this, the circuit takes as initial input a list $\mathcal{L}$ which contains the N initial array values, encoded as $\mathcal{M}$, followed by the T access tuples (ordered according to $t \in [N+1, N+T]$). The circuit C_{check} verifies the consistency of the accesses by checking that every read access returns the last value written to the same address.

To do so, following the same approach by Franzese et al., it requires a second list $\mathcal{L}'$ that is a permutation of the initial list $\mathcal{L}$ with the difference that it is sorted first according to the address l, and then according to the timestamp t. That is, within $\mathcal{L}'$, all accesses to the same address are grouped together, and then sorted chronologically. Given such a list $\mathcal{L}'$, the circuit checks for the following criteria:

1. $\mathcal{L}'$ is a permutation of $\mathcal{L}$.
2. Every adjacent pair of access tuple concerns either the same address, or two adjacent ones; i.e. for $([l'_i], [t'_i], *, *)$ and $([l'_{i+1}], [t'_{i+1}], *, *)$ in $\mathcal{L}'$, it holds that
$$((l'_i = l'_{i+1}) \wedge (t'_i < t'_{i+1})) \vee (l'_i + 1 = l'_{i+1}).$$
3. All accesses are made to addresses within bounds; i.e. $l'_{N+T} = N$. (Combined with the adjacency requirement from the previous step this implies all addresses are bounded by N.)
4. All operations are either reads or writes; i.e. $\mathsf{op}_i \in \{0, 1\}$ for $i \in [N+T]$.
5. All read tuples contain the same value as the last one to be written at that address; this is checked pair-wise by evaluating
$$(l'_i + 1 = l'_{i+1}) \vee (d'_i = d'_{i+1}) \vee (\mathsf{op}_{i+1} = \mathsf{write}).$$

The differences with the check performed by the protocol of Franzese et al. are three fold. First, all of our checking circuit is arithmetic whereas only criteria 1, i.e. the permutation check, is performed with an arithmetic circuit in [9]. Second, we do not pack our values ahead of the permutation check as this would require operations over $\mathbb{F}^4$ which would be too big for fields of high prime characteristic; instead we use an inner-product compression technique to reduce this to the one-dimensional case. Finally, we do not check that the first access at every address is a write operation since this is enforced by the structure of $\mathcal{M}$ within $\mathcal{L}$; and we also additionally check that op_i is a bit which is not necessary in [9] as they work with fields of characteristic 2.

In order to evaluate these consistency criteria, we present three arithmetic sub-circuits, EqCheck, BdCheck and PermCheck, which respectively verify equality, upper and lower bounds, and permutation of sensitive values while preserving zero-knowledge. A detailed description of these circuits is given in Sect. 3. As outlined above, only the equivalent of PermCheck is computed as an arithmetic circuit by Franzese et al. These three circuits are designed using standard arithmetic operations (addition, multiplication and equality check against a public constant) and also contain the following additional commands.

- Input: this command allows the prover to give additional inputs to C_{check}, such as the permuted version of an array. We include it in the description of the sub-circuits to highlight that some additional inputs are required at certain points. As the prover is free to input arbitrary values, those inputs, which must satisfy certain properties, must then also be checked.
- Rand: this command produces one or more uniformly random elements of $\mathbb{F}$. It represents randomness needed for statistical verification of properties (such as polynomial equality). Looking ahead, such randomness must be produced only after the inputs of the circuits have been committed to so that they cannot be selected such that verification incorrectly succeeds with non-negligible probability.

Organization. After preliminaries on zero-knowledge and commitment functionalities, MPC-in-the-Head protocols and RAM-based computation in Sect. 2, Sect. 3 presents and analyzes our three sub-circuits and the final C_{check} circuit. Section 4 then presents our Π_{ZKArray} protocol and the functionalities that it uses and realizes; it also presents how these can be extended to realize ZK proofs of RAM programs. Section 5 presents a generalization of the Limbo protocol for the UC framework and shows that is realizes the $\mathcal{F}_{\mathsf{ZKin}}$ functionality required by the Π_{ZKArray} protocol. Finally, Sect. 6 discusses our C++ implementation and the results that we obtained.

2 Preliminaries

We use bold letters to denote vectors and matrices, e.g., $\mathbf{a}$, $\mathbf{B}$; the operator $*$ denotes the inner product of two vectors. We denote by $[d]$ the set of integers $\{1, \ldots, d\}$, and by $[e, d]$ the set of integers $\{e, \ldots, d\}$ with $1 < e < d$. The notation $\langle \cdot \rangle$ stands for secret-shared values, and $\langle \cdot \rangle_i$ is used for the share held by party P_i; the notation $[\,\cdot\,]$ denotes sensitive data that should not be publicly revealed.

2.1 MPC-in-the-Head

In [20], Ishai, Kushilevitz, Ostrovsky and Sahai introduced the MPC-in-the-Head framework to build zero-knowledge proofs for NP-relations from secure multiparty computation. Let $\mathcal{P}$ be a prover and $\mathcal{V}$ a verifier with common input the statement x, and $\mathcal{P}$'s private input the witness w; and let f be the function which checks if w is a valid witness, i.e. $f_x(w) = \mathcal{R}(x, w)$. At a high level, an MPC-in-the-Head protocol will work as follows: the prover emulates "in its head" an MPC protocol between n parties that computes f, i.e. $\mathcal{P}$ generates a sharing $\langle w \rangle$ of the witness and distributes the corresponding shares as private inputs to the parties, and then simulates the evaluation of $f(\langle w \rangle) = \mathcal{R}(x, \langle w \rangle)$ by choosing uniformly random coins r_i for each party P_i, $i \in [n]$. This emulation yields one transcript of the protocol execution per party. After this "MPC evaluation", $\mathcal{P}$ and $\mathcal{V}$ can interact to reveal a subset of transcripts, which the verifier can check for consistency. If the consistency check succeeds, and the output of f is correct, then the verifier will be convinced that the prover knows w. Intuitively, the privacy of the MPC protocol ensures that this procedure does not leak any information about the witness if not too many transcripts are revealed.

Limbo. In our work we consider Limbo [7], an efficient instantiation of the MPC-in-the-Head framework which achieves good concrete prover performance, including for medium-large circuits.

Recall that Limbo is constructed from a client-server ρ-round MPC protocol Π_f, for a function f as described above, between a sender client P_S, computation servers $P_1, \ldots, P_n$, and a receiver client P_R. The authors present a zero-knowledge interactive oracle proof (ZK-IOP) protocol for arithmetic or Boolean circuit satisfiability based in part on a multiplication-checking MPC protocol, MultCheck, provided in [7, Section 4.2].

The client-server MPC protocol used by the ZK-IOP protocol can be divided in the following two phases. First, the sender client P_S sends the inputs of the circuit to the servers, together with the outputs of every multiplication gate; using these, the servers perform a local computation of the circuit with secret-shared values. In the second phase, the servers use MultCheck to verify that P_S sent correct multiplication gate outputs. To do so, they first package the multiplication tuples[1] into randomised inner-product tuples using a public random-coin functionality. These inner-product tuples are then compressed repeatedly, again using a public random-coin functionality, until a single tuple of low dimension is left to be verified. This is done by P_R who receives every secret share of the tuple from the servers and can output 0 or 1 based on its correctness. To amplify the soundness this basic protocol needs to be repeated a certain number of times. In the paper, the authors show an improvement to this naïve approach.

Theorem 1 ([7]). *If δ is the probability that* MultCheck *fails, i.e., an incorrect triple remains undetected, the basic version of* Limbo, *with τ repetitions, is a (honest-verifier) ZK-IOP with soundness error $\epsilon = (1/n + (1 - 1/n) \cdot \delta)^\tau$.*

2.2 RAM-Based Computation

We follow the RAM-based computation model described by Gordon et al. [13]. We focus on RAM program for computing a function $f(x, M)$, where x is a

[1] A multiplication tuple is a tuple (x, y, z) which is correct if $x \cdot y = z$, or incorrect otherwise. Here the goal of the servers is to verify that the z values given by P_S form correct tuples.

Functionality $\mathcal{F}_{\mathsf{ZK\text{-}RAM}}$

Prove: On input $(\mathsf{sid}, \mathsf{Prove}, \Pi, \mathsf{type}, N, M)$ from $\mathcal{P}$, compute $y = \Pi(M)$. Send (Prove, Π) to $\mathcal{V}$ and $\mathcal{S}$ and store (Π, y).

Verify: On input $(\mathsf{sid}, \mathsf{Verify}, \Pi, \mathsf{type})$ from $\mathcal{V}$, query $\mathcal{S}$; if $\mathcal{S}$ returns fail, or if (Π, y) has not been stored, send $(\mathsf{sid}, \Pi, 0)$ to $\mathcal{V}$. Otherwise, send (sid, Π, y) to $\mathcal{V}$.

Fig. 1. Ideal functionality for RAM-based ZK proofs

small, possibly public, input, and M is a large dataset, which can be viewed as stored in a memory array $M_1, \ldots, M_N$, and accessed through read or write instructions. More formally, a RAM program is defined by a "next instruction" circuit Π which, given its current state state and a value d (that will always be equal to the last-read element), outputs the next instruction and an updated state state'. Thus, if M is an array of N entries, each ν bits long, we can view an execution of a RAM program proceeding as follows. First, set $\mathsf{state} = \mathsf{start}$ and $d = 0^\nu$, and secondly, until termination, compute $(\mathsf{op}, l, d', \mathsf{state}') = \Pi(\mathsf{state}, d)$ and update $\mathsf{state} = \mathsf{state}'$. Then: (1) if $\mathsf{op} = \mathsf{stop}$, terminate with output d'; (2) if $\mathsf{op} = \mathsf{read}$, set $d = M_l$; (3) if $\mathsf{op} = \mathsf{write}$, set $M_l = d'$ and $d = d'$.

The *space complexity* of a RAM program on initial inputs x, M is the maximum number of entries used by the memory array M during the course of the execution. The *time complexity* is the number of instructions issued in the execution as described above.

In this work we focus on public-coin ZK proofs for RAM programs Π representing an NP relation $\mathcal{R}(x, M)$, where $\mathcal{R}$ and x are public and M is a large private dataset (which acts as a witness for x). In Fig. 1 we describe an ideal functionality for RAM-based ZK proof, and in Sect. 4.3 we give a protocol realizing it.

3 Arithmetic Circuit for ZK Verification of Array Access

In this section we construct an arithmetic circuit C_{check} (over a binary or prime field $\mathbb{F}$) which verifies the consistency of a series of T read or write accesses to an initial array $\mathcal{M}$ of size N.

We denote by $[x]$ wire values in C_{check} that are sensitive and should not be revealed when C_{check} is proven in zero-knowledge. Each entry in the initial array is of the form $(i, i, \mathsf{write}, [M_i])$ for $i \in [N]$, where $M = (M_1, \ldots, M_N)$ is an arbitrary initial state. Contrary to Franzese et al. [9], here our circuit assumes that the each of the first N tuples of the list $\mathcal{L}$ contains a hard-coded write operation (with unknown data values); this implies that our circuit does not need to verify that the first access to an index is always a write operation.

3.1 Constant Overhead Equality Check

Our first sub-circuit verifies the equality of two hidden values without leaking the result; this allows the equality bit to continue to be used as a hidden value

Circuit 1. $\mathsf{EqCheck}([x],[y])$

1: **Input** $[r] = \begin{cases} ([x]-[y])^{-1} & \text{if } x \neq y \\ \text{random non-zero} & \text{if } x = y \end{cases}$
2: **Input** $[r^{-1}]$
3: Check that $[r]\cdot[r^{-1}]$ is equal to 1; if not, set circuit output to 0.
4: $[b] \leftarrow ([x]-[y])\cdot[r]$
5: Check that $(1-[b])\cdot[b]$ is equal to 0; if not, set circuit output to 0.
6: **return** $1-[b]$

within C_{check}. To obtain the result of the equality test within a hidden value, the EqCheck sub-circuit shown in Circuit 1 makes use of an auxiliary value r which, when $x \neq y$, is set to $(x-y)^{-1}$ such that $b = (x-y)\cdot r = 1$. When $x = y$, $b = (x-y)\cdot r = 0$ for any r. The circuit then returns $1-b$ so that 1 is output in case of equality.

Since this r requires a precise value, it must be input into the circuit using the `Input` command. However, this allows for dishonest behaviour, so the circuit must also check that: 1. r is non-zero and 2. the final result b is indeed a bit (if r was non-zero but also not equal to $(x-y)^{-1}$ when $x \neq y$, then b would not be a bit). To perform the first check, EqCheck requires r^{-1} to be input so that $r\cdot r^{-1}$ can be verified to equal 1. For the second check, $(1-b)\cdot b$ is tested to be equal 0, which implies $b \in \{0,1\}$.

Zero-Knowledge. If correct, both $r\cdot r^{-1}$ and $(1-b)\cdot b$ always evaluate to the same value, independently of r or b, so they can be safely checked against a constant (1 or 0) without leaking information.

Soundness. Both checks are deterministic, therefore if r and r^{-1} are incorrectly input, either of these will fail and C_{check} will output 0 with probability 1.

Cost. This circuit requires a constant number of `Input`, multiplication and constant checks (resp. 2, 3 and 2) to evaluate the equality bit of two values.

3.2 Permutation Check

Our second sub-circuit probabilistically checks that two arrays of S (tuples of) field elements are permutations of one another without revealing either the content of the arrays or the permutation that links them. We first describe the procedure in the one- and multi-dimensional case before formally presenting the PermCheck sub-circuit.

Checking a One-Dimensional Permutation. We first present the checking procedure in the one-dimensional case, as described in [6]. Let $[A] = [[a_1]\cdots[a_S]]$ and $[B] = [[b_1]\cdots[b_S]]$ be two arrays in $\mathbb{F}^S$; to show that there exists a secret permutation π such that $B = \pi(A)$, we use the fact that polynomials are identical under permutation of the roots [14,24]. In other words, we define two polynomials $P_A, P_B \in \mathbb{F}[x]$ such that their zeros are exactly the elements of the respective arrays:

$$[P_A(x)] = \prod_{i=1}^{S}(x - [a_i]) \qquad \text{and} \qquad [P_B(x)] = \prod_{i=1}^{S}(x - [b_i]).$$

If the arrays are indeed permutations of one another, then the polynomials are defined identically and it holds that $P_A = P_B$. We check this probabilistically using the Schwartz–Zippel Lemma.

1: Receive public random challenge $r \in \mathbb{F}$.
2: Compute $r - [a_i]$ and $r - [b_i]$ for $i \in [S]$.
3: Compute the values $[P_A(r)] = \prod_{i=1}^{S}(r - [a_i])$ and $[P_B(r)]$ similarly.
4: Check that $P_A(r) - P_B(r)$ is equal to 0.

Given that P_A and P_B are both of degree S, the Schwartz–Zippel Lemma states that, if $P_A \neq P_B$, then the check in Step 4 will incorrectly pass with probability at most $S/|\mathbb{F}|$.

Checking a Multi-dimensional Permutation. In our application, as the two lists $\mathcal{L}$ and $\mathcal{L}'$ contain tuples of 4 elements we instead need to consider matrices. However, the following analysis can be generalized to matrices of higher dimension. Let $[\mathbf{A}] = [[\mathbf{a}_1] \cdots [\mathbf{a}_S]]$ and $[\mathbf{B}] = [[\mathbf{b}_1] \cdots [\mathbf{b}_S]]$ be matrices in $\mathbb{F}^{4 \times S}$; we wish to prove that the columns of $\mathbf{B}$ are a permutation of the columns of $\mathbf{A}$, i.e. there exists a permutation π such that $\mathbf{A}P_\pi = \mathbf{B}$, where P_π is the matrix permutation associated to π.

To do so, we reduce the question to the one-dimensional case using randomized inner products. First, a random challenge $\mathbf{s} \in \mathbb{F}^4$ is sampled. Then, $\mathbf{A}$ is compressed to a one-dimensional array $\mathbf{a}$ by setting $(\mathbf{a})_i = a_i = \mathbf{s} * \mathbf{a}_i$, for $i \in [S]$, where $*$ denotes the inner product of two vectors. Similarly, $\mathbf{B}$ is compressed to $\mathbf{b}$ using the same $\mathbf{s}$. (Using the same challenge $\mathbf{s}$ for all columns of both matrices is necessary since the permutation must remain secret.) Now, the procedure for the one-dimensional case presented above can be used to check that $\mathbf{b}$ is a permutation of $\mathbf{a}$.

To show that this procedure correctly checks that the columns of $\mathbf{B}$ are a permutation of the columns of $\mathbf{A}$, we show that any difference is preserved by the randomized inner product except with some probability.

Lemma 1. *Given two matrices* $\mathbf{A}, \mathbf{B}$ *as above, if there does not exist a column permutation matrix* P_π *such that* $\mathbf{A}P_\pi = \mathbf{B}$ *then the sets* $\{a_1, \ldots, a_S\}$ *and* $\{b_1, \ldots, b_S\}$ *are different except with probability at most* $1/|\mathbb{F}|$ *over the random choice of* $\mathbf{s} \in \mathbb{F}^4$.

Proof. We can consider the linear map $f_{\mathbf{a}-\mathbf{b}}(\mathbf{s})$, defined by the matrix $\mathbf{D} = (\mathbf{A} - \mathbf{B})^T \in \mathbb{F}^{M \times 4}$. If $\mathbf{A}$ and $\mathbf{B}$ are correctly generated, $\mathbf{D} = \mathbf{0}$ and the condition $f_{\mathbf{D}}(\mathbf{s}) = 0$ holds $\forall \mathbf{s} \in \mathbb{F}^4$.
If the adversary cheated, i.e., $\mathbf{D} \neq \mathbf{0}$, we can have the following different cases:

Circuit 2. $\mathsf{PermCheck}(\nu \in \{1,4\}, [\mathcal{L}], [\mathcal{L}'])$

1: **if** $\nu = 4$ **then**
2: $\quad \mathbf{s} \leftarrow \mathtt{Rand}(\mathbb{F}^\nu)$
3: **for** $i \in [S]$ **do**
4: $\quad$ **if** $\nu = 1$ **then**
5: $\quad\quad [a_i] \leftarrow [\mathcal{L}[i]]$ and $[b_i] \leftarrow [\mathcal{L}'[i]]$
6: $\quad$ **else**
7: $\quad\quad [a_i] \leftarrow \mathbf{s} * [\mathcal{L}[i]]$ and $[b_i] \leftarrow \mathbf{s} * [\mathcal{L}'[i]]$
8: $r \leftarrow \mathtt{Rand}(\mathbb{F})$
9: $[P_A(r)] \leftarrow \prod_{i=1}^{S}(r - [a_i])$ and $[P_B(r)] \leftarrow \prod_{i=1}^{S}(r - [b_i])$
10: Check that $[P_A(r)] - [P_B(r)]$ is equal to 0; if not, set circuit output to 0.

- If only one row is incorrect, then rank $\mathbf{D} = 1$ and the rank-nullity theorem tells us $\dim(\ker f_{\mathbf{D}}) = 3$. This means that the probability that $\mathbf{s} \in \ker f_{\mathbf{D}}$ is $|\mathbb{F}^3|/|\mathbb{F}^4| = 1/|\mathbb{F}|$.
- If two rows are incorrect, then rank $\mathbf{D} \leq 2$. If it is 1, then we are in the same situation as before, otherwise $\dim(\ker f_{\mathbf{D}}) = 2$ and the probability that $\mathbf{s} \in \ker f_{\mathbf{D}}$ is $|\mathbb{F}^2|/|\mathbb{F}^4| = 1/|\mathbb{F}^2|$.
- If three rows are incorrect, then rank $\mathbf{D} \leq 3$, hence either we are in one of the situations described above or $\dim(\ker f_{\mathbf{D}}) = 1$ and the probability that $\mathbf{s} \in \ker f_{\mathbf{D}}$ is $|\mathbb{F}|/|\mathbb{F}^4| = 1/|\mathbb{F}^3|$.
- If we have more than 3 incorrect rows and rank $\mathbf{D} = 4$, then $f_{\mathbf{D}}$ is injective and $\ker f_{\mathbf{D}} = \{\mathbf{0}\}$. Hence, the probability of passing the test is $1/|\mathbb{F}^4|$.

Given that the number of erroneous rows fixes the rank of $\mathbf{D}$ to exactly one of the four cases above, the overall probability of passing the test is at most $1/|\mathbb{F}|$. This concludes the proof.

Constructing the Circuit. We now present the PermCheck sub-circuit in Circuit 2. This takes $\nu \in \mathbb{N}$ as parameter to indicate the row-dimension of the arrays $\mathcal{L}$ and $\mathcal{L}'$; if $\nu = 4$ then we use the multi-dimensional check described above and sample a random vector $\mathbf{s} \in \mathbb{F}^\nu$. Then, the circuit performs the Schwartz–Zippel test by requiring a random $r \in \mathbb{F}$, evaluating the polynomials P_A and P_B on r and checking that they are equal, i.e. that their difference is 0.

Zero-Knowledge. The only revealed information is that $P_A(r) - P_B(r)$ is equal to 0; however, this is always the case when $[\mathcal{L}']$ is a permutation of $[\mathcal{L}]$, therefore no information is leaked.

Soundness. When $\nu = 1$, the one-dimensional case is sufficient to show that PermCheck incorrectly passes with probability at most $S/|\mathbb{F}|$. When $\nu = 4$, Lemma 1 gives us that, if $\mathcal{L}'$ is not a permutation of $\mathcal{L}$, $\{a_i\}$ and $\{b_i\}$ will be different except with probability at most $1/|\mathbb{F}|$. If the sets are different, the one-dimensional case then again implies that the last check will incorrectly pass

Circuit 3. $\mathsf{BdCheck}(\{[x_i]\}_1^T, B_1, B_2)$

1: Arrange initial array $[\mathcal{L}] = [B_1, B_1+1, \ldots, B_2, [x_1], [x_2], \ldots, [x_T]]$ of size $S = B_2 - B_1 + 1 + T$.
2: $\mathtt{Input}[\mathcal{L}']$ containing entries of $\mathcal{L}$ sorted from lowest to highest.
3: $\mathsf{PermCheck}([\mathcal{L}], [\mathcal{L}'])$ ▷ Sets the circuit output to 0 if it fails.
4: **for** $i \in [S-1]$ **do**
5: $[\alpha_i] \leftarrow [\mathcal{L}'[i+1]] - [\mathcal{L}'[i]]$
6: Check that $[\alpha_i] \cdot (1 - [\alpha_i])$ is equal to 0; if not, set circuit output to 0.
7: Check that $[\mathcal{L}'[1]] = B_1$ and that $[\mathcal{L}'[S]] = B_2$; if not set circuit output to 0.

with probability at most $S/|\mathbb{F}|$. Therefore, when $\nu = 4$, the probability that PermCheck incorrectly passes is at most

$$\Pr_{\mathbf{s}}[\{a_i\} = \{b_i\}] + \Pr_{\mathbf{s}}[\{a_i\} \neq \{b_i\}] \cdot \Pr_{r}[P_A(r) = P_B(r)]$$
$$\leq \frac{1}{|\mathbb{F}|} + \left(1 - \frac{1}{|\mathbb{F}|}\right)\frac{S}{|\mathbb{F}|} \leq \frac{S+1}{|\mathbb{F}|}.$$

Cost. When $\nu = 1$, this circuit requires one `Input` command, one `Rand` command, $2(S-1)$ multiplications gates and one constant equality check. When $\nu = 4$, it requires an additional ν `Rand` commands as well as $2\nu S$ multiplications to compute the inner products.

3.3 Amortized Constant Overhead Bound Test

Our third sub-circuit BdCheck, shown in Circuit 3, verifies in zero-knowledge that a set $\{[x_i]\}$ of T values are all contained within specified public bounds B_1 and B_2.

To do so, it first creates an array $\mathcal{L}$ of all values from B_1 to B_2, both included, and then appends all T values to be checked, forming an array of size $S = B_2 - B_1 + 1 + T$. Using `Input` commands, it then requires an array $[\mathcal{L}']$ of same size S which is expected to be an ordered permutation of $\mathcal{L}$. (Even though the values $B_1, \ldots, B_2$ were not hidden in $\mathcal{L}$, all of the values of $\mathcal{L}'$ must now remain hidden so that no information is leaked about $\{[x_i]\}$.) By verifying that the first entry of $\mathcal{L}'$ is equal to B_1 and the last entry of $\mathcal{L}'$ is equal to B_2, the circuit verifies that $B_1 \leq x_i \leq B_2$ for all $i \in [T]$.

As in the circuit for equality checking, the `Input` commands allow for dishonest behaviour so several properties of $\mathcal{L}'$ must additionally be checked. First, BdCheck calls PermCheck to verify that $\mathcal{L}'$ is indeed a permutation of $\mathcal{L}$ and therefore that no value has been modified.

Second, the circuit checks that successive entries in $\mathcal{L}'$ are either equal to each other or differ by exactly 1. In a correctly input $\mathcal{L}'$, this is always the case as every value $[x_i]$ should be equal to one value between B_1 and B_2.

It does so by first computing $\alpha_i = \mathcal{L}'[i+1] - \mathcal{L}'[i]$ and then checks that $\alpha_i \in \{0, 1\}$ by making sure α_i is a root of $X \cdot (X-1)$.

Finally, $\mathsf{BdCheck}$ verifies that $\mathcal{L}'[1] = B_1$ and that $\mathcal{L}'[S] = B_2$. This, combined with the second check, implies that $B_1 \leq x_i \leq B_2$ for all $i \in [T]$.

Zero-Knowledge. First, $\mathsf{PermCheck}$ guarantees zero-knowledge of $[\mathcal{L}']$ during the first check. Next, if $[\mathcal{L}']$ was input correctly, then $[\alpha_i]$ should always be a root of $X \cdot (X-1)$ and therefore no information is leaked by checking this. Finally, given that B_1 and B_2 are public values and included in $[\mathcal{L}]$, checking the first and last entry of $[\mathcal{L}']$ does not reveal any information on any $[x_i]$ if $[\mathcal{L}']$ was input correctly.

Soundness. The checks on $[\alpha_i]$ and the first and last entries of $[\mathcal{L}']$ are all deterministic, so $\mathsf{BdCheck}$ makes C_{check} output 0 with probability 1 if any of these fail. $\mathsf{PermCheck}$ is probabilistic in nature, however, so $\mathsf{BdCheck}$ has the same soundness error overall, i.e. $S/|\mathbb{F}|$ since $\mathcal{L}$ is one-dimensional here.

Cost. This circuit amortizes the cost of checking whether $B_1 \leq x \leq B_2$ by checking T values at the same time. This requires S calls to `Input`, one $\mathsf{PermCheck}$ call, $S-1$ multiplications and $S+2$ constant equality checks.

3.4 Putting Everything Together

We now present the complete C_{check} circuit which verifies the consistency of accesses, held as tuples $([l], t, [op], [d])$ within the list $\mathcal{L}$. Recall that it does so by requiring a second list $\mathcal{L}'$ to be an ordering of $\mathcal{L}$ and by verifying that (1) $\mathcal{L}'$ is a permutation of $\mathcal{L}$; (2) $\mathcal{L}'$ is correctly ordered, first according to l and then according to t for entries concerning the same address; (3) all addresses are within bounds; (4) all operations are either reads or writes; and (5) all read tuples contain the same value as the last one written to the same address.

Checking (1) and (3). The first is done by calling $\mathsf{PermCheck}(4, [\mathcal{L}], [\mathcal{L}'])$ and the second is done by checking that $[l'_{N+T}] = N$.

Checking (2). Here we check equalities, which is done using $\mathsf{EqCheck}$, but also the inequalities $t'_i < t'_{i+1}$, in the case where $l'_i = l'_{i+1}$. Since the t_i values are public within $\mathcal{L}$, and we know that $\mathcal{L}'$ is a permutation of $\mathcal{L}$, it holds that $1 \leq [t'_i] \leq N+T$ for all $i \in [N+T]$. Letting $[\tau_i] = [t_{i+1}] - [t_i]$, we see that $0 < [\tau_i] \implies [t_i] < [t_{i+1}]$. Therefore, calling $\mathsf{BdCheck}([\tau_i], 1, N+T-1)$ would allow to test this (setting 1 as the lower bound ensures the strict inequality; setting $N+T-1$ as the upper bound ensures all values of τ_i are included). However, if successive tuples access different addresses, then successive values of t are not ordered in this way; e.g. with the tuples $(1, 2, *, *)$ and $(2, 1, *, *)$. Therefore calculating τ_i in this manner does not yield the correct check.

To fix this, we include only the τ_i values for accesses to the same address, i.e. those for which the equality $l'_i = l'_{i+1}$ holds. Setting $[\alpha_i] \leftarrow \mathsf{EqCheck}([l'_i], [l'_{i+1}])$, we can instead let $[\tau_i] \leftarrow [\alpha_i]([t'_{i+1}] - [t'_i]) + (1 - [\alpha_i])$. The first summand includes $[t'_{i+1}] - [t'_i]$ when the equality holds, and nullifies it otherwise, and the second summand ensures $\tau_i > 0$ when the equality does not hold. Now, $\mathsf{BdCheck}(\{\tau_i\}, 1, N+T-1)$ will pass exactly when the t values are correctly ordered within groups of accesses to the same address l.

Circuit 4. $C_{\mathsf{check}}([\mathcal{L}])$

1: Assume initial array is of the form

$$[\mathcal{L}] = [(1, 1, \mathsf{write}, [M_1]), \ldots, (N, N, \mathsf{write}, [M_N]), \ldots$$
$$\ldots ([\ell_{N+1}], N+1, [\mathsf{op}_{N+1}], [d_{N+1}]), \ldots, ([\ell_{N+T}], N+T, [\mathsf{op}_{N+T}], [d_{N+T}])]$$

2: $\texttt{Input}[\mathcal{L}']$ containing entries of $\mathcal{L}$ sorted first by ℓ then by t.
3: $\mathsf{PermCheck}(4, [\mathcal{L}], [\mathcal{L}'])$
4: **for** $i \in [N+T-1]$ **do**
5: Set $[\alpha_i] \leftarrow \mathsf{EqCheck}([\ell'_i], [\ell'_{i+1}])$
6: Set $[\lambda_i] \leftarrow [\ell'_{i+1}] - [\ell'_i]$
7: Set $[\tau_i] \leftarrow [\alpha_i] \cdot ([t'_{i+1}] - [t'_i]) + (1 - [\alpha_i])$
8: Check that $[\alpha_i] + [\lambda_i]$ is equal to 1; if not, set circuit output to 0.
9: Check that $(1 - [\mathsf{op}'_i]) \cdot [\mathsf{op}'_i]$ is equal to 0; if not, set circuit output to 0.
10: $[\beta_i] \leftarrow \mathsf{EqCheck}([d'_i], [d'_{i+1}])$
11: Set $[\gamma_i] \leftarrow 1 - [\alpha_i] \cdot (1 - [\beta_i]) \cdot (1 - [\mathsf{op}'_{i+1}])$
12: Check $[\gamma_i]$ is equal to 1; if not, set circuit output to 0.
13: $\mathsf{BdCheck}(\{[\tau_i]\}_{i=1}^{N+T-1}, 1, N+T-1)$
14: Check $[\ell'_{N+T}]$ is equal to N; if not, set circuit output to 0.
15: If circuit output was not set to 0 at any point, output 1.

To finally check the ordering of the addresses, similarly to the $\mathsf{BdCheck}$ circuit, verifying that $[l'_{i+1}] = [l'_i]+1$ when $[l'_{i+1}] \neq [l'_i]+1$ does not require a second $\mathsf{EqCheck}$. Instead we compute $[\lambda_i] \leftarrow [l'_{i+1}] - [l'_i]$ and check that $[\alpha_i] + [\lambda_i]$ is equal to 1. If $[l'_{i+1}] \notin \{[l'_i], [l'_i]+1\}$, this will not pass.

Checking (4). For every $i \in [N+T]$, as $[op'_i]$ should be a bit, representing either read or write, we check that $(1 - [\mathsf{op}'_i])[\mathsf{op}'_i] = 0$.

Checking (5). We check that adjacent tuples contain either (a) different addresses, (b) equal memory values, or (c) a write operation. As $[\alpha_i]$ already contains the equality bit of the two addresses, and (2) checked that addresses either are equal or differ by one, then $1 - [\alpha_i]$ is exactly the truth value required for (a). For (b) we set $[\beta_i] \leftarrow \mathsf{EqCheck}([d'_i], [d'_{i+1}])$. Finally for (c), $[op'_{i+1}]$ is its own equality bit with respect to the write operation. To evaluate $(a) \vee (b) \vee (c)$, we then compute $\neg(\neg(a) \wedge \neg(b) \wedge \neg(c))$:

$$[\gamma_i] \leftarrow 1 - [\alpha_i] \cdot (1 - [\beta_i]) \cdot (1 - [\mathsf{op}'_{i+1}]),$$

and check that $[\gamma_i]$ is equal to 1 for every $i \in [N+T-1]$.

The C_{check} Circuit. The final circuit is presented in Circuit 4; it performs checks (1) through (5) as described above and, if the output was never set to 0 by a failed constant check, then it outputs 1 to signify that all accesses contained in $\mathcal{L}$ are consistent with the initial memory and one another.

Correctness. We first note that, if all $\texttt{Input}$ gates are given correctly, then the C_{check} circuit will always output 1, independently of the output of the $\texttt{Rand}$ gates.

Zero-Knowledge. The zero-knowledge properties of the EqCheck, PermCheck and BdCheck sub-circuits was argued in previous sections. As for the C_{check} circuit, the check of step 8 is always equal to 1 if $\mathcal{L}'$ was input correctly, and so is the check of step 12, therefore no information is leaked by either. Similarly, $[\mathsf{op}'_i]$ should always be a bit, so step 9 also does not leak information. Finally, N is already publicly contained in $\mathcal{L}$ as the address of the last tuple, so step 14 does not reveal information either if $\mathcal{L}'$ was input correctly.

Soundness. PermCheck is the only non-deterministic check performed in the circuit, at steps 3 and 13 (within BdCheck). We therefore have the following.

Lemma 2. *If* $[\mathcal{L}]$ *is a inconsistent list of array accesses, then* C_{check} *will output 1 with probability at most* $2(N+T-1)/|\mathbb{F}|$.

Proof. Given that $[\mathcal{L}]$ is inconsistent, C_{check} will output 1 in the following cases:

1. $[\mathcal{L}']$ is consistent, and PermCheck at step 3 fails to detect that it is not a permutation of $[\mathcal{L}]$; this happens with probability at most $(N+T+1)/|\mathbb{F}|$.
2. $[\mathcal{L}']$ is a permutation of $[\mathcal{L}]$ and the checks at steps 8, 9, 12, 13 and 14 fail to detect that it is inconsistent. Of these, only step 13 is probabilistic and the assumption that $[\mathcal{L}']$ is inconsistent implies one of these checks must set the output to 0.
   - If $[\mathcal{L}']$ is "consistent enough" that the *deterministic* checks of steps 8, 9, 12 and 14 pass, then it must be inconsistent only in the ordering of the t' values and it will pass the probabilistic check of step 13 with probability at most $2(N+T-1)/|\mathbb{F}|$.
   - If $[\mathcal{L}']$ is inconsistent in any other way, the probability of C_{check} outputting 1 is 0.

   Thus, the probability of C_{check} outputting 1 when $[\mathcal{L}']$ is a permutation of an inconsistent $[\mathcal{L}]$ is at most $2(N+T-1)/|\mathbb{F}|$.
3. $[\mathcal{L}']$ is inconsistent, but is also not a permutation of $[\mathcal{L}]$. In this case, $[\mathcal{L}']$ would need to pass the checks of both case 1 and case 2 above so the probability of C_{check} outputting 1 would be at most $p_1 \times p_2$ where p_i is the probability of case i.

Since these three cases are mutually exclusive, when $[\mathcal{L}]$ is inconsistent C_{check} will output 1 with probability at most $2(N+T-1)/|\mathbb{F}|$.

Cost. Since PermCheck and BdCheck are called outside of the **for** loop, the execution of C_{check} costs $O(N+T)$ standard arithmetic operations with $O(N+T)$ additional inputs.

4 Zero-Knowledge Proof of Array Access

The standard (stateless) zero-knowledge proof functionality for Boolean or arithmetic circuits is only suitable for deterministic circuits. As described in Sect. 3, our C_{check} circuit probabilistically verifies the consistency of the access list. To ensure soundness, this requires that the verification randomness be generated

Functionality $\mathcal{F}_{\mathsf{ZKin}}$

The functionality runs with a prover $\mathcal{P}$, a verifier $\mathcal{V}$ and an adversary $\mathcal{S}$.
It is parametrized by $\mathsf{type} = \{\mathsf{Boolean}, \mathsf{Arithmetic}\}$.

Init: On input $(\mathsf{sid}, \mathsf{Init}, \mathsf{type}, \mathcal{L})$ from $\mathcal{P}$, if no previous initialization command has been given, and if $\mathcal{L}$ matches type, store type and $\mathcal{L}$ and send $(\mathsf{sid}, \mathsf{Initialized}, \mathcal{P})$ to $\mathcal{V}$ and $\mathcal{S}$. Otherwise, ignore this command.

Input: On input $(\mathsf{sid}, \mathsf{Input}, v)$ from $\mathcal{P}$, append v to $\mathcal{L}$ if the type of v matches type and send $(\mathsf{sid}, \mathsf{Input})$ to $\mathcal{V}$. If Init has not been given, or if Prove has already been given, ignore this command instead.

Prove: Receive $(\mathsf{sid}, \mathsf{Prove}, \mathcal{P}, \mathcal{V}, C, x)$ from the prover. If Init has not been given, if the type of C or x does not match type, or if $(C, *)$ is already stored, ignore this command. Otherwise, compute $y = C(\mathcal{L}, x)$, send (Prove, C) to $\mathcal{S}$ and $\mathcal{V}$, and store (C, y).

Verify: On input $(\mathsf{sid}, \mathsf{Verify}, C)$ from $\mathcal{V}$, query $\mathcal{S}$. If $\mathcal{S}$ sends fail, or if (C, y) is not stored, send $(\mathsf{sid}, C, 0)$ to $\mathcal{V}$. Otherwise, send (sid, C, y) to $\mathcal{V}$.

Fig. 2. Ideal functionality for circuit-based ZK proof with separate input command.

only *after* the inputs have been committed to, as otherwise the prover could use the randomness to commit to incorrect inputs which would nonetheless satisfy the checks.

In this section, we first introduce an "input" extension of the $\mathcal{F}_{\mathsf{ZK}}$ functionality which then accepts circuits to be evaluated both on stored and fresh input values. Alongside, we also present the version of $\mathcal{F}_{\mathsf{ZKArray}}$ that our initial protocol realizes and discuss the differences with the version of Franzese et al. Then we present Π_{ZKArray}, our zero-knowledge protocol for private read/write array access, which realizes our $\mathcal{F}_{\mathsf{ZKArray}}$ using the extended zero-knowledge functionality, and prove its security in the UC framework. Finally, we discuss how our $\mathcal{F}_{\mathsf{ZKArray}}$ and Π_{ZKArray} can both be extended to provide stateless proofs for richer circuits that include both arithmetic operations and array accesses.

4.1 $\mathcal{F}_{\mathsf{ZKin}}$ and $\mathcal{F}_{\mathsf{ZKArray}}$ Functionalities

Figure 2 describes the $\mathcal{F}_{\mathsf{ZKin}}$ functionality for (stateless) zero-knowledge proof of Boolean or arithmetic circuit with a separate **Input** command. This functionality must be initialized once with sid and $\mathsf{type} \in \{\mathsf{Boolean}, \mathsf{Arithmetic}\}$. Since the aim is to allow for inputs to be given ahead of the **Prove** command, the initialization also accepts a list $\mathcal{L}$ of values, which the functionality stores. Afterwards, the **Input** command may be called several times to append values v to the initial list $\mathcal{L}$; the verifier $\mathcal{V}$ is informed of each of these calls.

The **Prove** command may then be called once, during which $\mathcal{P}$ specifies the circuit C and any additional input x. The functionality then evaluates C jointly on $\mathcal{L}$ and x, stores the result, and informs $\mathcal{S}$ and $\mathcal{V}$.

Finally, the verifier may call the **Verify** command, specifying the circuit C; this ensures that $\mathcal{P}$ and $\mathcal{V}$ agree on the circuit that should be proven. If $C(\mathcal{L}, x)$

Functionality $\mathcal{F}_{\mathsf{ZKArray}}$

The functionality runs with $\mathcal{P}, \mathcal{V}$ and an adversary $\mathcal{S}$.
PARAMETERS: The functionality is parametrized by a flag $\mathsf{f} \in \{0, 1\}$, the size N of the array, and an upper bound T on the number of memory accesses.

Init: On input $(\mathsf{sid}, \mathsf{Init}, \mathsf{type}, M, N, T)$ from $\mathcal{P}$, if no previous initialization command has been given, and if the entries of M match type, store type and M; send $(\mathsf{sid}, \mathsf{Initialized}, \mathsf{type}, \mathcal{P}, N, T)$ to $\mathcal{V}$ and $\mathcal{S}$. Set $\mathsf{f} = 1$. Otherwise, ignore this command.

Access: On input $(\mathsf{sid}, \mathsf{Access}, l, \mathsf{op}, d)$ from $\mathcal{P}$, if $l \geq N$ set $\mathsf{f} = 0$, otherwise:
- if $\mathsf{op} = \mathsf{Read}$: if $M_l \neq d$ then set $\mathsf{f} = 0$;
- if $\mathsf{op} = \mathsf{Write}$: set $M_l = d$.

In all cases, send $(\mathsf{sid}, \mathsf{Access})$ to $\mathcal{V}$ and $\mathcal{S}$.

Check: Upon receiving $(\mathsf{sid}, \mathsf{Check}, T)$ from $\mathcal{V}$, query $\mathcal{S}$. If $\mathcal{S}$ sends fail, return $(\mathsf{sid}, 0)$ to $\mathcal{V}$; otherwise, when $\mathcal{S}$ sends Deliver, if $\mathsf{f} = 0$ then send $(\mathsf{sid}, 0)$ to $\mathcal{V}$, otherwise send $(\mathsf{sid}, 1)$ and halt.

Fig. 3. Functionality for *stateless* ZKP for private read/write array access

has not been proven by $\mathcal{P}$, or if $\mathcal{S}$ decides to interrupt, then $\mathcal{F}_{\mathsf{ZKin}}$ informs $\mathcal{V}$ of the failure and stops. Otherwise, it sends $(\mathsf{sid}, C, 1)$ to $\mathcal{V}$ and stops.

Figure 3 presents a *stateless* version of the $\mathcal{F}_{\mathsf{ZKArray}}$ functionality. As opposed to the stateful one presented by Franzese et al. [9], this functionality does not extend $\mathcal{F}_{\mathsf{ZKin}}$, and therefore does not have a **Prove** command for arbitrary circuits, but only provides commands to initialize and access a memory array in zero-knowledge and also check the consistency of the accesses that were made. We discuss the extension of our $\mathcal{F}_{\mathsf{ZKArray}}$ functionality with a **Prove** command in Sect. 4.3.

4.2 ZKArray Protocol

We provide a protocol for private read/write array access, which first allows the prover $\mathcal{P}$ to commit to an array of values, and then to read or write values from or to the committed data structure in such a way that the verifier $\mathcal{V}$ does not learn the address being accessed, nor the operation being performed or the value being written.

Our protocol Π_{ZKArray}, described in Fig. 4, makes use of C_{check} presented in Sect. 3 to realize $\mathcal{F}_{\mathsf{ZKArray}}$. At **Init**, the prover receives the initial memory array $M = [M_1, \ldots, M_N]$. From it, it creates a list of initial access tuples $\mathcal{M}[i] = (i, i, \mathsf{write}, M_i)$ which enforces that every address is written to according to the entry in the array and that the first N memory accesses are write operations. After initializing the access counter at $t = N$, ready to be incremented, and creating an empty list $\mathcal{L}$ to contain the future accesses, $\mathcal{P}$ commits to the initial memory by sending $(\mathsf{sid}, \mathsf{Init}, \mathsf{type}, \mathcal{M})$ to $\mathcal{F}_{\mathsf{ZKin}}$. Afterwards, for each **Access** operation and its corresponding (ℓ, op, d) input, $\mathcal{P}$ increments t and appends $(\ell, t, \mathsf{op}, d)$ to the list $\mathcal{L}$.

Protocol Π_{ZKArray}

PARAMETERS: N is the size of the array, and T an upper bound on the number of accesses.

Init: On input a memory array M with contents $M_1, \ldots, M_N$, and a type, $\mathcal{P}$ creates a list $\mathcal{M} = [(1, 1, \mathsf{write}, M_1), \ldots, (N, N, \mathsf{write}, M_N)]$, initializes a counter $t = N$ and creates two empty lists $\mathcal{L}, \mathsf{AuxIn}$. It then sends $(\mathsf{sid}, \mathsf{Init}, \mathsf{type}, \mathcal{M})$ to $\mathcal{F}_{\mathsf{ZKIn}}$.

Access: On input (l, op, d), $\mathcal{P}$ increments t and appends (l, t, op, d) to $\mathcal{L}$.

Check: $\mathcal{P}$ and $\mathcal{V}$ perform the following steps:

1. $\mathcal{P}$ parses $C_{\mathsf{check}}(\mathcal{M}||\mathcal{L})$ and for each $\mathtt{Input}(x)$ command it appends x to AuxIn.
2. $\mathcal{P}$ sends $(\mathsf{sid}, \mathsf{Input}, \mathcal{L}||\mathsf{AuxIn})$ to $\mathcal{F}_{\mathsf{ZKIn}}$ which then sends $(\mathsf{sid}, \mathsf{Input})$ to $\mathcal{V}$.
3. $\mathcal{V}$ sends r_i to $\mathcal{P}$ for each $\mathtt{Rand}$ command in C_{check}.
4. $\mathcal{P}$ sends $(\mathsf{sid}, \mathsf{Prove}, \mathcal{P}, \mathcal{V}, C_{\mathsf{check}}^{\{r_i\}}, \emptyset)$ to $\mathcal{F}_{\mathsf{ZKIn}}$.
5. $\mathcal{V}$ sends $(\mathsf{sid}, \mathsf{Verify}, C_{\mathsf{check}}^{\{r_i\}})$ to $\mathcal{F}_{\mathsf{ZK}}$. It returns whatever $\mathcal{F}_{\mathsf{ZKIn}}$ returns and stops.

Fig. 4. Protocol realizing $\mathcal{F}_{\mathsf{ZKArray}}$ in the $\mathcal{F}_{\mathsf{ZKIn}}$-hybrid model.

When T access operations have been completed, the **Check** procedure begins. First, $\mathcal{P}$ parses C_{check} for $\mathtt{Input}$ gates and computes the required value for each, appending it to AuxIn each time. Note that no such auxiliary input within C_{check} is dependent on the output of a $\mathtt{Rand}$ gate, therefore all values can be computed by $\mathcal{P}$ before receiving the outputs for the $\mathtt{Rand}$ gates. After parsing all $\mathtt{Input}$ gates, $\mathcal{P}$ commits to these values by sending $(\mathsf{sid}, \mathsf{Input}, \mathcal{L}||\mathsf{AuxIn})$ to $\mathcal{F}_{\mathsf{ZKIn}}$.

The verifier receives confirmation of the commitment from the functionality and proceeds to sampling a random value r_i for each $\mathtt{Rand}$ within C_{check} before sending all of them to $\mathcal{P}$.

Now, both $\mathcal{P}$ and $\mathcal{V}$ can replace the output of the $\mathtt{Rand}$ gates by the values sampled above to specify the circuit to a deterministic one, which we label $C_{\mathsf{check}}^{\{r_i\}}$. Finally, it is this circuit, without additional input, that $\mathcal{P}$ proves with $\mathcal{F}_{\mathsf{ZKIn}}$ and that $\mathcal{V}$ asks to verify. In the full version, we prove the following theorem.

Theorem 2. *Protocol Π_{ZKArray} securely realizes $\mathcal{F}_{\mathsf{ZKArray}}$ in the $\mathcal{F}_{\mathsf{ZKIn}}$-hybrid model with statistical error at most $2(N + T - 1)/|\mathbb{F}|$.*

4.3 Realizing $\mathcal{F}_{\mathsf{ZK}}$-RAM

Here we show how to extend $\mathcal{F}_{\mathsf{ZKArray}}$ to be able to describe a protocol for RAM-based computation and implement the ideal functionality $\mathcal{F}_{\mathsf{ZK}}$-RAM given in Fig. 1.

To accept richer circuits, constructed from both arithmetic or Boolean operations and array accesses, we modify our functionality and protocol as follows.

Functionality. To extend our $\mathcal{F}_{\mathsf{ZKArray}}$ with a **Prove**(C) command, we merge the **Access** commands into the computation of C. That is, when given (C, x) from **Prove** and M from **Init**, the extended functionality $\mathcal{F}_{\mathsf{ZKArray}}^{\mathsf{ex}}$ computes

$C(M, x)$ and, every time an $\texttt{Access}$ is encountered within C, it queries $\mathcal{P}$ to input (l, op, d) as the access operation.

The corresponding **Verify** command then supersedes **Check** and performs the following operations. As **Check**, it first of all verifies that all the accesses given by $\mathcal{P}$ are consistent with the initial M and with each other. Additionally, it also verifies that the accesses given by $\mathcal{P}$ are consistent with C; i.e. that $\mathcal{P}$ provided the correct l, op and d that C instructed to perform at that moment. Finally, as for $\mathcal{F}_{\mathsf{ZKin}}$, it stores the result $y = C(M, x)$ in order to validate, or not, the successful computation of C.

Protocol. To extend Π_{ZKArray} to handle richer circuits, we expand the circuit that $\mathcal{P}$ submits to $\mathcal{F}_{\mathsf{ZKin}}$. Namely, $\mathcal{P}$ constructs the same list $\mathcal{L}$ of access tuples and, in addition to $C^{\{r_i\}}_{\mathsf{check}}$, also proves (1) the arithmetic or Boolean circuits which output the tuples that C is expecting and (2) C itself, simplified to an arithmetic or Boolean circuit by using the tuples in $\mathcal{L}$ as constant wire values.

Realizing $\mathcal{F}_{\mathsf{ZK\text{-}RAM}}$ in the $\mathcal{F}^{\mathsf{ex}}_{\mathsf{ZKArray}}$-Hybrid Model. Given the command (sid, Prove, $\mathcal{P}, \mathcal{V}, \Pi, \mathsf{type}, N, M$), $\mathcal{P}$ sends $(\mathsf{sid}, \mathsf{Init}, \mathsf{type}, M, N, T)$ to $\mathcal{F}_{\mathsf{ZKArray}}$ where T is an upper bound on the time complexity of the program . It then sends $(\mathsf{sid}, \mathsf{Prove}, \mathcal{P}, \mathcal{V}, C_\Pi, \emptyset)$ to $\mathcal{F}^{\mathsf{ex}}_{\mathsf{ZKArray}}$ where C_Π is the circuit built as a succession of next-instruction circuits $\Pi(\mathsf{state}, d)$ interleaved with $\texttt{Access}$ instructions. We note that, with this formulation of a RAM program as a sequence of next-instruction circuits, only $\mathsf{op} \in \{\mathsf{read}, \mathsf{write}\}$ operations are written into $\mathcal{F}_{\mathsf{ZKArray}}$, all other operations are translated into arithmetic circuits; in particular $\mathsf{op} = \mathsf{stop}$ is a circuit that preserves the last state, such that once stop is reached, all the remaining evaluations of the next-instruction circuit to reach the upper bound T will also yield stop.

5 Realizing $\mathcal{F}_{\mathsf{ZKin}}$ with Limbo

In this section, we show how the ZK proof system Limbo [7] can be generalized to securely realize $\mathcal{F}_{\mathsf{ZKin}}$ in the $\mathcal{F}_{\mathsf{Commit}}$-hybrid model. In the full version, we also present a small optimization that we extensively use in our implementation.

Handling Init and Input Commands. Recall that the MPC protocol used by Limbo is divided into two phases; a first where P_S sends the inputs of the circuit and the outputs of the multiplication gates to the computation servers, and a second where servers, using $\mathcal{F}_{\mathsf{Rand}}$ and helped by P_S, execute the MultCheck protocol and send the output to P_R.

To realize $\mathcal{F}_{\mathsf{ZKin}}$, we let the Limbo prover $\mathcal{P}$ perform the following before beginning the first phase. When the **Init** command is given, $\mathcal{P}$ commits to $\mathcal{L}$ as the beginning of the input, and waits. For every **Input** command given afterwards, $\mathcal{P}$ commits to v and appends it to $\mathcal{L}$ and waits further. When the **Prove** command is given, $\mathcal{P}$ appends x to $\mathcal{L}$ and considers this final $\mathcal{L}$ as the input to the circuit C given by **Prove**.

UC Security in the $\mathcal{F}_{\mathsf{Commit}}$-Hybrid Model. In the full version, we present the Limbo$_{\mathsf{UC}}$ protocol, the generalized version of Limbo described above which we also rephrase for the UC framework. For the detailed description of the protocol and the relevant definitions, we refer the reader to [7].

Non-Interactive Proof. As our Π_{ZKArray} protocol is entirely stateless and uses only public randomness, it can be compiled to a non-interactive (NI) proof in the $\mathcal{F}_{\mathsf{ZKin}}$-hybrid model according to the Fiat–Shamir transform.

Furthermore, the Limbo protocol for $\mathcal{F}_{\mathsf{ZKin}}$ can itself be compiled to an NI proof with the same methodology. However, due to its high number of interaction rounds between the prover and the verifier, the soundness analysis of the resulting protocol is non-trivial [7, Section 6].

Similarly, our generalized $\mathsf{Limbo}_{\mathsf{UC}}$ protocol can be transformed to an NI proof where each call to $\mathcal{F}_{\mathsf{Commit}}$ is replaced by calls to a random oracle that generates randomness in place of $\mathcal{V}$. Combined with an NI version of Π_{ZKArray}, the random oracle would then generate the randomness for the Rand gates on behalf of $\mathcal{V}$ between the Input and Prove calls to $\mathcal{F}_{\mathsf{ZKin}}$. We leave the exact soundness analysis and parameter generation to further work.

6 Implementation Results

We implemented our protocol in C++, using a slightly modified version of Limbo as described in the full version. We first added support for arbitrary fields on top of the implementation for binary fields of [7], and then expanded the Bristol Format of circuits by adding Access gates.

The circuit is represented as a text file which specifies the size of the memory that will be needed, the number of input wires, output wires and hardcoded wires. For each hardcoded wire, the value is also specified. Finally, the file also contains a list of gates in topological order where each gate specifies the operation it performs and the wires it operates on.

We start by parsing the circuit in order to propagate hardcoded wires. Then, we transform every Access gate into a set of new input wires which will define the lists $\mathcal{L}$ and $\mathcal{L}'$. Everywhere it can be done, we apply the *Equality with constant check* trick described in the full version, effectively achieving a 1.5x speed-up and halving the size of the proofs. Once the whole circuit has been analysed, we build C_{check} using the newly defined wires. At this point, we have a circuit composed only of *standard* arithmetic gates which Limbo can evaluate.

As an additional improvement with respect to the original code, we also support Rand gates. These gates are implicitly used in our protocol every time the Verifier needs to send a challenge to the Prover in the PermCheck circuit. However, if the need arises for a specific use case, our implementation can handle such Rand gates within the circuit itself, thus giving more freedom for future implementation of statistical check in the spirit of PermCheck.

Finally, we also propose a multi-threaded implementation, where each repetition of the proof is run on its own thread. As for the original Limbo, this trivial parallelization does not allow us to divide the running time by the number of threads, because there are some places where threads have to join, but it nonetheless gives a significant improvement.

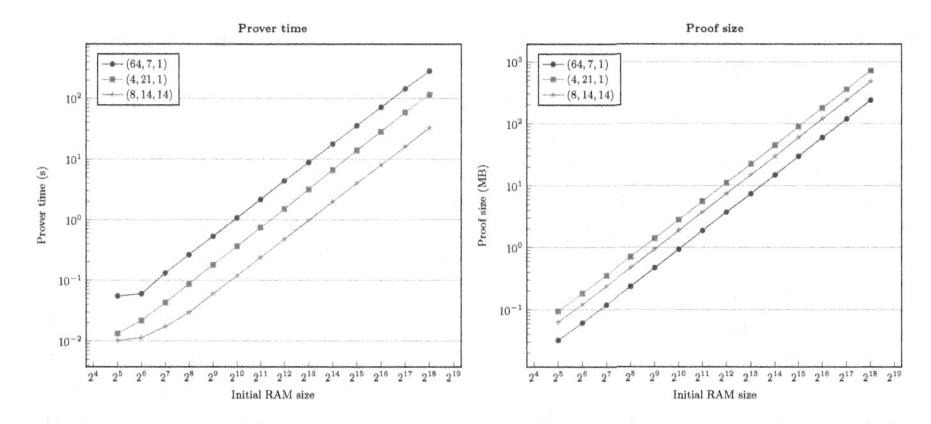

Fig. 5. Prover time and proof size in the interactive case for initialization of different sizes of RAM. We specify (#parties, #repetitions, #threads).

Table 1. Comparison of our protocol with previous work in the designated-verifier setting. For our scheme we specify (#parties, #repetitions, #threads).

Scheme	Algebraic Structure	Asymptotic Complexity	Access Time (ms)	Access Size (KB)
BubbleRAM [16][a]	$GF(2^{40}-87)$	$O(log^2(N))$	0.15	1.5
PrORAM [17][a]	$GF(2^{40}-87)$	$O(log(N))$	0.01	0.4
Franzese et al. [9]	$\mathbb{Z}_{2^{32}}$	$O(1)$	0.01	0.031
Ours (64, 7, 1)	$GF(2^{61}-1)$	$O(1)$	1.11	0.920
Ours (4, 21, 1)	$GF(2^{61}-1)$	$O(1)$	0.42	2.82
Ours (8, 14, 1)	$GF(2^{61}-1)$	$O(1)$	0.44	1.82
Ours (8, 14, 14)	$GF(2^{61}-1)$	$O(1)$	0.12	1.82

[a] Access Time and Access Size are considered for a RAM of size 2^{18} elements.

6.1 Performance

All benchmarks were done on a desktop computer with an Intel i9-9900 (3.1 GHz) CPU and 128 GB of RAM. We only provide proving times and proof size; and do not take into account communication time between parties. In all cases, we show the running time of our implementation using $\mathbb{F} = GF(2^{61}-1)$ averaged over 20 runs for varying RAM sizes.

In Fig. 5, we show figures for the initialization phase of the array for three parameter sets to emphasize potential trade-off between running time and proof size as well as the benefit of multi-threading; all sets provide statistical security of 40 bits for interactive proofs. In the case of multi-threading, we selected 8 parties and 14 repetitions because we had 14 threads available on our CPU.

With all optimizations implemented, we observe that the initialization phase of the array costs an amortized 8 `Mult` gates and 6 constant checks per memory slot. Subsequent accesses, with sensitive operations and memory location also cost an amortized 8 `Mult` gates and 6 constant checks per access. In terms of concrete performance, when focusing on better runtime for a single thread, each access amounts to roughly 0.4 ms and 1.8 KB. For the multi-threaded case, each access costs 0.12 ms and 1.8 KB.

In Table 1, we summarize our comparison with other work. We compare our results to Franzese et al. [9], noting that their performance is measured for proofs using rings of 32-bit integers, whereas our implementation uses $GF(2^{61}-1)$ which is 30 bits larger. On a single thread, using parameters optimizing for running time, we are about 40 times slower with proof sizes 60 times bigger; if we instead trade-off running time for better proof size, we are about 110 times slower with proof sizes 30 times bigger.

We also compare with BubbleRAM and the more recent PrORAM [16,17], both are tailored for private-coin protocols in the prime field setting. For a RAM size of 2^{18} elements in $GF(2^{40} - 87)$, BubbleRAM (resp. PrORAM) achieves an amortized access time of 0.15 ms (resp. 0.01 ms) and communication size of 1.5 KB (resp. 0.4 KB). While providing memory elements that are 21 bits larger (about 1.5x), our protocol is therefore only 3 times slower with 1.2 times bigger proof size than BubbleRAM and 40 times slower with 5 times bigger proof size than PrORAM. In light of these comparisons, we emphasize that MPCitH protocols are designed to be public-coin and therefore inherently produce slower and bigger proofs than protocols that exploit private coins.

Finally, we remark that multi-threaded implementations can significantly speed up MPCitH protocols. If hardware allows, each repetition of the proof can run on a separate thread. We report that with 14 threads we can match the running time of BubbleRAM with a proof size only 1.2 times bigger.

Acknowledgements. This work has been supported in part by ERC Advanced Grant ERC-2015-AdG-IMPaCT, by the Defense Advanced Research Projects Agency (DARPA) under contract No. HR001120C0085, by CyberSecurity Research Flanders with reference number VR20192203, and by the FWO under Odysseus project GOH 9718N. Any opinions, findings and conclusions or recommendations expressed in this material are those of the authors and do not necessarily reflect the views of any funding body. The U.S. Government is authorized to reproduce and distribute reprints for governmental purposes notwithstanding any copyright annotation therein.

References

1. Ames, S., Hazay, C., Ishai, Y., Venkitasubramaniam, M.: Ligero: lightweight sublinear arguments without a trusted setup. In: Thuraisingham, B.M., Evans, D., Malkin, T., Xu, D. (eds.) ACM CCS 2017, pp. 2087–2104. ACM Press, October/November 2017. https://doi.org/10.1145/3133956.3134104
2. Baum, C., Malozemoff, A.J., Rosen, M.B., Scholl, P.: Mac'n'Cheese: zero-knowledge proofs for boolean and arithmetic circuits with nested disjunctions. In: Malkin, T., Peikert, C. (eds.) CRYPTO 2021, Part IV. LNCS, vol. 12828, pp. 92–122. Springer, Cham (2021). https://doi.org/10.1007/978-3-030-84259-8_4
3. Ben-Sasson, E., Chiesa, A., Genkin, D., Tromer, E., Virza, M.: SNARKs for C: verifying program executions succinctly and in zero knowledge. In: Canetti, R., Garay, J.A. (eds.) CRYPTO 2013, Part II. LNCS, vol. 8043, pp. 90–108. Springer, Heidelberg (2013). https://doi.org/10.1007/978-3-642-40084-1_6

4. Ben-Sasson, E., Chiesa, A., Riabzev, M., Spooner, N., Virza, M., Ward, N.P.: Aurora: transparent succinct arguments for R1CS. In: Ishai, Y., Rijmen, V. (eds.) EUROCRYPT 2019, Part I. LNCS, vol. 11476, pp. 103–128. Springer, Cham (2019). https://doi.org/10.1007/978-3-030-17653-2_4
5. Ben-Sasson, E., Chiesa, A., Tromer, E., Virza, M.: Succinct non-interactive zero knowledge for a von neumann architecture. In: Fu, K., Jung, J. (eds.) USENIX Security 2014, pp. 781–796. USENIX Association, August 2014
6. Bootle, J., Cerulli, A., Groth, J., Jakobsen, S., Maller, M.: Arya: nearly linear-time zero-knowledge proofs for correct program execution. In: Peyrin, T., Galbraith, S. (eds.) ASIACRYPT 2018, Part I. LNCS, vol. 11272, pp. 595–626. Springer, Cham (2018). https://doi.org/10.1007/978-3-030-03326-2_20
7. de Saint Guilhem, C., Orsini, E., Tanguy, T.: Limbo: efficient zero-knowledge MPCitH-based arguments. In: Vigna, G., Shi, E. (eds.) ACM CCS 2021, pp. 3022–3036. ACM Press, November 2021. https://doi.org/10.1145/3460120.3484595
8. Dittmer, S., Ishai, Y., Ostrovsky, R.: Line-point zero knowledge and its applications. In: Tessaro, S. (ed.) 2nd Conference on Information-Theoretic Cryptography, ITC 2021, Virtual Conference. LIPIcs, vol. 199, pp. 5:1–5:24. Schloss Dagstuhl - Leibniz-Zentrum für Informatik (2021). https://doi.org/10.4230/LIPIcs.ITC.2021.5
9. Franzese, N., Katz, J., Lu, S., Ostrovsky, R., Wang, X., Weng, C.: Constant-overhead zero-knowledge for RAM programs. In: Vigna, G., Shi, E. (eds.) ACM CCS 2021, pp. 178–191. ACM Press, November 2021. https://doi.org/10.1145/3460120.3484800
10. Gennaro, R., Gentry, C., Parno, B., Raykova, M.: Quadratic span programs and succinct NIZKs without PCPs. In: Johansson, T., Nguyen, P.Q. (eds.) EUROCRYPT 2013. LNCS, vol. 7881, pp. 626–645. Springer, Heidelberg (2013). https://doi.org/10.1007/978-3-642-38348-9_37
11. Goldberg, L., Papini, S., Riabzev, M.: Cairo - a turing-complete STARK-friendly CPU architecture. Cryptology ePrint Archive, Report 2021/1063 (2021). https://eprint.iacr.org/2021/1063
12. Goldwasser, S., Micali, S., Rackoff, C.: The knowledge complexity of interactive proof-systems (extended abstract). In: 17th ACM STOC, pp. 291–304. ACM Press, May 1985. https://doi.org/10.1145/22145.22178
13. Gordon, S.D., et al.: Secure two-party computation in sublinear (amortized) time. In: Yu, T., Danezis, G., Gligor, V.D. (eds.) ACM CCS 2012, pp. 513–524. ACM Press, October 2012. https://doi.org/10.1145/2382196.2382251
14. Groth, J.: Linear algebra with sub-linear zero-knowledge arguments. In: Halevi, S. (ed.) CRYPTO 2009. LNCS, vol. 5677, pp. 192–208. Springer, Heidelberg (2009). https://doi.org/10.1007/978-3-642-03356-8_12
15. Groth, J.: On the size of pairing-based non-interactive arguments. In: Fischlin, M., Coron, J.-S. (eds.) EUROCRYPT 2016, Part II. LNCS, vol. 9666, pp. 305–326. Springer, Heidelberg (2016). https://doi.org/10.1007/978-3-662-49896-5_11
16. Heath, D., Kolesnikov, V.: A 2.1 KHz zero-knowledge processor with BubbleRAM. In: Ligatti, J., Ou, X., Katz, J., Vigna, G. (eds.) ACM CCS 2020, pp. 2055–2074. ACM Press, November 2020. https://doi.org/10.1145/3372297.3417283
17. Heath, D., Kolesnikov, V.: PrORAM - Fast P(log n) authenticated shares ZK ORAM. In: Tibouchi, M., Wang, H. (eds.) ASIACRYPT 2021, Part IV. LNCS, vol. 13093, pp. 495–525. Springer, Cham (2021). https://doi.org/10.1007/978-3-030-92068-5_17

18. Heath, D., Yang, Y., Devecsery, D., Kolesnikov, V.: Zero knowledge for everything and everyone: fast ZK processor with cached ORAM for ANSI C programs. In: 2021 IEEE Symposium on Security and Privacy, pp. 1538–1556. IEEE Computer Society Press, May 2021. https://doi.org/10.1109/SP40001.2021.00089
19. Hu, Z., Mohassel, P., Rosulek, M.: Efficient zero-knowledge proofs of non-algebraic statements with sublinear amortized cost. In: Gennaro, R., Robshaw, M. (eds.) CRYPTO 2015, Part II. LNCS, vol. 9216, pp. 150–169. Springer, Heidelberg (2015). https://doi.org/10.1007/978-3-662-48000-7_8
20. Ishai, Y., Kushilevitz, E., Ostrovsky, R., Sahai, A.: Zero-knowledge from secure multiparty computation. In: Johnson, D.S., Feige, U. (eds.) 39th ACM STOC, pp. 21–30. ACM Press, June 2007. https://doi.org/10.1145/1250790.1250794
21. Jawurek, M., Kerschbaum, F., Orlandi, C.: Zero-knowledge using garbled circuits: how to prove non-algebraic statements efficiently. In: Sadeghi, A.R., Gligor, V.D., Yung, M. (eds.) ACM CCS 2013, pp. 955–966. ACM Press, November 2013. https://doi.org/10.1145/2508859.2516662
22. Katz, J., Kolesnikov, V., Wang, X.: Improved non-interactive zero knowledge with applications to post-quantum signatures. In: Lie, D., Mannan, M., Backes, M., Wang, X. (eds.) ACM CCS 2018, pp. 525–537. ACM Press, October 2018. https://doi.org/10.1145/3243734.3243805
23. Mohassel, P., Rosulek, M., Scafuro, A.: Sublinear zero-knowledge arguments for RAM programs. In: Coron, J.-S., Nielsen, J.B. (eds.) EUROCRYPT 2017, Part I. LNCS, vol. 10210, pp. 501–531. Springer, Cham (2017). https://doi.org/10.1007/978-3-319-56620-7_18
24. Neff, C.A.: A verifiable secret shuffle and its application to e-voting. In: Reiter, M.K., Samarati, P. (eds.) ACM CCS 2001, pp. 116–125. ACM Press, November 2001. https://doi.org/10.1145/501983.502000
25. Setty, S.: Spartan: efficient and general-purpose zkSNARKs without trusted setup. In: Micciancio, D., Ristenpart, T. (eds.) CRYPTO 2020, Part III. LNCS, vol. 12172, pp. 704–737. Springer, Cham (2020). https://doi.org/10.1007/978-3-030-56877-1_25
26. Weng, C., Yang, K., Katz, J., Wang, X.: Wolverine: fast, scalable, and communication-efficient zero-knowledge proofs for boolean and arithmetic circuits. In: 2021 IEEE Symposium on Security and Privacy, pp. 1074–1091. IEEE Computer Society Press, May 2021. https://doi.org/10.1109/SP40001.2021.00056
27. Weng, C., Yang, K., Xie, X., Katz, J., Wang, X.: Mystique: efficient conversions for zero-knowledge proofs with applications to machine learning. In: Bailey, M., Greenstadt, R. (eds.) USENIX Security 2021, pp. 501–518. USENIX Association, August 2021
28. Yang, K., Sarkar, P., Weng, C., Wang, X.: QuickSilver: efficient and affordable zero-knowledge proofs for circuits and polynomials over any field. In: Vigna, G., Shi, E. (eds.) ACM CCS 2021, pp. 2986–3001. ACM Press, November 2021. https://doi.org/10.1145/3460120.3484556

Inner Product Functional Commitments with Constant-Size Public Parameters and Openings

Hien Chu[1], Dario Fiore[2], Dimitris Kolonelos[2,3](✉), and Dominique Schröder[1]

[1] Friedrich Alexander Universität Erlangen-Nürnberg, Erlangen, Germany
{hien.chu,dominique.schroeder}@fau.de
[2] IMDEA Software Institute, Madrid, Spain
{dario.fiore,dimitris.kolonelos}@imdea.org
[3] Universidad Politenica de Madrid, Madrid, Spain

Abstract. Functional commitments (Libert et al. [ICALP'16]) allow a party to commit to a vector $\boldsymbol{v}$ of length n and later open the commitment at functions of the committed vector succinctly, namely with communication logarithmic or constant in n. Existing constructions of functional commitments rely on trusted setups and have either $O(1)$ openings and $O(n)$ parameters, or they have short parameters generatable using public randomness but have $O(\log n)$-size openings. In this work, we ask whether it is possible to construct functional commitments in which both parameters and openings can be of constant size. Our main result is the construction of the first FC schemes matching this complexity. Our constructions support the evaluation of inner products over small integers; they are built using groups of unknown order and rely on succinct protocols over these groups that are secure in the generic group and random oracle model.

1 Introduction

Commitments are one of the most fundamental cryptographic primitives having important implications in both theory and practice. In a classical commitment scheme, the sender commits to some value and hands it over to the receiver. The security of commitments guarantees that the receiver learns nothing about the committed value (hiding), while the sender cannot change the committed value afterward (binding). Commitments are one of the best-studied primitives, both in terms of underlying assumptions, integration into more complex cryptographic schemes, and several generalizations were proposed. In this work, we study *functional commitments* (FC), proposed by Libert, Ramanna, and Yung [30], that follow the goal of providing advanced functionalities while minimizing

---

The full version of the paper can be found at https://eprint.iacr.org/2022/524.pdf
Dimitris Kolonelos—The third author is the contact author.

C. Galdi and S. Jarecki (Eds.): SCN 2022, LNCS 13409, pp. 639–662, 2022.
https://doi.org/10.1007/978-3-031-14791-3_28

communication complexity. In FC, the sender commits to a vector $\boldsymbol{v}$ of length n and can later open the commitment to *functions* $f(\boldsymbol{v})$ of the committed vector. A distinguishing feature of FCs is that commitment and openings should be short, namely of size logarithmic or constant in n. In terms of security, binding for FCs means that the sender cannot open the same commitment to two different outputs of the same function, i.e., to prove that both y and $y' \neq y$ are $f(\boldsymbol{v})$. Functional commitments generalize other commitments notions in prior work that are concerned with short commitments and openings, such as vector commitments (VC) [17,31] and polynomial commitments (PC) [28]. In a vector commitment, one opens single (or multiple [9,29]) positions of the committed vector, i.e., a VC is an FC where the class of functions is specified as the projections $f_i(\boldsymbol{v}) = v_i$. In a polynomial commitment, one commits to a polynomial $p(X)$ and opens to evaluations of p on given points z, i.e., a PC is an FC where $\boldsymbol{v}_p$ is the vector of $p(X)$'s coefficients and one opens to $f_z(\boldsymbol{v}_p) = p(z)$.

In terms of realizations, Libert et al. [30] proposed an FC construction for linear functions. More recently, Lipmaa and Pavlyk [34] showed an FC for a class of arithmetic circuits[1]. Both these constructions [30,34] rely on groups with pairings, and they have public parameters that must be generated in a trusted manner and whose length is at least linear in the length of the vector.

In this work, we consider the problem of realizing functional commitments that admit constant-size public parameters generated using a transparent public-coin setup. It is not hard to see that this question has a positive answer if one is willing to rely on the random oracle heuristic. In this case, one can build a functional commitment by using a succinct commitment scheme and a SNARK with transparent setup [1,4,5,18,35,37–39,42] thanks to which one can generate an opening through a SNARK proof for the NP statement that $y = f(\boldsymbol{v})$ and the commitment C opens to $\boldsymbol{v}$. However, for an NP statement of size N, all existing SNARKs with a transparent setup have proofs of length at least $O(\lambda \log N)$, where λ stands for the security parameter. Therefore, this construction implies functional commitments with logarithmic-size openings. And logarithmic opening size is the best one can achieve in the literature even if one considers FCs for a simple functionality like inner products. Indeed, an inner product argument such as Bulletproofs [13] yields an FC for linear functions in which openings consist of $2 \cdot \log n$ elements of a group $\mathbb{G}$ where the discrete logarithm problem is hard.

To summarize, to the best of our knowledge, there is no functional commitment (including polynomial commitments) that admits constant-size and transparent public parameters and constant-size openings in the literature. The only exceptions are a few vector commitment constructions [9,16] in groups of unknown order, which, however, are functional commitments for a very specific, non-algebraic, functionality. Therefore, the main question we ask in this work is:

Can we build functional commitments with constant-size public parameters consisting of a uniformly random string and with constant-size openings?

[1] It is also easy to note that it is possible to construct an FC for polynomials from one for linear functions, by linearizing the polynomial.

1.1 Our Contributions

The main result of our paper is the construction of the first functional commitments that answer the above question in the affirmative.

FC for Binary Inner Products with Constant-Size Openings. Our first result is a functional commitment that supports the evaluation of binary inner products over the integers. Namely one can commit to a vector $\boldsymbol{v} \in \{0,1\}^n$ and, for any $\boldsymbol{f} \in \{0,1\}^n$, open the commitment to $\langle \boldsymbol{v}, \boldsymbol{f} \rangle$ computed over $\mathbb{Z}$. The scheme works over groups of unknown order and, due to the use of succinct proofs of exponentiation from [9], relies on the random oracle and generic group models. The scheme's public parameters are four group elements, while openings consist of 21 elements of the hidden-order group, and 14λ bits.

While all prior FCs for inner products use techniques that somehow rely on the homomorphic property of an underlying vector commitment, our construction departs from this blueprint and shows a new set of techniques for proving an inner product. In a nutshell, we start from the first vector commitment of Campanelli et al. [16], which uses an encoding of a vector based on two RSA accumulators, and then we show how to reduce the problem of proving an inner product with a public function to that of proving that a certain exponent lies in a range. To the best of our knowledge, this technique is novel. Also, a core part of this technique is a way to succinctly prove the cardinality of a set in an RSA accumulator, which we believe can be of independent interest.

FC for Integer Inner Products. Our second result is a collection of transformations that lift an FC for binary inner products, like the one above, to one that supports the computation of inner products over the integers and over finite rings. More in detail, we show two main transformations for the following functionality: one can commit to a vector $\boldsymbol{v} \in (\mathbb{Z}_{2^\ell})^n$ and, for any $\boldsymbol{f} \in (\mathbb{Z}_{2^m})^n$, open the commitment to $\langle \boldsymbol{v}, \boldsymbol{f} \rangle$ computed over $\mathbb{Z}$.

Through the first transformation, we obtain an FC whose openings have size of $O(\ell + m)$ group elements and additive $(\ell + m)\log(\ell n)$ bits, and whose algorithms running time is approximately $(\ell+m)$ times that of the FC for binary inner products.

Through the second transformation, we achieve a different tradeoff: the algorithms' running time grow by a factor $2^{\ell+m}$ but openings have a fixed size $O(1)$ group elements.

We also show analogues of both transformations for the case of inner products modulo any integer p, i.e., for $\langle \cdot, \cdot \rangle : \mathbb{Z}_p^n \times \mathbb{Z}_p^n \to \mathbb{Z}_p$, that yield FCs with the same complexity as the ones above, considering ℓ and m as the bitsize of p.

Among the two, the second transformation is of particular interest because, in the case of $\ell, m = O(\log \lambda)$ (resp. $p = \mathsf{poly}(\lambda)$) it yields functional commitment schemes with constant-size openings.

Finally, due to the known construction of polynomial commitments from functional commitments for inner products (see above), our FCs also imply polynomial commitments with transparent setup for polynomials in $\mathbb{Z}_p[X]$.

Comparison and Concrete Interpretation of our Results. As mentioned above, the objective of our work is to eliminate any dependence on the size of the parameters and proofs on the vector length n. Our constructions have sizes dependent only on the security parameter λ. When concretely instantiating the group of unknown order these sizes get $O(\lambda^2)$ for class groups [7,22,27] or $O(\lambda^3)$ for RSA groups.

On the other hand, elliptic curve group elements typically have size $O(\lambda)$. Therefore, if we consider polynomial lengths $n = \mathsf{poly}(\lambda)$ then elliptic curve-based functional vector commitments as Bulletproofs [13] have proof size $O(\lambda \log n) = O(\lambda \log \lambda)$, which are concretely more efficient. For this, our results firstly serve as feasibility results for the complexity of the sizes of functional vector commitments. We note, however, that our solutions would still be asymptotically better if different unknown order group instantiations with optimal $O(\lambda)$ size were introduced, or in complexity leveraging scenarios where one considers super-polynomial vector sizes, $n > \mathsf{poly}(\lambda)$.

This asymptotic drawback of constant-sized constructions is typical for many primitives based on groups of unknown order such as RSA accumulators [3,6,9,33], vector commitments [9,16,17,29] or SNARKs [29].

Therefore, if we compare to the functional commitment built using the Bulletproofs inner product argument [13] (which to the best of our knowledge is currently the most efficient one that admits constant-sized and transparent parameters) the proof sizes of our schemes are concretely larger (for $n = \mathsf{poly}(\lambda)$). On the other hand, our FC has two main advantages. The first one is *flexibility*. Our FC "natively" supports inner products over $\mathbb{Z}_p$ for *any* integer p, whereas Bulletproofs only supports inner products over $\mathbb{Z}_q$ where q is the prime modulus of a group $\mathbb{G}$ where discrete logarithm holds[2]. The second advantage is that in our FC the verification algorithm admits *preprocessing*, that is, after spending $O(n)$ group exponentiations for a deterministic preprocessing of the function $\boldsymbol{f}$, the rest of the verification has a fixed cost $O(\lambda)$. Notably, inner product arguments based on the folding techniques of Bootle et al. [10] do not admit this preprocessing, as their verification time is $O(n)$ independently of the time to read the statement.

1.2 Other Related Work

As mentioned earlier, functional commitments [30] are related to the notion of vector commitments [17,31] and polynomial commitments [28].

In recent work, Peikert, Pepin and Sharp [36] propose a new lattice-based vector commitment and also show an extension of their construction to support opening to functions, expressed as boolean circuits, of the committed vector. However, their construction works in a weaker model that assumes the availability of a trusted authority that uses a *secret key* to generate functional keys that allow one to create the opening. We argue that this is a much weaker model than

[2] One could use Bulletproofs arithmetic circuit protocol in order to simulate $\bmod p$ algebra over $\mathbb{Z}_q$, at the price of a prover's overhead.

the one from [30] that we use in our work, where anyone can generate openings given a set of public parameters. Furthermore, the model of [36] seems impossible to achieve if one aims to use public parameters generated using a public-coin setup.

Concurrent Work. In a very recent work, Arun et al. [2] also propose a functional commitment construction for inner products with transparent setup and constant-size openings, and show extensions and applications of their scheme to building constant-size SNARKs with transparent setup. Although the scheme of [2] gives a solution to the same problem addressed in this paper, we emphasize that their work is fully concurrent to ours. In fact, except for sharing the fact of relying on groups of unknown order, the techniques are very different. They use extremal combinatorics techniques, whereas we rely on a new technique for proving the cardinality of a set in an RSA accumulator.

2 Preliminaries

Notation. We denote by λ the security parameter. The set of all polynomial functions is denoted by $\mathsf{poly}(\lambda)$. We write $\epsilon(\lambda) \in \mathsf{negl}(\lambda)$ for a function $\epsilon(\lambda)$ if it vanishes faster than the inverse of any polynomial and we call it *negligible*. An algorithm $\mathcal{A}$ is said PPT if it is modeled as a probabilistic Turing machine that runs in time $\mathsf{poly}(\lambda)$.We use bold lowercase letters to denote a vector, e.g. $\boldsymbol{v} = (v_1, \ldots, v_n)$. With $[n]$ we denote $\{1, \ldots, n\}$ and with $[A, B]$ the set $\{A, A+1, \ldots, B-1, B\}$ where $A, B \in \mathbb{Z}, A < B$. The operator $\|\cdot\|$ is used for the bit-size, i.e. $\|x\| = \lceil \log(x) \rceil$, for $x \in \mathbb{N}$. $\mathsf{Primes}(\lambda)$ stands for the set of all primes of size λ, i.e. $\mathsf{Primes}(\lambda) = \{p : p \text{ prime } \wedge \|p\| = \lambda\}$. $O_\lambda(n)$ will mean $O(\lambda n)$ (and *not* $O(\mathsf{poly}(\lambda) n)$).

2.1 Functional Commitments

Functional commitments (FC), introduced by Libert, Ramanna and Yung [30], allow a sender to commit to a vector $\boldsymbol{v}$ and then to open the commitment to a function $y = f(\boldsymbol{v})$. As in vector commitments [17], what makes this primitive non-trivial is a succinctness property, which requires commitments and openings to be "short", that is constant or logarithmic in the length of $\boldsymbol{v}$. In our work we use a slight generalization of the FC notion of [30] considering *universal specializable public parameters*. This is a model, akin to the universal CRS of [26], where Setup creates length-independent public parameters pp, which one can later specialize to a specific length n by using a deterministic algorithm $\mathsf{Specialize}$.

Definition 1 (Functional Commitments). *A functional commitment scheme for a class of functions $\mathcal{F}$ is a tuple of algorithms* $\mathsf{FC} = (\mathsf{Setup}, \mathsf{Specialize}, \mathsf{Com}, \mathsf{Open}, \mathsf{Ver})$ *with the following syntax and that satisfies correctness, succinctness, and function binding.*

$\mathsf{Setup}(1^\lambda) \to \mathsf{pp}$ *given the security parameter* λ*, outputs public parameters* pp*, which contain the description of a domain* $\mathcal{D}$ *and a universal class of functions* $\mathcal{F} = \{\mathcal{F}_n\}_{n\in\mathbb{N}}$*, where* $\mathcal{F}_n$ *is a class of* n*-input functions* $\{f : \mathcal{D}^n \to \mathcal{R}\}$.

$\mathsf{Specialize}(\mathsf{pp}, \mathcal{F}_n) \to \mathsf{pp}_n$ *given public parameters* pp *and a description of the function class* $\mathcal{F}_n$*, outputs specialized parameters* pp_n.

$\mathsf{Com}(\mathsf{pp}_n, \boldsymbol{v}) \to C$ *on input a vector* $\boldsymbol{v} \in \mathcal{D}^n$ *outputs a commitment* C.

$\mathsf{Open}(\mathsf{pp}_n, \boldsymbol{v}, f) \to \Lambda$ *on input a vector* $\boldsymbol{v} \in \mathcal{D}^n$ *and an admissible function* $f \in \mathcal{F}_n$*, outputs an opening* Λ.

$\mathsf{Ver}(\mathsf{pp}_n, C, f, y, \Lambda) \to b \in \{0, 1\}$ *on input a commitment* C*, a function* $f \in \mathcal{F}_n$*, a value* $y \in \mathcal{R}$*, and an opening* Λ*, accepts* ($b = 1$) *or rejects* ($b = 0$).

Correctness. FC *is correct if, for any public parameters* $\mathsf{pp} \leftarrow \mathsf{Setup}(1^\lambda)$*, any length* $n \in \mathbb{N}$ *and specialized* $\mathsf{pp}_n \leftarrow \mathsf{Specialize}(\mathsf{pp}, n)$*, any vector* $\boldsymbol{v} \in \mathcal{D}^n$ *and any admissible function* $f \in \mathcal{F}_n$*, it holds*

$$\mathsf{Ver}(\mathsf{pp}_n, \mathsf{Com}(\mathsf{pp}_n, \boldsymbol{v}), f, f(\boldsymbol{v}), \mathsf{Open}(\mathsf{pp}_n, \boldsymbol{v}, f)) = 1$$

Succinctness. FC *is* succinct *if there exists a fixed polynomial* $p(\cdot)$ *such that for any* $n = \mathsf{poly}(\lambda)$*, commitments and openings generated in the scheme have size at most* $p(\lambda, \log n)$.

Function Binding. *For any PPT adversary* $\mathcal{A}$ *and any* $n = \mathsf{poly}(\lambda)$*, we have*

$$\Pr\left[\begin{array}{c} \mathsf{Ver}(\mathsf{pp}_n, C, f, y, \Lambda) = 1 \\ \wedge\ y \neq y' \wedge \\ \mathsf{Ver}(\mathsf{pp}_n, C, f, y', \Lambda') = 1 \end{array} : \begin{array}{r} \mathsf{pp} \leftarrow \mathsf{Setup}(1^\lambda) \\ (C, f, y, \Lambda, y', \Lambda') \leftarrow \mathcal{A}(\mathsf{pp}) \\ \mathsf{pp}_n \leftarrow \mathsf{Specialize}(\mathsf{pp}, \mathcal{F}_n) \end{array}\right] = \mathsf{negl}(\lambda)$$

Remark 1. The $\mathsf{Specialize}$ algorithm is deterministically computed from pp and $\mathcal{F}_n$. For this reason, it suffices for Function Binding that the adversary $\mathcal{A}$ takes as input pp (instead of pp_n).

Remark 2 (Preprocessing-based verification). Our FC constructions enjoy a preprocessing model of verification, similar to that of preprocessing SNARKs [26]. This means that one, given pp_n and a function f, can generate a verification key vk_f and the latter can be later used to verify any opening for f. In particular, while the cost of computing vk_f can depend on the complexity of the function, e.g., it is $O(n)$ for a linear function with n coefficients, the subsequent cost of verifying openings using vk_f depends only on the succinctness of the scheme, e.g., it is a fixed $p(\lambda)$.

2.2 Groups of Unknown Order

For our constructions we use groups of unknown order $\mathbb{G}$, i.e., groups where computing the order is hard. Throughout this work we will assume an efficient group sampling probabilistic algorithm $\mathsf{Ggen}(1^\lambda)$ that generates such a group $\mathbb{G}$. Potential candidates are class groups of imaginary quadratic order [12] and

RSA groups where the factorization is unknown. The instantiation through class groups is the one that admits a public-coin (aka transparent) setup.

Hardness Assumptions. Below we recall the 2-Strong RSA assumption [14], the Adaptive Root assumption [41] and the Low Order assumption [8].

Definition 2 (2-Strong RSA assumption [14]). *We say that the* 2-strong RSA assumption *holds for* Ggen *if for any PPT adversary* $\mathcal{A}$*:*

$$\Pr\left[\begin{array}{c} u^e = g \\ \wedge e \neq 2^k,\ k \in \mathbb{N} \end{array} : \begin{array}{c} \mathbb{G} \leftarrow \mathsf{Ggen}(\lambda) \\ g \leftarrow_{\$} \mathbb{G} \\ (u, e) \leftarrow \mathcal{A}(\mathbb{G}, g) \end{array}\right] = \mathsf{negl}(\lambda)$$

The 2-Strong RSA assumption is a special case of r-Strong RSA assumption, introduced in [14]. The latter is in turn a generalization of (and trivially reduces to) the standard Strong RSA assumption [3] (where $r = 1$). Taking square roots can be done efficiently in Class Groups of imaginary quadratic order [11], but for higher order roots it is believed to be hard. Thus 2-Strong RSA assumption is believed to hold. For RSA groups the (plain) Strong RSA is a standard assumption.

Definition 3 (Adaptive Root assumption [40]). *We say that the* adaptive root assumption *holds for* Ggen *if for any PPT adversary* $(\mathcal{A}_1, \mathcal{A}_2)$*:*

$$\Pr\left[\begin{array}{c} u^\ell = w \\ \wedge w \neq 1 \end{array} : \begin{array}{c} \mathbb{G} \leftarrow \mathsf{Ggen}(\lambda) \\ (w, \mathsf{state}) \leftarrow \mathcal{A}_1(\mathbb{G}) \\ \ell \leftarrow_{\$} \mathsf{Primes}(\lambda) \\ u \leftarrow \mathcal{A}_2(\ell, \mathsf{state}) \end{array}\right] = \mathsf{negl}(\lambda)$$

The Adaptive Root assumption is believed to hold on Class Groups and RSA groups[3]. For completeness we also recall the Low Order assumption, which is implied by the Adaptive Root assumption (see [8] for the reduction).

Definition 4 (Low Order assumption [8]). *We say that the* low order assumption *holds for* Ggen *if for any PPT adversary* $\mathcal{A}$*:*

$$\Pr\left[\begin{array}{l} u^\ell = 1 \\ \wedge u \neq 1 \\ \wedge 1 < \ell < 2^{\mathsf{poly}(\lambda)} \end{array} : \begin{array}{c} \mathbb{G} \leftarrow \mathsf{Ggen}(\lambda) \\ (u, \ell) \leftarrow \mathcal{A}(\mathbb{G}) \end{array}\right] = \mathsf{negl}(\lambda)$$

2.3 Arguments of Knowledge

Let $R \subset \mathcal{X} \times \mathcal{W}$ be an NP relation for a language $\mathcal{L} = \{x : \exists w \text{ s.t. } (x, w) \in R\}$. An argument system for $\mathcal{L}$ is a triple of algorithms $(\mathsf{Setup}, \mathsf{P}, \mathsf{V})$ where: $\mathsf{Setup}(1^\lambda)$

[3] In fact over the quotient group $\mathbb{G}/\{1, -1\}$ of an RSA group, since we need to exclude the element $-1 \in \mathbb{G}$ whose order is known.

takes a security parameter λ and outputs a common reference string crs; $\mathsf{P}(\mathsf{crs}, x, w)$ takes the crs, a statement x and a witness w; $\mathsf{V}(\mathsf{crs}, x)$ takes the crs, a statement x, interacts with the prover, and finally accepts or rejects. We denote an execution between the prover and verifier with $\langle \mathsf{P}(\mathsf{crs}, x, w), \mathsf{V}(\mathsf{crs}, x)\rangle = b$, with $b \in \{0, 1\}$ being the verifier's output. When V uses only public randomness, the protocol is called public coin.

Completeness. For all $(x, w) \in R$ we have

$$\Pr\left[\langle \mathsf{P}(\mathsf{crs}, x, w), \mathsf{V}(\mathsf{crs}, x)\rangle = 1 : \mathsf{crs} \leftarrow \mathsf{Setup}(1^\lambda)\right] = 1.$$

Let $\mathcal{A} = (\mathcal{A}_0, \mathcal{A}_1)$ be an adversary modeled as a pair of algorithms such that $\mathcal{A}_0(\mathsf{crs}) \rightarrow (x, \mathsf{state})$ (i.e. outputs an instance $x \in \mathcal{X}$ after $\mathsf{crs} \leftarrow \mathsf{Setup}(\lambda)$ is run) and $\mathcal{A}_1(\mathsf{crs}, x, \mathsf{state})$ interacts with a honest verifier. Then an argument of knowledge must satisfy the following properties:

Soundness. For all PPT $\mathcal{A} = (\mathcal{A}_0, \mathcal{A}_1)$ we have

$$\Pr\left[\begin{array}{c} \langle \mathcal{A}_1(\mathsf{crs}, x, \mathsf{state}), \mathsf{V}(\mathsf{crs}, x)\rangle = 1 \\ \text{and } \nexists w : R(x, w) = 1 \end{array} \middle| \begin{array}{c} \mathsf{crs} \leftarrow \mathsf{Setup}(\lambda) \\ (x, \mathsf{state}) \leftarrow \mathcal{A}_0(\mathsf{crs}) \end{array}\right] \in \mathsf{negl}(\lambda).$$

Knowledge Extractability. For all polynomial time adversaries $\mathcal{A}_1$ there exists a polynomial time extractor Ext such that, for all PPT $\mathcal{A}_0$ it holds

$$\Pr\left[\begin{array}{c} \langle \mathcal{A}_1(\mathsf{crs}, x, \mathsf{state}), \mathsf{V}(\mathsf{crs}, x)\rangle = 1 \\ \text{and } (x, w') \notin \mathcal{R} \end{array} \middle| \begin{array}{c} \mathsf{crs} \leftarrow \mathsf{Setup}(\lambda) \\ (x, \mathsf{state}) \leftarrow \mathcal{A}_0(\mathsf{crs}) \\ w' \leftarrow \mathsf{Ext}(\mathsf{crs}, x, \mathsf{state}) \end{array}\right] \in \mathsf{negl}(\lambda).$$

Succinctness. Informally, an argument system is succinct if the communication and the verifier's running time in an execution of the protocol are constant or polylogarithmic in the witness length. Note that in our work, we do not need zero-knowledge arguments.

2.4 Succinct Proofs of Exponentiation

We make use of the following succinct arguments of knowledge of exponents over groups of unknown order. Below we describe the protocols' functionalities and defer their description to the full version [19].

PoKE. First we recall the proof of knowledge of exponent (PoKE) of [9] for the language:

$$\mathcal{L}_{\mathsf{PoKE}} = \left\{(Y, u; x) \in \mathbb{G}^2 \times \mathbb{Z} : Y = u^x\right\}$$

parametrized by a group $\mathbb{G} \leftarrow\$ \mathsf{Ggen}(\lambda)$ and a group element $g \leftarrow\$ \mathbb{G}$. The protocol is succinct: it consists of 3 $\mathbb{G}$-element and 1 $\mathbb{Z}_{2^\lambda}$-element and the verification time is $O(\lambda)$, both regardless of the size, $\|x\|$, of the witness.

PoDDH. We also recall the proof of knowledge of a Diffie-Hellman tuple (PoDDH) of [16], for the language:

$$\mathcal{L}_{\mathsf{PoDDH}} = \left\{(Y_0, Y_1, Y; x_0, x_1) \in \mathbb{G}^3 \times \mathbb{Z}^2 : g_0^{x_0} = Y_0 \wedge g_1^{x_1} = Y_1 \wedge g^{x_0 x_1} = Y\right\}$$

parametrized by a group $\mathbb{G} \leftarrow\$ \mathsf{Ggen}(\lambda)$ and three group elements $g, g_0, g_1 \leftarrow\$ \mathbb{G}$. Notice that, unlike the usual DH-tuple, in the above protocol the bases are different and honestly generated in the setup. However, the same protocol can work for the same base, $g = g_0 = g_1$. Similarly to the PoKE, the protocol is succinct: 3 $\mathbb{G}$-elements and 2 $\mathbb{Z}_{2^\lambda}$-elements and $O(\lambda)$.

PoRE. We wil make use of a succinct protocol (PoRE) proving that the exponent of an element $Y = g^x$ lies in a certain range, $x \in [L, R]$.

$$\mathcal{L}_{\mathsf{PoRE}} = \left\{(Y, L, R; x) \in \mathbb{G} \times \mathbb{Z}^3 : L < x < R \wedge g^x = Y\right\}.$$

parametrized by a group $\mathbb{G} \leftarrow\$ \mathsf{Ggen}(\lambda)$ and a group element $g \leftarrow\$ \mathbb{G}$.

For this we rely on the square-decomposition technique [25,32]. That is, an integer x is in the range $[L, R]$ if and only if there exist $(x_1, x_2, x_3) \in \mathbb{Z}^3$ such that $4(x-L)(R-x)+1 = \sum_{i=1}^{3} x_i^2$. The proof consists of the following subprotocols (run in parallel):

- For each $i = 1, 2, 3$, the prover computes x_i, sends $Z_i = g^{x_i^2}$ for $i \in [3]$ and involves with the verifier in a succinct argument of knowledge of square exponent (PoSE) proving the validity of the last:

$$\mathcal{L}_{\mathsf{PoSE}} = \left\{(Z_i; x_i) \in \mathbb{G} \times \mathbb{Z} : g^{x_i^2} = Z_i\right\}.$$

  PoSE is presented as a stand-alone protocol in the full version of the paper.
- The prover sends $Y' = g^{(x-L)(R-x)}$ and involves in a PoDDH protocol with the verifier for the tuple (g^{x-L}, g^{R-x}, Y'). Observe that g^{x-L}, g^{R-x} can be computed homomorphically by the verifier from $Y = g^x$, thus don't have to be sent.
- Finally, the verifier merely checks if $Y'^4 \cdot g = \prod_{i=1}^{3} Z_i$.

All the above protocols are knowledge-extractable in the generic group model for groups of unknown order [9,21].

Non-interactive Versions. All protocols can be made non-interactive by the standard Fiat-Shamir transformation [23][4].

3 Our Functional Commitment for Binary Inner Products

In this section we present our core construction of Functional Commitments for binary inner products with constant-size parameters and openings. Precisely, in the scheme we commit to binary vectors $\boldsymbol{v} = (v_1, \ldots, v_n) \in \{0,1\}^n$ and the class of functions is $\mathcal{F} = \{\mathcal{F}_n\}$ where, for every positive integer n, $\mathcal{F}_n = \{f : \{0,1\}^n \to \mathbb{Z}\}$ such that f is a linear function represented as a vector of binary

[4] In these types of proofs though one should set ℓ to be of size 2λ for the non-interactive case [8].

coefficients, i.e., $\boldsymbol{f} = (f_1, \ldots, f_n) \in \{0,1\}^n$, and computes the result as the inner product

$$y = \langle \boldsymbol{f}, \boldsymbol{v} \rangle = \sum_{i=1}^{n} f_i \cdot v_i \in \mathbb{Z}.$$

Note that, for a fixed n, every possible result y is an integer in $\{0, \ldots, n\}$. Our starting point is the vector commitment (VC) of Campanelli et al. [16], which is based on RSA accumulators [3,6,9,33]. In [16], each position of $\boldsymbol{v}$ is encoded as a prime, via a collision-resistant hash-to-prime function $\mathsf{Hprime}(i) \rightarrow p_i$ for each $i \in [n]$. Then, in order to commit to $\boldsymbol{v}$, one creates two RSA accumulators, C_0, C_1: the former that accumulates all primes corresponding to zero-values of $\boldsymbol{v}$ ($\{p_i = \mathsf{Hprime}(i) : v_i = 0\}$), and the latter for one-values ($\{p_i = \mathsf{Hprime}(i) : v_i = 1\}$) respectively. That is merely, $C_0 = g_0^{\prod_{v_i=0} p_i}$ and $C_1 = g_1^{\prod_{v_i=1} p_i}$. Observe that these two sets of primes form a partition of all the primes corresponding to positions $\{1, \ldots, n\}$. For binding of the commitment, they also add a succinct proof PoDDH to show that the sets in C_0 and C_1 are indeed a partition.

Starting from this vector commitment, our contribution is a new technique that allows us to create inner product opening proofs. To this end, our first key observation is that:

$$y = \langle \boldsymbol{v}, \boldsymbol{f} \rangle = \sum_{i} v_i f_i = \sum_{f_i=0} v_i \cdot 0 + \sum_{f_i=1} v_i \cdot 1 = \sum_{f_i=1} v_i = |\{i \in [n] : f_i = 1, v_i = 1\}|$$

since both v_i and f_i are binary. Then the prover commits to the subvector of $\boldsymbol{v}$ corresponding to positions where $f_i = 1$. This is done by using the same vector commitment described previously. That is, we compute $F_0 = g_0^{\prod_{f_i=1,v_i=0} p_i}$ and $F_1 = g_1^{\prod_{f_i=1,v_i=1} p_i}$, accompanied with a PoDDH proof π'_{PoDDH} of Diffie-Hellman tuple for the tuple (F_0, F_1, F), for $F = g^{\prod_{f_i=1} p_i}$. Notice that F can be computed by only knowing $\boldsymbol{f}$, without knowledge of $\boldsymbol{v}$.

The next step to prove the inner product is to show that (F_0, F_1) is actually a commitment to a subvector of $\boldsymbol{v}$. This is done by showing that F_0 accumulates a subset of the primes of C_0, and similarly F_1 accumulates a subset of the primes of C_1. Putting it in other words, the 'exponent' of F_b is contained in the accumulator C_b: there is a W_b such that $W_b^{\prod_{f_i=1,v_i=b} p_i} = C_b$ and $F_b = g_b^{\prod_{f_i=1,v_i=b} p_i}$, for $b = 0, 1$. The last can be proven in a succinct way via a simple concatenation of two PoKE proofs, π_0, π_1.

Observe now that the F_1 accumulates exactly the (primes corresponding to) positions that contribute to the inner product $\{i \in [n] : f_i = 1, v_i = 1\}$. The number of primes that F_1 contains in its 'exponent' is exactly y. All that is missing now is a way to convince the verifier about the number of primes in the exponent of F_1. For this, we set the size of each prime p_i to be such that the range of any product $\prod_{i \in \mathcal{I}} p_i$ determines uniquely the cardinality of $\mathcal{I}$ (i.e., the number of primes in the product). This way, a range proof for the 'exponent' of F_1 can convince the verifier about the cardinality of the accumulated set, which is the inner product result y. For this, we generate a succinct range proof π_{PoRE} using our protocol of Sect. 2.4.

The verifier, holding the commitment $(C_0, C_1, \pi_{\mathsf{PoDDH}})$, receives the opening proof $(F_0, F_1, \pi'_{\mathsf{PoDDH}}, W_0, \pi_0, W_1, \pi_1, \pi_{\mathsf{PoRE}})$. It is important to make sure that F_1 contains exactly the primes of positions where $f_i = 1$ and $v_i = 1$. The (F_1, C_1)-'subvector' proof π_1 ensures that $v_i = 1$ for all its primes (since C_1 contains only primes for $v_i = 1$). For the $f_i = 1$ part, the verifier herself computes $F = g^{\prod_{f_i=1} p_i}$ and verifies that (F_0, F_1, F) is a DH tuple through π'_{PoDDH}. This ensures that (1) all the primes in the exponents of F_0, F_1 are for $f_i = 1$ and (2) no position i for $f_i = 1$ was excluded maliciously; all of them were either put in F_0 or F_1. This convinces the verifier that exactly the positions i where $f_i = 1, v_i = 1$ are in the 'exponent' of F_1.

3.1 Functional VCs for Binary Linear Functions from Range Proofs

Here we formally describe our construction. We simplify the notation omitting the indicator $i \in [n]$ from the sums and the products below. For example $\sum_i x_i$ would implicitly mean $\sum_{i \in [n]} x_i$ and $\prod_{v_i=1} x_i$ would implicitly mean $\prod_{i \in [n], v_i=1} x_i$. Furthermore, we use abbreviations for some products we will use that can be found in Fig. 1.

$\mathsf{prod} = \prod_i \mathsf{Hprime}(i)$	$\mathsf{fprod} = \prod_{f_i=1} \mathsf{Hprime}(i)$
$\mathsf{prod}_0 = \prod_{v_i=0} \mathsf{Hprime}(i)$	$\mathsf{fprod}_0 = \prod_{f_i=1, v_i=0} \mathsf{Hprime}(i)$
$\mathsf{prod}_1 = \prod_{v_i=1} \mathsf{Hprime}(i)$	$\mathsf{fprod}_1 = \prod_{f_i=1, v_i=1} \mathsf{Hprime}(i)$

Fig. 1. Summary of symbols for the products used in the construction.

$\mathsf{Setup}(1^\lambda) \to \mathsf{pp}$: The setup algorithm generates a hidden order group $\mathbb{G} \leftarrow \mathsf{Ggen}(1^\lambda)$ and samples three generators $g, g_0, g_1 \leftarrow \$ \mathbb{G}$. It determines a collision-resistant function Hprime that maps integers to primes and it returns $\mathsf{pp} = (\mathbb{G}, g, g_0, g_1)$.

$\mathsf{Specialize}(\mathsf{pp}, n) \to \mathsf{pp}_n$: The algorithm samples a collision-resistant function Hprime that maps integers to primes[5]. Computes $\mathsf{prod} = \prod_i \mathsf{Hprime}(i)$ and sets $U_n = g^{\mathsf{prod}}$. Returns $\mathsf{pp}_n = (\mathsf{pp}, \mathsf{Hprime}, U_n)$.

$\mathsf{Com}(\mathsf{pp}_n, \boldsymbol{v}) \to C$: The commitment algorithm takes as input a vector of bits $\boldsymbol{v} = (v_1, \ldots, v_n) \in \{0,1\}^n$. It computes the product of all primes that correspond to a zero-value of the vector (i.e., $v_i = 0$) as $\mathsf{prod}_0 = \prod_{v_i=0} \mathsf{Hprime}(i)$, and similarly $\mathsf{prod}_1 = \prod_{v_i=1} \mathsf{Hprime}(i)$ for the one-values. Next, it computes the accumulators

$$C_0 = g_0^{\mathsf{prod}_0} \quad \text{and} \quad C_1 = g_1^{\mathsf{prod}_1}$$

and a PoDDH proof $\pi = \mathsf{PoDDH.P}((\mathbb{G}, g, g_0, g_1), (C_0, C_1, U_n), (\mathsf{prod}_0, \mathsf{prod}_1))$, which ensures that, given the above (C_0, C_1, U_n), it holds $\mathsf{prod} = \mathsf{prod}_0 \cdot \mathsf{prod}_1$:

$$\mathcal{L} = \left\{(C_0, C_1, U_n; \mathsf{prod}_0, \mathsf{prod}_1) : g_0^{\mathsf{prod}_0} = C_0 \wedge g_1^{\mathsf{prod}_1} = C_1 \wedge g^{\mathsf{prod}_0 \cdot \mathsf{prod}_1} = U_n\right\}$$

[5] As we discuss next and in more detail in Sect. 3.3, the choice of Hprime depends on n.

Returns $C = (C_0, C_1, \pi)$.
$\mathsf{Open}(\mathsf{pp}_n, C, \boldsymbol{v}, \boldsymbol{f}) \rightarrow (y, \Lambda)$: $\boldsymbol{f} = (f_1, \ldots, f_n) \in \{0,1\}^n$ is a vector of bits. The output of the function is

$$y = \langle \boldsymbol{v}, \boldsymbol{f} \rangle = \sum v_i f_i = \sum_{f_i=0} v_i \cdot 0 + \sum_{f_i=1} v_i \cdot 1 = \sum_{f_i=1} v_i$$

Let $\mathsf{fprod} = \prod_{f_i=1} \mathsf{Hprime}(i)$, $\mathsf{fprod}_0 = \prod_{f_i=1, v_i=0} \mathsf{Hprime}(i)$ and $\mathsf{fprod}_1 = \prod_{f_i=1, v_i=1} \mathsf{Hprime}(i)$. Computes $F = g^{\mathsf{fprod}}$ and

$$F_0 = g_0^{\mathsf{fprod}_0} \qquad \text{and} \qquad F_1 = g_1^{\mathsf{fprod}_1}$$

Then computes the following arguments of knowledge:

- π_0: a proof that F_0 contains a 'subvector' of C_0, i.e. a proof for the language:

$$\mathcal{L}_0 = \left\{ (F_0, W_0; \mathsf{fprod}_0) : W_0^{\mathsf{fprod}_0} = C_0 \wedge g_0^{\mathsf{fprod}_0} = F_0 \right\}$$

- π_1: a proof that F_1 contains a 'subvector' of C_1, i.e. a proof for the language:

$$\mathcal{L}_1 = \left\{ (F_1, W_1; \mathsf{fprod}_1) : W_1^{\mathsf{fprod}_1} = C_1 \wedge g_1^{\mathsf{fprod}_1} = F_1 \right\}$$

- π_2: a PoDDH for F_0, F_1, F:
$$\mathcal{L}_2 = \left\{ (F_0, F_1, F; \mathsf{fprod}_0, \mathsf{fprod}_1) : g_0^{\mathsf{fprod}_0} = F_0 \wedge g_1^{\mathsf{fprod}_1} = F_1 \wedge g^{\mathsf{fprod}_0 \cdot \mathsf{fprod}_1} = F \right\}$$

- π_3: a range proof that fprod_1 is in a certain range $L(y) < \mathsf{fprod}_1 < R(y)$, that is uniquely determined by y. L and R are public functions that depend on Hprime (see Fig. 2 for their concrete description).

$$\mathcal{L}_3 = \left\{ (F_1, y; \mathsf{fprod}_1) : L(y) < \mathsf{fprod}_1 < R(y) \wedge g_1^{\mathsf{fprod}_1} = F_1 \right\}$$

Returns $\Lambda = (F_0, F_1, W_0, W_1, \pi_0, \pi_1, \pi_2, \pi_3)$
$\mathsf{Ver}(\mathsf{pp}_n, C, \Lambda, \boldsymbol{f}, y) \rightarrow b$: It computes $F = g^{\mathsf{fprod}} = g^{\prod_{f_i=1} \mathsf{Hprime}(i)}$ that depends only on $\boldsymbol{f}$ and outputs 1 iff all $\pi, \pi_0, \pi_1, \pi_2, \pi_3$ verify. Notice that computing F is necessary as is an input to the proof π_2.

$\mathsf{Hprime} : [n] \rightarrow \left(2^{\kappa(\lambda)}, 2^{\kappa(\lambda) + \frac{\kappa(\lambda)}{n}}\right)$ collision-resistant hash-to-prime function.

$$L(y) = \begin{cases} 2^{\kappa(\lambda) y}, & y \in [n] \\ 1, & y = 0 \end{cases} \qquad \text{and} \qquad R(y) = \begin{cases} 2^{(\kappa(\lambda) + \frac{\kappa(\lambda)}{n}) y}, & y \in [n] \\ 1, & y = 0 \end{cases}$$

Fig. 2. Definitions of the range functions L, R. The functions depend on the range Hprime, which in turn depends on n and λ (specified in the setup and specialize phases respectively).

Remark 3. For ease of presentation, in the Open algorithm, we describe four distinct proofs, $\pi_0, \pi_1, \pi_2, \pi_3$. In order to optimize the proof size, they can be merged into a single proof avoiding redundancies. We present in details the (merged) protocol in Sect. 3.3.

Determining the Hash Function and the Range. We need to find a proper hash-to-prime function and a corresponding range $[L(y), R(y)]$ for fprod_1 such that for any $y = 1, \ldots, n$:

$$\mathsf{fprod}_1 := \prod_{v_i=1, f_i=1} \mathsf{Hprime}(i) \in [L(y), R(y)] \iff \left|\{i \in [n] : v_i = 1, f_i = 1\}\right| = y$$

meaning that a range for the product of the primes should translate to its number of prime factors. And the correspondence should be unique. E.g. $p_2 p_7 p_{11} \in [L, R] \iff 3$ factors $\iff y = 3$. For the degenerate case of $y = 0$, $\mathsf{fprod} = 1$.

The following lemma shows that such Hprime, L, R exist and specifies their parameters:

Lemma 1. *Assume a collsion-resistant function that maps integers to prime numbers,* $\mathsf{Hprime} : [n] \rightarrow \left(2^{\kappa(\lambda)}, 2^{\kappa(\lambda)+\frac{\kappa(\lambda)}{n}}\right)$*, parametrized by* λ *and* n*, and functions* $L : \{0, \ldots, n\} \rightarrow \mathbb{Z}$*,* $R : \{0, \ldots, n\} \rightarrow \mathbb{Z}$ *such that* $L(y) = 2^{\kappa y}$ *and* $R(y) = 2^{(\kappa + \frac{\kappa}{n})y}$ *respectively. Then for any* $\mathcal{I} \subseteq [n]$*:*

$$\prod_{i \in \mathcal{I}} \mathsf{Hprime}(i) \in [L(y), R(y)] \iff |\mathcal{I}| = y$$

Proof. For any number of factors $y = 1, \ldots, n$ we have $2^{\kappa y} < \prod_{i \in [y]} p_i < 2^{(\kappa + \frac{\kappa}{n})y}$. Since $\kappa y + \frac{\kappa y}{n} < \kappa(y+1)$ for any $y \in [n]$ all ranges are distinct. So the mapping is '1-1'.

In Sect. 3.3 we discuss concrete instantiations for the function Hprime and consequently L and R.

3.2 Security

Correctness. Follows from correctness of the [16] Vector Commitment, correctness of PoKE, PoDDH, PoRE arguments of knowledge and from Lemma 1.

Function Binding. Our proof strategy is the following. Given two openings Λ and Λ' of the same commitment C to distinct outputs y, y', we first use the 'subvector' proofs' extractors $\pi_0, \pi_1, \pi_0', \pi_1'$ to argue that (the exponents of) (F_0, F_1) and (F_0', F_1') are subvectors of C. Then we use the PoDDH's extractors π_2, π_2' to argue that in fact these subvectors are for the same subset of positions $\mathcal{I}_1 = \{i \in [n] : f_i = 1\}$. For the latter we also use the collision-resistance of Hprime. Then we use the extractors of PoRE π_3, π_3' for F_1 and F_1' resp., the fact that $y \neq y'$ (by definition of the game) and lemma 1 to argue that these subvectors (for the same positions) are different. Finally, we argue that this fact, having two different subvectors for the same subset of positions and commitment C, contradicts the position-binding property of the [16] Vector Commitment.

Theorem 1. *Let* Ggen *be a hidden order group generator where the [16] VC is position binding,* PoKE, PoDDH, PoRE *be succinct knowledge-extractable arguments of knowledge and* Hprime *be collision-resistant. Then our functional commitment for binary inner products is function binding.*

Due to space limitations we postpone the formal security proof for the full version.

3.3 Instantiation

Instatiation of Hprime. As stated in Lemma 1, Hprime should be a collision-resistant function with domain $[n]$ that outputs prime numbers in the range $\left(2^{\kappa(\lambda)}, 2^{\kappa(\lambda)+\frac{\kappa(\lambda)}{n}}\right)$. Here we specify the function $\kappa(\cdot)$ and show instantiations for Hprime under these restrictions.

Hashing to primes is a well studied problem [15,20,24]. A standard technique is rejection sampling: on input x it computes $y = F_K(x, 0)$, where F_K is a pseudorandom function with seed K and range $[A, B]$, and checks y for primality. If y is not prime it continues to $y = F_K(x, 1)$ and so on, until it finds a prime $F(x, j)$ for some j. From the density of primes the expected number of tries is $\log(B - A)$. As an alternative, F_K can also be a random oracle.

Assume a collision-resistant hash function H that we model as a random oracle and its outputs are in the range $\left(2^{\kappa(\lambda)}, 2^{\kappa(\lambda)+\frac{\kappa(\lambda)}{n}}\right)$[6]. For H to be collision resistant we require, due to the birthday bound, its range to contain at least $2^{2\lambda}$ prime numbers. From the density of primes we know that in the above range there are about:

$$\frac{2^{\kappa+\frac{\kappa}{n}}}{\kappa+\frac{\kappa}{n}} - \frac{2^{\kappa}}{\kappa} \approx \frac{2^{\kappa+\frac{\kappa}{n}}}{\kappa} - \frac{2^{\kappa}}{\kappa} = \frac{2^{\kappa}\left(2^{\frac{\kappa}{n}}-1\right)}{\kappa}$$

prime numbers, where for the first approximate equality we assumed that $\kappa \ll n$.

So if we set κ (depending on λ and n) to be the smallest positive integer such that:

$$\frac{2^{\kappa}\left(2^{\frac{\kappa}{n}}-1\right)}{\kappa} \geq 2^{2\lambda}$$

then H gives sufficiently many primes to instantiate Hprime (via the rejection sampling method we described above).

For example for $n = 2^{60}$ and $\lambda = 128$: $\kappa = 317$. So instantiating Hprime with the rejection sampling method based on the SHA512 (for F_K) fixing its output range to $(2^{317}, 2^{317+317/2^{60}})$ we get a sufficient Hprime for our functional vector commitment construction that satisfies lemma 1.

Instantiation of the Arguments of Knowledge. Here we present the merged argument of knowledge for our Open algorithm of Sect. 3.1. As noted, it was

[6] We can securely fix the range of a hash function (as SHA512) by fixing some of its bits and truncating others.

presented modularly in order to ease the presentation of the protocol and its security proof, however we can merge the proofs for the four languages $\mathcal{L}_0$ – $-\mathcal{L}_3$ into a single protocol, using standard composition techniques. The unified language of the Open algorithm is:

$$\mathcal{L} = \left\{ \begin{array}{r} (F_0, F_1, F, W_0, W_1, R, L; \mathsf{fprod}_0, \mathsf{fprod}_1) : \\ W_0^{\mathsf{fprod}_0} = C_0 \wedge g_0^{\mathsf{fprod}_0} = F_0 \wedge \\ \wedge W_1^{\mathsf{fprod}_1} = C_1 \wedge g_1^{\mathsf{fprod}_1} = F_1 \wedge \\ \wedge g^{\mathsf{fprod}_0 \cdot \mathsf{fprod}_1} = F \wedge L < \mathsf{fprod}_1 < R \end{array} \right\}$$

The description of the protocol can be found in the full version of the paper [19].

Concrete Security Assumptions. After the above instantiations we get that our overall binary inner product commitment is secure in the GGM and RO model assuming that H (used for Hprime as described above) is collision-resistant: the argument of knowledge is knowledge-extractable in the generic group model and gets non-interactive in the random oracle model and the [16] SVC is position binding under the 2-strong RSA and Low order assumptions (that are secure in the GGM).

3.4 Efficiency

Our FC for binary inner products has $O(1)$ public parameters, $O(1)$ commitment size and $O(1)$ openings proof size. More in detail, $|\mathsf{pp}_n|$ consists of 4 $|\mathbb{G}|$-elements and the descriptions of $\mathbb{G}$ and Hprime (which are concise). $|C|$ is 5 $|\mathbb{G}|$-elements and 2 $|\mathbb{Z}_{2^{2\lambda}}|$-elements. Finally the opening proof $|\Lambda|$ is 21 $|\mathbb{G}|$-elements and 7 $|\mathbb{Z}_{2^{2\lambda}}|$-elements[7].

Generating the public parameters, via Setup and Specialize, takes a $\mathbb{G}$-exponentiation of size $\kappa n = O_\lambda(n)$. The generation doesn't require any private coins and thus is transparent.

The prover's time (i.e. the running time of Open) is dominated by the exponentation $F_1' = g_1^{(\mathsf{fprod}_1 - L)(R - \mathsf{fprod}_1)}$, that is a $\mathbb{G}$-exponentation of size $2\kappa n = O_\lambda(n)$.

The verifier's running time (i.e. Ver) is dominated by the computation of $F = g^{\prod_{f_i=1} \mathsf{Hprime}(i)}$, which takes (in the worst case where $\boldsymbol{f} = (1, 1, \ldots, 1)$) a $\mathbb{G}$-exponentiation of size $\kappa n = O_\lambda(n)$. The rest of the computations, i.e. the verification of the argument of knowledge, take constant time $O(2\lambda) = O_\lambda(1)$ $\mathbb{G}$-exponentiations. However, below we make two observations that can speed up the verification in two useful ways.

Preprocessing-Based Verification. Our Functional Commitment construction allows preprocessing the verification (see Remark 2). The verifier can compute a-priori the function-dependent value F so that the online verification gets

[7] We do not consider optimizations for the arguments of knowledge with which we could reduce the size of $|C|$ by 1 and $|\Lambda|$ by 6 group elements respectively.

$O_\lambda(n)$. Notably, this preprocessing is deterministic and proof-independent, and thus can be reused to verify an unbounded number of openings for the same function f.

From Group-Based to Integers-Based Linear Work. Even without preprocessing, the prover can compute and send to the verifier a PoE proof [9,41] for $F = g^{\prod_{f_i=1} \mathsf{Hprime}(i)}$. Then the verifier verifies PoE instead of computing F herself. This takes $O_\lambda(n)$ integer operations and $O_\lambda(1)$ group exponentiations, in place of $O_\lambda(n)$ group operations, which concretely gives a significant saving.

4 Our FC for Inner Products over the Integers

In this section, we present two transformations that turn any functional commitment for binary inner products (like the one we presented in Sect. 3) into a functional commitment for inner products of vectors of (bounded) integers. Precisely, we build an FC where one commits to vectors $\boldsymbol{v} \in (\mathbb{Z}_{2^\ell})^n$ and the class of admissible functions is

$$\mathcal{F}_n = \{f : (\mathbb{Z}_{2^\ell})^n \rightarrow \mathbb{Z}\}$$

where each f is represented as a vector $\boldsymbol{f} \in (\mathbb{Z}_{2^m})^n$.

Consider an FC scheme bitFC for binary inner products, and let $t_{\mathsf{Com}}(n)$, $t_{\mathsf{Open}}(n)$, $t_{\mathsf{Ver}}(n)$ be the running times of its algorithms Com, Open and Ver respectively, and let $s(n)$ be the size of its openings.

Our two transformations yield FCs for the integer inner products functionality $\mathcal{F}$ that achieve different tradeoffs:

1. With our first transformation we obtain an FC where

$$t'_{\mathsf{Com}}(n) = t_{\mathsf{Com}}(n\ell),\ t'_{\mathsf{Open}}(n) = (\ell+m)\cdot t_{\mathsf{Com}}(n\ell),\ t'_{\mathsf{Ver}}(n) = (\ell+m)\cdot t_{\mathsf{Ver}}(n\ell),$$

$$s'(n) = (\ell+m)\cdot(s(n\ell) + \log(n\ell))$$

2. With our second transformation we obtain an FC where

$$t'_{\mathsf{Com}}(n) = t_{\mathsf{Com}}(n\ell 2^{\ell+m}),\ t'_{\mathsf{Open}}(n) = t_{\mathsf{Com}}(n\ell 2^{\ell+m}),\ t'_{\mathsf{Ver}}(n) = t_{\mathsf{Ver}}(n\ell 2^{\ell+m}),$$

$$s'(n) = s(n\ell 2^{\ell+m})$$

Given the tradeoffs, and considering instantiations of bitFC like ours, in which $s(n)$ is a fixed value in the security parameters, then the second transformation is particularly interesting in the case $\ell, m = O(1)$ are constant or $O(\log\lambda)$ as it yields an FC with constant, or polynomial, time overhead and constant-size openings.

4.1 Our Lifting to FC for Integer Inner Products with Logarithmic-Size Openings

We start by providing here an intuitive description of our transformation. We give a formal description of the FC scheme slightly below.

For our transformation, we use a binary representation of the vectors of integers $\boldsymbol{v} \in (\mathbb{Z}_{2^\ell})^n$ and $\boldsymbol{f} \in (\mathbb{Z}_{2^m})^n$, that is:

$$\boldsymbol{v} = (v_1, \dots, v_n) \in (\{0,1\}^\ell)^n \quad \text{and} \quad \boldsymbol{f} = (f_1, \dots, f_n) \in (\{0,1\}^m)^n$$

Denote $v_i = \sum_{j=0}^{\ell-1} v_i^{(j)} 2^j$ and $f_i = \sum_{k=0}^{m-1} f_i^{(k)} 2^k$ the bit decomposition of v_i, f_i respectively. Then we can rewrite the inner product of $\boldsymbol{v}$ and $\boldsymbol{f}$ as

$$y = \langle \boldsymbol{f}, \boldsymbol{v} \rangle = \sum_{i=1}^{n} v_i f_i = \sum_{i=1}^{n} \left(\sum_{j=0}^{\ell-1} \sum_{k=0}^{m-1} v_i^{(j)} f_i^{(k)} 2^{j+k} \right). \tag{1}$$

If we swap the counters we conclude to:

$$y = \sum_{j=0}^{\ell-1} \sum_{k=0}^{m-1} \left(\sum_{i=1}^{n} v_i^{(j)} f_i^{(k)} \right) 2^{j+k} = \sum_{j=0}^{\ell-1} \sum_{k=0}^{m-1} \langle \boldsymbol{v}^{(j)}, \boldsymbol{f}^{(k)} \rangle 2^{j+k}$$

where above $\boldsymbol{v}^{(j)} = (v_1^{(j)}, \dots, v_n^{(j)}) \in \{0,1\}^n$ is a bit-vector of the j-th bits of all entries v_i (and similarly for $\boldsymbol{f}^{(k)}$). The inner product y of $\boldsymbol{v}$ and $\boldsymbol{f}$ is hereby broken into the above sum of ℓm binary inner products. So, a first idea to open the inner product over the integers would be to let one create ℓ commitments, one for each $\boldsymbol{v}^{(j)}$ of length n, and then open to the inner product y by revealing all the ℓm binary inner products, each with its corresponding opening proof. The issue with this idea is that it yields an $O(\ell m \log n)$-size opening.

Next, we show a more efficient way to use an FC for binary inner product that avoids this quadratic blowup.

To this end, we show that y can also be represented as the sum of $\ell + m$ binary inner products between vectors of length $n\ell$. We start observing that we can rewrite (1) as

$$y = \sum_{i=1}^{n} \sum_{j=0}^{\ell-1} v_i^{(j)} \cdot \left(\sum_{k=0}^{m-1} f_i^{(k)} 2^{j+k} \right) = \sum_{i=1}^{n} \sum_{j=0}^{\ell-1} v_i^{(j)} \cdot \hat{f}_i^{(j)} \tag{2}$$

where, for every i, j, each $\hat{f}_i^{(j)}$ is the integer $\sum_{k=0}^{m-1} f_i^{(k)} \cdot 2^{j+k} \in [0, 2^{\ell+m-1}]$. Now the inner product y over integers is reshaped as an inner product between an $n\ell$-long binary vector

$$\boldsymbol{v}' = \boldsymbol{v}^{(0)} \| \dots \| \boldsymbol{v}^{(\ell-1)}$$

and an $n\ell$-long function with coefficients in $[0, 2^{\ell+m-1}]$. It is left to appropriately grind this inner product into binary inner products. We are about to show that those binary inner products are between $\boldsymbol{v}'$ and the following binary vectors

$$f'_h = f^{(h)} \| f^{(h-1)} \| \dots \| f^{(h-\ell+1)}$$

where $h \in [0, \ell + m - 2]$, $f^{(k)} = (0, \dots, 0)$ for all $k \notin [0, m-1]$.

Indeed, let $y'_h = \langle v', f'_h \rangle$. Then by changing the variable $k = h - j$ and rearranging the summation of j, we can rewrite (1) as

$$y = \sum_{h=0}^{\ell+m-2} \sum_{j=0}^{\ell-1} \langle v^{(j)}, f^{(h-j)} \rangle \cdot 2^h = \sum_{h=0}^{\ell+m-2} \langle v', f'_h \rangle \cdot 2^h = \sum_{h=0}^{\ell+m-2} y'_h \cdot 2^h.$$

Using as a building block the binary functional vector commitment we get a functional vector commitment for bounded-integers as follows: only one commitment C is needed for the concatenating vector v'. Then the opening proof consists of the partial outputs $\{y_h\}_{h\in[0,\ell+m-2]}$ together with their corresponding functional opening proofs $\{\Lambda_h\}_{h\in[0,\ell+m-2]}$, one for each binary inner product $\langle v', f'_h \rangle$. For verification, one is checking that each Λ_h verifies with respect to C and f'_h, to ensure that y_h are the correct partial outputs. Then it reconstructs $y = \sum_{h=0}^{\ell+m-2} y_h 2^h$ according to the above equality.

FC Scheme. Consider bitFC as an arbitrary FC for binary inner products, we present below a formal description of the transformation.

$\mathsf{Setup}(1^\lambda) \to \mathsf{pp}$: runs $\mathsf{pp} = \mathsf{bitFC.Setup}(1^\lambda)$. Returns pp

$\mathsf{Specialize}(\mathsf{pp}, \mathcal{F}_n) \to \mathsf{pp}_{\mathcal{F}_n}$: given the description of the functions class $\mathcal{F}_n$, which includes the bounds ℓ, m and the vector length n, the specialization algorithms sets $N = n\ell$ and returns $\mathsf{pp}_{\mathcal{F}_n} = \mathsf{bitFC.Specialize}(\mathsf{pp}, N)$.

$\mathsf{Com}(\mathsf{pp}_{n,\ell}, v) \to C$: Let $v = (v_1, \dots, v_n) \in (\{0,1\}^\ell)^n$ be a vector of ℓ-bit entries, and let $v^{(j)} = (v_1^{(j)}, \dots, v_n^{(j)})$ be the binary vector expressing the j-th bit of all entries in v, i.e., it holds $v = \left(\sum_{j=0}^{\ell-1} v_1^{(j)} 2^j, \dots, \sum_{j=0}^{\ell-1} v_n^{(j)} 2^j\right)$.

The commitment algorithm computes the commitment

$$C = \mathsf{bitFC.Com}(\mathsf{pp}_{\mathcal{F}_n}, v'), \text{ s.t. } v' = v^{(0)} \| \dots \| v^{(\ell-1)}$$

and returns C.

$\mathsf{Open}(\mathsf{pp}_{\mathcal{F}_n}, C, v, f) \to (y, \Lambda)$: $f = (f_1, \dots, f_n) \in (\{0,1\}^m)^n$ is a vector of m-bit entries.

If $f = \left(\sum_{k=0}^{m-1} f_1^{(k)} 2^k, \dots, \sum_{k=0}^{m-1} f_n^{(k)} 2^k\right)$ then $f^{(k)} = (f_1^{(k)}, \dots, f_n^{(k)})$ is the binary vector of the k-th bit of all entries of f.

The opening algorithm proceeds as follows. For each $h = 0, \dots, \ell + m - 2$:

$$\text{set } f'_h = f^{(h)} \| f^{(h-1)} \| \dots \| f^{(h-\ell+1)}, \text{ where } f^{(i)} = (0, \dots, 0) \forall i \notin [0, m-1],$$

$$\text{and compute } y_h = \langle v', f'^h \rangle \text{ and } \Lambda_h = \mathsf{bitFC.Open}(\mathsf{pp}_{\mathcal{F}_n}, C, v', f'_h),$$

Return $\Lambda = \{y_h, \Lambda_h\}_{h\in[0,\ell+m-2]}$.

$\mathsf{Ver}(\mathsf{pp}_{\mathcal{F}_n}, C, \Lambda, f, y) \to b$: returns 1 iff:

1. $\mathsf{bitFC.Ver}(\mathsf{pp}_{\mathcal{F}_n}, C, \Lambda_h, f'_h, y_h) = 1$, for each $h \in [0, \ell + m - 2]$.
2. $y = \sum_{h=0}^{\ell+m-2} y_h 2^h$.

Theorem 2. *If the binary functional vector commitment is functional binding, then our bounded-integer functional vector commitment is functional binding.*

Proof. The proof is straightforward from the fact that two valid openings y, z over integer imply immediately that there exists at least an index h for which there are two valid openings for distinct binary inner products $y_h \neq z_h$.

4.2 Our Lifting to FC for Integer Inner Products with Constant-Size Openings

Here we provide a different method to lift an FC for binary inner products to an FC for integer inner products that achieves a different tradeoff. The prover time and verification time are $2^{\ell+m}$ times those of the bitFC scheme, while openings are exactly the same as those of bitFC (and thus constant-size using our scheme of Sect. 3).

Intuition. In the transformation of the previous section we showed how how to express the inner product $y = \langle \boldsymbol{v}, \boldsymbol{f} \rangle$ of n-long vectors of integers into the weighted sum of $\ell + m - 1$ binary inner products of vectors of length $n\ell$:

$$y = \sum_{h=0}^{\ell+m-2} \langle \boldsymbol{v}', \boldsymbol{f}'_h \rangle \cdot 2^h = \sum_{h=0}^{\ell+m-2} y_h \cdot 2^h$$

The drawback of this transformation is that we need to include all the y_h in the opening, and each of this integer is up to $\log n$-bits long.

It turns out that we can iterate the same idea and encode the above weighted sum into a single inner product $\langle \tilde{\boldsymbol{v}}, \tilde{\boldsymbol{f}} \rangle$ of binary vectors of length $n\ell H$ with $H = \sum_{h=0}^{\ell+m-2} 2^h = 2^{\ell+m-1} - 1$.

For every $h \in [0, \ell+m-2]$, define the vector $\tilde{\boldsymbol{f}}_h = \boldsymbol{f}'_h \| \cdot \| \boldsymbol{f}'_h \in \{0,1\}^{n\ell 2^h}$, that is the concatenation of 2^h copies of $\boldsymbol{f}'_h$. Similarly, set $\tilde{\boldsymbol{v}}_h = \boldsymbol{v}' \| \cdots \| \boldsymbol{v}' \in \{0,1\}^{n\ell 2^h}$. Next, if we define

$$\tilde{\boldsymbol{v}} = \tilde{\boldsymbol{v}}_h \| \cdots \| \tilde{\boldsymbol{v}}_h \in \{0,1\}^{n\ell H} \text{ and } \tilde{\boldsymbol{f}} = \tilde{\boldsymbol{f}}_0 \| \cdots \| \tilde{\boldsymbol{f}}_{\ell+m-2} \tag{3}$$

it can be seen that

$$\langle \tilde{\boldsymbol{v}}, \tilde{\boldsymbol{f}} \rangle = \sum_{h=0}^{\ell+m-2} \langle \tilde{\boldsymbol{v}}_h, \tilde{\boldsymbol{f}}_h \rangle = \sum_{h=0}^{\ell+m-2} \langle \boldsymbol{v}', \boldsymbol{f}'_h \rangle \cdot 2^h = y$$

FC Scheme. More in detail the FC scheme works as follows.

$\mathsf{Setup}(1^\lambda) \rightarrow \mathsf{pp}$: runs $\mathsf{pp} = \mathsf{bitFC.Setup}(1^\lambda)$. Returns pp

$\mathsf{Specialize}(\mathsf{pp}, \mathcal{F}_n) \rightarrow \mathsf{pp}_{\mathcal{F}_n}$: given the description of the functions class $\mathcal{F}_n$, which includes the bounds ℓ, m and the vector length n, the specialization algorithms sets $N = n\ell H$, with $H = 2^{\ell+m-1} - 1$, and returns $\mathsf{pp}_{\mathcal{F}_n} = \mathsf{bitFC.Specialize}(\mathsf{pp}, N)$.

$\mathsf{Com}(\mathsf{pp}_{\mathcal{F}_n}, \boldsymbol{v}) \rightarrow C$: Given $\boldsymbol{v} = (v_1, \ldots, v_n) \in (\{0,1\}^\ell)^n$, compute a vector $\tilde{\boldsymbol{v}} \in \{0,1\}^{n\ell H}$ as in Eq. (3), and return the commitment

$$C = \mathsf{bitFC.Com}(\mathsf{pp}_{\mathcal{F}_n}, \tilde{\boldsymbol{v}}).$$

$\mathsf{Open}(\mathsf{pp}_{\mathcal{F}_n}, C, \boldsymbol{v}, \boldsymbol{f}) \rightarrow \Lambda$: Given $\boldsymbol{f} = (f_1, \ldots, f_n) \in (\{0,1\}^m)^n$, compute vectors $\tilde{\boldsymbol{v}}, \tilde{\boldsymbol{f}} \in \{0,1\}^{n\ell H}$ as in Eq. (3), and return the opening

$$\Lambda = \mathsf{bitFC.Open}(\mathsf{pp}_{\mathcal{F}_n}, \tilde{\boldsymbol{v}}, \tilde{\boldsymbol{f}}).$$

$\mathsf{Ver}(\mathsf{pp}_{\mathcal{F}_n}, C, \Lambda, \boldsymbol{f}, y) \rightarrow b$: returns 1 iff $\mathsf{bitFC.Ver}(\mathsf{pp}_{\mathcal{F}_n}, C, \Lambda, \tilde{\boldsymbol{f}}, y) = 1$.

Theorem 3. *If* bitFC *is functional binding, then the FC described above is functional binding.*

The proof is straightforward based on the observation that two valid openings for distinct $y \neq y'$ of our FC are also two valid proofs, for the same commitment and outputs, for the bitFC scheme.

5 Our FC for Inner Products Mod p

In this section, we show how to extend the transformations of the previous section in order to build FCs for inner products modulo an integer p, starting from an FC for binary inner products. Namely we build FCs for

$$\mathcal{F}_{p,n} = \{f : (\mathbb{Z}_p)^n \rightarrow \mathbb{Z}_p\}.$$

Solutions with Logarithmic-Size Openings. For the FC of our first transformation of Sect. 4.1, the adaptation to support the inner product mod p is easy. The only change is to run that construction by setting $\ell = m = \|p\|$ and by letting the second verification check be: $y = \sum_{h=0}^{\ell+m-2} y_h \cdot 2^h \bmod p$. Notice that the FC scheme has exactly the same complexity analysis, considering $\ell = m = \|p\|$.

More in general, given any FC for integer inner products it is possible to construct one for inner products modulo an integer p, at the cost of additionally including $\log(np^2)$ bits in the opening: one simply adds to the opening the result y over the integers, and the verifier additionally checks that $y_p = y \bmod p$.

Solutions with Constant-Size Openings. To build an FC for $\mathcal{F}_{p,n}$ in which openings remain of constant size, we discuss two solutions based on our second transformation of Sect. 4.2.

The first solution is described in the full version of the paper. It shows how to use an FC for integer inner products to obtain an FC for inner products modulo p, for $p = \mathsf{poly}(\lambda)$, with no overhead in the size of openings. This construction can be instantiated using the FCs obtained with our second transformation of Sect. 4.2. To avoid a quadratic blowup in verification time, this construction can start from FC for integer inner products that enjoy preprocessing-based verification. This way, the verification of the resulting FC remains $O(n)$; as drawback, however the resulting FC does not have preprocessing anymore.

FC *for* $\mathbb{Z}$ *inner products, with* $O(1)$ *proofs and preprocessing*	$\Longrightarrow$	FC *for* $\mathbb{Z}_p$ *inner products, with* $O(1)$ *proofs (no preprocessing)*

More concretely, by applying the first solution to an instantiation of intFC obtain by applying the transformation of Sect. 4.2 to the FC of Sect. 3 we obtain, for $p = O(1)$ ($p = O(\log \lambda)$), an FC for inner products $\pmod p$ in which openings have fixed size $O_\lambda(1)$ and verification is $O_\lambda(n)$ ($O_\lambda(n \log \lambda)$ resp.).

The second solution consists into using the same transformation of Sect. 4.2 with the following differences: set $\ell = m = \|p\|$ and, as a building block, use an FC for binary inner products modulo p, i.e., for computing $\langle \boldsymbol{v}, \boldsymbol{f} \rangle \pmod p$ for $\boldsymbol{v}, \boldsymbol{f} \in \{0,1\}^n$. If such a building block is available and it has constant size proofs, it is easy to see that this variant of the transformation is correct and secure. Clearly, due to the complexity of the transformation we can only use it for small integers $p = O(1), O(\log \lambda)$.

The only missing piece for this construction is showing this building block. In the full version of the paper we describe a construction of such a scheme, obtained by tweaking our scheme of Sect. 3. This solution preserves preprocessing verification.

FC *for* $\mathbb{Z}_2$ *inner products mod* p, *with* $O(1)$ *proofs*	$\Longrightarrow$	FC *for* $\mathbb{Z}_p$ *inner products, with* $O(1)$ *proofs*

The modification we mention before adds up the opening size for binary inner products an $O_\lambda(\log p + \lambda)$ complexity. It also takes time $O_\lambda(\log p + \lambda) + t_{\mathsf{Ver}}(n)$ to verify, where $t_{\mathsf{Ver}}(n)$ is the verification time of intFC.

Considering an instantiation of intFC deriving from applying the transformation of Sect. 4.2 to the FC of Sect. 3 we then, for $p = O(1)$, obtain an FC for inner products modulo p in which openings are of size $O_\lambda(1)$ and verification is in time $O_\lambda(1)$ with preprocessing.

For lack of space we refer to the full version for the formal description of the constructions.

Acknowledgements. The second and third authors received funding from the European Research Council (ERC) under the European Union's Horizon 2020 research and innovation program under project PICOCRYPT (grant agreement No. 101001283), by the Spanish Government under projects SCUM (ref. RTI2018-102043-B-I00) and RED2018-102321-T, and by the Madrid Regional Government under project BLOQUES (ref. S2018/TCS-4339). This work is also supported by a research grant (ref. PL-RGP1-2021-051) from Protocol Labs.

References

1. Ames, S., Hazay, C., Ishai, Y., Venkitasubramaniam, M.: Ligero: lightweight sublinear arguments without a trusted setup. In: Thuraisingham, B.M., Evans, D., Malkin, T., Xu, D. (eds.) ACM CCS 2017, pp. 2087–2104. ACM Press (Oct/Nov 2017). https://doi.org/10.1145/3133956.3134104
2. Arun, A., Ganesh, C., Lokam, S., Mopuri, T., Sridhar, S.: Dew: transparent constant-sized zksnarks. Cryptology ePrint Archive, Report 2022/419 (2022)
3. Barić, N., Pfitzmann, B.: Collision-free accumulators and fail-stop signature schemes without trees. In: Fumy, W. (ed.) EUROCRYPT 1997. LNCS, vol. 1233, pp. 480–494. Springer, Heidelberg (1997). https://doi.org/10.1007/3-540-69053-0_33
4. Ben-Sasson, E., Bentov, I., Horesh, Y., Riabzev, M.: Scalable zero knowledge with no trusted setup. In: Boldyreva, A., Micciancio, D. (eds.) CRYPTO 2019. LNCS, vol. 11694, pp. 701–732. Springer, Cham (2019). https://doi.org/10.1007/978-3-030-26954-8_23
5. Ben-Sasson, E., Chiesa, A., Riabzev, M., Spooner, N., Virza, M., Ward, N.P.: Aurora: transparent succinct arguments for R1CS. In: Ishai, Y., Rijmen, V. (eds.) EUROCRYPT 2019. LNCS, vol. 11476, pp. 103–128. Springer, Cham (2019). https://doi.org/10.1007/978-3-030-17653-2_4
6. Benaloh, J., de Mare, M.: One-way accumulators: a decentralized alternative to digital signatures. In: Helleseth, T. (ed.) EUROCRYPT 1993. LNCS, vol. 765, pp. 274–285. Springer, Heidelberg (1994). https://doi.org/10.1007/3-540-48285-7_24
7. Biasse, J.-F., Jacobson, M.J., Silvester, A.K.: Security estimates for quadratic field based cryptosystems. In: Steinfeld, R., Hawkes, P. (eds.) ACISP 2010. LNCS, vol. 6168, pp. 233–247. Springer, Heidelberg (2010). https://doi.org/10.1007/978-3-642-14081-5_15
8. Boneh, D., Bünz, B., Fisch, B.: A survey of two verifiable delay functions. Cryptology ePrint Archive, Report 2018/712 (2018)
9. Boneh, D., Bünz, B., Fisch, B.: Batching techniques for accumulators with applications to IOPs and stateless blockchains. In: Boldyreva, A., Micciancio, D. (eds.) CRYPTO 2019. LNCS, vol. 11692, pp. 561–586. Springer, Cham (2019). https://doi.org/10.1007/978-3-030-26948-7_20
10. Bootle, J., Cerulli, A., Chaidos, P., Groth, J., Petit, C.: Efficient zero-knowledge arguments for arithmetic circuits in the discrete log setting. In: Fischlin, M., Coron, J.-S. (eds.) EUROCRYPT 2016. LNCS, vol. 9666, pp. 327–357. Springer, Heidelberg (2016). https://doi.org/10.1007/978-3-662-49896-5_12
11. Bosma, W., Stevenhagen, P.: On the computation of quadratic 2-class groups. J. de théorie des nombres de Bordeaux **8**(2), 283–313 (1996)
12. Buchmann, J., Hamdy, S.: A survey on IQ cryptography (2001). http://tubiblio.ulb.tu-darmstadt.de/100933/
13. Bünz, B., Bootle, J., Boneh, D., Poelstra, A., Wuille, P., Maxwell, G.: Bulletproofs: short proofs for confidential transactions and more. In: 2018 IEEE Symposium on Security and Privacy, pp. 315–334. IEEE Computer Society Press (2018). https://doi.org/10.1109/SP.2018.00020
14. Bünz, B., Fisch, B., Szepieniec, A.: Transparent SNARKs from DARK compilers. In: Canteaut, A., Ishai, Y. (eds.) EUROCRYPT 2020. LNCS, vol. 12105, pp. 677–706. Springer, Cham (2020). https://doi.org/10.1007/978-3-030-45721-1_24
15. Cachin, C., Micali, S., Stadler, M.: Computationally private information retrieval with polylogarithmic communication. In: Stern, J. (ed.) EUROCRYPT 1999.

LNCS, vol. 1592, pp. 402–414. Springer, Heidelberg (1999). https://doi.org/10.1007/3-540-48910-X_28
16. Campanelli, M., Fiore, D., Greco, N., Kolonelos, D., Nizzardo, L.: Incrementally aggregatable vector commitments and applications to verifiable decentralized storage. In: Moriai, S., Wang, H. (eds.) ASIACRYPT 2020. LNCS, vol. 12492, pp. 3–35. Springer, Cham (2020). https://doi.org/10.1007/978-3-030-64834-3_1
17. Catalano, D., Fiore, D.: Vector commitments and their applications. In: Kurosawa, K., Hanaoka, G. (eds.) PKC 2013. LNCS, vol. 7778, pp. 55–72. Springer, Heidelberg (2013). https://doi.org/10.1007/978-3-642-36362-7_5
18. Chiesa, A., Ojha, D., Spooner, N.: FRACTAL: post-quantum and transparent recursive proofs from holography. In: Canteaut, A., Ishai, Y. (eds.) EUROCRYPT 2020. LNCS, vol. 12105, pp. 769–793. Springer, Cham (2020). https://doi.org/10.1007/978-3-030-45721-1_27
19. Chu, H., Fiore, D., Kolonelos, D., Schröder, D.: Inner product functional commitments with constant-size public parameters and openings. Cryptology ePrint Archive (2022)
20. Cramer, R., Shoup, V.: Signature schemes based on the strong RSA assumption. In: Motiwalla, J., Tsudik, G. (eds.) ACM CCS 99, pp. 46–51. ACM Press (1999). https://doi.org/10.1145/319709.319716
21. Damgård, I., Koprowski, M.: Generic lower bounds for root extraction and signature schemes in general groups. In: Knudsen, L.R. (ed.) EUROCRYPT 2002. LNCS, vol. 2332, pp. 256–271. Springer, Heidelberg (2002). https://doi.org/10.1007/3-540-46035-7_17
22. Dobson, S., Galbraith, S.D., Smith, B.: Trustless unknown-order groups. Cryptology ePrint Archive (2020)
23. Fiat, A., Shamir, A.: How to prove yourself: practical solutions to identification and signature problems. In: Odlyzko, A.M. (ed.) CRYPTO 1986. LNCS, vol. 263, pp. 186–194. Springer, Heidelberg (1987). https://doi.org/10.1007/3-540-47721-7_12
24. Gennaro, R., Halevi, S., Rabin, T.: Secure hash-and-sign signatures without the random oracle. In: Stern, J. (ed.) EUROCRYPT 1999. LNCS, vol. 1592, pp. 123–139. Springer, Heidelberg (1999). https://doi.org/10.1007/3-540-48910-X_9
25. Groth, J.: Non-interactive zero-knowledge arguments for voting. In: Ioannidis, J., Keromytis, A., Yung, M. (eds.) ACNS 2005. LNCS, vol. 3531, pp. 467–482. Springer, Heidelberg (2005). https://doi.org/10.1007/11496137_32
26. Groth, J., Kohlweiss, M., Maller, M., Meiklejohn, S., Miers, I.: Updatable and universal common reference strings with applications to zk-SNARKs. In: Shacham, H., Boldyreva, A. (eds.) CRYPTO 2018. LNCS, vol. 10993, pp. 698–728. Springer, Cham (2018). https://doi.org/10.1007/978-3-319-96878-0_24
27. Hamdy, S., Möller, B.: Security of cryptosystems based on class groups of imaginary quadratic orders. In: Okamoto, T. (ed.) ASIACRYPT 2000. LNCS, vol. 1976, pp. 234–247. Springer, Heidelberg (2000). https://doi.org/10.1007/3-540-44448-3_18
28. Kate, A., Zaverucha, G.M., Goldberg, I.: Constant-size commitments to polynomials and their applications. In: Abe, M. (ed.) ASIACRYPT 2010. LNCS, vol. 6477, pp. 177–194. Springer, Heidelberg (2010). https://doi.org/10.1007/978-3-642-17373-8_11
29. Lai, R.W.F., Malavolta, G.: Subvector commitments with application to succinct arguments. In: Boldyreva, A., Micciancio, D. (eds.) CRYPTO 2019. LNCS, vol. 11692, pp. 530–560. Springer, Cham (2019). https://doi.org/10.1007/978-3-030-26948-7_19

30. Libert, B., Ramanna, S.C., Yung, M.: Functional commitment schemes: from polynomial commitments to pairing-based accumulators from simple assumptions. In: Chatzigiannakis, I., Mitzenmacher, M., Rabani, Y., Sangiorgi, D. (eds.) ICALP 2016. LIPIcs, vol. 55, pp. 30:1–30:14. Schloss Dagstuhl (2016). https://doi.org/10.4230/LIPIcs.ICALP.2016.30
31. Libert, B., Yung, M.: Concise mercurial vector commitments and independent zero-knowledge sets with short proofs. In: Micciancio, D. (ed.) TCC 2010. LNCS, vol. 5978, pp. 499–517. Springer, Heidelberg (2010). https://doi.org/10.1007/978-3-642-11799-2_30
32. Lipmaa, H.: On diophantine complexity and statistical zero-knowledge arguments. In: Laih, C.-S. (ed.) ASIACRYPT 2003. LNCS, vol. 2894, pp. 398–415. Springer, Heidelberg (2003). https://doi.org/10.1007/978-3-540-40061-5_26
33. Lipmaa, H.: Secure accumulators from euclidean rings without trusted setup. In: Bao, F., Samarati, P., Zhou, J. (eds.) ACNS 2012. LNCS, vol. 7341, pp. 224–240. Springer, Heidelberg (2012). https://doi.org/10.1007/978-3-642-31284-7_14
34. Lipmaa, H., Pavlyk, K.: Succinct functional commitment for a large class of arithmetic circuits. In: Moriai, S., Wang, H. (eds.) ASIACRYPT 2020. LNCS, vol. 12493, pp. 686–716. Springer, Cham (2020). https://doi.org/10.1007/978-3-030-64840-4_23
35. Micali, S.: CS proofs (extended abstracts). In: 35th FOCS, pp. 436–453. IEEE Computer Society Press (1994). https://doi.org/10.1109/SFCS.1994.365746
36. Peikert, C., Pepin, Z., Sharp, C.: Vector and functional commitments from lattices. In: Nissim, K., Waters, B. (eds.) TCC 2021. LNCS, vol. 13044, pp. 480–511. Springer, Cham (2021). https://doi.org/10.1007/978-3-030-90456-2_16
37. Setty, S.: Spartan: efficient and general-purpose zkSNARKs without trusted setup. In: Micciancio, D., Ristenpart, T. (eds.) CRYPTO 2020. LNCS, vol. 12172, pp. 704–737. Springer, Cham (2020). https://doi.org/10.1007/978-3-030-56877-1_25
38. Setty, S., Lee, J.: Quarks: quadruple-efficient transparent zkSNARKs. Cryptology ePrint Archive, Report 2020/1275 (2020)
39. Wahby, R.S., Tzialla, I., Shelat, a., Thaler, J., Walfish, M.: Doubly-efficient zkSNARKs without trusted setup. In: 2018 IEEE Symposium on Security and Privacy, pp. 926–943. IEEE Computer Society Press (2018). https://doi.org/10.1109/SP.2018.00060
40. Wesolowski, B.: Efficient verifiable delay functions. Cryptology ePrint Archive, Report 2018/623 (2018). https://eprint.iacr.org/2018/623
41. Wesolowski, B.: Efficient verifiable delay functions. In: Ishai, Y., Rijmen, V. (eds.) EUROCRYPT 2019. LNCS, vol. 11478, pp. 379–407. Springer, Cham (2019). https://doi.org/10.1007/978-3-030-17659-4_13
42. Zhang, J., Xie, T., Zhang, Y., Song, D.: Transparent polynomial delegation and its applications to zero knowledge proof. In: 2020 IEEE Symposium on Security and Privacy, pp. 859–876. IEEE Computer Society Press (2020). https://doi.org/10.1109/SP40000.2020.00052

MyOPE: Malicious SecuritY for Oblivious Polynomial Evaluation

Malika Izabachène[1], Anca Nitulescu[2], Paola de Perthuis[1,3](✉), and David Pointcheval[3]

[1] Cosmian, Paris, France
[2] Protocol Labs, Paris, France
[3] DIENS, École normale supèrieure, CNRS, Inria, PSL University, Paris, France
paola.de.perthuis@ens.fr

Abstract. Oblivious Polynomial Evaluation (OPE) schemes are interactive protocols between a sender with a private polynomial and a receiver with a private evaluation point where the receiver learns the evaluation of the polynomial in their point and no additional information. In this work, we introduce MyOPE, a "short-sighted" non-interactive polynomial evaluation scheme with a poly-logarithmic communication complexity in the presence of malicious senders. In addition to strong privacy guarantees, MyOPE enforces honest sender behavior and consistency by adding verifiability to the calculations.

The main building block for this new verifiable OPE is an inner product argument (IPA) over rings that guarantees an inner product relation holds between committed vectors. Our IPA works for vectors with elements from generic rings of polynomials and has constant-size proofs that consist in one commitment only while the verification, once the validity of the vector-commitments has been checked, consists is one quadratic equation only.

We further demonstrate the applications of our IPA for verifiable OPE using Fully Homomorphic Encryption (FHE) over rings of polynomials: we prove the correctness of an inner product between the vector of powers of the evaluation point and the vector of polynomial coefficients, along with other inner-products necessary in this application's proof.

MyOPE builds on generic secure encoding techniques for succinct commitments, that allow real-world FHE parameters and Residue Number System (RNS) optimizations, suitable for high-degree polynomials.

1 Introduction

1.1 Oblivious Polynomial Evaluation

Oblivious Polynomial Evaluation (OPE) is a protocol that allows two parties, the sender and the receiver, to evaluate a polynomial $\mathsf{f}(X)$ of fixed public degree N secretly chosen by the sender in a point m known only by the receiver. The receiver obtains the value $\mathsf{f}(\mathsf{m})$ without learning anything else about the polynomial f and without giving the sender any information about the point m.

C. Galdi and S. Jarecki (Eds.): SCN 2022, LNCS 13409, pp. 663–686, 2022.
https://doi.org/10.1007/978-3-031-14791-3_29

OPE is an important building block for various 2-party computation (2-PC) schemes that generally require multiple executions of an OPE protocol for the same polynomial and different evaluation points, such as for Private Set Intersection (PSI), data mining [31], privacy-preserving keyword search [29], set membership (related to PSI) or and RSA key generation [24], to mention a few. Our building blocks for OPE can also be used to attain Symmetric Private Information Retrieval (SPIR). However, the standard definition of receiver privacy does not preclude the sender from cheating by using a polynomial of higher degree than expected, changing the polynomial between multiple executions, or sending polynomial evaluation results in a wrong order, thus potentially easily leaking private information if the protocol includes a step to return the intersection result to the sender in the PSI application. Therefore, extending the security to malicious senders is essential in practical contexts.

With generic 2PC techniques in the malicious setting, some efficiency overheads incur, with the cut-and-choose technique or an expensive preprocessing to generate correlated randomness, that needs to be regularly repeated, and for the techniques using FHE ciphertexts to get better asymptotic communication and less interaction, this level of security had not yet been guaranteed.

1.2 Inner-Product Arguments over Rings

An inner product argument ensures the correctness for an inner product evaluation between two committed vectors. Following the observation that a polynomial evaluation can be written as an inner product between the vector of its coefficients and the vector of the consecutive powers of the evaluation point, we can use such protocols to enforce honest behavior in OPE schemes.

Inner-product arguments [7,9–11,16,30,37] are core components of many other primitives, including zero-knowledge proofs and polynomial/vector commitment schemes. While all of these IPAs follow the same strategy using folding techniques, they only achieve logarithmic-size proofs without privacy, and they support only inner product of vectors with elements from a field. While the verification time is linear in most of the mentioned works, the recent results by [11,16] achieve logarithmic-time verification using a trusted setup.

We design a new ring Inner-Product Argument (ring-IPA) that allows the verification of inner product evaluations for vectors with elements from a ring. Our scheme relies on a trusted setup in order to achieve succinct proofs and verification. We also offer a new commitment scheme for vectors with elements from generic rings of polynomials, compatible with FHE ciphertexts, as an improvement to previous such schemes that only work for vectors over fields or groups of elliptic curve elements.

Our ring-IPA construction improves on proof sizes and verification times achieving constant-size proofs and constant-time verification, independent of the size of the vectors. Moreover, the ring-IPA can be used for vectors over rings of polynomials, compatible with the rings used by various FHE schemes, providing proofs for the evaluation of inner products over ciphertexts, which can then also be seen as ciphertexts of inner products, from their homomorphic properties.

1.3 Related Work

Despite its broad applicability, the study of the OPE functionality includes few practical and secure protocols, initiated in [33] and further continued in works like [13,27,38].

While [33] proposed a first construction for OPE, it relies on a newly introduced intractability assumption: the noisy polynomial interpolation. Naor and Pinkas conjectured that it could be reduced to a more widely studied assumption, the polynomial reconstruction problem. Nevertheless, as shown in [5], this conjecture seems not to hold in general.

OPE Schemes with Active Security. Among recent OPE schemes, to the best of our knowledge, some of the best schemes with security against malicious adversaries are given by [26,27]. However, [27] has at least 17 rounds of interaction and the parties send each other $\mathcal{O}(\lambda N)$ Paillier encryptions, where λ is the security parameter and N the degree of the polynomial, and their claimed efficiency holds only for sufficiently low degree polynomials. [26] shows an OPE scheme for polynomial evaluation in the exponent of a DLog group using algebraic Pseudo-Random Functions (PRF). They focus on improving the computational efficiency of [27] by reducing the number of modular exponentiations, and removing the trusted setup requirement, while preserving the same number of rounds of interaction and communication complexity as in [27], and apply their scheme to private set membership 2PC. [35] gives malicious security for PSI with symmetric set sizes, but the communication is linear in the set sizes. There are also efficient schemes like [8], but they don't have the sublinear communication complexity and reduced interactivity we get with FHE methods.

Verifiable Computation (VC). Introduced by [20], VC schemes are cryptographic systems that enable checking the integrity of results from delegated computations. More recent works [6,18] have improved the efficiency of VC schemes to work for computations over encrypted data. These schemes, however, require proving the entire FHE circuit evaluation which is very expensive. Moreover, they neither allow using practical parameters for the FHE scheme, nor speedups through classical optimizations such as Residue Number System (RNS).

Then, [19] also gives constructions for general algebraic circuits over ring elements, but using a general approach which is not optimized for our inner-product and OPE application, which we can instantiate with a small cleartext modulus $t = 3$ (when theirs are greater to have big enough ideal subsets), and for which we select parameters compatible with OPE requirements like the computation privacy, when this other work is focused on non-private algebraic circuit calculations, and would thus not hide the polynomial.

1.4 Our Contribution

Our first contribution is a generic framework based on any secure encoding that allows building an inner product argument (IPA) over vectors with elements coming from wider spaces, not only from fields as defined in prior works. Depending on the instantiation of the underlying secure encoding scheme, we are able to obtain IPA schemes for vectors of ciphertexts from Fully Homomorphic Encryption (FHE) schemes, such as the Fan-Vercauteren scheme [17], that can provide privacy under the Ring-LWE (RLWE) assumption. Other FHE schemes relying on the RLWE assumption could also be used.

Equipped with our new constant-size and constant-time inner product argument, we next apply our techniques to enhance the security of OPE schemes to malicious senders, by enforcing an honest behavior when evaluating the polynomial. We focus on OPE schemes with minimal communication requirements and without an offline pre-processing phase, based on Fully Homomorphic Encryption (FHE) on an encrypted point.

More precisely, we introduce MyOPE, a scheme for verifiable oblivious evaluation of polynomials of high degrees N that achieves $\mathcal{O}((\log(N))^2)$ communication cost, for a constant security level (when considering the privacy, correctness, and soundness properties). This sublinear communication improves on the state-of-the-art, with just a $\log N$ factor with respect to schemes without an active security.

As a straightforward use case, we illustrate our verifiable OPE application to Private Set Intersection (PSI) in the unbalanced-set setting: basically, the sender, who owns the larger set $\mathcal{X} = \{x_1, \ldots, x_N\}$, defines the polynomial $\mathsf{f} = \prod_{i=1}^{N}(X - x_i)$, and the receiver asks for evaluations $\mathsf{f}(y_j)$ for each element in $\mathcal{Y} = \{y_1, \ldots, y_K\}$ to detect the common roots. Our communication complexity then becomes $\mathcal{O}(K \cdot (\log(N))^2)$, with just a $\log N$ factor compared to the most efficient PSI algorithm [14] without verifiability, where K is the size of the small set and N is the size of the large set.

Our scheme guarantees the client's privacy with post-quantum FHE ciphertexts, under the Ring-LWE assumption, while the soundness of the proof can rely on a variety of secure encoding schemes, from pairings (under the Power Knowledge of Exponent Assumption) to any linear-only encryption scheme such as the Paillier scheme [34] (under the integer factoring) and the Castagnos-Laguillaumie scheme [12] (under some class group problems), but also based on the post-quantum Learning With Errors (LWE) problem [22], thus making the entire scheme post-quantum secure.

1.5 Technical Overview

Inner Product Argument. Our first tool is of independent interest: it allows to prove inner-product evaluation of two vectors $\boldsymbol{u}$ and $\boldsymbol{v}$, with respect to their commitments U and $\bar{V}$ respectively. Our vector commitments will be based on commitments keys that encode powers of a secret point s, using any secure encoding scheme, $[1], [s], \ldots, [s^{n-1}]$, defined and published once for all. We define $U = [\sum_i u_i s^i] = \sum_i u_i[s^i]$ while $\bar{V}$ will be in the reverse order: $\bar{V} = \sum_i v_i[s^{n-i}]$. The notation $[.]$ is an informal representation of a secure encoding, that leads to a computationally binding commitment. The hiding property is achieved with an additional secret component and Schnorr-like proofs. It will additionally have bilinear properties, which lead to $U \times \bar{V} = \sum_{i,j}(u_i v_j)[s^{n+i-j}] = \langle \boldsymbol{u}, \boldsymbol{v}\rangle[s^n] +$

$\sum_{i \neq j}(u_i v_j)[s^{n+i-j}]$. By showing $U \times \bar{V} - \alpha[s^n]$ has no term in $[s^n]$, one proves that $\langle \boldsymbol{u}, \boldsymbol{v} \rangle = \alpha$. Whereas the analysis will be performed on polynomials evaluated in a secret point s, the Schwartz-Zippel lemma [36,39] will lift the relations on the polynomials, as non-zero polynomials are unlikely evaluated to 0. But this assumes good properties for the algebraic structures, which are not always satisfied. A favorable situation is considered first, in fields of large characteristic, then more complex structures are discussed in the full version [28], in rings. Globally, the soundness of the proofs relies on the secure encodings (which can require the Power Knowledge of Exponent Assumption when pairings are used, or the linear-only property of any encryption scheme) and the Schwartz-Zippel lemma (that requires no computational assumption, but appropriate algebraic structures)

Verifiable Polynomial Evaluation. Now, from a polynomial $\mathsf{f} = \sum \mathsf{f}_i X^i$, which can be encoded as a vector $\boldsymbol{v} = (\mathsf{f}_i)_i$, and thus committed as $\bar{V}$ (in reverse order), and an element m, which can be encoded as a vector $\boldsymbol{u} = (\mathsf{m}^i)_i$, and thus committed as U, $\mathsf{f}(\mathsf{m}) = \langle \boldsymbol{u}, \boldsymbol{v} \rangle$, correctness can be proven as above with respect to the binding commitments U and $\bar{V}$. Again, efficiency will depend on the actual algebraic structures. For the reader's convenience, indices for vectors start at 0, to consider the constant monomial in polynomials.

Receiver Privacy: Fully Homomorphic Encryption. When both f and m are public, which easily allows getting confidence in U and $\bar{V}$, the above approach is convincing. When receiver privacy is expected, with a private point m, the receiver could send encryptions M_i of the m^i under an additively homomorphic encryption scheme: if W is a commitment of the vector $\boldsymbol{w} = (\mathsf{M}_i)_i$, using the linear property of the encryption scheme, $\langle \boldsymbol{w}, \boldsymbol{v} \rangle = \sum \mathsf{f}_i \mathsf{M}_i$ is the encryption of $\mathsf{f}(\mathsf{m}) = \sum \mathsf{f}_i \mathsf{m}^i$, which can be proven with respect to W and $\bar{V}$, as above. Once convinced, the receiver can decrypt it to get $\mathsf{f}(\mathsf{m})$. Their privacy is guaranteed by the semantic security of the encryption scheme. But sending all the M_i's implies a huge communication cost. One can then use a Fully Homomorphic Encryption (FHE) to let the sender generate the vector: the receiver provides M as an encryption (under their own key) of m, and FHE allows the sender to compute M_i. The additive homomorphism allows continuing as above.

But why should the receiver trust the sender to have correctly computed the M_i's as the encryptions of the successive powers of m and the commitment W correctly? Let us assume each M_i, in $\boldsymbol{w}$ committed in W, encrypts the plaintext m_i. One can use another verifiable inner product to check $\mathsf{m}_i = \mathsf{m}^i$: from a random common public element n, chosen after the publication of W, and the vector $\boldsymbol{z} = (\mathsf{n}^i)_i$ publicly committed into $\bar{Z}$ (in reverse order), the receiver can verifiably compute the inner product $\langle \boldsymbol{w}, \boldsymbol{z} \rangle$ with respect to W and $\bar{Z}$. Since it is proven correct, it decrypts to $\sum \mathsf{m}_i \mathsf{n}^i$, while one would like it to be $\sum \mathsf{m}^i \mathsf{n}^i$. In case of equality, this means that polynomials $\sum \mathsf{m}_i X^i$ and $\sum \mathsf{m}^i X^i$ evaluate the same way on the random point n. By applying the Schwartz-Zippel lemma in the plaintext-space, this means that $\mathsf{m}_i = \mathsf{m}^i$ with overwhelming probability. This concludes the security analysis.

To draw the above conclusion, we assumed the Schwartz-Zippel lemma could be applied in both the plaintext-space (for getting $\mathsf{m}_i = \mathsf{m}^i$) and the ciphertext-space (for verifying the two inner product evaluations between $(\mathsf{M}_i)_i$ and $(\mathsf{f}_i)_i$, and between $(\mathsf{M}_i)_i$ and $(\mathsf{n}^i)_i$). Furthermore, for effective application of FHE, additional constraints might be added to the ciphertext-space, such as Residue Number System (RNS) representation. All these questions will be addressed below, dealing with arbitrary rings.

Sender Privacy: Noise-Flooding and Hiding Commitments. OPE also expects sender privacy, with no leakage about the polynomial f. However, the commitment U might leak some information, unless it guarantees the additional *hiding* property. Furthermore, the homomorphic evaluation $\mathsf{f}(\mathsf{m})$ in the ciphertexts may leak more than just the result, and possibly the evaluation steps, as the final noise in $\langle \boldsymbol{w}, \boldsymbol{v} \rangle$ leaks them. To avoid such a leakage, the sender can add extra super-polynomial noise to $\langle \boldsymbol{w}, \boldsymbol{v} \rangle$. This is the so-called *noise-flooding* technique [23]. One will of course have to prove this does not impact the decrypted result, requiring a small enough norm for the added noise. Which results in another inner-product proof, as the L_2-norm is an inner product square root.

Efficiency for two Secure Encoding Instantiations. Any Secure Encoding scheme can be used in our construction: depending on the instantiation choice different assumptions will be used, and if the Secure Encoding scheme uses a modulus which is not a multiple of q, then the size will have a $\mathcal{O}(\log(N))$ complexity. We compare two example instantiations in Fig. 1.

Secure Encoding	Pairings	Paillier Encryption
Assumptions	Power Knowledge of Exponent	Hardness of Integer Factoring + Linear-Only Encryption
Field/Ring Modulus q	prime	composite (for RNS)
Size complexity	$\mathcal{O}(1)$	$\mathcal{O}(\log(N))$

Fig. 1. Comparison of pairing and Paillier encryption instantiations of the secure encoding scheme. The size complexity (of both the individual encodings and the total proof) is given in N, the size of the inner-product vectors.

Efficiency in Practice. With the Fan-Vercauteren FHE scheme [17], from the plaintext ring $\mathcal{R}_t = \mathbb{Z}_t[X]/\mathsf{r}(X)$, where $\mathsf{r}(X) = X^n + 1$, into the ciphertext ring $\mathcal{R}_q = \mathbb{Z}_q[X]/\mathsf{r}(X)$, the core parameters are the integers n, q, and t, to guarantee the semantic security under the Ring-LWE assumption. For the PSI application, one needs to encode elements from $\mathcal{X}$ and $\mathcal{Y}$ into $\mathcal{R}_t$. Since $n > 128$, $t = 3$ will be big enough. Each ciphertext is $2n \log_2 q$ bits long.

With a MyOPE instantiation for polynomials of degree $N = 2^{30}$, we set $n = 2^{14}$ which leads to q over 610 bits to obtain an appropriate FHE semantic security (according to the LWE estimator [1]) and decryption correctness, including with noise-flooding. To exploit RNS optimizations [2], as proposed in SEAL[1], q can be the product of 11 primes on less than 60 bits each.

[1] https://github.com/microsoft/SEAL.

Then, the size of the FHE ciphertext to be sent is of about 3 MBytes. The result of the sender and proof of their honest behavior consists of about 5 MBytes, for a prime q and soundness of 2^{-128}. If RNS is used, with a composite q, the Schwartz-Zippel guarantees are lower, and our commitments will have to be repeated several times for the soundness: the result and proof then consists of some 170MBytes, from our analysis in the full version [28].

2 Preliminaries

2.1 MyOPE: Verifiable OPE

We first formalize the notion of *verifiable oblivious polynomial evaluation.* A $\mathsf{MyOPE} = (\mathsf{OPE.Setup}, \mathsf{OPE.KeyGen}, \mathsf{OPE.QueryGen}, \mathsf{OPE.Compute}, \mathsf{OPE.Verify}, \mathsf{OPE.Decode})$ scheme for polynomial evaluation consists of the following algorithms:

$\mathsf{OPE.Setup}(1^\lambda) \to (\mathsf{PK}, \mathsf{SK})$: Given the security parameter λ, output a pair of keys independent on polynomials to compute. The public key PK will be provided as input to all the subsequent algorithms.
$\mathsf{OPE.KeyGen}(\mathsf{PK}, f) \to \mathsf{pk}_f$: Given the polynomial f, output a public key pk_f.
$\mathsf{OPE.QueryGen}(\mathsf{PK}, \mathsf{pk}_f, x) \to \sigma_x$: Given the public key pk_f and the input x, encode the evaluation point x into σ_x, and output it.
$\mathsf{OPE.Compute}(\mathsf{PK}, f, \sigma_x) \to \sigma_y$: Given the polynomial f and the encoded input, output an encoded value σ_y of the result y.
$\mathsf{OPE.Verify}(\mathsf{PK}, [\mathsf{SK}], \mathsf{pk}_f, \sigma_x, \sigma_y) \to acc$: Given the secret key SK, in case of designated-verifier scheme, the public key pk_f for polynomial f, and the encoding σ_x of the evaluation point, accept (with $acc = 1$) or reject (with $acc = 0$) an output encoding σ_y.
$\mathsf{OPE.Decode}(\mathsf{SK}, \sigma_y) \to y$: Given the secret key SK for polynomial f, and an output encoding σ_y, output the result y.

For concrete use, between a sender with input polynomial f and a receiver with evaluation point x:

- The Setup algorithm is first run by the receiver (in case of designated-verifier) or a trusted party.
- The Sender executes the KeyGen algorithm with their input polynomial f.
- The Receiver runs QueryGen on their input x.
- The Sender runs Compute algorithm to obtain an encoding of the result σ_y.
- The Receiver can verify and decode the result with algorithms Verify and Decode.

Note that the QueryGen and Decode correspond to the encryption and decryption algorithms of a (fully) homomorphic encryption scheme.

$\mathsf{Exp}^{\mathsf{SND}}_{\Pi,\mathcal{A}}(\lambda)$:
$(\mathsf{PK},\mathsf{SK}) \leftarrow \mathsf{Setup}(1^\lambda)$; $(f, x, \mathsf{st}) \leftarrow \mathcal{A}_1(\mathsf{PK})$
$\mathsf{pk}_f \leftarrow \mathsf{KeyGen}(\mathsf{PK}, f)$; $\sigma_x \leftarrow \mathsf{QueryGen}(\mathsf{PK}, \mathsf{pk}_f, x)$; $\sigma_y \leftarrow \mathcal{A}_2(\mathsf{PK}, \mathsf{pk}_f, \sigma_x, \mathsf{st})$;
if $\mathsf{Verify}(\mathsf{PK}, [\mathsf{SK}], \mathsf{pk}_f, \sigma_x, \sigma_y) = 1$ and $\mathsf{Decode}(\mathsf{SK}, \sigma_y) \neq f(x)$, then return 1
else return 0.

$\mathsf{Exp}^{\mathsf{R\text{-}Privacy}}_{\Pi,\mathcal{A}}(\lambda)$:
$b \xleftarrow{\$} \{0,1\}$; $(\mathsf{PK},\mathsf{SK}) \leftarrow \mathsf{Setup}(1^\lambda)$; $(f, x_0, x_1, \mathsf{st}) \leftarrow \mathcal{A}_1(\mathsf{PK})$
$\mathsf{pk}_f \leftarrow \mathsf{KeyGen}(\mathsf{PK}, f)$; $\sigma_b \leftarrow \mathsf{QueryGen}(\mathsf{PK}, \mathsf{pk}_f, x_b)$; $b' \leftarrow \mathcal{A}_2(\mathsf{PK}, \sigma_b, \mathsf{st})$
if $f(x_0) \neq f(x_1)$, then return $\perp$ else return $(b = b')$

$\mathsf{Exp}^{\mathsf{S\text{-}Privacy}}_{\Pi,\mathcal{A}}(\lambda)$:
$b \xleftarrow{\$} \{0,1\}$; $(\mathsf{PK},\mathsf{SK}) \leftarrow \mathsf{Setup}(1^\lambda)$; $(f_0, f_1, \mathsf{st}) \leftarrow \mathcal{A}_1(\mathsf{PK})$
$\mathsf{pk}_f \leftarrow \mathsf{KeyGen}(\mathsf{PK}, f_b)$; $b' \leftarrow \mathcal{A}_2^{\mathsf{CO}(.)}(\mathsf{PK}, \mathsf{SK}, \mathsf{pk}_f, \mathsf{st})$
if f_0 or f_1 invalid functions, if some σ_x asked to CO decodes to an x such that $f_0(x) \neq f_1(x)$, then return $\perp$ else return $(b = b')$

$\mathsf{CO}(\sigma_x)$: return $\sigma_y \leftarrow \mathsf{Compute}(\mathsf{PK}, f_b, \sigma_x)$

Fig. 2. Security Games

Correctness. The *correctness* of a MyOPE scheme requires that if one runs Compute on an honestly generated query encoding of x, after honest Setup and KeyGen executions for f, then the output must verify and its decoding should be $y = f(x)$.

Soundness. The verifiability of a MyOPE guarantees the receiver of correct computation, even in front of a malicious sender, once Setup and KeyGen have been run honestly. This is done by means of a proof, the encoded value of the result σ_y should contain a proof of correctness of y. The soundness (SND) experiment (with other privacy experiments) is described in Fig. 2.

Definition 1 (Soundness (SND)). *Let Π be an instance of our VC protocol and $\mathcal{A} = (\mathcal{A}_1, \mathcal{A}_2)$ a two-stage adversary. Protocol Π is SND-secure if the advantage $\mathsf{Adv}^{\mathsf{SND}}_{\Pi,\mathcal{A}}(\lambda) = \Pr[1 \leftarrow \mathsf{Exp}^{\mathsf{SND}}_{\Pi,\mathcal{A}}(1^\lambda)]$ is negligible.*

However, one may also expect some privacy properties which are now defined.

Receiver Privacy. This notion ensures that the input x of the receiver remains hidden during the protocol execution, for an honestly generated pk_f.

Definition 2 (Receiver Privacy (R-Privacy)). *Let Π be an instance of our MyOPE protocol and $\mathcal{A} = (\mathcal{A}_1, \mathcal{A}_2)$ a two-stage adversary, where $\mathcal{A}_2$ has adaptive access to the Compute-oracle on legitimate queries only. Protocol Π is R-Privacy-secure if the advantage $\mathsf{Adv}^{\mathsf{R\text{-}Privacy}}_{\Pi,\mathcal{A}}(\lambda) = \Pr[1 \leftarrow \mathsf{Exp}^{\mathsf{R\text{-}Privacy}}_{\Pi,\mathcal{A}}(1^\lambda)]$ is negligible.*

Sender Privacy. This notion ensures that the polynomial f of the sender remains hidden during the protocol execution, for adaptive legitimate requests by the receiver. We indeed exclude Compute-queries that trivially help to distinguish between two functions.

Definition 3 (Sender Privacy (S-Privacy)). *Let Π be an instance of our* MyOPE *protocol and $\mathcal{A} = (\mathcal{A}_1, \mathcal{A}_2)$ a two-stage adversary, where $\mathcal{A}_2$ has adaptive access to the* Compute*-oracle on legitimate queries only. Protocol Π is* S-Privacy*-secure if the advantage $\mathsf{Adv}^{\mathsf{S\text{-}Privacy}}_{\Pi,\mathcal{A}}(\lambda) = \Pr[1 \leftarrow \mathsf{Exp}^{\mathsf{S\text{-}Privacy}}_{\Pi,\mathcal{A}}(1^\lambda)]$ is negligible.*

2.2 Building Blocks

Let us recall the generic definitions of verifiable computation to illustrate our inner-product argument and verifiable oblivious polynomial evaluation, with fully homomorphic encryption. First we will need compact binding encodings with verifiable commitments.

Verifiable Commitments. A first tool is verifiable commitments $\mathsf{Com} = (\mathsf{Setup}, \mathsf{Commit}, \mathsf{Verify}, \mathsf{Open})$ for elements in a space $\mathcal{X}$:

$\mathsf{Com.Setup}(1^\lambda) \rightarrow (\mathsf{ck}, [\mathsf{vk}])$: Given the security parameter, output the commitment key ck and possibly a secret verification key vk in case of designated-verifier proof.

$\mathsf{Com.Commit}(\mathsf{ck}, x) \rightarrow (c_x, w)$: Given the commitment key and an element $x \in \mathcal{X}$, output a commitment c_x and an opening value w.

$\mathsf{Com.Verify}(\mathsf{ck}, [\mathsf{vk}], c) \rightarrow acc$: Given the commitment key, optionally the verification key, and a commitment c, accept (with $acc = 1$) or reject (with $acc = 0$) a commitment c.

$\mathsf{Com.Open}(\mathsf{ck}, x, c, w) \rightarrow acc$: Given the commitment key, an element x, a commitment c, and the opening value w, accept (with $acc = 1$) or reject (with $acc = 0$) the commitment c for x.

The *correctness* property means that the Verify and Open algorithms accept when commitments have been honestly generated on inputs in the appropriate space $\mathcal{X}$. On the other hand, the *binding* property means that no adversary can make Verify accept on committed elements that open outside the appropriate space $\mathcal{X}$ nor make Open accept on two different values. Additionally, one may expect the *hiding* property which means that c_x does not reveal any information about x (at least computationally). We stress that the target space $\mathcal{X}$ is verified: an acceptable commitment necessarily encodes an element in $\mathcal{X}$.

rIPA: Inner Product Argument for Rings. We are first interested in the verifiable computation of inner products between committed vectors. As already noted, when there is no privacy issue, the commitment algorithm can simply be the identity function. But for efficiency reasons, we expect a more compact binding verifiable commitment to encode inputs. Then, from $\mathsf{pk}_x \leftarrow c_x$ with a commitment c_x of $\boldsymbol{x}$ (from $\mathsf{Com.Commit}(\mathsf{ck}, x)$) and $\sigma_y \leftarrow (\boldsymbol{y}, c_y)$ with a commitment c_y of $\boldsymbol{y}$, the sender generates $\sigma_z = (z, \pi)$, where π is a proof of $z = \langle \boldsymbol{x}, \boldsymbol{y} \rangle$, when c_x and c_y are valid commitments of appropriate vectors $\boldsymbol{x}$ and $\boldsymbol{y}$ (in the correct vector spaces). One may additionally expect receiver and/or sender privacy, with private $\boldsymbol{y}$ and/or $\boldsymbol{x}$.

Verifiable OPE: Oblivious Polynomial Evaluation. This is another case of VC, with a polynomial $\mathsf{f}(X) \in \mathsf{R}[X^n]$ as function, and $\mathsf{m} \in \mathsf{R}$ as evaluation point. Only $\mathsf{f}(\mathsf{m})$ is learnt by the receiver, and no other information leaks. It also ensures the computations were executed as pledged in the protocol by providing verifiability.

FHE: Fully Homomorphic Encryption. We will achieve privacy-preserving VCs using Fully Homomorphic Encryption (FHE). FHE has been introduced in [23]. This is particular case of classical public-public encryption, with a KeyGen algorithm that generates a key-pair $(\mathsf{pk}, \mathsf{sk})$ as well as encryption and decryption algorithms Enc and Dec, but with an additional Eval algorithm to operate on ciphertexts to build a ciphertext of $f((x_i)_i)$ from the ciphertexts of the x_i's. Since the initial construction, major improvements have been made, with now practical and efficient solutions. In this work we will use the Fan-Vercauteren (FV) FHE scheme [17] for our analyses, with $\mathcal{R}_t = \mathbb{Z}_t[X]/\mathsf{r}(X)$ as the plaintext message space and $\mathcal{R}_q \times \mathcal{R}_q$ as the ciphertext space, where $\mathcal{R}_q = \mathbb{Z}_q[X]/\mathsf{r}(X)$, with $\mathsf{r}(X) = X^n + 1$ for some well-chosen integer n (usually a power of 2). Semantic security relies on the Ring-LWE assumption. To enable some optimizations as the RNS representation used in SEAL, we will allow q with small prime factors on 60 bits. Detail about this FHE scheme is given in the full version [28]. We use the notation $[a]_q = a \mod q$ for $a \in \mathbb{Z}$, and, for a ring element a, $[\mathsf{a}]_q$ will represent the ring element with $[\cdot]_q$ applied to all its coefficients. Essentially, the public key is then $\mathsf{pk} = (\mathsf{p}, \mathsf{p}') = ([-(\mathsf{a} \cdot \mathsf{s} + \mathsf{e})]_q, \mathsf{a}) \in \mathcal{R}_q^2$, for random polynomials $\mathsf{a} \overset{\$}{\leftarrow} \mathcal{R}_q$, $\mathsf{s}, \mathsf{e} \leftarrow \chi$ (for χ a discrete centered Gaussian distribution in $\mathcal{R}_q$), while the secret key is $\mathsf{sk} = \mathsf{s}$. To encrypt a message $\mathsf{m} \in \mathcal{R}_t$, one computes $(\mathsf{c}, \mathsf{c}') = ([\mathsf{p} \cdot \mathsf{u} + \mathsf{e}_1 + \Delta \cdot \mathsf{m}]_q, [\mathsf{p}' \cdot \mathsf{u} + \mathsf{e}_2]_q)$ with small noises $\mathsf{u}, \mathsf{e}_1, \mathsf{e}_2 \leftarrow \chi$, where $\Delta = \lfloor q/t \rfloor$. One can see that with $\mathsf{d} = [\mathsf{c} + \mathsf{c}' \cdot \mathsf{s}]_q = [\Delta \cdot \mathsf{m} - \mathsf{e} \cdot \mathsf{u} + \mathsf{e}_2 \cdot \mathsf{s} + \mathsf{e}_1]_q = \Delta \cdot \mathsf{m} + \mathsf{v}$, with $||\mathsf{v}||$, the resulting noise vector, having a small enough norm for correct decryption, $\mathsf{m}' = [\lfloor \mathsf{d}/\Delta \rceil]_t = [\mathsf{m} + \lfloor \mathsf{v}/\Delta \rceil]_t$ leads to m, if the error term v is small enough (with an infinity norm $||\mathsf{v}||_\infty$ less than $\Delta/2$). We do not detail Eval, but for our analysis to hold, we will need the following property, in the particular case where $L = 2N$ (N being the maximal degree of our OPE polynomial), which can be guaranteed with an appropriate parameter choice, for d one less than the minimal circuit depth enabling bootstrapping:

Definition 4 **((L, d)-$\mathcal{R}_t$-Linear-Homomorphism).** *For any $\mathsf{a}_i, \mathsf{m}_i \in \mathcal{R}_t$, and some ciphertexts $(\mathsf{c}_i, \mathsf{c}_i') \in \mathcal{R}_q^2$ of m_i obtained from a circuit of multiplicative depth at most d,*

$$\mathsf{Dec}\left(\mathsf{sk}, \sum_{i=1}^{L} \mathsf{a}_i \cdot (\mathsf{c}_i, \mathsf{c}_i')\right) = \sum_{i=1}^{L} \mathsf{a}_i \cdot \mathsf{m}_i \in \mathcal{R}_t$$

2.3 Secure Encoding Schemes

Our main ingredient will be secure, or linear-only, encodings introduced by [3,21] for succinct non-interactive arguments of knowledge (SNARKs). We provide a general definition over rings. An encoding scheme over a ring R consists in a tuple of algorithms:

- $(\mathsf{pk}, \mathsf{sk}, \mathsf{vk}) \leftarrow \mathsf{Gen}(1^\lambda)$, a key generation algorithm that takes as input a security parameter and outputs public information pk, a secret key sk, and a verification key vk, that can be either public or private;
- $E \leftarrow \mathsf{E}_{\mathsf{sk}}(a)$, a (probabilistic) encoding algorithm mapping a ring element $a \in \mathsf{R}$ in the encoding space $\mathcal{E}$, using the secret key sk.

It should then satisfy a few properties:

- L-Linearly homomorphic, with an algorithm $\mathsf{Eval}_{\mathsf{pk}}$ that homomorphically combine encodings into the encoding of the same linear combination of the inputs;
- L-Quadratic root verification, with an algorithm $\mathsf{QCheck}_{\mathsf{vk}}$ that can check a quadratic relation between the encoded elements, just from the encodings;
- Image verification, with an algorithm $\mathsf{Verify}_{\mathsf{vk}}$ that check the validity of the encoding. This certifies the membership of the encoded element in the appropriate space.

According to the verification key that can be either public or private, the verification processes will be either public or private. The encoding is linearly-homomorphic, but for a *secure* encoding, one expects no one to be able to derive new valid encodings except from linear combinations, hence the *linear-only* property: any new *valid* encoding E of some $a \in \mathsf{R}$ will necessarily satisfy $a = \sum_i c_i a_i$, for extractable elements $c_i \in \mathsf{R}$. Intuitively, when an encoding E passes the verification test, one can extract the linear combination of the given initial encodings.

The above properties will be enough for a binding commitment, but additional blinding factors will be required for hiding commitments, together with zero-knowledge proofs to keep the above verifications possible, without leaking more information.

In the full version [28], we provide a more formal definition, with two illustrations. First, encodings over $\mathbb{Z}_q$, with q a prime large enough, in a pairing-friendly setting $\mathsf{pk} = (\mathbb{G}_1, \mathbb{G}_2, \mathbb{G}_T, q, g, \mathfrak{g}, e)$, using the Knowledge of Exponent Assumption [15]. If we denote $G = e(g, \mathfrak{g})$ and $\mathsf{vk} = \mathfrak{g}^\alpha$ for the secret key $\alpha \xleftarrow{\$} \mathbb{Z}_q$, the encoding function can be defined as $\mathsf{E}_{\mathsf{sk}}(a) = (g^a, g^{\alpha \cdot a}, \mathfrak{g}^a) \in \mathbb{G}_1^2 \times \mathbb{G}_2$. Image verification can be publicly done with $e(g^a, \mathfrak{g}) = e(g, \mathfrak{g}^a)$ and $e(g^a, \mathsf{vk}) = e(g^{\alpha \cdot a}, \mathfrak{g})$. It is clearly L-linearly-homomorphic for any L. The bilinear map e allows public quadratic root verification, on the elements g^a and $\mathfrak{g}^a$. To hide the content of an encoding, one just needs the encoding $E' = (g, g^\alpha, \mathfrak{g})$ of 1, multiplied by a private random factor in $\mathcal{M} = \mathbb{Z}_q$. Classical Schnorr-proof can then be applied. Such encodings just consist of three group elements (2 in $\mathbb{G}_1$ and 1 in $\mathbb{G}_2$).

We then discuss the situation where q is the product of smaller primes. Then, the hardness of discrete logarithm does not hold anymore, but one can use linear-only encryption schemes, which limit to linear combinations only. We develop more the case of the Paillier encryption scheme [34] with large RSA modulus $\mathcal{N}$. Such secure encodings just consist of two Paillier ciphertexts in $\mathbb{Z}_{\mathcal{N}^2}$ each.

We could also use a secure encoding scheme based on the Learning With Errors (LWE) problem to make the whole scheme post-quantum secure.

When the receiver has published secure encodings of successive powers $\mathsf{E}_{\mathsf{sk}}(1)$, $\mathsf{E}_{\mathsf{sk}}(s), \ldots, \mathsf{E}_{\mathsf{sk}}(s^{n-1})$, for a random secret point s, the sender can only generate valid commitments of polynomials f of degree at most $n-1$, as $\mathsf{E}_{\mathsf{sk}}(\mathsf{f}(s))$, thanks to the linear property of the encoding and the image verification. Quadratic root verification allows the sender to verify any quadratic relations between polynomials committed by the sender. Note that the initial secure encodings of successive powers can either be generated by a trusted third party, when using the above pairing-based secure encodings that are publicly verifiable, or by the receiver when using a linear-only encryption scheme.

In the body of the paper, for the sake of clarity, hiding commitments and zero-knowledge proofs will be ignored, as their computational and communication impacts are minimal, since they only deal with few scalars.

3 Verifiable Commitments

A major contribution of this paper is the construction of commitments of multivariate polynomials over rings so that succinct proofs can later be described. This is in the same vein as in [18], but the latter is only defined for secure encodings based in pairings, whereas we describe here the construction from any secure encodings. With a linear-only encryption scheme, they will not be publicly verifiable anymore, but this will be useful to build compact commitments of polynomials over $\mathbb{Z}_q$ in 2PC protocols, whatever the integer q (large prime or composite).

We provide here the intuition of our approach for polynomials in $\mathcal{R}_1 = \mathbb{Z}_q[X^{n-1}]$ (polynomials of degree at most $n-1$), while more polynomial spaces will be used in the global protocol. We stress again that commitments are specific to a space $\mathcal{X}$ and when valid they ensure the committed element actually lies in $\mathcal{X}$. The verifier first generates secure encodings $E_i \leftarrow \mathsf{E}_{\mathsf{sk}}(s^i)$, for $i \in [\![0; n-1]\!]$ and a random secret element $s \stackrel{\$}{\leftarrow} \mathbb{Z}_q^*$. Thanks to the linear-only extractability, when a player generates a valid encoding E, being only given $(E_0, \ldots, E_{n-1})$, one can extract (c_i) such that E is an encoding of $c_0 + c_1 s + \ldots c_{n-1} s^{n-1}$ in $\mathbb{Z}_q$, and thus of the polynomial $\mathsf{c} = \sum_i c_i X^i$ in $\mathcal{R}_1$. The encoding E is thus a commitment of $\mathsf{c} \in \mathcal{R}_1$: the list of initial encodings E_i specifies a basis of the exact space $\mathcal{X}$ we target. Here, $\mathcal{R}_1$ is spanned by $(1, X, \ldots, X^{n-1})$ in $\mathbb{Z}_q$.

In addition, thanks to the quadratic verification on the encodings, if we have four polynomials u, v, m and r such that $\mathsf{m} = \mathsf{u} \cdot \mathsf{v} \bmod \mathsf{r}$, which means that $\mathsf{m} = \mathsf{u} \cdot \mathsf{v} + \mathsf{r} \cdot \mathsf{q}$ for some polynomial q, where all the polynomials are of degree at most $n-1$, we can check such a product: from valid commitments U and V of u and v, R and Q of r and q, respectively, and M of the polynomial m, all of degree at most $n-1$, as they are all simple encodings, $\mathsf{QCheck}_{\mathsf{vk}}(X_1 X_2 + X_3 X_4 - X_5, U, V, R, Q, M) = \mathsf{true}$ implies that $\mathsf{m}(s) = \mathsf{u}(s) \cdot \mathsf{v}(s) + \mathsf{r}(s) \cdot \mathsf{q}(s)$.

Under the Schwartz-Zippel lemma, if q is a large prime, the probability to have this equality in a random point $s \in \mathbb{Z}_q$ whereas $\mathsf{m} \neq \mathsf{u} \cdot \mathsf{v} + \mathsf{r} \cdot \mathsf{q}$ in $\mathbb{Z}_q[X]$ is bounded by $2n/q$, as the total degree of the relation is at most $2n$. Hence, the probability over s to have a false positive is bounded by $2n/q$. This is negligible in the large prime case but if we want to use RNS optimizations when computing modulo q, we need to take q a product of primes, and will hence need more repetitions with probability bounds stated by the Schwartz-Zippel lemma. Detail about this case is given in the full version [28], along with a complete description of binding and hiding polynomial commitments, for univariate and bivariate polynomials, with multiple evaluation points when necessary.

4 Inner Product Arguments

4.1 Description of Our Ring-IPA

Our main tool is verifiable computation of inner products, from commitments on vectors, in various structures. To this aim, we convert vectors in polynomials to commit them as explained above. We stress that for the moment, we do not consider privacy, nor FHE ciphertexts, but just vectors in clear.

To start off, let us consider vectors in a field $\mathbb{Z}_q$ (with a prime q). We will extend our method to the case where q is a product of primes, and $\mathbb{Z}_q$ a ring, in the full version [28], adding necessary repetitions. To commit such vectors, we will consider them as coefficients of a polynomial, and then commit the corresponding polynomials, as above. Let us consider $\mathsf{A} = (a_0, \dots, a_N)$ and $\mathsf{B} = (b_0, \dots, b_N)$ in $\mathbb{Z}_q^{N+1}$ (equivalent to $\mathcal{R}_3 = \mathbb{Z}_q[Y^N]$, as defined in the full version [28]), two vectors whose inner-product is equal to $c = \langle \mathsf{A}, \mathsf{B} \rangle$ in $\mathbb{Z}_q$. As explained in Sect. 1.4, the commitments $\bar{A}$ of A and B of B with secure encodings are $\bar{A} = \bar{\mathsf{a}}(s)$ and $B = \mathsf{b}(s)$ for the polynomials $\bar{\mathsf{a}}(Y) = \sum_{j=0}^{N} a_j Y^{N-j}$ and $\mathsf{b}(Y) = \sum_{j=0}^{N} b_j Y^j$ in $\mathcal{R}_3$. Note that coefficients of A are set into $\bar{\mathsf{a}}$ in a reversed order:

$$\bar{\mathsf{a}}(Y) \cdot \mathsf{b}(Y) = \sum_{i,j=0}^{N} a_i b_j \cdot Y^{N+j-i} = \sum_{j=0}^{N} a_j b_j Y^N + \sum_{0 \le i \ne j \le N} a_i b_j Y^{N+j-i}.$$

Let us define the polynomial $\mathsf{d}(Y) = \bar{\mathsf{a}}(Y) \cdot \mathsf{b}(Y) - cY^N$ of degree at most $2N$. If c is correct, d is in the subspace $\mathcal{R}_4 = \mathbb{Z}_q[Y^{2N \setminus N}]$ (the polynomials of degree at most $2N$, without monomial of degree N). By publishing a commitment D of d, that is verifiably in $\mathcal{R}_4$, one can verify the above quadratic relation, using $\bar{A}$, B, c, and D, and get convinced of the inner product value c. The proof of correct computation of $c = \langle \mathsf{A}, \mathsf{B} \rangle$ with respect to the given commitments $\bar{A}$ and B just consists of $\pi = \{D\}$ (1 commitment only), and the verification consists in checking the validity of the commitments and one quadratic relation.

Inner-Product Arguments Algorithms. More generally, one can define rIPA scheme on vectors $\mathsf{A}, \mathsf{B} \in \mathcal{X}^{N+1}$ and the result $c = \langle \mathsf{A}, \mathsf{B} \rangle$ in a space $\mathcal{X}$ for which $\mathcal{X}^{N+1}$ has either vectorial space (when $\mathcal{X}$ is a field) or module (when $\mathcal{X}$ is a ring) structure:

$\mathsf{rIPA.Setup}(1^\lambda)$ generates the verifiable commitment keys for the acceptable bases for $\mathcal{R}_3$ and $\mathcal{R}_4$ in PK to allow verifying commitments in these spaces. According to the encoding, verification will need SK or not;

$\mathsf{rIPA.KeyGen}(\mathsf{PK}, \mathsf{A})$, from a vector A, outputs $\bar{A}$, a commitment of A (in the reverse order) using the commitment scheme Com;

$\mathsf{rIPA.QueryGen}(\mathsf{PK}, \mathsf{B})$, from a vector B, outputs (B, B), where B is a commitment of B;

$\mathsf{rIPA.Compute}(\mathsf{PK}, \mathsf{A}, (\mathsf{B}, B))$, from the two vectors A and B, outputs $c = \langle \mathsf{A}, \mathsf{B} \rangle$ and $\pi = \{D\}$ (where D is a commitment of d, as defined above);

$\mathsf{rIPA.Verify}(\mathsf{PK}, [\mathsf{SK}], \bar{A}, B, (c, \pi))$, with $\pi = \{D\}$, checks the relation $\mathsf{d}(Y) = \mathsf{a}(Y) \cdot \mathsf{b}(Y) - c \cdot Y^N$ from $\bar{A}$, B, D and c.

Since there is no privacy in this protocol, $\mathsf{rIPA.Compute}$ directly outputs the result $c = \langle \mathsf{A}, \mathsf{B} \rangle$: there is no need of private $\mathsf{rIPA.Decode}$.

Polynomial Evaluation. It can be turned into a polynomial evaluation $y = P(x)$, with one vector A containing the coefficients of P and the other vector B built from the powers of x, and the expected inner product being y.

Infinity Norm Evaluation. It also provides a setting to compute the L_2-norm $\|\mathsf{e}\|_2$, of $\mathsf{e} \in \mathbb{Z}_q[X^{n-1}]$, as $\|\mathsf{e}\|_2^2 = \langle \mathsf{E}, \mathsf{E} \rangle$, for the vector E of the polynomial's coefficients. This leads to an approximation of the infinity norm with $\|\mathsf{e}\|_\infty \leq \|\mathsf{e}\|_2 \leq \sqrt{n} \cdot \|\mathsf{e}\|_\infty \leq \sqrt{n} \cdot \|\mathsf{e}\|_2$. One just needs $E = \mathsf{e}(s)$ and $\bar{E} = \bar{\mathsf{e}}(s)$, where

$$\mathsf{e}(X) = \sum_0^{n-1} e_i X^i \qquad \bar{\mathsf{e}}(X) = \sum_0^{n-1} e_i X^{n-1-i} = X^{n-1} \cdot \mathsf{e}(1/X)$$

which can be verified with the existence, for a random challenge $\beta \xleftarrow{\$} \mathbb{Z}_q^*$, of polynomials e' and $\bar{\mathsf{e}}'$ that satisfy, with $e = \mathsf{e}(1/\beta)$,

$$\mathsf{e}(X) - e = \mathsf{e}(X) - \mathsf{e}(1/\beta) = (X - 1/\beta) \cdot \mathsf{e}'(X)$$
$$\bar{\mathsf{e}}(X) - \beta^{n-1} \cdot e = \bar{\mathsf{e}}(X) - \beta^{n-1} \cdot \mathsf{e}(1/\beta) = \bar{\mathsf{e}}(X) - \bar{\mathsf{e}}(\beta) = (X - \beta) \cdot \mathsf{e}''(X).$$

Indeed, as e and $\bar{\mathsf{e}}$ have been committed in E and $\bar{E}$ before the random choice of β, the first equation guarantees that $e = \mathsf{e}(1/\beta)$ while the second equation guarantees $\bar{\mathsf{e}}(\beta) = \beta^{n-1} e = \beta^{n-1} \mathsf{e}(1/\beta)$. The Schwartz-Zippel lemma ensures that the polynomials e and $\bar{\mathsf{e}}$, of degree $n-1$, satisfy with high probability $\bar{\mathsf{e}}(X) = X^{n-1} \mathsf{e}(1/X)$: $\bar{\mathsf{e}}$ is indeed e with order of coefficients reversed. From the commitment E of e and the result $\|\mathsf{e}\|_2$ to be proven (or a commitment of it), the proof consists of the commitments $E' = \mathsf{e}'(s)$ and $E'' = \mathsf{e}''(s)$ (to verify the two above equations), plus the inner-product proof (with the commitment D as above) with the additional commitment $\bar{E}$ and the scalar e. The validity of the proof requires the verification of the validity of the commitments and three quadratic relations (the two above, and the one for the inner product). For strong privacy, one can first commit the scalar $\|\mathsf{e}\|_2^2$, prove the correct computation of this hidden value with the above approach, and then perform a zero-knowledge range proof for the committed value, to show it is of appropriate size.

4.2 Inner Product Arguments with Privacy

If we now consider vectors $\mathsf{A} = (\mathsf{a}_0, \ldots, \mathsf{a}_N)$ and $\mathsf{B} = (\mathsf{b}_0, \ldots, \mathsf{b}_N)$ in $\mathcal{R}_t^{N+1}$, where $\mathcal{R}_t = \mathbb{Z}_t[X]/\mathsf{r}(X)$, they can be committed with bivariate polynomials in $\mathbb{Z}_t[X, Y]$, using secure encodings with monomials $s^i s'^j$: $\bar{A} = \bar{\mathsf{a}}(s, s')$ and $B = \mathsf{b}(s, s')$, where $\bar{\mathsf{a}}(X, Y) = \sum_{i=0}^{n-1} \sum_{j=0}^{N} a_{j,i} X^i Y^{N-j}$ and $\mathsf{b}(X, Y) = \sum_{i=0}^{n-1} \sum_{j=0}^{N} b_{j,i} X^i Y^j$. One can get $\mathsf{p} = \langle \mathsf{A}, \mathsf{B} \rangle \in \mathcal{R}_t$. If one wants to keep vector B private, the latter can be encrypted with the FV FHE scheme, in $(\mathsf{c}_i, \mathsf{c}'_i) \in \mathcal{R}_q \times \mathcal{R}_q$, for $i = 0, \ldots, N$. Thanks to the linear-homomorphism of the FHE, $\mathsf{Dec}(\langle \mathsf{A}, \mathsf{C} \rangle, \langle \mathsf{A}, \mathsf{C}' \rangle) = \langle \mathsf{A}, \mathsf{B} \rangle$, where $\mathsf{C} = (\mathsf{c}_0, \ldots, \mathsf{c}_N)$ and $\mathsf{C}' = (\mathsf{c}'_0, \ldots, \mathsf{c}'_N)$ are in $\mathcal{R}_q^{N+1}$ (equivalent to $\mathcal{R}_2 = \mathbb{Z}_q[X^{n-1}, Y^N]$, as denoted in the full version [28]). One now needs the verifiability of $\langle \mathsf{A}, \mathsf{C} \rangle$ and $\langle \mathsf{A}, \mathsf{C}' \rangle$ in $\mathcal{R}_q$: we consider $\mathsf{A} = (\mathsf{a}_0, \ldots, \mathsf{a}_N) \in \mathcal{R}_t^{N+1}$ and $\mathsf{C} = (\mathsf{c}_0, \ldots, \mathsf{c}_N) \in \mathcal{R}_q^{N+1}$, and we want to compute $\mathsf{d} = \langle \mathsf{A}, \mathsf{C} \rangle \in \mathcal{R}_q$ and prove it. One can similarly operate to compute and prove $\mathsf{d}' = \langle \mathsf{A}, \mathsf{C}' \rangle$.

We set both polynomials in $\mathcal{R}_2 = \mathbb{Z}_q[X^{n-1}, Y^N]$,

$$\bar{\mathsf{a}}(X, Y) = \sum_{i=0}^{n-1} \sum_{j=0}^{N} a_{j,i} X^i Y^{N-j} \qquad \mathsf{c}(X, Y) = \sum_{i=0}^{n-1} \sum_{j=0}^{N} c_{j,i} X^i Y^j.$$

They are committed as $\bar{A} = \bar{\mathsf{a}}(s, s')$ and $C = \mathsf{c}(s, s')$. The result of the inner product $\mathsf{d} \in \mathcal{R}_q$ is committed into D. However, in $\mathbb{Z}_q[X]$, the result of the inner product is equal to $\mathsf{d} + \mathsf{q} \cdot \mathsf{r}$, where r is the public quotient polynomial in rings $\mathcal{R}_t$ and $\mathcal{R}_q$, and q is the quotient, committed into Q. We want to prove $\langle \mathsf{A}, \mathsf{C} \rangle = \mathsf{d} + \mathsf{q} \cdot \mathsf{r}$ in $\mathbb{Z}_q[X]$.

Then, for a random scalar $\sigma \in \mathbb{Z}_q$, one has the following relations, with $\bar{\mathsf{a}}'(Y) = \bar{\mathsf{a}}(\sigma, Y)$ and $\mathsf{c}'(Y) = \mathsf{c}(\sigma, Y)$, committed into $\bar{A}', C'$,

$$\bar{\mathsf{a}}(X, Y) - \bar{\mathsf{a}}'(Y) = (X - \sigma) \cdot \bar{\mathsf{a}}''(X, Y) \quad \mathsf{c}(X, Y) - \mathsf{c}'(Y) = (X - \sigma) \cdot \mathsf{c}''(X, Y)$$

for some polynomials $\bar{\mathsf{a}}''$ and c'' that can be computed from $\bar{\mathsf{a}}, \bar{\mathsf{a}}', \mathsf{c}, \mathsf{c}'$ and committed into $\bar{A}'', C''$, as well as the polynomial $X - \sigma$, so the receiver can check the above quadratic relations. Then, we also have

$$\bar{\mathsf{a}}'(Y) \cdot \mathsf{c}'(Y) = \sum_{j=0}^{N} a'_j \cdot c'_j \cdot Y^N + \sum_{0 \le i \ne j \le N} a'_i \cdot c'_j \cdot Y^{N+j-i}$$

$$\text{and} \sum_{j=0}^{N} a'_j \cdot c'_j = \sum_{j=0}^{N} \mathsf{a}_j(\sigma) \cdot \mathsf{c}_j(\sigma) = \mathsf{d}(\sigma) + \mathsf{q}(\sigma) \cdot \mathsf{r}(\sigma)$$

Setting $\delta = \mathsf{d}(\sigma)$, $\phi = \mathsf{q}(\sigma)$ and $\rho = \mathsf{r}(\sigma)$, the values can be sent and checked with respect to d, Q, and r, as $\mathsf{q}(X) - \phi = (X - \sigma) \cdot \mathsf{q}'(X)$. If we additionally set $\mathsf{e}(Y) = \bar{\mathsf{a}}'(Y) \cdot \mathsf{c}'(Y) - (\delta + \phi \cdot \rho) \cdot Y^N$, committed in E, by proving it relies in $\mathcal{R}_4 = \mathbb{Z}_q[Y^{2N \setminus N}]$, this proves the result d of the inner product in $\mathcal{R}_q$.

The proof of correct computation of $\mathsf{d} = \langle \mathsf{A}, \mathsf{C} \rangle$ in $\mathcal{R}_q$, with respect to the given commitments $\bar{A}$ and C just consists of $\pi = \{Q, Q', \bar{A}', \bar{A}'', C', C'', E, \phi\}$ (7 commitments and a scalar), for publicly generated or computed σ, δ and ρ, and the verification consists in checking the validity of the commitments and four quadratic relations. The same is needed for $\mathsf{d}' = \langle \mathsf{A}, \mathsf{C}' \rangle$. By then decrypting $(\mathsf{d}, \mathsf{d}')$ one should get $\mathsf{p} = \langle \mathsf{A}, \mathsf{B} \rangle \in \mathcal{R}_t$.

Inner-Product Arguments with Privacy. More formally, we can define a inner products argument with privacy for one of the vectors rIPAwP. Given vectors A, B in the ring $\mathcal{R}_t^{N+1}$ we prove the correctness of their inner product result $\mathsf{p} \in \mathcal{R}_t$, while keeping B private:

rIPAwP.Setup(1^λ) generates the parameters for the FV FHE with plaintext space $\mathcal{R}_t$ and cyphertext space $\mathcal{R}_q$. The secure encodings on the acceptable bases for $\mathcal{R}_1$, $\mathcal{R}_2$ and $\mathcal{R}_4$ with the FHE encryption key are put in PK to allow encryption and evaluations on ciphertexts, as well as the generation of commitments in these spaces. The verification key of the secure encodings (if needed) and the FHE decryption key are put in SK;

rIPAwP.KeyGen(PK, A), from a vector A, outputs $\bar{A}$, a commitment of A (in the reverse order);

rIPAwP.QueryGen(PK, B), from a vector B, outputs $((\mathsf{C}, \mathsf{C}'), (C, C'))$, where in $\mathsf{C} = (\mathsf{c}_i)_i$, $\mathsf{C}' = (\mathsf{c}'_i)_i$ with $(\mathsf{c}_i, \mathsf{c}'_i)$ the ciphertext of b_i, for $i = 0, \ldots, N$, and then C, C' the commitment of C and C′ respectively;

rIPAwP.Compute(PK, A, $(\mathsf{C}, \mathsf{C}', C, C')$), from the two pairs of vectors (A, C) and (A, C′), outputs $\mathsf{d} = \langle \mathsf{A}, \mathsf{C} \rangle$ and $\mathsf{d}' = \langle \mathsf{A}, \mathsf{C}' \rangle$ and π, for proving the correct inner-product evaluations;

rIPAwP.Verify(PK, [SK], $\bar{A}$, (C, C'), $(\mathsf{d}, \mathsf{d}', \pi)$), checks the proof π from the initial commitments $\bar{A}$, (C, C') and the additional ones in π;

rIPAwP.Decode(SK, $(\mathsf{d}, \mathsf{d}', \pi)$), from the FHE decryption key, decrypts the pair $(\mathsf{d}, \mathsf{d}')$ to get $\mathsf{p} = \langle \mathsf{A}, \mathsf{B} \rangle$.

In this case, rIPAwP.Compute outputs an encryption of the expected result, hence the need of the private rIPAwP.Decode. We used again the Schwartz-Zippel lemma to translate equalities between evaluated polynomials into equalities between polynomials, based on the unpredictability of σ. But according to q (large prime or product of smaller primes), one may reduce the bad cases by using multiple σ_κ's.

4.3 Verifiability of the Committed Ciphertext

As already explained in the overall description of our protocol in Sect. 1.4, before verifying the correct inner products $\mathsf{d} = \langle \mathsf{A}, \mathsf{C} \rangle$ and $\mathsf{d}' = \langle \mathsf{A}, \mathsf{C}' \rangle$ and decrypt the pair $(\mathsf{d}, \mathsf{d}')$ to get $\langle \mathsf{A}, \mathsf{B} \rangle$, one may want to be sure that each $(\mathsf{c}_i, \mathsf{c}'_i)$, ciphertext that would decrypt to m_i, is actually a correct encryption of m^i in $\mathcal{R}_t$. This means that B should be the vector $(\mathsf{m}^0, \ldots, \mathsf{m}^N)$ in $\mathcal{R}_t^{N+1}$. Indeed, the sender receives an encryption of m (and possibly some additional information) and generates the vectors C and C′ thanks to the linearity of the FHE scheme. Why would they be honest?

To verify that, we use the above inner-product proof between each vector of ciphertexts $\mathsf{C} = (\mathsf{c}_0, \ldots, \mathsf{c}_N)$ or $\mathsf{C}' = (\mathsf{c}'_0, \ldots, \mathsf{c}'_N)$ and a vector of powers

$\mathsf{N} = (\mathsf{n}^0, \mathsf{n}^1, \ldots, \mathsf{n}^N)$ derived from a public random $\mathsf{n} \in \mathcal{R}_t$ drawn by the verifier (or generated from a hash). Neither of these vectors need to be kept private as they are generated from information both parties have.

Let $\mathsf{u} = \langle \mathsf{N}, \mathsf{C} \rangle$ and $\mathsf{u}' = \langle \mathsf{N}, \mathsf{C}' \rangle$ be the results of the inner products in $\mathcal{R}_q$, proven as above (with 12 commitments and 2 scalars, and 8 quadratic relations to check). From the linear-homomorphism of the FHE, with appropriate parameters, $\mathsf{Dec}(\mathsf{u}, \mathsf{u}') = \sum_{j=0}^{N} \mathsf{n}^j \cdot \mathsf{m}_j$. The verifier checks this decryption is $\sum_{j=0}^{N} \mathsf{n}^j \cdot \mathsf{m}^j$, with appropriate error (bounded as expected). This leads to $\sum_{j=0}^{N} \mathsf{n}^j \cdot \mathsf{m}_j = \sum_{j=0}^{N} \mathsf{n}^j \cdot \mathsf{m}^j$ in $\mathcal{R}_t$. Note that $\mathcal{R}_t$ is unfortunately not a field, but possibly a ring that is the product of large fields only: $\mathsf{r} = X^{2^k} + 1$ is not irreducible in any $\mathbb{Z}_t[X]$ for a prime t, but for well-chosen prime, all the factors of $X^n + 1$ may have large degrees in $\mathbb{Z}_t[X]$: according to [4], with $t+1 = 2^\alpha(2\tau+1)$, for any integer τ, $\alpha \geq 2$, and $n = 2^k$, then all the factors of $X^{2^k} + 1$ have degree $2^{k+1-\alpha}$. If one chooses $t = 3 \bmod 8$, $\alpha = 2$, and in particular $t = 3$ (with $\tau = 0$), there are just two irreducible factors of degree $2^{k-1} = n/2$ in $\mathbb{Z}_t[X]$: the above polynomial thus has all zero coefficients by the Schwartz-Zippel lemma, excepted with probability $2N/t^{n/2}$, as the polynomial is of degree N and n is randomly chosen among $t^{n/2}$ possible values in each of the two fields. Hence, $\mathsf{m}_i = \mathsf{m}^i$ in $\mathcal{R}_t$, excepted with probability bounded by $2N/t^{n/2}$, which is clearly negligible. Note that one cannot use $t = 2$ as $\mathsf{r}(X) = X^n + 1$ is divisible by $X + 1$ in $\mathbb{Z}_2[X]$.

By checking the noise in $(\mathsf{u}, \mathsf{u}')$, as expected with reasonable margin, as one knows the expected plaintext, one gets an upper-bound on individual errors. Even if this might be larger than initially expected, one can guarantee appropriate noise in the $(\mathsf{c}_i, \mathsf{c}'_i)$'s to satisfy the linear-homomorphism, as we will take additional margin to take care of the noise-flooding. If the sender tries to cheat with larger noise in the $(\mathsf{c}_i, \mathsf{c}'_i)$'s, they may reduce the privacy impact of the noise-flooding. But soundness remains guaranteed.

5 Verifiable OPE with Privacy

We now have the tools to allow the receiver/verifier with their private input message m to learn in a verifiable way the inner product of the vector $\mathsf{M} = (\mathsf{m}^j)_j$ with a private vector $\mathsf{F} = (\mathsf{f}_j)_j$, for indices j in $[\![0; N]\!]$, both committed by the sender/prover.

5.1 Complete Protocol

More details and more applications are provided in the full version [28], but we sketch here a full verifiable OPE protocol, where we assume all the global parameters set, and the sender's polynomial $\mathsf{F} = (\mathsf{f}_j)_j$ committed in a hiding way in $\bar{F}$. Once the receiver has encrypted the input $\mathsf{m} \in \mathcal{R}_t$ under their own FHE key and sent $\mathsf{Enc}(\mathsf{m}) = (\mathsf{c}, \mathsf{c}') \in \mathcal{R}_q^2$ to the sender, the latter

- computes the $(\mathsf{u}_j, \mathsf{u}'_j) = \mathsf{Enc}(\mathsf{m}^j)$, for $j \in [\![0; N]\!]$, from $(\mathsf{c}, \mathsf{c}')$ thanks to the homomorphic properties of the encryption scheme; generates the vectors $\mathsf{U} =$

(u_j) and $\mathsf{U}' = (\mathsf{u}'_j)$ as well as their commitments U and U'; and provides a proof of valid computation of the inner products $\mathsf{b} = \langle \mathsf{N}, \mathsf{U} \rangle$ and $\mathsf{b}' = \langle \mathsf{N}, \mathsf{U}' \rangle$, for a common vector $\mathsf{N} = (\mathsf{n}^j)_j$ for a random $\mathsf{n} \xleftarrow{\$} \mathcal{R}_t$ (chosen with a random hash function on the previous information), with respect to the commitments U, U': ignoring scalars, the proof consists of 12 commitments (to be sent and checked), the ciphertext $(\mathsf{b}, \mathsf{b}')$, and 6 quadratic relations to be verified;
- generates a zero-ciphertext $(\mathsf{z}, \mathsf{z}')$ with a proof of small norm of the error, and provides a proof of valid computation of the noisy inner products $\mathsf{d} + \mathsf{z}$ and $\mathsf{d}' + \mathsf{z}'$, where $\mathsf{d} = \langle \mathsf{F}, \mathsf{U} \rangle$ and $\mathsf{d}' = \langle \mathsf{F}, \mathsf{U}' \rangle$, with respect to the commitments $\bar{F}, U, U'$: the proof consists of 9 new commitments (and also the original commitment of the polynomial) (to be sent and checked) and 5 quadratic relations to be verified, along with the result $(\mathsf{d}, \mathsf{d}')$, once the noise-flooding has been proven. The latter consists of 15 commitments (to be sent and checked) and 9 quadratic relations to be verified;

By first verifying $\mathsf{Dec}(\mathsf{b}, \mathsf{b}') = \sum (\mathsf{nm})^j$ and the appropriate noise, the receiver gets convinced (U, U') commits to correct encryptions of the powers m^j. Then, with the verification of the inner products and the small noise, one gets the guarantee that $\mathsf{Dec}(\mathsf{d} + \mathsf{z}, \mathsf{d}' + \mathsf{z}') = \langle \mathsf{F}, \mathsf{M} \rangle = \mathsf{F}(\mathsf{m})$. As there are common commitments in the successive phases and one actually considers the noise components of $(\mathsf{z}^*, \mathsf{z}'^*)$ instead of these directly in practical applications, the global proof consists of 33 commitments and the verification checks them plus 20 quadratic relations (ignoring scalars and zero-knowledge proofs on scalars), as shown in the full version [28]. This is thus independent of the degree of the polynomials.

5.2 Security Remarks

The soundness of this protocol is guaranteed by the proofs of valid computations of inner products, first to ensure the content of the commitments U and U' (with 2 inner products), and then to convince of the correct computation of the ciphertext $(\mathsf{d}+\mathsf{z}, \mathsf{d}'+\mathsf{z}')$ (with 2 inner products). The small additional noise $(\mathsf{z}, \mathsf{z}')$ is also proven by inner products to bound the infinity norms of the 3 polynomials $\mathsf{u}, \mathsf{e}_1, \mathsf{e}_2$ involved in $(\mathsf{z}, \mathsf{z}') = (\mathsf{p} \cdot \mathsf{u} + \mathsf{e}_1 \bmod q, \mathsf{p}' \cdot \mathsf{u} + \mathsf{e}_2 \bmod q)$, and proven with linear relations:

Theorem 5. *Our MyOPE scheme is* SND*-secure against malicious adversaries (see Definition 1), under the security of the secure encoding (and namely the quadratic root verification and the image verification properties).*

The complete proof is provided in the full version [28], together with the analysis of the privacy properties, as stated in Definitions 2 and 3. First, the receiver's privacy is ensured by the semantic security of the FHE encryption of m that protects its input. This is a computational security, under the Ring-LWE assumption. Second, the sender's privacy is guaranteed by the hiding commitment $\bar{F}$ and the noise $(\mathsf{z}, \mathsf{z}')$ that hides the evaluated circuit. They both provide statistical privacy to the sender.

For a non-interactive proof, the random elements chosen by the receiver can be generated by a hash function, using the Fiat-Shamir paradigm. Then, the security holds in the random oracle model.

5.3 FHE Security Analysis

Semantic Security. [17] gives us a condition in the relationship between parameters q, σ, n that will grant us the security relying on the difficulty of the RLWE problem. For a fixed root-Hermite factor δ, which we take such that $\log_2(\delta) = 1.8/(\lambda + 110)$, where λ is the security parameter, that we will take equal to $\lambda = 128$ in our applications, and if ε is the advantage of the distinguishing attack in [32], which we take equal to $\varepsilon = 2^{-64}$ for a corresponding $\lambda = 128$ in applications, and $\alpha = \sqrt{\ln(1/\varepsilon)/\pi}$ ($\varepsilon = 2^{-64}$ leads to $\alpha \approx 3.758$), we then have the condition:

$$\alpha \cdot \frac{q}{\sigma} < 2^{2\sqrt{n \log_2(q) \log_2(\delta)}}. \tag{1}$$

So that a parameter n can be derived from a (q, σ) pair and reciprocally. In particular, taking $\sigma = \alpha q = \sqrt{n}$ meets the above condition, thus granting the asymptotic security. For the practical security, in order to grant privacy with specific parameter sets, we will use [1]'s estimator, with results shown in Fig. 3.

Correctness. We now study the parameters needed for the correctness of the computations on FV ciphertexts.

Correctness for Basic FV. From [17], assuming χ is B-bounded, we find that the decryption of ciphertexts obtained from a d-depth circuit of somewhat homomorphic operations will be correct if d verifies: $4\beta(\epsilon)\delta_{\mathcal{R}}^{d} \cdot (\delta_{\mathcal{R}} + 1.25)^{d+1} \cdot t^{d-1} < \frac{q}{\sigma}$, where $\beta(\epsilon)$ is drawn from the security parameter for [32]'s distinguishing attack ϵ, taken equal to $\epsilon = 2^{-64}$ when $\lambda = 128$ which yields $\beta(\epsilon) \approx 9.2$. For a cyclotomic polynomial r in $\mathcal{R}$, the above becomes:

$$4\beta(\epsilon)n^{d} \cdot (n + 1.25)^{d+1} \cdot t^{d-1} < \frac{q}{\sigma} \tag{2}$$

Which gives an upper bound on d. Then, if we want full FHE capabilities from bootstrapping, [17], we will need the minimum allowed circuit depth d_{min} to verify the above equation, where $d_{\text{min}} = d_{\text{bs}} + 1$ (where d_{bs} is the depth of the bootstrapping operation) is given in [17]'s third theorem to have full FHE bootstrapping capacities with the condition: $d_{\text{min}} \geq \mathsf{BitSize}(\lceil \nu \cdot t \rceil) + \mathsf{HammingWeight}(t) + 2$, with $\nu = \gamma \cdot (H(\mathsf{r}) \cdot h + 1)$ with $2 < \gamma < 3$, $H(\mathsf{r}) = 1$ for r a cyclotomic polynomial, and h the hamming weight of the FV scheme's secret key s, for which we can take $h = 63$ according to [17]. Taking some margin on h, that we can consider as high as $h = 169$ for better security, with $t = 3$ in our scheme, and using a cyclotomic polynomial ring, we can thus take $d_{\text{min}} = 12$. Replacing relation (1) in Eq. (2), with a security parameter $\lambda = 128$, $\beta(\epsilon) \approx 9.2$, $\alpha \approx 3.8$, $t = 3$, we find the relation: $4\alpha \cdot \beta(\epsilon) \cdot \delta_{\mathcal{R}}^{d_{\text{min}}}(\delta_{\mathcal{R}} + 1.25)^{d_{\text{min}}+1} t^{d_{\text{min}}-1} < 2^{2\sqrt{n \log_2(q) \log_2(\delta)}}$ is verified with: $25 + 25\log_2(n) < 0.1743 \cdot \sqrt{n \log_2(q)}$. So if we choose $n = 2^{14}$, then FHE capabilities will be granted with q on 283 bits or more.

Correctness with $2N$-Linearity. Then, as we also want to be able to perform $L = 2N$ additions (N being the public degree of the sender's polynomial) on

FV ciphertexts without additional bootstrapping in our protocol, we need to check that the error growth they give on bootstrapped ciphertexts still allows decryption. In a nutshell, we will need the $(L, d_{\text{min}}-1)$-$\mathcal{R}_t$ linear homomorphism property: $\mathsf{Dec}\left(\sum_{i=1}^{L} \mathsf{a}_i \cdot (\mathsf{c}_i, \mathsf{c}'_i)\right) = \sum_{i=1}^{L} \mathsf{a}_i \cdot \mathsf{m}_i$ for any $\mathsf{a}_i \in \mathcal{R}_t$ and ciphertexts $(\mathsf{c}_i, \mathsf{c}'_i) \in \mathcal{R}_q^2$ generated with a circuit of multiplicative depth $d_{\text{min}} - 1$ (applying the bootstrapping operation), encrypting $\mathsf{m}_i \in \mathcal{R}_t$.

In order to decrypt the linear combination, we compute: $\left[\sum_{i=1}^{L} \mathsf{a}_i \cdot \mathsf{c}_i + \mathsf{s} \cdot \sum_{i=1}^{L} \mathsf{a}_i \cdot \mathsf{c}'_i\right]_q = \left[\sum_{i=1}^{L} \mathsf{a}_i \left(\mathsf{c}_i + \mathsf{s} \cdot \mathsf{c}'_i\right)\right]_q = \left[\sum_{i=1}^{L} \mathsf{a}_i (\Delta \cdot \mathsf{m}_i + \mathsf{v}_i)\right]_q = \left[\Delta \cdot \sum_{i=1}^{L} \mathsf{a}_i \cdot \mathsf{m}_i + \sum_{i=1}^{L} \mathsf{a}_i \cdot \mathsf{v}_i\right]_q$, where each v_i is the noise contained on the bootstrapped ciphertext $(\mathsf{c}_i, \mathsf{c}'_i)$, of infinite norm bounded by $2\beta(\epsilon)\sigma \cdot \delta_{\mathcal{R}}^{d_{\text{min}}-1} \cdot (\delta_{\mathcal{R}} + 1.25)^{d_{\text{min}}} \cdot t^{d_{\text{min}}-3}$.

The decryption will be correct if:

$$\|\sum_{i=1}^{L} \mathsf{a}_i \cdot \mathsf{v}_i\|_\infty \le \sum_{i=1}^{L} n\|\mathsf{a}_i\|_\infty \cdot \|\mathsf{v}_i\|_\infty \le nt \sum_{i=1}^{L} \|\mathsf{v}_i\|_\infty \le ntL\|\mathsf{v}\|_\infty \le \Delta/2,$$

for a noise bounded by $\|\mathsf{v}\|_\infty \le 2\beta(\epsilon)\sigma \cdot \delta_{\mathcal{R}}^{d_{\text{min}}-1} \cdot (\delta_{\mathcal{R}} + 1.25)^{d_{\text{min}}} \cdot t^{d_{\text{min}}-3}$.

So the decryption works if: $4nL\beta(\epsilon)\sigma \cdot \delta_{\mathcal{R}}^{d_{\text{min}}-1} \cdot (\delta_{\mathcal{R}} + 1.25)^{d_{\text{min}}} \cdot t^{d_{\text{min}}-1} \le q$. With a cyclotomic polynomial ring $\mathcal{R}$, and approximating $\beta(\epsilon)$ with 9.2 this becomes:

$$36.8 \times L\sigma \cdot n^{d_{\text{min}}} \cdot (n + 1.25)^{d_{\text{min}}} \cdot t^{d_{\text{min}}-1} \le q \tag{3}$$

With $\sigma \le \sqrt{n}$, $n \ge 2^9$, $t = 3$ and d_{min} from the above calculations, we get the previous inequality with the following condition, with $L = 2N$: $23.8 + \log_2(N) + 24.5\log_2(n) \le \log_2(q)$. As an example, if $N = 2^{40}$ and $n = 2^{14}$, then taking q on 407 bits or more will grant this condition.

Correctness with Noise-Flooding. A linear combination of ciphertexts can leak the coefficients, from the evolution of the final noise, which can be recovered by the owner of the decryption key. To avoid this leakage, one can add super-polynomial noise to the result, this is the so-called *noise-flooding* technique: the sender will generate encryption of 0, *i.e.* polynomials $(\mathsf{z}^*, \mathsf{z}'^*)$ of the form

$$(\mathsf{z}^*, \mathsf{z}'^*) = (\mathsf{p} \cdot \mathsf{u} + \mathsf{e}_1 \bmod q, \mathsf{p}' \cdot \mathsf{u} + \mathsf{e}_2 \bmod q),$$

with coefficients of $\mathsf{u}, \mathsf{e}_1, \mathsf{e}_2$ follow the appropriate distribution for their own privacy: according to a Gaussian distribution on $\mathbb{Z}$ with standard deviation 2^λ larger than the error in the result, that we bounded by $B' = 2Ln\beta(\epsilon)\delta_{\mathcal{R}}^{d_{\text{bs}}} \cdot (\delta_{\mathcal{R}} + 1.25)^{d_{\text{bs}}+1} \cdot t^{d_{\text{bs}}-1} \cdot \sigma$. Using the verifiable inner-product for provable L_2-norm, one can prove that $\|\mathsf{u}\|_2, \|\mathsf{e}_1\|_2, \|\mathsf{e}_2\|_2$ are lower than $2^\lambda B'$, which guarantees the infinity norms are also lower than that.

Asymptotic Parameters. One now needs $q \geq 2^\lambda \times 2tB'$: With the above B', this means that

$$4Ln2^\lambda \beta(\epsilon)\delta_{\mathcal{R}}^{d_{\text{bs}}} \cdot (\delta_{\mathcal{R}} + 1.25)^{d_{\text{bs}}+1} \cdot t^{d_{\text{bs}}} \cdot \sigma \leq q \tag{4}$$

guarantees the (L, d_{bs})-$\mathcal{R}_t$ linear homomorphism property and noise-flooding, and combined with the required hardness of the RLWE problem in Eq. 1, we now require: $4\alpha Ln2^\lambda \beta(\epsilon)\delta_{\mathcal{R}}^{d_{\text{bs}}} \cdot (\delta_{\mathcal{R}} + 1.25)^{d_{\text{bs}}+1} \cdot t^{d_{\text{bs}}} < 2^{2\sqrt{n \log_2(q) \log_2(\delta)}}$, with $L = 2N$ (N being the public degree of the sender's polynomial), a cyclotomic polynomial ring, $\lambda = 128$, $t = 3$, $n \geq 2^9$, $d_{\text{bs}} = 11$ (from the above $d_{\min} = 12$ calculation in Sect. 5.3), $\alpha \approx 3.8$, $\beta(\epsilon) \approx 9.2$, the above equation is verified if:

$$151.7 + 28\log_2(n) + \log_2(N) < 0.1743 \cdot \sqrt{n \log_2(q)}$$

So for instance for $n = 2^{14}$ and $N = 2^{40}$, we are sure that q on 685 bits or more will grant full FHE functionalities, and we also get the following FHE ciphertext size complexity: $n \log_2(q) = \mathcal{O}(\log(N)^2)$.

5.4 Succinctness

As explained above, the proof is succinct, with a constant number of elements, and independent of the degree of the polynomial, but the size of the commitments may depend on q for some choices of Secure Encodings. In Sect. 5.3, we studied asymptotic bounds for q and n, to get correctness, and get $\log q = \mathcal{O}(\log N)$, and $n = \mathcal{O}(\log N)$. Then the size of a ciphertext is in $\mathcal{O}(n \log q) = \mathcal{O}((\log N)^2)$ bits and this gives the receiver's communication complexity. Then, the sender essentially sends back the result (1 ciphertext $= \mathcal{O}((\log N)^2)$) and the proof which consists in a constant number of commitments in $\mathcal{O}(\log q) = \mathcal{O}(\log N)$. So, globally, the communication complexity is in $\mathcal{O}((\log N)^2)$.

We estimated practical sizes using security bounds on the privacy of FHE given by the LWE estimator [1]. For N between 2^{20} and 2^{40}, a prime q should be on 600 to 620 bits, which would lead to 3MBytes for the FHE ciphertext to be sent, and about 5MBytes for the result and its proof.

In the full version [28], we give more details with a composite q, which allows RNS optimizations for FHE. Then, the size of the proof increases because of the repetitions of the commitments, as the Schwartz-Zippel lemma provides a smaller soundness, but it remains in a 90 to 520MBytes range for N less than 2^{40}, from our analysis using our correctness formula, the [1] estimator, and the Schwartz-Zippel lemma for the proof soundness. In Fig. 3, we give parameters and resulting sizes for our OPE construction. We achieve the correctness from inequality (4)'s exact requirements (without the following approximations), and the privacy provided by the FHE security is calculated using [1]'s estimator. Soundness requirements given by the Schwartz-Zippel lemma then provide the number of required repetitions on which the number of commitments ν_c and the number of checked equations ν_e depend.

$\lvert N\rvert$	$\lvert n\rvert$	$\lvert q\rvert$	Receiver Communications		Sender Communications		
			FHE Security	Total Size	ν_c	ν_e	Total Size
20	14	600	115	3 MB	33	20	5 MB
30	14	610	113	3 MB	33	20	5 MB
40	14	620	110	3 MB	33	20	5 MB

Fig. 3. Parameters and security bounds for the FHE ciphertexts and the proof, with a prime ciphertext modulus q and the plaintext modulus $t = 3$. The proof size column encompasses all the elements communicated by the sender, including the result. This is for a 2^{-128}-soundness. $|x|$ is the bit-length of x. As q is a large prime, one can use an encoding scheme based on pairings: $\mathbb{G}_2$ elements are encoded on 880 bits for a 128-bit security, as in [25]'s recommendations.

Acknowledgments. This work was supported in part by the European Community's Horizon 2020 Project CryptAnalytics (Grant Agreement No. 966570)

References

1. Albrecht, M.R., Player, R., Scott, S.: On the concrete hardness of learning with errors. J. Math. Cryptol. **9**(3), 169–203 (2015)
2. Bajard, J.-C., Eynard, J., Hasan, M.A., Zucca, V.: A full RNS variant of FV like somewhat homomorphic encryption schemes. In: Avanzi, R., Heys, H. (eds.) SAC 2016. LNCS, vol. 10532, pp. 423–442. Springer, Cham (2017). https://doi.org/10.1007/978-3-319-69453-5_23
3. Bitansky, N., Chiesa, A., Ishai, Y., Paneth, O., Ostrovsky, R.: Succinct non-interactive arguments via linear interactive proofs. In: Sahai, A. (ed.) TCC 2013. LNCS, vol. 7785, pp. 315–333. Springer, Heidelberg (2013). https://doi.org/10.1007/978-3-642-36594-2_18
4. Blake, I.F., Gao, S., Mullin, R.C.: Explicit factorization of $x^{2^k} + 1$ over $\mathbb{F}_p$ with prime $p = 3 \bmod 4$. Appl. Algebra Eng. Commun. Comput. **4**, 89–94 (1993). https://doi.org/10.1007/BF01386832
5. Bleichenbacher, D., Nguyen, P.Q.: Noisy polynomial interpolation and noisy Chinese remaindering. In: Preneel, B. (ed.) EUROCRYPT 2000. LNCS, vol. 1807, pp. 53–69. Springer, Heidelberg (2000). https://doi.org/10.1007/3-540-45539-6_4
6. Bois, A., Cascudo, I., Fiore, D., Kim, D.: Flexible and efficient verifiable computation on encrypted data. In: Garay, J.A. (ed.) PKC 2021, Part II. LNCS, vol. 12711, pp. 528–558. Springer, Cham (2021). https://doi.org/10.1007/978-3-030-75248-4_19
7. Bootle, J., Cerulli, A., Chaidos, P., Groth, J., Petit, C.: Efficient zero-knowledge arguments for arithmetic circuits in the discrete log setting. In: Fischlin, M., Coron, J.-S. (eds.) EUROCRYPT 2016, Part II. LNCS, vol. 9666, pp. 327–357. Springer, Heidelberg (2016). https://doi.org/10.1007/978-3-662-49896-5_12
8. Bui, D., Couteau, G.: Private set intersection from pseudorandom correlation generators. Cryptology ePrint Archive, Report 2022/334 (2022). https://ia.cr/2022/334
9. Bünz, B., Bootle, J., Boneh, D., Poelstra, A., Wuille, P., Maxwell, G.: Bulletproofs: short proofs for confidential transactions and more. In: 2018 IEEE Symposium on

Security and Privacy, pp. 315–334. IEEE Computer Society Press (2018). https://doi.org/10.1109/SP.2018.00020
10. Bünz, B., Chiesa, A., Mishra, P., Spooner, N.: Recursive proof composition from accumulation schemes. In: Pass, R., Pietrzak, K. (eds.) TCC 2020, Part II. LNCS, vol. 12551, pp. 1–18. Springer, Cham (2020). https://doi.org/10.1007/978-3-030-64378-2_1
11. Bünz, B., Maller, M., Mishra, P., Tyagi, N., Vesely, P.: Proofs for inner pairing products and applications. In: Tibouchi, M., Wang, H. (eds.) ASIACRYPT 2021, Part III. LNCS, vol. 13092, pp. 65–97. Springer, Cham (2021). https://doi.org/10.1007/978-3-030-92078-4_3
12. Castagnos, G., Laguillaumie, F.: Linearly homomorphic encryption from DDH. In: Nyberg, K. (ed.) CT-RSA 2015. LNCS, vol. 9048, pp. 487–505. Springer, Cham (2015). https://doi.org/10.1007/978-3-319-16715-2_26
13. Chang, Y.-C., Lu, C.-J.: Oblivious polynomial evaluation and oblivious neural learning. In: Boyd, C. (ed.) ASIACRYPT 2001. LNCS, vol. 2248, pp. 369–384. Springer, Heidelberg (2001). https://doi.org/10.1007/3-540-45682-1_22
14. Chen, H., Laine, K., Rindal, P.: Fast private set intersection from homomorphic encryption. In: Thuraisingham, B.M., Evans, D., Malkin, T., Xu, D. (eds.) ACM CCS 2017, pp. 1243–1255. ACM Press (2017). https://doi.org/10.1145/3133956.3134061
15. Damgård, I.: Towards practical public key systems secure against chosen ciphertext attacks. In: Feigenbaum, J. (ed.) CRYPTO 1991. LNCS, vol. 576, pp. 445–456. Springer, Heidelberg (1992). https://doi.org/10.1007/3-540-46766-1_36
16. Daza, V., Ràfols, C., Zacharakis, A.: Updateable inner product argument with logarithmic verifier and applications. In: Kiayias, A., Kohlweiss, M., Wallden, P., Zikas, V. (eds.) PKC 2020, Part I. LNCS, vol. 12110, pp. 527–557. Springer, Cham (2020). https://doi.org/10.1007/978-3-030-45374-9_18
17. Fan, J., Vercauteren, F.: Somewhat practical fully homomorphic encryption. Cryptology ePrint Archive, Report 2012/144 (2012). https://eprint.iacr.org/2012/144
18. Fiore, D., Nitulescu, A., Pointcheval, D.: Boosting verifiable computation on encrypted data. In: Kiayias, A., Kohlweiss, M., Wallden, P., Zikas, V. (eds.) PKC 2020, Part II. LNCS, vol. 12111, pp. 124–154. Springer, Cham (2020). https://doi.org/10.1007/978-3-030-45388-6_5
19. Ganesh, C., Nitulescu, A., Soria-Vazquez, E.: Rinocchio: SNARKs for ring arithmetic. Cryptology ePrint Archive, Report 2021/322 (2021). https://eprint.iacr.org/2021/322
20. Gennaro, R., Gentry, C., Parno, B.: Non-interactive verifiable computing: outsourcing computation to untrusted workers. In: Rabin, T. (ed.) CRYPTO 2010. LNCS, vol. 6223, pp. 465–482. Springer, Heidelberg (2010). https://doi.org/10.1007/978-3-642-14623-7_25
21. Gennaro, R., Gentry, C., Parno, B., Raykova, M.: Quadratic span programs and succinct NIZKs without PCPs. In: Johansson, T., Nguyen, P.Q. (eds.) EUROCRYPT 2013. LNCS, vol. 7881, pp. 626–645. Springer, Heidelberg (2013). https://doi.org/10.1007/978-3-642-38348-9_37
22. Gennaro, R., Minelli, M., Nitulescu, A., Orrù, M.: Lattice-based zk-SNARKs from square span programs. In: Lie, D., Mannan, M., Backes, M., Wang, X. (eds.) ACM CCS 2018, pp. 556–573. ACM Press (2018). https://doi.org/10.1145/3243734.3243845
23. Gentry, C.: Fully homomorphic encryption using ideal lattices. In: Mitzenmacher, M. (ed.) 41st ACM STOC, pp. 169–178. ACM Press (2009). https://doi.org/10.1145/1536414.1536440

24. Gilboa, N.: Two party RSA key generation. In: Wiener, M. (ed.) CRYPTO 1999. LNCS, vol. 1666, pp. 116–129. Springer, Heidelberg (1999). https://doi.org/10.1007/3-540-48405-1_8
25. Guillevic, A.: Pairing friendly curves (2021). https://members.loria.fr/AGuillevic/pairing-friendly-curves/
26. Hazay, C.: Oblivious polynomial evaluation and secure set-intersection from algebraic PRFs. J. Cryptol. **31**(2), 537–586 (2017). https://doi.org/10.1007/s00145-017-9263-y
27. Hazay, C., Lindell, Y.: Efficient oblivious polynomial evaluation with simulation-based security. Cryptology ePrint Archive, Report 2009/459 (2009). https://eprint.iacr.org/2009/459
28. Izabachène, M., Nitulescu, A., de Perthuis, P., Pointcheval, D.: MyOPE: malicious securitY for oblivious polynomial evaluation. Cryptology ePrint Archive, Report 2021/1291 (2021). https://eprint.iacr.org/2021/1291
29. Jarecki, S., Liu, X.: Efficient oblivious pseudorandom function with applications to adaptive OT and secure computation of set intersection. In: Reingold, O. (ed.) TCC 2009. LNCS, vol. 5444, pp. 577–594. Springer, Heidelberg (2009). https://doi.org/10.1007/978-3-642-00457-5_34
30. Lai, R.W.F., Malavolta, G., Ronge, V.: Succinct arguments for bilinear group arithmetic: practical structure-preserving cryptography. In: Cavallaro, L., Kinder, J., Wang, X., Katz, J. (eds.) ACM CCS 2019, pp. 2057–2074. ACM Press (2019). https://doi.org/10.1145/3319535.3354262
31. Lindell, Y., Pinkas, B.: Privacy preserving data mining. In: Bellare, M. (ed.) CRYPTO 2000. LNCS, vol. 1880, pp. 36–54. Springer, Heidelberg (2000). https://doi.org/10.1007/3-540-44598-6_3
32. Lindner, R., Peikert, C.: Better key sizes (and attacks) for LWE-based encryption. In: Kiayias, A. (ed.) CT-RSA 2011. LNCS, vol. 6558, pp. 319–339. Springer, Heidelberg (2011). https://doi.org/10.1007/978-3-642-19074-2_21
33. Naor, M., Pinkas, B.: Oblivious transfer and polynomial evaluation. In: 31st ACM STOC, pp. 245–254. ACM Press (1999). https://doi.org/10.1145/301250.301312
34. Paillier, P.: Public-key cryptosystems based on composite degree residuosity classes. In: Stern, J. (ed.) EUROCRYPT 1999. LNCS, vol. 1592, pp. 223–238. Springer, Heidelberg (1999). https://doi.org/10.1007/3-540-48910-X_16
35. Pinkas, B., Rosulek, M., Trieu, N., Yanai, A.: PSI from PaXoS: fast, malicious private set intersection. In: Canteaut, A., Ishai, Y. (eds.) EUROCRYPT 2020, Part II. LNCS, vol. 12106, pp. 739–767. Springer, Cham (2020). https://doi.org/10.1007/978-3-030-45724-2_25
36. Schwartz, J.T.: Fast probabilistic algorithms for verification of polynomial identities. J. ACM **27**(4), 701–717 (1980)
37. Wahby, R.S., Tzialla, I., Shelat, A., Thaler, J., Walfish, M.: Doubly-efficient zkSNARKs without trusted setup. In: 2018 IEEE Symposium on Security and Privacy, pp. 926–943. IEEE Computer Society Press (2018). https://doi.org/10.1109/SP.2018.00060
38. Zhu, H., Bao, F.: Augmented oblivious polynomial evaluation protocol and its applications. In: di Vimercati, S.C., Syverson, P., Gollmann, D. (eds.) ESORICS 2005. LNCS, vol. 3679, pp. 222–230. Springer, Heidelberg (2005). https://doi.org/10.1007/11555827_13
39. Zippel, R.: Probabilistic algorithms for sparse polynomials. In: Ng, E.W. (ed.) Symbolic and Algebraic Computation. LNCS, vol. 72, pp. 216–226. Springer, Heidelberg (1979). https://doi.org/10.1007/3-540-09519-5_73

NIWI and New Notions of Extraction for Algebraic Languages

Chaya Ganesh[1], Hamidreza Khoshakhlagh[2(✉)], and Roberto Parisella[3]

[1] Indian Institute of Science, Bengaluru, India
chaya@iisc.ac.in
[2] Aarhus University, Aarhus, Denmark
hamidreza@cs.au.dk
[3] Simula UiB, Bergen, Norway
robertoparisella@hotmail.it

Abstract. We give an efficient construction of a computational non-interactive witness indistinguishable (NIWI) proof in the plain model, and investigate notions of extraction for NIZKs for algebraic languages. Our starting point is the recent work of Couteau and Hartmann (CRYPTO 2020) who developed a new framework (CH framework) for constructing non-interactive zero-knowledge proofs and arguments under falsifiable assumptions for a large class of languages called algebraic languages. In this paper, we construct an efficient NIWI proof in the plain model for algebraic languages based on the CH framework. In the plain model, our NIWI construction is more efficient for algebraic languages than state-of-the-art Groth-Ostrovsky-Sahai (GOS) NIWI (JACM 2012). Next, we explore knowledge soundness of NIZK systems in the CH framework. We define a notion of strong f-extractability, and show that the CH proof system satisfies this notion.

We then put forth a new definition of knowledge soundness called *semantic extraction*. We explore the relationship of semantic extraction with existing knowledge soundness definitions and show that it is a general definition that recovers black-box and non-black-box definitions as special cases. Finally, we show that NIZKs for algebraic languages in the CH framework cannot satisfy semantic extraction. We extend this impossibility to a class of NIZK arguments over algebraic languages, namely quasi-adaptive NIZK arguments that are constructed from smooth projective hash functions.

1 Introduction

Zero-knowledge proofs, introduced by Goldwasser, Micali and Rackoff [28], are cryptographic primitives that allow a prover to convince a verifier that a statement is true without revealing any other information. Zero-knowledge proof systems have a rich history in cryptography [8,21,26] finding numerous applications in cryptographic constructions such as identification schemes [20], public-key encryption [37], signature schemes [14], anonymous credentials [13], secure multi-party computation [27], and a wide variety of emerging applications.

C. Galdi and S. Jarecki (Eds.): SCN 2022, LNCS 13409, pp. 687–710, 2022.
https://doi.org/10.1007/978-3-031-14791-3_30

The notion of zero-knowledge proof was later extended to non-interactive zero-knowledge (NIZK) proofs by Blum, Feldman and Micali [10] where there is a single message sent from the prover to the verifier. NIZKs are particularly useful in low-interaction settings, and feasibility is known for all of NP in the common reference string (CRS) model.

Pairing-Based NIZKs. Starting from the work of Groth and Sahai [31], many pairing-based NIZK proof systems have been constructed. These proof systems avoid the need for expensive reductions to NP-complete languages and can directly handle a large class of languages over abelian groups.

Another line of work for constructing pairing-based NIZKs is via a smooth projective hash function (SPHF) [17]. For a language over some abelian group $\mathbb{G}_1$, a secret hashing key is embedded in group $\mathbb{G}_2$, and this NIZK proof can be verified via a pairing operation between $\mathbb{G}_1$ and $\mathbb{G}_2$. The SPHF-based approach leads to very efficient proofs for linear languages. However, they only provide a quasi-adaptive type of soundness, where the CRS can depend on the language.

NIWIs. One can relax the security of a NIZK argument to a Non-Interactive Witness Indistinguishable (NIWI) argument by replacing the zero-knowledge property with a weaker witness indistinguishability (WI) property. Unlike NIZKs for which we know impossibility in the plain model [10], and can therefore only exist in the CRS model, NIWIs are possible in the plain model. Informally, witness indistinguishability means that the verifier at the end of protocol, cannot guess which of the possible witnesses the prover used to compute the proof.

The general idea to construct a NIWI in the plain model, is to start from zero-knowledge proofs that are perfectly sound for some choice of the verifier randomness (or some choice of the CRS). Namely, we let the prover sample the randomness by itself and include additional checks to force the prover to compute at least one proof for such choice of randomness. The first NIWI construction in the plain model was proposed by Barak et al. [6] obtained by derandomizing any two-round zero-knowledge proof (ZAP) [18]. The idea behind the construction is to let the prover send a "high enough" number of proofs, each for a different choice of randomness, such that it is hard to cheat for all of them. There are however drawbacks that make such NIWI schemes unsuitable in practical applications. In the NIWI of [6], the prover has to compute logarithmically many proofs, which leads to inefficient schemes, both in terms of computation and communication, even starting from efficient, say, linear ZAPs. Also, security is based on a complexity theoretic assumption (namely $\mathbf{E} = \mathbf{DTIME}(2^{O(n)})$ has a function of circuit complexity $2^{\Omega(n)}$) that implies $\mathbf{BPP} = \mathbf{P}$.

Groth, Ostrovsky and Sahai [30] proposed a different framework for NIWI proofs, which leads to more efficient proofs for concrete languages (instead of circuit satisfiability). The key idea in [30] is to force the prover to produce two CRSs, such that at least one of them guarantees perfect soundness. Moreover, the structure of the CRS is such that multiplication of one element can always transform a computationally sound CRS into a perfectly sound CRS. The NIWI proof system can now take advantage of the structure in the CRS as follows: the prover generates a CRS on its own and provides proofs under both the chosen

CRS and its transformation. Perfect soundness holds by the fact that at least one of the two CRSs guarantees this property. Some of the issues in the construction of [6] mentioned above are overcome by the NIWI proof system of [30], thanks also to further optimizations [39]. Namely, it is based on well-established assumptions, and the number of proof elements is constant instead of logarithmic in the security parameter. However, for some applications, communication complexity that is twice the size of a Groth-Sahai (GS) proof is still not practical, particularly considering that GS NIZK, and consequently the NIWI often comes with a drastic efficiency reduction due to the need for reducing the original language to an intermediate language supported by the GS proof system.

In this work, we construct more efficient computational NIWI proofs in the plain model for a larger class of languages.

CH Framework. Recently, Couteau and Hartmann [16] developed a new framework (henceforth referred to as the CH framework) for constructing non-interactive zero-knowledge proofs and arguments for a broad class of languages under a falsifiable assumption. They provide several constructions whose efficiency is satisfactory for many applications and enjoy a number of interesting features such as having proofs that are as short as proofs resulting from the Fiat-Shamir transformation applied to Σ-protocols. Their approach, at a very high level, consists of compiling a Σ-protocol over an abelian group $\mathbb{G}_1$ into a non-interactive zero-knowledge argument over Type III pairings by embedding the challenge e into a group $\mathbb{G}_2$ and adding the embedded challenge to the CRS.

The work of [16] also obtains a simple and efficient ZAP argument in the plain model where the WI property holds statistically as opposed to all previous pairing-based constructions that satisfy computational WI. While this ZAP argument can be compiled directly into a non-interactive ZAP using the compiler of [6], the prover, as mentioned above, needs to send logarithmically many proofs, hence decreasing the efficiency of the original scheme.

CH Framework with Knowledge Soundness. All aforementioned proof systems based on CH framework only guarantee soundness meaning that accepting proofs cannot be computed for false statements. Typically, applications require a stronger notion of soundness called *knowledge soundness* which guarantees that the prover *knows* a witness for a statement if it can make the verifier accept. This notion of knowledge soundness is formalized by the existence of an efficient extractor that can extract a valid witness from the prover whenever the prover provides a valid proof. Given that the NIZK systems in [16] only guarantee soundness, we investigate the possibility of knowledge soundness of the CH protocol, and pairing-based arguments in general.

Can we construct NIZK proofs in the CH framework with knowledge soundness?

A naïve solution to provide extractability in the CRS model is to use well-known techniques to augment the statement with a trapdoor for extraction. In particular, given a CRS that contains a public key pk, the most efficient currently known approach is to ask the prover to encrypt the witness under pk and then prove that the ciphertext is computed correctly. The extractor can then use the secret key of pk to recover a valid witness from the proof. This however makes the proof size much larger. On a high level, this is because existing algebraic encryption schemes are not friendly enough with the CH framework, unless we perform the encryption bit-by-bit as in [9], which makes the construction undesirable. More importantly, the underlying NP relation is now changed into an augmented relation that should also manage the correctness of ciphertext computations. Our goal is however to study the (im)possibility of extractability for the standard CH framework without changing the underlying relation.

Another solution is to show extractability under knowledge assumptions, or in idealized models such as generic group model (GGM) [42] or algebraic group model (AGM) [22]. Indeed, it is not hard to show that CH NIZKs are knowledge sound in the AGM[1]. Gentry and Wichs [25] show impossibility of a black-box reduction to a falsifiable assumption to prove soundness for succinct arguments, where the proof size is logarithmic in the size of the witness and the statement. However, the use of idealized models or knowledge assumptions to prove knowledge soundness of *non-succinct* proof systems seems to be less justifiable.

At first look, it might seem like knowledge assumptions for extraction are justified since soundness of some CH NIZK is already based on a *non-falsifiable* version of the **extKerMDH** assumption. As per Naor's classification [36], knowledge assumptions are a class of non-falsifiable assumptions. However, since knowledge assumptions stipulate "feasibility" of efficient extraction, they do not fit within a taxonomy of *intractability* assumptions [38]. On the other hand, an assumption such as **extKerMDH**, while non-falsifiable, is still an intractability assumption that can be phrased as a game between an adversary and a challenger, albeit with an inefficient challenger.

1.1 Our Contributions

We study NIZK and NIWI constructions in the pairing-based setting and make the following contributions.

NIWI in the Plain Model. Different from the aforementioned idea of constructing NIWI in the plain model based on the CH framework [16] using the compiler of [6], we investigate a more efficient strategy inspired by the approach of [30] which allows the verifier to verify if, given a (small) set of CRSs, at least one of them is perfectly binding, without breaking soundness.

Our construction is based on the existence of an efficient algorithm that, given one CRS of the NIZK proof of [16], allows the verifier to check if it is a perfectly binding one without compromising the soundness property. The key idea in constructing such an algorithm is, at a high level, to add two additional group elements to the CRS, chosen such that assuming the existence of Type III pairings, it allows the verifier to (efficiently) check the distribution of the

[1] We show knowledge soundness of the CH argument in the AGM in the full version [24].

CRS (with a technique similar to what was done in [1]) while not compromising the WI property. Now, with the verifier equipped with such an algorithm, we construct a non-interactive ZAP by letting the prover compute this CRS and output it together with the proof.

We need additional ideas to prove security of the resulting construction. First, as noted in [16], the soundness of the resulting NIZK proof is based on the special soundness property of the underlying Σ-protocol. Soundness of our NIWI proof follows from the same reasoning and from the correctness of the algorithm that checks the distribution of the CRS. Indeed, if the verifier accepts, then the prover correctly sampled a perfectly binding CRS and thus soundness holds. To show WI, we rely on a new decisional assumption, which we validate in the AGM. The ability of the verifier to check the distribution of the CRS relies on DDH being easy, and therefore it is not possible to rely on DDH for WI.

CH Framework with Knowledge Soundness. The proof and argument systems presented in [16] and our NIWI construction ensure only soundness. As our second contribution, we investigate knowledge soundness of NIZK systems in the CH framework.

f-extractability. We define a notion of *strong f-extractability* that extends related notions of partial extraction used in literature. Informally, an argument system satisfies f-extractability if there exists an efficient extractor that outputs $\widetilde{\mathtt{w}}$ whenever the verifier accepts the proof for statement $\mathtt{x}$, where $\widetilde{\mathtt{w}} = f(\mathtt{w})$ and $\mathtt{w}$ is a valid witness for $\mathtt{x}$. We extend the notion to strong f-extractability where we ask that the partial witness $\widetilde{\mathtt{w}}$ allows for efficiently deciding membership of the statement. We show that the CH proof system satisfies this notion where the extracted value is the encoding of a witness to $\mathbb{G}_2$.

Semantic Extraction. We then investigate the possibility of *knowledge soundness* of the CH NIZKs, and pairing-based arguments in general. We show that the CH argument is knowledge sound in the Algebraic Group Model (AGM), and then ask the following question: can we show knowledge soundness in the standard model without relying on knowledge assumptions or show impossibility of extraction? Towards this end, we put forth a notion of extraction called *semantic extraction*, and prove that this notion of extraction is impossible for the CH argument. The intuition behind the definition of semantic extraction is to consider the random coins of the adversary as an input from a certain distribution. This makes it possible to associate a function to each adversary: the function that it computes on certain inputs including its random coins. We then require that adversaries that implement the same function, have the same extractor. We allow the flexibility to split the random coins in two distinct portions, and then allow the extractor to see only one of the two portions. This gives a general definition that, depending on how much randomness we allow the extractor to see, gradually makes the extractor more powerful. We then investigate the relationship between semantic extraction and classic notions of extraction. We show that semantic extraction is a *general* definition, that captures both white-box(n-BB) and black-box(BB) extraction. In particular, BB extraction trivially implies semantic extraction. Also a slightly weaker version of the other direction is true, when we give no randomness to the semantic extractor. Moreover, semantic extraction is equivalent to n-BB extraction, where we give to the extractor all the random coins of the adversary. Finally, we show impossibility of semantic extraction for CH argument: that no extractor that sees only a portion of the adversary's randomness can succeed. We then generalize this impossibility to a class of NIZK arguments over algebraic languages, namely *quasi-adaptive* NIZK arguments based on SPHFs. As a concrete case, we show that the most efficient Quasi-Adaptive NIZK construction of Kiltz and Wee [34] cannot be semantically extractable. While black-box extraction is impossible since the arguments are shorter than the witnesses, the impossibility of semantic extraction is a stronger result. We present this in the full version [24].

1.2 Technical Overview

In this section we provide a technical overview of our results. We start with an overview of our NIWI construction in the plain model. Then we discuss our definition of semantic extraction and sketch our impossibility result for semantic extractability of CH NIZKs.

NIWI in the Plain Model. The starting point of our construction is the NIZK proof for algebraic languages in [16] which is based on a compiler that converts a Σ-protocol with linear answers over a group $\mathbb{G}_1$ into a NIZK argument by embedding the verifier's challenge into a group $\mathbb{G}_2$ in the CRS.
Σ-Protocols for Linear Languages. A linear language with language parameter $[\mathbf{M}]_1 \in \mathbb{G}_1^{n\times k}$ is defined as $\mathcal{L}_\mathbf{M} = \{[\mathbf{x}]_1 \in \mathbb{G}_1^n | \exists \mathbf{w} \in \mathbb{Z}_p^k : [\mathbf{x}]_1 = [\mathbf{M}]_1 \cdot \mathbf{w}\}$. A Σ-protocol for a linear language $\mathcal{L}_\mathbf{M}$ with corresponding relation $\mathcal{R}_\mathbf{M}$ is a three-move honest-verifier zero-knowledge (HVZK) proof system between a prover $\mathcal{P}$ and a verifier $\mathcal{V}$ with the following syntax. First, $\mathcal{P}$ with an input pair $([\mathbf{x}]_1, \mathbf{w})$ selects $\mathbf{r} \leftarrow \mathbb{Z}_p^k$ and sends a first message $[\mathbf{a}]_1 := [\mathbf{M}]_1 \cdot \mathbf{r} \in \mathbb{G}_1^n$ to $\mathcal{V}$. Next, $\mathcal{V}$ sends a random string $e \in \mathbb{Z}_p$ to $\mathcal{P}$. Finally, $\mathcal{P}$ sends a reply $\mathbf{d} := \mathbf{w}e + \mathbf{r} \in \mathbb{Z}_p^k$ to $\mathcal{V}$, who accepts the proof if $[\mathbf{M}]_1 \cdot \mathbf{d} = [\mathbf{x}]_1 e + [\mathbf{a}]_1$. The *special soundness* property states that for any $[\mathbf{x}]_1$ and any pair of accepting conversations $([\mathbf{a}]_1, e, \mathbf{d}), ([\mathbf{a}]_1, e', \mathbf{d}')$ on $[\mathbf{x}]_1$ where $e \neq e'$, one can efficiently compute a valid witness $\mathbf{w}$ for $[\mathbf{x}]_1$.

CH Compiler. Couteau and Hartmann [16] proposed the following approach to compile a Σ-protocol into a NIZK in the CRS model: the setup algorithm picks a random $e \in \mathbb{Z}_p$ and sets $[e]_2$ as the CRS. The prover computes $[\mathbf{a}]_1$ as in the Σ-protocol, and an embedding of $\mathbf{d}$ in $\mathbb{G}_2$ by computing $[\mathbf{d}]_2 := \mathbf{w} \cdot [e]_2 + \mathbf{r} \cdot [1]_2$. The proof can (publicly) be verified by checking if the pairing equation $[\mathbf{M}]_1 [\mathbf{d}]_2 = [\mathbf{x}]_1 [e]_2 + [\mathbf{a}]_1 [1]_2$ holds. While this leads to an argument system with computational soundness, [16] further shows how to turn the argument into a proof by providing two challenges with two different generators in the CRS and having the prover answer both with the same randomness. The (unconditional) special soundness property of the underlying Σ-protocol now guarantees that a witness exists, resulting in perfect soundness.

The idea behind our NIWI construction is as follows: consider the CRS of the CH NIZK proof $[s_1, s_2, e_1 s_1, e_2 s_2]_2 \in \mathbb{G}_2^4$, where $e_1, e_2, s_1, s_2 \in \mathbb{Z}_p$, and $[e_1, e_2]_2$ play the role of the two challenges (embedded in $\mathbb{G}_2$) in the underlying Σ-protocol. Now, we have the prover pick the CRS and the verifier checks that this CRS computed by a potentially malicious prover is such that $e_1 \neq e_2$, so we can rely on the special soundness of the underlying Σ-protocol. We then prove that the proof is witness-indistinguishable by relying on a new decisional assumption that we show secure in the AGM. This observation leads us to a NIWI proof in the plain model, where we let the prover to choose the "crs" parameters by itself, such that it is verifiable that $e_1 \neq e_2$.

Extractability in the CH Framework. We now give an overview of the extractability notions we explore, the new notion of *semantic extraction* we propose, and the impossibility of semantic extraction for CH NIZKs.

The standard definition of knowledge extraction asks for the existence of an efficient algorithm called *extractor* that takes as input a proof π of a statement $\mathtt{x}$ and returns a value $\mathtt{w}'$ such that $\mathtt{w}'$ is a witness for the truth of $\mathtt{x}$, i.e., $(\mathtt{x}, \mathtt{w}') \in \mathcal{R}$. While such *full extractability* captures the fact that the prover must have known the witness, there are instances where the existence of such a powerful extractor is unlikely; however, it is still possible to extract some partial information about the witness. One concrete example is the Groth-Sahai non-interactive proof of knowledge [31] from which one can only extract a one-way function of the witness $f(\mathtt{w})$ where $f : \mathbb{F} \to \mathbb{G}$ is the encoding of the witness in the underlying group. The barrier to full extractability is the fact that there does not seem to be a trapdoor that can be used to compute, in an efficient way, a witness $\mathtt{w}$ from $f(\mathtt{w})$ (i.e., discrete logarithm problem). To capture this notion of *partial extractability*, Belenkiy et al. [7] formalized the notion of f-extractability by the existence of an efficient algorithm that outputs $\widetilde{\mathtt{w}}$ such that there exists some $\mathtt{w}$ with $(\mathtt{x}, \mathtt{w}) \in \mathcal{R}$ and $\widetilde{\mathtt{w}} = f(\mathtt{w})$[2]. In their context of constructing anonymous credentials, f-extractability is used by relaxing the notion of unforgeability to f-unforgeable signatures where the adversary produces $(f(m), \sigma)$ pair (as opposed to (m, σ)) without previously obtaining a signature on m. Since then, f-extractability has been used as a standard property in many privacy-preserving authentication mechanisms [3,12,19,29,33,40].

We begin with this observation that the CH NIZK proof is not only f-extractable for $f := [\cdot]_2$, but the extracted value also allows to decide the membership of the statement via pairing checks. To see this, let $([\mathbf{x}]_1, \mathbf{w})$ be a pair of statement-witness in the linear relation $\mathcal{R}_{\mathbf{M}}$ that returns 1 if $[\mathbf{x}]_1 = [\mathbf{M}]_1 \cdot \mathbf{w}$. One can observe that extracting $[\mathbf{w}]_2$ suffices to decide the membership of $[\mathbf{x}]_1$ by checking if $[\mathbf{M}]_1[\mathbf{w}]_2 = [\mathbf{x}]_1[1]_2$. The primary distinction between partial and full extractability is in the ability to decide membership of the statement being proven via the extracted value. We fill the gap between the two notions by defining a stronger form of partial extractability called *strong f-extractability* which guarantees the existence of an efficient procedure D that for any given statement

[2] Note that this a generalization of the standard notion as the identity function $f(\cdot)$ implies full extractability.

$\mathtt{x}$ and f-extracted value $\widetilde{\mathtt{w}} := f(\mathtt{w})$, $\mathsf{D}(\mathtt{x}, \widetilde{\mathtt{w}})$ can decide the membership of $\mathtt{x}$. Note that $\widetilde{\mathtt{w}}$ still falls short of being a full witness for the relation; assuming that f is one-way, $\widetilde{\mathtt{w}}$ cannot be used to produce a valid proof for $\mathtt{x}$. This is what separates strong f-extractability from full extractability.

Impossibility of Semantic Extraction. We show impossibility of semantic extraction for the CH NIZK argument for algebraic languages. Note that this is a stronger result than ruling out BB extraction. Our impossibility holds only for semantic extraction where there exists a portion of the adversary's randomness that the extractor cannot see.

We now articulate the implications of ruling out semantic extraction for pairing-based arguments. In these systems, a proof consists *only* of group elements, while witnesses are elements of the underlying field[3]. Soundness relies on the hardness of discrete logarithm in order to argue that the exponents of elements in the CRS remain hidden from the prover. As a concrete example, let us consider the CH NIZK argument that essentially compiles a Σ-protocol with three-round messages $([\mathbf{a}], e, \mathbf{d})$ into a NIZK argument in the CRS model in such a way that the CRS includes $[e]_2$ and the proof consists of two (vector of) group elements $([\mathbf{a}]_1, [\mathbf{d}]_2)$. Informally, the security relies on the fact that the prover cannot compute e (or $[e]_1$) and the second component $[\mathbf{d}]_2$ should have been computed as $[\mathbf{d}]_2 = \mathbf{d}_0[1]_2 + \mathbf{d}_1[e]_2$. But now, one can observe that from a *semantic* point of view, there is no distinction between the case that $[\mathbf{d}]_2$ is computed honestly as above and the case where the CRS trapdoor e is used for generating $[\mathbf{d}]_2$ as $\mathbf{d}_0[1]_2 + e[\mathbf{d}_1]_2$. In fact, if an extractor Ext that is limited to being *semantic* is able to extract the witness $\mathbf{d}_1$, then one can invoke Ext to break the discrete logarithm in $\mathbb{G}_2$ by sampling e in the reduction. The above reduction does not go through if Ext is a semantic extractor that has access to all the adversary random coins (we show that such Ext is equivalent to a classic white-box extractor). But as soon as some randomness is hidden from the extractor, we can define an adversary that embeds a DL challenge in this hidden part of the execution, for which no extractor can exist. This means that a valid proof in such argument systems does not prove "knowledge" of $\mathbf{w}$, but only knowledge of $[\mathbf{w}]_1, [\mathbf{w}]_2$, and in order to extract $\mathbf{w}$, one must rely on the hypothesis of asymmetric pairings to conclude that the prover actually knew $\mathbf{w}$ as a field element, which is essentially a knowledge-of-exponent type assumption.

Our results suggest that for most algebraic languages, extracting a witness given the statement $[\mathbf{x}]_1$ is as hard as extracting a witness given $[\mathbf{x}]_1$, a valid proof π together with used randomness r and trapdoor of the CRS e. Thus, if an extractor that is *not* based on knowledge assumption exists, it completely ignores the proof and just recomputes sampling a true statement together with its relative witness. This can also be seen in the following way: consider a language whose hardness relies on the hardness of discrete logarithm. Now, computing the witness from the statement is as hard as discrete logarithm; computing the

[3] In structure preserving systems, the witness can be group elements as well, but in this work, we are only interested in proof systems where witnesses are field elements.

witness given the statement, a proof, randomness used to compute the proof, and trapdoor is (in the case of CH20) as hard as symmetric discrete logarithm (SDL). This implies that either there is a gap between DL and SDL; or computing $\mathbf{w}$ from $[\mathbf{x}]_1$ is as hard as computing $\mathbf{w}$ from $([\mathbf{x}]_1, r, \pi, e)$. In the case of SPHF, both hardness of the language and our result rely on hardness of discrete logarithm, implying that computing $\mathbf{w}$ from $[\mathbf{x}]_1$ is as hard as computing $\mathbf{w}$ from $([\mathbf{x}]_1, \pi, r, \mathtt{td})$. This gives an explanation for why in the pairing-based setting, we have perfect soundness and f-extractability, like we show the CH proof is, while no fully extractable scheme exists under falsifiable assumptions.

2 Preliminaries

Notation. For any positive integer n, $[n]$ denotes the set $\{1, \ldots, n\}$. Let $k \in \mathbb{N}$ be the security parameter. Let $\mathsf{negl}(k)$ be an arbitrary negligible function. We write $a \approx_k b$ if $|a - b| \leq \mathsf{negl}(k)$. Moreover a is a negligible function if $a \approx_k 0$. When a function can be expressed in the form $1 - \mathsf{negl}(k)$, we say that it is overwhelming in k. We use DPT (resp. PPT) to mean a deterministic (resp. probabilistic) polynomial time algorithm. We write $Y \leftarrow \mathsf{F}(X)$ to denote an algorithm with input X and output Y. Further, we write $a \stackrel{\$}{\leftarrow} S$ to denote that a is sampled according to distribution S, or uniformly randomly if S is a set. For two interactive machines $\mathcal{P}$ and $\mathcal{V}$, we denote by $\langle \mathcal{P}(\alpha), \mathcal{V}(\beta) \rangle(\gamma)$ the output of $\mathcal{V}$ after running on private input β with $\mathcal{P}$ using private input α, both having common input γ. All adversaries will be stateful. To represent matrices and vectors, we use bold upper-case and bold lower-case letters, respectively.

2.1 Bilinear Groups

We use additive notation for groups. Throughout the paper we let $\mathcal{G}$ be a bilinear group generator that on input security parameter k returns $(p, \mathbb{G}_1, \mathbb{G}_2, \mathbb{G}_T, \hat{e}, [1]_1, [1]_2) \leftarrow \mathcal{G}(1^k)$, where $\mathbb{G}_1, \mathbb{G}_2, \mathbb{G}_T$ are groups of prime order p, $[1]_1$ and $[1]_2$ are respectively the generators for $\mathbb{G}_1$ and $\mathbb{G}_2$, and $\hat{e} : \mathbb{G}_1 \times \mathbb{G}_2 \rightarrow \mathbb{G}_T$ is a non-degenerate efficiently computable bilinear map such that $\forall [u]_1 \in \mathbb{G}_1, \forall [v]_2 \in \mathbb{G}_2, \forall a, b \in \mathbb{Z}_p : \hat{e}(a[U]_1, b[V]_2) = (ab)\hat{e}([U]_1, [V]_2)$.

We denote $\hat{e}([U]_1, [V]_2)$ as $[U]_1[V]_2$. We consider only type III pairings, where there does not exist an efficient isomorphism between $\mathbb{G}_1$ and $\mathbb{G}_2$.

2.2 Algebraic Languages

We refer to algebraic languages as the set of languages associated to a relation that can be described by algebraic equations over an abelian group. More precisely, let $\mathtt{gpar} = (p, \mathbb{G}_1, \mathbb{G}_2, \mathbb{G}_T, \hat{e}, [1]_1, [1]_2) \leftarrow \mathcal{G}(1^k)$. For the rest of the paper, we suppose that these global parameters $\mathtt{gpar}$ are implicitly given as input to each algorithm. Let $\mathtt{lpar} = (\mathbf{M}, \boldsymbol{\theta})$ be a set of language parameters generated by a polynomial-time algorithm $\mathtt{setup.lpar}$ which takes $\mathtt{gpar}$ as input. Here,

$\mathbf{M} : \mathbb{G}^\ell \mapsto \mathbb{G}^{n\times k}$ and $\boldsymbol{\theta} : \mathbb{G}^\ell \mapsto \mathbb{G}^n$ are linear maps such that their different coefficients are not necessarily in the same algebraic structures. Namely, in the most common case, given a bilinear group $\mathtt{gpar} = (p, \mathbb{G}_1, \mathbb{G}_2, \mathbb{G}_T, \hat{e}, [1]_1, [1]_2)$, they can belong to either $\mathbb{Z}_p$, $\mathbb{G}_1$, $\mathbb{G}_2$, or $\mathbb{G}_T$ as long as the equation $\boldsymbol{\theta}(\mathbf{x}) = \mathbf{M}(\mathbf{x}) \cdot \mathbf{w}$ is "well-consistent". However, in this paper we only use algebraic languages where the statement is defined as elements in $\mathbb{G}_1$. Formally, we define the algebraic language $\mathcal{L}_{\mathtt{lpar}} \subset \mathcal{X}_{\mathtt{lpar}}$ as

$$\mathcal{L}_{\mathtt{lpar}} = \left\{[\mathbf{x}]_1 \in \mathbb{G}_1^\ell | \exists \mathbf{w} \in \mathbb{Z}_p^k : [\boldsymbol{\theta}(\mathbf{x})]_1 = [\mathbf{M}(\mathbf{x})]_1 \cdot \mathbf{w}\right\} . \quad (1)$$

An algebraic language where $\mathbf{M}$ is independent of $\mathbf{x}$ and $\boldsymbol{\theta}$ is the identity is called a *linear language.* We sometimes require algebraic languages to satisfy a property we call 1DL-friendly. Roughly, this is to enable the embedding of a symmetric simple discrete logarithm challenge, which is given as a pair of group elements, into an algebraic statement in the reduction. We give the formal definition of this property in the full version [24]. We note that algebraic languages are as expressive as NP, since every Boolean circuit can be represented by sets of linear equations.

2.3 Non-interactive Zero-knowledge Arguments

A NIZK (non-interactive zero-knowledge) argument Π, for a family of languages $\mathcal{L}_{\mathtt{lpar}}$ consists of four PPT algorithms.

- CRSGen on input a security parameter 1^k generates a pair $(\mathtt{crs}, \mathtt{td})$.
- $\mathcal{P}$ on input a $\mathtt{crs}$, a statement $\mathtt{x}$ and a witness $\mathtt{w}$, computes a proof π.
- $\mathcal{V}$ on input a $\mathtt{crs}$, a statement $\mathtt{x}$ and a proof π outputs 1 (accept) or 0 (reject).
- Sim on input $\mathtt{td}$, a true statement $\mathtt{x}$ computes a simulated proof π.

Here we are implicitly supposing that $\mathtt{lpar}$ is always given as input. We assume that each $\mathtt{td}$ corresponds to only one $\mathtt{crs}$ and also that given $\mathtt{td}$ it is possible to efficiently and deterministically compute the corresponding $\mathtt{crs}$. This is w.l.o.g., since it is always possible to define the trapdoor in a way that the previous property is satisfied. The following properties are required for a NIZK argument:

- *Perfect completeness*: for any pair of true statement $\mathtt{x}$ with a relative witness $\mathtt{w}$, for any $\mathtt{crs}$ computed by CRSGen

$$\Pr\left[\mathcal{V}(\mathtt{crs}, \mathtt{x}, \pi) = 1 | \pi \leftarrow \mathcal{P}(\mathtt{crs}, \mathtt{x}, \mathtt{w})\right] = 1.$$

- *Computational soundness*: for any PPT adversary $\mathcal{A}$

$$\Pr\left[\begin{array}{c|c} \mathcal{V}(\mathtt{crs}, \mathtt{x}, \pi) = 1 & (\mathtt{crs}, \mathtt{td}) \leftarrow \mathsf{CRSGen}(1^k); \\ \mathtt{x} \notin \mathcal{L}_{\mathtt{lpar}} & (\mathtt{x}, \pi) \leftarrow \mathcal{A}(\mathtt{crs}) \end{array}\right] \leq \mathsf{negl}(k)$$

- *(Perfect) zero-knowledge*: for any true statement, witness pair $(\mathtt{x}, \mathtt{w})$, for any $(\mathtt{crs}, \mathtt{td}) \leftarrow \mathsf{CRSGen}(1^k)$ the following distributions are identical

$$\mathcal{P}(\mathtt{crs}, \mathtt{x}, \mathtt{w}) \equiv \mathsf{Sim}(\mathtt{crs}, \mathtt{td}, \mathtt{x}).$$

If the zero-knowledge property requires the two distributions to only be computationally insitinguishable, then we get a computational NIZK. If soundness holds even against unbounded adversaries, we say that the protocol is a NIZK proof system, with perfect soundness. We say that Π is black-box knowledge sound if there exists an efficient extractor that computes a witness, given a statement, an accepting proof and the $\texttt{crs}$ trapdoor.

Definition 1 (BB Knowledge soundness). *Let $\Pi = (\mathsf{CRSGen}, \mathcal{P}, \mathcal{V}, \mathsf{Sim})$ be a NIZK argument for the relation $\mathcal{R}_{\texttt{lpar}}$, defined by some language parameter $\texttt{lpar}$. We say that Π is black-box knowledge sound, if there exists an extractor $\mathsf{Ext}_{\mathsf{bb}}$ such that, for any PPT adversary $\mathcal{A}$:*

$$\Pr\left[\begin{array}{l|c} \mathcal{V}(\texttt{crs}, \texttt{x}, \pi) = 1 & (\texttt{crs}, \texttt{td}) \leftarrow \mathsf{CRSGen}(1^k); \\ \wedge(\texttt{x}, \texttt{w}) \notin \mathcal{R}_{\texttt{lpar}} & (\texttt{x}, \pi) \leftarrow \mathcal{A}(\texttt{crs}, \texttt{lpar}; r); \texttt{w} \leftarrow \mathsf{Ext}_{\mathsf{bb}}(\texttt{td}, \texttt{x}, \pi) \end{array}\right] \leq \mathsf{negl}(k)$$

where r is the random coins of the adversary.

If the extractor is allowed to depend on the adversary and we also give it as additional input, the random coins used by the adversary, we say that Π is white-box knowledge sound.

Definition 2 (n-BB Knowledge soundness). *Let $\Pi = (\mathsf{CRSGen}, \mathcal{P}, \mathcal{V}, \mathsf{Sim})$ be a NIZK argument for the relation $\mathcal{R}_{\texttt{lpar}}$, defined by some language parameter $\texttt{lpar}$. We say that Π is white-box knowledge sound, if for any PPT adversary $\mathcal{A}$, there exists an efficient extractor $\mathsf{Ext}_{\mathsf{wb},\mathcal{A}}$ such that:*

$$\Pr\left[\begin{array}{l|c} \mathcal{V}(\texttt{crs}, \texttt{x}, \pi) = 1 & (\texttt{crs}, \texttt{td}) \leftarrow \mathsf{CRSGen}(1^k); \\ \wedge(\texttt{x}, \texttt{w}) \notin \mathcal{R}_{\texttt{lpar}} & (\texttt{x}, \pi) \leftarrow \mathcal{A}(\texttt{crs}, \texttt{lpar}; r); \texttt{w} \leftarrow \mathsf{Ext}_{\mathsf{wb},\mathcal{A}}(\texttt{td}, \texttt{x}, \pi, r) \end{array}\right] \leq \mathsf{negl}(k)$$

where r is the random coins of $\mathcal{A}$.

We also consider the concrete security variants of the above definitions. The formal definitions are given in the full version [24]. Roughly, Π is (t, ϵ)-BB knowledge sound if the extraction property holds with respect to all $t(k)$-time bounded provers (as opposed to all PPT provers), and that the extractor succeeds except with probability ϵ (as opposed to being negligible).

Lastly, we state the witness indistinguishability definition for non-interactive protocols. Recall that we are interested in non-interactive witness indistinguishable proof systems in the plain model without a trusted setup.

Definition 3 (Witness Indistinguishability (WI)). *A non-interactive proof system $\Pi = (\mathcal{P}, \mathcal{V})$ for language $\mathcal{L}_{\texttt{lpar}}$ is WI if for every PPT verifier $(\mathcal{V}_1^*, \mathcal{V}_2^*)$, for all $(\texttt{x}, \texttt{w}_1, \texttt{w}_2)$ such that $(\texttt{x}, \texttt{w}_1) \in \mathcal{R}_{\texttt{lpar}}, (\texttt{x}, \texttt{w}_2) \in \mathcal{R}_{\texttt{lpar}}$, we have*

$$\Pr\left[b \leftarrow \mathcal{V}_2^*(\mathsf{st}, \pi) \middle| (\texttt{x}, \texttt{w}_1, \texttt{w}_2, \mathsf{st}) \leftarrow \mathcal{V}_1^*(\texttt{lpar}); b \xleftarrow{\$} \{0,1\}; \pi \leftarrow \mathcal{P}(\texttt{lpar}, \texttt{x}, \texttt{w}_b)\right] \approx_k \frac{1}{2}$$

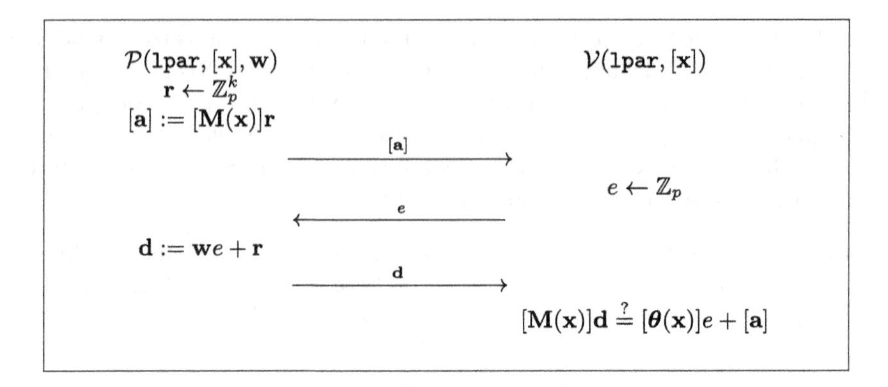

Fig. 1. Σ-protocol for algebraic language $\mathcal{L}_{\mathtt{lpar}}$ with $\mathtt{lpar} = (\mathbf{M}, \boldsymbol{\theta})$

$\mathsf{CRSGen}(1^k)$	$\mathcal{P}(\mathtt{lpar}, \mathtt{crs}, [\mathbf{x}]_1, \mathbf{w})$
$\mathtt{gpar} \leftarrow \mathsf{setup.gpar}(1^k)$	$\mathbf{r} \leftarrow \mathbb{Z}_p^k$
$e \leftarrow \mathbb{Z}_p$	$[\mathbf{a}]_1 := [\mathbf{M}(\mathbf{x})]_1\mathbf{r}$
$\mathtt{crs} := (\mathtt{gpar}, [e]_2); \mathtt{td} := e$	$[\mathbf{d}]_2 := \mathbf{w}[e]_2 + [\mathbf{r}]_2$
return $(\mathtt{crs}, \mathtt{td})$	**return** $\pi := ([\mathbf{a}]_1, [\mathbf{d}]_2)$
$\mathsf{Sim}(\mathtt{lpar}, \mathtt{crs}, e, [\mathbf{x}]_1)$	$\mathcal{V}(\mathtt{lpar}, \mathtt{crs}, [\mathbf{x}]_1, \pi = ([\mathbf{a}]_1, [\mathbf{d}]_2))$
$([\mathbf{a}]_1, \mathbf{d}) := \mathcal{S}_\Sigma([\mathbf{x}]_1, e)$	$[\mathbf{M}(\mathbf{x})]_1 \cdot [\mathbf{d}]_2 \stackrel{?}{=} [\boldsymbol{\theta}(\mathbf{x})]_1 \cdot [e]_2 + [\mathbf{a}]_1 \cdot [1]_2$
return $\pi := ([\mathbf{a}]_1, [\mathbf{d}]_2)$	

Fig. 2. NIZK argument for algebraic language $\mathcal{L}_{\mathtt{lpar}}$ with $\mathtt{lpar} = (\mathbf{M}, \boldsymbol{\theta})$ [16]

2.4 From Σ-protocols to NIZKs

Recently, Couteau and Hartmann [16] propose a new approach for building pairing-based non-interactive zero-knowledge arguments for algebraic languages. At a high level, their approach is based on compiling a Σ-protocol (see full version [24]) into a non-interactive zero-knowledge argument by embedding the challenge in $\mathbb{G}_2$ and publishing it once in the $\mathtt{crs}$. The NIZK argument is depicted in Fig. 2, where we denote as $\mathcal{S}_\Sigma$ the simulator for special honest verifier zero-knowledge property of the Σ-protocol. A variant of their compiler yields NIZK *proofs*, depicted in Fig. 3, based on standard assumptions. We refer to the full version [24] for more details.

2.5 Cryptographic Assumptions

The DL (discrete logarithm) assumption in group $\mathbb{G}_\iota$ of order p states that it is hard to compute the discrete logarithm of a random element in $\mathbb{G}_\iota$.

$\mathsf{CRSGen}(1^k)$	$\mathcal{P}(\mathtt{lpar}, \mathtt{crs}, [\mathbf{x}]_1, \mathbf{w})$
$s_1, s_2, e_1, e_2 \leftarrow \mathbb{Z}_p$	$\mathbf{r} \leftarrow \mathbb{Z}_p^k$
$\mathtt{crs} := ([s_1, s_2, s_1e_1, s_2e_2]_2)$	$[\mathbf{a}]_1 := [\mathbf{M}(\mathbf{x})]_1\mathbf{r}$
$\mathbf{return\ crs}$	$[\mathbf{d}_i]_2 := \mathbf{w}[s_ie_i]_2 + \mathbf{r}[s_i]_2$
	$\mathbf{return}\ \pi := ([\mathbf{a}]_1, [\mathbf{d}_1, \mathbf{d}_2]_2)$
$\mathsf{Sim}(\mathtt{lpar}, [\mathbf{x}]_1)$	$\mathcal{V}(\mathtt{lpar}, \mathtt{crs}, [\mathbf{x}]_1, \pi = ([\mathbf{a}]_1, [\mathbf{d}_1, \mathbf{d}_2]_2))$
$e, s_1, s_2 \leftarrow \mathbb{Z}_p$	**for** $i \in \{1, 2\}$ check
$([\mathbf{a}]_1, \mathbf{d}) := \mathcal{S}_\Sigma([\mathbf{x}]_1, e)$	$[\mathbf{M}(\mathbf{x})]_1 \cdot [\mathbf{d}_i]_2 \stackrel{?}{=} [\boldsymbol{\theta}(\mathbf{x})]_1 \cdot [s_ie_i]_2 + [\mathbf{a}]_1 \cdot [s_i]_2$
$\mathtt{crs} = ([s_1, s_2, s_1e, s_2e]_2)$	
$\pi := ([\mathbf{a}]_1, [\mathbf{d}s_1, \mathbf{d}s_2]_2)$	
$\mathbf{return}\ (\mathtt{crs}, \pi)$	

Fig. 3. NIZK proof for algebraic language $\mathcal{L}_{\mathtt{lpar}}$ with $\mathtt{lpar} = (\mathbf{M}, \boldsymbol{\theta})$ [16]

Assumption 1 (Discrete logarithm assumption). *For any PPT adversary $\mathcal{A}$, it holds that:*

$$\Pr\left[w[1]_\iota = [x]_\iota \middle| \ w \leftarrow \mathcal{A}([1, x]_\iota) \right] \leq \mathsf{negl}(k)$$

where x is sampled from the uniform distribution over $\mathbb{Z}_p$.

Assumption 2 (Symmetric discrete logarithm assumption). *For any PPT adversary $\mathcal{A}$, it holds that:*

$$\Pr\left[w[1]_\iota = [x]_\iota \ ; \ \iota = 1, 2 \middle| \ w \leftarrow \mathcal{A}([1, x]_1, [1, x]_2) \right] \leq \mathsf{negl}(k)$$

where x is sampled from the uniform distribution over $\mathbb{Z}_p$.

The co-CDH assumption was first proposed in [11]. Later a modified version of the assumption was proposed in [32] which we adapt as follows.

Assumption 3 (Computational co-Diffie-Hellman (co-CDH) assumption). *For any PPT adversary $\mathcal{A}$, it holds that:*

$$\Pr\left[[xy]_2 \leftarrow \mathcal{A}([1, x]_1, [1, x, y]_2) \right] \leq \mathsf{negl}(k)$$

where x, y are sampled from the uniform distribution over $\mathbb{Z}_p$.

3 NIWI Proof in the Plain Model

Our NIWI proof system in the plain model is given in Fig. 4. We show that our construction is perfectly sound and computationally WI. To show WI, we rely on a new assumption that we validate in the algebraic group model (AGM) in

$\mathcal{P}(\mathtt{lpar}, [\mathbf{x}]_1, \mathbf{w})$	$\mathcal{V}(\mathtt{lpar}, [\mathbf{x}]_1, \pi)$
$s_1, s_2, e_1, e_2 \leftarrow \mathbb{Z}_p$ s.t $e_1 \neq e_2$	parse π as $\Big([\mathbf{a}, c_1, c_2]_1, [s_1, s_2, E_1, E_2, \mathbf{d}_1, \mathbf{d}_2]_2\Big)$
$\mathbf{r} \leftarrow \mathbb{Z}_p^k$	accept if all the following checks pass
$[\mathbf{a}]_1 := [\mathbf{M}(\mathbf{x})]_1 \mathbf{r}$	$[c_i]_1[1]_2 \stackrel{?}{=} [1]_1[s_i]_2$ **for** $i \in \{1,2\}$ (1)
$\mathbf{d}_i := s_i e_i \mathbf{w} + s_i \mathbf{r}$ **for** $i = 1, 2$	$[c_2]_1[E_1]_2 \stackrel{?}{\neq} [c_1]_1[E_2]_2$ (2)
return $\pi := \Big([\mathbf{a}, s_1, s_2]_1,$	**for** $i \in \{1,2\}$:
$[s_1, s_2, s_1e_1, s_2e_2, \mathbf{d}_1, \mathbf{d}_2]_2\Big)$	$[\mathbf{M}(\mathbf{x})]_1[\mathbf{d}_i]_2 \stackrel{?}{=} [\boldsymbol{\theta}(\mathbf{x})]_1[E_i]_2 + [\mathbf{a}]_1[s_i]_2$ (3)

Fig. 4. NIWI proof for algebraic language $\mathcal{L}_{\mathtt{lpar}}$ with $\mathtt{lpar} = (\mathbf{M}, \boldsymbol{\theta})$

$G_{\mathbf{ADHR},b}(\mathcal{A}, \mathtt{lpar})$
$([\mathbf{x}]_1, \mathbf{w}_0, \mathbf{w}_1) \leftarrow \mathcal{A}([1]_1, [2]_2, \mathtt{lpar});$
$s_1, s_2, e_1, e_2 \leftarrow \mathbb{Z}_p; \mathbf{r} \leftarrow \mathbb{Z}_p^k; (e_1 \neq e_2);$
$\pi = ([\mathbf{M}(\mathbf{x})\mathbf{r}, s_1, s_2]_1, [s_1, s_1e_1, s_2, s_2e_2, s_1e_1\mathbf{w}_b + s_1\mathbf{r}, s_2e_2\mathbf{w}_b + s_2\mathbf{r}]_2);$
$b' \leftarrow \mathcal{A}([\mathbf{M}(\mathbf{x})]_1, \mathbf{w}_0, \mathbf{w}_1, \pi);$
if $b = b'$ **then return** 1; **else return** 0 **fi** ;

Fig. 5. Algebraic decisional hidden range games $G_{\mathbf{ADHR},i}$.

the full version [24]. While it might seem like we can show WI by relying on DDH in the second group and then invoking the WI of the underlying sigma protocol, the presence of $[s_2]_1$ in the proof makes this impossible. In fact, we rely on DDH being easy for perfect soundness by enabling the verifier to check that the two challenges are indeed distinct. We show that the new assumption holds in the AGM introduced by Fuchsbauer, Kiltz and Loss [22]. The model is a relaxation of the generic group model [42] that captures adversaries exploiting the representation of the underlying group, and has been shown to be useful in reasoning about security properties of various constructions [15,23,35]. The work of [41] extends this model to handle decisional assumptions by introducing the notion of algebraic distinguishers. We use this model to show the algebraic equivalence between our assumption and *symmetric power discrete logarithm* (SPDL) assumption. While the assumption we make is a tautological assumption, we hope it will be analysed further and will find other applications, just like the tautological Kiltz-Wee assumption for QA-NIZK [2,34]. We believe it is an interesting open problem to prove the security of our construction under standard decisional assumptions.

Assumption 4 (Algebraic decisional hidden range). *Let* $\mathtt{lpar} = (\mathbf{M}, \boldsymbol{\theta})$ *be any pair of language parameter that defines the algebraic language* $\mathcal{L}_{\mathtt{lpar}}$. *Let*

*$G_{ADHR,i}$, for $i \in \{0,1\}$ be the games depicted in Fig. 5. The $(\mathbf{M}, \boldsymbol{\theta})$-**ADHR** assumption states that for any PPT adversary $\mathcal{A}$,*

$$\mathbf{Adv}_{\mathcal{A},\mathtt{lpar}}^{G_{ADHR,0,1}} = |\Pr[G_{ADHR,0}(\mathcal{A}, \mathtt{lpar}) = 1] - \Pr[G_{ADHR,1}(\mathcal{A}, \mathtt{lpar}) = 1]| \leq \mathsf{negl}(k).$$

Theorem 1. *For any algebraic language $\mathcal{L}_{\mathtt{lpar}}$, with $\mathtt{lpar} = (\mathbf{M}, \boldsymbol{\theta})$, the protocol in Fig. 4 is a non-interactive witness indistinguishable proof under the $(\mathbf{M}, \boldsymbol{\theta})$-**ADHR** assumption.*

Proof. (Perfect completeness). We show that an honest prover convinces an honest verifier with probability 1. For an honestly generated proof $\pi = ([\mathbf{a}, c_1, c_2]_1, [s_1, s_2, E_1, E_2, \mathbf{d}_1, \mathbf{d}_2]_2)$, by construction, we have that $c_i = s_i^{-1}$, $E_i = s_i e_i$ and $\mathbf{d}_i = s_i(e_i \mathbf{w} + \mathbf{r})$. It is easy to see that all the verifier checks pass.

1. $[c_i]_1[s_i]_2 = [s_i^{-1}]_1[s_i]_2 = [1]_T$.
2. $[c_1]_1[E_1]_2 = [s_1^{-1}]_1[s_1 e_1]_2 = [e_1]_T$, and $[c_2]_1[E_2]_2 = [s_2^{-1}]_1[s_2 e_2]_2 = [e_2]_T$, and since $e_1 \neq e_2$, we have $[c_1]_1[E_1]_2 \neq [c_2]_1[E_2]_2$.
3. $\mathbf{M}(\mathbf{x})\mathbf{d}_i = s_i e_i \mathbf{M}(\mathbf{x})\mathbf{w} + s_i \mathbf{M}(\mathbf{x})\mathbf{r} = E_i \boldsymbol{\theta}(\mathbf{x}) + \mathbf{a} s_i$.

(Perfect soundness). Let $\mathcal{A}$ be any (possibly unbounded) adversary that breaks the soundness property by outputting a proof $\tilde{\pi} = ([\tilde{a}, \tilde{c}_1, \tilde{c}_2]_1, [\tilde{s}_1, \tilde{s}_2, \tilde{E}_1, \tilde{E}_2, \tilde{d}_1, \tilde{d}_2]_2)$ relative to an (adaptively) chosen statement $\mathtt{x} = [\mathbf{x}]_1 \notin \mathcal{L}_{\mathtt{lpar}}$, such that the NIWI verifier accepts $\tilde{\pi}$. We show that such an accepting proof contradicts with the assumption that $\mathtt{x} \notin \mathcal{L}_{\mathtt{lpar}}$. In what follows, the index i will always be used as for each $i \in \{1, 2\}$.

From the verifier's check (1), it must be that $\tilde{c}_i = \tilde{s}_i$. Moreover, from check (3) we have that $\mathbf{M}(\mathbf{x})\tilde{d}_i = \boldsymbol{\theta}(\mathbf{x})\tilde{E}_i + \tilde{a}\tilde{s}_i$, which means that $\mathbf{M}(\mathbf{x})\tilde{d}_i/\tilde{c}_i = \boldsymbol{\theta}(\mathbf{x})\tilde{E}_i/\tilde{c}_i + \tilde{a}$. Now, since the NIWI verifier accepts the proof, from check (2), we have that $\tilde{c}_2\tilde{E}_1 \neq \tilde{c}_1\tilde{E}_2$. Therefore, there exists a pair of valid transcripts $([\tilde{a}]_1, \tilde{E}_i/\tilde{c}_i, \tilde{d}_i/\tilde{c}_i)$ for $\mathtt{x}$, with the same first message $[\tilde{a}]_1$ and different challenges. From special soundness of the underlying Σ-protocol, there exists an extractor that outputs a witness for $\mathtt{x}$ given two such transcripts. This contradicts the assumption that $\mathtt{x} \notin \mathcal{L}_{\mathtt{lpar}}$.

(Witness indistinguishability). Let $\mathcal{L}_{\mathtt{lpar}}$ be an algebraic language with $\mathtt{lpar} = (\mathbf{M}, \boldsymbol{\theta})$. Let $\mathcal{A}$ be a PPT adversary that wins the WI game with non-negligible probability ϵ. We build an efficient adversary $\mathcal{B}$ against $(\mathbf{M}, \boldsymbol{\theta})$-**ADHR** assumption as follows: $\mathcal{B}$ first calls $\mathcal{A}$ and obtains $\mathsf{st} = ([\mathbf{x}]_1, \mathbf{w}_0, \mathbf{w}_1)$. It then outputs st and receives π from the challenger. Lastly, $\mathcal{B}$ calls $\mathcal{A}$ on π and returns $\mathcal{A}$'s decision bit. Since the challenger of $G_{\mathbf{ADHR},i}$ computes π exactly as the honest prover of the NIWI in Fig. 4, $\mathcal{B}$ breaks the assumption with the same non-negligible probability ϵ. □

We discuss the efficiency of our construction and applications of NIWI in the plain model in the full version [24].

4 Partial Extractability for the CH Framework

In this section, we first recall the definition of f-extractability and show the NIZK proof system in Fig. 3 is $[\cdot]_2$-extractable. Next, we strengthen this property by introducing a new notion called *strong f-extractability* where the partial witness $\widetilde{\mathtt{w}}$ can be used by an efficient algorithm to decide membership of the statement. In more detail, here we also require the existence of an efficiently computable decision procedure D such that for $\widetilde{\mathtt{w}} = f(\mathtt{w})$ output by the extractor, $\mathsf{D}(\mathtt{x}, \widetilde{\mathtt{w}})$ decides membership of $\mathtt{x}$ (i.e., $(\mathtt{x}, \mathtt{w}) \in \mathcal{R}$ iff $\mathsf{D}(\mathtt{x}, \widetilde{\mathtt{w}}) = 1$). However, $\widetilde{\mathtt{w}}$ falls short of being a witness for the relation; assuming that f is one-way, $\widetilde{\mathtt{w}}$ cannot be used to produce a valid proof for $\mathtt{x}$.

Definition 4 (f-extractability [7]). *Let $\Pi = (\mathsf{CRSGen}, \mathcal{P}, \mathcal{V}, \mathsf{Sim})$ be a NIZK argument for the relation $\mathcal{R}$, defined by some language parameter* $\mathtt{lpar}$. *Let f be an efficiently computable function. We say that Π is (black-box) f-extractable if there exists a PPT extractor* Ext *such that for any PPT adversary that returns an accepting proof π for a statement $\mathtt{x}$,* Ext *outputs a value $\widetilde{\mathtt{w}}$ for which there exists some $\mathtt{w}$ such that $(\mathtt{x}, \mathtt{w}) \in \mathcal{R}$ and $\widetilde{\mathtt{w}} = f(\mathtt{w})$ with overwhelming probability. More formally, for any PPT adversary $\mathcal{A}$, we have*

$$\Pr\left[\begin{array}{c} \mathcal{V}(\mathtt{crs}, \mathtt{x}, \pi) = 1 \\ \wedge(\mathtt{x}, f^{-1}(\widetilde{\mathtt{w}})) \notin \mathcal{R} \end{array}\middle| \begin{array}{c} (\mathtt{crs}, \mathtt{td}) \leftarrow \mathsf{CRSGen}(1^k); \\ (\mathtt{x}, \pi) \leftarrow \mathcal{A}(\mathtt{crs}, \mathtt{lpar}; r); \widetilde{\mathtt{w}} \leftarrow \mathsf{Ext}(\mathtt{td}, \mathtt{x}, \pi) \end{array}\right] \leq \mathsf{negl}(k)$$

where r is the random coins of the adversary.

We show that the CH proof system satisfies f-extractability where $f(x)$ is the encoding of x to $\mathbb{G}_2$. We state the lemma below and give the proof in the full version [24].

Lemma 1. *The NIZK proof system of [16] depicted in Fig. 3 is $[\cdot]_2$-extractable.*

4.1 Strong f-extractability

We now define strong f-extractability as an strengthening of f-extractability where the extracted value further allows to decide membership of the statement (although it cannot be used to produce a valid proof for it).

Definition 5 (Strong f-extractability). *Let $\Pi = (\mathsf{CRSGen}, \mathcal{P}, \mathcal{V}, \mathsf{Sim})$ be a NIZK argument for the relation $\mathcal{R}$, defined by some language parameter* $\mathtt{lpar}$. *Let f be an efficiently computable function. We say that Π is strong f-extractable if the following properties hold:*

Extractability. *Π is f-extractable (see Definition 4).*

Decidability. *There exists a DPT algorithm* D*, such that for any statement* $\mathtt{x}$ *and string $\widetilde{\mathtt{w}}$, it holds that $\mathsf{D}(\mathtt{x}, \widetilde{\mathtt{w}}) = 1$ iff $(\mathtt{x}, \mathtt{w}) \in \mathcal{R}$, where $\widetilde{\mathtt{w}} = f(\mathtt{w})$.*

One-wayness. *For any $(\mathtt{x}, \widetilde{\mathtt{w}})$ sampled uniformly at random s.t $\mathsf{D}(\mathtt{x}, \widetilde{\mathtt{w}}) = 1$, if there exists a PPT adversary $\mathcal{A}$ and a polynomial $p(\cdot)$, such that*

$$\Pr\left[\mathcal{V}(\mathtt{crs}, \mathtt{x}, \pi') = 1 \middle| \pi' \leftarrow \mathcal{A}(\mathtt{crs}, \mathtt{x}, \widetilde{\mathtt{w}})\right] \geq \frac{1}{p(k)},$$

there exists a PPT algorithm $\mathcal{I}$, and polynomial $q(\cdot)$ such that

$$\Pr\left[f(\bar{\mathtt{w}}) = \widetilde{\mathtt{w}} \middle| \bar{\mathtt{w}} \leftarrow I(\widetilde{\mathtt{w}})\right] \geq \frac{1}{q(k)}.$$

Remark 1. Similar to Definition 4, strong f-extractability is defined without any restriction on f and hence it can recover full extractability for the case when f is the identity function. However, we only focus on strong f-extractability for non-trivial f in this work. Having no restriction on f in Definition 4 and 5 makes strong f-extractability a middle ground between full and f-extractability.

We show in the full version [24] that the proof system in Fig. 3 is strong $[\cdot]_2$-extractable under a standard hardness assumption.

5 Full Extractability for the CH Framework

The CH argument system from Fig. 2 is knowledge sound in the AGM (see the full version [24]). Now, we turn to showing limitations of proving knowledge soundness.[4] We begin this section by defining a notion of knowledge soundness called *semantic extraction.* We study the relationship between semantic knowledge soundness and standard notions of black-box (BB) and white-box (n-BB) knowledge soundness. Then, we show impossibility of the existence of semantic extractors for the CH argument system in Fig. 2. The generalization of this impossibility to quasi-adaptive NIZK arguments constructed from SPHFs is in the full version [24].

Notation. We introduce some additional notation for this section. We denote by **CRS** the set of all possible $\mathtt{crs}$'s. We denote by χ the set of the statements $\mathtt{x}$ and by Ψ the set of all possible proofs π We also split the randomness of PPT-s into two strings s and t. We denote by $\mathbf{\Gamma_t}$ the set of all possible strings t and by $\mathbf{\Gamma_s}$ the set of all possible strings s. Looking ahead, for adversarial provers, this split, at a high level, is to distinguish between the portion of randomness that is provided to the semantic extractor (t), and the portion that is not (s). Note that, while **CRS**, χ, Ψ are defined by the NIZK construction, the randomness spaces are not fixed by the NIZK. We only assume that s, t have polynomial size.

5.1 Semantic Extractor

We now define our new notion of extraction. Informally, this extractor inverts the "semantic" function implemented by an adversarial prover regardless of *how*

[4] Recently, [4] instantiated AGM under falsifiable assumptions. However, their construction relies on indistinguishability obfuscation. It is inherently inefficient and not a practical group for applications. Here, we focus on feasibility of knowledge soundness of the CH framework as is in the standard model, without compromising on the efficiency.

the computation was done. The key difference from n-BB notion is that we will not ask for a different extractor for every PPT $\mathcal{A}$, instead, we ask for an extractor associated with a function f; this extractor is universal for all TMs (even unbounded ones) that implement f. We begin by modeling the function implemented by a knowledge soundness adversary. To capture any possible adversarial strategy, we consider functions f and a distribution D from which random coins are sampled for a machine that implements f.

Definition 6 (Knowledge soundness strategy (KSS)). *Consider NIZK $\Pi = (\mathsf{CRSGen}, \mathcal{P}, \mathcal{V}, \mathsf{Sim})$. Let $f : \mathbf{CRS} \times \mathbf{\Gamma_s} \times \mathbf{\Gamma_t} \rightarrow \chi \times \Psi$ be a function, and D be the uniform distribution over $\mathbf{\Gamma_s} \times \mathbf{\Gamma_t}$. f is said to be a knowledge soundness strategy for Π if*

$$\Pr\left[\mathcal{V}(\mathtt{crs}, \mathtt{x}, \pi) = 1 \middle| \begin{array}{r}(\mathtt{crs}, \mathtt{td}) \leftarrow \mathsf{CRSGen}(1^k); (s||t) \leftarrow D \\ f(\mathtt{crs}; (s,t)) = (\mathtt{x}, \pi)\end{array}\right] = \eta(k)$$

where $\eta(k)$ is non-negligible. We say that a TM $\mathcal{A}$ implements the knowledge soundness strategy f, if for any $\mathtt{crs} \in \mathbf{CRS}$ and $(s,t) \leftarrow D$, we have $z \leftarrow \mathcal{A}(\mathtt{crs}; s, t)$, where $z = f(\mathtt{crs}, s, t)$. If there exists a PPT $\mathcal{A}$ that implements a knowledge soundness strategy f, we say that f is efficiently implementable.

We now define semantic knowledge soundness for a KSS.

Definition 7 (Semantic knowledge soundness). *Consider a NIZK argument $\Pi = (\mathsf{CRSGen}, \mathcal{P}, \mathcal{V}, \mathsf{Sim})$. Let D be the uniform distribution over $\mathbf{\Gamma_s} \times \mathbf{\Gamma_t}$. We call Π semantic knowledge sound if for every efficiently implementable KSS f, there exists a PPT extractor $\mathsf{Ext} = \mathsf{Ext}_f$, such that, for each (even unbounded) TM $\mathcal{A}^*$ that implements f, we have*

$$\Pr\left[\begin{array}{r}\mathcal{V}(\mathtt{crs}, \mathtt{x}, \pi) = 1 \\ \wedge (\mathtt{x}, \mathtt{w}) \notin \mathcal{R}\end{array} \middle| \begin{array}{r}(\mathtt{crs}, \mathtt{td}) \leftarrow \mathsf{CRSGen}(1^k); (s||t) \leftarrow D \\ (\mathtt{x}, \pi) \leftarrow \mathcal{A}^*(\mathtt{crs}; (s,t)); \boxed{\mathtt{w} \leftarrow \mathsf{Ext}(\mathtt{td}, \mathtt{x}, \pi, t)}\end{array}\right] \leq \mathsf{negl}(k)$$

Remark 2. We note that asking for extraction only against provers that implement a KSS is *not* a weakening of the extraction definition, since we only care about extracting from provers that make the verifier accept with non-negligible probability.

Remark 3. Note that this definition is a generalization of the usual knowledge soundness definitions. In particular, if we hide all the randomness from the extractor (that is $\mathbf{\Gamma_t}$ is the set that contains only the empty string), then we recover the usual black-box knowledge soundness. On the other hand, if we give the extractor all the randomness used by the adversary (that is $\mathbf{\Gamma_s}$ is the set that contains only the empty string), then we recover the canonical white-box knowledge soundness. We discuss these connections formally in the full version [24]. We define semBB and semn-BB exactly as in Definition 7 with the boxed part replaced with $\mathtt{w} \leftarrow \mathsf{Ext}(\mathtt{td}, \mathtt{x}, \pi)$, and $\mathtt{w} \leftarrow \mathsf{Ext}(\mathtt{td}, \mathtt{x}, \pi, s||t)$ respectively.

Remark 4 (Canonical knowledge soundness adversary). The usual definition of knowledge soundness naturally handles the existence of an extractor for the honest prover. Our definition handles the case of the honest prover too; we show the honest efficiently implementable KSS for a NIZK Π below:

1. Sample uniformly random strings $(s, t) \leftarrow \mathbf{\Gamma_s} \times \mathbf{\Gamma_t}$.
2. Sample a true statement $\mathtt{x}$ together with $\mathtt{w}$, from the uniform distribution over pair of $(\mathtt{x}, \mathtt{w}) \in \mathcal{R}$, using random seed s. Note that this can be done efficiently. That is, there exists a PPT $\mathcal{A}$ that computes $(\mathtt{x}, \mathtt{w})$ on random coins s. Let us define the function $g : \mathbf{\Gamma_s} \rightarrow \chi \times \{0,1\}^*$ as $g(s) = (\mathtt{x}, \mathtt{w})$.
3. Run the honest prover algorithm on input $(\mathtt{crs}, \mathtt{x}, \mathtt{w})$ and random coins t, to compute a proof π. Define the function $g' : \mathbf{CRS} \times \chi \times \{0,1\}^* \times \mathbf{\Gamma_t} \rightarrow \Psi$ as $g'(\mathtt{crs}, \mathtt{x}, \mathtt{w}, t) = \mathcal{P}(\mathtt{crs}, \mathtt{x}, \mathtt{w}; t)$.
4. Define $f : \mathbf{CRS} \times \mathbf{\Gamma_s} \times \mathbf{\Gamma_t} \rightarrow \chi \times \Psi$ as $f(\mathtt{crs}, (s, t)) = (\mathtt{x}, \pi)$ where $(\mathtt{x}, \mathtt{w}) = g(s)$ and $\pi = g'(\mathtt{crs}, \mathtt{x}, \mathtt{w}, t)$.

We call this f the canonical knowledge soundness strategy, and a PPT algorithm that implements it the *canonical adversary* of knowledge soundness.

We illustrate the meaningfulness of the new notion by showing relationships of semantic extraction with BB and n-BB extraction definitions in the full version [24]. Here we point out that the notion of semantic extraction has been implicitly used in other works. For instance, standard Σ-protocols satisfy the semantic extraction notion. By special soundness, given a certain number of accepting transcripts for the same statement, and the same prover's first message, an extractor exists that outputs a valid witness. The extractor, therefore, does not depend on the prover's computation, instead, on a "semantic" function: one that outputs two different accepting transcripts relative to the same statement, and the same first message. One advantage in thinking of an extractor as a semantic one is the possibility to use it in a reduction, without its relative "native" adversary. This is indeed what is done in the proof of soundness for the NIZK proof of [16] described in Fig. 3, which is based on the existence of an (unbounded) TM that computes a valid input for the special soundness extractor, and then relying on the implicit semantic property of the latter.

The non-black-box nature of the semantic definition is limited to making non-black-box use of the malicious prover's randomness, but otherwise the prover's TM is treated as a black-box. There are instances in literature where a n-BB technique in fact corresponds to a semantic technique. Consider the case of simulation – Barak's non-black-box zero-knowledge protocol [5]. Though simulation is defined to make non-black-box use of the verifier's TM, it can be modified to only make non-black-box use of the auxiliary input and running time of the verifier, and not its TM. The property needed to define the simulator is the existence of an efficient (with bounded-length description) adversary. Then in the security proof, the next-message function implemented by the adversary is used, together with the ability to choose its random coins. This means that the security proof works for any adversary (even an unbounded one) that computes the same next-message function. Moreover, the zero-knowledge simulator for each of these adversaries would be exactly the same simulator as the one defined for the efficient adversary. For concreteness, we may think that, given the code of one efficient adversary, we define a simulator that works for each TM that computes the same function, in the sense that we use the code in a black-box way; by just fixing the random coins and taking partial outputs.

5.2 Impossibility of Semantic Knowledge Soundness for CH-NIZK

In this section we focus on semantic knowledge soundness of NIZK argument in Fig. 2 for a large and useful class of algebraic languages. We show in the full version [24] that when the adversary is algebraic, knowledge soundness holds in the AGM for this NIZK argument. We ask for knowledge soundness in the standard model, and show that CH NIZK argument cannot be semantic knowledge sound. The impossibility can be interpreted as an adversary explicitly violating AGM rules by hiding some exponent about the statement, and thus making the extractor fail. We refer to Remark 5, for more remarks on the interpretation of this result, while we focus on technical details for the rest of this section.

We now show the impossibility proof of semantic knowledge soundness of CH arguments for linear languages $\mathcal{L}_{\mathtt{lpar}}$, where $\mathtt{lpar} = [\mathbf{M}]_1$ is a constant matrix. The proof of Theorem 2 for general case of 1DL-friendly languages is provided in the full version [24].

Lemma 2. *Let $\mathcal{L}_{\mathtt{lpar}}$ be a linear language defined by constant matrix $\mathtt{lpar} := [\mathbf{M}]_1$. The NIZK argument in Fig. 2 cannot be semantic knowledge sound for $\mathcal{L}_{\mathtt{lpar}}$ under the SDL assumption.*

Proof. We denote as w_i components of the vector $\mathbf{w}$. The description of the canonical prover adversary on input ($\mathtt{crs} = [e]_2$) and random coins (s, t), where $t = (\mathbf{r}, r')$ is given in Fig. 6a. Let Ext_f be the semantic extractor for the function $f([e]_2; (s, t)) = ([\mathbf{x}]_1, \pi)$, with $\pi = ([\mathbf{a}]_1, [\mathbf{d}]_2)$ that is implemented by the canonical prover adversary. By completeness of the NIZK argument, $\mathsf{Ext}_f(e, [\mathbf{x}, \mathbf{a}]_1, [\mathbf{d}]_2, t)$ outputs a valid witness $\mathbf{w}$ for $[\mathbf{x}]_1$ with overwhelming probability. Let us consider the (not polynomial-time) TM $\mathcal{P}^*$ as in Fig. 6b that implements f. $\mathcal{P}^*$ implements the same f of the canonical adversary and therefore its output can be used to feed the same extractor Ext_f.

We now exploit Ext_f to define an adversary $\mathcal{A}$ against SDL assumption. On input an SDL challenge $([w_1]_1, [w_1]_2)$, $\mathcal{A}$ is defined as in Fig. 6c. Since $\mathcal{A}$ computes inputs of Ext_f exactly as $\mathcal{P}^*$ does, they are correctly distributed, and hence $\mathcal{A}$ breaks SDL with the same probability that Ext_f succeeds.

Theorem 2. *Let $\mathcal{L}_{\mathtt{lpar}}$ be a 1DL-friendly algebraic language defined by language parameters $\mathtt{lpar} := (\mathbf{M}, \boldsymbol{\theta})$. The NIZK argument in Fig. 2 cannot be semantic knowledge sound for $\mathcal{L}_{\mathtt{lpar}}$ under the SDL assumption.*

Remark 5. Since our reduction exploits the knowledge of the trapdoor to compute a proof, (as a typical ZK simulator would do), it might seem like we are arguing about extracting from the simulator. However this is not the case, at

1. Sample uniformly random w_1 using random coins s.
2. Sample other components of $\mathbf{w}$, w_i for $i \neq 1$, using random coins r'.
3. Compute $[\mathbf{x}]_1 = [\mathbf{M}]_1\mathbf{w}$.
4. Compute $[\mathbf{a}]_1 = [\mathbf{M}]_1\mathbf{r}$.
5. Compute $[\mathbf{d}]_2 = \mathbf{w}[e]_2 + \mathbf{r}[1]_2$.
6. Output $([\mathbf{x}]_1, \pi = ([\mathbf{a}]_1, [\mathbf{d}]_2))$.

(a) Canonical prover adversary

1. Use random coins s to sample w_1 and compute $[w_1]_1, [w_1]_2$.
2. Compute (inefficiently) e from $[e]_2$.
3. Sample other components of $\mathbf{w}$ using random coins r'.
4. Compute $[\mathbf{x}]_1 = [\mathbf{Mw}]_1$.
5. Compute $[\mathbf{a}]_1 = [\mathbf{Mr}]_1$.
6. Compute $[\mathbf{d}]_2 = e[\mathbf{w}]_2 + \mathbf{r}[1]_2$.

(b) Unbounded adversary

1. Sample $e, \mathbf{r}, r'$.
2. Sample other components of $\mathbf{w}$, w_i for $i \neq 1$, using random coins r'.
3. Compute $[\mathbf{x}]_1 = [\mathbf{Mw}]_1$.
4. Compute $[\mathbf{a}]_1 = [\mathbf{Mr}]_1$.
5. Compute $[\mathbf{d}]_2 = e[\mathbf{w}]_2 + \mathbf{r}[1]_2$.
6. Compute $\mathbf{w} \leftarrow \mathsf{Ext}_f(([\mathbf{a}]_1, [\mathbf{d}]_2), e, [\mathbf{x}]_1, (\mathbf{r}, r'))$.
7. Output w_1.

(c) SDL adversary

Fig. 6. Procedures for Fig. 2

least in general. We note that the procedure defined by the SDL adversary is very different from the zero-knowledge simulator. First, the adversary knows something that the simulator does not, which is $[\mathbf{x}]_2$. Moreover, the adversary is able to compute $[\mathbf{a}]_1$ before computing $[\mathbf{d}]_2$ as the honest prover; while the simulator, in order to compute a proof must compute $\mathbf{d}$ before. This can be also seen as the fact that the honest prover and simulator do not implement the same function. In fact, given the language parameter $\mathbf{M} \in \mathbb{Z}_p^{n \times m}$ the prover computes a proof π as a function of $\mathbf{x}, \mathbf{w}, r$ where $r \in \mathbb{Z}_p^{n \times 1}$, while the simulator computes a proof which is a function of random coins $r_{\mathsf{Sim}} \in \mathbb{Z}_p^{m \times 1}$. In order to invoke the semantic extractor associated to the honest prover, we must have a function that defines a relation between the two randomness. This, for instance, can be done (inefficiently) only in some particular cases, like when $\mathbf{M}$ is a square invertible matrix. Finally, the existence of such cases is evidence towards the impossibility of extraction. In fact, given the latter case, since we have perfect zero-knowledge for a relation that defines only true statement, given a proof from the NIZK argument, it is impossible to distinguish the case when the prover was honest, from the case when a powerful adversary just computes the discrete logarithm of the CRS and runs the simulator. Furthermore, it is impossible to distinguish the case that adversary had $[\mathbf{w}]_2$ and the trapdoor e, instead of $\mathbf{w}$ without relying on knowledge-type assumptions.

References

1. Abdolmaleki, B., Baghery, K., Lipmaa, H., Zając, M.: A subversion-resistant SNARK. In: Takagi, T., Peyrin, T. (eds.) ASIACRYPT 2017. LNCS, vol. 10626, pp. 3–33. Springer, Cham (2017). https://doi.org/10.1007/978-3-319-70700-6_1
2. Abdolmaleki, B., Lipmaa, H., Siim, J., Zając, M.: On QA-NIZK in the BPK model. In: Kiayias, A., Kohlweiss, M., Wallden, P., Zikas, V. (eds.) PKC 2020. LNCS, vol. 12110, pp. 590–620. Springer, Cham (2020). https://doi.org/10.1007/978-3-030-45374-9_20
3. Acar, T., Nguyen, L.: Revocation for delegatable anonymous credentials. In: Catalano, D., Fazio, N., Gennaro, R., Nicolosi, A. (eds.) PKC 2011. LNCS, vol. 6571, pp. 423–440. Springer, Heidelberg (2011). https://doi.org/10.1007/978-3-642-19379-8_26
4. Agrikola, T., Hofheinz, D., Kastner, J.: On instantiating the algebraic group model from falsifiable assumptions. In: Canteaut, A., Ishai, Y. (eds.) EUROCRYPT 2020. LNCS, vol. 12106, pp. 96–126. Springer, Cham (2020). https://doi.org/10.1007/978-3-030-45724-2_4
5. Barak, B.: How to go beyond the black-box simulation barrier. In: 42nd FOCS, pp. 106–115. IEEE Computer Society Press, October 2001. https://doi.org/10.1109/SFCS.2001.959885
6. Barak, B., Ong, S.J., Vadhan, S.: Derandomization in cryptography. In: Boneh, D. (ed.) CRYPTO 2003. LNCS, vol. 2729, pp. 299–315. Springer, Heidelberg (2003). https://doi.org/10.1007/978-3-540-45146-4_18
7. Belenkiy, M., Chase, M., Kohlweiss, M., Lysyanskaya, A.: P-signatures and noninteractive anonymous credentials. In: Canetti, R. (ed.) TCC 2008. LNCS, vol. 4948, pp. 356–374. Springer, Heidelberg (2008). https://doi.org/10.1007/978-3-540-78524-8_20
8. Ben-Or, M., et al.: Everything provable is provable in zero-knowledge. In: Goldwasser, S. (ed.) CRYPTO 1988. LNCS, vol. 403, pp. 37–56. Springer, New York (1990). https://doi.org/10.1007/0-387-34799-2_4
9. Benhamouda, F., Pointcheval, D.: Trapdoor smooth projective hash functions. Cryptology ePrint Archive, Report 2013/341 (2013). http://eprint.iacr.org/2013/341
10. Blum, M., Feldman, P., Micali, S.: Non-interactive zero-knowledge and its applications (extended abstract). In: 20th ACM STOC, pp. 103–112. ACM Press, May 1988. https://doi.org/10.1145/62212.62222
11. Boneh, D., Gentry, C., Lynn, B., Shacham, H.: Aggregate and verifiably encrypted signatures from bilinear maps. In: Biham, E. (ed.) EUROCRYPT 2003. LNCS, vol. 2656, pp. 416–432. Springer, Heidelberg (2003). https://doi.org/10.1007/3-540-39200-9_26
12. Bootle, J., Cerulli, A., Chaidos, P., Ghadafi, E., Groth, J., Petit, C.: Short accountable ring signatures based on DDH. Cryptology ePrint Archive, Report 2015/643 (2015). http://eprint.iacr.org/2015/643
13. Camenisch, J., Lysyanskaya, A.: An efficient system for non-transferable anonymous credentials with optional anonymity revocation. In: Pfitzmann, B. (ed.) EUROCRYPT 2001. LNCS, vol. 2045, pp. 93–118. Springer, Heidelberg (2001). https://doi.org/10.1007/3-540-44987-6_7
14. Camenisch, J., Stadler, M.: Efficient group signature schemes for large groups. In: Kaliski, B.S. (ed.) CRYPTO 1997. LNCS, vol. 1294, pp. 410–424. Springer, Heidelberg (1997). https://doi.org/10.1007/BFb0052252

15. Chiesa, A., Hu, Y., Maller, M., Mishra, P., Vesely, N., Ward, N.: Marlin: preprocessing zkSNARKs with universal and updatable SRS. In: Canteaut, A., Ishai, Y. (eds.) EUROCRYPT 2020. LNCS, vol. 12105, pp. 738–768. Springer, Cham (2020). https://doi.org/10.1007/978-3-030-45721-1_26
16. Couteau, G., Hartmann, D.: Shorter non-interactive zero-knowledge arguments and ZAPs for Algebraic languages. In: Micciancio, D., Ristenpart, T. (eds.) CRYPTO 2020. LNCS, vol. 12172, pp. 768–798. Springer, Cham (2020). https://doi.org/10.1007/978-3-030-56877-1_27
17. Cramer, R., Shoup, V.: Universal hash proofs and a paradigm for adaptive chosen ciphertext secure public-key encryption. In: Knudsen, L.R. (ed.) EUROCRYPT 2002. LNCS, vol. 2332, pp. 45–64. Springer, Heidelberg (2002). https://doi.org/10.1007/3-540-46035-7_4
18. Dwork, C., Naor, M.: Zaps and their applications. In: 41st FOCS, pp. 283–293. IEEE Computer Society Press, November 2000. https://doi.org/10.1109/SFCS.2000.892117
19. Faonio, A., Fiore, D., Herranz, J., Ràfols, C.: Structure-preserving and re-randomizable RCCA-secure public key encryption and its applications. In: Galbraith, S.D., Moriai, S. (eds.) ASIACRYPT 2019. LNCS, vol. 11923, pp. 159–190. Springer, Cham (2019). https://doi.org/10.1007/978-3-030-34618-8_6
20. Feige, U., Fiat, A., Shamir, A.: Zero knowledge proofs of identity. In: Aho, A. (ed.) 19th ACM STOC, pp. 210–217. ACM Press, May 1987. https://doi.org/10.1145/28395.28419
21. Fortnow, L.: The complexity of perfect zero-knowledge (extended abstract). In: Aho, A. (ed.) 19th ACM STOC, pp. 204–209. ACM Press, May 1987. https://doi.org/10.1145/28395.28418
22. Fuchsbauer, G., Kiltz, E., Loss, J.: The Algebraic group model and its applications. In: Shacham, H., Boldyreva, A. (eds.) CRYPTO 2018. LNCS, vol. 10992, pp. 33–62. Springer, Cham (2018). https://doi.org/10.1007/978-3-319-96881-0_2
23. Gabizon, A., Williamson, Z.J., Ciobotaru, O.: PLONK: Permutations over Lagrange-bases for Oecumenical Noninteractive Arguments of Knowledge. Cryptology ePrint Archive, Report 2019/953 (2019). https://eprint.iacr.org/2019/953
24. Ganesh, C., Khoshakhlagh, H., Parisella, R.: NIWI and new notions of extraction for Algebraic languages. Cryptology ePrint Archive, Report 2022/851 (2022). https://eprint.iacr.org/2022/851
25. Gentry, C., Wichs, D.: Separating succinct non-interactive arguments from all falsifiable assumptions. In: Fortnow, L., Vadhan, S.P. (eds.) 43rd ACM STOC, pp. 99–108. ACM Press, Jun 2011. https://doi.org/10.1145/1993636.1993651
26. Goldreich, O., Micali, S., Wigderson, A.: Proofs that yield nothing but their validity and a methodology of cryptographic protocol design (extended abstract). In: 27th FOCS, pp. 174–187. IEEE Computer Society Press, October 1986. https://doi.org/10.1109/SFCS.1986.47
27. Goldreich, O., Micali, S., Wigderson, A.: How to play any mental game or a completeness theorem for protocols with honest majority. In: Aho, A. (ed.) 19th ACM STOC, pp. 218–229. ACM Press, May 1987. https://doi.org/10.1145/28395.28420
28. Goldwasser, S., Micali, S., Rackoff, C.: The knowledge complexity of interactive proof-systems (extended abstract). In: 17th ACM STOC, pp. 291–304. ACM Press, May 1985. https://doi.org/10.1145/22145.22178
29. Green, M., Hohenberger, S.: Practical adaptive oblivious transfer from simple assumptions. In: Ishai, Y. (ed.) TCC 2011. LNCS, vol. 6597, pp. 347–363. Springer, Heidelberg (2011). https://doi.org/10.1007/978-3-642-19571-6_21

30. Groth, J., Ostrovsky, R., Sahai, A.: New techniques for noninteractive zero-knowledge. J. ACM **59**(3), 1–35 (2012)
31. Groth, J., Sahai, A.: Efficient non-interactive proof systems for bilinear groups. In: Smart, N. (ed.) EUROCRYPT 2008. LNCS, vol. 4965, pp. 415–432. Springer, Heidelberg (2008). https://doi.org/10.1007/978-3-540-78967-3_24
32. Hu, J., Khalil, I., Tari, Z., Wen, Sh. (eds.): MONAMI 2017. LNICST, vol. 235. Springer, Cham (2018). https://doi.org/10.1007/978-3-319-90775-8
33. Izabachène, M., Libert, B., Vergnaud, D.: Block-wise P-signatures and Non-interactive anonymous credentials with efficient attributes. In: Chen, L. (ed.) IMACC 2011. LNCS, vol. 7089, pp. 431–450. Springer, Heidelberg (2011). https://doi.org/10.1007/978-3-642-25516-8_26
34. Kiltz, E., Wee, H.: Quasi-adaptive NIZK for linear subspaces revisited. In: Oswald, E., Fischlin, M. (eds.) EUROCRYPT 2015. LNCS, vol. 9057, pp. 101–128. Springer, Heidelberg (2015). https://doi.org/10.1007/978-3-662-46803-6_4
35. Maller, M., Bowe, S., Kohlweiss, M., Meiklejohn, S.: Sonic: zero-knowledge SNARKs from linear-size universal and updatable structured reference strings. In: Cavallaro, L., Kinder, J., Wang, X., Katz, J. (eds.) ACM CCS 2019, pp. 2111–2128. ACM Press, November 2019. https://doi.org/10.1145/3319535.3339817
36. Naor, M.: On cryptographic assumptions and challenges. In: Boneh, D. (ed.) CRYPTO 2003. LNCS, vol. 2729, pp. 96–109. Springer, Heidelberg (2003). https://doi.org/10.1007/978-3-540-45146-4_6
37. Naor, M., Yung, M.: Public-key cryptosystems provably secure against chosen ciphertext attacks. In: 22nd ACM STOC, pp. 427–437. ACM Press, May 1990. https://doi.org/10.1145/100216.100273
38. Pass, R.: Unprovable security of perfect NIZK and non-interactive non-malleable commitments. In: Sahai, A. (ed.) TCC 2013. LNCS, vol. 7785, pp. 334–354. Springer, Heidelberg (2013). https://doi.org/10.1007/978-3-642-36594-2_19
39. Ràfols, C.: Stretching Groth-Sahai: NIZK proofs of partial satisfiability. In: Dodis, Y., Nielsen, J.B. (eds.) TCC 2015. LNCS, vol. 9015, pp. 247–276. Springer, Heidelberg (2015). https://doi.org/10.1007/978-3-662-46497-7_10
40. Rial, A., Kohlweiss, M., Preneel, B.: Universally composable adaptive priced oblivious transfer. In: Shacham, H., Waters, B. (eds.) Pairing 2009. LNCS, vol. 5671, pp. 231–247. Springer, Heidelberg (2009). https://doi.org/10.1007/978-3-642-03298-1_15
41. Rotem, L., Segev, G.: Algebraic distinguishers: from discrete logarithms to decisional Uber assumptions. In: Pass, R., Pietrzak, K. (eds.) TCC 2020. LNCS, vol. 12552, pp. 366–389. Springer, Cham (2020). https://doi.org/10.1007/978-3-030-64381-2_13
42. Shoup, V.: Lower bounds for discrete logarithms and related problems. In: Fumy, W. (ed.) EUROCRYPT 1997. LNCS, vol. 1233, pp. 256–266. Springer, Heidelberg (1997). https://doi.org/10.1007/3-540-69053-0_18

Succinct Attribute-Based Signatures for Bounded-Size Circuits by Combining Algebraic and Arithmetic Proofs

Yusuke Sakai(✉)

AIST, Tokyo, Japan
yusuke.sakai@aist.go.jp

Abstract. Attribute-based signatures allow fine-grained attribute-based authentication and at the same time keep a signer's privacy as much as possible. While there are constructions of attribute-based signatures allowing arbitrary circuits or Turing machines as an authentication policy, none of them is practically very efficient. Some schemes have long signatures or long user secret keys which grow as the sizes of a policy or attributes grow. Some scheme relies on a vast Karp reduction which transforms public-key and secret-key operations into an arithmetic circuit. We propose an attribute-based signature scheme for bounded-size arbitrary arithmetic circuits with constant-size signatures and user secret keys without relying on such a Karp reduction. The scheme is based on bilinear groups and is proven secure in the generic bilinear group model. To achieve this we develop a new extension of SNARKs (succinct non-interactive arguments of knowledge). We formalize this extension as *constrained SNARKs*, which can be seen as a simplification of commit-and-prove SNARKs both in syntax and technique. In a constrained SNARK, one can force a prover to use a witness satisfying some constraint by announcing a *succinct* constraint string which encodes a constraint on a witness. If a proof is valid under some constraint string, it is ensured that the witness behind the proof satisfies the constraint that is behind the constraint string. By succinct, we mean that a constraint string has a constant length independent of the length of the plain description of the constraint, and notably a verifier need not know the (potentially long) plain description of the constraint for verifying a proof. We construct a constrained SNARK in the generic bilinear group model.

1 Introduction

Attribute-based signatures are a powerful cryptographic primitive for privacy-preserving authentication. They allow a signer in possession of a set of attributes to sign on a message while revealing only the fact that his attributes satisfy a public policy. More concretely, in the set-up phase, an authority generates a master secret key together with some public parameters, and publicizes the public parameter. Each signer having some attributes is issued a user secret key associated with his attributes. Using this user secret key he can generate a signature on

C. Galdi and S. Jarecki (Eds.): SCN 2022, LNCS 13409, pp. 711–734, 2022.
https://doi.org/10.1007/978-3-031-14791-3_31

a message with a policy. Such a signature is publicly verifiable using the message and the policy, and the fact that the verification passes discloses that the signer of the signature has some attributes that satisfy the public policy. More importantly, any information on the attributes beyond this fact is completely hidden from the verifier. This primitive has multiple applications, such as anonymous credentials [19], attribute-based messaging [15], and secret leaking [15].

One of the active lines of research in attribute-based signatures is to extend the class of the policies that a scheme supports. Research along this line includes a scheme for non-monotone span programs [16], for bounded-depth circuits [20], for unbounded circuits [17], for bounded-depth circuits from lattices [21], for unbounded circuits from lattices (in the random oracle model) [8], for Turing machines [18], and for unbounded arithmetic branching programs [7]. In this line of research, two extremes of the classes of policies, that is, unbounded circuits and Turing machines, are both achieved.

However, such schemes are not necessarily very efficient. For example, the scheme for unbounded circuits [17] has a long signature size linear in the number of the NAND gates, while the scheme for Turing machines [18] has a signature size quadratic to the running time of the Turing machine. The two lattice-based schemes for bounded-depth circuits [21] have constant-size signatures and constant-size user secret keys, respectively, but these schemes do not achieve constant-size user secret keys and signatures simultaneously. Namely, even in these two schemes either keys or signatures grow depending on the sizes of a policy or attributes. Besides, these two schemes only achieve relatively weaker security notions.

Succinct functional signatures [4] use SNARKs (succinct non-interactive arguments of knowledge) to have very short (succinct in their terminology) signatures. A drawback of this scheme is to require a vast Karp reduction for generating a signature, and thus it is not very efficient in running time.

One may think that this use of a Karp reduction is not a weakness of their scheme, since a Karp reduction from a circuit to, say, a quadratic arithmetic program is trivial. However, in their scheme, a SNARK needs to prove not only the satisfiability of a policy by attributes but also the validity of a (secret) digital signature on a (secret) encoding of the signer's attributes. For the satisfiability of a policy, the Karp reduction (from a circuit to a quadratic arithmetic program) is straightforward. In contrast, for the validity of a signature, the Karp reduction is not so easy to carry on, since we need to express many of *public-key and secret-key operations* (modular arithmetic, elliptic curve operations, bilinear maps, hashing, and so on) *in a quadratic arithmetic program.* Expressing public-key and secret-key operations in a quadratic arithmetic program is very costly, and this hinders practical applications of their functional signature scheme.

We summarize these schemes in Table 1.

This current situation is not satisfactory, since in applications of attribute-based signatures policies and attributes can be both very large, and thus the lack of constant-size keys and signatures restricts potential applications of

Table 1. Comparison among expressive attribute-based signature schemes.

	Policy	Sig. size[a]	Key size[a]	Param. size[a]	Karp reduc.	Assump	Security[b]
OT11 [16]	Non-mono. SP	$O(\ell)$	$O(d)$	$O(d)$		DLIN	
TLL14 [20]	Bound.-depth cir	$O(1)$	$O(\|C\|)$	$O(\|x\|)$		MLM	Selec. unforge
SAH16 [17]	Unbound. cir	$O(\|C\|)$	$O(1)$	$O(\|x\|)$		SXDH	
T17 (1) [21]	Bound.-depth cir	$O(1)$	$O(\text{poly}(\|C\|))$	$O(\text{poly}(\|C\|_{\max}))$		SIS	Weak. ano
T17 (2) [21]	Bound.-depth cir	$O(\text{poly}(\|x\|))$	$O(1)$	$O(\|x\|)$		SIS	Selec. unforge
EK18 [8]	Unbound. cir	$O(\|C\|)$	$O(1)$	$O(\|x\|)$		SIS and LWE in ROM	
SKAH18 [18]	Unbound. TM	$O(T^2)$	$O(\|\Gamma\|)$	$O(1)$		SXDH	
DOT19 [7]	Unbound. ABP	$O(m)$	$O(n)$	$O(1)$		SXDLIN	
BGI14 [4]	Unbound. cir	$O(1)$	$O(1)$	$O(1)$	Required	zk-SNARKs	
Ours	Bound. cir	$O(1)$	$O(1)$	$O(\|C\|_{\max} \log\|C\|_{\max})$		GGM	

[a] [1] The dependencies on the security parameter is ignored.
[b] [2] The blanks mean the "full" security, i.e., the same level of security as in the definition in this paper.
Non-mono. SP : Non-monotone span programs.
Bound.-depth cir .: Bounded-depth circuits (the bound is fixed at the set-up phase).
Unbound. cir .: Circuits with no size bounds.
Unbound. TM .: Turing machines with no bounds on the descriptions and time/space complexity.
Unbound. ABP : Unbounded arithmetic branching programs.
Bound. cir .: Bounded-size circuits (the bound is fixed at the set-up phase).
ℓ: The number of the rows of the non-monotone span program.
d: The number of the variables of non-monotone span programs.
$|C|$: The size of the circuit.
$|x|$: The number of the input wires of circuits.
$|C|_{\max}$: The upper bound for the sizes of circuits.
T: The running time of the Turing machine.
$|\Gamma|$: The cardinality of the tape alphabet.
m: The number of the vectors representing the arithmetic span programs.
n: The length of the input to arithmetic span programs.
DLIN : The decision linear assumption over pairing groups.
MLM : Multilinear maps.
SXDH : The symmetric external Diffie-Hellman assumption.
SIS : The short integer solution assumption.
LWE : The learning with errors assumption.
ROM : The random oracle model.
SXDLIN : The symmetric external decision linear assumption.
zk-SNARKs: Zero-knowledge SNARKs.
GGM : The generic bilinear group model.
Selec. unforge.: Selective unforgeability.
Weak ano.: Weak anonymity.

attribute-based signatures. The only known scheme that avoids long signature and user secret key, i.e., the scheme by Boyle et al. [4], suffers from a Karp reduction in the above sense.

1.1 Our Contribution

In this paper, we construct the first *succinct* attribute-based signature scheme for bounded-size arithmetic circuits *without Karp reductions*. Here, by bounded-size circuits, we mean that the family of arbitrary circuits with polynomially upper-bounded sizes where the polynomial is specified at the set-up phase of attribute-based signatures. The sizes of user signing keys and signatures are independent of the size of the circuits and the bound of the circuit size. A drawback of our construction is that the public parameters grow linearly in the upper bound of circuit sizes. The security of the scheme is proven in the generic bilinear group model.

When instantiated in asymmetric bilinear groups, our scheme has a signature size of 18 $\mathbb{G}_1$ elements and 14 $\mathbb{G}_2$ elements. A signing key includes three $\mathbb{G}_1$ elements and one $\mathbb{G}_2$ elements. (For details on the instantiation, see Sect. 4.3.) Compared with the attribute-based signature schemes supporting arbitrary circuits except for Boyle et al.'s (i.e., Sakai et al.'s [17] and El Kaafarani and Katsumata's [8]), our scheme drastically reduces the size of signatures.

Compared with Boyle et al.'s scheme [4] (instantiated with Groth's SNARK [11] and a standard RSA signature scheme), the number of exponentiations in our signing algorithm is roughly 300 times fewer than that of Boyle et al.'s. Our signing algorithm includes roughly 100 exponentiations plus additional ones whose number is dependent on the size of the circuit. In contrast, the signing algorithm of Boyle et al.'s includes roughly 330,000 exponentiations plus almost the same additional exponentiations as ours. This estimation comes from (i) xJsnark's optimization [13, Table III], in which verifying a standard signature, e.g., an RSA exponentiation and hashing, requires about 110,000 constraints of a quadratic arithmetic program, and (ii) the estimation that Groth's SNARK requires roughly three exponentiations for one constraint.[1]

Table 1 compares our scheme with the above-mentioned existing schemes. Compared with others, our scheme achieves another trade-off between expressiveness of policies and efficiency. For example, while our scheme can only accept bounded-size circuits as a policy, it can avoid Karp reductions. In contrast, the functional signature scheme accepts unbounded-size circuits as a policy at the cost of a Karp reduction. In particular, our scheme is the first scheme that achieves constant-size signatures and user secret key while simultaneously avoiding Karp reductions for public-key and secret-key operations.

In order to make a signature succinct and to avoid a Karp reduction, we combine SNARKs and structure-preserving cryptography [1]. Our first observation is that some SNARKs have verification equations expressed as pairing-product equations [12], which leads us to the possibility of proving the knowledge of a SNARK in a structure-preserving manner. Remember that one of the general approaches to construct an expressive attribute-based signature scheme is to sign on attributes and prove the knowledge of the signature together with proving the satisfiability of a policy by the same attributes [15,17,18]. We separately construct these two proofs by Groth-Sahai proofs [12] and SNARKs.

To combine these two proofs, we need to extend the syntax of SNARKs. We name it as *constrained (preprocessing)*[2] *SNARKs*.[3] We formalize the syntax and security notion of constrained SNARKs as an independent cryptographic primitive for a modular construction of succinct attribute-based signatures. Constrained SNARKs allow a third party to force a prover to use a witness of some type by publicizing a *constraint string* which is generated from a constraint on a witness. A proof is verified under the CRS and a constraint string. If a proof is valid under a constraint string, the witness behind the proof is ensured to

[1] This instantiation is optimized for the signature length. Boyle et al.'s construction requires the SNARK to be "trapdoor extractable" [10], but we ignore this requirement and assume that Groth's SNARK has this property (Instead, to avoid this extra assumption, one may attach an encryption of the part of the witness that needs to be extracted to a signature). Furthermore, Groth's SNARK is not necessarily optimized for RSA exponentiation, as it only supports arithmetic circuits of a prime modulus. Still, we adopt this SNARK for optimization for the signature length.

[2] A (constrained) SNARK is preprocessing if the sizes of the statements that can be proved are bounded at the time of generating a common reference string (CRS).

[3] Constrained SNARKs can be seen as a simplification of commit-and-prove SNARKs [5]. For a comparison between these two types of formalization, see Sect. 1.3.

satisfy the constraint behind the constraint string. The point is that the constraint string is *succinct*, namely, the size of a constraint string is independent of the size of the constraint from which the constraint string is generated (up to a factor polylogarithmic to the maximal size of constraints). This succinctness enables us to have a succinct attribute-based signature scheme when we combine constrained SNARKs with standard non-interactive zero-knowledge proofs. In our implementation of constrained SNARKs, the class of constraints is relatively restricted, namely, the class of prefix constraints (a witness satisfies a constraint if and only if it has a specific prefix). We remark that while this is less expressive, this class of constraints is sufficient for our purpose.

Formally, we provide a generic construction of attribute-based signatures from constrained SNARKs, non-interactive witness-indistinguishable extractable proofs, and digital signatures. These ingredients are all instantiated using asymmetric bilinear groups, and their security is proven in the generic bilinear group model. Furthermore, since the constrained SNARK has succinct proofs and succinct constraint strings, the resulting attribute-based signature scheme is also succinct (in terms of the user secret key and signature sizes).

1.2 Difficulty and Our Technique

In this subsection, we explain the main obstacle in our construction, that is, how to avoid Karp reductions.

Let us remind the readers of one of the general approaches to construct an attribute-based signature scheme [15,17,18]. In this approach, an authority sets up a standard signature scheme and a non-interactive zero-knowledge proof system. The verification key and the CRS constitute the public parameter, and the signing key is the master secret key. To issue a user signing key for some attributes, the authority generates a signature on the attributes, and issues this signature as a user signing key. To issue an attribute-based signature, a user proves the knowledge of a signature that is valid on some attributes and proves that the same attributes satisfy the policy.

Dividing a Proof. The first step toward succinct attribute-based signatures without Karp reductions is observing the fact that the first statement, the validity of a signature, can be efficiently proven by Groth-Sahai proofs, while the other statement, the satisfiability of the policy, can be efficiently proven by some SNARKs. Implementing this idea is not straightforward, because it is non-trivial to prove the consistency between two proofs. By consistency between the two proofs, we intend that the witnesses behind the proofs, the one behind the Groth-Sahai proof and the one behind the SNARK, are the same. If this consistency is not ensured by any means, it results in an insecure scheme.

A naive way to ensure consistency is to add a third non-interactive proof. Namely, this third proof proves that the Groth-Sahai proof and the SNARK are computed correctly by proving the knowledge of the witnesses behind them. In addition, the third proof simultaneously proves that the two sets of attributes (one is included in the witness of the Groth-Sahai proof, and the other is included in the witness of the SNARK) are identical. However, this approach does not work well. For example, let us consider instantiating the third proof by SNARKs. In that case, while it can achieve succinctness, it again introduces a Karp reduction. This is because the well-formedness Groth-Sahai proofs and SNARKs can be expressed as pairing product equations, but no known SNARKs can deal with such equations directly. Therefore, we need to express such equations in a Boolean circuit. Another choice for instantiating the third proof is to use Groth-Sahai proofs. While this may eliminate the need for a Karp reduction, it happens not to be succinct, since the size of the witness of the SNARK grows as the sizes of the policy and the attributes grow.

Constraining a SNARK. To overcome this difficulty, we introduce a mechanism to constrain the witness of a SNARK to follow a prescribed constraint, in which a prover is unable to generate a proof without following the prescribed constraint. We name SNARKs with this mechanism as constrained SNARKs. We remark that this formalism can be seen as a simplification of the syntax and technique of commit-and-prove SNARKs [5,6,9] but for efficiency we deviate from their formalization. More precisely, using constrained SNARKs, anyone can generate a *constraint string* which encodes a prescribed constraint on a witness. A proof is verified under the CRS and such a constraint string. If a proof is valid under the CRS and a constraint string, it ensures that the prover knows a witness which is valid for the statement and simultaneously satisfies the prescribed constraint. An important property of constrained SNARKs is that the prescribed constraint can be fixed before fixing the statement to be proven. More importantly, a constraint string should be succinct for the reasons mentioned later (If a constraint string is not succinct, the construction is trivial). Moreover, the verifier does not need to know the constraint in the plain form, but only needs to know its succinct encoding, namely, the constraint string.

More formally, constrained SNARKs are used in the following scenario. In the set-up phase, a third party generates a CRS. After seeing the CRS, given a constraint on a witness, any party can generate a constraint string. Given the CRS, the constraint string, a statement, and a witness satisfying the constraint, a prover can generate a proof. The proof is verified using the CRS, the constraint string, and the statement. If a proof is verified as valid, this fact ensures that the prover knows a witness that is for the statement and satisfies the constraint that is behind the constraint string.

Replacing the above use of a SNARK with a constrained SNARK, we can establish consistency between a Groth-Sahai proof and a (constrained) SNARK. For this purpose, we use the equality constraints (which is a subclass of the prefix constraints) as the class of constraints for the constrained SNARK. Namely, a constraint is described by attributes, and some given witness (attributes) satisfies a constraint, if and only if they are identical. With these constraints, we can implement attribute-based signatures as follows. We let an authority generate a CRS of Groth-Sahai proofs, a CRS for the constrained SNARKs, and a key pair of a signature scheme. To issue a user signing key, the authority computes a constraint string for the constraint described by the user's attributes. Then the authority signs on that constraint string, and issues the user with the constraint string and the signature as the user signing key. Given the constraint string and the signature on it, the user generates an attribute-based signature as follows. The user firstly generates a SNARK which proves that his attributes satisfy the policy. Note that this SNARK is valid under the constraint string given as a part of the user signing key. Then the user generates a Groth-Sahai proof which proves that (i) the knowledge of a SNARK that is valid under a constraint string and (ii) the knowledge of a signature on that constraint string. The user issues this Groth-Sahai proof as an attribute-based signature.

The important point for the security is that the Groth-Sahai proof ensures that the constraint strings used in the above two statements (i) and (ii) are identical. By this, if a malicious user tries to use different attributes than his own attributes for a witness of a SNARK, the malicious user needs to "disobey" the constraint string that was signed on by the authority (or needs to forge a signature on a maliciously chosen constraint string).

We remark that the succinctness of constraint strings is also important. This is because an attribute-based signature includes a Groth-Sahai proof with witness a constraint string. Therefore, an attribute-based signature grows linearly to the size of a constraint string. Thus, to have a succinct attribute-based signature, we need to have a succinct constraint string.

We also remark that in many SNARKs which can prove circuit satisfiability a witness is divided into two parts: The assignment to input wires and that of internal wires. If we implement a constraint mechanism into such a SNARK and apply it to attribute-based signatures, it is convenient to be able to constrain only the input-wire part. This is because even a single user may use different circuits for different signatures, and then the user may use different witnesses for different signatures. Such a partial constraint is expressed as a prefix constraint. Namely, a constraint is described by assignment to input wires. A witness (assignment to input wires and that of internal wires) satisfies a constraint if these two sets of assignment to input wires are equal. Such a constraint can be seen as a "prefix" constraint.

1.3 Related Work

On Expressive Attribute-Based Signatures. The research of attribute-based signatures was initiated by Maji, Prabhakaran, and Rosulek [15]. They proposed three constructions (all on bilinear groups), which have different advantages and disadvantages. The first two schemes rely on the approach of proving the knowledge of signature on attributes.

Among the schemes on bilinear groups, this approach has been the most effective way to construct a very expressive attribute-based signature scheme, despite its relative inefficiency. For example, Sakai, Attrapadung, and Hanaoka [17] and Sakai et al. [18] both use this approach to construct schemes for unbounded circuits and Turing machines, respectively. These two schemes obtain their expressiveness at the cost of very long signatures (and user signing keys for the latter), as mentioned in Table 1.

A different and complemental approach is to base an attribute-based signature scheme on (the techniques of) attribute-based encryption scheme, and, more concretely, those of dual system encryption. The Okamoto-Takashima scheme [16] and the Datta-Okamoto-Takashima scheme [7] fall into this category. In both schemes, both the signature and user secret key sizes are not fully dependent on the complexity parameters of policies. For example, in the Okamoto-Takashima scheme (see Table 1), the complexity of a policy is measured by the parameters ℓ and d but the signature and user secret key sizes are dependent on only ℓ and d, respectively. In addition, these two schemes allow us to use large-universe policies.

The currently known lattice-based schemes also have the above contrast. El Kaafarani and Katsumata used a technique similar to that of Sakai, Attrapadung, and Hanaoka [17] (for an attribute-based signature scheme for circuits), that is, to commit to wire assignment and prove the relations imposed on wires by each gate. In contrast, Tsabary's scheme [21] is very specific to lattice assumptions but obtains performance and assumption advantages.

If we are willing to employ multilinear maps, we can adopt the scheme by Tang, Li, and Liang [20].

Boyle, Goldwasser, and Ivan [4] introduced a related primitive called functional signatures. Notably, one of their instantiations of functional signatures achieves succinctness, however, this instantiation relies on a Karp reduction, which we want to avoid.

On SNARKs Related to Constrained SNARKs. Commit-and-prove SNARKs (Geppetto [6], LegoSNARK [5], implicitly Fiore et al. [9], also implicitly Agrawal et al. [3], etc.) allow a prover to commit to (a part of) a witness and later to prove that the witness that was committed to satisfies a statement (together with the rest of a witness). This type of abstraction can replace constrained SNARKs in our construction, however, the abstraction of the commit-and-prove SNARKs is rather too rich for our purpose. More concretely, while commit-and-prove SNARKs provide the zero-knowledge property in general, our construction *does not* require that constrained SNARKs (and commit-and-prove SNARKs) be zero-knowledge. Instead, privacy is obtained by wrapping a constrained SNARK by a Groth-Sahai proof.[4] In fact, constrained SNARKs can be seen as a simplification of commit-and-prove SNARKs. This simplification is not only of the syntax but our construction can be seen as an adoption of Geppetto's idea to Groth's SNARK. For a detailed discussion, see the last paragraphs of Sect. 3.3.

LegoSNARK [5] uses a commit-and-prove technique to combine different proof systems for different models of computations (arithmetic/Boolean circuits, state machines, random access machines, etc.). Since this goal of LegoSNARK

[4] The point that we need to "wrap" a constrained SNARK is to avoid the following linkability issue: In our construction, a signer reuses his constraint string that encodes his attributes and was signed on by the authority every time he wants to issue an attribute-based signature; thus, making this constraint string public allows an adversary to track all the attribute-based signatures issued by him.

is exactly what our construction wants to achieve, i.e., combining proof systems for arithmetic circuits and pairing-product equations, then one may think that LegoSNARK can be used to construct an attribute-based signature scheme without Karp reductions. However, this is not straightforward. This is because LegoSNARK does not support pairing-based statements, which are vital for letting signers prove the knowledge of a signature on attributes.

Agrawal et al. [3] also presented a method for proving a "composite" statement that consists of both arithmetic equations and group-based equations. Again, one may think that this can be used for our purpose. However, this is also not straightforward. The reason is that their method uses elliptic-curve groups of a large order (for dealing with an addition formula of an elliptic curve in the exponent and in particular dealing with modular reductions involved in computing the formula). Thus the resulting attribute-based signature scheme is not very efficient.

Fiore et al. [9] introduced the abstraction of online-offline verification of SNARKs. This abstraction is quite similar to our abstraction of constrained SNARKs. In our terminology, their formulation additionally allows a malicious prover to generate a constraint string maliciously and further requires that the corresponding extractor be able to extract a consistent constraint in the plain form. In our application, we do not need this stronger knowledge soundness, and hence we adopt our weaker version of knowledge soundness.

2 Preliminary

We give the necessary definitions used in this paper. We omit the standard definitions of bilinear groups, the generic bilinear groups, signatures, and a hash function family for the space limitation.

Witness-Indistinguishable and Extractable Proof Systems. A non-interactive proof system consists of the following algorithms.

$\mathsf{WI.Setup}(1^\lambda) \to \mathsf{crs}$. The setup algorithm takes as input a security parameter 1^λ and outputs a CRS crs.

$\mathsf{WI.Prove}(\mathsf{crs}, x, w) \to \pi$. The proving algorithm takes as input a CRS crs, a statement x, and a witness w and outputs a proof π.

$\mathsf{WI.Verify}(\mathsf{crs}, x, \pi) \to 0$ **or** 1. The verification algorithm takes as input a CRS crs, a statement x, and a proof π and outputs a bit 0 or 1.

$\mathsf{WI.ExtSetup}(1^\lambda) \to (\mathsf{crs}, \mathsf{xk})$. The extractable setup algorithm takes as input a security parameter 1^λ and outputs a CRS crs and an extraction trapdoor xk.

$\mathsf{WI.Extract}(\mathsf{crs}, \mathsf{xk}, x, \pi) \to w$. The extraction algorithm takes as input a CRS crs, an extraction trapdoor xk, a statement x, and a proof π and outputs a witness w.

We say that $(\mathsf{WI.Setup}, \mathsf{WI.Prove}, \mathsf{WI.Verify}, \mathsf{WI.ExtSetup}, \mathsf{WI.Extract})$ is a non-interactive proof system for relation R, if for all $\lambda \in \mathbb{N}$, all $\mathsf{crs} \leftarrow \mathsf{WI.Setup}(1^\lambda)$, all $(x, w) \in R$, and all $\pi \leftarrow \mathsf{WI.Prove}(\mathsf{crs}, x, w)$, it holds that $\mathsf{WI.Verify}(\mathsf{crs}, x, \pi) = 1$.

We define two security requirements for non-interactive proofs, witness indistinguishability and extractability.

Definition 1. *A non-interactive proof system is witness indistinguishable, if for all probabilistic polynomial-time adversaries $\mathcal{A}$ it holds that*

$$2 \cdot \left| \Pr[b \leftarrow \{0,1\}; \mathsf{crs} \leftarrow \mathsf{WI.Setup}(1^\lambda); b' \leftarrow A^{\mathcal{O}_b}(\mathsf{crs}) : b = b'] - \frac{1}{2} \right|$$

is negligible in λ where $\mathcal{O}_b$ is an oracle that given (x, w_0, w_1) returns $\pi \leftarrow \mathsf{WI.Prove}(\mathsf{crs}, x, w_b)$ if (x, w_0), $(x, w_1) \in R$ and returns $\perp$ if $(x, w_0) \notin R$ or $(x, w_1) \notin R$.

Definition 2. *A non-interactive proof system is extractable, if for all probabilistic polynomial-time adversaries $\mathcal{A}$ it holds that*

$$|\Pr[\mathsf{crs} \leftarrow \mathsf{WI.Setup}(1^\lambda); b' \leftarrow \mathcal{A}(\mathsf{crs}) : b' = 1] \\ - \Pr[(\mathsf{crs}, \mathsf{xk}) \leftarrow \mathsf{WI.ExtSetup}(1^\lambda); b' \leftarrow \mathcal{A}(\mathsf{crs}) : b' = 1]|$$

is negligible in λ, and for all probabilistic polynomial-time adversaries $\mathcal{A}$ it holds that

$$\Pr\left[\begin{array}{l} (\mathsf{crs}, \mathsf{xk}) \leftarrow \mathsf{WI.ExtSetup}(1^\lambda); \\ (x^*, \pi^*) \leftarrow \mathcal{A}(\mathsf{crs}); w^* \leftarrow \mathsf{WI.Extract}(\mathsf{crs}, \mathsf{xk}, x^*, \pi^*) \\ : \mathsf{WI.Verify}(\mathsf{crs}, x^*, \pi^*) = 1 \wedge (x^*, w^*) \notin R \end{array}\right]$$

is negligible in λ.

Attribute-Based Signatures. An attribute-based signature scheme consists of the following algorithms.

$\mathsf{ABS.Setup}(1^\lambda) \rightarrow (\mathsf{pp}, \mathsf{mk})$. The setup algorithm takes as input a security parameter 1^λ and outputs a public parameter pp and a master secret key mk.

$\mathsf{ABS.Kg}(\mathsf{pp}, \mathsf{mk}, u) \rightarrow \mathsf{uk}$. The key generation algorithm takes as input a public parameter pp, a master secret key mk, and attributes u and outputs a user secret key uk.

$\mathsf{ABS.Sign}(\mathsf{pp}, u, \mathsf{uk}, C, m) \rightarrow \Sigma$. The signing algorithm takes as input a public parameter pp, attributes u, a user secret key uk, a policy C, and a message m and outputs an attribute-based signature Σ.

$\mathsf{ABS.Verify}(\mathsf{pp}, C, m, \Sigma) \rightarrow 0$ **or** 1. The verification algorithm takes as input a public parameter pp, a policy C, a message m, and an attribute-based signature Σ and outputs a bit 0 or 1.

We say that $(\mathsf{ABS.Setup}, \mathsf{ABS.Kg}, \mathsf{ABS.Sign}, \mathsf{ABS.Verify})$ is an attribute-based signature scheme, if for all $\lambda \in \mathbb{N}$, all $(\mathsf{pp}, \mathsf{mk}) \leftarrow \mathsf{ABS.Setup}(1^\lambda)$, all sets of attributes u, all $\mathsf{uk} \leftarrow \mathsf{ABS.Kg}(\mathsf{pp}, \mathsf{mk}, u)$, all policies C satisfying $C(u) = 1$, all messages m, and all $\Sigma \leftarrow \mathsf{ABS.Sign}(\mathsf{pp}, u, \mathsf{uk}, C, m)$, it holds that $\mathsf{ABS.Verify}(\mathsf{pp}, C, m, \Sigma) = 1$.

We define two security requirements for attribute-based signatures, anonymity and unforgeability.

Definition 3. *An attribute-based signature scheme is anonymous, if for all probabilistic polynomial-time stateful adversaries $\mathcal{A}$ it holds that*

$$2 \cdot \left| \Pr \begin{bmatrix} b \leftarrow \{0,1\}; (\mathsf{pp}, \mathsf{mk}) \leftarrow \mathsf{ABS.Setup}(1^\lambda); \\ (u_0, u_1, C, m) \leftarrow \mathcal{A}(\mathsf{pp}, \mathsf{mk}); \mathsf{uk} \leftarrow \mathsf{ABS.Kg}(\mathsf{pp}, \mathsf{mk}, u_b); \\ \Sigma^* \leftarrow \mathsf{ABS.Sign}(\mathsf{pp}, u_b, \mathsf{uk}, C, m); b' \leftarrow \mathcal{A}(\Sigma^*) \\ : b = b' \end{bmatrix} - \frac{1}{2} \right|$$

is negligible in λ where $\mathcal{A}$ is required to output u_0, u_1, and C satisfying that $C(u_0) = C(u_1) = 1$.

Definition 4. *An attribute-based signature scheme is unforgeable, if for all probabilistic polynomial-time adversaries $\mathcal{A}$ it holds that*

$$\Pr \begin{bmatrix} (\mathsf{pp}, \mathsf{mk}) \leftarrow \mathsf{ABS.Setup}(1^\lambda); (C^*, m^*, \Sigma^*) \leftarrow \mathcal{A}^{\mathcal{O}}(\mathsf{pp}) \\ : \mathsf{ABS.Verify}(\mathsf{pp}, C^*, m^*, \Sigma^*) = 1 \wedge \bigwedge_{u \in K} (C^*(u) \neq 1) \wedge (C^*, m^*) \notin Q \end{bmatrix}$$

is negligible in λ. The oracle $\mathcal{O}$ records pairs (u, uk) of attributes u and a corresponding user signing key uk in which the record is initially empty and accepts the following two types of queries:

1. *When a key generation query u is issued by $\mathcal{A}$, the oracle searches for a recorded tuple (u, uk) for some uk and returns uk if the tuple is found; if not found, the oracle computes $\mathsf{uk} \leftarrow \mathsf{ABS.Kg}(\mathsf{pp}, \mathsf{mk}, u)$, records the tuple (u, uk), and returns uk;*
2. *when a signing query (u, C, m) is issued by $\mathcal{A}$, the oracle searches for a recorded tuple (u, uk) for some uk; it computes $\mathsf{uk} \leftarrow \mathsf{ABS.Kg}(\mathsf{pp}, \mathsf{mk}, u)$ and records (u, uk) if not found; it computes $\Sigma \leftarrow \mathsf{ABS.Sign}(\mathsf{pp}, u, \mathsf{uk}, C, m)$, and returns Σ.*

The set K is the set of attributes u that is issued as a key generation query, and the set Q is the set of the tuples (C, m) that is issued as a signing query (u, C, m) with some u.

Universal Arithmetic Circuits. A universal arithmetic circuit is an arithmetic circuit over a field $\mathbb{F}$ that takes as input a description C of an arithmetic circuit over the same field $\mathbb{F}$ and an input u for C and outputs $C(u)$. A universal arithmetic circuit can be constructed by generalizing a Boolean universal circuit [22,23]. Such a generalization was briefly mentioned by Lipmaa et al. [14]. In this paper, sometimes we need to mention the wire assignment v for a universal arithmetic circuit U. To explicitly mention this, we use the notation $U(C, u; v) = y$, which denotes that the universal arithmetic circuit U outputs y when evaluated on C and u, and v is the wire assignment of the universal arithmetic circuit U for that evaluation.

3 Constrained SNARKs

In this section, we firstly describe a technical overview of our construction of constrained SNARKs. Then we describe the syntax and requirements of constrained (preprocessing) SNARKs as well as our construction of it. While our syntax and technique can be seen as a simplification of those of commit-and-prove SNARKs [5,6,9], we do not follow their formalization for efficiency reasons.

3.1 Technical Overview

In this subsection, we explain a technical overview of our construction of constrained SNARKs. We base our constrained SNARK on Groth's SNARK [11]. Recall that Groth's SNARK can prove satisfiability of the following equation:

$$\Big(\sum_{i=0}^{m} a_i u_i(X)\Big) \cdot \Big(\sum_{i=0}^{m} a_i v_i(X)\Big) \equiv \sum_{i=0}^{m} a_i w_i(X) \bmod t(X) \quad (1)$$

where X is an indeterminate, $u_i(X)$, $v_i(X)$, and $w_i(X) \in \mathbb{Z}_p[X]$ are public polynomials of degree $n-1$ and $t(X) \in \mathbb{Z}_p[X]$ is a public polynomial of degree n. The coefficients $a_0, \ldots, a_{\ell'}$ ($\ell' < m$) are a statement, and $a_{\ell'+1}, \ldots, a_m$ are a witness.

We reinterpret this assignment of coefficients to a statement and a witness as below. We regard $a_0, \ldots, a_\ell$ ($\ell < \ell'$) as a statement and $a_{\ell+1}, \ldots, a_{\ell'}$, $a_{\ell'+1}, \ldots, a_m$ as a witness, and regard $a_{\ell+1}, \ldots, a_{\ell'}$ as the prefix part. This way, the prefix part will be treated as a public statement by Groth's SNARK . This can be slightly confusing at first glance but simplifies the construction. This reinterpretation leaks the prefix of the witness to the verifier. This does not cause a problem, because of two reasons. Firstly, the existence of a prefix constraint itself leaks the information of the prefix of the witness on its own. Secondly, we do not intend to achieve the zero-knowledge property in the constrained SNARK, because, in our construction of attribute-based signatures, we wrap a SNARK by a Groth-Sahai proof. This use of a Groth-Sahai proof ensures the anonymity of the attribute-based signature scheme.

Now we provide a quick and necessary review of Groth's SNARK . In Groth's SNARK, the verifier checks the following equation for verifying a proof $\pi = (A, B, C)$:

$$\begin{aligned} &e(A, B) \\ &\quad = e([\alpha]_1, [\beta]_2) \cdot e\bigg(\bigg[\sum_{i=0}^{\ell'} a_i \frac{\beta u_i(x) + \alpha v_i(x) + w_i(x)}{\gamma}\bigg]_1, [\gamma]_2\bigg) \cdot e(C, [\delta]_2) \end{aligned}$$

where $e\colon \mathbb{G}_1 \times \mathbb{G}_2 \to \mathbb{G}_T$ is a bilinear map, $[a]_1 = g^a$ for some generator $g \in \mathbb{G}_1$, $[b]_2 = h^b$ for some generator $h \in \mathbb{G}_2$, and $[\alpha]_1$, $[\beta]_2$, $[\gamma]_2$, $[\delta]_2$, and $[(\beta u_i(x) + \alpha v_i(x) + w_i(x))/\gamma]$ for $i = 1, \ldots, \ell'$ are included in the CRS .

We divide the summation in the above verification equation into the product of the following two group elements:

$$\left[\sum_{i=0}^{\ell} a_i \frac{\beta u_i(x) + \alpha v_i(x) + w_i(x)}{\gamma}\right]_1 \cdot \left[\sum_{i=\ell+1}^{\ell'} a_i \frac{\beta u_i(x) + \alpha v_i(x) + w_i(x)}{\gamma}\right]_1.$$

Noticing that the first group element can be computed from the statement (of our constrained SNARK) and that the second group element can be computed from the constraint, we let the constraint string be

$$\rho = \left[\sum_{i=\ell+1}^{\ell'} a_i \frac{\beta u_i(x) + \alpha v_i(x) + w_i(x)}{\gamma}\right]_1.$$

We first remark that this obviously achieves succinctness. A constraint $(a_{\ell+1}, \ldots, a_{\ell'})$ is compressed into a constraint string of just a single group element. The size of a constraint string does not grow depending on the size of statements, witnesses, and constraints.

We then give intuition on why this compression is secure. The following intuition does not directly correspond to the actual proof. However, since our formal proof seems to hide intuition on why our compression is secure, we elaborate a more intuitive explanation below (by deviating from the formal proof).

The very basic intuition is seeing the above compression as a commitment to $(a_{\ell+1}, \ldots, a_{\ell'})$, albeit it is not hiding. Note that we know a "genuine" opening $(a_{\ell+1}, \ldots, a_{\ell'})$ of the above commitment. Then if an adversary produces a proof whose corresponding witness does not satisfy the genuine constraint, it can be plausible for the adversary to have made use of another opening $(a^*_{\ell+1}, \ldots, a^*_{\ell'})$ of the very same commitment. Furthermore, in the generic bilinear group model, if the adversary has made use of a different opening, we can hope that the adversary's opening can be extracted.

Therefore, if the above commitment is binding, we can hope for the security of the constrained SNARK . A subtlety is that this commitment is not always binding. Alternatively, we claim as follows: If the adversary produces two openings $(a_{\ell+1}, \ldots, a_{\ell'})$ and $(a^*_{\ell+1}, \ldots, a^*_{\ell'})$, such a pair of openings is benign in the sense that $(a_0, \ldots, a_\ell, a_{\ell+1}, \ldots, a_{\ell'}, a_{\ell'+1}, \ldots, a_m)$ satisfies Eq. (1) if and only if so does $(a_0, \ldots, a_\ell, a^*_{\ell+1}, \ldots, a^*_{\ell'}, a_{\ell'+1}, \ldots, a_m)$. To see this, assuming that there are two openings $(a_{\ell+1}, \ldots, a_{\ell'})$ and $(a^*_{\ell+1}, \ldots, a^*_{\ell'})$ satisfying that

$$\left[\sum_{i=\ell+1}^{\ell'} a_i \frac{\beta u_i(x) + \alpha v_i(x) + w_i(x)}{\gamma}\right]_1 = \left[\sum_{i=\ell+1}^{\ell'} a^*_i \frac{\beta u_i(x) + \alpha v_i(x) + w_i(x)}{\gamma}\right]_1,$$

let us consider the following two cases.

- The polynomial

$$\sum_{i=\ell+1}^{\ell'} (a_i - a_i^*) \frac{\beta u_i(x) + \alpha v_i(x) + w_i(x)}{\gamma} \tag{2}$$

is identically zero, when we see α, β, γ, and x as indeterminates.
- The same polynomial is not identically zero, when we see α, β, γ, and x as indeterminates.

Let us consider the first case. Due to the existence of α and β factors, this case can be rephrased as follows: The polynomials

$$\sum_{i=\ell+1}^{\ell'} (a_i - a_i^*) u_i(x), \qquad \sum_{i=\ell+1}^{\ell'} (a_i - a_i^*) v_i(x), \qquad \sum_{i=\ell+1}^{\ell'} (a_i - a_i^*) w_i(x)$$

are all identically zero, when we see x as an indeterminate. In this case, even though $(a_{\ell+1}, \ldots, a_{\ell'}) \neq (a_{\ell+1}^*, \ldots, a_{\ell'}^*)$, these two openings are benign in the above sense. This is because, in Eq. (1), we can substitute the appearance of

$$\sum_{i=\ell+1}^{\ell'} a_i u_i(X), \qquad \sum_{i=\ell+1}^{\ell'} a_i v_i(X), \qquad \sum_{i=\ell+1}^{\ell'} a_i w_i(X)$$

with

$$\sum_{i=\ell+1}^{\ell'} a_i^* u_i(X), \qquad \sum_{i=\ell+1}^{\ell'} a_i^* v_i(X), \qquad \sum_{i=\ell+1}^{\ell'} a_i^* w_i(X)$$

without changing the (un)satisfiability of Eq. (1). Then in the first case any two different openings are benign. The second case, in fact, occurs only with negligible probability. This is because of the fact that Eq. (2) is not identically zero as a polynomial of α, β, γ and x, but is equal to zero for random assignment to α, β, γ, and x. This fact implies that such random assignment is a root of the polynomial Eq. (2). Since the degree of this polynomial is small, the probability that random assignment becomes a root of such a polynomial is negligible, due to the Schwartz-Zippel lemma.[5]

More General Cases. Finally, we remark that it can be the case that adversary may use a malicious opening $(a_0^*, \ldots, a_\ell^*, a_{\ell+1}^*, \ldots, a_{\ell'}^*)$ of a commitment

$$\rho = \left[\sum_{i=\ell+1}^{\ell'} a_i \frac{\beta u_i(x) + \alpha v_i(x) + w_i(x)}{\gamma} \right]_1$$

[5] One may think that the adversary knows the assignment to the polynomial before fixing a polynomial, and thus we cannot apply the Schwartz-Zippel lemma. This is not the case in the formal security proof. In the formal proof, which is carried on in the generic bilinear group model, the group operation oracles are simulated with polynomials and indeterminates, and the assignment is chosen after the adversary fixes a polynomial in question.

satisfying

$$\rho = \left[\sum_{i=0}^{\ell} a_i^* \frac{\beta u_i(x) + \alpha v_i(x) + w_i(x)}{\gamma}\right]_1 \cdot \left[\sum_{i=\ell+1}^{\ell'} a_i^* \frac{\beta u_i(x) + \alpha v_i(x) + w_i(x)}{\gamma}\right]_1$$

to "cancel out" the statement term in the verification equation. However, even to that case the following argument applies with an appropriate modification. Remember that the verification equation may have a form of

$$e(A, B) = e([\alpha]_1, [\beta]_2) \cdot e\left(\left[\sum_{i=0}^{\ell} a_i \frac{\beta u_i(x) + \alpha v_i(x) + w_i(x)}{\gamma}\right]_1, [\gamma]_2\right) \cdot (\rho, [\gamma]_2) \cdot e(C, [\delta]_2).$$

Here, (the unconstrained part of) the witness $w = (a_{\ell'+1}^*, \ldots, a_m^*)$ that is extracted from the adversary's proof is consistent with $(a_0 + a_0^*, \ldots, a_\ell + a_\ell^*, a_{\ell+1}^*, \ldots, a_{\ell'}^*)$. We claim that even in that case w is a witness for $(a_0, \ldots, a_\ell, a_{\ell+1}^*, \ldots, a_{\ell'}^*)$ if and only if w is one for $(a_0 + a_0^*, \ldots, a_\ell + a_\ell^*, a_{\ell+1}^*, \ldots, a_{\ell'}^*)$. This is because in that case the equalities

$$\sum_{i=0}^{\ell}(a_i - (a_i + a_i^*))u_i(x) + \sum_{i=\ell+1}^{\ell'}(a_i - a^*)u_i(x) = 0,$$
$$\sum_{i=0}^{\ell}(a_i - (a_i + a_i^*))v_i(x) + \sum_{i=\ell+1}^{\ell'}(a_i - a^*)v_i(x) = 0,$$
$$\sum_{i=0}^{\ell}(a_i - (a_i + a_i^*))w_i(x) + \sum_{i=\ell+1}^{\ell'}(a_i - a^*)w_i(x) = 0,$$

hold for an indeterminate x. Thus we can substitute $\sum_{i=0}^{\ell} a_i u_i(x) + \sum_{i=\ell+1}^{\ell'} a_i u_i(x)$ with $\sum_{i=0}^{\ell}(a_i + a_i^*)u_i(x) + \sum_{i=\ell+1}^{\ell'} a_i^* u_i(x)$ and the same holds for $v_i(x)$ and $w_i(x)$.

3.2 Syntax and Security Definitions of Constrained SNARKs

The syntax and security definitions of constrained SNARKs are as follows.

Let $\mathcal{R}$ be the algorithm that takes as input a security parameter 1^λ and outputs a tuple (R, P, z) where R is an NP relation, P is a predicate on the tuples (r, w) of a constraint r and a witness w, and z is an auxiliary input. A constrained SNARK consists of the following algorithms.

$\mathsf{cSNARK.Setup}(R, P) \to \sigma$. The setup algorithm takes as input an NP relation R and a constraint predicate P and outputs a CRS σ.

$\mathsf{cSNARK.Constrain}(\sigma, r) \to \rho$. The *deterministic* constraining algorithm takes as input a CRS σ, and a constraint r and outputs a constraint string ρ.

$\mathsf{cSNARK.Prove}(\sigma, r, x, w) \to \pi$. The proving algorithm takes as input a CRS σ, a constraint r, a statement x, and a witness w and outputs an argument π.

$\mathsf{cSNARK.Verify}(\sigma, \rho, x, \pi) \to 0$ **or** 1. The verification algorithm takes as input a CRS σ, a constraint string ρ, a statement x, and an argument π and outputs a bit 0 or 1.

We say that ($\mathsf{cSNARK.Setup}, \mathsf{cSNARK.Constrain}, \mathsf{cSNARK.Prove}, \mathsf{cSNARK.Verify}$) is a constrained SNARK for $\mathcal{R}$, if for all $(R, P, z) \leftarrow \mathcal{R}(1^\lambda)$, all $\sigma \leftarrow \mathsf{cSNARK.Setup}(R, P)$, all constraints r, all $(x, w) \in R$ satisfying $(r, w) \in P$, $\rho \leftarrow \mathsf{cSNARK.Constrain}(\sigma, r)$, and all $\pi \leftarrow \mathsf{cSNARK.Prove}(\sigma, r, x, w)$, it holds that $\mathsf{cSNARK.Verify}(\sigma, \rho, x, \pi) = 1$.

We require a constrained SNARK to be constrained knowledge sound and succinct, which we define below.

Definition 5. *We say that a constrained SNARK* ($\mathsf{cSNARK.Setup}, \mathsf{cSNARK.Constrain}, \mathsf{cSNARK.Prove}, \mathsf{cSNARK.Verify}$) *is constrained knowledge sound if for all non-uniform polynomial-time adversaries $\mathcal{A}$ there exists a non-uniform polynomial-time extractor $\mathcal{X}_\mathcal{A}$ satisfying that*

$$\Pr\left[\begin{array}{l}(R, P, z) \leftarrow \mathcal{R}(1^\lambda); \sigma \leftarrow \mathsf{cSNARK.Setup}(R, P); \\ ((x, r, \pi); w) \leftarrow (\mathcal{A} \| \mathcal{X}_\mathcal{A})(R, P, z, \sigma); \rho \leftarrow \mathsf{cSNARK.Constrain}(\sigma, r) \\ : \mathsf{cSNARK.Verify}(\sigma, \rho, x, \pi) = 1 \wedge \neg((x, w) \in R \wedge (r, w) \in P)\end{array}\right]$$

is negligible.

This definition requires that whenever an adversary outputs a valid SNARK, its corresponding extractor can output a witness. The important point is that the extracted witness should satisfy both the relation R and the extra constraint imposed by r.

Definition 6. *We say that a constrained SNARK* ($\mathsf{cSNARK.Setup}, \mathsf{cSNARK.Constrain}, \mathsf{cSNARK.Prove}, \mathsf{cSNARK.Verify}$) *is succinct if there is a polynomial* $\mathrm{poly}(\lambda)$ *satisfying that for all $\lambda \in \mathbb{N}$, all $(R, P, z) \leftarrow \mathcal{R}(1^\lambda)$, all $\sigma \leftarrow \mathsf{cSNARK.Setup}(R, P)$, all constraints r, all $(x, w) \in R$ satisfying $(r, w) \in P$, all $\rho \leftarrow \mathsf{cSNARK.Constrain}(\sigma, r)$ and $\pi \leftarrow \mathsf{cSNARK.Prove}(\sigma, r, x, w)$ it holds that $|\rho| \leq \mathrm{poly}(\lambda + \log \ell_x + \log \ell_r)$ and $|\pi| \leq \mathrm{poly}(\lambda + \log \ell_x + \log \ell_r)$ where ℓ_x and ℓ_r are the maximum sizes of the descriptions of the statements x and the constraints r that R and P can take as input, respectively.*

We remark that as mentioned in the introduction, we do not require a constrained SNARK to be zero-knowledge. This is because we hide the knowledge on a witness and a constraint by wrapping a SNARK with another non-interactive proof which is witness indistinguishable.

3.3 Constrained SNARKs for QAPs and Prefix Constraints

In this subsection, we describe our construction of a constrained SNARK .

The relation R and the predicate P that the construction supports are defined as follows. The relation R has a form of $R = (\mathsf{gk}, \ell, \ell', (u_i(X), v_i(X), w_i(X))_{i=0}^m, t(X))$, and a statement $x = (a_1, \ldots, a_\ell) \in (\mathbb{Z}_p)^\ell$ is in the language if and only if there is a witness $w = (a_{\ell+1}, \ldots, a_{\ell'}, a_{\ell'+1}, \ldots, a_m) \in (\mathbb{Z}_p)^{m-\ell}$ satisfying

$$\Big(\sum_{i=0}^m a_i u_i(X)\Big) \cdot \Big(\sum_{i=0}^m a_i v_i(X)\Big) = \sum_{i=0}^m a_i w_i(X) + h(X)t(X)$$

with $a_0 = 1$ and some $h(X) \in \mathbb{Z}_p[X]$. This relation is called quadratic arithmetic programs (QAPs). We assume that the gk component of R is generated by a bilinear group generator $\mathcal{G}$. A constraint $r = (a'_{\ell+1}, \ldots, a'_{\ell'}) \in (\mathbb{Z}_p)^{\ell'-\ell}$ and a witness $w = (a_{\ell+1}, \ldots, a_{\ell'}, a_{\ell'+1}, \ldots, a_m) \in (\mathbb{Z}_p)^{m-\ell}$ satisfy $(r, w) \in P$ if and only if $(a_{\ell+1}, \ldots, a_{\ell'}) = (a'_{\ell+1}, \ldots, a'_{\ell'})$.

The construction is as follows.

$\mathsf{cSNARK.Setup}(R, P)$. Choose α, β, γ, δ, $x \leftarrow \mathbb{Z}_p \setminus \{0\}$ and compute σ as

$$\Bigg([\alpha]_1, [\beta]_1, ([x^i]_1)_{i=0}^{n-1}, \left(\left[\frac{\beta u_i(x) + \alpha v_i(x) + w_i(x)}{\gamma}\right]_1\right)_{i=0}^{\ell'},$$
$$\left(\left[\frac{\beta u_i(x) + \alpha v_i(x) + w_i(x)}{\delta}\right]_1\right)_{i=\ell'+1}^{m}, \left(\left[\frac{x^i t(x)}{\delta}\right]_1\right)_{i=0}^{n-2},$$
$$[\beta]_2, [\gamma]_2, [\delta]_2, ([x^i]_2)_{i=0}^{n-1}\Bigg).$$

Then output σ.

$\mathsf{cSNARK.Constrain}(\sigma, r)$. Parse r as $(a_{\ell+1}, \ldots, a_{\ell'})$. Compute

$$\rho \leftarrow \left[\sum_{i=\ell+1}^{\ell'} a_i \frac{\beta u_i(x) + \alpha v_i(x) + w_i(x)}{\gamma}\right]_1$$

and output ρ.

$\mathsf{cSNARK.Prove}(\sigma, r, x, w)$. Parse x as $(a_0, \ldots, a_\ell)$ and w as $(a_{\ell+1}, \ldots, a_{\ell'}, a_{\ell'+1}, \ldots, a_m)$. Compute

$$A \leftarrow \Big[\alpha + \sum_{i=0}^m a_i u_i(x)\Big]_1, \qquad B \leftarrow \Big[\beta + \sum_{i=0}^m a_i v_i(x)\Big]_2,$$

and

$$C \leftarrow \left[\sum_{i=\ell'+1}^{m} a_i \frac{\beta u_i(x) + \alpha v_i(x) + w_i(x)}{\delta} + \frac{h(x)t(x)}{\delta}\right]_1$$

where $h(X)$ is the polynomial that satisfies

$$\sum_{i=0}^{m} a_i u_i(X) \cdot \sum_{i=0}^{m} a_i v_i(X) = \sum_{i=0}^{m} a_i w_i(X) + h(X)t(X).$$

Then output (A, B, C).

$\mathsf{cSNARK.Verify}(\sigma, \rho, x, \pi)$. Parse x as $(a_0, \ldots, a_\ell)$ and π as (A, B, C). Verify that

$$e(A, B) = e([\alpha]_1, [\beta]_2) \cdot e\left(\left[\sum_{i=0}^{\ell} a_i \frac{\beta u_i(x) + \alpha v_i(x) + w_i(x)}{\gamma}\right]_1, [\gamma]_2\right)$$
$$\cdot e(\rho, [\gamma]_2) \cdot e(C, [\delta]_2).$$

If it holds, output 1, and output 0 otherwise.

Comparison with Geppetto [6]. In our construction, we "separated" a set of polynomials $\beta u_i(x) + \alpha v_i + w_i(x)$ where $i = \ell + 1, \ldots, \ell'$ from another set of polynomials $\beta u_i(x) + \alpha v_i(x) + w_i(x)$ where $i = \ell' + 1, \ldots, m$ by multiplying them with different reciprocals $1/\gamma$ and $1/\delta$. This is important for forbidding an adversary from including in a proof some value that cancels out the constraint string and thereby proving a false statement or proving a statement without the knowledge of a witness. In fact, if we set $\gamma = \delta$, then the summation in C could run over $\{\ell + 1, \ldots, \ell'\}$ and this way C would cancel out the constraint string.

This idea already appeared in Geppetto [6]. In Geppetto, a set of QAP coefficients $(a_0, \ldots, a_m)$ is split into sub-sequence and for each sub-sequence, a prover can generate a commitment to that sub-sequence. In order to be secure against the attacks of the above type, in the Geppetto construction, polynomials $u_i(x)$, $v_i(x)$, and $w_i(x)$ are multiplied by some integers which are different for each sub-sequence. Our idea can be seen as a simplification of this and adaptation to Groth's SNARK.

3.4 Security

We describe the security of this construction. The correctness of this construction can be obtained from calculation. The constrained knowledge soundness is shown in the following theorem. The proof is postponed to the full version.

Theorem 7. *The construction is constrained knowledge sound against all generic adversaries with a polynomial number of group operation queries.*

4 Succinct Attribute-Based Signatures for Bounded-Size Circuits

In this section, we apply our constrained SNARK to a construction of a practical attribute-based signature scheme for bounded-size arithmetic circuits.

4.1 Construction

For constructing such an attribute-based signature scheme we employ a constrained SNARK $(\mathsf{cSNARK.Setup}, \mathsf{cSNARK.Constrain}, \mathsf{cSNARK.Prove}, \mathsf{cSNARK.Verify})$, a non-interactive proof system $(\mathsf{WI.Setup}, \mathsf{WI.Prove}, \mathsf{WI.Verify}, \mathsf{WI.ExtSetup}, \mathsf{WI.Extract})$, a signature scheme $(\mathsf{Sig.Kg}, \mathsf{Sig.Sign}, \mathsf{Sig.Verify})$, a hash function family $(\mathcal{H}, \mathsf{Hash})$, and a universal arithmetic circuit U for the field $\mathbb{Z}_p$ where p is the order of the bilinear groups. The constrained SNARK needs to support the relation R of

$$(\langle C, h\rangle, \langle t, u, v\rangle) \in R \iff (t = \bot \wedge U(C, u; v) = 1) \vee (t = h) \tag{3}$$

where C is the circuit that describes the policy to be proven, h is some hash value, t is a hash value or a special symbol $\bot$, u is input to the circuit C, and v is wire assignment of the evaluation of $U(C, u)$. In addition, the constrained SNARK needs to support the predicate P of

$$(\langle t', u'\rangle, \langle t, u, v\rangle) \in P \iff (t = t') \wedge (u = u')$$

where t' is a hash value or a special symbol $\bot$, and u' is input to the circuit C. The non-interactive proof system needs to support the relation

$$\mathsf{cSNARK.Verify}(\sigma, \rho, \langle C, h\rangle, \pi) = 1 \wedge \mathsf{Sig.Verify}(\mathsf{vk}, \rho, \theta) = 1 \tag{4}$$

where $\langle \sigma, \mathsf{vk}, C, h\rangle$ is the statement and $\langle \rho, \theta, \pi\rangle$ is the witness.

An overview of the construction is as follows.

In the set-up phase, an authority sets up a constrained SNARK and a non-interactive proof system, together with a digital signature scheme. The signing key of the digital signature scheme serves as a master secret key. To generate a user secret key uk, the authority generates a constraint string ρ that constrains the prefix of the witness to be the user's attributes. Then the authority signs on that constraint string ρ and issues the user with the constraint string and the signature as the user secret key. As discussed in the introduction, a constraint string can be seen as a commitment to a constraint, thus this procedure is essentially the same as signing on the attributes of the user.

To sign anonymously, a user generates a constrained SNARK proving that his attributes satisfy the policy, and also generates a non-interactive proof of knowledge of the signature, the constraint string, and the constrained SNARK proving the satisfiability of the policy by his attributes. This non-interactive proof is used as an attribute-based signature.

This attribute-based signature ensures that there are attributes that satisfy the policy and that such attributes are certified by the authority, which in turn ensures the unforgeability. The former is ensured simply by the knowledge of the SNARK. The latter is ensured by the combination of the knowledge of the authority's signature and the constrained knowledge soundness of the constrained SNARK. These two facts in combination ensure that the attributes that satisfy the policy are certified by the authority.

To bind a message into a signature, we use the pseudo-attribute technique [15]. In this technique, the user proves the knowledge of a signature by the authority which is on his attributes or on the message itself. This way, if an adversary sees an attribute-based signature on a message m and tries to forge another attribute-based signature on m', the adversary needs to forge a standard signature on the attributes or one on a message m'. This is infeasible due to the unforgeability of the standard signature scheme. This technique is implemented by the existence of the witness t in Eq. (3) and Eq. (4).

Finally, the anonymity of an attribute-based signature is ensured by the witness indistinguishability of the non-interactive proof system. The relation of Eq. (4) is designed so that the public statement is identical whenever the policy and the message used to generate a signature are identical regardless of what attributes are used to generate a signature. This fact directly ensures the anonymity of an attribute-based signature, since an attribute-based signature is exactly the witness-indistinguishable non-interactive proof.

The construction is as follows.

$\mathsf{ABS.Setup}(1^\lambda)$. Compute CRSs $\sigma \leftarrow \mathsf{cSNARK.Setup}(R, P)$ and $\mathsf{crs} \leftarrow \mathsf{WI.Setup}(1^\lambda)$ of the constrained SNARK and the non-interactive proof system. Generate a verification key and a signing key $(\mathsf{vk}, \mathsf{sk}) \leftarrow \mathsf{Sig.Kg}(1^\lambda)$ of a signature scheme and a hashing key $\mathsf{hk} \leftarrow \mathcal{H}(1^\lambda)$ of a collision-resistant hash function family. Set $\mathsf{pp} \leftarrow (\sigma, \mathsf{crs}, \mathsf{vk}, \mathsf{hk})$ and $\mathsf{mk} \leftarrow \mathsf{sk}$ and output $(\mathsf{pp}, \mathsf{mk})$.

$\mathsf{ABS.Kg}(\mathsf{pp}, \mathsf{mk}, u)$. Compute a constraint string

$$\rho \leftarrow \mathsf{cSNARK.Constrain}(\sigma, \langle \bot, u \rangle)$$

of $\langle \bot, u \rangle$ and generate a signature

$$\theta \leftarrow \mathsf{Sig.Sign}(\mathsf{vk}, \mathsf{sk}, \rho)$$

on ρ. Set $\mathsf{uk} \leftarrow (\rho, \theta)$ and output uk.

$\mathsf{ABS.Sign}(\mathsf{pp}, u, \mathsf{uk}, C, m)$. Compute the wire assignment v of the evaluation of $U(C, u)$ and a hash value $h \leftarrow \mathsf{Hash}(\mathsf{hk}, \langle C, m \rangle)$. Generate a constrained SNARK

$$\pi \leftarrow \mathsf{cSNARK.Prove}(\sigma, \langle \bot, u \rangle, \langle C, h \rangle, \langle \bot, u, v \rangle)$$

and a non-interactive proof

$$\pi' \leftarrow \mathsf{WI.Prove}(\mathsf{crs}, \langle \sigma, \mathsf{vk}, C, h \rangle, \langle \rho, \theta, \pi \rangle). \quad (5)$$

Set $\Sigma \leftarrow \pi'$ and output Σ.

$\mathsf{ABS.Verify}(\mathsf{pp}, C, m, \Sigma)$. Compute a hash value $h \leftarrow \mathsf{Hash}(\mathsf{hk}, \langle C, m \rangle)$ and verify the proof π' by running $\mathsf{WI.Verify}(\mathsf{crs}, \langle \sigma, \mathsf{vk}, C, h \rangle, \pi')$. If the verification passes, output 1. Otherwise output 0.

On Benign Openings. As we remarked in Sect. 3.1, a constraint string in our constrained SNARKs may have a pair of different but benign openings. Here, for a sanity check, we remark that such a benign pair of openings do not make a security issue to our construction.

To explain this, let us consider the following adversarial strategy: An adversary corrupts a signer with attribute u and obtains a signing key $\theta = \mathsf{Sig.Sign}(\mathsf{vk}, \mathsf{sk}, \mathsf{cSNARK.Constrain}(\sigma, \langle \bot, u \rangle))$; then the adversary somehow finds a different opening $\langle t^*, u^* \rangle$ of $\mathsf{cSNARK.Constrain}(\sigma, \langle \bot, u \rangle)$, that is, $\langle t^*, u^* \rangle$ satisfying $\mathsf{cSNARK.Constrain}(\sigma, \langle \bot, u \rangle) = \mathsf{cSNARK.Constrain}(\sigma, \langle t^*, u^* \rangle)$; using this opening $\langle t^*, u^* \rangle$, the adversary generates an attribute-based signature on a circuit C.

This strategy does not produce a successful forgery. To see this, let us consider the two cases: (i) $t^* = \bot$ and (ii) $t^* \neq \bot$. Remember that the different openings $\langle \bot, u \rangle$ and $\langle t^*, u^* \rangle$ should be benign, namely, for all C, h, and v, it holds that $(\langle C, h \rangle, \langle \bot, u, v \rangle) \in R \iff (\langle C, h \rangle, \langle t^*, u^*, v \rangle) \in R$. Then, in the case (i), the benign property tells us that $C(u) = C(u^*)$ for all circuits C. Thus, the adversary can generate a signature for a circuit C if and only if $C(u) = 1$. Since the adversary already knows a signing key θ of attributes u, such an attribute-based signature is not counted as a forgery. For the case (ii), the opening $\langle t^*, u^* \rangle$ is simply not benign, and thus is infeasible to compute. This is because for C, h and v such that $U(C, u; v) = 1$ and $h \notin \{\bot, t^*\}$, it holds that $(\langle C, h \rangle, \langle \bot, u, v \rangle) \in R$ and $(\langle C, h \rangle, \langle t^*, u^*, v \rangle) \notin R$.

4.2 Security

We then prove the security of this construction. The proofs are postponed to the full version.

Theorem 8. *Assuming the non-interactive proof system is witness indistinguishable, the attribute-based signature scheme is anonymous.*

Theorem 9. *Assuming the constrained SNARK is constrained knowledge sound, the non-interactive proof system is witness indistinguishable and extractable, the signature scheme is unforgeable, and the hash function family is collision resistant, the attribute-based signature scheme is unforgeable.*

4.3 Instantiation

Now we discuss an instantiation of this generic construction.

Universal Arithmetic Circuit. A universal arithmetic circuit U can be constructed by extending Valiant's construction of a (Boolean) universal circuits [22, 23]. Such an extension was briefly mentioned by Lipmaa et al. [14]. We quickly review their argument. To extend Valiant's construction to a universal arithmetic circuit, we need to implement a universal gate

$$U_0(c, x_0, x_1) = \begin{cases} x_0 + x_1 & (c = 0), \\ x_0 x_1 & (c = 1), \end{cases}$$

the X switching gate

$$X(c, x_0, x_1) = \begin{cases} (x_0, x_1) & (c = 0), \\ (x_1, x_0) & (c = 1), \end{cases}$$

and the Y switching gate

$$Y(c, x_0, x_1) = \begin{cases} x_0 & (c = 0), \\ x_1 & (c = 1). \end{cases}$$

They can be implemented by the following arithmetic computation:

$$\begin{aligned} U_0(c, x_0, x_1) &= (1 - c)(x_0 + x_1) + c x_0 x_1, \\ X(c, x_0, x_1) &= ((1 - c)x_0 + c x_1, (1 - c)x_1 + c x_0), \\ Y(c, x_0, x_1) &= (1 - c)x_0 + c x_1. \end{aligned}$$

Using these implementations, we can implement a universal arithmetic circuit.

Constrained SNARKs. For the constrained SNARK, we can use our construction in Sect. 3. To use this construction, we need to express the relation Eq. (3) in a quadratic arithmetic program. Clearly, the relation $U(C, u; v) = 1$ can be expressed as a set of quadratic equations, in which each variable corresponds to an outgoing wire of an addition or multiplication gate. Thus to express the entire relation of Eq. (3), we need to express the conjunction and disjunction in Eq. (3). While a generic conversion (through NAND gates, for example) suffices, we mention a more dedicated conversion. Since the relation in Eq. (3) is equivalent to

$$((t = \bot) \lor (t = h)) \land ((U(C, u; v) = 1) \lor (t = h)),$$

we can translate this to the following quadratic arithmetic program:

$$\begin{cases} (t - 0) \cdot (t - h) = 0, \\ (v_{\mathrm{out}} - 1) \cdot (t - h) = 0, \end{cases}$$

where v_{out} is the variable that corresponds to the output wire of the universal arithmetic circuit U. Here, we abuse 0 for the special symbol $\bot$ and assume that the range of the hash function is $\mathbb{Z}_p \setminus \{0\}$. This can be ensured by prepending 1 to the output of hash function, for example. This way, the size of the quadratic arithmetic programs that the constrained SNARK needs to support is just the size of the universal arithmetic circuit U plus two extra equations.

Non-interactive Proofs and Signatures. While we can use any non-interactive proof system and signature scheme, for efficient and practical instantiation, we choose to use the Groth-Sahai proof system [12] and structure-preserving signatures [1]. The relation of Eq. (4) falls into the category of the pairing product equations, thus we can apply structure-preserving cryptography. The choice for the structure-preserving signature scheme is arbitrary, however, we choose Abe et al.'s scheme [2] to instantiate the signature scheme, for concreteness and efficiency. A signature includes two $\mathbb{G}_1$ elements and one $\mathbb{G}_2$ element, and the verification equations include one linear pairing product equation and one quadratic pairing product equation. The security is proven in the generic bilinear group model.

Signature Size. When instantiated as above, a signature of our attribute-based signature scheme includes five commitments to $\mathbb{G}_1$ elements, two commitments to $\mathbb{G}_2$ elements, and proofs for one linear pairing product equation with $\mathbb{G}_1$ variables and two (quadratic) pairing product equations. Thus a signature includes 18 $\mathbb{G}_1$ elements and 14 $\mathbb{G}_2$ elements in total.

Acknowledgments. This work was supported by JSPS KAKENHI Grant Numbers JP18K18055 and JP19H01109. This work was partially supported by JST AIP Acceleration Research JPMJCR22U5, Japan.

References

1. Abe, M., Fuchsbauer, G., Groth, J., Haralambiev, K., Ohkubo, M.: Structure-preserving signatures and commitments to group elements. J. Cryptol. **29**(2), 363–421 (2016). https://doi.org/10.1007/s00145-014-9196-7
2. Abe, M., Groth, J., Haralambiev, K., Ohkubo, M.: Optimal structure-preserving signatures in asymmetric bilinear groups. In: Rogaway, P. (ed.) CRYPTO 2011. LNCS, vol. 6841, pp. 649–666. Springer, Heidelberg (2011). https://doi.org/10.1007/978-3-642-22792-9_37
3. Agrawal, S., Ganesh, C., Mohassel, P.: Non-interactive zero-knowledge proofs for composite statements. In: Shacham, H., Boldyreva, A. (eds.) CRYPTO 2018. LNCS, vol. 10993, pp. 643–673. Springer, Cham (2018). https://doi.org/10.1007/978-3-319-96878-0_22
4. Boyle, E., Goldwasser, S., Ivan, I.: Functional signatures and pseudorandom functions. In: Krawczyk, H. (ed.) PKC 2014. LNCS, vol. 8383, pp. 501–519. Springer, Heidelberg (2014). https://doi.org/10.1007/978-3-642-54631-0_29
5. Campanelli, M., Fiore, D., Querol, A.: LegoSNARK: modular design and composition of succinct zero-knowledge proofs. In: Proceedings of the 2019 ACM SIGSAC Conference on Computer and Communications Security, pp. 2075–2092. ACM (2019)
6. Costello, C., et al.: Geppetto: Versatile verifiable computation. In: 2015 IEEE Symposium on Security and Privacy, pp. 944–961 (2018)
7. Datta, P., Okamoto, T., Takashima, K.: Efficient attribute-based signatures for unbounded arithmetic branching programs. In: Lin, D., Sako, K. (eds.) PKC 2019. LNCS, vol. 11442, pp. 127–158. Springer, Cham (2019). https://doi.org/10.1007/978-3-030-17253-4_5
8. El Kaafarani, A., Katsumata, S.: Attribute-based signatures for unbounded circuits in the rom and efficient instantiations from lattices. In: Abdalla, M., Dahab, R. (eds.) PKC 2018. LNCS, vol. 10770, pp. 89–119. Springer, Cham (2018). https://doi.org/10.1007/978-3-319-76581-5_4

9. Fiore, D., Fournet, C., Ghosh, E., Kohlweiss, M., Ohrimenko, O., Parno, B.: Hash first, argue later: adaptive verifiable computations on outsourced data. In: Proceedings of the 2016 ACM SIGSAC Conference on Computer and Communications Security, pp. 1304–1316. ACM (2016)
10. Fiore, D., Nitulescu, A.: On the (in) security of SNARKs in the presence of oracles. In: Hirt, M., Smith, A. (eds.) TCC 2016. LNCS, vol. 9985, pp. 108–138. Springer, Heidelberg (2016). https://doi.org/10.1007/978-3-662-53641-4_5
11. Groth, J.: On the size of pairing-based non-interactive arguments. In: Fischlin, M., Coron, J.-S. (eds.) EUROCRYPT 2016. LNCS, vol. 9666, pp. 305–326. Springer, Heidelberg (2016). https://doi.org/10.1007/978-3-662-49896-5_11
12. Groth, J., Sahai, A.: Efficient noninteractive proof systems for bilinear groups. SIAM J. Comput. **41**(5), 1193–1232 (2012)
13. Kosba, A., Papamanthou, C., Shi, E.: xJsnark: a framework for efficient verifiable computation. In: 2018 IEEE Symposium on Security and Privacy (SP), pp. 944–961. IEEE (2018)
14. Lipmaa, H., Mohassel, P., Sadeghian, S.: Valiant's universal circuit: improvements, implementation, and applications. Cryptology ePrint Archive, Report 2016/017 (2016). https://eprint.iacr.org/2016/017
15. Maji, H.K., Prabhakaran, M., Rosulek, M.: Attribute-based signatures. In: Kiayias, A. (ed.) CT-RSA 2011. LNCS, vol. 6558, pp. 376–392. Springer, Heidelberg (2011). https://doi.org/10.1007/978-3-642-19074-2_24
16. Okamoto, T., Takashima, K.: Efficient attribute-based signatures for non-monotone predicates in the standard model. In: Catalano, D., Fazio, N., Gennaro, R., Nicolosi, A. (eds.) PKC 2011. LNCS, vol. 6571, pp. 35–52. Springer, Heidelberg (2011). https://doi.org/10.1007/978-3-642-19379-8_3
17. Sakai, Y., Attrapadung, N., Hanaoka, G.: Attribute-based signatures for circuits from bilinear map. In: Cheng, C.-M., Chung, K.-M., Persiano, G., Yang, B.-Y. (eds.) PKC 2016. LNCS, vol. 9614, pp. 283–300. Springer, Heidelberg (2016). https://doi.org/10.1007/978-3-662-49384-7_11
18. Sakai, Y., Katsumata, S., Attrapadung, N., Hanaoka, G.: Attribute-based signatures for unbounded languages from standard assumptions. In: Peyrin, T., Galbraith, S. (eds.) ASIACRYPT 2018. LNCS, vol. 11273, pp. 493–522. Springer, Cham (2018). https://doi.org/10.1007/978-3-030-03329-3_17
19. Shahandashti, S.F., Safavi-Naini, R.: Threshold attribute-based signatures and their application to anonymous credential systems. In: Preneel, B. (ed.) AFRICACRYPT 2009. LNCS, vol. 5580, pp. 198–216. Springer, Heidelberg (2009). https://doi.org/10.1007/978-3-642-02384-2_13
20. Tang, F., Li, H., Liang, B.: Attribute-based signatures for circuits from multilinear maps. In: Chow, S.S.M., Camenisch, J., Hui, L.C.K., Yiu, S.M. (eds.) ISC 2014. LNCS, vol. 8783, pp. 54–71. Springer, Cham (2014). https://doi.org/10.1007/978-3-319-13257-0_4
21. Tsabary, R.: An equivalence between attribute-based signatures and homomorphic signatures, and new constructions for both. In: Kalai, Y., Reyzin, L. (eds.) TCC 2017. LNCS, vol. 10678, pp. 489–518. Springer, Cham (2017). https://doi.org/10.1007/978-3-319-70503-3_16
22. Valiant, L.G.: Universal circuits (preliminary report). In: Proceedings of the Eighth Annual ACM Symposium on Theory of Computing, pp. 196–203. ACM (1976)
23. Wegener, I.: The Complexity of Boolean Functions. John Wiley & Sons Inc., Hoboken (1987)

What Makes Fiat–Shamir zkSNARKs (Updatable SRS) Simulation Extractable?

Chaya Ganesh[1], Hamidreza Khoshakhlagh[2](✉), Markulf Kohlweiss[3], Anca Nitulescu[4], and Michał Zając[5]

[1] Indian Institute of Science, Bengaluru, India
chaya@iisc.ac.in

[2] Aarhus University, Aarhus, Denmark
hamidreza@cs.au.dk

[3] University of Edinburgh and IOHK, Edinburgh, UK
mkohlwei@inf.ed.ac.uk

[4] Protocol Labs, San Francisco, USA
anca@protocol.ai

[5] Nethermind, London, UK

Abstract. We show that three popular universal zero-knowledge SNARKs (Plonk, Sonic, and Marlin) are updatable SRS simulation extractable NIZKs and signatures of knowledge (SoK) out-of-the-box avoiding any compilation overhead.

Towards this we generalize results for the Fiat–Shamir (FS) transformation, which turns interactive protocols into signature schemes, non-interactive proof systems, or SoK in the random oracle model (ROM). The security of the transformation relies on rewinding to extract the secret key or the witness, even in the presence of signing queries for signatures and simulation queries for proof systems and SoK, respectively. We build on this line of work and analyze multi-round FS for arguments with a structured reference string (SRS). The combination of ROM and SRS, while redundant in theory, is the model of choice for the most efficient practical systems to date. We also consider the case where the SRS is updatable and define a strong simulation extractability notion that allows for simulated proofs with respect to an SRS to which the adversary can contribute updates.

We define three properties (trapdoor-less zero-knowledge, rewinding-based knowledge soundness, and a unique response property) that are sufficient for argument systems based on multi-round FS to be also simulation extractable in this strong sense. We show that Plonk, Sonic, and Marlin satisfy these properties, and conjecture that many other argument systems such as Lunar, Basilisk, and transparent variants of Plonk fall within the reach of our main theorem.

1 Introduction

Zero-knowledge proof systems, which allow a prover to convince a verifier of an NP statement $\mathbf{R}(\mathsf{x}, \mathsf{w})$ without revealing anything else about the witness w

C. Galdi and S. Jarecki (Eds.): SCN 2022, LNCS 13409, pp. 735–760, 2022.
https://doi.org/10.1007/978-3-031-14791-3_32

have broad application in cryptography and theory of computation [7,26,33]. When restricted to computationally sound proof systems, also called *argument systems*[1], proof size can be shorter than the size of the witness [16]. Zero-knowledge Succinct Non-interactive ARguments of Knowledge (zkSNARKs) are zero-knowledge argument systems that additionally have two succinctness properties: small proof sizes and fast verification. Since their introduction in [47], zk-SNARKs have been a versatile design tool for secure cryptographic protocols. They became particularly relevant for blockchain applications that demand short proofs and fast verification for on-chain storage and processing. Starting with their deployment by Zcash [9], they have seen broad adoption, e.g., for privacy-preserving cryptocurrencies and scalable and private smart contracts in Ethereum.

While research on zkSNARKs has seen rapid progress [10,12,13,31,36,37,42, 43,49] with many works proposing significant improvements in proof size, verifier and prover efficiency, and complexity of the public setup, less attention has been paid to non-malleable zkSNARKs and succinct signatures of knowledge [18,20] (sometimes abbreviated SoK or referred to as SNARKY signatures [4,39]).

Relevance of Simulation Extractability. Most zkSNARKs are shown only to satisfy a standard knowledge soundness property. Intuitively, this guarantees that a prover that creates a valid proof in isolation knows a valid witness. However, deployments of zkSNARKs in real-world applications, unless they are carefully designed to have application-specific malleability protection, e.g. [9], require a stronger property – *simulation-extractability* (SE) – that corresponds much more closely to existential unforgeability of signatures.

This correspondence is made precise by SoK, which uses an NP-language instance as the public verification key. Instead of signing with the secret key, SoK signing requires knowledge of the NP-witness. Intuitively, an SoK is thus a proof of knowledge (PoK) of a witness that is tied to a message. In fact, many signatures schemes, e.g., Schnorr, can be read as SoK for a specific hard relation, e.g., DL [23]. To model strong existential unforgeability of SoK signatures, even when given an oracle for obtaining signatures on different instances, an attacker must not be able to produce new signatures. Chase and Lysyanskaya [20] model this via the notion of simulation extractability which guarantees extraction of a witness even in the presence of simulated signatures.

In practice, an adversary against a zkSNARK system also has access to proofs computed by honest parties that should be modeled as simulated proofs. The definition of knowledge soundness (KS) ignores the ability of an adversary to see other valid proofs that may occur in real-world applications. For instance, in applications of zkSNARKs in privacy-preserving blockchains, proofs are posted on-chain for all blockchain participants to see. We thus argue that SE is a much more suitable notion for robust protocol design. We also claim that SE has primarily an intellectual cost, as it is harder to prove SE than KS—another analogy here is IND-CCA vs IND-CPA security for encryption. However, we will show that the proof systems we consider are SE out-of-the-box.

[1] We use both terms interchangeably.

Fiat–Shamir-Based zkSNARKs. Most modern zkSNARK constructions follow a modular blueprint that involves the design of an information-theoretic interactive protocol, e.g. an Interactive Oracle Proof (IOP) [11], that is then compiled via cryptographic tools to obtain an interactive argument system. This is then turned into a zkSNARK using the Fiat-Shamir transform. By additionally hashing the message, the Fiat-Shamir transform is also a popular technique for constructing signatures. While well-understood for 3-message sigma protocols and justifiable in the ROM [6], Fiat–Shamir should be used with care because there are both counterexamples in theory [34] and real-world attacks in practice when implemented incorrectly [48].

In particular, several schemes such as Sonic [46], Plonk [28], Marlin [21] follow this approach where the information-theoretic object is a multi-message algebraic variant of IOP, and the cryptographic primitive in the compiler is a polynomial commitment scheme (PC) that requires a trusted setup. To date, this blueprint lacks an analysis in the ROM in terms of simulation extractability.

Updatable SRS zkSNARKs. One of the downsides of many efficient zkSNARKs [22,31,36,37,42,43,49] is that they rely on a *trusted setup*, where there is a structured reference string (SRS) that is assumed to be generated by a trusted party. In practice, however, this assumption is not well-founded; if the party that generates the SRS is not honest, they can produce proofs for false statements. If the trusted setup assumption does not hold, knowledge soundness breaks down. Groth et al. [38] propose a setting to tackle this challenge which allows parties – provers and verifiers – to *update* the SRS.[2] The update protocol takes an existing SRS and contributes to its randomness in a verifiable way to obtain a new SRS. The guarantee in this *updatable setting* is that knowledge soundness holds as long as one of the parties updating the SRS is honest. The SRS is also *universal*, in that it does not depend on the relation to be proved but only on an upper bound on the size of the statement's circuit. Although inefficient, as the SRS size is quadratic in the size of the circuit, [38] set a new paradigm for designing zkSNARKs.

The first universal zkSNARK with updatable and linear size SRS was Sonic proposed by Maller et al. in [46]. Subsequently, Gabizon, Williamson, and Ciobotaru designed Plonk [28] which currently is the most efficient updatable universal zkSNARK. Independently, Chiesa et al. [21] proposed Marlin with comparable efficiency to Plonk.

The Challenge of SE in the Updatable Setting. The notion of simulation-extractability for zkSNARKs which is well motivated in practice, has not been studied in the updatable setting. Consider the following scenario: We assume a "rushing" adversary that starts off with a sequence of updates by malicious parties resulting in a subverted reference string srs. By combining their trapdoor contributions and employing the simulation algorithm, these parties can easily compute a proof to obtain a triple $(\mathsf{srs}, \mathsf{x}, \pi)$ that convinces the verifier of

[2] This can be seen as an efficient player-replaceable [32] multi-party computation.

a statement x without knowing a witness. Now, assume that at a later stage, a party produces a triple $(\mathsf{srs}', \mathsf{x}, \pi')$ for the same statement with respect to an updated srs' that has an honest update contribution. We want the guarantee that this party must know a witness corresponding to x. The ability to "maul" the proof π from the old SRS to a proof π' for the new SRS without knowing a witness would clearly violate security. The natural idea is to require that honestly *updated* reference strings are indistinguishable from honestly *generated* reference strings even for parties that previously contributed updates. However, this is not sufficient as the adversary can also rush toward the end of the SRS generation ceremony to perform the last update.

A definition of SE in the updatable setting should take these additional powers of the adversary, which are not captured by existing definitions of SE, into consideration. While generic compilers [1,41] can be applied to updatable SRS SNARKs to obtain SE, not only do they inevitably incur overheads and lead to efficiency loss, we contend that the standard definition of SE does not suffice in the updatable setting.

1.1 Our Contributions

We investigate the non-malleability properties of zkSNARK protocols obtained by FS-compiling multi-message protocols in the updatable SRS setting and give a modular approach to analyze their simulation-extractability. We make the following contributions:

- *Updatable simulation extractability (USE).* We propose a definition of simulation extractability in the updatable SRS setting called USE, that captures the additional power the adversary gets by being able to update the SRS.
- *Theorem for USE of FS-compiled proof systems.* We define three notions in the updatable SRS and ROM, *trapdoor-less zero-knowledge*, a *unique response* property, and *rewinding-based knowledge soundness.* Our main theorem shows that multi-message FS-compiled proof systems that satisfy these notions *are USE out-of-the box.*
- *USE for concrete zkSNARKs.* We prove that the most efficient updatable SRS SNARKS – Plonk/Sonic/Marlin – satisfy the premises of our theorem. We thus show that these zkSNARKs are updatable simulation extractable.
- *SNARKY signatures in the updatable setting.* Our results validate the folklore that the Fiat–Shamir transform is a natural means for constructing signatures of knowledge. This gives rise to the first SoK in the updatable setting and confirms that a much larger class of zkSNARKs, besides [39], can be lifted to SoK.
- *Broad applicability.* The updatable SRS plus ROM includes both the trusted SRS and the ROM model as special cases. This implies the relevance of our theorem for transparent zkSNARKs such as Halo2 and Plonky2 that replace the polynomial commitments of Kate et al. [40] with commitments from Bulletproof [17] and STARKs [8], respectively.

1.2 Technical Overview

At a high level, the proof of our main theorem for updatable simulation extractability is along the lines of the simulation extractability proof for FS-compiled sigma protocols from [24]. However, our theorem introduces new notions that are more general to allow us to consider proof systems that are richer than sigma protocols and support an updatable setup. We discuss some of the technical challenges below.

Plonk, Sonic, and Marlin were originally presented as interactive proofs of knowledge that are made non-interactive via the Fiat–Shamir transform. In the following, we denote the underlying interactive protocols by P (for Plonk), S (for Sonic), and M (for Marlin) and the resulting non-interactive proof systems by P_{FS}, S_{FS}, M_{FS} respectively.

Rewinding-Based Knowledge Soundness (RBKS). Following [24], one would have to show that for the protocols we consider, a witness can be extracted from sufficiently many valid transcripts with a common prefix. The standard definition of special soundness for sigma protocols requires the extraction of a witness from any two transcripts with the same first message. However, most zkSNARK protocols do not satisfy this notion. We put forth a notion analogous to special soundness that is more general and applicable to a wider class of protocols. Namely, protocols compiled using multi-round FS that rely on an (updatable) SRS. P, S, and M have more than three messages, and the number of transcripts required for extraction is more than two. Concretely, $(3\mathsf{n} + 6)$ for Plonk, $(\mathsf{n} + 1)$ for Sonic, and $(2\mathsf{n} + 3)$ for Marlin, where n is the number of constraints in the proven circuit. Hence, we do not have a pair of transcripts but a *tree of transcripts.*

Furthermore, the protocols we consider are arguments and rely on a SRS that comes with a trapdoor. An adversary in possession of the trapdoor can produce multiple valid proof transcripts potentially for false statements without knowing any witness. This is true even in the updatable setting, where a trapdoor still exists for any updated SRS. Recall that the standard special soundness definition requires witness extraction from *any* suitably structured tree of accepting transcripts. This means that there are no such trees for false statements.

Instead, we give a rewinding-based knowledge soundness definition with an extractor that proceeds in two steps. It first uses a tree building algorithm $\mathcal{T}$ to obtain a tree of transcripts. In the second step, it uses a tree extraction algorithm $\mathsf{Ext}_{\mathsf{ks}}$ to compute a witness from this tree. Tree-based knowledge soundness guarantees that it is possible to extract a witness from all (but negligibly many) trees of accepting transcripts produced by probabilistic polynomial time (PPT) adversaries. That is, if extraction from such a tree fails, then we break an underlying computational assumption. Moreover, this should hold even against adversaries that contribute to the SRS generation.

Unique Response Protocols (UR). Another property required to show simulation extractability is the unique response property which says that for 3-message sigma protocols, the response of the prover (3-rd message) is determined by the first message and the challenge [25] (intuitively, the prover can only employ fresh randomness in the first message of the protocol). We cannot use this definition since the protocols we consider have multiple rounds of randomized prover messages. In Plonk, both the first and the third messages are randomized. Although the Sonic prover is deterministic after it picks its first message, the protocol has more than 3 messages. The same holds for Marlin. We propose a generalization of the unique response property called k-UR. It requires that the behavior of the prover be determined by the first k of its messages. For our proof, it is sufficient that Plonk is 3-UR, and Sonic and Marlin are 2-UR.

Trapdoor-Less Zero-Knowledge (TLZK). The premises of our main theorem include two computational properties that do not mention a simulator, RBKS and UR. The theorem states that together with a suitable property for the simulator of the zero-knowledge property, they imply USE. Our key technique is to simulate simulation queries when reducing to RBKS and UR. For this it is convenient that the zero-knowledge simulator be trapdoor-less, that is can produce proofs without relying on the knowledge of the trapdoor. Simulation is based purely on the simulators early control over the challenge. In the ROM this corresponds to a simulator that programs the random oracle and can be understood as a generalization of honest-verifier zero-knowledge for multi-message Fiat–Shamir transformed proof systems with an SRS. We say that such a proof system is k-TLZK, if the simulator only programs the k-th challenge and we construct such simulators for P_{FS}, S_{FS}, and M_{FS}.

Technically we will make use of the k-UR property together with the k-TLZK property to bound the probability that the tree produced by the tree builder $\mathcal{T}$ of RBKS contains any programmed random oracle queries.

1.3 Related Work

There are many results on simulation extractability for non-interactive zero-knowledge proofs (NIZKs). First, Groth [35] noticed that a (black-box) SE NIZK is universally-composable (UC) [19]. Then Dodis et al. [23] introduced a notion of (black-box) *true simulation extractability* (i.e., SE with simulation of true statements only) and showed that no NIZK can be UC-secure if it does not have this property.

In the context of zkSNARKs, the first SE zkSNARK was proposed by Groth and Maller [39] and a SE zkSNARK for QAP was designed by Lipmaa [44]. Kosba et al. [41] give a general transformation from a NIZK to a black-box SE NIZK. Although their transformation works for zkSNARKs as well, the succinctness of the proof system is not preserved by this transformation. Abdolmaleki et al. [1] showed another transformation that obtains non-black-box simulation extractability but also preserves the succinctness of the argument. The zkSNARK of [37] has been shown to be SE by introducing minor modifications to the construction and making stronger assumptions [2,15]. Recently, [4] showed that the Groth's original proof system from [37] is weakly SE and randomizable. None of these results are for zkSNARKs in the updatable SRS setting or for zkSNARKs obtained via the Fiat–Shamir transformation. The recent work of [30] shows that Fiat–Shamir transformed Bulletproofs are simulation extractable. While they show a general theorem for multi-round protocols, they do not consider a setting with an SRS, and are therefore inapplicable to zkSNARKs in the updatable SRS setting.

2 Definitions and Lemmas for Multi-message SRS-Based Protocols

Simulation-Extractability for Multi-message Protocols. Most recent SNARK schemes follow the same blueprint of constructing an interactive information-theoretic proof system that is then compiled into a public coin computationally sound scheme using cryptographic tools such as polynomial commitments, and finally made non-interactive via the Fiat–Shamir transformation. Existing results on simulation extractability (for proof systems and signatures of knowledge) for Fiat–Shamir transformed systems work for 3-message protocols without reference string that require two transcripts for standard model extraction, e.g., [24,45,50].

In this section, we define properties that are necessary for our analysis of multi-message protocols with a universal updatable SRS. In order to prove simulation-extractability for such protocols, we require more than just two transcripts for extraction. Moreover, in the updatable setting we consider protocols that rely on an SRS where the adversary gets to contribute to the SRS. We first recall the updatable SRS setting and the Fiat-Shamir transform for $(2\mu + 1)$-message protocols. Next, we define trapdoor-less zero-knowledge and simulation-extractability which we base on [24] adapted to the updatable SRS setting. Then, to support multi-message SRS-based protocols compiled using the Fiat–Shamir transform, we generalize the unique response property, and define a notion of computational special soundness called rewinding-based knowledge soundness.

Let P and V be PPT algorithms, the former called the *prover* and the latter the *verifier* of a proof system. Both algorithms take a pre-agreed structured reference string srs as input. The structured reference strings we consider are (potentially) updatable, a notion we recall shortly. We focus on proof systems made non-interactive via the multi-message Fiat–Shamir transform presented below where prover and verifier are provided with a random oracle $\mathcal{H}$. We denote by π a proof created by P on input $(\mathsf{srs}, \mathsf{x}, \mathsf{w})$. We say that proof is accepting if $\mathsf{V}(\mathsf{srs}, \mathsf{x}, \pi)$ accepts it.

Let $\mathsf{R}(\mathcal{A})$ denote the set of random tapes of correct length for adversary $\mathcal{A}$ (assuming the given value of security parameter λ), and let $r \leftarrow\!\!\$\, \mathsf{R}(\mathcal{A})$ denote the random choice of tape r from $\mathsf{R}(\mathcal{A})$.

$\mathsf{UpdO}(\mathtt{intent}, \mathsf{srs}_n, \{\rho_j\}_{j=1}^n)$

```
if srs ≠ ⊥ : return ⊥
if (intent = setup) :
  (srs', ρ') ← GenSRS(R)
  Q_srs ← Q_srs ∪ {(srs', ρ')}
  return (srs', ρ')

if (intent = update) :
  b ← VerifySRS(srs_n, {ρ_j}_{j=1}^n)
  if (b = 0) : return ⊥
  (srs', ρ') ← UpdSRS(srs_n, {ρ_j}_{j=1}^n)
  Q_srs ← Q_srs ∪ {(srs', ρ')}
  return (srs', ρ')

if (intent = final) :
  b ← VerifySRS(srs_n, {ρ_j}_{j=1}^n)
  if (b = 0) ∨ Q_srs^(2) ∩ {ρ_j}_i = ∅ :
  return ⊥
    srs ← srs_n, return srs
else return ⊥
```

Fig. 1. The oracle defines the notion of updatable SRS setup.

2.1 Updatable SRS Setup Ceremonies

The definition of updatable SRS ceremonies of [38] requires the following algorithms.

- $(\mathsf{srs}, \rho) \leftarrow \mathsf{GenSRS}(\mathbf{R})$ is a PPT algorithm that takes a relation $\mathbf{R}$ and outputs a reference string srs, and correctness proof ρ.
- $(\mathsf{srs}', \rho') \leftarrow \mathsf{UpdSRS}(\mathsf{srs}, \{\rho_j\}_{j=1}^n)$ is a PPT algorithm that takes a srs, a list of update proofs and outputs an updated srs' together with a proof of correct update ρ'.
- $b \leftarrow \mathsf{VerifySRS}(\mathsf{srs}, \{\rho_j\}_{j=1}^n)$ takes a reference string srs, a list of update proofs, and outputs a bit indicating acceptance or not.[3]

In the next section, we define security notions in the updatable setting by giving the adversary access to an SRS update oracle UpdO, defined in Fig. 1. The oracle allows the adversary to control the SRS generation. A trusted setup can be expressed by the updatable setup definition simply by restricting the adversary to only call the oracle on $\mathtt{intent} = \mathtt{setup}$ and $\mathtt{intent} = \mathtt{final}$. Note that a soundness adversary now has access to both the random oracle $\mathcal{H}$ and UpdO: $(\mathsf{x}, \pi) \leftarrow \mathcal{A}^{\mathsf{UpdO},\mathcal{H}}(1^\lambda; r)$.

Remark on Universality of the SRS. The proof systems we consider in this work are universal. This means that both the relation $\mathbf{R}$ and the reference string srs allows to prove arithmetic constraints defined over a particular field up to some size bound. The public instance x must determine the constraints. If $\mathbf{R}$ comes with any auxiliary input, the latter is benign. We elide public preprocessing of constraint specific proving and verification keys. While important for performance, this modeling is not critical for security.

2.2 Multi-message Fiat-Shamir Compiled Provers and Verifiers

Given interactive prover and (public coin) verifier P', V' that exchange messages resulting in transcript $\tilde{\pi} = (a_1, c_1, \ldots, a_\mu, c_\mu, a_{\mu+1})$, where a_i comes from P' and c_i comes from V', the $(2\mu + 1)$-message Fiat-Shamir heuristic defines non-interactive provers and verifiers P, V as follows:

[3] For instance Plonk and Marlin will use the GenSRS, UpdSRS and VerifySRS algorithms in Fig. 2.

$\mathsf{GenSRS}(1^\lambda, \mathsf{max})$	$\mathsf{UpdSRS}(\mathsf{srs}, \{\rho_j\}_{j=1}^n)$
$\chi \leftarrow\!\$\ \mathbb{F}_p$ $\mathsf{srs} := \left(\left[\{\chi^i\}_{i=0}^{\mathsf{max}}\right]_1, [\chi]_2\right);$ $\rho = ([\chi, \chi]_1, [\chi]_2)$ **return** (srs, ρ)	Parse srs as $([\{A_i\}_{i=0}^{\mathsf{max}}]_1, [B]_2)$ $\chi' \leftarrow\!\$\ \mathbb{F}_p$ $\mathsf{srs}' := \left(\left[\{\chi'^i A_i\}_{i=0}^{\mathsf{max}}\right]_1, [\chi' B]_2\right);$ $\rho' = ([\chi' A_1, \chi']_1, [\chi']_2)$ **return** (srs', ρ')

$\mathsf{VerifySRS}(\mathsf{srs}, \{\rho_j\}_{j=1}^n)$

Parse srs as $([\{A_i\}_{i=0}^{\mathsf{max}}]_1, [B]_2)$ and $\{\rho_j\}_{j=1}^n$ as $\left\{\left(P_j, \bar{P}_j, \widehat{P}_j\right)\right\}_{j=1}^n$

Verify Update proofs:

$\bar{P}_1 = P_1$

$P_j \bullet [1]_2 = P_{j-1} \bullet \widehat{P}_j \quad \forall j \geq 2$

$\bar{P}_n \bullet [1]_2 = [1]_1 \bullet \widehat{P}_n$

Verify SRS structure:

$[A_i]_1 \bullet [1]_2 = [A_{i-1}]_1 \bullet [B]_2$ for all $0 < i \leq \mathsf{max}$

Fig. 2. Updatable SRS scheme SRS for $\mathbf{PC_P}$

- P behaves as P′ except after sending message a_i, $i \in [1\,..\,\mu]$, the prover does not wait for the message from the verifier but computes it locally setting $c_i = \mathcal{H}(\tilde{\pi}[0..i])$, where $\tilde{\pi}[0..j] = (\mathsf{x}, a_1, c_1, \ldots, a_{j-1}, c_{j-1}, a_j)$.[4]
  P outputs the non-interactive proof $\pi = (a_1, \ldots, a_\mu, a_{\mu+1})$, that omits challenges as they can be recomputed using $\mathcal{H}$.
- V takes x and π as input and behaves as V′ would but does not provide challenges to the prover. Instead it computes the challenges locally as P would, starting from $\tilde{\pi}[0..1] = (\mathsf{x}, a_1)$ which can be obtained from x and π. Then it verifies the resulting transcript $\tilde{\pi}$ as the verifier V′ would.

We note that since the verifier can compute the challenges by querying the random oracle, they do not need to be sent by the prover. Thus the π - $\tilde{\pi}$ notational distinction.

Notation for $(2\mu + 1)$*-message Fiat–Shamir transformed proof systems.* Let $\mathsf{SRS} = (\mathsf{GenSRS}, \mathsf{UpdSRS}, \mathsf{VerifySRS})$ be the algorithm of an updatable SRS ceremony. All our definitions and theorems are about non-interactive proof systems $\boldsymbol{\Psi} = (\mathsf{SRS}, \mathsf{P}, \mathsf{V}, \mathsf{Sim})$ compiled via the $(2\mu + 1)$-message FS transform. That is $\pi = (a_1, \ldots, a_\mu, a_{\mu+1})$ and $\tilde{\pi} = (a_1, c_1, \ldots, a_\mu, c_\mu, a_{\mu+1})$, with $c_i = \mathcal{H}(\tilde{\pi}[0..i])$. We use $\tilde{\pi}[0]$ for instance x and $\tilde{\pi}[i]$, $\tilde{\pi}[i].\mathsf{ch}$ to denote prover message a_i and challenge c_i respectively.

[4] For Fiat–Shamir based SoK the message signed m is added to x before hashing.

$\mathsf{SimO}.\mathcal{H}(x)$	$\mathsf{SimO}.\mathsf{Prog}(x, h)$	$\boxed{\mathsf{SimO}.\mathsf{P}(\mathsf{x},\mathsf{w})}$ $\mathsf{SimO}.\mathsf{P}'(\mathsf{x})$
if $H[x] = \bot$ **then**	**if** $H[x] = \bot$ **then**	$\boxed{\textbf{assert } (\mathsf{x},\mathsf{w}) \in \mathbf{R}}$
$\quad H[x] \leftarrow\!\!\$\ \mathsf{Im}(\mathcal{H})$	$\quad H[x] \leftarrow h$	$\pi \leftarrow \mathsf{Sim}^{\mathsf{SimO}.\mathcal{H},\mathsf{SimO}.\mathsf{Prog}}(\mathsf{srs},\mathsf{x})$
return $H[x]$	$\quad Q_{\mathsf{prog}} \leftarrow Q_{\mathsf{prog}} \cup \{x\}$	$Q \leftarrow Q \cup \{(\mathsf{x},\pi)\}$
	return $H[x]$	**return** π

Fig. 3. Simulation oracles: srs is the finalized SRS, only SimO.P′ allows for simulation of false statements

2.3 Trapdoor-Less Zero-Knowledge (TLZK)

We call a protocol *trapdoor-less zero-knowledge* (TLZK) if there exists a simulator that does not require the trapdoor, and works by programming the random oracle. Moreover, the simulator may only be allowed to program the random oracle on point $\tilde{\pi}[0, k]$, that is the simulator can only program the challenges that come after the k-th prover message. We call protocols which allow for such a simulation *k-programmable trapdoor-less zero-knowledge.*

Our definition of zero-knowledge for non-interactive arguments is in the programmable ROM. We model this using the oracles from Fig. 3 that provide a stateful wrapper around Sim. $\mathsf{SimO}.\mathcal{H}(x)$ simulates $\mathcal{H}$ using lazy sampling, $\mathsf{SimO}.\mathsf{Prog}(x, h)$ allows for programming the simulated $\mathcal{H}$ and is available only to Sim. $\mathsf{SimO}.\mathsf{P}(\mathsf{x},\mathsf{w})$ and $\mathsf{SimO}.\mathsf{P}'(\mathsf{x})$ call the simulator. The former is used in the zero-knowledge definition and requires the statement and witness to be in the relation, the latter is used in the simulation extraction definition and does not require a witness input.

Definition 1 (Updatable k-Programmable Trapdoor-Less Zero-Knowledge). *Let* $\mathbf{\Psi}_{\mathsf{FS}} = (\mathsf{SRS}, \mathsf{P}, \mathsf{V}, \mathsf{Sim})$ *be a* $(2\mu+1)$*-message FS-transformed NIZK proof system with an updatable SRS setup. We call* $\mathbf{\Psi}_{\mathsf{FS}}$ trapdoor-less zero-knowledge *with security* $\varepsilon_{\mathsf{zk}}$ *if for any adversary* $\mathcal{A}$, $|\varepsilon_0(\lambda) - \varepsilon_1(\lambda)| \le \varepsilon_{\mathsf{zk}}(\lambda)$, *where*

$$\varepsilon_0(\lambda) = \Pr\left[\mathcal{A}^{\mathsf{UpdO},\mathcal{H},\mathsf{P}}(1^\lambda)\right], \varepsilon_1(\lambda) = \Pr\left[\mathcal{A}^{\mathsf{UpdO},\mathsf{SimO}.\mathcal{H},\mathsf{SimO}.\mathsf{P}}(1^\lambda)\right].$$

If $\varepsilon_{\mathsf{zk}}(\lambda)$ *is negligible, we say* $\mathbf{\Psi}_{\mathsf{FS}}$ *is trapdoor-less zero-knowledge. Additionally, we say that* $\mathbf{\Psi}_{\mathsf{FS}}$ *is k-programmable, if* Sim *before returning a proof* π *only calls* SimO.Prog *on* $(\tilde{\pi}[0..k], h)$*. That is, it only programs the k-th message.*

Remark 1 (TLZK vs HVZK). We note that TLZK notion is closely related to honest-verifier zero-knowledge in the standard model. That is, if we consider an interactive proof system $\mathbf{\Psi}$ that is HVZK in the standard model then $\mathbf{\Psi}_{\mathsf{FS}}$ is TLZK. This comes as the simulator Sim in $\mathbf{\Psi}$ produces a valid simulated proof by picking verifier's challenges according to a predefined distribution and $\mathbf{\Psi}_{\mathsf{FS}}$'s simulator $\mathsf{Sim}_{\mathsf{FS}}$ produces its proofs similarly by picking the challenges and additionally programming the random oracle to return the picked challenges. Importantly, in both $\mathbf{\Psi}$ and $\mathbf{\Psi}_{\mathsf{FS}}$ success of the simulator does not depend on access to an SRS trapdoor.

We note that Plonk is 3-programmable TLZK, and Sonic and Marlin are 2-programmable TLZK. This follows directly from the proofs of their standard model zero-knowledge property in Lemma 5 and lemmas 11 and 14 in the full version [29].

2.4 Updatable Simulation Extractability (USE)

We note that the zero-knowledge property is only guaranteed for statements in the language. For *simulation extractability* where the simulator should be able to provide simulated proofs for false statements as well, we thus use the oracle $\mathsf{SimO.P'}$[5].

Definition 2 (Updatable Simulation Extractability). *Let* $\mathbf{\Psi}_{\mathsf{NI}} = (\mathsf{SRS}, \mathsf{P}, \mathsf{V}, \mathsf{Sim})$ *be a NIZK proof system with an updatable SRS setup. We say that* $\mathbf{\Psi}_{\mathsf{NI}}$ *is* updatable simulation-extractable *with security loss* $\varepsilon_{\mathsf{se}}(\lambda, \mathsf{acc}, q)$ *if for any* PPT *adversary* $\mathcal{A}$ *that is given oracle access to setup oracle* UpdO *and simulation oracle* SimO *and that produces an accepting proof for* $\mathbf{\Psi}_{\mathsf{NI}}$ *with probability* acc, *where*

$$\mathsf{acc} = \Pr\left[\begin{matrix}\mathsf{V}(\mathsf{srs}, \mathsf{x}, \pi) = 1 \\ \wedge (\mathsf{x}, \pi) \notin Q\end{matrix} \;\middle|\; \begin{matrix} r \leftarrow\!\$\, \mathsf{R}(\mathcal{A}) \\ (\mathsf{x}, \pi) \leftarrow \mathcal{A}^{\mathsf{UpdO}, \mathsf{SimO}.\mathcal{H}, \mathsf{SimO.P'}}(1^\lambda; r)\end{matrix}\right]$$

there exists an expected PPT extractor $\mathsf{Ext}_{\mathsf{se}}$ *such that*

$$\Pr\left[\begin{matrix}\mathsf{V}(\mathsf{srs}, \mathsf{x}, \pi) = 1, \\ (\mathsf{x}, \pi) \notin Q, \\ \mathbf{R}(\mathsf{x}, \mathsf{w}) = 0\end{matrix} \;\middle|\; \begin{matrix} r \leftarrow\!\$\, \mathsf{R}(\mathcal{A}), (\mathsf{x}, \pi) \leftarrow \mathcal{A}^{\mathsf{UpdO}, \mathsf{SimO}.\mathcal{H}, \mathsf{SimO.P'}}(1^\lambda; r) \\ \mathsf{w} \leftarrow \mathsf{Ext}_{\mathsf{se}}(\mathsf{srs}, \mathcal{A}, r, Q_{\mathsf{srs}}, Q_{\mathcal{H}}, Q)\end{matrix}\right] \le \varepsilon_{\mathsf{se}}(\lambda, \mathsf{acc}, q)$$

Here, srs *is the finalized SRS. List* Q_{srs} *contains all* (srs, ρ) *of update SRSs and their proofs, list* $Q_{\mathcal{H}}$ *contains all* $\mathcal{A}$*'s queries to* $\mathsf{SimO}.\mathcal{H}$ *and the (simulated) random oracle's answers,* $|Q_{\mathcal{H}}| \le q$, *and list* Q *contains all* (x, π) *pairs where* x *is an instance queried to* $\mathsf{SimO.P'}$ *by the adversary and* π *is the simulator's answer.*

2.5 Unique Response (UR) Protocols

A technical hurdle identified by Faust et al. [24] for proving simulation extraction via the Fiat–Shamir transformation is that the transformed proof system satisfies a unique response property. The original formulation by Fischlin, although suitable for applications presented in [24,25], does not suffice in our case. First, the property assumes that the protocol has three messages, with the second being the challenge from the verifier. That is not the case we consider here. Second, it is not entirely clear how to generalize the property. Should one require that after the first challenge from the verifier, the prover's responses are fixed? That does

[5] Note, that simulation extractability property where the simulator is required to give simulated proofs for true statements only is called *true simulation extractability*.

not work since the prover needs to answer differently on different verifier's challenges, as otherwise the protocol could have fewer messages. Another problem is that the protocol could have a message, beyond the first prover's message, which is randomized. Unique response cannot hold in this case. Finally, the protocols we consider here are not in the standard model, but use an SRS.

We work around these obstacles by providing a generalized notion of the unique response property. More precisely, we say that a $(2\mu + 1)$-message protocol has *unique responses from* k, and call it a k-UR-protocol, if it follows the definition below:

Definition 3 (Updatable k-Unique Response Protocol). *Let* $\mathbf{\Psi}_{\mathsf{FS}} = (\mathsf{SRS}, \mathsf{P}, \mathsf{V}, \mathsf{Sim})$ *be a* $(2\mu + 1)$*-message FS-transformed NIZK proof system with an updatable SRS setup. Let* $\mathcal{H}$ *be the random oracle. We say that* $\mathbf{\Psi}_{\mathsf{FS}}$ *has* unique responses for k *with security* $\varepsilon_{\mathsf{ur}}(\lambda)$ *if for any* PPT *adversary* $\mathcal{A}_{\mathsf{ur}}$*:*

$$\Pr\left[\begin{array}{l}\pi \neq \pi', \tilde{\pi}[0..k] = \tilde{\pi}'[0..k], \\ \mathsf{V}'(\mathsf{srs}, \mathsf{x}, \pi, c) = \mathsf{V}'(\mathsf{srs}, \mathsf{x}, \pi', c) = 1\end{array} \middle| \; (\mathsf{x}, \pi, \pi', c) \leftarrow \mathcal{A}_{\mathsf{ur}}^{\mathsf{UpdO}, \mathcal{H}}(1^\lambda) \right] \leq \varepsilon_{\mathsf{ur}}(\lambda)$$

where srs *is the finalized SRS and* $\mathsf{V}'(\mathsf{srs}, \mathsf{x}, \pi = (a_1, \ldots, a_\mu, a_{\mu+1}))$ *behaves as* $\mathsf{V}(\mathsf{srs}, \mathsf{x}, \pi)$ *except for using* c *as the* k*-th challenge instead of calling* $\mathcal{H}(\tilde{\pi}[0..k])$*. Thus,* $\mathcal{A}$ *can program the* k*-th challenge. We say* $\mathbf{\Psi}_{\mathsf{FS}}$ *is* k-UR*, if* $\varepsilon_{\mathsf{ur}}(\lambda)$ *is negligible.*

Intuitively, a protocol is k-UR if it is infeasible for a PPT adversary to produce a pair of accepting proofs $\pi \neq \pi'$ that are the same on the first k messages of the prover.

The definition can be easily generalized to allow for programming the oracle on more than just a single point. We opted for this simplified presentation, since all the protocols analyzed in this paper require only single-point programming,

2.6 Rewinding-Based Knowledge Soundness (RBKS)

Before giving the definition of rewinding-based knowledge soundness for NIZK proof systems compiled via the $(2\mu + 1)$-message FS transformation, we first recall the notion of a tree of transcripts.

Definition 4 (Tree of accepting transcripts, cf. [14]). *A* $(n_1, \ldots, n_\mu)$*-tree of accepting transcripts is a tree where each node on depth* i*, for* $i \in [1 \mathinner{..} \mu + 1]$*, is an* i*-th prover's message in an accepting transcript; edges between the nodes are labeled with challenges, such that no two edges on the same depth have the same label; and each node on depth* i *has* $n_i - 1$ *siblings and* n_{i+1} *children. The tree consists of* $N = \prod_{i=1}^{\mu} n_i$ *branches, where* N *is the number of accepting transcripts. We require* $N = \mathsf{poly}(\lambda)$*. We refer to a* $(1, \ldots, n_k = n, 1, \ldots, 1)$*-tree as a* (k, n)*-tree.*

The existence of simulation trapdoor for P, S and M means that they are not special sound in the standard sense. We therefore put forth the notion of rewinding-based knowledge soundness that is a computational notion. Note that in the definition below, it is implicit that each transcript in the tree is accepting with respect to a "local programming" of the random oracle. However, the verification of the proof output by the adversary is with respect to a non-programmed random oracle.

Definition 5 (Updatable Rewinding-Based Knowledge Soundness). *Let* $n_1, \dots, n_\mu \in \mathbb{N}$. *Let* $\mathbf{\Psi}_{\mathsf{FS}} = (\mathsf{SRS}, \mathsf{P}, \mathsf{V}, \mathsf{Sim})$ *be a* $(2\mu+1)$*-message FS-transformed NIZK proof system with an updatable SRS setup for relation* $\mathbf{R}$. *Let* $\mathcal{H}$ *be the random oracle. We require existence of an expected PPT tree builder* $\mathcal{T}$ *that eventually outputs a* T *which is either a* $(n_1, \dots, n_\mu)$*-tree of accepting transcript or* $\perp$ *and a PPT extractor* $\mathsf{Ext}_{\mathsf{ks}}$. *Let adversary* $\mathcal{A}_{\mathsf{ks}}$ *be a PPT algorithm, that outputs a valid proof with probability at least* acc, *where*

$$\mathsf{acc} = \Pr\left[\begin{array}{c} \mathsf{V}(\mathsf{srs}, \mathsf{x}, \pi) = 1 \\ \wedge (\mathsf{x}, \pi) \notin Q \end{array} \middle| \begin{array}{c} r \leftarrow\!\$\, \mathsf{R}(\mathcal{A}_{\mathsf{ks}}) \\ (\mathsf{x}, \pi) \leftarrow \mathcal{A}_{\mathsf{ks}}^{\mathsf{UpdO}, \mathcal{H}}(1^\lambda; r) \end{array}\right].$$

We say that $\mathbf{\Psi}_{\mathsf{FS}}$ *is* $(n_1, \dots, n_\mu)$*-rewinding-based knowledge sound with security loss* $\varepsilon_{\mathsf{ks}}(\lambda, \mathsf{acc}, q)$ *if*

$$\Pr\left[\begin{array}{c} \mathsf{V}(\mathsf{srs}, \mathsf{x}, \pi) = 1, \\ \mathbf{R}(\mathsf{x}, \mathsf{w}) = 0 \end{array} \middle| \begin{array}{l} r \leftarrow\!\$\, \mathsf{R}(\mathcal{A}_{\mathsf{ks}}), \\ (\mathsf{srs}, \mathsf{x}, \cdot) \leftarrow \mathcal{A}_{\mathsf{ks}}^{\mathsf{UpdO}, \mathcal{H}}(1^\lambda; r) \\ \mathsf{T} \leftarrow \mathcal{T}(\mathsf{srs}, \mathcal{A}_{\mathsf{ks}}, r, Q_{\mathsf{srs}}, Q_{\mathcal{H}}), \mathsf{w} \leftarrow \mathsf{Ext}_{\mathsf{ks}}(\mathsf{T}) \end{array}\right] \leq \varepsilon_{\mathsf{ks}}(\lambda, \mathsf{acc}, q).$$

Here, srs *is the finalized SRS. List* Q_{srs} *contains all* (srs, ρ) *of updated SRSs and their proofs, and list* $Q_{\mathcal{H}}$ *contains all of the adversaries queries to* $\mathcal{H}$ *and the random oracle's answers,* $|Q_{\mathcal{H}}| \leq q$.

3 Simulation Extractability—The General Result

Equipped with the definitional framework of Sect. 2, we now present the main result of this paper: a proof of simulation extractability for multi-message Fiat–Shamir-transformed NIZK proof systems.

Without loss of generality, we assume that whenever the accepting proof contains a response to a challenge from a random oracle, then the adversary queried the oracle to get it. It is straightforward to transform any adversary that violates this condition into an adversary that makes these additional queries to the random oracle and wins with the same probability.

The core conceptual insight of the proof is that the k-unique response and k-programmable trapdoor-less zero-knowledge properties together ensures that the k-th move challenges in the trees of rewinding-based knowledge soundness are fresh and do not come from the simulator. This allows us to eliminate the simulation oracle in our rewinding argument and enables us to use the existing results of [3] in later sections.

Theorem 1 (Simulation-extractable multi-message protocols). *Let* $\mathbf{\Psi}_{\mathsf{FS}} = (\mathsf{SRS}, \mathsf{P}, \mathsf{V}, \mathsf{Sim})$ *be a* $(2\mu+1)$*-message FS-transformed NIZK proof system with an updatable SRS setup. If* $\mathbf{\Psi}_{\mathsf{FS}}$ *is an updatable* k*-unique response protocol* *with security loss* $\varepsilon_{\mathsf{ur}}$*, updatable* k*-programmable trapdoor-less zero-knowledge, and updatable rewinding-based knowledge sound with security loss* $\varepsilon_{\mathsf{ks}}$*; Then* $\boldsymbol{\Psi}_{\mathsf{FS}}$ *is* updatable simulation-extractable *with security loss*

$$\varepsilon_{\mathsf{se}}(\lambda, \mathsf{acc}, q) \leq \varepsilon_{\mathsf{ks}}(\lambda, \mathsf{acc} - \varepsilon_{\mathsf{ur}}(\lambda), q)$$

against any PPT *adversary* $\mathcal{A}$ *that makes up to* q *random oracle queries and returns an accepting proof with probability at least* acc.

Proof. Let $(\mathsf{x}, \pi) \leftarrow \mathcal{A}^{\mathsf{UpdO}, \mathsf{SimO}.\mathcal{H}, \mathsf{SimO}.\mathsf{P}'}(r_{\mathcal{A}})$ be the USE adversary. We show how to build an extractor $\mathsf{Ext}_{\mathsf{se}}(\mathsf{srs}, \mathcal{A}, r_{\mathcal{A}}, Q, Q_{\mathcal{H}}, Q_{\mathsf{srs}})$ that outputs a witness w, such that $\mathbf{R}(\mathsf{x}, \mathsf{w})$ holds with high probability. To that end we define an algorithm $\mathcal{A}_{\mathsf{ks}}^{\mathsf{UpdO}, \mathcal{H}}(r)$ against rewinding-based knowledge soundness of $\boldsymbol{\Psi}_{\mathsf{FS}}$ that runs internally $\mathcal{A}^{\mathsf{UpdO}, \mathsf{SimO}.\mathcal{H}, \mathsf{SimO}.\mathsf{P}'}(r_{\mathcal{A}})$. Here $r = (r_{\mathsf{Sim}}, r_{\mathcal{A}})$ with r_{Sim} the randomness that will be used to simulate $\mathsf{SimO}.\mathsf{P}'$.

The code of $\mathcal{A}_{\mathsf{ks}}^{\mathsf{UpdO}, \mathcal{H}}(r)$ hardcodes Q such that it does not use any randomness for proofs in Q as long as statements are queried in order. In this case it simply returns a proof π_{Sim} from Q but nevertheless queries $\mathsf{SimO}.\mathsf{Prog}$ on $(\tilde{\pi}_{\mathsf{Sim}}[0..k], \tilde{\pi}_{\mathsf{Sim}}[k].ch)$, i.e. it programs the k-th challenge. While it is hard to construct such an adversary without knowing Q, it clearly exists and $\mathsf{Ext}_{\mathsf{se}}$ has the necessary inputs to construct $\mathcal{A}_{\mathsf{ks}}$. This hardcoding guarantees that $\mathcal{A}_{\mathsf{ks}}$ returns the same (x, π) as $\mathcal{A}$ in the experiment. Eventually, $\mathsf{Ext}_{\mathsf{se}}$ uses the tree builder $\mathcal{T}$ and extractor $\mathsf{Ext}_{\mathsf{ks}}$ for $\mathcal{A}_{\mathsf{ks}}$ to extract the witness for x. Both guaranteed to exist (and be successful with high probability) by rewinding-based knowledge soundness. This high-level argument shows that $\mathsf{Ext}_{\mathsf{se}}$ exists as well.

We now give the details of the simulation that guarantees that $\mathcal{A}_{\mathsf{ks}}$ is successful whenever $\mathcal{A}$ is—except with a small security loss that we will bound later: Since $\mathcal{A}_{\mathsf{ks}}$ runs $\mathcal{A}$ internally, it needs to take care of $\mathcal{A}$'s oracle queries. $\mathcal{A}_{\mathsf{ks}}$ passes on queries of $\mathcal{A}$ to the update oracle UpdO to its own UpdO oracle and returns the result to $\mathcal{A}$. $\mathcal{A}_{\mathsf{ks}}$ internally simulates (non-hardcoded) queries to the simulator $\mathsf{SimO}.\mathsf{P}'$ by running the Sim algorithm on randomness r_{Sim} of its tape. Sim requires access to oracles $\mathsf{SimO}.\mathcal{H}$ to compute a challenge honestly and $\mathsf{SimO}.\mathsf{Prog}$ to program a challenge. Again $\mathcal{A}_{\mathsf{ks}}$ simulates both of these oracles internally, cf. Fig. 4, this time using the $\mathcal{H}$ oracle of $\mathcal{A}_{\mathsf{ks}}$. Note that queries of $\mathcal{A}$ to $\mathsf{SimO}.\mathcal{H}$ are not programmed, but passed on to $\mathcal{H}$.

Importantly, all challenges in simulated proofs, up to round k are also computed honestly, i.e. $\tilde{\pi}[i].\mathsf{ch} = \mathcal{H}(\tilde{\pi}[0..i])$, for $i < k$.

$\mathsf{SimO}.\mathcal{H}(x)$	$\mathsf{SimO}.\mathsf{Prog}(x, h)$
if $H[x] = \bot$ **then**	**if** $H[x] = \bot$ **then**
$\quad H[x] \leftarrow \mathcal{H}(x)$	$\quad H[x] \leftarrow h$
return $H[x]$	$\quad Q_{\mathsf{prog}} \leftarrow Q_{\mathsf{prog}} \cup \{x\}$
	return $H[x]$

Fig. 4. Simulating random oracle calls.

Eventually, $\mathcal{A}$ outputs an instance and proof (x, π). $\mathcal{A}_{\mathsf{ks}}$ returns the same values as long as $\tilde{\pi}[0..i] \notin Q_{\mathsf{prog}}$, $i \in [1, \mu]$. This models that the proof output by $\mathcal{A}_{\mathsf{ks}}$ must not contain any programmed queries as such a proof would not be consistent to $\mathcal{H}$ in the RBKS experiment. If $\mathcal{A}$ outputs a proof that does contain programmed challenges, then $\mathcal{A}_{\mathsf{ks}}$ aborts. We denote this event by E.

Lemma 1. *Probability that* E *happens is upper-bounded by* $\varepsilon_{\mathsf{ur}}(\lambda)$.

Proof. We build an adversary $\mathcal{A}_{\mathsf{ur}}^{\mathsf{UpdO}, \mathcal{H}}(\lambda; r)$ that has access to the random oracle $\mathcal{H}$ and update oracle UpdO. $\mathcal{A}_{\mathsf{ur}}$ uses $\mathcal{A}_{\mathsf{ks}}$ to break the k-UR property of $\boldsymbol{\Psi}_{\mathsf{FS}}$.

When $\mathcal{A}_{\mathsf{ks}}$ outputs a proof π for x such that E holds, $\mathcal{A}_{\mathsf{ur}}$ looks through lists Q and $Q_{\mathcal{H}}$ until it finds $\tilde{\pi}_{\mathsf{Sim}}[0..k]$ such that $\tilde{\pi}[0..k] = \tilde{\pi}_{\mathsf{Sim}}[0..k]$ and a programmed random oracle query $\tilde{\pi}_{\mathsf{Sim}}[k].\mathsf{ch}$ on $\tilde{\pi}_{\mathsf{Sim}}[0..k]$. $\mathcal{A}_{\mathsf{ur}}$ returns two proofs π and π_{Sim} for x, and the challenge $\tilde{\pi}_{\mathsf{Sim}}[k].\mathsf{ch} = \tilde{\pi}[k].\mathsf{ch}$. Importantly, both proofs are w.r.t the unique response verifier. The first, since it is a correctly computed simulated proof for which the unique response property definition allows any challenges at k. The latter, since it is an accepting proof produced by the adversary. We have that $\pi \neq \pi_{\mathsf{Sim}}$ as otherwise $\mathcal{A}$ does not win the simulation extractability game as $\pi \in Q$. On the other hand, if the proofs are different, then $\mathcal{A}_{\mathsf{ur}}$ breaks k-UR-ness of $\boldsymbol{\Psi}_{\mathsf{FS}}$. This happens only with probability $\varepsilon_{\mathsf{ur}}(\lambda)$. □

We denote by $\widetilde{\mathsf{acc}}$ the probability that $\mathcal{A}_{\mathsf{ks}}$ outputs an accepting proof. We note that by up-to-bad reasoning $\widetilde{\mathsf{acc}}$ is at most $\varepsilon_{\mathsf{ur}}(\lambda)$ far from the probability that $\mathcal{A}$ outputs an accepting proof. Thus, the probability that $\mathcal{A}_{\mathsf{ks}}$ outputs an accepting proof is at least $\widetilde{\mathsf{acc}} \geq \mathsf{acc} - \varepsilon_{\mathsf{ur}}(\lambda)$. Since $\boldsymbol{\Psi}_{\mathsf{FS}}$ is $\varepsilon_{\mathsf{ks}}(\lambda, \widetilde{\mathsf{acc}}, q)$ rewinding-based knowledge sound, there is a tree builder $\mathcal{T}$ and extractor $\mathsf{Ext}_{\mathsf{ks}}$ that rewinds $\mathcal{A}_{\mathsf{ks}}$ to obtain a tree of accepting transcripts T and fails to extract the witness with probability at most $\varepsilon_{\mathsf{ks}}(\lambda, \widetilde{\mathsf{acc}}, q)$. The extractor $\mathsf{Ext}_{\mathsf{se}}$ outputs the witness with the same probability.

Thus $\varepsilon_{\mathsf{se}}(\lambda, \mathsf{acc}, q) = \varepsilon_{\mathsf{ks}}(\lambda, \widetilde{\mathsf{acc}}, q) \leq \varepsilon_{\mathsf{ks}}(\lambda, \mathsf{acc} - \varepsilon_{\mathsf{ur}}, q)$. □

Remark 2. Observe that our theorem does not depend on $\varepsilon_{\mathsf{zk}}(\lambda)$. There is no real prover algorithm P in the experiment. Only the k-programmability of TLZK matters.

Remark 3. Observe that the theorem does not prescribe a tree shape for the tree builder $\mathcal{T}$. Interestingly, in our concrete results $\mathcal{T}$ outputs a $(k, *)$-tree of accepting transcripts.

4 Concrete SNARKs Preliminaries

Bilinear groups. A bilinear group generator $\mathsf{Pgen}(1^{\lambda})$ returns public parameters $\mathsf{p} = (p, \mathbb{G}_1, \mathbb{G}_2, \mathbb{G}_T, \hat{e}, [1]_1, [1]_2)$, where $\mathbb{G}_1$, $\mathbb{G}_2$, and $\mathbb{G}_T$ are additive cyclic groups of prime order $p = 2^{\Omega(\lambda)}$, $[1]_1, [1]_2$ are generators of $\mathbb{G}_1$, $\mathbb{G}_2$, resp., and $\hat{e} : \mathbb{G}_1 \times \mathbb{G}_2 \to \mathbb{G}_T$ is a non-degenerate PPT-computable bilinear pairing. We assume the bilinear pairing to be Type-3, i.e., that there is no efficient isomorphism from $\mathbb{G}_1$ to $\mathbb{G}_2$ or from $\mathbb{G}_2$ to $\mathbb{G}_1$. We use the by now standard bracket notation, i.e., we write $[a]_\iota$ to denote $a[1]_\iota$. We denote $\hat{e}([a]_1, [b]_2)$ as $[a]_1 \bullet [b]_2$. Thus, $[a]_1 \bullet [b]_2 = [ab]_T$. Since every algorithm $\mathcal{A}$ takes as input the public parameters we skip them when describing $\mathcal{A}$'s input. Similarly, we do not explicitly state that each protocol starts by running Pgen.

4.1 Algebraic Group Model

The algebraic group model (AGM) of Fuchsbauer, Kiltz, and Loss [27] lies somewhat between the standard and generic bilinear group model. In the AGM it is assumed that an adversary $\mathcal{A}$ can output a group element $[y] \in \mathbb{G}$ if $[y]$ has been computed by applying group operations to group elements given to $\mathcal{A}$ as input. It is further assumed, that $\mathcal{A}$ knows how to "build" $[y]$ from those elements. More precisely, the AGM requires that whenever $\mathcal{A}([\boldsymbol{x}])$ outputs a group element $[y]$ then it also outputs $\boldsymbol{c}$ such that $[y] = \boldsymbol{c}^\top \cdot [\boldsymbol{x}]$. Plonk, Sonic and Marlin have been shown secure using the AGM. An adversary that works in the AGM is called *algebraic*.

Ideal Verifier and Verification Equations. Let $(\mathsf{SRS}, \mathsf{P}, \mathsf{V}, \mathsf{Sim})$ be a proof system. Observe that the SRS algorithms provide an SRS which can be interpreted as a set of group representation of polynomials evaluated at trapdoor elements. That is, for a trapdoor χ the SRS contains $[\mathsf{p}_1(\chi), \dots, \mathsf{p}_\mathsf{k}(\chi)]_1$, for some polynomials $\mathsf{p}_1(X), \dots, \mathsf{p}_\mathsf{k}(X) \in \mathbb{F}_p[X]$. The verifier V accepts a proof π for instance x if (a set of) verification equation $\mathsf{ve}_{\mathsf{x},\pi}$ (which can also be interpreted as a polynomial in $\mathbb{F}_p[X]$ whose coefficients depend on messages sent by the prover) zeroes at χ. Following [28] we call verifiers who check that $\mathsf{ve}_{\mathsf{x},\pi}(\chi) = 0$ *real verifiers* as opposed to *ideal verifiers* who accept only when $\mathsf{ve}_{\mathsf{x},\pi}(X) = 0$. That is, while a real verifier accepts when a polynomial *evaluates* to zero, an ideal verifier accepts only when the polynomial *is* zero.

Although ideal verifiers are impractical, they are very useful in our proofs. More precisely, we show that the idealized verifier accepts an incorrect proof (what "incorrect" means depends on the situation) with at most negligible probability (and in many cases—never); when the real verifier accepts, but not the idealized one, then a malicious prover can be used to break the underlying security assumption (in our case—a variant of dlog.)

Analogously, idealized verifier can be defined for polynomial commitment schemes.

4.2 Dlog Assumptions in Standard and Updatable Setting

Definition 6 (**(q_1, q_2)-dlog assumption**). *Let $\mathcal{A}$ be a* PPT *adversary that gets as input $[1, \chi, \dots, \chi^{q_1}]_1, [1, \chi, \dots, \chi^{q_2}]_2$, for some randomly picked $\chi \in \mathbb{F}_p$, the assumption requires that $\mathcal{A}$ cannot compute χ. That is*

$$\Pr[\chi = \mathcal{A}([1, \chi, \dots, \chi^{q_1}]_1, [1, \chi, \dots, \chi^{q_2}]_2) \mid \chi \leftarrow\!\!\$\, \mathbb{F}_p] \leq \mathsf{negl}(\lambda).$$

Since all our protocols and security notions are in the updatable setting, it is natural to define the dlog assumptions also in the updatable setting. That is, instead of being given a dlog challenge the adversary $\mathcal{A}$ is given access to an update oracle as defined in Fig. 1. The honestly generated SRS is set to be a dlog challenge and the update algorithm UpdSRS re-randomizing the challenge. We define this assumptions and show a reduction between the assumptions in the updatable and standard setting.

Note that for clarity we here refer to the SRS by Ch. Further, to avoid cluttering notation, we do not make the update proofs explicit. They are generated in the same manner as the proofs in Fig. 2.

Definition 7 **((q_1, q_2)-udlog assumption).** *Let $\mathcal{A}$ be a PPT adversary that gets oracle access to UpdO with internal algorithms $(\mathsf{GenSRS}, \mathsf{UpdSRS}, \mathsf{VerifySRS})$, where GenSRS and UpdSRS are defined as follows:*

- $\mathsf{GenSRS}(\lambda)$ *samples* $\chi \leftarrow\$ \mathbb{F}_p$ *and defines* $\mathsf{Ch} := ([1, \chi, \ldots, \chi^{q_1}]_1, [1, \chi, \ldots, \chi^{q_2}]_2)$.
- $\mathsf{UpdSRS}(\mathsf{Ch}, \{\rho_j\}_{j=1}^{n})$ *parses* Ch *as* $([\{A_i\}_{i=0}^{q_1}]_1, [\{B_i\}_{i=0}^{q_2}]_2)$, *samples* $\widetilde{\chi} \leftarrow\$ \mathbb{F}_p$, *and defines* $\widetilde{\mathsf{Ch}} := \left(\left[\{\widetilde{\chi}^i A_i\}_{i=0}^{q_1}\right]_1, \left[\{\widetilde{\chi}^i B_i\}_{i=0}^{q_2}\right]_2\right)$.

Then $\Pr\left[\bar{\chi} \leftarrow \mathcal{A}^{\mathsf{UpdO}}(\lambda)\right] \leq \mathsf{negl}(\lambda)$, *where* $\left(\left[\{\bar{\chi}^i\}_{i=0}^{q_1}\right]_1, \left[\{\bar{\chi}^i\}_{i=0}^{q_2}\right]_2\right)$ *is the final* Ch.

Remark 4 (Single adversarial updates after an honest setup.). As an alternative to the updatable setting defined in Fig. 1, one can consider a slightly different model of setup, where the adversary is given an initial honestly-generated SRS and is then allowed to perform a malicious update in one-shot fashion. Groth et al. show in [38] that the two definitions are equivalent for polynomial commitment based SNARKs. We use this simpler definition in our reductions.

In the full version [29], we show a reduction from (q_1, q_2)-dlog assumption to its variant in the updatable setting (with single adversarial update).

Generalized Forking Lemma. Although dubbed "general", the forking lemma of [5] is not general enough for our purpose as it is useful only for protocols where a witness can be extracted from just two transcripts. To be able to extract a witness from, say, an execution of $\mathbf{P}$ we need at least $(3\mathsf{n}+6)$ valid proofs (where n is the number of constrains), $(\mathsf{n}+1)$ for $\mathbf{S}$, and $2\mathsf{n}+3$ for $\mathbf{M}$. Here we use a result by Attema et al. [3][6] which lower-bounds the probability of generating a tree of accepting transcripts T. We restate their Proposition 2 in our notation:

Lemma 2 (Run Time and Success Probability). *Let $N = n_1 \cdot \cdots \cdot n_\mu$ and $p = 2^{\Omega(\lambda)}$. Let $\varepsilon_{\mathsf{err}}(\lambda) = 1 - \prod_{i=1}^{\mu}\left(1 - \frac{n_i - 1}{p}\right)$. Assume adversary $\mathcal{A}$ that makes up to q random oracle queries and outputs an accepting proof with probability at least acc. There exists a tree building algorithm $\mathcal{T}$ for $(n_1, \ldots, n_\mu)$-trees that succeeds*

[6] An earlier versions had its own forking lemma generalization. Attema et al. has a better bound.

in building a tree of accepting transcripts in expected running time $N + q(N-1)$ *with probability at least*

$$\frac{\mathsf{acc} - (q+1)\varepsilon_{\mathsf{err}}(\lambda)}{1 - \varepsilon_{\mathsf{err}}(\lambda)}.$$

Opening Uniqueness of Batched Polynomial Commitment Openings. To show the unique response property required by our main theorem we show that the polynomial commitment schemes employed by concrete proof systems have unique openings, which, intuitively, assures that there is only one valid opening for a given committed polynomial and evaluation point:

Definition 8 (Unique opening property). *Let* $m \in \mathbb{N}$ *be the number of committed polynomials,* $l \in \mathbb{N}$ *number of evaluation points,* $\boldsymbol{c} \in \mathbb{G}^m$ *be the commitments,* $\boldsymbol{z} \in \mathbb{F}_p^l$ *be the arguments the polynomials are evaluated at,* K_j *set of indices of polynomials which are evaluated at* z_j*,* $\boldsymbol{s}_i$ *vector of evaluations of* f_i*, and* $\boldsymbol{o}_j, \boldsymbol{o}'_j \in \mathbb{F}_p^{K_j}$ *be the commitment openings. Then for every* PPT *adversary* $\mathcal{A}$

$$\Pr\left[\begin{array}{c|c} \mathsf{Verify}(\mathsf{srs}, \boldsymbol{c}, \boldsymbol{z}, \boldsymbol{s}, \boldsymbol{o}) = 1, & \\ \mathsf{Verify}(\mathsf{srs}, \boldsymbol{c}, \boldsymbol{z}, \boldsymbol{s}, \boldsymbol{o}') = 1, & (\boldsymbol{c}, \boldsymbol{z}, \boldsymbol{s}, \boldsymbol{o}, \boldsymbol{o}') \leftarrow \mathcal{A}^{\mathsf{UpdO}}(\mathsf{max}) \\ \boldsymbol{o} \neq \boldsymbol{o}' & \end{array}\right] \leq \mathsf{negl}(\lambda).$$

We show that the polynomial commitment schemes of Plonk, Sonic, and Marlin satisfy this requirement in the full version [29].

Remark 5. In the full version [29], we presents efficient variants of KZG [40] polynomial commitment schemes used in Plonk, Sonic and Marlin that support batched verification. Algorithms Com, Op, Verify take vectors as input and receive an additional arbitrary auxiliary string. This adversarially chosen string only provides additional context for the computation of challenges and allows reconstruction of proof transcripts $\tilde{\pi}[0..i]$ for batch challenge computations. We treat auxiliary input implicitly in the definition above.

5 Non-malleability of Plonk

In this section, we show that $\mathbf{P}_{\mathsf{FS}}$ is simulation-extractable. To this end, we first use the unique opening property to show that $\mathbf{P}_{\mathsf{FS}}$ has the 3-UR property, cf. Lemma 3. Next, we show that $\mathbf{P}_{\mathsf{FS}}$ is rewinding-based knowledge sound. That is, given a number of accepting transcripts whose first 3 messages match, we can either extract a witness for the proven statement or use one of the transcripts to break the udlog assumption. This result is shown in the AGM, cf. Lemma 4. We then show that $\mathbf{P}_{\mathsf{FS}}$ is 3-programmable trapdoor-less ZK in the AGM, cf. Lemma 5.

Given rewinding-based knowledge soundness, 3-UR and trapdoor-less zero-knowledge of $\mathbf{P}_{\mathsf{FS}}$, we invoke Theorem 1 and conclude that $\mathbf{P}_{\mathsf{FS}}$ is simulation-extractable.

5.1 Plonk Protocol Description

The Constraint System. Assume C is a fan-in two arithmetic circuit, whose fan-out is unlimited and has n gates and m wires ($\mathsf{n} \le \mathsf{m} \le 2\mathsf{n}$). The constraint system of Plonk is defined as follows:

- Let $\boldsymbol{V} = (\boldsymbol{a}, \boldsymbol{b}, \boldsymbol{c})$, where $\boldsymbol{a}, \boldsymbol{b}, \boldsymbol{c} \in [1\,..\,\mathsf{m}]^{\mathsf{n}}$. Entries $\boldsymbol{a}_i, \boldsymbol{b}_i, \boldsymbol{c}_i$ represent indices of left, right and output wires of the circuit's i-th gate.
- Vectors $\boldsymbol{Q} = (\boldsymbol{q_L}, \boldsymbol{q_R}, \boldsymbol{q_O}, \boldsymbol{q_M}, \boldsymbol{q_C}) \in (\mathbb{F}^{\mathsf{n}})^5$ are called *selector vectors*: (a) If the i-th gate is a multiplication gate then $\boldsymbol{q_L}_i = \boldsymbol{q_R}_i = 0$, $\boldsymbol{q_M}_i = 1$, and $\boldsymbol{q_O}_i = -1$. (b) If the i-th gate is an addition gate then $\boldsymbol{q_L}_i = \boldsymbol{q_R}_i = 1$, $\boldsymbol{q_M}_i = 0$, and $\boldsymbol{q_O}_i = -1$. (c) $\boldsymbol{q_C}_i = 0$ for multiplication and addition gates.[7]

  We say that vector $\boldsymbol{x} \in \mathbb{F}^{\mathsf{m}}$ satisfies constraint system if for all $i \in [1\,..\,\mathsf{n}]$

$$\boldsymbol{q_L}_i \cdot \boldsymbol{x}_{\boldsymbol{a}_i} + \boldsymbol{q_R}_i \cdot \boldsymbol{x}_{\boldsymbol{b}_i} + \boldsymbol{q_O} \cdot \boldsymbol{x}_{\boldsymbol{c}_i} + \boldsymbol{q_M}_i \cdot (\boldsymbol{x}_{\boldsymbol{a}_i} \boldsymbol{x}_{\boldsymbol{b}_i}) + \boldsymbol{q_C}_i = 0.$$

  Public inputs $(\mathsf{x}_j)_{j=1}^{\ell}$ are enforced by adding the constrains

$$\boldsymbol{a}_i = j, \boldsymbol{q_L}_i = 1, \boldsymbol{q_M}_i = \boldsymbol{q_R}_i = \boldsymbol{q_O}_i = 0, \boldsymbol{q_C}_i = -\mathsf{x}_j\,,$$

for some $i \in [1\,..\,\mathsf{n}]$.

Algorithms Rolled Out. Plonk argument system is universal. That is, it allows to verify computation of any arithmetic circuit which has up to n gates using a single SRS. However, to make computation efficient, for each circuit there is a preprocessing phase which extends the SRS with circuit-related polynomial evaluations.

For the sake of simplicity of the security reductions presented in this paper, we include in the SRS only these elements that cannot be computed without knowing the secret trapdoor χ. The rest of the preprocessed input can be computed using these SRS elements. We thus let them to be computed by the prover, verifier, and simulator separately.

Plonk *SRS generating algorithm* $\mathsf{GenSRS}(\mathbf{R})$*:* The SRS generating algorithm picks at random $\chi \leftarrow\!\$\, \mathbb{F}_p$, computes and outputs $\mathsf{srs} = \left(\left[\{\chi^i\}_{i=0}^{\mathsf{n}+5}\right]_1, [\chi]_2\right)$.

Preprocessing: Let $H = \{\omega^i\}_{i=1}^{\mathsf{n}}$ be a (multiplicative) n-element subgroup of a field $\mathbb{F}$ compound of n-th roots of unity in $\mathbb{F}$. Let $\mathsf{L}_i(X)$ be the i-th element of an n-elements Lagrange basis. During the preprocessing phase polynomials $\mathsf{S}_{\mathsf{id}\mathsf{j}}, \mathsf{S}_{\sigma\mathsf{j}}$, for $\mathsf{j} \in [1\,..\,3]$, are computed:

$$\begin{aligned} \mathsf{S}_{\mathsf{id}1}(X) &= X, & \mathsf{S}_{\sigma 1}(X) &= \textstyle\sum_{i=1}^{\mathsf{n}} \sigma(i)\mathsf{L}_i(X), \\ \mathsf{S}_{\mathsf{id}2}(X) &= k_1 \cdot X, & \mathsf{S}_{\sigma 2}(X) &= \textstyle\sum_{i=1}^{\mathsf{n}} \sigma(\mathsf{n}+i)\mathsf{L}_i(X), \\ \mathsf{S}_{\mathsf{id}3}(X) &= k_2 \cdot X, & \mathsf{S}_{\sigma 3}(X) &= \textstyle\sum_{i=1}^{\mathsf{n}} \sigma(2\mathsf{n}+i)\mathsf{L}_i(X). \end{aligned}$$

[7] The $\boldsymbol{q_C}_i$ selector vector is meant to encode (input independent) constants.

Coefficients k_1, k_2 are such that $H, k_1 \cdot H, k_2 \cdot H$ are different cosets of $\mathbb{F}^*$, thus they define $3 \cdot \mathsf{n}$ different elements. Gabizon et al. [28] notes that it is enough to set k_1 to a quadratic residue and k_2 to a quadratic non-residue.

Furthermore, we define polynomials $\mathsf{q_L}, \mathsf{q_R}, \mathsf{q_O}, \mathsf{q_M}, \mathsf{q_C}$ such that

$$\mathsf{q_L}(X) = \sum_{i=1}^{\mathsf{n}} q_{L_i} \mathsf{L}_i(X), \qquad \mathsf{q_O}(X) = \sum_{i=1}^{\mathsf{n}} q_{O_i} \mathsf{L}_i(X),$$
$$\mathsf{q_R}(X) = \sum_{i=1}^{\mathsf{n}} q_{R_i} \mathsf{L}_i(X), \qquad \mathsf{q_C}(X) = \sum_{i=1}^{\mathsf{n}} q_{C_i} \mathsf{L}_i(X).$$
$$\mathsf{q_M}(X) = \sum_{i=1}^{\mathsf{n}} q_{M_i} \mathsf{L}_i(X),$$

Proving Statements in $\mathbf{P}_{\mathsf{FS}}$. We show how prover's algorithm $\mathsf{P}(\mathsf{srs}, \mathsf{x} = (\mathsf{w}'_i)_{i=1}^{\ell}, \mathsf{w} = (\mathsf{w}_i)_{i=1}^{3\cdot\mathsf{n}})$ operates for the Fiat–Shamir transformed version of Plonk. Note that for notational convenience w also contains the public input wires $\mathsf{w}'_i = \mathsf{w}_i$, $i \in [1 \mathinner{..} \ell]$.

Message 1. Sample $b_1, \ldots, b_9 \leftarrow\$ \mathbb{F}_p$; compute $\mathsf{a}(X), \mathsf{b}(X), \mathsf{c}(X)$ as

$$\mathsf{a}(X) = (b_1 X + b_2)\mathsf{Z_H}(X) + \sum_{i=1}^{\mathsf{n}} \mathsf{w}_i \mathsf{L}_i(X)$$
$$\mathsf{b}(X) = (b_3 X + b_4)\mathsf{Z_H}(X) + \sum_{i=1}^{\mathsf{n}} \mathsf{w}_{\mathsf{n}+i} \mathsf{L}_i(X)$$
$$\mathsf{c}(X) = (b_5 X + b_6)\mathsf{Z_H}(X) + \sum_{i=1}^{\mathsf{n}} \mathsf{w}_{2\cdot\mathsf{n}+i} \mathsf{L}_i(X)$$

Output polynomial commitments $[\mathsf{a}(\chi), \mathsf{b}(\chi), \mathsf{c}(\chi)]_1$.

Message 2. Compute challenges $\beta, \gamma \in \mathbb{F}_p$ by querying random oracle on partial proof, that is, $\beta = \mathcal{H}(\tilde{\pi}[0..1], 0)$, $\gamma = \mathcal{H}(\tilde{\pi}[0..1], 1)$.
Compute permutation polynomial $\mathsf{z}(X)$

$$\mathsf{z}(X) = (b_7 X^2 + b_8 X + b_9)\mathsf{Z_H}(X) + \mathsf{L}_1(X) +$$
$$+ \sum_{i=1}^{\mathsf{n}-1} \left(\mathsf{L}_{i+1}(X) \prod_{j=1}^{i} \frac{(\mathsf{w}_j + \beta\omega^{j-1} + \gamma)(\mathsf{w}_{\mathsf{n}+j} + \beta k_1 \omega^{j-1} + \gamma)(\mathsf{w}_{2\mathsf{n}+j} + \beta k_2 \omega^{j-1} + \gamma)}{(\mathsf{w}_j + \sigma(j)\beta + \gamma)(\mathsf{w}_{\mathsf{n}+j} + \sigma(\mathsf{n}+j)\beta + \gamma)(\mathsf{w}_{2\mathsf{n}+j} + \sigma(2\mathsf{n}+j)\beta + \gamma)} \right)$$

Output polynomial commitment $[\mathsf{z}(\chi)]_1$

Message 3. Compute the challenge $\alpha = \mathcal{H}(\tilde{\pi}[0..2])$, compute the quotient polynomial

$$\begin{aligned}
&\mathsf{t}(X) = \\
&(\mathsf{a}(X)\mathsf{b}(X)\mathsf{q_M}(X) + \mathsf{a}(X)\mathsf{q_L}(X) + \mathsf{b}(X)\mathsf{q_R}(X) + \mathsf{c}(X)\mathsf{q_O}(X) + \mathsf{PI}(X) + \mathsf{q_C}(X))/\mathsf{Z_H}(X) + \\
&+ ((\mathsf{a}(X) + \beta X + \gamma)(\mathsf{b}(X) + \beta k_1 X + \gamma)(\mathsf{c}(X) + \beta k_2 X + \gamma)\mathsf{z}(X))\alpha/\mathsf{Z_H}(X) \\
&- (\mathsf{a}(X) + \beta \mathsf{S}_{\sigma 1}(X) + \gamma)(\mathsf{b}(X) + \beta \mathsf{S}_{\sigma 2}(X) + \gamma)(\mathsf{c}(X) + \beta \mathsf{S}_{\sigma 3}(X) + \gamma)\mathsf{z}(X\omega))\alpha/\mathsf{Z_H}(X) \\
&+ (\mathsf{z}(X) - 1)\mathsf{L}_1(X)\alpha^2/\mathsf{Z_H}(X)
\end{aligned}$$

Split $\mathsf{t}(X)$ into degree less then n polynomials $\mathsf{t_{lo}}(X), \mathsf{t_{mid}}(X), \mathsf{t_{hi}}(X)$, such that $\mathsf{t}(X) = \mathsf{t_{lo}}(X) + X^{\mathsf{n}}\mathsf{t_{mid}}(X) + X^{2\mathsf{n}}\mathsf{t_{hi}}(X)$. Output $[\mathsf{t_{lo}}(\chi), \mathsf{t_{mid}}(\chi), \mathsf{t_{hi}}(\chi)]_1$.

Message 4. Get the challenge $\mathfrak{z} \in \mathbb{F}_p$, $\mathfrak{z} = \mathcal{H}(\tilde{\pi}[0..3])$. Compute opening evaluations $\mathsf{a}(\mathfrak{z}), \mathsf{b}(\mathfrak{z}), \mathsf{c}(\mathfrak{z}), \mathsf{S}_{\sigma 1}(\mathfrak{z}), \mathsf{S}_{\sigma 2}(\mathfrak{z}), \mathsf{t}(\mathfrak{z}), \mathsf{z}(\mathfrak{z}\omega)$, Compute the linearization polynomial

$$\mathsf{r}(X) = \begin{array}{l}
\mathsf{a}(\mathfrak{z})\mathsf{b}(\mathfrak{z})\mathsf{q_M}(X) + \mathsf{a}(\mathfrak{z})\mathsf{q_L}(X) + \mathsf{b}(\mathfrak{z})\mathsf{q_R}(X) + \mathsf{c}(\mathfrak{z})\mathsf{q_O}(X) + \mathsf{q_C}(X) \\
+ \alpha \cdot ((\mathsf{a}(\mathfrak{z}) + \beta\mathfrak{z} + \gamma)(\mathsf{b}(\mathfrak{z}) + \beta k_1 \mathfrak{z} + \gamma)(\mathsf{c}(\mathfrak{z}) + \beta k_2 \mathfrak{z} + \gamma) \cdot \mathsf{z}(X)) \\
- \alpha \cdot ((\mathsf{a}(\mathfrak{z}) + \beta \mathsf{S}_{\sigma 1}(\mathfrak{z}) + \gamma)(\mathsf{b}(\mathfrak{z}) + \beta \mathsf{S}_{\sigma 2}(\mathfrak{z}) + \gamma)\beta \mathsf{z}(\mathfrak{z}\omega) \cdot \mathsf{S}_{\sigma 3}(X)) \\
+ \alpha^2 \cdot \mathsf{L}_1(\mathfrak{z}) \cdot \mathsf{z}(X)
\end{array}$$

Output $\mathsf{a}(\mathfrak{z}), \mathsf{b}(\mathfrak{z}), \mathsf{c}(\mathfrak{z}), \mathsf{S}_{\sigma 1}(\mathfrak{z}), \mathsf{S}_{\sigma 2}(\mathfrak{z}), \mathsf{t}(\mathfrak{z}), \mathsf{z}(\mathfrak{z}\omega), \mathsf{r}(\mathfrak{z})$.

Message 5. Compute the opening challenge $v \in \mathbb{F}_p$, $v = \mathcal{H}(\tilde{\pi}[0..4])$. Compute the openings for the polynomial commitment scheme

$$\mathsf{W}_{\mathfrak{z}}(X) = \frac{1}{X - \mathfrak{z}} \begin{pmatrix} \mathsf{t}_{\mathsf{lo}}(X) + \mathfrak{z}^{\mathsf{n}} \mathsf{t}_{\mathsf{mid}}(X) + \mathfrak{z}^{2\mathsf{n}} \mathsf{t}_{\mathsf{hi}}(X) - \mathsf{t}(\mathfrak{z}) + v(\mathsf{r}(X) - \mathsf{r}(\mathfrak{z})) + v^2(\mathsf{a}(X) - \mathsf{a}(\mathfrak{z})) \\ + v^3(\mathsf{b}(X) - \mathsf{b}(\mathfrak{z})) + v^4(\mathsf{c}(X) - \mathsf{c}(\mathfrak{z})) + v^5(\mathsf{S}_{\sigma 1}(X) - \mathsf{S}_{\sigma 1}(\mathfrak{z})) \\ + v^6(\mathsf{S}_{\sigma 2}(X) - \mathsf{S}_{\sigma 2}(\mathfrak{z})) \end{pmatrix}$$

$$\mathsf{W}_{\mathfrak{z}\omega}(X) = (\mathsf{z}(X) - \mathsf{z}(\mathfrak{z}\omega))/(X - \mathfrak{z}\omega)$$

Output $[\mathsf{W}_{\mathfrak{z}}(\chi), \mathsf{W}_{\mathfrak{z}\omega}(\chi)]_1$.

Plonk verifier $\mathsf{V}(\mathsf{srs}, \mathsf{x}, \pi)$**:** The Plonk verifier works as follows

1. Validate all obtained group elements.
2. Validate all obtained field elements.
3. Parse the instance as $\{\mathsf{w}_i\}_{i=1}^{\ell} \leftarrow \mathsf{x}$.
4. Compute challenges $\beta, \gamma, \alpha, \mathfrak{z}, v, u$ from the transcript.
5. Compute zero polynomial evaluation $\mathsf{Z}_\mathsf{H}(\mathfrak{z}) = \mathfrak{z}^{\mathsf{n}} - 1$.
6. Compute Lagrange polynomial evaluation $\mathsf{L}_1(\mathfrak{z}) = \frac{\mathfrak{z}^{\mathsf{n}} - 1}{\mathsf{n}(\mathfrak{z} - 1)}$.
7. Compute public input polynomial evaluation $\mathsf{PI}(\mathfrak{z}) = \sum_{i \in [1\,..\,\ell]} \mathsf{w}_i \mathsf{L}_i(\mathfrak{z})$.
8. Compute quotient polynomials evaluations

$$\mathsf{t}(\mathfrak{z}) = \Big(\mathsf{r}(\mathfrak{z}) + \mathsf{PI}(\mathfrak{z}) - (\mathsf{a}(\mathfrak{z}) + \beta \mathsf{S}_{\sigma 1}(\mathfrak{z}) + \gamma)(\mathsf{b}(\mathfrak{z}) + \beta \mathsf{S}_{\sigma 2}(\mathfrak{z}) + \gamma)(\mathsf{c}(\mathfrak{z}) + \gamma)\mathsf{z}(\mathfrak{z}\omega)\alpha - \mathsf{L}_1(\mathfrak{z})\alpha^2\Big)/\mathsf{Z}_\mathsf{H}(\mathfrak{z}).$$

9. Compute batched polynomial commitment $[D]_1 = v\,[r]_1 + u\,[z]_1$ that is

$$[D]_1 = v \begin{pmatrix} \mathsf{a}(\mathfrak{z})\mathsf{b}(\mathfrak{z}) \cdot [\mathsf{q_M}]_1 + \mathsf{a}(\mathfrak{z})\,[\mathsf{q_L}]_1 + \mathsf{b}\,[\mathsf{q_R}]_1 + \mathsf{c}\,[\mathsf{q_O}]_1 + \\ + ((\mathsf{a}(\mathfrak{z}) + \beta\mathfrak{z} + \gamma)(\mathsf{b}(\mathfrak{z}) + \beta k_1 \mathfrak{z} + \gamma)(\mathsf{c} + \beta k_2 \mathfrak{z} + \gamma)\alpha + \mathsf{L}_1(\mathfrak{z})\alpha^2) + \\ - (\mathsf{a}(\mathfrak{z}) + \beta \mathsf{S}_{\sigma 1}(\mathfrak{z}) + \gamma)(\mathsf{b}(\mathfrak{z}) + \beta \mathsf{S}_{\sigma 2}(\mathfrak{z}) + \gamma)\alpha\beta \mathsf{z}(\mathfrak{z}\omega)\,[\mathsf{S}_{\sigma 3}(\chi)]_1) \end{pmatrix} + \\ + u\,[\mathsf{z}(\chi)]_1\,.$$

10. Computes full batched polynomial commitment $[F]_1$:

$$[F]_1 = ([\mathsf{t}_{\mathsf{lo}}(\chi)]_1 + \mathfrak{z}^{\mathsf{n}}\,[\mathsf{t}_{\mathsf{mid}}(\chi)]_1 + \mathfrak{z}^{2\mathsf{n}}\,[\mathsf{t}_{\mathsf{hi}}(\chi)]_1) + u\,[\mathsf{z}(\chi)]_1 + \\ + v \begin{pmatrix} \mathsf{a}(\mathfrak{z})\mathsf{b}(\mathfrak{z}) \cdot [\mathsf{q_M}]_1 + \mathsf{a}(\mathfrak{z})\,[\mathsf{q_L}]_1 + \mathsf{b}(\mathfrak{z})\,[\mathsf{q_R}]_1 + \mathsf{c}(\mathfrak{z})\,[\mathsf{q_O}]_1 + \\ + ((\mathsf{a}(\mathfrak{z}) + \beta\mathfrak{z} + \gamma)(\mathsf{b}(\mathfrak{z}) + \beta k_1 \mathfrak{z} + \gamma)(\mathsf{c}(\mathfrak{z}) + \beta k_2 \mathfrak{z} + \gamma)\alpha + \mathsf{L}_1(\mathfrak{z})\alpha^2) + \\ - (\mathsf{a}(\mathfrak{z}) + \beta \mathsf{S}_{\sigma 1}(\mathfrak{z}) + \gamma)(\mathsf{b}(\mathfrak{z}) + \beta \mathsf{S}_{\sigma 2}(\mathfrak{z}) + \gamma)\alpha\beta \mathsf{z}(\mathfrak{z}\omega)\,[\mathsf{S}_{\sigma 3}(\chi)]_1) \end{pmatrix} \\ + v^2\,[\mathsf{a}(\chi)]_1 + v^3\,[\mathsf{b}(\chi)]_1 + v^4\,[\mathsf{c}(\chi)]_1 + v^5\,[\mathsf{S}_{\sigma 1}(\chi)]_1 + v^6\,[\mathsf{S}_{\sigma 2}(\chi)]_1\,.$$

11. Compute group-encoded batch evaluation $[E]_1$

$$[E]_1 = \frac{1}{\mathsf{Z}_\mathsf{H}(\mathfrak{z})} \begin{bmatrix} \mathsf{r}(\mathfrak{z}) + \mathsf{PI}(\mathfrak{z}) + \alpha^2 \mathsf{L}_1(\mathfrak{z}) + \\ - \alpha\,((\mathsf{a}(\mathfrak{z}) + \beta \mathsf{S}_{\sigma 1}(\mathfrak{z}) + \gamma)(\mathsf{b}(\mathfrak{z}) + \beta \mathsf{S}_{\sigma 2}(\mathfrak{z}) + \gamma)(\mathsf{c}(\mathfrak{z}) + \gamma)\mathsf{z}(\mathfrak{z}\omega)) \end{bmatrix}_1 \\ + \left[v\mathsf{r}(\mathfrak{z}) + v^2\mathsf{a}(\mathfrak{z}) + v^3\mathsf{b}(\mathfrak{z}) + v^4\mathsf{c}(\mathfrak{z}) + v^5\mathsf{S}_{\sigma 1}(\mathfrak{z}) + v^6\mathsf{S}_{\sigma 2}(\mathfrak{z}) + u\mathsf{z}(\mathfrak{z}\omega)\right]_1.$$

12. Check whether the verification equation holds

$$\left([\mathsf{W}_{\mathfrak{z}}(\chi)]_1 + u \cdot [\mathsf{W}_{\mathfrak{z}\omega}(\chi)]_1\right) \bullet [\chi]_2 - \\ \left(\mathfrak{z} \cdot [\mathsf{W}_{\mathfrak{z}}(\chi)]_1 + u\mathfrak{z}\omega \cdot [\mathsf{W}_{\mathfrak{z}\omega}(\chi)]_1 + [F]_1 - [E]_1\right) \bullet [1]_2 = 0\,. \quad (1)$$

The verification equation is a batched version of the verification equation from [40] which allows the verifier to check openings of multiple polynomials in two points (instead of checking an opening of a single polynomial at one point).

Plonk simulator $\mathsf{Sim}_\chi(\mathsf{srs}, \mathsf{td} = \chi, \mathsf{x})$**:** We describe the simulator in Lemma 5.

5.2 Simulation Extractability of Plonk

Due to lack of space, we provide here only theorem statements and intuition for why they hold. Full proofs are given in the full version [29].

Unique Response Property

Lemma 3. *Let* $\mathsf{PC_P}$ *be a polynomial commitment that is* $\varepsilon_{\mathsf{bind}}(\lambda)$*-binding and has unique opening property with loss* $\varepsilon_{\mathsf{op}}(\lambda)$*. Then* $\mathsf{P_{FS}}$ *is* 3-UR *against algebraic adversaries, who makes up to* q *random oracle queries, with security loss* $\varepsilon_{\mathsf{bind}}(\lambda) + \varepsilon_{\mathsf{op}}(\lambda)$.

Proof (Intuition). We show that an adversary who can break the 3-unique response property of $\mathsf{P_{FS}}$ can be either used to break the commitment scheme's evaluation binding or unique opening property. The former happens with the probability upper-bounded by $\varepsilon_{\mathsf{bind}}(\lambda)$, the latter with the probability upper bounded by $\varepsilon_{\mathsf{op}}(\lambda)$.

Rewinding-Based Knowledge Soundness

Lemma 4. $\mathsf{P_{FS}}$ *is* $(3, 3\mathsf{n}+6)$*-rewinding-based knowledge sound against algebraic adversaries who make up to* q *random oracle queries with security loss*

$$\varepsilon_{\mathsf{ks}}(\lambda, \mathsf{acc}, q) \le \left(1 - \frac{\mathsf{acc} - (q+1)\left(\frac{3\mathsf{n}+5}{p}\right)}{1 - \frac{3\mathsf{n}+5}{p}}\right) + (3\mathsf{n}+6) \cdot \varepsilon_{\mathsf{udlog}}(\lambda)\,,$$

Here acc *is a probability that the adversary outputs an accepting proof, and* $\varepsilon_{\mathsf{udlog}}(\lambda)$ *is security of* $(\mathsf{n}+5, 1)$-udlog *assumption.*

Proof (Intuition). We use Attema et al. [3, Proposition 2] to bound the probability that an algorithm $\mathcal{T}$ does not obtain a tree of accepting transcripts in an expected number of runs. This happens with probability at most

$$1 - \frac{\mathsf{acc} - (q+1)\left(\frac{3\mathsf{n}+5}{p}\right)}{1 - \frac{3\mathsf{n}+5}{p}}$$

Then we analyze the case that one of the proofs in the tree T outputted by $\mathcal{T}$ is not accepting by the ideal verifier. This discrepancy can be used to break an instance of an updatable dlog assumption which happens with probability at most $(3\mathsf{n}+6)\cdot\varepsilon_{\mathsf{udlog}}(\lambda)$.

Trapdoor-Less Zero-Knowledge of Plonk

Lemma 5. P_{FS} *is 3-programmable trapdoor-less zero-knowledge.*

Proof (Intuition). The simulator, that does not know the SRS trapdoor can make a simulated proof by programming the random oracle. It proceeds as follows. It picks a random witness and behaves as an honest prover up to the point when a commitment to the polynomial $\mathsf{t}(X)$ is sent. Since the simulator picked a random witness and $\mathsf{t}(X)$ is a polynomial only (modulo some negligible function) when the witness is correct, it cannot compute commitment to $\mathsf{t}(X)$ as it is a rational function. However, the simulator can pick a random challenge $\mathfrak{z}$ and a polynomial $\tilde{\mathsf{t}}(X)$ such that $\mathsf{t}(\mathfrak{z})=\tilde{\mathsf{t}}(\mathfrak{z})$. Then the simulator continues behaving as an honest prover. We argue that such a simulated proof is indistinguishable from a real one.

Simulation Extractability of P_{FS}

Since Lemmas 3 to 5 hold, P is 3-UR, rewinding-based knowledge sound and trapdoor-less zero-knowledge. We now make use of Theorem 1 and show that P_{FS} is simulation-extractable as defined in Definition 2.

Corollary 1 (Simulation extractability of P_{FS}). P_{FS} *is* updatable simulation-extractable *against any* PPT *adversary* $\mathcal{A}$ *who makes up to* q *random oracle queries and returns an accepting proof with probability at least* acc *with extraction failure probability*

$$\varepsilon_{\mathsf{se}}(\lambda,\mathsf{acc},q)\le\left(1-\frac{\mathsf{acc}-\varepsilon_{\mathsf{ur}}(\lambda)-(q+1)\varepsilon_{\mathsf{err}}(\lambda)}{1-\varepsilon_{\mathsf{err}}(\lambda)}\right)+(3\mathsf{n}+6)\cdot\varepsilon_{\mathsf{udlog}}(\lambda),$$

where $\varepsilon_{\mathsf{err}}(\lambda)=\frac{3\mathsf{n}+5}{p}$, $\varepsilon_{\mathsf{ur}}(\lambda)\le\varepsilon_{\mathsf{bind}}(\lambda)+\varepsilon_{\mathsf{op}}(\lambda)$, *$p$ is the size of the field, and* n *is the number of constrains in the circuit.*

References

1. Abdolmaleki, B., Ramacher, S., Slamanig, D.: Lift-and-shift: obtaining simulation extractable subversion and updatable SNARKs generically. In: Ligatti, J., Ou, X., Katz, J., Vigna, G. (eds.) ACM CCS 20, pp. 1987–2005. ACM Press (2020). https://doi.org/10.1145/3372297.3417228
2. Atapoor, S., Baghery, K.: Simulation extractability in groth's zk-SNARK. Cryptology ePrint Archive, Report 2019/641 (2019). https://eprint.iacr.org/2019/641
3. Attema, T., Fehr, S., Klooß, M.: Fiat-shamir transformation of multi-round interactive proofs. Cryptology ePrint Archive, Report 2021/1377 (2021). https://ia.cr/2021/1377

4. Baghery, K., Kohlweiss, M., Siim, J., Volkhov, M.: Another look at extraction and randomization of groth's zk-SNARK. Cryptology ePrint Archive, Report 2020/811 (2020). https://eprint.iacr.org/2020/811
5. Bellare, M., Neven, G.: Multi-signatures in the plain public-key model and a general forking lemma. In: Juels, A., Wright, R.N., De Capitani di Vimercati, S. (eds.) ACM CCS 2006, pp. 390–399. ACM Press (2006). https://doi.org/10.1145/1180405.1180453
6. Bellare, M., Rogaway, P.: Random oracles are practical: a paradigm for designing efficient protocols. In: Denning, D.E., Pyle, R., Ganesan, R., Sandhu, R.S., Ashby, V. (eds.) ACM CCS 93, pp. 62–73. ACM Press (1993). https://doi.org/10.1145/168588.168596
7. Ben-Or, M., et al.: Everything provable is provable in zero-knowledge. In: Goldwasser, S. (ed.) CRYPTO 1988. LNCS, vol. 403, pp. 37–56. Springer, New York (1990). https://doi.org/10.1007/0-387-34799-2_4
8. Ben-Sasson, E., Bentov, I., Horesh, Y., Riabzev, M.: Scalable, transparent, and post-quantum secure computational integrity. Cryptology ePrint Archive, Report 2018/046 (2018). https://eprint.iacr.org/2018/046
9. Ben-Sasson, E., et al.: Zerocash: decentralized anonymous payments from bitcoin. In: 2014 IEEE Symposium on Security and Privacy, pp. 459–474. IEEE Computer Society Press (2014). https://doi.org/10.1109/SP.2014.36
10. Ben-Sasson, E., Chiesa, A., Genkin, D., Tromer, E., Virza, M.: SNARKs for C: verifying program executions succinctly and in zero knowledge. In: Canetti, R., Garay, J.A. (eds.) CRYPTO 2013. LNCS, vol. 8043, pp. 90–108. Springer, Heidelberg (2013). https://doi.org/10.1007/978-3-642-40084-1_6
11. Ben-Sasson, E., Chiesa, A., Spooner, N.: Interactive oracle proofs. In: Hirt, M., Smith, A. (eds.) TCC 2016. LNCS, vol. 9986, pp. 31–60. Springer, Heidelberg (2016). https://doi.org/10.1007/978-3-662-53644-5_2
12. Ben-Sasson, E., Chiesa, A., Tromer, E., Virza, M.: Succinct non-interactive zero knowledge for a von neumann architecture. In: Fu, K., Jung, J. (eds.) USENIX Security 2014. pp. 781–796. USENIX Association (2014)
13. Bitansky, N., Chiesa, A., Ishai, Y., Paneth, O., Ostrovsky, R.: Succinct non-interactive arguments via linear interactive proofs. In: Sahai, A. (ed.) TCC 2013. LNCS, vol. 7785, pp. 315–333. Springer, Heidelberg (2013). https://doi.org/10.1007/978-3-642-36594-2_18
14. Bootle, J., Cerulli, A., Chaidos, P., Groth, J., Petit, C.: Efficient zero-knowledge arguments for arithmetic circuits in the discrete log setting. In: Fischlin, M., Coron, J.-S. (eds.) EUROCRYPT 2016. LNCS, vol. 9666, pp. 327–357. Springer, Heidelberg (2016). https://doi.org/10.1007/978-3-662-49896-5_12
15. Bowe, S., Gabizon, A.: Making groth's zk-SNARK simulation extractable in the random oracle model. Cryptology ePrint Archive, Report 2018/187 (2018). https://eprint.iacr.org/2018/187
16. Brassard, G., Chaum, D., Crépeau, C.: Minimum disclosure proofs of knowledge. J. Comput. Syst. Sci. **37**(2), 156–189 (1988)
17. Bünz, B., Bootle, J., Boneh, D., Poelstra, A., Wuille, P., Maxwell, G.: Bulletproofs: short proofs for confidential transactions and more. In: 2018 IEEE Symposium on Security and Privacy, pp. 315–334. IEEE Computer Society Press (2018). https://doi.org/10.1109/SP.2018.00020
18. Camenisch, J., Stadler, M.: Efficient group signature schemes for large groups. In: Kaliski, B.S. (ed.) CRYPTO 1997. LNCS, vol. 1294, pp. 410–424. Springer, Heidelberg (1997). https://doi.org/10.1007/BFb0052252

19. Canetti, R.: Universally composable security: a new paradigm for cryptographic protocols. Cryptology ePrint Archive, Report 2000/067 (2000). http://eprint.iacr.org/2000/067
20. Chase, M., Lysyanskaya, A.: On signatures of knowledge. In: Dwork, C. (ed.) CRYPTO 2006. LNCS, vol. 4117, pp. 78–96. Springer, Heidelberg (2006). https://doi.org/10.1007/11818175_5
21. Chiesa, A., Hu, Y., Maller, M., Mishra, P., Vesely, N., Ward, N.: Marlin: preprocessing zkSNARKs with universal and updatable SRS. In: Canteaut, A., Ishai, Y. (eds.) EUROCRYPT 2020. LNCS, vol. 12105, pp. 738–768. Springer, Cham (2020). https://doi.org/10.1007/978-3-030-45721-1_26
22. Danezis, G., Fournet, C., Groth, J., Kohlweiss, M.: Square span programs with applications to succinct NIZK arguments. In: Sarkar, P., Iwata, T. (eds.) ASIACRYPT 2014. LNCS, vol. 8873, pp. 532–550. Springer, Heidelberg (2014). https://doi.org/10.1007/978-3-662-45611-8_28
23. Dodis, Y., Haralambiev, K., López-Alt, A., Wichs, D.: Efficient public-key cryptography in the presence of key leakage. In: Abe, M. (ed.) ASIACRYPT 2010. LNCS, vol. 6477, pp. 613–631. Springer, Heidelberg (2010). https://doi.org/10.1007/978-3-642-17373-8_35
24. Faust, S., Kohlweiss, M., Marson, G.A., Venturi, D.: On the non-malleability of the fiat-shamir transform. In: Galbraith, S., Nandi, M. (eds.) INDOCRYPT 2012. LNCS, vol. 7668, pp. 60–79. Springer, Heidelberg (2012). https://doi.org/10.1007/978-3-642-34931-7_5
25. Fischlin, M.: Communication-efficient non-interactive proofs of knowledge with online extractors. In: Shoup, V. (ed.) CRYPTO 2005. LNCS, vol. 3621, pp. 152–168. Springer, Heidelberg (2005). https://doi.org/10.1007/11535218_10
26. Fortnow, L.: The complexity of perfect zero-knowledge (extended abstract). In: Aho, A. (ed.) 19th ACM STOC, pp. 204–209. ACM Press (1987). https://doi.org/10.1145/28395.28418
27. Fuchsbauer, G., Kiltz, E., Loss, J.: The algebraic group model and its applications. In: Shacham, H., Boldyreva, A. (eds.) CRYPTO 2018. LNCS, vol. 10992, pp. 33–62. Springer, Cham (2018). https://doi.org/10.1007/978-3-319-96881-0_2
28. Gabizon, A., Williamson, Z.J., Ciobotaru, O.: PLONK: permutations over lagrange-bases for oecumenical noninteractive arguments of knowledge. Cryptology ePrint Archive, Report 2019/953 (2019). https://eprint.iacr.org/2019/953
29. Ganesh, C., Khoshakhlagh, H., Kohlweiss, M., Nitulescu, A., Zajac, M.: What makes fiat-shamir zksnarks (updatable srs) simulation extractable? Cryptology ePrint Archive, Report 2021/511 (2021). https://ia.cr/2021/511
30. Ganesh, C., Orlandi, C., Pancholi, M., Takahashi, A., Tschudi, D.: Fiat-shamir bulletproofs are non-malleable (in the algebraic group model). Cryptology ePrint Archive, Report 2021/1393 (2021). https://ia.cr/2021/1393
31. Gennaro, R., Gentry, C., Parno, B., Raykova, M.: Quadratic span programs and succinct NIZKs without PCPs. In: Johansson, T., Nguyen, P.Q. (eds.) EUROCRYPT 2013. LNCS, vol. 7881, pp. 626–645. Springer, Heidelberg (2013). https://doi.org/10.1007/978-3-642-38348-9_37
32. Gilad, Y., Hemo, R., Micali, S., Vlachos, G., Zeldovich, N.: Algorand: Scaling byzantine agreements for cryptocurrencies. Cryptology ePrint Archive, Report 2017/454 (2017). http://eprint.iacr.org/2017/454
33. Goldreich, O., Micali, S., Wigderson, A.: Proofs that yield nothing but their validity and a methodology of cryptographic protocol design (extended abstract). In: 27th FOCS, pp. 174–187. IEEE Computer Society Press (1986). https://doi.org/10.1109/SFCS.1986.47

34. Goldwasser, S., Kalai, Y.T.: On the (in) security of the Fiat-Shamir paradigm. In: 44th FOCS, pp. 102–115. IEEE Computer Society Press (2003). https://doi.org/10.1109/SFCS.2003.1238185
35. Groth, J.: Fully anonymous group signatures without random oracles. In: Kurosawa, K. (ed.) ASIACRYPT 2007. LNCS, vol. 4833, pp. 164–180. Springer, Heidelberg (2007). https://doi.org/10.1007/978-3-540-76900-2_10
36. Groth, J.: Short pairing-based non-interactive zero-knowledge arguments. In: Abe, M. (ed.) ASIACRYPT 2010. LNCS, vol. 6477, pp. 321–340. Springer, Heidelberg (2010). https://doi.org/10.1007/978-3-642-17373-8_19
37. Groth, J.: On the size of pairing-based non-interactive arguments. In: Fischlin, M., Coron, J.-S. (eds.) EUROCRYPT 2016. LNCS, vol. 9666, pp. 305–326. Springer, Heidelberg (2016). https://doi.org/10.1007/978-3-662-49896-5_11
38. Groth, J., Kohlweiss, M., Maller, M., Meiklejohn, S., Miers, I.: Updatable and universal common reference strings with applications to zk-SNARKs. In: Shacham, H., Boldyreva, A. (eds.) CRYPTO 2018. LNCS, vol. 10993, pp. 698–728. Springer, Cham (2018). https://doi.org/10.1007/978-3-319-96878-0_24
39. Groth, J., Maller, M.: Snarky signatures: minimal signatures of knowledge from simulation-extractable SNARKs. In: Katz, J., Shacham, H. (eds.) CRYPTO 2017. LNCS, vol. 10402, pp. 581–612. Springer, Cham (2017). https://doi.org/10.1007/978-3-319-63715-0_20
40. Kate, A., Zaverucha, G.M., Goldberg, I.: Constant-size commitments to polynomials and their applications. In: Abe, M. (ed.) ASIACRYPT 2010. LNCS, vol. 6477, pp. 177–194. Springer, Heidelberg (2010). https://doi.org/10.1007/978-3-642-17373-8_11
41. Kosba, A., et al.: How to use SNARKs in universally composable protocols. Cryptology ePrint Archive, Report 2015/1093 (2015). http://eprint.iacr.org/2015/1093
42. Lipmaa, H.: Progression-free sets and sublinear pairing-based non-interactive zero-knowledge arguments. In: Cramer, R. (ed.) TCC 2012. LNCS, vol. 7194, pp. 169–189. Springer, Heidelberg (2012). https://doi.org/10.1007/978-3-642-28914-9_10
43. Lipmaa, H.: Succinct non-interactive zero knowledge arguments from span programs and linear error-correcting codes. In: Sako, K., Sarkar, P. (eds.) ASIACRYPT 2013. LNCS, vol. 8269, pp. 41–60. Springer, Heidelberg (2013). https://doi.org/10.1007/978-3-642-42033-7_3
44. Lipmaa, H.: Key-and-argument-updatable QA-NIZKs. Cryptology ePrint Archive, Report 2019/333 (2019). https://eprint.iacr.org/2019/333
45. Malkin, T., Peikert, C. (eds.): CRYPTO 2021. LNCS, vol. 12825. Springer, Cham (2021). https://doi.org/10.1007/978-3-030-84242-0
46. Maller, M., Bowe, S., Kohlweiss, M., Meiklejohn, S.: Sonic: Zero-knowledge SNARKs from linear-size universal and updatable structured reference strings. In: Cavallaro, L., Kinder, J., Wang, X., Katz, J. (eds.) ACM CCS 2019, pp. 2111–2128. ACM Press (2019). https://doi.org/10.1145/3319535.3339817
47. Micali, S.: CS proofs (extended abstracts). In: 35th FOCS, pp. 436–453. IEEE Computer Society Press (1994). https://doi.org/10.1109/SFCS.1994.365746
48. Miller, J.: Coordinated disclosure of vulnerabilities affecting girault, bulletproofs, and plonk (2022). https://blog.trailofbits.com/2022/04/13/part-1-coordinated-disclosure-of-vulnerabilities-affecting-girault-bulletproofs-and-plonk/
49. Parno, B., Howell, J., Gentry, C., Raykova, M.: Pinocchio: nearly practical verifiable computation. In: 2013 IEEE Symposium on Security and Privacy, pp. 238–252. IEEE Computer Society Press (2013). https://doi.org/10.1109/SP.2013.47
50. Pointcheval, D., Stern, J.: Security arguments for digital signatures and blind signatures. J. Cryptol. **13**(3), 361–396 (2000). https://doi.org/10.1007/s001450010003

Zero-Knowledge for Homomorphic Key-Value Commitments with Applications to Privacy-Preserving Ledgers

Matteo Campanelli[1], Felix Engelmann[2(✉)], and Claudio Orlandi[3]

[1] Protocol Labs, San Francisco, USA
matteo@protocol.ai
[2] IT University of Copenhagen, Copenhagen, Denmark
fe-research@nlogn.org
[3] Aarhus University, Aarhus, Denmark
orlandi@cs.au.dk

Abstract. Commitments to key-value maps (or, authenticated dictionaries) are an important building block in cryptographic applications, including cryptocurrencies and distributed file systems.

In this work we study short commitments to key-value maps with two additional properties: double-hiding (both keys and values should be hidden) and homomorphism (we should be able to combine two commitments to obtain one that is the "sum" of their key-value openings). Furthermore, we require these commitments to be short and to support efficient transparent zero-knowledge arguments (i.e., without a trusted setup).

As our main contribution, we show how to construct commitments with the properties above as well as efficient zero-knowledge arguments over them. We additionally discuss a range of practical optimizations that can be carried out depending on the application domain. Finally, we formally describe a specific application of commitments to key-value maps to scalable anonymous ledgers. We show how to extend QuisQuis (Fauzi et al. ASIACRYPT 2019). This results in an efficient, confidential multi-type system with a state whose size is independent of the number of transactions.

Keywords: Zero-knowledge · Key-Value map · Commitments

1 Introduction

In this work we propose constructions for efficient commitments to key-value maps (with specific features) and for efficient zero-knowledge arguments that can prove properties on committed key-value maps.

KEY-VALUE MAPS. We can loosely consider a key-value map as the equivalent of a dictionary in some programming languages (e.g., Python): a way to map

C. Galdi and S. Jarecki (Eds.): SCN 2022, LNCS 13409, pp. 761–784, 2022.
https://doi.org/10.1007/978-3-031-14791-3_33

arbitrary keys—e.g., strings—to values—e.g., scalars. For example, the balance of a user in a wallet application could be represented by a key-value map as $\mathsf{kv} = \{(\mathsf{USD}, 100), (\mathsf{BTC}, 10)\}$, where each of the different asset types (the keys) are associated to an amount (the values). In this paper we will generally assume that values are in an algebraic group endowed with an addition operation $+$.

Our Focus: Short, Homomorphic, Doubly-Hiding Commitments. A commitment to a key-value map is roughly similar to an ordinary commitment: it cannot be opened to two different key-value maps (binding) and it should not leak anything about neither the keys nor the values in it. In the case of key-value maps, however, we are interested in some additional functional and efficiency-related requirements:

- *Large key universe:* our commitments should support a large universe of keys, potentially superpolynomial in the security parameter[1]. This implies that the algorithms of the commitment scheme should have a runtime independent of (or logarithmic in) the size of the key universe.
- *Short commitments:* our commitments should have size independent not only of the size of the key universe, but also of the *density* of the key-value map. The density is the number of elements whose value is not zero (e.g., the density of kv in the example above was 2).
- *Homomorphic commitments:* we require our commitments to support an homomorphic operation $\circ$. For example assume each commitment encodes a wallet and that we have two wallets c, c' with $c = \mathsf{Com}(\{(\mathsf{USD}, 100), (\mathsf{BTC}, 10)\})$ and $c' = \mathsf{Com}(\{(\mathsf{USD}, 20), (\mathsf{ETH}, 1)\})$. Then we can compute the commitment $c^* \leftarrow c \circ c' = \mathsf{Com}(\{(\mathsf{USD}, 120), (\mathsf{BTC}, 10), (\mathsf{ETH}, 1)\})$ without knowing the opening of any of the commitments. Requiring homomorphism rules out Merkle Trees as a solution. Homomorphic properties of commitments to "structured objects" have wide applications in cryptography (see, e.g., [27] for homomorphic polynomial commitments). The homomorphic property is a natural one and allows many useful applications: as an example we describe applications to privacy-preserving cryptocurrencies in Sect. 7 and an additional class of application scenarios in Sect. 1.1.
- *Efficient and transparent*[2] *zero-knowledge proofs*: we should be able to prove (and verify) efficiently arbitrary properties over commitments of key-value maps. We are interested in zero-knowledge proofs—which allow to prove properties over a secret value without leaking it—and where both keys and values are part of the secret. For example, one can prove that two committed key-value maps hold the same value for some (hidden) key $\tilde{k}$. More formally, given as public input commitments c, c' and a public function f, one can prove knowledge of a key $\tilde{k}$ such that c, c' are commitments to key-value maps $\mathsf{kv}, \mathsf{kv}'$ respectively and $\mathsf{kv}[\tilde{k}] = f(\mathsf{kv}'[\tilde{k}])$.

[1] This is a way to describe our setting asymptotically. We stress, however, that is not necessary: an interesting setting for our constructions is just one where the universe of keys is *concretely* large.

[2] In a *transparent* argument system the setup does not need to be produced by a trusted party. This property is interesting in the case of *non-interactive* argument systems, which are the focus of this work.

While different subsets of these properties have been studied in literature, our contribution is to investigate constructions that require them *all*. Our goal is to provide concretely efficient tools useful in different application domains.

KEY-HIDING PROPERTIES. Here we clarify what we mean by key-hiding properties and discuss how existing solutions fail to solve our problem. We have three *key sets* of interest: the set of all the keys in the universe (which we will assume to be $\{0,1\}^*$ or a field $\mathbb{F}$ from now on), the set K_{active} of *active keys*, defined as all the keys that are being used in the system, and the set K_{com} of *committed keys*, defined as the non-zero keys in any *given* commitment. As our commitment scheme always supports an exponentially large key space, the notion of active and committed keys is only relevant for commitments which require a NIZK about their opening. For example, in a wallet setting, K_{active} consists of all the keys (asset types) encoded in *some* wallet, while K_{com} would consist of those encoded in a *specific given* wallet. Depending on whether we want to hide the active or the committed keys or both we get four different settings, which we discuss below (see also Fig. 1).

PUBLIC ACTIVE KEYS. In the case where both the active keys and the committed keys are public, Pedersen commitments are already a solution to our problem. The system parameters will contain group elements $h, g_1, \ldots, g_n$ where there is a known association between k_i and g_i for all active keys k_i. E.g. A public coin setup process generates $g_i = \mathcal{H}(k_i)$ with a hash function $\mathcal{H}$. Thereby the association is known by all participants. We commit by computing $c = h^r \prod_i g_i^{v_i}$, and proving properties of values is trivial to do using existing sigma protocols since the verifier is allowed to learn the keys. In the case in which the active keys are public but the committed keys are private, Pedersen commitment can still be used but the (proving) complexity of the ZK proof would be linear in the number of active keys[3]. One of our contributions is to show how to bring this down to the size of the committed set.

PRIVATE ACTIVE KEYS. It does not make sense to consider the case where the set of active keys are private but the committed keys are public. The most interesting case is the one in which both of these sets are private. In this setting, it would be possible to commit using a non-homomorphic version of Pedersen commitment. We thus have $2n+1$ generators $(h, g_1, f_1, \ldots, g_n, f_n)$ and we commit computing $c = h^r \Pi g_i^{v_i} f_i^{k_i}$. Now it is possible to efficiently prove statements but the commitment is not homomorphic (and therefore not applicable in our settings of interest). Our main contribution is to provide a better solution for this case.

1.1 Applications of Our Work

APPLICATION: MULTI-TYPE QUISQUIS. The privacy-preserving transaction system QuisQuis [23] crucially relies commitments endowed with an homomorphic

[3] This is true for the aforementioned approach with sigma-protocols as well as for other straightforward applications of NIZKs.

property. It builds upon accounts to which tokens are deposited in a transaction without interaction of the receiver. A crucial performance consideration is the storage needed for a client to participate in the system. This corresponds to the local state necessary to validate arising updates (i.e. transactions). Compared to other privacy-preserving transaction systems like Zcash [11] or Monero [31], the design of QuisQuis achieves a state size linear in the number of participants instead of monotonically growing over time (i.e. requiring clients to store the full history). We extend this system through a notion of currency types such that different currencies share a common anonymity set. This allows for a dynamic creation of confidential tokens by any participant without setting up a full separate system. For this application, we also present a secret key based key-value map commitment[4]. In combination with efficient NIZKs, to show that transactions conserve all value, we achieve small transaction sizes. We formally describe this application in Sect. 7.

APPLICATION: PUBLICLY VERIFIABLE EVOLVING DATABASE. Consider a database (representable as key-value store) which receives numerous updates and where we want the content of the database to remain private but we also are interested in the database publicly "evolving through time".

As an example of the above, consider a register of tax-related information where users are identified by their SSN. The set of valid identities grows dynamically, which results in a high overhead if the public parameter changes every time. Users provide their SSN to their employer who uses it to report the salary. At the end of the month, each employer creates a hiding key-value map commitment with one key per employee and their earned amount as value, e.g. $\delta C_{\text{Corp X,May}} = \mathsf{Com}(\{\text{SSN}_{\text{Alice}} : 3142, \text{SSN}_{\text{Bob}} : 2718\})$. The company may either prove that for the employee's identity the correct amount was committed (without revealing the identities of co-workers), or reveal the full opening to their employees. Every company publishes these commitments to a persistent log. At the end of the year, the tax authority homomorphically adds all published commitments and can then generate proofs on a single commitment instead of all commitments from all companies. The required value opening is provided by the tax payers and the randomness by the companies. Employees with multiple sources of income get the amounts homomorphically added. Different categories of income may be separated by namespaces in the key.

1.2 Technical Overview

OUR CONSTRUCTION OF KEY-VALUE MAP COMMITMENTS. In order to commit to a key-value map $\{v_k\}_{k \in K}$ we assume a group $\mathbb{G}$ where the discrete logarithm is hard and a hash function $\mathcal{H}$ modeled as a random oracle mapping keys to group elements. We then compute a commitment as $c = \prod_{k \in K} \mathcal{H}(k)^{v_k} h^r$ where h is a random generator of the group and r is a random scalar. This can be seen as a (vector) Pedersen commitment with random key-dependent generators and it

[4] I.e., a commitment which can be opened using a secret key in place of the randomness.

has short homomorphic commitments. In the next paragraphs, we show how we can construct efficient zero-knowledge proofs for circuits over such commitments.

MODULAR TRANSPARENT ZERO-KNOWLEDGE ARGUMENTS FOR COMMITTED KEY-VALUE MAPS. Fix a (large) field $\mathbb{F}$ and consider a circuit C over key-value maps (we assume that $\mathbb{F}$ is also both the key and the value space of the key-value map). We assume the syntax of C to be of the type $C(\mathsf{kv}_1, \ldots, \mathsf{kv}_\ell, \omega)$, the kv_i-s as private key-value maps and ω as an additional private witness (ω is a vector of field elements). Given such a circuit we are interested in proving an augmented circuit that takes as public input commitments to the ℓ key-value maps and proves their opening in addition to the relation from circuit C. More specifically, we propose an argument system for:

$$C^*(c_1, \ldots, c_\ell; (\mathsf{kv}_1, \rho_1), \ldots, (\mathsf{kv}_\ell, \rho_\ell), \omega) := C(\mathsf{kv}_1, \ldots, \mathsf{kv}_\ell, \omega) \wedge \bigwedge_{i \in [\ell]} c_i = \mathsf{Com}(\mathsf{kv}_i, \rho_i) \quad (1)$$

where the part after the semicolon is considered the private witness. A more concrete intuition on the circuit above is: given committed key–value pairs we can prove properties of their values, their keys and any relation between these and other private values (contained in ω).

OUR TEMPLATE FOR ZERO-KNOWLEDGE ARGUMENTS ON COMMITTED KEY-VALUE MAPS. We now describe how to prove properties on committed key-value maps. The following refers to the setting with private-active-keys/private-committed-keys (see lower-right quadrant in Fig. 1). We denote the construction for the doubly-private case by **Z●-dp** (first part alternatively spelled "ZKeyWee", as a pun on "ZK for KV", and pronounced "*zee-kee-wee*"; "dp" stands for doubly-private).

	Public K_{active}	Private K_{active}
Public K_{com}	$c = h^r \prod_i g_i^{v_i}$ & Σ-protocols	*(Uninteresting case)*
Private K_{com}	c as in Fig. 2 & Z●-set (Sec. 1.2)	c as in Fig. 2 & Z●-dp (Sec. 4)

Fig. 1. How to construct commitments to key-value maps & NIZKs over them within our settings and with our requirements of interests. (K_{active}: "*active*" keys set, i.e., all the keys committed somewhere; K_{com} *committed* keys set, i.e. those that open the commitments we are using in a proof *right now*). The related constructions are specified in the second lines with our two contributions **Z●-set** and **Z●-dp**.

Our construction follows a basic blueprint, which we now exemplify through a concrete case. Consider a committed key-value map $\{v_k\}_{k \in K}$ and the problem of proving in zero-knowledge that all its values v_k are in some range $\{0, \ldots 2^{\mu} - 1\}$. We proceed in two steps: we first let the prover send the verifier what we call *key-tags*, these are masked versions of the non-zero keys in the committed key-value map. The prover will also show that they are valid maskings of some set of keys. By providing key-tags, we can then break the rest of the relation in two parts: *a)* showing knowledge of values (and randomness) that combined with the key-tags produce the commitment c (part of the public input); *b)* showing that these values are in range. We now elaborate on each of these steps.

Given a key-value map $\{v_k\}_{k \in K}$ with density n (the number of non-zero keys[5]) we provide n key-tags by sending $b_k = \mathcal{H}(k)h^{r_k}$ for a random r_k. The prover should also prove that each of them is of the prescribed form. We stress that, in order to do this, *we use the heuristic technique of proving a random oracle in zero-knowledge by assuming there exists a circuit for it* (a non-standard but common technique; see, e.g., [36]). Next, the prover would show knowledge of values $v_1, \ldots, v_n$ and an appropriate r' such that $c = b_{k_1}^{v_1} \cdots b_{k_n}^{v_n} h^{r'}$ and $v_i \in \{0, \ldots 2^{\mu} - 1\}$ for all $i \in [n]$. The latter relation—comprising reconstructing the commitment from the key-tags and the range proof—can for example be performed through a system like the generalized Bulletproofs in LMR [28] or compressed Σ-protocols [10]. These provide interfaces to prove bilinear circuits, of which we only use the non-bilinear gates, with logarithmic proof sizes. We stress that our focus is on *transparent* solutions, i.e., without a trusted setup; all our constructions can be instantiated in a fully transparent manner. We discuss an experimental evaluation in Sect. 6. We estimate our system can open $n = 100$ values and prove they are in range in approximately one minute. A very loose estimate for the size of the corresponding proof is $<$ 6KB using [28] in the Ristretto curve (see also Table 1 and Sect. 4.3).

We remark on two properties of the template of our construction above. *First*, we can easily reduce its amortized cost by splitting it into an offline stage (independent of the commitments on which we are carrying out proofs) and an online stage. We further discuss these improvements in Sect. 5. Second, we adapt and optimize our construction to the scenario with *public* active keys and private committed keys (lower-left quadrant in Fig. 1). We describe this next.

A 2ND CONSTRUCTION WITH REGISTRATION OF ACTIVE KEYS. In some settings, although the whole universe of keys can be extremely large, the set of active keys K_{active} at any given time can have a manageable size and be publicly known. Consider for example applications (e.g. multi-asset transaction system) where there is an exponentially large set of potential asset types (keys), but only a manageable subset of them are present in the system (active) at any given time. Moreover, before becoming active in the system they plausibly need to be registered (for example, through a first "genesis" transaction for that specific asset type). In such settings we can leverage the partial knowledge on existing

[5] Here we consider the case where leaking the density of the key-value map is not a problem. We will also adapt our construction where this leakage does not occur if an upper bound on this density is known.

keys to improve efficiency. We do this by introducing an operation that preprocesses the parameters of the system (or CRS) specializing them for a specific set of active keys. Our proposed construction for this setting—denoted by Z●-set (for "registered *set*" of keys) and discussed in more detail in the full version [17]—assumes the specialized CRS for the set K_{active} to contain an accumulator[6] to the set of (unmasked) key-tags corresponding to K_{active}, i.e., to the set $B_{\text{active}} = \{\mathcal{H}(k) : k \in K_{\text{active}}\}$. Thus, in the online stage, we can produce a proof on a commitment $c = \mathsf{Com}(\{v_k\}_{k \in K})$ by: 1) producing masked key-tags $B' = \{\mathcal{H}(k)h^{r_k} : k \in K\}$ produced with some fresh randomness r_k; 2) showing that each $b'_k \in B'$ is of the form $b \cdot h^{r_k}$ for some b in the accumulator; 3) showing knowledge of v_k-s such that $c = h^r \prod_k b'^{v_k}_k$.

The main advantage of the construction above, Z●-set , is that it does not require the hashing $\mathcal{H}(k)$ for the key-tags to be proven in zero-knowledge (by exploiting the fact that the keys are public and "pre-registered"). This can result in savings in verification time of one order of magnitude compared to Z●-dp (we elaborate in the full version [17]); such savings also apply to the multi-type transaction systems Multi-type QuisQuis (Sect. 7) and can be extended to other transaction systems (our techniques in Z●-set are compatible with other frameworks besides QuisQuis and they could be straightforwardly applied, e.g., to obtain a multi-type version of Veksel [19]).

MULTI-TYPE QUISQUIS. In contrast to the original QuisQuis where an account stored a scalar value representing an amount, we generalize accounts to store tokens of different types in a key-value map. Each key corresponds to a type, also known as currency, and the value specifies how many tokens of the specific type are held by the account. An account acct holds a balance kv, represented as a key-value map. To transfer tokens from one account to another, a transaction includes both accounts as active inputs, denoted by the set $\mathcal{P}$. The transaction subtracts tokens from one account with a secret index s and adds them to the other one. The output of the transaction are two updated accounts belonging to the same users as the inputs; the input accounts are discarded. To achieve anonymity, the input consists of $\mathcal{P}$ together with a potentially large anonymity set of accounts $\mathcal{A}$ which keep their balance unchanged but provide set anonymity for the active accounts. The sender uses Z●-set with a circuit to prove that they have enough funds (knowledge of secret key and positive balance) and that the updates are consistent.

1.3 Related Work

Authenticated Data Structures. Besides the aforementioned straw-man schemes based on Pedersen, a common approach to succinct key-value commitments uses Merkle trees. They are not homomorphic and opening them in

[6] An accumulator is a cryptographic data structure that allows to commit to a set in a binding manner and to prove membership of an element efficiently. NB: we can compute accumulators *deterministically* from a set, i.e., without a trusted authority.

zero-knowledge requires proving a number of hashes logarithmic in the number of committed elements, which can be expensive.

A related primitive is that of vector commitments [20]. A limitation of using vector commitments as key-value map commitments in general is that values need to be stored at positions that have already been agreed upon. That is, since we need to know for each key k what is the index i_k it refers to in the vector. This type of common agreement may be achieved in the setting in the bottom left quadrant in Fig. 1 (public active keys) but not in the bottom right one (private active keys). Also, while some constructions of vector commitments are homomorphic (e.g., [20]) they lose this property when hiding is added to them (which is usually achieved by storing hiding commitments to the values of interest). Other constructions do not have this limitation [14,30] but, like vector commitments in general, only support public active keys. We finally remark that, vector commitments focus on a different notion of *succinctness* than the one that is the focus in this paper. Our focus is on a proof size that is sublinear in the size of the circuit we apply on the opening, but not necessarily sublinear in the number of committed elements.

There is a large body of work on succinct commitments to key-value maps, e.g.[7], [5,13,18,35]. Differently from our work, constructions in literature are not homomorphic and do not directly support hiding of keys/values. We observe, however, that if one could do without homomorphism the latter problem could be mitigated for some of these constructions by applying masking of keys/values and zero-knowledge. This is true for example for some of the works based on groups of unknown-order [13,18] where we can use techniques to compose algebraic accumulators proofs and succinct zero-knowledge proof systems described in [12].

The work in [4] formalizes encryption on distributed key-value maps with consistency properties; it is not concerned with homomorphism or efficient zero-knowledge. Other works on efficient Zero-Knowledge and key-value maps include Spice [33]. The authors use data-structures that hide the key but that are not homomorphic. Their constructions use a trusted setup.

Confidential Transaction Systems and Multiple Token Types. Here we describe works related to our application, a multi-type version of QuisQuis.

Works on confidential transaction systems include Zcash [11], Monero [31], Omniring [29], and Veksel [19]. We now compare these works against the QuisQuis framework, which we extend in this work. The most critical aspect is sender anonymity. Zcash obtains the largest anonymity set among these works (as large as the UTXO set), but it does not have plausible deniability[8] and requires a trusted setup. Monero does not have these limitations; it is unclear how the anonymity in Monero fares against that in QuisQuis (see Discussion in [23]). Omniring improves the transaction size from being linear in the size of the anonymity set (Monero) to a logarithmic size. Both Zcash and Monero style systems, however, have transaction outputs that can (essentially) never be

[7] We refer the reader to [35] for a survey of this rapidly growing field.

[8] Plausible deniability: no one can tell if a user meant to be involved in a transaction.

removed from the UTXO set. The payment system in $\mathbb{V}$eksel, like QuisQuis, does not have this drawback. Differently from QuisQuis, $\mathbb{V}$eksel achieves $O(1)$ transaction sizes, but at the price of weaker anonymity guarantees. In all these systems amounts are confidential, yet they lack a notion of type/currency.

The work in [32] introduces confidential types by using homomorphic commitments whose construction is the "single key" version of ours. Their design has also been used in SwapCT [21] and integrated in MimbleWimble [37]. Another construction of confidential types is that of Cloaked Assets developed by Stellar, which separates types and values in two different data structures, similar to our non-homomorphic example. Therefore a transactor requires the openings of all inputs to create a conservation proof, providing no sender anonymity.

2 Notation and Preliminaries

Preliminaries on (Sparse) Key-Value Maps. We assume a universe of keys $\mathcal{K}$ and a universe of values $\mathcal{V}$ such that in a key-value map, keys are a subset of $\mathcal{K}$ and values are any element in $\mathcal{V}$; they may be of size superpolynomial in a security parameter λ. We assume $\mathcal{V}$ to be an additive group endowed with some operation $+$. A key-value map is defined as a function $\mathsf{kv} : \mathcal{K} \to \mathcal{V}$. We call its *density* the number of elements that are mapped to a non-zero value in $\mathcal{V}$. Our focus is on *sparse* key-value maps whose density grows asymptotically with $\mathsf{poly}(\lambda)$ (and in practice may be concretely small). We can represent a sparse key-value map as a set of pairs $\{(k, v_k)\}_{k \in K}$ where $K \subseteq \mathcal{K}$: this maps each element $k \in K$ to v_k and any other element to $0 \in \mathcal{V}$. We often use the more succinct notation $\{v_k\}_{k \in K}$ for a key-value map $\{(k, v_k)\}_{k \in K}$ over the set K (we assume that the set K is implicitly part of the description of $\{v_k\}_{k \in K}$). Hence the empty set $\emptyset$ represents the key-value map with all elements in the universe initialized to zero; we denote the latter empty key-value map $\emptyset_{kv}$ to be explicit. We denote by $-\mathsf{kv}$ the key-value map associating the value $-\mathsf{kv}(k)$ to each key k; we define a sum of key-value maps as follows: $\{v_k\}_{k \in K} + \{v'_{k'}\}_{k' \in K'} := (k, v_k + v'_{k'})_{k \in K \cup K'}$. A partition of a key-value map $\{v_k\}_{k \in K}$ is a pair of key-value maps $(\{v'_{k'}\}_{k' \in K'}, \{v''_{k''}\}_{k'' \in K''})$ such that (K', K'') is a partition of K.

Cryptographic Assumptions. For convenience we use a different, but equivalent, formulation of the discrete logarithm assumption. Below $\mathcal{G}$ denotes a group generator.

Assumption 1 (Generalized DLOG [16]). $\forall$ PPT $\mathcal{A}, m \geq 2$:

$$\Pr\left[\begin{array}{c} \mathbb{G} \leftarrow \mathcal{G}(1^\lambda); (g_1, \ldots, g_m) \leftarrow_{\$} \mathbb{G} \\ (a_1, \ldots, a_m) \leftarrow \mathcal{A}(\mathbb{G}, g_1, \ldots, g_m) \end{array} : \begin{array}{c} \exists j^* \in [m]\ a_{j^*} \neq 0\ \wedge \\ \prod_{j \in [m]} g_j^{a_j} = 1_{\mathbb{G}} \end{array}\right] \leq \mathsf{negl}(\lambda)$$

NIZKs. Here we describe the basic notion of non-interactive zero-knowledge. In Sect. 4 we provide explicit syntax for the specific setting of NIZKs over committed key-value maps.

Definition 1. *A NIZK for a relation family* $\mathcal{R} = \{R_\lambda\}_{\lambda \in \mathbb{N}}$ *is a tuple of algorithms* $\mathsf{NIZK} = (\mathsf{Setup}, \mathsf{Prove}, \mathsf{VerProof})$ *with the following syntax:*

- $\mathsf{NIZK.Setup}(1^\lambda) \to \mathsf{crs}$ *outputs a common-reference string* crs*; if the argument system is transparent this can consist of uniform random elements.*
- $\mathsf{NIZK.Prove}(\mathsf{crs}, \mathbb{x}, \mathbb{w}) \to \pi$ *takes as input a string* crs*, an input description* $\mathbb{x}$ *(in which we embed the whole public input), a witness* $\mathbb{w}$ *such that* $R_\lambda(\mathbb{x}, \mathbb{w})$*; it returns a proof* π*.*
- $\mathsf{NIZK.VerProof}(\mathsf{crs}, \mathbb{x}, \pi) \to b \in \{0,1\}$ *takes as input a string* crs*, a public input* $\mathbb{x}$*, a proof* π*; it accepts or rejects the proof.*

Whenever the relation family is obviously defined, we talk about a "NIZK for a relation R". We require a NIZK to be *complete*, that is, for any $\lambda \in \mathbb{N}$ and $(\mathbb{x}, \mathbb{w}) \in R_\lambda$ it holds with overwhelming probability that $\mathsf{VerProof}(\mathsf{crs}, \mathbb{x}, \pi)$ where $\mathsf{crs} \leftarrow \mathsf{Setup}(1^\lambda)$ and $\pi \leftarrow \mathsf{Prove}(\mathsf{crs}, \mathbb{x}, \mathbb{w})$. Other properties we require are: *knowledge-soundness* and *zero-knowledge*. Informally, the former states we can efficiently "extract" a valid witness from a proof that passes verification; the latter states that the proof leaks nothing about the witness (this is modeled through a simulator that can output a valid proof for an input in the language without knowing the witness). Notationally, we separate public and private inputs in relations and proving algorithm through a semicolon.

Knowledge-Soundness. For all $\lambda \in \mathbb{N}$ and for all (non-uniform) efficient adversaries $\mathcal{A}$, auxiliary input $z \in \{0,1\}^{\mathsf{poly}(\lambda)}$, there exists a (non-uniform) efficient extractor $\mathcal{E}$ such that

$$\Pr\left[\begin{array}{l} \mathsf{crs} \leftarrow \mathsf{Setup}(1^\lambda); (\mathbb{x}, \pi) \leftarrow \mathcal{A}(z, \mathsf{crs}) \\ \mathbb{w} \leftarrow \mathcal{E}(z, \mathsf{crs}) \end{array} : \begin{array}{r} R_\lambda(\mathbb{x}, \mathbb{w}) \neq 1 \wedge \\ \mathsf{Vfy}(\mathsf{crs}, \mathbb{x}, \pi) = 1 \end{array}\right] \leq \mathsf{negl}(\lambda)$$

Zero-Knowledge. There exists a PPT simulator $\mathcal{S}$ such that for any $\lambda \in \mathbb{N}$, PPT $\mathcal{A}$, auxiliary input $z \in \{0,1\}^{\mathsf{poly}(\lambda)}$, and it holds $p_0 = p_1$ where

$$p_b := \Pr\left[\begin{array}{c} \mathsf{crs} \leftarrow \mathsf{Setup}(1^\lambda); (\mathbb{x}, \mathbb{w}) \leftarrow \mathcal{A}(z, \mathsf{crs}) \\ \pi \leftarrow X_b(\mathsf{crs}, \mathbb{x}, \mathbb{w}) \text{ if } R_\lambda(\mathbb{x}, \mathbb{w}) \text{ o.w. } \bot \end{array} : \mathcal{A}(z, \mathsf{crs}, \pi) = 1\right]$$

$X_0(\mathsf{crs}, \mathbb{x}, \mathbb{w}) := \mathcal{S}(z, \mathsf{crs}, \mathbb{x})$ and $X_1(\mathsf{crs}, \mathbb{x}, \mathbb{w}) := \mathsf{Prove}(\mathsf{crs}, \mathbb{x}, \mathbb{w})$.

On Efficiency of NIZKs. The efficiency (proving/verification runtimes and proof size) of a NIZK often depends on the size of the description of a relation in *constraints* (these roughly correspond to the multiplication gates of its circuit representation). We will refer to this notion later in the text. See also [16].

3 Key-Value Commitments

Here we define homomorphic commitments to key-value maps where both keys and values are hidden. To the best of our knowledge this definition is new, but it straightforwardly extends homomorphic commitments with key-value maps as message space. In the full version [17], we also present an extended construction, which we use to build Multi-Type Quis-Quis.

Definition 2 (Commitment to Key-Value Maps (kvC)). *The following is a syntax for our key-value maps*

$\mathsf{Setup}(1^\lambda) \rightarrow \mathsf{pp}$ *generates public parameters.*
$\mathsf{Com}(\mathsf{pp}, \{v_k\}_{k\in K}; r) \rightarrow c$ *commits to the key-value map with randomness* r. *We keep the randomness implicit whenever it does not affect clarity and we assume it to be sampled from an additive group.*[9]

Definition 3 (Hiding). *A key-value map commitment is hiding if for all key-value maps* $\{v'_{k'}\}_{k'\in K'}, \{v''_{k''}\}_{k''\in K''}$ *(even of different size), for* $\mathsf{pp} \leftarrow \mathsf{Setup}(1^\lambda)$ *the following two distributions are computationally indistinguishable:*

$$\{\mathsf{Com}(\mathsf{pp}, \{v'_{k'}\}_{k'\in K'})\} \approx \{\mathsf{Com}(\mathsf{pp}, \{v''_{k''}\}_{k''\in K''})\}$$

Definition 4 (Binding). *A key-value map commitment is (computationally) binding if for any PPT adversary* $\mathcal{A}$, *it holds that*

$$\Pr\left[\begin{array}{ll} \mathsf{pp} \leftarrow \mathsf{Setup}(1^\lambda) & c = \mathsf{Com}(\mathsf{pp}, \{v'_{k'}\}_{k'\in K'}, r') \wedge \\ (c, \{v'_{k'}\}_{k'\in K'}, r', & : \; c = \mathsf{Com}(\mathsf{pp}, \{v''_{k''}\}_{k''\in K''}, r'') \wedge \\ \quad \{v''_{k''}\}_{k''\in K''}, r'') \leftarrow \mathcal{A}(\mathsf{pp}) & \{v'_{k'}\}_{k'\in K'} \neq \{v''_{k''}\}_{k''\in K''} \end{array}\right] \leq \mathsf{negl}(\lambda)$$

Definition 5 (Homomorphism). *We say a commitment to a key-value map is homomorphic if there exists an operation* $\circ$ *such that* Setup *always produces* pp *such that for all maps* $\{v_k\}_{k\in K}, \{v'_{k'}\}_{k'\in K'}$ *and randomness* r, r' *it holds that*

$$\mathsf{Com}(\{v_k\}_{k\in K}; r) \circ \mathsf{Com}(\{v'_{k'}\}_{k'\in K'}; r') = \mathsf{Com}(\{v^*_{k^*}\}_{k^*\in K^*}; r + r')$$

$$\text{where } K^* = K \cup K' \text{ and } (k^*, v^*_{k^*}) = \begin{cases} (k^*, v_{k^*}) \text{ if } k^* \in K \setminus K' \\ (k^*, v'_{k^*}) \text{ if } k^* \in K' \setminus K \\ (k^*, v_{k^*} + v'_{k^*}) \text{ if } k^* \in K \cap K' \end{cases}$$

3.1 Construction

We recap some of the properties we are interested in obtaining in our construction: (i) support large key universe; (ii) small commitments and

[9] We will use this when defining the homomorphic property of commitments.

$\mathsf{Setup}(1^\lambda) \to \mathsf{pp}$: samples group $\mathbb{G}$; $g, h \leftarrow\$ \mathbb{G}$; return $\mathsf{pp} = (\mathbb{G}, g, h)$.
$\mathsf{Com}(\mathsf{pp}, \{v_k\}_{k \in K}; r) \to c$: return $\prod_{k \in K} \mathcal{H}(k)^{v_k} h^r$.

Fig. 2. Our construction for kvC.

small parameters; (iii) homomorphic (Definition 5); (iv) support efficient non-interactive zero-knowledge proof of knowledge of opening (in particular they should run in time linear in the density of the key-value map).

In Fig. 2 we propose a construction based on random-oracle with the properties above. Our commitment construction is an extension to key-value maps of the one in [32]. Given a prime p we consider the universe of values $\mathcal{V} = \mathbb{Z}_p$, a group $\mathbb{G}$ isomorphic to it and for which the GDLOG assumption holds, a hash function $\mathcal{H}$ modeled as a random oracle and an arbitrary key universe $\mathcal{K}$ such that $\mathcal{H} : \mathcal{K} \to \mathbb{G}$. We prove Theorem 1 in the full version [17].

Theorem 1. *If $\mathcal{H}$ is a random oracle and under the GDLOG assumption the construction in Fig. 2 is a kvC with value universe $\mathbb{Z}_p$.*

4 Arguments on Key-Value Commitments (Doubly-Private Setting)

Here we formalize and construct zero-knowledge arguments over key-value map commitments for the setting in which there is no information on the keys available in the system and those we are using in our proof.

Circuits over Key-Value Maps. To support arbitrary computation on committed key-value maps, we provide an interface which supports any arithmetic circuit of the following form. The keys and values kv as well as an additional witness ω are field elements in $\mathbb{F}$. The circuit consists of multiplication gates of the form $\mathbb{F} \times \mathbb{F} \to \mathbb{F}$. They have an unbounded outbound degree and any linear relations are directly expressed between outputs and inputs.

We write any circuit using multiplication gates in the domain $\mathcal{KV}^\ell \times \mathbb{F}^{n_\omega}$ as $C^{\mathbb{F}}(\mathsf{kv}_1, \ldots, \mathsf{kv}_\ell, \omega)$. This circuit depends on the desired property the openings should have. Here ω is an additional private witness that may not depend on the opening to the key-value maps.

4.1 Arguments for Circuits over Committed Key-Value Maps

Here we present the overview of our argument system which works over committed key-value maps and takes an arbitrary inner circuit operating on the openings of the commitments. To be clear, we spell out its formalization explicitly but it is a special case of Definition 1. Given an inner circuit $C^{\mathbb{F}}$ as described above, our high level interface for proofs has the following form:

$\mathsf{kvNIZK.Setup}(1^\lambda) \rightarrow \mathsf{crs}$ takes a security parameter λ and outputs a crs.

$\mathsf{kvNIZK.Prove}(\mathsf{crs}, C^{\mathbb{F}}, c_1, \ldots, c_\ell, (\mathsf{kv}_1, \rho_1), \ldots, (\mathsf{kv}_\ell, \rho_\ell), \omega) \rightarrow \pi$ takes the crs and a circuit $C^{\mathbb{F}}$ as well as ℓ commitments c_i and their openings (kv_i, ρ_i) and an auxiliary witness ω. It outputs a proof π

$\mathsf{kvNIZK.VerProof}(\mathsf{crs}, C^{\mathbb{F}}, c_1, \ldots, c_\ell, \pi) \rightarrow b \in \{0, 1\}$ takes the crs, a circuit $C^{\mathbb{F}}$, and ℓ commitments c_i. The output bit b returns the validity of the proof π.

The relation we want to prove is defined by the circuit C^* in Eq. (1). To clarify our notation we re-define correctness for arguments for committed key-value maps.

Definition 6 (kvNIZK Correctness). *A* kvNIZK *is correct if, for any* $\lambda \in \mathbb{N}$ *with* $\mathsf{crs} \in \mathsf{kvNIZK.Setup}(1^\lambda)$*, circuit* $C^{\mathbb{F}}$*, key-value maps* $\vec{\mathsf{kv}} \in \mathcal{KV}^\ell$ *and randomness* $\vec{\rho} \in \mathbb{F}^\ell$ *with* $\forall i \in [\ell] : c_i = \mathsf{Com}(\mathsf{kv}_i, \rho_i)$ *and any* $\omega \in \mathbb{F}^{n_\omega}$ *for which* $C^*(c_1, \ldots, c_\ell; (\mathsf{kv}_1, \rho_1), \ldots, (\mathsf{kv}_\ell, \rho_\ell), \omega) = 1$ *it holds that*

$$\mathsf{kvNIZK.VerProof}(\mathsf{crs}, C^{\mathbb{F}}, c_1, \ldots, c_\ell, \pi) = 1 \textit{ where}$$
$$\pi \leftarrow \mathsf{kvNIZK.Prove}(\mathsf{crs}, C^{\mathbb{F}}, c_1, \ldots, c_\ell, (\mathsf{kv}_1, \rho_1), \ldots, (\mathsf{kv}_\ell, \rho_\ell), \omega).$$

As for NIZKs, we require knowledge-soundness and zero-knowledge.

4.2 Construction with Intermediate Key-Tags

Our construction has two stages. First the prover creates some key-tags b_k and proves that they are well formed (i.e., they are obtained by hashing a key and masking with a random group element, both known to the prover). These key-tags are then used in a subsequent proof for the opening of the commitment and the actual relation. Intuitively, since the prover knows how the key-tags have been produced, the prover is able to compute openings of the input commitments under the new "base" $(h, b_1, \ldots, b_n)$—as opposed to the original base $(g, \mathcal{H}(k_1), \ldots, \mathcal{H}(k_n))$—by appropriately computing the randomizers as a function of the values in the commitment and the randomness used for producing the key-tags. This allows to avoid proving properties of the hash function in the second part of the proof. The full construction Z●-dp is presented in Fig. 3. For sake of presentation and w.l.o.g., in the construction we assume that all our key-value maps include the same keys $k_1, \ldots, k_n$.

Theorem 2. *Under the GDLOG assumption, if* NIZK_{tags} *and* NIZK_C *are secure (correct, zero-knowledge, knowledge-sound) NIZKs for their required relation families, then the construction* Z●-dp *is a secure kvNIZK for arbitrary circuits over the key-value map commitment in Fig. 2.*

Proof. Correctness: Correctness follows by inspection. In particular, note that when proving R_C the prover "opens" the commitments c_i under the base defined by the key-tags b_k's. Since the b_k's are generated with the same h as the original commitment and the prover knows the openings of the b_k's, the prover can find the right value to be used as exponent for h.

The protocol is described in the random oracle model where all parties have access to $\mathcal{H} : \{0,1\}^* \rightarrow \mathbb{G}$.

$\mathsf{Setup}(1^\lambda)$: 1. compute $\mathsf{crs}_{\mathsf{tags}} \leftarrow \mathsf{NIZK.Setup}_{\mathsf{tags}}(1^\lambda)$, $\mathsf{crs}_{\mathrm{C}} \leftarrow \mathsf{NIZK.Setup}(1^\lambda)$.

2. generate the commitment key $h \xleftarrow{\$} \mathbb{G}$ (setup for kv commitments).
3. sample random generators $\vec{g} \xleftarrow{\$} \mathbb{G}^n$ where n is the maximum number of committed keys ($\leq$ number of active keys) in a commitment.
4. Output $\mathsf{crs} = (\mathsf{crs}_{\mathsf{tags}}, \mathsf{crs}_{\mathrm{C}}, h, \vec{g})$

$\mathsf{Prove}(\mathsf{crs}, C^{\mathbb{F}}, c_1, \ldots, c_\ell, (\mathsf{kv}_1, \rho_1), \ldots, (\mathsf{kv}_\ell, \rho_\ell), \omega)$:

1. From all key-value maps kv_i, extract the set of non-zero keys K_i and define $(k_1, \ldots, k_n) := \bigcup_{i \in [\ell]} \{k \in K_i\}$. Parse $\mathsf{kv}_i = \{(k, v_{i,k}) : k = k_1, \ldots, k_n\}$ for each $i = 1, \ldots, \ell$
2. Sample random values $\vec{r} \xleftarrow{\$} \mathbb{F}^n$ and create the key-tags $b_{k_i} = \mathcal{H}(k_i) h^{r_i}$. Additionally, create a vector Pedersen commitment to all keys (called pre-image commitment) $c^* = h^s \prod_{i=1}^n g_i^{k_i}$ with randomness $s \xleftarrow{\$} \mathbb{F}$.
3. Generate a proof that the key-tags are well formed by proving knowledge of the pre-images k_i i.e., generate a proof

$$\pi_{\mathsf{tags}} \leftarrow \mathsf{NIZK.Prove}_{\mathsf{tags}}(\mathsf{crs}, b_{k_1}, \ldots, b_{k_n}, c^*; k_1, \ldots, k_n, \vec{r}, s)$$

for the relation

$$R_{\mathsf{tags}}(b_{k_1}, \ldots, b_{k_n}, c^*; k_1, \ldots, k_n, \vec{r}, s) := \left(c^* = h^s \prod_{i=1}^n g_i^{k_i} \wedge \forall i \in [n] : b_{k_i} = \mathcal{H}(k_i) h^{r_i}\right)$$

4. Generate a proof

$$\pi_{\mathrm{C}} \leftarrow \mathsf{NIZK.Prove}_{\mathrm{C}}(\mathsf{crs}, C^{\mathbb{F}}, c_1, \ldots, c_\ell, b_{k_1}, \ldots, b_{k_n}, c^*; (\mathsf{kv}_1, \rho_1), \ldots, (\mathsf{kv}_\ell, \rho_\ell), \vec{r}, s, \omega)$$

for the relation

$$R_{\mathrm{C}}(C^{\mathbb{F}}, c_1, \ldots, c_\ell, b_{k_1}, \ldots, b_{k_n}, c^*; (\mathsf{kv}_1, \rho_1), \ldots, (\mathsf{kv}_\ell, \rho_\ell), \vec{r}, s, \omega) := c^* = h^s \prod_{i=1}^n g_i^{k_i} \wedge \forall i \in [\ell] : c_i = h^{\rho_i - \sum_{j=1}^n r_j v_{i,k_j}} \prod_{j=1}^n b_{k_j}^{v_{i,k_j}} \wedge C^{\mathbb{F}}((\mathsf{kv}_i)_{i \in [\ell]}, \omega) = 1 \quad (2)$$

5. Return both proofs including the key-tags and the pre-image commitment $\pi := (b_{k_1}, \ldots, b_{k_n}, c^*, \pi_{\mathsf{tags}}, \pi_{\mathrm{C}})$

$\mathsf{VerProof}(\mathsf{crs}, C^{\mathbb{F}}, c_1, \ldots, c_\ell, \pi)$:

1. Parse π as $(b_{k_1}, \ldots, b_{k_n}, c^*, \pi_{\mathsf{tags}}, \pi_{\mathrm{C}})$.
2. Verify $b_0 \leftarrow \mathsf{NIZK.VerProof}_{\mathsf{tags}}(\mathsf{crs}, b_{k_1}, \ldots, b_{k_n}, c^*, \pi_{\mathsf{tags}})$
3. Verify $b_1 \leftarrow \mathsf{NIZK.VerProof}_{\mathrm{C}}(\mathsf{crs}, C^{\mathbb{F}}, c_1, \ldots, c_\ell, b_{k_1}, \ldots, b_{k_n}, c^*, \pi_{\mathrm{C}})$
4. return $b_0 \wedge b_1$

Fig. 3. Z●-dp, our construction for kvNIZK

Knowledge-Soundness: To prove knowledge-soundness, assume the existence of extractors $\mathcal{E}_{\text{tags}}, \mathcal{E}_{\text{C}}$ for the two sub-relations. We build an extractor $\mathcal{E}^*$ that on input a statement $(C^{\mathbb{F}}, c_1, \ldots, c_\ell)$ and accepting proof $(b_1, \ldots, b_n, c^*, \pi_{\text{tags}}, \pi_{\text{C}})$, outputs $((\mathsf{kv}_1, \rho_1), \ldots, (\mathsf{kv}_\ell, \rho_\ell), \omega)$. Our $\mathcal{E}^*$ works as follows. It first extracts through $(k'_1, \ldots, k'_n, \vec{r}r', s') \leftarrow \mathcal{E}_{\text{tags}}(b_1, \ldots, b_n, c^*, \pi_{\text{tags}})$ and then the rest through $((\mathsf{kv}_1, \rho'_1), \ldots, (\mathsf{kv}_\ell, \rho'_\ell), \vec{r}, s, \omega) \leftarrow \mathcal{E}_{\text{C}}(C^{\mathbb{F}}, c_1, \ldots, c_\ell, b_1, \ldots, b_n, c^*, \pi_{\text{C}})$ such that the two relations hold for the extracted witnesses. We first argue it holds that $(k'_1, \ldots, k'_\ell, s') = (k_1, \ldots, k_\ell, s)$, since otherwise we can construct an adversary that breaks the binding property of the Pedersen commitment c^*. Then, we show how to extract valid openings for the input commitments c_i. Remember that thanks to the knowledge-soundness of the second proof system (for relation R_{C}) we know that for all commitments c_i it holds $c = h^{\rho' - \sum_{j=1}^{n} r_j v_{k_j}} \prod_{j=1}^{n} b_{k_j}^{v_{k_j}}$ (we remove the index i here to improve readability) .

Thanks to the knowledge soundness of the first proof system (for relation R_{tags}) we know that $b_{k_j} = \mathcal{H}(k_j) h^{r'_j}$, thus we can rewrite c as

$$c = h^{\rho' - \sum_{j=1}^{n} r_j v_{k_j}} \prod_{j=1}^{n} \mathcal{H}(k_j)^{v_{k_j}} h^{r'_j \cdot v_{k_j}} \quad = h^{\rho' - \sum_{j=1}^{n} (r_j - r'_j) v_{k_j}} \prod_{j=1}^{n} \mathcal{H}(k_j)^{v_{k_j}}$$

Thus our extractor can output $((\mathsf{kv}_1, \rho_1), \ldots, (\mathsf{kv}_\ell, \rho_\ell), \omega)$ with $\rho_i = \rho'_i - \sum_{j=1}^{n} (r_j - r'_j) v_{k_{i,j}}$ as the witness for the overall relation. Note that the proof does not guarantee that $\vec{r} = \vec{r'}r'$. However this is not a problem since we are still guaranteed that the extracted witness for the overall relation is a valid one.
Zero-Knowledge: follows from the ZK property of the underlying arguments and the hiding property of the commitments. Details can be found in the full version [17].

4.3 How to Instantiate the Subprotocols in Z●-dp

To instantiate the well formedness of the tags, i.e. the relation R_{tags}, we propose to use a cryptographic hash function such as MiMC [7], Poseidon [25], GMiMC [6], or Marvellous [8] which are optimized for zero-knowledge proofs. They provide hashing to a field element ($\mathcal{H}^{\mathbb{F}} : \{0,1\}^* \rightarrow \mathbb{F}$) which can be leveraged to obtain random group elements through some of the techniques in [15,22,34]. A subsequent circuit then proves this hashing and the rerandomization of the group element as key-tags, i.e., $[b_{k_i}] = [\mathcal{H}(k_i)] + r_i \cdot [h]$, where brackets enclose group elements. The combined constraints can then proven by e.g. Bulletproofs [16] or [9].

The circuit for the relation R_{C} can be implemented through a generalization of Bulletproofs [28][10]. They provide an interface supporting bilinear circuits with five gates to enable arbitrary computation of which we use a subset of gates

[10] If malleability is a concern, Bulletproofs are proven to be non-malleable in the AGM [24].

for non-bilinear circuits only. Given a circuit C constructed from the available gates, they then provide an efficient protocol with communication complexity $6\lceil \log_2(|C|) \rceil + 28$ group elements.

5 Improvements in Practice: Offline/Online Stages

The proving algorithms of our constructions (both **Z◉-dp** and **Z◉-set**) follow a two-step template. In step *(a)* the prover provides key-tags b_k-s and proves they are valid. This can be done independently of the commitment. In a following step *(b)* we compute a proof about properties of the commitment opening (and that actually depends on the commitments). Crucially, in the latter step, the prover uses the key-tags as (rerandomized) "anchors" to the keys. We observe that we can exploit the fact that *(a)* does not depend on the commitments to the key-value maps (but only on the keys that they will contain) to preprocess this step.

Consider, for instance, the running example from the introduction where the commitments contain multi-currency wallets. Assume that the prover knows that *in the future* they will want to prove some properties about some of their wallets (which are expected to keep changing between now and the proving time). Moreover, while a large set K_{active} of asset types might be circulating in the system, the prover knows that they will only hold a very specific and relatively small subset K_{pre} of these keys (e.g., maybe only ETH, USD and EUR). If that is the case they can preemptively perform an "offline proving stage" that would be valid for all of the *online* proofs they will have to carry out later. Specifically, in **Z◉-dp** the prover performs step *(a)* above offline as follows. On input set K_{pre}, the prover provides a set of $|K_{\text{pre}}|$ key-tags $B = \{b_k : k \in K_{\text{pre}}\}$, defined as usual as $b_k = \mathcal{H}(k)h^{r_k}$ together with a proof π_{tags} that they were constructed honestly. The output of this step is therefore $\pi_{\text{offl}} = (B, \pi_{\text{tags}})$. At a later time, when input commitments $c_1, \ldots, c_\ell$ are available, the prover uses the pre-computed set of key-tags B to produce a step (a) (the production of key-tags) for each of the commitments c_i. In order to preserve zero-knowledge, step (b) is modified to rerandomize the related b_k-s first. The rerandomization hides the mapping between online proofs, however the verifier learns that all commitments of the online phase contain the same set of keys. We can similarly adapt **Z◉-set** by performing a proof of membership and masking before hand.

The advantage of this approach is to use a single offline stage for many proofs. The efficiency savings of this stage (both for proving and verification time) can be significant since it involves proving/verifying hashing in zero-knowledge. For example, we conservatively estimate approximately 5k constraints using Poseidon hashing on a Ristretto curve [25]. Each of these hashes can be proved in the order of hundreds of milliseconds (see, e.g., Table 5 in [25]). For $n \approx 100$ this involves for example saving half a million constraints[11] amounting to around half a minute of proving time. Savings for verification time are comparable.

[11] For some applications this can be huge—for comparison, the ZCash circuit [26] has approximately 100k constraints.

Naturally the offline stage preprocesses an *upper bound* U on the total number of active keys, since each commitment may have openings to key-value maps of different density. This may incur a high overhead cost if U is far from the actual densities (because we still need to process U key-tags as input to the circuit). The gains from an offline stage can differ accordingly and should be weighed depending on the application.

Efficiency Summary of our Constructions. We summarize the (asymptotic) efficiency of our constructions in Table 1. We present it for the case with offline processing, but summing the offline and online columns corresponds to the setting without an offline stage.

Table 1. Efficiency of our constructions and comparison with non-homomorphic solutions (when they are applicable). Above we describe proof sizes, proving time and verification times during offline and online stage. We also describe the additional costs for proving the homomorphism in zero-knowledge with a non-homomorphic solution ($\mathsf{kv}_{\mathsf{add}}(n)$). All values are implicitly in big O notation and denote operations in a prime-order group unless underlined. Rows marked with $\star$ refer to this work. The construction of Z🌑-dp is in Fig. 3. "Z🌑-set (Acc)" refers to the instantiation of Z🌑-set with NIZKs over accumulators in unknown-order groups we describe in the full version [17]. "Pedersen (Non-Hom.)" refers to the non-homomorphic solution based on Pedersen described in the introduction. Typical values for our parameters could be $M \approx 1000$ and $n \approx 100$.

K_{active}	K_{com}	Construction	$\lvert\pi_{\text{offl}}\rvert$	$\lvert\pi_{\text{onl}}\rvert$	$\lvert\pi(\mathsf{kv}_{\mathsf{add}}(n))\rvert$
priv	priv	Z🌑-dp $\star$	$\log(n(\lvert\mathcal{H}\rvert + \lvert\mathbb{G}_{\text{add}}\rvert))$	$\log(\lvert C\rvert)$	—
priv	priv	Pedersen (Non-Hom.)	—	$\log(\lvert C\rvert)$	$\log(n)$
publ	priv	Z🌑-set (Acc) $\star$	$n + \log(n\lvert\mathbb{G}_{\text{add}}\rvert)$	$\log(\lvert C\rvert)$	—

K_{active}	K_{com}	Construction	$\mathcal{V}_{\text{offl}}$	$\mathcal{V}_{\text{onl}}$	$\mathcal{V}(\mathsf{kv}_{\mathsf{add}}(n))$
priv	priv	Z🌑-dp $\star$	$n(\lvert\mathcal{H}\rvert + \lvert\mathbb{G}_{\text{add}}\rvert)$	$\lvert C\rvert$	—
priv	priv	Pedersen (Non-Hom.)	—	$\lvert C\rvert$	n
publ	priv	Z🌑-set (Acc) $\star$	$\underline{n\lvert\mathbb{G}_?\rvert} + n\lvert\mathbb{G}_{\text{add}}\rvert$	$\lvert C\rvert$	—

K_{active}	K_{com}	Construction	$\mathcal{P}_{\text{offl}}$	$\mathcal{P}_{\text{onl}}$	$\mathcal{P}(\mathsf{kv}_{\mathsf{add}}(n))$
priv	priv	Z🌑-dp $\star$	$n(\lvert\mathcal{H}\rvert + \lvert\mathbb{G}_{\text{add}}\rvert)$	$\lvert C\rvert$	—
priv	priv	Pedersen (Non-Hom.)	—	$\lvert C\rvert$	n
publ	priv	Z🌑-set (Acc) $\star$	$\underline{(M - n + n\log n)\lvert\mathbb{G}_?\rvert}$ $+n\lvert\mathbb{G}_{\text{add}}\rvert$	$\lvert C\rvert$	—

N :	Size of key universe $\mathcal{K}$
M :	Number of active / registered keys (K_{active})
n :	Number of keys in the opening of a key-value map commitment
	$N >> M \geq n$
$\lvert\mathcal{H}\rvert$:	Number of constraints for hashing to a group element
$\lvert\mathbb{G}_{\text{add}}\rvert$:	Number of constraints for summing two group elements
$\lvert\mathbb{G}_?\rvert$:	Cost of exponentiation in unknown-order group
$\mathsf{kv}_{\mathsf{add}}(n)$:	Sum operation among key-value maps of size n
C :	Circuit computed on key-value map.

6 Experimental Evaluation

Here we show the practical feasibility of our construction. Our focus is on Z-dp; we compare its efficiency to that of Z-set in the full version [17].

Recall that our construction-template uses two separate steps (see also beginning of Sect. 5 and Fig. 3): *(a)* validity of key-tags and *(b)* actual property on opening of commitment. We evaluate our construction on a representative application setting for cryptocurrencies, that is a 64-bit range proof as a circuit proven in step *(b)*.

Let n be the size of the opening of the commitment (also equal to the number of elements we are showing are in range). We estimate the following runtimes. For step *(a)*: $\approx n \cdot 700\,\text{ms}$ for proving and $n \cdot 100\,\text{ms}$ for verification; for step *(b)* $\approx n \cdot 235\,\text{ms}$ for proving and $n \cdot 89\,\text{ms}$ verification. We stress that proving times for step *(a)* are fully parallelizable (as we generate n independent proofs for key-tags).

These timings refer to those for a common laptop (i7-6820HQ CPU at 2.70 GHz) and aim at estimating an efficient instantiation through the zero-knowledge scheme LMR [28] as $\mathsf{NIZK}_{\mathsf{tags}}$ and $\mathsf{NIZK}_{\mathrm{C}}$ using Ristretto Curve as an underlying group.

How we Derive Timings. A similar derivation for Bulletproof timings was previously used in [29]. For each timing we use the formula $T(n) \approx n \cdot \mathsf{num\_of\_constraints\_circuit}_{\mathrm{LMR}} \cdot \mathsf{cost\_per\_constraint}$.

Deriving Step *(a)*: for proving, $\mathsf{cost\_per\_constraint}$ is measured to be $\approx 8.97/64$ ms/constraint (our experimental finding) for the implementation in [2]. For verification 1.22/64 ms/constraint. We estimate $\mathsf{num\_of\_constraints\_circuit}_{\mathrm{LMR}}(\mathsf{tag}) \approx 5k$: for a circuit for Poseidon hash [25] and fixed base exponentiation (for rerandomization) of curve points[12][13] requires $L = 2806$ multiplicative constraints. To use this in LMR [28] we need to encode this as a witness vector (a very conservative upper bound is $2L$, which we approximate to $5k$). **Deriving step *(b)*:** for proving, $\mathsf{cost\_per\_constraint}$ is measured to be $\approx 232/64$ ms/constraint. For verification 88/64 ms/constraint. We derive these estimations from BL12-381[14]; we know this to be a fair estimate for Ristretto [2]. $\mathsf{num\_of\_constraints\_circuit}_{\mathrm{LMR}}(\mathsf{range}_{64}) \approx 65$ constraints.

7 Application: Multi-type QuisQuis

QuisQuis [23] is a privacy-preserving transaction system which allows for pruning old transactions, keeping the state of each participant linear in the number of

[12] This is a lower bound but we expect it be a reasonable estimate (up to approximately a factor 2) of hashing-to-group techniques close to those in Sect. 1.1 in [15].

[13] Since there is no public circuit implementation for Ristretto operations for this, we use arkworks [1] BL12-381 implementation for this estimate. We expect this to be an upper bound on Ristretto points given their smaller field size—$\frac{255}{381}$x smaller, more precisely. We measure this number using the implementation in [1].

[14] We use a different implementation [3] on BL12-381 points as the implementation in [2] is not compatible with BL12-381.

users. This is a major advantage over other privacy-preserving transaction systems, which require a state size linear in the number of transactions. A QuisQuis transaction is a redistribution of tokens among a set of accounts. An account belongs to an owner and stores their tokens. Instead of consuming accounts and creating new ones, QuisQuis updates the accounts. These update operations need to change the balance of a peer without knowing their total balance. This is achieved with homomorphic commitments.

In contrast to the original QuisQuis where an account stored a scalar value representing an amount, we generalize accounts to store tokens of different types in a key-value map. Each key corresponds to a type, also known as currency, and the value specifies how many tokens of the specific type are held by the account. An account acct then belongs to a secret key sk and holds a balance kv, represented as a key-value map. To transfer tokens from one account to another, a transaction includes both accounts as active inputs, denoted by the set $\mathcal{P}$. The transaction subtracts tokens from one account with a secret index s and adds them to the other one. The output of the transaction are two updated accounts belonging to the same users as the inputs; the input accounts are discarded. To achieve anonymity, the input consists of $\mathcal{P}$ together with a potentially large anonymity set of accounts $\mathcal{A}$ which keep their balance unchanged but provide set anonymity for the active accounts.

As the central building block of our multi-type QuisQuis system, we present an updatable account based on our key-value commitments.

7.1 Multi-type QuisQuis: Syntax

The original QuisQuis transaction protocol consists of the three algorithms $(\mathsf{Setup}, \mathsf{Trans}, \mathsf{Verify})$. Their multi-type equivalent is as follows:

$\mathsf{Setup}(1^\lambda, \vec{\mathsf{kv}}) \rightarrow \mathsf{state}$**:** takes the security parameter λ and a vector of key-value balances $\vec{\mathsf{kv}}$ and outputs an initial state state. One part of the state is a set of unspent accounts where each key-value balance has an account.

$\mathsf{Trans}(\mathsf{sk}, \mathcal{P}, \mathcal{A}, \delta\vec{\mathsf{kv}}) \rightarrow \mathsf{tx}$**:** takes a secret key sk which corresponds to one account in the set of active accounts $\mathcal{P}$ and an anonymity set $\mathcal{A}$ with a vector of key-value maps $\delta\vec{\mathsf{kv}}$ to update tokens. Trans outputs a transaction tx.

$\mathsf{Verify}(\mathsf{state}, \mathsf{tx}) \rightarrow \bot/\mathsf{state}'$**:** takes a state and a transaction tx and outputs a new state' or fails with $\bot$.

To support dynamic registration of new types, we require an additional algorithm $\mathsf{Register}$, which is defined as:

$\mathsf{Register}(\mathsf{acct}, k, v_k) \rightarrow \mathsf{tx}$ takes an account acct and a new type k with amount v_k and outputs a transaction tx.

A registration transaction is accepted by Verify if the type k has not been registered before. We define the correctness of a transaction system more formally. Let for all $\lambda \in \mathbb{N}$ and $\vec{\mathsf{kv}}$ with $R^{\mathsf{kv}}_{\mathsf{rng}}(\mathsf{kv}_i) = 1$ be $\mathsf{state} \leftarrow \mathsf{Setup}(1^\lambda, \vec{\mathsf{kv}})$. For all accounts in $\mathcal{P}, \mathcal{A}$ with index sets $\mathcal{P}^* := \{i \in [|\mathsf{Sort}(\mathcal{P} \cup \mathcal{A})|] : \mathsf{acct}_i \in \mathcal{P}\}$ and $\mathcal{A}^*$

accordingly in a canonically ordered form with Sort. All accounts in $\mathcal{P} \cup \mathcal{A}$ are part of the UTXO set in state, all $\delta\vec{\mathsf{kv}}$ with $R^{\mathsf{kv}}_{\mathsf{rng}}(-\mathsf{kv}_s) = 1$ and $R^{\mathsf{kv}}_{\mathsf{rng}}(\mathsf{kv}_i) = 1$ for $i \in \mathcal{P}^*\{s\}$ and $\mathsf{kv}_i = \emptyset_{kv}$ for $i \in \mathcal{A}^*$ and sk corresponding to an account $\mathsf{acct}_s \in \mathcal{P}$ with enough tokens such that after the transaction there is no negative type $R^{\mathsf{kv}}_{\mathsf{rng}}(\mathsf{kv}_s + \delta\mathsf{kv}_s) = 1$, it holds that $\mathsf{Verify}(\mathsf{state}, \mathsf{Trans}(\mathsf{sk}, \mathcal{P}, \mathcal{A}, \delta\vec{\mathsf{kv}})) = \mathsf{state}'$ where $\mathsf{state}' \neq \perp$ and contains an updated UTXO set with all inputs $\mathcal{P} \cup \mathcal{A}$ removed and the transaction outputs added.

Multi-type QuisQuis: Security. The security of a QuisQuis-like transaction system consists of two main properties. The first property we need to achieve is *anonymity.* A transaction system is anonymous if an adversary cannot successfully distinguish two transactions. The transactions are created according to malicious instructions after the adversary has interacted with an oracle signing transactions on behalf of uncompromised participants.

The second property is *theft prevention.* This entails that *(i)* the adversary cannot steal tokens from uncompromised accounts; *(ii)* the adversary cannot create tokens out of thin air. Slightly more formally, we model these properties as follows. While interacting with the aforementioned signing oracle the balance of honest accounts (not controlled by the adversary) must not decrease. Additionally, the total amount of tokens must not increase from transaction to transaction. Notice, however, the number of tokens may increase as the result of mining or a token registration—the latter counts as a "genesis" transaction.

Our variant of QuisQuis with multiple token types shares many of the same properties as the non-type aware system. We refer the reader to the original QuisQuis paper [23] for details.

7.2 Construction

We construct the multi token QuisQuis scheme following the original QuisQuis but with two main adaptations: each account holds tokens in multiple types and making sure a transaction guarantees that the amounts of tokens are balanced for each of the token types.

The details of updatable accounts for key-value maps are presented in the full version [17]. In a nutshell they have the same algorithms as the original QuisQuis construction but allow for multiple kinds of tokens.

Setup. The setup algorithm generates a list of updatable accounts, one for each initial balance key-value map.

Trans. Our transaction structure follows that in QuisQuis where a "transaction" denotes a redistribution of wealth among all accounts involved ($\mathcal{P} \cup \mathcal{A}$). The transaction takes a vector of key-value maps, one for each account. The account is then updated according to the key-value map. Key-value maps that contain only valid positive values ($R^{\mathsf{kv}}_{\mathsf{rng}}(\delta\mathsf{kv}_i) = 1$) are used to deposit tokens to receiving accounts. In order to ensure that the total number of tokens is preserved, we require that one key-value map holds negative values. This is to satisfy that the sum of all key-value maps is zero, or $\sum_{i=1}^{|\vec{\delta kv}|} \delta \mathsf{kv}_i = \emptyset_{kv}$. For the account with the negative key-value map (indexed by s in the canonically ordered set $\mathcal{P} \cup \mathcal{A}$), the transaction signature ensures that the owner of the account acct_s authorizes the spending by proving knowledge of the matching secret key sk. The algorithm $\mathsf{Trans}((s, \mathsf{sk}_s, \mathsf{kv}_s), \mathcal{P}, \mathcal{A}, \vec{\mathsf{kv}})$ performs the following steps:

1. Parse all input accounts $\mathcal{P} \cup \mathcal{A} = \{\mathsf{acct}_1, \ldots, \mathsf{acct}_n\}$ and check the spending account is valid by $\mathsf{VerifyAcct}(\mathsf{acct}_s, (\mathsf{sk}_s, \mathsf{kv}_s)) = 1$. The transaction needs to be balanced: $\sum_{i=1}^{|\vec{\delta kv}|} \delta \mathsf{kv}_i = \emptyset_{kv}$ and all key-value maps other than the spending account must be non-negative $\forall i \neq s : R^{\mathsf{kv}}_{\mathsf{rng}}(\delta \mathsf{kv}_i) = 1$. To support large anonymity sets $\mathcal{A}$, we choose to disclose the upper bound on active accounts by showing that $\delta \mathsf{kv}_i = \emptyset_{kv}$ for $i \in \mathcal{A}^*$ instead or a range proof. The spending account must be negative $R^{\mathsf{kv}}_{\mathsf{rng}}(-\delta \mathsf{kv}_s) = 1$ and the resulting account must be valid $R^{\mathsf{kv}}_{\mathsf{rng}}(\mathsf{kv}_s + \delta \mathsf{kv}_s) = 1$, to prevent overspending.
2. Let $\mathsf{outputs} = (\mathsf{acct}_1^{\mathcal{T}}, \ldots, \mathsf{acct}_n^{\mathcal{T}})$ be a canonical order of the accounts generated by $\mathsf{UpdateAcct}(\mathcal{P} \cup \mathcal{A}, \vec{\delta \mathsf{kv}}; r)$.
3. Let $\psi : [n] \to [n]$ be the permutation that maps the canonically ordered inputs to the canonically ordered outputs, i.e. input i has the same secret key as output $\psi(i)$.
4. Create a zero knowledge proof π showing that the transaction is well formed, i.e. that it satisfies the following relation:

$$R_{\mathsf{tx\text{-}wf}} : \begin{cases} \mathbb{x} = (\mathsf{inputs}, \mathsf{outputs}), \mathbb{w} = (\mathsf{sk}, \mathsf{kv}_s, \vec{\delta \mathsf{kv}}, r = (r_1, r_2), \psi) \text{ s.t.} \\ \mathsf{VerifyUpdateAcct}(\mathsf{acct}_i^{\mathcal{S}}, \mathsf{acct}_{\psi(i)}^{\mathcal{T}}, \delta \mathsf{kv}_i) = 1 \forall i \in \mathcal{P}^* \\ \wedge R^{\mathsf{kv}}_{\mathsf{rng}}(\delta \mathsf{kv}_i) = 1 \forall i \in \mathcal{P}^*/\{s\} \wedge R^{\mathsf{kv}}_{\mathsf{rng}}(-\delta \mathsf{kv}_s) = 1 \\ \wedge \delta \mathsf{kv}_i = \emptyset_{kv} \forall i \in \mathcal{A}^* \wedge \sum_{i=1}^{n} \delta \mathsf{kv}_i = \emptyset_{kv} \\ \wedge \mathsf{VerifyAcct}(\mathsf{acct}_{\psi(s)}^{\mathcal{T}}, \mathsf{sk}, \mathsf{kv}_s + \delta \mathsf{kv}_s) = 1. \end{cases}$$

The relation ensures that the permuted output account is correctly updated by the transferred balance $\delta \mathsf{kv}_i$ for all active accounts. It then ensures that the updated key-value maps are valid, i.e. there is one spending account at index s and no value is taken from other accounts. The balances of the accounts in the anonymity set must not change. To ensure that the spender has enough tokens, the proof checks that the updated spender account has no negative balance. The transaction consists of the inputs, outputs and the proof π.

Verify. A transaction is valid in respect to a state if all accounts in inputs have not been used in another transaction and the proof π is valid.

Security Analysis. Our key-value commitments provide the same hiding and binding properties as the commitments to single scalars used in QuisQuis. The construction is a parallel version of the single type case and thereby the theft security holds also for all keys in parallel. Regarding anonymity, we achieve the same properties as QuisQuis, if we define an upper bound of the number of types involved in a transaction. For transactions with few different types, we achieve this through padding. With a constant size transaction proof, our new transactions are as indistinguishable as the original QuisQuis transactions.

Acknowledgements. Research supported by: the Concordium Blockhain Research Center, Aarhus University, Denmark; the Carlsberg Foundation under the Semper Ardens Research Project CF18-112 (BCM); the European Research Council (ERC) under the European Unions's Horizon 2020 research and innovation programme under grant agreement No 803096 (SPEC). This work was partly produced while Matteo Campanelli and Felix Engelmann were affiliated with Aarhus University.

References

1. Ark-works. http://arkworks.rs
2. Dalek bulletproofs implementation. https://github.com/zkcrypto/bulletproofs.git
3. Zengo-x bulletproofs implementation. https://github.com/ZenGo-X/bulletproofs
4. Agarwal, A., Kamara, S.: Encrypted key-value stores. In: Bhargavan, K., Oswald, E., Prabhakaran, M. (eds.) INDOCRYPT 2020. LNCS, vol. 12578, pp. 62–85. Springer, Cham (2020). https://doi.org/10.1007/978-3-030-65277-7_4
5. Agrawal, S., Raghuraman, S.: KVaC: key-value commitments for blockchains and beyond. In: Moriai, S., Wang, H. (eds.) ASIACRYPT 2020, Part III. LNCS, vol. 12493, pp. 839–869. Springer, Cham (2020). https://doi.org/10.1007/978-3-030-64840-4_28
6. Albrecht, M.R., et al.: Feistel structures for MPC, and more. In: Sako, K., Schneider, S., Ryan, P.Y.A. (eds.) ESORICS 2019, Part II. LNCS, vol. 11736, pp. 151–171. Springer, Cham (2019). https://doi.org/10.1007/978-3-030-29962-0_8
7. Albrecht, M., Grassi, L., Rechberger, C., Roy, A., Tiessen, T.: MiMC: efficient encryption and cryptographic hashing with minimal multiplicative complexity. In: Cheon, J.H., Takagi, T. (eds.) ASIACRYPT 2016, Part I. LNCS, vol. 10031, pp. 191–219. Springer, Heidelberg (2016). https://doi.org/10.1007/978-3-662-53887-6_7
8. Aly, A., Ashur, T., Ben-Sasson, E., Dhooghe, S., Szepieniec, A.: Design of symmetric-key primitives for advanced cryptographic protocols. Cryptology ePrint Archive, Report 2019/426 (2019). https://eprint.iacr.org/2019/426
9. Attema, T., Cramer, R.: Compressed Σ-protocol theory and practical application to plug & play secure algorithmics. In: Micciancio, D., Ristenpart, T. (eds.) CRYPTO 2020, Part III. LNCS, vol. 12172, pp. 513–543. Springer, Cham (2020). https://doi.org/10.1007/978-3-030-56877-1_18
10. Attema, T., Cramer, R., Rambaud, M.: Compressed sigma-protocols for bilinear circuits and applications to logarithmic-sized transparent threshold signature schemes. Cryptology ePrint Archive, Report 2020/1447 (2020). https://eprint.iacr.org/2020/1447
11. Ben-Sasson, E., et al.: Zerocash: decentralized anonymous payments from bitcoin. In: 2014 IEEE Symposium on Security and Privacy, pp. 459–474. IEEE Computer Society Press, May 2014. https://doi.org/10.1109/SP.2014.36
12. Benarroch, D., Campanelli, M., Fiore, D., Kolonelos, D.: Zero-knowledge proofs for set membership: efficient, succinct, modular. Cryptology ePrint Archive, Report 2019/1255 (2019). https://eprint.iacr.org/2019/1255

13. Boneh, D., Bünz, B., Fisch, B.: Batching techniques for accumulators with applications to IOPs and stateless blockchains. In: Boldyreva, A., Micciancio, D. (eds.) CRYPTO 2019, Part I. LNCS, vol. 11692, pp. 561–586. Springer, Cham (2019). https://doi.org/10.1007/978-3-030-26948-7_20
14. Bootle, J., Groth, J.: Efficient batch zero-knowledge arguments for low degree polynomials. In: Abdalla, M., Dahab, R. (eds.) PKC 2018, Part II. LNCS, vol. 10770, pp. 561–588. Springer, Cham (2018). https://doi.org/10.1007/978-3-319-76581-5_19
15. Brier, E., Coron, J.-S., Icart, T., Madore, D., Randriam, H., Tibouchi, M.: Efficient indifferentiable hashing into ordinary elliptic curves. In: Rabin, T. (ed.) CRYPTO 2010. LNCS, vol. 6223, pp. 237–254. Springer, Heidelberg (2010). https://doi.org/10.1007/978-3-642-14623-7_13
16. Bünz, B., Bootle, J., Boneh, D., Poelstra, A., Wuille, P., Maxwell, G.: Bulletproofs: short proofs for confidential transactions and more. In: 2018 IEEE Symposium on Security and Privacy, pp. 315–334. IEEE Computer Society Press, May 2018. https://doi.org/10.1109/SP.2018.00020
17. Campanelli, M., Engelmann, F., Orlandi, C.: Zero-knowledge for homomorphic key-value commitments with applications to privacy-preserving ledgers. Cryptology ePrint Archive, Report 2021/1678 (2021). https://eprint.iacr.org/2021/1678
18. Campanelli, M., Fiore, D., Greco, N., Kolonelos, D., Nizzardo, L.: Incrementally aggregatable vector commitments and applications to verifiable decentralized storage. In: Moriai, S., Wang, H. (eds.) ASIACRYPT 2020, Part II. LNCS, vol. 12492, pp. 3–35. Springer, Cham (2020). https://doi.org/10.1007/978-3-030-64834-3_1
19. Campanelli, M., Hall-Andersen, M.: Veksel: simple, efficient, anonymous payments with large anonymity sets from well-studied assumptions. IACR Cryptology ePrint Archive 2021/327 (2021)
20. Catalano, D., Fiore, D.: Vector commitments and their applications. In: Kurosawa, K., Hanaoka, G. (eds.) PKC 2013. LNCS, vol. 7778, pp. 55–72. Springer, Heidelberg (2013). https://doi.org/10.1007/978-3-642-36362-7_5
21. Engelmann, F., Müller, L., Peter, A., Kargl, F., Bösch, C.: SwapCT: Swap confidential transactions for privacy-preserving multi-token exchanges. PoPETs **2021**(4), 270–290 (2021). https://doi.org/10.2478/popets-2021-0070
22. Farashahi, R.R., Fouque, P.A., Shparlinski, I., Tibouchi, M., Voloch, J.: Indifferentiable deterministic hashing to elliptic and hyperelliptic curves. Math. Comput. **82**(281), 491–512 (2013)
23. Fauzi, P., Meiklejohn, S., Mercer, R., Orlandi, C.: Quisquis: a new design for anonymous cryptocurrencies. In: Galbraith, S.D., Moriai, S. (eds.) ASIACRYPT 2019, Part I. LNCS, vol. 11921, pp. 649–678. Springer, Cham (2019). https://doi.org/10.1007/978-3-030-34578-5_23
24. Ganesh, C., Orlandi, C., Pancholi, M., Takahashi, A., Tschudi, D.: Fiat-Shamir bulletproofs are non-malleable (in the algebraic group model). In: Dunkelman, O., Dziembowski, S. (eds.) EUROCRYPT 2022, Part II. LNCS, vol. 13276, pp. 397–426. Springer, Heidelberg (2022). https://doi.org/10.1007/978-3-031-07085-3_14
25. Grassi, L., Khovratovich, D., Rechberger, C., Roy, A., Schofnegger, M.: Poseidon: a new hash function for zero-knowledge proof systems. In: 30th USENIX Security Symposium (2021)
26. Hopwood, D., Bowe, S., Hornby, T., Wilcox, N.: Zcash protocol specification, version 2021.1.15 (2021)
27. Kate, A., Zaverucha, G.M., Goldberg, I.: Constant-size commitments to polynomials and their applications. In: Abe, M. (ed.) ASIACRYPT 2010. LNCS, vol.

6477, pp. 177–194. Springer, Heidelberg (2010). https://doi.org/10.1007/978-3-642-17373-8_11
28. Lai, R.W.F., Malavolta, G., Ronge, V.: Succinct arguments for bilinear group arithmetic: practical structure-preserving cryptography. In: Cavallaro, L., Kinder, J., Wang, X., Katz, J. (eds.) ACM CCS 2019, pp. 2057–2074. ACM Press, November 2019. https://doi.org/10.1145/3319535.3354262
29. Lai, R.W.F., Ronge, V., Ruffing, T., Schröder, D., Thyagarajan, S.A.K., Wang, J.: Omniring: scaling private payments without trusted setup. In: Cavallaro, L., Kinder, J., Wang, X., Katz, J. (eds.) ACM CCS 2019, pp. 31–48. ACM Press, November 2019. https://doi.org/10.1145/3319535.3345655
30. Libert, B., Yung, M.: Concise mercurial vector commitments and independent zero-knowledge sets with short proofs. In: Micciancio, D. (ed.) TCC 2010. LNCS, vol. 5978, pp. 499–517. Springer, Heidelberg (2010). https://doi.org/10.1007/978-3-642-11799-2_30
31. Noether, S., Mackenzie, A., et al.: Ring confidential transactions. Ledger **1**, 1–18 (2016)
32. Poelstra, A., Back, A., Friedenbach, M., Maxwell, G., Wuille, P.: Confidential assets. In: Zohar, A., et al. (eds.) FC 2018. LNCS, vol. 10958, pp. 43–63. Springer, Heidelberg (2019). https://doi.org/10.1007/978-3-662-58820-8_4
33. Setty, S., Angel, S., Gupta, T., Lee, J.: Proving the correct execution of concurrent services in zero-knowledge. In: 13th USENIX Symposium on Operating Systems Design and Implementation, OSDI 2018, pp. 339–356 (2018)
34. Tibouchi, M., Kim, T.: Improved elliptic curve hashing and point representation. Des. Codes Cryptogr. **82**(1), 161–177 (2017)
35. Tomescu, A., Xia, Y., Newman, Z.: Authenticated dictionaries with cross-incremental proof (dis)aggregation. Cryptology ePrint Archive, Report 2020/1239 (2020). https://eprint.iacr.org/2020/1239
36. Valiant, P.: Incrementally verifiable computation or proofs of knowledge imply time/space efficiency. In: Canetti, R. (ed.) TCC 2008. LNCS, vol. 4948, pp. 1–18. Springer, Heidelberg (2008). https://doi.org/10.1007/978-3-540-78524-8_1
37. Yi, Z., Ye, H., Dai, P., Tongcheng, S., Gelfer, V.: Confidential assets on MimbleWimble. Cryptology ePrint Archive, Report 2019/1435 (2019). https://eprint.iacr.org/2019/1435

Author Index